# The Wiley-Blackwell Companion to the Anglican Communion

# The Wiley-Blackwell Companions to Religion

The Wiley-Blackwell Companions to Religion series presents a collection of the most recent scholarship and knowledge about world religions. Each volume draws together newly commissioned essays by distinguished authors in the field, and is presented in a style which is accessible to undergraduate students, as well as scholars and the interested general reader. These volumes approach the subject in a creative and forward-thinking style, providing a forum in which leading scholars in the field can make their views and research available to a wider audience.

**Recently Published**

**The Blackwell Companion to the Qur'ān**
Edited by Andrew Rippin

**The Blackwell Companion to Contemporary Islamic Thought**
Edited by Ibrahim M. Abu-Rabi′

**The Blackwell Companion to the Bible and Culture**
Edited by John F. A. Sawyer

**The Blackwell Companion to Catholicism**
Edited by James J. Buckley, Frederick Christian Bauerschmidt, and Trent Pomplun

**The Blackwell Companion to Eastern Christianity**
Edited by Ken Parry

**The Blackwell Companion to the Theologians**
Edited by Ian S. Markham

**The Blackwell Companion to the Bible in English Literature**
Edited by Rebecca Lemon, Emma Mason, John Roberts, and Christopher Rowland

**The Blackwell Companion to the New Testament**
Edited by David E. Aune

**The Blackwell Companion to Nineteenth-Century Theology**
Edited by David Fergusson

**The Blackwell Companion to Religion in America**
Edited by Philip Goff

**The Blackwell Companion to Jesus**
Edited by Delbert Burkett

**The Blackwell Companion to Paul**
Edited by Stephen Westerholm

**The Blackwell Companion to Religion and Violence**
Edited by Andrew R. Murphy

**The Blackwell Companion to Christian Ethics, Second Edition**
Edited by Stanley Hauerwas and Samuel Wells

**The Wiley-Blackwell Companion to Practical Theology**
Edited by Bonnie J. Miller-McLemore

**The Wiley-Blackwell Companion to Religion and Social Justice**
Edited by Michael D. Palmer and Stanley M. Burgess

**The Wiley-Blackwell Companion to Chinese Religions**
Edited by Randall L. Nadeau

**The Wiley-Blackwell Companion to African Religions**
Edited by Elias Kifon Bongmba

**The Wiley-Blackwell Companion to Christian Mysticism**
Edited by Julia A. Lamm

**The Wiley-Blackwell Companion to the Anglican Communion**
Edited by Ian S. Markham, J. Barney Hawkins IV, Justyn Terry, and Leslie Nuñez Steffensen

# The Wiley-Blackwell Companion to the Anglican Communion

*Edited by*

Ian S. Markham, J. Barney Hawkins IV,
Justyn Terry, and Leslie Nuñez Steffensen

WILEY-BLACKWELL

A John Wiley & Sons, Ltd., Publication

*Library of Congress Cataloging-in-Publication Data*

The Wiley-Blackwell Companion to the Anglican Communion / Edited by The Rev. Dr. J. Barney Hawkins IV, The Very Rev. Dr. Ian S. Markham, The Rev. Leslie Nuñez Steffensen, The Very Rev. Dr. Justyn Terry.
          pages cm
   Includes bibliographical references and index.
   ISBN 978-0-470-65634-1 (cloth)
   1. Anglican Communion.   I. Hawkins, J. Barney (James Barney), editor of compilation.
   BX5005.W55 2013
   283–dc23

                              2012046828

A catalogue record for this book is available from the British Library.

Cover image: Lambeth Conference, 2008. Photo © Susan L. Shillinglaw of Virginia Theological Seminary.
Cover design by Nicki Averill Design

Set in 10/12.5pt Photina by Toppan Best-set Premedia Limited
Printed and bound in Singapore by Markono Print Media Pte Ltd

1   2013

# Contents

# Notes on Contributors

**Titre Ande** is the Bishop of Aru Diocese in the Democratic Republic of the Congo and a member of the Inter-Anglican Standing Commission for Unity, Faith and Order (IASCUFO). He was principal of the Anglican Theological College in Congo and has a doctorate from Birmingham University in the United Kingdom.

**The Most Rev. Dr. Mouneer Hanna Anis** is currently the Bishop of the Episcopal/Anglican Diocese of Egypt with North Africa and the Horn of Africa, as well as the President Bishop of the Episcopal/Anglican Province of Jerusalem and the Middle East. He is married and has two sons.

**Katharine E. Babson** is a priest of the Episcopal Church, past Episcopal Church missionary to the Church of the Province of Myanmar, adjunct faculty member in Mission and World Religion at Virginia Theological Seminary, and trustee of the Cetana Foundation, which supports advanced educational opportunity for Myanmar students whose professional skills will enhance their country's future hope. She has worked and traveled extensively in Myanmar since 1994.

**The Rev. Dr. Ricardo F. Blanco-Beledo** is a priest in the Diocese of Mexico, Anglican Church of Mexico. He is ecumenical chaplain of the Theological Community of Mexico; professor in the College of Philosophy, Faculty of Philosophy and Letters, at UNAM (Autonomous National University of Mexico); and a clinical psychologist and psychoanalyst. He is the author or editor of numerous books and articles in national and international journals.

**A. Hugo Blankingship, Jr.** is the chancellor and deputy chair for the Anglican Church in North America. He trained and practiced as a lawyer in Northern Virginia for 55 years, and is a past president of both the Virginia Bar Association and the Virginia Board of Bar Examiners. He is the son of the Rt. Rev. Alexander Hugo Blankingship, who was Bishop of Cuba from 1939 to 1961. He has earned a BA from the University of Virginia and an LLB from the University of Virginia School of Law. Previously, he served on the boards of trustees for Episcopal High School, Virginia

Theological Seminary, and Trinity School for Ministry, and as chancellor for the Episcopal Diocese of Virginia.

**The Rev. Gustavo L. Castello Branco** is Brazilian and is currently the rector of *Paroquia Anglicana Cristo Libertador* (Anglican Parish of Christ the Liberator), in the city of João Pessoa, in the Diocese of Recife. He also works as a lawyer. Gustavo earned his masters' degree in theology (Church History Concentration) in 2007 at Trinity School for Ministry, Ambridge, PA.

**Christopher Byaruhanga** is the professor of historical and systematic theology at Uganda Christian University. He holds a ThD from the General Theological Seminary in New York City. His publications include *Bishop Alfred Robert Tucker and the Establishment of the African Anglican Church* (Nairobi: WordAlive, 2008); *Christian Theology for University Students* (Kampala: Wavah Books Limited, 2005). Awards he has received include the 2005/06 Saint Luke Project Scholar (OMSC, New Haven, CT); 2009 John Jay Institute of Faith, Law and Society fellow (Colorado Springs, CO); and 2010 Washington Scholar (Family Research Council, Washington, DC).

**Gregory K. Cameron** is the Bishop of St. Asaph in the Church in Wales. He was deputy general secretary of the Anglican Communion between 2003 and 2009, in which capacity he served as director of Ecumenical Relations, and secretary of the Lambeth Commission on Communion which produced the Windsor Report. In 2007, he was awarded an honorary Doctorate of Divinity by the Episcopal Divinity School in honor of his commitment to reconciliation in the Anglican Communion.

**George L. Carey**, Baron Carey of Clifton, was the Archbishop of Canterbury from 1991 to 2002. While he was archbishop, the first women were ordained priests in the Church of England. During his tenure, there was a lively debate about homosexuality, especially at the Lambeth Conference of 1998. He graduated from King's College, London. He is married to Eileen Hood, and they have two sons and two daughters.

**Mark Chapman** is vice principal of Ripon College Cuddesdon, Oxford, and reader in modern theology at the University of Oxford. He has written widely on many different aspects of church history and theology. Among his books are *Anglicanism: A Very Short Introduction* (Oxford: Oxford University Press, 2006) and *Anglican Theology* (London: T & T Clark, 2012). He is a priest in the Church of England and a member of its General Synod.

**Bishop Timothy J. Dakin** is a former head of the Church Mission Society (2000–2012) and was previously the principal of Carlile College, a theology and business training college in Nairobi, from 1993 to 2000. He was born in East Africa but received his theological education in the United Kingdom. He was an elected member of the General Synod of the Church of England and an honorary Canon Theologian of Coventry Cathedral (2001–2012). He became the Bishop of Winchester in December 2011.

**Duleep de Chickera**, the former Bishop of Colombo, holds a BTh (Serampore) and an MSc (Oxn). He is a founder member of the Congress of Religions and the Friday Forum in Sri Lanka; serves on the Anglican Oriental Orthodox Conversations and the Palestine Israel Ecumenical Forum of the World Council of Churches; and is a moderator of the IR Working Group of the Churches Commission for International Affairs of the World Council of Churches. His ministerial interests include Inter-Religious dialogue, Just peace, and an Asian spirituality.

**Norman Doe** is a professor of law and director of the Centre for Law and Religion at Cardiff Law School. He was a member of the Lambeth Commission, and has served as a consultant in canon law to the Anglican Communion Primates' Meeting, Lambeth Conference, Covenant Design Group, and Legal Advisers' Network. In 2010, he was president of the European Consortium for Church and State Research, and in 2011 a visiting fellow at Trinity College, Oxford.

**Mary Jane L. Dogue-is** is a priest in the Episcopal Church in the Philippines, the Diocese of North Central Philippines. She was baptized Roman Catholic, but was confirmed and received in the Episcopal Church. She studied theology at St. Andrew's Theological Seminary and is now finishing her MA at Virginia Theological Seminary. She is married with three daughters.

**Andrew Goddard** is associate director of the Kirby Laing Institute of Christian Ethics based in Cambridge. He also teaches Christian ethics part-time at Trinity College, Bristol, England and Anglican History and Polity for Fuller Theological Seminary's Anglican Studies Program. He is a fellow of the Anglican Communion Institute. He has written on both ethics and Anglicanism, most recently *Rowan Williams: His Legacy* (Lion, 2013). He is married to Lis, who is also ordained, and they have two grown-up children.

**Alan L. Hayes** (BA, Pomona College; BD, PhD, McGill University) is Bishops Frederick and Heber Wilkinson Professor of the History of Christianity at Wycliffe College in the University of Toronto, and director of the Toronto School of Theology. He is the author of *Anglicans in Canada: Controversies and Identity in Historical Perspective* (University of Illinois Press, 2004). He is an Anglican priest in the diocese of Niagara.

**The Rev. Dr. Robert S. Heaney** is an Anglican priest–scholar ordained in the Church of Ireland. He is director of postgraduate studies and research at St. John's University of Tanzania, and senior lecturer and MA course co-coordinator in the School of Theology and Religious Studies.

**The Rev. Dr. Elizabeth Hoare** teaches spirituality and worship at Wycliffe Hall, Oxford, and oversees missions and prayer. She is ordained with over 17 years of parish experience, all in rural ministry. Her original area of research was the English Reformation. She is currently writing a book on the link between the Desert Fathers and Celtic Christianity. She is married to an Anglican priest, and they have one son.

**Christopher Honoré** is a lecturer in Anglican studies at the Theological College of St John the Evangelist, Auckland, New Zealand. His interests include New Zealand Church History, the work of the CMS in New Zealand, and the craft of teaching and learning. He has been a priest of the Diocese of Auckland since 1980.

**Nancy Carol James** has a PhD in religious studies from the University of Virginia. An Episcopal priest, she is the rector of Trinity Parish in Charles County, MD. She has published widely on the French mystic Madame Jeanne de la Mothe Guyon, including *The Complete Madame Guyon* (Brewster, MA: Paraclete Press, 2011) and *Bastille Witness: The Prison Autobiography of Madame Guyon 1648–1717* (Lanham, MD: University Press of American, 2012). Now writing about the Anglican Communion, she has published *The Developing Schism Within the Episcopal Church 1960–2010* (Lewiston, NY: Mellen Press, 2010).

**The Most Rev. Benjamin A. Kwashi**, D.Min, DD, is Archbishop, Diocese of Jos, Nigeria. He is a well-known preacher and evangelist. He was ordained in 1982 after attending the Theological College of Northern Nigeria, Bukuru, Jos. In 1987, his church and vicarage were totally burned down in Christian–Muslim riots. He has a long association with ANITEPAM (African Network of Institutions of Theological Education Preparing Anglicans for Ministry). He is married to Gloria, and they have six children.

**Paul Kwong** was born and bred in Hong Kong. He read theology in the United States of America and United Kingdom, and is now the Anglican Archbishop and Primate of Hong Kong. He also serves as a member of the Standing Committee of the Anglican Consultative Council.

**Grant LeMarquand** is assistant bishop in the Anglican/Episcopal Diocese of Egypt with North Africa and the Horn of Africa and area bishop for the Horn of Africa. Previously, he taught New Testament and Mission at Trinity School for Ministry in Ambridge, PA. He is a Canadian and a graduate of both McGill University in Montreal and Wycliffe College in Toronto. He is married to Wendy, and they have two grown children.

**Julian Linnell**, PhD, is executive director of Anglican Frontier Missions, member of the Evangelism and Church Growth Initiative of the Anglican Communion, and adjunct professor of Global Missions at Trinity School for Ministry.

**The Rev. Canon Dr. John A. Macdonald** is associate professor of mission and evangelism and director of the Stanway Institute for World Mission and Evangelism at Trinity School for Ministry in Ambridge, PA. He was a former missionary to Honduras for 12 years, and has also served in parishes in the United States. In 2008, Dr. Macdonald spent a sabbatical year doing research in Spain and working with the Spanish Reformed Episcopal Church. Additionally, in recent years, he has made five trips to

Mexico to teach at the Seminario San Andrés in Mexico City and at clergy gatherings in other parts of the province.

**The Rt. Rev. Dr. Azad Marshall** is Bishop of the Diocese of Iran and Assistant Bishop of Cyprus and the Gulf. He graduated from Sherbourne College in England. He is a supporter of the Anglican Covenant and served as president of the National Council of Churches in Pakistan.

**Moses Matonya** is a priest in the Diocese of Central Tanganyika, assistant lecturer at St. John's University of Tanzania, and director of the Diocese of Central Tanganyika Msalato Theological College, Dodoma, Tanzania. He is married to Ruth and has five children.

**The Rev. Dr. Saw Maung Doe** studied at Holy Cross Theological College and the Myanmar Institute of Theology in Yangon, Myanmar, and received his Doctorate in Religion from the Oxford Center for Mission Studies in England. Professor of church history at Holy Cross Theological College since his ordination to priesthood in 1990, he served as the college's principal from 1998 to 2006, and serves to date as its academic dean and as associate priest of the college parish, Holy Cross Church. He also serves as priest-in-charge of St. Andrew's Church, Yangon, and as assistant at the Church of the Resurrection and at Holy Trinity Cathedral, both in Yangon.

**Bishop Godfrey Mdimi Mhogolo** is the current Bishop of the Anglican Diocese of Central Tanganyika. With its half-million Anglicans, in 256 parishes with 1,000 growing congregations, it is numerically the largest Anglican diocese in the Anglican Communion. Most of his publications have targeted Swahili-speaking audiences for both academics and theologians. Among his publications are *Elendelea Kukua* (growing in the faith) – Christian ethics (Dodoma: Central Tanganyika Press, 1985); *Huduma ya Kanisa* (Christian ministry) (Dodoma: Central Tanganyika Press, 1996); *Utawala Bora* (good church governance) (Dodoma: Central Tanganyika Press, 2004); *Ibada* (liturgy and African culture) (Dodoma: Central Tanganyika Press, 2012); and, in publication, *Neema ya Kutosha* (abundant grace) 23 years of Cooperation and Service in the Diocese of Central Tanganyika (Dodoma: Central Tanganyika Press, forthcoming). Bishop Mhogolo studied for his bachelors and masters degrees at Ridley College, University of Melbourne, in the period 1976–1981.

**Barry Morgan**, Bishop of Bangor (1993–1999), Bishop of Llandaff since 1999, is also Archbishop of Wales since 2003. A graduate in history and theology from London University and Cambridge University, respectively, he gained a doctorate from the University of Wales in 1986 and is its current Pro Chancellor. A Fellow of many Welsh universities, he served on the Primates Standing Committee from 2003 to 2011, and has written many articles and books, most recently on the poet R.S. Thomas entitled *Strangely Orthodox*.

**Emmanuel Mukeshimana** is a priest in the Anglican Province of Rwanda, Cyangugu diocese. He worked as vicar and diocesan secretary of the diocese. He holds a Bachelor of Divinity from Uganda Christian University and a Master of Arts in Theology from joint studies between Trinity School for Ministry in Ambridge (PA) and Uganda Christian University (UCU) – Mukono. Currently, he is a PhD candidate at the UCU. He is married to Emilienne Nyiraburanga, and they have two children, Davis and Annabella.

**Phanuel L. Mung'ong'o** is the sub-dean of the Cathedral of the Holy Spirit in Dodoma. He has taught at St. Philip's Theological College and continues to teach at DCT Msalato Theological College. He is married to Flora, and they have three children – two daughters and a son.

**Bishop Michael Nazir-Ali** was the 106th Bishop of Rochester for 15 years, until 1 September, 2009. He is originally from Asia and was the first non-white diocesan bishop in the Church of England. Before that, he was the general secretary of CMS from 1989 to 1994, and prior to holding this position was Bishop of Raiwind in Pakistan. He holds both British and Pakistani citizenships, and from 1999 was a member of the House of Lords where he was active in a number of areas of national and international concern. He has both a Christian and a Muslim family background, and is now president of the Oxford Centre for Training, Research, Advocacy and Dialogue (OXTRAD). Michael's secondary education was in Pakistan. He read Economics, Sociology and Islamic History at the University of Karachi, and Theology at Fitzwilliam College and Ridley Hall, Cambridge. He has taught at colleges and universities in the United Kingdom and Pakistan. He is an Honorary Fellow of St. Edmund Hall, Oxford, and Fitzwilliam College, Cambridge, and is Senior Fellow of Wycliffe Hall, Oxford. He is Visiting Professor of Theology and Religious Studies in the University of Greenwich, and on the faculty of the London School of Theology (LST), affiliated to the Universities of Brunel and Middlesex. Michael is the author of ten books and of numerous articles on mission, ecumenism, the Anglican Communion, and relations with people of other faiths (particularly Islam).

**Robyn M. Neville** is currently visiting professor of church history at the General Theological Seminary in New York. After earning a BA with honors in religion at the College of William and Mary in Virginia, Robyn went on to Virginia Theological Seminary, where she earned the MDiv degree with honors. After two years of full-time parochial ministry, Robyn returned to graduate study, obtaining the ThM degree at Harvard Divinity School and then a PhD in historical theology through the Graduate Division of Religion at Emory University. Robyn has won several research awards, including Emory's Arts and Sciences fellowship and a grant to study at Oxford University through the National Endowment for the Humanities. Her current scholarship focuses on the history of Christianity in Ireland, with a special interest in medieval hagiography. An ordained Episcopal priest, Robyn has served parishes in Virginia, Massachusetts, and Georgia.

**The Rt. Rev. Abraham Yel Nhial** is the Bishop of the Diocese of Aweil, and the first bishop of this diocese. He holds a Bachelor of Biblical Studies from Atlanta Christian College, now Point University, in Atlanta, GA, and a Master of Divinity from Trinity School for Ministry, in Ambridge, PA. Bishop Nhial is a former Lost Boy from Sudan (the war orphan children). He is a co-author of *Lost Boy No More*. He is a former pastor of the South Sudanese in the Episcopal Church in Atlanta. He is married and has four children.

**Renta Nishihara** was born in 1962 in Kyoto, Japan. Nishihara graduated from Kyoto University, where he majored in technology. He finished at the Central Theological College, the Graduate School of Christian Studies of the Rikkyo University, with a focus on the theology of Richard Hooker. He is now a professor in the Graduate School of Christian Studies of the Rikkyo University and the vice president of the Rikkyo University. His research and teaching activities have focused on issues of Anglicanism and ecumenism. He is a member of the Central Committee of the World Council of Churches (WCC) and the Anglican–Lutheran International Commission (ALIC).

**Shourabh Pholia** is a leader in the Church of Bangladesh. He has been involved in the worldwide Anglican network which supports youth work.

**The Rev. Canon Professor Emeritus John S. Pobee** is vicar general of the Diocese of Accra, CPWA. Canon Pobee, a Ghanaian, studied at University College of Ghana, which was then in a special relationship with the University of London and Selwyn College, University of Cambridge. His priestly formation was at Westcott House, Cambridge. He has to his name 24 monographs including *The Anglican Story in Ghana, from Mission Beginnings to Province of Ghana* (Accra: Amanza Ltd., 2010); *Invitation to Be African Anglican* (Accra: Asempa Press, 2000); and *Christ Would Be an African Too* (Geneva: WCC, 1996). He has edited 22 books, and has written 120 chapters in books edited by others and 117 articles in refereed journals.

**Titus Presler**, ThD, DD, is a priest of the Episcopal Church USA, and principal of Edwardes College in Peshawar, Pakistan. A graduate of Harvard, General Theological Seminary (GTS), and Boston University, he has mission experience in India, Zimbabwe, and Pakistan and has chaired the Episcopal Church's Standing Commission on World Mission. Holding a doctorate in missiology, he was academic dean at GTS and president of the Seminary of the Southwest. His publications include *Transfigured Night: Mission and Culture in Zimbabwe's Vigil Movement* (Pretoria: UNISA Press, 1999), *Horizons of Mission* (Cambridge, MA: Cowley, 2001), and *Going Global with God: Reconciling Mission in a World of Difference* (New York: Morehouse, 2010). He was a researcher for the Global Anglicanism Project and consultant to the Anglican Indaba Project.

**Robert W. Prichard** is the Arthur Lee Kinsolving Professor of Christianity in America and instructor in liturgics at the Virginia Theological Seminary, where he has been a member of the faculty since 1983. A graduate of Princeton (AB), Berkeley at Yale (MDiv), and Emory (PhD) universities, he is the author or editor of nine books, including

*A History of the Episcopal Church.* He is a priest of the Diocese of Virginia and the current president of the Historical Society of the Episcopal Church.

**William Bradley Roberts**, DMA, is professor of church music and director of chapel music at Virginia Theological Seminary, Alexandria. Previously, he was director of music at St. John's, Lafayette Square, in Washington, DC; he also held similar positions in Tucson, AZ, Newport Beach, CA, Louisville, KY, and Houston TX. Active in the work of the national Episcopal Church, he has served as chair of the Standing Commission on Church Music, the AAM Mentoring Task Force, and chair of the Leadership Program for Musicians (LPM), for which he authored the original LPM curriculum *Voice Training for Choirs.* Dr. Roberts is a composer of choral music with works published by Augsburg-Fortress, Church Publishing, Paraclete, St. James Music Press, and Selah. He is author of the book *Music and Vital Congregations: A Practical Guide for Clergy.*

**William L. Sachs** directs the Center for Interfaith Reconciliation in Richmond, VA, which promotes understanding and cooperation between faiths, especially Christians and Muslims. He also serves as a Chabraja Fellow for Seabury Western Seminary in Chicago, where he consults and teaches on leadership and Anglican history. Previously, Sachs was vice president of the Episcopal Church Foundation in New York, and served as a parish priest in Virginia, Chicago, and Connecticut. He is the author of four books, namely *Homosexuality and the Crisis of Anglicanism* (Cambridge, UK: Cambridge University Press, 2009), *The Transformation of Anglicanism* (Cambridge, UK: Cambridge University Press, 1993, 2002), and *Restoring the Ties That Bind* (New York: Church Publishing, 2004); a contributor to the *Oxford Guide to the Book of Common Prayer*; and an editor of the *Oxford History of Anglicanism*. In addition, he is the author of over 150 articles, reviews, reports, workbooks, and chapters on Anglicanism, pluralism, minority rights, and leadership. His work has been cited by and he has been interviewed in major media. He has helped to lead and has spoken at interfaith events in Egypt, Jordan, Oman, Qatar, and Turkey. Sachs received his PhD from the University of Chicago, after earning degrees from Baylor, Vanderbilt, and Yale. He has been a visiting faculty member at various institutions, including Yale Divinity School in 2006.

**Bishop Dhirendra Kumar Sahu** comes from Khurda, Odisha, in India. He obtained economics (Hons) from Utkal University, BD from Serampore, MA in theology from the University of Oxford, and PhD from Birmingham University. Thirty-five years of his ordained ministry includes positions such as Presbyter of the Diocese of Cuttack, professor of theology at Serampore College, Bishop of the Church of North India's Diocese of the Eastern Himalayas, and general secretary of National Council of Churches in India.

**Brian Smith** was born in Edinburgh, and until 2011 was Bishop of Edinburgh. Before that, he held appointment as Bishop of Tonbridge in the Church of England. He was educated at the Edinburgh and Cambridge universities. He has held a number of posts in parochial and sector ministry, and taught in Oxford as senior tutor at Ripon College Cuddesdon. He is currently retired and lives in Edinburgh.

**Cameron J. Soulis** is a postulant for holy orders in the Diocese of Washington (DC), an MDiv student at Virginia Theological Seminary, and assists in the Center of Anglican Communion Studies at Virginia Theological Seminary. A former high school teacher, she has a BA from Hood College, Frederick, MD.

**The Rev. Dr. Leon Spencer**, an Episcopal priest in the United States, served the Anglican Church of Kenya as Dean of Studies at the Diocese of Nairobi's theological college, Trinity; administered an African Anglican theological education network, ANITEPAM; became the first dean of the School of Ministry of the Episcopal Diocese of North Carolina; and is on the adjunct faculty at the Wake Forest University Divinity School. He has been a consultant for the Diocese of Botswana on their plans for an Anglican house of studies, and was a part of an ANITEPAM deputation on post-genocide theological education to the Province of Rwanda. He investigated global partnerships in theological education for the Seminary Consultation on Mission. He earned a doctorate in African history from Syracuse University in the United States and taught African history at an historic African American degree institution, Talladega College, in Alabama, for 16 years. Much of his research and writing concerned the church and issues of justice in the colonial period, principally regarding Kenyan history. He discerned a calling to the ordained ministry, earning an MDiv (and later receiving an honorary DD) from Virginia Theological Seminary.

**Andrew Bennett Terry** holds a BA in religious studies from the College of William and Mary, a post-graduate certificate in ministry from Ripon College Cuddesdon, and an MDiv from Virginia Theological Seminary. He is a priest in the Diocese of Virginia serving at Richmond Hill, an ecumenical Christian community.

**Mark D. Thompson** serves in the Anglican Diocese of Sydney, and is principal of Moore Theological College. He is a member of the General Synod of the Anglican Church of Australia, and of the Synod and Standing Committee of the Diocese of Sydney. He attended GAFCON and was a member of its Theological Resource Group.

**The Rev. Marcus Throup** is British and has worked in the Anglican Church in North East Brazil since the year 2000. He has published books and articles in both Portuguese and English and is presently completing a PhD in New Testament Studies at the University of Nottingham.

**The Rev. Canon Noel Titus** has the degrees of BA and MA in theology (Durham), and MA and PhD in history (University of the West Indies). He was a lecturer, then principal, of Codrington College. He is a Fellow of the Royal Historical Society, and has served on various commissions/committees of the Diocese of Trinidad and Tobago, the Diocese of Barbados, and of the Province of the West Indies. He has given public lectures in various places including, in 2002, the inaugural Bray Lecture of the SPCK and the SPG. He has a number of publications to his name, and his current research is for a book to be titled *Religion and Toleration in 17th century Barbados*. He has served, including service as chair or president, on the Association of Caribbean Tertiary Institutions, the Caribbean Association of Theological Schools, and the Executive of the World Conference of Associations of Theological Institutions, a department of the World Council of Churches.

**Dr. Robert Tong** is deputy chancellor and a member of the Standing Committee of the Diocese of Sydney. Nationally, he is a member of the General Synod Standing Committee and the Church Law Commission. Internationally, he represented Australia on the Anglican Consultative Council, attended Lambeth 1998, GAFCON 2008, and the Global South Encounter 2010. His contribution to the Anglican Church was recognized by appointment as a Member of the Order of Australia.

**Janet Trisk** is rector of St. David's parish in Pietermaritzburg, South Africa, and an honorary lecturer at the University of Kwa Zulu Natal. She is editor of the *Journal of Theology for Southern Africa* and regional editor for the *Journal of Anglican Studies*. She holds degrees in law and theology from the KwaZulu Natal, Cape Town, and Rhodes universities. She has published in a variety of journals in her areas of interest, including identity, Anglicanism, and theological education.

**The Rev. Canon Samuel Van Culin** is canon ecumenist at the Washington National Cathedral, Washington, DC. A native of Honolulu, Hawaii, he is a graduate of Princeton University and the Virginia Theological Seminary. He was awarded an honorary Doctorate of Divinity from that institution in 1977. Canon Van Culin has worked as a priest in parishes in Honolulu, Hawaii, and Washington, DC. He has also spent much of his career working in mission organizations, including the Unit for National and World Mission at the Episcopal Church Center in New York City. In 1976, he was appointed executive for world mission for the Episcopal Church USA. Canon Van Culin served as secretary general of the Anglican Consultative Council from 1983 until 1994, and was secretary to the Lambeth Conference in 1988. In addition to many other honors, he is a canon of Canterbury Cathedral, England, and Saint George's Cathedral, Jerusalem.

**Emma Wild-Wood** is director of the Henry Martyn Centre for the Study of Mission and World Christianity. She teaches in the Cambridge Theological Federation and the Divinity Faculty of Cambridge University. Previously, she taught at the Anglican Theological College in Congo.

**Katherine L. Wood** is associate director of the Center for Anglican Communion Studies at Virginia Theological Seminary in Alexandria, VA, where she is responsible for the seminary's international and inter-religious programs. She has more than two decades of professional experience in international relations, educational exchange, and public affairs, and has held leadership positions in government, the arts, and higher education. Her research interests include the role of faith-based organizations and civil society in countries undergoing democratic transitions, religion and culture in international affairs, and multi-track diplomacy. She is a consultant for civil society organizations and serves on advisory commissions in higher education, the arts, and public broadcasting. She has a Master of Divinity degree *cum laude* from the Harvard University Divinity School, a Master of Music degree from Boston University, and a Bachelor of Arts in History from St. Olaf College in Northfield, MN.

**J. Robert Wright**, D.Phil (Oxon), is Professor Emeritus of Ecclesiastical History at the General Theological Seminary of the Episcopal Church, New York City, and a life fellow of the Royal Historical Society in London. In addition to the 17 books of which he is the author or editor, he has published over 200 articles that have appeared in various scholarly or popular journals in the historical, ecumenical, and liturgical fields. He has been awarded the Cross of St. Augustine of Canterbury by Archbishop Rowan Williams, as well as five honorary doctorates and five Orthodox patriarchal crosses. From 2000 to 2012, he served as historiographer of the Episcopal Church by appointment of the presiding bishop.

**Yang Guen-Seok** (PhD) is the president of (Anglican) SungKongHoe University in Seoul. He also teaches mission and biblical hermeneutics in the Post-graduate School of Theology in the university and serves as an assistant priest for the Anglican Cathedral of Seoul.

# Preface

*The Wiley-Blackwell Companion to the Anglican Communion* is a reference volume concerned with every aspect of the Anglican Communion. The volume results from a project supported and undertaken by two Episcopal seminaries in the United States. These two seminaries, Trinity School for Ministry in Ambridge, PA, and Virginia Theological Seminary in Alexandria, VA, incarnate the wide spectrum of theological perspectives in the diverse Anglican Communion.

Trinity School for Ministry sees itself as "a global center for Christian formation, producing outstanding leaders who can plant, renew and grow churches that make disciples of Jesus Christ." Trinity welcomes faculty and students who are "evangelical in faith, catholic in order, alive in the Holy Spirit and committed to mission." It is a seminary founded in 1976 to keep the Episcopal Church in the United States mindful of its evangelical heritage.

Virginia Theological Seminary seeks "to form men and women for leadership in the Episcopal Church." Founded in 1823, Virginia affirms the "richness of the orthodox Christian tradition" and recognizes that "Christians disagree." The seminary sees itself in the center of the Episcopal Church in the United States and keeps central the Holy Scriptures and the historic creeds as "Christians across the spectrum are welcome."

The editors and writers for *The Wiley-Blackwell Companion to the Anglican Communion* reflect the theological perspectives of Trinity School for Ministry and Virginia Theological Seminary and many others. Primates, bishops, academics, theologians, and church leaders lay and ordained have contributed to this reference volume. The contributors, like the seminaries which nurtured this project, are both conservative and liberal with many different positions on the "cultural war issues" which consume the worldwide Anglican Communion. The spectrum of writers reflects the reality that the Anglican Communion is in a season of disagreement and conflict. The biographies of the editors and writers reveal a group of distinguished leaders and scholars as rich and diverse as the Communion they serve in Christ's name.

It is worth being clear what this book is not. It is not a comprehensive survey of Anglican history. There is not, for example, an article on one of its greatest theologians, Richard Hooker. It is not focused exclusively on the immediate problems of the communion. It is much bigger than that. Instead, the editors hope to provide a definitive reference work on the communion – a reference work that captures the remarkable way that Anglicanism has adapted around the globe. In this book, you will read of missionaries, clergy, and laypeople who wanted to serve. And the result is a tradition which is both faithful and generous.

This reference volume is divided into four sections: History; Structures of the Communion; Provinces; and Themes (covering thematic topics such as theology, liturgy, inter-religious relations, and spirituality in the Communion). The section on history connects the Communion to Anglicanism and its theological moorings. The section on Communion structures gives careful consideration to the so-called instruments of unity which have been under great stress in a new century of Anglicanism. The section on Anglican provinces reveals a geography of faith which is worldwide and increasingly acculturated. The provinces are divided by continent, with a map for each area. Each contributor was encouraged to write about the history, organization, and contemporary challenges, and to anticipate the future a little. Each contributor was also given discretion to facilitate the distinctive nature of their province and therefore the distinctive content of their article. The final section provides the themes or discussion topics which keep Anglicans connected as the Christian faith is practiced in Anglican ways. The themes emerge from the intersection of theology and practice in a modern day Communion.

The Anglican Communion is the third largest family in Christendom, after the Roman Catholics and the Orthodox. It is a family with a rich history which is storied, yet troubled and complex. *The Wiley-Blackwell Companion to the Anglican Communion* will serve a very large family of Christians whose faith is seeking understanding in a myriad of cultural contexts.

Ian S. Markham, J. Barney Hawkins IV, Justyn Terry, and Leslie Nuñez Steffensen

# Acknowledgements

The editors are deeply grateful to all those who made this project possible. First and foremost, we are grateful to our contributors, and overwhelmed by their willingness to write for this book. We are very conscious of how busy and distinguished our contributors are, and it is great that they found time in their busy lives to write for this Companion. It reflects the significance and affection that our contributors have for the Anglican Communion.

Working with Wiley-Blackwell has been a delight. Rebecca Harkin, who commissioned the volume, gave sound advice and followed the project closely. At the copy editing and proof stage, the editors were extremely grateful to Aravind Kannankara and Fiona Screen for their professionalism and competence.

We are grateful to our internal editing team made up of Linda Hawkins and Cameron Soulis. As manuscripts arrived, they were responsible for working with the text to ensure consistency and clarity. Lesley Markham helped put the final manuscript together. Christine Faulstich did an outstanding job on the index.

Finally, we are grateful to our colleagues and friends, who understood that a project of this scale makes demands. We thank them for their understanding and support.

Ian S. Markham
J. Barney Hawkins IV
Justyn Terry
Leslie Nuñez Steffensen

PART I

# History

# CHAPTER 1

# Locating the Anglican Communion in the History of Anglicanism

## Gregory K. Cameron

## 1867 and All That

On September 24, 1867, at 11 o'clock in the morning, 76 bishops representing Anglican and Episcopal Churches across the globe gathered without great ceremony for a quiet said Service of Holy Communion in Lambeth Palace Chapel. They were keenly observed – from outside the Palace – by press and commentators alike, because this was the opening service of the first Lambeth Conference. This gathering of bishops marks the self-conscious birth of the Anglican Communion. Bringing together a college of bishops from around the world, the Conference was a step unprecedented outside the Roman Catholic Church in the second millennium of Christianity, as bishops of three traditions within Anglicanism were consciously gathered together in what we can now recognize as a "Christian World Communion."[1] The 76 constituted only just over half of the bishops who had been invited, but they had deliberately been invited as being in communion with the See of Canterbury, and they now began to understand themselves as belonging to one family.

Groundbreaking as it was, the calling of the first Lambeth Conference by Charles Longley, the 92nd Archbishop of Canterbury, represented the culmination of a process of self-understanding which had been developing rapidly over the previous 100 years. In the previous decades, many had articulated a vision intended to draw the growing diversity of Anglican Churches and dioceses into one fellowship and communion. In a seminal moment some 16 years before, for example, 17 bishops had processed together at the invitation of the then Archbishop of Canterbury, John Sumner, at a Jubilee

---

[1] This term has become widely accepted in the ecumenical world to describe those councils, federations, or gatherings of families of churches which share a common heritage or point of origin, namely, the World Methodist Council (1881), Lutheran World Federation (1947), and the Reformed Ecumenical Council (1946).

---

*The Wiley-Blackwell Companion to the Anglican Communion*, First Edition. Edited by Ian S. Markham, J. Barney Hawkins IV, Justyn Terry, and Leslie Nuñez Steffensen.
© 2013 John Wiley & Sons, Ltd. Published 2013 by John Wiley & Sons, Ltd.

Service to mark 150 years of the Society for the Propagation of the Gospel. It was an event which had been enthusiastically greeted at the time as the dawn of a new age and a harbinger of things to come. Henry Caswell, one of the first American clerics to take up a ministry in England, had taken inspiration from the Jubilee Service, seeing the presence of the bishops there as a trailblazer for "the 108 bishops of the Anglican Communion whom they may be considered to represent" (see Stephenson 1967, 43).

However, the opening of the first Lambeth Conference may be reliably taken as the first occasion when the Churches of the Anglican Communion – in the persons of their bishops at least – acted deliberately and consciously as a worldwide communion. The Archbishop of Canterbury presided, the Archbishops of Dublin and Armagh read the lessons, and the Bishop of Illinois preached the sermon. The first Lambeth Conference formalized a profound change in the consciousness of Anglicanism, acknowledging its evolution from an essentially British Protestantism into something which could identify itself as a global expression of the Church Catholic. Now, an episcopally ordered communion could claim to reach out as an equal partner to the Orthodox Churches and the episcopal Lutheran Churches of Scandinavia with a vision of an episcopally ordered global family to rival that of the Roman Catholic Church. As a result of the first Lambeth Conference, Anglicanism gained the confidence to become a global communion in which diversity of church life, adapted to local cultures and increasingly pluralistic in its expression, could flourish; an international movement in which the voices and expressions of church life far removed from the established Church of England could contribute to and shape a distinctive form of Christianity.

## Early Diversity: A Prehistory of the Anglican Communion, 1530–1776

While the Anglican Communion as a self-conscious entity belongs to the second half of the nineteenth century, its origins lie alongside the very roots and foundations of Anglicanism. It is possible to talk of two distinct periods in the history of Anglicanism prior to the emergence of the Anglican Communion, with each contributing philosophical and theological understandings to shape the later reality.

Between 1530 and 1776, Anglicans defended their faith as a national expression of Christian discipleship lived out in the realms of a monarch who ruled "by the grace of God," and who was therefore correctly acknowledged as the supreme head or governor of the church as well as the state in the territories subject to him.[2] The early architects of Anglicanism did not see themselves as establishing a new branch of Christianity, but

---

[2] Article 37 of the Articles of 1571: "The King's Majesty hath the chief power in this Realm of England, and other his Dominions, unto whom the chief Government of all Estates of this Realm, whether they be Ecclesiastical or Civil, in all causes doth appertain, and is not, nor ought to be, subject to any foreign Jurisdiction. Where we attribute to the King's Majesty the chief government, by which Titles we understand the minds of some slanderous folks to be offended; we give not our Princes the ministering either of God's Word, or of the Sacraments, the which thing the Injunctions also lately set forth by Elizabeth our Queen do most plainly testify; but that only prerogative, which we see to have been given always to all godly Princes in holy Scriptures by God himself; that is, that they should rule all estates and degrees committed to their charge by God, whether they be Ecclesiastical or Temporal, and restrain with the civil sword the stubborn and evil-doers."

as discharging their responsibility, under God and the monarch, to order church life in their nations in a way which conformed to the will of God expressed in Holy Scripture. It was essentially a political vision of Christian faith, justifiable to the rest of Christendom on the grounds that it was right for the British and Irish peoples, under a Christian monarch, to determine and establish for themselves the form of their church and worship.

Such an explicit nationalism, however, also meant that, from its very beginning, Anglicanism carried the seed of the idea that there should be autonomy for each church in each nation, governing itself in a way which was authentic for that people. This principle was from the first acknowledged quite naturally beyond the English realm. In the sixteenth century, the Protestant Churches of the European continent were natural partners in faith and life. In the seventeenth century, political necessity allowed established religion to take very different paths north and south of the English–Scottish border. Anglicanism has always understood itself as belonging to a wider family of churches rather than as constituting a self-sufficient church, and this was particularly true as it developed distinct and separate expressions of Christian life in the different nations of the British Isles. The theological principle that each people was competent to decide its own religion and liturgy formed part of the foundations of Anglicanism, and this bore fruit centuries later as national and regional churches were formed to sustain Anglicanism in very different environments.

Even in the earliest period, this diversity was apparent in the distinct Anglican Churches of the Atlantic Isles. The four dioceses of Wales were part of the Province of Canterbury, and the nation of Wales had been united to the Crown of England by the will of the Westminster Parliament in 1536. There was nevertheless a real sense that religious provision for the people of Wales should be adapted to their own language and culture. This contrasted with the way in which the institutions of civil government imposed English methods of state control. While the officers of the state were required to govern Wales through the medium of English, Welsh remained the language of faith. The Bible was rapidly translated by a series of Welsh scholars in the late sixteenth century, and a Welsh Prayer Book followed a decade later.[3] Care was taken to promote Welsh speakers to the episcopate in Wales,[4] and Anglicanism was adapted to an indigenous form.

Across the Irish Sea, the Church of Ireland was established by the Irish Parliament as a separate and independent church in 1536, and survived as such until Ireland was itself united politically with Great Britain in 1801, and a United Church of England and Ireland created. In 1615, the Church of Ireland created its own body of doctrine with the publication of the 104 Articles of Religion, which were more explicit in their Calvinism, even if the Thirty-Nine Articles were also adopted alongside them in 1634.

---

[3] The 1599 translation of the 1552 Book of Common Prayer, and the 1667 translation of the 1662 Book of Common Prayer.

[4] Richard Davies, who assisted in the translation of the New Testament, was Bishop of St. David's between 1561 and 1581. William Morgan, principal translator of the Bible into Welsh, was both Bishop of Llandaff (1595–1601) and Bishop of St. Asaph (1601–1604). He was succeeded by his fellow translator, Richard Parry, who was Bishop of St. Asaph between 1604 and 1622.

The translation of the Scriptures into Irish was promoted by the Irish episcopate between 1580 and 1680, although the episcopate came to be dominated increasingly by English or Scottish clergy. This independent life was extinguished with the political union of England and Ireland, but it remained as a clear precedent that Anglicanism was a faith capable of expression in more than one church.

The early chapters of the life of the Scottish Episcopal Church were much stormier, being bound up with the battle between the king and "covenanters" in the early seventeenth century. When the bishops refused to accept the legitimacy of King William III in the Revolution of 1688 and were ejected from the Church of Scotland, forming their own Scottish Episcopal Church, the Church of England was unsure whether its true partner in Scotland was the (Presbyterian) Church of Scotland or the tiny remaining Episcopal Church – a tension exacerbated by the severe legal penalties imposed on the nonjuring church. While there could be said to be at least two Anglican Churches in Great Britain, they were not regarded as being in communion. Nevertheless, it was the independent existence of a form of Anglicanism north of the English border which was ultimately to be a vital catalyst in the development of the Anglican Communion, since a distinct and separate hierarchy survived, not bound by the structures or doctrine of the larger church to the south. From its very beginnings, Anglicanism existed as a family of churches.

The seventeenth and eighteenth centuries saw the exploration of the globe by British soldiers, merchants, and adventurers, and the expansion of British rule across vast swathes of North America, Southern Africa, and India. However, there was no attempt at this stage to plant anything like autonomous churches in these lands. Rather, while the practice of Anglicanism was propagated, it was seen as an extension of the Church of England. Indeed, the Bishop of London was nominally the Bishop of all these territories and responsible for the deployment of clergy across the burgeoning Empire, sending out Commissaries as necessary to order the life of scattered congregations. It was often the mission societies that provided the links between the churches, and at the turn of the eighteenth century, societies such as the Society for the Promotion of Christian Knowledge (SPCK, founded in 1698) and the Society for the Propagation of the Gospel in Foreign Parts (SPG, founded in 1701) set the tone for links within Anglicanism in different parts of the globe. There were occasional attempts to provide bishops in North America – but politics on one side of the Atlantic or the other tended to frustrate all schemes (see Neill 1958, 222f).

The Church of England had become a global institution. Nonetheless, the pattern of the four home nations set the tone for an underlying acknowledgement of the importance of diversity, and seeds were sown which would sustain a more federated polity in the future. All this was to be radically realized when part of His Majesty's dominions asserted their independent status in the American Revolution.

## Parallel Tracks 1776–1867

Anglicanism arrived in North America with the first English settlers. Although the majority of settlers tended to be those seeking an escape from Anglican conformity, the pattern was far from uniform, and many settlers remained part of structures that understood themselves as part of the Church of England. Indeed, the second Charter of the London and Plymouth Virginia Company, granted by King James in 1606, specifically provided that the established religion of the new colony should be that of the same church established in England.

Even so, Anglican Churches in North America tended to be left to their own devices, apart from the occasional ordination of a cleric for service in North America, and the occasional Commissary acting in North America on behalf of the Bishop of London. Thomas Bray, a founding figure in both the SPCK and the SPG, was one such Commissary. He operated in Maryland by license of the Bishop of London, but spent little more than a year at the task before returning to London. More effective was James Blair, a Scotsman, who was appointed as Commissary in Virginia, and stuck to the task between 1689 and 1743. Anglican Churches in North America were, however, without the direct ministrations of bishops, and aspiring clergy would have to seek ordination from any bishop they could find back in the "old country." Thus, Samuel Seabury, who would become a pivotal player in forthcoming events, was deaconed by the Bishop of Lincoln and priested by the Bishop of Carlisle.

Following the American Revolution and the establishment of an independent United States of America, one of the chief challenges for Anglicans in North America was to determine their future and polity and to define their relationship with the Church of England. The decisions to be "Episcopal" and to seek a catholicity which maintained links with the Church of England was to have profound consequences for the future.

Early leaders of Anglicanism in the newly independent United States, such as William White, were keen to ensure that "as far as possible [the liturgy of the Episcopal Church] should conform to that of the Church of England" (see Stephenson 1967, 37). White advanced his views in books such as *The Case of the Episcopal Churches in the United States Considered*, published in 1782, and through meetings of the churches in New York and Pennsylvania congregational conventions. In October 1784, a particularly significant meeting was held prior to the first General Convention. In setting out their hopes for the church whose shape was to be decided at the General Convention, the meeting resolved thus: "4th. That the said Church shall maintain the doctrines of the gospel, now held by the Church of England, and shall adhere to the liturgy of the said Church, as far as shall be consistent with the American Revolution, and the constitutions of the respective states" (Resolution for an Episcopal Church in the United States of America, New York, 1784, recorded in William White, *Memoirs*, quoted in Evans and Wright 1991, 289).

Such arguments proved to be persuasive at the General Conventions of 1785 and 1786. By 1801, the General Convention had already met nine times (the second and third General Conventions both met in two separate sessions), and had shown itself ready to adopt the historic formularies of the Church of England, the Thirty-Nine Articles, as the basis of its own faith, although with appropriate revisions for a republic. In doctrine, therefore, the North American Episcopalians set out their faith in continuity with the Church of England. In discipline, as well, North American Anglicans chose to be episcopal in governance, and the first General Convention had made it clear that it was "requesting due episcopal succession" (see Perry 1874, 25) in its life, even if it took until 1789 to secure the establishment of a House of Bishops as a separate entity within the polity of the church.

The story leading to the ordination of Samuel Seabury as Bishop of Connecticut in 1784 is well known, but it is important to note that the refusal of the bishops of the Church of England to consecrate Seabury did not arise out of any inherent hostility to the idea, but because the English bishops were all too stuffily conscious that, as part of a church by law established, they were limited by that law and could only consecrate bishops by the sovereign's mandate and only then for service in his realms. The law was in fact quickly changed (the Consecration of Bishops Abroad Act, 1786, 26 George III, c.84), and the next two bishops for the United States (William White, Bishop of Pennsylvania, and Samuel Provoost, Bishop of New York) were ordained by the Archbishop of Canterbury acting with the Archbishop of York and the Bishop of Bath and Wells in Lambeth Palace Chapel in 1787. To these was added James Madison, consecrated at Lambeth Palace in 1790 as Bishop of Virginia. From this point on, the new Episcopal Church had its own line of bishops in historic succession.

By 1808, the House of Bishops could write a pastoral letter to the members of the new Protestant Episcopal Church that rehearsed a history referring to the "connections speedily created of our churches until then detached from one another, in terms which contemplated the perpetuating of the communion [a use of the term which was to become highly significant, *vide infra*], with all the distinguishing properties of the Church of England" (The Pastoral Letter of the House of Bishops [Baltimore, 1808] quoted in Evans and Wright 1991, 298).

Even so, from the first there was uncertainty in the English episcopate as to the implications of their participation in the consecration of bishops for the American Church. Although the authority to consecrate had been conferred by Act of Parliament, the act of consecration was not seen as constitutive of interchangeability of ministries. Consecration was seen as an exceptional action, and the legislation passed specifically excluded the possibility of bishops and clergy ordained for and in the Protestant Episcopal Church of the United States serving in His Majesty's domains.[5] When Bishop Hobart of New York was present at a consecration in Lambeth Palace Chapel in 1824, he was not permitted to participate in the actual laying on of hands (see Bosher 1962, 28, note 65). It took until 1840 and another Act of Parliament to introduce interchangeability of ministers (see Podmore 2005, 29). This uncertainty did not, however, focus solely on the American Church; even those ordained for work in the colonial church had been placed in a separate category from those ordained for ministry in England.[6]

---

[5] Section 3 of the Act: "no person or persons consecrated to the office of a bishop in the manner aforesaid nor any person or persons deriving their consecration from or under any of the bishops so consecrated nor any person or persons admitted to the office of deacon or priest by any bishop or bishops so consecrated shall be thereby enabled to exercise his or their office or offices within his Majesty's domains." Quoted in Chapter 3 of Colin Podmore's *Aspects of Anglican Identity*, 2005, p. 28.

[6] The Ordination for the Colonies Act, 1819: "in every such case it shall be distinctly stated in the letters of ordination of every person so admitted to holy orders that he has been ordained for the cure of souls in his Majesty's foreign possessions." Quoted in Evans and Wright, *The Anglican Tradition*, p. 302.

The story of Anglicanism in the early nineteenth century becomes, therefore, a story of three communions – the first centered on the now United Church of England and Ireland, and the second centered on the Protestant Episcopal Church, which soon began to spread its wings and commitment to overseas mission. The Scottish Episcopal Church constituted a third element in the growing families of churches. However, it remained the junior partner given its reduced numbers, and different writers of the period varied in their opinions as to whether there were now two or three branches of Anglicanism.

Having consecrated bishops for the United States, the Church of England woke up to the importance of providing episcopal ministry for the other territories in which Anglicanism now flourished and that remained part of the British Empire. The United States had not only created its own indigenous form of Anglicanism; it triggered the development of such structures right across the British Empire. Bishops were provided in sharp order for newly erected dioceses in Nova Scotia (1787), Quebec (1793), Calcutta (1814), Barbados and Jamaica (1824), Madras (1835), Australia (1836), Bombay (1837), and Newfoundland and Toronto (1839). The process was unsteady, and the strange nature of episcopal governance envisaged for these territories may be gauged from the fact that, between 1824 and 1836, the entire landmass of Australia had been seen to comprise merely part of the Archdeaconry of Calcutta in a diocese which spanned most of South East Asia and Australasia.

The Episcopal Church also became committed to vigorous overseas development, and a firmly grounded missionary impulse led to outreach across the globe. At first, their missionary society, founded in 1821, had an independent existence, but General Convention decided in 1835 that membership of the Church and the Missionary Society was to be identical: mission was the responsibility of the whole church. Indeed, the legal corporate name of the national body of the Episcopal Church remains to this day the "Domestic and Foreign Missionary Society of the Protestant Episcopal Church in the United States of America."

Having secured its own episcopate in the historic succession through the consecrations of 1784 and 1787, the Episcopal Church was confident in establishing the episcopate in other places where it now began to spread its wings, both within the United States and without. In 1834, James Otey was consecrated for the new Diocese of Tennessee, a state in which there was not a single existing Anglican congregation. In 1844, the Episcopal Church appointed Horatio Southgate as Bishop of the Dominions and Dependencies of the Sultan of Turkey, and William Boone as Bishop of China. In 1851, John Payne was consecrated to be Bishop of Cape Palmas and to lead the work of the Episcopal Church in Liberia.

There were indeed three families of Anglicans now spreading across the globe. However, how exactly were these three branches related?

## Envisioning an Anglican Communion

When William White published *The Case of the Episcopal Churches in the United States Considered* in 1782, he had argued persuasively that both the liturgy and the polity of the newly emerging Episcopal Church should continue to be modeled closely on the Church of England. White was insistent that there could be no question of any continuing subjection for the Episcopalians of the United States "to any spiritual jurisdiction connected with the temporal authority of a foreign state" (accessed on February 25, 2012, from the online version of the book at http://anglicanhistory.org/usa/wwhite/case1782.html). Although the North American Church would be independent like the new United States, it was intended that it would live in the closest association with the Church of England.

In the description that William White offers of his own church, White has to reach out to forge a new vocabulary for the way in which the emerging network of Anglican congregations were related to one another. It was in this context that White repeatedly referred to the network of congregations and parishes as "a communion," which seems to have functioned for White in the way in which the term "connexion" has functioned for Methodists. In other words, the continuing unity of the congregations of the various parishes depended on the "communion" they shared. Such a communion flowed from the common bonds of faith and polity. Woven into the foundation of the Episcopal Church was an understanding that it sustained its being through the communion it shared. William White's own usage of "communion" as the way to describe what binds Anglican Churches together forms the true backdrop to all later usage of this term.

The argument that the two "communions" or branches on both sides of the Atlantic did belong together was timely and welcome, at least as far as the leaders of the High Church movement in England were concerned. This movement, which had inherited the more Catholic approach of the Caroline divines, included a fierce anti-Erastianism and wanted to exalt the independent credentials of the Church of England over and against a view which treated it as a department of state entirely subject to parliamentary control. The recognition that there were Anglican Churches which stood outside the British political system and yet were able to be recognized as part of a wider communion with the Church of England, therefore, fitted the agenda of the High Church party. From 1790 onward, clergy, including, for example, the Bishop of St. Asaph, Samuel Horsley, agitated for increasing recognition of Anglicanism outside England as a step toward establishing Anglican ecclesiastical autonomy within the state. Horsley argued first for the relief of the clergy of the Scottish Episcopal Church, facing severe penalties under the law – a goal which was achieved in an Act of Parliament of 1792 – and then for the recognition and interchangeability of their orders. For such churchmen, the reality of an episcopally ordered and catholically minded church north of the border was far more important than an alliance of the two established churches: the Church of England and the Presbyterian Church of Scotland.

The journals and publications of the High Church movement now became the articulators of a new vision for Anglicanism – one which was international and comprehended the different branches of Anglican Churches. For the Church of England, the *Colonial Church Chronicle and Missionary Journal*, a newspaper published from 1847 under the editorship of Francis Fulford, a Devonshire cleric who was to go on to be the first Bishop of Montreal in 1850, was a primary organ by which the vision of a worldwide association of Anglican Churches was advanced. Its very first edition was entitled "The Extension of the Reformed Episcopal Church" (see Podmore 2005,

34), a name then being favored and advocated in some quarters for international Anglicanism.

One of the foremost advocates of a global vision of Anglicanism in England was the cleric Walter Farquhar Hook (1798–1875). In 1825, Hook preached the sermon at the Consecration of Matthew Luscombe in Stirling, Scotland. The bishops of the Scottish Episcopal Church were taking the lead once again, consecrating Luscombe, a Church of England cleric, as a missionary Bishop for Europe. Luscombe was the Anglican Chaplain in Paris and had been given a ministry of superintendence of European Anglican congregations. With the connivance of the then foreign secretary, George Canning, Luscombe followed the path pioneered by Seabury and received episcopal ordination from the Scottish bishops. In the sermon, Hook sought to defend and advance "the Catholicism of the Church of England and the other branches of the Episcopal Church" and spoke of a "reformed Catholic Church" held together by a bond of union which transcended human organization or state boundaries. This one church existed "in England, in Ireland, in presbyterian Scotland [and] republican America, in the regions of the East, and the islands of the West" (Hook 1825, 24).

Sixteen years later, Hook as Vicar of Leeds oversaw the construction of the new Parish Church, a magnificent neo-Gothic creation, and at its consecration ensured that his bishop (the then Bishop of Ripon, Charles Longley, who was to go on to call the first Lambeth Conference) was joined not only by the Metropolitan, the Archbishop of York, but also by the Bishop of Ross, Argyll and the Isles, and by the Bishop of New Jersey to represent the other two Anglican traditions.

Another of the chief advocates of association at this time was Henry Caswell. Caswell had been ordained for ministry in the United States. Arriving in the United Kingdom in 1843, Caswell had required a private Act of Parliament to be allowed to become an incumbent in the Church of England (see Podmore 2005, 28), but he never ceased to be a warm advocate of "America and the American Church," a phrase which became the title of his bestselling work published in 1839, and which was re-issued in a second edition in 1851. Caswell worked tirelessly in support of a vision of a worldwide family of churches. In the second edition, issued after the SPG Jubilee Service, Caswell spoke of his hopes for the future, that "They [the bishops] might devise measures for adapting the church to its enlarged sphere" (Caswell 1851, 395). For Caswell, the future of Anglicanism lay in Catholic order and a united episcopal college.

This movement in England was also supported across the Atlantic. William Whittingham, Bishop of Maryland, wrote in 1851 to urge a revision of the 1604 Canons of the Church of England in order to fit them for the present age and as something which could be recognized as Canon law "by the whole of the Churches of the two Communions" (letter of William Whittingham, Bishop of Maryland, quoted in Stephenson 1967, 49). By the middle of the nineteenth century, it became commonplace to refer to the growing family of Anglican and Episcopal Churches as "two communions," and talk of there being a single communion was not slow in following.

In 1843, John Jebb, another high-churchman, gave his book – an overview of the cycle of worship in the great Anglican ecclesial foundations of Britain and Ireland – the title *The Church Service of the United Church of England and Ireland, Being an Enquiry into the Liturgical Systems of the Cathedral and Collegiate Foundations of the Anglican*

*Communion*. In such an offhand way was the future name given birth, and it expressed what was a growing vision in the minds of many people. Although the book was confined to the foundations of the United Church, Jebb was consciously invoking the wider loyalties that were now being generated.

In 1847, Horatio Southgate, the Missionary Bishop of the Episcopal Church in the Dominions of the Sultan, writing to the *Colonial Church Chronicle* about his plans to record his presentations to explain Anglicanism to the Church of Constantinople, expressed himself in these terms: "I next spoke of each of the three branches of the Anglican Communion separately, namely, the English, the Scotch, and the American . . . I then combined the three under the title, 'The Anglican Branch of the Church of Christ'"(*Colonial Church Chronicle*, 1, 1847/1848, 396, quoted in Podmore 2005, 36).

These ideas were finding favor in high places. In 1851, when Archbishop Sumner invited the American bishops to the service to celebrate the sesquicentenary of the Society for the Propagation of the Gospel, he spoke of "the close communion binding the Churches of America and England" and of the "two branches" (see Stephenson 1967, 43) of Anglicanism. However, the Archbishop was already behind the curve of the developing language by which this "close communion" was now being described as one family and one global communion.

## The Emergent Communion and the Path to Lambeth

As ever in the history of Christianity, it was the mission field that generated urgent questions for the organization and corporate life of the church. China was the most obvious arena in which the two communions of Anglicanism came into competition with one another. Like Japan, China had turned against the presence of Christian missionaries toward the end of the seventeenth century, and the country remained closed to foreign mission until 1844. Almost as soon as this policy of exclusion was relaxed with the accession of the Daoguang Emperor, the Episcopal Church sent Bishop Boone to Shanghai to establish a Christian mission. This was followed by a similar mission from the Church of England, which established a See of Hong Kong in 1848, to be followed by another in Ningpo in 1872, and a third for North China in 1880. With two expanding missionary episcopates, the mission of the church would not be best served by two competing and mutually exclusive jurisdictions. In 1852, therefore, the General Convention of the Episcopal Church called for closer cooperation among the Anglican Churches and for the clergy domiciled in the other's jurisdictions to be allowed to minister in all the jurisdictions in China. It was clear that steps would have to be taken to bring the two branches closer together.

In 1852, the Canadian bishops met in Quebec as the Synod of the United Church of England and Ireland in Canada and passed resolutions which included in Article 12 their desire that "there should be no let or hindrance to a full and free communion between ourselves and the other Reformed Episcopal Churches" (see Stephenson 1967, 52).

Alongside these growing aspirations, others warmed to the idea that the best way forward would be a council of all the bishops in communion with the See of Canterbury. Bishop Hopkins of Vermont wrote to the Archbishop of Canterbury in 1851, speaking of the communion shared by "these two branches" and expressing the hope that "we shall prove the reality of that communion in the primitive style by meeting in the good old fashion of synodical action" (see Stephenson 1967, 43). Similarly, Bishop Whittingham of Maryland wrote a letter published in the *Colonial Church Chronicle* (July 1852, 32) to commend "An assemblage of the whole episcopate, either absolutely or representatively, in council, for organization as one branch of the Church Catholic."

Furthermore, as relations developed, and bishops from one family of Anglicanism visited another, old scruples were breaking down. In 1853, Bishop McIlvaine of Ohio was permitted to participate in the consecration of John Jackson as Bishop of Lincoln in the Church of England, contrary to the precedent set in 1824 when Bishop Hobart had been able to preach but not participate in the laying on of hands. As the potential for easier travel across the globe increased, so did the visits that were paid by bishops from one territory to another. This created a momentum for further change.

The immediate cause of the first Lambeth Conference lay, of course, in the objections that the conservatively minded bishops of North America had against the liberal attitudes of the African bishops. The challenges that Bishop John William Colenso, a Cornishman appointed by the Crown as Bishop of Natal in South Africa, provided to the church by his writings would be regarded as mild today, but they were enough to excite comment and outrage in the growing Anglican communities across the globe then. The Provincial Synod of the United Church of England and Ireland in Canada, meeting in Montreal in September 1865, addressed a letter to the Convocation of Canterbury following a motion introduced by the Bishop of Ontario. This suggested, as a direct response to the Colenso affair, that the growing relations between Anglican Churches across the globe "would be most effectually preserved and perpetuated if means could be adopted by which the members of our Anglican Communion in all quarters of the world should have a share in the deliberations for her welfare, and be permitted to have representation in one General Council of her members gathered from every land" (see Neill 1958, 360).

However, the questions arising from the mission fields also had a key role in persuading the bishops of the different churches to cooperate. In the event, the first two resolutions of the 1867 Conference and two others (four of the thirteen passed) would focus not on the Colenso affair, but on questions of the coordination of mission activity and the system of jurisdictions most fitting to support it. This meant that the participation of the bishops of all three Anglican traditions was vital. In February 1867, the letters of invitation went out with this crucial addition:

> both Houses of the Convocation of my Province have addressed to me their dutiful request that I would invite the attendance, not only of our Home and Colonial Bishops, but of all who are avowedly in communion with our Church. The same request was unanimously preferred to me at a numerous gathering of English, Irish, and Colonial Archbishops and Bishops recently assembled at Lambeth; at which – I rejoice to record

it – we had the counsel and concurrence of an eminent Bishop of the Church in the United States of America – the Bishop of Illinois (the Archbishop of Canterbury's Letter of Invitation to the 1867 Lambeth Conference, reproduced in Evans and Wright 1991, 329).

So it was that when 76 bishops of the Anglican Communion met in London in September 1867, the hopes and aspirations of many to see one communion which drew all the branches of Anglicanism together were realized. Of course, the Anglican Communion did not emerge fully formed from the 1867 Lambeth Conference. However, the value and impact of the Conference was considerable, and there was an immediate desire to meet again. By the time Archbishop Archibald Tait came to invite the bishops for the second Conference which was convoked in 1878, his letter of July 19, 1877 (quoted in Neill 1958, 363) was confidently addressed "to the Bishops of the Anglican Communion."

## Bibliography

Bosher, R. 1962. *The American Church and the Formation of the Anglican Communion.* Illinois: Seabury-Weston.

Buchanan, Colin. 2006. *Historical Dictionary of Anglicanism.* Lanham, MD; Toronto; Oxford: Scarecrow Press.

Caswell, Henry. 1839/1851. *America and the American Church,* 2nd Ed. London: Rivington, John and Charles Mozley.

*Colonial Church Chronicle and Missionary Journal* (1847–1874). London: various publishers.

Evans, G. R. and Wright, J. Robert. 1991. *The Anglican Tradition.* London: SPCK.

Garbett, Cyril. 1947. *The Claims of the Church of England.* London: Hodder & Stoughton.

Kaye, Bruce. 2008. *An Introduction to World Anglicanism.* Cambridge: Cambridge University Press.

Hook, W. F. 1825. *An Attempt to Demonstrate the Catholicism of the Church of England and the Other Branches of the Episcopal Church in a Sermon preached in the Episcopal Chapel at Stirling, on Sunday March XX, MDCCCXXV, at the Consecration of the Right Rev. Matthew Luscombe.* London.

Neill, Stephen. 1958. *Anglicanism.* London: Mowbrays.

Perry, William Stevens. 1874. *Journals of the General Conventions of the Protestant Episcopal Church, 1785–1835.* Claremont, NH: Claremont Manufacturing Company.

Podmore, Colin. 2005. *Aspects of Anglican Identity.* London: Church House Publishing.

Stephenson, Alan. 1967. *The First Lambeth Conference.* London: SPCK.

White, William. 1782. *The Case of the Episcopal Churches in the United States Considered.* Philadelphia: David Claypoole.

White, William. 1836. *Memoirs of the Protestant Episcopal Church in the United States of America,* 2nd Ed. New York: Swords, Stanford and Co.

Wilson, A. N. 2011. *The Elizabethans.* London: Hutchinson.

CHAPTER 2

# The History of Mission in the Anglican Communion

## Titus Presler

In this historical overview, Christian mission is understood as the phenomenon of sending and being sent by God and by communities over boundaries of difference in order to bear witness in word and deed to the initiative of God in Jesus Christ in the power of the Holy Spirit. This understanding includes major historical features of Anglican mission thought and activity and alludes to tensions that have been perceived among them: mission as God's initiative and mission as the church's activity; mission as working at home within a given people, and mission as working with groups and peoples different from the sending group; mission as proclamation in word and mission as service in deed; and mission as grounded in Trinitarian faith, and mission as humanitarian work in the service of God more broadly conceived.

This understanding of mission is more comprehensive than "the propagation of the Christian faith" (Cross and Livingstone 1997, s.v.), "Christian expansion" (Neill 1986, 9), or "converting people" in popular discourse, although propagation has been a central modality and conversion and church extension have been major results. It is narrower than contemporary "mission of God" theology, which encompasses the totality of God's vision for humanity and humanity's participation in that vision. It is more differentiated than a recent standard definition, "the dimension of Christian witness concerned with outreach to the world" (Johnson and Ross 2009, 327).

This survey focuses, therefore, on Anglicans' attempts to reach beyond their ethnic, socio-economic, linguistic, and national contexts to bear witness to the gospel through proclamation, service, and church formation – the New Testament trio of *kerygma*, *diakonia*, and *koinonia* – and prophetic justice. It includes major trends in mission thought that have influenced Anglican work. Initiatives from multiple centers are included, especially in view of Anglicanism's demographic shift to the Global South in the twentieth century.

*The Wiley-Blackwell Companion to the Anglican Communion*, First Edition. Edited by Ian S. Markham,
J. Barney Hawkins IV, Justyn Terry, and Leslie Nuñez Steffensen.
© 2013 John Wiley & Sons, Ltd. Published 2013 by John Wiley & Sons, Ltd.

The existence of the Anglican Communion in the twenty-first century – a community of 44 regional and national churches with over 86 million members in over 165 countries – is due to many and diverse initiatives in mission over the centuries. Mission is thus not an ancillary aspect of the world's third largest Christian communion but the central movement that brought the communion into being. This is true of all Christian communions, but it is nevertheless important to recognize at the outset.

The specifically Anglican mission story begins with the separation of the Church of England (CofE) from the Roman Catholic Church in 1536, but the CofE inherited a considerable mission tradition from its Celtic and Roman antecedents, both as a recipient and as an agent of mission. While little is known about Christianity in Britain during Roman times, it may be presumed to have been the fruit of mission, and later it was pushed to the margins by incoming pagan Saxons. The first great mission figure was Patrick, a Briton credited with the conversion of Ireland in the fifth century, and he appears to have been motivated both by divine call and, remarkably, love for the people whom he had served as a captive.

What became the mainstream of British Christianity began with the direct mission initiative of Pope Gregory I in 596 when he sent the Benedictine monk Augustine with companions to seek the conversion of the Saxons, beginning with Kent through King Ethelbert, whose wife Bertha was already a Christian. While far from determining the character of Anglican mission a thousand years later, three features of this successful effort were harbingers. Augustine's opening liturgical procession into Canterbury anticipated Anglicans' emphasis on patterned worship in mission. Second, Gregory's famous directive in 601 to adapt pagan sites and practices to Christian devotion rather than destroy them suggested a creative stance toward preexisting religions and cultures for mission in and from Britain, and it anticipated discussions of the scope and limits of syncretism and enculturation that have recurred in Anglican mission. Third, the strategy of reaching people through their monarchs, determined by hierarchical structures of the time, anticipated Anglican mission's frequent and ambiguous relationship with state power.

The tradition of Celtic missions from Ireland stimulated British Christianity to mission initiative during the early medieval period. Leaders included Willibrord (c. 658–739), who evangelized and established the church among the Frisians of present-day Holland and Belgium, and Boniface (c. 680–754), who did the same to dramatic effect in Germany. Also following the Celtic example, English missionaries founded monasteries in newly evangelized areas of Europe as stable sources of continuing mission energy and vision. Engaging a perennial issue in Western mission, English abbot Alcuin (730–804) strongly advised Charlemagne, the first emperor of the Franks, against the policy of military force he adopted in the Christianization of Saxons in Germany. The Crusades launched between 1096 and 1291 to recover Christian holy sites from Muslims in Palestine drew in English leaders – for instance, Robert of Normandy in the First Crusade and King Richard in the Third – and thereby involved English Christianity in a dark saga of Christian mission that has challenged Christian–Muslim relations to the present day.

While heir to exemplary models of mission vision, in the sixteenth and seventeenth centuries, the Church of England, now separated from Rome, shared with other

European Protestant bodies a lack of mission emphasis as the church sought to establish itself amid conflicts with Roman Catholic and Puritan rivals, both ecclesiastical and
political. Further, Henry VIII's suppression of monasteries, 1536–1540, removed the
traditional source of mission vision and personnel. As he defended the Elizabethan Settlement against Puritan detractors in *Of the Lawes of Ecclesiastical Politie* at the turn of
the seventeenth century, theologian Richard Hooker compared the religious authority
of the Christian monarch with that of a "heathen" monarch, but religio-political
controversies about internal religious conformity inhibited consideration of a call or
duty of a Christian monarch or society to present the gospel in non-Christian settings.
Notwithstanding the global initiative of Jesuits, Franciscans, and Dominicans in the
Roman Counter-Reformation, continental Calvinism's stress on the sovereignty of God
expressed through predestination encouraged among reformed churches a confidence
that non-Christian peoples' relation to Christ would be determined by God alone and
even that human initiative could be presumptuous.

Significant for Anglican mission was the English Reformation's emphasis on presenting scripture and liturgy in the vernacular of the people. Although Bible translator
William Tyndale was executed by the English church in 1536, Anglicans built on his
work to produce, among other translations, the Bishops' Bible of 1568 and the King
James Version of 1611, and had a major role in distributing the latter throughout the
world. The Book of Common Prayer (BCP) was premised on the commitment "that all
things shall be read and sung in the Church in the English Tongue." Alongside the rule
that "all the whole Realm shall have but one Use" were hints of the principle of localization for worship language and form. "[E]very country should use such Ceremonies as
they shall think best to the setting forth of God's honour and glory," declared Thomas
Cranmer in the 1549 BCP. The Preface to the 1662 BCP acknowledged that changes
could be made "according to the various exigency of times and occasions" and anticipated use in regions beyond England "for the baptizing of Natives in our Plantations,
and others converted to the Faith" (*Book of Common Prayer*, v–xiii).

English commerce and settlement outside Britain raised the possibility of mission
and engaged a relationship with colonialism that dogged Anglican mission into the
twentieth century. The perennial but not early perceived issue for mission from Western
colonial nations was the integrity of gospel presentation where it is made possible by
the projection of a nation's power through imperial rule and where the presenters
either are or may be perceived to be part of an imperial structure. The issue is sharpened
for the mission of all state-established churches such as the Church of England, where
the monarch is formally known as "Defender of the Faith."

The charter for the Virginia colony granted by King James I in 1606 commended
the adventurers' desire "in propagating of Christian Religion to such People, as yet live
in Darkness and miserable Ignorance of the true Knowledge and Worship of God, and
may in time bring the Infidels and Savages, living in those Parts, to human Civility, and
to a settled and quiet Government" (Eliot 1910, 50). In this formulation, a religious
mandate to present Christian truth was accompanied by a comparably urgent cultural
mandate to "civilize" other peoples, the latter premised on an assumption of European
cultural superiority that recurred throughout the mission history of British and North
American Anglicans. While widely celebrated, the conversion of Pocahontas in 1613

occurred while the colonists held her hostage, and their relations with the Powhatan Indians were dominated by intermittent warfare in which forcible conversion was an accepted motive, albeit secondary to rivalry over land.

Chartered by Queen Elizabeth I in 1600, the East India Company gradually became an instrument of British imperialism in India, first in fact and later in law. Its chaplains served the expatriate community, were occasionally encouraged to present Christian faith to Indians, and some missionaries were employed as chaplains. In a significant counterpoint of the colonial period, however, the company generally sought, with varying success until its dissolution in 1858, to prevent or inhibit missionary work in India in the interest of avoiding cultural disturbance that could, in turn, destabilize imperial rule. Churches and mission societies opposed the policy, and the advocacy of evangelicals secured greater freedom through parliamentary measures in 1814 and 1833. Queen Victoria's 1858 proclamation of religious liberty in India was important as an aspiration of colonial and government policy, though it could not at once satisfy the grievances of either the opponents or advocates of mission in India and elsewhere:

> Firmly relying ourselves on the truth of Christianity, and acknowledging with gratitude the solace of religion, we disclaim alike the right and desire to impose our convictions on any of our subjects. We declare it to be our royal will and pleasure that none be in anywise favoured, none molested or disquieted, by reason of their religious faith or observances, but that all alike shall enjoy the equal and impartial protection of the law; and we do strictly charge and enjoin all those who may be in authority under us that they abstain from all interference with the religious belief or worship of any of our subjects on pain of our highest displeasure. (*Annual Register* 1858, 258–9)

As concern for stability functioned earlier, so later the growing ecclesial diversity of England inhibited the established church's mission activity because church legislation required approval from a denominationally diverse Parliament unlikely to sponsor specifically Anglican initiatives in mission. The bulk of CofE mission initiative therefore was undertaken by voluntary societies of concerned individuals. Interest in BCP and literature dissemination lay behind the founding by Thomas Bray (1656–1730) of the Society for Promoting Christian Knowledge (SPCK) in 1698. Initially concerned with neglected Anglican clergy in the American colonies, SPCK grew to become a major publisher and book distributor, ultimately facilitating over 200 translations of various BCP editions into other languages. The second SPCK was founded in India in 1710, and today it is the most prolific of the autonomous SPCK houses – others being in Australia, Ireland, New Zealand, and the United States – as it publishes about 75 titles a year to support the mission of Indian churches.

The Society for the Propagation of the Gospel in Foreign Parts (SPG) was founded in 1701, also at the initiative of Thomas Bray, both to minister to Britons overseas and to evangelize non-Christians living under the British crown. It became a major missionary-sending agency with an initial focus on the American colonies, where it worked with American Indians and African Americans and founded some of the oldest parishes of what is now the Episcopal Church. Gradually, its work spread: for instance, to the

West Indies in 1712, Ghana in 1751, Canada in 1759, Australia in 1793, and India and South Africa in 1821. In accord with its royal charter, SPG initiative tended to follow the establishment of British commercial and imperial presence.

SPG's handling of a 1710 bequest of two sugar plantations in Barbados illustrates the complicit side of Anglican mission's relation to colonialism. Christopher Codrington willed that SPG establish a missionary college on the land and that the resident 300 slaves be provided religious instruction as their plantation labor supported the college. The resulting grammar school and later Codrington College is the oldest continuing Anglican educational institution in the Western hemisphere, but it never focused on missionary education, though today it is the seminary of the Anglican Church of the West Indies. Religious instruction for the slaves was weak and intermittent, and SPG did not significantly challenge the institution of slavery or its own participation in it at Codrington right up to the abolition of slavery in the British Empire in 1834.

In 1965, SPG merged with the Universities Mission to Central Africa (UMCA), the society founded in 1857 through the initiative of David Livingstone and focused on Nyasaland (Malawi today), and the two became the United Society for the Propagation of the Gospel (USPG, renamed simply "Us" in 2012). Influenced by the Anglo-Catholic revival of the nineteenth century, SPG's promotion of High Church style in such areas as the Caribbean and southern Africa nurtured liturgical ceremonial, highlighted the missional role of bishops, slowed affirmation of women's ordination, and encouraged comparative receptivity in the communion's recent sexuality debates.

The nineteenth-century blossoming of CofE mission work was energized by the founding of more voluntary societies, the fruit of a general evangelical awakening in the eighteenth century. A group of evangelicals known as the Clapham Sect founded the Church Missionary Society (CMS) in 1799. Best known among them was William Wilberforce, who as a member of Parliament was active in the abolition of the slave trade and slavery itself in the empire. The CMS both addressed such injustices in the international system and pursued world evangelization with a vision of the inauguration of God's kingdom in a coming millennial age. CMS sought to initiate work outside the British colonial structure and so express the universality of mission. It worked extensively in China, Japan, Persia, the Middle East, India, and west and east Africa. While lamenting the imperial circumstances of the 1842 "unequal" Nanking Treaty that concluded the Opium War, CMS and the Episcopal Church USA joined numerous other bodies in using the treaty to initiate work in China and thereby incurred hostility to Christian mission that ultimately contributed to the Maoist suppression of mission churches in the mid-twentieth century. While initially distrusted as an autonomous society, by the mid-1800s CMS had the support of numerous bishops and was infusing world mission into the ethos of the CofE. CMS promoted a Low Church style, so that Anglicans in areas of CMS work such as east Africa tend to be more revivalist, less eucharistic, readier to affirm women's ordination, and more opposed to the acceptance of homosexuality.

The major policy-maker in nineteenth-century CofE mission was Henry Venn, who directed CMS from 1841 to 1872. His principles for missionaries stressed preaching the cross of Christ, learning local languages, translating scripture into vernaculars, providing schools, and cooperating with Protestant denominations. Aware of the twin perils of missionary paternalism and indigenous dependency, Venn promoted the goal of "establishing a Native Church upon the principles of self-support, self-government, and self-extension," which continues to be popular today and was influential in China's Three-Self Patriotic Movement. Venn recommended that

> It is important ever to keep in view what has been happily termed "the Euthanasia of a Mission" where the Missionary is surrounded by well-trained Native congregations under Native Pastors, when he gradually and wisely abridges his own labours, and relaxes his superintendence over the Pastors till they are able to sustain their own Christian ordinances, and the District ceases to be a Missionary field, and passes into Christian parishes under the constituted ecclesiastical authorities. (Warren 1971, 63)

Venn emphasized that authentic church life among newly evangelized peoples would express their cultural particularities and should not be expected to reproduce the church life of missionaries. Such principles prompted CMS to initiate in 1864 the first Anglican mission venture to be directed by a non-European bishop, Samuel Adjai Crowther, a former slave, in the Niger River delta in eastern Nigeria. In the imperial "Scramble for Africa" that commenced in 1885, however, Venn's successors were not as open to indigenous leadership, and the three bishops who followed Crowther after his death in 1891 were Europeans. Indigenization of leadership became an issue for all Western mission organizations, especially in the twentieth century as they were slow to train leaders and reluctant to cede leadership even when indigenous capacity was clear. While most missionaries affirmed "the euthanasia of a mission" in principle, reasons were usually found to extend missionaries' superintendence indefinitely, as pointed out by SPG missionary Roland Allen in his 1912 critique, *Missionary Methods: St. Paul's or Ours?* (84–93).

Beyond the initial three major Anglican societies, a proliferation of voluntary societies for specific mission emphases at home in Britain and abroad testified to the mutual missional stimulation of domestic and international concern. Anglicans comprised half of the committee of 30 for the interdenominational British and Foreign Bible Society, founded in 1804, which worked both at home and abroad, as did the Home and Colonial School Society. Societies with a domestic mission focus included, among many others, the Church Pastoral Aid Society, the National Society for Promoting the Education of the Poor, the Church of England Sunday School Institute, and the London Diocesan Home Mission. Groups focused abroad included, among many others, the Colonial and Continental Church Society (CCCS), founded in 1823 and now the Intercontinental Church Society; South American Missionary Society (SAMS), established in 1844 and merged with CMS in 2010; the London Society for Promoting Christianity amongst the Jews; the Colonial Bishoprics' Fund; the Mackenzie Memorial Mission to Zululand; the Association for the Furtherance of Christianity in Egypt; and the Church of England Zenana Missionary Society (CEZMS). The scale of these efforts may be gauged by the fact that, in 1884, four years after its founding, the Zenana society had 100 women missionaries, 1,785 so-called harems under visitation, and over 2,000 pupils in what is now India and Pakistan. Evangelism and education were its main emphases, the latter empowering women quite

beyond the categories of benevolence and charity. Clearly, ordinary Anglicans understood that mission was relevant both at home and abroad as they reached beyond
their communities to engage others with proclamation, service, church formation,
and justice.

Many Anglican congregations in the American colonies were founded by, and continued to benefit from, the ministrations of SPG and SPCK. During the revolutionary
period, Anglicans' identity as members of the state-established Church of England was
a liability that prompted loyalty questions, the abandonment of some churches, and
the emigration of many Anglicans to Canada or England. For the few who remained
after the Revolutionary War, founding the Episcopal Church USA as an autonomous
body, not governed from England and yet in full communion with the Archbishop of
Canterbury, was a survival strategy motivated by desire both to maintain Anglican
identity and to be accepted as loyal citizens of the new United States. This American
innovation formed the first non-British province of what came to be known as the
Anglican Communion and developed the missionally important concept of Anglican
Christianity outside Britain free of colonial ties. The consecration of its first bishop in
1784 was followed by an act of Parliament in 1786 that authorized the consecration
in England of bishops for dioceses abroad.

As with the post-Reformation Church of England, stabilizing its existence as a church
in a hostile environment, not mission, was the Episcopal Church's initial preoccupation.
Episcopalians adapted the Book of Common Prayer to their situation, organized dioceses and established a more centralized polity modeled on the United States Congress.
The 1792 General Convention adopted a short-lived plan to direct and raise funds "for
supporting missionaries to preach the Gospel on the frontiers," and most of the early
frontier work was carried out by dioceses. During his episcopate in New York, for
instance, John Henry Hobart (1775–1830) increased the number of diocesan missionaries from two to fifty, planted a church in almost every town, and began work among
the Oneida Indians. The global horizon was highlighted by the founding of Protestant
mission societies and by CMS, which from 1815 on urged the Episcopal Church to
promote world mission, termed "the advancement of the Kingdom of Christ among the
heathen."

Establishment of the Domestic and Foreign Missionary Society (DFMS) by the 1821
General Convention combined the voluntary and centralized modes of missionary initiative, for it was an official organ of the church, but members paid voluntary dues.
After this version faltered, the 1835 General Convention amended the DFMS constitution to read, "The Society shall be considered as comprehending all persons who are
members of this Church" (Constitution 1835, 129). The theological basis was articulated by George Washington Doane:

> In an address of great power, he argued "that by the original constitution of Christ, the
> Church as the Church, was the one great Missionary Society; and the Apostles, and the
> Bishops, their successors, his perpetual trustees; and this great trust could not, and should
> never be divided or deputed." The duty, he maintained, to support the Church in preaching
> the Gospel to every creature, was one which passed on *every Christian by terms of his bap-*
> *tismal vow,* and from which he could never be absolved. (Stowe 1935, 176)

In a move facilitated by centralized Episcopal polity, mission was thus institutionalized as defining the nature of the church and the vocation of all its members, rather than as a function of the voluntary inclinations of especially interested persons. Moreover, the 1835 DFMS constitution declared the unity of the mission field:

> For the guidance of the Committees [for Domestic Missions and for Foreign Missions] it is declared that the missionary field is always to be regarded as one, the world – the terms domestic and foreign being understood as terms of locality adopted for convenience. *Domestic* missions are those which are established *within*, and *foreign* missions are those that are established *without*, the territory of the United States. (Constitution 1835, 131)

The 1835 convention went on to institute the office of missionary bishop, which, Doane explained,

> . . . is a bishop *sent forth* by the Church, *not sought for* of the Church; going before to organize the Church, not waiting till the Church has partially been organized; a leader not a follower, in the march of the Redeemer's conquering and triumphant Gospel . . . sent by the Church, even as the Church is sent by Christ. (Stowe 1935, 171)

While CMS held that the episcopate should be the culmination, not the foundation, of church growth and that the first bishop in a newly evangelized area should be an indigenous Christian, not a missionary, the Episcopal stance was premised on a High Church view that the presence of a bishop meant that the church itself was present and that a bishop therefore had apostolic responsibility to preach and grow the church. Jackson Kemper was appointed bishop for the Midwest in 1835, and William Boone was elected in 1844 as Bishop of "Amoy and Other Parts of China," where Episcopal missionaries had arrived in 1835. Liberia and Japan were the other major areas of nineteenth-century Episcopal mission. Contributions for international mission were voluntary until the twentieth century, so numbers of missionaries were not large, but women played a major role in funding mission throughout the century. The 1871 formation of the Women's Auxiliary to the Board of Missions focused their efforts, which gained strength with the leadership of Mary Emery Twing and Julia Chester Emery, and by 1898 the Auxiliary was funding 40 women missionaries, both domestic and foreign.

As the United States became an international power after the Spanish–American War and World War I, Episcopal mission in the Caribbean and Central and South America accelerated the establishment of missionary districts, then Episcopal missionary dioceses with missionary bishops in much of the region and in Taiwan and the Philippines. CofE chaplaincies were often absorbed, but dioceses in what is now the Province of the Southern Cone of South America were established by the CofE through SAMS. Indigenous peoples were reached with the gospel – Charles Henry Brent's work among Filipino hill tribes being an outstanding example – but Episcopal mission soon experienced the weight of imperial entanglement, especially as the United States' economic dominance grew and the US military undertook numerous interventions and occupations.

Canadian evangelicals, dioceses, and internal provinces formed several mission societies in the nineteenth century while SPG and CMS continued substantial work in the country. In 1902, the church's General Synod established the centralized Missionary Society of the Church of England in Canada, which incorporated the provincial and evangelical societies. It oversaw the church's residential schools for First Nations children, where abuses became controversial at the end of the twentieth century, and initiated work in India, China, and Japan. In Australia, CMS chaplain Samuel Marsden (1765–1838) oversaw the establishment of a CMS Auxiliary in Sydney in 1825. Although CMS mission among Aboriginal people had only limited success, CMS associations were founded in various parts of the country, and the groups' first international missionary, Helen Philips, went to Ceylon in 1892. In 1916, the CMS of Australia was formed as an indigenous society, and it continued work in China, India, Palestine, Iran, Tanganyika, and North Australia.

Meanwhile, beginning with the authorization of overseas dioceses by Parliament in 1786, the CofE institutionalized the mission presence of the church by establishing dioceses and appointing bishops around the world. Nova Scotia in 1787 was the first such diocese, followed in 1814 by Calcutta, where Thomas Middleton and Reginald Heber, the first two bishops, provided outstanding leadership. The dioceses of Jamaica and Barbados were established in 1824; Sydney in 1836; New Zealand and Jerusalem in 1841; Gibraltar in 1842; Cape Town in 1847, where the first bishop, Robert Gray, was a formidable controversialist; Victoria, for Hong Kong, in 1849; Central Africa in 1861, where Charles Mackenzie, William Tozer, and Edward Steele were notable bishops under the auspices of the UMCA; North China in 1872; and Eastern Equatorial Africa in 1884, where James Hannington and his companions were martyred.

In some localities such as Gibraltar, Hong Kong, and Jerusalem, Anglican ministry began as chaplaincy to resident expatriates and then expanded to reach local populations. In others such as Uganda, Central Africa, and Mashonaland, where George Knight-Bruce visited chiefs prior to the Rhodesian settlement, pioneering bishops worked directly with indigenous people. During the second half of the nineteenth century, Anglicanism was disestablished in most colonies where it had been the state church, and complex and piecemeal measures gradually fixed the principle that Anglican churches outside of Britain were self-governing. Nevertheless, mission tensions inherent in the colonial dispensation persisted, for instance in the work of New Zealand's first bishop, George Augustus Selwyn, who dedicated himself to Maori work and in the long-running New Zealand Wars between the Maori and the colonial government sought to minister to both sides – and elicited both praise and criticism from each.

Generally, Anglican growth resulted in exponential diocesan multiplication, so that by 1892 the Colonial Bishoprics' Council could report 77 overseas dioceses. Sample membership figures from that decade include Calcutta, 75,000; Cape Town, 46,360; Colombo, 23,000; Jamaica, 200,000; Japan, 2,500; Madagascar, 25,000; mid-China, 1,065; Madras, 128,000; Melbourne, 283,000; Newfoundland, 69,000; and Rangoon, 10,386. In Japan, simultaneous Anglican mission efforts from the United States, Britain, and Canada resulted in confusion that was clarified by their union as Nippon Sei Ko Kai, the Holy Catholic Church of Japan, in 1887. The 76 bishops who gathered for the first Lambeth Conference of bishops in 1867 were convened substantially to address missional concerns raised by Natal Bishop John Colenso's accommodating response to African polygamy and by his liberal theology and biblical exegesis, which he argued was vital for credible gospel presentation to non-Christians.

Anglican missionaries were a considerable proportion of the global total at the end of the nineteenth century. In 1896, SPG counted 782 missionaries (including 170 "natives" and 63 single women); CMS, 903 (including 93 lay, 274 wives, and 192 single women); CCCS, 266; SAMS, 41; UMCA, 82; CEZMS, 170; and there were others. The total under the auspices of British Anglicans, about 2,500, was about one-third the total for all of Europe, and the money contributed totaled about £750,000 (equivalent to about £75 million today). In North America, by contrast, DFMS supported 103 missionaries in 1899, a total that increased to 371 in 1919, and a peak of 486 in 1933; whereas in 1896 the Congregationalists supported 557, the Methodists 600, and the Presbyterians 623.

Language acquisition was a priority for many Anglican missionaries. In some contexts, they were among those who committed languages to writing for the first time. Whether working with small language groups or in huge populations, many undertook to translate the Bible and BCP into other languages in the Americas, Africa, Asia, and the Pacific. Henry Martyn (1771–1812), the first English CMS missionary, translated the New Testament and BCP into Hindi and Persian. Joseph Schereshewsky (1831–1906), originally a Lithuanian Jew, became the Bishop of Shanghai as an Episcopalian and translated the Bible and BCP into Mandarin and Wenli. Making scripture accessible in local languages affirmed the dignity of cultures, stimulated indigenous theological reflection on the interchange between religion and culture, and deepened missionaries' understanding of their contexts.

Revived by the Anglo-Catholic movement of the mid-nineteenth century, Anglican religious orders reengaged the missional emphasis of their medieval forebears. The Society of St. John the Evangelist, founded in 1866 near Oxford, had significant work in South Africa, and the American house had for some time a base in Japan. The American branch of the Society of St. Margaret, founded in 1873, has maintained a number of well-known ministries in Haiti since 1927. Founded in 1884 in the state of New York, the Order of the Holy Cross had missionaries in Liberia, and its recently established house in Grahamstown, South Africa, has founded a school. The South African work of the Community of the Resurrection in Mirfield, England, counted among its members Trevor Huddleston (1913–1998), who was an important influence for Desmond Tutu (1931–), the first African Archbishop of Cape Town and winner of the Nobel Peace Prize for anti-apartheid work. New Anglican orders in various parts of the world are strongly missional through evangelism, orphanages, schools, and healthcare – for instance, the Community of the Holy Transfiguration, a women's order founded at Bonda in Zimbabwe.

In most geographical areas, the evangelization that resulted in the Anglican Communion was the work of indigenous people who, having become Christian, then shared their faith with others either through vocations as evangelists, catechists, and teachers, or in the run of daily life. Missionaries and their supporting societies catalyzed this development through initial proclamation and the establishment of churches, schools, and hospitals, but their relatively small numbers in any period cannot account for the exponential Anglican growth as a proportion of populations in Africa and, to a lesser extent, Asia and Latin America. The example of the 32 young men martyred for their faith in the court of the king of Buganda in 1886 prompted many conversions. The mass movements into mission churches that occurred on the Indian subcontinent in the later decades of the nineteenth century and the early decades of the twentieth were energized by indigenous mission enthusiasts, largely among the low castes for whom the gospel signaled social as well as spiritual liberation. Marveling at a popular movement into Anglicanism in eastern Rhodesia in the early 1900s, a missionary wrote, "The movement is obviously of God: we can do, and have done, extraordinarily little" (Broderick 1953, 269–73). Assisted by a twentieth-century revival movement of allnight *pungwe* vigils, today's Zimbabwean celebrations of the martyrdom of catechist Bernard Mizeki in 1896 are the world's largest annual Anglican gatherings. The East African Revival, the *Balokole* movement, was energized by Semyoni Nsibambi and others in the 1920s in Rwanda, and it spread over the next quarter century in Uganda, Kenya, and Tanzania, strengthening Anglican and other churches and nurturing leaders such as Festo Kivengere (1919–1988), who became a global evangelist as Bishop of Kigezi in Uganda.

There were many indigenous catalysts apart from mass movements. The mission societies' "Bible Women" served as evangelists and teachers, often preaching and baptizing as well. Damari Sagatwa (1875–1960), an outstanding example in central Tanzania, served with CMS but illustrated that such affiliation simply supported an essentially indigenous mission impulse. Muslim scholar Imad-ud-din became a Christian in 1866 and then was a prominent preacher and Christian apologist in India. An Afghan, Fazl Haqq, served as evangelist to Nuristan in the mountains of the Hindu Kush. Pandita Ramabai (1858–1922) converted from Brahmanic Hinduism, served widowed women, and became a social reformer known in both India and the West. The site of the death of Manche Masemola, a 14-year-old killed by her parents for her faith in 1928 in South Africa's Sekhukuneland, draws pilgrims to this day. Lucien Tapiedi, a catechist killed by Japanese soldiers in Papua New Guinea in 1942, is now virtually the patron saint of Anglicans in that country.

The founding of the Indian Missionary Society in south India in 1903 was especially notable, for today the group supports over 650 evangelistic and church-planting missionaries in 20 Indian states, especially in the north. Its principal founder was Vedanayakam Samuel Azariah (1874–1945), who in 1912 became the first Indian bishop, serving the new Diocese of Dornakal. He and others began the transition to the entirely indigenous presbyterate and episcopate typical of Anglicanism today. In 1918, Tsae Seng Sing, whose father was the first Chinese Anglican clergyperson, became assistant bishop in the Diocese of Chekiang. In 1923, Joseph Sakunoshin Motoda, with a doctorate from the University of Pennsylvania, became the Bishop of Tokyo.

In keeping with SPG's 1706 instructions to missionaries "that they encourage the setting up of Schools for the teaching of Children," Anglican mission, like that of other communions, emphasized education in all locales, beginning with primary and then secondary schools, which both promoted general learning and assisted evangelization through religious instruction of the young. Local languages typically were the medium of instruction at the primary level, and English was taught in preparation for that being the medium at the secondary level. Recognizing that the churches' schools were fulfilling a governmental responsibility, colonial administrations in many places made operational subsidies available that buttressed the churches' schools but provoked church–state conflict amid rising nationalist resistance to colonialism in Africa and Asia in the twentieth century.

Anglican higher education often focused on preparation of clergy, such as at Bishop's College, Calcutta, established in 1820, and continuing as a seminary today among scores of Anglican seminaries worldwide. Some seminaries expanded to become universities: St. Michael's Theological Institute, founded in Korea in 1923, became Sungkonghoe University in 1992; and Bishop Tucker Theological College in Uganda, founded in 1913, became Uganda Christian University in 1997. Other institutions were founded with a range of disciplines, for example, Boone University, Wuchang, China, 1871; Rikkyo University, Tokyo, 1874; St. John's University, Shanghai, 1879, reconstituted in Taiwan in 1967; Cuttington College, Liberia, 1889, to which a seminary was added in 1897; Edwardes College, Peshawar, 1900; and a large number of colleges in India. Anglican institutions typically maintained high standards and contributed to their churches' mission directly through education and indirectly through scholarship and the public standing of their faculties. Today, the Colleges and Universities of the Anglican Communion (CUAC) network has 125 member institutions.

As with other mission churches, medical work was the third major institutional focus of Anglican mission, with clinics and hospitals too numerous to name established throughout the world. Viewed as an expression of Christ's compassion and healing ministry, medical work was valued also for its evangelistic potential, as expressed by Florence Nightingale Main from CMS Hospital, Hangchow, China, in 1890:

> There have been many opportunities for "telling out among the heathen that the Lord is King"; and we feel very grateful for the willing reception the good news has had from them. . . . One of the advantages of the hospital is that it brings us into contact with rich and poor alike; it gives us an entrance into the houses of the better classes which many others find difficult to obtain; and it helps us to retain our hold of the old patients who have given evidence of their interest in the Gospel. (Main 1890, 69)

Such focus on gospel proclamation was evident in the first missionary conference for the Anglican Communion as a whole, held in London in 1894, at which the topics illustrated how mission was conceptualized: "The Missionary's Vocation and Training"; "The Religions to be Dealt With," focused on Asia's major religions and Judaism, with minor notice of African religions; "The Presentation of Christianity"; "Problems to be Solved," arranged regionally but with polygamy addressed separately; "Dangers to be Avoided," which included "Undue Introduction of Western Ways"; "Methods to be Employed," citing family life, education and industry, medicine, and translation; "The Building Up of the Church," which included church organization and native agency; "Relations of Mission to the Church at Home"; and a "Women's Section" which addressed similar topics from a female perspective (Spottiswoode 1894, ix–xvi). The watchword of the Student Volunteer Movement, "The Evangelization of the World in

This Generation," similarly underlay the pivotal ecumenical World Missionary Conference of 1910 in Edinburgh, in which many Anglicans participated.

The religious and cultural self-confidence that supported Western mission's emphasis on evangelization and "civilization" was shaken, however, by further events and intellectual developments in the twentieth century, mission's Century of Self-Criticism. Appreciation of other religions was growing both through missionaries' experience on the ground and through the inquiries of such theologians as Anglican F. D. Maurice, who declared that there must be light in other religions, or they could not persist, and suggested that Christ was at work in other religions and cultures (Maurice 1854, 32, 195–6). As with religious competition, denominational competition among churches in mission was critiqued as hindering Christian witness. The mutual destruction wrought by so-called Christian nations in World War I brought the supposed superiority of Western religion and civilization into question. Long-festering skepticism about the benefits and justice of Western colonial projects was sharpened by the growing strength of independence movements such as the Indian National Congress, founded in 1885; the All India Muslim League, 1906; the African National Congress in South Africa, 1912; and several similar groups in Kenya in the 1920s. Insofar as Anglican mission benefited from British and American imperialism and from Canadian and Australian spheres of influence, and sometimes actively cooperated with them, it was criticized both inside and outside the churches. The growing maturity of the "younger churches" in numerical and institutional strength, leadership capacity, and theological sophistication elicited declarations that continuing missionary superintendence was paternalistic and colonial.

Responding to the ecumenical imperative, the 1910 Edinburgh conference birthed the Faith and Order movement, which drew Anglican participation and resulted in the World Council of Churches (WCC) in 1948. Anglicans were active in the International Missionary Council stemming from Edinburgh and in the conferences that continued after its incorporation into the WCC in 1960. Having explored since the 1920s how their mission as a small minority presence could be ecumenically strengthened, Anglicans in south Asia joined with other churches in organic unions: the Church of South India in 1947, the Church of North India and the Church of Pakistan in 1970, and the Church of Bangladesh in 1971.

The independence of new nations out of the British Empire after World War II prompted a corresponding devolution of Anglican provinces such as Central Africa, West Africa, and East Africa out of colonial church jurisdictions, and some of the large African provinces subdivided several times. Although Latin American nations became independent in the nineteenth century, it was in the late twentieth that an autonomy movement for the relatively small Anglican churches in the region issued in new provinces from international jurisdictions of the Episcopal Church USA, such as Brazil, the Philippines, Mexico, and Central America. These developments were regarded as fulfilling the longstanding goal that mission should culminate in self-governing, self-supporting, and self-propagating churches.

Meanwhile, Anglicans sought to forge appropriate relationships between older and newer churches in an era where the former were no longer founding or superintending but were relatively affluent, though declining in membership, and the latter were self-governing, often spectacularly self-propagating through evangelistic revivalism, but poor enough that self-support was difficult, especially for the large numbers of schools, clinics, and hospitals they inherited from Western mission agencies. An immediate shift was that Western Anglican missionary numbers plummeted after mid-century as inter-religious dialogue replaced evangelization as the theological priority of the day, Western agencies distanced themselves from a perceived equivalence of mission with colonialism, and the new churches' surge suggested that Western mission, at least as traditionally conceived, was redundant in the Two-Thirds World.

The convergence of independence movements with exponential Anglican growth in the Two-Thirds World, especially in Africa, in the latter half of the twentieth century suggested a complex relationship between Anglican mission and Anglo-American colonialism. While colonial power ostensibly had given missionaries an unfair advantage, perceived connections between missionaries and the imperial establishment had actually hampered gospel reception. Christian and Anglican growth flourished after national and ecclesial independence, and Christianity's center of gravity shifted to the Global South.

The concept of shared partnership in mission among Anglican churches around the world was promoted by Max Warren of CMS in the mid-1950s. "Mutual Responsibility and Interdependence in the Body of Christ" (MRI), the theme of the 1963 Anglican Congress in Toronto, was championed by Stephen Bayne, later executive officer of the communion, as heralding a new era of parity and interchange, although it quickly focused on a "directory of projects" which the richer churches would fund for the poorer. More fruitful was the Companion Diocese Movement (CDM) that began in the 1960s and that, up to the present, brought Anglicans of almost every diocese into some form of direct and often multi-faceted relationship with Anglicans in some other diocese in the world. The CDM intensified the now-ongoing democratization of mission initiative from centralized church and agency structures to dioceses and congregations, where mission was localized, deprofessionalized, and diversified. Old mistakes were often repeated as inexperienced players plunged into international mission, but the CDM multiplied personal relationships among Anglicans at the grassroots and de-bureaucratized the effort.

Partnership in Mission (PIM), as adopted in 1971 by the Anglican Consultative Council, became extraordinarily popular as a guiding model at all ecclesial levels for mutual mission across cultures and socio-economic divides, though the interprovincial "PIM consultations" were only marginally helpful. PIM's initial articulation was memorable for transcending dichotomies and providing grounds for continuing mutual investment in relationship:

> The emergence everywhere of autonomous churches in independent nations has challenged our inherited idea of mission as a movement from "Christendom" in the West to the "non-Christian" world. In its place has come the conviction that there is but one mission in all the world, and that this one mission is shared by the world-wide Christian community. The responsibility for mission in any place belongs *primarily* to the church in that place. However, the universality of the gospel and the oneness of God's mission mean also that this mission must be shared in each and every place with fellow-Christians from

each and every part of the world with their distinctive insights and contributions. If we once acted as though there were only givers who had nothing to receive and receivers who had nothing to give, the oneness of the missionary task must make us all both givers and receivers. (Anglican Consultative Council 1973, 53)

Following the new paradigm, Global North Anglican missionaries, now sometimes termed "mission partners" or "mission companions," worked under indigenous leaders in congregations, schools, hospitals, seminaries, and micro-enterprises and sought to strengthen relations between the sending and receiving churches. Shifting priorities meant that their numbers in 2000 were about one-fifth of what they were in 1900, and "volunteer" rather than stipendiary status became the norm, with missionaries obliged to raise their own support. Meanwhile the "short-term mission teams" sent by congregations and dioceses exposed many thousands of British and North American Anglicans annually to the enculturated vitality of Global South Anglicanism. The transformation of the mission pilgrim became a common theme for these and for long-term missionaries.

Pilgrimage among the communion's churches emerged as an aspiration as Anglicans recognized that gospel understanding in any one culture is both uniquely revelatory and inevitably limited, and that therefore Christians need one another across ethnicities and nationalities in order, in the words of the writer to the Ephesians, "to grow into the full stature of Christ." At the turn of the twenty-first century, companionship, typically in a journey of mutual spiritual and practical discovery, was being suggested as a helpfully relational mode of mission, more appropriate to the time than partnership, which tended to focus on the organization and funding of projects. A related theological tendency was to characterize Christian mission not so much as obedience to God's will – identified, for instance, in Jesus' various commissions to his disciples – but as participation in the missional movement of God evident in the entire history of salvation. This contribution of "mission of God" theology was sometimes interpreted so broadly, however, that the mission distinctive of encounter with difference was blurred, strengthening a perennial tendency to question engagement beyond boundaries when much remains to be done in the home community. Meanwhile, BCP revisions around the world after the mid-twentieth century made mission more prominent, especially in collects, eucharistic prayers, and dismissals.

The Decade of Evangelism adopted communion-wide in the 1990s highlighted mission distinctives of Global North and Two-Thirds-World Anglicans, the former cautious about the role of evangelism amid postmodern pluralism, the latter embracing and implementing it with zeal. A new Office of Mission and Evangelism (renamed simply Mission in 2008) was established to coordinate the decade, and its successive officers have been Africans, Cyril Okorocha of Nigeria and John Kafwanka of Zambia. The year 1996 saw the founding of the Church of Nigeria Missionary Society "to select, train, and send forth Mission Partners to unreached parts of Nigeria, Africa and the rest of the World." An early action was the consecration of nine bishops specifically for evangelism in the Muslim-predominant north of Nigeria, and the society undertook work in north Africa in concert with Anglican Frontier Missions, an American initiative intended for "unreached peoples" of the world. The united churches of south Asia, full members of the Anglican Communion, had quiet but significant initiatives in both evangelism and inter-religious collaboration underway in their minority contexts. The Al Qaeda attacks of September 11, 2001, in the United States and subsequent events prompted Anglicans both to reflect on aspects of Christian mission history that provoked religious hostility and to realize anew that Muslims – and members of other world religions as well – had their own visions and programs of global propagation. Two archbishops of Canterbury, George Carey and Rowan Williams, pursued conversations with Muslim leaders beginning in the 1990s, principally through Al-Azhar University in Cairo. A Muslim–Christian dialogue specifically about mission was planned by Episcopal agencies in the United States.

Missionary sending from Two-Thirds World churches to the West was widely promoted, especially since 60 percent of Anglicans were now located in the Global South and their fresh spirituality and missional zeal were anticipated to revitalize Global North churches afflicted by declining numbers, colonial guilt, affluent complacency, and theological uncertainty. Significant leadership posts in Western churches were filled by leaders with non-Western origins: for instance, the appointment of two Pakistanis to head British mission societies – Michael Nazir Ali at CMS, 1989–1994, and Munawar Rumalshah at USPG, 1998–2003 – and the appointment of Ugandan John Sentamu as Archbishop of York in 2005. Western churches diversified significantly through immigration from the Two-Thirds World, but financial obstacles and limited vision have kept the broader hope for intentional south-to-north mission largely unfulfilled.

After World War II, Western Anglican churches focused mission increasingly on what came to be called "development," the strengthening of educational, healthcare, and economic structures in societies, more recently adding environmental sustainability, in an overall effort to alleviate poverty, currently within the framework of the United Nations' Millennium Development Goals (MDGs). Liberation theology and its concern to challenge unjust structures strengthened biblical foundations already buttressed earlier by the Christian Socialism and Social Gospel movements. Major efforts of the past decades include Anglican response to the AIDS crisis, support for ending apartheid in South Africa, advocacy for reducing Two-Thirds-World debt, and reflection on economic and cultural dimensions of globalization. The 2007 Boksburg international conference, Toward Effective Anglican Mission, convened by Archbishop Njongonkulu Ndungane of South Africa, galvanized MDG enthusiasm under the rubric of God's mission. Instrumentalities of the churches include the Council of Anglican Provinces in Africa, the Synodical Board of Social Services for the Church of North India, Christian Aid for the CofE, Episcopal Relief and Development in the United States, and the Canadian Primate's Fund for World Relief and Development, and in 2010 many joined in a consultative and coordinating network, the "Anglican Alliance: Relief, Development, Advocacy." While many Western Anglicans see "development" as mission's center of gravity, Two-Thirds-World Anglicans tend to affirm it in holistic union with their spiritual outreach.

In recent decades, mission has been a rallying cry amid Anglican dissensions. A number of voluntary mission entities were founded by evangelicals in the late twentieth century in the American and Canadian churches because they believed the centralized structures were deficient in evangelism and missionary deployment. While both Ameri-can sides cooperated in the Episcopal Partnership for Global Mission beginning in 1990, the sexuality controversy fractured the network in 2004, and conservative agencies gathered under a new network, Anglican Global Mission Partners. In 2000, the Angli-can Mission in the Americas was initiated by the Anglican Church of Rwanda as a missionary outreach in North America because the Episcopal and Canadian Anglican churches were viewed as contravening historic norms of biblical interpretation with reference to human sexuality, and it claimed to have established a new congregation every three weeks during its first eight years. Conversely, those advocating the affirma-tion of homosexuality in the church's life often did so in the name of advancing the inclusivity and justice of God's mission. Given such broad-based invocation of mission as central in the nature and purpose of the church, mission naturally became promi-nent in efforts to bridge divisions. Mission and identity were the twin themes of the 2008 Lambeth Conference. Mission is a prominent criterion of Christian faithfulness in the Anglican Communion Covenant currently under consideration by Anglican provinces as a means of sustaining unity amid divisive issues. The Anglican Indaba Project similarly stresses missional activity as a potential ground of unity between dioceses that might differ in their biblical and theological orientations.

Coming to the fore in the second decade of the twenty-first century are the Five Marks of Mission developed by the Anglican Consultative Council in the 1980s and 1990s, and since then affirmed by the Lambeth Conference and numerous provinces:

To proclaim the Good News of the Kingdom;
To teach, baptise and nurture new believers;
To respond to human need by loving service;
To seek to transform unjust structures of society; and
To strive to safeguard the integrity of creation and sustain and renew the life of the earth.
    (Reflections Group, 13)

The first three recapitulate the triad of *kerygma*, *diakonia*, and *koinonia* that has defined mission since Jesus. The justice emphasis of the fourth resonates with both biblical witness and many initiatives throughout mission history. While reflecting the present-day ecological crisis, the fifth is biblically grounded and connects with both service and justice. Reflecting a conviction that reconciliation is the central movement of God's work in Christ and thus essential to mission, the Anglican Consultative in 2012 revised the Fourth Mark of Mission to read: "To seek to transform unjust structures of society, to challenge violence of every kind and to pursue peace and reconciliation."

Several concerns and developments are likely to condition Anglican mission work and reflection in the future. Continuing evolution in the theology of religions will influence the respective emphases of evangelization and inter-religious collaboration, especially in relation to Islam. The vision and priorities of Global South Anglicans, now the majority, will increasingly define the communion's mission theology, vision, and program. Future divergence and convergence about human sexuality will affect whether Anglican mission initiatives collaborate or become increasingly fractured. Longstand-ing concerns for poverty alleviation and economic justice are likely to become more focused through the lens of the ecological crisis and its effects on human populations.

Reconciliation will grow as an emphasis as the increasing interconnectedness of the world appears not only to deepen community but also to aggravate ethnic, religious, and economic polarization. Overall, mission is likely to intensify as a commitment that can integrate Anglicans amid their alienations and energize them to participate in God's work in the world.

## Bibliography

Allen, Roland. 1962. *Missionary Methods: St. Paul's or Ours?* Grand Rapids: Eerdmans.

Anglican Consultative Council. 1973. *Partnership in Mission: Anglican Consultative Council: Second Meeting, Dublin, Ireland, 1973.* London: SPCK.

Broderick, George E. P. 1953. History of the Diocese of Southern Rhodesia (formerly the Diocese of Mashonaland). Typescript. Zimbabwe National Archives.

Constitution of the Domestic and Foreign Missionary Society. 1835. *Journal of the Proceedings of the Bishops, Clergy, and Laity of the Protestant Episcopal Church in the United States of America in General Convention.* New York: Protestant Episcopal Press.

Cross, F. L. and E. A. Livingstone. 1997. *The Oxford Dictionary of the Christian Church*, 3rd Ed. Oxford and New York: Oxford University Press.

Eliot, Charles W., ed. 1910. *American Historical Documents, 1000–1904.* The Harvard Classics, vol. 43. New York: P. F. Collier & Son.

Johnson, Todd M. and Kenneth R. Ross. 2009. *Atlas of Global Christianity, 1910–2010.* Edinburgh: Edinburgh University Press.

Main, Florence Nightingale. 1890. Hospital notes, from the Hang-chow Mission Hospital. *The Church Missionary Gleaner*, vol. 17, no. 197 (May 1890).

Maurice, Frederick Denison. 1854. *The Religions of the World and Their Relations to Christianity.* Boston: Gould and Lincoln.

Neill, Stephen. 1986. *A History of Christian Missions.* Revised edition. New York: Penguin.

Spottiswoode, George A. 1894. *The Official Report of the Missionary Conference of the Anglican Communion.* London: SPCK.

Stowe, Walter Herbert. 1935. A Turning Point: General Convention of 1835. *Historical Magazine of the Protestant Episcopal Church*, vol. 4 (September 1935).

*The Annual Register, or a View of the History and Politics of the Year 1858.* 1859. London: Longman & Co.

*The Book of Common Prayer and Administration of the Sacraments and Other Rites and Ceremonies of the Church according to the Use of the Church of England.* n.d. Cambridge: Cambridge University Press.

Warren, Max, ed. 1971. *To Apply the Gospel: Selections from the Writings of Henry Venn.* Grand Rapids: William B. Eerdmans.

CHAPTER 3

# The Emergence of the Anglican Communion in the Nineteenth and Twentieth Centuries

William L. Sachs

## Introduction

Between 1800 and 2000, the Church of England gave rise to a global family of churches that became known as the Anglican Communion. The transformation of religious establishment into a series of churches rooted in various cultures but linked by English precedent was unanticipated. As a matter of sheer expansion, it was not unique. All major Christian bodies that originated in the global North expanded substantially. However, Anglicans have claimed that their rise into a "communion" of churches is unique. Anglicans rooted themselves in disparate contexts with local oversight while preserving lines of continuity with their English precedent. They envisioned a bond among themselves that would both honor and transcend locality. In this chapter, I consider how these claims fostered global communion.

The emergence of the Anglican Communion could seem inevitable because the church followed the British flag. However, the appearance of the empire was hardly uniform. As John Seeley wrote in 1883, the British Empire "was acquired in a fit of absence of mind." This was true of Anglicanism as well, but the church expanded beyond British colonialism. For example, in the nineteenth century, Anglicanism gained a lasting presence in Japan and found initial footing in Latin America. Church growth in these settings followed a pattern seen in colonial contexts, but without the imprint of empire. Evangelism blended with efforts to build the church. Conversions led to worship according to the Book of Common Prayer and the ministries of bishops, priests, and deacons, as well as laity. There were efforts to better local societies through education and amelioration of distress. Governance by synods became common. Anglicans created a distinct footprint reflective of the English example, but adapted to contextual realities. They presumed to incorporate what was local through worship and ministry

*The Wiley-Blackwell Companion to the Anglican Communion*, First Edition. Edited by Ian S. Markham,
J. Barney Hawkins IV, Justyn Terry, and Leslie Nuñez Steffensen.
© 2013 John Wiley & Sons, Ltd. Published 2013 by John Wiley & Sons, Ltd.

of apostolic origin. Anglicans also grounded their life in an evolving coherence with one another. Communion emerged from efforts to realize catholicity inspired by the English example and rooted in local ethos.

"Emergence" is a philosophical reference that explains how social systems arise. It depicts complexity that grows from simplicity compounded. Inconsequential steps prompt interactions that encourage patterns of organization. Clear intentions become overshadowed by consequences that prove more extensive than anticipated. The emergence of communion began as Anglican leaders made responses to particular circumstances that proved far reaching. Communion was not inevitable, but steps toward elaboration of church identity can be gleaned. Anglicans created a myriad of indigenous churches outside Britain. The meaning of being "indigenous" took shape as religious ideals met social realities. The communion's emergence reflected encounters between the English experience and different contextual norms.

Anglicans sought a balance between indigenous organization and linkages which reflected being in communion. Both the hope of being indigenous in new contexts and of being linked grew profound in the nineteenth century. Expansion encouraged fresh expressions of historic forms. For example, the ideal of the National Church extended the legacy of establishment to new circumstances where Anglicans aspired to function as pastor and conscience of society. The English precedent guided expansion and shaped the creation of communion. Anglicans created linkages that would serve as instruments of unity, though it did not seem at issue initially. However, as Anglicanism became a quilt of varied cultures, English influence alone could not knit it together. Unity required that as Anglicans faced comparable challenges they posed similar responses. It was possible to build links and to forge continuity when Anglicans saw their circumstances in similar terms. Eventually, uniting Anglicanism's varieties amid lessened deference to England proved daunting.

Anglicans prized a balance between contextual adaptation and governance and wider loyalty that would prove elusive. Anglican life became fractious as it diversified. Indigenous authority fueled contextual movements for independence from the empire and from the church and cultural influences that symbolized it. By the early twenty-first century, the meaning of being Anglican was contested and the unity of Anglicanism fragmented. How communion arose and how its unity became imperiled are the themes that frame this chapter.

## The Rise of Indigenous Anglican Churches

The origin of the Anglican Communion lay in the creation of indigenous churches in varied contexts. Mission began as extensions of the Church of England to British subjects in colonial areas. The first locus was North America, where settlement began in the seventeenth century. By the eve of revolution, the colonial church had a notable presence. Growth relied in part on being the established church of the colonial power. However, mission outpaced imperial assumptions. The basis of communion lay in work by the Society for the Propagation of the Gospel (SPG), founded in 1701 by Thomas Bray, who saw a need for extension of religious instruction and of the church's ministries. The result was concerted effort to building the church, with early results in New England, and to developing society and commerce as forms of religious purpose. Not all commerce was endorsed; SPG leaders were uneasy about slavery. The SPG extended the church apart from the empire, a basis of the rise of communion.

The other pillar of indigenous Anglicanism was evangelism, proclaiming the Gospel to unsaved populations. Organization of the Church Mission Society (CMS) in 1799 injected evangelicals into the mission field. Evangelicalism was a trans-Atlantic movement that initially focused on unchurched segments of the English population. Late in the eighteenth century, the next generation of evangelical leaders embraced a wider view of mission. At the center of this vision was the Clapham Sect, a lay coterie influential in policy considerations. Avowed opponents of slavery, they looked to spread Christian influence throughout the emerging empire and beyond. In the nineteenth century, when the CMS and other agencies sent missionaries to Africa and Asia, global expansion was underway. What had been solely the Church of England became a series of Anglican churches in disparate locations. An emphasis on mission was apparent, though it resisted consensus. High Church Anglicans sent bishops and built church life while Low Church Anglicans sent missionaries who sought conversions. In the 1830s and 1840s, these approaches became compatible.

Missionary bishops embodied church extension. In 1835, the American Episcopal Church consecrated Jackson Kemper for such service. He launched the church's ministry in the Midwest of the United States. He extended this work to Native Americans and ordained the first Native American in holy orders. Emphasis on mission launched by a bishop moved Anglicans and German Lutherans to create an episcopal see at Jerusalem in 1841. In the same year, Charles Blomfield, Bishop of London, and William Howley, Archbishop of Canterbury, launched the Colonial Bishoprics Fund, to extend the episcopate beyond Britain. Beyond the bounds of establishment, the church raised its resources and generated its organization.

Anglicanism required leadership suitable for particular contexts and structures of governance. Both were necessary, but both fostered controversy. The rise of indigenous leadership benefitted from the work of Henry Venn, Secretary of the CMS from 1841 to 1872. Venn encouraged creation of a "Native Pastorate" in mission fields. Missionary work intended to create an indigenous, self-supporting church. It would generate its own resources and leadership, and govern itself apart from missionary oversight. This intention prompted Venn to create the Sierra Leone Native Pastorate in 1851, a leadership formation program. Venn facilitated the consecration of Samuel Crowther as Bishop of West Africa, the first indigenous bishop, in 1864. Crowther embodied an emerging Anglicanism that transcended English origins without relinquishing them. He represented the intention of transferring authority from missionaries to local leaders.

Indigenous Anglicanism arose as the faith was translated into contextual forms. Scripture and the Book of Common Prayer were conveyed in recognizable forms for different cultures. This meant instruction in reading and writing, which prompted formation of schools and colleges to train leaders. An indigenous church required self-government, and circumstances encouraged its rise. The American Revolution left Anglicanism there in a precarious state, but the Episcopal Church achieved self-organization along democratic lines that reflected the new nation's government. Authority was rooted in the deliberations of elected, representative bodies. There was recognition that the church needed local oversight.

The rise of synodical government was clearly outlined in Australia, Canada, New Zealand, and South Africa. In each place, the combination of church growth and distance from England argued for local governance. Similarly, in the 1830s, the British government began to shift authority to colonial legislatures under the oversight of local governors. Provision of colonial bishops also made the rise of synods seem a natural step. William Broughton, the first Bishop of Australia, became a vigorous advocate of synods, for he feared for a church dependent on oversight from afar. Like Broughton, George Selwyn, Bishop of New Zealand, and Robert Gray, Bishop of Cape Town, advanced governance by synods. This trend was opposed in the 1840s and 1850s by Anglican evangelicals who valued the church's link to the Crown. Yet, the rise of synods continued. A synod was formed in Nova Scotia in 1856 despite opposition from three parishes. Over evangelical opposition, Australian dioceses convened conferences of clergy and laity that created synodical governance. Anglicans emphasized local authority while a communion of dispersed Anglican churches began to emerge. This ironic turn would become the basis of both church growth and conflict.

Two contentious clergy in South Africa illustrated the challenges that Anglicans would face. William Long, a priest in Cape Town, refused to participate in church synods. For his opposition to the 1860 synod, Bishop Gray deprived him of his post. Long appealed, and the Privy Council in London reversed the South African decision in 1863. Long argued that the synod had no authority. The South African church was an extension of the Church of England, and could not act apart from it. The Privy Council recognized Gray's right to supervise his clergy; Long could be suspended. However, the authority of a synod rested on the consensus between bishop, clergy, and lay leaders. Synods could not claim English legal authority. The need for consensus also fueled conflict in the 1850s and 1860s when J. W. Colenso, Bishop of Natal, challenged conventional theological views. Colenso endorsed a theological liberalism that seemed scandalous at the time. Implicitly, he challenged Gray's authority as the South African metropolitan. Again, uncertainty arose about the limits of belief and practice, and how iconoclastic individuals could be disciplined. Deprived of his see, Colenso clung to it, heightening questions of governance and authority. The emergence of communion rested on the need for consensus.

## National Churches and International Links

By the middle of the nineteenth century, Anglicanism had expanded. Secure in North America and the West Indies, the church grew in Australia and New Zealand. Efforts in Sierra Leone and the Niger Delta held West African promise, while South Africa was turning inland from Cape Town. South Asia seemed a region of promise, and East Asia loomed. It was not clear how extensive Anglicanism would become, but there were 45 bishops in colonial areas and another 34 in the United States. The church's growth and dispersal were welcomed, but tensions accompanied them. The issues raised by Long and Colenso would resurface. The juxtaposition of opportunity and challenge was significant. Anglicans saw themselves as more than disjointed regional churches; they held an ideal of catholicity. While building indigenous local churches, they shaped the linkages of communion.

One of the pillars of communion has been the Lambeth Conference, a decennial meeting of bishops. Its rise followed diminished reliance on the English establishment. By 1850, the Colonial Office ceased to issue letters patent for overseas bishops and deferred to local synods. Already, the term "Anglican Communion" was used, and calls for a council of bishops had surfaced. When Canadian bishops made a proposal in 1865, the idea grew. There was need of a forum to address variations and to build unity. Anglicanism was changing, and differences were apparent. Archbishop of Canterbury Charles Longley called a meeting of bishops in 1867. He cautioned that this assembly had no authority to impose standards. It would seek the mind of the church on crucial issues and encourage consensus.

Several dozen bishops declined to attend; some feared the gathering would weaken the Church of England, while some quibbled with theological references in the invitation. Although unity seemed within reach in subsequent Lambeth Conferences, later controversies surfaced similar fragmentation. The Lambeth Conference offered a forum for the resolution of discrepancies in faith and practice. However, its consensual authority could be undermined by concerted resistance. Nevertheless, Lambeth became Anglicanism's largest regular forum for addressing key issues. The range of issues and the positions formulated mark the emergence of the communion. Particular theological and cultural questions surfaced as the church grew. One of the most vexing was polygamy.

For a century, Lambeth Conferences returned to this issue. It became a source of tension between local church life and wider church ties, between the global North's sense of moral primacy and the global South's cultural energy. Missionaries tended to reject many cultural customs they encountered. However, African tribal leaders framed polygamy as a basic social unit that extended group identity and security. Missionaries countered that Christianity upheld only monogamy and that polygamous converts should not be baptized. Over time, some missionaries tacitly accepted polygamy. A few, starting with Colenso, even endorsed polygamy in a burst of cultural relativism. Eventually, in 1988, the Lambeth Conference reached a pastoral compromise. Polygamists and their spouses could be baptized if care was extended to all, and no further spouses were added. However, the ability of Lambeth to enforce this decision was problematic. The communion rested on consensus about faith and practice.

Yet, consensus grounded in a distinctive appropriation of faith tradition seemed within reach, and the Lambeth Conference was its catalyst. Concerns about variation in belief and practice prompted broad conversations about Anglicanism's nature. Then, in 1876, William Reed Huntingdon's *The Church Idea* proposed a new basis of unity. When adopted by the Lambeth Conference in 1888, Huntingdon's four marks of identity became known as the Chicago–Lambeth Quadrilateral for their origin in the American church and affirmation at Lambeth. Anglican identity now rested on the Scriptures of the Old and New Testaments, the Apostles and Nicene Creeds, the sacraments of Baptism and Holy Communion, and the historic episcopate "locally adapted in the methods of its administration to the varying needs of the nations and peoples of God into the Unity of the Church."

The power of consensus became apparent. Consensus among Anglicans permitted far-reaching ecumenical conversations. It drew Anglicans into prominent roles in global mission consultations such as the Edinburgh Conference of 1910, where American bishop Charles Brent became a leading voice. The new tone was echoed in the Church of England, especially by William Temple, who would become the Archbishop of Canterbury. Temple recast Anglicanism's approach to industrial society. He focused the church's life on the Kingdom of God as an ideal society. United by this vision and defined by four tenets, Anglicans faced social needs, took ecumenical roles, and criticized the mores of industrial society. The Anglican social voice sharpened, and with it the rise of being a communion of churches was clear. Lambeth Conference encouraged an infrastructure that began with a committee on the organization of communion. At the 1897 conference, thought was given to a central consulting body and to the relations of Anglican primates outside Britain to Canterbury. A process of organization was underway.

That process, and the linkages that arose from it, proved necessary as Anglicans framed church life along national lines. This had been foreshadowed by the Episcopal Church in the United States, and, once again, American priest William Reed Huntington sensed this development. His *A National Church*, published in 1898, argued for grounding religious life in national identity. However, this idea was problematic. Vast areas of the Anglican world remained colonial and, however appealing, the ideal of a national church faltered while missionary control remained, as was the case well into the twentieth century. Missionaries fretted that indigenous leadership and resources were inadequate, and that continued dependence on direction from the global North was necessary. The Anglican world was being knit together, but not on equitable terms. The experience of Samuel Crowther was illustrative. The first African bishop was treated by missionaries more as an African than as a bishop. Similarly, in the nineteenth century, James Johnson, an African in the employ of the CMS, agitated against missionary control and for an indigenous church. He faltered when summoned to London, but later founded an independent African congregation.

Anglicanism became a series of national churches vesting authority in synodical governance, and posing high ideals based on fragile consensus in the vision of a wider communion. How to balance indigenous life with being linked became the source of tension. The case for an indigenous church was clear, but the case for indigenous churches being linked, and ceding their authority to external structures, became problematic.

## Wresting Control Yet Aspiring to Communion

For ten days in the summer of 1908, the Anglican Communion saw itself as something of a whole. It was not the first time as Lambeth Conferences had convened every ten years since 1867, and the fifth one would convene in July. However, that summer it was preceded by the Pan-Anglican Congress, a large conference of bishops, clergy, and lay leaders from every continent. From June 15 to 24, they met in sessions addressing religious, economic, and social trends. They considered whether Anglican Christians should be polygamists or socialists or any of a myriad of other cultural and political identities. They discussed techniques of evangelism and church growth in scores of countries. Above all, they considered how they were linked. Being in communion had become a key issue.

By the time of the Congress, being in communion meant forging a distinctive Anglican response to modern life and finding a consistent church identity across a myriad of contexts. As these challenges were addressed in 1908, the priority of the English example and the guidance of the global North were presumed. Anglicans were not averse to self-criticism, nor to critiques of mores in powerful nations. However, the Anglican sense of catholicity presumed the authority of Britain and North America, and the deference of Anglicans elsewhere. Yet, diffuse ideals of church authority were posed, all failing to commend centralized forms. Anglican authority was depicted as consensual, synodical, and rooted in essentials of faith, worship, and ministry. Nevertheless, the manner of consensus reflected global North influence. Being in communion took form, but not along equitable lines.

Yet, like the Lambeth Conference, the Pan-Anglican Congress afforded a valuable, if quite occasional forum. The process of addressing issues and seeking collaboration advanced intramural links. These were necessary as the perennial tension of local initiative versus wider linkage intensified. Anglicanism's growth in varied situations challenged its ability to sustain consistent norms of religious community and identity. Soon after the Congress, this tension erupted as a dispute between missionary bishops. In 1913, W. G. Peel of Mombasa and J. J. Willis of Uganda participated in an ecumenical communion service at a Church of Scotland congregation in Kikuyu, Kenya. Bishop Frank Weston of Zanzibar demanded church proceedings against them. He appealed to the English authority, where the matter was quietly put to rest.

Nevertheless, Weston forged innovations of his own. In 1919, he published the Zanzibar Rite, an adaptation of the Prayer Book to a missionary context. Controversy greeted the rite, for it reflected adaptive work in one setting presented as widely definitive. Indeed, the rite informed African Prayer Books as national churches arose in former colonies. In the mission field, innovative patterns of church life arose as responses to local circumstances. Nevertheless, how local initiative embodied coherent Anglican identity was a troubling question. In part, this was because the missionary hold on church life was slipping. The East Africa Revival, a series of religious awakenings that peaked in the 1930s, made this plain. The Revival injected new fervor into Anglican life. It encouraged growth and surfaced affective norms of church life. Some missionaries decried it, while others endorsed it. Eventually it ebbed, but revivals among Anglicans recurred. Local fervor challenged communion-wide relations in new ways.

At the time, religious revivals seemed more transient than Anglicanism's major challenges: global war and the end of colonialism. The two were inextricably linked, for war made empire's continuance impossible and transitions of colonies into nations followed after hostilities ceased. These transitions preoccupied Anglican leaders, and Lambeth Conferences became crucial for posing responses. Economic and social challenges were considerable, and tested the capacity of Anglicans to work together as their center of gravity shifted. Long foreseen, then suddenly necessary, political and religious self-governance in the former colonies challenged Anglicanism's coherence in ways that continue to be addressed. Yet continued deference to England permitted consensus about being in communion for the time being. The readiness of Anglicans in the global North to criticize the moral shortcomings of their own societies also encouraged a common mind. Never apologetic for modern life, Anglicans in more developed nations sharpened their social critique before economic downturn and war. A readiness to speak critically built a common mind among Anglicans. A broad swath welcomed fresh political and ecclesiastical arrangements as necessary replacements for the empire.

Unprecedented organization of church life in South Asia after World War II dramatized Anglican life after the empire. In India, Pakistan, Ceylon, and later Bangladesh, Protestant Christians formed union churches. The Anglican stamp was clear as these churches preserved the episcopate and diocesan organization. Continuity facilitated recognition by the Anglican Communion and incorporation of their bishops into the Lambeth Conference. South Asia epitomized the new shape of communion as colonial churches became national ones. Elsewhere, independent Anglican branches arose as independent national churches appeared. The power of context to shape church life was apparent.

Anglicans in wealthier nations offered resources for development, and the Church of England took precedence. At Canterbury, creation of St. Augustine's College in 1948 offered a center for leadership training. Later, the College became a fund to finance aspects of communion life including gatherings that provided vital linkages. Anglicans in the global North supplied resources in various ways. Trinity Church, Wall Street, in New York, took special interest in equipping African Anglicans. The historic, English societies added their emphasis on social development as a key feature of mission. However, Anglicans in the developing world chafed at the inequity of their ties, even as they welcomed resources. The reality was that more voices were at the table, and finding parity among them was crucial to the future.

Yet, Anglicans pulled together in various ways. There was fresh emphasis on ecumenical relations and dialogue with non-Christian faiths. There also was profound emphasis on social justice. Opposition to apartheid in South Africa and support for Anglicans there became widespread. The rise of Desmond Tutu as a peacemaker brought Anglicans renown. Anglicans also rallied when Ugandan dictator Idi Amin oppressed church leaders. Some Ugandan bishops and their families fled to Britain and North America, where they were welcomed. Meanwhile, global North Anglicans were vigorous in opposing racial discrimination in their homelands. Social justice became a clear, uniting goal.

Liturgical revision also played a role in enhancing communion bonds. Anglican theology had depicted the church as embodiment of the Kingdom of God. The quest for just societies encouraged this ideal as distinctions between the church and the world became urgent, and the image of the Kingdom dramatized the difference. As liturgical scholars discovered early church emphasis on the Eucharist, a basis for liturgical revision coalesced. It found broad appeal, and a movement for revision emerged among Anglicans from the 1950s onward. This consensus was incomplete, but a tipping point was reached, and Eucharistic emphasis informed new versions of the Prayer Book in much of the Anglican world. Even so, Anglican unity would prove fragile.

## The Erosion of Consensus

In the second half of the twentieth century, Anglicans devoted creative attention to forging the unity of their communion. When 326 bishops representing over 40 million Anglicans gathered for the Lambeth Conference of 1948, they were strangers to one another. Because of war, there had been no Lambeth since 1930. Meanwhile, the church and the world had changed decisively, and the implications were clear. Colonies were becoming nations, and the churches within them were assuming self-direction. The meaning of being in communion focused on being better organized and uniting in mission. New initiatives were apparent across the Anglican world. In 1948, American Presiding Bishop Henry Knox Sherrill created a fund for world relief as a sign of commitment to desperate needs. The Lambeth Conference echoed this initiative by creating an Advisory Council on Mission Strategy to coordinate mission work. It met only once, but the ideal it symbolized would take hold.

By the 1958 Lambeth Conference, Anglicans were ready to unify. There had been a Congress in 1954, and it had been a joyous family reunion. The breadth of church life loomed as a basis for mission if coordination could be developed. Anglicans could act effectively if they could create centralized structures focused on internal relations. Proposals emerged for regular meetings of representatives of all provinces and for a central office to join mission efforts. Influential leaders endorsed these steps. Max Warren, head of the CMS, called for partnership and equity in Anglican relations. These hopes were clouded by economic and cultural disparities. Advocates of unity tried to address these realities, but tensions remained between local contexts and larger ties. Both were needed, and they seemed compatible.

In part, the Anglican world required disentangling. The church in some nations such as Liberia, Taiwan, and Mexico remained under the aegis of the Episcopal Church. Britain still had colonial territories including portions of the West Indies and Hong Kong. The Anglican ideal remained creation of independent branches along national lines united by consensus on key aspects of faith and practice. To this end, the Lambeth Conference of 1958 moved to create an executive secretary of the communion who proved to be the American bishop Stephen Bayne. Widely respected, Bayne took energetic steps to build mission. One result was a church Congress in Toronto in 1963. It extended attention to mission amid the challenges of national development after colonialism. At the Congress, a new initiative, "Mutual Responsibility and Interdependence," was announced. It proposed communion-wide resource sharing for local mission. Partnership and contextual priorities were central. Dioceses in the developed nations built companion relations with those in new nations. A sense of stitching the Anglican quilt together was apparent, and response was enthusiastic.

"MRI" proved to be the peak of Anglican global coordination. It created new ties and fresh appreciation for mutual mission. MRI represented a decisive turn from the colonial outlook and toward the realization of the ideal of communion. In its wake, new forms of common life followed. In 1968, the Lambeth Conference created the Anglican Consultative Council led by a secretary general in succession to Stephen Bayne. The Council usually meets every three years and includes delegations of bishops, clergy, and laity from each of the church's provinces. It has no authority to legislate, but has offered a forum for addressing major issues and encouraged coordinated approaches to mission. Various provinces launched mission initiatives as a result, notably Partners in Mission which several provinces, notably the Canadian church, have sustained. The American Episcopal Church launched Venture in Mission in 1976, committing nearly $100 million to new grassroots initiatives.

Like the Anglican Consultative Council, every two years Anglican primates, heads of the various provinces, meet in different sites around the world. The Primates' Meeting was established in 1978 by then Archbishop of Canterbury Donald Coggan. These meetings permit discussion of key issues and efforts to build consensus around them. Though public interest has been intense at times, press coverage is limited to permit candid exchanges. The need for such candor soon became acute.

Communion-wide emphasis on mission produced impressive results. In some parts of the Anglican world, there were striking examples of growth, notably in Africa. By the twenty-first century, Nigeria reported over 18 million Anglicans and Uganda more than 8 million. Less dramatically, the church grew in Spanish, French, and Portuguese-speaking nations, especially in Latin America, clear signs that Anglicanism had transcended British origin. Numbers could be small and resources scant, but steady leadership built congregations and church infrastructure. In some places, there were fresh spiritual energies, and the charismatic movement of the late twentieth century stamped church life in parts of Asia and Africa. Meanwhile, Anglicans generally continued to build social-service ministries and to be known for providing education and healthcare. Indigenous leadership had become the norm, and missionaries from highly developed nations served rather than set contextual priorities.

However, the results of Anglicanism's mission efforts were ragged. Though emphasis was similar across the communion, different local circumstances prompted different styles and priorities. Worse, theological and cultural divergence was apparent. Being Anglican did not mean the same thing everywhere. Specific issues surfaced fault lines and undercut being in communion. Anglicanism had been prone to splinter groups over theological differences and innovations in church life. However, in the late twentieth century, proponents and opponents of change became mobilized. The ordination of women to priesthood and episcopate has gained momentum among global North Anglicans and gradually in some African, Asian, and Latin American provinces. Opposition was concerted when the American Church approved women in holy orders in 1976. There had been women priests in Hong Kong, but the American step, and a generation later, the Church of England's approval, seemed decisive.

A few Anglicans around the world left to form dissident groups or even to join the Roman Catholic or Orthodox churches in protest. However, over time, an Anglican *modus vivendi* arose. Some provinces refused to ordain women; some opened ordained ministry to women but few bishops and dioceses acted; other provinces readily opened the clergy ranks and many women were ordained. Lay leadership roles for women also expanded in most of the Anglican world. By the twenty-first century, notable numbers of women had been ordained in some places but not in others. Yet, this reality did little to fracture the Anglican Communion.

The issue of sexuality was more vexing, especially the question of homosexuality. Public consensus in the global North moved toward acceptance, and advocacy groups mobilized to secure it. Similarly, the presence of gay people in the church, always tacitly understood, became public, especially in ordained ministry. Homosexuality as an open, affirmed lifestyle became an issue which threatened to split the communion.

Homosexuality subsumed other Anglican tensions. It posed the global North against the global South in multiple ways. It entwined with the "culture wars" fragmentation. It tapped conflict over mission priorities and resource disparity. It surfaced differences over the authority of the Bible, and the shape of faith tradition and faith community. Differences over homosexuality fostered alternative definitions of communion and of Anglicanism itself. Late in the twentieth century, opposition coalitions united wide segments of the Anglican world. When the American church consecrated an openly gay, partnered man as bishop in 2003, opposition became concerted.

Following the lines of disagreement, separate ideals of communion took shape. Opponents of accepting homosexuality formed networks and even held an alternative to the Lambeth Conference in 2008 in Jerusalem and Jordan. Yet, efforts to sustain communion persisted. There was talk of a Covenant which would restrict participation in communion to provinces which adhered to the majority consensus of faith and practice. In the early twenty-first century, this meant no approval for gay persons in leadership roles or for the blessing of same-sex unions as many global North Anglicans intended. Meant to bolster communion, pursuit of a Covenant faltered at Anglicanism's ideological divide. Additional steps appeared necessary because Anglicanism's instruments of unity – the Lambeth Conference, the Primates' meetings, the Anglican Consultative Council, and the Archbishop of Canterbury – seemed insufficient. The balance between local adaptation and catholic ideals that made it possible eroded amid divergent views of Anglicanism and even of Christianity itself. The future of communion seemed in doubt.

## Bibliography

Cox, Jeffrey. 2009. *The British Missionary Enterprise Since 1700*. New York: Routledge.

Cox, R. David. 1987. *A Vision to Fulfill: Mutual Responsibility and Interdependence in the Anglican Communion*. STM Thesis, Yale University Divinity School.

Goldstein, Jeffrey. 1999. Emergence as a Construct: History and Issues. *Emergence*, vol. 1, no. 1 (April 1999), 49–72.

Huntington, W. R. 1872. *The Church Idea*. New York: Hurd and Houghton.

Huntington, W. R. 1898. *A National Church*. New York: Scribner's.

Jacob, W. M. 1997. *The Making of the Anglican Church Worldwide*. London: SPCK.

Kaye, Bruce. 2008. *An Introduction to World Anglicanism*. Cambridge: Cambridge University Press.

Mullin, Robert Bruce. 1986. *Episcopal Vision/American Reality*. New Haven: Yale University Press.

*Pan-Anglican Congress*. 1908. London: SPCK.

Porter, Andrew. 2004. *Religion Versus Empire?* Manchester: Manchester University Press.

Sachs, William L. 1993/2002. *The Transformation of Anglicanism*. Cambridge: Cambridge University Press.

Sachs, William L. 2009. *Homosexuality and the Crisis of Anglicanism*. Cambridge: Cambridge University Press.

Stanley, Brian. 1990. *The Bible and the Flag*. England: Apollos Press.

Stephenson, Alan M. G. 1978. *Anglicanism and the Lambeth Conferences*. London: SPCK.

Sundkler, Bengt. 1954. *Church of South India: The Movement Toward Union*. London: Lutterworth Press.

Ward, Kevin. 2006. *A History of Global Anglicanism*. Cambridge: Cambridge University Press.

Ward, Kevin and Brian Stanley, ed. 2000. *The Church Mission Society and World Christianity, 1799–1999*. Grand Rapids: Eerdmans.

Woolverton, John F. 1984. *Colonial Anglicanism in North America*. Detroit: Wayne State University Press.

# PART II

# Structures of the Communion

CHAPTER 4

# The Instruments of Unity and Communion in Global Anglicanism

## Norman Doe

The Anglican Communion is a worldwide fellowship of 44 churches in communion with the See of Canterbury (TACC, 4.1.1).[1] It has no formal body of law applicable to these churches. Each church (or province) is autonomous and has its own legal system. Rather, classically, the communion has been understood to be held together by "bonds of affection," by the shared loyalty of its churches to scripture, creeds, baptism, Eucharist, and historic episcopate, and by its institutional "instruments of unity" – Archbishop of Canterbury, Lambeth Conference, Anglican Consultative Council, and Primates' Meeting; but these institutions cannot make decisions binding on churches (Anglican Communion Network of Legal Advisers 2008, Principle 11.2).[2] However, the Lambeth Commission on Communion, in its Windsor Report (2004), called for an appraisal of these instruments of unity and communion. The Commission was established by the Archbishop of Canterbury in 2003 to address "the legal and theological implications" of the decisions of the Episcopal Church (USA) to select a priest in a committed same-sex relationship as one of its bishops, and of the Diocese of New Westminster (Canada) as to services for use in connection with same-sex unions; its mandate was also to make "practical recommendations for maintaining the highest degree of communion possible in the circumstances resulting from these decisions" (*The Windsor Report* 2004, 13, Mandate 1 and 2). The Commission recommended three key

---

[1] Moreover: "The Anglican Communion is a fellowship, within the One, Holy, Catholic and Apostolic Church, of national or regional Churches, in which each recognises in the others the bonds of a common loyalty to Christ expressed through a common faith and order, a shared inheritance in worship, life and mission, and a readiness to live an interdependent life".

[2] Principle 11.2: "Each church recognises that the churches of the Anglican Communion are bound together, not juridically by a central legislative, executive, or judicial authority, but by mutual loyalty maintained through the instruments of Anglican unity as an expression of that communion"; see Principle 11.1 for adherence to scripture, creeds, baptism, Eucharist, the threefold ministry of bishops, priests and deacons, and common patterns of worship; see Principle 10 for the nature of the Anglican Communion.

---

*The Wiley-Blackwell Companion to the Anglican Communion*, First Edition. Edited by Ian S. Markham, J. Barney Hawkins IV, Justyn Terry, and Leslie Nuñez Steffensen.

normative developments designed to maintain the creative tension between provincial autonomy (locally) and ecclesial communion (globally): a clarification of the roles of the institutional instruments of unity (or communion); the completion of a statement of principles of canon law common to the churches of the Anglican Communion; and the adoption by each church of an Anglican Communion Covenant (and it offered a draft). This chapter explores the key elements of these developments, as well as the plethora of instruments within these developments and the relations between them.

## The Institutional Instruments of Unity and Communion

Historically, the institutional instruments of the global Anglican Communion (the Archbishop of Canterbury, Lambeth Conference, Anglican Consultative Council, and Primates' Meeting) developed as mechanisms by which the churches could engage in common counsel in matters of mutual concern; and they were understood to represent a form of dispersed, moral, "complex and still-evolving" authority (*The Virginia Report*, Ch. 3, 42).[3] These bodies had all been regarded classically as "instruments of unity," but the Lambeth Commission recommended a change in usage – that the Archbishop of Canterbury be regarded as the "focus of unity" and that the Lambeth Conference, Anglican Consultative Council, and Primates' Meeting be regarded as "the instruments of communion"; it also called for greater clarity about the respective responsibilities of each instrument and "the expectations placed on provinces in responding to the decisions of these Instruments"; but it did not favor the accumulation of formal power by the instruments or the establishment of any kind of central curia for the worldwide Anglican Communion (*The Windsor Report* 2004, para. 106).[4] Indeed, the draft covenant proposed by the Windsor Report required that the instruments of communion set out formally their composition, functions, and relations one with another, and that they be empowered to resolve contentious issues (*The Windsor Report* 2004, Appendix Two, Arts. 23 & 26). Today, canonically, these institutional instruments of unity and communion enjoy only such binding authority within a church as may be prescribed by the law of that church (Anglican Communion Network of Legal Advisors 2008, Principle 11.5).[5] They exist to assist in the discernment, articulation, and exercise of the shared faith and common life and mission of Anglicans and express this cooperative service in the life of communion.[6] In short, as a fundamental principle consonant with provincial autonomy, they enjoy moral authority and not coercive jurisdiction (see

[3] The Anglican Communion Office (in London) acts as the secretariat to the instruments, though technically it is the secretariat only to the Anglican Consultative Council): see TWR Appendix One (8).
[4] See para. 106 as to whether they should be ranked in terms of their respective authorities.
[5] See also 11.4, which classifies the Archbishop of Canterbury as "the focus of unity" and the Lambeth Conference, Anglican Consultative Council, and Primates' Meeting as the "instruments of communion."
[6] TACC, s. 3.1.4: moreover, "The life of communion includes an ongoing engagement with the diverse expressions of apostolic authority, from synods and episcopal councils to local witness, in a way which continually interprets and articulates the common faith of the Church's members (*consensus fidelium*). In addition to the many and varied links which sustain our life together, we acknowledge four particular Instruments at the level of the Anglican Communion."

following text on Section III, titled "Our Unity and Common Life," for the procedures applicable under the Anglican Communion Covenant).

The Archbishop of Canterbury (both office and person) is seen classically as "the pivotal instrument and focus of unity" and "relationship to him became a touchstone of what it was to be Anglican" (*The Windsor Report* 2004, para. 99; see also LC 1988, Resolution 18; and Podmore 2005, 65). In turn, the laws of some communion churches around the world, variously, recognize that the archbishop enjoys "the first place" among Anglican metropolitans (Sudan, Const., Art. 4.2; Central Africa, Fundamental Declarations, II), is owed deference (West Indies, Canon 8), has a limited jurisdiction exercisable in relation to disputes about doctrine and liturgy (see Doe 1998, Chs. 7 and 8), or the appointment of bishops in the event of failure by an electoral college to elect (Central Africa, Canon 3), or has a wider and more general metropolitical authority (e.g., Puerto Rico, Const., II.5; Lusitanian Catholic Apostolic and Evangelical Church, Const., Preamble, 7; see Doe 1998, 344–5). However, the Lambeth Commission proposed that the Archbishop of Canterbury must not be regarded as a figurehead but as "the central focus of both unity and mission within the Communion." Moreover, the office has a very significant teaching role to articulate the mind of the communion, especially in controversial matters. Accordingly, it recommended the establishment of a Council of Advice to assist in the worldwide ministry of the Archbishop, and that "[t]he Communion should be able to look to the holder of this office to speak directly to any provincial situation on behalf of the Communion when this is deemed advisable" – but that "[s]uch action should not be viewed as outside interference in the exercise of autonomy by any province" (*The Windsor Report* 2004, para. 109; see para. 11 for the suggested Council of Advice). Moreover, the draft covenant appended to the Windsor report provided that, as part of its process in contentious communion matters, the Archbishop of Canterbury "may issue such guidance as he deems fit, or, as appropriate, refer the matter to the Council of Advice for guidance" (*The Windsor Report* 2004, Appendix Two, Art. 26.3).[7]

The Windsor Report stimulated extensive debate about whether the Archbishop of Canterbury should exercise a wider coercive jurisdiction globally in the communion (see Doe 2008, 122, 123, 130, 133, 141, 160, 196; see also Kuehn 2008, 161 at 166). However, the Nassau draft covenant (2007), the St. Andrews draft covenant (2008), and the Ridley-Cambridge draft covenant (2009) (Doe 2008, 130 (Nassau, Art. 5), 141 (St. Andrews, Cl. 3.1.4 and Ridley-Cambridge, 3.1.4), all dealt with the moral (and not coercive) authority of the office of Archbishop of Canterbury in broadly the same terms as it is treated in the (final) Anglican Communion Covenant, which provides: "We accord the Archbishop of Canterbury, as the Bishop of the See of Canterbury with which Anglicans have historically been in communion, a primacy of honour and respect among the college of bishops in the Anglican Communion as first among equals

---

[7] The Archbishop would also have been given the duty to "decide all questions of interpretation of this Covenant, consulting the Council of Advice, and seeking the advice of any other body as he deems appropriate" – if approved by the Joint Standing Committee of the Primates' Meeting and Anglican Consultative Council, the decision of the Archbishop was to be "regarded as authoritative in the Communion until altered in like manner": Art. 27.1–2.

(*primus inter pares*)." Thus, in terms of functions: "As a focus and means of unity, the Archbishop gathers and works with the Lambeth Conference and Primates' Meeting, and presides in the Anglican Consultative Council" (TACC, 3.1.4.I; for antecedents to this in earlier drafts of the covenant, see Doe 2008). It may be noted that the Covenant does not expressly incorporate the recommendations of the Windsor Report about (a) the significant teaching role of the archbishop, (b) the establishment of a Council of Advice (to assist the archbishop), or (c) the recognition of a right in the archbishop to speak directly to controversial provincial affairs. The high level of generality in the treatment of the functions of the Archbishop of Canterbury in the Anglican Communion Covenant is echoed in the principles of canon law common to the churches of the communion (for which see following text on Section II, titled "The Life We Share with Others: Our Anglican Vocation").[8]

The first Lambeth Conference of 1867 brought together bishops from around the world, and it has met since at intervals of roughly ten years (for the controversy surrounding its convening, see *The Windsor Report* 2004, para. 100; see also Podmore 2005, 36–7). Since then, Lambeth Conferences have sought to unify the global Anglican family of churches, to develop a consensus in matters of faith and order, to promote ecumenical dialogue, and to stimulate action in the world on moral and political issues: international conflict (1930); racial discrimination (1948); capital punishment (1978); human rights, poverty, debt (1988); and HIV/AIDS, the environment, and human sexuality (1998). Similarly, issues with a legal dimension have never been very far below the surface: disciplining bishops (1867); missionary jurisdictions (1878); doctrinal dispute (1867–1897); liturgical reform (1908, 1948); marriage and divorce (1958); female ordination (1948–1988); provincial autonomy and communion structures (1948–1978); ordination and homosexuality (1998); and the structures of the Anglican Communion (2008).

The Lambeth Conference is not a pan-Anglican synod with legislative or judicial powers, but an advisory body.[9] The Conference has no formal constitution as such, and attendance is by invitation of the Archbishop of Canterbury (*The Windsor Report* 2004, para. 110). Its resolutions are not binding but enjoy a moral authority.[10] However, the Lambeth Commission recommended clarification of the role of the Lambeth Conference in terms of its provision of worldwide leadership and the nature of its authority; moreover, the "provinces of the Communion should not proceed with controversial developments in the face of teaching to the contrary from all the bishops gathered

[8] Anglican Communion Network of Legal Advisers 2008, Principle 11.4: the Archbishop of Canterbury is (simply) "the focus of unity."
[9] See also LC 1867, Res. 9: the conference suggested that "a committee [of bishops] be instructed to consider the constitution of a voluntary spiritual tribunal, to which questions of doctrine might be carried by appeal"; this never came to pass. However, in his letter of invitation, Archbishop Longley stressed that "Such a Meeting would not be competent to make declarations, or lay down definitions on points of doctrine" (Stephenson 1967, 188).
[10] Doe (1998) 346–8: this discusses the dominant view that its resolutions do not bind the churches and the minority view that they represent a form of ecclesiastical "quasi-legislation" (and many are actually incorporated in provincial laws); for the minority view that they are "more than 'not binding'" and constitute a "new body of legislation," see Chadwick 1992, xv–xvii.

together in Lambeth Conferences" (*The Windsor Report* 2004, Appendix One (3)). While it did not propose changing the formal status of Conference resolutions, the Commission suggested "that there should be some level of distinction between different kinds of motion at the Conference" – in particular, resolutions which touch upon the definition of Anglicanism or the authentic proclamation of the Gospel should be subject to a distinctive procedure and therefore require the special attention of the communion.[11] The Windsor Report stimulated widespread debate on the role of the Lambeth Conference (and its teaching authority) (see Doe 2008, 122, 124, 141, 168); but the terms of the Nassau, St. Andrews, and Ridley-Cambridge draft covenants, and their provisions on the Lambeth Conference (Doe 2008, 130), are generally mirrored in the Anglican Communion Covenant: "The Lambeth Conference expresses episcopal collegiality worldwide, and brings together the bishops for common worship, counsel, consultation and encouragement in their ministry of guarding the faith and unity of the Communion and equipping the saints for the work of ministry (Eph 4.12) and mission"(TACC, 3.1.4.II).

The Anglican Consultative Council (established in 1967) was the result of a call for greater lay participation in synodical government at provincial level and the resolution of the Lambeth Conference 1897 to establish a permanent consultative body as developed subsequently.[12] In point of fact, the laws of some churches already enable recourse to the Council (by various means) in disputed matters of faith and order (e.g., Kenya, Const., Art. II; Sudan, Const., Art. 2; Tanzania, Const., Art. IV; Uganda, Const., Art. II). In turn, the Windsor Report proposed consideration of whether the Council, given its composition of laity, clergy, and bishops, should become "more appropriately the body which can take something approaching binding decisions for the Communion" (*The Windsor Report* 2004, para. 106).[13] The terms of the Nassau, St. Andrews, and Ridley-Cambridge draft covenants, and their provisions on the Council (Doe 2008, 130–1, 141), are generally mirrored in the Anglican Communion Covenant: the Anglican Consultative Council is comprised of lay, clerical, and episcopal representatives from our Churches. The Council facilitates the cooperative work of the Churches of the Anglican Communion, coordinates aspects of international Anglican ecumenical and mission work, calls the Churches into mutual responsibility and interdependence, and advises on developing provincial structures (TACC, s. 3.1.4; see also Constitution of the ACC, Arts. 2, 3, and Schedule; Report of the Windsor Continuation Group, 69; IATDC, para. 113.).[14] The Covenant does not provide that ACC decisions bind the churches.

---

[11] *The Windsor Report* 2004, Appendix One (4): "Such motions would also require a clear process by which they could be adopted – the extended consideration of the whole conference; to require an increased majority for passing or to trigger stated methods of reception in order to be seen as the 'definitive teaching' of the Communion."

[12] LC 1897, Res. 5; LC 1908, Res. 54; LC 1920, res. 44: the consultative body is "a purely advisory body . . . and neither possesses nor claims any executive or administrative power"; see also LC 1930, Res. 50; LC 1948, Res. 80 and 81; LC 1958, Res. 61.

[13] The Commission also proposed consideration of widening membership of the Council to Primates and about the meetings of the Primates' and Council's Standing Committees: TWR, Appendix One (1) and (2).

[14] TACC, s. 3.1.4; see also Constitution of the ACC, Arts. 2, 3, and Schedule; Report of the Windsor Continuation Group, 69; IATDC, Communion, Conflict and Hope, para. 113.

The establishment of the Primates' Meeting was the result of a recommendation of the Lambeth Conference in 1978 to the Archbishop of Canterbury to collaborate with all the primates of the Anglican Communion to consider how "to relate together the international conferences, councils and meetings within the Anglican Communion so that the Anglican Communion may best serve God within the context of one, holy, catholic and apostolic church" (LC 1978, Res. 12). The Primates' Meeting continues to act as a consultative and advisory body though there has been much debate as to whether it should exercise "an enhanced responsibility in offering guidance on doctrinal, moral and pastoral matters" (LC 1988, Res. 18.2(a), 1998, Res. III.6; see also Gomez and Sinclair 2001). Indeed, the laws of some churches enable recourse to the Primates' Meeting in disputed matters of faith and order (e.g., South East Asia, Fundamental Declarations, 4). The Lambeth Commission proposed that the Primates' Meeting should function as "the primary forum for the strengthening of the mutual life of the provinces, and be respected by individual primates and the provinces they lead as an instrument through which new developments may be honestly addressed"; moreover, the Meeting should serve as the Standing Committee of the Lambeth Conference and as such "should monitor developments in furtherance of resolution of the Lambeth Conference in addition to the process of reception."[15] The terms of the Nassau, St. Andrews, and Ridley-Cambridge draft covenants, and their provisions on the Primates' Meeting (Doe 2008, 130), are generally mirrored in the Anglican Communion Covenant: the Primates' Meeting is convened by the Archbishop of Canterbury for mutual support, prayer, and counsel. The authority that primates bring to the meeting arises from their own positions as the senior bishops of their provinces, and the fact that they are in conversation with their own Houses of Bishops and located within their own synodical structures. In the meeting, the primates and moderators are called to work as representatives of their provinces in collaboration with one another in mission and in doctrinal, moral, and pastoral matters that have communion-wide implications (TACC, 3.1.4).

The Anglican Communion Covenant also provides that it is the responsibility of each instrument to consult with, respond to, and support each other instrument and the churches of the communion. Each instrument may initiate and commend a process of discernment and a direction for the communion and its churches (TACC, 3.1.4.IV). This, and the role of the instruments in processes to resolve controversial communion issues, is discussed more fully in the following text on Section III, titled "Our Unity and Common Life." However, in addition to these four institutions with a worldwide ministry, there are networks, commissions, and other bodies charged with a wide range of tasks to be carried out at the global level.[16] Perhaps the institutional instrument of unity

---

[15] *The Windsor Report* 2004, Appendix One (5): The Commission also proposed consideration of the organization of the Primates' Meeting "to facilitate greater participation by the primates and to provide for more formal and businesslike sessions": ibid.; for the idea that the Primates' Meeting serve as the Standing Committee of the Lambeth Conference, see LC 1978, Res. 11.

[16] These include, for example, Anglican Health Network, Anglican Peace and Justice Network, Anglican Communion Environmental Network, Network for Interfaith Concerns, Inter-Anglican Standing Commission on Unity, Faith and Order (and its work includes addressing issues related to the institutional instruments of unity communion), Inter-Anglican Standing Commission on Ecumenical Relations, and the Inter-Anglican Theological and Doctrinal Commission.

and communion which was most neglected in the Windsor reception process was that of each church itself – it is at the provincial level that juridical activity takes place within the worldwide communion, and it is in this activity that we might identify the contribution of provincial laws to the promotion and maintenance of global ecclesial communion – and it is to this we now turn.

## The Canonical Instruments of Unity and Communion

Each autonomous church in the Anglican Communion has its own legal system. Each legal system is to be found in a variety of different sources. Typically, each church has a constitution, canons, and other regulatory instruments including rules, decrees, regulations, and liturgical directives; there are also normative instruments in the form of codes of practice, guidance, and policy documents (which constitute what might be styled ecclesiastical quasi-legislation). These sources exist in the form of the general law of a provincial, national, or regional church (applicable to each of its component territorial units), as well as laws at the diocesan level. Their function is to order and facilitate common life and communion within each church (Doe 1998). The laws of each province not only function as an instrument of unity or communion within the province. Indeed, recent tensions in the communion have stimulated discussion of the ways in which these laws of churches may contribute to more visible international ecclesial unity in global Anglicanism in terms of the common principles they share.

The Primates' Meeting of 2001 discussed a paper on the role of canon law in the Anglican Communion – how there is no global canon law in Anglicanism, how provincial laws acknowledge membership of the communion but deal in the main with domestic provincial matters, and how exploration of these laws reveals fundamental shared principles of Anglican canon law (Doe 2002, 241; see also Doe 2003, 4). In consequence, the Primates' Meeting decided to explore whether there is an unwritten common law (or *ius commune*) shared by the churches of the communion. In March 2002, an Anglican Communion Legal Advisers Consultation, the first of its type, accepted the hypothesis on the basis of a study of 44 possible candidate principles prepared in advance for discussion at the event. The following month, the Primates' Meeting discussed a report on the Consultation and concluded: "The Primates recognized that the unwritten law common to the Churches of the Communion and expressed as shared principles of canon law may be understood to constitute a fifth 'instrument of unity'"; the Primates' Meeting also recommended the establishment of an Anglican Communion Network of Legal Advisers to produce "a statement of principles of Canon Law common within the Communion." The Network was set up at a meeting of the Anglican Consultative Council (ACC) in September 2002. In October 2003, an extraordinary Primates' Meeting urged completion of the work as did the Lambeth Commission in 2004. A drafting group of the Network met in 2005 (at Toronto) and 2006 (at Nassau), and after extensive consultation *The Principles of Canon Law Common to the Churches of the Anglican Communion* was launched at the Lambeth Conference in 2008 (Anglican Communion Network of Legal Advisers 2008). In 2009, the ACC thanked the Network for its work, commended the principles for study in every province, invited the provinces to submit comments on the document, requested a report on these, and encouraged provinces to use the Network as a resource in dealing with legal issues in those provinces (ACC-14, Res.14.20; resolved May 5, 2009).

That the Principles of Canon Law are recognized as an instrument of unity of communion is clearly expressed in the six conclusions formulated by the Legal Advisers Consultation of 2002 and repeated in the document launched by the Network of Legal Advisers in 2008.[17] First, there are principles of canon law common to the churches within the Anglican Communion. Indeed, the category "the principles of canon law" had previously been formally recognized by at least four Anglican churches as well as by other churches (West Indies, Const. Art. 6.2(1); Southern Africa, Canon 50; Central Africa, Canon 32.1; Nigeria, Const., Art. XIX.V; see also Roman Catholic Code of Canon Law 1983, c. 9; Eastern Catholic Churches, Code 1990, c.1501). Moreover, the provincial laws of many churches in the Anglican Communion commonly invoke explicit principles as the foundation for more detailed rules which function to enable communion within those churches. These principles give the more detailed rules shape, coherence, meaning, and purpose. Principles of canon law are in the form of general propositions or maxims; they express fundamental ecclesial or theological values, and are often rooted in the canonical tradition inherited by the churches of the Anglican Communion. As such, *principles* differ from *rules* (particular norms on particular factual situations). They also enjoy a dimension of weight and may indeed be shared with secular legal systems (such as the principle of the rule of law). Secondly, the existence of the principles can be factually established. The principles of canon law are induced from the factual similarities between the actual laws of each church of the Anglican Communion. Their recognition is a scientific task – an exercise in careful observation and comparison of the legal texts of the provinces of the communion. These similarities are often generated by churches using a common historical source, such as a Lambeth Conference resolution, rubrics of the Book of Common Prayer 1662, or even the Canons Ecclesiastical 1603 (of the Church of England).

Thirdly, for the consultation and network, each church contributes through its own legal system to the principles of canon law common within the communion. The Anglican *ius commune* represents the collective effect of similarities between provincial legal systems – it is not imposed from above – nor could it be, as no global institutional instrument in the communion has the jurisdictional competence to legislate for the autonomous churches. That the common principles are immanent in actual legal similarities means that each church is the legislator of the *ius commune*. When a church legislates on a particular matter, that church contributes to the store of principles. Moreover, the law of a church may function as a precedent which other churches employ in their own legislative activity – legal reform in the provinces often involves exploration of how other churches in the communion approach a particular matter. While churches are autonomous, as a matter of practice they often adopt or adapt provisions from the legal systems of fellow churches; and unilateral legislative adoption from another church may augment the authority of the principle. Fourthly, the principles have a strong persuasive authority and are fundamental to the self-understanding of each church in

---

[17] See the website of the Consultation: www.acclawnet.co.uk; see also Anglican Communion Network of Legal Advisers 2008, p.17.

the communion. While most principles may derive from similarities between written laws, some are based on unwritten assumptions implicit in written laws, and churches frequently portray a legal principle as having a deeper authority, beyond that of the formal law in which it appears.[18] Accordingly, the principles have the appearance of laws (they may be preceptive, prohibitive, or permissive), but they are not themselves laws: they are principles of law.

Fifthly, the principles have a living force, and contain in themselves the possibility of further development. Each church through its own legislative activity may contribute to or subtract from the store of principles, particularly when such developments are replicated around the communion. For example, churches are increasingly legislating to forbid racial discrimination in church membership and government; churches are developing rules on the admission of the unconfirmed to Holy Communion, particularly children; and many churches today are introducing norms to protect children from abuse in the exercise of ministry. Examples such as these may indicate the evolutionary character of the *ius commune* of the Anglican Communion. Finally, the existence of the principles both demonstrates unity and promotes unity within the Anglican Communion. The principles might be perceived by some as a threat to the autonomy of the member churches, or as a stimulus for global divisions (see also Jones 2005, 117 at 129). However, the principles are themselves a product of the exercise of the autonomy of churches. That they are created locally by the churches also underscores how the churches themselves use their legislative autonomy to shape the juridical unity in global Anglicanism which is present in the similarities exhibited in the articulation of the principles. Provincial autonomy is unaffected: as we have seen, churches remain free legally to depart from or to add to the principles of canon law. Indeed, that legal systems converge in shared principles of canon law is a concrete expression of the very character of Anglicanism internationally, its commitment to the values presented in them, and, in so far as each church contributes to the principles, the individual responsibility of each church for the shape and maintenance of Anglican identity. Also, first principles may be a useful resource for churches seeking to reform their own legal systems not least to test the innovativeness of the reform.[19]

The Legal Advisers Consultation 2002 was not particularly concerned with the methodological question of what test should be employed to determine whether a principle is one common to the churches.[20] However, *The Principles of Canon Law Common to the Churches of the Anglican Communion* provides that: "A 'principle of canon law' is a foundational proposition or maxim of general applicability which has a strong dimension of weight, is induced from the similarities of the legal systems of churches, derives

---

[18] The former Church of India, Pakistan, Burma and Ceylon, Constitution (1930), Declaration 11: "Of the authority of the principles and customs set out in the preceding Declarations"; the church has received these "from the Holy Catholic Church of ages past" and "believes that it was by the guidance of the Holy Spirit that those principles came to be recognised and those customs adopted."

[19] The principles were invoked in a property dispute by the Supreme Court of British Columbia in *Bentley v Anglican Synod of the Diocese of New Westminster* [2009] BCSC 1608.

[20] Anglican Communion Network of Legal Advisers 2008, 101; namely: unanimity; majority; face validity; reversal; common source; canonical tradition; fundamental ecclesial value; theological dimension; perception; and consensus.

from the canonical tradition or other practices of the church, expresses a basic theological truth or ethical value, and is about, is implicit in, or underlies canon law" (Anglican Communion Network of Legal Advisers 2008, Definitions, 95). There are 100 principles in the document. They are arranged under eight parts – and the 100 macroprinciples consists of over 600 micro-principles. Part I, "Order in the Church" (Principles 1–8), deals with the necessity for law in ecclesial society; law as the servant of the church; the conditional nature of church law; the sources, subjects, and forms of church law; the rule of law in the church; the requirement of authority; and the effect, application, and interpretation of law. The preamble to Part I emphasizes that the laws from which these principles are induced are "never the last word in determining the will of God, though they will often encapsulate the accumulated wisdom and discernment of people living within a certain Christian tradition during the church's long history" (Anglican Communion Network of Legal Advisers 2008, 17).

Part II concerns 'The Anglican Communion' (Principles 9–14) and includes principles relating to the nature of the communion, the instruments of communion, provincial autonomy, mutual respect, juridical presumptions, and the mutual availability of ministrations. The preamble to this part stresses that: "The strict legal autonomy of each church is seen not as being an end in itself"; rather, it is a means to provide "the greatest possible liberty to order its life and affairs, appropriate to its people in their geographical, cultural and historical context," while at the same time "living in interdependence with other Anglican churches who share the same historic identity and calling" (Anglican Communion Network of Legal Advisers 2008, 23). The principles set out in Part III (Principles 15–25) indicate the profound juridical unity throughout the Anglican Communion in relation to "Ecclesiastical Government": polity, leadership and authority, administration, delegation, representative government, legislative competence, lay participation in church government, visitations, and judicial process in courts and tribunals. Part IV carries principles of "Ministry" (Principles 26–46): the threefold ordained ministry of bishops, priests, and deacons; primates, archbishops, admission to the episcopate, the ministry of diocesan and assistant bishops, ordination, authority to minister in a diocese, ministry of priests and deacons, termination of ordained ministry; and the laity, church membership rolls, rights and duties of the faithful, lay ministers and officers, and professional and personal relationships in ministry. As the preamble to this part explains, the laws from which these principles are induced are themselves designed to engage, enable, and enlist "human resources in service of their mission to the world, promotion of fellowship of the faithful and witness to the gospel" (Anglican Communion Network of Legal Advisers 2008, 37).

"Doctrine and Liturgy," Part V, includes principles (47–59) on profession of the faith; the sources and development of doctrine; preaching, teaching, and outreach; doctrinal discipline; and public worship and liturgy – making and authorizing forms of service, the administration of public worship, and liturgical discipline. Throughout these principles runs "the certainty that in Christ, God's revelation is made known, controlling the Church's faith, commanding the worship of the faithful, and energising the whole body" of the communion of churches so that they may better "illuminate, challenge and transform cultures, structures, thinking and doing" in the wider world (Anglican

Communion Network of Legal Advisers 2008, 55). Principles on baptism, confirmation, Holy Communion, marriage, confession, and burial are set out in Part VI, 'The Rites of the Church' (Principles 60–79). Interestingly, the preamble to this part provides that: "Perhaps unsurprisingly within a worldwide Communion whose liturgical life was essentially shaped by . . . the Book of Common Prayer (1662), there has been widespread agreement over matters of form, including agreement about the principles of liturgical revision in individual churches"; however, "at the same time, historic tensions between the Catholic and Protestant emphases within Anglicanism are never far from the surface" (Anglican Communion Network of Legal Advisers 2008, 65).

Part VII (Principles 80–92) reflects the juridical unity in Anglicanism as to "Church Property" – it presents principles on, amongst other things, ownership and administration, responsible stewardship, places of worship, clergy residences, registers and records, the distribution and control of funds, sources of income, investments, insurance, and clergy stipends and pensions. According to the preamble to this part: "The recurrent theme is the church's interest in ensuring that property be set aside, used and maintained with reverence and integrity to further the mission of the church" (Anglican Communion Network of Legal Advisers 2008, 79). The final section, Part VIII on "Ecumenical Relations," features principles relating to ecumenical responsibilities, freedom, recognition, agreements, collaboration, admission, and reception, as well as the admission of non-Anglicans to Holy Communion (Principles 93–100). The preamble to this part proposes that these juridical principles underline how "[t]he Anglican Communion has never seen itself as a complete and self-sufficient entity, but as an expression of Communion within the One Holy Catholic and Apostolic Church which takes seriously its vocation to reach out beyond its own life to the greater unity of the Church" (Anglican Communion Network of Legal Advisers 2008, 89).

With the exception of Parts I and II (on church order and the Anglican Communion), the grouping of principles into these parts is shaped by the systematization of laws employed by the churches of the communion, treating as they do governance, ministry, doctrine and liturgy, rites, property, and, increasingly, ecumenical relations. The principles are derived from various formal sources. Most are from constitutions and canons, and many from the liturgical norms of service books (which themselves enjoy canonical authority) (e.g., Principle 69 on the nature of marriage), and historical sources (the authority of which may be canonically recognized by the churches), such as the Book of Common Prayer 1662 (e.g., Principle 64.6: on baptism and confirmation of mature persons), the canonical tradition (e.g., Principle 25.6: *nemo iudex in sua causa* [an aspect of judicial impartiality]), divine law (e.g., Principle 47.2: the duty to proclaim the Gospel), or the practice of the church universal (e.g., Principle 60.1: baptism effects incorporation into the church of Christ). Others are rooted in a theological idea expressed in laws (e.g., Principle 53: worship as a fundamental action of the church), or from guidance issued by ecclesiastical authorities to supplement church law (e.g., Principle 43: the professional ethic of public ministry). While the vast majority derives from similarities between the written laws of churches, some are based on unwritten assumptions, general propositions implicit in church laws. The juridical values of clarity, conciseness, and consistency govern the form of the principles which themselves are cast in a variety of juridical formulae: most are permissions ("may"); many are precepts ("shall," "must"); some are prohibitions ("shall not," "no one shall"); many are exhortations ("should": aspirational); and some are maxims ("is").

The document *The Principles of Canon Law Common to the Churches of the Anglican Communion* has appeared at a time of great tension in the worldwide Anglican Communion. However, as the preface to the document states: "this work is still far from being set in stone: these principles are by their nature organic and open to development and refinement"; they map out the main legal themes of the Anglican inheritance "when some of the peripheral local detail is stripped away"; and their articulation is "to stimulate reflection on what it is to be a Communion of ordered churches, seeking to live out the Anglican tradition in a world of intensely rapid communication" (Anglican Communion Network of Legal Advisers 2008, 14–15). Indeed, this project might have been undertaken, with the exactly the same results, at any time. The underlying idea is not revolutionary. For the most part, the document is simply a statement or description of facts derived from the convergences of Anglican legal systems. The *ius commune* is not an instrument of unity in the sense of a "top-down" binding global legal system imposed by a central Anglican authority (none is competent to create such a system). Rather, it is an instrument of unity in the sense of a "grassroots" development growing from the exercise by each church of its own autonomy through its legal system. The statement clearly shows how much Anglicans are united by way of what they share in common, using local provincial laws and the global principles they reveal as the medium. The principles also provide an accessible resource for ecumenical partners in developing their own understanding of Anglicanism from a global perspective. As such, the *ius commune*, as a global canonical instrument of unity and communion, enriches rather than undermines traditional Anglican ecclesiology in its historical theological form (see Cameron 2008, 69 at 76).

## The Covenant as Instrument of Unity and Communion

The *Windsor Report* (2004) proposed, *inter alia*, the adoption by the churches of the Anglican Communion of a covenant,[21] and the report included a draft covenant (hereafter, the Windsor Draft Covenant [WDAC]) (*The Windsor Report* 2004, Appendix Two, 81; see Doe 2004, 147). *Towards an Anglican Covenant*, published in 2006 to take the proposal forward, was endorsed later that year by the Joint Standing Committee of the ACC and Primates' Meeting. A Covenant Design Group was set up, offered its first draft covenant in 2007 (the Nassau Draft Covenant [NDC]), and following a provincial consultation in 2007 revised this in its St. Andrews draft covenant (SADC) in 2008 (see Doe 2008). The latter was discussed at the Lambeth Conference in the summer of 2008. The Covenant Design Group met in September 2008 to consider the reflections

---

[21] The Primates' Meeting in 2001 considered a paper which (along with the principles of canon law project) proposed adoption of "a concordat for incorporation by individual churches in their own canonical systems" seeking "to increase the profile of communion, to define their inter-church relations, and for the resolution of inter-Anglican conflict"; the paper was subsequently published as Doe 2002, 241 esp. 262.

of the Lambeth Conference and produced its Ridley-Cambridge draft in 2009 (RCDC).[22] Section 4 of the RCDC was revised after discussion by the ACC in May 2009 (ACC-14, Res. 14.11; May 8, 2009). Once the Standing Committee of the Anglican Communion agreed upon the final text in December 2009, the Anglican Communion Covenant was circulated to the churches of the communion for ratification or rejection in accordance with their own particular formal processes.[23] The Covenant is understood to reflect the call of Anglicans to be in communion in witness and mission so as to enrich the common life of the communion; enabling "the Churches to live together in mutual care and affection as one Communion . . . to witness . . . to the biblical commands of charity and unity" (TACC:QAA, sect. 3; see also sect. 4 on how the covenant will "deepen" communion life for background, see Doe 2008, Ch. 3).

The Anglican Communion Covenant consists of a preamble, four sections, and a declaration. While the covenant is itself an instrument of unity and communion, it also points to other instruments of unity and communion in global Anglicanism. The preamble sets out the reasons for covenanting: to proclaim the grace of God revealed in the gospel, to respond to the needs of the world, to maintain unity, and to attain the full stature of Christ. The first three sections, on faith, mission, and unity, consist of affirmations followed by commitments arising from those affirmations; it is each church of the communion that makes the affirmation and the commitment – as with the Principles of Canon Law, this approach once more underscores how each of the churches is itself an instrument of communion (and is responsible for its continued maintenance). The first section is entitled "Our Inheritance of Faith." Each church affirms its communion in the one, holy, catholic, and apostolic church, the catholic and apostolic faith revealed in scripture and set out in the catholic creeds and historic formularies of the Church of England (where acknowledged provincially), the Chicago-Lambeth Quadrilateral (on scripture, creeds, sacraments, and historic episcopate), shared patterns of worship, and its participation in the mission of the people of God (TACC, 1.1).[24] The covenantal commitments address a common approach to the contextual application of the shared inherited faith. In living out the inheritance together in their varying contexts, each church commits itself, *inter alia*, to teach and act in continuity and consonance with scripture and the catholic and apostolic faith, order, and tradition, as received by the churches, to faithful, coherent, and respectful interpretation of scripture, and to nurture and sustain Eucharistic communion (TACC, 1.2.1–8; see also TACC:ASG, 6: the commitments spell out "a way of" teaching, etc.).

The second section, titled "The Life We Share with Others: Our Anglican Vocation," deals with mission. Mission itself is presented as an instrument of communion insofar as it brings each of the churches together in its promotion – mission is by nature a collaborative process. Each church affirms that communion is not an end in itself but

[22] The Framework Procedures for the Resolution of Covenant Disagreements appended to SADC was dropped after criticism of it at the Lambeth Conference as too juridical; for the procedure, see Doe 2008, Ch. 4.
[23] The Anglican Communion Office issued "The Anglican Communion Covenant: A Study Guide" (TACC:ASG), and "The Anglican Communion Covenant: Questions and Answers" (TACC:QAA). As of May 2011, the covenant has been adopted by Mexico, West Indies, Myanmar, and Ireland.
[24] The footnotes to 1.1 refer to the Thirty-Nine Articles of Religion, 1662 Book of Common Prayer, and Ordering of Bishops, Priests, and Deacons, and Chicago-Lambeth Quadrilateral 1886/1888.

seeks to proclaim and witness to God and that God has been at work in Anglican history in shaping its worldwide mission; each church also confesses its failure to live up to that calling and undertakes to cooperate with other Anglicans in mission and with other Christians ecumenically. In turn, each church commits itself to share its resources to evangelize, heal, and reconcile the broken world; to engage in mission; to be humble and open to conversion; to renew structures for mission; and to root mission in the worship of God (particularly in Eucharistic communion) (TACC, 2.2.1–5).[25]

The third section, "Our Unity and Common Life," deals with the exercise of provincial autonomy in the context of ecclesial communion.[26] Each church affirms its call to live in peace and build up the common life of the communion, its resolve to live in a communion of churches, its autonomy (its own system of government and law), the absence of a central global authority in Anglicanism, the role of bishops and the three-fold ministry, and the importance of the instruments of communion in global Anglicanism (Archbishop of Canterbury, Lambeth Conference, Anglican Consultative Council, and Primates' Meeting) (TACC, 3.1.1–4).[27] Next, each church commits itself to having regard for the common good of the communion in the exercise of its autonomy, to support the work of the instruments of communion, and to receive their work with a readiness to reflect on their counsels and endeavor to accommodate their recommendations. Moreover, each church must respect the constitutional autonomy of all the churches of the communion; uphold mutual responsibility and interdependence; seek to discern the will of God through listening, prayer, study, and debate; and seek a shared mind (consistent with canon law) in matters of common concern through consultation. Each church must also act with diligence, care, and caution in matters which may provoke controversy "which by its intensity, substance or extent threaten the unity of the Communion and the effectiveness of its mission." In conflicts, a church must participate in mediated conversations and bear in mind that the bonds of affection and love of Christ require maintenance of "the highest degree of communion possible" (TACC, 3.2.1–7).

Section four is entitled "Our Covenanted Life Together." This sets out the procedures for adopting the covenant and living together by it, and includes rudimentary procedures for conflict resolution. Each church affirms a set of principles and procedures and, reliant on the Holy Spirit, commits itself to their implementation. By adopting the covenant, a church freely offers a commitment to other churches "to live more fully into

[25] A prominent place is given to the Five Marks of Mission as found in the MISSIO Report 1999 and set out in ACC-6 and 8.

[26] It builds on the principle of autonomy-in-communion developed in *The Windsor Report* 2004, para. 76, *The Windsor Report* 2004, Appendix Two, Pt. IV. However, the section was substantially modified (from SADC) in the light of suggestions received from the Provinces and the Lambeth Conference: CDG, Commentary on RCDC (April 1, 2009).

[27] Interestingly, while each church is party to the covenant, the covenant provides that: "It is the responsibility of each Instrument to consult with, respond to, and support each other Instrument and the Churches of the Communion. Each Instrument may initiate and commend a process of discernment and a direction for the Communion of Churches." In other words, the covenant provides for a persuasive authority (or jurisdiction) for the instruments (even though they are not themselves signatories to it). One task of the Inter-Anglican Standing Commission on Unity, Faith and Order is to study the role and responsibilities of the Instruments of Communion: ACC-14, Res. 14.09 and 10.

the ecclesial communion and interdependence which is foundational to the Churches of the Anglican Communion" (TACC, 4.1.1).[28] Adoption means that a church recognizes that the covenantal statement of faith, mission, and interdependence of life is consistent with its own life, but such mutual commitment does not represent submission to any external ecclesiastical jurisdiction. Every church of the communion, as recognized under the ACC Constitution (i.e., those churches listed on the schedule of membership of the ACC), is invited to enter the covenant according to its own constitutional procedures. However, if a church does not adopt the Covenant, this does not mean that it is no longer a part of the Anglican Communion; it still retains its Anglican identity (TACC:QAA, sect. 6.).[29] The Covenant is active for a church when it adopts the Covenant through the procedures contained in its own constitution and canons (TACC, 4.1.6).[30]

The next set of provisions deals with maintenance of the covenant and resolution of disputes; the covenanted position may be summed up in the maxim: the communion guides; each church decides (CDG Report on the RCDC 2009; April 1, 2009); in relation to its Section 3), thus protecting provincial autonomy and giving no coercive jurisdiction to the central instruments of communion. Each church has a duty of "fidelity" to the Covenant. The Standing Committee of the Anglican Communion (responsible to the ACC and Primates' Meeting) must monitor "the functioning of the Covenant in the life of the Anglican Communion on behalf of the Instruments [of Communion]." When questions arise about "the meaning of the Covenant, or about the compatibility of an action by a covenanting Church with the Covenant, it is the duty of each covenanting Church to seek to live out the commitments [of mutual accountability and interdependence]." When a shared mind has not been reached, the Standing Committee must make every effort to facilitate agreement. The Covenant does not provide a system of sanctions in the event of breach of covenant by a signatory church. The Committee may request a church to defer a controversial action; if the church declines to do so, the Committee may recommend to any Instrument of Communion "relational consequences" which may specify a provisional limitation of participation in or suspension from that instrument until completion of the following process. The Committee may also (on the advice of the ACC and the Primates' Meeting) make a declaration that an action or decision is "incompatible with the Covenant." On the advice received, the

[28] Moreover: "The Anglican Communion is a fellowship, within the One, Holy, Catholic and Apostolic Church, of national or regional Churches, in which each recognises in the others the bonds of a common loyalty to Christ expressed through a common faith and order, a shared inheritance in worship, life and mission, and a readiness to live an interdependent life".

[29] However, see also the Covenant Working Party Commentary on Revisions to Section 4 (2009): "The question has also been raised about the status of Churches of the Anglican Communion who choose not to enter the Anglican Communion Covenant. The working Group considers that it is not appropriate to address this question within the text of the Covenant. Rather, there should be the flexibility for the Instruments of Communion to determine an appropriate response in the evolving situation that would accompany a process of reception and adoption of the Covenant." For earlier debate about tiers of membership, see N. Doe, *An Anglican Covenant* (2008) Ch. 8.

[30] *The Windsor Report* had proposed that each church enacts its own brief communion law authorizing its primate (or equivalent) to sign the covenant on behalf of that church and commit the church to adhere to the terms of the covenant: *The Windsor Report* 2004, para. 118.

Committee must make recommendations to the churches and instruments as to relational consequences which flow from such incompatibility – namely, the extent which
the decision of the covenanting church in question impairs or limits the communion
between that church and other churches of the communion and the practical consequences of this. Each church or instrument then determines whether or not to accept
the recommendations. Each church must also have its own structures to oversee the
maintenance of the Covenant in the life of that church and to relate to the instruments
of communion on matters pertinent to the Covenant (TACC, 4.2.9; for the original idea,
see *The Windsor Report* 2004, Appendix Two, Art. 25: the Anglican Communion officer).
Finally, any covenanting church may decide to withdraw from the Covenant, the Covenant may be amended with the consent of three-quarters of the covenanting churches
(TACC, 4.4.2),[31] and the signatories declare their churches "to be partakers in this
Anglican Communion Covenant" (TACC, "Our Declaration": this also invokes Hebrews
13.10, 21). That the Covenant is an instrument which binds a church is in line with
the canonical principle (with its long historical and theological pedigree) *pacta sunt
servanda*: agreements must be kept (see Doe 2008, Ch. 9).

The Covenant represents a major historical development for worldwide Anglicanism. It raises a host of both theological and legal issues, ranging from the theological
nature of communion, through the legal character of provincial autonomy, to the
theological and juridical implications of covenanting. The initial Windsor proposal and
draft covenant were not universally welcomed: some accepted the covenant principle
and the draft; others, the principle but not the draft; and some rejected both (for
rejection of the idea see, e.g., Adams 2004, 9; see also Adams 2005, 70). Following
publication of the Nassau, St. Andrews, and Ridley-Cambridge drafts, responses indicated a greater general sympathy for a covenant, and voices rejecting the principle
became fewer.[32] Respondents generally agreed about the voluntary and relational
character of a covenant with commitments (see, e.g., Goddard 2008, 47; see also The
Inter-Anglican Standing Commission on Mission and Evangelism, Covenant for Communion in Mission 2005, 3, 7; Williams 2006), though several attacked analogies
between a covenant and a contract as too juridical and likely to undermine the consensual character of Anglicanism (see, e.g., Lewis 2005, 601 at 604). Many respondents
felt that a covenant accords with the notion of the communion as a consensual family
of churches (see Radner 2005, 609; Gladwin 2008, 3), but for the critics a covenant
is at odds with the spirit of Anglicanism, crisis-driven, a "quick fix" which would translate the bonds of affection into a formal (juridical) commitment (see Chapman 2008,
33; see also, e.g., the studies in Bolt et al. 2005), that there are too many practical
obstacles in the process of adoption in each church (Tong 2005, 58), that it will make
divisions within the communion even more visible, and that it makes new demands
on the instruments of communion (see, e.g., TACC:QAA, sect. 10 and *The Anglican*

[31] The requirement for altering or adding to the Schedule of member churches of the ACC is approval by
two-thirds of the Primates of the Anglican Communion: ACC Const., Articles of Association, Art. 7.2.
[32] See, for example, Covenant Working Party Commentary on Revisions to Section 4 (2009): "The clear
majority of responses demonstrated that a section of the Covenant which seeks to provide an ordered way
for the Communion to approach disagreement remains a necessary feature of the Covenant."

*Covenant: A Church Times Guide* 2011). However, much depends on how it will be received in the life of the communion (TACC:QAA, sect. 10).

The Covenant project should not be seen in isolation. It may usefully be measured against covenant models in scripture, sacramental theology, ecumenism, and comparable global ecclesial communities (see generally Doe 2008, 47–51). First, prior to circulation of the Covenant, much was made of the idea that existing covenantal relationships in Anglicanism have biblical foundations, and it was often proposed that scriptural covenants may provide an inspiration for development of an ecclesial covenant (Seitz 2008, 81). Indeed, covenantal theology (particularly in Protestant tradition) maintains that scriptural covenants may legitimately function as models for ecclesiastical polity: covenants associate an ecclesial community. Secondly, in the sacramental covenants of baptism, marriage, and ordination, the parties are called to covenant, exchange promises, undertake commitments, and limit their autonomy by the duty to have regard for others; the sacramental covenants are entered solemnly, bind the parties, and are regulated by canon law (with consequences for non-compliance with their commitments). Thirdly, ecumenical covenants and other agreements are today normal vehicles by which Anglican churches enter and regulate their relationships of communion or inter-communion with other churches, often after negotiation following a call to covenant; they are voluntarily entered, involve affirmations of common identity, and prescribe commitments through pledges and other solemn undertakings. They enable shared ministry, worship and mission, and represent a witness to the unity for which Christ prayed. Often, provision is made in them for their own development, for tiered membership and differentiated commitments. They may be unilateral, bilateral, or multilateral, but generally recognize and protect the autonomy of the partner churches as compatible with being in communion. Finally, in addition to parallels which may be drawn with historical and contemporary covenants entered between Anglicans,[33] the Anglican covenant shares many similarities with the instruments of unity and communion of comparable international ecclesial communities in the Orthodox, Lutheran, Methodist, and Reformed traditions (Doe 2008, Ch. 3).

## Conclusion

Needless to say, theologically, the principal instrument of unity and communion for Anglicans as for other Christians is the unity provided by the loving activity of God in the lives of the faithful. The institutional, canonical, and covenantal instruments outlined here are merely functional, humanly created instruments designed to promote and support ecclesial unity and communion. They represent a means to an end – the deeper unity and communion for which Christ prayed for his church. Nevertheless, as instruments operative in the visible structures of global Anglicanism, they play their part as obvious mechanisms to enable and order the visible relations between Anglicans

---

[33] For the *Concordate* of 1784 between Samuel Seabury, for the diocese of Connecticut, and the Scottish bishops, see Thomas 2004, 9; for the idea presented at the Lambeth Conference 1988 of a "common declaration," see Hind 2008, 112 at 121.

in their common service of God. The Archbishop of Canterbury, Lambeth Conference, Anglican Consultative Council, and Primates' Meeting are all important deliberative facilities to enable Anglicans to unite one with another in a global institutional framework. In these institutions, Anglicans take common counsel and encouragement in their individual and collaborative promotion of the mission of the church universal – and the institutions themselves exercise an important moral authority for the global family of churches in terms of their shared faith and order. Moreover, the principles of canon law represent a canonical instrument of unity and communion not in the sense of a binding global legal system but in terms of the juridical unity which Anglicans share on the basis of the profound similarities which exist between those legal systems. The principles do not achieve spiritual communion but provide a juridical framework within which Anglicans may recognize among themselves the marks of their shared ecclesial heritage. In this sense, the principles and the juridical unity they reveal also underscore that the primary responsibility for the shape and maintenance of communion in global Anglicanism resides with the provincial church – and that the legislative activity of each church locally is a place from which juridical unity globally emanates. Similarly, the Anglican Communion Covenant represents a historical landmark in the development of ecclesial unity and communion in global Anglicanism. The covenant represents a way of setting out the basic ground rules by which the worldwide Anglican family should achieve its objectives and how it should address making decisions on difficult issues of common concern. The Covenant sees partnership between the communion (the family) and each autonomous church as the primary manifestation of Anglicanism, one which protects the autonomy of the province (its legal freedom) subject to the competence of the communion (through its instruments) to guide in a limited field of highly contentious matters of common concern: the communion guides; each church decides. That is the modest function which any instrument of unity is able to serve.

## Bibliography

ACC Constitution.

ACC-14.

Adams, M. 2004. How to Quench the Spirit. *Church Times*, vol. 9 (October 29, 2004).

Adams, M. 2005. Faithfulness in Crisis. In *Gays and the Future of Anglicanism: Responses to the Windsor Report*, eds. A. Linzey and R. Kirker. Winchester: O Books.

Anglican Communion Network of Legal Advisers. 2008. *Principles of Canon Law Common to the Churches of the Anglican Communion (PCLCCAC)*. London: Anglican Communion Office.

*Bentley v. Anglican Synod of the Diocese of New Westminster* [2009] BCSC 1608.

Bolt, P. G., M. D. Thompson, and R. Tong, eds. 2005. *The Faith Once For All Delivered*. Camperdown, NSW: The Australian Church Record in conjunction with the Anglican League.

Cameron, G. K. 2008. A Tortoise in a Hurry: The Ordering of the Anglican Communion. *International Journal for the Study of the Christian Church*, vol. 8 (2008), 69 at 76.

CDG Report on the RCDC 2009 (April 1, 2009).

Central Africa. The Province of. Canons.

Central Africa. Fundamental Declarations.

Chadwick, O. 1992. Introduction. In *Resolutions of the Twelve Lambeth Conferences*

1867–1988, ed. E. Coleman. The Anglican Communion, Lambeth Reports. London.

Chapman, Mark D. 2008. *The Anglican Covenant: Unity and Diversity in the Anglican Communion*. London: Mowbray.

Doe, N. 1998. *Canon Law in the Anglican Communion*. Oxford: Clarendon Press.

Doe, N. 2002. Canon Law and Communion. *Ecclesiastical Law Journal*, vol. 6 (2002), 241.

Doe, N. 2003. The Common Law of the Anglican Communion. *Ecclesiastical Law Journal*, 7 (2003), 4.

Doe, N. 2004. The Anglican Covenant proposed by the Lambeth Commission. *Ecclesiastical Law Journal*, 17 (2004), 147.

Doe, N. 2008. *An Anglican Covenant: Theological and Legal Considerations for a Global Debate*. London: Canterbury Press.

Eastern Catholic Churches, Code 1990, c.1501.

Gladwin, J. 2008. The Local and the Universal and the Meaning of Anglicanism: Kenya. In *A Fallible Church: Lambeth Essays*, ed. K. Stevenson. London: Darton, Longman & Todd.

Goddard, A. 2008. Unity and Diversity, Communion and Covenant: Theological, Ecclesiological, Political and Missional Challenges for Anglicanism. In *The Anglican Covenant*, ed. M. Chapman. London: Mowbray.

Gomez, D. W. and M. W. Sinclair, eds. 2001. *To Mend the Net: Anglican Faith and Order for Renewed Mission*. Carolton TX: Ekklesia Society.

Hind, J. 2008. The Idea of an Anglican Covenant: A Faith and Order Perspective. *International Journal for the Study of the Christian Church*, vol. 8 (2008), 112 at 121.

IATDC. Communion, Conflict and Hope.

Jones, G. 2005. Thy Grace Shall Always Prevent. . . . In *Gays and the Future of Anglicanism: Responses to the Windsor Report*, eds. A. Linzey and R. Kirker. Winchester: O Books.

Kenya, The Anglican Church of. Constitution.

Kuehn, E. F. 2008. Instruments of Faith and Unity in Canon Law: the Church of Nigeria Constitutional Revision of 2005. *Ecclesiastical Law Journal*, vol. 10 (2008), 161 at 166.

Lambeth Conference (LC). 1867.

Lambeth Conference (LC). 1908.

Lambeth Conference (LC). 1920.

Lambeth Conference (LC). 1930.

Lambeth Conference (LC). 1948.

Lambeth Conference (LC). 1958.

Lambeth Conference (LC). 1978.

Lambeth Conference (LC). 1988.

Lambeth Conference (LC). 1998

Lewis, H. T. 2005. Covenant, Contract and Communion: Reflections on a Post-Windsor Anglicanism. *Anglican Theological Review*, 87 (2005), 601 at 604.

Lusitanian Catholic Apostolic and Evangelical Church, Constitution.

Nigeria, Church of. Constitution.

Podmore, C. 2005. *Aspects of Anglican Identity*. London: Church House Publishing.

Puerto Rico, The Diocese of. Constitution.

Radner, E. 2005. Freedom and Covenant: The Miltonian Analogy Transfigured. *Anglican Theological Review*, vol. 87 (2005), 609.

Report of the Windsor Continuation Group.

Roman Catholic Church. 1983. Roman Catholic Code of Canon Law 1983.

Seitz, C. 2008. Canon, Covenant and Rule of Faith – The Use of Scripture. *International Journal for the Study of the Christian Church*, vol. 8 (2008), 81.

South East Asia, The Province of. Fundamental Declarations.

Southern Africa, Anglican Church of. Canons.

Stephenson, A. M. G. 1967. *The First Lambeth Conference*. London: SPCK.

Sudan, The Episcopal Church of. Constitution.

Tanzania, The Anglican Church of. Constitution.

The Anglican Communion Covenant (TACC).

The Anglican Communion Covenant: A Study Guide (TACC:ASG). The Anglican Communion Office.

The Anglican Communion Covenant: Questions and Answers (TACC:QAA). The Anglican Communion Office.

*The Anglican Covenant: A Church Times Guide.* 2011. Church Times, March 18, 2011.

The Inter-Anglican Standing Commission on Mission and Evangelism. 2005. Covenant for Communion in Mission.

*The Virginia Report.*

*The Windsor Report (TWR).* 2004. London: Anglican Communion Office.

The Windsor Report, Appendix Two: Proposal for the Anglican Covenant, The Anglican Covenant (hereafter WDAC)

Thomas, P. H. E. 2004. Unity and Concord: An Early Anglican "Communion". *Journal of Anglican Studies*, vol. 21 (2004), 9.

Tong, R. 2005. How Would the Anglican Church of Australia Commit Itself to an Anglican Covenant? In *The Faith Once for All Delivered*, eds. P. G. Bolt, M. D. Thompson and R. Tong. Camperdown, NSW: The Australian Church Record in Conjunction with the Anglican League.

Uganda, The Province of. Constitution.

West Indies, The Province of. Canons.

West Indies, Constitution.

Williams, Rowan. 2006. The Challenge and Hope of Being Anglican Today: A Reflection for the Bishops, Clergy and Faithful of the Anglican Communion (June 27, 2006): Anglican Communion News Service 4161.

CHAPTER 5

# The Archbishops of Canterbury, Past and Current

## Nancy Carol James

### The Role of the Archbishop of Canterbury

After the 2011 Occupy protests at St. Paul's Cathedral in London, a reporter asked Archbishop of Canterbury Rowan Williams a question about the slogan WWJD (What would Jesus do?) to which Williams gave the answer, "WWJD? He'd first of all be *there*: sharing the risks, asking the long and hard questions. Not just taking sides but steadily changing the entire atmosphere by the questions he asks of everybody involved. . . . What changes the world isn't a single formula for getting the right answer but a willingness to stop and let yourself be challenged right to the roots of your being" (Radio Times 2011).

In this answer, Williams captures the essence of the role of the Archbishop of Canterbury. For this position requires one who stands strong in times of crisis, shares the risks of life, and asks the difficult questions to all involved. The archbishop serves all people throughout the globe in the name of Christ and has become an international person who speaks truth without reservations and who offers himself as a trustworthy spiritual guide. At times of crisis and tragedy, many turn to the Archbishop of Canterbury for help and assistance.

The archbishop functions as the head of the Diocese of Canterbury in England, and yet has assumed responsibility for the entire Anglican Communion as well as the Church of England. He exercises the complex role of spiritual leader for this global church with 38 provinces.

Through the work of the archbishops, the faithful passion of Jesus' first apostles has been sustained, and so global Anglicans still affirm the succession from the time of the apostles. Apostolic succession in the Anglican Communion helps guarantee the continuation of this church, with the Archbishop of Canterbury assessing situations from the perspective of how to ensure truth and justice. Indeed, the Archbishop of

*The Wiley-Blackwell Companion to the Anglican Communion*, First Edition. Edited by Ian S. Markham,
J. Barney Hawkins IV, Justyn Terry, and Leslie Nuñez Steffensen.
© 2013 John Wiley & Sons, Ltd. Published 2013 by John Wiley & Sons, Ltd.

Canterbury promises to seek the divine will in the light of scriptures and revelation and to pronounce the Word of God faithfully to a world in need.

### Serving the monarch of England: sharing the risks

Right from the first Archbishop of Canterbury, all have worked closely with the English monarchy. Throughout history, the king or queen has wanted a holy person with integrity to crown him or her to ensure that his or her temporal power would be accepted. The monarch was responsible for keeping people safe as well as ensuring that a healthy church served the people. With their close relationships with the heads of state, these archbishops have developed a faith that is not separated from the troubling and harsh human reality of maintaining political power amidst frequently difficult circumstances.

One symbol of the close relationship between the monarch and the Archbishop of Canterbury can literally be seen in the staircase physically added to Lambeth Palace, the official residence for the archbishop, for Queen Victoria's room when she spent the night. This queen rightly feared the danger of fires and always had a fire exit planned. For her room at Lambeth Palace, they built a special fire escape staircase for her that still graces the sidewall. Through the centuries, the Archbishop of Canterbury and the monarch have experienced a close and productive collaboration.

Enthroned archbishops have also fulfilled their role by helping the monarch and political leaders interpret history. At their best, the many and varied Archbishops of Canterbury have struggled for truth and justice in particular historical events while serving a dual function with both ecclesiastical and secular authority. Success in this complicated role seems partially dependent on personal qualities of courage, judgment, eloquence, and self-control, because while the Archbishop of Canterbury has access to worldly power and a public voice, in modern times he possesses little or no legal power or coercive capability.

Compounding the responsibilities of the Archbishop of Canterbury is the unstated expectation of utilizing diplomatic and even legal skills in the Anglican Communion and in international relationships. Indeed, before being granted this position, many of the archbishops were tested with a secular or church diplomatic mission. The Archbishops of Canterbury also served many monarchs as chancellors and, while doing so, helped define the legal and complicated relationship between church and crown. Hence, the Archbishop of Canterbury is a complex position with spiritual goals, all of which need to be applied in immediate historical situations with public results.

### The risks of involvement: accepting the challenges

The current Archbishop is Justin Welby. He was appointed to what is universally described as one of the hardest positions in the church. His predecessor, Rowan Williams, in his discussion of St. Antony of Egypt and the Desert Fathers once described bishops as the "bearers of dangerous possibilities" (Williams 2003, 66). Indeed, the Archbishop of Canterbury does carry dangerous possibilities. The archbishop carries within his own being the potential to bring affliction upon himself as he speaks the Word of God. The archbishop also carries dangerous possibilities for others as he ordains them into the church and as they engage with the demands of historical action within the Anglican Communion.

Throughout the centuries, the Archbishops of Canterbury have had to deal with a wide variety of historical difficulties, including church intrigue with the antipopes, revolutions in the English Court, numerous Viking invasions, charges of treason, the demand for church lands and money, exorbitant clergy taxation, and personal violence. They struggled against pressure to subordinate the English Church to Roman Catholic authority. They needed to enforce unpopular clergy discipline and provide supervision for lax religious houses. In some troublesome eras, they have become clerical states-men. They needed to defend the rights of the church amidst struggles to decide which had precedence, canon law or English common law. Manifold dangers abounded for such diplomatic, prophetic, and spiritual roles residing in one person.

The great truth upon which the role of the Archbishop of Canterbury is based is that religious and political realms are inextricably combined. They are, so to speak, two sides of the same coin. The political realm makes decisions for the well-being (or lack thereof) of society. The religious realm seeks the will of God and faithfully voices and records what its perceptions are. If one separates from the other, this becomes a dangerous relationship between the two realms. One example of this is seen in the conflict between Archbishop Thomas Becket and King Henry II that led to Becket's martyrdom.

And yet, in modern times, the archbishop's actual power is quite limited: he has no army, no ability to arrest people, no authority over different provinces in the Anglican Communion, and no power over other primates with whom he disagrees. With all of these limitations, he is fully vulnerable to the sweeps of historical activity that all experi-ence. Examples of the exigent problems associated with historical events abound. During World War II, Lambeth Palace was hit by many bombs and severely damaged. In 1987, Archbishop Runcie's envoy Terry Waite went to Lebanon for a diplomatic mission and, sadly, Waite was kidnapped and held until 1991.

In contrast, the pope as head of the Roman Catholic Church lives and works in a much more protected environment. He is the head of a sovereign city-state called Vatican City which has land separated by walls and surrounded by Rome. The pope also enjoys the protection of the Swiss Guard. In the nineteenth century, the decision was made that if the Pope speaks *ex cathedra*, the words are infallible, which grants him additional authority.

Yet, those who have been placed in the role of the Archbishop of Canterbury under-stand the value of living a public yet vulnerable life and do not seek additional control. In 1989, Archbishop Runcie wrote, "We have no intention of developing an alternative papacy" (1989, 7). Faith is needed to fulfill this vital position.

### Asking the long and hard questions

Because of his limited power, the life of the Archbishop of Canterbury as lived in modern times is not unlike the life of the common man or woman. The questions the person in this position has to struggle with are ones all humanity needs to face. On what spiritual authority, if any, do I rest my life? How will I achieve integrity or happiness? How do I serve my country? If I am a faithful person, what role will this faith take in my life? The life that each Archbishop of Canterbury develops helps reveal not only a potential revelation of God, but also how that man deals with the very real dangers and stresses of the era in which he lives. As Anglicans see the public life of the Archbishop of Canterbury, they engage with and have the possibility of pondering their own historical choices made in the rush of time.

Yet, every archbishop faces different challenges and asks different questions depending on the tenor of the times. During World War II, Archbishop Temple asked how faith can survive when the civilization itself is under attack. Rowan Williams asks about what spiritual grounding we can find for the Christian faith in a postmodern culture that questions all authority. The genius of the position is that so much depends on the qualities of the man who directly interacts and struggles with the world surrounding him.

That every person faces the difficulties of these questions has helped the role of the Archbishop of Canterbury survive. Faithful Anglicans look to him for guidance and hope while living through similar challenges of human life.

## Augustine, the First Archbishop of Canterbury

From the beginning, the Archbishop of Canterbury did not know a place of peace and concord, but maybe that is the secret of its strength and survival. Friction and disagreement open and allow the space of new voices and ideas to surface that the faithful believe can be the voice of God.

The Christian faith came to the British Isles in the second century with the beginning of the Celtic Church; the Anglo-Saxons arrived later, in the sixth century. The Celtic Church became established and fruitful, yet at times they were reluctant to send missionaries to convert the Anglo-Saxons because of the existing conflicts between the two groups. The Celtic Church, though, did convert the northern half of Anglo-Saxon Britain.

The sixth-century tradition says that Bishop Gregory of Rome saw three Yorkshire youths for sale in the slave market of Rome and immediately hoped for their conversion. Upon finding out where they were from, he desired to help and planned to send missionaries to them. According to scholar Bishop Walter Hook, Gregory asked who they were and was told that they were Angles from Deira under the rule of King Ella. A man who liked puns, Gregory said that "the Angles should become angels"; that "the Deirans must be rescued *de irâ*"; and that "the subjects of King Ella should be made to sing Alleluia" (1882, Vol. I, 48). Hence, Gregory sent the monk Augustine along with 40 monks to work for the conversion of the Anglo-Saxons and had them prepared for the unusual task of entering England armed only with the gospel message.

In about 596, this group of missionaries left on their call and entered into their courageous work. Bishop Gregory sent them a letter encouraging them, "to accomplish the good work which, by the help of our Lord, you have undertaken" (Hook 1882, Vol.

I, 51). The missionaries went to Kent, England, and there met King Ethelbert and his wife Queen Bertha, daughter of the King of Paris, who still practiced her Christian religion. At their meeting, Augustine told the king that, "How the merciful Jesus, by his own passion, redeemed this guilty world, and opened to believing men an entrance into the kingdom of heaven" (Hook 1882, Vol. I, 54).

King Ethelbert became Christian and the faith spread rapidly with Augustine working among the other peoples in the British Isles, including those worshipping the gods Wodon and Frigga. Augustine quickly came into dispute with the Welch bishops as he too confidently tried to claim authority over them. Hence, the role of Archbishop of Canterbury and the Anglican Communion began with this loosely knit alliance between the distant pope in Rome, pagan worshippers, and Celtic Christianity.

Augustine asked Gregory about the liturgy, and Gregory wisely told Augustine to make "an English one" (Hook 1882, Vol 1, 62). This powerful decision opened the door for a worship liturgy different from the Roman one. In 601, Gregory proclaimed Augustine the Archbishop of Canterbury and sent others to help with this mission. In 604, Laurentius, one of the first monks, succeeded Augustine as the next archbishop. This tradition of choosing a monk that had arrived with Augustine continued for the first six Archbishops of Canterbury, many of whom were canonized as Catholic saints.

The baptism by fire for these archbishops was frequently the long journey to Rome to get the symbol of authority, the pallium, which established the wearer's participation in full apostolic succession. This pallium, a cross-shaped vestment, granted the wearer the sign of apostolic succession. Hence, this church from its beginning drew upon the apostolic foundation derived from the Bishop of Rome, yet also appreciated the deep roots of Celtic spirituality, which created a double-pronged foundation for the Archbishops of Canterbury.

## Distinctive Men Serving as Archbishops of Canterbury

A brief overview of the Archbishops of Canterbury shows the role's many changes for the men who have served, although, with the ordination of women, a woman might grace this position in the future. The first archbishops were unmarried monks who lived an ascetic life while serving the Church of England. Throughout the Middle Ages, the archbishops actively served the king or queen and frequently became part of the inner workings of the royal court. In 1534, King Henry VIII destroyed the relationship with the pope in Rome. Hence the Archbishop of Canterbury became the ultimate leader in the Church of England. In the sixteenth century, Reformation ideals became the dominant power of the church under the leadership of the archbishops. In 1867, the newly begun Lambeth Conferences added additional responsibility to the archbishop. In the twentieth and twenty-first centuries, the archbishop became an international figure to whom many turn for wisdom and assistance.

The genius of the position of Archbishop of Canterbury lies in its attempt to retain spiritual authority while not retreating from worldly affairs. Many Archbishops of Canterbury have served well and are remembered for distinctive contributions as they identified and defended the Anglican faith in their eras. To critique them, the following questions were asked. Did they accurately identify the issues of their time? Did they rally others to help address these issues and keep the faith while doing so? These following examples give the flavor of the office when held by a person with faith and passion.

*Archbishop Oda* lived a bold life defending his country and church. The son of a Dane, Oda became a Christian and subsequently was disinherited by his father, but his adopted Anglo-Saxon father gave Oda the benefit of an excellent education. Oda's religious fervor was sincere, yet his genius for military work was recognized. Even after becoming Bishop of Ramsbury, he fought in battles with a club studded with spikes. In one battle, when King Athelstan lost his sword, Oda moved in quickly to give him a new sword, hence saving the king's life.

This decisive action aided his selection as the Archbishop of Canterbury in 942. Following this, Oda threw himself into this position with passion and restored the Canterbury Cathedral while undertaking serious reforms with both the monks and clergy, including enforcing married clergy to leave their wives. He applied the Benedictine Rule to the monasteries, a reformation principle that a successor, Dunstan, continued. Dunstan intensified this Benedictine reform and, along with like-minded bishops, their work survived and hence is called a tenth-century reformation.

*Archbishop Lanfranc* was called the apostolic man who worked for the independence of the Church of England from Rome. As a young man, he gained a reputation as an eloquent lawyer, yet he left his native Italy and moved to Normandy, where he continued his successful career. Unexpectedly, Lanfranc experienced a sudden conversion and joined a monastery. Later, in 1070, the Norman William the Conqueror, to whom Lanfranc had a long allegiance, appointed him as the Archbishop of Canterbury. After he became the Archbishop of Canterbury, he converted the monastery into a Benedictine one and worked for the restoration of the church.

A friend of Lanfranc, *Archbishop Anselm* in 1093 was also appointed to this position by William the Conqueror. He developed the theological system called Scholasticism that greatly influenced the European mind until the sixteenth century. During his time as archbishop, the primacy of Canterbury over the other English bishoprics was confirmed *in perpetuum* by Pope Paschal. Even at the end of his life, Anselm's theological passion continued. In Holy Week, 1109, Anselm said to a friend, "I should also feel grateful, if He would vouchsafe me a longer time with you, and permit me to solve a question, in which I feel a lively interest, on the origin of the soul" (Hook 1884, Vol. II, 275). Five days later, he died.

*Archbishop Thomas Becket* became archbishop in 1162 and struggled for a church autonomous from the powers of the English king. After this, King Henry II suggested to four knights that his honor had been besmirched by Becket. Because of this, the knights confronted Becket and murdered him in the Canterbury Cathedral. He died for the freedom of the spiritual authority of the church and was made a saint shortly afterwards. Because of his martyrdom, pilgrims frequently traveled to Canterbury and, in the fourteenth century, Geoffrey Chaucer memorialized this saint as the foundation for the position of the Archbishop of Canterbury.

*Archbishop Stephen Langton*, enthroned in 1207, helped in a dispute that led to the achievement of the freedoms specified in the Magna Carta. Langton also developed the popular biblical structure of dividing the scriptures into chapter and verse.

As Bishop of Ely, *Thomas Arundel* loaned money to the King Richard II to help save England from bankruptcy. Arundel subsequently became the chancellor for England. After becoming the Archbishop of Canterbury in 1396, he provided aid at the meeting between the kings of France and England. Yet, even after this loyal service, the archbishop along with his beloved brother, the Earl of Arundel, and the Duke of Gloucester were unfairly charged with treason. Indeed, Richard tricked the archbishop into inviting his brother to dinner and then arresting the Earl of Arundel. Subsequently, Thomas Arundel was banished from England, and his brother was beheaded. Arundel traveled to Rome to seek justice and on the way was nearly murdered, probably by a man sent by King Richard. The pope appointed Roger Walden to become the new Archbishop of Canterbury and gave another bishopric to Arundel. After this, Arundel worked for the Revolution of 1399. Arundel cast the first vote in Parliament accepting Richard II's renunciation of the crown and later conducted the coronation of King Henry IV. After this, Arundel was again recognized as the Archbishop of Canterbury. An intelligent man, Arundel protected the rights of the church from a state confiscation of church lands and is quoted, "You will find an invasion of the rights and possessions of the Church no very easy matter" (Hook 1865, Vol. IV, 488).

*Archbishop Thomas Cranmer* was appointed in 1533 and worked with King Henry VIII as they struggled to allow for Henry to be divorced. After the pope denied this, the Act of Royal Supremacy Act in 1534 declared that the king was the Supreme Head of the English Church, thus completing the division from the Roman Catholic Church. The king, though, did not want new worship services and liturgy. Following his death and the ascension of King Edward VI, Cranmer wrote a new liturgy. He welcomed Reformation ideas and worked to free people from a powerful medieval church structure. To support this, Cranmer researched the early church and wrote the liturgy of the 1549 Book of Common Prayer that preserved the real presence of the Lord himself in the sacrament without affirming transubstantiation. When receiving the sacrament, the priest said, "The body of our Lord Jesus Christ which was given for thee, preserve thy body and soul unto everlasting life." Written in a small study in Lambeth Palace, Cranmer created a liturgy in which the people fully participated.

Later, Cranmer wrote in 1552 a more Protestant version of the Book of Common Prayer. Cranmer advocated for a married priesthood.

Queen Mary repealed the Act of Royal Supremacy. In 1555, Cranmer was arrested and accused of "blasphemy, incontinency, and heresy" (Hook 1868, Vol. VII, 355). At his trial, his judge, the Bishop of Gloucester, Dr. Brookes, sat below an ornate altar with the Catholic reserved sacrament exposed, revealing to Cranmer the already guilty judgment that awaited him. Cranmer wore the robes of the Archbishop of Canterbury and refused to remove his cap to this bishop representing the pope and said that he would never "consent to the admitting of the Bishop of Rome's authority into this realm of England again" (Hook 1868, Vol. VII, 355). Cranmer was burned at the stake in Oxford, England, where a memorial garden still remembers the place of his death.

After the ascension of the Roman Catholic Queen Mary to the throne, Reginald Pole became the Archbishop of Canterbury in 1556. Pole had accused Cranmer of perjury and heresy and so was implicated in Cranmer's death. *Archbishop Reginald Pole* himself was accused of heresy by Pope Paul IV and summoned before the Inquisition, but

Queen Mary intervened on his behalf. Pole actively served in Queen Mary's councils during the religious persecutions and killings for which this era is known. Queen Mary died in 1558 and Archbishop Pole died 12 hours after her.

Becoming the archbishop in 1559, *Archbishop Matthew Parker* actualized the Elizabethan Settlement that based the Church's structure on the early church. Parker directed the completion of the influential Thirty-Nine Articles of Religion still accepted in the Anglican Communion. He helped establish Protestantism in England and defended the rights of the clergy to marry. His scholarship included collecting and researching manuscripts from the Anglo-Saxons to prove that the Protestant influence dated from the early church. Parker was rewarded by Queen Elizabeth for his "excellent endowments of mind, and great dexterity in managing affairs," yet in all humbleness he chose his motto as "The world passeth away and the lust thereof" (Hook 1872, Vol. IX, 523).

*Archbishop Whitgift*, enthroned in 1583, took strong measures to suppress the Puritans. He struggled against popular preacher and Puritan Thomas Cartwright, known as the "Chief of the Nonconformists," who wrote *Admonition to the Parliament* (Hook 1875 Vol. X, 151). Whitgift reconciled with Cartwright before the latter's death.

Enthroned in 1633, *Archbishop William Laud* worked to establish the Catholic theology of King Charles I. He was disliked for his extreme Catholic tendencies and persecution of the Protestants. In 1637, Laud had three Puritans, William Prynne, John Bastwick, and Henry Burton, arrested. When convicted of seditious libel, their ears were cut off and their faces branded with SL. In 1640, the Parliament had Laud arrested and he was beheaded in 1645. King Charles I was convicted of treason and killed in 1649.

The Commonwealth of England ruled from 1645 to 1660. During this time, there was no Archbishop of Canterbury.

Becoming the archbishop in 1862, *Archbishop Charles Longley* began the Lambeth Conferences in 1867 after he prosecuted a heated heresy trial and international bishops wanted to consult about this case.

Beginning his time as archbishop in 1868, *Archbishop Archibald Tait*, a Scotsman, was very concerned about the living conditions and poverty in London and, along with his wife, worked in London in dire conditions.

Enthroned in 1903, *Archbishop Randall Davidson* spoke out in concern about World War I when many church leaders on both sides of the Atlantic were spearheading support for the "Great War." He attempted to achieve a revision of the English prayer book, but this was narrowly defeated in Parliament. After this, he became the first archbishop to resign.

*Archbishop Cosmo Lang* became archbishop in 1928 and was concerned about the conditions of the working class. Early on, he became involved with the twentieth-century ecumenical movement. He is also remembered for his actions in trying to help the Jewish people avoid the holocaust in World War II.

*Archbishop William Temple* served from 1942–1944. The son of Archbishop of Canterbury Frederick Temple, William led during World War II. An influential author, he created a synthesis between theology and the world as he worked to keep the Christian faith connected to society.

*Archbishop Geoffrey Fisher* was enthroned in 1945 and performed the 1953 corona-tion of Queen Elizabeth II. In 1960, he visited Pope John XXIII which was the first meeting between a pope and the Archbishop of Canterbury since the Reformation.

*Archbishop Michael Ramsay* became the 100th Archbishop of Canterbury in 1961. Possessing a strong personality, Ramsay's actions created stories that still circulate about his passion for the gospel and bold theological understandings. Archbishop Ramsay came from the Anglo-Catholic heritage and understood the worship experience itself as the essence of the faith. He possessed a natural spiritual authority that others respected, including Pope Paul VI. On July 20, 1965, Ramsay gave a speech in the House of Lords that helped pass the Abolition of the Death Penalty Bill. Ramsay cor-rectly identified the declining Anglican identity following World War II.

Many admired Ramsay, including Episcopal theologian Charles P. Price who wrote about Ramsay's involvement at a World Council of Churches meeting in New Delhi, "There was a protracted discussion of the identity of the apostolic tradition. At a crucial point, after debate had gone on for some time and was threatening to bog down in uncertainty and disagreement, Archbishop Ramsay strode to the platform and said, 'I am the apostolic tradition'" (James 2010, 17). Archbishop Rowan Williams writes that the holy person is one who does difficult tasks and yet makes them look easy. This seems to describe Ramsay, who walked into difficult situations and yet made it look natural and easy.

After becoming the archbishop in 1974, *Archbishop Donald Coggan*, helped produce the new biblical translation titled *The New English Bible*.

*Archbishop Robert Runcie* was enthroned in 1980. At Lambeth 1988, he maintained unity that helped preserve the Anglican Communion. He wrote, "Although we have machinery for dealing with problems within a diocese and within a Province, we have few for those which exist with the Communion as a whole" (1989, 9). He pre-sented a stark decision for the Anglican Communion, writing that we have a "choice between unity or gradual fragmentation" (1989, 11). Hoping for a diplomatic break-through in 1987, one of Runcie's emissaries, Terry Waite, went to Lebanon to help negotiate the release of hostages where Waite himself was kidnapped. After Waite's release in 1991, the two men had a thankful reunion.

Becoming *Archbishop George Carey* in 1991, he was from the evangelical wing of the Church of England and understood the dynamics of personal faith. He described one experience, "I felt the love of God and His tenderness towards me. As I prayed out loud – a practice I strongly recommend – I felt a sense of joy and elation, of reassurance and hope as I resumed my walk with God" (2004, 72). During his 1998 Lambeth Conference, prohibitions against non-celibate homosexual clergy were passed that have caused controversy.

Becoming archbishop in 2002, *Archbishop Rowan Williams* understood the postmod-ern era and moves with dignity in this culture. A well-respected theologian, he placed emphasis on understanding the spiritual implications of Christian theology.

In 2009, Williams released a covenant proposal to create a new structure of rela-tionships among the provinces in the Anglican Communion. In this brilliant plan, Williams advocated for a two-tiered approach; the first tier required assent to state-ments of faith, while the second tier was loosely connected and allowed a province to make decisions with which others disagreed. If this structure were applied, then the individual province could choose to consecrate non-celibate homosexuals and remain in the second tier. Williams' covenant proposal has been rejected by some provinces at the time of publication, and it appears it will not pass the voting process. However, his covenant proposal has begun global dialogue and seeded other ideas of how the Anglican Communion can retain its unity.

Williams protected the traditional spiritual authority of this position without seeking increased power, and even those who disagreed with him respected his integrity. Ugandan Archbishop Henry Luke Orombi described Williams saying, "He is a wonderful, godly man and has passion" (James 2010, 175). Williams resigned and left office at the end of 2012.

## The Vows

The earliest Archbishops of Canterbury were initially chosen by the pope and later by the monarch of England. In modern times though, the holder of this office is nominated by the Crown Appointments Commission, elected by the College of Canons, and certified by the Confirmation of Election.

The Archbishop of Canterbury takes vows at his public enthronement, with church and state leaders attending this public ceremony. At the beginning of Williams' enthronement, the Dean of the Canterbury Cathedral stated, "Let us join our Archbishop in prayer for God's blessing on his ministry in this Diocese, in the Province of Canterbury and throughout the world-wide Anglican Communion" (Enthronement 2003, 14).

The Archbishop of York asked Rowan Williams, "In the declaration you are about to make will you affirm your loyalty to this inheritance of faith as your inspiration and guidance under God in bringing the grace and truth of Christ to this generation and making him known to those in your care?" (Enthronement 2003, 15).

The Archbishop of Canterbury replied, "I, Rowan Douglas Williams, do so affirm, and accordingly declare my belief in the faith which is revealed in the Holy Scriptures and set forth in the catholic creeds and to which the historic formularies of the Church of England bear witness; and in public prayer and administration of the sacraments, I will use only the forms of service which are authorised or allowed by Canon" (Enthronement 2003, 16).

The Dean received the Canterbury Gospels and presented them to the archbishop, saying, "You, Most Reverend Father, shall make your corporal oath on these Holy Gospels of God which you thus hold, that you will inviolably observe the ancient and approved customs of this Cathedral and Metropolitical Church of Christ, Canterbury, and that to your best ability you will give help and assistance in defending the rights, statutes and liberties of this Church" (Enthronement 2003, 16).

The archbishop then kissed the book which the Dean held.

The archbishop swore, "As I shall answer the same to Almighty God I hereby make this my corporal oath" (Enthronement 2003, 16).

Following the taking of the vows, the Archbishop of Canterbury proclaimed his first sermon to the people in attendance.

## The Future of the Role of Archbishop of Canterbury

In the twentieth and twenty-first centuries, social changes have caused controversy in the Anglican Communion, which has challenged the very role of the archbishop. The ordination of women as well as non-celibate homosexuals and lesbians has caused great dissension. With this current disagreement impacting all levels in the Anglican Communion, some groups seek an Archbishop of Canterbury who agrees with and will enforce their positions, yet debate has ensued about the appropriateness of enforcing any position.

In the late twentieth century, some international leaders asked for the position of the Archbishop of Canterbury to be a moving position and be capable of locating in any diocese in the globe. It is too early to predict whether such a change will continue to be discussed.

At times, these men in their spiritual role have brought the mighty acts of God before an unbelieving world in person, presence, acts, and words. They have proclaimed the remembrance of the redemption possible in Jesus Christ. For some, their lives and actions have been graced by their own blood in martyrdom, as in the lives of Thomas Becket and Thomas Cranmer. In the intricate ministry of the Archbishop of Canterbury, he strives to console, to bring wisdom, to reconcile, to sacrifice, and to speak words of faith in all times. He hopes to show the overcoming of tragedy by eternal faith. Living in the Word of God, the Archbishop of Canterbury speaks words of faith that establishes human dignity and freedom.

With a long history of distinguished service in dangerous historical situations, the Archbishop of Canterbury has become a revered, spiritual person seen as the center and focus of the Anglican Communion. The archbishops' clear and worthy contributions to the Christian faith and to global humanity have been recognized throughout history. The Archbishops of Canterbury experience fully the historical world or, to paraphrase Rowan Williams, they have shared the risks while steadily changing the atmosphere by their questions. From Augustine to the present, those gifted with this high calling have worked for the realization of God's will in the Anglican Communion as they "lived and moved and had their being" as the influential Archbishop of Canterbury (Acts of the Apostles 17:28).

## Timeline of First Years for the Archbishops of Canterbury

| Year | Dioceses created |
| --- | --- |
| 597 | Augustine |
| 604 | Laurentius |
| 619 | Mellitus |
| 624 | Justus |
| 627 | Honorius |
| 655 | Deusdedit |
| 668 | Theodore |

*(Continued)*

| Year | Dioceses created |
|------|------------------|
| 693 | Brehtwald |
| 731 | Tatwine |
| 735 | Nothelm |
| 740 | Cuthbert |
| 761 | Bregowine |
| 765 | Jaenbert |
| 793 | Ethelhard |
| 805 | Wulfred |
| 832 | Feologeld |
| 833 | Ceolnoth |
| 870 | Ethelred |
| 890 | Plegmund |
| 914 | Athelm |
| 923 | Wulfhelm |
| 942 | Oda |
| 959 | Brithelm |
| 959 | Aelfsige |
| 960 | Dunstan |
| 988 | Ethelgar c. |
| 990 | Sigeric |
| 995 | Elfric |
| 1005 | Alphege |
| 1013 | Lyfing |
| 1020 | Ethelnoth |
| 1038 | Eadsige |
| 1051 | Robert of Jumieges |
| 1052 | Stigand |
| 1070 | Lanfranc |
| 1093 | Anselm |
| 1114 | Ralph d'Escures |
| 1123 | William de Corbeil |
| 1139 | Theobald |
| 1162 | Thomas Becket |
| 1174 | Richard of Dover |
| 1184 | Baldwin |
| 1193 | Hubert Walter |
| 1207 | Stephen Langton |
| 1229 | Richard le Grant |
| 1234 | Edmund of Abingdon |
| 1245 | Boniface of Savoy |
| 1273 | Robert Kilwardby |
| 1279 | John Peckham |
| 1294 | Robert Winchelsey |
| 1313 | Walter Reynolds |
| 1328 | Simon Mepeham |
| 1333 | John de Stratford |

| Year | Dioceses created |
| --- | --- |
| 1349 | Thomas Bradwardine |
| 1349 | Simon Islip |
| 1366 | Simon Langham |
| 1368 | William Whittlesey |
| 1375 | Simon Sudbury |
| 1381 | William Courtenay |
| 1396 | Thomas Arundel |
| 1398 | Roger Walden |
| 1399 | Thomas Arundel (restored) |
| 1414 | Henry Chichele |
| 1443 | John Stafford |
| 1452 | John Kemp |
| 1454 | Thomas Bouchier |
| 1486 | John Morton |
| 1501 | Henry Deane |
| 1503 | William Warham |
| 1533 | Thomas Cranmer |
| 1556 | Reginald Pole |
| 1559 | Matthew Parker |
| 1576 | Edmund Grindal |
| 1583 | John Whitgift |
| 1604 | Richard Bancroft |
| 1611 | George Abbot |
| 1633 | William Laud |
| 1645–1660 | No Archbishop from |
| 1660 | William Juxon |
| 1663 | Gilbert Sheldon |
| 1678 | William Sancroft |
| 1691 | John Tillotson |
| 1695 | Thomas Tenison |
| 1716 | William Wake |
| 1737 | John Potter |
| 1747 | Thomas Herring |
| 1757 | Matthew Hutton |
| 1758 | Thomas Secker |
| 1768 | Frederick Cornwallis |
| 1783 | John Moore |
| 1805 | Charles Manners-Sutton |
| 1828 | William Howley |
| 1848 | John Bird Sumner |
| 1862 | Charles Thomas Longley |
| 1868 | Archibald Campbell Tait |
| 1883 | Edward White Benson |
| 1896 | Frederick Temple |
| 1903 | Randall Davidson |

(*Continued*)

| Year | Dioceses created |
|------|------------------|
| 1928 | Cosmo Gordon Lang |
| 1942 | William Temple |
| 1945 | Geoffrey Francis Fisher |
| 1961 | Arthur Michael Ramsay |
| 1974 | Frederick Donald Coggan |
| 1980 | Robert Alexander Kennedy Runcie |
| 1991 | George Leonard Carey |
| 2002 | Rowan Douglas Williams |
| 2013 | Justin Portal Welby |

## Bibliography

*Archbishop Asks 'What Would Jesus Do?' in Christmas Issue of Radio Times.* December 5, 2011. archbishopofcanterbury.org

Bellenger, Dominic Aidan and Stella Fletcher. 2005. *The Mitre & the Crown: A History of the Archbishops of Canterbury.* England: Sutton Publishing Limited.

Carey, George. 2004. *Know the Truth: A Memoir.* London: HarperCollins.

Enthronement of the One Hundred and Fourth Archbishop of Canterbury Rowan Douglas Williams. February 27, 2003. anglicancommunion.org.

Hook, Walter Farquhar. 1865–1884. *Lives of the Archbishops of Canterbury.* Volumes I–XII. London: Richard Bentley & Son.

James, Nancy. 2010. *The Developing Schism within the Episcopal Church.* New York: Edwin Mellen Press.

Maxwell-Stuart, P. G. 2006. *The Archbishops of Canterbury.* Great Britain: Tempus Publishing Limited.

Runcie, Robert. 1989. *The Unity We Seek.* Harrisburg, Pennsylvania: Morehouse Publishing.

Williams, Rowan D. 2003. *Silence and Honey Cakes: The Wisdom of the Desert.* Oxford: Lion Publishing.

CHAPTER 6

# The Book of Common Prayer

## J. Robert Wright

The Anglican Communion has a unity based more upon worship than upon doctrinal statements or confessional formulas or any single definitive theologian, important though they be, and thus in a very real sense its focus and source of identity have been defined by the Book of Common Prayer. Anglican doctrine, indeed its fundamental consensus so far as there be one, is derived from its worship, and most Anglicans, but not all, would tend to agree that the most important thing that the church does is to worship God, and that all its other activities are derived from or related to that. There are certainly other things, such as the so-called Instruments of Communion (also called Instruments of Unity), the Chicago-Lambeth Quadrilateral, and even the subsequent drafts of the proposed Covenant, all of which are historically important or even authoritative in various ways, but to most Anglicans these would probably seem somehow slightly less definitive or visible, and not of the first order. It is liturgy that is needed to give them life. One reason for this, as has been well said (by no less than Archbishop Michael Ramsey), is that the supremely important point about worship is not what we make of it but what it makes of us.

Thus it is, for example, that the first characteristic of Anglican churches in communion with the see of Canterbury that was stipulated in the semi-official definition of the Anglican Communion at the Lambeth Conference of 1930, was that they "uphold and propagate the Catholic and Apostolic Faith and Order as they are generally set forth in the Book of Common Prayer as authorized in their several Churches." Likewise, the Report of the Lambeth Conference of 1978 on the Basis of Anglican Unity devoted its major attention to the Book of Common Prayer and concluded: "Accordingly, in order to find out what characterizes Anglican doctrine, the simplest way is to look at Anglican worship and deduce Anglican doctrine from it." In another way, this principle was already enunciated centuries earlier by Prosper of Aquitaine in the fifth

*The Wiley-Blackwell Companion to the Anglican Communion*, First Edition. Edited by Ian S. Markham,
J. Barney Hawkins IV, Justyn Terry, and Leslie Nuñez Steffensen.
© 2013 John Wiley & Sons, Ltd. Published 2013 by John Wiley & Sons, Ltd.

century: *Legem credendi lex statuat supplicandi*, or *Lex orandi lex credendi*, or, put more simply, "the law of prayer determines the law of belief," or "the rule of prayer is the rule of faith."

And so we can observe that virtually every one of the more than 40 national or regional churches that now constitute the Anglican Communion has had and does have a Book of Common Prayer that is more or less recognizably "Anglican" on the basis of the definitive English Book of 1662 or other related books that are easily and recognizably traceable back to the original English Book of Common Prayer of 1549, which was in turn an English distillation of the later medieval English service books under the patristic, biblical, and humanistic revivals that flourished in the period of the Western Renaissance and Reformation. In recent times, to be sure, this fundamental consensus has been challenged from the modern liturgical movement that has continually stretched and strained the scope and content of Anglican unity over the last century or so by producing many new Books of Common Prayer for different countries and regions that are increasingly different from one another. Particular details of many of these various books, when appropriate, are given under the sections of this volume devoted to each Anglican province around the world, whereas this present chapter is concerned primarily about the Anglican concept of prayer in common from one book, its origins, and early development. Deviations from whatever version of the Book that is official in a particular area at a given time are occasionally tolerated in local situations for a while, but generally Anglicans would say that their worship is to be conducted from it, Anglican doctrine to be derived from it, Anglican life to be lived by it, and Anglican clergy must be prepared to use its contents and to say and lead its words in public worship with a consenting mind.

Given the profusion of liturgical books that flourished in late medieval England, it does seem nonetheless probable that the notion or concept of one book of common prayer was largely the original proposal of Archbishop Thomas Cranmer, and it eventually gained acceptance and approbation, even if not all at once. It is noteworthy that the most important prelude to the appearance in 1549 of the first Book of Common Prayer, in addition to the repudiation of papal jurisdiction and the establishment of royal supremacy, was the appearance of the Bible in the English vernacular tongue which had clearly matured by the early decades of the sixteenth century. Change was underway as early as 1544 when the first English Litany was occasioned by the command of Henry VIII for litanies, understandable by the people, to be said or sung in English to seek divine assistance as he prepared to invade France. Composed by Cranmer from materials in the Sarum Processional, Luther's Litany, and the Orthodox Liturgy of John Chrysostom, the litany was revised in 1547, omitting the invocation of saints, and in that revised form it entered the 1549 Book. From its beginning, though, it carried the clause "From all sedition and privy conspiracy, from the tyranny of the Bishop of Rome and all his detestable enormities," which was finally removed in 1559 and never since restored. By the death of Henry VIII in 1547, though, the earliest stage of the English Reformation was over, leaving a continuity of traditional catholic faith and practice, the redefinition of past history in a way that enabled changes to seem like restorations, and the concept of one national commonwealth, both state and church, with a quasi-episcopal king replacing the pope.

Beginning in 1547 with Edward VI (king at the age of nine), a second stage commenced, with reforms in doctrine and liturgy, but not so far reaching or radical as on the European continent, and with English bishops continuing to take the lead in both stages. Early in the new reign there appeared "The Order of the [people's] Communion," derived both from reformation sources and from medieval forms for communion from the reserved sacrament outside Mass, all published in English in 1548 by royal proclamation. Just as people were now reading and speaking in English, so also it seemed logical for them to want "but one use" (as Cranmer explained in his preface) so that they could pray in their own tongue. To be inserted into the Latin Mass after the priest's communion and before the ablutions, the unusual feature of this "Order of Communion," in addition to the liturgical English and the restoration of the chalice to the laity, was the assumption that the normal lay communicant could achieve repentance without the sacrament of Penance, which was now made optional.

The chief author of the first Book of Common Prayer was not some rebellious and bombastic monk but the Archbishop of Canterbury, formerly a fellow at Cambridge University. Cranmer had first experienced Lutheran worship in Lent of 1532 at Nuremberg (where he secretly married the niece of Andreas Osiander, a lesser figure in the German reforms), and subsequently he encouraged various continental reformers to seek refuge in England. In 1533, he became Archbishop of Canterbury, and his liturgical aptitude, linguistic felicity, and reforming tendencies began to be obvious in many endeavors. After the death of Henry VIII in early 1547 and the accession of Edward VI as a minor, Cranmer's ability to cause and direct the course of religious reform was greatly strengthened. By Cranmer and his carefully selected committee, the Book of Common Prayer was produced by January of 1549 and in the same month officially endorsed by Parliament for use throughout the realm. Replacing the plurality of medieval usages that included but was not limited to the dominant use of Sarum (Salisbury), henceforth "but one use" in the English vernacular was to be observed throughout the realm, all contained within this one volume. Issued under authority of the king in Parliament, its use was made obligatory in all churches, with penalties for disobedience, beginning on Whitsunday of the same year. Most of the early printings were in folio format (about 12 inches high), and clearly intended for use of the clergy in chancels, not for the laity to carry around with them. Conservative reaction and revolts began almost immediately, there was confusion as to what the new services meant theologically, and the way some priests celebrated the new English was equally as incomprehensible as the old Latin. Most laity, however, would not have recognized that very much had changed, for they would not have known what the Latin had said in the first place.

Although the 1662 revision of the English prayer book is widely recognized as being authoritative for the worldwide Anglican Communion today, it must be recognized that the very first Book of 1549 was the one that marked a fundamental break from the patterns of English worship of the first 1,500 years and the Book of Common Prayer from which the 1662 revision and all editions that followed were in some sense derived. Since the Book of 1549 set the standard from which they have come, considerable attention must be given to the changes that were made in it. The length of this chapter is far too brief to note all the subsequent versions over the globe and over time and history, of course, but we note that already in 1549 the Calendar of the new book contained no festival commemorations except of the Lord and of New Testament saints (no longer called "saints"), the table of Scripture lessons followed the calendar year and not the ecclesiastical one, the many daily offices of the medieval church were combined into two, Matins and Evensong, and clergy with cure of souls were required to say both these offices daily in public with tolling of the bell. Whole chapters of Scripture were to be read at each service. Patterns of Reformation were thus being established in the 1549 Book that would forever claim the attention of all subsequent liturgical revisers of the Anglican Communion in the ages to follow. Baptism was now normally to be a public act on Sunday, the threefold renunciation no longer being from Satan, his works, and his pomps but from the devil, the world, and the flesh. At the end of the Baptismal service, the godparents were required to see that the child learns the Creed, the Lord's Prayer, and the Ten Commandments; that is to say, the godparents not only make answers on behalf of the infant but also enter into a contract about the child's Christian future. The Catechism (new in 1549 and replacing entirely an earlier one issued separately in 1548) is included along with the Confirmation service, and the latter is tied closely to the ministry of the bishop but without the use of chrism. The marriage rite is linked to a public celebration of the Eucharist, and the newlyweds are required to receive communion on that day. In its preface, also penned by the first Archbishop of Canterbury to be married, the reasons given for matrimony now include not only the procreation of children and the avoidance of sin but also "for the mutual society, help, and comfort that the one ought to have of the other." The ring is no longer blessed, but there is now a promise by the man "to love and to cherish" and by the woman "to love, cherish, and obey." The burial rite is now linked to a public celebration of the Eucharist. Special services are also provided for Ash Wednesday (with a nodding reference to the discipline of public penance in the early church, but without ashes, which had already been abolished by order of Privy Council in 1548), and for the Purification of Women. The Psalms, although part of the Bible, were not initially printed with the Prayer Book. One appendix to the 1549 Book, "Of Ceremonies," stated that an excess of ceremonies was wrong but it gave no principle for determination which should be abolished and which retained. Already then, in 1549, fundamental changes were being made to Anglican worship that would set the patterns from which much else would flow.

The title given to the 1549 Eucharist is "The Supper of the Lorde, and the Holy Communion, commonly called the Masse," the term "Mass" being the third alternative and placed in diminutive type. The terms "altar" (less often "Goddes borde") and "priest" were retained, and authority was granted only to bishops and priests to absolve, bless, and preside at Mass. A role for a deacon is provided at the reading of the Gospel, bidding the Eucharistic prayer, and administering the chalice. Such facts as these, which are now fundamentals in Anglican polity and ecclesiology, coupled with the reference in the preface to the role of "the bishop of the diocese" in settling disputes, prompt the observation that the very first Anglican Prayer Book in one sense offered a synthesis of the traditional catholic doctrine of Holy Orders, as Anglicans see it, with a strong reformation doctrine of Justification by Faith, as applied to the Eucharist itself.

The 1549 Book assumes that a choral service will be the norm, and a group of clerks are expected to sing the Introit, the private prayers of the priest having been eliminated. The Collect for Purity had been part of the daily monastic office in England ever since it was prescribed by the "Monastic Agreement of the Monks and Nuns of the English Nation" in the year 970; now, however, it was revised according to reformed doctrine and made part of the opening of the new Mass in English. Its previous conclusion ("*ut te perfecte diligere et digne laudare mereamur*"), which would have translated literally as "that we may merit to love you perfectly and praise you worthily," was now shorn of any implication of "earned merit," the concept that all reformers vigorously rejected, and was given the form that Anglicans have known ever since. The Kyrie (ninefold) and Gloria follow, although the Graduals, Alleluias, Sequences, Tracts, offertory sentences and prayers, and postcommunion sentences and prayers, were all omitted. There was to be only one collect of the day, crafted invariably with a superior sense of English rhythm and cadence, to be followed by either of two collects for the king (with unmistakable allusions to the royal supremacy). In the Nicene Creed, for curious reasons, the phrase "whose kingdom shall have no end" was omitted, and the word "holy" from the description of the church. Every Sunday, "the sermon or homily, or some portion of one of the homilies," was required (the First Book of Homilies having appeared in 1547), followed by an exhortation to worthily receiving the communion. A longer exhortation commended private confession and absolution (but optional) for those who could not relieve their consciences through private prayer or general confession. There is an Offertory but no longer any offertory prayer. The offertory sentences no longer bear any relation to the liturgical season, but are a collection of biblical texts exclusively concerned with the offering of alms, the ceremony they are intended to cover. A series of collects is provided to be said after the Offertory on days where there is no communion. Only five proper prefaces are retained, those for Christmas and Whitsunday being freshly written.

Although the Sanctus is introduced by the Sursum Corda, the 1549 "Canon" is introduced by a bidding from the priest or deacon to pray for the whole state of Christ's Church. (In 1552, the words "militant here in earth" were added, reflecting the more protestant view that there was no point to pray for those who were already dead.) The medieval Sarum Canon by contrast had six paragraphs, each really a separate prayer concluded by an "Amen," with the Lord's Prayer said after the fifth. The Canon of 1549 is to be said or sung "playnly and distinctly," not silently as in the medieval tradition, and it was not to begin until the clerks had finished singing the Sanctus. The king is prayed for by name in the Canon, as are "all Bishops, Pastors, and Curates" (an interesting nonreference to the threefold order, which would later become "all bishops and other ministers"). Reference is made to "this congregation which is here assembled in thy name, to celebrate the commemoration of the most glorious death of thy son," but the resurrection and ascension are "remembered" only later, after the words of institution. There is a commemoration of saints, although only Mary is named, and there is a commendation of the faithful departed. Insertion of the phrase "until his coming again," not in the Sarum Canon, carried the implication that, just as Christ's passion was a thing of the past, so his "coming again" would be in the future. Exactly what was happening "here and now" was not precisely specified, although the phrase "perpetual memory" is in fact very close to the concept of "vital recall" or "anamnesis," which certainly indicated more than a mere backward glance. By adding the clause "with thy Holy Spirit and Word vouchsafe to bless and sanctify these thy gifts and creatures of bread and wine," Cranmer inserted an almost consecratory epiclesis before the words of institution, specifying and even printing two signs of the cross at the words "bless and sanctify."

It was Cranmer's conviction that humankind could do, and need do, nothing to move God to forgiveness, for God had already done the one thing that was necessary. In place of our offering of beauty or music or ritual, therefore, which are indeed expressions of our gratitude, all that we can plead is a spiritual remembrance of the one perfect offering of Christ. In a transformation of the medieval doctrine of Eucharistic sacrifice, therefore, whereas the old Sarum Latin Canon had begun with a prayer offering the unconsecrated gifts and then continued after the words of institution with a further prayer offering the gifts now consecrated, Cranmer's new Canon began with the offering of intercessory prayers and reference to the "one oblation once offered, a full, perfect, and sufficient sacrifice, oblation, and satisfaction, for the sins of the whole world," in language reminiscent of the epistle to the Hebrews. Then, after the institution narrative, the prayer merely said that we make, "with these thy holy gifts, the memorial that thy Son hath willed us to make." No "gifts" are actually offered, the one sacrifice of Calvary is re-presented rather than repeated, and the only sacrifice we offer is praise and thanksgiving, ourselves, our souls, and bodies, our bounden duty and service. Near the end, God is asked to bring, not the oblation or the holy gifts that had just been consecrated as in the old Canon, but "these our prayers and supplications," by the ministry of the Holy Angels up into the Holy Tabernacle in the sight of the divine majesty (with no references to the sacrifices of Abel, Abraham, and Melchizedek, or to God's altar on high, as in the old Latin Canon). And in a requirement that tore at the heart of medieval devotion to the real presence in the consecrated Host, the central elevations at the words of institution, whereby the consecrated gifts were then adored, frequently accompanied by bells, incense, and candles, are now prohibited. Common since the twelfth and thirteenth centuries, these were the only ceremonial actions of the priest to be explicitly forbidden in the new prayer book. At the words of institution, however, the new Book directed that the priest "must" take the bread into his hands (and "shall" take the cup), as the narration of the prayer itself changed from third person plural to first person singular in the words of Christ coupled with the second person of address. In this way, the traditional catholic doctrine of the priest as an image of Christ, acting "in persona Christi," was retained, as it would be in subsequent Anglican Prayer Books (except for 1552), a doctrine that would have been obfuscated if the priest were allowed merely to read Jesus' words from the lectern or pulpit or elsewhere. As Canon Geoffrey Cuming observed of the 1549 Canon, "Its most remarkable feature is its mere existence," since "The abolition of the Canon was an article of faith with all the continental

Reformers," the old Canon being "normally replaced by the Words of Institution, read as a lesson."

The 1549 Canon was followed immediately by the Lord's Prayer, a typically Cran-merian touch, and then the peace. (There is no indication that it was to be done manu-ally.) Next comes the text "Christ our paschal lamb is offered up for us, once for all." Although the sacrificial implications of this statement can be variously interpreted in the light of Reformation theology, one must note that the phrase "once for all" is absent in the scriptural verse of I Cor. 5:7 from which the text is taken. There is no fraction or commixture, although one of the final rubrics required that each consecrated wafer be divided (it does not say when) into at least two parts. The communion of priest and people is preceded by an invitation, general confession (the only place where the con-gregation is directed to kneel), the absolution, the "Comfortable Words," and the Prayer of Humble Access, all taken from the 1548 Order of Communion but now placed before the priest's communion and not after it. The general confession was directed to be said "in the name of all those that are minded to receive the Holy Communion, either by one of them, or else by one of the ministers, or by the priest himself" because very few of the congregation would yet have had or been able to own their own copies of the new book itself. The rubrics directed that those intending to communicate were to hand in their names on the night before or at Matins on the morrow, and then at commun-ion-time to sit "in the quire, or in some convenient place nigh the quire, the men on the one side, and the women on the other side."

The priest communicates first, and then the "other ministers." Communion is to be in both kinds, and it was specified that the bread be made throughout the realm in the same way, unleavened and round and "without all manner of print" and larger and thicker than before so that it could be divided into several pieces. Even though it is acknowledged that "people many years past received . . . in their own hands, no com-mandment of Christ to the contrary," people in 1549 are still to receive the bread into their mouths, in order to prevent theft and superstition. It is specified that "all must attend [this service] weekly, but need communicate but once a year." Noncommunicat-ing attendance is not forbidden, but no priest may "solemnise so high and holy myster-ies" unless there are at least some who will communicate. In the words of administration are found the two phrases of the 1549 Book that are most directly traceable to any Lutheran source (and already present since March of 1548 in "The Order of the Com-munion"): the words "given for thee" and "shed for thee," which Cranmer derived directly from the catechism of the Lutheran theologian Justus Jonas, personally known to him, which he translated. The threefold Agnus Dei is sung during communion, and afterward there are some sentences from Scripture to be said or sung which are called "the post Communion." There is a fixed final prayer of thanksgiving, probably adapted from one composed by Cranmer's chaplain Thomas Becon in 1542 and incorporating the understanding that the church, not the Eucharist, is the "mystical body, the blessed company of all faithful people." The cryptic "*Ite missa est*" dismissal of the medieval rite is omitted, and instead the blessing begins with "The peace of God" which is probably an adaptation of the previous phrase "Go in peace." The priest alone gives the blessing, just as earlier it is the prerogative of a priest to preside at the Eucharistic prayer and to give the absolution. A rubric allows that the Gloria, Creed, Homily, and Exhortation may be omitted at celebrations on weekdays or in private homes. No provision is made for verbal repetition if there is insufficient sacramental species for all to communicate, as there had been in the 1548 "Order of the Communion." No instructions at all are given as to what should be done with any of the sacramental elements that remain. With 1549, overall, it is clear that the emphasis is less upon the change effected in the Eucharistic elements during the Canon and more upon the act of communion and the consequent change in the faithful believers who receive. As Luther also had taught, the Body and Blood of Christ are offered not to God but to those who communicate. "The miraculous working of Christ is not in the bread, but in them that duly eat the bread and drink the drink," Cranmer said.

An Ordinal was not published until March of 1550, its preface stressing continuity with the time of the apostles. In it, the subdiaconate and minor orders were omitted, but an "Oath of the King's Supremacy" was required that included renunciation of "the Bishop of Rome and his authority, power, and jurisdiction." The Ordinal, revised, was annexed to the next official Book, that of 1552, now with the tradition of instruments deleted and priests and bishops given only a Bible and deacons the New Testament. Constant in both versions, however, is the use of the term "priest," a real role for deacons, and the understanding that the church is episcopally governed with ordination the prerogative of bishops rather than a delegation of authority from the local congregation.

It has well been said that Cranmer in the first Prayer Book blended the traditional "catholic" doctrine of Holy Orders with the reformed doctrine of justification, as he dealt with that which was in many ways the central issue of the Reformation and secured its acceptance for the Church of England more by liturgical subtlety than by lengthy doctrinal treatises. A prime example of the way in which he achieved this synthesis can be seen in his alterations of the 66 collects that he took over from the medieval Latin church, as he removed all references to human merit in them, saving the merits of Christ alone. For this very reason, Anglicans all over the world resonate as their prayers conclude with the phrase (actually adapted in part from the old Roman canon) "not weighing our merits but pardoning our offenses" as they follow the middle way between what was perceived to be the Roman overemphasis upon good works as a means of earning forgiveness or merit from God, and the seeming rejection, attributed to Luther, of any significant role for good works in the life of faith.

Already the Anglican Communion was in process of birth as evidenced by the various translations of the Book beginning to appear, the earliest being the Latin translation of 1551, then the French of 1553, the Welsh of 1567, and the Greek of 1569, to be followed in the seventeenth and eighteenth centuries by translations into Irish-Gaelic, Arabic, Italian, Hebrew, and Manx. As is well known, the second English edition of the Prayer Book, that of 1552, moved along a more protestant direction, although historians differ as to whether this move was encouraged by Cranmer himself, or merely tolerated by him under various outside pressures. Already observed earlier, though, the major change had been that of 1549 itself, which gave birth to something radically new in liturgy, in English religion, and in the

Anglicanism that was being born at that very time. There would be hundreds if not thousands of changes in subsequent issues of the prayer book, far too many for even the most significant changes to be enumerated in detail here, and it must suffice merely to list the major issues that flowed in the ages that followed. Including the 1549 and the 1552, there were thereafter three more major editions, those of 1559, 1604 (stemming from the Hampton Court Conference), and that of 1662, which is widely regarded as definitive. However, to say this is not by any means to complete the picture, which can fortunately now be traced in much greater scope thanks to modern research and many recent publications. Fundamental is *The Bibliography of the Book of Common Prayer 1549–1999* by David N. Griffiths, published in 616 pages by the British Library in 2002, which catalogues some 4,810 issues within its scope, including some 1,200 translations into no less than 199 foreign languages other than English, both classical and vernacular, from Acholi to Zulu. Griffiths' work, being a bibliography, is somewhat tedious to read, even though most of the essential facts are there in a way that only detailed research could reveal. Somewhat lighter, but much more readable and even breathtaking in its worldwide scope, is *The Oxford Guide to The Book of Common Prayer: A Worldwide Survey*, edited by Charles Hefling and Cynthia Shattuck and published in 614 pages by Oxford University Press in 2006.

All told, then, the Anglican prayer book tradition was founded by Thomas Cranmer as he sought to provide "but one use" in a single volume in the magnificent English prose of that era, which he knew so well, which was intended to purge the church in that land of what were perceived to be medieval corruptions in doctrine and practice and thus to return to what was thought to be a more primitive and scriptural usage. Already the Anglican prayer book tradition was clearly capable of differing doctrinal interpretations and thus focused towards a broad and comprehensive approach, for no specific reformed doctrines other than the removal of "some things untrue, some uncertain, some vain and superstitious" had been given in the preface as reasons for introducing the 1549 Book in the first place. Nevertheless, howsoever mixed this Book's intentions may have been, howsoever subject to continuing development its author's theological convictions were, the legacies of the prayer book tradition were already being set for subsequent ages and indeed for the entire Anglican Communion: (1) prayer in the English vernacular, (2) prayer in a language both contemporary and dignified without being commonplace or sentimental, (3) prayer from one book for all the services of the church and all occasions of life, (4) prayer that could be doctrinally comprehensive without causing overmuch offense, and (5) prayer in common with both clergy and laity as members of the same mystical body receiving in both kinds.

## Bibliography

Buchanan, Colin O., ed. 1959, etc. *Modern Anglican Liturgies* (several volumes with slightly different titles).

*But One Use: An Exhibition Commemorating the 450th Anniversary of the Book of Common Prayer.* The St. Mark's Library, General

Theological Seminary, New York, NY, 1999.

Griffiths, David N. 2002. *The Bibliography of the Book of Common Prayer 1549–1999*. London: British Library.

Hefling, Charles and Cynthia Shattuck, ed. 2006. *The Oxford Guide to The Book of Common Prayer: A Worldwide Survey*. New York: Oxford University Press.

Wright, J. Robert. 2009. Iconography and Eucharistic Ecclesiology in the Apse Mosaics of San Vitale, Ravenna, and Their Distant Liturgical Echo in the First Anglican Canon of 1549. *Anglican and Episcopal History*, vol. 78, no. 2, 219–26.

Complete texts of hundreds of Anglican prayer books and the liturgies therein can be found transcribed online at http://justus.anglican.org/resources/BCP.

CHAPTER 7

# The Lambeth Conferences

## Robert W. Prichard

The Lambeth Conference is a roughly decennial gathering of the bishops of the various provinces of the Anglican Communion. Most gatherings take place in years ending with eight (1878, 1888, etc.), but there are exceptions: two nineteenth-century gatherings that met on years ending in seven (1867 and 1897) and a twentieth-century disruption in schedule caused by the World Wars (1920 and 1930, followed by a return to the usual pattern in 1948). The gathering takes its name from Lambeth Palace, the London residence of the Archbishop of Canterbury in which the meetings initially took place. As the bishops in the Anglican Communion have grown more numerous, meetings have taken place in other venues, through always in England.

## Origin

The first gathering of the Lambeth Conference took place in 1867 at the invitation of Archbishop of Canterbury Charles Longley (1794–1868). Longley's invitation was, however, the result of earlier developments in the British Isles, North America, Australia, New Zealand, and South Africa.

In the first half of the nineteenth century, two obstacles existed to any kind of international Anglican gathering. The first problem was the lack of provincial and diocesan structures in England and her colonial dependencies. It would be difficult to call for an international gathering at a point in which there were no diocesan and provincial synods. In the case of the Church of England, King George I had suspended the convocations of Canterbury and York in 1717. In most colonial dioceses, synods had simply not been created.

This situation began to change in mid-nineteenth century, as dioceses responded to increasing secularization, of which British Reform Act of 1832 and the disestablishment of the Anglican Church in Nova Scotia (1850), Upper Canada (1854), and Ireland

*The Wiley-Blackwell Companion to the Anglican Communion*, First Edition. Edited by Ian S. Markham,
J. Barney Hawkins IV, Justyn Terry, and Leslie Nuñez Steffensen.
© 2013 John Wiley & Sons, Ltd. Published 2013 by John Wiley & Sons, Ltd.

(1869) were examples. No longer certain of the support of secular governments, bishops began to call diocesan and provincial synods to make their own plans independent of state policy. Early diocesan synods met in Toronto (1854); Nova Scotia, Adelaide, and Melbourne (1856); Tasmania and Capetown (1857); and Montreal and Quebec (1859). These were followed by provincial synods in New Zealand (1859) and Canada (1861). The Canterbury Convocation began to meet again in 1852, and York in 1861. (Stephenson 1978, 13–15; *Oxford Companion* 2002, s.v. Convocations of Canterbury and York).

The second obstacle to reunion was the status of the Scottish Episcopal Church and Protestant Episcopal Church in the United States. Unlike the Church of England and its various dependencies, the churches in these two areas had self-governing synods that dated to the eighteenth century. The exact relationship of these two churches to the Church of England was, however, not entirely clear. British Parliamentary actions following the Glorious Revolution (1688) and the American Revolution (1775–83) prevented interchangeability of clergy of these two churches with the Church of England, arguably implying less than full communion between the three churches (Podmore 2005, 29–31).

In the 1820s, members of the so-called "Hackney Phalanx" in England began to theorize about closer relationship between the Church of England (and its colonial dependencies), the Scottish Episcopal Church, and the Protestant Episcopal Church in the United States. Henry Handley Norris (1771–1850) met with visiting Bishop of New York John Henry Hobart (1775–1830) in 1823–1824, and Walter Farquhar Hook (1798–1875) preached an 1825 ordination sermon titled "An Attempt to Demonstrate the Catholicism of the Church of England and the Other Branches of the Episcopal Church" (Podmore 2005, 31).

In the following three decades, American Episcopalians issued repeated calls for some kind of meeting of Anglican leaders. One key American involved was the Bishop of Vermont and later Presiding Bishop John Henry Hopkins (1792–1868). Hopkins was, among other things, an apologist and controversialist; he was particularly interested in supporting the claims of the Episcopal Church in the face of the rapidly growing Roman Catholic Church in the United States. Hopkins argued in his *Primitive Church* (1835) that the Episcopal Church more closely resembled the Early Church than did the Roman Catholic Church or any Protestant body. Part of his claim was that the primitive church was divided into patriarchies and governed by general councils in which bishops met as equals, an order that, Hopkins suggested, the Church of England had retained (Hopkins 1835, Vol. 1, 192–3). In 1838, Hopkins and fellow bishop Charles Pettit McIlvaine (1799–1873) of Ohio convinced the American House of Bishops to form a committee to investigate contacting "the foreign Protestant Episcopal churches" (*Journal of the General Convention* 1838, 93–5). McIlvaine's participation was significant. Much of the early support for an international Anglican synod came from High Church leaders; McIlvaine was an evangelical Episcopalian, making the project appear as less of a party project. The House of Bishops' committee, on which both Hopkins and McIlvaine served, asked then Presiding Bishop Alexander Griswold (1766–1843) to communicate with the Archbishops of Canterbury and Armagh, and the Primus of Scotland.

Hopkins repeated the request for a meeting of bishops in a personal letter to the Archbishop of Canterbury, asking for "communion in the primitive style, by meeting in the good old fashion of synodical action" (1851). Bishop of Montreal Francis Fulford (1803–1868) used a visit to the United States to preach at an ordination service to add his voice to the American request (1853). These individual requests were followed by resolutions at the House of the Bishops of the Episcopal Church (1859) and at the first Canadian General Synod (1861) (*Journal of the General Convention* 1862, 345).

Archbishop of Canterbury John Bird Sumner (1780–1862) offered a partial response to these continuing requests for a common gathering by including representative bishops from the United States and Scotland among those invited to the anniversary celebration of the Society for the Proclamation of the Gospel held at Westminster Abbey in 1852 (Podmore 2005, 33). During his archiepiscopate, Sumner was supportive of the revival of the convocations of Canterbury and York (*Oxford Companion* 2002, s.v. Convocations of Canterbury and York).

A fight that was brewing in the colonial church in South Africa in the early 1860s also contributed to the growing interest in an international gathering of Anglican bishops. Bishop John Colenso (1814–83) of Natal and Archbishop Robert Gray (1809–72) reached a standstill in their fight over biblical interpretation and missionary strategy. A church court in South Africa found Colenso guilty of heresy and deposed him in 1853, but the judicial committee of the English Privy Council ruled in 1865 that Gray and the church court that had heard the case had no authority over Colenso. The confusion over the status of colonial churches and the frustration about the inability to silence the unpopular Colenso added to the call for an international gathering of Anglican bishops. In 1865, the Canadian bishops repeated their request for such a gathering (Sachs 1993, 199–201). In February of 1867, the Convocation of Canterbury, augmented by the presence of eight colonial, four Irish, and one American bishop, unanimously approved "a Petition of the Colonial Bishops for a General Synod" asking Archbishop Sumner's successor at Canterbury Charles Thomas Longley (Archbishop, 1862–68) "to invite a meeting of all the bishops of the various Churches holding full communion with the United Church of England and Ireland" (Stephenson 1978, 29–30).

## The First Lambeth Conference

Seventy-six bishops attended the first meeting in September of 1867. As with all new endeavors, there was some confusion about the purpose and character of the gathering. Archbishop Gray of South Africa was anxious to gain support in the continuing fight with Bishop Colenso. When the Conference as a whole did not agree to deal with the matter in a way that met his satisfaction, he organized his own unofficial committee of 12 colonial bishops. In the end, the Conference adopted resolutions suggested by that committee, which bemoaned the "present condition of the Church in Natal" without explaining what that condition was (1867 Resolution 6), and suggested that "if it be decided that a new bishop [of Natal] should be consecrated," that "every bishop, priest and deacon to be appointed to office should be required to subscribe" to "a formal instrument, declaratory of the doctrine and discipline of the Church of South Africa" (1867 Resolution 7).

There was residual confusion about the status of the Scottish Episcopal Church and the Protestant Episcopal Church in the United States. American Presiding Bishop John Henry Hopkins, for example, felt he could not participate in the Gray committee, because he was not a colonial bishop (Stephenson 1978, 34–5). The conference did, however, address a major concern of the Scots and the Americans by calling for letters of transfer for clergy and laity seeking to move among the various Anglican provinces (1867 Resolution 2). The British Colonial Clergy Act of 1874 would later clarify matters further, providing the procedure by which clergy from bishops outside of England might be allowed to serve within it.

At the time of the 1867 Conference the language used for those churches that descended from the Church of England was still in flux. By choosing the relatively new term "Anglican Communion" (1867 Resolutions 1, 4, 6, and 8), the Conference fixed that language for later generations. The final resolution adopted by the council gave thanks to God for the Conference and expressed the hope for "other meetings to be conducted in the same spirit of brotherly love" (1867 Resolution 13). The conference of 1897 later added what would by that time be the established practice—i.e. that such other meetings be held "at intervals of about ten years, on the invitation of the Archbishop" (1897 Resolution 2).

## The Work of the Lambeth Conferences

Lambeth Conferences provide an opportunity for the Bishops of the Anglican Communion "to come together for common counsel, encouragement and fellowship" (*Truth Shall Make You Free* 1988, 295). They worship together, create and maintain friendships with one another, communicate about events and issues in their individual provinces and national churches, and hear from the Archbishop of Canterbury and other important Anglican leaders. The bishops typically divide into committees or sections that consider individual issues. They reflect upon working papers that have been prepared in advance and prepare reports on the results of their deliberations. The assembly as a whole then usually votes on resolutions that are suggested by those committees or sections. Resolutions were relatively few in number at the first three conferences (13, 12, and 19, respectively), but since 1897 have been considerably more numerous. Conferences generally issue encyclical or pastoral letters directed to members of the Anglican Communion, and on occasion (e.g., "An Appeal to All Christian People" of 1920 Resolution 9) address the Christian population at large.

There is considerable disagreement among Anglicans about the authority of the resolutions adopted by Lambeth. Indeed, the Conferences themselves are not in entire agreement. Some Conferences make what sound like very definitive statements (1948 Resolutions 113–115 on the status of women, or 1998 Resolution I.10 on homosexuality), while other Conferences stress the advisory character of all Lambeth resolutions. The 1878 and 2008 Conferences, which took the latter position, did not adopt any formal resolutions at all.

The two areas in which it is most clear, however, that the Lambeth Conferences do speak with authority are in regard to relationships of the various provinces within the Anglican Communion and in regard to ecumenical relationships on an international level, matters about which no single province or national church can speak definitively. The 1998 Lambeth Conference recognized the appropriateness of this approach, affirming "the principle of 'subsidiarity,' . . . which provides that 'a central authority should have a subsidiary function, performing only those tasks which cannot be performed at a more immediate or local level', provided that these tasks can be adequately performed at such levels" (1998 Resolution III.3).

In other matters, however, Lambeth Conferences adopt positions that are reflective of the attitudes of the majority of bishops present at certain times but which are advisory in character and binding only if adopted on a provincial level. Such statements, which are often corrected by later Conferences, serve as benchmarks, however, of changing attitudes in the Anglican Communion.

## Anglican Structures

The Lambeth Conferences over the years have devoted a great deal of attention to organization of the Communion. Communications among the various provinces and dioceses was an important starting point. The first two Lambeth resolutions called upon provinces to notify "all archbishops and metropolitans, and all presiding bishops of the Anglican Communion" in "all cases of establishment of new sees, and appointment of new bishops" (1867 Resolution 1, reaffirmed by 1896 Resolution 25), and for the creation of letters commendatory for clergy and laity traveling from their dioceses and visiting others (1867 Resolution 2).

Conferences made suggestions about how the churches in various provinces might best be organized. They suggested hierarchical patterns by which diocesan bishops were subordinate to a "primate or metropolitan" (1897 Resolution 10) and diocesan synods subject to "a synod or synods above them" (1867 Resolution 4). Where provinces were not yet in existence, Lambeth Conferences favored their creation (1878 Resolution 2), but later made it clear that four or more dioceses were needed for this process to take place (1930 Resolution 53). In nations where there were several provinces, Lambeth approved the formation of "the larger unity of a 'national Church,'" even if that national church did not have the civil status of an established church (1930 Resolution 52). Conferences have taken note of the success of individual parts of the church in provincial organization, noting, for example, the efforts in Japan and China (1930 Resolution 57) and the progress in East Africa (1930 Resolution 58) in 1930, and the "the steps . . . taken in East, West and Central Africa, and the Pacific" in 1948 (1948 Resolution 79).

Conference worried about conflicts that might take place when two or more different provinces established congregations in overlapping areas. They worried, for example, about the potential for conflict created by competing American and British émigré congregations on the European continent (1867 Resolutions 12, 1878 Resolution 12) and established it as a basic principle that "independent Churches of the Anglican

Communion ought to recognise the equal rights of each other when establishing foreign missionary jurisdictions, so that two bishops of that Communion may not exercise jurisdiction in the same place" (1897 Resolution 24).

The participants in the 1867 Conference seemed to have envisioned Lambeth or a subcommittee of Lambeth playing a major role in defining and safeguarding the common "faith and discipline" of "the several branches of the Anglican Communion." That gathering's reference to the canonical subordination of synods "to the higher authority of a synod or synods above them" was drafted in such a way as to leave open the possibility that it referred to centralization beyond the provincial level (1867 Resolution 4). The same 1867 gathering called for a committee to "consider the constitution of a voluntary spiritual tribunal, to which questions of doctrine may be carried by appeal from the tribunals for the exercise of discipline in each province of the colonial Church" (1867 Resolution 9). The committee established to consider the idea reported back in 1878, however, that it was "not prepared to recommend that there should be any one central tribunal of appeal from . . . provincial tribunals," and that it believed that every ecclesiastical province "should be held responsible for its own decisions" (1878 Recommendation 8; reaffirmed by 1930 Resolution 51).

The idea of some central authority never entirely disappeared, however, and later Conferences have called for scaled-down versions of the idea. Lambeth 1897, for example, suggested that it was "advisable that a consultative body should be formed to which resort may be had, if desired, by the national Churches, provinces, and extraprovincial dioceses of the Anglican Communion either for information or for advice" (1897 Resolution 5). The Archbishop of Canterbury subsequently created a Central Consultative Body (later also called the Lambeth Consultative Body), which was periodically reorganized (1920 Resolution 30, 1958 Resolution 61) until 1968, when it was superseded by other bodies.

Subsequent meeting of the Conference have called for or expressed approval of other organizations for Anglican cooperation. Lambeth 1948 called for the creation of the Advisory Council on Missionary Strategy (1948 Resolution 80) in a period in which former British colonial mission churches were moving toward independence. Lambeth 1968 endorsed plans for an Anglican Consultative Council (1968 Resolution 69), which soon replaced both the Lambeth Consultative Body and the Advisory Council on Missionary Strategy as the major body planning for the Anglican Communion between Lambeth Conferences. That leadership role was soon to be shared, however, with the formation of a regular Primates' Meeting (implied by 1978 Resolutions 11–14; clarified by 1988 Resolutions 18 and 52). A report adopted at the 1988 Lambeth Conference identified the Lambeth Conference, the two bodies of which it had approved (Anglican Consultative Council, the Primates' Meeting), and Archbishop of Canterbury as the four "instruments of Communion" that "have now become established" (*The Truth Shall Make You Free*, 294).

In addition to these general continuing bodies, Lambeth Conferences have called for a variety of commissions to address specific issues. These include the Inter-Anglican Theological and Doctrinal Commission (1978 Resolution 25; 1988 Resolution 18), the "Eames Commission" to consider the ordination of women to the episcopate (1988

Resolution 1; 1998 Resolutions 111.2 and 4), and the Inter-Anglican Standing Commission on Ecumenical Relations (1998 Resolution IV.3).

Lambeth Conferences have also offered a useful definition of the Anglican Communion: "a fellowship, within the one Holy Catholic and Apostolic Church, of those duly constituted dioceses, provinces or regional Churches in communion with the See of Canterbury, which have the following characteristics in common: a. they uphold and propagate the Catholic and Apostolic faith and order as they are generally set forth in the Book of Common Prayer as authorised in their several Churches; b. they are particular or national Churches, and, as such, promote within each of their territories a national expression of Christian faith, life and worship; and c. they are bound together not by a central legislative and executive authority, but by mutual loyalty sustained through the common counsel of the bishops in conference" (1930 Resolution 49).

## Mission

The question of foreign mission has often been closely linked with the discussion of structure, for it is in the newly established missions that the structure is least clear, most in flux, and the most in need of definition. In addition to calling for cooperation of churches that send missionaries, Lambeth Conference have called for supporting (1897 Resolution 55) and serving in the mission field (1920 Resolution 32; 1948 Resolution 84). Lambeth 1920 identified the "ultimate aim of all mission work" as "the establishment of self-governing, self-supporting, and self-extending Churches, from which outside control has been withdrawn at the earliest moment, so as to allow the free expression of their national character" (1920 Resolution 34). The Conference of 1968 endorsed the principle of Mutual Responsibility and Interdependence by which the younger churches of the former mission field and the more established provinces of the Communion pledged to work with one another on an equal footing (1968 Resolution 67).

## Ecumenism

Another issue to which Lambeth Conferences have devoted considerable attention over the years is ecumenism, with particular attention paid to the topic at the Conferences of 1897, 1920, 1958, and 1968. Early resolutions called for members of the Anglican Communion to pray for unity (1878 Recommendation 6; 1897 Resolution 59; 1908 Resolution 59), and encouraged conversation with Christians of other denominations, beginning with those who were English speakers (1888 Resolution 12). The Conference of 1920 issued its own "Appeal to all Christian People" on the matter of unity (1920 Resolution 9; reaffirmed by 1948 Resolution 56).

Conferences have supported participation in international ecumenical bodies such as the International Congress in Vienna (1897 Resolution 33), the Faith and Order Commission (1920 Resolution 16), and the World Council of Church (1948 Resolution

75; 1958 Resolutions 55–56). They have also focused on bi-lateral conversation with other denominations. Dialogue with the Old Catholic Churches was perhaps the earliest (1888 Resolution 15; 1897 Resolutions 28–29, etc.) with those discussions leading eventually to a full communion relationship.

Calls for discussion with Orthodox Churches began in 1897 (1897 Resolution 36; 1908 Resolution 60, 62; 1920 Resolution 19; 1948 Resolution 66, etc.). The 1908 conference approved of conversations with the non-Chalcedonian Churches of the East (1908 Resolutions 61 and 63), with the 1920 Conference declaring in Resolution 21 that the resultant discussions had "have gone far towards showing that any errors as to the incarnation of our Lord, which may at some period of their history have been attributed to them, have at any rate now passed away" (1920 Resolution 21).

Resolutions concerning discussion with Lutherans began with the Church of Sweden (1897 Resolution 39; 1908 Resolution 74), but subsequently expanded at the Conferences of 1930 and 1948 to include other Scandinavian countries, Finland, and Lativia (1930 Resolution 37–38; 1948 Resolutions 69–71). The Conference of 1998 noted with approval that many provinces of the Anglican Communion had established or were nearing the establishment of full-communion relationships with the Lutherans (1998 Resolution IV.16).

Resolutions for conversations with Moravians began at the Conference of 1888 (1888 Resolution 16), and those regarding relationships with Presbyterians in 1908 (1908 Resolution 75). Other conversation partners named in resolutions include the Evangelical Free Churches of England (1930 Resolution 44), the Methodists (1958 Resolutions 29–30), and the Baptist World Alliance (1988 Resolution 10).

The Conference of 1930 took notice of the movement to create a United Church in South India and the subsequent Conference expressed support for that effort and for parallel efforts elsewhere in South Asia (1930 Resolution 40; 1948 Resolutions 52–55; 1948 Resolutions 52–55, and 62–63).

The 1948 Conference asked the Archbishop of Canterbury to call for a conference of Anglican Bishops with the bishops of other churches with whom the Anglican Church was in communion (1948 Resolution 74). Although this request was repeated (1958 Resolution 15), such a conference has not taken place. The 1988 Conference, however, partially addressed the issue by endorsing a proposal from the Anglican Consultative Congress that the bishops from United Churches in full communion (Church of South India, etc.) be invited to Lambeth and to the Primates' Meeting (1988 Resolution 12).

Conferences said relatively little about the Roman Catholic Church until the middle of the twentieth century, and the few statements adopted prior to that time were largely negative. Conferences complained about the Roman Catholic policy of requiring that all children of mixed marriage be raised as Roman Catholics (1908 Resolution 67; 1948 Resolution 98). They did applaud the work of Cardinal Mercier (1851–1926) and the informal Malines Conversations on Anglican–Roman Catholic reunion, but regretted "that by the encyclical 'Mortalium animos' members of the Roman Catholic Church are forbidden to take part in the World Conference on Faith and Order and other similar conferences" (1930 Resolution 32). That largely negative attitude changed after Vatican II (1962–65), with later Conferences applauding the creation (1968, Resolution 52) and supporting the work (1978 Resolution 33; 1988 Resolution 8, etc.) of the Anglican–Roman Catholic International Commission (ARCIC).

Conferences in the early twentieth century were critical of Hinduism and Buddhism (1897 Resolution 15), and Theosophy, Spiritualism, and Christian Science (1920 Resolution 55–65). It was only in the last third of the twentieth century that Conferences began to speak in more favorable terms about inter-religious dialogue (1968 Resolution 11; 1978 Resolution 37).

## Liturgy

Lambeth Conferences have tried to balance an appreciation for the value of the historic editions of the *Book of Common Prayer*, which the Conference of 1930 identified as the first characteristic of the Anglican Communion (1930 Resolution 49), with the need to adapt the liturgy to the needs of individual nations and cultures. The Conference of 1878, for example, recognized the need for forms of the "Books of Common Prayer, suitable to the needs of native congregations in heathen countries," but cautioned "that the principles embodied in such books should be identical with the principles embodied in the Book of Common Prayer; and that the deviations from the Book of Common Prayer in point of form should only be such as are required by the circumstances of particular Churches" (1878 Recommendation 10).

In questions of ritual, the Conferences have tried to remain aloof of the debates that at times have troubled the various Anglican provinces. The conference 1878, for example, balanced a warning that "communion in worship may be endangered by excessive diversities of ritual" with an acknowledgement that some Anglicans argued that "such large elasticity in the forms of worship is desirable as will give wide scope to all legitimate expressions of devotional feeling." The Conference then passed on the problem to the various provinces and national churches, the members of which it hoped would "recognise the duty of submitting themselves, for conscience' sake, in matters ritual and ceremonial, to the authoritative judgements of [their] particular or national Church" (1878 Resolution 7).

Twentieth-century Conferences have recognized the need for some revision in the form of the *Book of Common Prayer*. The Conference of 1908 suggested seven principles that might be followed in the revision of the prayer book (1908 Resolution 27), and noted the need for more hopeful prayers in the Visitation of the Sick (1908 Resolution 35).

Some resolutions did support existing practice in the face of call for change, such as resolutions denying that infectious disease created the need to abandon the common cup (1908 Resolution 31), and affirming the necessity of confirmation prior to reception of the Eucharist (1948 Resolution 103). By 1958, however, the Conference gave full support to revision of the prayer book, calling for that work, however, to be done thoughtfully and in inter-Anglican and ecumenical conversation (1958 Resolutions 73–80). The 1988 Conference asked the Archbishop of Canterbury to appoint a committee to offer "encouragement, support and advice to Churches of the Communion in their work of liturgical revision as well as facilitating mutual consultation concerning, and review of, their Prayer Books as they are developed" (1988 Resolution 18). This resolution led to the appointment of a "coordinator of the Liturgy" (1998 Resolution III.15).

The single liturgical issue that has consumed the greatest amount of time at Lambeth Conferences has been consideration of the possibility of women serving in the ordained ministry. The Conference of 1897 gave thanks for "revival alike of brotherhoods and sisterhoods and of the office of deaconess in our branch of the Church" (1897 Resolution 11). The Conferences of 1920 declared that "women should be admitted to those councils of the Church to which laymen are admitted, and on equal terms" (1920 Resolution 46), and that the time had come when "the diaconate of women should be restored formally and canonically, and should be recognized throughout the Anglican Communion" (1920 Resolution 47). It also declared, however, that "the order of deaconesses [was] for women the one and only order of ministry which has the stamp of apostolic approval" (1920 Resolution 48). Nonetheless, Bishop Ronald Owen Hall (1895–1975) of Hong Kong ordained Deaconesses Florence Li Tim-Oi (1907–1992) as a priest during the extraordinary circumstances of World War II. When the Chinese Church requested permission to continue ordination of women to priesthood for a period of 20 years, the Conference of 1948 responded that such a move would be "against the tradition and order and would gravely affect the internal and external relations of the Anglican Communion" (1948 Resolution 113). By 1968, however, the bishops at the Lambeth Conference suggested that "the theological arguments at present presented for and against the ordination of women to the priesthood are inconclusive," and asked individual provinces to study the matter (1968 Resolutions 34–35). By 1978, four provinces were ordaining women to the presbyterate, and eight others were moving in that direction. The Conference suggested that the decision on the matter was up to each province and urged mutual respect for those with differing opinions (1978 Resolution 21). It also urged provinces considering the consecration of women to the episcopate not to act "without consultation with the episcopate through the primates and overwhelming support in any member Church and in the diocese concerned, lest the bishop's office should become a cause of disunity instead of a focus of unity" (1978 Resolution 22). The 1988 Conference requested the Archbishop of Canterbury to appoint a commission to discuss the possibility and results of consecrating women the episcopate (1988 Resolution 1). By 1998, some provinces had already consecrated women as bishops. The Conference in that year noted "although some of the means by which communion is expressed may be strained or broken, there is a need for courtesy, tolerance, mutual respect, and prayer for one another" (1998 Resolution III.2 quoting the Eames Report), and called provinces that ordained women to "make such provision, including appropriate episcopal ministry" for members of the church who opposed the decisions reached (1998 Resolution III.2).

## Theology

In matters of theology, Conferences have generally focused on basic creedal principles, such as the four propositions of the Chicago-Lambeth Quadrilateral (Resolution 11 of

1888; 1948 Resolution 59; 1998 Resolution IV.2), or the proposition that religious training "which limits itself to historical information and moral culture" is inadequate (1908 Resolution 12). Some individual Conferences have developed particular themes such as that of 1948, which devoted attention to the "Christian doctrine of Man", affirming the existence of "a spiritual as well as a material nature" in the face of growing materialism (1948 Resolution 1), and the 1958 Conference, which devoted its first 12 resolutions to the place of Scripture, which it held "discloses the truths about the relation of God and man which are the key to the world's predicament and is therefore deeply relevant to the modern world" (1958 Resolution 1). In general, however, Conferences have avoided the creation of detailed statements of faith. This minimalist approach may be one of the reasons why theological statements have not been the occasion for great dispute at Lambeth Conferences.

## Ethics

Conferences have addressed a variety of ethical issues, particularly those that have international connotations. The Conferences at the end of the nineteenth and the early twentieth century worried about the effect of international trade in alcohol (1897 Resolution 23) and opium (1908 Resolution 44; 1930 Resolution 28). Conferences have generally opposed racial discrimination; that of 1920, for example, protested "against the colour prejudice among the different races of the world, which not only hinders intercourse, but gravely imperils the peace of the future" (1920 Resolution 7). Early conference often, however, nuanced their opposition to racial segregation with other concerns. The Conference of 1897 accepted the possibility of "separate modes of administration" for different ethnic groups so long as they did not "obscure the fact that the many races form but one Church" (1897 Resolution 21). The Conference of 1930 accepted the "ruling of one race by another," provided that the ruling race kept in mind "the highest welfare of the subject race" (1930 Resolution 21). The same Conference called for "interdependence and not competition" among races, but noted that "interdependence does not itself involve intermarriage" (1930 Resolution 23). Subsequent conferences have been less nuanced in their positions. The 1948 Conference declared "that discrimination between men on the ground of race alone is inconsistent with the principles of Christ's religion" (1948 Resolution 43). The Conference of 1988 singled out one nation for criticism, noting that "the system of apartheid in South Africa is evil and especially repugnant "(1988 Resolution 39).

Other resolutions have criticized economic exploitation, noting the Church's teaching that "property is a trust held for the benefit of the community, and its right use be insisted upon as a religious duty" (1908, Resolution 48), and that investments involve "moral responsibility" to employees and society (1908 Resolution 49). The 1930 Conference adopted a statement that war "as a method of settling international disputes is incompatible with the teaching and example of our Lord Jesus Christ" (1930 Resolution 25; reaffirmed by 1958 Resolution 106). Conferences have expressed sympathy for those who were the victims of war and violence, especially Christians facing discrimination, as was the case with Armenian, Assyrian, and Syrian Jacobite Christians (1920

Resolution 20), the Church of Russia (1930 Resolution 34), and the Church in Persia (1930 Resolution 41).

Although Lambeth Conferences have declared "that the Church is not to be identified with any particular political or social system" (1958 Resolution 104), some ethical pronouncements make clear political references. Various Conferences expressed support for the ideals of the League of Nations (1920 Resolution 78; 1930 Resolution 26), called for just treaties for Japan and Germany after the end of World War II (1948 Resolution 12), called the United Nations to place the city of Jerusalem under international control (1948 Resolution 16), declared "that Marxian Communism is contrary to the Christian faith and practice" (1948 Resolution 25), criticized the racial policy of South Africa (1988 Resolution 39), called for the "the abolition by international agreement of nuclear bombs and other weapons of similar indiscriminate destructive power, the use of which is repugnant to the Christian conscience," and pointed to the "the obligations of states to maintain peace and security in accordance with the United Nations Charter" (1958 Resolution 106).

The largest number of ethical resolutions have, however, dealt with personal morality, sexuality, and family life. The Conference of 1888 declared that "our Lord's words expressly forbid divorce, except in the case of fornication or adultery" (1888 Resolution 4). The Conference of 1908 warned about "the growing prevalence of disregard of the sanctity of marriage" and the "terrible evils which have grown up from the creation of facilities for divorce" (1908 Resolution 37–38), a theme to which later Conferences returned. That of 1948, for example, urged states that adopted lenient divorce laws to reconsider their legislation (1948 Resolution 97). The 1958 Conference modified the Conferences' stance on divorce, however, admitting that "in certain cases where a decree of divorce has been sought and may even have been granted, there may in fact have been no marital bond in the eyes of the Church," and therefore called for consideration of "a procedure for defining marital status" (1958 Resolution 118). Conferences since that time have been largely silent on the morality of divorce and remarriage.

The 1908 and 1920 Conferences opposed the use of birth control "as demoralising to character and hostile to national welfare" (1908 Resolutions 41–42; 1920 Resolution 68). The Conference of 1930 reversed that opinion, however, allowing for the use of birth control in those limited circumstances in which there was "clearly felt moral obligation to limit or avoid parenthood, and where there is a morally sound reason for avoiding complete abstinence" (1930 Resolution 15).

The question of polygamy has been discussed in the relationship to African Missions and to the discipline of baptism. Samuel Crowther (c. 1807–1891), the first African to be an Anglican bishop, brought the matter for discussion at the Lambeth Conference of 1888; that Conference adopted the position that "persons living in polygamy be not admitted to baptism . . . until such time as they shall be in a position to accept the law of Christ." The conference held, however, that local authorities could decide on the baptism of the "wives of polygamists" (1888 Resolution 5). The Conferences of 1958 and 1968 asked for a further investigation of the question (1958 Resolution 120; 1968 Resolution 23), with the Conference of 1988 ultimately suggesting that men who were polygamists prior to joining the church might under some circumstances be baptized (1988 Resolution 26).

The Lambeth Conference of 1998 considered the morality of gay and lesbian behavior. While recognizing that "there are among us persons who experience themselves as having a homosexual orientation," the Conference adopted the position that "abstinence is right for those who are not called to marriage," and that it could not, therefore, "advise the legitimising or blessing of same sex unions nor ordaining those involved in same gender unions" (1998 Resolution I.10).

## The Future of the Lambeth Conference

Decisions made by the Anglican Church in Canada and the Episcopal Church to marry and ordain gay and lesbian persons, in opposition to the advice of the 1998 Conference (1998 Resolution I:10), have led to considerable unhappiness in the Anglican Communion, particularly on the part of the provinces of the Global South. The Primates' Meeting called for the establishment of a Lambeth Commission (2003) to consider a response to the American and Canadian actions. That Commission issued the *Windsor Report* (2004), which proposed the creation of an Anglican Covenant that would provide a mechanism for dealing with doctrinal disagreements in the Anglican Communion. A Covenant Design Group then developed various drafts of the proposed covenant, which, as of this writing, has received a mixed response from the provinces and national churches of the Anglican Communion.

Much of the leadership for the so called "Windsor Process" has come from the Primates' Meeting, rather than from the Lambeth Conference. The Conference has not, however, remained unaffected. Concern about growing division in the Anglican Communion led the 2008 Conference to forego the adoption of any resolutions and simply to organize in unofficial Indaba discussion groups. Some bishops from the Global South, unhappy with the failure to take concrete action to enforce the 1998 resolution on homosexuality, boycotted the 2008 Lambeth Conference, participating instead in a Global Anglican Future Conference (GAFCON) that met in the same year in Jerusalem.

Such opposition is unlikely to bring an end to the Lambeth Conferences. Indeed, the tensions in the Anglican Communion in the early twenty-first century are very much like those of the mid-nineteenth century that gave rise to the Lambeth Conferences in the first place.

## Bibliography

The Resolutions of the several Lambeth Conferences can be found online at www.lambethconference.org.

Cannon, John, ed. 2002. *The Oxford Companion to British History*. New York: Oxford University Press.

Hopkins, John Henry. 1835. *The Primitive Church Compared with the Protestant Episcopal Church of the Present Day*, 2 vols. Burlington: Smith and Harrington.

*Journal of the Proceeding of the Bishops Clergy, and Laity of the Protestant Episcopal Church* in the United States of America Assembled in General Convention. 1838. New York: printed for the convention.

*Journal of the Proceeding of the Bishops Clergy, and Laity of the Protestant Episcopal Church in the United States of America Assembled in General Convention.* 1862. New York: printed for the convention.

*The Truth Shall Make You Free: The Lambeth Conference 1988.* London: Church for the Anglican Consultative Council.

Podmore, Colin. 2005. *Aspects of Anglican Identity.* London: Church House Publishing.

Sachs, William L. 1993. *The Transformation of Anglicanism: From State Church to Global Communion.* Cambridge: Cambridge University Press.

Stephenson, Alan M. G. 1978. *Anglicanism and the Lambeth Conferences.* London: SPCK.

CHAPTER 8

# Anglican Consultative Councils

## Samuel Van Culin and Andrew Bennett Terry

Any consideration and discussion of the Anglican Consultative Council (ACC) will have to begin with a recognition of the fact that the Anglican Communion, in these early years of the twenty-first century, is engaged in a deep and contentious debate about the nature of its life and message as an historical Christian community. A careful reading of the Acts of the Apostles reminds us that deep and contentious debate within the Christian community is nothing new. Each age in the church's life is confronted with its own particular issues. The church must undertake to form its own view on those issues and try (indeed struggle) to discern how the Holy Spirit is moving the church toward a deeper understanding of God's truth. This call to discern God's truth is a vocational task for the church in every place at every time. For a communion of churches, there is the compelling impulse of the Holy Spirit to discover and embrace a common point of recognition, understanding, and acceptance of each other in bonds of affection and common commitment. For the Anglican Communion, these bonds are expressed and sustained through the office and ministry of the Archbishop of Canterbury, the Lambeth Conference, the Primates' Meeting, and the Anglican Consultative Council. They are in place to help maintain the "communion of churches."

Once asked "What is the job of the Archbishop of Canterbury?" Archbishop Robert Runcie answered, "My job is to *gather* the Communion not to *rule* it." Since the 1867 Lambeth Conference, the archbishop has gathered the communion – first the Bishops to Lambeth, as host, then the Primates as chairman, then the ACC as president.

In several respects, the Anglican Consultative Council (ACC) is unique in the history of the Anglican Communion (Howe 1985, 985). It is the only Inter-Anglican Body with a constitution. Its constitution was drafted at an Inter-Anglican meeting in Ceylon (now Sri Lanka) and presented to the Lambeth Conference in 1968 (Howe 1985, 110). The conference accepted and endorsed the proposed constitution and submitted it to the

*The Wiley-Blackwell Companion to the Anglican Communion*, First Edition. Edited by Ian S. Markham, J. Barney Hawkins IV, Justyn Terry, and Leslie Nuñez Steffensen.
© 2013 John Wiley & Sons, Ltd. Published 2013 by John Wiley & Sons, Ltd.

member churches of the Communion for review and approval. The replies from the churches were unanimous. Each church had endorsed the constitution in accordance with its own synodical arrangements. With these approvals, the ACC met for the first time at Limuru Conference Center in Kenya in February 1971.

As a consultative body, the ACC does not rule or govern the communion. Its consultative character provides the member churches with the opportunity to share, plan, and undertake joint action for mission. It is an instrument of common action. Its activities, programs, initiatives, reports, and resolutions provide opportunity for widespread discussion, study, and prayer and reflection within the member churches.

There are critics who say that the consultative process is not adequate to provide that "common point of commitment" for a body of almost 80 million Christians who are members of 34 independent provinces, four united churches, and six "other churches" spread across the globe. The united churches included are those formed between Anglican and several other Protestant traditions (i.e., Church of South India). "Other churches" include the Spanish Reformed Church and the Lusitanian Church of Portugal. The critics insist that what is needed is a direct and mutually recognizable point of authority, direction, and discipline, i.e., a joint confessional statement or covenant of understanding and belief. This debate is proceeding within the Anglican Communion. It is the responsibility of the ACC to service this debate, keep open the lines of communication, compile and circulate information about the debate, and compile the responses. It is also the responsibility of the ACC to reflect and comment on the process but not to decide! Not to decide is, of course, a decision. It is a decision to let the Holy Spirit move through the consultative process at every level, deepening insight, opening understanding, and building new and more comprehensive consensus. It is a recognition that distinctive histories and experiences operate with powerful influence in the churches in every different culture. Through patience, thoughtful consideration, and prayer, these experiences can be integrated into a new "point of commitment."

It has been said there are two key ways to do something: coercion and persuasion. The ACC is an instrument of persuasion. Its consultative character is open to the leading of the Holy Spirit. Anglicans have always safeguarded this work of the Holy Spirit and are trying to learn how the consultative process enables the building of new relationships within the churches at this time of history. The ACC is a kind of "midwife" in bringing new relationships to life, thus assisting the Archbishop of Canterbury in his "gathering" vocation.

As a consultative organ of the communion, the ACC can trace its lineage to the Lambeth Conference of 1878, when a committee was formed to develop a scheme of subjects to be discussed at the next Lambeth Conference – this initiated a process of planning ahead within the Lambeth Conference system. By the Lambeth Conference 1930, duties were given to this formally recognized "consultative body," and its membership was defined. Its responsibilities were described as "to direct, consider, advise, and to take action in an advisory capacity only without executive or administrative powers" (Bayne 1964, 5). This body was joined by an "advisory council on missionary strategy." With the Archbishop of Canterbury, these two bodies functioned in partnership as review and planning instruments for the communion supported by the archbishop's staff at Lambeth Palace.

Following the conclusion of World War II, the Lambeth Conference of 1958 recognized the increase in mission, and ecumenical and social challenges for all the Anglican churches. The conference authorized the archbishop to appoint a full-time secretary for the consultative body. Bishop Stephen Bayne (United States) accepted this appointment.

On assuming office, Bayne inaugurated an extensive and comprehensive series of consultations throughout the communion in an effort to consolidate a picture of changing missionary, ecumenical, and developmental opportunities and difficulties. The fruit of these five years was presented to the Anglican Conference in Toronto, Canada, 1963, in a document entitled "Mutual Responsibility and Interdependence in the Body of Christ" (MRI) (Project Canterbury 2009). It was endorsed by the Primates, the Advisory Council on Missionary Strategy, the Lambeth Consultative Body, and the full membership of the Anglican Congress 1963.

The Lambeth Conference in 1968 explicitly endorsed the MRI document in authorizing the establishment of the ACC. It made mission the central focus of its work and responsibilities and emphasized the fact that the ACC was the direct heir to the theology and strategy outlined in MRI. It transferred all the responsibilities of both the Lambeth Consultative Body and the Advisory Council on Missionary Strategy to the ACC itself.

The ACC employs a staff at the Anglican Communion Office in London. It holds funds for financing its operations. It is a registered charity functioning within the regulations of The Charity Commissioners of England and Wales. The location of the staff away from Lambeth Palace was specifically designed to avoid any suggestion that the Anglican Communion was seeking to establish an "Anglican Vatican." At the same time, regular cooperative meetings between the Secretary General and staff and the Archbishop of Canterbury and staff are a necessary and established practice.

The membership of the ACC is composed of bishops, priests, deacons, and laypersons, all of whom are elected by each member church as representatives on the council. From its beginning, ecumenical representatives have been in attendance. A steering committee functions between full meetings of the ACC. By a recent change in the constitution of the ACC, the members of the Primates Standing Committee were made *ex-officio* members of the ACC and its Standing Committee. This Standing Committee meets annually, now, in an effort to strengthen the quality of the relationship between the Primates' meeting and the ACC. The membership of the ACC has grown from 22 provinces at ACC 1 in 1971 to 44 provinces, united churches, and "other" churches at ACC 14 in 2009. The staff of the Secretary General has grown from three at ACC 1 in 1971 to 21. The Secretary General's duties have dramatically increased, with the expanded responsibilities of serving the work and meetings of the Lambeth Conference, the Primates' meeting, in addition to the ACC and its Commissions, Networks, and research initiatives.

## The ACC and the "Arc of Mission"

A reading of the first ACC report from Limuru, Kenya, in 1971, "The Time is Now," reveals the wide range of subjects discussed and the significant resolutions endorsed

(ACC 1971). The work of the meeting was divided into four major areas of effort, "Unity and Ecumenical Affairs," "Renewal—Church and Society," "Renewal—Order and Organization in the Anglican Church," and "Mission and Evangelism." These four general themes continue to provide the structure within which the ACC does its work and undertakes its initiatives.

It was Resolution 31 at this first ACC meeting which was the most explicit response to MRI, calling, as it does, for the Secretary General to initiate actions that would lead eventually to a series of "partnership discussions" on the subject of mission in the local church (ACC 1971, 52). In 1973, following two years of concentrated work, the staff was able to report to ACC 2, in Dublin, Scotland. In Resolution 27 of the Dublin Report, a new pattern of missionary planning, implementation, and support was recognized (ACC 1973, 59).

Following the Dublin meeting, the Secretariat initiated a series of "Partners in Mission" Consultations (PIM), drawing together leadership in missionary societies and agencies, supporting churches, provinces, dioceses, and councils. At its third meeting in Trinidad in 1976, the Council affirmed its pleasure with the results of the "Partnership in Mission" process as an "important cooperative and educational experiment which should continue to be developed" (ACC 1976, 58).

This partnership initiative of the ACC has led to the dramatic opening of many companionships and partnerships across the Anglican Communion over the years. They surely have deepened and strengthened the "Bonds of Affection" that sustain the Communion. By the fourth meeting of the ACC in Canada, the PIM Consultations had identified shared mission challenges and opportunities for the Communion. The report from the meeting identified "the need to explore more strategic use of our resources and experiences to meet new challenges for mission. The PIM process has taken us one stage further, but there have been few opportunities for – planning as a whole" (ACC 1979, 26). It instructed the Secretary General to "establish a procedure whereby – more serious study and review can be undertaken" (ACC 1979, 927).

The major initiative undertaken by the Secretary General was the establishment of the "Mission Issues and Strategy Group" (MISAG). MISAG undertook a review of mission issues and strategy, identifying development needs and finding ways and means for collaboration with other Christian bodies in mission and evangelism. The MISAG opened new procedures for cooperative planning and action between all societies, agencies, provinces, dioceses, and councils of the Communion, and with widespread ecumenical agencies.

The MISAG report "Progress in Partnership" was received by ACC 7 in Singapore in 1987, and its strategic observations and proposals were referred to the ACC Standing Committee for "appraisal and appropriate action" (ACC 1987, 31). The most important result was the appointment for five years of an Inter-Anglican Standing Commission on Mission and Evangelism (IASCOMBE). From its appointment in 2000 to the presentation of its final report at ACC 13 in Nottingham in 2005, it provided the Communion with a continuing network of planning and initiatives for mission.

In the words of Archbishop Williams, the report demonstrated "how much both the global nature of the conversation and local contexts of encounter inform how we understand not only our missionary work but the apostolic purpose of our Communion" (ACC 2005, 195).

One of the important contributions to the understanding and embrace of the missionary vocation of the church was presented at ACC 8 in Wales (ACC 1990, 101). These "Five Marks of Mission" continue to provide a framework for reflecting and acting across the Communion.

They are:

1.   To proclaim the good news of the Kingdom
2.   To teach, baptize, and nurture new believers
3.   To respond to human need by loving service
4.   To seek to transform unjust structures of society
5.   To strive to safeguard the integrity of creation and renew the life of the earth

A proposal has been made by the church in Canada to add a sixth mark of mission, which relates to peace, conflict transformation, and reconciliation, to the current list of five. No decision has yet been made by the ACC itself.

A "Mission Cluster" has been established within the Secretariat to coordinate the continuing implications of mission for the Communion. The Cluster includes ACC staff, Lambeth Palace staff, and representatives working on behalf of the "Five Marks."

## The Ecumenical Dimension of Mission

In the resolution endorsing the establishment of the ACC, the Lambeth Conference 1968 identified as one of its major functions "to encourage and guide Anglican participation in the ecumenical movement and the ecumenical organizations; to cooperate with the World Council of Churches and the World Confessional Bodies – and to make arrangements for the conduct of Pan-Anglican Conversations with the Roman Catholic Church and the Orthodox Churches" (Coleman 1992, 172).

The concern for and commitment to the ecumenical dimension of mission were not new for the Anglican Communion when it established the ACC. These concerns had been carried by the Lambeth Conference since 1887. Until the establishment of the ACC, the staff responsibilities were carried out by the "Archbishop's Counselors on Foreign Relations" at Lambeth Palace. With the transfer of these responsibilities to the ACC, a new dynamic emerged in the staffing relationships. With regard to the ecumenical responsibilities which had been assigned to them, the ACC staff worked cooperatively with the Lambeth Palace staff and the various participants in ecumenical bodies and in bilateral dialogues and united churches. In all of these situations, divergent histories and traditions had to be integrated.

At ACC 1 in Limuru in 1971, the rich history of the ecumenical dimensions of mission became evident. At this inaugural session of the ACC, it received and reviewed reports from the united churches, bilateral dialogues, and ecumenical bodies, and referred them to the churches. It took action to invite united churches in full communion with Anglican churches to join the ACC as full members. It affirmed its commitment to church union and invited the member churches to consider the theology of full communion. By ACC 3 in 1976 a significant number of negotiations toward church union had collapsed, and the Council undertook an examination of the causes and consequences (ACC 1976, 9).

At ACC 4 in 1979, some of the practical challenges that exist between churches in bilateral dialogue emerged, both in discussions of the Anglican–Orthodox Dialogue regarding the omission of the *filioque* clause and in discussion of the Anglican Roman Catholic International Commission (ARCIC) regarding the way in which the Anglican Communion can make an authoritative response to the three agreed statements from ARCIC (ACC 1979, 4). By ACC 6 in 1984, a report by the Anglican/Lutheran working group highlighted the fact that Anglican/Lutheran agreements were progressing through regional dialogues, particularly in the United States, Europe, and Africa.

By 1987, it was evident that a comprehensive report on all bilateral dialogues and on the essential elements that Anglicans should consider for churches in full communion needed to be inaugurated. The "Emmaus Report" provided this comprehensive overview and was submitted to ACC 7 in Singapore in 1987 and was forwarded to the Lambeth Conference in 1988 (Anglican Ecumenical Consultation 1987). It was prepared by a number of bishops and ecumenical officers from the Anglican Communion and provided a framework for the ecumenical section at Lambeth 1988.

The 1988 Lambeth Conference proposed as the next step the establishment of an Inter-Anglican Commission on Ecumenical Relations (IASCER) to offer advice to provinces on ecumenical projects and agreements and to help coordinate the various bilateral developments. At ACC 14 in Jamaica, 2009, the Council received and commended the IASCER book "The Vision Before Us," describing its work between the years 2000 and 2008, including an analysis of the entire breadth of ecumenical engagements in the Anglican Communion (ACC 2009, Resolution 14.01). Within that vision, one finds principals of ecumenical engagement. These provide a short benchmark of Anglican ecumenical work in a parallel way to the "Five Marks of Mission."

At present, all concerns for the Anglican ecumenical mission are placed in the staff of unity, faith, and order at the Secretariat. This staff provides the necessary services for the Inter-Anglican Standing Committee on Unity, Faith, and Order (IASCUFO), which was established by the Lambeth Conference, the Primates' Meeting, and the ACC. It integrates the work done by the former doctrinal commission, the ecumenical relations commission, and the Windsor Continuing Group.

## The Secretariat

While the Secretary General and staff were originally responsible for the servicing of the work of the ACC itself, the need to build stronger relations between the "Instruments of Unity" has required an expansion of the responsibilities of the Secretariat. The office today is responsible for planning and managing the meetings and programs of the Primates' Meeting, the Lambeth Conference, and the ACC itself. As the preceding description of the "Arc of Mission" demonstrates, a process of gradual transfer of some responsibilities from the staff from Lambeth Palace to the ACC staff has occurred over the years. This has resulted in the need to adopt working procedures that integrate the work and responsibilities of the Instruments of Unity. The Standing Committee now is composed of ACC and Primates (as noted in the preceding text).

The Secretariat is now the Anglican Communion Office (ACO), serving the Lambeth Conference, the Primates' Meeting, and the ACC. It is divided into eight departments:

The Secretary General's Office
Communications
Unity, Faith, and Order
Finance and Administration
Mission
Theological Studies
Continuing Indaba
The Office of the Anglican Observer at the UN

With the growth of the requirements for communications, the ACO has expanded its facilities dramatically. The website www.anglicancommunion.org carries all the reports, resolutions, studies, and news items of the ACC, the Primates' Meetings, the Lambeth Conference, and the Archbishop of Canterbury. It also provides news of activities and issues arising in various churches. The communications department works through the Internet as well as with television, radio, and news services to interpret the life and work of the Communion accurately. It coordinates a network of Anglican Church communicators around the world and helps with the training of bishops and others in raising awareness of the values and dangers in modern communication.

The Unity, Faith, and Order department is referred to earlier in the ecumenical section. It is important to add that its responsibilities have increased with establishment of individual working groups on the Anglican Covenant, ecumenical consistency and policy, reception, the definition of "church," and the theological understanding of the "Instruments of Communion."

The finance and administration department is responsible for maintaining the necessary resources to support the extensive network of consultation required by the ACO. A review of the Inter-Anglican budget will reveal the nature of this support. Contributions from member churches provide the major support, with special fundraising as the second most important. Details can be seen in the report of ACC 13 (ACC 2005, 627). At this meeting, the Council took note of the special importance of "The Compass Rose Society" for its fundraising and mission support (ACC 2005, 27). The Society is a network of members committed to the mission of the Anglican Communion and the work of the Archbishop of Canterbury and the ACO.

The Mission Department has responsibility for the "Evangelism and Church Growth Initiative" (ECGI), working toward the development of a databank of resources in evangelism and church growth models. Within the department, the "Anglican Alliance" is seeking to establish a new way for Anglicans to work together globally for relief and development. The department also manages the Networks of the Anglican Communion (see Anglican Communion Networks in the following text).

Theological Studies is chiefly responsible for "theological education for the Anglican Communion" (TEAC), which was established by the Anglican Primates. They have established goals and priorities and educational materials for all institutions training people for ordained Anglican ministries. This department also oversees a major project on "The Bible in the Life of the Church," which was endorsed by ACC 14 in 2009 (ACC 2009, Resolution 14.06). The project seeks to discover how Anglicans read the Bible, reading the very diverse contexts that are inevitably brought to this reading. The Network for Interfaith Concerns (NIFCON) is a working part of the department. It produced a document on theology of interfaith dialogue entitled "Generous Love" reflecting on the rationale for interfaith dialogue. Regular issues of the Christian–Muslim Digest have been produced.

The Continuing Indaba is a project that began at the Lambeth Conference in 2008 (Lambeth Conference). "Indaba" is a Zulu word for discernment by consensus which is common in many African cultures with parallels in many societies throughout the world. It is intended to strengthen relationships for local and global mission across the communion. It is interesting to note that this project is being funded by a grant from the Satcher Health Leadership Institute at the Morehouse School of Medicine. The project demonstrates how mutual listening across a range of topics can open the church to a deeper understanding of the "holistic" dimensions of mission outlined in "Five Marks of Mission."

The Office of the Anglican Observer at the United Nations has Category 2 consultative status with UN Economic and Social Council (ECOSOC), which permits consultation with the UN on matters of mutual concern. This has provided the Communion with important opportunities to engage jointly with such UN commissions as the one on the "Status of Women" and on "Sustainable Development." The Anglican Observer has continued to highlight specific issues such as the "Millennium Development Goals," "Violence against Women," "Human Trafficking," and the "Impact of the Financial and Economic Crisis." Finance for the office is provided by extra-budgetary funds.

## The Networks

Just as the conclusion of World War II had required the churches of the Anglican Communion to review and reorganize their arrangements for mission planning and management (see the ACC and the "Arc of Mission" in the preceding text), so the development of the Internet and revolutionary new modes of electronic communication have required a reconsideration of communication and coordination for the ACC and wider communion. The result has been the evolution and development of the Anglican Communion Networks.

Participation in a wide range of mission activities throughout the world requires aggregation of mission and ministry initiatives from the grassroots level. The Anglican Communion Networks serve to aggregate the various forms of God's mission and ministry throughout the communion and bring them before the ACC. They also serve to knit the communion together around these common mission and ministry initiatives, thus helping to animate the communion.

There are eleven official Networks of the Anglican Communion. They comprise the Anglican Communion Environmental Network (ACEN), the Anglican Health Network (AHN), the International Anglican Women's Network (IAWN), the Anglican Indigenous Network (AIN), Le Reseau francophone de la Communion anglicane (the Francophone Network), the International Anglican Youth Network (IAYN), the International Anglican Family Network (IAFN), Anglican Communion Legal Advisers (ACLAN), Anglican Peace and Justice Network (APJN), Anglican Refugee and Migrant Network (ARMN), and Colleges and Universities of the Anglican Communion (CUAC). The Anglican Safe Church Consultation may seek formal Network status at ACC 15 and become the Communion's twelfth Network. These Networks share five areas which are of central importance to the future and well-being of the Networks individually and collectively: communication, gathering, fundraising, leadership, and guidelines.

## Communication

Communication is of central importance to all of the Networks. This includes both mechanisms for reporting back from a Network gathering, disseminating information into the provinces, as well as communication internally within networks. Reporting back to a province seems to work best when a primate appoints a representative to a Network and then expects that representative to report back both to the primate and to the rest of the province. Structures must also be put in place for this provincial dissemination of information.

Communication within Networks is also of central importance. Many networks utilize email listservs to share information within the Network. It is important to recognize that there are cultural differences within this electronic exchange. For instance, a woman in an African village might carefully craft an email response to the listserv, beginning with greetings. A woman walking down the street in New York City who receives the listserv message on her Blackberry might respond with a few words typed quickly. These cultural differences must be taken into account within electronic communication. The Internet communication for Networks will be improved as the new Director for Communications in the Anglican Communion Office, Jan Butter, is able to streamline the Anglican Communion's communication, as funding support is available. It will be important to watch how other forms of social networking such as Linkedin and Facebook continue to interplay with and shape the work of the Anglican Communion Networks.

## Gathering

There are five key aspects for Network gathering and consultation:

a.  Grounding in local context – This includes visits to local missions and ministries during the consultation as well as having local experts participate in exploring the designated topic.

   b.   Time for provincial reporting – This is a key opportunity for the dissemination of information about various mission and ministry initiatives from various local contexts.

   c.   Theological reflection/Bible study – Strong network gatherings incorporate some form of theological reflection on the issue at hand and opportunities for participants themselves to reflect theologically.

   d.   Clear actionable items – There must be time left for conversation and creation of a plan for action following the consultation.

   e.   Clear guidelines for reporting – Part of this action plan must be about how to disseminate information when returning to the province.

### Fundraising

With the current economic climate, fundraising is a major challenge facing all the Networks. The Episcopal Church USA has been a significant financial supporter of several of the Networks, but is being affected by the economic downturn also. Networks are broadening their field of fund searching more widely and asking questions about how they operate in terms of coordination and publishing. The church in Hong Kong is funding a coordinator for the Refugee and Migrant Network, which means that the Network has some grounding in the Eastern world. The St. Luke's Health System, an influential Episcopal health system in the Diocese of Texas, helps to fund the Anglican Health Network, while the AHN being based in Geneva allows the Network to be in partnership with the World Health Organization. The Anglican Youth Network has taken the tack in the past of sending out a message to the provinces that if they are serious about their youth then they need to support the Youth Network financially. The International Anglican Family Network has worked diligently in seeking out funding from provinces, theological education institutions, and grant-making bodies to fund a coordinator, print the newsletter, and gather for consultation.

One of the greatest expenses facing these Networks is in gathering for consultation. The importance of face-to-face interaction for the life of the Networks cannot be over-estimated. A significant portion of the expense for consultation simply comes down to paying for travel and the increasingly prevalent problems with visas. Therefore, regional gatherings, with sponsorship locally, may become an increasingly valuable model.

### Leadership

Network leadership is an important component for the future of the Networks. When a Network emerges, the Network's leadership tends to emerge with it. Leadership is typically made up of a coordinator or coordinators who are surrounded by a steering committee or reference group. This steering committee or reference group is made up of laity, priests, and bishops who have some organic connection to the mission of the Network through their vocational work and ministry. One key aspect of leadership is how the coordinators, whether paid or unpaid, lead those who gather around as a steering committee or reference group. The Rev. Terrie Robinson, the coordinator at the Anglican Communion Office for all of the Anglican Networks, envisions each Network coordinator as "chief enabler" within a team of Network "animators." The coordinator, therefore, leads through facilitating the leadership and work of the steering committee and members of the Network.

## Guidelines

The guidelines currently in place for the Networks were adopted in Resolution 7 at ACC 10 in Panama (ACC 1996, 180–1). These guidelines focus on the relationship of the Networks to the ACC and on fundraising practices. ACC 15, which will take place in 2012 in Auckland, New Zealand, may be an opportunity for the ACC to give feedback to the Networks and provide clarity in terms of what defines an Anglican Communion Network in an age when "networks" and "networking" are used in a variety of different ways and contexts. In this current age, are the Anglican Communion Networks migrating toward being fully Internet based? This is an important question for the future of the Networks. Internet-based activity can be done using small amounts of funding. However, by becoming Internet-based social networking sites, the Anglican Communion Networks would lose the value of face-to-face interaction in consultation. Therefore, the Networks cannot solely be Internet-based sites to share information about a particular mission or ministry, although this must certainly be a part of a Network's function.

The Anglican Communion Networks must also be oriented toward action. To be action oriented, there must be clearly specified goals and expectations. This clarity and focus will allow for effective advocacy in the world and greater influence on the instruments of communion. Resolutions put forward at ACC must be clear and actionable. Similarly, action items and tasks emerging from Consultations must be clear and concise. Yet another key component of successful Consultations is theological reflection and bible study. Emerging from consultation, networks will also do the wider communion service in providing theological educational materials in their field of mission and ministry. Therefore, perhaps, the Networks can be conceived of as communities of praxis, action, and reflection, building on the conceptions of community and praxis models developed through liberation theology.

One recent movement within the Anglican Communion may help shed light on the expanding understanding of mission and the future role of the Anglican Communion Networks.

## Acting against gender–based violence, a communion–wide movement

In 2009, the ACC passed a resolution stating that it "unequivocally supports the elimination of all forms of violence against women and girls, including trafficking, and encourages all Provinces to participate in programmes and events that promote the rights and welfare of women, particularly as expressed in the Beijing Platform for

Action and the United Nations Millennium Development Goals" (ACC 2009, Resolution 14.33). In Lambeth 2008, bishops and their spouses held a session entitled "Equal in God's Sight: When Power is Abused" which voiced concern about violence against women. In 2009, the Archbishop of Canterbury made a statement together with the Archbishop of Congo against the violence in the Congo, particularly violence against women and children. Finally, in 2011, the primates sent a letter out to the churches of the Anglican Communion committing to affirm, pray for, and bless "initiatives already in place within dioceses and parishes in response to violence against women and girls" (Primates 2011). They further committed to trainings for clergy and pastors and liturgies for events such as "November 25: The International Day for the Elimination of Violence against Women."

However, what role did the Anglican Communion Networks play in these actions of the instruments of communion? According to Networks' coordinator Terrie Robinson, the Networks created a "groundswell of consciousness-raising" around violence against women and girls. This was a concerted effort of multiple networks: the Women's Network, the Family Network, the Indigenous Network, the Francophone Network, the Peace and Justice Network, and the Youth Network all addressed the issue. The Women's Network and the Family Network were particularly instrumental in raising awareness around violence against women. The IAWN is helping to promote the "Sixteen Days of Activism against Gender Violence" and has been tasked with tracking how the letter from the primates is implemented on the ground. The Family Network published three newsletters in succession on the issues of violence in the family. The Networks' Coordinator also played a direct role by carrying the message to the instruments of communion and other bodies in the Anglican Communion, making presentations to the primates and to the provincial secretaries on the issue of violence against women and girls.

Network collaboration must continue to be facilitated and encouraged on mission and ministry that are shared among multiple Networks. Possible areas of future movement may involve the environment, following on the 2011 gathering of the Environmental Network in Lima, Peru, and in accord with the fifth mark of mission. The environment is of concern to multiple networks including the Environmental Network and the Indigenous People's Network. Another possible area of future movement may be around maternity and newborns, which is of concern both to the Health Network and to the Family Network. Future movements of the Spirit must be listened for and discerned among the Networks as this model of grassroots gathering and consciousness-raising in concert with other actors in mission throughout the Anglican Communion will be an important future role for the Networks.

## Officers of the ACC

*Presidents*

The Most Rev. & Rt. Hon. Michael Ramsay [1969–1973]
The Most Rev. & Rt. Hon. Donald Coggan [1974–1979]

The Most Rev. & Rt. Hon. Robert Runcie [1980–1990]
The Most Rev. & Rt. Hon. George Carey [1991–2001]
The Most Rev. & Rt. Hon. Rowan Williams [2002– 2012] The Most Rev. & Rt. Hon. Justin Welby [2013–Present]

## Secretaries general

The Rt. Rev. John Howe [1969–1982]
The Rev. Canon Samuel Van Culin [1983–1994]
The Rev. Canon John L. Peterson [1995–2004]
The Rev. Canon Kenneth Kearon [2005–Present]

## Chairs

Sir Louis Mbanefo (West Africa) [1971–1976]
Mrs. Harold C. Kelleran (USA) [1976–1981]
Mr. John Denton (Australia) [1981–1987]
The Ven. Yong Ping Chung (East Asia) [1987–1993]
The Rev. Canon Colin Craston (England) [1993–1999]
The Rt. Rev. Simon Chiwanga (Tanzania) [1999–2005]
The Rt. Rev. John Paterson (Aotearoa, New Zealand, and Polynesia) [2005–2009]
The Rt. Rev. James Tengatenga (Central Africa) [2009–Present]

## Bibliography

ACC. 1971. *The Time is Now: ACC First Meeting, Limuru*. London: SPCK.

ACC. 1973. *Partners in Mission: ACC Second Meeting, Dublin*. London: SPCK.

ACC. 1976. *ACC 3 Trinidad*. Canley, Coventry: Coventry Printers.

ACC. 1979. *ACC 4 London, Ontario, Canada*. Cowley, Oxford: Bocardo and Church Army Press.

ACC. 1987. *Many Gifts One Spirit: Report of ACC 7*. London: Church House Publishing.

ACC. 1990. *Mission in a Broken World: Report of ACC 8*. London: Church House Publishing.

ACC. 1996. *Being Anglican in the Third Millennium: The Official Report of the Tenth Meeting of the Anglican Consultative Council*. Harrisburg, PA: Morehouse Publishing.

ACC. 2005. *Living Communion: The Official Report of the Thirteenth Meeting of the Anglican Consultative Council Nottingham 2005*. New York: Church House Publishing.

ACC. 2009. Anglican Consultative Council – ACC 14. Accessed January 11, 2012. http://www.anglicancommunion.org/communion/acc/meetings/acc14/index.cfm.

Anglican Ecumenical Consultation. 1987. *The Emmaus Report*. London: Church House Publishing.

Bayne, Stephen Fielding, Jr. 1964. *An Anglican Turning Point: Documents and Interpretations*. Austin, Texas: The Church Historical Society.

Coleman, Roger, ed. 1992. *Resolutions of the Twelve Lambeth Conferences*. Toronto: Anglican Book Center.

Howe, John. 1985. *Highways and Hedges: Anglicanism and the Universal Church*. London: CIO Publishing.

Lambeth Conference. *Lambeth Indaba*. Pamphlet published by the Lambeth Conference.

Primates. 2011. A Letter to the Churches of the Anglican Communion from the Primates of the Anglican Communion following their Primates' Meeting in Dublin, Ireland, between 24 and 30 January 2011. Accessed January 24, 2012. http://www.aco.org/communion/primates/resources/downloads/prim_gbv.pdf.

Project Canterbury. 2009. Mutual Responsibility and Interdependence in the Body of Christ. Accessed January 11, 2012. http://anglicanhistory.org/canada/toronto_mutual1963.html.

CHAPTER 9

# The Anglican Communion Covenant

## Andrew Goddard

On December 18, 2009, Kenneth Kearon, secretary general of the Anglican Communion, sent the final text of the Anglican Communion Covenant to each communion province for formal consideration for adoption. By late 2012, it had been accepted fully in some form by seven provinces. Others had been less positive and many had not reported progress. Most notably and significantly, the Church of England's diocesan synods failed to give it the support necessary for General Synod to consider adopting it.

Whatever happens in coming years, the covenant represents a significant development in the life of the Anglican Communion. Although it has generated much discussion online, only a few publications address it in detail (see Chapman 2008; Doe 2008; Hill 2008; Guyer 2012). This chapter seeks to explain and assess the final text by setting it in a broader context. It explores the covenant's origins, noting attempts to address the same issues before the 2004 Windsor Report that have often been forgotten or ignored (Section One). It then charts its development, the changing content, and debates as the Covenant Design Group produced three drafts before the agreed final text (Section Two). The content of that final text is set out (Section Three) before a short concluding assessment of the covenant's impact on the Communion (Section Four).

## Section One – The Path to the Covenant Proposal

The Anglican Covenant was proposed by the Lambeth Commission on Communion in The Windsor Report (TWR) of 2004 (Lambeth Commission on Communion 2004). The Commission was established by the Archbishop of Canterbury in 2003 to report "on the legal and theological implications flowing from the decisions of the Episcopal Church (USA) to appoint a priest in a committed same sex relationship as one of its

*The Wiley-Blackwell Companion to the Anglican Communion*, First Edition. Edited by Ian S. Markham,
J. Barney Hawkins IV, Justyn Terry, and Leslie Nuñez Steffensen.
© 2013 John Wiley & Sons, Ltd. Published 2013 by John Wiley & Sons, Ltd.

bishops, and of the Diocese of New Westminster to authorise services for use in connection with same sex unions," and specifically on issues related to impaired and broken communion. It was mandated "to include practical recommendations . . . for maintaining the highest degree of communion that may be possible in the circumstances resulting from these decisions, both within and between the churches of the Anglican Communion" (Lambeth Commission on Communion 2004, 13). Section C examined "Our Future Life Together" and addressed the issue of "Canon Law and Covenant" (paras 113–20), while Appendix Two proposed "a preliminary draft and discussion document" (para 118).

Among what TWR described as the "overwhelming" arguments for adopting a covenant, the Commission gave priority to the fact that "it is our shared responsibility to have in place an agreed mechanism to enable and maintain life in communion, and to prevent and manage communion disputes" (para 119). It also pointed to a covenant embodying "communion as a visible foundation around which Anglicans can gather to shape and protect their distinctive identity and mission" and providing "an accessible resource for our ecumenical partners in their understanding of Anglicanism" (para 119).

Although goals such as these remained paramount, this context of the original proposal has had a number of consequences in relation to the covenant's reception and how it has been interpreted, particularly by its critics. First, it has been closely tied to disputes about sexuality, despite the fact that another section of TWR (Section D) addressed these matters, and at no point did any draft of the covenant address the issue. Nevertheless, broadly speaking, those most sympathetic to Anglicans blessing same-sex relationships were most skeptical or hostile to the idea of a covenant. Second, by combining the covenant with a proposal in relation to canon law and offering a draft with a strong legal tone, the covenant was portrayed as marking a shift from a communion held together by relational "bonds of affection" to one whose focus was more juridical and canonical. Third, the question of the relationship between the covenant and membership of the communion was raised in such a way that the covenant could be portrayed as seeking to exclude current members of the communion: "it may be that the Anglican Consultative Council could encourage full participation in the Covenant project by each church by constructing an understanding of communion membership which is expressed by the readiness of a province to maintain its bonds with Canterbury, and which includes a reference to the Covenant" (para 120). Fourth, although it was stressed that the covenant should be "largely descriptive of existing principles" (para 118), the TWR draft proposed (in Article 27) a new power – "The Archbishop of Canterbury shall decide all questions of interpretation of this Covenant" and, if approved by the Joint Standing Committee, "the decision of the Archbishop shall be regarded as authoritative in the Communion." This ignited concerns that the covenant represented a centralizing, authoritarian vision, undermining or even destroying traditional provincial autonomy. All four of these concerns were taken on board during the covenant's redrafting, but they remain at the heart of many doubts about the covenant proposal.

Within the Windsor Report, the covenant was clearly a response to a much wider and more fundamental challenge than divisions over sexuality – "how to make the principles of inter-Anglican relations more effective at the local ecclesial level" (para 117). It sought a covenant which would deal with "the acknowledgement of common identity; the relationships of communion; the commitments of communion; the exercise of autonomy in communion; and the management of communion affairs (including disputes)" (para 118). These are longstanding challenges the Anglican Communion has faced and sought to address in ways similar to the covenant.

The most recent attempt to address them prior to the Windsor Report was from Professor Norman Doe, who served on the Commission. At the Primates' Meeting in 2001, Doe gave a presentation on canon law in the communion (Doe 2001) which led to a consultation that identified 44 shared principles of canon law across the communion and gave background to the content of TWR's draft covenant (the final principles are in Anglican Communion Office 2008). Although undeveloped, his paper referred to a possible concordat between provinces, a precursor of the later covenant proposal.

Doe's proposed concordat and Windsor's covenant are simply new ways of addressing concerns already identified in the 1980s. Similar solutions had already been considered. In 1986, a group chaired by Archbishop Robin Eames (who chaired the Lambeth Commission over 15 years later) produced a paper for ACC-7 in Singapore in 1987. This recommended that the provinces "should adopt a common *Declaration*" as "a sign of the Church's adherence to apostolic faith and order" and also "a sign of communion between the Churches" (Lambeth Conference 1988, para 20). This proposed Declaration appears not to have been taken forward at the time (although it was discussed in some provinces), but ACC-7 agreed unanimously to a more tentative report produced in Singapore, introducing the concept of the Instruments of Unity and entitled "Unity in Diversity within the Anglican Communion: A Way Forward" (Anglican Consultative Council 1987). The ideas in the Declaration proposal derive from the same principles which shape the covenant. This is evident in the Discussion Paper for Lambeth 1988 which notes that "if communion between Provinces is to be maintained and nurtured then there must be some limits to autonomy in areas of theological and moral significance" (Lambeth Conference 1988, para 24), and that "at the very least the areas covered by the Chicago-Lambeth Quadrilateral and by the proposed declaration should be matters of Communion-wide significance" (para 25).

The next stage appears to have been a paper entitled "Provincial Constitutions: Autonomy and Interdependence" commissioned by the secretary general and written by David Chaplin for ACC-8 in 1990. It revived the idea of a Draft Common Declaration to be included in provincial constitutions along with a suggested article "on the relation of the Province to other Provinces of the Anglican Communion" (Chaplin 1990). It also proposed that provincial constitutions "could at least ensure that inter-Anglican consultation takes place by permitting reference or appeal outside the Province when matters of doctrine and discipline are in dispute". It suggested the Primates' Meeting as "the appropriate body to become the Committee of Reference for the Communion to which disputed doctrinal, moral and pastoral matters might be referred" (paras 17–18). The document, however, gained minimal support. Mentioned only in passing in the ACC report – "there was no high level of enthusiasm in any Section for the Common Declaration" (Anglican Consultative Council 1990, 143) – resolution 21 stated that it regarded "the document 'Provincial constitutions: autonomy and interdependence', circulated to the Council, as premature" (Anglican Consultative Council 1990, 162–3). It appears this judgment brought to an end for over a decade serious plans for institutional developments akin to the covenant. Attention turned instead to developing a theology of communion through *The Virginia Report*.

This brief historical sketch demonstrates that the covenant proposal was not as novel as first appeared to most people in 2004. It is rather the fruit of bringing together that theological reflection on communion from the 1990s with these earlier, forgotten institutional proposals that sought to give expression to what unites Anglicans and outlines how they should live out their autonomy-in-communion when facing difficult decisions.

## Section Two – Designing the Covenant

The covenant idea was quickly supported by the Archbishop of Canterbury in his 2004 Advent Letter and by the 2005 Primates' Meeting, but one-third of the responses to the Windsor Report proposal did not support a covenant. A consultation paper, "Towards An Anglican Covenant," was prepared for the March 2006 Joint Standing Committee which was then circulated for consultation (Anglican Communion Office 2006). This asked whether the concept of an Anglican Covenant was still viable and its summary of responses captures well what would remain the main areas of disagreement about the covenant. It noted (para 5) that opponents "worry that a covenant might be seen to alter the nature of the Communion towards that of a narrowly confessional family, with the attendant danger that preparedness to sign up to the covenant becomes a test of authentic membership." They fear "establishing a bureaucratic and legalistic foundation at the very heart of the Communion," risking "inspired and prophetic initiatives in God's mission," "threatening Anglican comprehensiveness" and establishing "a centralised jurisdiction." Supporters argued (para 6) that a covenant "would clarify the identity and mission of the Churches of, or in association with, the Anglican Communion" and "by articulating our ecclesiological identity . . . help the Anglican Communion in self-understanding and in ecumenical relationships." It could provide "a fundamental basis of trust, co-operation and action" among Anglican churches and "express what is already implicit, by articulating the 'bonds of affection', that is, the 'house rules' by which the family of Anglican churches wishes to live together" so as "to develop a disciplined and fulfilling life in communion." The paper set out three goals for the covenant – relational (para 8, assisting reconciliation), educational (para 9), and institutional (para 10, "providing what is currently lacking – an agreed framework for common discernment, and the prevention and resolution of conflict").

It soon became clear that the hope of establishing agreed moratoria on controversial actions would not happen to the satisfaction of many in the communion. Following the American church's General Convention, Archbishop Rowan published a reflection in June 2006 entitled "The Challenge and Hope of being an Anglican Today" (Archbishop of Canterbury 2006). In this, he acknowledged that "there is no way in which the

Anglican Communion can remain unchanged by what is happening at the moment" and spoke in more detail about the covenant proposal. He included the following important passage highlighting that the covenant could bring about differentiation among Anglicans:

> The idea of a 'covenant' between local Churches (developing alongside the existing work being done on harmonising the church law of different local Churches) is one method that has been suggested, and it seems to me the best way forward. It is necessarily an 'opt-in' matter. Those Churches that were prepared to take this on as an expression of their responsibility to each other would limit their local freedoms for the sake of a wider witness; and some might not be willing to do this. We could arrive at a situation where there were 'constituent' Churches in covenant in the Anglican Communion and other 'churches in association', which were still bound by historic and perhaps personal links, fed from many of the same sources, but not bound in a single and unrestricted sacramental communion, and not sharing the same constitutional structures.

In this continuing fraught context, in January 2007, the Archbishop of Canterbury announced the membership of a Covenant Design Group (CDG). It comprised 11 members from across the communion, with a leading Global South primate and member of the Lambeth Commission (Archbishop Drexel Gomez of the West Indies) as Chair. Meeting four times between January 2007 and April 2009, the CDG produced three draft texts, each refined in the light of feedback from provinces, individuals, and organizations across the communion. What follows highlights key elements in the covenant's evolution, with special reference to the most controversial elements: who would be given oversight of the covenant, what powers they would have, and what processes would be followed when a breach of the covenant was alleged.

### The Nassau Draft (January 2007)

At their first meeting, rather than working with the draft in the Windsor Report, the CDG drew on work by Australia (Anglican Church of Australia 2006) and, in particular, the Global South (Global South 2006), to produce a quite different first official draft covenant (Covenant Design Group 2007a). In addition, they were resourced by various responses to "Towards An Anglican Covenant" and input from appointed consultants.

The CDG vision was to "hold together and strengthen the life of the Communion" by offering a "clarification of a process of discernment which was embodied in the Windsor Report and in the recent reality of the life of the Instruments of Communion, and which was founded in and built upon the elements traditionally articulated in association with Anglicanism and the life of the Anglican Churches" (Covenant Design Group 2007b). The group, however, stressed their perception of urgency – the communion's life "would suffer irreparably if some measure of mutual and common commitment to the Gospel was not reasserted in a short time frame."

This first draft introduced two central features of all future drafts – the fundamental structure of affirmations and commitments and a threefold focus on faith, mission, and shared life situated between a preamble and concluding declaration. One notable feature which did not survive in future drafts was the extensive citation of biblical texts in each section.

The sixth section, in which each church made commitments with regard to the unity of the communion, opens with commitments to the communion's common good, consultation, and seeking of a common mind about matters of essential concern. These would remain central features in all future drafts. It also proposed, however, that adopting churches commit "to heed the counsel of our Instruments of Communion in matters which threaten the unity of the Communion and the effectiveness of our mission" (Covenant Design Group 2007a, 6.4). This implied an unqualified commitment to their judgment overriding provincial autonomy. Furthermore, within the Instruments, the Primates were given a special status (reflecting requests of the 1988 and 1998 Lambeth Conferences). The guidance of the Instruments was to be sought in matters of serious dispute "by submitting the matter to the Primates Meeting" who would "offer guidance and direction" (6.5). Finally, the Nassau draft called on provinces to "acknowledge that in the most extreme circumstances, where member churches choose not to fulfil the substance of the covenant as understood by the Councils of the Instruments of Communion, we will consider that such churches will have relinquished for themselves the force and meaning of the covenant's purpose, and a process of restoration and renewal will be required to re-establish their covenant relationship with other member churches" (6.6).

This draft was considered at the February 2007 Primates' Meeting in Tanzania which also established the timetable for revision and final agreement on a covenant text at ACC-14 in 2009. That meeting also had to monitor responses to Windsor's moratoria requests and the increasing divisions within the American church. Its proposals for a Primates' Pastoral Council to address these, and its insistence on clarification of the church's commitment to the moratoria led to concerns in some circles about how the Primates might use the powers offered in the Nassau Draft. As a result, Kathy Grieb, one of the two Americans on the CDG, warned ECUSA's House of Bishops in March that "the best source for understanding the logic of the proposed Anglican Covenant and the best evidence for how it is likely to be interpreted in the future is the recent Communiqué of the Primates"(Grieb 2007).

## The St. Andrew's Draft (February 2008)

In early 2008, the CDG met in the context of ongoing division over the American church's response to the Windsor moratoria. As Archbishop Rowan stated in his Advent 2007 letter, "we have no consensus" (Archbishop of Canterbury 2007) about whether the response was adequate. In addition, a number of provinces, unhappy about the Archbishop's decision to invite American bishops (apart from Gene Robinson) to Lambeth but not to invite "missionary bishops" consecrated by other provinces to serve in America, announced their bishops would not attend Lambeth. Instead, they began planning the Global Anglican Future Conference (GAFCON) for just before Lambeth.

The second St. Andrew's Draft drew on responses from 13 provinces and many other bodies (see Covenant Design Group 2008a, 2008c). The CDG considered whether to abandon the title of 'covenant' and return to some of the earlier terms used prior to Windsor (such as 'common declaration'), but unanimously favored retaining 'covenant.' Its overall vision and rationale remained clearly one of "autonomy-in-communion."

The draft (Covenant Design Group 2008d) made the threefold structure of affirmations and commitments much more explicit and added explanatory notes, highlighting the use of traditional sources such as the Chicago-Lambeth Quadrilateral and the Church of England's Declaration of Assent. It also removed the biblical references and instead offered an eight-paragraph introduction providing a biblical and theological rationale drawing on ecumenical agreements (Covenant Design Group 2008e).

Unsurprisingly, it was the final sixth section of Nassau (now section 3.2) which required most work and saw most change. There was a stronger emphasis on autonomy with the provinces being described as "autonomous-in-communion" (3.1.2) and committing to "respect the constitutional autonomy of all of the Churches of the Anglican Communion, while upholding the interdependent life and mutual responsibility of the Churches, and the responsibility of each to the Communion as a whole" (3.2.2., drawing on words from the Primates' Communique in Tanzania). One effect of this was that, rather than committing to heed any advice from the Instruments, it was clearly stated that any request "would not be binding on a Church unless recognised as such by that Church" (3.2.5e). It was, however, still held that not adopting such advice "may be understood by the Church itself, or by the resolution of the Instruments of Communion, as a relinquishment by that Church of the force and meaning of the covenant's purpose, until they re-establish their covenant relationship with other member Churches" (3.2.5e).

The significant position of the Primates' Meeting was removed from this draft. In a provisional draft appendix offering "Framework Procedures for the Resolution of Covenant Disagreements" (Covenant Design Group 2008b), it was the Archbishop of Canterbury and Anglican Consultative Council (ACC) which took the central roles in overseeing and resolving conflict. The CDG acknowledged that this procedural appendix "will need much scrutiny and careful analysis" and encouraged "comments and response" (Covenant Design Group 2008a, on clause 3.2.5). The appendix set out principles of informal conversation and of consultation. If the former failed, the archbishop, advised by three assessors, would determine the seriousness of the situation and whether he should issue an urgent request to a church or refer the matter to another instrument, a commission, or mediation. Timetabled processes were set out for each of these routes, and churches would have to respond to any request from an instrument within six months. A failure to accept the request would be referred to the ACC. It would determine whether or not such rejection by the church concerned was compatible with the covenant. If not, the ACC or the church itself could determine whether it had "relinquished the force and meaning of the purposes of the Covenant" (Covenant Design Group 2008b, 8.4).

## The Ridley Cambridge Draft (April 2009)

The St. Andrew's Draft was widely discussed, particularly at the Lambeth Conference. A meeting of the CDG in Singapore in September 2008 was presented with a 75-page summary of responses from bishops (Cooper 2008). This showed about two-thirds being very or reasonably content with the concept of a covenant but about 10 percent with serious reservations about the concept and whether the covenant expressed a firm foundation for Anglicans' common life. The vision of interdependence in Section 3 caused the greatest concern. However, the more conservative bishops who were absent from Lambeth largely failed to respond to this survey (there are no replies from either Uganda or Nigeria). The CDG produced a 33-page commentary responding to Frequently Asked Questions, commenting on the current draft text and signaling likely changes in the third and final draft (Covenant Design Group 2008f).

The third Ridley Cambridge Draft (Covenant Design Group 2009) was further shaped by 21 provincial responses, and many from other interested parties. It retained the introduction (though clarified it was not formally part of the covenant, 4.4.1) and the preamble largely unchanged. Section One included the full Lambeth Quadrilateral and made other revisions, ensuring its content drew on established Anglican texts and thought. Section Two on mission was strengthened and expanded. Section Three – subject to most comment – was significantly reworded. Its overall vision of autonomy and interdependence was retained although "autonomous–in–communion" was replaced with "in communion with autonomy and accountability" (3.1.2). The overall principle remained "the Communion guides, each Church decides." Additions included an outline of the characteristics of issues likely to threaten the communion's unity and common mission (3.2.5), and a commitment to mediated conversations (3.2.6).

The most significant development was the inclusion of a fourth section titled "Our Covenanted Life Together." This set out procedures for adoption of the covenant, its maintenance and conflict resolution, withdrawal from the covenant, and amendment of the text. Although addressing matters covered by the second draft's appendix, it did so in significantly different ways. First, and most strongly, it made clear that provinces remained autonomous. They were not subject to "any external ecclesiastical jurisdiction" (4.1.1), not limiting their "autonomy of governance" (4.1.3), and not granting to anybody the power or authority to "exercise control or direction" over their internal life (4.1.3). Second, the oversight of the covenant was granted to the Joint Standing Committee, comprising representatives elected by the ACC and the Primates. Third, the juridical and punitive tone many discerned and objected to in the earlier appendix was replaced with a focus on discerning together and proposing the "relational consequences" of controversial actions. The idea of "relinquishment" of the covenant by a province was also replaced with a possible declaration that a particular action was "incompatible with the covenant."

*The Final Text (December 2009)*

The Ridley Cambridge Draft was presented to ACC-14 in Jamaica in May 2009. Faced with a new and controversial section, the ACC accepted the first three sections, but asked the Archbishop of Canterbury "to appoint a small working group to consider and consult with the Provinces on Section 4 and its possible revision" (Resolution 14.11, Anglican Consultative Council 2009, 46) before sending the text for approval. A sub-group of the CDG met and, after considering responses to Section 4 from over 20 provinces, made some minimal revisions, including the renaming of the Joint Standing Committee as the Standing Committee of the Anglican Communion, a consequence of changes to the ACC Constitution (Covenant Working Party 2009a, 2009b).

## Section Three – The Anglican Communion Covenant Text

The preceding section has traced some of the key themes, areas of contention, and developments that occurred in the process of producing the final text (Covenant Working Party 2009a). This section summarizes its content through an overview of each of the seven parts, particularly the four central sections and their affirmations and commitments.

### Introduction

Although the introduction is always annexed to the covenant, it is not part of it but "shall be accorded authority in understanding the purpose of the Covenant" (4.4.1). It opens with 1 John 1.2–4 in which our communion together is rooted in our communion with the Father and the Son who has revealed eternal life to us. Its eight paragraphs draw particularly on Ephesians and the Corinthian letters to offer a Trinitarian-based communion ecclesiology, citing the 2007 Cyprus Statement of the International Commission for Anglican Orthodox Theological Dialogue. God's covenants are traced through salvation history, and the responsibilities arising from the call and gift of communion are summarized. This situates the history of the Anglican family of churches and the step of covenanting together "as churches of this Anglican Communion to be faithful to God's promises through the historic faith we confess, our common worship, our participation in God's mission, and the way we live together." Different aspects of this faith, worship, mission, and common life are then described with the clear statement that "to covenant together is not intended to change the character of this Anglican expression of Christian faith" but to renew our commitment.

### Preamble

The Preamble names the covenanting bodies as "Churches of the Anglican Communion," highlights their global sweep with reference to Revelation 7.9, and states a threefold goal – more effective proclamation in different contexts of God's grace revealed in the gospel, offering God's love in responding to need and maintaining unity – in the context of seeking wider growth and unity in Christ.

*Section one – our inheritance of faith*

Each covenanting church makes an eight-fold affirmation of faith and eight commitments as to how to live this out contextually in the power of the Spirit. Our communion is not ultimately Anglican but in the one, holy, catholic, and apostolic church worshipping the triune God (1.1.1). The catholic and apostolic faith is summarized in words from the Church of England's Declaration of Assent, and its formularies are acknowledged alongside their varied appropriation among Anglicans (1.1.2). The Chicago-Lambeth Quadrilateral is then affirmed (1.1.3–6), as is the importance of "shared patterns" of "common prayer and liturgy" (1.1.7) and our joining, with other churches, in the apostolic mission of all God's people (1.1.8).

The commitments begin by agreeing to teach and act "in continuity and consonance" with Scripture and received faith, order, and tradition, "mindful of" Anglican councils and ecumenical agreements (1.2.1). Theological and moral reasoning and discipline are similarly to be "rooted in and answerable to" Scripture and tradition (1.2.2), a witness to Christ-centered renewal, and a reflection of God's gift and call to holiness (1.2.3). There is commitment to contextual appropriation of Scripture informed by wider communal reading, teaching, study, and the fruits of scholarship (1.2.4), so that it can illumine and transform (1.2.5). Living out our inheritance also requires "prophetic and faithful leadership" (1.2.6) and sustaining Eucharistic communion (1.2.7) in the context of the whole body of Christ seeking "to discern the fullness of truth into which the Spirit leads us, that peoples from all nations may be set free to receive new and abundant life in the Lord Jesus Christ" (1.2.8).

The section thus seeks to enable churches to express their shared Anglican identity in the context of wider Christian identity and the transforming mission of God. It relates Scripture, tradition, and reason, recognizing the need for a common affirmation of inherited faith and shared pattern of ecclesial discernment alongside contextual and developing expressions of this faith.

*Section two – the life we share with others: our anglican vocation*

The five affirmations and commitments open with affirmations echoing elements of the introduction – communion as God's gift within his global transforming mission (2.1.1), and thanks for the historic development of this among Anglicans as mission created a global communion (2.1.2). There needs, however, to be humility and penitence (2.1.3) alongside acknowledging the communion's call into God's mission (2.1.4) with other churches and traditions (2.1.5).

Churches therefore commit to evangelization and healing and reconciling mission marked by mutual accountability in sharing resources (2.2.1). The mission is that of

God in Christ and is summarized (2.2.2) in the Five Marks of Mission now widely accepted among Anglicans. Drawing on ecumenical agreements, these were originally set out in the MISSIO Report of 1999 following ACC-6 (1984) and ACC-8 (1990). There is again recognition of the need for humility, openness, and ongoing conversion (2.2.3), and a commitment to revive and renew mission structures (2.2.4) and order mission Christo-centrically and Eucharistically "in the joyful and reverent worship of God" (2.2.5).

Once again, the covenant seeks to draw on well-known words and principles. Its affirmations and commitments enable local churches to locate themselves, as the fruit of mission, in a wider global Anglican and ecumenical context, through understanding their holistic mission as a sharing together in God's mission.

### Section three – our unity and common life

As noted earlier, this section underwent significant revision throughout the drafting process as it sought to give expression to the vision of communion life developed in recent decades in a manner that gained wide support. It now contains four affirmations and seven commitments.

Each church affirms its sacramental incorporation into one body and the call to peace and building each other up (3.1.1). That takes shape in a resolve "to live in a Communion of Churches." The character of this is described in terms of each church ordering its own life "in communion with autonomy and accountability" (3.1.2), a key phrase capturing the covenant's vision. This requires trust in the Spirit's work and seeking to affirm our common life through the instruments of communion which enable us "to be conformed together to the mind of Christ" in a distinctively Anglican pattern of shared life summarized in words from the 1930 Lambeth Conference (3.1.2). There follows an affirmation of "the central role of bishops" in key aspects of this life together as a communion of churches (3.1.3) before the final, longest affirmation. This states the importance of communion instruments in "the discernment, articulation and exercise of our shared faith and common life and mission" (3.1.4), and describes the four particular instruments that exist and their responsibilities (3.1.4).

Affirmation of this interdependent life entails commitment to a pattern of life marked by certain virtues, practices, and disciplines. These are set out in the commitments. Churches commit to exercising autonomy with "regard for the common good of the Communion" and to work with the instruments (3.2.1), respecting other churches' autonomy and upholding mutual responsibility and interdependence (3.2.2, a reference to the 1963 Toronto Congress). In areas of theological debate, there is commitment to a pattern of shared discernment (3.2.3) and to "wide consultation" in the quest for "a shared mind . . . about matters of common concern" (3.2.4). Diligence, care, and caution will be shown when an action "may provoke controversy, which by its intensity, substance or extent could threaten the unity of the Communion and the effectiveness or credibility of its mission" (3.2.5). Should conflict arise, there is commitment to "mediated conversations" (3.2.6), recognizing we are compelled "always to uphold the highest degree of communion possible" (3.2.7).

This section thus sets out a practical vision of life in communion, drawing on the theological work of recent decades and the often painful experiences of recent divisions. It seeks agreement on how as Anglicans in autonomous churches we live and discern the leading of the Spirit together across cultural and theological diversity.

*Section four – our covenanted life together*

This is undoubtedly the most contentious of the covenant's sections. Rather than being structured around affirmations and commitments, each church affirms principles and procedures and commits to implement them. These cover four areas. The least contentious will be noted first. In freely adopting the covenant "to live more fully into the ecclesial communion and interdependence which is foundational to the Churches of the Anglican Communion" (4.1.1), each church "recognises in the preceding sections a statement of faith, mission and interdependence of life which is consistent with its own life and with the doctrine and practice of the Christian faith as it has received them," and recognizes these elements as foundational (4.1.2). Autonomy is clearly and repeatedly safeguarded (4.1.3). Members of the communion are invited to enter by their own procedures (4.1.4), and other churches may be invited to adopt it (a contentious issue, given the new Anglican province in North America). Adoption does not grant a church recognition by or membership of the instruments (4.1.5) but makes the covenant active for the adopting church (4.1.6), although it remains free to withdraw (4.3.1). The relationship of the introduction to the covenant is explained (4.4.1) and a process of amendment laid down, with three-quarters of covenanting churches needing to ratify any proposal before it has force (4.4.2).

Section 4.2 addresses the thorny issue of "the maintenance of the covenant and dispute resolution" stressing the covenant's role in enabling "mutual recognition and communion" and the responsibilities undertaken by participation (4.2.1). It authorizes "The Standing Committee of the Anglican Communion, responsible to the Anglican Consultative Council and the Primates' Meeting" to monitor its functioning "on behalf of the Instruments," supported where necessary by other bodies (4.2.2). In the face of questions of interpretation or application, churches have a duty to live out the covenant commitments (4.2.3) and, where a shared mind has not been reached, questions are referred to the Standing Committee which will "make every effort to facilitate agreement" and take advice (4.2.4). It may request deferral of a controversial action. If this request is declined, it may recommend "relational consequences" to any instrument "which may specify a provisional limitation of participation in, or suspension from" the instrument while processes continue (4.2.5). Advised by ACC and Primates, it may declare an action or decision "incompatible with the Covenant" (4.2.6) and recommend relational consequences resulting from such incompatibility. However, "each Church or each Instrument shall determine whether or not to accept such recommendations" (4.2.7). Decisions relating to the covenant are limited to members whose churches "have adopted the Covenant, or who are still in the process of adoption" (4.2.8). In addition to these communion-wide processes, each church undertakes to establish its own means of overseeing the covenant's maintenance in its own life and to relate to the instruments on covenant matters (4.2.9).

This section therefore seeks to be faithful to the vision of Section Three, respecting the autonomy of provinces and the instruments (hence the emphasis on recommendations and requests), while enabling greater coordination of communion responses faced with the consequences of controversial actions.

### Declaration

The closing declaration is in the form of a prayer expressing resolve to partake in the covenant "for fruitful service" and "binding ourselves more closely in the truth and love of Christ." It concludes with the blessing of Hebrews 13.20–21.

## Section Four – Concluding Assessment

It is too soon to determine the Anglican Communion Covenant's impact on the life and future of the communion. As we have seen, since it was proposed, the covenant has had its stern critics but has based itself on decades of Anglican and ecumenical reflection, agreement, and experience, and, as it took shape from 2004, intensive consultation and revision. It articulates a vision of what it would mean to be a communion of autonomous but interdependent Anglican churches within the one holy, catholic, and apostolic church, seeking to live in deepening communion. What is less clear is whether or how this vision will become a reality.

The covenant is already in force between adopting provinces but the Church of England (and perhaps some other significant provinces) will not be immediately adopting it. As was recognized from the start, the covenant alone cannot solve the tensions and divisions within the communion. In the short term, differing responses to it may even increase these. There are at least two major alternative visions of being a communion of Anglican churches. One is the confessional vision focused on GAFCON and its Jerusalem Declaration. This has the support of a number of Southern primates, the new non-communion province in North America and, through the Fellowship of Confessing Anglicans, congregations, and networks in Northern provinces. The other vision is of a looser association (sometimes described as a federation) where autonomy and diversity are privileged and there is less concern with seeking and sharing a common mind.

As the Archbishop of Canterbury foresaw in 2006, the communion is therefore going to be marked by both covenanting and non-covenanting provinces for some time. The final balance or fragmentation between these may take some time to become clear. The response of African and wider Global South provinces, most of which have yet to decide whether or not to adopt the covenant, will be crucial. In particular, it remains to be seen whether a new Archbishop of Canterbury, the other instruments, and the standing committee, which oversees the covenant on their behalf, can keep or regain the confidence of sufficient provinces, reform communion structures, and so facilitate a relatively smooth transition to a covenantal Anglican Communion.

## Bibliography

The texts relating to the covenant are available on the Anglican Communion Office website at www.anglicancommunion.org/commission/covenant/index.cfm.

Anglican Church of Australia. 2006. A Covenant for the Anglican Communion: Draft Submitted by the Anglican Church of Australia.

Anglican Communion Office. 2006. Towards an Anglican Covenant: A Consultation Paper on the Covenant Proposal of the Windsor Report.

Anglican Communion Office. 2008. *The Principles of Canon Law Common to the Churches of the Anglican Communion.* London: ACO.

Anglican Consultative Council. 1987. Unity in Diversity within the Anglican Communion: A Way Forward. In *Many Gifts, One Spirit: Report of ACC-7: Singapore 1987*, ed. Anglican Consultative Council. London: Church House Publishing, 129–34.

Anglican Consultative Council. 1990. *Mission in a Broken World: Report of ACC-8 Wales 1990.* London: Church House Publishing.

Anglican Consultative Council. 2009. *One Love: The Official Report of the 14th Meeting of the ACC, Jamaica 2009.* London: Anglican Communion Office.

Archbishop of Canterbury. 2006. The Challenge and Hope of Being an Anglican Today.

Archbishop of Canterbury. 2007. Archbishop of Canterbury's Advent Letter, 14th December 2007.

Chaplin, David. 1990. Provincial Constitutions: Autonomy and Interdependence. Paper for ACC-8.

Chapman, Mark D., ed. 2008. *The Anglican Covenant: Unity and Diversity in the Anglican Communion.* London: Mowbray.

Cooper, Steven. 2008. Lambeth 2008 – Comments on the St Andrew's Draft: Report to the Covenant Design Group.

Covenant Design Group. 2007a. Draft Anglican Covenant (Nassau Draft).

Covenant Design Group. 2007b. Preliminary Report of the Covenant Design Group.

Covenant Design Group. 2008a. An Anglican Covenant – Commentary to the St Andrew's Draft.

Covenant Design Group. 2008b. An Anglican Covenant – Draft Appendix: Framework Procedures for the Resolution of Covenant Disagreements.

Covenant Design Group. 2008c. An Anglican Covenant – St Andrew's Communique.

Covenant Design Group. 2008d. An Anglican Covenant – St Andrew's Draft Text.

Covenant Design Group. 2008e. Introduction to the Anglican Covenant – St Andrew's Draft.

Covenant Design Group. 2008f. A Lambeth Commentary on the St. Andrew's Draft for an Anglican Covenant.

Covenant Design Group. 2009. The Ridley Cambridge Documents.

Covenant Working Party. 2009a. Anglican Communion Covenant – Final Text.

Covenant Working Party. 2009b. Commentary on Revisions to Section Four.

Doe, Norman. 2001. Canon Law and Communion. Given in 2001 at Primates. A paper was published under this title in *Ecclesiastical Law Journal* 6 (2002), 241–63.

Doe, Norman. 2008. *An Anglican Covenant: Theological and Legal Considerations for a Global Debate.* Norwich: Canterbury Press.

Global South. 2006. Draft Anglican Covenant.

Grieb, Katherine. 2007. Interpreting the Proposed Anglican Covenant through the Communique: Presentation to ECUSA Bishops.

Guyer, Benjamin M., ed. 2012. *Pro Commun-ione: Theological Essays on the Anglican Cove-nant.* Eugene, Oregon: Pickwick Publications, Wipf and Stock.

Hill, Mark, ed. 2008. *International Journal for the Study of the Christian Church: Commun-ion, Covenant and Canon Law,* vol. 8, no. 2.

Lambeth Commission on Communion. 2004. *The Windsor Report.* London: Anglican Com-munion Office.

Lambeth Conference. 1988. Instruments of Communion and Decision-Making: The Development of the Consultative Process in the Anglican Communion. In *The Truth Shall Make You Free: The Lambeth Conference 1988,* ed. Anglican Consultative Council. London: Church House Publishing, 293–8.

# PART III

# Provinces

# Africa

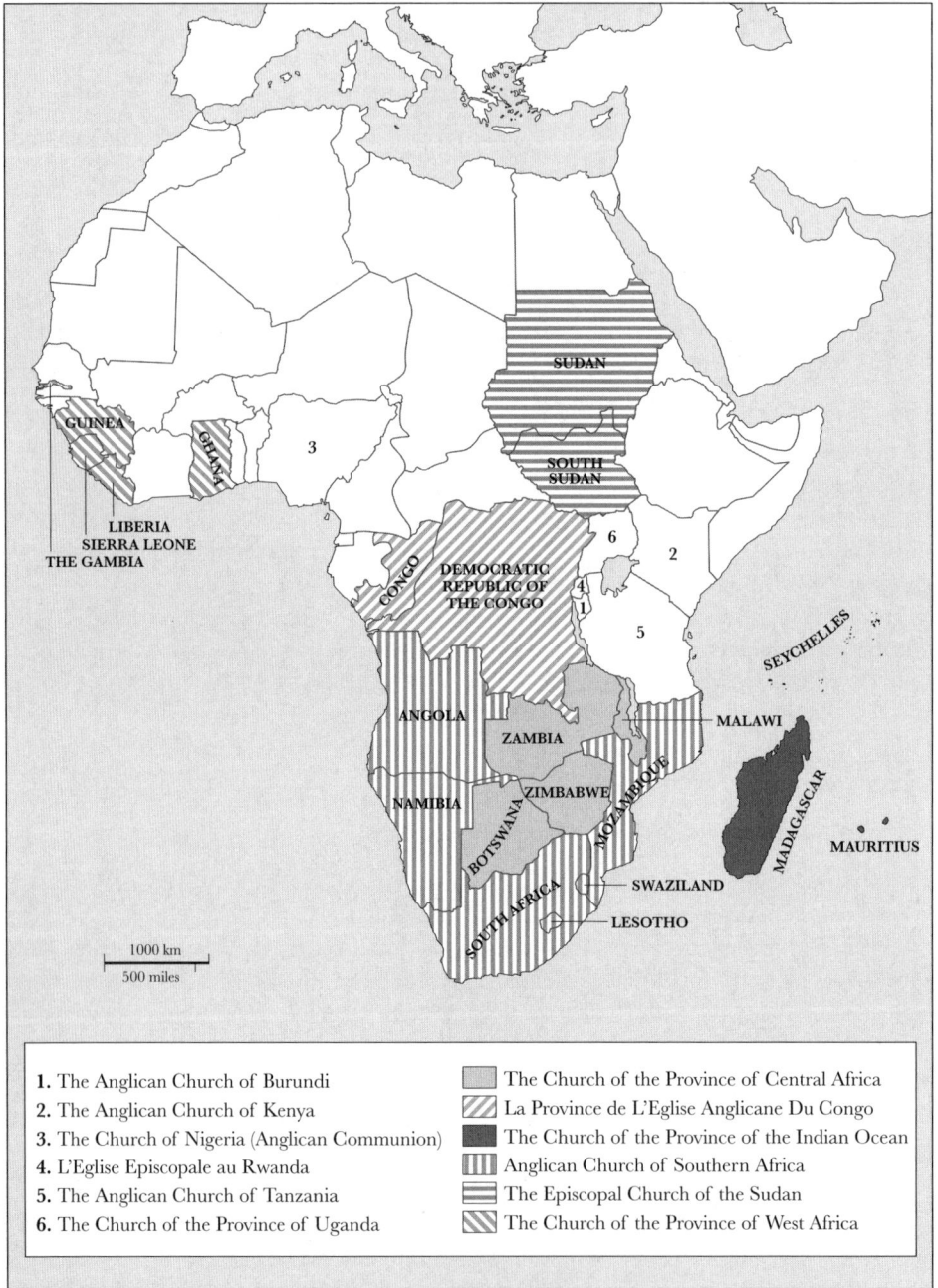

1000 km
500 miles

1. The Anglican Church of Burundi
2. The Anglican Church of Kenya
3. The Church of Nigeria (Anglican Communion)
4. L'Eglise Episcopale au Rwanda
5. The Anglican Church of Tanzania
6. The Church of the Province of Uganda

The Church of the Province of Central Africa
La Province de L'Eglise Anglicane Du Congo
The Church of the Province of the Indian Ocean
Anglican Church of Southern Africa
The Episcopal Church of the Sudan
The Church of the Province of West Africa

# CHAPTER 10
# The Anglican Church of Burundi

## Katherine L. Wood

The Province of the Anglican Church of Burundi was established in 1992, making it a relatively young jurisdiction in the Communion. Indeed, Anglicanism itself has only a brief history in this part of Africa compared to some other areas of the continent. Geographically, the boundaries of the province are identical to those of the country of Burundi, and the history of the province and nation are closely intertwined. This chapter will briefly survey the history of the Anglican Church in Burundi prior to the country's political independence in 1962 and in the period from independence to the outbreak of civil war in 1993. It then will provide a more in-depth look at the Anglican Church of Burundi during and after the war.

The land that now comprises Burundi was occupied by Belgian troops in 1916. Following World War I, the League of Nations granted Belgium an administrative mandate over the territory of Ruanda-Urundi, which comprised today's nations of Rwanda and Burundi. The Belgians brought with them French-speaking, Roman Catholic missionaries who built schools and hospitals with Belgian government support. Thus, Roman Catholicism grew rapidly, and it remains the dominant form of Christianity in Burundi.

The first Anglican missions were led by the Church Missionary Society and were established at Buhiga in the north and Matana in the south in 1935. Another mission site at Buye became the home of a theological college in the late 1930s. These missions came about during the early days of the East African Revival, the evangelical movement that fueled rapid church growth in the twentieth century and that continues to influence Anglicanism in Burundi and the wider East African region. In this early period, the Church Missionary Society joined with the Danish Baptist Missionary Society, the Friends Africa Gospel Mission, the Free Methodist Mission, and the World Gospel Mission in Ruanda-Urundi to form the Protestant Alliance. The Alliance promoted teacher training, represented educational institutions before the government, and sponsored interdenominational evangelistic meetings (Hohensee 1977, 41–2).

*The Wiley-Blackwell Companion to the Anglican Communion*, First Edition. Edited by Ian S. Markham, J. Barney Hawkins IV, Justyn Terry, and Leslie Nuñez Steffensen.
© 2013 John Wiley & Sons, Ltd. Published 2013 by John Wiley & Sons, Ltd.

Following World War II, the United Nations made Ruanda-Urundi a UN Trust Territory, again under Belgian administration. Momentum for the territory's independence grew, and on July 1, 1962, Burundi and Rwanda separated from Belgium and each other to become two newly independent nations. For Burundi, independence marked the beginning of a 30-year period (1962–1992) of political instability, multiple coups, and ongoing ethnic conflict between the Hutu majority and the dominant Tutsi minority.

This conflict was felt within Burundi's Anglican community. In 1962, the year of Burundi's independence, a group of Hutus seceded from the Church, obtained legal recognition, and became known as the *Église de Dieu* (Church of God). "About eighty percent of the Anglican Church around Matana joined this movement. . . . At its height it claimed 8,000 members and a total of 20,000 adherents. It became involved in politics and was accused of subversion. It was forcefully suppressed by the government; worship ceased in 1966. The Church fell apart [and] many returned to the Anglican Church" (Hohensee 1977, 45, see also Barrett 1971, 199).

The first three decades of political independence were a time of significant growth for the Anglican Church in Burundi, which then belonged to the Province of Uganda, Rwanda, Burundi, and Boga-Zaire (now the Democratic Republic of Congo). In 1965, the Rt. Rev. John Nkuzumwami was consecrated as the Burundi church's first bishop and the 1936 mission site of Buye was chosen as the new diocese for the entire country. During the 1960s and 1970s, the Church Missionary Society continued to send physicians and educators, who built hospitals and schools and encouraged widespread Bible study and prayer. By 1973, membership in the Anglican Church was the largest in Burundi's Protestant Alliance, numbering "approximately the same as the combined totals of the other four Churches within the Alliance" (Hohensee 1977, 92). In 1975, a second diocese was created in Bujumbura. Two more dioceses followed: Gitega in 1985 and Matana in 1990. The Anglican Church of Burundi became an autonomous province in 1992, and the Dioceses of Makamba and Muyinga were added in 1997 and 2005, respectively.

One year after the new province was established, Burundi's continuing ethnic strife turned into a long and bloody civil war. During the conflict, the presidency was seized several times by force, an estimated 300,000 people were killed, and more than a million were displaced, many becoming refugees in neighboring Tanzania. A transitional constitution was adopted in 1998, and in 2003 the government and the main armed rebel group signed a peace agreement in Arusha, Tanzania, that had been mediated by South Africa. Another rebel group continued fighting until a final ceasefire was signed in 2006, officially ending the war.

The war was traumatic for the province. Many Anglicans were among those who lost their lives or who fled the country. The Bishop of Bjumbura was abducted at gunpoint and later escaped (Letter from the Bishop 2004). In Buta, 40 Hutu and Tutsi seminarians who chose to die together were slaughtered (EAB Press 2007).

Other Burundian Anglicans intervened politically. According to the report of a delegation of the Anglican Peace and Justice Network, during a presidential coup in 1996, the Anglican Church of Burundi along with other Christian churches intervened, so that Parliament could resume its functions. The religious leaders served as facilitators between the parliamentarians hiding in various embassies and the coup leaders, helping to prevent further chaos. The church further influenced governance through asserting its moral authority and by preaching peace, reconciliation, and healing to the congregations (APJN Visit 1999).

The Rt. Rev. Martin Nyaboho, Bishop of Makamba, commenting in 2004 on the previous decade, said, "Initially, the Church felt paralysed. Its buildings were destroyed, its members killed or fled, to say nothing of the feeling of hopelessness caused by the conflict. . . . but despite the fear and despair the Church remained and persisted with its message." At the height of the war, he held worship services in the road, bringing people together in the middle of the countryside because the towns and villages were too dangerous. "Ironically, the trauma that Burundi has gone through has started to show positive effects. The refugees have evangelised those that they fled to, new churches are springing up as those previously shattered communities restore meaning to their lives. . . . one of the major aspects of the revival has been the new energy that Church members have given to theological education" (Craske 2004).

Further examples appear in a research report by a Burundian priest who was a student at the time and in 2009 conducted field research on the church's actions from 1993 to 2008 in the Diocese of Gitega (Kimararungu 2009). Gitega is predominantly Roman Catholic, but the report nevertheless indicates how the Anglican Church tried to cope with wartime trauma at the local level, both politically and pastorally. In the political realm, "the Diocese of Gitega did not stop and would have been unable to stop the massacres of 1993 if it had tried. . . . Tutsi pastors fled to save their lives . . . while their fellow Hutu pastors did not have any courage to stand firm and denounce the killings, because of fearing the murderers" (Kimararungu 2009, 34–5). However, on the pastoral side, the diocese was very much involved in providing support for war victims' physical and spiritual needs. Churches and church-affiliated schools provided shelter for those fleeing their villages and provided food, clothes, and blankets (Kimararungu 2009, 38). Pastors, including those who had fled, provided counseling, led worship, and preached to traumatized persons. The diocese also organized seminars and workshops on forgiveness, love, and peace building that helped foster repentance, forgiveness, and reconciliation (Kimararungu 2009, 40–1).

Following the war's official end in 2006, the first direct presidential election in more than a decade took place in 2010. Pierre Nkurunziza – whom Parliament had chosen as president in 2005 – won an uncontested race when the opposition boycotted the election. He remains in office. Since then, there have been periodic outbreaks of violence. Burundi remains one of the poorest countries in the world, ranking number 185 out of 187 countries on the 2011 UN Human Development Index (UN Index 2011, 126). Many of those displaced by the war have yet to return home. In 2012, Human Rights Watch reported an increase in political killings by both state agents and armed opposition groups since the 2010 election, and documented the government's efforts to restrict independent media and civil society activists (Burundi 2011).

In this environment, the Province of the Anglican Church of Burundi is now committed "to the rebuilding of the country around the following issues:

- Evangelism and mission alongside faith-building, training, and education.
- Development programs as communities try to provide clean water, decent housing, schools, hospitals and clinics. To encourage income-generating projects, micro-credit schemes, effective agriculture, and fair distribution of food.
- Current issues relating to gender, illiteracy, and care of the environment.
- Advocacy for those who suffer from poverty, HIV/AIDS, and other diseases such as malaria which is endemic in the country. To speak on behalf of the many who continue to suffer as a result of the war, orphans, widows, the displaced, and refugees. To ensure that those being repatriated receive the basics for survival, and promote human rights.
- The process of peace and reconciliation in order to bring hope for a better, more secure future. To encourage negotiation and dialogue between different groups and factions. To find ways to help the traumatized and bereaved, the returnees and the internally displaced. To encourage the youth to be peace-builders."
(Overview of Province 2012)

This agenda is being implemented by the Most Rev. Bernard Ntahoturi, who became primate in 2005. He also serves as bishop of the province's Diocese of Matana. Under his leadership, the province is taking a visible role in Anglican affairs on the African continent and strengthening its international ties. Archbishop Ntahoturi was chosen in 2012 to chair the Council of Anglican Provinces of Africa, an organization that works to address Africa's governance, human rights, economic, and social problems from a faith-based perspective. Within Burundi, he and other clergy meet with the president and other political leaders and civil society groups to monitor implementation of the peace agreement.

The province leans toward the conservative side of the theological spectrum, a reflection of its East African Revival roots. It signed the 2008 Global Anglican Future Conference (GAFCON) Jerusalem Declaration. However, it is one of the few provinces in Africa that ordains women, and Archbishop Ntahoturi has urged the Church to lead the way in speaking out against gender-based violence.

Archbishop Ntahoturi has developed strong ties with the Church of England and the Episcopal Church in the United States. The Most Rev. Rowan Williams preached at Archbishop Ntahoturi's enthronement, marking the first time any Archbishop of Canterbury visited the Province of Burundi. The province works on multiple development projects with the British charity Christian Aid and with Episcopal Relief and Development, the Episcopal Church's aid agency. It has provided capacity-building workshops for 500 clergy and laypersons to promote peace-building and reconciliation, with funding from Trinity Church in New York (Role of the Church 2007, Pastors Gather 2007).

An exemplary project where the Anglican Church of Burundi has partnered successfully with British and American organizations is the Mothers' Union Literacy and Development Programme (MULDP), conducted by the London-based NGO with funding from Trinity Church. In a country where violence has disrupted schooling and 67 percent are illiterate (Celebrating Literacy 2008), MULDP has helped 26,000 persons – three-quarters of them women – to acquire literacy skills. Participants also have had the opportunity to discuss gender equality issues, HIV/AIDS prevention, the environment, human rights, and family planning. They have gone on to run small businesses and join community leadership groups. MULDP is so successful that the government of Burundi is seeking to make it the national model for its literacy program (Province of Burundi).

The Province of the Anglican Church of Burundi is thus a key player in post-war reconstruction and contemporary Burundian nation-building, working with the government, other elements of civil society, and the international community. In a country whose total population numbers 10.5 million, only 5 percent, or 500,000, are Protestant, including Anglicans and other denominations. Roman Catholics number 62 percent of the populace, Muslims 10 percent, and 23 percent of the people follow indigenous beliefs (World Factbook 2012). Thus, the province's influence inside and outside the country that shares its name is larger than what its relative size or youthful history would suggest.

## Bibliography

APJN Visit to Burundi and Pastoral Letter to the Church in Burundi, 1999. Accessed August 2012. http://apjn.anglicancommunion.org/reports/visittoburundi.cfm.

Barrett, David. 1971. *African Initiatives in Religion*. Nairobi: East African Publishing House.

Burundi: Escalation of Political Violence in 2011. Human Rights Watch. Accessed August 2012. http://www.hrw.org/news/2012/05/02/burundi-escalation-political-violence-2011.

Celebrating Eight Years of Literacy and Development in Burundi. EAB Press September 26, 2008. Accessed August 2012. http://www.anglicancommunion.org/provincialnews/eab/client/news/client_news_detail.cfm?naid=1445.

Craske, Michael. 2004. Out of the Fire. *Anglican Episcopal World Trinitytide*. Accessed August 2012. http://www.anglicancommunion.org/ministry/mission/resources/stories/burundi.cfm.

EAB Press October 9, 2007. Anglican Peace and Justice Network in Burundi 27 September to 3 October, 2007. Accessed August 2012. http://www.anglicancommunion.org/provincialnews/eab/client/news/client_news_detail.cfm?naid=1226.

Hohensee, Donald. 1977. *Church Growth in Burundi*. South Pasadena, CA: William Carey Library.

Kimararungu, Aimé Joseph. 2009. The Response of the Anglican Church of Burundi to the Politico-Ethnic Crisis (1993–2008) with Particular Reference to the Diocese of Gitega. Unpublished research paper, Uganda Christian University, Mukono, Uganda.

Letter from the Bishop of Bjumbura on his Recent Attempted Abduction by the FNL. *Anglican Communion News Service*, August 16, 2004. Accessed August 2012. http://www.anglicancommunion.org/acns/news.cfm?mode=entry&entry=CB20C8EF-A73E-20C5-302ABBFF03F22DAA.

Overview of Province. Province of the Anglican Church of Burundi website. Accessed August 2012. http://www.anglicanburundi.org/about_us.shtml

Pastors Gather to Consider their Role as Peacemakers. EAB Press November 24, 2007. Accessed August 2012. http://www.anglicancommunion.org/provincialnews/eab/client/news/client_news_detail.cfm?naid=1264.

The Province of Burundi. Mothers' Union: Christian Care for Families website. Accessed

August2012.http://www.themothersunion. org/province_burundi.aspx.

The Role of the Church in the building and consolidation of peace in Burundi. EAB Press July 21, 2007. Accessed August 2012, http://www.anglicancommunion.org/ provincialnews/eab/client/news/client_ news_detail.cfm?naid=1167.

The World Factbook. Accessed August 2012. http://www.cia.gov/library/publications/ the-world-factbook/geos/by.html.

United Nations Human Development Index, Statistical Annex 2011.UN Development Programme website 2012. Accessed August 2012. http://www.undp.org/content/dam/ undp/library/corporate/HDR/2011%20 Global%20HDR/English/HDR_2011_EN_ Tables.pdf.

CHAPTER 11

# The Church of the Province of Central Africa

## Katherine L. Wood

The Province of Central Africa has 15 dioceses that cover the Anglican Church in the nations of Botswana, Malawi, Zambia, and Zimbabwe. Geographically, the Diocese of Botswana is the country with the same name. The dioceses of Lake Malawi, Northern Malawi, Southern Malawi, and Upper Shire are all located in Malawi. The dioceses of Central Zambia, Eastern Zambia, Luapula, Lusaka, and Northern Zambia cover the country of Zambia. The remaining dioceses are all in Zimbabwe: Central Zimbabwe, Harare, Manicaland, Masvingo, and Matabeleland. National councils have been created in Malawi, Zambia, and Zimbabwe, since these countries have multiple dioceses.

This chapter briefly recounts the history of the province and describes its current features and key issues. Special attention is given to the Diocese of Harare, where a schismatic bishop has aligned himself with Zimbabwe's despotic ruler. This development is significant both for the province and on the world stage.

The first Anglican missionary to arrive in the area was Bishop Charles Mackenzie, who traveled with the Scottish explorer Dr. David Livingstone in Nyasaland (now Malawi) in 1861 under the auspices of the newly founded Universities' Mission to Central Africa. This organization became known for its medical work, promotion of education, and opposition to the slave trade.

Another British explorer active in the region was Cecil John Rhodes, whose British South Africa Company colonized what became Southern Rhodesia (later Zimbabwe) in 1889. The company administered the territory until it became a self-governing British colony in 1922. In 1953, the British government joined Southern Rhodesia, Northern Rhodesia (later Zambia), and Nyasaland (later Malawi) into the Central African Federation, foreshadowing the establishment of the Province of Central Africa in 1955. Except for the addition of Botswana, the new province mirrored the consolidation of several British colonies into a single political unit. In subsequent decades, these colonies each

*The Wiley-Blackwell Companion to the Anglican Communion*, First Edition. Edited by Ian S. Markham,
J. Barney Hawkins IV, Justyn Terry, and Leslie Nuñez Steffensen.
© 2013 John Wiley & Sons, Ltd. Published 2013 by John Wiley & Sons, Ltd.

gained their independence, but the province has remained intact with a movable arch-bishopric. In a part of the world known for its religious pluralism (predominantly Christian, Muslim, and indigenous traditions), the province's Anglicans number about 600,000 out of 14.9 million Christians in a total population of 31.8 million (Provincial Directory 2012).

African opposition to colonial rule increased in the 1930s and further intensified after World War II. During the mid-twentieth century, notable members of the English clergy such as Bishop Kenneth Skelton of Southern Rhodesia strongly advocated for African participation in local governance, while other whites worked just as ardently to preserve the status quo. Racial tension and efforts to ease it remain a factor in provincial affairs.

Theologically, the Province of Central Africa is evangelical and conservative. It participates in the Anglican Global South movement and does not ordain women. Its current primate is the Most Rev. Albert Chama, who was installed in 2011. He concurrently serves as Bishop of the Diocese of Northern Zambia and is the first Zambian to hold the office of archbishop (Anglican Communion News Service 2011). The province's component dioceses and national councils carry out programs with other Anglican Communion–affiliated organizations to address development issues such as poverty and health. For example, the Zambian Anglican Council has an anti-malaria initiative underway in partnership with the British NGO Christian Aid. The council's presiding bishop, William Mchombo, described additional health programs in a 2010 speech in Lusaka, noting the Church's shared African and English heritage (Bishop's Centenary Address 2010). At the provincial level, the Central Africa bishops have pledged to support efforts to halt the spread of HIV/AIDS, including prevention and counseling (Bishops Retreat 2004).

As in other parts of the Anglican Communion, the subject of homosexuality has fostered divisiveness. The province severed all ties with the American Diocese of New Hampshire in 2003 when it elevated the Rev. Gene Robinson, an openly gay priest, to the episcopate. In the Diocese of Botswana, a group of clergy and laypersons called for the resignation of Bishop Trevor Mwamba in 2008, accusing him "of taking a very vocal pro-homosexuality stance" (Anglicans Petition 2008).

A crisis erupted in Zimbabwe in September 2007, when Dr. Nolbert Kunonga, then the Bishop of Harare, openly broke with the province on grounds that it had become sympathetic towards homosexuals – although it neither conducts same-sex marriages nor ordains gay priests. In fact, Dr. Kunonga directly benefited from the ruling party's seizures of white-owned commercial farms and had aligned himself politically with President Robert Mugabe, the strongman who has ruled the country since it became independent in 1980 (Dugger 2008). Mugabe's rabid anti-homosexual views may have provided a needed smokescreen for Kunonga. Several months before he severed his relationship with the Central Africa province, Archbishop of Canterbury Rowan Williams and the then-Provincial Primate Bernard Malango met with Dr. Kunonga to share their concerns about the deteriorating economic and human rights situation in Zimbabwe and to encourage the church in Harare to respond with a more independent voice (Zimbabwe's Anglican Church). Later, instead of speaking out against the government, Dr. Kunonga resigned from the province to form his own Anglican Church of

Zimbabwe, naming himself as archbishop and putting himself squarely in the Mugabe camp. He took church funds and properties with him.

Provincial leaders appointed Bishop Sebastian Bakare as Acting Bishop of Harare and announced their excommunication of Dr. Kunonga in May 2008. In the meantime, Kunonga loyalists, government security forces, and the police engaged in a campaign of violence, harassment, and intimidation against Anglicans who remained with the Province of Central Africa. Worship services were interrupted, access to churches was blocked, and people were beaten and killed. The violence escalated after the March 2008 election that threatened President Mugabe's hold on power and led to a contested runoff vote in June that he won under irregular circumstances.

In October 2011, at the invitation of Archbishop Chama, the Archbishop of Canterbury made a week-long pastoral visit to the province. The visit began in Malawi with a special service celebrating the 150th anniversary of the Anglican Church there, and it ended in Zambia. The most reported part of the trip took place in Harare, where Archbishop Williams met for two hours with President Mugabe. In a statement issued after the meeting, the Archbishop said, "We strongly and unequivocally support the efforts of ordinary Anglicans to worship in peace and to minister to the spiritual and material needs of their communities. Today we were able to present President Mugabe with a dossier compiled by the bishops in Zimbabwe which gives a full account of the abuses to which our people and our church has been subject. We have asked, in the clearest possible terms, that the President use his powers as Head of State to put an end to all unacceptable and illegal behaviour" (Archbishops Meet). President Mugabe in return "delivered a history lesson on Anglo-Zimbabwean relations, detailed his own [Roman Catholic] religious upbringing, and reminded Williams that the Church of England is 'a breakaway group' from the Catholic Church" (When Anglican Archbishop Meets 2011).

In a May 2011 interview with the *New York Times*, Dr. Kunonga indicated that he aims to control "about 3,000 churches, schools, hospitals and other properties in Zimbabwe, Zambia, Botswana and Malawi"– in other words, in the four countries of the Anglican Province of Central Africa. He continues to rally against homosexuals, and like President Mugabe, he "casts himself as a nationalist leader who is Africanizing a church associated with British colonialism" (Dugger 2011).

Meanwhile, Dr. Chad Gandiya, who was elected and consecrated in 2009 as the new Bishop of Harare, is trying to bring normalcy to his diocese against the odds. Dr. Kunonga and the Zimbabwean government continue to persecute Anglicans loyal to his diocese and the province. In late 2011, Bishop Gandiya reported that Dr. Kunonga was evicting Anglican clergy from their homes (Conger August 2011), and Bishop Gandiya himself was arrested after performing a confirmation service (Conger 2012). As of June 2012, Bishop Gandiya's spokesperson said that President Mugabe had not yet acted on the dossier presented to him by the Archbishop of Canterbury eight months earlier (Special Coverage 2012). In November 2012, Zimbabwe's Supreme Court ruled that the church properties previously seized by Dr. Kunonga belonged to the Province of Central Africa, and ordered Dr. Kunonga to return them.

In sum, the Province of Central Africa is a geographically complex structure that works across the national boundaries of four countries. The province's history and its race relations are part of the legacy of the British Empire. The province is working to improve people's lives but problems emanating from the Diocese of Harare are impeding progress. When Archbishop Albert Chama was elected in 2011, the *Church of England Newspaper* noted that "high on the agenda for Archbishop-elect Chama will be the on-going dispute in the Diocese of Harare and the persecution of the church in Zimbabwe, the church's role in politics, and pressures for the division of the province with Zambia, Malawi and Zimbabwe forming their own Anglican provinces – a move that has been on hold since the collapse of Zimbabwe" (Conger March 2011). These matters will remain troublesome for some time to come.

## Bibliography

Anglican Communion News Service. 2011. Zambian Bishop Installed as Sixth Archbishop of Central Africa Province. March 23. Accessed August 2012. http://www.aco.org/acns/news.cfm/2011/3/23/ACNS4826.

Anglican Communion News Service. 2012. Zimbabwe Anglicans to Return to Their Churches After Supreme Court Ruling. November 19. Accessed November 30, 2012. http://www.anglicancommunion.org/acns/news.cfm/2012/11/19/ACNS5249.

Anglicans Petition Mwamba. 2008. *The Botswana Gazette*. November 13. Accessed August 2012. http://www.gazettebw.com/index.php?option=com_content&view=article&id=1907:anglicans-petition-mwamba&catid=18:headlines&Itemid=2.

Archbishops Meet with Zimbabwean President. October 10, 2011. Archbishop of Canterbury website. Accessed August 2012. http://www.archbishopofcanterbury.org/articles.php/2209/archbishops-meet-with-zimbabwean-president.

Bishop's Centenary Address Celebrates Zambia Church's Role in Society and Communion. 2010. Anglican Communion News Service. November 2. Accessed August 2012. http://www.anglicancommunion.org/acns/digest/index.cfm/2010/11/2/Bishops-centenary-address-celebrates-Zambia-Churchs-role-in-society-and-Communion.

Bishop's Retreat – The Province of Central Africa Bishops Retreat. July 13–14, 2004.

World Council of Churches website. Accessed August 2012. http://www.oikoumene.org/de/dokumentation/documents/other-ecumenical-bodies/church-statements-on-hivaids/archbishop-of-the-anglican-province-of-central-africa.html.

"Christian Aid Launches New Malaria Initiative in Zambia." September 2010. Christian Aid website. Accessed August 2012. http://www.christianaid.org.uk/pressoffice/pressreleases/september-2010/new-malaria-initiative-launched-in-zambia.aspx.

Conger, George. March 2011. Central Africa Archbishop Elected. *The Church of England Newspaper*. March 4. Conger blogpost March 8. Accessed August 2012. http://geoconger.wordpress.com/2011/03/08/central-african-archbishop-elected-the-church-of-england-newspaper-march-4-2011-p-7/.

Conger, George. August 2011. Anglican Clergy Under Siege in Harare. *The Church of England Newspaper*. August 21. Accessed August 2012. http://religiousintelligence.org/churchnewspaper/?p=18762.

Conger, George. 2012. Harare Bishop Arrested for Holding Confirmation Service. *The Church of England Newspaper*. January 20. Conger blogpost January 25. Accessed August 2012. http://geoconger.wordpress.com/tag/chad-gandiya/.

Dugger, Celia. 2008. Zimbabwe's Rulers Unleash Police on Anglicans. *The New York Times*. May 16. Accessed August 2012. http://www.nytimes.com/2008/05/16/world/africa/16zimbabwe.html.

Dugger, Celia. 2011. Mugabe Ally Escalates Push to Control Anglican Church. *The New York Times.* May 29. Accessed August 2012. http://www.nytimes.com/2011/05/30/world/africa/30zimbabwe.html.

Provincial Directory: The Church of the Province of Central Africa. Anglican Communion website. Accessed August 2012. http://www.anglicancommunion.org/tour/province.cfm?ID=C2.

Special Coverage of the Anglican Crisis in Zimbabwe. Religion in Zimbabwe. Accessed August 2012. http://relzim.org/major-religions-zimbabwe/anglicans/kunonga-crisis/.

When Anglican Archbishop Meets Catholic President. October 11, 2011. Religion in Zimbabwe. Accessed August 2012. http://relzim.org/news/2788/.

Zimbabwe's Anglican Church Encouraged to Develop "Independent Voice" on Human Rights. Anglican Communion News Service. March 7, 2007. Accessed August 2012. http://www.anglicancommunion.org/acns/news.cfm?mode=entry&entry=6F75FD7E-F85C-3937-610B9A6929190D93.

CHAPTER 12

# The Province of the Anglican Church of the Congo

## Emma Wild-Wood and Titre Ande

During the closing ceremony of the All Africa Bishops Conference in Kampala in September 2010, the Archbishop of Congo, Isingoma Kahwa, stated proudly, "We have no theological problem in Congo and we are not concerned by what is going on in the Anglican Communion, because our church was not founded by a European missionary, but a Ugandan." This bold statement indicates how many Congolese Anglicans have perceived their church and its place in the world: as both African initiated and globally connected, desirous of carrying out God's mission through worship, service, and proclamation rather than focusing upon complex discussions. In the small chapels of remote villages, at its most local and indigenous, there is a recognition that the church is in fellowship with Christians worldwide and has a long Christian heritage. Belonging to the Anglican Communion has been a point of succor, pride, and encouragement, but in recent years it has also caused bewilderment and confusion. The history of La Province de l'Eglise Anglicane du Congo (PEAC) demonstrates both its sense of proud independence and also its feeling of connection to the wider Christian church within Congo and within the Anglican Communion. The contemporary issues facing the PEAC demonstrate the difficulties of comprehending the concerns of others in the communion when responding to a protracted internal war and its aftermath.

## History of the Anglican Church in the Congo

Anglicans in Congo consider Saint Apolo Kivebulaya to be the founder of their church. Although he was not the only, nor indeed the first, Ugandan evangelist to work in Congo, he became the best loved and most greatly respected. In 1896, he arrived in the village of Boga on the escarpment west of the Semeliki River for the first time. By his death in 1933, he had been instrumental in planting 50 small churches within a

*The Wiley-Blackwell Companion to the Anglican Communion*, First Edition. Edited by Ian S. Markham,
J. Barney Hawkins IV, Justyn Terry, and Leslie Nuñez Steffensen.
© 2013 John Wiley & Sons, Ltd. Published 2013 by John Wiley & Sons, Ltd.

60-mile radius of Boga and training 88 catechists. Over 1,500 Christians had been baptized among seven ethnic groups, including the Mbiti pygmies, with whom he was associated in missionary literature of the time (Lloyd 1923, 1928, 1934). An employee of the Church Missionary Society (CMS), he worked closely with British missionaries when he was in Toro, Uganda. He worked more independently when the area west of the Semeliki came under Belgian control from 1910 and access by British CMS missionaries was limited. In Catholic and Belgian Congo, this small, geographically isolated church led by an African priest was viewed with suspicion by colonial authorities. It maintained its links with Uganda and developed its own local identity, but colonial and missionary restrictions on growth, coupled with a desire to sacralize the tradition which Apolo had introduced, meant that the Anglican Church did not spread from the Boga area until after political independence in 1960.

Apolo and his early converts appear to have welcomed the novelties of literacy, healthcare, and Anglican liturgy as signs of a socio-spiritual power which demonstrated potency for sustaining life in the insecurity of early colonialism. Initially, in their enthusiasm for the new ways of Christianity, some rejected traditional religious practices, seeking new forms of worship and of healing, and emphasizing the transformation of behavior. The evangelical Anglicanism they adopted had already been adapted by Ugandan Christians, and thus the Hema in Boga began to understand the Anglican structure as being analogous to their own social structure. A co-existence developed in Boga between traditional rites and Anglican rites, with the chief playing a significant role in both. For some, this parallel relationship was acceptable; for others, it was suggestive of a lack of proper commitment. For other ethnic groups of the escarpment, the close relationship between Anglicanism and Hema culture appeared to bolster the unequal client relations already at work in the area.

Apolo developed around him teams of young people, many of whom became prominent in the church after his death and ensured that his memory lived on. The first two Congolese priests, Nasani Kabarole and Yusufu Limenya, ordained in 1937, had both known Apolo well. Although the ordination of local priests is often recognized as a sign of the health of a local church, it often coincides with a diminution of leadership by women. The early Anglican Church was one of the few churches in Congo that had accepted women catechists. They led chapels and taught literacy, but their numbers dwindled over time. Apolo had also gained a reputation among Ugandans as an exceptional missionary, and after his death the appeal to continue his work in the Boga area caused a number of Ugandans to offer their services to Congo. Prominent among them was Nasanari Mukasa, who spent nearly 50 years connected with the Anglican Church of Congo, even coming out of retirement to be the first Archdeacon of Aru in the 1980s.

After 1960, Anglican members used their greater freedoms of movement and religious expression to expand into the country beyond the Ituri region. In doing so, they understood that they were following the intention of Apolo's dying wish to be buried with his head towards the west, rather than towards his home in the east. Anglicans who had already migrated from the rural Semeliki escarpment to take advantage of the economic possibilities in the growing towns of Congo requested evangelists to join them in establishing chapels. Subsequent growth meant that the first diocese, Boga-Zaire, was created when Philip Ridsdale, a CMS missionary, was consecrated in 1972. The early connection with CMS has continued throughout the history of the church. From 1934 to 1960 and from 1972 until the present day, it has welcomed mission partners from CMS UK, Ireland, Australia, and New Zealand. There have also been some from the ECUSA. The importance of providing Congo with its own diocese was recognized in 1969 by the Rev. Ted L. Lewis, an American Foreign Service officer attached to the US Embassy in Kinshasa. He visited Boga and was greatly impressed by the vitality of the church and the commitment of Archdeacon Festo Byakisaka. Lewis petitioned members of the communion to provide support for Congolese Anglicans. Deaconess Lucy Ridsdale accompanied her husband and temporarily re-established the training of female catechists. She and Byakisaka facilitated the translation of the Prayer Book in a form of Swahili common in Congo. The church no longer needed to rely on the luToro/kiHema version of the Prayer Book, familiar only to the Hema people, or the more complex Kenyan Swahili. A new Prayer Book in a common language undoubtedly aided the establishment of the church in new areas and among new peoples.

The second diocese was established in Bukavu in 1976, with Ndahura Bezaleri as its first bishop. A native of the village of Boga, he was an able young man who became a schools' inspector and then, identified as possessing episcopal gifts, rose rapidly through the ecclesiastical ranks. He was an enthusiastic exponent of Anglicanism in Congo, encouraging members to plant churches in new locations and supporting independent churches to join the Anglican Church. In 1981, he became archbishop of the newly formed Francophone Province of Rwanda, Burundi, and Boga-Zaire, but died suddenly the following year.

Kisangani and Katanga became dioceses in 1980. The Anglican Church in Katanga had a distinct genesis. It emerged from a Bemba congregation of migrant copper mine workers around Lubumbashi, initially supported by the Anglican Church in Northern Rhodesia/Zambia. Migrants to the Congo have enriched the Anglican Church. The church in the north-east corner of the country developed as a result of the forced migration of Ugandans at the end of Idi Amin's brutal regime in 1979, and migration from the protracted Sudanese civil war. The Diocese of Aru was inaugurated in 2005. A number of the migrants were influenced by the East African Revival and placed great emphasis on evangelism and church planting. The flight of Rwandan refugees across the vast country after the genocide in 1994 not only bolstered the small Anglican congregations around the capital, Kinshasa, but took Anglicanism over the Congo River, into Brazzaville and the Republic of Congo where a number of parishes now form an archdeaconry in the Kinshasa diocese.

The second significant factor for the growth of the church, particularly in Katanga and Kindu (diocese inaugurated 1997) and the Kasais (Diocese of Mbuji-Mayi inaugurated 2011), was through the affiliation of whole denominations to the EAC because of a restriction on independent congregations in the country. In 1973, it became imperative for all congregations to gain civil status or belong to one of three legal entities: the Roman Catholic Church, the largest church in DRC with a membership of about 49 percent of the population; the Kimbanguist Church with 18 percent of the population, arising from the short ministry of Simon Kimbangu and long years as an underground movement during the colonial regime; and the Eglise du Christ au

Congo/Zaïre (ECC/Z),with 29 percent of the population, the organization for Protestant churches formed from the missionary council, and of which the Anglican Church was a member (Barrett et al. 2001, 211–6). Some congregations chose to become members of the Anglican Church rather than disband. It appears that some made this decision because they knew least about it, and its center was a great distance away! Some church leaders were dismayed when Anglican pastors arrived to initiate them into Anglican ways. The Anglican Church was willing to embrace a wide variety of different Christian groups because it perceived its ecumenical contribution to ". . . help this body of Christians in Congo, who . . . have been left with no historic Church or affiliations of a true nature with other world wide Churches" (Ridsdale 1961, 10): a statement which indicates a perception of the role of the Anglican Communion in Congolese Christian relationships. Administration and leadership have played important roles in the coordination of the disparate migrant groups and independent churches.

In August 1981, Ndahura demitted the Anglican Church from the ECZ and for five years it existed outside it. Although it could not sustain its non-membership of the ECZ in the closely controlled political climate of Zaïre, the attempt of the Anglican Church to leave the Protestant organization illustrates its relation with the Congo state and the Anglican Communion. The move was not intended to break relations with other Protestant denominations, although the growing Anglican Church wanted to abolish the missionary comity boundaries that it perceived to restrict its geographical spread. The decision was more significantly a criticism of an organization that failed to respect the priority of Anglican theology, practice, and structures and insisted on imposing a different administrative structure. Other members were concerned about mismanagement, malpractice, and bureaucracy in the ECZ. Some were also wary of the consequences of an ecclesiastical loyalty which was limited to the nation-state. The Anglican Church wanted to be part of a council of churches but disliked the development of what it described as a "super-church," appearing to serve the purposes of the state bureaucracy. It wished to maintain a single "spiritual" allegiance, "to the Archbishop of Canterbury, spiritual head of the Anglican Communion" (Balufuga 1982, 7). The Anglican Church sought fellowship, prayer, aid, and guidance from outside Congo and appreciated practical forms of support and the sense of spiritual kinship with a wider Christian movement. This incident demonstrates a desire to be an autonomous national church within a worldwide communion. In the 1980s, membership in the Anglican Communion appeared to offer the Anglican Church in Zaïre an opportunity to be flexible, free and take local initiative.

To achieve initiative and independence within Congo, the Anglican Church appreciated its involvement in the formal, transnational networks that facilitate communication between provinces of the Anglican Communion, such as the Lambeth Conference, the Mothers' Union, and the Anglican Consultative Council. Yet, its relationship to these networks is constantly informed by local concerns emerging within its congregations, parishes, and dioceses (Wild-Wood 2011). In the early 1990s, awareness of differences within the Anglican Communion helped negotiate change within the Anglican Church of Congo. The knowledge of charismatic movement in other provinces, for example, influenced its reception of new Pentecostal churches and the introduction of some charismatic practices in some of its own congregations. The call for the ordination of women came from an awareness of women priests elsewhere in the communion.

## The Story of the Contemporary Church

In 1992, the church became an autonomous province within the Anglican Communion, and Patrice Njojo, the second Bishop of Boga, became its first archbishop. The PEAC deemed it strategic to locate its dioceses in cities, and the second archbishop, Dirokpa Balufuga, moved the seat of the archbishopric and the provincial headquarters from Bunia in the east of the country to the capital, Kinshasa. Yet, the majority of Anglican Christians are to be found in rural areas. Like many of the people in Congo, they are poor, subsistence farmers who are often at the mercy of political and economic forces beyond their control.

President Mobutu Sese Seko ruled the country from 1965 until 1997, using its natural resources to finance a lavish lifestyle while greatly restricting the autonomy and prosperity of the Congolese people. Mobutu was deposed by Laurent Kabila whose son, Joseph, was elected as president in 2005. While the country is rich in natural resources, the benefits of these are rarely seen by the population. More often, the desire to control the mineral wealth of the country causes instability and violence. Since 1996, there has been a series of wars and conflicts which have killed about 5.4 million people. The wars were precipitated by the genocide in Rwanda in 1994 and the escape of the perpetrators into Congo, pursued by the armies of Rwanda and Uganda. The majority of the country has returned to some form of stability but violence against civilians by the army, Ugandan and Rwandan rebels, and local militia erupts frequently in North and South Kivu, and the Lord's Resistance Army, now banished from Uganda, operates in the northern border area of the country. Two of the most horrific aspects of the continual violence are the systematic rape of women and girls and the use of children as soldiers. Many people remain internally displaced and traumatized by brutality. Nevertheless, in the last ten years, there has been a deliberate attempt to develop a civil society. Despite ongoing concerns about governance, church leaders have a made prominent contribution to the rebuilding of society, including Bishop Masimango (Kindu), a *senateur* between 2003 and 2006 who contributed to the writing of the constitution. Chinese companies are now particularly active in the country, mining the mineral resources. There is ambivalence about their presence; some welcome the improvements they bring to the infrastructure, some fear a neo-colonial situation.

It is in this complex situation of grave poverty, outbreaks of violence, and muted optimism for the future that the PEAC seeks to carry out God's mission. It recognizes itself as a poor church among the poor, a situation of frustration and of suffering. It is made more acute by the rise of new Pentecostal churches offering easy routes to "material blessings," a theology the PEAC cannot espouse. It is grateful for the work of advocacy that it can effect on behalf of Congo through relations in the Anglican Communion, significant among them the support of Michael Scott-Joynt, until recently Bishop of Winchester, in Britain, who sits on the Great Lakes Region all-party parliamentary committee advising the British government. Inadequate as the PEAC sometimes feels its response to be to the suffering and injustice that its members experience, it often makes a significant difference in the lives of communities among whom it is present. Like many churches in Congo, the PEAC plays a prominent role in local development and runs projects in the fields of education, healthcare, humanitarian aid, agriculture, micro-business, training, and peace and reconciliation.

Pastors are expected to be prominent community leaders, and many of them inspire their communities to build churches, schools and health centers, or to protect springs to provide clean water. Although the majority of Anglican pastors are men, women can be ordained. The first female priest, Muhindo Tsongo, was ordained in 2003. Dioceses have Bible schools in which pastors and evangelists are trained. Those who have their secondary school leavers' certificate are often trained at the small provincial theological college in Bunia. In 2010, the college became the Université Anglicane du Congo (UAC) inaugurated by the Most Rev. Rowan Williams in June 2011. This development follows a trend seen in other African nations to create Christian universities and is in part a response to the increasing need for higher education after years of instability, and in part, an income-generating measure. Ministerial formation at degree level was under threat because of the withdrawal of funds from overseas partners. It is hoped that the courses in development, applied sciences and psychology, and education will flourish and support the training of clergy at a level which enables them to engage critically with the Christian tradition and with contemporary issues.

The PEAC has a network of primary and secondary schools, clinics, and hospitals. It has trained nurses for decades and, in 2010, opened the Institut Supérieur Medical in Aru, offering a degree course in nursing. A return to stability in some areas has increased the aspirations for education and seen women returning to school to complete their education. Each diocese has a development office which runs a number of different projects. Some function better than others, but in the archdeaconry of Goma, for example, which has seen some of the very worst violence, there is a thriving development office which, under the leadership of the Rev. Desiré and Claudaline Mukanirwa, runs a number of small projects intended to help the most vulnerable, including micro-credit projects, counseling and healthcare for survivors of rape and their children, agricultural support for those returning home after displacement, and reconciliation workshops. Various partner organizations are involved in supporting these activities, prominent among them the Congo Church Association and the Semiliki Trust.

Forty-seven percent of Congo's 64.3 million people are under 14 years of age. Thus, the work of Agape, the youth wing of the Anglican Church, is crucial. Originally the initiative of CMS mission partner Judy Acheson, and now led by Rev. Balikenga Bisoke it has, over 20 years, trained diocesan youth co-ordinators and developed a network of youth groups which provide leisure activities, skills for work, and opportunities for discussion and Bible study, and encourage the participation of young people in the life of church and society. A focus on rebuilding the country is visible in the Agape youth manuals *Young People, with God Let's Rebuild our Beautiful Country* (2006), *Stand up Young Congolese, with God Let's Fight Poverty* (2009), which have been adopted by the Congolese government for use throughout the country in order to encourage young people to take a proud civic role. Agape has also developed a youth training college in Mahagi which is committed to the formation of both young men and young women.

The work of the Mothers' Union (MU) is significant in the PEAC. Women come together for mutual support and prayer. They share small business skills and are often responsible for the pastoral care of their communities, organizing visits to local families. They welcome the support of the wider MU and appreciate being part of a worldwide movement. Many MU groups are also linked to local branches of the Féderation des Femmes Protestantes of the ECC. Often the most lively of ecumenical organizations at a grassroots level, the Féderation des Femmes holds regular services and literacy classes and provides a forum for women to meet across denominations. Mbambu Dorcas is an outstanding example of the care that Anglican women often show in their communities. A trained midwife who worked for the Anglican medical service in Butembo, she and husband took care of abandoned babies. When local authorities heard of her work, they brought to her children who had been orphaned or abandoned in recent conflicts, but she received no financial support for their care. Many of the children were HIV+. Faced with social stigma and an inability to pay school fees, she opened a school which now has 300 pupils. Now Compassion Orphanage and school are supported by the Diocese of Nord Kivu, and other church members are encouraged to give homes to orphans.

The call to follow Jesus Christ and to preach the Gospel that has power to transform lives is central to the mission of the PEAC. While the majority of Congolese citizens proclaim a Christian faith, during years of war some have been involved in practices that are morally questionable. Ise-somo Muhindo, the provincial evangelist until 2010 when he became Bishop of Nord Kivu, developed a ministry among the military during the conflicts. He was invited to preach in barracks and gave out Bibles to soldiers, challenging the predatory behavior of soldiers towards civilians. Other groups have worked to rehabilitate child-soldiers back into local communities.

A revised Swahili Prayer Book was published in 1998 after widespread consultation. It included important ceremonies like prayers for the lifting of the mourning period after a person has died. In most churches across the province, the 1998 Prayer Book is used with different degrees of flexibility. Archbishop Dirokpa (2005–2010) was committed to further inculturation of worship and devised his own liturgy with more radical innovations which was used in Bukavu. It has had limited acceptance among ordinary Anglicans, many of whom wish to maintain the distinctiveness of Anglican worship and, in so doing, its associations with membership of a transnational communion. Such an approach is also seen in the various reactions to the influence of Pentecostal belief and practice: some embrace a more spontaneous form of worship and welcome a greater emphasis on the work of the Holy Spirit to inspire and to heal as signs of reconnection with a god-given African spirituality, others link it to a global charismatic movement, while others are suspicious of forms of worship redolent of traditional practices they thought that Christianity had eschewed. Nevertheless, worship in PEAC services is often dynamic. It rejoices in the traditions of song and song-writing that have developed in Congo. Church choirs make a significant contribution to worship and community life. A single congregation may have several choirs, and the most talented of these will compose their own songs and organize *soirées musicales*, evenings of entertainment and evangelism. "Animation" is also popular part of

Congolese worship, in which a singer will lead a congregation in lively singing of popular choruses.

## Contemporary Issues Facing the Province

The PEAC would like to improve its service to Congolese society. It grapples with the practical ways in which it can be a church beyond the local parish and how it participates in the worldwide body of Christ. However, its leadership often feels hampered by the lack of resources, lack of confidence, and lack of education and theological reflection. The controversies within the Anglican Communion often appear distant to the concerns of Congo and detrimental to its mission.

The PEAC is a small church in a vast country. Many pastors are responsible for geographically large parishes which are divided into sub-parishes and single congregations. They have a team of catechists and evangelists, some of who have had only the most rudimentary formation. Pastors usually have to support themselves and families by growing food, but it is hard work and the weather and seasons are increasingly unpredictable. The poor infrastructure and lack of communication systems ensure that the church is internally disconnected and lacks sustained contact with the Anglican Communion. There is limited access to electricity and to the Internet, and diocesan staff often have to rely on the vagaries of a few Internet cafés. The provincial office has no efficient network with which to communicate with the dioceses, and a lack of resources limit the frequency of provincial synods to every five or six years. There is frustration at the inability to operate in a collegial manner, consulting and informing one another. Such problems are heightened in communication with the Anglican Communion. Many articles are in English, but French is widely used in Congo. *Réseau Francophone* within the Anglican Communion offers a limited resource to overcome this problem. The PEAC has felt proud to be part of the Anglican Communion but feels unable to fully contribute to the communion or to understand entirely its debates. Many of the problems of poverty, war, hunger, and sickness that are so pressing for the Congolese nation do not appear to be prominent in inter-communion discussions. In terms of human sexuality, all dioceses have stated that they support the traditional view of marriage as being between a man and a woman, and the PEAC's priority is to address sexual violence, usually meted out to women by men, particularly as a systemic act of war.

The leadership of the PEAC has steadily strengthened over the last two decades, yet there is a need for more confident leaders who are both humble people and visionaries, properly able to serve the church and society and demonstrate how all Christians can become active participants in the economic, political, and social development of their nation (Ande 2009, 167). At times the PEAC seems rudderless; its leaders, having grown up under the intimidating dictatorship of Mobutu and operating in the context of political instability, often find it difficult to give a clear direction during crisis. By their own admission, some draw back from making judgments in order to avoid problems with local authorities. Their theology should be informed by an understanding of the dynamics of political power and not simply of culture. A recognition of the misuses of power would present a challenge to church leaders, some of whom have used the church authority to maintain their own status and develop coercive relationships (Ande 2010, 25–6). Leaders have been encouraged to use a philosophy for grassroots transformational development, known as *Ensemble Nous Pouvons*, which uses a series of Biblical reflections and seminars to enable congregations and communities to discover for themselves their potential to bring about change and build a better future using their own capacities and resources.

Greater attention to education and theological reflection would greatly enhance the PEAC. If "we have no theological problem," it may be because we do not address issues in a theological way. Teaching methods rarely encourage reflection, and theological formation faces a lot of challenges. The completion of primary school is often the academic qualification required to attend a Bible school. It is vital that ordinands can relate theological and biblical understanding to practical situations in preaching, pastoral care, and ethics, and so refresh theology and practice.

Theology is not often on the agenda while discussing church issues, and the PEAC lacks a Theological and Doctrinal Commission in order to discuss theological issues needed for mission in Congo. One such area of attention is ecclesiology. While Anglicans in Congo are proud of their identity as Anglicans, they have little doctrinal understanding of what they mean by "church"; and it becomes very difficult to decide with whom to be in communion and with whom to exchange ministers and sacraments within the Anglican Communion and within the ECC. The PEAC has good relationships with other churches in Congo. It shares ministry, sacraments (although without formal discussion and agreements), and significant events with other members of the ECC and has cordial relationships with the Roman Catholic Church. These relationships are under severe strain because of the prominence of the homosexuality debate within the Anglican Communion. Other churches are beginning to see the PEAC as a "wolf among lambs." The controversy impacts negatively upon the Christian testimony in the PEAC, and upon collaboration in ministry and mission with other churches in Congo. Some PEAC members have begun to be ashamed of their Anglican identity and either attempt to hide it or to leave the PEAC. The PEAC has worked hard at developing ecumenical relationships, particularly in areas where it has recently developed its ministry. It has understood Anglicanism as a *via media* which promotes understanding among different denominations, and it is saddened by the diminution of this role in Congolese society.

After the war, as the PEAC attempts to play its part in civil society and the rebuilding of the country, the language of mission is about "holistic ministry," a need for a "social gospel," and the place of "material blessing" as signs of God's abundant love. However, in aiming to provide an effective and practical response to the discomforting situations in society, mission can become a problem-solving activity. There is little theological framework to provide the basis for mission. It also often depends on the calling, the motivation, and energy for mission of individual Christians rather than planned and coordinated action. The PEAC must participate in the continual and transformational character of God's mission in order to experience what Emil Brunner said, "Mission is to the Church what combustion is to fire." Theological formation, contextual awareness, and prayerfulness are important for all Christians so they may discern where and how to participate in God's mission.

Long-term poverty and acute personal and corporate suffering and trauma are the most significant issues that the PEAC and its people face. It affects all the issues mentioned earlier. Such poverty is exacerbated by the disintegration of traditional cultures, values, and social structures. It exists in a world of enormous technological and scientific advances, where there is a greater understanding of human psychology and greater economic prosperity. Members of the PEAC are acutely aware of the inequalities of wealth and power in the world, and they are grateful for the support of Christian brothers and sisters, to whom they have felt a great attachment. Yet, there are murmurs of complaint too. Some say, "we have not benefited from the Anglican Communion as others have done." Others weigh up the debates within the Anglican Communion and take a pragmatic approach: "We are poor and if we stop working with the Episcopal Church, who will help us?" At the same time, the PEAC wants to be "evangelical" and its developing sense of identity brings it closer to other African provinces which claim to "evangelical." The PEAC is faced with a painful dilemma and tries to maintain a balanced position between extremes. It is a position full of ambiguity and uncertainty. If it is true that "we are not concerned by what is going on in the Anglican Communion," it may be because we feel unable to address sufficiently the live debates within it.

## Conclusion

It is said that the twenty-first century will be the century of African energy, growth, and vision in the Christian church. Archbishop Rowan Williams noted during the All Africa Bishops' conference in Uganda that God raises up different countries and cultures in different seasons to bear witness to his purpose in a special way. He said, "If the churches of Africa are going to be for this time a city set on a hill, how very important it will be for the health and growth of all God's churches throughout the world that this witness continues at its best and highest." The question is how the PEAC will be a city set on a hill. That is, how will it develop a graceful interdependence and unity in faith and doctrine among Anglicans? How will it be faithful to the gospel in its historical and cultural context? And how will it face moral, doctrinal, social, and economic exigencies which demand discernment and response in order to maintain its identity as a Christian community?

## Bibliography

Agape manual. 1994 Swahili, 2004 French. *Rejouis-toi dans ta jeunesse*. Kampala: Leading Edge.

Agape manual. 2006, 1st ed.; 2008, 2nd ed. *Jeunes, avec Dieu reconstruisons notre beau pays*. Lubumbashi: Mediaspaul.

Agape manual. 2009. *Debout Jeunes Congolais, avec Dieu luttons contre la pauvreté en RDC.* Foreword by the minister for youth and sport. Lubumbashi: Mediaspaul.

Ande, Titre. 2009. *Leadership and Authority, Bula Matari and Life Community Ecclesiology in Congo*. Oxford: Regnum International.

Ande, Titre. 2010. *A Guide to Leadership*. London: SPCK.

Balufuga, Dirokpa Fidèle. 1982. Autonomie de L'Eglise Anglicane du Zaire. *Fraternité, Bulletin d'Information Provincial*. 3e trimester 1982.

Balufuga, Dirokpa Fidèle. 2001. Liturgie Anglicane at Inculturation Hier, Aujourd'hui et Demain: Regard sur la Célébration eucharistique en République Démocratique du Congo. PhD Université Laval.

Barrett, David, George Thomas Kurian, and Todd M. Johnson. 2001. *World Christian Encyclopaedia: A Companion Study of Churches and Religions in the Modern World, AD 1900–2000*, vol. 1. Oxford: Oxford University Press, 211–6.

Congo Church Association http://www.congo-churchassn.org.uk/ Liturgy in Swahili and abridged text in English can be found on this website.

Lloyd, A. B. 1923. *Apolo of the Pygmy Forest*. London: CMS.

Lloyd, A. B. 1928. *More About Apolo*. London: CMS.

Lloyd, A. B. 1934. *Apolo the Pathfinder – Who Follows?* London: CMS.

Luck, Anne. 1963. *African Saint: The Story of Apolo Kivebulaya*. London: SCM.

Ridsdale, Philip. 1962. Report on Mboga, 1961. Church of Uganda archives, UCU, Mukono.

Roome, W. J. 1934. *Apolo, the Apostle to the Pygmies*. London: Morgan & Scott.

Semiliki Trust http://www.semiliki-trust.org.uk.

United Nations Statistics http://data.un.org/CountryProfile.aspx?crName=Democratic%20Republic%20of%20the%20Congo

Wild-Wood, Emma. 2008. *Migration and Christian Identity in Congo (DRC)*. Leiden: Brill.

Wild-Wood, Emma. 2011. Attending to Translocal Identities: How Congolese Anglicans Talk about their Church. *Journal of Anglican Studies*, vol. 9, no. 1, pp. 80–99.

CHAPTER 13

# The Church of the Province of the Indian Ocean

## Cameron J. Soulis

The Province of the Indian Ocean is made up of islands located off the eastern coast of Tanzania and Mozambique. The province, founded in 1973, covers the countries of Madagascar, Mauritius, and the Seychelles. There are seven dioceses in the province: five are on Madagascar, Mauritius is another, and the Seychelles forms the last diocese. The see of the province depends on where the primate resides. The current primate is the Most Rev. Ian Gerald James Ernest. Currently, the see is in Mauritius.

The Anglican presence in this province began in 1810 when the British captured Mauritius from the French. The British took control of the Seychelles from the French the next year. Initially, the Church of England sent chaplains to the colonial administrators; it was not until the 1830s and 1840s that missionary work began in Mauritius and the Seychelles. The first Anglican missionaries arrived in Madagascar in 1864. Both the Society for the Propagation of the Gospel (SPG) and the Church Missionary Society (CMS) sent missionaries to these islands. The Diocese of Mauritius (covering Mauritius and the Seychelles) was established in 1854. The Diocese of Seychelles was separated from it in 1973 when the province was formed. The Diocese of Madagascar was established in 1874. This diocese was divided into three in 1969, and another two dioceses were created in 2003 (CAPA 2012).

The population of this province is ethnically and religiously diverse. The people of these islands are of Indian, Arab, African, Asian, and European descent. As a result, there is a mix of cultures and faiths. The CIA Factbook website lists the following faiths present among the populations of these countries: indigenous religions, Hindu, Muslim, and Christian (both Roman Catholic and Protestant). Whereas Christians are in the minority in Mauritius and Madagascar (in Mauritius, the population is majority Hindu, and in Madagascar, the population is majority indigenous religions), they are in the

*The Wiley-Blackwell Companion to the Anglican Communion*, First Edition. Edited by Ian S. Markham,
J. Barney Hawkins IV, Justyn Terry, and Leslie Nuñez Steffensen.
© 2013 John Wiley & Sons, Ltd. Published 2013 by John Wiley & Sons, Ltd.

majority in the Seychelles. Roman Catholics make up the largest percentage of Seychellois at 82 percent (CIA Factbook Seychelles 2012). Anglicans are in the minority in all three countries. The Anglican Communion website reports 120,000 Anglicans among the nearly 7 million Christians in this province (Anglican Communion 2012). Taylor, in his history of the Anglican Church in the Seychelles, states that growth of the Church of England was slow in Mauritius and the Seychelles in the first 40 years of British control. Among the reasons he gave for this was a lack of funds for clergy and for building churches or schools. Another was the tendency of the French inhabitants to stick with their Roman Catholicism (even in the years when there were an inadequate number of Roman Catholic priests), and an unwillingness on the part of the Anglicans to proselytize Roman Catholics. As a result, the number of Anglicans on Mauritius and the Seychelles are small (Taylor 2005, 134–7). Not surprisingly, the Anglican Church in this province is committed to ecumenical and interfaith dialogue (WCC 2012a).

Clergy in this province are trained at St. Paul's Theological College in Madagascar, St. Paul's College in Mauritius, and St. Philip's Theological College in Seychelles. The dioceses have a number of ministries for social benefit. The Diocese of Seychelles has men's ministry, youth ministry, and friends of prison ministry (Diocese of Seychelles 2008). The church in Madagascar runs schools, orphanages, and health centers. The church in Mauritius runs centers for the care of the elderly, blind people, and unwanted children, plus two secondary schools. Also, the Mothers' Union is present and active in the dioceses of Seychelles and Mauritius (CAPA 2012).

## Bibliography

Anglican Communion. 2012. Provincial Directory: The Church of the Province of the Indian Ocean. Accessed August 20, 2012. http://www.anglicancommunion.org/tour/province.cfm?ID=I1.

Central Intelligence Agency (US). July 5, 2012. Seychelles. *The CIA World Factbook.* Accessed August 20, 2012. https://www.cia.gov/library/publications/the-world-factbook/geos/se.html.

Central Intelligence Agency (US). July 17, 2012. Madagascar. *The CIA World Factbook.* Accessed August 20, 2012. https://www.cia.gov/library/publications/the-world-factbook/geos/ma.html.

Central Intelligence Agency (US). July 31, 2012. Mauritius. *The CIA World Factbook.* Accessed August 20, 2012. https://www.cia.gov/library/publications/the-world-factbook/geos/mp.html.

Council of Anglican Provinces of Africa (CAPA). 2012. Province of the Indian Ocean. Accessed August 19, 2012. http://www.capa-hq.org/index.php/provinces/indian-ocean.

Seychelles, Diocese of. 2008. Welcome to Anglican Diocese of Seychelles. Accessed August 19, 2012. http://netministries.org/frames.asp?ch=ch00757&st=Seychelles&name=Anglican%20Diocese%20of%20Seychelles&city=Victoria.

Taylor Donald. 2005. *Launching Out into the Deep: The Anglican Church in the History of Seychelles.* Victoria, Seychelles: The Board of Church Commissioners, Diocese of Seychelles.

World Council of Churches. 2012a. Church of the Province of the Indian Ocean. Accessed August 19, 2012. http://www.oikoumene.org/en/member-churches/regions/africa/

madgascar/church-of-the-province-of-the-indian-ocean.html.

World Council of Churches. 2012b. Theological Colleges in Africa. Accessed August 21, 2012. http://www.oikoumene.org/en/programmes/education-and-ecumenical-formation/ecumenical-theological-education/wcc-partners-in-theological-education/international-directory-of-theological-schools/theological-colleges-in-africa.html?tx_pagebrowse_pi1[page]=3&cHash=eb30bfc6e48f235a632b56924810a81b.

# CHAPTER 14
# The Anglican Church of Kenya

## J. Barney Hawkins IV

The Anglican Church of Kenya has a long and rich history and traces its beginnings in the middle of the nineteenth century to the arrival of Anglican missionaries at the port city of Mombasa on the Indian Ocean. In 1895, the first Africans were ordained to the priesthood. The Anglican Church grew rapidly in Kenya, due in part to mass conversions associated with the East Africa Revival Movement. The first Kenyan bishops were consecrated in 1955. Five years later, the Anglican Church of Kenya became part of the Province of East Africa. In 1970, the Anglican Church of Kenya became one of the provinces of the Anglican Communion. The constitution for the new province was revised in 1979. The constitution set forth the boundaries of the several dioceses in the province, including the Diocese of Nairobi, the Diocese of Mombasa, the Diocese of Mount Kenya South, the Diocese of Mount Kenya East, the Diocese of Nakuru, the Diocese of Maseno South, and the Diocese of Maseno North (Church of the Province of Kenya 1979). In 2012, there are 30 dioceses in a geographical area of 580,400 sq km (Anglican Communion website 2012).

It is estimated that there are over 1,500,000 Anglicans in Kenya with its population of 31,000,000. This chapter will consider the early days of the Anglican Church of Kenya and its association with the slave trade; the liturgical renewal which has honored the indigenous culture; and the church's conversation with Islam in diverse, modern-day Kenya.

The early history begins with a moving story about a young boy of the Yao people who was sold into slavery by his uncle at the slave market on the island of Zanzibar in Tanzania in about 1840. The ship bearing the slave-to-be was intercepted by the British Royal Navy. Zoom forward. In 1904, a "revered clergyman died at Rabai, near the town of Mombasa, Kenya" (Reed 1997, 1). This early saint of the Kenyan Church, one of the first African clergy in Kenya, adopted the name William Jones. His African name is lost to history. A contemporary of the Rev. William Jones was the Rev. Ishmael Semler.

*The Wiley-Blackwell Companion to the Anglican Communion*, First Edition. Edited by Ian S. Markham, J. Barney Hawkins IV, Justyn Terry, and Leslie Nuñez Steffensen.
© 2013 John Wiley & Sons, Ltd. Published 2013 by John Wiley & Sons, Ltd.

These two priests anchor Anglicanism in Kenya and with them the story of a dynamic church begins.

The Church Missionary Society (CMS) advanced the Christian faith in Kenya. From 1841 to 1871, the leader of the CMS was Canon Henry Venn. He "became famous for his policies of establishing a 'Native Church'." Venn was convinced that the Anglican Church would prevail if it were led, organized, and supported by the local people. For decades, there was tension in the Anglican Church of Kenya between those who supported a church led by African leaders and those who sought a European-dominated Anglican mission in Kenya. If the CMS and other missionary organizations were divided on best practices for the fledgling Anglican Church of Kenya, they were united in their determination to the end the slave trade in East Africa. The British government succumbed to pressure from the CMS and, in 1873, the Frere treaty was signed. Unfortunately, the treaty addressed the export of slaves. Domestic slaves were still allowed (Reed 2003, 25).

The CMS connected its concerns about the slave trade to the need for education. In 1888, the Rev. E. A. Fitch promoted theological education for freed slaves and, for the first time, there was training for the ordained ministry in Kenya. In 1903, the cornerstone was laid for St. Paul's Divinity School at Frere Town, Mombasa. That divinity school is now St. Paul's University, an ecumenical institution serving and encouraged by the National Council of Churches of Kenya.

The Frere Treaty and the establishment of St. Paul's Divinity School may have been the high point of the relationship between the CMS and African Anglicans. By the end of the nineteenth century, cohabitation was stormy between the Europeans and the Africans. One sticky point was that the CMS in London saw itself as having authority over the bishops in matters relating to the local church and the selection of ordinands. "The heavy-handed control from London is evident in such insignificant details as a query over the price of a door paid for a building at Frere Town, and the purchase price for a donkey" (Reed 1997, 132). The paternalistic rule by the CMS and other missionary organizations of the Anglican Church in Kenya, however, would not last forever; yet, Kenyan bishops were not consecrated until 1955.

The late-twentieth, early-twenty-first century Anglican Church in Kenya is theologically conservative and concerned about the state of the Anglican Communion. Of course, this could be said for most of Africa. The late-nineteenth-century missionaries who served in Kenya were influenced by the likes of the American evangelist D. L. Moody. Moody was well known in the United States but also had an impact on students being educated for the mission field at such places as Cambridge University in England. Moody took a pre-millennial view that the coming of God's Kingdom would provoke a crisis. Jesus Christ would come as Judge and Savior, and rule for a thousand years on earth. All that was not of the Kingdom would be destroyed. Society is corrupt for those who hold a pre-millennial viewpoint, and the only hope is the intervention of God in human history, the *parousia* of Christ. Such a theology of the end of history has shaped Kenyan theology and the way the church should serve in the world. The Anglican Church in Kenya is both evangelical and fundamentalist. The East Africa Revival Movement is rooted in a pre-millennial view of history and the final, triumphant reign of God on earth as God reigns in heaven.

Kenya's Anglican theology has influenced its liturgy and worship. In Kenyan worship, Anglican identity meets and embraces the African tradition. The Prayer Book is a blend of cultures African and European. "African oral culture and memory have much to teach the Western church" (Kings and Morgan 2001, 6). In "A Kenyan Service of Holy Communion," the Prayer of Thanksgiving reveals the collaborative, interactive nature of Eucharistic worship in Kenya. There are a series of questions and answers for the Sanctus and Benedictus:

"Is the Father with us? (Minister)
He is. (People)
Is Christ among us? (Minister)
He is. (People)
Is the Spirit here? (Minister)
He is. (People)
This is our God. (Minister)
Father, Son and Holy Spirit. (People)"

The Anglican Church of Kenya has found a distinctive voice in its liturgy and, particularly, in its music. The rich culture of Kenya is clearly celebrated in Kenya's Anglican churches. Biblical truths are interpreted by the local experience. The Anglican Church of Kenya is very much an African Church – which understands its European heritage and legacy.

Anglicanism flourishes in Kenya, which is culturally and religiously diverse. Kenya has always been a multi-faith society. The "return to fundamentalism in Islam and the missionary zeal which accompanies it" have made conversations between Christians and Muslims much more difficult (Church of the Province of Kenya Provincial Unit of Research 1994, 177). Anglicans engage Muslims in Kenya – yet are clear about its own community of faith and the need to be "the light of the world and the salt of the earth" (Church of the Province of Kenya Provincial Unit of Research 1994, 178). Both the value of conversation and the need for conversion motivate Anglicans in their discourse with Islam.

## Bibliography

Anglican Communion website. 2012.

Church of the Province of Kenya. 1979. *Constitution.*

Church of the Province of Kenya Provincial Unit of Research. 1994. *Rabai to Mumias: A Short History of the Church of the Province of Kenya 1844 to 1994.* Nairobi: Uzima.

Kings, Graham and Geoff Morgan. 2001. *Offerings from Kenya to Anglicanism: Liturgical Texts and Contexts Including "A Kenyan Service of Holy Communion".* Cambridge: Grove Books Limited.

Reed, Colin. 1997. *Pastors, Partners and Paternalists: African Church Leaders and Western Missionaries in the Anglican Church in Kenya, 1850–1900.* Leiden: E. J. Brill.

Reed, Colin. 2003. *Founded in Faith: The Early Years of the Anglican Church in Kenya.* Nairobi: Uzima.

# CHAPTER 15

# The Church of Nigeria (Anglican Communion)

## Benjamin A. Kwashi

## Introduction

The gray old cathedral at Canterbury has witnessed many wonderful events, but St. Peter's Day, 29 June, 1864, will rank as a red-letter day in its annals. It was no ordinary occasion. Special trains were run from London and elsewhere. This letter patent was read: "We do by this our licence, under our Royal signet and sign manual, authorize and empower you, the said Samuel Adjai Crowther, to be Bishop of the United Church of England and Ireland, in the said countries of Western Africa beyond the limits of our dominions." (Page 1908, 186—8)[1]

The consecration of Bishop Samuel Adjai Crowther was a turning point in the history of the Anglican Church and a landmark moment in the story of the Christian gospel in Africa, and in Nigeria in particular. Could an African be capable of holding such a high office? Could, indeed should, such a risk be taken? A black man would be able to withstand the virulent attacks of malaria better than a white man, but could a black man's brain, integrity, and personality be equal to the task? Such were the concerns, the questions, and the matters for debate in the early 1860s, as the first-ever black bishop was consecrated. Crowther's nomination had been strongly urged by Henry Venn, the Church Mission Society (CMS) general secretary (1842–1872), but had met with stiff opposition, especially from white priests serving in Nigeria. To appoint a black bishop over a white priest was unheard of: the Europeans would lose prestige!

Crowther's mandate was to be bishop "in the countries of Africa beyond the limits of our dominions," that is, excluding those areas which were already British colonies, or dominated by white workers, notably (in Nigeria) Lagos, together with Abeokuta and

---

[1] Page, J. 1908 *The Black Bishop Samuel Adjai Crowther*. London: Hodder & Stoughton. Reprinted in 1979. Connecticut: Greenwood Press, pp.186–8.

---

*The Wiley-Blackwell Companion to the Anglican Communion*, First Edition. Edited by Ian S. Markham, J. Barney Hawkins IV, Justyn Terry, and Leslie Nuñez Steffensen.

Ibadan. This definition of his role ensured that expatriate staff and white clergy were not expected to work under the authority of a black bishop. The festering sore of this thoroughly unbiblical attitude again came to a head at the end of Bishop Crowther's ministry with the disgraceful, arrogant behavior of a group of young, inexperienced, white "missionaries" who seemed to think that their lack of experience and lack of understanding of language, culture, history, and tradition were somehow more than compensated for by their white skin which thus gave them authority to discredit and discard the life, work, and ministry of the elderly Bishop Crowther. To the glory of God, however, the seeds of an indigenous African church had been planted; it was this which ensured that, unlike the abortive short-lived work by Portuguese missionaries in Benin and Warri in the sixteenth century, and even the North African Church of the fourth century, Christianity had now come to stay.

It is noted with sadness, however, that even today a lack of trust, cooperation, care, and concern between the hundreds of tribes in Nigeria has slowed down or even destroyed the growth of the church. Augustine's fourth-century church failed to reach out to the surrounding indigenous peoples in their own language, and so the church eventually died. Today, it is still possible to find many "chaplaincy" churches situated in one part of the country but existing exclusively for people who come from a different region. How much more, sometimes obviously but sometimes as an underground current, has the antipathy between black and white continued to mar the spread of the gospel? Thank God that the white man brought the gospel to these shores; our gratitude for their sacrifice is endless. In time, however, the work of missionaries became intertwined with the advent of colonial power, with trade and commerce. Some trade was beneficial, some, such as the spread of alcohol, led to the destruction of lives and communities. Many who came as missionaries were wonderful, godly people, but some others, and many who came primarily as colonial officials or traders, refused to listen to, or be led by Africans. The work of mission was often directed by decisions made in far-away London, by those who had never set foot in Africa and who knew little or nothing about life here. The shift of authority from white to black, from expatriate to indigenous people, was bound to take time. Even today, the resentment on the one hand, and the ignorant arrogance on the other, may still be perceived, even if it is as an inherited, almost unconscious and unrecognized attitude. All such residual attitudes are a sore in the body of the church.

## The First Beginnings

The preface to the story of the Church of Nigeria began in 1841 with the British government's First Niger Expedition, which included among its personnel two from the CMS, Mr. Samuel A. Crowther and the Rev. J. F. Schön (seconded from the Basel Missionary Society). Despite elaborate plans and preparations, the expedition had to be aborted because so many of the European members of the party died of fever. What may be regarded as the real opening chapter of the story of the Anglican Church came in the next year, 1842, when Henry Townsend of the CMS left Freetown, Sierra Leone, and landed at Badagry before proceeding to Abeokuta. He was the first missionary in the Yoruba Mission. When he landed, he met the first Methodist missionary to Nigeria, the Rev. Thomas Birch Freeman, and they celebrated the Eucharist together under a tree on Christmas Day 1842. This is held to mark the establishment of the Anglican Church in Nigeria.

Crowther, meanwhile, having surprised and greatly impressed his English university examiners with his academic ability, was ordained deacon in England in 1843. This was almost exactly 21 years after he had been rescued as a small boy from a slave ship and put ashore at Freetown, Sierra Leone, where he had studied and eventually taught. After ordination, he quickly returned to Africa, stopping at Freetown, from where he joined a missionary party who reached Badagry in January 1845. From there, they moved to Abeokuta, where the work bore fruit and a number of other mission stations were opened, including Ibadan, Oyo, Ife, and Ilesha. When a mission party was sent from Britain in 1854, Crowther was asked to join them. This expedition proved much more successful than that of 1841, and they reached some distance beyond the confluence of the Niger and Benue rivers. Therefore, in 1857, a further mission was sent to the Niger River. Crowther was appointed to lead this mission: they were to establish the Niger Mission and evangelize the people. Crowther took with him six other African teachers and clergy. The Rev. J. C. Taylor, Catechist Simon Jonas, and three young traders (all Africans) were left at Onitsha, to establish a base there. The other members of the team continued up the Niger, starting mission work in various centers, including Rabba, the capital of the Nupe Kingdom. Before they could reach Jebba, their vessel struck a rock and sank, causing them to spend almost two years there before another ship could come for them. On their return, the work at Onitsha was found to have prospered and about 500 people were attending Sunday services. Thanks to the tireless travels of Crowther and his colleagues, the work was further consolidated by subsequent expeditions, often under difficult, exhausting conditions.

The vision of Henry Venn, the CMS secretary, was that as converts are gathered together into a congregation, the aim should always be to make them self-supporting, self-propagating, and eventually self-governing. Attention was therefore paid to the selection and training of local leaders, to education (for women as well as for men!), to healthcare and to trade. Crowther's work was consistently in line with this, but sadly, this vision died when Africa moved into the colonial era: racial pride took over and the prospects of an indigenous church receded.

In 1864, after many years of faithful missionary service under all kinds of conditions, Crowther was consecrated as bishop. Immediately thereafter, he returned to Sierra Leone and thence to Lagos. He made Lagos his headquarters, even though it was actually outside his diocese. From there, he continued his mission work, traveling up and down the Niger, a region which was not his by birth. Thus, the unwillingness of white mission personnel to have a black bishop over them led to an unsatisfactory situation whereby Crowther was excluded from work in the Yoruba mission (his native area) which was supervised by the English Bishop of Sierra Leone, and instead he, together with his assistants, was working as a missionary along the river, where there were the many peoples of the delta in the south, the Igbo in the middle, the Nupe and other more Islamicized peoples, including some Hausa, in the north. Nevertheless, much was achieved, except that the Niger diocese never became self-supporting and was completely financially dependent on CMS in London. Therefore, when the CMS finance committee was suddenly dominated by young, inexperienced, white, hotheaded missionaries, the bishop and the diocese were in a very vulnerable position. The resulting "Niger Purge," as it has come to be known, was a disaster and ruined the end of the elderly bishop's long and faithful service, "damaging black–white Church relations for many years all along the west coast, and ensuring a misguided caution whereby there would be no other African diocesan bishop for forty years, until another such landmark was consecrated in 1939, this time not in Canterbury Cathedral, but in St. Peter's Rome" (Hastings 1994, 392). Meanwhile, the area supervised by the bishop's son, the Ven. Dandeson Crowther, separated to become the "Niger Delta Pastorate," becoming reconciled with the main diocese only in 1933.

## Northern Nigeria

Towards the end of the nineteenth century, various small groups of Christians in England became concerned about the "Sudan belt" of Africa, and Bishop Tugwell made exploratory journeys, reaching Bida and Bassa country in 1895, Keffi in 1896, and the Bassa Komo area in 1897. In 1899, Dr. Miller and his party set out from England to Nigeria in the hope of evangelizing the Hausa people; at Lagos, they were joined by Bishop Tugwell. In 1900, the British Protectorate of Northern Nigeria was proclaimed, with Sir Frederick Lugard as the first high commissioner. Thus, the gospel and the colonial powers arrived in the north of Nigeria at about the same time. This was in many ways unfortunate, as the two were often presumed to be one. This opened the way to a mistaken understanding of the gospel, and of Christian behavior and morals, to an equating of Christianity with colonialism, and also to the notion that Christianity was primarily for the white man.

As Tugwell, Miller, and their party moved north, they were generally well received, even by the Emir of Zaria. Unfortunately, they did not stay long in Zaria, but against the advice of the emir and contrary to the wishes of Lugard, rushed on to Kano. In Kano, they were humiliated and summarily sent away. On their return to Zaria, their reception now was not so friendly, and they were requested to move further south. It has been suggested that the unsatisfactory relationship between Lugard and the missionaries dates from this time. In his speech at the installation of the newly appointed Sultan of Sokoto in March 1903, Lugard promised that his rule would be just and fair and that all men should be free to worship God as they pleased; the government would not interfere with the Muslim religion.[2]

The extent to which Lugard's policy assisted Islam and prohibited the spread of the gospel has been much debated. It is true that the Christian missions did not have enough resources to spread far and wide, and therefore it has been suggested that their being restricted to the "pagan" areas was actually beneficial. Lugard, too, was limited in his resources, but his wish to disturb things as little as possible and the resultant

---

[2] Parliamentary Papers. 1904. *LVII Northern Nigeria: Report for 1902*, Appendix 3, pp. 104, 106, quoted in Crampton 45.

policy of placing large numbers of "pagans" under Fulani district heads who were supported by the government must have been to the benefit of Islam. Much would seem to
depend on the understanding of "tolerance." To the Christian missionaries, this meant
freedom to practice and to propagate their faith, whereas to the Muslims it meant that
non-Muslims were free to practice their faith, but not to seek to evangelize others. It is
interesting to note that these differing attitudes are still present today in attempts to
legislate against proselytization of Muslims, against any criticism of Islam, and against
any perceived jokes about the Islamic faith (e.g., the debates over the "freedom clauses"
of the Serious Organised Crime and Police Act 2005 and the Racial and Religious
Hatred Act 2005 in the British Parliament (see Cox and Marks 2003, 132–3). Sadly, at
the time of Lugard, there may well also have been other more racist factors at work,
such as the idea that if the missionaries' system of education could be kept out of the
north, there would be little chance of the "natives" being able to take over administrative positions from the white men. Miller strongly criticized those who felt that Islam
was more suitable for "native subject peoples." He wrote, "It is surely necessary to be
convinced that Islam is more suitable for *everyone* before using a phrase suggestive of
contempt in speaking of its value to subject peoples."[3]

At the first International Missionary conference held at Lokoja in 1920, a series of
resolutions was agreed upon. The seventh read, "That this conference does not consider
that the pledge of non-interference with religion given by Government to the Moham-
medan rulers is in any way violated by the presence of Christian missionaries peacefully
and tactfully setting forth the claims of their faith."[4]

The extent to which the government officials may or may not have encouraged and
increased the emirs' opposition to the presence of missionaries will never be known,
but whatever the case, the policy of exclusion continued in general. Only in the early
1930s did the situation improve.

Lugard's term of office ended in 1906, but he returned in 1912 to assist in preparing
for the amalgamation of the various regions into the one country Nigeria, which came
into existence on January 1, 1914. Thereafter, the north and the south were under one
government, but some policies differed between the two regions. It would appear that
Lugard's successors and especially the colonial office were largely against the presence
of missionaries in the north. It is of course noted that missionaries were a potential
source of embarrassment to the government as they were the only people capable of
bringing to the attention of the public in Britain any act of injustice on the part of the
administration or the emirs!

### Zaria–Wusasa (see Kwashi 2000)

Zaria is one of the very old, walled cities of Northern Nigeria, ruled over by a Muslim
emir. Zaria and Kano were, and still are, two of the main Hausa-speaking Islamic
centers. Dr. Walter R. S. Miller spent his life working in and around Zaria and Kano,

---

[3] Miller, Walter R. 1947. *Have We Failed in Nigeria?* London: Lutterworth Press, p. 82, quoted in Crampton 49.
[4] CMS G3/A9/1910, no 74, Resolutions of United Missionary Conference no.7, quoted in Crampton 60.

before retiring to Bukuru, near Jos, where he died in 1952. He was responsible for the translation of the Bible into Hausa and for the fact that it uses Roman script, and not Arabic. Gradually, other missionaries joined him, including Guy Bullen (later bishop) and Max Warren, later general secretary of CMS. It was generally felt that the mission should move out of the city to a square mile of land which would be allocated to them at Wusasa (about three miles away). This did not meet with the agreement of the most senior missionary, Dr. Miller, and he long opposed the idea. Nonetheless, he eventually gave in and wrote (on March 21, 1926) to the Africa secretary of CMS headquarters, London, indicating his agreement but "not without much misgivings, to throw in my lot with Bullen and Warren to come to an agreement with Government on the lines suggested." According to the minutes of the executive committee of CMS in London, meeting on July 11, 1928, the members of that committee "record their approval of the proposal and authorize the Acting secretary of the Mission to go forward with the negotiations with the Nigerian Government to this end."

It may be noted that a major policy decision was taken, or at least given final approval, in London. No reference was made to ecclesiastical authority in Nigeria.

Work at Wusasa began in earnest in late 1929, with the building of a church, schools, and hospital. It was to this mission center that the Anglicans from Ngasland came some few years later. One of those who moved to Wusasa was Pa Yohanna Gowon (the father of Gen. Yakubu Gowon, later head of state), who went there with his family in 1936. He was employed, like certain other Ngas Christians, as an evangelist in that area.

### The plateau

"About the year 1904, a small band of young Cambridge men whose hearts had been moved by the call from unevangelized races associated themselves in an effort, independent of any other organisation, to plant a Mission in some place which had never been reached by the Gospel of Christ" (Stock 1916, 72). The impetus for this may be attributed in part to the Student Volunteer Conference held in Edinburgh in January 1904; the result was the formation of the Cambridge University Missionary Party (CUMP). This was an association formed among friends at Cambridge in which those who stayed at home agreed to support those who went to the mission field. The chosen sphere of work was the "Bauchi Highlands" in Northern Nigeria, an area now part of Plateau State. Of the two main centers of work, Panyam is some 80 kilometers from Jos, the present state capital, and Kabwir some 160 kilometers from Jos.

The CUMP took on an Anglican character and as such entered into a relationship with the CMS. The memorandum drawn up after a meeting between the officials of the two societies reads:

The C.U.M.P. propose that Northern Nigeria should be their first objective; that their Mission there should be conducted on Church of England lines; that their men should be as far as possible associated together in an assigned district; and that they should be on the roll of C.M.S. Missionaries, conform to its regulations and, under certain conditions, work under its administration. The C.U.M.P. will be free at any future time after due notice, to withdraw their men and money or to modify their agreement as may be mutually agreed upon.[5]

The first CUMP missionary to sail for Nigeria was the Rev. John Wheeler Lloyd, who left England on October 20, 1906, together with Dr. W. R. S. Miller. Lloyd spent some time in Zaria, learning the Hausa language, before proceeding to his area of assignment. The Rev. G. T. Fox left England in December 1906, and finally joined Lloyd in Panyam on Christmas Eve 1907. Missionaries from the Sudan United Mission (SUM – now "Action Partners") had arrived on the Plateau in 1904 and had done much good work, but had not reached Panyam or Kabwir, the main center of the Ngas people and the place which subsequently (1910) became a center of CUMP/CMS work.

Some years ago, the late Josiah Zhim (already an elderly man) related his memories of the first coming of white people to his village of Kabwir. It is interesting to hear this story in his own words:

We heard that men with white skins were conquering the land, and that they had more powerful weapons than any we had seen. One day a messenger came to tell us that a white man with a small force of soldiers was coming from Bauchi to visit Chief Bewarang. Bewarang consulted with his elders. Should they prepare to fight the stranger, or should they receive him in peace? They discussed what they had heard and decided that to act peacefully was the wiser course to take.

I can still remember something of that day. We all gathered round the sides of the big court-yard in the middle of the chief's compound. The stranger arrived with his soldiers, entered and talked with Bewarang and his men. We were all very frightened as we looked at the man's strange white skin, his queer clothes and the big white hat on his head. Little did we realize that in time to come we should be sitting down in white people's houses having fellowship with them because of our one heavenly Father!

The European left on friendly terms. The year, I believe was 1905. Our lives changed little, however, for the next two years; until the arrival of more strangers who brought news which was quite different from anything we had ever heard before.[6]

The next white man and the first missionary to reach Kabwir was Mr. T. E. Alvarez, the secretary of the Niger Mission of the CMS In order to decide whether or not to welcome him and his message, Chief Bewarang consulted his advisers who in turn consulted the Tuwan people who resolved the matter through an oracle: if a particular bird appeared during the next three nights to "coo," then there was danger and the message was to be rejected. If the bird did not appear, the conclusion would be that the stranger had come with good news from God. The bird did not appear, so the missionaries were

[5] CMS Archives: *Hausaland Mission*.
[6] Unpublished interview with Josiah Zhim, conducted by Miss E. O. Crane of SUM (date unknown, probably 1960s).

welcomed. As a result, a Yoruba man named Moses was sent to live and work amongst
the people. After some three years, the Rev. Lloyd moved from Panyam to Kabwir. He
took with him Dr. J. C. Fox, the younger brother of the Rev. G. T. Fox, who had left
England for Nigeria in November 1909.

Both these men made major contributions to the work of the gospel: in addition to
his translation work, the Rev. Lloyd was a committed evangelist, constantly going out
on preaching expeditions and living for some time at Per (Amper); Dr. Fox built at
Kabwir what was actually the first hospital in Northern Nigeria. Sadly, Rev. Lloyd died
at Kabwir of blackwater fever on October 20, 1916. Dr. Fox, after leave of absence to
serve in World War I, returned to Nigeria against medical advice, and died on August
16, 1919 (aged 37) at Panyam, trying to reach Kabwir. Meanwhile, his older
brother, the Rev. G. T. Fox had died at Kano on March 12, 1912, aged 31. The faith and
commitment of families such as that of the Fox brothers can only be wondered at.
When their father, Prebendary Fox heard that he had now lost two sons on the mission
field, he offered to finance another missionary who would go out to replace Dr. Fox. He
said, "It is probable that he contracted the fatal fever on his way up the river. Great as
the blow is to us, I mourn as much the loss to the Mission. The call of Africa was upon
him. But the Great director of all Christian missions has his plans, with which he works
his purpose out."[7]

The Rev. C. H. Wedgewood had first left England for Nigeria in 1907. He spent many
years at Panyam, and then at Kabwir. The Anglican Church at Panyam, named the
Church of St. John the Evangelist, opened at Christmas 1916: eight people were present
for Holy Communion; 229 attended morning service. Miss E. M. Webster ("Nakam")
came to Panyam in 1919 and spent a great many years there, refusing to move even
after the work was transferred to SUM.

Despite the initial acceptance of the missionaries, the relationship between the new
Ngas Christians and those who continued in their traditional pagan beliefs was not
always easy. This was highlighted by the problem brought about by an Ngas interpreter,
Mallam Goyan. Instead of translating correctly, he added his own words on top of what
the missionaries said concerning the punishment to be inflicted on anyone who committed adultery. This condemnation of adultery was in fact helpful to the promotion of
Christianity because traditionally any Ngas person who stole or who committed adultery was cast out of the tribe. Later, however, when Goyan himself committed adultery
and did not receive the punishment he (but not the missionaries) had stipulated, the
Ngas people turned against the missionaries: they were apparently condoning a recognized sin, and on top of that they had not kept their word. The Ngas people were so
noted for keeping their word that the Hausas had a saying, *Aska daya, magana daya*, that
is, "one tribal mark (which was what the Ngas had), one word." This situation therefore
resulted in a large-scale return to traditional religion. The chief, however, refused to
break his word and so refused to give up his Christian faith, choosing instead to give up
the chiefdom[8].

[7] Notice of the death of Dr. J. C. Fox in *the C.M.S. Gleaner* for October 1, 1919, p.138.
[8] It is interesting to note that today there are three young ordained Anglican clergy from this family, one of
whom (a great-grandson of Chief Bewarang) is presently Bishop of Langtang.

From the outset, the CUMP had been concerned about teaching the people to read and write, to provide education, and to train evangelists. In addition to the provision of medical care, they also helped with the digging of bore holes and the planting of fruit trees and various improved crops.

Eventually, the acute shortage of European staff was such that an approach was made by CUMP, through CMS, to the SUM, concerning a possible take-over of the work at Panyam and Kabwir by the SUM. This was eventually agreed upon, and the transfer officially took place on April 19, 1930. It should be noted that these negotiations and decisions were made without reference to the local people, or to the diocesan authority. The diocesan authority was based far away in Lagos (with an assistant bishop at Ilorin), but following on from the first baptisms in Kabwir in October 1913, Bishop Tugwell had confirmed 22 persons including seven young married couples in Kabwir in April 1915. Confirmations were also held in Panyam on various occasions including 1915 and 1918, and in 1922 Bishop Melville-Jones visited Panyam on a motorbike. This means that the work in this area was by no means unknown to the Anglican authorities in Nigeria. At the time of transfer, there were some 48 communicant members at Panyam, and 101 at Kabwir.

The Ngas people in particular did not like the handover to SUM. Many of them walked over 400 kilometers to Zaria, the headquarters of the CMS in Northern Nigeria, to register a protest before Bishop Alfred Smith. A considerable number moved from the Plateau to Zaria and Wusasa to live and work there.

## The Province of West Africa

Until 1951, the two dioceses in Nigeria (Lagos covering the whole of the north as well as Yoruba land), together with the dioceses of Sierra Leone, Accra, Gambia, and Rio Pongas, were under the supervision of the Archbishop of Canterbury. In 1951, however, they were constituted into the Province of West Africa, under the leadership of Archbishop Leslie G. Vining. This province stretched over the entire area of Anglophone West Africa and included hundreds of different tribes, languages, and cultures, as well as different styles of churchmanship. When inaugurating the province, Archbishop Geoffrey Fisher predicted that the province was to become the mother of new dioceses and new provinces. The speed with which this has become true has increased as the years have passed by!

In 1945, the whole of Northern Nigeria was constituted into an archdeaconry; in January 1950, this was divided into the two archdeaconries of Kano and Jos. The first ordination of men from the Plateau area, however, did not take place until 1976 when the Rt. Rev. M. K. Maza and the Ven. D. Sila were ordained as deacons.

Crowther had been consecrated bishop in 1864, and it had been expected by many that another African would succeed him. No other African was consecrated bishop until 1952, when Bishop A. B. Akinyele was appointed to the see of Ibadan, and Bishop Dimieari to that of Niger Delta. By this time, the number of dioceses was beginning to increase, as may be seen in the following table:

**Table 15.1:**  Timeline of the creation of dioceses in
Nigeria 1919–1977.

| Year | Dioceses created | Total |
|------|------------------|-------|
| 1919 | Lagos | 1 |
| 1922 | Diocese on the Niger (1864) | 1 |
| 1952 | Niger Delta; Ibadan; Ondo-Benin | 3 |
| 1954 | Northern Nigeria | 1 |
| 1959 | Owerri | 1 |
| 1962 | Benin | 1 |
| 1966 | Ekiti | 1 |
| 1970 | Enugu | 1 |
| 1972 | Aba | 1 |
| 1974 | Kwara; Ilesha | 2 |
| 1976 | Egba-Egbado; Ijebu | 2 |
| 1977 | Asaba | 1 |
| | **TOTAL** | **16** |

Nigeria is itself a large country, covering over 923,750 sq. km. (with a population in 2011 of over 150 million). It must therefore be recognized that the size of some of these dioceses, and the consequent determination needed by the bishop to supervise the entire area under his charge, was still very demanding. The following extract from the farewell address in 1996 of the then Bishop of Kaduna (formerly Bishop of Northern Nigeria) speaks for itself:

I was enthroned on 6th of July, 1975. . . . In the 1978 Lambeth Conference, I uniquely stood alone by the map of my Diocese, the whole of the geographical and political area known as Northern Region less what we now have as Kwara and Kogi States, with people asking if I had aeroplanes that I travelled with to reach parts of my diocese. But in my bid to cover every part of the diocese as much as was then practicable, I went by air, rail, motor cars of various types, sometimes on foot where roads were not available which involved having to wade bare-footed across streams where bridges did not exist, and my request for a Land Rover turned down. 1980 saw the first division of the extensive Diocese of the North into three, by carving out Kano and Jos Dioceses, leaving the residue as Kaduna Diocese. In 1982 the Diocese of Abuja was created with me as the supervising Bishop. So it was again that at the 1988 Lambeth Conference I had to carry the flags of two Dioceses, and so was again faced with having to explain to those who asked, how I was able to own and run two dioceses. In 1989, the Diocese of Abuja was formally inaugurated after the consecration of her bishop. The Decade of Evangelism coupled with the progressive vision of the Archbishop, the Most Rev. J. A. Adetiloye saw the consecration of eight Bishops for eight Missionary Dioceses, with another one for Kano Diocese, But the recent consecration of 5 other bishops for 5 newly created Missionary dioceses further puts the church of Nigeria (Anglican Communion) ahead of all other Denominations in expansion through-out the country, in fact she has been ably described as the fastest growing Church in the world.

And so it is . . . that the Diocese handed to us as one by the Province of West Africa under the Arch-Episcopacy of the then Archbishop of West Africa, the Most Rev. Moses Omobiala Scott, is what I now leave for the Church of Nigeria (Anglican communion) as 17 Dioceses. Yes, this is the Lord's Doing, and it is marvellous in our eyes. (Ogbonyomi 1996, 8–9)

## The Province of Nigeria

According to the constitution, any group of four contiguous dioceses could become a province, and therefore, on February 24, 1979, the Province of Nigeria was born with the Most Rev. Timothy O. Olufosoye as the first archbishop. His pioneering work bore much fruit and after his retirement he was followed by the man who has been rightly called the Visionary Primate, The Most Rev. Joseph Abiodun Adetiloye, *DD* (1988–1999). Adetiloye was determined to open up unreached areas to the gospel as part of the church's response to the Decade of Evangelism proclaimed at Lambeth in 1988. A significant achievement of his tenure was the creation of ten missionary dioceses in 1990 (namely, Minna, Kafanchan, Katsina, Sokoto, Makurdi, Maiduguri, Bauchi, Yola, Calabar, and Uyo), and the subsequent creation of three internal provinces covering the three broad geographical regions of Nigeria. These earned the Church of Nigeria the reputation of being the fastest-growing province in the Anglican Communion.

In March 2000, the Most Rev. Peter J. Akinola, *DD, CON* (2000–2010) was presented as the third primate of the Church of Nigeria, Anglican Communion. On the assumption of his primacy of the church, Archbishop Akinola made clear his commitment to pursue evangelism vigorously, and the number of dioceses rose astronomically from 76 in year 2000, to 121 in May 2007, and 164 in 2011! Some were initially created as "missionary dioceses," that is, they received financial support from an older diocese or from another source for an initial period. The following table shows the timeline of the creation of these dioceses, in the period 1980–2009.

In addition to the creation of more dioceses, the creation of more provinces assisted episcopal supervision by reducing some of the traveling with the attendant hazards and dangers of the roads, and also making administration more localized and therefore easier. At first, the country was split into three provinces on September 20, 1997: Province One, consisting of the dioceses in the west, was headed by Archbishop Adetiloye, who remained Primate of All Nigeria; Province Two, consisting of the Eastern dioceses, had the Rt. Rev. Ben. Nwankiti of Owerri and, after his retirement in 1998, J. A. Onyemelukwe, Bishop on the Niger, as archbishop; while Province Three, consisting of the northern dioceses, had the Bishop of Abuja, the Rt. Rev. Dr. Peter J. Akinola, as archbishop. Subsequently, for the sake of evangelism and for ease of administration, a ten-province structure was proclaimed at the Cathedral Church of Christ, Marina Lagos, on January 19, 2003. The provinces were: Lagos, Ibadan, Ondo, Bendel, the Niger, Niger Delta, Owerri, Abuja, Kaduna, and Jos. Four more provinces were subsequently proclaimed: Lokoja, Kwara, Aba, and Enugu, giving a total of 14.

The mission to the Province of Congo began in 2005, with the Rt. Rev. A. Olaoye as the missionary.

**Table 15.2:**    Timeline of the creation of dioceses in Nigeria 1980–2009.

| Year | Dioceses created | Total |
|------|------------------|-------|
| 1980 | Kano; Jos; Warri | 3 |
| 1983 | Akoko; Owo; Akure | 3 |
| 1984 | Remo; Okigwe-Orlu | 2 |
| 1987 | Awka; Osun | 2 |
| 1989 | Abuja | 1 |
| 1990 | Egbado; Ife; Minna; Kafanchan; Katsina; Sokoto; Makurdi; Maiduguri; Bauchi; Yola; Calabar; Uyo | 12 |
| 1992 | Mbaise | 1 |
| 1993 | Oke-Osun; Sabongidda-Ora | 2 |
| 1994 | Okigwe North; Okigwe South; Umuahia; Ukwa; Nsukka; Lokoja | 6 |
| 1995 | Ikale-Ilaje | 1 |
| 1996 | Kabba; Nnewi; Egbu; Niger Delta North; Kebbi; Dutse; Damaturu; Jalingo; Otukpo | 9 |
| 1997 | Abakaliki; Wusasa | 2 |
| 1998 | Ughelli; Ibadan North | 2 |
| 1999 | Offa; Ibadan South; Igbomina; Oji River; Ideato; Gombe; Niger Delta West; Bida; Gusau; Lafia; Lagos West; Gwagwalada; Ekiti West; Oleh | 14 |
| 2001 | Esan; Ika | 2 |
| 2003 | Oyo; Okrika | 2 |
| 2004 | Ahoada; Ekiti-Oke | 2 |
| 2005 | Kubwa; Idah; Isuikwuato; Arochukwu; Ikwuano; Ogoni; Badagry; Ogbomoso; Zonkwa; Western Izon; Aguata; Ijebu North | 12 |
| 2006 | Lagos Mainland | 1 |
| 2007 | Pankshin; Bukuru; Zaria; Kontagora; New Bussa; Omu-Aran; Ajayi Crowther; Oke-Ogun; Ifo; Akoko Edo; Etsako; Ogbaru; Enugu North (Ngwo); Awgu/Aninri; Ikwo; Ngbo; Afikpo; Isiala-Ngwa South; Etche; Nike; Aba-Ngwa North; Isiala-Ngwa; Ikwerre; Egba West | 24 |
| 2008 | Bari; Langtang; Kwoi; Kutigi; Jebba; Ekiti Kwara; Ijumu; Okene; Ife East; Awori; Ndokwa; Northern Izon; Ogbia; Ohaji/Egbema; On the Lake; Ihiala; Niger West; Mbamili; Oru; Osun North | 20 |
| 2009 | Sapele; Okigwe; Amichi; Udi; Eha-Amufu; Zaki-Biam; Gboko; Ikara; Ogori-Magongo; Ilesa-South; Ijesha North; Ilaje; Irele-Ese-Odo; Evo; Ikeduru; Osun North-East; Ile-Oluji; Doko; Ijesha North East; Ijebu South West; Igbomina West; Idoani | 22 |
| | Total | 145 |
| | Total dioceses as in July 2011, including those created before 1979 | 162 |

In his opening remarks at the standing committee of the Church of Nigeria, held in Ibadan in February 2006, the primate, the Most Rev. Peter J. Akinola, said, "I have just discovered that there are over twelve million Fulani herdsmen in various parts of this country who have not heard the gospel. As we speak, there are only 3,000 Fulani Christians in Nigeria of which Anglicans are said to number about 200. This is for me an indictment. Therefore we are poised to radically change the unacceptable situation.

I seek your understanding and mandate to create immediately a non-geographic Fulani Missionary Diocese." The "Nomadic Mission" was born with the Rt. Rev. Simon Mutum as bishop.

In America, there are Episcopalians who have found it increasingly difficult to identify with the churches of which they had formerly been a part. In the Episcopal Church in the United States, the divergence in Biblical teaching and the appointment of practicing homosexuals as bishops have raised alarms in some quarters. The Church of Nigeria has been determined to assist Nigerians who were clamoring for help. Announcing the formation of the Convocation for Anglicans in North America (CANA) in April 2005, Archbishop Akinola, the then primate, wrote, "Our intention is not to challenge or intervene in the churches of the Episcopal Church in the United States of America (ECUSA) and the Anglican Church of Canada but rather to provide safe harbour for those who can no longer find their spiritual home in those churches."[9] In November 2005, the Church of Nigeria entered into a covenant agreement with the Reformed Episcopal Church and the Anglican Province of America, two churches which had separated from ECUSA on doctrinal issues. Their bishops were supportive of the Nigerian initiative, but the need to have an American-based bishop for the growing CANA became increasingly apparent. The first CANA bishop, the Rt. Rev. Martyn Minns, was therefore consecrated on August 20, 2006.

## GAFCON

In view of the discussion in the preceding text, it is not surprising that the vast majority of the Nigerian Bishops attended GAFCON (Global Anglican Future Conference) 2008. The Primate of Nigeria at the time, the Most Rev. Peter J. Akinola, the chairman of GAFCON, said in his opening address on Sunday, June 22, 2008:

Our beloved Anglican Communion must be rescued from the manipulation of those who have denied the gospel and its power to transform and to save; those who have departed from the scripture and the faith "once and for all delivered to the saints" from those who are proclaiming a new gospel, which really is no gospel at all . . . In the wisdom and strength God supplies we must rescue what is left of the Church from error of the apostates.

Brethren, we are here

- Because we are bound together in a godly fellowship by the Gospel – the gospel that shaped the theological and ecclesiological foundations of our Church – the same gospel with its transforming power that made the difference in the lives of our heroes like Thomas Cranmer, William Wilberforce, the Clapham brothers and Ajayi Crowther.

[9] Periodical, *Church of Nigeria Today*, August 20, 2006.

- Because we are convinced that GAFCON is a veritable tool within the Communion which God is using to bring together all who are concerned not only about the need to preserve the faith, but also to persevere and bequeath a legacy of wholesome, undiluted faith to future generations of Anglicans. It is God's gift to the Anglican Communion and to the world.
- To draw fresh inspiration to enable us to "contend for the faith once and for all delivered to the saints" both for our sake and for the sake of future generations of Anglicans.
- Because we want to renew our commitment to our sacred duty to preserve and proclaim uncompromisingly, the undistorted word of God written to a sinful and fragmented world. GAFCON is a meeting of ordained and lay leaders concerned about the mission of the Church and how best to carry it out and be poised to address the ever-present challenges of self-reliance, good governance, overcoming corruption and to prepare a strong and stable platform for upcoming generations.
- Yes, GAFCON offers fresh hope for a meaningful spiritual haven for orthodox Anglicans who can no longer hold out and be truly Anglican under revisionist leadership.
- We are here because we know that in God's providence GAFCON will liberate and set participants [particularly Africans] free from spiritual bondage which TEC and its Allies champion. Having survived the inhuman physical slavery of the 19th century, the political slavery called colonialism of the 20th century, the developing world economic enslavement, we cannot, we dare not allow ourselves and the millions we represent to be kept in religious and spiritual dungeon.
- Because we know that together as lay leaders, clergy and bishops of our Church we can banish the errors plaguing our beloved Communion – for we will not abdicate our God-given responsibility and simply acquiesce to destructive modern cultural and political dictates.
- We are here because we know that in spite of the fractures in our Communion, as orthodox Anglicans, we have a future and so we are here in the holy land to inaugurate and determine the roadmap to that future.

And from what better place in the world could we take the fullest advantage of the most powerful reminders of the life and ministry of our Lord and only Saviour Jesus the Christ than here in the holy land where he was born, grew up, served; was killed, rose again for our justification, ascended to heaven, and now seated at the right hand of God the Father, interceding for us."[10]

As he concluded, Akinola emphasized again that all at GAFCON were Anglican Christians by conviction, determined to uphold the tenets of Anglican Biblical orthodoxy, but having no intention at all of starting another church. This remains the stand of the Church of Nigeria in its relationships with other churches in the Anglican Communion as well as with other denominations.

---

[10] http://www.gafcon.org/news/a_rescue_mission_-_archbishop_akinolas_opening_address.

## Vision and Challenges

When the Most Rev. Peter J. Akinola retired in 2009, he was succeeded as primate by the Most Rev. Nicholas D. Okoh, who was presented on March 25, 2010. In the *Nigeria Anglican Church Daily* (vol.1, no. 1) of September 14, 2010, the new primate wrote:

> I thank God for our former Primate, the Most Rev. Dr. Peter J. Akinola DD, who worked tirelessly during his tenure in office. He has indeed left a very big shoe for me to step into and fill. I believe that with God, we will improve on the legacy left behind. Towards this, I put together a committee to review the vision of the church and come up with a revised vision. This committee met over a period of time to deliberate and come up with this vision.

The overall vision statement of the Church of Nigeria remains as before:

> The Church of Nigeria shall be Bible-based, spiritually dynamic, united, disciplined, self-supporting, committed to pragmatic evangelism, social welfare and a Church that epitomizes the genuine love of Christ.

In order to implement this vision more effectively, the following have been established:

1. Directorate of Social and Political Affairs
2. Directorate of Women, Youth and Children
3. Directorate of Theological and Doctrinal Matters
4. Directorate of Mission and Evangelism
5. Directorate of Communication
6. Finance/Investment Committee
7. Committee on Ecumenical Relations
8. Committee on Global Inter-Anglican Relations
9. Committee of Reference
10. Liturgical, Prayer and Spirituality Committee
11. Committee on Social welfare and Emergency Relief
12. Vision Implementation and Monitoring Committee

### Mission

The Church of Nigeria has been called the fastest-growing Anglican Church, but it should be remembered that the population of Nigeria is also increasing rapidly, and recent figures show that the population of persons under 35 years of age is 50 percent of the entire population of the country.[11] Herein lies one of the greatest hopes for

---

[11] Kwashi, Benjamin A. 2011. *Bishop's Charge 2011*. Anglican Diocese of Jos.

Nigeria. Statistics put the youth in this country at between 60 and 70 million. This means that for a long time in the history of this country there will be a growing generation. That generation needs to be guided, nurtured, trained, and established on a firm foundation for the building of this nation. The church is therefore put in an advantageous position, and we must see the opportunity ahead and be willing to seize it for times like this. There is also data showing that the number of street children in Nigeria is over 10 million. The question is therefore: is the church running ahead of the population explosion, is it even keeping up with it, or is it lagging behind?

At the heart of what it means to be Anglican is a burning concern for mission. The Church of Nigeria is therefore not only encouraging all church members to be evangelists and missionaries in their own house, compound, village, or town, but is also training and sending missionaries further and further afield, for example, reaching into the nooks and crannies of the north of Nigeria and then from there over the border into Niger, Cameroon, and even Kazakhstan, with some missionaries working from their diocese and others through the Church of Nigeria Missionary Society (CNMS). For many years, there has been a Nigerian priest working with students at the Nigerian Chaplaincy in London.

### Youth

Within this most urgent need for mission and evangelism of a manner and type which will change the lives of churches, communities, and of the nation is the outstanding need for work among the youth. The youths are the foundation of our society. Their energy, inventiveness, character, and orientation define the pace of development and the security of the church and of the nation. In comparison with the West, Nigeria has a young church, young in its existence and young in its membership.[12] The youth are much involved in the life of the church, through such organizations as Anglican Youth Fellowship, EFAC, Boys' Brigade, Girls' Brigade, Girls' Guild, and other local organizations such as Youth on Mission. It is pertinent to note that the Nigerian Youth are very intelligent, highly endowed, but they need avenues, opportunities, and encouragement to put their talents into use. The range, extent, and magnitude of the problems which confront the Nigerian youth require a committed and determined effort on the part of the church and all stakeholders in order to help them to achieve their potential and to make them appropriate partners in the task of mission and development.

### Persecution

Outside the church, however, there still remains a vast throng of unemployed, unemployable, and leaderless youths who are bored and poverty-stricken. They are easily drawn into the excitement and potential profit of riots and corruption. The church in

[12] Kwashi, Benjamin A. 2007a. *The Anglican Communion: An African Perspective*. Paper presented at the Anglican Mainstream Fringe meeting at the General Synod of the Church of England held in York.

various parts of Nigeria, and particularly the north, is suffering persecution and hostilities and is not free to build structures or to buy land. This church is also facing the growth and development of Islam. Thousands have been killed, and hundreds of homes, businesses, and places of worship destroyed in a growing cycle of violence during the last quarter of a century or so. It is true that the situation is complex, but those who might claim that it is in no way religious have not taken cognizance of the many heartbreaking stories of those who have watched their father or other family member being viciously killed before their eyes, just because he or she refused to renounce Christ. In many places, there are local initiatives in reconciliation and reconstruction, but wounds take a long time to heal, and the fear and the threat remain.

## Education

The Church of Nigeria is much involved in education at primary, secondary, and tertiary levels. When the gospel first came to this country, the mission schools were in content and purpose theological. They taught children how to pray, taught children to have respect for humanity, for the environment, and, most of all, taught children how to serve God and one another. The graduates of these schools became catechists, evangelists, clinic attendants and dispensers, teachers, and assistants in various forms to the missionaries. Much later, the colonial officers came, and many were stark unbelievers and pagans. They required from the missionaries a manpower supply of honest, dedicated, and educated locals who had received mission education. These were to be clerks, storekeepers, and account clerks in the treasury. Such people were readily at hand and were faithful in the discharge of their duties – so much so that the colonial officers always looked up to the mission for the supply of manpower.[13] The church today is seeking to restore and develop these standards which were largely lost after many of the original mission schools were taken over by government in the 1970s. Most dioceses now have their own schools and colleges (those owned by the church as well as those owned privately by committed Christians) where children are not only given a good academic training, but are also brought up with Christian standards of morality, discipline, and courtesy. This is essential in a society where corruption is rife, bribery is a normal practice, and dishonesty is endemic.

## Social concern

The Church of Nigeria faces huge social concerns in addition to those mentioned in the preceding text, for example, poverty, orphans and widows, refugees, HIV/AIDS patients and their families, and the very many families who simply cannot afford education or healthcare. The church has set up various local, diocesan, and national specialist ministries to teach, to care for, and to support patients, families, and communities suffering

---

[13] Kwashi, Benjamin A. 2007b. *Raising the Bar in Good Governance: The Imperative of Deepening the Discourse for National Unity and Mutual Co-existence.* J. D. Gomwalk Memorial Lecture.

from AIDS. Similarly, specialist ministries and dedicated workers are assisting those whose lives have been devastated, their homes and livelihoods destroyed, and the loved ones massacred in riots and violence.

In a country as vast as Nigeria, it is perhaps not surprising that there are over 300 different racial and tribal groups, many of whom have fought each other in the past and who now have to learn to live and grow together. With the increase in transport and communications systems, the youth in particular are meeting and sometimes marrying their age-mates from many different regions and backgrounds, despite the difficulties of language. The church has a big role to play here as the gospel is the one unifying factor in the midst of this diversity. It is therefore essential that older "colonial" or the later "one tribe" churches open their doors and their hearts to all.

### Women's work

The Church of Nigeria is blessed with a very strong Mothers' Union (MU) and Women's Guild, with the Girls' Guild coming behind them. These organizations are very active in mission, in teaching and in social concerns, as well as in the development of the spiritual and Christian life of their members. The MU in Nigeria was founded by Mrs. Abigail Oluwole in 1908. Today, it covers the 14 ecclesiastical provinces of the Church of Nigeria, with Mrs. Nkasiobi Okoh, the primate's wife, as president of the women's and girls' organizations. Awareness is being created about the MU's concern for families, emphasizing the need for Christian homes. Vibrant activities, including training programs, are organized for both young and old, married and unmarried, female and male alike, all in an effort to equip and encourage people to build and maintain stable Christian homes. The MU has provincial trainers who organize leadership training programs for members, with skill acquisition for self-reliance always included in such training programs.

## Conclusion

The Church of Nigeria, with its estimated membership of over 18 million, is reputed to be the second-largest province in the Anglican Communion. This fact is not a reason for self-congratulation or a sense of achievement; rather, it must be a catalyst to spur us on to a greater dedication, a more urgent evangelism, and an ever-deeper concern for God's world. What has been achieved so far, in roughly 160 years, is just a beginning!

### Bibliography

Akamisoko, D. 2002. *Samuel Ajayi Crowther in the Lokoja Area*. Ibadan: Sefer.

Church of Nigeria. 1992. *150 Years of Christianity in Nigeria 1842–1992*. Souvenir Brochure. Nigeria: CSS Press.

Church of Nigeria. 2006. *Church of Nigeria Today*. August 20, 2006.

Church of Nigeria. 2010. *The New Vision of the Church of Nigeria 2010*. Uchac Productions.

Church of Nigeria. *Nigerian Anglican Church Daily*, vol. 1, no. 1.

Church of Nigeria. *Nigerian Anglican Church Daily*, vol. 1, no. 4.

Church of Nigeria. Church of Nigeria website: www.anglican-nig.org. Accessed 2011.

Church Mission Society 2007. *Yes*. May–August.

Cox, C. and J. Marks. 2003/2006. *The West, Islam and Islamism*, 2nd ed. London: Civitas.

Crowder, M. 1996. *The Story of Nigeria*. London: Faber & Faber.

GAFCON. 2008. *Pilgrimage Guide, 2008*. London, Latimer Trust.

GAFCON. GAFCON website: http://www. gafcon.org. Accessed 2011.

Hastings, A. 1994. *The Church in Africa 1450–1950*. Oxford History of the Christian Church. Oxford: Clarendon Press.

Kwashi, B. A. 2000. An Analysis of the Mission Movement from Plateau to Wusasa by the C.U.M.P./C.M.S. and its effect on Anglicanism in Plateau State Today. Trinity Episcopal School for Ministry.

Kwashi, B. A. 2007a. The Anglican Communion: An African Perspective. A Paper presented at the Anglican Mainstream Fringe meeting at the General Synod of the Church of England held in York on July 9, 2007.

Kwashi, B. A. 2007b. Raising the Bar in Good Governance: The Imperative of Deepening the Discourse for National Unity and Mutual Co-Existence. Joseph Deshi Gomwalk Memorial Lecture, Jos, Nigeria, 2007.

Kwashi, B. A. 2011. *Bishop's Charge 2011*. Nigeria: Jos Diocesan Printers.

Nwankiti, B. C. 1996. *The Growth and Development of the Church of Nigeria*. Owerri, Nigeria: Ihem Davis Press.

Ogbonyomi, T. E. 1996. *Bishop's Charge at Farewell Synod, 1996*. Nigeria: Kaduna.

Omoyajowo, A., ed. 1994. *The Anglican Church in Nigeria (1842–1992)*. Nigeria: Macmillan.

Page, J. 1908/1979. *The Black Bishop, Samuel Adjai Crowther*. London: Hodder & Stoughton. Reprinted Connecticut: Greenwood Press.

Stock, E. 1916. *The History of the Church Missionary Society*. Vol.4. London: The Church Missionary Society.

CHAPTER 16

# L'Eglise Episcopale au Rwanda

## Emmanuel Mukeshimana

## History of the Anglican Church of Rwanda

The Anglican Church of Rwanda has its origin from the time of British missionaries under the Church Missionary Society (CMS). It was under the Diocese of Uganda in 1897 when Alfred Tucker became the first Bishop of Uganda. The Diocese of Uganda at that time covered Western Kenya, Central, Western, and Eastern Uganda, part of Sudan, and Boga in Congo (Byaruhanga 2008, 16). In 1951, it became the Archdeaconery of Ruanda-Urundi with the assistant bishop, the Rt. Rev. Jim Brazier (UCU Archive 1950), who was replaced by the Rt. Rev. Lawrence Barham in 1964 with the mission to create two dioceses with native bishops, respecting the political boundaries. In 1965, the first Rwandan bishop was elected under the Anglican Church of Rwanda, "Eglise Anglicane du Rwanda" (EAR). In 1966, the church had its official inauguration as the Diocese of Rwanda with its native bishop, the Rt. Rev. Adony Sebununguri (Osborn 2000, 185). In 1979, the name was changed to "Eglise Episcopale au Rwanda" (EER). In May 1980, the Francophone Province of Burundi, Rwanda, and Zaire was inaugurated under the Congolese Archbishop Bezareli Ndahura of the Diocese of Bukavu. One year later, following his death, he was replaced by a Rwandan Bishop of the Diocese of Butare, the Most Rev. Justin Ndandali (Surton n.d.).

In 1992, Rwanda became a province of its own under the Most Rev. Augustine Nshamihigo. In 1998, the Most Rev. Emmanuel Kolini was enthroned as the second Archbishop of the Province of Rwanda. By November 2007, the college of bishops of the Episcopal Church of Rwanda changed the name of the province to the Province of the Anglican Church of Rwanda or "Province de l'Eglise Anglicane au Rwanda" (Anglican Communion 2011). On September 18, 2008, the province published its first constitution and canons, replacing those of the Francophone province, which were in use until then (PEAR, History 2011). On January 28, 2011, the Most Rev. Onesphore

*The Wiley-Blackwell Companion to the Anglican Communion*, First Edition. Edited by Ian S. Markham, J. Barney Hawkins IV, Justyn Terry, and Leslie Nuñez Steffensen.
© 2013 John Wiley & Sons, Ltd. Published 2013 by John Wiley & Sons, Ltd.

Rwaje was enthroned as the third primate of the Province of the Anglican Church of Rwanda.

## The Anglican Church of Rwanda and the Revival Movement

Two missionary doctors from CMS, Dr. Arthur Stanley Smith and Dr. Leonard Sharp, explored Rwanda between 1914 and 1916; these laymen wanted to start something different from the previous missionaries. They wanted to make a full impact upon the local community by working with the unevangelized people. Therefore, they formed Rwanda Mission, which covered Rwanda, Burundi, and south-western Uganda – "Kigezi-Ankole" (Ward 2011, 14). In 1922, along with Captain Holmes of the British Army, they established a mission in Rwanda. In 1925, they started a missionary station which included building a hospital at Gahini. By 1926, the first indigenous Christians were being baptized by the Rev. Harold Guillebaud.

Other missionaries joined the team of Rwanda Mission as time went on. These were the Rev. Bert Jackson, Dr. Joe Church, and a Ugandan of Rwandan origin named Kosiya Shalita, who remained at Gahini (Church 1981, 33). With the permission of the Belgian authorities, other missionaries spread throughout the country with new mission stations. In 1931, the Rev. Geoffrey Holmes moved to the west and began a mission center in Kigeme, while Dr. Tarbot was stationed in Shyira in the north (Osborn 2000, 57).

From 1929, the revival spirit grew tremendously. Joe Church, Bert Jackson, Lawrence Barham, and indigenous men, mainly Ugandans, such as Yosiya Kinuka, Blasio Kigozi, Erica Sabiti, Simeoni Nsibambi, William Nagenda, and Kosiya Shalita, started prayer meetings asking God for a revival in this region. It is said, "In Revival, God leads people to pray; and, when people pray, God brings Revival" (Osborn 2000, 70).

The revival which began in Gahini spread to all Eastern African countries with the help of Rwandan missionaries and indigenous people. It extended to Uganda, Kenya, Burundi, Tanzania, Sudan, and South Africa from 1937 to 1945. There was no segregation of religion, tribes, colors, or country. For many living through this period, this was seen as a period of unity.

At the end of World War II, the team was invited to England and Switzerland in 1947; to Switzerland, France, and Germany in 1949; to Malawi in 1951; to Angola in March 1952; and to India in May 1957. The team went to the United States from May to August 1953; to Israel in September 1953; India and Pakistan from January to April 1954; Ethiopia from November to December 1954; Angola in 1956; and to South America in January 1959 (Osborn 2000, 83–4). In all these remarkable tours of these men from the smallest country of East Africa, their aim was to preach the gospel of the crucified and risen Christ, and to bring their hearers to acknowledge and repent of their sin, be baptized by the Holy Spirit, and seek sanctification (Ward 2011, 5). Dr. Church gives a profound definition of revival in the following words:

A God-given hunger for more holiness and Christ-likeness had come upon us and what is known as revival followed. We looked at revival in panorama through the Old and New

Testaments. Mankind was created to walk with God. Revival is a walk or a way and we are people of the way. God is holy God. Man is made to walk with him. But fallen man has a bias to fall away and can only come back through repentance and cleansing from sin. The joy of that forgiveness and the new love for the Lord Jesus and for one's neighbor that follows is revival. It is 'the burning heart'; it is the 'first love'! (Church 1981, 126)

The fruits of revival are still seen worldwide. The children of the revivalists are active in today's church leadership in all denominations in Rwanda. In the Anglican Church of Rwanda, both the former and the current archbishops are descendants of this movement.

## The Influence of the Church on the Indigenous/Traditional Cultures and Religion

The Anglican Church of Rwanda has had a great impact on the people of Rwanda and the culture in general. Its impact is mainly related to the teaching of the revival movement. The church, since the beginning, wanted to have people changed socially and physically, as well as spiritually. It encouraged the indigenous people to be "saved" partly to get rid of poverty. They believed that people were poor because they were not repenting (Osborn 2000, 89). In what is a characteristic of many renewal movements, converts were encouraged to improve their lifestyle.

The church founders had a "three-legged-stool" picture to represent the main departments of the church's work and orientation. Their objectives were to have schools, hospitals, and churches. If a leg is missing, cracked, too long or too short, the stool is unsteady and unreliable to sit on (Church 1981, 24). In fact, before teaching the word of God, they would remove jiggers (little fleas that burrow into human flesh) from the people by distributing soft pins and teaching proper hygiene.

The church played a big role in education and health. In each missionary center, there was a school and a health center which have become today's prominent secondary schools and hospitals. The local people were able to study and got good health facilities. The elite leadership of the country was produced by the church's missionary schools.

The church encouraged indigenous people to attend Sunday worship regularly, get baptized and baptize their children, be married to one wife in the church, and to receive the sacrament of Holy Communion. The church emphasized that people should not rejoice in the mere fact that they have been baptized, or to see this as a guarantee of being saved. They were told to leave the traditional religion which was practiced by a large number of people in the region. Today, only one-tenth of 1 percent is practicing traditional religion (Theodora 2011).

The theology was a traditional evangelical approach. So, for example, on the question of salvation, the church emphasized that it was by the blood of Christ. Salvation comes only through being washed in the blood of Christ, the bloodshed on the cross of Calvary. The centrality of the atonement is a classic feature of evangelical revivalism (Church 1981, 128). From the perspective of the Rwandan church, this was in contrast to the traditional religion teaching in which, to get right with the gods, one had to sacrifice an animal and sprinkle the blood on the ground or in the water. The daily teaching of the church was about sin, repentance, and new birth, separation from traditional religion, the victorious life, and being filled with the Holy Spirit.

The church emphasized the need for the recognition of sin and for repentance to be done in a public confession. The experience of being saved in the blood comes through a deep awareness of one's own sinfulness, often expressed by the "Abakijijwe or Abalokole" (literally, "the saved ones," i.e., the people of the revival movement) as being broken. After recognizing sin, someone was to confess it in public to the brothers and sisters as witnesses. Going back to it would be a shame to the whole society. In the case of stealing or misappropriation of funds, it was expected that a personal confession be made to whoever was wronged, and that restitution be made (Ward 2011).

About family life, the church stood for the dignity of women. Monogamy is an important principle. Polygamy was strongly opposed and discouraged from the beginning of the revival movement. The openness, integrity, and honesty which characterize relations between the believers should apply even within the marriage relationship so that there is a real sharing, and mutual love and respect. The fellowship also gives women a role in their own right. Women can confess, testify, preach, and pray on an equal basis with the men. Today, several women are ordained to the priestly order in the Anglican Church of Rwanda.

Personal piety is stressed. The church sees all believers as a living testimony, which involves witness to those outside the fellowship, in the market-place, outside the church, at the bus garage, in the bus or taxi, outside the chief's enclosure, and in their homes. While speaking of the joys of salvation, they were also a decisive warning to those who were perishing. This was "walking in the light" which involves being completely open and honest about your attitude to your brother or sister, sharing what you have found offensive, and not holding grudges or letting them go undisclosed.

The church was distancing itself from the political arena but could give guidance in one way or another. The preaching of the gospel, since the time of the revival, was that the Abakijijwe had no political parties; whoever is saved was to be looked at as a brother or sister. The division of Hutu, Tutsi, and Twa which characterized Rwanda since 1959 did not affect the Abakijijwe. They went in a different direction, sheltering their neighbors and helping them to get refuge, and sometimes going with them to neighboring countries (Church 1981, 251). There is some evidence that the church plays an important role in finding peaceful resolutions to conflicts found in the Great Lakes Region.

## Anglican Church Before and After the Genocide

Though the church and the revival movement sowed good seeds in the people of Rwanda, the tensions between politicians and the divisions among the people of Rwanda persisted. That is why Rwanda had several ethnic killings where the Hutu killed their Tutsi neighbors and sometimes forced them to flee into neighboring countries. This is a tragedy. The precise causes of these ethnic killings are complex. A factor was the poor leadership which characterized Rwanda in 1994; this weak leadership led to the genocide, and a number of Christians and church leaders were involved (Byham 2011). Some bishops were implicated before and during the genocide. Yet, the church has been involved in the work of peace, healing, repentance, forgiveness, reconciliation, unity, and justice after the genocide (Mukeshimana 2006, 89).

Since the genocide, the Anglican Church has been at the forefront of working to resolve ethnic divisions and noticed the errors committed by its previous leadership. The former Archbishop of Rwanda, Emmanuel Kolini, for the first time as a senior church leader publicly apologized on behalf of the Anglican Church in Rwanda for its silence during the genocide.

This public confession brought all churches together to follow this trend, for Christians to acknowledge their participation and to point out what their fellow brothers and sisters did during the genocide. Through the community-based courts known as "Gacaca," Christians participated willingly in public confession "revival movement style," and now most of the prisoners have been tried, and the innocent have been set free.

The Anglican Church has initiated centers for seminars on healing, peace, forgiveness, reconciliation, and unity in every diocese. The National Unity and Reconciliation Commission is led by an Anglican bishop, the retired bishop of Shyira diocese, the Rt. Rev. John Rucyahana (Nurc 2011).

Upon his enthronement on January 23, 2011, Archbishop Onesphore Rwaje emphasized in his speech that the Anglican Church of Rwanda will make every effort to promote unity in Rwanda and spread it to all other religious denominations within the country and abroad. He said, "We will continue to collaborate with other religious Dominions, including Islam, in fighting against the HIV/AIDS scourge, dealing with its effects and caring for the already affected, the orphans and widows." The archbishop also offered this reassurance: "I desire to follow God's will in encouraging Christians to fight poverty and laziness, having people work hard and fight ignorance, beginning at home" (January 23, 2011).

It is widely recognized that the church is doing important work in terms of support programs for orphans, widows, and genocide survivors emotionally, spiritually, and physically. The church does this through prayer meetings, seminars, visitations; by providing school fees; and by building homes for those who do not have them or whose homes were destroyed during the genocide. Also, the role of the church extends to the integration of the repentant perpetrators who are released from jail so that they may live in harmony with the survivors.

In this respect, it is interesting how the church in Rwanda combines a commitment to traditional evangelism with social programs. For the leadership of the church, there is a recognition that although the church's first purpose is to spread the gospel of Jesus and care for the spiritual life of its people, the church feels that its mission must go beyond that, aiming also to meet the intellectual and physical needs of the people in the context of their own culture.

One good illustration of this commitment to social programs is the work on such problems as HIV/AIDS, malaria, and other diseases, through awareness campaigns and teaching. Its health centers and social workers are working tirelessly to fight such epidemics. The church is committed to providing spiritual and healthcare to all residents in order to care for the body and the soul. Christians are receiving bed nets to prevent mosquito bites, water purification syrup to get clean drinking water, and condoms as well as teaching on abstinence and faithfulness to fight the spread of HIV/AIDS.

## The Growth of the Province of the Anglican Church of Rwanda

At the time of its establishment in 1992, the Province of Rwanda had the four dioceses: Kigali, Butare, Syira, and Byumba. By 2011, it had seven more dioceses: Syogwe, Kigeme, Cyangugu, Kibungo, Gahini, Kivu, and Gasabo. Out of a population of 11 million, 16 percent are Anglicans (i.e., 1.8 million), dispersed all over the country.

The church is involved in education from nursery level to secondary schools. The province is also training its workers in Bible schools, and it is running a Bible college in Kigali, soon to become Rwanda Christian University. The church has hospitals and health centers in all corners of the country to provide good-quality health facilities. It ordains women and has lay leaders heavily involved in its services.

In every diocese of the province, there is the rural development service. The vision of this service is holistic and aims to meet the physical and spiritual needs of the people. It provides regular training of church and group leaders. Through this service, the church trains people in food security, agriculture, farming, and environmental protection. The core of this program is to develop spiritual church members who can self-sustain to help eradicate poverty.

## The Province of the Anglican Church of Rwanda and AMiA

The Anglican Mission to the Americas (formerly called the Anglican Mission in America) was formed in response to the appeal of American Christians who wanted freedom from what it saw as rebellion against biblical teaching. It started with Little Rock Church in Arkansas in 1997. With the growth and endless consultation meetings of primates in Singapore and Kampala in 1999, Archbishop Kolini of Rwanda and Archbishop Moses Tay of South East Asia consecrated the Rev. Chuck Murphy and the Rev. Dr. John Rodgers as missionary bishops to look after the congregations of the United States. The retired Archbishop of Rwanda, Emmanuel Kolini, said that he was originally moved to respond to America because of the pain suffered in the horrific genocide in Rwanda that left 1 million people dead in 100 days. In his view, the United States was experiencing a "spiritual genocide" while the world was watching, as was the case for Rwanda (The Amia, Rwanda Connection).

The AMiA leadership is fully under the Province of the Anglican Church of Rwanda where Chuck Murphy is the overseer of the organization as the primeval vicar appointed by the House of Bishops of the Province of Rwanda (Wikipedia 2011). In 2007, the Anglican Mission in the Americas, with the advice of the Archbishop of Rwanda, formed an umbrella of Anglicans detached from the Episcopal Church of America and Canada, the Anglican Church of North America (ACNA). The Anglican Mission is composed of the Anglican Mission in the Americas (AMiA), the Anglican Coalition in America (ACiA), and the Anglican Coalition in Canada (ACiC) (PEAR, the Amia 2011).

As part of the PEAR, the AMiA is against the ordination of homosexuals to the priestly order. It is a partner of the Anglican Church in the north of America (ACNA) but remains fully under the supervision, spiritually and canonically authoritative, of the Province of Rwanda while the ACNA responds directly to GAFCON (Wikipedia 2011).

While the Province of Rwanda ordains women into full priesthood with the ACiA and ACiC, AMiA ordains women to the diaconate. "The Anglican Mission in the Americas provides a way to maintain the integrity, and honor the consciences of those with differing positions and policies on women's ordination" (The Amia, Identity 2011). The Anglican Mission is under the authority of the Church of the Province of Rwanda, a member church of the Anglican Communion. Its clergy are ordained under the oversight of the Archbishop of Rwanda and other participating Anglican primates and Rwandan bishops.

The Anglican Mission would like to remain under the Rwanda province because of the global connection of close partnership in mission and ministry, fueled by a shared passion and vision for reaching those outside the church in the United States and Canada. Its main purpose is to reach out in evangelism without borders of culture and geographical limitations.

## The Doctrine, Faith, and Order of the Anglican Church of Rwanda

The Anglican Province of Rwanda is a church in full communion with all Anglican churches, dioceses, and provinces that hold and maintain the orthodox historic faith, doctrine, sacraments, and discipline of the one holy, catholic, and apostolic faith in the name of our Lord and Savior Jesus Christ.

The Anglican Province of Rwanda affirms the Holy Scriptures composed of 66 books of the Bible as the complete foundation and the authority of faith. They were inspired by God and contain all the necessary instruction required to lead a person to salvation. The church adopts the Christian faith, which is summarized in the Creedal Statements found in the Apostles, Nicene, and Athanasian Creeds. The church confirms the sacraments as instituted by our Lord Jesus Christ, namely, Holy Baptism and Holy Eucharist. Finally, the Anglican Church of Rwanda accepts the Thirty-Nine Articles of Religion as adapted through the ages (PEAR, Promulgation 2011).

## The Province of the Anglican Church of Rwanda and the Anglican Communion

The Anglican Province of Rwanda is a member of the Anglican Communion and has been from its creation. With the current controversial matter of blessing same-sex marriage facing the Anglican Communion, the Province of Rwanda is distancing itself from what is not "scriptural" in this trend. The House of Bishops in March 2009 pointed out that "we hold very strongly, that as we continue to engage and develop this Anglican Covenant, we shall be identified by the Anglican Faith and Practice, based upon the Holy Scriptures, Doctrine and the Anglican Tradition as passed on by the early church" (Anglican Communion 2011).

However, the Anglican Church of Rwanda is still a member of the Anglican Communion as jurisdiction, not in practice. After refusing to attend Lambeth 2008 and deciding to be part of GAFCON/Jerusalem, the Province of the Anglican Church of Rwanda is part of the growing conservative Global South Anglicans which in April 2011 have confirmed the creation of a general office in London and in Nairobi as a sign of a new Anglican movement split from Lambeth (GAFCON 2011).

## The Anglican Province of Rwanda and Current Issues

From its beginning, the Anglican Church of Rwanda has been strongly opposed to the ordination of any person of same-sex marriage (gay and lesbians). In 2009, the House of Bishops' declaration made it clear that the Province of the Anglican Church of Rwanda believes the office of the bishop is one that develops from the office of the deacon and priest; however, the House of Bishops was also concerned with the previous orders (Anglican Communion 2011). The new archbishop, the Most Rev. Onesphore Rwaje, declared that he will step in the footsteps of his predecessor on the issue of gay marriage. "Anything that is contrary to God's family set-up is not acceptable; there is nowhere in the Bible where same-sex marriage is encouraged. God created a man and woman to be the basis of a family" (All Africa 2011).

The Anglican Province of Rwanda has problems of marriage related to polygamy and many widows left by the genocide of 1994. The East African Revival focused on "one man one wife" as it is recommended in the Bible, based on heterosexual blessing. Culturally, homosexuality is a taboo; therefore, there is no possibility of this new trend of homosexuality penetrating into the Anglican Church of Rwanda. It is what former Archbishop of Rwanda Emmanuel Kolini described as "cultural imperialism." He said, "They [Western Missionaries] asked us to read the Bible with them, but the difference is culture; it is not the understanding of the Bible. . . . If they interpret it in their own cultural contexts, let them keep it that way with themselves. It is not supposed to be imposed upon us" (Anglicans United 2011). The Bible is read with much authority, in reflection and respect to the people's culture. There is no culture in its formation which supports same-sex union except the new human's thinking.

## Conclusion

It is hard to compare the legacy of the revival and the hell of genocide in Rwanda because both happened to the people in this country. The work done by the Anglican Province of Rwanda is remarkable; it has combined a traditional evangelical emphasis on conversion with a deep commitment to social programs. The church in Rwanda is deeply committed to the emergence of AMiA. From the perspective of the church in

Rwanda, all Anglican groups in North America are advised to form one entity and to be fully under one leadership as one church of Christ with one mission to evangelize and re-evangelize the unreached.

Many in Rwanda believe that the time has come to bring the energy and passion of the church in Africa back to the West. The same spirit that enabled the continent of Africa to be touched by the gospel is needed in the West.

## Bibliography

All Africa. 2011. *Story*. Web. July 10, 2011. http://allafrica.com/stories/2010093 00297.html.

Anglican Communion. 2011. *Province*. Web. June 24, 2011. http://www.anglican communion.org/tour/province.cfm?ID=U1.

Anglicans United. 2011. Web. July 10, 2011. http://www.anglicansunited.com/?p= 6781.

Barrett, B. David, George T. Kuriam, and Todd M. Johnson, ed. 2001. *World Christian Encyclopedia: A Comparative Survey of Churches and Religions in the Modern World*, 2nd Ed. Vol. 1: The World by Countries: Religionists, Churches Ministries. Oxford: Oxford University Press, pp. 629–32.

Byaruhanga, Christopher. 2008. *Bishop Alfred Robert Tucker and the Establishment of the African Anglican Church*. Nairobi: WordAlive Publishers.

Byham, Kim. 2011. *Anglican Complicity in the Genocide in Rwanda and Lessons for the Anglican Communion Today*. Web. June 29, 2011. http://www.rci.rutgers.edu/~lcrew/ dojustice/j245.html.

Church, E. Joe. 1981. *Quest for the Highest: An Autobiographical Account of the East African Revival*. Exeter: Paternoster Press.

GAFCON. 2011. Web. July 5, 2011 http:// www.gafcon.org/news/plans_announced_ for_gafcon_2_and_london_and_africa offices/.

Jack, Campbell and Gavin J. McGrath, ed. 2006. *New Dictionary of Christian Apologetics*. Downers Grove: Intervarsity Press.

Mukeshimana, Emmanuel. 2006. MAT Dissertation: Christian Perspective on Comfort in

2 Cor. 1.3-7 in the Light of Suffering Endurance and Hope in the Post-Genocide Rwanda. UCU, Mukono.

Mukeshimana, Emmanuel. 2011. Eye Witness of the Enthronement Ceremony of the Most Rev. Rwaje Onesphore in Kigali on January 23, 2011.

NURC. 2011. Web. June 29, 2011. http:// www.nurc.gov.rw/.

Osborn, H. H. 2000. *Pioneers in the East African Revival*. Winchester: Apologia Publications.

PEAR. 2011. *History*. Web. June 27, 2011. http://www.pear-hq.org.rw.

PEAR. 2011. *Promulgation*. Web. July 10, 2011. http://www.pear-hq.org.rw/ promulgation.htm.

PEAR. 2011. *The Amia*. Web. July 2, 2011. http://www.pear-hq.org.rw/amia.htm.

Surton, S. E. n.d. *Congo Mission Archives: The Papers of Bishop Ridsdale (1916–2000)*. Missionary to the Eastern Congo. Archivist: Henry Martyn Center. Web. July 8, 2011. http://www.ampltd.co.uk/digital_guides/ congo_mission_archive/ EditorialIntroduction.aspx.

The AMIA. *Identity*. Web. July 3, 2011. http:// www.theamia.org/identity/our-story/.

The AMIA. *Rwanda-Connection*. Web. July 3, 2011. http://www.theamia.org/identity/ rwandaconnection/.

Theodora. 2011. *Rwanda People 2011*. World Fact Book and Other Sources. Web. June 29, 2011. http://www.theodora.com/ wfbcurrent/rwanda/rwanda_people.html.

UCU Archive. 1950. Regional Activities/Associated Regions. Rwanda Correspondences: Minutes of the Standing Committee of the

Diocesan Council Met in Buhiga, July 11–14, 1950.

Ward, Kevin. 2011. *Tukutendereza Yesu: The Balokole Revival in Uganda*. Dacb. Web. June 20, 2011. http://www.dacb.org/history/uganda-balokole%20print-friendly.html.

Ward, Kevin and Emma Wild-Wood. 2010. *The East African Revival: History and Legacies*. Kampala: Fountain Publishers.

Wikipedia. 2011. *Anglican Mission in the Americas*. Web. July 2, 2011. http://en.wikipedia.org/wiki/Anglican_Mission_in_the_Americas.

CHAPTER 17

# The Anglican Church of Southern Africa

## Ian S. Markham

Originally it was the Portuguese, and then the Dutch East India Company that settled the south of Africa. When the French and the British were in conflict, the British wanted to protect the trade route to India and keep it open. So it was in 1795 that the Dutch forces left the Cape Town Castle and the British arrived. It was 19 years later that the first Church of England church opened at Simonstown, which was a naval base.

The Cape Articles of Capitulation of 1806 allowed Dutch Reformed Church to continue to be the established church. The Dutch Reformed Church was the cradle of the Afrikaners theology. The Afrikaners were the new white Africans, with family roots in seventeenth-century Holland. They had their own distinctive narrative of oppression and journey, which shaped the history of South Africa in a very dramatic way (see Battle 1997). Out of this narrative emerged in the twentieth century the apartheid doctrine of white domination and racial separation.

## Anglican Development

The first Anglican bishop was Robert Gray (1809–1872). It was a turbulent and significant episcopate. He was the son of the Bishop of Bristol; he studied at Oxford University; and he was consecrated bishop for the Diocese of South Africa in June 1847 at Westminster Abbey.

Gray is a controversial bishop. Anthony Ive is on one side when he writes:

A determined Tractarian, he came to South Africa resolved to establish an Anglo-Catholic church, free from the doctrinal standards of the Church of England. . . . Evangelical churchmen were to be eliminated. . . . Gray had very strong opinions on the power and position of bishops, whom he regarded as essential to the existence of the Church of Christ.

*The Wiley-Blackwell Companion to the Anglican Communion*, First Edition. Edited by Ian S. Markham, J. Barney Hawkins IV, Justyn Terry, and Leslie Nuñez Steffensen.
© 2013 John Wiley & Sons, Ltd. Published 2013 by John Wiley & Sons, Ltd.

Characteristically, his sermon on the first Sunday after landing in South Africa, which could be expected to set the tone of his ministry, was on the theme not of the Christian gospel but of the necessity of episcopacy. (Ive 1966, 9)

Meanwhile, on the other side, we have Peter Hinchliff who writes:

Gray was not a product of the Tractarian movement. He read their works and sympathised with their aims. But it is an oversimplification of things to treat him as a "Tractarian" pure and simple. Gray was in age and outlook more akin to Bishop Samuel Wilberforce, and Wilberforce was perhaps the greatest single influence on Gray's ideas and policy. (Hinchliff 1963, 30)

Interestingly, Gray's primary conflict was not with the evangelicals, but with his fellow Bishop Colenso. In respect to his Anglo-Catholic propensities, these were largely confined to the wearing of the surplice, the "use of the prayer for the Church Militant, and the regular 'offertory'." (Hinchliff 1963, 49). However, Bishop John William Colenso posed a different problem. Influenced by the writings of F. D. Maurice, Colenso, in 1861, published *St. Paul's Epistle to the Romans: Newly Translated, and Explained from a Missionary Point of View*. In it, Colenso argued that the atonement had already done the work of redemption and therefore baptism is simply an invitation into a reality already made real by God. Gray wanted Colenso to withdraw his commentary on Romans. Then, in 1862, Colenso published *The Pentateuch and the Book of Joshua Critically Examined*. This book emerged as he translated the Old Testament into a Zulu language; it was the close reading of the text that led Colenso to struggle with the historicity of the narrative.

Gray moved against Colenso. The Archbishop of Canterbury, in consultation with 33 English, Irish, and colonial bishops, felt that Colenso should resign his see. So Gray put Colenso on trial in November 1863. Colenso was found guilty of nine charges, which included bringing the Book of Common Prayer into disrepute and questioning the authenticity of scripture.

Colenso is an important person for the Anglican Communion. It was this controversy which inspired the first Lambeth Conference. Harold T. Lewis describes Colenso as the "unwitting architect of the Anglican Communion" (Lewis 2007, 12). A number of overseas bishops petitioned the Archbishop of Canterbury to discuss this controversy as a communion. Hence, the first Lambeth Conference was held in 1867.

This issue shaped the South Africa Church in important ways. Looking back on the issue now, most theologians agree that Colenso was right on biblical criticism and perhaps wrong on his Christology (which tended to be very low).

There is no doubt that Colenso's missionary activities were affected by this controversy. However, the church did grow significantly over these initial decades. And from 1870 onward, growth proved dramatic. In the first provincial synod of 1870, none of the clergy attending were born in South Africa, but after 1870, "South African-born clergy were educated and ordained, South African clergy were consecrated as bishops . . . , and finally as archbishop of the province" (Suberq 1999, 43). The dioceses of Zululand, Bloemfontein, and Pretoria flourished. The Anglican Church attracted members from both white and black communities. And slowly it became increasingly indigenized. This was helped by the emergence of theological colleges (e.g., St. Paul's in Grahamstown opened in 1902, and St. Bede's emerged in 1899). The Order of Ethiopia has deep links with the Anglican Church and started in 1892, which after some initial difficulties around its constitution became an important part of the church. The Book of Common Prayer was constantly being revisited from the very earliest days. Special services, which were necessary for the indigenous population, were created. In 1954, *A Book of Common Prayer: South Africa* (normally called the South African Prayer Book) was published. And in 1993, after a gradual and growing recognition of the significance of women in the church, the ordination of women to priesthood was permitted.

## The Struggle against Apartheid

It was when the National Party was able to get a majority in the 1940s that the system of apartheid was established. In 1948, apartheid laws were institutionalized. Marriage between whites and non-whites was illegal; and "white-only" positions were allowed. In 1950, the Population Registration Act established three categories for all South Africans – white, black (which meant African), or colored (this applied to persons of mixed descent). Strangely, the colored category also included all Indians and Asians. The Department of Home Affairs determined the classification of all persons; and all blacks had to carry "pass books" which contained fingerprints, photo, and information.

The idea of "homelands" was intended to create jurisdictions for the different tribes which were separate. Ostensibly, these homelands were independent states; each African was assigned to a homeland; it was here that each individual was allowed to vote. And once in a homeland, you would need a passport to travel to the rest of Africa. By 1981, four homelands had been created, and 9 million South Africans were foreigners in their own country.

The whole system was kept in place by a brutal police state, which took full advantage of the 1953 Public Safety Act and Criminal Law Amendment Act. This allowed the government to declare a state of emergency and hand down harsh penalties on protests. So, for example, when Africans in Sharpeville refused the humiliation of carrying their pass books, a state of emergency was declared, which left 187 people wounded and 69 dead.

Trevor Huddleston (1913–1998) went to South Africa in 1943. Huddleston was perhaps the leading opponent of apartheid as these policies were developed and implemented. He had a significant impact on Bishop Ambrose Reeves, who became the third Bishop of Johannesburg in 1948. In Huddleston's famous book *Naught for your comfort*, he writes:

> I believe that, because God became Man, therefore human nature in itself has a dignity and a value which is infinite. . . . Any doctrine based on racial or color prejudice and enforced by the State is therefore an affront to human dignity and *ipso facto* an insult to God himself. It is for this reason that I feel bound to oppose not only the policy of the present

government of the Union of South Africa, but the legislation which flows from this policy. (Huddleston 1958, 17–18)

When Huddleston published a series of articles on South Africa in 1953 in the London newspaper *The Observer*, it was arguments such as these he made central. Although the Anglican Church was officially against apartheid, there was some anxiety among the bishops about this explicit approach. Archbishop Clayton, for example, thought that such tactics were unwise. Clayton did, however, support the creation of a defense fund for the anti-apartheid activists who were arrested in 1956. Clayton also opposed Clause 29(c) of the Native Laws Amendment Bill, which would have prohibited an African from attending a church in a white area.

Meanwhile, Bishop Reeves was an activist. He worked with other social groups and supported bus boycotts and opposed the removal of people under the Group Areas Act. He did flee the country and head back to Britain when he was worried about being arrested, which ultimately led to his resignation from his diocese in March 1961.

## Archbishop Tutu

Desmond Tutu came to prominence in South Africa in the 1970s. He was born in Klerksdorp in 1931. Initially he was a teacher, who later trained for ordination at St. Peter's Theological College in Johannesburg. In 1962, he worked on a BA degree and then a master's at King's College, London. In 1966, he joined the faculty at the Federal Theological Seminary in Alice; and then, in 1970, he moved to the University of Botswana, Lesotho and Swaziland.

It was in 1976 that Tutu became the Bishop of Lesotho. He moved in March 1978 to become the general secretary of the South African Council of Churches. It was in this role that his political activism became more prominent. The combination of a compelling mind and distinguished oratory meant that he was a powerful critic of the government. In October 1984, he was awarded the Nobel Peace Prize. A month later, Tutu was elected the Bishop of Johannesburg, and then made the first black Archbishop of South Africa. He was a strong advocate of sanctions, which ultimately undermined the apartheid regime.

Tutu was not brave simply in opposing the authorities, but also in opposing the brutal liberation movement practice of "necklacing," which involved taking an informer and "putting a car tire around the victim's neck, filling it with petrol, and setting it ablaze" (Sparks and Tutu 2011, 7). On two occasions, Tutu bravely confronted groups of young men who wanted to necklace an informer. He was seen as too moderate by the liberationists and as a supporter of terrorism by the government.

With the dramatic announcement of President de Klerk in 1990 that Nelson Mandela would be released, the world slowly started to change. The friendship between Desmond Tutu and Nelson Mandela played an important role in creating a new South Africa. Tutu was universally acclaimed for the important role he played in the Truth and Reconcilation Commission. Tutu himself described this work as the hardest job he had ever done. Sparks and Tutu describe his role thus:

Tutu's main contribution to the TRC process was that he gave it a clear ethical framework in which to operate. This was the twenty-first such commission established in the post-World War II world to probe a nation's own human rights violations, but it was by far the most textured, sophisticated, and purposeful. Tutu gave it a clear objective, which was not only to establish the truth of what happened during those years of vicious racial violence but to lay the basis for the start of an ongoing process of national reconciliation. (Sparks and Tutu 2011, 214)

It was a major political contribution, by a great and prophetic leader of the church.

## Conclusion

Harold Lewis is probably right. There is a sense that South Africa might well be the crucible for Anglicanism in a new century (see Lewis 2007). It is a province which has forced the church to struggle against a great injustice. Under the inspiring leadership of Archbishop Tutu, the themes of reconciliation and justice have been prominent. There have been determined overtures to the white population to stay in the country. The province has supported the ordination of women, and some (such as Archbishop Tutu) have supported the full recognition of gays and lesbians.

South Africa continues to have problems. The legacy of apartheid left the majority of the land and wealth in the hands of a small white minority. This will need to be addressed. There is hope: the transition from apartheid to majority rule was handled well. And with the inspiration of such great leadership, there is hope that the continuing challenges facing that nation will be handled well.

### Bibliography

Battle, Michael. 1997. *Reconcilation: The Ubuntu Theology of Desmond Tutu*. Cleveland, Ohio: The Pilgrim Press.

Hinchliff, Peter. 1963. *The Anglican Church in South Africa: An Account of the History and Development of the Church of the Province of South Africa*. London: Darton, Longman and Todd.

Huddleston, Trevor. 1958. *Naught for Your Comfort*. New York: Doubleday.

Ive, Anthony. 1966. *The Church of England in South Africa: A Study of its History, Principles and Status*. Cape Town: The Church of England Information Office.

Lewis, Harold T. 2007. *A Church for the Future: South Africa as the Crucible for Anglicanism in a New Century*. New York: Church Publishing.

Sparks, Alister and Mpho Tutu. 2011. *Tutu Authorized*. New York: HarperCollins.

Suberq, O. M. 1999. *The Anglican Tradition in South Africa: A Historical Overview*. Pretoria: University of South Africa.

CHAPTER 18

# The Episcopal Church of Sudan

## Abraham Yel Nhial

## History of the Anglican Church in the Province of the Episcopal Church of Sudan

The history of the Province of the Episcopal Church of Sudan includes a long struggle with Christian identity in the old Sudan. It is a painful and tragic story. We start with the history.

The missionaries from Church Mission Society (CMS) established the Episcopal Church of Sudan (ECS) in 1899. The missionaries established several mission stations, about 17, in southern and northern Sudan, beginning in 1906 with Malek mission station in Bor, which is now part of South Sudan. These mission stations grew into a few parishes and eventually grew into a diocese with two archdeaconries in northern and southern Sudan. The ECS is more than 100 years old and has grown into 31 dioceses across Sudan and South Sudan, and we expect more dioceses in the near future. The majority of these dioceses are in the south; there are only four in the north.

Until 2011, South Sudan was part of the Republic of Sudan. The vast majority of the population in the north is Muslim. The tensions between Muslims and Christians are the backdrop for the growth of the province. Prior to 2011, the church had been adversely affected by a government policy that was heavily influenced by Islam, which made life difficult for non-Muslims. People of other faiths, other than Islam, were not allowed to preach the gospel openly or to worship. Freedom for Christians was extremely limited. Freedom of religion, or rather, the lack thereof, became one of the major root causes of the long civil war in Sudan. The predominately Muslim government did not recognize sufficiently the existence of Christian faith in the old Sudan. In addition, the decision in 1983 of the Islamic government in Khartoum to impose Sharia law even on the southern region was very contentious. In summary, from the perspective of the

*The Wiley-Blackwell Companion to the Anglican Communion*, First Edition. Edited by Ian S. Markham, J. Barney Hawkins IV, Justyn Terry, and Leslie Nuñez Steffensen.
© 2013 John Wiley & Sons, Ltd. Published 2013 by John Wiley & Sons, Ltd.

Christian south, since the independence of Sudan in 1956, the central government had been marginalizing the Christians politically, economically, and religiously.

A good illustration of the problems facing the church was the decision of the government to expel missionaries from Sudan in 1962. Deng explains:

> In March 1964 the Sudan government took the final step of expelling all foreign missionaries from the South. "Foreign Missionary organizations have gone beyond the limits of their sacred mission," the government explained in a policy statement on its decision, arguing that the missionaries had "exploited the name of religion to impart hatred and implant fear and animosity in the minds of the Southerners against their fellow countrymen in the North with the clear object of encouraging the setting up of a separate political status for the southern provinces thus endangering the integrity and unity of the country." (Deng 2001)

This was interpreted by the south as a determined attempt to eliminate Christianity. This was at a time when the church was very small, and it was not clear that the church could survive the severe oppression from the north. However, the result of this suffering was church growth. And the growth was dramatic.

In *Suffering and God*, Isaiah Majok Dau says:

> In spite of all this suffering, the church in the Sudan is experiencing substantial growth. . . . These churches faced the serious challenges of Islamisation and Arabisation from 1956 to 1964. At the height of the Abboud regime's repressive Islamic policies, foreign missionaries were expelled from the south in 1964, accused of supporting southern agitation for secession or autonomy. Arabic was imposed as the language of communication and learning. Quranic schools were established everywhere in the south and the process of cultural repression was imposed. Many Southern Sudanese Christians who voiced concern were subjected to increasing harassment and harsh restrictions despite the fact that Sudan's constitution enshrined freedom of worship. With the intensification of the civil war in the years that followed and due to the reign of terror that the Abboud military government inflicted on the south, many people, including church leaders, were forced into exile. Here, they came in contact with the great East Africa revival of the 1950s and 1960s. Many were converted or revitalized. When the Addis Ababa peace accord was signed in 1972, they came back to the country with great evangelistic zeal and vigor. As a result, the church in the south, which had been greatly impeded by the expulsion of missionaries and persecution, but still maintained a presence, sometimes with great difficulty, began to grow again. (Dau 2002, 56–7)

The church grew rapidly and suffered at the same time; for many in Sudan, this was much like the early Christians after Jesus' resurrection.

## Relationship of Church with Indigenous/Traditional Cultures

One irony of the decision of the government to expel the missionaries is that the ECS has been an indigenous church since the 1960s. A result of the missionaries being exiled from Sudan was that indigenous leadership arose, which made a difference. The church has been training indigenous people to reach their own tribes with the gospel of Christ and has helped tribes to translate the Bible into their languages. Thus, they can read and understand the Bible in order to strengthen their faith. The indigenous leadership sent native missionaries to witness and plant new churches throughout the country among unreached people more quickly than Western missionaries. Native leaders and native missionaries are now carrying the entire ministry of the ECS. The result is an indigenous church.

## Ecumenical History

The ECS is a founding member of the Sudan Council of Churches (SCC), an ecumenical council in Sudan that represents the churches in Sudan both nationally and interna-tionally. It links South and North Sudan with the All African Conference of Churches (AACC), World Council Churches (WCC), and Council of Anglican provinces of Africa (CAPA), just to mention a few. One good example of the ecumenical history is a recent South Sudan Catholic and Episcopal meeting in Yei to pray together and commit them-selves to working together for peace to be realized in South and North Sudan. Also, the Province of the Episcopal Church of Sudan has an Interfaith and Ecumenical Relations Commission.

## Outstanding Leadership Both Ordained and Lay

The church has been fortunate with its leadership. The leaders of the ECS, led by Arch-bishop Dr. Daniel Deng Bul, are recognized locally, nationally, and internationally for their outstanding leadership in both South and North Sudan. Because of their dedi-cated leadership and work for peace for many years, President Salva Kiir Mayardit of the Republic of South Sudan has recently appointed Archbishop Daniel Deng Bul to be a chairperson for the peace committee in Jongeli State. The ECS has been honored with the trust that the president has bestowed upon ECS.

The church in both South and North Sudan is faced with two major problems, the conflicts/war and poverty. As part of our ministry in South Sudan, all the bishops, priests and laypeople are committed to work for reconciliation in our communities and nation. We want all people of South Sudan to live in peace and be involved in peace building. The long history of conflict in Sudan has created deep wounds of hatred within our communities and provinces. The church understands that it is called not only to reconcile broken relationships between South and North, and Chris-tians and Muslims, but also broken relationship between our communities, neighbors, families, and people of different ethnic backgrounds. There is a distinctive ethos emerging: we believe we should not be divided along political lines. The Church of God in North and South Sudan is united for justice and peace for all through the work of reconciliation.

## Description of Schools, Hospitals, Colleges, and Other Services / Outreach

During the long civil war, church buildings and the church compounds were used as temporary hospitals for wounded soldiers, civilians, and relief centers. Despite the civil war and all the associated difficulties, the church has continued its outreach services to those in need. It is widely understood that the purpose of the ECS is to honor God by bringing people into His Kingdom through His Son Jesus Christ. The priorities of the church are missions and providing services to all the people of God. Our mission is expressed as love and servant love for one another.

The lack of education in South Sudan has caused unparalleled illiteracy and continues to exacerbate severe poverty. There are few universities or colleges and even fewer hospitals, as even high schools or primary schools are essentially nonexistent in the region.

## Connection with the Worldwide Anglican Communion

The ECS is part of the Anglican Communion. The Anglican Book of Common Prayer is what defines us as one communion worldwide. The Book of Common Prayer came from the same root, even though every province translated it into their own language.

Hefling says, "The Prayer Book restored to use in 1662 was to all intents the same as the one restored at the beginning of Queen Elizabeth's reign. Many small improvements had been made, but none was of much doctrinal significance" (Hefling and Shattuck 2006, 61).

Because of the Book of Common Prayer, the Anglican Church sees itself as unified globally for the glory of God and the transforming power of our Lord Jesus Christ. As a result, all the provinces in the worldwide Anglican Communion are united through our Lord and Savior Jesus Christ. In Him, we are brothers and sisters. This sense of tangible unity with a global Anglican tradition is an important part of the Church of Sudan's self-understanding.

## Conclusion / Possible Future

The Province of the Episcopal Church of Sudan has a distinctive past made up of both pain and hope. For the Church of Sudan, it is considered almost miraculous that, despite the 50 years of Islamic government in Khartoum, which wanted an Islamic state to emerge throughout Sudan, the church has flourished.

For more than 50 years, the church in former Sudan faced persecution; many of the church leaders/members were killed, wounded, imprisoned, enslaved, denied food, water, medication, and education because they refused to become Muslims. More than 2 million people have died. As a result of the long civil war, Sudan was officially divided into two nations in 2011: the Republic of Sudan and the Republic of South Sudan. However, the church has remained as one church, the Episcopal Church of Sudan, covering both north and south, under the leadership of the Most Rev. Canon Dr. Daniel Deg Bul, the archbishop and primate of the Province of the Episcopal Church of Sudan. The future of the Province of the Episcopal Church of Sudan is hopeful. It has come this far. The hope in the church is that it will continue to grow and offer a vision of peace and hope for all the people of Sudan.

## Bibliography

Dau, Isaiah. 2002. *Suffering and God: A Theological Reflection on the War in Sudan*. Nairobi: Paulines Publications Africa.

Deng, Francis M. 2001. Civil War and Genoicide: Disappearing Christians in the Middle East. *The Middle East Quarterly*, vol. 8, no. 1. Available at http://www.meforum.org/22/sudan-civil-war-and-genocide.

Hefling, Charles and Cynthia Shattuck ed. 2006. *The Oxford Guide to the Book of Common Prayer*. New York: Oxford University Press.

CHAPTER 19

# The Anglican Church of Tanzania

## Phanuel L. Mung'ong'o and Moses Matonya

### Introduction

The Anglican Church of Tanzania (ACT) is a member of the Anglican Communion, the World Council of Churches (WCC), and the Christian Council of Tanzania, with its headquarters in the capital city of Dodoma. It seceded from the Province of East Africa in 1970, and until 1997 it was called the Church of the Province of Tanzania. Today, it is known as the Anglican Church of Tanzania or ACT in short, with the Most Rev. Valentino Mokiwa as archbishop.

Uniquely, the ACT has a history of two distinct church traditions: the evangelical and the Anglo-Catholic traditions, the product of the work of two missionary societies in the mid-nineteenth century, namely the Universities' Mission to Central Africa (UMCA) and the Church Missionary Society (CMS). It has 26 dioceses – 25 on the mainland and one in the Zanzibar Islands. Eight are Anglo-Catholic, and 18 are Evangelical in their church tradition. Membership is estimated at around 5 million people, the third biggest denomination. The church is actively involved in ecumenism and participates in various ecumenical and interfaith initiatives between Christians and Muslims.

### Structure

The church follows Episcopalian church government, which follows the "Apostolic succession." It maintains a system of geographical parishes, which are organized into dioceses, each headed by a bishop. Nationally, ACT is led by an archbishop, who is elected every five years by the Provincial Synod. His roles include chairing meetings

*The Wiley-Blackwell Companion to the Anglican Communion*, First Edition. Edited by Ian S. Markham, J. Barney Hawkins IV, Justyn Terry, and Leslie Nuñez Steffensen.
© 2013 John Wiley & Sons, Ltd. Published 2013 by John Wiley & Sons, Ltd.

with fellow bishops in the House of Bishops, the Provincial Synod, and General Council. He leads the church as *primus inter pares*, Latin for "first among equals," and continues as bishop of his diocese. Daily administration of Anglican affairs is the responsibility of the secretariat in Dodoma, headed by the general secretary.

The Provincial Synod is the main governing body, divided into the House of Bishops, House of Clergy, and House of Laity. Policy changes need a majority agreement of all three houses. Diocesan synods and bishops are in charge of their dioceses, which maintain a semi-autonomous status, and the archbishop's role is advisory rather than authoritative over the dioceses.

## Vision

To be a sustainable church working together for the growth of God's Kingdom through prayer, worship, preaching, teaching, pastoral care, and the provision of social services.

## Mission

To proclaim the kingdom of God through spiritual and socio-economic transformation by the empowerment of individuals and communities, so that they may experience the fullness of life in God.

## Doctrine and Practice

The center of the ACT's teaching is the life, ministry, death, and resurrection of Jesus Christ. The following statements are part of the teaching:

- Jesus Christ is fully human and fully God.
- He died and was raised from the dead by God the Father.
- Jesus is the savior who provides the way of eternal life for those who believe.
- The Old and New Testaments of the Bible were written by people "inspired by the Holy Spirit." The Apocrypha are additional books that are used in Christian teaching, but not for the formation of doctrine.
- The two great and necessary sacraments are Holy Baptism and Holy Eucharist.
- Other sacramental rites include confirmation, ordination, marriage, reconciliation of a penitent, and unction.
- Belief in heaven, hell, resurrection of the dead, and Jesus' return in glory to judge the world.

The threefold sources of authority typical of Anglicanism (scripture, tradition, and reason, which critique each other in a dynamic way, as proposed by Richard Hooker in the sixteenth century) determine ACT's doctrine. Scripture is primary with tradition and reason augmenting the threefold doctrine, and things stated plainly in scripture are accepted as true. Issues that are ambiguous are determined by tradition, which is checked by reason.

## Early Origins of the ACT

As mentioned in the preceding text, the Anglican Church in Tanzania is the product of two main missionary societies from England. The first Anglican missionaries were from CMS, which was founded in 1799 in England, for the purpose of propagating the gospel of Jesus Christ in Africa and the Far East. The first missionaries to East Africa were Johann Ludwig Krapf and his wife Rosina who arrived in Zanzibar on January 7, 1844. They stayed there for four months before moving to Mombassa on May 5, 1844. However, Krapf's wife and little baby died shortly after their arrival in Mombassa in July 1844. Krapf stayed there for two years to translate the New Testament into Swahili and to write a Swahili dictionary of 4,000 words. In 1846, Rev. Johannes Rebman was sent by CMS to join Krapf. Krapf and Rebman made several tours inland from 1847 to 1852. They opened a center at Rabai Mpya and Mwala in 1847. Rebman arrived in Taita in early 1848 and reached Mt. Kilimanjaro on April 27, 1848. Krapf on his side arrived in Vuga in Usambara uplands in 1848 and the Kamba region in 1849.

Krapf had to return to Europe on September 23, 1853, due to serious illness. Rebman continued for 20 years before returning home due to blindness. From 1876, expeditors Henry Speke and James Burton started their expedition from Bagamoyo, going to Kigoma and Buganda to trace slave trade routes. They followed this route and opened the first mission stations at Mamboya in Morogoro, and Mpwapwa and Buigiri in Dodoma.

The Archbishop of Canterbury suggested to CMS to form a new diocese for East Africa. The Diocese of East Equatorial Africa was started in June 1884, and James Hannington was consecrated as the first bishop of the diocese with its headquarters in Mombassa. Unfortunately, Bishop Hannington served only for two years and was assassinated by Kabaka Mwanga II of Buganda on February 8, 1886.

Bishop Tucker, the third Bishop of the Diocese of East Equatorial Africa, decided to divide the diocese into two – the Diocese of Mombassa under Bishop William George Peel, who was consecrated on June 28, 1899, and the Diocese of Uganda under Bishop Tucker himself. In 1927, the new Diocese of Central Tanganyika was born out of the mother Diocese of Mombassa. Its new bishop, the Rt. Rev. George Alexander Chambers, was consecrated on All Saints' Day, 1927. This is the background of the evangelical part of the Anglican Church in Tanzania

The Universities Mission to Central Africa (UMCA), born out of Dr. David Livingstone's appeal to the students of Oxford, Cambridge, Durham, London, Dublin, and Edinburgh universities to come to Africa for commerce instead of the slave trade and to spread Christianity, is behind the birth of Anglo-Catholic Anglicanism in Tanzania.

The first mission station was opened in Malawi at Magomero near River Shire. This place, however, was not very safe because of tribal fighting and infectious diseases. Bishop William Tozer, accompanied by Rev. C. A. Allington and Rev. Edward Steere, decided to move to a safe and healthy site in Zanzibar. They arrived in Zanzibar on August 31, 1864, and opened the first UMCA station on September 4, 1864. Sultan Majid of Zanzibar presented Bishop William Tozer with five boys who were freed from slavery. With those boys, Bishop Tozer began to build the first church in Zanzibar. In June 1865, five boys and nine girls were presented by the sultan to Bishop Tozer. There were 23 people altogether in the UMCA mission under Bishop Tozer.

While in Zanzibar, Rev. Steere learned Swahili and worked on a handbook of Swahili language, the translation of the Bible into Swahili, and the translation of the UMCA hymn book, famous as "Nyimbo za Dini" (religious hymns), which remains the principal hymn book for the Anglo-Catholic part of the ACT to date.

The Rev. C. A. Allington made his first visit inland in Usambara area in August 1867 and a mission station was begun at Magila in Muheza in 1868. From Magila, Bishop Charles Smithies (who succeeded Bishop Steere) traveled to Ruvuma in south-west Tanganyika in 1884. On his return to Zanzibar from Ruvuma, he traveled through Masasi and opened several mission stations between Ruvuma and Usambara in the north-east of Tanganyika.

The UMCA Diocese of Zanzibar was started in 1892. Four years later, the diocese was divided into two – Zanzibar itself to serve the Zanzibar Islands, and mainland Tanganyika. In 1926, Masasi was born as a new separate diocese independent of Zanzibar. Its first bishop was the Rt. Rev. Vincent Lucas, who is remembered for advocating the use of local cultural rituals in Christian mission so as to root the faith of the converts in their own culture. In 1952, the Diocese of South West Tanganyika was born, carved from Masasi, under Bishop Leslie Sterling. Briefly, this gives the early origins of the Anglo-Catholic section of the church and explains why the tradition is mainly confined to the south and south-west areas of the country.

Theological differences between CMS and UMCA existing in England were imported into Tanganyika and Zanzibar, dividing the church into two parts. One of the tasks of the newly formed Province of Tanzania was to look for ways of uniting the church, and the project of forming one liturgy and prayer book uniting the two traditions was launched. Today, the ACT has one prayer book and liturgy, although each tradition can choose and use aspects from the old prayer books.

## The Birth of the Province of the Church of Tanzania

There were only five dioceses in Kenya, Zanzibar, and Tanganyika in 1960 – the dioceses of Zanzibar (1892), Mombassa (1898), Masasi (1926), Central Tanganyika (1927), and South West Tanganyika (1952). These dioceses sought permission from the Archbishop of Canterbury to start a new Province of East Africa, which was formed on August 3, 1960. The synod of the Province of East Africa, held in Dodoma from February 3 to 8, 1969, decided to divide the province into two – for Kenya and Tanzania, and the new Province of the Church of Tanzania was born on July 3, 1970, with eight dioceses under the Most Rev. John Sepeku as the first archbishop. These dioceses were: the Diocese of Zanzibar and Tanga (1892), the Diocese of Masasi (1926), the Diocese of Central Tanganyika (1927), the Diocese of South West

Tanganyika (1952), the Diocese of Dar Es Salaam (1963), the Diocese of Victoria Nyanza (1963), the Diocese of Morogoro (1965), and the Diocese of Western Tanganyika (1966).

By 2011, ACT had 26 dioceses: 25 on the mainland and one in Zanzibar. The increase in the number of dioceses is attributed to the increase in the number of new churches as a result of evangelistic work in dioceses and pastoral demands necessitated by the increase in numbers of new Christians and their physical and spiritual needs. Social concern and action, especially in the areas of health, education, and relief work, have gone hand-in-hand with evangelism. Currently, the 26 dioceses of ACT are: the Diocese of Zanzibar and Tanga (1892), the Diocese of Masasi (1926), the Diocese of Central Tanganyika (1927), the Diocese of South West Tanganyika (1952), the Diocese of Dar Es Salaam (1963), the Diocese of Victoria Nyanza (1963), the Diocese of Morogoro (1965), the Diocese of Western Tanganyika (1966), the Diocese of Ruvuma (1977), the Diocese of Mount Kilimanjaro (1982), the Diocese of Kagera (1985), the Diocese of Mara (1985), the Diocese of Tabora (1989), the Diocese of Ruaha (1990), the Diocese of Mpwapwa (1991), the Diocese of the Rift Valley (1991), the Diocese of Southern Highlands (1999), the Diocese of Tanga (2000), the Diocese of Kondoa (2001), the Diocese of Shinyanga (2005), the Diocese of Lweru (2006), the Diocese of Kiteto (2009), the Diocese of Newalla (2009), the Diocese of Rorya (2010), the Diocese of Tarime (2010), and the Diocese of Lake Rukwa (2010).

## ACT's Relationship with Indigenous Cultures and Religions

Many Anglicasns come from a background of traditional cultures and religions. They were either followers of traditional religions and converted to Christianity, or born of Christian parents who had practiced traditional religions prior to their conversion. The ACT is friendly to followers of traditional religions but is strongly opposed to any syncretism among Anglicans.

Christians live within clans and families who still believe in traditional religions and other religions such as Islam, Sikhism, and Hinduism, and do things together at family, community, and national levels. They are together in social and community activities, such as weddings, funerals, and businesses. However, Christians are not supposed to take part in other religious matters. Some Anglicans regard traditional religions as pagan, superstitious, and even devilish, and tend to ignore and dismiss any element of practice in the Church which seems to relate to traditional religion and culture. However, some turn to traditional religion secretly in times of difficulty.

Others do respect the traditionalists and are open to dialogue for a richer understanding of their beliefs and an effective way of reaching them with the gospel of Christ. Inculturation and indigenization of the gospel compels the Anglican Church to incorporate some cultural practices into Christianity. Traditional musical instruments and traditional ways of singing are allowed in the Church. Traditional styles of blessing farms and praying for the livestock and properties of individual Christians in their respective places and homes are adapted, in the name of Christ.

Paul in his missionary endeavors found the Athenians had dedicated their temples "TO THE UNKNOWN GOD." He saw this as an opportunity to make their knowledge of God the bridge to Christianity (Acts 17:22–23). African knowledge of God expressed in traditional religions in Tanzania can similarly provide bridges for the gospel, making the Christian faith relevant to the Tanzanian context, answering questions which people ask about life. African Christian theology is taught in Anglican theological institutions so as to make the church truly Tanzanian. Christian theology must not be based on speculation about God in the abstract. Its task is interpreting the different ways in which God has revealed himself in the history of the people.

Emil Brunner suggests that revelation is "encounter"; hence theology has to be existential, resulting from people's life experiences. Experiences differ from place to place and from culture to culture. Theology deals with suffering and death. Life requires theological reflection. If "theology is the imagination for the kingdom of God," it is necessarily missionary in its character, seeking to proclaim the gospel to the world in a way that links the church with society in their various environments (see Moltmann 2000, xx).

The ACT has to interpret the Christian faith in the context of the cultural–religious and socio-political experiences of its people to remain relevant and is, therefore, involved in religious dialogue and ecumenism. This is important. Although it is good to stress unique efforts to root Christian faith and theology in the African religio-cultural and socio-political context for an authentic African Christianity, care needs to be taken so as not to end up with a Christianity that is completely divorced from its rightful place within the apostolic and universal scheme.

## Departments and Institutions of the ACT

### Health Department

Through the programs of its Health Department, run in collaboration with a number of local and international partners, the ACT has been able to provide quality and holistic curative, preventive, and rehabilitative healthcare and social services to the Tanzanian community, especially to those in most need. Some recent programs under the Health Department include: Living with Hope, funded by EED-Germany; Youth Training on HIV/AIDS Program, funded by the Anglican Church of Canada; and the KIVUKO Programme (Training of Youth on HIV/AIDS), funded by the Rapid Funding Envelope (see ACT's main website). The department also coordinates health projects at the diocesan level, albeit in an advisory role, in dioceses that provide health and education services.

The church must work with the government in this area without compromising its values. Some church hospitals have been made District Designated Hospitals with some funding from the government, but they operate with a Christian ethos, and the dioceses owning them have a say in their daily operations. The following is a list of health facilities run by Anglican dioceses:

1. Buguruni Health Centre (Diocese of Dare es Salaam)
2. Berega Hospital (Diocese of Morogoro)
3. Tunguli Dispensary (Diocese of Morogoro)
4. Mvumi Hospital (Diocese of Central Tanganyika
5. Mackay House Health Centre (Diocese of Central Tanganyika)
6. Hombolo Health Centre (Diocese of Central Tanganyika)
7. Kilimatinde Hospital (Diocese of the Rift Valley)
8. Misenye Dispensary (Diocese of Mara)
9. A.C.T. Health Centre (Diocese of Masasi)
10. Matyazo Health Centre (Diocese of Western Tanganyika)
11. A.C.T. Dispensary (Diocese of Victoria Nyanza)
12. Murugwanza Hospital (Diocese of Kagera)
13. A.C.T. Health Centre (Diocese of Shinyanga)
14. St. Anne Hospital Liuli (Diocese of Ruvuma)
15. St. Luke's Dispensary (Diocese of Mpwapwa)
16. A.C.T. Health Centre (Diocese of South West Tanganyika)
17. Milo Hospital (Diocese of South West Tanganyika)
18. St. Luke's Dispensary (Diocese of Tabora)
19. Teule Hospital (Diocese of Tanga)
20. St. Raphael Health Centre (Diocese of Tanga)
21. St. Luke's Dispensary (Tanga)
22. Kwa Mkono Hospital (Diocese of Tanga)
23. Uhambingeto Dispensary (Diocese of Ruaha)
24. St. Luke's Dispensary Mboliboli (Diocese of Ruaha.)

The Anglican Church health facilities are said to contribute up to 15 percent of the health services in the country, mostly in rural areas, providing a lifeline to many poor people who would otherwise have no access to health services at affordable costs. Costs are subsidized in a number of the health services through funding from overseas partners.

### Education department – theological institutions

**St Philip's Theological College, Kongwa**   With an evangelical emphasis, St. Philip's was started in 1913 with the purpose of training Christians who felt called to the ordained and non-ordained ministry within the Anglican Church (and from other denominations). The college offers two courses in theology, the certificate (in Kiswahili) and the diploma course (in English).

Known as Huron College when it started, it has trained clergy and non-clergy students for close to a century. The whitewashed Westgate building (built in 1913 by Rev. Westgate, a Canadian pastor) is an impressive site as you drive into the college. A number of prominent church leaders of the evangelical dioceses were trained there, including many bishops and the fourth Archbishop of the ACT, the Most Rev. Dr. Donald L. Mtetemela (founder and current chancellor of St. John's University of Tanzania).

Sadly, the current state of this great historical institution is discouraging, and unless urgent steps are taken to rescue it, the future of St. Philip's looks bleak.

*St. Mark's Theological College, Dar es Salaam*   With an Anglo-Catholic emphasis, St. Mark's College is situated in Dar es Salaam. It started in about 1908 in Zanzibar, with Rev. Frank Weston as its principal. Then it moved to Kalole in Dar es Salaam and then to Minaki, where it provided theological training, a medical school for medical assistants, as well as teachers' training, before moving to its current location. Minaki TTC wing was moved to Korogwe (Tanga) to become Korogwe Teachers College, with John Ramadhan (later Bishop of Zanzibar and Tanga, and third Archbishop of the ACT) as its first African principal. Bishop John Ramadhan also worked as principal for St. Mark's College before becoming bishop.

Many Anglo-Catholic priests and bishops of the ACT are the products of St. Mark's. The Most Rev. Dr. Valentino Mokiwa, once a student at St. Mark's, later became a teacher and principal there, before being elected Bishop of Dar es Salaam and then the fifth Archbishop of the ACT. From 2010, it became St. John's University of Tanzania Teaching Center, offering other courses such as bachelor's degrees in education, and business administration, open to all.

*Other institutions*   Dioceses have their own local Bible schools/colleges which serve them and their neighbors, training pastors, evangelists, and laypeople for ministry. DCT Msalato Theological College, which started as an institution for the Diocese of Central Tanganyika (as a Bible school) in 1961, celebrated its fiftieth anniversary in 2011, having grown from very humble beginnings to being part of St. John's University of Tanzania, offering a bachelor's degree and diploma in Applied Theology. In 2011–2012, it began offering a BA in Education (Holistic Child Development).

*Education department – primary schools, secondary schools, teachers' colleges, and universities*

The Anglican Church in Tanzania has been involved in the provision of education services for a long time. In its efforts to eradicate ignorance and enable Christians to read the Bible, the starting of Bush schools and primary schools went together with evangelism and church planting during the missionary period. Catechists performed the double role of planting churches and leading worship as well as teaching children how to read and write. Slowly, primary schools were built, which offered education up to Std IV, after which those who passed went on to middle school. Children traveled long distances on foot to these schools, which were mainly boarding schools. On completing Std VIII, they sat for exams, and those who passed went on to secondary school, while others were employed by the colonial government and the church in various capacities.

*Primary schools*   Important primary schools run by the Anglican Church in pre-independence times include St. Paul's Middle School Liuli (Boys) and St. Anne's Middle School (Girls) on the shores of Lake Nyasa. Mavala Middle School in Njombe and

Madilu Primary School in Ludewa (Southern Highlands) were started in the 1950s by Fr Joseph Mlele (later the first African bishop for South West Tanganyika). Pupils completing Std IV went on to Mavala Middle School, which catered to Std V–VII education, and St. Mary's Girls' School Ndwika (Masasi).

Magila Boys' Middle School (Tanga) was situated at Magila Mission Centre to cater to education, alongside the Magila Hospital, which catered to health services. A theological college was also started there for training clergy, and John Sepeku, the first Archbishop of the ACT, was a product of this college. Kiwanda Middle School (Muheza) was a boys' school which also served as a teachers' college, as well as a trade school for carpentry and tailoring, with Canon A .B. Hellier as its first principal. These were in areas where the UMCA started the Anglican Church. Mvumi Boys' Primary School in Dodoma served the central part of Tanganyika, and was owned by the Diocese of Central Tanganyika, which also owns DCT Holy Trinity English Medium Primary School, Bishop Stanway English Medium Primary School, and Canon Andrea Mwaka International School. The list is not comprehensive.

*Secondary schools*    Secondary schools run by the Anglican Church include Dodoma Alliance Secondary School (later Mazengo Secondary School and now St. John's University of Tanzania) in Dodoma, Chidya Secondary School (Masasi), Minaki Secondary School (Kisarawe), Korogwe Girls' Secondary School (Tanga), Msalato Girls' Secondary School (Dodoma), Musoma Alliance Secondary School, and Kigoma Alliance Secondary School. DCT also owns Jubilee Secondary School and Mvumi Secondary School.

Loleza Girls' School (Mbeya) was started by the colonial government in 1929 at Kimbila, Tukuyu. In 1961, it was moved to Mbeya, and taken over by the Anglican Church to be both a secondary school and teachers' college, with Sister Marina of the Order of Christ's Sacred Passion (CSP) as its first principal/headmistress. Students completing Loleza Girls' Secondary School went on to train as teachers at Loleza Teachers' College. The list is by no means comprehensive.

Many government and church leaders involved in achieving Tanzanian independence were the products of these Anglican institutions, which shows how the church has played a very important part in the eradication of illiteracy in the country over the years.

*Teachers' training colleges*    To provide the schools with qualified teachers, the church had its own teacher training colleges. These include Korogwe Teachers' College (moved from Minaki, as mentioned in the preceding text), Katoke Teachers' College (Bukoba), and Kiwanda Teachers' College (Tanga). Ndwika Teachers' College (Masasi) was started in 1911 to train girls to become primary school teachers. However, World War I disrupted the program, and the girls had to be sent home. When it was resumed in 1918 and the original students recalled, it was discovered that most of them had become married or moved elsewhere. In 1961, Loleza Girls' Secondary School became both a secondary school and a Girls' Teachers' College, as mentioned in the preceding text. Teachers from these colleges were later to play a very important role in the country in the area of education, as Tanzanian independence was achieved.

Many of these institutions were nationalized by the government in the early 1970s. Although the intention was to prevent segregation of children based on religious or racial grounds, this proved to be a great mistake, because the schools became so run-down and poorly managed that the quality of education provided dropped considerably. In recent years, the government has been encouraging private and religious schools to meet the great demand for education facilities due to population growth and the government's inability to provide.

*St. John's University of Tanzania, Dodoma*   St John's University of Tanzania (SJUT) started in September 2007, under the initiative and tireless efforts of the fourth Archbishop of the ACT, Dr. Donald Leo Mtetemela, the university's first chancellor. In November 2010, the first graduation took place, and about 1,250 graduates joined the labor market. The university is situated at what used to be Dodoma Alliance Secondary School (later Mazengo Secondary School). Some church theological institutions have also been made the university's teaching centers, i.e., St. Mark's and DCT Msalato Theological Colleges. The university also runs a town center, providing courses in various disciplines at different levels.

## The development department

The Provincial Development Policy, which seeks to remove the dichotomy between provision of spiritual ministry and social concerns, has the following as its Vision and Mission statements:

- Vision: "ACT – a Province realizing holistic development that proclaims the kingdom of Christ and empowers communities to experience the fullness of life characterized by culture of service, justice, love, freedom, hope and diversity."
- Mission: "To facilitate and provide holistic and sustainable development that empowers and enables communities in their environment to realize their potential and build capacity for transformation and advocacy."

## The Mothers' Union

The Mothers' Union (MU) is a worldwide Anglican organization of Christian women. It was founded in England in 1876 by Mary Elizabeth Sumner, who was a pastor's wife. The union was established in 1918 in Tanzania. Membership is open to both men and women who have been baptized and agree with and support its objectives. The MU was started as a semi-independent organization within the Church of the Province of Tanzania in 1970, with the wife of the first archbishop, Mrs. Sepeku, as its chairperson.

The aim of the MU is to promote Christianity in marriage and family life, through the development of women physically, spiritually, mentally, and economically. In Tanzania, the MU is under the patronage of the Archbishop of ACT and diocesan bishops. It has a national office, with a paid executive secretary who coordinates the union's activities from ACT's headquarters in Dodoma. The MU network starts at the provincial level and extends to every diocese. In each diocese, the MU is represented in all levels of church life.

The Mtumba Rural Women Training Centre was started in 1996 as part of the MU's efforts to train and empower rural women with entrepreneurial skills, as well as to train young men and women in children's work. The center has a modern conference facility which serves as an income-generating project for the MU at the provincial level.

### The Anglican Evangelistic Association (AEA)

Founded by Bishop Dr. Alpha Mohammed in Arusha in 1989, its office at ACT head office was opened in 1990. AEA works with churches in evangelistic endeavors in the dioceses. Under Lay Canon D. Haji, AEA is involved in direct preaching and teaching, as well as healing and deliverance ministry. When non-Christians see people being healed and delivered from spiritual oppression, they are attracted to the faith and become believers. Healing and deliverance ministry is among the concerns of African Christian theology which seeks a theological praxis that answers the questions asked by Africans.

### The Tanzania Anglican Youth Organization (TAYO)

The organization was formed in the 1980s as the umbrella organization which brings together all youth in the ACT as a reflection of the church's recognition of the important role the youth can play in its mission. It has a provincial coordinator housed at the ACT headquarters in Dodoma. Young people are involved in evangelism through youth camps, youth concerts, drama, sports, and gospel music. People of different religious backgrounds buy these gospel music audio cassettes, CDs, video cassettes, DVDs, and VCDs. Some of them end up going to church and eventually become Christians.

### Central Tanganyika Press (CTP)

This is an Anglican publishing company now based at St. John's University of Tanzania. It was at first based in Morogoro, before being moved to Msalato, Dodoma, where it was housed until 2009, when it moved to its current location at the university. Before becoming a provincial institution, it operated for some years under the Diocese of Central Tanganyika.

### ACT leadership

The following is a listing of the archbishops of the ACT:

1. The Most Rev. John Sepeku (1970–1978)
2. The Most Rev. Mussa Kahurananga (1979–1983)

3. The Most Rev. John Ramadhan (1984–1998)
4. The Most Rev. Donald Mtetemela (1998–2008)
5. The Most Rev. Dr. Valentino Mokiwa (2008–to date)

The following is a listing of the general secretaries of the ACT:

1. Rev. Canon Martin Mbwana (1970–1985/1986)
2. Rev. Simon Chiwanga (1986–1990)
3. Rev. Canon Dr. Mkunga Mtingele (1990–2001)
4. Rev. Canon Dr. Raphael Mwita Akiri (2001–2010)
5. Rev. Canon Dr. Dickson Chilongani (2010–to date)

Rev. Canon Martin Mbwana first worked at St. Mark's College, Dar es Salaam, from 1970 to 1977, part time, and moved to the headquarters in Dodoma in 1977 to work full time as general secretary, until 1985–1986, when the Rev. Simon Chiwanga, general secretary until 1990, took over. Simon Chiwanga then became Bishop of the Diocese of Mpwapwa, and Rev. Canon Mkunga Mtingele, a lawyer, took over and worked as general secretary until 2001, when he left for his doctorate studies in the United Kingdom. Dr. M. Mtingele is now general secretary of the Bible Society of Tanzania. Rev. Canon Dr. R. Mwita Akiri then took over as ACT general secretary until 2010, when he became bishop of the new Diocese of Tarime, handing over the baton to Rev. Canon Dr. Dickson Chilongani.

## Contemporary Issues Facing the Church

### Within the ACT – leadership

The ACT has witnessed a period of uncertainty and unhappiness revolving around leadership changes in the dioceses, when the old crop of bishops retires and heirs are required. The system of electing bishops needs reviewing.

Currently, a diocesan bishop is elected by the diocesan synod. In the past, the diocesan council voted for a candidate who was then endorsed by the Provincial Electoral College. The old system seemed sometimes to impose bishops on the dioceses by outsiders, while the new system is aimed at making the election of a bishop as representative as possible from within the diocese. However, since members of the diocesan synod are known beforehand, the system is vulnerable to politicking and corruption by dishonest candidates. Problems around disputed election results for bishops have seriously weakened church unity and mission, and marred ACT's integrity in and outside the country.

### With the worldwide communion

The Anglican Church in Tanzania has found itself caught up in the controversies facing the Anglican Communion. The ordination of openly homosexual persons has been a source of friction between the southern and the northern church. Africans feel that Western missionaries misled Africa when they taught that the Bible is the Word of God, and hence authoritative. Scripture is central in Anglicanism. Different approaches to its interpretation have contributed to the current woes of the communion, threatening to tear it apart.

The Lambeth Quadrilateral affirms that "The Holy Scriptures of the Old and the New Testaments" contain all things "necessary to salvation," and is the "rule and ultimate standard of faith." Anglicans have continually asserted that the Bible points us to Christ, through whom God has revealed to the world what he is like and what he has done, and how therefore we should respond to him. The Virginia Report states: "Anglicans affirm the sovereign authority of the Holy Scriptures as the medium through which God by the Holy Spirit communicates his word and thus enables people to respond with understanding and faith. The Scriptures are the 'uniquely inspired witness to divine revelation' and the primary norm for Christian faith and life" (Lambeth Report 1998, 32).

Therefore, the Bible "is regarded by Anglicans not simply as a static source of abstract theological information, but as the living Word of God by means of which we may learn the salvation that God offers to us and how we should live in light of that salvation" (*Some Issues in Human Sexuality*, 38). The Lambeth Conference in 1998 turned to this view of scripture when Resolution 1.10 (Archbishop Donald Mtetemela of ACT was instrumental in drafting it) was drafted, upholding faithfulness in marriage between a man and a woman, and sexual abstinence for those not called to marriage. Although the resolution was passed by 526 to 70 votes with 45 abstentions, some Anglicans have refused to accept it "on the grounds that it does not adequately reflect the development of contemporary scientific and theological understandings of homosexuality" (*Some Issues in Human Sexuality*, 31).

In December 2006, the ACT declared itself to be in "impaired communion" with the Episcopal Church (USA) over the issue of the ordination of openly homosexual persons and the blessing of same-sex unions. Tanzanian Anglicans accept the authority of scripture, and the Tanzanian church may have to rethink whether to align itself with the Western church theologically and support the African Christian theology movement in the quest for an African theology that answers African questions from an African perspective.

It is argued that cultural and historical contexts affect the way we interpret scripture. However, Paul says "there is one body and one Spirit . . . one hope . . . one Lord, one faith one baptism; one God and Father of all" (Eph. 4:4). How can one faith have many interpretations? E. D. Hirsch rightly challenges theologians saying, "How important are theoretical disagreements that now divide serious students of interpretation? How true is the resigned opinion that our various schools and approaches are like a multitude of warring sects, each with its own uncompromising theology? Is it the destiny of those who practice interpretation never to achieve an ecumenical harmony of theoretical principles?" (Hirsch 1976, 74).

Interpretation of Biblical texts must take both *authorial* meaning and *Authorial* (God's) intentions seriously. We need to start from scripture to culture, because the gospel is characteristically counter-cultural, challenging and correcting our social and cultural norms and practices. If interpretation leads to disharmonious understanding of scripture, then "if that is our destiny, so much the worse for theory, which is then only the ideology of a sect, and so much the better for the common sense of the practitioner who disdains theory to get on with his work" (op. cit 74).

Meaning in a text is a principle of stability, but its significance to the interpreter embraces a principle of change, involving consideration of context. Rejection of Bible texts which show that homosexuality is not God's intention for humanity implies knowledge of what is being rejected. As Hirsch says, "When an interpreter emphatically rejects the attitudes of a speaker or writer, he/she also adopts those attitudes in order to reject them" (op. cit.). The intentions of the author are not to give way to the reader's ability to "select and organize, anticipate and modify expectations, and create meaning" (see Davies 1990, 580). Any meaning divorced from the intentions of the author can lead to a completely new text being created by the reader.

## Conclusion / Possible Future

Internally, the ACT needs to take the challenges to Christianity seriously, taking the threat of poverty (both physical and spiritual) to society seriously, and come up with the relevant theologies that will address these challenges according to the Tanzanian context without losing sight of the universal nature of the Christian faith. Current proposals for the inauguration of an Anglican Micro-Finance Bank and Savings and Credit Co-operative Societies (SACCOS) at the parish level will help address physical poverty levels which hamper economic and spiritual emancipation of the individual and the church at large. To avoid dependency, it needs to revisit Henry Venn's "three-self's policy" in mission to attain economic autonomy for an independent voice internationally.

ACT theologians need to participate fully in the quest for an African Christian theology that answers questions being asked by Tanzanians if the church is to remain relevant to the Tanzanian context. Or else it will have to sit and watch many people return to traditional religion for answers to their contemporary religious, social, political, and economic problems.

The ACT currently is without a provincial education coordinator, both for theological education and secular education, an omission that weakens the coordination of education activities in the church. This causes the ACT not to have a unified course of action in this key mission area. Urgent remedial steps are needed to remedy this.

## At Anglican Communion Level

The Anglican Communion as a whole is now facing a crisis of identity, which is theological and institutional. As Metz suggests, "The crisis of identity in Christianity is not primarily a crisis of the Christian message, but rather a crisis of its subjects and institutions" (Metz 1980, ix). Also, Avis says that "The source of the problem lies in our perception of the identity of the gospel and the nature of the church" (Avis 1989, 2). He suggests that "What is needed is a complex and detailed clarification regarding the standpoint of doctrine and the real nature of the churches of the Anglican Communion" (op. cit., 298–9). The Christian community is no longer certain of its identity. Certainly, scripture has lost its impact and gone silent in such debates, and the church has become confused in its statements and practices.

Personal and corporate identities which come out of a living relationship with God through Christ bring us into the church. Anglicanism can only be justified by reference to Christianity, and ultimately to Jesus Christ. We have lost Christian identity by reverting to sociological and philosophical narratives neglecting and abandoning our Christian narrative. As Stroup points out, "the personal identity of many Christians is no longer shaped by Christian faith and the narratives that articulate that faith, but by other communities and other narratives . . . neither the language of Christian faith nor the fact of participation in the Christian communities seem to play prominent roles in those identity narratives" (Stroup 1984, 36ff). Any hope for the Anglican Church in Tanzania and the communion hinges on the current identity "dying and being born anew." It may have to accept the idea of "walking apart" if need be. The rebirth of identity means that it has to come through "death and resurrection, and there is no road to resurrection except by dying first" (Avis 1989, 20). This will have to include the way the church is governed at local and international levels. It will be painful, but the outcome will be worth the pain – a stronger and more alive Anglican Church worldwide.

Archbishop Rowan Williams called an emergency Primates Meeting at Lambeth Palace on October 15–16, 2003, at the end of which a statement was issued: "The recent actions in New Westminster and ECUSA do not express the mind of our Communion as a whole, and these decisions jeopardize our sacramental fellowship." It renewed the request made by the 1998 Lambeth Conference, Resolution IV.13, for the Archbishop of Canterbury to "establish a Commission *to consider his own role in maintaining the Communion within and between provinces when grave difficulties arise*" (Podmore 2005, 76). This led to the formation of the Lambeth Commission on Communion, which produced the Windsor Report (2004).

The House of Bishops of the Church of England "also recognizes that there are structural issues that will need to be resolved with some urgency in relation to how the Anglican Communion expresses its mind," supports the idea of an Anglican Covenant, and commends an enhanced and properly resourced role for the Archbishop of Canterbury in fostering the unity and mission of the Anglican Communion (House of Bishops Report 2005, 3). We cannot afford to do away with the unity of the church because that will not help our witness. Jesus prayed for that unity, and the world will find it hard to receive our message when we do not seem to agree among ourselves as to what the core message of the gospel is.

We believe that the leadership should beware of compromise. People who are elected to hold key leadership positions at all levels should be chosen carefully so that they may boldly lead the church in righteousness. Otherwise, "ordinary moral cowardice" will always be "represented as wise judgment"; where "equivocation and economy in the construction of compromise formulae is second nature to leaders who attain their positions in the church by avoidance of ideological coherence" (Norman 2004, 7).

In both the ACT and the communion, compromise is destroying the church, and "with each fudge, the institution supposedly being preserved stands for less and less" (op. cit. 7). Michael Ramsey said this about unity:

> The world does not hear the call to holiness and does not care for the truth of Christ. But the world has its own care for unity . . . longing for peace, it desires that peoples and nations shall be joined to each other and the forces which separate them removed. And the world, caring thus for unity, is shocked when the church fails to manifest it. (Ramsey, Canterbury Essays & Addresses, SPCK 1964, quoted by Redfern 2000, 124)

Christian unity is not only togetherness with one another, Ramsey says. It is unity in holiness and truth. The church unity which Anglicans should seek is a Christ-centered unity, not unity at the expense of Christian identity and values. Controversies will always be part of Christian life. It is as a result of controversies that many of our theological and doctrinal positions held in the church were thrashed out. The Jerusalem Council recorded in Acts 15 was the result of controversy on the mission field, as was the first Lambeth Conference in 1867. History teaches that doctrines have been formulated as the result of controversies.

We believe that the current controversy on human sexuality in the Anglican Communion, and problems faced by the Anglican Church in Tanzania are there to help the church thrash out once for all what the teaching of the church should be. In 325CE at Nicaea, the Arian controversy led to the formulation of the Creeds that resolved heresy about the two natures of Christ. The Lambeth Conference is like the Jerusalem Council of Acts 15. The Kikuyu Conference of 1913 was a result of problems on the mission field and issues of ecumenism. With prayerful dialogue and listening to God and to each other, the controversy threatening to break up the communion can be resolved, as the Virginia Report says: "From the earliest time in the history of the Christian community, an admonishing voice has been heard exhorting believers to maintain agreement with one another and thereby avert divisions. From almost equally early date they have found consensus, even on apparently major matters, singularly difficult to achieve" (Lambeth Report 1998, 21).

The recommendations of the Windsor Report could provide the starting point toward a much stronger unity within the Anglican Communion. The idea of an Anglican Covenant will increase commitment and accountability among members, and a more defined role of the Archbishop of Canterbury (and that of provincial primates and diocesan bishops) will provide the communion with a much stronger leadership that could help avert similar problems in the future. It is our hope that there is a future for the Anglican Church in Tanzania and the communion. However, it will have to come at the price of having to go through a very painful process – dying for resurrection to take place.

## Bibliography

Anglican Church of Tanzania. 2007. *Development Policy of the Anglican Church of Tanzania* (booklet). Dodoma: CTP, pp. 2–4.

The Anglican Church of Tanzania. Website.

Anglican Communion. 1930. *Official Report of the Lambeth Conference 1930*. London: Morehouse.

Anglican Communion. 1999. *The Official Report of the Lambeth Conference 1998*. London: Morehouse.

Anglican Communion. 2004. *The Windsor Report 2004*. London: Morehouse.

Archbishop's Council, The. 2003. *Some Issues in Human Sexuality*. London: Church House Publishing.

Archbishop's Council, The. 2005. *The Windsor Report: Report by the House of Bishops*. London: Church House Publishing.

Avis, P. 1989. *Anglicanism and the Christian Church*. Edinburgh: T&T Clark.

Bates, S. 2004. *A Church at War – Anglicans and Homosexuality*. London and New York: I. B. Tauris.

Davies, M. 1990. Reader Response Criticism. In *A Dictionary of Biblical Interpretation*, eds. R. J. Coggins and J. L. Houlden. London: SCM and Philadelphia: Trinity Press International, pp. 578–9.

Hirsch, E. D. Jr. 1976/1978. *The Aims of Interpretation*. Chicago: University of Chicago Press.

Metz, J. P. 1980. *Faith in History and Society: Towards a Practical Fundamental Theology*. London: Burns & Oates.

Moltmann, J. 2000. *Experiences in Theology: Ways and Forms of Christian Theology*. London: SCM.

Norman, E. 2004. *Anglican Difficulties: A New Syllabus of Errors*. London: Morehouse.

Podmore, C. 2005. *Aspects of Anglican Identity*. London: Church House.

Redfern, A. 2000. *Being Anglican*. London: Darton, Longmann and Todd.

Sahlberg, C. E. 1986. *From Krapf to Rugambwa – A Church History of Tanzania*. Nairobi: Evangel Publishing House.

Stroup, G. 1984. *The Promise of Narrative Theology*. London, 36ff; Quoted in Avis 1989, 3.

*The Anglican Church of Tanzania*. Wikipedia – A Free Encyclopedia.

Willis, J. J. 1947. *The Kikuyu Conference: Towards a United Church, 1913–1947*. London: Edinburgh House Press.

Oral interviews with:

Bishop Philip Baji (former Bishop of Tanga and principal of St. Mark's College)

Bishop John Simalenga (Diocese of South West Tanganyika)

Ms. Christine Kilipamwambu (former student of Loleza Girls' Secondary School and teacher at Ndwika TTC)

CHAPTER 20

# The Church of the Province of Uganda

## Christopher Byaruhanga

## Introduction

Anglicanism accompanied Christian missionaries when they opened churches outside Britain. As British Anglicans took their faith around the world, churches were established in many countries. British Anglicans encouraged autonomy and collegiality with these daughter churches, and over time, many separate "provinces" of the Anglican Church were established around the world. Inevitably, this transplanted Anglicanism took on aspects of the new contexts. In these new contexts, the earlier concept of an Anglican Church as a particular church, identified with the national life, traditions, and institutions of the English people, changed. English and Anglican were no longer equivalent terms. Anglican came to be equal to the national church established by missionaries from England and in communion with the See of Canterbury.

The Province of the Church of Uganda is a member of the Anglican Communion whose headquarters are in Kampala, Uganda. It consists of 34 dioceses that are headed by their respective bishops. The Province of the Church of Uganda traces its origins back to the Diocese of Eastern Equatorial Africa (Uganda, Kenya, and Tanzania) that was established in 1884 with James Hannington as its first bishop. However, Anglican missionary activity had been present in Uganda since the arrival of the Church Missionary Society (CMS) missionaries in 1877. In 1897, the Diocese of Eastern Equatorial Africa was split into two, with the new Diocese of Mombasa covering Kenya East of the Rift Valley and Central Tanganyika (Tanzania) and the Diocese of Uganda covering Western Kenya; Central, Western, and Eastern Uganda; Rwanda; Burundi; Boga in Congo; and part of Southern Sudan.

*The Wiley-Blackwell Companion to the Anglican Communion*, First Edition. Edited by Ian S. Markham, J. Barney Hawkins IV, Justyn Terry, and Leslie Nuñez Steffensen.
© 2013 John Wiley & Sons, Ltd. Published 2013 by John Wiley & Sons, Ltd.

# The Native Anglican Church (NAC) of Uganda (1877–1897)

The introduction of the Anglican Church in Uganda began with a quaint map of Equatorial Africa drawn by James Erhardt and sent to England in 1856 by Johannes
Rebmann. The map showed a great inland sea stretching across the interior of East
Africa. It was in response to this map that, in 1857, the Royal Geographical Society
sponsored an exploratory expedition to Central Africa by Captain John Speke and
Captain Richard Burton. The two explorers reported the existence of well-organized
kingdoms on the more distant shores of a great lake. Regarding the conditions for
mission work, Speke wrote that "of all places in Africa by far the most inviting to missionary enterprise are the kingdoms of . . . Uganda [Buganda] and Unyoro [Bunyoro]"
(Speke 1863, 366).

While Uganda became known to Britain geographically through the expedition of
Speke, the discovery of her people was through David Livingstone, despite the fact that
his journeys did not take him to Uganda itself. What Uganda owes to Livingstone is the
visit of Henry Morton Stanley to Uganda in 1875. Two newspapers, namely *The New
York Herald* and London's *Daily Telegraph*, sponsored Stanley's expedition across Africa
with one of the aims being to look for Livingstone, whom he eventually met on November 10, 1871. It was during this time that Stanley visited Uganda and spent several
months at King Mutesa's palace. Upon Mutesa's request, Stanley wrote his famous
letter that appeared in the *Daily Telegraph* of November 15, 1875, asking for missionaries to come to Uganda. Stanley's letter was "a spark that kindled the emotions that had
already been stirred by Livingstone's publications" (Byaruhanga 2008, 53).

On April 27, 1876, the CMS sent to Uganda a party of seven missionaries, but only
two of them, namely the Rev. C. T. Wilson and Shergold Smith, arrived at Mutesa's court
on June 30, 1877. The two were "helped by Dallington Scorpion Muftaa in conducting
regular Christian services" (Byaruhanga 2008, 55) at Mutesa's court.

While it is difficult to tell whether Mutesa's desire for European missionary presence
in his kingdom was primarily a political one or not, what is clear is that at first he had
a genuine intellectual curiosity with regard to the gospel. On several occasions, the
missionaries preached and Mutesa himself translated from Swahili to Luganda for the
chiefs and pages at his court.

On February 23, 1879, a party of Roman Catholic French priests arrived in Uganda.
As the number of European missionaries increased, Mutesa decided to make a choice
between the Roman Catholic party and the Anglican party. His attitude toward the
Anglican party cooled visibly, and he began to show much interest in the Roman Catholic party. However, Mutesa did not want the CMS missionaries to leave his country. He
therefore allowed them to continue with their normal activities without any hindrance.
In March 1882, the first official baptism by the Anglican Church in Uganda took place.
By the time Mutesa died on October 9, 1884, "eighty-eight natives had been baptized
in the native congregation of the Church of England" (Byaruhanga 2008, 67).

King Mutesa was succeeded in 1884 by Mwanga II, who was not in favor of Christianity. Mwanga's reign was characterized by a fierce struggle between the traditional

authority of kingship and the challenges of Christianity. In the early days of his reign, dark clouds hung over Buganda because, having no experience in political administration, Mwanga was always hasty in his judgments. On January 31, 1885, three Anglican Ugandans whom he accused of insubordination were killed by Mwanga. As Mwanga's hostility turned against the Christians, the CMS missionaries decided to elect a church council so that if they themselves had to leave the country, the new converts would have an organization of their own. The council members were taught how to lead worship and counsel their fellow Christians. On October 29, 1885, Mwanga ordered the killing of Bishop James Hannington, the first Bishop of the Diocese of Eastern Equatorial Africa. On November 15, 1885, Mwanga killed Joseph Mukasa Balikuddembe, the leading Roman Catholic convert in Buganda. Balikuddembe had rebuked Mwanga for having ordered the killing of Hannington. Mwanga's anger came to a climax on June 30, 1886, when 23 Anglicans were executed. Referring to Christian persecution during Mwanga's reign, J. F. Faupel wrote, "had there been a strong ruler, bloodshed might have been avoided, but with one of Mwanga's weakness of character an explosion was inevitable" (Faupel 1962, 64–5). The Christians who were killed during Mwanga's reign are remembered as the Martyrs of Uganda whose life is celebrated every year on June 3.

Many Anglicans died in many parts of Buganda between 1885 and 1886. As a result of these deaths, Anglicans were scattered into the far corners of Uganda. This enabled the Native Anglican Church to spread in places where it had never reached before. The 1885–1886 persecutions therefore achieved the opposite of what they were intended to do. The storm of persecution having blown over, Anglican Ugandans were convinced that there was no future for the Native Anglican Church in Uganda unless the Christians themselves secured political and military power. At this time, Mwanga began to rely on the younger generation that was comprised of the three religious groups in his kingdom, namely the Muslims, the Roman Catholics, and the Anglicans. He also founded three new chieftaincies whose leaders were appointed directly by him. One of these new chieftaincies he gave to Apolo Kagwa, the leading Anglican.

In the new class of a younger generation of leaders was a combination of two elements, namely new weapons and new religious beliefs. When the new generation of chiefs became too powerful to control, Mwanga organized a plan to get rid of both Christianity and Islam. Instead, he was overthrown through a joint conspiracy of both groups in September 1888. He was replaced on the throne by Kiwewa, his elder brother. Kiwewa expelled the CMS missionaries and ousted many of the Christian chiefs and established Muslim supremacy in Buganda. The Muslims tried to force Kiwewa to become a Muslim; however, he refused and was arrested and burned to death. Kiwewa was replaced on the throne by Kalema, his younger brother, whom the Muslims circumcised by force. On February 11, 1890, Apolo Kagwa led the victorious Christian army into Mengo and reinstalled Mwanga as the King of Buganda. It was the state of affairs existing in Uganda, namely the war between the Christians and Muslims on one hand, and the fight for political positions between the Roman Catholics and the Anglicans on the other, that forced the Bishop of the Diocese of Uganda, Alfred Robert Tucker, to encourage Britain to assume direct control of Uganda in 1894.

## The Consolidation of the Native Anglican Church – the Diocese of Uganda (1897–1961)

In 1897, the Diocese of Eastern Equatorial Africa was divided into two, from which was carved the Diocese of Uganda. Bishop Tucker chose to serve as Bishop of Uganda. As Bishop of Uganda, Tucker was determined to organize the growing Christian congregation into an African Anglican Church independent of the Church of England and yet an integral part of the Anglican Communion. Tucker's vision of consolidating the Anglican Church in Uganda had two phases, the first of which was church planting. Until 1891, the Christian missionaries were confined to the vicinity of the capital of the Buganda kingdom. Thereafter, Ugandan catechists and teachers began to spread Christianity to the neighboring regions. In most of the evangelized areas of Uganda, the CMS missionaries came to consolidate the newly converted Africans already evangelized by their fellow Africans.

The second phase was the creation of an indigenous ministry. It was clear to Tucker that, within a few years, the Anglican Church in Uganda would grow in numbers. The questions were how the sacraments were to be administered, and how the work of an organized church was to be done. According to Tucker, it was difficult enough to get ordained men from England for missionary work. In 1896, he ordained the first Ugandan priests.

With the creation of an indigenous ministry, there was need for:

(a) Church constitution. The drawing of the constitution of the African Anglican Church was based on the conviction that Ugandan Christians and CMS missionaries should have equal status in the Anglican Church in Uganda. The church constitution was aimed at granting considerable power to the indigenous Anglicans in what was known as the Native Anglican Church.

(b) Formal education. One of the most notable contributions of the Anglican Church was in the area of education. A well-organized formal education began with the arrival of the first party of ladies in 1895, who developed a network of schools at nearly every place where a church station was opened. At first, the CMS missionaries' efforts were focused on making the African converts literate so that they could read religious books. By 1901, the missionaries had recognized the need for a form of education designed to achieve two goals. First, there was the goal to help build the character of learners so as to make them useful citizens of their country. The second was the goal to prepare Africans for the wider world in which they would soon live. This was the beginning of high school education in 1905. In 1913, the Bishop Tucker Theological College was established in Mukono, and this institution was eventually expanded into what is now today the Uganda Christian University.

(c) Scientific medicine. The CMS missionaries took a lead in public health with the establishment of the Mengo Hospital in 1897. Traditional medicine could not deal effectively with the kind of diseases Africans were suffering from. Information to the effect that there existed an institution in Uganda that could relieve suffering spread throughout East Africa. The impact of modern medical and surgical knowledge on the Africans' old methods of treatment changed their attitude toward diseases; henceforth, disease was no longer interpreted in terms of witchcraft.

## East African Revival Movement

One of the truly remarkable revival movements in the history of the church is that of East Africa. It is one of the most amazing forces that have shaped the Christian faith in Africa. In its patterns of thinking and action, the East African Revival Movement is a genuinely African expression of Christianity. The first manifestations of a large-scale revival occurred at the CMS mission hospital at Gahini, Rwanda, which was an outpost of the Anglican Diocese of Uganda in 1921. Most of the hospital staff at Gahini and most of the leaders of the awakening were from Uganda. Serious revival began in 1931 when the first evangelistic team of the revival was formed. With the formation of more evangelistic teams in the subsequent years, the revival spread from personal dedication to evangelistic zeal.

The entire Great Lakes Region was transformed by the East African Revival Movement. Since there were already deeply converted and mature Christians in East Africa, the East African Revival movement worked alongside the churches and avoided schism. For instance, Bishop Stuart, Bishop of Uganda since 1934, had a warm sympathy for what had been happening in Gahini and Kigezi. He had trained Kigozi as a deacon and shared his concern to bring the fruits of the awakening back into the center of the Church of Uganda. He hoped that the celebrations for the diamond jubilee of the church in 1937 would be the occasion for a general renewal of the church. In pursuit of this aim, he organized a series of evangelistic missions to take place in every parish as a climax to the celebrations. In preparation for this, Stuart invited Joe Church to bring a team from Ruanda to hold a mission at Bishop Tucker College late in 1936.

Although receiving, at first, a mixed reception from church leaders,[1] the sense of having a mission from God to the whole church, of being a critical witness from within the church, is a dominant theme throughout the history of the East African Movement.

With the rise of African nationalism, relationships between the white missionaries and the Africans were often strained. Nevertheless, the East African Revival brought healing and unity everywhere, and this was one of its great achievements. Missionaries were humbled, stripped of racial pride, and able to enjoy deep Christian fellowship with African leaders, who also had such a deep understanding of Jesus' reconciling death as to free them from resentment against the whites. The revival bridged racial as well

[1] Revivals were by no means unknown in Africa in the early part of the twentieth century. However, with very few exceptions, they led almost immediately to schism and were often linked with anti-colonial feeling. The Africans, understandably, wanted a church of their own without interference from missionaries. In East Africa at this time, there was much nominal Christianity, with low moral standards and a great deal of corruption.

as spiritual divisions. Its teaching centered on the cleansing Jesus achieved for us when he died.

The East African Revival Movement's effects have been more lasting than almost any other revival in history. In some parts of the Great Lakes Region, the East African Movement has become the dominant expression of African Christianity, permeating the life of the church to such an extent that it is difficult to distinguish revival and church from each other. A person who wishes to train for the ministry of the church must be a saved person, and thus the church as an organization has become permeated with the East African Revival Movement ethos. The fact that revival and the church have become so closely identified has stamped a strong evangelical theology on the church; it has also prevented the movement from becoming a small inward-looking sect and has given the revival a relative openness to the world. In places where there were kingdoms, many people had nominally identified themselves with the religion of the king. It was the evangelistic zeal of the saved (Balokole) that transformed the situation.

The East African Revival Movement is essentially a lay movement, African in style and control, which has transcended tribal, racial, and church divisions, and has produced its own theology. However, the movement's lack of a formal organization has led, in some parts of East Africa, to the revival being superseded by the Pentecostal movement.

## The Province of the Church of Uganda, Rwanda-Burundi and Boga-Zaire (1961–1980)

The 1909 Tucker Constitution did not only give Ugandans access to modern democracy but also taught them the value of respecting their inalienable right to freedom. It had a creative role in fostering intellectual awakening that eventually enhanced a new self-understanding and self-appreciation beyond the immediate traditional circles of tribal identity. The 1909 constitution provided a structure in which the Church of Uganda could exercise genuine unity and responsibility, but it required trust on the part of all Church of Uganda Christians to ensure that this was the case. It was precisely this point that caused the 1961 Church of Uganda constitutional crisis.

Tucker's constitution was succeeded by the 1961 Church of the Province of Uganda and Rwanda-Burundi constitution. The 1961 constitution was accepted and approved by the Synod and the Diocesan Council of the Upper Nile on April 27–28, 1960, and came into effect in 1961. Article 1 of the 1961 constitution reads, "The Church of this Province shall be named the Church of the Province of Uganda and Ruanda-Urundi and shall consist in the first instance of the following dioceses . . . Northern Uganda . . . Soroti . . . Mbale . . . Namirembe . . . West Buganda . . . Ankole-Kigezi . . . Ruanzori . . . Ruanda-Urundi" (Constitution 1961). Like Tucker's 1909 constitution, the 1961 constitution had a built-in ability of weakening tribal boundaries and barriers, thus creating a comprehensive church. However, this idea of a comprehensive Church of Uganda was counterbalanced by a contrary factor in 1965 when the first Archbishop of the Province of Uganda, Rwanda-Burundi and Boga Zaire, Leslie Brown, retired. Like the colonial government which tended to favor the Buganda region, the CMS missionaries who came after Tucker also tended to favor Buganda. This created a situation where the dioceses in Buganda considered themselves special, and the rest of the dioceses had the feeling of deprivation. This horizontal conflict within the Church of Uganda compromised Tucker's idea of a comprehensive church.

The horizontal conflict within the Church of Uganda came to a climax at the time of Bishop Brown's resignation in 1965. Archbishop Brown was British and had been Bishop of Namirembe, the cathedral headquarters of the Church of the Province of Uganda. Apart from housing the "archiepiscopal" throne, the 1961 constitution did not say that the Diocese of Namirembe should be the Archdiocese of the Church of the Province of Uganda. However, it made it clear that the archbishop shall be a diocesan bishop of a diocese in the province and shall have a house at Namirembe. The 1961 constitution, Article VII (a) states:

> There shall be an Archbishop of the Church of Uganda and Ruanda-Urundi who shall be a Diocesan Bishop of a Diocese in the Province and who whilst normally residing in his Diocese shall have a house at Namirembe, Kampala, provided for him where he shall reside at regular intervals together with such offices as may be necessary for his work as Archbishop. An Archiepiscopal throne shall be provided for him in the Cathedral Church of Saint Paul, Namirembe. (Constitution 1961)

So long as Bishop Brown was Archbishop of the Church of the Province of Uganda and Rwanda-Burundi and the Diocesan Bishop of Namirembe, it (Namirembe) also functioned as archdiocese of the province. And Namirembe Cathedral was popularly regarded by all Christians in Uganda, Rwanda and Burundi as the Cathedral of the Church of the Province of Uganda.

As soon as Bishop Brown announced his resignation, the question of who was to succeed him became one of the hottest issues in the province. Was it going to be a muganda bishop or a bishop from another tribe? At this time, Brown was disillusioned with the Baganda who had accused him of conspiring with the British governor Sir Andrew Cohen and Obote to deport the King of Buganda (Kabaka) Mutesa II to the United Kingdom.[2] This incident "united both traditionalists and progressive nationalists, Buganda and the rest of Uganda, in opposition to British colonial arrogance. The authorities of the Church of Uganda, still dominated at its higher levels by missionaries, including the newly arrived Leslie Brown, came under strong attack for their close alliance with the colonial government" (Ward 2005, 111).

Secondly, he was accused of being Obote's friend, the great enemy of the Baganda. Brown was a strong supporter of Uganda People's Congress and Kabaka Yeeka party, and when the coalition won the election he was the first to congratulate Obote and invited him to a "Thanksgiving Service" for the National Assembly. In July 1962, Brown again invited Obote to a service, and in his opening speech Brown requested Obote to make the Church of Uganda a national church of Uganda. However, this was

---

[2] On the deportation of the Kabaka to Britain and the bad feelings of the Baganda toward the archbishop and Obote, see Ewechue, R. ed. 1991. *Makers of Modern Africa*, 2nd Ed. London: Africa Books, 16.

not in Obote's political agenda. The reason for Brown's close relationship with Obote was that he did not want the church to lose the benefits which the unique collaboration of church and state had produced in Uganda.[3]

By 1965, there were three Baganda bishops out of nine bishops in Uganda. Two of them were very old, and one by the name of Dunstan Nsubuga was very junior. Nsubuga had been consecrated in 1965 as Bishop of the Diocese of Namirembe just before Brown's departure. Although Nsubuga succeeded Brown as Bishop of the Diocese of Namirembe, he could not automatically claim to be the Archbishop of the Church of the Province of Uganda since there were other bishops who could claim to the post of archbishop on the basis of their experience and seniority. Again, the 1961 constitution did not state that the Bishop of the Diocese of Namirembe could automatically become the Archbishop of the Church of the Province of Uganda and Rwanda-Burundi.

In 1965, seniority was not an issue, but tribe was. By showing tribal sentiments in 1965, the Baganda lost any possible support from their colleagues for the post of archbishop. Nsubuga got three votes (including his own vote) from Buganda and one more vote from the Bishop of Ankole-Kigezi. In the spirit of democracy, Bishop Erica Sabiti from the Diocese of Rwenzori was elected archbishop. The vice of negative tribal sentiments that started in the 1960s was improved in the 1980s and perfected by the Church of Uganda in the 1990s where, apart from the Kampala and Northern Uganda dioceses, all dioceses have tribal bishops.

In the past, the Church of the Province of Uganda was a flagship against any negative tribal sentiments, but now it is in the danger of becoming the drag-ship which pulls the ideals of 1909 Tucker constitution behind. The issue of comprehensiveness can be addressed thoroughly if the Church of the Province of Uganda asks hard questions such as: How is tribal loyalty understood by the Christians in Uganda today? How is tribal loyalty related to the loyalty to the church and to Jesus Christ? Has the Church of the Province of Uganda managed to stand above negative tribal loyalty?

The origin of the negative tribal sentiments is difficult to understand unless one relates it to the ecclesiastical and political changes that have been taking place in Uganda. Negative tribal sentiments have their origins in pre-colonial, colonial, and post-colonial periods. In pre-colonial Uganda, tribes were homogeneous, and there was less competition between them for power. As J. Lonsdale argues, there was an "art of living in a reasonably peaceful way" (Lonsdale 1981, 139). When tribes were forced to merge during the colonial period, they attained new structures and definitions. Power and authority were vested in few ecclesiastical officers. Due to limited centers of ecclesiastical power and authority, Christians tend to fight to have an archdeacon, bishop, or archbishop coming from their tribe. For Christians to fight among themselves over leadership and for dioceses to be created on tribal lines is known to happen from time to time in the Church of Uganda. The competition for the limited centers of ecclesiastical power and authority within the Church of the Province of Uganda has changed what Tucker hoped to be a comprehensive church.

[3] For a detailed account of the relationship between Archbishop Brown and Obote's government, see Uganda Argus, February 16, 1962.

The problem of negative tribal sentiments in the Church of the Province of Uganda is linked with the question of competing loyalties. In Uganda, tribal loyalties have risen above other loyalties. While in the missionary era there were very few ecclesiastical incentives which tribes could offer, today tribal loyalty may mean a quick promotion in one's ecclesiastical status. Even the internal administration of church institutions has shown that their loyalty often lies more with their tribal groupings rather than with Christ.

The challenge of the Church of the Province of Uganda is how to appeal to the gospel values to construct a comprehensive church as Tucker saw it. This is a serious challenge because the Church of the Province of Uganda is considered to be a part of the problem of negative tribal sentiments, and as such it has failed to stand above this situation. The question is: is the Church of the Province of Uganda based on a sufficiently coherent form of authority that can attract a viable spiritual fellowship of tribal bishops, or does its understanding of the idea of comprehensiveness conceal internal divisions which may cause disruption in its mission? Can we say that, as understood by many Christians, comprehensiveness is a clever way to explain and cover up inconsistencies that exist within the Church of the Province of Uganda?

## Indigenous Ministry

By 1891, the number of those attending Sunday services was about a thousand people. The missionaries had been impressed by the inquiring spirit of the Africans and the way in which those who could read took it upon themselves to teach those who wanted to learn, and quickly acted on their potential as teachers and catechists. In January 1893, six African catechists were ordained deacons. Some of the six deacons were ordained priests in 1896.

The missionaries' model of an African ministry culminated in October 1947 in the consecration of the Rev. Aberi Balya of Toro as the first African Anglican Bishop in East Africa. When the Diocese of Uganda was divided into five dioceses in 1957, the Rev. Hosea Shalita was consecrated bishop in May that year. Upon the retirement of Bishop Balya in March 1960, the Rev. Erica Sabiti was appointed the Bishop of Rwenzori diocese. In 1966, Sabiti became the Archbishop of the Province of the Church of Uganda. In the 1960s, "the Church in Uganda slowly moved from an African congregation of the Church of England to the Anglican Church in Uganda" (Byaruhanga 2008, 169).

## Church of Uganda during Idi Amin's Regime

In 1971, Idi Amin, who had Islamic sympathies, became the president of Uganda in a coup d'état. The Church of Uganda became more outspoken in opposition to the policies of Amin. In reply, renewed persecution of Christians broke out again. The Christian resilience in the face of brutal torture and death demonstrated the continued influence of the Namugongo martyrs and the deep, vital, and abiding faith among so many who had been influenced by the East African Revival Movement. Among the many people who were brutally tortured and killed was the Anglican Archbishop of the Church of Uganda, Janani Jakayo Luwum, in 1977.

## Province of Uganda (1980–Present)

The Church of the Province of Uganda's inheritance in both doctrine and church practice is irrevocably tied to the cause of the Protestant Reformation. According to the Fathers of the Protestant Reformation, what makes a Christian tradition an authentic church is the faithful proclamation of the gospel. Paul Avis says: "where the Gospel is, Christ is; and where Christ is, there is the Church. All that is necessary to authentic 'church-hood' is the possession of the gospel" (Avis 1981, 221). The Church of Uganda is theologically conservative and deeply opposed to what it views as departures from orthodoxy in the Episcopal Church. The Church of Uganda derives her mandate and authority from the canonical scriptures of the Old and New Testaments, as the ultimate rule and standard of faith, given by inspiration of God and containing all things necessary for salvation.

The Church's position on human sexuality is consistent with its basis of faith and doctrine, and has been stated very clearly over the years as reflected in various documents. From a plain, careful, and critical reading of scripture, homosexual practice has no place in God's design of creation, the continuation of the human race through procreation, or His plan of redemption. Even natural law reveals that the very act of sexual intercourse is an experience of embracing the sexual "other." The Church of Uganda, therefore, believes that "Homosexual practice is incompatible with Scripture" (Lambeth 1998).

After the 2003 decision of the Episcopal Church in the United States of America (TEC) to consecrate as bishop a divorced man living in a same sex relationship, TEC's action "tore the fabric of the Anglican Communion at its deepest level" (Church of Uganda 2007). The Church of Uganda has been active in the leadership of southern hemisphere churches who have agreed to provide pastoral oversight and support to new Anglican churches in North America in the ongoing Anglican realignment.

In 2004, the Church of Uganda responded to the first appeal from biblically faithful congregations in America to receive them as members of the Church of Uganda. After the March 2007 TEC's House of Bishops' rejection of the pastoral scheme presented to them unanimously by the primates of the Anglican Communion, the House of Bishops elected the Rev. John Guernsey, a former priest in TEC and now a priest of the Church of Uganda, as bishop to provide episcopal oversight to the growing number of congregations in the United States that had not departed from orthodoxy, as understood by the Church of Uganda, and were seeking refuge in the Church of Uganda. The consecration of Guernsey on September 2, 2007, was an important statement to the Anglican Communion. The consecration was unprecedented in the history of the Church of Uganda. In addition to the 25 active and retired bishops of the Church of Uganda, there was significant international participation from the global Anglican Communion. The Primates of Kenya, Rwanda, and the Southern Cone (South America), and a representative of the Primate of Nigeria participated in the service, along with 14 other bishops from Kenya, Congo, Brazil, Australia, England, Canada, and the United States.

The Church of Uganda responded to TEC's action by declaring itself on June 23, 2009, to be in full communion with the American and Canadian Anglican churches, which are opposed to their national churches' actions regarding homosexuality. By her actions, the Church of Uganda is not seceding from the Anglican Communion, and is still very much a part of it. In her opinion, it is the Episcopal Church that has seceded from the Anglican Communion because of its teaching that has departed dramatically from the historic faith, teaching, and practice of the Bible and the Anglican Communion.

## Bibliography

"1961 Constitution" in File IPS 226/16, Uganda Christian University Archives.

Avis, Paul. 1981. *The Church in the Theology of the Reformers.* London: Marshall Morgan and Scott.

Byaruhanga, Christopher. 2008. *Bishop Alfred Robert Tucker and the Establishment of the African Anglican Church.* Nairobi: WordAlive.

The Church of Uganda, The. 2007. The Church of Uganda Consecrates Two Bishops. *Press Release by the Church of Uganda,* September 6, 2007.

Faupel, J. F. 1962. *African Holocaust: The Story of the Uganda Martyrs.* Kampala: St. Paul's Publications.

Lambeth Conference. 1998. Resolution 1.10.

Lonsdale, J. 1981. States and Social Process in Africa: A Histographical Survey. *African Studies Review,* vol. 3, no. 2 (June–September 1981), p. 139.

Speke, John Hannington. 1863. *What Led to the Discovery of the Source of the Nile.* Edinburgh: Blackwood and Sons.

Ward, Kevin. 2005. Eating and Sharing: Church and State in Uganda. *Journal of Anglican Studies,* vol. 3, no. 1 (June), p. 111.

CHAPTER 21

# The Church of the Province of West Africa

## John S. Pobee

## English Provenance

The designation of an ecclesial body as *Ecclesia Anglicana*, English/Anglican Church, is evidence of her English provenance and naissance. Because of the Christian core message of the incarnation, the construct was informed by English culture and idiom, epistemology, and ontology. It is a contextual construct.

## Changing Profile

The missionary movement which befits a church that defines herself by mission, and the scramble for Africa and the colonial expansion that began with the Berlin Conference of 1884–1885 (Kwarteng 2011, 273–97), set the stage for a revisit of the English model when she got to non-English soil (Sachs 1993). It was one story in countries like Australia, Canada, and South Africa, which have an English stamp, but quite another when she reached non-Anglo lands like China, Japan, Africa, Pacific Islands, and other Asian countries (Pobee 1988, 428–41). In the nineteenth century, the Ethiopianists had been articulating that "to render Christianity indigenous to Africa it must be watered by native hands, turned by native hatchet and tended with native soil. . . . It is a curse if we intend for ever to hold at the apron strings of foreign teachers doing the baby for aye" (Vincent 1889). As the nationalist and independence movements gathered momentum, foreign and colonial associations, trappings with paternalistic style, and the Peter Pan syndrome became more and more unpalatable to the native lands and a liability (Pobee 1986). The up-to-then "Overseas Bishops of the Canterbury Jurisdiction" was no longer suitable.

*The Wiley-Blackwell Companion to the Anglican Communion*, First Edition. Edited by Ian S. Markham, J. Barney Hawkins IV, Justyn Terry, and Leslie Nuñez Steffensen.
© 2013 John Wiley & Sons, Ltd. Published 2013 by John Wiley & Sons, Ltd.

The Anglican Communion was exhibiting dynamism and sensitivity to changing times. In 1947, the Church of Australia enjoyed "complete spiritual autonomy, with freedom to revise its formularies and to determine its laws of worship in accordance with its own desires" (Carpenter 1991, 485). On the African continent itself, the first province was in South Africa with its metropolitan see in Cape Town. Indeed, its constitution became the model for subsequent developments on the continent. This development was the implementation of Resolution 43 of Lambeth 1920, which encouraged "the gradual creation of new provinces" (Coleman 1992, 59–8).

## The Mission Society Factor

In addition to the changing demands at the global level, there were internal factors calling for such developments. Africa was evangelized by differing missionary societies, principally the Church Missionary Society (CMS) in Nigeria, Sierra Leone, Kenya, and Uganda; the Society for the Propagation of the Gospel in Foreign Lands (SPG) in Gold Coast/Ghana; the Universities Mission to Central Africa (UMCA) in Tanganyika; and the Bible Churchman's Missionary Society. By virtue of the different and differing churchmanships they represented, the multi-headed Anglican ecclesial life potentially complicated and compounded the already ethnic, religious, etc., divisions on the continent and within countries. It has sometimes resulted in the "obfuscation of the sense of unity within the one denomination . . . and segregated uniformity" (Pobee 1986, 99). The idea of province was envisaged as a help in overcoming isolationism, monolithic situations, and introspection arising from isolation. The above-mentioned Resolution 43 of Lambeth 1920 stated it clearly: "the fact that dioceses proposing to form a province owe their origin to missions of different branches of the Anglican Communion need be no bar to such action" (Coleman, ibid).

## Mooting of Idea of CPWA

In 1944, the 98th Archbishop of Canterbury, William Temple (1942–1944), had suggested the idea of a CPWA. However, his untimely death in 1944 left the next archbishop, Geoffrey Francis Fisher (1945–1961), to pursue the project. He did it carefully and with sensitivity. In an encounter with Bishop Sherwood Jones of Lagos, Nigeria, Archbishop Fisher stated: "it is essential that the constitutional foundations shall be well and truly laid. It is my bounden duty to see that every care is taken to secure a workable and fool-proof Constitution of the Province which will not lead it subsequently in legal difficulties with Dioceses."

In 1944, the bishops of West Africa met in conference in Accra to discuss the issue. Before Fisher moved to Canterbury, a special committee under the chairmanship of Bishop Palmer of Bombay, India, had been set up to advise Cantaur. Lambeth Resolution 43 had suggested a minimum of four dioceses as the basis of a province. The 1944 Accra meeting included the Dioceses of Lagos, founded 1919; Sierra Leone, founded 1858; Accra, founded 1909, the Niger, founded 1921; and Gambia and Rio Pongas, founded 1935. Hence, they fulfilled all righteousness in respect to the minimum number of dioceses in a province.

However, there was some resistance to the move from within West Africa. Canon Howells of Lagos, in a meeting at Lambeth with Cantaur on April 30, 1947, cautioned that the Africans had little or no sense, let alone understanding, of the idea of province. It was both resistance to change and the fear that Cantaur wanted to wash his hands off his daughter church.

Bishop John Aglionby of Accra was strongly against the idea of a province, and had influenced his diocese to argue that such a scheme would be encouragement for "unwise ecumenical schemes for reunion." Such was his opposition to a province that Cantaur had to orchestrate Aglionby's retirement from the West African scene (Carpenter 1991, 504).

In the autumn of 1950, Bishop John Daly of the Gambia, Bishop Leslie Vining of Lagos, and Bishop John Horstead of Sierra Leone met in Lambeth Palace to confer on the details of the inauguration of the province. The constitution was ready. The venue for inauguration was fixed for Freetown, Sierra Leone, which had been the seat of the mother Diocese of Western Equatorial Guinea. The date was fixed for April 17, 1951, and His Grace and Rt. Hon. Geoffrey Fisher would come in person to inaugurate the province at a Eucharistic celebration according to the 1652 Rite at St. George's Cathedral, Freetown.

## Changing Composition of CPWA

As a living organization, CPWA's composition did not remain static. Today, following the creation of more dioceses in the geographical area of West Africa, the CPWA is comprised of 16 dioceses: Accra, Bo, Cameroon, Cape Coast, Dunkwa-on-Offin, Freetown, Gambia, Guinea, Ho, Koforidua, Kumasi, Liberia, Sekondi, Sunyani, Tamale, and Wiawso.

At its inception, Nigeria was included. However, in 1975, it applied to leave the province, and the Province of Nigeria came into being on February 24, 1979, under the name of the Church of Nigeria, with Timothy Olufosoye as the first archbishop. Liberia joined as an associate member of the CPWA in 1970, still enjoying a special relationship with the ECUSA (now TEC).

Thus, to start with, the CPWA was contiguous with the geographical and political area of West Africa. It was co-extensive with British Colonial West Africa and had a very Anglo-culture. Now Francophone West Africa is being added, thus making the province a laboratory for Francophone-Anglicanism.

## Province of Ghana

In 1992, Bishop Theophilus Annobil of Sekondi proposed to the Joint Anglican Diocesan Council (JADC) of Ghana, a putative province, to consider the "Ghanaian National Church forming a Province . . . to enable the God-given genius of a Nation to find its appropriate expression in the worship and work of the Church. Again, because of the intimate connection with the nation as a whole, the national Church could effectively influence national life." The visit of the ACC in 2004 showed that no preparations had been made for a viable ongoing province. Following decisions of the Provincial Synod, Liberia in September 2012, the Administrative Province of Ghana with First Administrative Archbishop Daniel Yinka Sarfo of Kumasi came into being on December 16th, 2012.

The foregoing story is the tip of an iceberg of issues. The first issue is the role of the ACC. It does not have juridical authority; it has authority of spiritual and moral suasion. The ACC, like the Archbishop of Canterbury, has "authority of influence not of decree." The second is an unarticulated issue of the style of the incumbent primate. When, at a JADC assembly at St. Stephen's Church in 1997, I articulated a concern about the move, people said to me in the corridors that they did not see and feel the role of the primate; it was as if he were more visible outside Ghana than inside it. This in my view unconsciously underlined a gem in the Hurd Report that "the ability of the Archbishop to gather and lead, however, is most effective when he has the kind of understanding of the needs and circumstances of the Church that can only come by personal contact." Personal relationships, and not just institutional–structural relationships, are key to generating and undergirding the bonds of affection in a communion/province.

At the above-mentioned Congress, I made a second argument: Outside Ghana, the remaining dioceses were small islets in a sea of Muslim predominance, and therefore, could become most vulnerable.

## Finances

A third consideration is the track record vis-à-vis the financial viability of the province. The financial story of CPWA as of JADC is simple to summarize and creates an underlying difficulty.

The financial strength of the dioceses varies considerably. And the total holdings of all the dioceses combined have grown slowly. In 2006, it was £89,425. It saw significant growth in 2007 to £115,334. Inevitably, it slowed in 2008, but still grew a little to £121,152. In 2009, it reached £134,448; and in 2010, it was £160,287. However, the assessment to support the activities of the province has been very small. In 2006, the amount required from the dioceses was £23,370; in 2010, the amount was £28,830. Hence, while the total funds held by the diocese have grown by 79%, the funds going to the province have only increased by 23%.

It turns out that, in the politics of succession to the archepiscopacy after the Most Rev. Okine, a candidate had stated that there was no need to pay assessment to the province. The story raises two issues: the sense of corporate ownership of the project, and the sense of a diocese and/or province. Equally worrying is the fact that, time and again, decisions at the diocesan and provincial synods are honored in breach. This might point the finger at a more basic issue of whether the structures inherited are really in sync with the minds of West Africans.

## Primates of West Africa

According to the statutes of the CPWA, the official face of the province is the archbishop and primate. Since the creation of the province in 1951, there have been eight arch-bishops with the designation "Most Reverend." To this, some add "Metropolitan," which is clearly a misnomer in the context. The following table lists the archbishops of the province from 1951 till date.

Some lessons may be drawn from this list. First, being diocesan bishop is prerequisite for becoming a primate. Second, the primatial seat has rotated between Nigeria, Sierra Leone, and Ghana. If Ghana were to become a province, would the rotation of the archiepiscopal seat change to become metropolitan archiepiscopal at the capital of Ghana? Third, since 1969, Africans have been primates in consistency with the changed political climate, i.e., African nationalism and independence. Whether native bodies are equal to the mind of the context is another matter, because some natives of West Africa are in North Atlantic captivity. However, it is a step in the right direction for fulfilling the missiological principle of being self-governing. Have the province and its institu-tions been "recast in patterns that answer to the African contexts or have they become square pegs in round holes, expressing foreign patterns in a different cultural and reli-gious landscape?" (Pobee 2010, 84).

The founding of historic churches by missionary societies and the continuing con-nection with them has come with a system of grants which holds the African dioceses in a bondage of sorts. Such grants are made according to the needs of institutional self-interest and perpetuated denominationalism, *à la* the ethos of the particular mis-sionary society (Pobee and Oshitelu 1988, 55).

The combination of obscurity regarding African personality and identity, and captiv-ity to the institutional self-interest of mission boards results in the short changing of the three-self principles established by Rufus Anderson (1792–1880), American congrega-tional administrator and theorist of foreign missions, and Henry Venn, general secretary of CMS (1796–1873) (Anderson 1998, 20), i.e., self-governing, self-supporting, and self-propagating. In the light of experiences gained through encounters with African

**Table 21.1:**   Archbishops of the Province of West Africa from 1951 to present.

| Dates of Service | Name | Diocesan Seat |
| --- | --- | --- |
| 1951–1955 | Leslie Gordon Vining | Bishop of Lagos, Nigeria |
| 1955–1961 | John L. C. Horstead | Bishop of Freetown, Sierra Leone |
| 1961–1969 | Cecil J. Patterson | Bishop of Niger, Nigeria |
| 1969–1981 | Moses N. C. O. Scott | Bishop of Freetown, Sierra Leone |
| 1981–1982 | Ishmael S. M. LeMaire | Bishop of Accra, Ghana |
| 1982–1983 | George D. Brown | Bishop of Monrovia, Liberia |
| 1993–2003 | Robert G. A. Okine | Bishop of Koforidua, Ghana |
| 2004–2012 | Justice Ofei Akrofi | Bishop of Accra, Ghana |
| 2012–present | Solomon Tilewa Johnson | Bishop of Gambia |

initiatives in Christianity, the three principles need to be revisited, for self-supporting has often become self-serving and self-perpetuating. In its place is needed a more dynamic concept like self-motivating. Self-propagating should become self-contextualizing, and self-governing should become self-critical (Nussbaum 1994, 2; Pobee and Oshitelu 1998, 55–6).

## African Province for the Sake of Anglican Communion with Integrity

Without African identity, the idea of a communion and *Una Sancta* will be shortchanged and unfulfilled. Catholicity has often been explained in terms of the spread of the faith throughout the world and the fullness of the truth handed down from the Apostles. However, in the face of the unprecedented communications revolution of our time, "communication – including issues of culture, identity and social change – becomes a third and necessary addition to catholicity. . . . This theological addendum gives the new catholicity concreteness" (Schreiter 1997, xi). In other words, the CPWA should manifest African identity for the sake of a genuine Anglican Communion that has integrity as communion.

## Anglicanism and Dispersed Authority

Anglicanism upholds dispersed authority (Sykes 1978), and thus the primate of the province is *Primus inter Pares*. On the ground, one senses the frustration of the faithful as regards the apparent helplessness of the primate in exercising power and authority. On the other hand, there are, at times, signs of a primate wielding more power than he is entitled to claim. Hence, it is very much on the agenda of the CPWA to discover the right model of dispersed authority. In an area which has been subjected to painful, ruthless power politics, the issue is a measure of the moral authority of the Church to respond to the ruthless and cruel use of power in a secular society.

## Provincial Power and Authority vis-à-vis Diocesan Power and Authority

Since the diocese constitutes the basic unit, there is a constant issue of how decisions at the provincial/communion level may be received at the diocesan level. "These things affect harmonious and efficient running of a diocese and/or can help minimize and/or maximize distrust and conflicts. The Province needs to be more intentional in working at Reception" (Pobee 2010, 84).

## Education and Formation

The agenda of church, namely mission, evangelism, and liturgy, and procedures of administration and governance, are issues of education and formation. However, these have been in North Atlantic, especially English, captivity. Further, the liturgical emphasis of the High Church tradition has tended to shortchange the consciousness of African identity. The "as it was in the beginning, is now and ever shall be" has been interpreted literally and has not been conducive to developing an African identity in the CPWA. There is an additional consideration, since a sizeable part of the church is non-literate, that the received artifacts are not exactly at the wavelength of *homo africanus*. Vital, vibrant, and viable education and formation need development which pays serious attention to the interior environment.

## Bibliography

African Independent Churches and a Call for a New Three-Self Formula. 1994. In *Freedom and Independence 2*, ed. Stan Nussbaum. Nairobi: OAIC.

Anderson, Gerald H. 1998. *Biographical Dictionary of Christian Missions*. New York: Simon and Schuster.

Ayandele, E. A. 1966. *The Missionary Impact of Modern Nigeria 1842–1914*. London: Longmans, Green & Co. Ltd.

Ayandele, E. A. 1979. *The African Historical Studies*. London: Frank Cass.

Booty, John E. and Stephen Sykes, eds. 1988. *The Study of Anglicanism*. London: SPCK.

Carpenter, Edward. 1991. *Archbishop Fisher. His Life and Times*. Norwich: Canterbury Press.

Coleman, Roger. 1992. *Resolutions of the Twelve Lambeth Conferences 1867–1988*. Toronto: Anglican Book Center.

Kwarteng, Kwasi. 2011. *Ghosts of Empire, Britain's Legacies in the Modern World*. London: Bloomsbury.

Nussbaum, Stan, ed. 1994. *Freedom and Independence 2*. Nairobi: OAIC.

Pobee, John S. 1986. Mission, Paternalism and Peter Pan Syndrome. In *Crossroads Are For Meeting. Essays on the Mission and Common Life of the Church in a Global Society*, eds. Philip Turner and Frank Sugeno. Sewanee: SPCK/USA. 91–108.

Pobee, John S. 1988. Non-Anglo-Saxon Anglicanism Communion. In *The Study of Anglicanism*, eds. John E. Booty and Stephen Sykes. London: SPCK, pp. 428–41.

Pobee, John S. 2010. *The Anglican Story in Ghana. From Mission Beginnings to Province of Ghana*. Kaneshie-Accra: Amanza Ltd.

Pobee, John S. and Gabriel Ositelu II. 1998. *African Initiatives in Christianity*. Geneva: WCC.

Sachs, William S. 1993. *The Transformation of Anglicanism from State Church to Global Communion Custody*. Cambridge: Cambridge University Press.

Schreiter, Robert J. 1997. *The New Catholicity Theology Between the Global and the Local*. MaryKnoll, NY: Orbis.

Sykes, Stephen. 1978. *The Integrity of Anglicanism*. London: Mowbray.

Turner, Philip and Frank Sugeno, eds. 1986. *Crossroads Are for Meeting. Essays on the Mission and Common Life of the Church in a Global Society*. Sewanee: SPCK/USA.

Vincent, David Brown a.k.a Mojola Agbebi. 1889. cited in E. A. Ayandele. 1966. *The Missionary Impact of Modern Nigeria 1842–1914*. London: Longmans, Green & Co. Ltd., p. 200.

# Asia

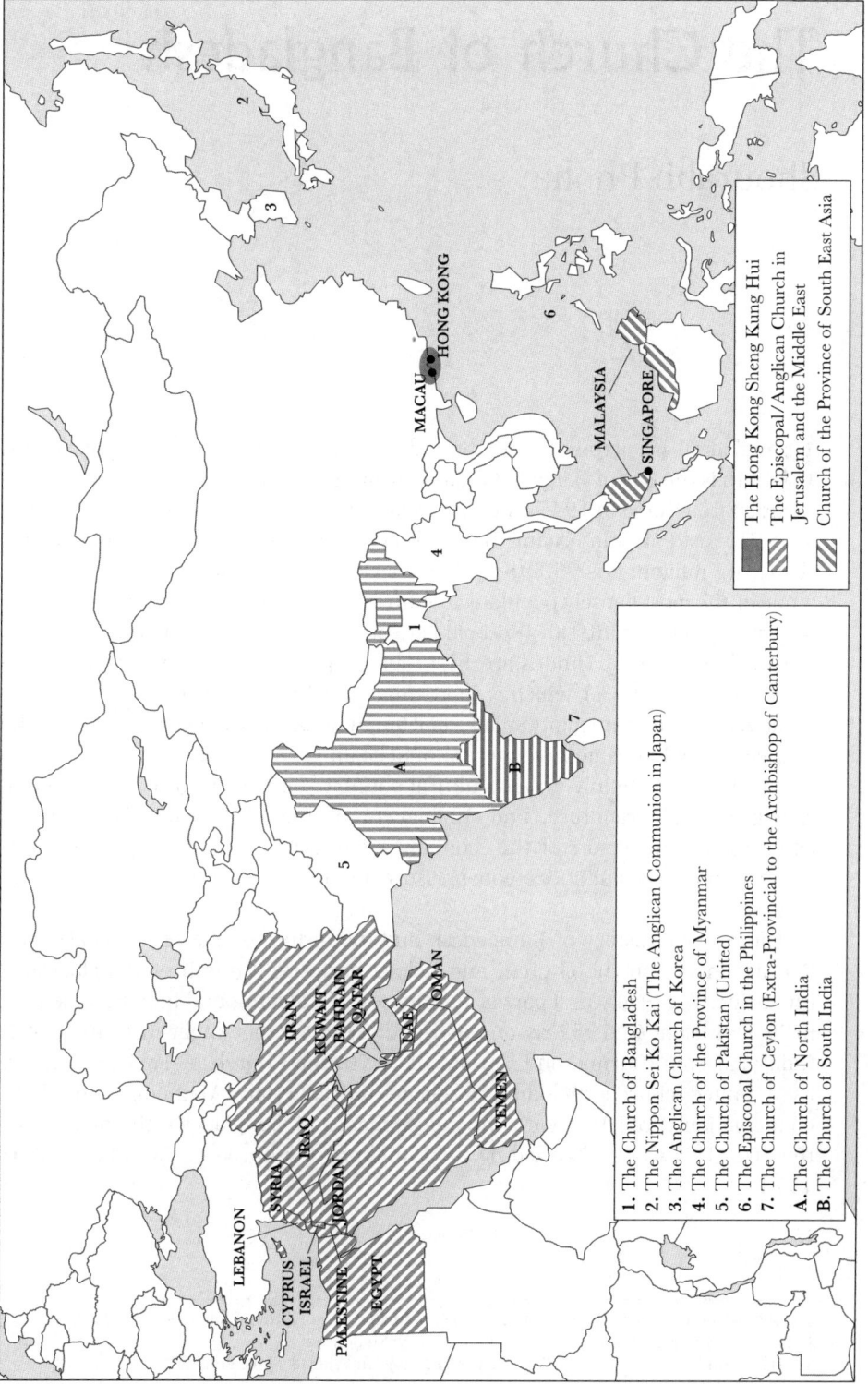

The Hong Kong Sheng Kung Hui

The Episcopal/Anglican Church in Jerusalem and the Middle East

Church of the Province of South East Asia

1. The Church of Bangladesh
2. The Nippon Sei Ko Kai (The Anglican Communion in Japan)
3. The Anglican Church of Korea
4. The Church of the Province of Myanmar
5. The Church of Pakistan (United)
6. The Episcopal Church in the Philippines
7. The Church of Ceylon (Extra-Provincial to the Archbishop of Canterbury)

A. The Church of North India
B. The Church of South India

CHAPTER 22

# The Church of Bangladesh

## Shourabh Pholia

Bangladesh is surrounded by the India; to the southeast is Myanmar, and on its south is the Bay of Bengal. Bangladesh was part of Pakistan, which was formed by partition from India in 1947. After the civil war between East and West Pakistan ended in 1971, East Pakistan became Bangladesh. It is a country with a total population of about 142 million. It is 55,598 square miles (143,998 square kilometers) in size, and is one of the most densely populated countries in the world, with nearly 3,000 persons per square mile (about 1,000 people per square kilometer). A majority of the people are Muslims (86.6%). Hindus are 12.1% of the population, and Christians are a very small minority (0.05%), which is approximately 500,000 people. The official language is Bangla, but there are many small tribal language groups. English is not widely known or used except in business or international dealings.

Bangladesh is mainly an agricultural country; 64 percent of the total population is engaged in agriculture, and 32 percent of the GDP comes from agriculture. Other prominent sectors of the economy are pisciculture and the garment industry. Frequent natural calamities create pressure on the existing infrastructure and agricultural sector.

The political history of Bangladesh and the history of the ecumenical movement had an impact on the church, and helped bring the Church of Bangladesh (COB) into being. The COB was a part of the Diocese of Calcutta, and then became a diocese in its own right in 1952 as one of the dioceses of the Anglican Church of North India, Pakistan, Burma, and Ceylon. In 1970, the Church of Pakistan was created as a united church including Anglican, Presbyterian, Methodist, and Lutheran congregations. In 1971, with the independence of Bangladesh, the diocese became the COB. This was recognized by the synod of the Church of Pakistan on April 24, 1974.

*The Wiley-Blackwell Companion to the Anglican Communion*, First Edition. Edited by Ian S. Markham,
J. Barney Hawkins IV, Justyn Terry, and Leslie Nuñez Steffensen.
© 2013 John Wiley & Sons, Ltd. Published 2013 by John Wiley & Sons, Ltd.

As a result, the COB is one of the United Churches, formed by a union of Anglicans with Christians of other traditions.

## Short History of the Church of Bangladesh

The church grew out of the work started in the late nineteenth century by the Church Missionary Society (CMS), the Oxford Mission to Calcutta, and the English Presbyterian Society. Until 1951, the Anglican Church in East Pakistan was under the Diocese of Calcutta. Under the church union plan of North India and Pakistan of 1965, the Church of Pakistan was created on November 1, 1970. The Anglican Church, United Church, United Methodist Church, and Lutheran Church in Pakistan all merged to form the Church of Pakistan. After the liberation war, the COB became a church of the Anglican Communion, formed by the union of Christian churches in the region, principally Anglican, Methodist, and Presbyterian.

In 1952, the Diocese of Dhaka was created, and Oxford Mission brother the Rev. James D. Blair was consecrated as its first bishop. Being the first Bishop of the Diocese of Dhaka, Bishop Blair played a vital role in helping the church grow for the glory of God. He was very keen to raise up native church leaders. Due to his prayer and efforts, the first indigenous Bishop of the Diocese of Dhaka, the Rt. Rev. B. D. Mondal, was consecrated. He continued in the path of Bishop Blair by encouraging more active participation of lay leaders from all sections of the COB.

Toward the end of 1980s, because of the scattered geographical set-up of the church, the increased volume of work, the need for more effective social ministry, and more efficient supervision of the pastoral work, the leadership of COB realized the need for a second diocese. Thus, a second diocese was established in the district town of Kushtia. The Rt. Rev. Michael S. Baroi was consecrated as the Bishop of the Diocese of Kushtia on November 30, 1990. This new diocese also provided a national church status for the COB.

Following the creation of the independent COB, efforts were made to increase local leadership. After the creation of the synod, the Rt. Rev. B. D. Mondal became the first moderator of the COB, and the Rt. Rev. Michael S. Baroi the deputy moderator. At the time of the Rt. Rev. B. D. Mondal's retirement, a new bishop was elected, and in January 2003 the Rt. Rev. Paul S. Sarkar became the third national bishop of the COB. Although the title "archbishop" is not employed in this province, due to the acknowledgement of the Bishop of Dhaka as a primate within the Anglican Communion, he is entitled to the title "Most Reverend." The current primate is the Most Rev. Paul S. Sarkar. The fourth national bishop is the Rt. Rev. Samuel Sunil Mankhin, who is from the Garo tribe and is now the deputy moderator of the COB.

The church understands its mission as proclaiming the good news of Jesus Christ, responding to human needs, striving to build a more just society, and preserving the integrity of God's creation. In the aftermath of the war for independence which caused enormous damage to the country and the people, and while the nation was just starting its recovery process, the newly emerged leadership of the COB had to face these realities and give shape to the solidarity and participation of the church in the reconstruction of the country, according to the teachings of the Lord Jesus Christ. As a result, the church started its social development service alongside the process of deepening its spiritual ministry. Relationships of cooperation were established with new partners in Europe and North America as well as in Asia. The work went beyond the church's own constituency to all people in need and became registered with the government as a separate entity. Today, the Church of Bangladesh Social Development Programme (CBSDP) operates projects in different regions of the country, along with relief and rehabilitation activities. All the projects are situated in the rural areas, and the activities are being implemented among the poorest sectors in the community, irrespective of religion, tribe, or caste.

## Structure of the Church of Bangladesh

The COB has two dioceses, the Diocese of Dhaka and the Diocese of Kushtia. The Diocese of Dhaka is further broken down into three deaneries (Dhaka, Jobarpar, and Haluaghat), the Chittagong City Pastorate, and the English Congregation. The Diocese of Kustia is made up of the Bollovhpur and the Rajshashi deaneries.

## Statistics of the Dioceses of Dhaka and Kushtia

There are 94 congregations in total; 63 are in the Diocese of Dhaka and 31 are in the Diocese of Kushtia. Average weekly church attendance is 60 percent for the Diocese of Dhaka and 62 percent for the Diocese of Kushtia. The total number of families in the church is 4,035; there are 2,460 families in the Diocese of Dhaka and 1,575 families in the Diocese of Kushtia. The occupations of the members break down as follows. In the Diocese of Dhaka, 50 percent of the members are service holders, 25 percent are farmers/fishermen, 10 percent are day laborers, 3 percent are small businessmen, with the last 12 percent holding other kinds of jobs. In the Diocese of Kushtia, 20 percent of the members are service holders, 35 percent are farmers/fishermen, 35 percent are day laborers, 2 percent are small businessmen, with the last 8 percent holding other kinds of jobs. The COB has 34 active priests and 45 active catechists/evangelists, along with two bishops in two dioceses. Also, there are two retired bishops and seven retired priests.

The COB will have another diocese in the near future named the Diocese of Barisal, which was inaugurated in 2011 by the Rt. Rev. Barry Morgan, Archbishop of Wales. The COB has membership in many church bodies and mission partners. This includes the World Council of Churches, as well as a whole host of more local organizations.

The COB has five deaneries. Short descriptions of each are given in the following text.

# Rajshahi Deanery

## A Santali congregation

As far as we know, the Santal ethnic group is one of the oldest existing in the Indian subcontinent, and their "Adivasi" (or aboriginal) culture predates that of the Bengalis, the predominant group in Bangladesh, who are racially a mix of the Hindu Aryan invaders who came from the northeast about 1,000 BC and the Adivasis who originally inhabited the Bengal. In the north of Bangladesh, there are some very ancient Santali communities, but in the Rajshahi area they were brought by the British colonial administration of the Indian Empire to build the railways in the 1920s. Most of these Santals came from what is now known as Jharkhand and Bihar provinces in India. The first missionaries from the English Presbyterian Church came to them in 1949, establishing the first church congregation in 1951 in Belghoria, a village where CBSDP-Rajshahi presently has one of its sub-centers.

The COB sees itself as bringing about the kingdom of God in Bangladesh. Pioneers like the Rev. P. K. Baroi, a Bengali, and the Rev. Salku Murmo, a Santali priest, began to plant churches after 1965. Today, the Rajshahi deanery has 17 parishes, and out of them 14 parishes (2,500 members) belong to the Santal people. The Santal congregations are today the most vibrant part of the COB, as they have a deep spirituality and are still growing in number.

Every year, we have a spiritual revival meeting for three to four days, known as *Helmel Sova. Helmel* is a Santali word which means "fellowship." This *Sova* is held in February or March. During the *Sova*, people from the whole Rajshahi deanery come together to hear the word of God and sing to rejoice in the Lord.

Since 1997, four new churches have been planted and new church buildings constructed at Nasratpur, Bubuldung, Jhinafulbaria, and Nimghutu. More than 500 people have become Christians.

# Bollovepur Deanery

Bollovepur deanery is the largest of the deaneries in the COB. It is situated in the southwest part of Bangladesh, near the border with West Bengal, India. Most of its members live close to the border.

In the middle of the nineteenth century, the CMS started working in these areas. The CMS missionaries started a hospital at Bollovepur. They also started schools. The people of the area engage in agriculture and small-scale businesses. Many are day-laborers. The land in the area has a relatively high elevation but is fertile. The people of the deanery are very simple and God fearing. Churches arrange different programs for the children, young people, women, men, and the elderly. Bible studies, Christian teaching in the Sunday schools, meetings, and conferences are regularly organized for the spiritual well-being of the people.

*Dhannya Budhbar Savha* is a spiritual revival meeting held once a year in February. Some 112 years ago, in a place called Maliapota, in the district of Nadia, West Bengal, India, some very simple and dedicated village people received the Holy Spirit as the disciples received it on the day of Pentecost. To commemorate the great event, thousands of people (believers and non-believers) gather for two days from around Bangladesh, and even from India, to have simple meals, sing spiritual songs (Kirton), listen to the word of God, and be renewed through prayers. It has always been a joyous occasion for the people of the deanery. The secret of the success of this great event is the *Ujjiboni Sava* (prayer meetings). A group of people in each parish gather together on every Wednesday and pray for this event every week until it is held the following year. The whole thing is managed self-financed.

There are also groups like "Namjapo Dal" who sing, repeating the name of Jesus and giving glory to God for all His mercies. "Matirprodip dal" (light in the earthen pot) is another interdenominational group; members go to different houses and pray with the families.

## Jobarpar Deanery

The south part of Bangladesh, especially the vast areas of Barisal and Faridpur districts, is mainly low-lying and marshy land. Almost all the inhabitants were from the lower-caste Hindu communities. In 1875, the Rev. Berairo, a Baptist pastor, decided to join his congregation with the Anglican Church. Thus, the first Anglican Church was established in this area.

About 100 years ago, the English Brothers of the Epiphany Brotherhood of Oxford Mission started evangelical work among the people of these areas. They used bicycles and boats to go from one place to another. The first Anglican Church was established in the village called Dhamsor, about 20 kilometers from the town of Barisal. After this, many small parishes were established in different areas, and Jobarpar was considered the focal point of the Oxford Mission Brotherhood. Eventually, the Jobarpar deanery was formed, consisting of the parishes situated in the greater areas of Barisal, Faridpur, Jessore, and Khulna districts.

At present, there are 33 parishes in the Jobarpar deanery with about 7,000 members. Almost all the local parishes have a parish committee, programs for women and young people, Sunday schools, Boys' and Girls' Brigades, and programs for older people and the handicapped. The church also runs many institutions, such as schools, clinics, hostels, and social development programs alongside the church's pastoral and charitable activities.

The occupation of most of the people of this area is based on agriculture, yet there are also people with other occupations, such as fishermen, day-laborers, and NGO workers. Frequent natural calamities occur in these areas, causing suffering among the people and damage to the crops, which affects the economic stability of the people.

The congregations lead a purposeful spiritual life by participating in different spiritual activities, such as family prayer meetings, church congregational meetings, interdenominational prayer meetings, an annual revival meeting (*Boro Shava*), as well as attending regular church services, festivals, and other programs undertaken by the church.

The annual revival meeting (*Baro Shava*) is a great yearly event for this deanery. This *Baro Shava* was held first in 1917 at the Dhandoba parish. This is the occasion when people from other churches are also invited to take part. Many non-Christians also attend this meeting and want us to pray for them. Through prayers we have seen many miracles happen.

## Haluaghat Deanery

### A Garo congregation

According to anthropologists, the Garo people originated from the Mongol people of Tibet and China. They belong mainly to the Bormon and Bado communities of the people of Tibet. It is also said that they lived at first on the banks of Eang-Sikiang and the Huang-ho River of China. The scholars think that this community came to the Indian subcontinent around 400–500 years ago. The arrival of the Garos in Bangladesh is dated approximately in the Middle Ages, in the pre-Mughal period. In those days, according to the historians, Garos used to fight between their clans in the Garo Hills and Assam, and during that time, the peaceful-minded Garos came down to the plains of Bangladesh in search of peace. According to recent governmental data, there are more than 100,000 Garo people living in Bangladesh.

The main characteristic of Garo culture is that it is matriarchal. In a matriarchal society, the mother is the head of the family. However, if we closely examine the structure of the Garo families, we see that the mother is not the head of the family. Husbands also have authority and power over female members of the family. Some prefer the term "matrilineal" to "matriarchal" because the family property is passed down through the female line.

The Garos are a mainly agriculture-based community. During the East Pakistan time, most Garos had considerable property, which they have since lost, either because people cheated them or they were indifferent to property of any kind. Their social customs are such that they celebrate, eat, drink, spend money lavishly, and care very little about the future of themselves or their families. As a result, they have now become landless and destitute. One unique thing about them is that 90 percent of Garos are literate, and many have left their homes and have gone to cities and towns for different jobs.

Like the other deaneries, the Haluaghat deanery organizes a *Baro Shava* (annual revival meeting) every year. It was started in 1910. The brothers of the St. Andrew's Mission were the source of inspiration, and they took the initiative to start this kind of gathering for a spiritual revival. This becomes a major social and community event of the year.

One significant aspect of the *Baro Shava* of the Haluaghat deanery is that the participants who attend this spiritual meeting along with their family members or groups bring all their food and fuel for cooking. They build temporary shelters to spend the night and sleep on straw. The COB's Haluaghat deanery has about 3,000 members, almost all from the Garo tribe.

## Dhaka Deanery

The Dhaka City Pastorate Council was formally declared and inaugurated as the Dhaka deanery in St. Thomas Church, New Centre, Moghbazar, on July 22, 2011. The new deanery was consecrated in the Holy Communion Service in the morning, followed by the lighting of candles, cutting of a cake, and releasing a festoon by the moderator of the COB, the Rt. Rev. Paul S. Sarkar, the Rt. Rev. Michael S. Baroi, and the synod secretary, Mr. Joseph Sudhin Sarkar. The first council of the Dhaka deanery took place on the same day in St. Thomas Church, New Centre, Moghbazar.

## English Congregation

There is an English congregation at Moghbazar, Dhaka, where mission partners working in Dhaka and other foreigners living in Dhaka join the services. This congregation meets on Friday once a week. They worship in different houses for better communication with the members. Occasionally, they gather at the Armenian church, which is another old Orthodox church in Dhaka. Here, the membership always goes up and down, but it is a place where people from abroad are welcomed and can have good friends from all over the world. The Rev. Angela Robinson and Br. Jacques look after the congregation along with other Bengali priests who are working in Dhaka.

## Mission Partners

There are ten missionaries now working with the COB as experts in CBSDP and in the Health Ministry. They are from CMS and PCUSA. They meet once or twice a year in a seminar and retreat. The COB is happy to have them contributing in church and social development programs. They work as the key persons to sustain the relationship with the partners and to cooperate with each other to do mission work in Bangladesh.

## Key Institutions of the Church of Bangladesh

The COB has one brotherhood and two sisterhoods. They are the Brotherhood of the Epiphany, Christo Sevika Sangha, and St. Mary's Sisterhood.

### Brotherhood of the Epiphany, Barisal

The 100th year of the Oxford Mission was celebrated in 1995. All the English brothers have died. Brother Francis Panday, a national brother, is now in charge, and he is looking out for the possibility to organize a national brotherhood.

*Christo Sevika Sangha, Jobarpar, Barisal*

We have a National Sisterhood called the Christo Sevika Sangha (Handmaids of Christ), which was started on the January 25, 1970. They now have 12 sisters. The late Mother Sushila played a major role in nurturing the Sangha. She died in 2011, and now Sr. Jharna is in charge of the Sangha.

*St. Mary's Sisterhood, Haluaghat*

In 1930, Sister Eda came to Haluaghat from Barisal with two sisters, one of whom was a trained teacher, and began the sisterhood. There are now four sisters and two novices in the Sisterhood. Sister Mira is the superior.

*St. Andrew's Theological College*

The COB has its own theological college, St. Andrew's Theological College, where they train their priests, evangelists, church workers, and leaders. It also trains pastors and leaders for other churches. It was founded in 1976 and named in honor of a small theological college which had existed at St. Andrew's Mission, Haluaghat, in the 1930s. There are 62 Bachelor of Theology students, and 12 Diploma in Bible Translation students from different denominations like COB, BBCF, BBCS, Methodist, Lutheran, Isa E Jamat, and Free Churches.

At first, St. Andrew's was started with students who did not have enough academic qualifications or who could not go to Bishop's College, Calcutta, due to visa problems. Most of the former students are now potential priests of the church. Then it developed a B.Th. program, started different courses, and opened its programs to all denominations and both genders.

The college is now affiliated with the Senate of Serampore College and University, India. It offers courses of study for Christian believers in Bangladesh, such as Bachelor of Christian Studies (Serampore Course), Bachelor of Theology (Serampore Course), Diploma in Bible Translation (Serampore Course), Diploma in Social Ministry (College Course), and Lay People Course (College Course). The college is a member of the Theological Association of Bangladesh.

# Bible School and Brigades

Keeping the preceding objective in mind, our church considers it a priority to help boys and girls to become followers of the Lord Jesus Christ, and, through self-control, reverence, and a sense of responsibility, to find true enrichment of life from childhood onward. The COB has many programs for children. The work of the Sunday schools and the Girls' and Boys' Brigades go hand in hand. For example, they arrange seminars, Bible quizzes, games, and gatherings.

## Youth Fellowship

According to the constitution of the Youth Work Committee of the COB, "And You will bear witness for me" (Acts 1:8) is the principal aim and objective to be achieved by and for the young people. Youth are the future of the church. The COB believes they are not only the future but the present too. The Youth Work Committee of the COB has helped young people to be committed to their Savior and Redeemer, the Lord Jesus Christ.

## Women's Fellowship

Like many Christian congregations around the world, it is the women who are the real strength of our church. Their prayers, support for the families, and attendance at Sunday and other worship services help keep the church healthy and alive. Almost every parish has a women's fellowship and a number of part-time and full-time workers. Activities include prayer meetings, house visiting, collection of rice and money for the church, exchange programs, and helping the poor and the needy.

## Golden Age

In this program for elderly people, they meet twice a week for prayer meetings, cultural functions, storytelling, and singing. They also perform drama, do Bible study, and participate in indoor games and exchange programs. They make house visits and pray by the side of the sick and especially elderly people. They make handicrafts and sell them in local markets to earn money and as a result feel independent. Once a month, they hold a fellowship meal. Every week, they come to a center and have fellowship over a cup of tea, with light eats and seasonal fruits. They can have a health checkup from the nearest hospital or clinic or community health workers.

## Other Programs

The COB has its social development program, which is known as the Church of Bangladesh Social Development Programme (CBSDP). Through this, the COB primarily works with the local community, groups, and church congregations to promote holistic development for the poorest of the poor, disadvantaged, and vulnerable people, irrespective of religion, gender, or age. Through the CBSDP, the COB responds to the issues of women, children, ecological crisis, environmental issues, and food security. CBSDP also runs pre-primary schools, primary schools, and health centers. In the light of Christ's teaching (Jn.10:10), the CBSDP desires and seeks fulfilled communities living in justice and peace with all of God's creation. Its mission is to advocate for and work alongside people affected by poverty and injustice, striving for their liberation, building sustainable local capacity, and empowering communities to work together to claim their rights.

Another program of the COB is known as the Christian Ministry to Children and Youth (CMCY). Through this program, the COB provides residential care, education, health, early childhood development, day care services, and spiritual nurture to poor and needy children in Bangladesh, irrespective of their religion, race, or gender. The CMCY's vision is that every child, regardless of race, religion, and background may grow to his/her fullness by unleashing their God-given potential, and may experience the love of Christ. Its mission is to ensure the holistic development of poor children and youth through the provision of resident care, health care, nutritional feeding, education, skill training, day care services, and spiritual nurture, so that they may become self-reliant and contributing members of society.

The COB is involved in four major types of programs through the CMCY.

A.  Residential hostels – There are five girls' hostels and ten boys' hostels throughout Bangladesh. The goal is to ensure the holistic development of poor children with full residential care, safety, security, health, education, spiritual nurture, and cultural development to enable them to strive for a better life.
B.  Community intervention programs (CIPs) – There are five CIPs in the COB. They have the goal of ensuring the early childhood development of minor children, aged four to seven years, with day care services, safety and security, pre-school education, health and nutritional feeding, and cultural development, so that the children may continue their education after five years at the CIPs. Another goal of CIPs is to empower poor women, mothers, and adolescent girls through self-help groups that enhance their savings, economic condition, health, and rights and dignity in society.
C.  Vocational training programs – The COB has three vocational training institutes. One is under the government curriculum, and the other two are short-term courses, one for boys and one for girls. These are to ensure that the youths can be self-reliant and contribute to society.
D.  Child sponsorship programs (CSPs) – The COB has eight CSPs to ensure day care services for poor and needy children through health, education, social, and spiritual nurture activities. These will help them to become self-reliant and experience the love of Christ in their whole life and work.

*Health care program*   The COB continues its caring ministry through its two hospitals and many clinics throughout Bangladesh. It has two nursing institutes where young girls receive training, become self-reliant, and contribute to society. Many of them are working abroad and also working as missionaries. The COB continues its healthcare program through its ten clinics and many mobile clinics under its social development programs to reach out to the poor who cannot come to hospitals.

*Education program*   The COB has an education board under which there are four nursery and 44 primary schools, and three junior and four senior high schools. These schools serve poor children and those who cannot pay for education. There are other pre-primary schools under the CBSDP, which are for poor children to prepare them for further education and encourage them to continue their education in government-sponsored schools.

## Publications

The COB has two publications: *Kapot* (bi-monthly, in Bangla) and *Janasuna* (monthly, in Bangla). In addition, it has an English newsletter and a tabloid from the Diocese of Kushtia.

## Priorities of the COB

The main mission of the COB is the community life of its members, where the members share, care, pray, and worship for each other and for their neighbors. The main expression of its faith is to serve the poor and destitute through different programs which depend on foreign funds.

The priorities for the COB for the five years from 2007 were as follows:

1.  Ministry. The church endeavored to strengthen its pastoral ministry by the development of leadership through training locally and abroad, and by theological education at all levels and ages in both residential and extension programs. It also tried to strengthen its women's ministry by encouraging women's work at the synod and diocesan levels, and by increasing women's participation in the church at all levels. A goal was to increase women's participation by up to 30 percent within five years. It wanted to strengthen its Sunday school and Brigade programs by encouraging congregations, wardens of children's homes, heads of boarding schools, and mission school teachers to send more children to participate in these activities. It also wished to strengthen the Sunday school and Brigade programs by increasing the training of their leaders and teachers. It aimed to strengthen its ecumenical and interfaith relationships at the local and national levels.
2.  Self-reliance. Emphasis was given at all levels for the church to attain self-reliance.
3.  Education. The church tried to continue and increase its work in general education from the pre-primary to secondary school level, in technical and vocational training, and care for underprivileged children.
4.  Community health. The church wanted to continue to provide health services to the community. It set out to identify and meet the highest-priority health needs of the community through community participation. It tried to provide regular health education for common diseases, sanitation, hygiene, and nutritious food. It wanted to provide inpatient and outpatient services, backed up by diagnostic and therapeutic facilities.

5.  Socioeconomic development. The church decided to provide programs which improve socioeconomic standing to all, regardless of religion. Poverty was to be alleviated through credit and income-generating activities, and through projects to empower the marginalized. Other development projects included ecology and pollution control, integrated community development, community awareness building, motivation for the best use of one's materials and resources, meeting the challenges of growing urbanization, responding to natural calamities and disasters, empowerment of women at the grassroots level, advocacy and legal aid, and skill development and leadership training.

## Conclusion

The COB is one of the mainline churches in Bangladesh. It is contributing to the society in Bangladesh and witnessing to Christ through the lives and activities of its members. It is a church which is traditional and which sustains relationships with all the people in the society. Through its social, educational, and health programs, people are learning of the love of God and sharing in the life of Christ. It provides a voice for women, but it still has to be more open to women. It had only two women priests, who were ordained in 1997, but they are to be retired very soon as they were ordained at an older age. The COB has to be more open to women for pastoral ministry and other opportunities. The COB operates in a multi-religious context, so it takes initiatives to live in peace and harmony with people of other faiths in Bangladesh. It encourages ecumenical movements in Bangladesh among the Christian communities. The COB has given a permanent home to many ethnic and tribal groups, such as the Santali, Garos, and Tripuras. The COB is facing new challenges as people are migrating from rural to urban areas. It has to focus on urban ministry. To reach out to those in urban areas, its clergy people have to be more educated and better trained. People in urban areas are facing new issues, like the breakup of families. This is another challenge to which the church must respond. Finally, climate change is having a severe impact in Bangladesh, and the church must respond effectively.

## Bibliography

Anglican Communion. 2012. Website of the Anglican Communion. http://www.anglicancommunion.org.

Church of Bangladesh. 2003. *Constitution.* Dhaka: The Church of Bangladesh Publication Department.

Church of Bangladesh. 2003. *English Service Order Book.* Dhaka: The Church of Bangladesh Publication Department.

Church of Bangladesh. 2002. *The Church of Bangladesh Profile 2002.* Dhaka: The Church of Bangladesh Publication Department.

Church of Bangladesh. 2007. *The Church of Bangladesh Profile 2007.* Dhaka: The Church of Bangladesh Publication Department.

Church of Bangladesh. 2012. Website of the Church of Bangladesh. http://www.churchofbangladesh.org.

Church of Bangladesh. 2012. *The COB Diary – 2012*. Dhaka: The Church of Bangladesh Publication Department.

World Council of Churches. 2012. Church of Bangladesh. http://www.oikoumene.org/ en/member-churches/regions/asia/bangla-desh/church-of-bangladesh.html?print=1% 2525253Fprint%2525253D1print.

# CHAPTER 23
# The Hong Kong Sheng Kung Hui

## Paul Kwong

The Anglican Church in Hong Kong and Macau is a growing Christian community in a fast developing region of South China. We are known by our Chinese name, the Hong Kong Sheng Kung Hui (HKSKH), and we have a closely connected network of churches, schools, and social welfare centers. Our province was established in 1998, just over a year after the return of Hong Kong to Chinese sovereignty. Although we are the youngest province in the worldwide Anglican Communion, we have a history of more than 160 years. We also serve a large population in Hong Kong and Macau, and beyond. As we try to serve others, the HKSKH has sought to bear witness to God's love, follow Christ in mission, and, empowered by the Holy Spirit, respond to the challenges of the times.

The HKSKH is an urban church in a dynamic part of the world, standing at a crossroads between East Asia and other parts of the globe. We are an autonomous church within a Special Administrative Region (SAR) of the People's Republic of China, a Chinese church, but international in terms of our membership and global linkages. Although we have a long history, we are still challenged to root our church more deeply in the hybrid reality of Hong Kong and Macau, so that we can continue to be faithful to God, care for the people, and contribute to society.

In this chapter, after a brief consideration of our history and present situation, I want to focus on the challenge of what I call "identity in community," and in that context discuss the issues we face.

## Our History and Tradition

The story of the HKSKH began with the early efforts of the English clergy and laity who settled in Hong Kong after it became a British colony. Following the Treaty of Nanking

*The Wiley-Blackwell Companion to the Anglican Communion*, First Edition. Edited by Ian S. Markham,
J. Barney Hawkins IV, Justyn Terry, and Leslie Nuñez Steffensen.
© 2013 John Wiley & Sons, Ltd. Published 2013 by John Wiley & Sons, Ltd.

that ended the Opium War, Vincent Stanton was appointed the first colonial chaplain in 1843. The Diocese of Victoria (as it was then called) was established by Royal Letters Patent in 1849. That same year, St. John's Cathedral opened for Sunday worship and George Smith was consecrated as our first bishop. He presided over what was then the largest diocese in the world, including all of China as well as Japan. In 1851, after several years of preparatory work, St. Paul's College was started to educate young men for mission and ministry among the Chinese people.

The Church Missionary Society (CMS) began work in Hong Kong in 1862, and it remained the major Anglican mission body in Hong Kong and South China for the next century. The church developed slowly under a succession of bishops related to the CMS who were initially appointed by the colonial office. Lo Sam-yuen became the first Chinese deacon, and he helped start St. Stephen's Church, the first Chinese parish, which opened in 1865. Beginning in 1898, by which time the church was no longer receiving government subsidies, bishops were appointed by the Archbishop of Canterbury. Throughout the nineteenth century, the church continued to establish a foundation for education and social welfare in Hong Kong, two areas that have continued to be distinctive features of the church's mission up to the present.

By the early twentieth century, Anglican and Episcopal missionary work had developed in many parts of China through the efforts of English mission societies, the American Church Mission, and later the Canadian Church. To work for unity and enhance cooperation among the different dioceses and missionary areas, bishops and clergy met four times between 1897 and 1909. This led to the establishment of the Chung Hua Sheng Kung Hui (The Holy Catholic Church of China) in 1912, the first major Protestant (or Non-Roman) church in China, consisting of 11 dioceses. Hong Kong became part of the (Chinese) Diocese of South China that overlapped with the (English) Diocese of Victoria. The Chung Hua Sheng Kung Hui was recognized as an independent province at the Seventh Lambeth Conference in 1930. Its last general synod was in 1947, but the Sheng Kung Hui continued to function on the China mainland until 1958.

Bishop R. O. Hall (1932–1966) stands out as one of the great Anglican bishops of the last century, and the longest-serving bishop in Hong Kong. By the 1920s and 1930s, Chinese clergy and laity were increasingly setting the direction for our mission work. In response to Bishop Hall's vision, they further developed the work of the church in Hong Kong and South China before and after World War II, and established many churches, schools, and social welfare centers. In 1938, the diocese began mission work in Macau, which became an important center for refugees from the Japanese occupation. In 1944, Bishop Hall ordained Florence Tim-Oi Li to the priesthood to serve the pastoral and sacramental needs of the church there. She was the first woman priest in the Anglican Communion, and her ordination was then a source of great controversy.

After the establishment of the People's Republic of China in 1949, the Diocese of Hong Kong and Macau became a detached diocese of the Chung Hua Sheng Kung Hui. The church responded to the influx of refugees from the mainland by developing new social welfare initiatives and schools. During this time, "Hong Kongers" began to develop their own sense of identity, no longer simply subjects in a British colony, but not yet part of China. After the Limuru meeting of the Anglican Consultative

Conference in 1971, more women were ordained to the priesthood, establishing Hong Kong's place as a pioneer in the ordination of women.

Peter Kong-kit Kwong was elected our first Chinese bishop in 1981, just as Hong Kong was beginning its transition to the resumption of Chinese sovereignty. He saw that a detached diocese, working under the canons and constitution of a church that no longer existed, meant for an uncertain existence. Through his wise leadership, collaborative working style, clear vision, and evangelistic spirit, Bishop Peter worked for the establishment of the Province of Hong Kong and Macau, which became the 38th province in the Anglican Communion in 1998. Archbishop Peter retired in 2007. I was subsequently elected bishop of Hong Kong Island (2005) and archbishop and primate of the province (2007).

## The Church in Hong Kong Today

Our church has developed from the early efforts of English missionaries and Chinese Christians, making use of our Anglican and Chinese heritage to serve God and our community in our parishes, our schools, and welfare centers. We celebrate our history and tradition, but we are keenly aware of the challenges that lie before us. Allow me to introduce our context and our situation in the HKSKH today, so that these may be better understood.

The HKSKH is made of the three dioceses of Hong Kong Island, Eastern Kowloon, and Western Kowloon, and the missionary area of Macau. Hong Kong has a population of 7 million (95 percent Chinese), and Macau a population of 526,000 (also 95 percent Chinese). These two metropolitan areas are part of the rapidly developing region of the Pearl River Delta in South China that has achieved unprecedented levels of economic growth in the past two decades. The urban areas of Hong Kong are very densely populated. Families live in small spaces in soaring high rises and densely packed housing estates. Housing is at a premium, and housing prices are among the highest in the world. The Hong Kong SAR is economically strong, with a GDP of US$30,000 per capita in 2008, but there is a growing gap between the rich and the poor. Politically, Hong Kong has an executive-led government with a partially elected legislature, established under the "one country two systems" policy of the People's Republic of China and grounded in the Basic Law (1990). There is near-universal literacy and an excellent system of education in which school children learn in two or three languages. Hong Kong is a secular city with many religious communities. There are more than 640,000 Christians, which is about 9 percent of the population. Our religious communities live in harmony with one another, and there is little inter-religious tension or conflict.

In the colonial era, Christianity was given a privileged position. We do not seek to return to a time when Christianity held a special position in society, because we now see that this was a corrupting influence that in some ways inhibited the development of relationships with others. Christians are a minority community in Hong Kong, and in China as a whole. We cannot afford to be on our own, just as we cannot live for ourselves.

Hong Kong is a globalized city at the crossroads of the world. However, Hong Kong also brings together many local communities with particular characteristics, strong cultural roots, and pressing social needs. The 2008 economic crisis hit our city hard, dependent as it is on economic globalization. Although recovery has been rapid, many people were deeply affected, and the most vulnerable sectors of the population still have not shared in the recovery. We have a low unemployment rate, but more than 17 percent of the population lives below the official poverty line. The "post-eighties generation" (young people born after 1980) does not share the confidence or optimism that has traditionally characterized Hong Kong people. At the same time, young people and many others have called for a faster pace of democratization and have raised their voices on a variety of social issues. Journalists have written about the search for an authentic Hong Kong identity in a city that is no longer a British territory but where people are not yet ready to identify with China.

Over the last 15 years, the HKSKH has developed initiatives in lay ministry, theological training, evangelism, and social welfare, as well as outreach to mainland China. In the process, eight new missionary churches have been established, and 36 deacons and priests have been ordained. The HKSKH exists to serve all people in Hong Kong, and not just those who worship in our churches.

The laity plays a strong role in every aspect of the HKSKH. Not only are our schools and welfare centers lay led, but we depend on lay leaders in the day-to-day work of the church. We have many lay ministers and evangelists who assist in the work of our growing churches. The laity gives leadership to our synod meetings and church committees. Youth, women, and laymen have also taken on many mission projects at both the parish and diocesan levels.

We now have approximately 30,000 members worshipping in 53 churches, including five churches in Macau. We have 80 full-time clergy. The HKSKH operates 134 schools, from kindergartens to the tertiary level, and our primary and secondary schools are among the best in Hong Kong. We also operate 92 social welfare units related to the HKSKH Social Welfare Council. Many people in Hong Kong know about our church primarily through our work in education and social welfare. These have been the core areas of our mission from the earliest years of our church. More recently, we have established new initiatives in working with Hong Kong's growing population of migrant workers, people suffering from HIV/AIDS, and new immigrants from the mainland.

We are proud to be part of China. Now, 15 years after Hong Kong's return to Chinese sovereignty, our cooperation with the Church in China, with social welfare agencies, and with the Chinese government has increased. We regularly visit church leaders in China, we participate in numerous exchanges with churches on the mainland, and we respond to requests for disaster relief and assistance in programs of social service. We are also proud to be related to the Anglican Communion. Our clergy and laity play an active role in the communion. In 2007, Hong Kong hosted the meeting of Anglican provincial secretaries; our young people are fully involved in the continuing Indaba process; and some of our members have played leading roles in organizing Lambeth conferences and in the Compass Rose Society.

We have much to be thankful for in the HKSKH, but Hong Kong and our church are also facing many challenges.

## The Challenge of Identity in Community: Toward an Urban Theology of Mission for Hong Kong

The Church exists for the sake of mission. Mission in Hong Kong is in one sense the same as it has been at all times and in all places, to follow Jesus, inspired by the Holy Spirit as we proclaim the Reign of God to all people. However, Hong Kong is also unique, just as all contexts are unique. Here, I want to speak about contextualizing an urban theology of mission for Hong Kong and Macau, and particularly about how this affects our own identity in community.

What can be said about our Hong Kong context? *Culturally*, we are a Chinese city, but also a melting pot. Hong Kong attracts people from all over the world, but we remain fundamentally a Chinese city. We are post-colonial Chinese, but because of our history, we have been strongly influenced by the West, particularly Britain. Being both Chinese and Western is part of our common identity. As such, we are unlike any other city in the world.

*Politically*, Hong Kong is a SAR of the People's Republic of China. Our government is led by Hong Kong people under the "One Country, Two Systems" formula. In the years leading up to 1997 and Hong Kong's return to Chinese sovereignty, there were many conflicting views, but a general sense in which Hong Kong people felt that we were left out of the decision-making process about our own future. In the 15 years since the handover, our politics has been developing, with many contesting voices, combined with a growing sense that we have a special political role to play in Greater China.

*Economically*, we are a wealthy city, driven by the property, banking, and financial services sectors. However, there is a growing gap between rich and poor, a high level of unemployment, and we have a fragile economic place in an emerging China. Not all Hong Kong people have benefited from our city's prosperity, and this is why our HKSKH concern for programs in social welfare has increased. More generally, we see that many businesses have moved to other parts of China – or to other parts of the world – because of the high cost of living and doing business here. The property sector is the liveliest part of our market economy, but still many families are without adequate housing, and young people have been priced out of the over-heated market.

All these factors are part of our context. In response, the church needs an urban theology of mission that takes account of our hybrid Chinese identity, our political particularity, and our economic unease. We need a theology of *this* place, and like all good Anglican theology, it should be a theology of incarnation that takes context very seriously. Our identity as Hong Kong people and our community life are key aspects of this urban theology of mission.

In my recent book, I have explored the question of identity as an aspect of an authentic agenda for the church in Hong Kong (Kwong 2011). In the years leading up to 1997, the people of Hong Kong were uneasy at not being allowed by China to take part in the process of negotiation over their future. Hong Kong people were also disappointed with Britain for not being helpful in safeguarding their interests and for denying their rights of abode in the United Kingdom. This led them to identify themselves more with Hong Kong than with Britain or China. Hong Kong people feared China would come in after 1997 and take control of them and all they had. This further consolidated a new sense of Hong Kong ethnic identity, a "Hongkongese" identity. This identity has possessed at times an "anti-China" component that has been invoked to assert local identity against the taken-for-granted "Chinese" identity. The contest of these identities created conflicts after our return to China, but it also added a certain richness to who we are as Hong Kong people.

The people and the churches of Hong Kong have been challenged by questions of identity throughout our history. We have gone from being a "collaborated community" in the colonial era, to a "concerned community" in the transitional period (1985–1997), and to an increasingly "politicized community" in the post-colonial era. These identities brought with them conflicts and struggles, in relationship to the Hong Kong SAR government, and to some extent with China over our national identity. The church was challenged to learn how to show allegiance to the national identity on one hand while on the other to try to make an effort to affirm her own identity. Throughout, we have sought to remain faithful to God. Nevertheless, negotiating and transforming our identity remain continuing issues for Hong Kong people and pose a challenge to Christian theology.

What theological methodology should be used in negotiating identity? Our starting point should be the concrete concerns of Hong Kong people. What Hong Kong people are suffering on the ground, what they experience in their day-to-day lives, is at the center of our theological enterprise. Theology should speak for and identify with the people, people who are fragmented, broken, and searching for meaning in life. The search for a sense of community in the context of increasing tension and conflict among contested identities is central to our task. In our city, where conflict and exclusion are everyday realities, theology should give people a sense of purpose and help them develop a sense of community. It should also help people live peacefully with one another.

In developing this theology of mission in Hong Kong, our purpose is to encourage our church members to see themselves as "social agents." In other words, they should play an active role in church and society. This is why our concern for the laity and lay ministry was highlighted in the previous section. Social agents are active participants in the cultural, economic, and political order, not passive people who are acted upon. Social agency in the HKSKH is enhanced by a participatory sense of the liturgy as well as involvement by church members in mission programs and in their own places of work and involvement.

Second, a theology of mission should be based on Reason, the Bible, and Tradition, which have always been sources of Anglican theology. We seek to hold the three together. We interpret the Bible in light of both reason and tradition. The Bible is important for all Chinese Christians. And so, the HKSKH has supported the revision of the Chinese Union Version of the Bible, which, after 19 years of work, was published in the Fall of 2010. We are also supporting a project that will do a new Chinese translation of the deuterocanonical books. The HKSKH does not see the Bible as a rigid book of dogma or a static source of inherited wisdom, but as the living word of God that needs to be interpreted afresh in our urban setting.

Our emphasis on reason, practical and relational, enables us to communicate with non-Christians, who are in the majority in Hong Kong. Our church is small in numbers, but we are involved with all of the people of Hong Kong. At our last General Synod, we discussed ways of implementing our new education policy, which seeks to reclaim the core religious and humanistic values that should be at the heart of our schools. As noted in the preceding section, the HKSKH has been involved in education for a very long time, and our schools are held in very high regard. However, the sense in which they are explicitly Christian or Anglican schools, has been lost. Most of our students are non-Christians, and we need to help them see the values that we uphold, in the belief that these values are important in our world. Our education policy seeks to "promote the ethos of Christian whole-person education" by emphasizing God's love and the spiritual dimension of life in our work with students, teachers, and school administrators. To do so, we need to rely on right reason in the classroom, so as to encourage a greater concern for ethics, religious faith, and the concern for other people and for the environment.

Tradition is also important for the HKSKH. Recently, one of my priests wrote a book on the relevance of Charles Gore's theology of incarnation for Hong Kong today, exploring in depth one of our great Anglican thinkers (Fan 2009). I myself have been deeply influenced by the thought and spirituality of Bishop Gore, especially during the time I spent at the Community of the Resurrection after I was elected as bishop. Tradition (or, as we argue in the following text, traditions) is an important source for our theology. In HKSKH liturgy also, we deeply value our inherited tradition, even as we try to develop it further. This is why we have decided to produce a new *Book of Common Prayer of the Hong Kong Sheng Kung Hui* for use in public worship. A committee has begun work on this important task, which we envision will take many years to complete. The new *Book of Common Prayer* will draw on the richness of Anglican tradition, but it will also incorporate prayers and services that are important for Chinese culture, such as the Chinese Spring Festival (or Chinese New Year), the Mid-Autumn Festival, the Ching Ming Festival of sweeping the graves, and Chinese National Day.

We want our theology to grow out of the realities we experience today, in other words, out of the cultural, political, and economic realities we discussed earlier. This is a third aspect of our theological method. It is an aspect of contextual theology from every place and time. For Hong Kong, it means that we have to pay attention to the concrete living experiences of people in our place and in our time, as we attempt to discern the ways in which God is speaking to us. We need to analyze our social realities and see how they affect people. The post-eighties generation, the elderly, families struggling to make a living, the migrants among us – these are but some of the groups whom we seek to minister to, but we also hope to foster them as social agents, so that they can become part of God's mission in the world.

The contest of identities, as I have noted earlier, has been one of the major factors contributing to the cultural, political, and economic problems of Hong Kong. However, it is also a source of complexity, richness, diversity, and difference. Recent Biblical studies have emphasized the importance of difference in the early Christian communities. As Anglicanism spread around the world, the tradition developed in different ways, so it is now more appropriate to speak of Anglican traditions rather than Anglican tradition. We use reason to negotiate different Biblical understandings and different traditions within the broader Christian community. However, in Hong Kong, we also use reason to negotiate different understandings within the Chinese community, most of whom are not Christians. Our Hong Kong identities, cultural and religious, political and economic, are diverse, but overlapping.

We need to embrace our differences and learn to live with one another in the broader community of Hong Kong. Any practice that fosters prejudice and exclusivism ought to be overcome with the unity we have been given in Jesus Christ who undermines all cultural, political, and economic difference and pulls down the walls that people put up to preserve their identities. Identities are always contested, but never absolute. God in Jesus Christ affirms each identity, accepting all, Jew and Gentile, woman and man, slave and free. God welcomes God's children in the richness of their cultural diversity, calling them all into community.

The building up of a new community is an essential part of the mission of the church who needs to hear God's voice speaking through the experiences and perspectives of those whose identities are contested or denied. So we first need to listen to what the poor, the marginalized, and the weak are saying to the church. Sharing God's loving and embracing presence draws us of necessity into building a sustainable community where all can have different identities but be able to live together in harmony.

In my book, I emphasize that Hong Kong people are part of overlapping communities, local and global, cultural and religious, political and economic (Kwong 2011). We have different views on many subjects, but these do not inhibit our growing together into community. Our identities are never fixed, once and for all, but are always growing and evolving in relationship to the communities of which we are a part. We can see our contested identities in a different way. We identify ourselves as "Christian" and "Anglican," but we also identify ourselves as "Chinese" and "Hongkongese." Identity is a way of affirming who we are, not in an exclusive way, but in an embracing way. Our Christian identity is not meant to exclude "non-Christians," nor is our "Chinese" identity meant to exclude foreigners. Hong Kong is a Chinese city, but we are enriched by the presence of many nationalities and ethnicities among us. In our churches, we have historically had a strong Eurasian presence. We worship in Cantonese, but also in English, Mandarin, and Tagalog. As "Hongkongese," living together in this globalized metropolis, we need to affirm both the multiplicity and the hybridity of our identities. We recognize that all self-identifications are themselves social constructs, but our identities enhance rather than diminish who we are.

Two things about identity in community are distinctive for people in Hong Kong. First, as with Asia as a whole, we are traditionally more community oriented than the more individualistic West. Family and social networks are important part of who we are. We know who we are by the family of which we are part. The Chinese family is a source of cultural and community strength. True, the family structure has been challenged in the modern era, but in Chinese culture, the family endures and

continues to sustain us. Relationships within the family teach us to negotiate difference and practice love. This becomes the basis for tolerance, understanding, and
mutual respect.

I like to emphasize the HKSKH as a family. Christians are called to grow together in
love for one another. We get together frequently in clergy meetings, services of worship,
committee work, and times of celebration. As a family, we also reach out to others less
fortunate. We seek to be an inclusive, not an exclusive family and community.

A second aspect of our identity in community is adherence to the middle way. Comprehensiveness and the *via media* are important in Anglicanism. The Middle Way is also
important in Chinese tradition. *The Doctrine of the Mean* is a classic from the sixth
century B.C.E. attributed to Confucius. It is a short text that teaches forbearance and
gentleness in responding to others, harmony and equilibrium in society, and self-control and moderation in one's own life. Both *The Doctrine of the Mean* and the Anglican
*via media* can strengthen relations in community. They help us guard against going to
extremes and excessive self-expression in relationships with others.

Both of these aspects of identity in community help us to practice responsibility and
restraint for the common good. In a crowded city like Hong Kong, this helps us stay
together, despite all of our contested identities. As part of China, a sense of family and
the Middle Way can help Hong Kong people work together for the good of the nation,
even though we have different political and religious views on many things (one
country, two systems). In the HKSKH, comprehensiveness and an understanding of
church as extended family helps us build up the church, participate in mission, and
relate to the wider Anglican Communion.

## Conclusion: Facing the Future

The urban theology of mission we are seeking to develop for Hong Kong is only in its
formative stages. It will be expressed not only in our writings and church statements,
but in the work we do together in the HKSKH.

Hong Kong is at once a flourishing and prosperous global city, but politically and
economically we are also quite vulnerable. People see their lives as contingent and their
future as uncertain. I have not discussed the environment in this short chapter, but
this, too, is part of the agenda for an urban theology of mission. The HKSKH is already
taking steps toward a greener and more environmentally friendly approach to our life
in Hong Kong. In addition to our mission in the schools and welfare centers, and our
work with the most vulnerable members of our community, the environment will be
an important part of our work in the future.

The HKSKH strongly supports the Anglican Communion, and we hope that we can
move beyond the struggles that have divided us. The HKSKH has consistently advocated
the Middle Way so as to avoid the extreme positions and keep the communion together.
This means, at times, that we need to exercise restraint in relationships to others. I
realize that there are strongly held Christian beliefs, about which many believe there
can be no compromise. However, the differences that divide us should not break the
fellowship we have that has been given to us by God. I have spoken earlier about the

position of the HKSKH with regard to blessing same-sex unions and episcopal oversight by bishops in provinces other than their own (HKSKH Sentiments 2010).

My hope for the future is that our perspective on identity in community, with emphasis on the church as family and the *via media* in relationships with others, will help us put the issues we face in Hong Kong and in the Anglican Communion as a whole in a clearer perspective.

## Bibliography

Fan, Samson. 2009. *Incarnation: Charles Gore's Anglican Theology*. Hong Kong: Religious Education Resource Center (in Chinese).

HKSKH Sentiments with Respect to Certain Anglican Issues. 2010. *The English Echo*, vol. 266 (June 2010), 3–4.

Kwong, Paul. 2011. Identity *in Community: Toward a Theological Agenda for the Hong Kong SAR*. Münster: ContactZone/Lit Verlag.

CHAPTER 24

# The Nippon Sei Ko Kai (The Anglican Communion in Japan)

## Renta Nishihara

## The Arrival and Emergence of Anglicanism in Japan

The Rev. Channing Moore Williams, a missionary from the Episcopal Church in the United States of America, led the first full-fledged Episcopalian mission to Japan. In the autumn of 1852, Williams enrolled at the Virginia Theological Seminary where he cultivated a passion for preaching. Early on, he was committed to foreign missionary work. He graduated in 1855 and was sent to China along with his classmate John Liggins. The Episcopal Church in the United States of America was attempting to start up missions in China at the time. At first, Williams and Liggins were posted to Shanghai; but, in keeping with church policy, they traveled from there to Nagasaki in 1859. This was the beginning of the mission of the Anglican Church of Japan.

Unfortunately, Liggins, who came to Japan along with Williams, had to return home just after arriving due to illness. Williams settled in Sofukuji Temple in Nagasaki and, at first, he presided over worship for English and American merchants but was not preaching to Japanese people. In fact, in his first seven years in Japan, Williams was not able to preach directly to the Japanese people due to the Shogunate's anti-Christian policy. During these years, Williams lived at the Sofukuji Temple and spent all his time studying the Japanese language. He spent his days translating the Chinese version of the Book of Common Prayer into Japanese.

Williams did not know what the future would bring. He could not see what direction he would take, and he had no prospects for change – but he stayed looking for opportunities to preach to the Japanese.

Channing Moore Williams made a trip back to the United States in 1866 and was consecrated Bishop of China and Japan. The next year, with the 1867 Meiji Restoration, Bishop Williams was finally able to commence his full-fledged mission to Japan.

*The Wiley-Blackwell Companion to the Anglican Communion*, First Edition. Edited by Ian S. Markham, J. Barney Hawkins IV, Justyn Terry, and Leslie Nuñez Steffensen.
© 2013 John Wiley & Sons, Ltd. Published 2013 by John Wiley & Sons, Ltd.

In 1868, George Ensor, missionary from England's Church Missionary Society (CMS), came to Japan. William Ball Wright and Alexander Croft Shaw et al., missionaries from England's Society for the Propagation of the Gospel in Foreign Parts (SPG), came to Japan in 1873. Bishop Williams, relieved of his responsibility for China, moved to Edo (now Tokyo) in 1873, and the next year he was consecrated as the Bishop of Edo, not the Bishop of China. Bishop Williams established parishes and mission stations in Fukagawa, Kanda, and Asakusa. At the same time, he founded a small Anglican school, later to become Rikkyo University in Tsukiji.

In the 1880s, the size of the Anglican Church in Japan increased dramatically. However, at the same time, a number of issues with the Japanese missions of the Anglican Church came to light. In particular, the Anglican Church in Japan was served by three missionary groups: the Episcopal Church in the United States of America, SPG, and CMS from England (which later had the participation of the Anglican Church of Canada). These three missionary groups did not have cooperative relationships, and each conducted activities according to their own policies which led to discord and confusion.

The Church of England, through discussions with SPG and CMS, consecrated Edward Bickersteth as the Bishop of Japan. Bishop Bickersteth arrived in Japan in 1886 and had many discussions with Bishop Williams. In February 1887, the first general assembly of the Anglican Church in Japan was held. Through the cooperation of the three missionary groups in this assembly, the *Nippon Sei Ko Kai*; NSKK (the Anglican Church in Japan) was legally established (Tsukada 1978).

The first Japanese bishop, Sakunoshin Motoda, was consecrated in 1923, and NSKK became an official province of the Anglican Communion in 1930. In 2012, NSKK has approximately 55,500 members in 11 dioceses, with 313 parishes and about 300 clergy (2011).

To commemorate 150 years of the Anglican Mission in Japan, the Most Rev. Rowan Williams, the 104th Archbishop of Canterbury, was welcomed to Japan on September 23, 2009. Attendees included not only the Archbishop of Canterbury but also the Most Rev. Katharine Jefferts Schori, the presiding bishop of the Episcopal Church of the United States, all the diocesan bishops of the Anglican Church of Korea, and many guests from all over the world.

## Marginal Anglican Histories in Japan: A Case of Yukie Chiri

It is important for us to be grateful for, and also to commemorate, the work of famous historical leaders such as Bishop Williams and the missionaries from England, including Bishop Bickersteth. However, it is important to shine a light not only on mainstream history but also on each action which is recognized as marginal as exterior or external history and to learn from these. This makes it possible to understand the essence of what is really valued by the Anglican Church in Japan in each part of its history.

The Ainu are an indigenous people in Japan. The Rev. John Batchelor, a missionary from the CMS, undertook a mission in 1880 to the Ainu people in Hokkaido in the northern part of Japan. He was called the father of the Ainu. At that time, the Japanese discriminated against the Ainu, and Japan was implementing the so-called integration policy which usurped the Ainu language and culture. Batchelor edited the Ainu Language Dictionary and the Ainu Language Bible, and he worked to defend the rights of the Ainu people. Thanks to Batchelor, many Ainu were baptized. Among these was a young woman, Yukie Chiri, who transcribed the tales of the Ainu that had been handed down from generation to generation in the word-of-mouth culture of the Ainu and in the Ainu Epic Tales, *Yukar*.

Yukie Chiri was young when she worked to translate the *Yukar*. She was discovered by a Japanese linguist, Kyosuke Kindaichi, and following this, she moved from Hokkaido to Tokyo to stay at Kindaichi's house and put the Ainu Epic Tales or *Yukar* into writing, preserving them for future generations. Unfortunately, Yukie Chiri passed away from heart failure at the age of 19.

Until her death at 19 years of age, Yukie was extremely influenced by Christianity and the gospels, and she included in her diary in her last years quotes from the Bible and prayers to God. Kyosuke Kindaichi wrote the following of Yukie: "Every time she heard of a story in which someone was the victim, she prayed for them. Christ was also the victim of the people and was the most wonderful person. She was a girl who was jealous of people who were victimized."

There are many gods in the religious culture of the Ainu: trees are gods, bears are gods, and many other kinds of animals are gods. Many gods are worshipped. Yukie Chiri transcribed: "Where the silver droplets fall, where the golden droplets fall." This is about an owl which is a god. The tale of the owl god was her most prized tale. It is the first tale that appears in Yukie's Ainu Epic Tales, *Yukar*.

The tale is narrated by the owl god, and begins with him singing and flying over the heads of a group of children. The children, knowing the bird is a divine being, decide to shoot their arrows at it, saying that whoever hits the bird first is the bravest and most heroic among them. The first to try to shoot the owl were the children who were "of households which had once been poor but were now rich." They used fine metal arrows and bows and shot many arrows, but the owl "caused them [the arrows] to veer up or down and they all missed." Not all the children in the group were rich though.

Among them was one child who carried a bow and arrow made only of rough wood. I saw what the child was wearing and knew that he was from a poor household. This child also fit his wooden arrow into his wooden bow and aimed at me. As he did so, the children who had once been poor but were now rich laughed at him and said, "Now, that's really funny! You silly pauper, that's a divine bird. It will never accept your rotten wooden arrow when it won't even accept our shiny metal arrows. Not in a million years."

They kicked him with their legs and hit him with their fists. However, the poor boy ignored them and carefully aimed his arrow at me. I watched him and was moved.

"Where the silver droplets fall, where the golden droplets fall," I sang as I drew a circle slowly in the sky. The poor boy drew one leg back and set it firmly behind him while setting the other leg firmly in front of him. He bit on his lower lip and steadied his aim. The arrow was released in a whoosh of air.

The tiny arrow flew clean and straight towards me. I stretched out my claw and plucked that little arrow from the air. I sliced through the wind and was fluttering to the ground. "Where the silver droplets fall, where the golden droplets fall . . ." (Chiri 1978)

This poem of an owl god is the one which Yukie valued most. The owl god who could not be struck by the metal arrows of the rich children pitied the poor boy with his tattered kimono as he was ridiculed and kicked by the other children. So he deliberately aimed himself at the wooden arrow that the boy shot. In other words, "plucked" means that the owl aimed his body at the arrow that the poor boy had shot. The owl god fell to the ground dying. "Where the silver droplets fall, where the golden droplets fall." This is a *Yukar* in which the owl falls to the ground dying at its own behest for the sake of the poor child.

Why did Yukie choose this very beautiful, very sad *Yukar* for the first of the Ainu Epic Tales? For Yukie, the gospels of Jesus were present in this tale – the compassion for the pain of oppressed as an Ainu. It was her religious belief that Jesus lived along with oppressed people. She and her people read the gospel and the Bible. They learned from the missionaries that Jesus died for people who were persecuted and poor. Jesus then rose from the dead.

She told the stories from these gospels at the Anglican Sunday school at Asahikawa. An understanding of these gospels was incarnated in Yukie, and this led her to select the tale of the owl god as the most important *Yukar*. The gospels preached by the Anglican missionary were incarnated in Yukie, an Ainu woman. This is a valuable piece of history of Anglicanism in Japan.

## Marginal Anglican Histories in Japan: A Case of Okaya St. Barnabas Church (Nishihara 2010)

Next, there is the story about Okaya St. Barnabas Church on the banks of Lake Suwa in Nagano Prefecture, where I am the managing minister. In June 2008, Okaya Church celebrated the Eucharist to commemorate 80 years of the consecration of the church. The whole of the Chubu diocese, to which the Okaya Church belongs, was first set up by the Anglican Church of Canada, which also set up a mission to Okaya. The Okaya St. Barnabas Church was served by the Rev. Hollis Hamilton Corey, a priest from the Anglican Church of Canada.

When Corey decided to build a church in a place called Okaya, we wondered how many people believed in its future. Even now, it is an extremely small congregation. It is also a poor church. It has only 20 members, at most. We were still able to offer up prayers of thanks for our 80th anniversary. We believe that this is, in a way, a miracle.

When Corey conducted his missionary work in the Lake Suwa region and decided to build a church, he had trouble deciding where he should build. According to the instructions of the Canada Mission, the choice was between Shimosuwa, a bustling town, or Kamisuwa. Corey, however, wanted to establish a church for the people who faced the most hardship in the Suwa region. He wanted to build a place of worship for the people who had the most difficult lives. At the time, in 1928, Okaya was a silk-manufacturing town of 60,000. In fact, the population of Okaya has remained almost unchanged. However, population ratios were completely different, with 70 or 80 percent of the 60,000 population of the town of Okaya at the time being female factory workers aged from around 14 to 17 or 18 years of age. There is a famous book by Shigemi Yamamoto called *Ah! Nomugi Toge*. It is a sad tale of the maidens who cross the mountains from Hida to come to work in Okaya. At the time, Okaya was full of female factory workers. When I did some research at the public library in Okaya, I found documentation of a survey conducted by the Communist Party at the time entitled *The History of the Oppression of Female Factory Workers in Okaya*. It contains details of wretched conditions and unspeakable images that I cannot write about. It is all about the difficult experiences of the factory girls.

So, Corey decided to establish the church in Okaya. He wanted to build a place of worship for the female factory workers. That is why he decided he had to build the church in Okaya. The headquarters of the Canada Mission was against the location. The factory girls were seasonal workers who went home in the off-season. Of course, they were poor. They would not be able to support the church economically. They would not be regular members of the congregation either. The Canada Mission knew that there was no way that it was possible to maintain a church for such people.

However, Corey responded by saying that we should believe that God would provide everything. Koyoshi Fukazawa, a former female factory worker who is still a member of the congregation at the age of 98, says the following:

> When I ran to church clasping my non-existent pocket money in my hand as my offering, the tall blue-eyed priest was waiting for me at the bottom of the steps and hugged me and said "Thank you for coming." I didn't really understand the meaning of the sermons but my eyes spilled over with tears at the warmth of the hug I received from the priest. That church really was heaven.

The floor of the Okaya St. Barnabas Church is laid with Japanese traditional mats, *tatami*. This was a request from the female factory workers. Normally, they worked a 16-hour day, with a total of only 40 minutes break. The factory girls had to sit on hard wooden chairs without cushions at the factory. These women wanted to feel like they were coming home when they came to church which is why they made this request. In response to this request, Corey laid the floor of Okaya Church with *tatami*. In this way, the church was the women's home. The origin of the word "church" is the Greek *Oikos Ecclesia*, whose original meaning is "home."

This church soothed, comforted, and encouraged the women, becoming a place for them to regain their own dignity. The history of Okaya St. Barnabas Church appears as only a few lines in the official text of the history of the Chubu diocese. However, this is also an important case of the history of the NSKK.

The Anglican Church in Japan celebrated the 150th year anniversary of its mission in 2009. It is an extremely crucial task to shine a light on such a piece of valuable history that plucks at the heartstrings of the Japanese people – rather than just the history of famous ministers and theologians or great churches and schools or projects.

The gospel of the Holy Bible ran like living water through the people of Japan in a way that the foreign missionaries of the Anglican Church of the Meiji Period could never have imagined. For people like Yukie or the factory girls, the Bible was not a document that was written 2,000 years ago – but the food of life for living life today and in the future. Maybe those girls understood the real meaning of the gospel better than first-class theologians and famous ministers. It is important to position this miracle prominently in the history of the Anglican missions in Japan and the Anglican Church in Japan, NSKK.

## The Catastrophic Natural Disaster and the Responsibilities of the NSKK

The earthquake which struck the Tohoku regions and most of eastern Japan on March 11, 2011, registered a magnitude of 9.0 on the Richter scale, the strongest earthquake in the country's history. The enormous tsunami which resulted brought unprecedented death and destruction up and down the coast. Roughly 30,000 people were dead or missing. Many lost family and friends, homes, and savings. In 2012, many still have no choice but to stay in emergency shelters. This cataclysmic event seriously damaged the Fukushima nuclear power plant, resulting in radioactive pollution which has forced many people to leave the familiar surroundings of their homes.

I wrote a short reflection a few days after the earthquake on March 11. It has been introduced to the world by the Archbishop of Canterbury, The Most Rev. Rowan Williams, and placed on the official web site of the Anglican Communion. It has been included here as a way of reflecting on the earthquake which makes explicit a connection with the moment from a faith perspective.

"Do Not be Afraid"

On March 11th, the great earthquake took place. As it took place, I was at the university. My bookshelves were falling, lights were swaying wildly. Turning on a television, I saw a great tsunami about to swallow up some people. The city's public transport at Tokyo was paralyzed, so we opened up the university campus of Rikkyo for the public. I spent the night at the university together with about 5,000 people. The following morning, it was becoming clear that we were faced with a situation that far outstripped any words. We were experiencing that lamentation that the Psalmist felt as he faced intense hardship, so that his tongue stuck to the roof of his mouth, not even able to pray to God.

One woman's testimony still rings in my ears. As she was making her way to high ground, running from the great tsunami, she looked back; a number of elementary school students were crying out, running desperately. But when she looked back again, the children had vanished. One boy was going among the evacuation centers with a piece of cardboard on which he had written the names of his parent and his brothers and sisters. As we face this reality, all that is left to us is a dazed silence.

And then, in addition to the earthquake and the tsunami, we were gripped by an additional fear: fear due to the explosion of the reactors at the Fukushima Daiichi nuclear power plant, as they went out of control and spread abroad concentrated radioactivity. The Japanese scholars would tell us that these levels were "at levels that would not affect the human body," but the thing which I have learned when I was a student of the department of technology at Kyoto University is that there is no radioactivity which does not have influence in a human body.

Actually, four years ago, these Fukushima plants were brought up in the Diet as the possible site of a hideous accident produced by loss of coolants, should there be a Chile-class tsunami. In this sense, the accident at this reactor can be termed entirely man-made in nature. We should remember those people who have offered up themselves in the effort to wrest control of the situation, even as fierce radioactive rays rain down on them. One can only imagine what their families are thinking as they follow the events.

One after another, messages of encouragement have been coming in to me, sent by brothers and sisters around the world who are linked to me through the Anglican Communion and other international Christian networks. According to the Rev. Terrie Robinson, a secretary at the Anglican Communion Office, within the first thirty hours after the earthquake, hundreds of emails with encouragement and prayer had been delivered from various parts of the world.

The parishioners and clergy of the dioceses of Tohoku and Kita Kanto, along with all those who suffered this disaster, are still in extreme hardship and distress. But they are not the only ones; all of us sense a terror deeper than words. However, we are not alone. Our sisters and brothers throughout the world sense this pain together with us, feel the pain in their very bowels, and hold on to our hand and will not let us go, praying with a prayer that is a veritable shout.

In this very moment, our faith is being questioned. Didn't the risen Jesus give strength to Mary and the others as they shivered, saying "do not be afraid"? The name given by God to the resurrected Lord Jesus Christ, who changed despair to eternal life, is the name "Emmanuel." That name's meaning is "Lord is with us."

Amid the rubble of the devastated areas, there was a young boy who was gritting his teeth as he walked, holding a large container full of water in both hands. He was moving through the hopelessness of that rubble, yet moving forward with hope, the hope of life itself. With him, with all those who have been afflicted in this disaster, with each and every one of us, the resurrected Lord is walking as he did on that road to Emmaus, bringing warmth to our hearts.

This year's Easter will be a very special Lord's day. It will be a precious time when we take a new step toward hope, like a small shoot growing up amidst the rubble. Amen.

Faced with this earthquake and the accompanying tragedy, the Anglican Church in Japan realizes that it has a responsibility to deepen ties with the world, our society, and our neighbors.

The Fukushima Daiichi nuclear power plant tragedy has once again revealed how fragile our confidence must be in our "knowledge" and "science." Immediately after March 11, the nuclear power plants which were touted as being absolutely safe in the face of any natural disaster exploded one after another, and unbelievable amounts of radioactivity and radioactive substances were spread into the air, earth, and ocean. This catastrophe is on par with the Chernobyl disaster. The Japanese scholars who appeared on television repeated their view that "there is no immediate influence to the human body." It is fair to say that the Japanese government, power companies, and university experts who compose the so-called "nuclear village" hold vested interests in nuclear power. They often misrepresent the extent of the damage – despite knowing the immeasurable damage which will have an impact 10 years, 20 years, and many generations from now.

Japan has been a "victim" of radiation represented by "Hiroshima" and "Nagasaki." However, after "Fukushima," Japan was continuing to spread radiation across the world and subjectively must be seen as having become the "offender." Meanwhile, we, as an Anglican Church in Japan, must strongly reflect upon why we could not speak more prophetically. In light of Christian ethics, why does the Anglican Church in Japan not oppose Japanese nuclear energy administration and knowledge?

At the same time, from this disaster, we have recognized how important it is to encourage our congregations to be more sympathetic to the pain of others and to be able to have a concrete solidarity.

The NSKK started a project to support the victims of the disaster, called "Let Us Walk Together Project." NSKK is carrying out activities with attention to disaster victims facing particular hardship – elderly, children, those with disabilities, foreign residents, low-income people, and refugees.

## The Mission Statement of the NSKK

Actually, there are many achievements worthy of notice in the missionary history of the NSKK. However, it would be difficult to say that these valuable records had been treasured in the NSKK. Only since the 1990s has there been any fresh evaluation of these deeds. Only in that period was the NSKK able finally to discern the meaning of the expanded missiology of worldwide Anglicanism.

In August 1995, the NSKK Conference on Mission opened at the Seisenryō in Kiyosato. This meeting resulted from a resolution at the previous year's 46th regular general synod of the NSKK: "A Church whose life is Christ at work in history, the world, society and the people." The theme of the conference was "The Mission of the NSKK – Our responsibility to History and Outlook on the 21st Century." At this conference, the NSKK confessed with pain and sought forgiveness for its support of wars which have led to the invasion of various countries in Asia. The following year at its general synod, the NSKK formally adopted a resolution: "A Declaration concerning the war responsibility of the NSKK," which was highly regarded and talked about at the 1998 Lambeth Conference.

The Conference on Mission also announced the following definition of the NSKK's mission:

> In the middle year of the Decade of Evangelism, we affirm anew that the Church exists for God's Mission. Mission in this sense means that, under God's calling and guidance in history, we do not maintain the *status quo* as something fixed, but ceaselessly and boldly follow the process of reform. Human rights, justice and the environment represent the central issues of mission. We are resolved to become a Church whose purpose is the restoration of their rights and position in society to those who suffer and are despised as "little ones". We the NSKK must continually renew this response to mission. Together with those who have been excluded from society and those who are oppressed we will struggle against all situations of discrimination. And we will continue to listen, not to the stories of the rulers but to the stories of the people. Following them we will tell our own stories. In our own words we will tell about the history and the present of the NSKK, and also of its future. Through this effort we believe that we will be able for the first time to make incarnate the Gospel of Our Lord Jesus Christ. We are also being called to fulfil a prophetic mission in this world and this society. Above all, the NSKK must become the salt of the earth, the light of the world, to change the social order itself, that gives birth to and supports discrimination and oppression. We understand the Mission of God in which we have a part to include all of these things. (Executive Committee of the 1995 NSKK Conference on Mission 1995)

If this definition were merely a literary expression, it would be an altogether meaningless exercise. Is the NSKK prepared to build on this missiology by wrestling with issues and with regular concrete action and service?

## Bibliography

Chiri, Yukie. 1978. *Ainu Shin Yo Shu (Ainu Epic Tales)* [in Japanese]. Tokyo: Iwanami Shoten.

Executive Committee of the 1995 NSKK Conference on Mission. 1995. *Report of the '95 Conference on Mission* [in Japanese]. Tokyo: NSKK Provincial Office.

Nishihara, Renta. 2010. *Seikokai ga Taisetsuni Shitekita Mono (A Treasure of the Anglicanism)* [in Japanese]. Tokyo: Sei Ko Kai Shuppan.

Tsukada, Osamu. 1978. *Nippon Sei Ko Kai no Keisei to Kadai (The Formation and Issues of the NSKK)* [in Japanese]. Tokyo: Sei Ko Kai Shuppan.

CHAPTER 25

# The Episcopal/Anglican Church in Jerusalem and the Middle East

## Mouneer Hanna Anis

## Introduction

It all began here in the Middle East – the story of God's creation; the Covenant with Abraham; the story of the Exodus; the presence of God in the midst of His people; the failures and the victories of the People of God; the birth of Jesus Christ our Savior; His crucifixion, resurrection, and ascension; and the first Christian mission to the world – all began here on this land of the Middle East.

The first church of Christ was started here in the Middle East 2,000 years ago and continues to witness to the love of God today. Jerusalem was the birthplace of the church. Antioch in Syria was the place where people were first called "Christians." Alexandria was the place where St. Mark established the first church in Egypt and the first seminary in the world. Cyprus was at the heart of the missionary journeys of the Apostles. The Christian presence in Iran goes back to the day of Pentecost.

In this Middle Eastern context, the Anglican Church started through the combination of the zeal of Anglican missionaries to spread the gospel and through the generosity and welcome of the local Middle Eastern people. It is a great blessing and a great challenge to live and serve in the midst of churches that are 2,000 years old and have survived in spite of unbearable persecution over the centuries. The fathers of these churches were ready to shed their blood in order to keep the faith once received from Jesus Christ through the saints. They endured many hardships to combat heresies and to preserve the apostolic faith.

This history challenges us to continue in the faithful way of God without losing the flexibility of approach that is needed to address new generations. The first-century churches continue to shape our mind, teaching, and theology and remind us that when

*The Wiley-Blackwell Companion to the Anglican Communion*, First Edition. Edited by Ian S. Markham, J. Barney Hawkins IV, Justyn Terry, and Leslie Nuñez Steffensen.
© 2013 John Wiley & Sons, Ltd. Published 2013 by John Wiley & Sons, Ltd.

we say in the Nicene Creed, "we believe in one, holy, universal, and apostolic church" we need to strive to keep the oneness and unity of the church. Our history and the church in the Middle East teach us how to avoid unilateral decisions that may widen the gap between us as Anglicans and other churches.

On the other hand, our presence in the midst of our Muslim friends is also a helpful challenge. Every day, and five times a day, the Imam calls people to pray with the words "Allahu Akbar" meaning "God is the Greatest." These words remind Christians throughout the Middle East, five times a day, that God is here and that He is Great! These words also urge us to draw near to God at all times.

## History of the Episcopal/Anglican Church of Jerusalem and the Middle East

The Episcopal/Anglican Church of Jerusalem and the Middle East, created on January 6, 1976, is one of the largest and most diverse provinces in the Anglican Communion, stretching from Algeria in the west to Iran in the east and from Somalia in the south to Cyprus in the north. There are four dioceses: the Diocese of Jerusalem (Israel, Palestine, Jordan, Syria, and Lebanon), the Diocese of Cyprus and the Gulf (Cyprus, Bahrain, Iraq, Kuwait, Oman, Qatar, Saudi Arabia, United Arab Emirates, and Yemen), the Diocese of Iran (Iran), and the Diocese of Egypt with North Africa and the Horn of Africa (Egypt, Algeria, Tunisia, Libya, Ethiopia, Eritrea, Somalia, and Djibouti). Today, the province has over 50,000 baptized members in approximately 200 congregations, is led by a president bishop, and is governed by the provincial (central) synod.

The history of the Province of Jerusalem and the Middle East stretches back to when the Anglican presence in Jerusalem was started in 1841 as a joint venture between the Church of England (Queen Victoria) and the Lutheran Prussians (King Frederick William IV). In 1841, the Archbishop of Canterbury consecrated the Rev. Michael Solomon Alexander as the first Bishop of Jerusalem (1842–1845). Subsequent bishops were supposed to be nominated alternately by the English and Prussian sovereigns and to be consecrated by Anglican bishops.

On December 30, 1846, the second bishop arrived in Jerusalem, the Rt. Rev. Samuel Gobat, and he served there from 1846 to 1879. It is said that Bishop Gobat:

> believed that the way to evangelize the people of the Ottoman Empire was through the members of the Middle Eastern Churches. Since, however, he considered those churches to be wayward and in deep spiritual sleep, they had to be awakened and restored to the true and pure faith, namely, to the evangelical faith that is founded on the Bible alone, the sole authority for faith. (Frarah 2005, 729)

This approach to strengthening the Orthodox Churches concerned Dr. William Howley, the Archbishop of Canterbury from 1828 to 1848, who did not want the Anglican presence in the Middle East to create more divisions. He wrote that the Bishop of Jerusalem should play a bridging and healing role, "of putting an end to the divisions which had brought the most grievous calamities to the Church of Christ."

The Archbishop of Canterbury signed an agreement with the Patriarch of the Alexandria (of the Coptic Orthodox Church) in which he committed the Anglican Church to serve the Orthodox Churches. In 1842, the Anglican Church started a seminary for the Coptic Orthodox Church in the patriarchate in Cairo. The cooperation of the Anglican–Orthodox continued for five years during which one of the graduates of the seminary became the Pope of Alexandria. His name was Kyrilos (Cyril) the Reformer. Pope Kyrilos developed the Coptic Orthodox Church by building many Coptic schools and encouraged the education of girls.

The mission of the Anglican Churches in the Middle East continued with an emphasis on serving the local communities without any discrimination between Christians, Muslims, and Jews. The Archbishop of Canterbury appointed the Archbishop in Jerusalem who oversaw the whole region (the history of this period is mentioned in the individual diocese later on).

Archbishop Angus Campbell MacInnes, after serving from 1957 to 1968, resigned. It was announced that the Archbishop of Perth, George Appleton, had been appointed by the Archbishop of Canterbury and in consultation with the other metropolitans of the Anglican Communion, to fill the vacancy in Jerusalem (1969–1974). In early 1970, Archbishop George Appleton appointed a special committee to consider the future of the dioceses including the archbishopric. Discussion took place regarding a possible restructuring of the archdiocese and, during the interim, Bishop Albert Kenneth Cragg (1970–1974) served as the Assistant Bishop of Jerusalem and then Bishop Robert Stopford (1974–1976) served as the Vicar General of Jerusalem.

Finally, in 1976, the Episcopal Church in Jerusalem and the Middle East, also known today as the Episcopal/Anglican Province of Jerusalem and the Middle East, was inaugurated. Metropolitical authority was given from the Archbishop of Canterbury to the provincial (central) synod, and the following have served as its president bishop or primate: Hassan Dehqani-Tafti (1976–1986), Samir Kafity (1986–1996), Ghais Abdel Malik (1996–2000), Iraj Mottahedeh (2000–2002), Clive Handford (2002–2007), and Mouneer Hanna Anis (2007–present).

# The Diocese of Jerusalem

## The history of the Diocese of Jerusalem

The Anglican presence in Jerusalem goes back to 1841 even though Church Mission Society (CMS) missionaries began preparations to serve in the Middle East as early as 1821. In 1833, a CMS missionary station was established in Jerusalem with the support of the London Society for Promoting Christianity Amongst the Jews, now known as the Church's Ministry Amongst Jewish People, or CMJ.

Jerusalem's first bishop, the Rt. Rev. Michael Solomon Alexander, arrived in 1841 and, in 1845, dedicated Christ Church at Jaffa Gate to be the first Anglican church in Jerusalem. CMS sent missionaries to Israel from 1851 to 1879 to spread the gospel, from 1879 to 1905 to expand and grow, and from 1905 to 1918 to hand over the work to native leaders (cf. Murry 1985). CMS started its missionary work in Palestine and Jordan in 1848.

The Rt. Rev. Samuel Gobat, Jerusalem's second bishop, opened 42 schools and ordained the first-ever Palestinian priests. However, in 1881, after the failure to secure Episcopal orders for the Lutherans, the joint Anglican—Prussian bishopric was dissolved. Anglican bishop Joseph Barclay served from 1881 to 1887 and then, on March 25, 1887, the bishopric was reconstituted on a purely Anglican basis, with Archdeacon George Francis Popham Blythe, a Jewish convert to Christianity, consecrated as the first bishop (1887–1914). The Jerusalem Bishopric Fund was set up by Bishop Blythe, succeeded by the Jerusalem and East Mission Fund, now the Jerusalem and Middle East Church Association (JMECA), to maintain and develop the work of the diocese.

St. George's Cathedral in Jerusalem was built during the episcopacy of the Rt. Rev. George Blyth, Jerusalem's fourth bishop (1887–1914). Bishop Blythe was succeeded by the Rt. Rev. Rennie MacInnes (1914–1931), who served during the Great War. In 1915, the British congregations and their clergy all left Palestine. The Rt. Rev. George Francis Graham Brown served Jerusalem from 1932 to 1942, and then the Rt. Rev. Weston Henry Stuart became bishop (1943–1957).

In 1948, with the creation of the State of Israel and the ensuing war between the Arabs and the Jews, many were displaced, and refugees abounded. In 1956, "The Majma in Jordan unanimously passed a resolution advising the Archbishop of Canterbury to appoint an Arab priest from the diocese as the next Anglican Bishop in Jerusalem. The reaction of Archbishop Geoffrey Fisher of Canterbury was his decision to bring into existence the Jerusalem Archbishopric and a new diocese" (Every 4). In 1957, the Diocese of Jerusalem was elevated to an archbishopric under the extra-provincial jurisdiction of the Archbishop of Canterbury. A new diocese of Jordan, Lebanon, and Syria was formed, and the Archbishop of Jerusalem had oversight over the entire current province, with the inclusion of Sudan (five dioceses altogether). In 1957, Najib Cubain, the first Arab bishop, was consecrated as the Bishop of Jordan, Lebanon, the West Bank, and Syria. He served as an assistant to the Archbishop in Jerusalem.

From 1970 to 1976, the dioceses in the Middle East were restructured and, in 1976, the Diocese of Jerusalem (including Israel, Palestine, Jordan, Syria, and Lebanon) was created. Its bishop became both the "Bishop in Jerusalem," as he represented all Anglicans in Jerusalem, and the "Bishop of Jerusalem," as he represented the newly formed Diocese of Jerusalem. In 1976, church membership was approximately 7,500, composed mostly of Arabic-speaking congregations, some English-speaking congregations, and some Hebrew Christian congregations. In 1976, the Diocese of Jerusalem had 12 schools, hospitals in Nablus and Gaza, seven social institutions, and two youth hostels in Jerusalem (one at Christ Church, one at St. George's Cathedral).

Since the creation of the Province of Jerusalem and the Middle East in 1976, and restructure of the current Diocese of Jerusalem, there have been four Anglican Bishops of Jerusalem: Faik Ibrahim Haddad (1976–1984), who was the first Palestinian bishop; Samir Hanna Kafity (1984–1998), who raised up indigenous leaders and developed many institutions; Riah Hanna Abu el-Assal (1998–2007), who fought for justice and advocacy; and Suheil Salman Ibrahim Dawani (2007–present), who stands for peace and reconciliation, especially between Palestinians and Israelis.

*The story of the contemporary church*

The Diocese of Jerusalem is currently led by the Rt. Rev. Suheil Dawani, who was installed on April 15, 2007, at St. George the Martyr Cathedral in Jerusalem. The Diocese of Jerusalem includes Israel, Palestine, Jordan, Syria, and Lebanon, and has 27 parishes, approximately 30 priests, and includes over 7,000 Anglicans. The diocese meets the needs of its communities through its 33 institutions which include clinics, hospitals (over 200 beds), kindergartens and schools (over 6,400 students), vocational programs, and centers for the deaf, disabled, and elderly. It employs about 1,500 people.

While it is impossible to detail every institution, it is important to mention several of them. The Diocese of Jerusalem is proud of the Princess Basma Center for Disabled Children, which has more than 700 students, and St. George's College in Jerusalem, which continues to train lay and ordained people in theological education. St. Paul's in West Jerusalem, completed in 1873 with support from CMS and dedicated in 1874, served as a place of worship until the Palestinian displacement of 1948. In 2011, the church was reopened in the presence of Bishop Suheil Dawani, His Beatitude Theophilos III of the Greek Orthodox Church, Bishop Munib Younan of the Evangelical Lutheran Church, and His Grace Kamal Batheesh of the Latin Church.

In 2010, the Archbishop of Canterbury and the Bishop of Jerusalem rededicated St. Philip's Church in Gaza and visited Ahli Hospital in Palestine. On the same visit, Bishop Suheil and Archbishop Rowan laid the cornerstone of an Anglican Church at the baptismal site of Jesus Christ in Jordan. The land was a gift of His Majesty King Abdullah II of Jordan. Also in Jordan, Savior Church, founded in 1950 and relocated in 1960, was renovated and rededicated on April 11, 2010, by Bishop Suheil Dawani. The church serves approximately 200 people through its services, youth and women's meetings. On August 5, 2010, Bishop Suheil Dawani dedicated a new church, St. Mary the Virgin, in Irbid, Jordan. In nearby Amman, the Diocese of Jerusalem also runs the Ahliyyah School for Girls, and Church of the Redeemer. Also, in 2011, Bishop Suheil laid the foundation stone for a new school for children with special needs in Al Husn. This is in addition to the Schneller School, which is almost 50 years old and has 160 boarding students, 120 day students, and live-in educators.

# The Diocese of Cyprus and the Gulf

*The history of the Diocese of Cyprus and the Gulf*

Bishop Leonard Ashton, the first Bishop of the Diocese of Cyprus and the Gulf (1976–1983) wrote:

> Beyond the vast horizons of sand and dust, where the palm trees lean against the blue sides and the lazy waters, somewhere there is hidden the traditional site of the Garden of Eden . . . the place of Noah's Flood, the home of Abraham of Ur, the Tower of Babel, the ruins of Babylon and Ctesiphon. Across these lands the Queen of Sheba made her way to

visit King Solomon in Jerusalem, and the Magi brought gold and frankincense and myrrh to Bethlehem. From the great rivers Tigris and Euphrates through a thousand and one nights in Baghdad, leaning eastwards from the Holy Land to the Mediterranean, we approach the lovely land of Cyprus. This was a land of the Greek Gods, where Aphrodite, goddess of love and beauty, was said to have been born of the sea foam. In this place Saint Barnabas lived, and St. Paul began his missionary journeys. . . . Deep in these territories is the heart of Islam, where the Prophet Mohammed (upon whom be peace) rode to conquer. This is the geographical area of the Diocese of Cyprus and the Gulf rich with ancient history tradition and mythology where Christians of many nations are working and worshipping together.

The origins of the Anglican presence in the Gulf can be traced back to an Act of Parliament in 1877 which established the Diocese of Lahore and included Delhi, East Punjab, Kashmir, Pakistan, and the southern states of the Arabian Gulf. Its first bishop was Thomas Valpy French (1825–1888). "Although Anglicans were the first to point out that the Gulf was a rich mission field, they did not enter it themselves until well into the oil era (from the 1930s onward), and then not through their mission agencies but under ecclesiastical auspices" (Scudder 2005, 754).

Congregations continue to be predominately composed of expatriates except in Cyprus and Iraq, where there are large numbers of indigenous Christians.

Since the realignment of the Province of Jerusalem and the Middle East in 1976, the following have served as bishops of the Diocese of Cyprus and the Gulf: the Rt. Rev. Leonard J. Ashton (1976–1983), the Rt. Rev. Henry W. Moore (1983–1986), the Rt. Rev. John E. Brown (1987–1995), the Rt. Rev. George Clive Handford (1996–2007), and the Rt. Rev. Michael Augustine Owen Lewis (2007–present).

## The story of the contemporary church

The Diocese of Cyprus and the Gulf is currently led by the Rt. Rev. Michael Lewis and is divided into two archdeaconries (Cyprus and the Gulf) with two cathedrals: St. Paul's Cathedral in Nicosia, Cyprus, and St. Christopher's Cathedral in Manama, Bahrain. The Diocese of Cyprus and the Gulf primarily provides support for the expatriate communities except in Cyprus and Iraq, where there are thriving indigenous congregations. There are unique opportunities at the interface with Islam and great scope for ecumenical contact with Christian expatriate workers from the Indian sub-continent, Africa, and the Far East (cf. http://www.cypgulf.org).

The following churches exist in the Diocese of Cyprus and the Gulf: the Cathedral Church of St. Christopher in Bahrain; St. Andrew's (Abu Dhabi), Holy Trinity (Dubai), Christ Church (Jebel Ali), St. Luke's (Ras al Khaimah), St. Nicholas (Fujairah), and St. Martin's (Sharjah) in the United Arab Emirates; St George's (Baghdad) in Iraq; St. Paul's (Ahmadi) in Kuwait; congregations in Ruwi, Ghala, Salalah, and Sohar in the Sultanate of Oman; Church of the Epiphany (Doha) in Qatar; Christ Church (Aden) and congregations in Tawahi in Yemen; the Cathedral Church of St. Paul (Nicosia), St. George in the Forest (Troodos), St. Barnabas (Limassol), Panayia Chysopolitissa (Paphos), St. Helena's (Larnaca), St. Andrew's (Kyrenia), the Anglican Church in South East Cyprus and St. Mark's Anglican Chaplaincy (St. George the Foreigner) in Famagusta in Cyprus. In addition, there is the Mission to Seamen in Larnaca and Limassol (in Cyprus), in Manama (in Bahrain), and in Jumeira (in Dubai, the United Arab Emirates).

# The Diocese of Egypt with North Africa and the Horn of Africa

## The history of the Diocese of Egypt with North Africa and the Horn of Africa

The Anglican presence in Egypt owes itself to the Providence of God and great missionary evangelists. In 1819, the first CMS missionary to Egypt arrived and after meeting the Coptic Orthodox Patriarch and receiving letters of introduction to all monasteries in Egypt, set out to visit the monks and distribute copies of the four gospels in Arabic (Salamah 2005, 735). Land was given to the Anglican Church by Mohammed Ali Pasha, and St. Mark's Anglican Church in Alexandria, Egypt, was consecrated on December 17, 1839. On January 23, 1876, the Cathedral Church of All Saints' was consecrated in Cairo, Egypt, by Bishop Samuel Gobat of Jerusalem.

The Anglican presence grew through the ministry of CMS which during the late nineteenth and early twentieth centuries sent the Rev. Llewellyn Gwynne, Dr. Frank Harpur, the Rev. Douglas Thornton, the Rev. Canon Temple Gairdner, and Ms. Constance Padwick, among others. Their accomplishments, too numerous to recount here, cannot be understated and continues today, especially in the establishing of the *Orient & Occident Magazine*, Jesus Light of the World Church in Old Cairo, and Harpur Memorial Hospital in Menouf, among others. During this period, outreach to non-Christians and to Coptic Orthodox Christians grew considerably.

In 1920, the Diocese of Egypt and the Sudan was formed with the Rt. Rev. Llewelyn Gwynne as its first bishop (enthroned on November 21, 1921). On April 25, 1938, the Feast of St. Mark, the patron saint of Egypt, Bishop Gwynne established the first All Saints' Cathedral in Cairo, and the Archbishop of York, Dr. William Temple, consecrated it.

World War II brought many British to Egypt and North Africa, but also created a sense of colonialism. In 1950, to distance itself from the Church of England, the Episcopal Church in Egypt was formed under Bishop Geoffrey Allen (de Saram 1992, 80). In 1956, after a decade of political unrest in Egypt, the government forced all expatriates to repatriate, leaving only four Egyptian clergy, temporarily under the direct oversight of the Archbishop in Jerusalem, to maintain dozens of churches, schools, hospitals, and other institutions throughout Egypt. With great regret and sadness, many Anglican churches in Egypt were destroyed, some were taken by other denominations, and some were given to other denominations. Yet, God preserved the Anglican Church in Egypt, and we remember "blessed by Egypt my people."

A new era of training and equipping indigenous leaders, lay and ordained, was established, and in 1974, the first Egyptian bishop, Isaaq Musaad was consecrated. With the restructuring of the Province of Jerusalem and the Middle East and its dioceses in 1976, Algeria, Libya, and Tunisia became the "North Africa" part (now an Episcopal Area), and Ethiopia, Eritrea, Somalia, and Djibouti became the "Horn of Africa" part (now an Episcopal Area) of the Diocese of Egypt with North Africa and the Horn of Africa.

In 1984, Ghais Abdel Malik became the second Egyptian bishop of the diocese (1984–2000), and later the president bishop of the province (1996–2000). On the Feast of St. Mark, April 25, 1988, the third and present All Saints Cathedral in Cairo, whose shape can be described as either a Bedouin tent (because Christianity is mobile) or a lotus flower (because Christians are to offer the sweet fragrance of Christ), was consecrated.

In 2000, Bishop Mouneer Anis became the third Egyptian bishop of the diocese (2000–present), and in 2007 president bishop of the province (2007–present).

## The story of the contemporary church

The Diocese of Egypt with North Africa and the Horn of Africa is currently led by the Most Rev. Dr. Mouneer Hanna Anis, installed in 2000 at All Saints Cathedral, Cairo. As described in their literature:

> The Episcopal/Anglican Diocese of Egypt with North Africa and the Horn of Africa, a diocese within the Province of Jerusalem and the Middle East in the worldwide Anglican Communion, extends over eight countries including Algeria, Tunisia, Libya, Egypt, Ethiopia, Eritrea, Somalia and Djibouti. There are over 100 congregations throughout the Diocese, with All Saints Cathedral, Cairo being the spiritual centre. The Diocese supports over thirty institutions which include hospitals, clinics, nurseries, libraries, schools, a theological seminary, micro-enterprise ventures, vocational training programs, as well as institutions for refugees, the deaf, and the disabled. The five goals of the Diocese are: 1) to reach the unreached with the Gospel of Christ, 2) to grow Christ's church by making disciples and equipping leaders, 3) to serve our neighbours in Christ's name, 4) to work for unity among all Christians, and 5) to dialogue with other faith communities (www.dioceseofegypt.org).

Due to the large geographical area of the diocese, the varying cultures and languages, and the increase in ministry, Bishop Mouneer Anis started two Episcopal Areas with assistant (area) bishops in the diocese. In 2007, Bishop Mouneer consecrated Andrew Proud to be the first Area Bishop for the Horn of Africa, covering Ethiopia, Eritrea, Somalia, and Djibouti, and in 2009 Bishop Mouneer consecrated Dr. Bill Musk to be the first Area Bishop for North Africa, covering Algeria, Tunisia, and Libya. In 2012, Bishop Mouneer consecrated Dr. Grant LeMarquand to continue the work started by Bishop Andrew Proud. The goal for these Episcopal Areas is to develop local leaders to build up the local church.

The churches in the Diocese of Egypt with North Africa and the Horn of Africa are: All Saints Cathedral (Cairo), St. Mark's Pro-Cathedral (Alexandria), Christ the King (Ras el Soda), All Saints (Stanley Bay), St. John the Baptist (Maadi), St. Michael and All Angels (Heliopolis), Jesus Light of the World (Old Cairo), Church for the Deaf (Old Cairo), Church of the Good Shepherd (Giza), St. Mark's (Menouf), Church of our Saviour (Suez), Church of the Epiphany (Port Said), and St. Paul's Church (Ezbit el Nakhl) in Egypt; Christ the King Anglican Church (Tripoli, Libya), St George's (Tunis, Tunisia),

Holy Trinity Anglican Church (Algiers, Algeria), St George's (Asmara, Eritrea), St Matthew's (Addis Ababa, Ethiopia), St Luke's and over 70 congregations throughout Gambella, Ethiopia.

Of particular importance are the establishment of the Alexandria School of Theology in 2005; the centenary of Harpur Memorial Hospital in Menouf, and the founding of Harpur Memorial Hospital in Sadat City, both occurring in 2010; the opening of the Gambella Anglican Centre in 2011; and the creation in 2012 of the Vocational Training Centre for the Deaf in 6th of October City.

## The Diocese of Iran

### The history of the Diocese of Iran

The first religious services "according to the rites of the Church of England in Persia were held for [East India] company employees in the 17th Century" (Yarshaker 510). It was not until the Rev. Henry Martyn (1781–1812) came to Iran, as a chaplain of the East India Company, that the entire New Testament was translated into Persian and the Bible became accessible to Persian speakers around the world (cf. Padwick 1922, 291–7). Henry Martin, protégé of Charles Simeon, wrote in his journal on January 1, 1812, in Shiraz: "If I live to complete the Persian New Testament, my life after that will be of less importance. But whether life or death be mine, may Christ be magnified in me" (Padwick *Henry* 1922, 260).

Protestant missionary work in Iran began in the 1820s with a focus on evangelizing Jews by, among other groups, the London Missionary Society (Scudder 2005, 747). The first Bishop of Persia was the Rt. Rev. C. H. Stileman (1912–1919), and the second was the Rt. Rev. J. H. Linton (1919–1935). William James Thompson was consecrated the third Bishop of Iran at St. Paul's Cathedral, London, on October 18, 1935, and one of his pupils, Hassan Barnaba Dehqani-Tafti, became the next bishop on April 25, 1961.

The Rt. Rev. Hassan Dehqani-Tafti wrote in "Partners in Mission" while in Jerusalem in 1976:

> The present day Church in Iran grew out of the C.M.S. Mission . . . with medical service and later, schools. The first church building was put up in Isfahan in 1909, the first [indigenous] Persian pastor ordained in 1935, and Bishop Hassan Barnabas Dehqani-Tafti, consecrated in 1961 . . . is the first Persian bishop for over a thousand years, for in pre-Islamic days Iran was a country with a strong church with over eighty "bishops" and sent missionaries to India, China and the Far East.

The Revolution of 1979 brought new oppression to Christianity. After Bishop Hassan's retirement, Bishop Iraj Mottahedeh was consecrated as the fifth Bishop of Iran on June 11, 1986. He was the president bishop of the province between 2000 and 2002. Upon Bishop Iraj's retirement, Bishop Azad Marshall, the then assistant bishop for the Urdu-speaking congregations in the Gulf, having been consecrated on June 4, 1994, at the

Cathedral Church of the Resurrection in Lahore, Pakistan, was installed in 2007 as the sixth Bishop of Iran

At Bishop Azad's installation at St. Paul's Church in Iran on August 5, 2007, he said "My Christ did not come for only Christians; my Christ is for the whole world. With your help and cooperation I will seek to serve both Muslims and Christians because Christ came to serve all." The church in Iran continues faithfully to serve all people.

### The story of the contemporary church

The Diocese of Iran is currently led by the Rt. Rev. Azad Marshall, the sixth Bishop of Iran, with one cathedral, St. Luke's Cathedral in Isfahan, Iran. In addition to the work carried out in churches, the Diocese of Iran has hospitals, primary and middle schools, and hostels for boys and girls, and in engaged in blind welfare work. The Rt. Rev. Hassan Dehqani-Tafti epitomized the work of the Diocese of Iran by saying:

> In a vast and varied country such as Iran, the Episcopal Church, tiny though it is, has a very important part to play, especially at this particular time in the country's history. It is said that Iran is to be the most rapidly growing nation on earth; its people have to adapt themselves to three thousand years of progress within a period of thirty years. It is no wonder that they get tired, bewildered and lost. To those who feel lost, bewildered and tired, the Church can be a lighthouse, a haven in this journey which does exhaust mentally, spiritually and physically too. (Partners in Mission 9)

Currently, the Rev. Canon Nosratullah Sharifian and Mr. Baba Mohammadi are serving in Ishafan, the Rev. Christopher Edgar in Tehran, and Mr. Ashrafi in Shiraz.

## Outstanding Leadership in the Province

While it is very difficult to assess outstanding leadership, over the course of hundreds of years in European, Middle Eastern, and African countries, the following people were selected to show exemplary leadership and service to Jesus Christ and his church.

### The Rev. Canon Temple Gairdner (July 31, 1873–May 22, 1928)

William Henry Temple Gairdner was a pioneer for the Anglican Church in Egypt. Gairdner was an Arabist, and used drama, music, literature, and art as tools to share the Christian faith. With his love for literature, Gairdner "brought the Episcopal Publishing House into existence with the magazine *Orient and Occident* at its heart" (Rhodes 2005, 62). At the beginning, Gairdner supported the CMS policy of encouraging reform within the Coptic Orthodox Church and sending converts to them. However, over many years, he realized that the Coptic Orthodox Church was incapable of providing for

Muslim converts. This led Gairdner to develop the Arabic-speaking congregations and, in 1924, Gairdner supported the ordination of Egypt's first Anglican clergyman, Girgis Bishai, who was ordained a deacon in 1924 and a priest in 1925. Unfortunately, Gairdner died on May 22, 1928. Bishop Llewellyn Gwynne wrote that Gairdner "used to magnify my office for the sake of discipline. He was cleverer, more able, knew more than I, yet he served me." In 1934, Bishop Gwynne built the Jesus Light of the World Church in Old Cairo in Gairdner's memory.

### The Rt. Rev. Dr. Kenneth Cragg (March 8, 1913–November 13, 2012)

Albert Kenneth Cragg, born on March 8, 1913, was a significant figure in the province due to his love for the Middle East, understanding of Islam, interfaith dialogue, and Christian–Muslim relations. From 1970 to 1974, he was the Assistant Bishop of Jerusalem. Under his leadership, and with his sensitivity to cultural and religious issues, he paved the way for the restructuring of the new Province of Jerusalem and the Middle East in 1976. For another 30 years, he lectured all across the world. Even with his eyesight failing, he continued to write books and provide wise counsel. He published hundreds of articles and more than 40 books. His love for Muslims and the Middle East cannot be forgotten. It can be said that he was one of the few Christian theologians to have truly engaged with Islam.

### The Rt. Rev. Hassan Barnaba Dehqani–Tafti (May 14, 1920–April 29, 2008)

Hassan Dehqani-Tafti was the first Iranian to become a bishop since the seventh century. He was the Anglican Bishop of Iran from 1961 until 1990, and was the first President Bishop of the Province of Jerusalem and the Middle East from 1976 to 1986. Following the Revolution of 1979, when Christian schools and hospitals were taken, bank accounts frozen, missionaries were expelled or imprisoned, and many killed (including the Rev. Arastoo Sayaah whose throat was cut in Shiraz), there was an attempt on his life. Assassins shot six bullets from the end of his bed; four bullets hit his pillow, one hit the mattress, and one went into his wife Margaret's hand. However, God allowed him to live. Soon after this incident, he left Iran. His son, Bahram, was murdered on May 6, 1980. Bishop Hassan was not able to attend the funeral. He was forced to spend the last ten years of his episcopacy in exile.

### The Rt. Rev. John Edward Brown (July 13, 1930–October 23, 2011)

John Edward Brown was the third Bishop of Cyprus and the Gulf. Born on July 13, 1930, and ordained a priest in 1956, he became a curate at St. George's Cathedral in Jerusalem. He then returned to England to work in Reading before serving God for four years as a missionary in Sudan. From 1978 to 1987, he was the Archdeacon of Berkshire before becoming the Bishop of Cyprus in the Gulf (1987–1995). He will be remembered for creating the Diocesan Constitution, for uniting the two archdeaconries of "Cyprus" and "the Gulf" into one diocese, for his constant support of chaplaincies, and his establishing both lay and ordained training. He is remembered for obtaining a fatwa to re-open Christ Church in Aden, which is now thriving as a church and clinic. In 1995, he retired as an assistant bishop in the Diocese of Lincoln, yet he never failed to continue to share about the Middle East. In a letter to Bishop Mouneer Anis on February 8, 2011, he wrote:

> I think there cannot be anywhere else in the world . . . where there is so much suffering as a result of political turmoil as in the Province of Jerusalem and the Middle East; and the anguish is, especially for us who pray in hope and faith, that it has always been like this. I am persuaded that we have to live in God's time, and that in our earthly time we pray with love for all, however difficult this is for us, and with faith and hope that God's Will will be done.

## Challenges and Contemporary Issues Facing the Province

### Being a minority church

Anglicans in the Middle East are not only a minority, but a minority within the Christian minority living in an Islamic majority context. This is the main challenge facing the church in the Middle East. How can the church witness for the love of God in Christ and at the same time maintain good relations with its Muslim or Jewish neighbors? This challenge encouraged the Anglican Church in the Middle East to put emphases on serving the community through institutions such as schools, hospitals, clinics, and community development centers.

### Interfaith dialogue

When Jesus chose to speak with the Samaritan Woman (John 4:1–42), He chose to engage in "Interfaith Dialogue." Individual dioceses within the province also play important roles in facilitating the ongoing discussion between the Anglican Communion and Al Azhar Al Sherif (the world hub of Sunni Islam based in Cairo, Egypt), the use of *A Common Word* in interfaith dialogue, in relating to the World Islamic Call Society of Libya, in the work of peace and reconciliation in Jerusalem, and in participating in the Doha International Centre for Interfaith Dialogue.

However, Interfaith Dialogue can take another form called "life dialogue," which is a day-to-day practical interfaith dialogue at the grass-roots level. It happens through our Anglican ministries and institutions. That is why observers of the Anglican Church in the Middle East may be surprised to see more community centers than churches in the province. Recently, in different dioceses within the province, art and music is used as a medium for interfaith dialogue, such as the Caravan Festival of the Arts of St. John the Baptist Church in Maadi, Egypt.

*Evangelism*

While it is technically illegal in most Middle Eastern countries to openly share the Christian faith, the church continues to share the love of Christ through healing ministry, education, community development, etc.

*Emigration*

Although there are no reliable figures for emigration, emigration is a critical issue facing the people of the Middle East. It is said that in the one year following the January 2011 Revolution, more Christians emigrated from Egypt than in the previous ten years combined! And this phenomenon is not subject to Egypt alone. Due to political, religious, and economic reasons, some fear for the extinction of Christianity in the Middle East. In many places in the Middle East, Christian minorities are not able to fully participate in politics, government work, education, or the military. Most of the emigrants are young and highly educated Christians. This is not only a brain-drain, but also will lead to the witness of the church being diminished.

The two main reasons for emigration are: unemployment due to economic reasons and fanaticism, and the rise of political Islamists. This latter reason makes young people worried about their future in their own countries. The Anglican Church, as well as other churches, is now finding ways to minimize the rate of emigration through building up the capacity of young people in order to give them better chances for employment. The Arab Spring gave an opportunity for the church to call for more democracy, the abolition of discrimination, and freedom.

*Theological education*

With the growth of the indigenous membership of the church, theological education for locals became a major challenge. In the past, the Anglican churches sent students to be trained abroad. Since overseas training is very expensive and may not be relevant to the Middle Eastern context, the Diocese of Egypt established the first Anglican Arabic-speaking seminary in the Middle East in 2005.

*The ordination of women*

While always affirming the ministry of women, the province has historically not affirmed the ordination of women, citing biblical, cultural, and ecumenical reasons. Nevertheless, for many years, the Diocese of Cyprus and the Gulf, which has mainly expatriate congregations, has been given permission to license women ordained outside of the province to serve expatriate congregations within the diocese. In 2011, the provincial synod gave an exceptional permission for the ordination of women inside the Diocese of Cyprus and the Gulf, and on June 5, 2011, the first woman was ordained. The other three dioceses of the province do not permit the ordination of women.

### Identity

Anglicans in Egypt may exemplify the situation for Anglicans throughout the Middle East as they face an identity crisis. They are Christian but not part of the Orthodox majority; they are Anglican but not British; they are Arab but not Muslim; they are nationally Egyptian and continentally African but culturally Middle Eastern. All of these issues result in a complex identity crisis.

There is also another factor in the identity crisis. Since Anglicans (and Roman Catholics, Lutherans, or Presbyterians, for that matter) are not part of the Orthodox Church, they are seen as "Western" forms of Christianity in the Middle East. In other words, an Arab Anglican is often accused of being part of the Church of England, and is not seen as being part of a Middle Eastern or indigenous form of Christianity. This complicates the relationship that many Christians have in the Middle East, as one might be "Eastern" by race or nationality but "Western" by religion. The Anglican churches are trying to indigenize the church and acculturate its liturgy. This is done through the training and ordaining of local leaders across the countries of the Middle East.

## Relationship with Indigenous and/or Traditional Cultures and Religions

### The Province of Jerusalem and the Middle East

From its very beginning, the Anglican presence in the Middle East played not only a bridging role between the more Protestant and Reformed denominations and the Catholic and Orthodox churches, but also, in the words of Archbishop Runcie, the 102nd Archbishop of Canterbury, "our vocation as Anglicans was to put ourselves out of business. We were a part seeking to be united with the whole." In other words, the Anglican Church has never considered itself to be "The Church," but only a part of the one, holy, catholic, and apostolic church. In light of this, and because the unity which Jesus spoke about in John 17 does not mean uniformity, ecumenical relations are very important for the province.

In regard to the relationship between the Anglican Communion and other ecumenical churches, Dr. William Howley, the Archbishop of Canterbury from 1828 to 1848, wrote:

the Bishop [of Jerusalem] was charged not to intermeddle in any way with the jurisdiction of the Prelates of the Eastern Churches, and by all means in his power to promote an interchange of respect, courtesy and kindness, and a hearty desire was expressed to renew that amicable intercourse with the Churches of the East which had been suspended for ages, and which, if restored, may have the effect, with the blessing of God, of putting an end to the divisions which had brought the most grievous calamities to the Church of Christ.

The Province of Jerusalem and the Middle East continues to build bridges with other churches in the Middle East. The province is a founding member of the Middle East Council of Churches (MECC), created in 1974, and participates in the World Council of Churches (WCC).

The Diocese of Jerusalem has a very important role in securing freedom, peace, and reconciliation, especially in Jerusalem, with the Jewish people, the Muslims, and the 13 historic churches: Greek Orthodox, Latin Catholic, Armenian Orthodox, Coptic Orthodox, Ethiopian Orthodox, Armenian Catholic, Syrian Catholic, Maronite, Greek Catholic (Melkite), Franciscans (Custody of the Holy Land), Lutherans, and the Anglicans.

The Diocese of Cyprus and the Gulf maintains excellent relations with the Greek Orthodox Church and the Roman Catholic Church, among others. The Diocese of Iran relates to the Persian churches, St. Thomas (Mar Toma) and the Armenian Orthodox Church, among others.

In Egypt, Anglicans have a very special relationship with the Coptic Orthodox Church, the Roman Catholic Church, and other Protestant churches, because in 1923, the Rev. Canon Temple Gairdner drafted the policy which would be endorsed by the Archbishop of Canterbury, Randall Davidson:

> The primary aim of the Anglican Church in Egypt is the evangelisation of the non-Christian population and it does not desire to draw adherents from the Coptic or the Evangelical [Presbyterian] Churches. Those who, in sincerity find the Anglican Church their spiritual home are welcome to join it, but the Church does not set out to gain their allegiance. Instead it seeks to extend the hand of fellowship to the Coptic Church so as to render it every possible form of service, and at the same time it strives for closer cooperation and greater unity between all the churches in Egypt.

## Connection with the Worldwide Anglican Communion

The Episcopal/Anglican Province of Jerusalem and the Middle East is a member of the worldwide Anglican Communion. The province relates to the four instruments of unity within the Anglican Communion: the Archbishop of Canterbury, the Primates Meetings, the Lambeth Conference, and the Anglican Consultative Council (ACC). The province, or diocese(s) within the province, participates in various inter-Anglican councils and dialogues such as the International Commission for Anglican–Orthodox Theological Dialogue, the Anglican Communion–Al Azhar Al Sherif Dialogue, the Anglican–Lutheran Dialogue, the Network of Inter Faith Concerns (NIFCON), the

Council of Anglican Provinces of Africa (CAPA), and the Global South Anglican movement.

### Companion dioceses

The Diocese of Jerusalem has companionship relations with the Diocese of Los Angeles of the Episcopal Church (TEC). The Diocese of Iran has companionship relations with the Diocese of Peshawar of the Church of Pakistan. The Diocese of Cyprus and the Gulf has companionship relations with the Diocese of Exeter of the Church of England and the Diocese of Thika in the Anglican Church of Kenya. The Diocese of Egypt with North Africa and the Horn of Africa has companionship relations with the Diocese of Singapore and the Diocese of South Carolina of TEC.

## Conclusion / Possible Future

The Episcopal/Anglican Province of Jerusalem and the Middle East will continue to be an important and special part of the Anglican Communion. This is not only because of its geographical centrality, but also its presence in the midst of the oldest churches in the world. Because of this, the province plays an important role in the ecumenical relations with these churches and the whole Anglican Communion. The province also plays an important bridging role between East and West, and between Christians and other faiths.

## Bibliography

Ashton, Leonard. 1990. *Winged Words to Get It Across*. London: Churchman Publishing.

de Saram, B. 1992. *Nile Harvest: The Anglican Church in Egypt and the Sudan*. Bournemouth: Bourne Press Ltd.

Episcopal (Anglican) Church in Persia. 1996. In *Encyclopaedia Iranica*, ed. Ehsan Yarshaker. Centre for Iranian Studies, Columbia University, New York. Volume VIII. Fascilcles 5. Costa Mesa, California: Mazda Publishers, pp. 510–12.

Frarah, Rafiq. 2005. Evangelical Missions and Churches in the Middle East: II: Palestine and Jordan. In *Christianity: A History in the Middle East*, ed. Habib Badr. Lebanon: The Middle East Council of Churches.

Murry, Jocelyn. 1985. *Proclaim the Good News: A Short History of the Missionary Society*. London: Hodder and Stoughton.

Padwick, Constance E. 1922. *Henry Martyn: Confessor of the Faith*. London: George H. Doran Company, p. 260.

Padwick, Constance E. 1929. *Temple Gairdner of Cairo*. London: Society for Promoting Christian Knowledge (SPCK).

Rhodes, Matthew. 2005. The Anglican Church in Egypt 1936–1956 and its relationship with British Imperialism. Thesis submitted to the Graduate Institute of Theology's Faculty of Arts of the University of Birmingham for the degree of Doctor of Philosophy.

Rhodes, Matthew. CMS Archives G3/E/O/ 1925/15 at the University of Birmingham, UK.

Salamah, Adib Naguib. 2005. Evangelical Missions and Churches in the Middle East: III: Egypt and Sudan. In *Christianity: A History in the Middle East*, ed. Habib Badr. Lebanon: The Middle East Council of Churches.

Scudder, Jr., Lewis R. 2005. Evangelical Missions and Churches in the Middle East: IV: Iraq and the Gulf. In *Christianity: A History in the Middle East*, ed. Habib Badr. Lebanon: The Middle East Council of Churches.

# CHAPTER 26

# The Anglican Church of Korea

Yang Guen-Seok

## Historical Context of Anglican Mission in Korea

The Anglican Mission in Korea started in 1890 when English Bishop John Corfe landed at Incheon, a port city on the west coast of the Korean peninsula. Although the Anglican Church of Korea (ACK) is a small church, having a relatively short history within the Anglican Communion, its history of mission is filled with very colorful events and powerful experiences. At the end of the nineteenth century, the Korean peninsula began to be transformed into a battlefield of rising superpowers wanting to assert their colonial hegemony in Northeast Asia. The China–Japan War in 1894 and the Russia–Japan War in 1905 made the peninsula a battlefield which resulted in the devastation of the country of the morning calm. With Japan's victory in both wars, Korea was forcefully annexed to Japanese colonial rule from 1910 to 1945. At the end of World War II, the Korean people anticipated becoming an independent nation. But their hope for independence changed to frustration when the armies of the United States and the Soviet Union, claiming to be liberation armies for Korea, divided the peninsula into North and South; the Soviet Union occupying the North and the United States, the South. The Korean peninsula then became the Cold War confrontation line between the West and the East in Northeast Asia, and the war later developed into what is known as the Korean War. More than a civil war caused by internal conflicts, the tension was an international conflict because many countries from both the Western and Eastern blocks participated. Millions of people lost their lives, the whole country was completely ruined, and deep scars were left on both sides of the peninsula. Deep hostility and antagonism became the basis of the spirit and order of both societies. Following the war, the consequent militarization continued to take countless lives in the divided

*The Wiley-Blackwell Companion to the Anglican Communion*, First Edition. Edited by Ian S. Markham,
J. Barney Hawkins IV, Justyn Terry, and Leslie Nuñez Steffensen.
© 2013 John Wiley & Sons, Ltd. Published 2013 by John Wiley & Sons, Ltd.

territory. A military dictatorship was legitimized in South Korea, coupled with rapid industrialization that was carried out by military mobilization. Beginning in the 1960s, however, the people's resistance and democratic uprising continued. A nationwide civil struggle for democratization took place in June 1987, of which the Seoul Anglican Cathedral was the epicenter. In the late 1980s, the peoples' struggle reached its historical turning point with the democratization of South Korea. Finally, the first democratically elected civil government came into existence in 1993. Despite democratization, however, the Cold War division between North and South Korea continued and has not substantially changed. This was tragically illustrated in the sinking of a South Korean naval vessel and an artillery attack by the North in 2010 near the western sea border. The potential for military conflict with the loss of life continues.

In this historical context, the ACK consecrated their first Korean Bishop for the Diocese of Seoul in 1965. The Diocese of Daejeon was also established in the same year, and the Diocese of Pusan in 1974. In 1992, the national synod ratified the provincial canons of ACK and declared herself as independent province. Today, ACK has 50,000 church members in over 200 parish churches and more than 100 social mission centers in the three dioceses of South Korea. More than 200 clergy are currently engaged in ministry with the parish churches and social mission centers. One-third of the clergy works in social ministries, which demonstrates the Anglican Churches' commitment to social actions and community development.

## Historical and Theological Reflections

The ACK has strived to witness to the gospel in a country with such a very painful history. I believe, paradoxically, that such a painful history provided the very context for the Korean people to experience the saving and healing power of the gospel more deeply. As Bishop John Corfe confessed, embarking for a little-known country called Korea resembled a general going to battle with only a small boat (Jae-Jeong 1990, 32). By God's grace, the prayers of the Korean people coincided with Bishop Corfe's faithful answer to God's call. In order to encourage support for the mission, Bishop Corfe published a missionary magazine entitled *Morning Calm*, where he expressed his missionary convictions and principles. The cover art depicted a compass surrounded by the phrase from Acts 1:8. His missionary principle was expressed with the phrase *Nihil longe est Deo*, cited from Augustine, which depicted his missionary zeal in following God's call. For Koreans, living through the suffering of war, it was a very powerful consolation, vindication, and promise that God would be with them.

### Colonialism and Anglicanism

The first important point that needs to be considered about the Anglican mission in Korea was its relationship with colonialism. Unlike other countries colonized by Europe, the relationship in Korea was unique. Although it is not possible to claim that the relationship between colonization and evangelization was absolutely neutral or

antagonistic, it can be persuasively argued that there was no intimate religious cultural sympathy between Japanese colonialists and Christian missionaries. Because
Christian missionaries to Korea were relatively free from the pressure of the Japanese
colonizers, there was a possibility for Christian missionaries to look at the Korean
peoples' situation more objectively. However, it was not easy for the first missionaries
to fully comprehend that many people embraced Christianity as part of their yearning
for freedom, struggle for liberation, and desire for independence (Sharpe 1906, 182–3;
Turner 1907, 37). Christian missionaries adopted the separation between religion and
politics as a principle of Christian mission in Korea (Byung-Joon 2009). It was a principle reflecting the strategic intention to prevent Koreans' dangerous interpretation or
appropriation of biblical messages and motifs for their own liberation struggle and to
avoid the suspicion that missionaries were a foreign power collaborating with colonialism. However, communication is not only decided by the intention of the sender. In
fact, the rapid development of Christianity during the colonial period cannot be attributed solely to the missionaries' efforts. Koreans' receptiveness of the gospel should be
properly considered. The interaction and resonance of the gospel message was far
beyond the expectations of the missionaries.

A second contribution of the Anglican mission in colonial Korea was its efforts for
education and publishing. Christians' contribution for the socio-cultural transformation of Korea has already been well evaluated (Man-Yeol 1998). The translation of the
Bible into the Korean vernacular, *Hangul*, had been already started prior to the beginning of the Protestant (including Anglican) missions. In 1877, translation was begun
by the Scottish missionary, John Ross, who was living in Manchuria, China (SHCK
2011, 101–14). In 1887, a full translation of the New Testament was completed. Prior
to the establishment of the Anglican mission, around 50,000 *Hangul* Bibles were
already in the hands of Korean readers (SHCK 2011, 111). Anglicans, who valued the
importance of publication and translation into *Hangul*, spent a lot of energy in the
publication and translation of biblical, theological, and liturgical books (Jae-Jeong
1990, 55–8). The translation of the Bible and theological books meant more than
having an effective instrument of evangelization. It was also regarded as a transforming
event in Korean socio-cultural history. Prior to colonization, the *Hangul* was used by
the lower classes and women in the feudal system, while Chinese characters were used
in academic letters and by officials. Therefore, the *Hangul* rather than the Chinese
translation meant that the vernacular alphabet became a medium that bore divine
words. Additionally, the lower class, and especially women, had an instrument with
which to challenge the authority of works written with classical Chinese characters.
In colonial Korea, Christian groups, including Anglicans, played a significant role in
the development, promotion, and use of *Hangul*, despite it being severely suppressed by
colonial policy which imposed the use of Japanese.

The third important heritage of the colonial time was the very name of the Anglican
Church of Korea. From the beginning of the Anglican mission, missionaries used the
name *Jong Ko Seong Kyo-Hoe*, which was the *Hangul* pronunciation of the Chinese
translation of One, Holy, Catholic, and Apostolic Church. In 1910, the new name of
*Sung Kong Hoe* was adopted. It is the *Hangul* pronunciation of the Chinese translation
of Holy Catholic Church. This name had already been used in the Anglican Church in

Japan in the name *Sei Ko Kai*, which was the Japanese pronunciation of the same Chinese translation. Today, the Anglican Churches in Korea, Japan, Hong Kong, and Taiwan, which all inherited the culture of Chinese characters, use the same Chinese translation of Holy Catholic Church with their own country names. For example, the Anglican Church of Korea is called *Dae-Han (Korea) Sung Kong Hoe*, the Anglican Church of Japan is *Nippon (Japan) Sei Ko Kai*, and the Anglican Church in Hong Kong is *Hong Kong Sheng Kung Hui*. This name, which is a direct translation of the belief in the church as expressed in the Nicene Creed, has been clearly pointing to the goal and responsibility of those churches. It means that the creedal belief of the church is a common goal of their life and mission. It is their conviction that the Christian mission in Asia is not to implant the divisions of the confessional churches made in sixteenth-century Europe, but for a new journey toward one church. This catholic and ecumenical vision, including all the dimensions of the life of humanity, should always be remembered as a priority in all their efforts of mission and evangelization. It should never be interpreted as a narrow view of Catholicism, or the idea of a particular churchmanship of a group from the Anglican mother country.

### Anglicanism in the context of ideological conflict and war

The end of colonialism did not bring liberation or independence, but new division and conflict. The immediate occupation of the Korean peninsula by the Soviet Union and the United States following Japan's defeat in the Pacific War meant that a battle line between East and West was established on the peninsula. This radical change of political configuration ignited the ideological and political conflict in both parts of Korea. The conflict did not develop only into occasional physical confrontation, but it also brought a political situation where the dichotomy of the ideological and political choice was forced on all individuals and groups.

Christians became deeply involved in the political turmoil. In the North, the so-called pro-American or pro-West individuals and groups, including Christians and churches, were excluded and persecuted. In the South, the so-called pro-leftist or pro-communist individuals and groups had to face the same ordeal. The conflict and war in the 1950s caused the disappearance of churches and Christians in the North and escape to the South. ACK lost around 60 churches and chaplaincies in the North, more than half of all churches at that time (Jae-Jeong 1990, 216). Many clergy who tried to maintain their congregations in this very difficult situation were either arrested, imprisoned, or brought to the North and died as captives. For example, ACK Bishop Cecil Cooper was imprisoned in a North Korean prison camp for three years (Daily 2010, 234–44). This and the many compelling stories of the faithful clergy are the steadfast foundation of the Korean Anglican faith.

The experiences of persecution and suffering during the war resulted in both negative and positive consequences for the Anglicans in Korea. It was a period of trial through which genuine belief in God appeared as a ray of light in the darkness. However, it is also a regrettable past for Christians. It could have been an opportunity for them to work for the unity and reconciliation of the nation. However, in a situation where a neutral stand was not allowed for anyone, many Christians and churches did become accomplices in the division and conflict. Moreover, anti-communism and antagonism against the North was deeply internalized, and this has become the most distinctive character of Christian faith in Korea (In-Cheol 2006). This made the confession of sins a very delicate topic within Korean churches. The fact that Koreans once legitimized the killing of their brothers and sisters is a memory that will never be forgotten (NCCK 1988). The experience of deliverance and salvation from suffering has not necessarily led to efforts of reconciliation; rather, the experience fostered the potential for hatred and antagonism.

### Anglicans under division, military dictatorship, and industrialization

Sociologists agree that one of the most important developments on the Korean peninsula following the Korean War was the system of division, called *Bun Dan Che Je*, which literally means "division system" (Nak-Chong 1998). The political and ideological antagonism between the North and the South defined not only military and political decisions but also the values and social orders within both territories. The military dictatorship in both countries broadly accepted this division system, and the rapid industrialization in the South has been sustained and mobilized by it.

During this period, the Anglican Church of Korea poured all its efforts into becoming an independent and self-supporting church. Bishop John Daily, in his inaugural sermon in 1955, wrote:

> Our task is to build an indigenous Korean church, self-governing, self-propagating and self-supporting. We have no intention of running a Mission and a Church. Those of us who come from overseas must take our places within the framework of the indigenous church. The foundations of our diocese are the nineteen Korean clergy, the five Korean sisters and their three Novices and the company of the faithful laity; throughout the Anglican Communion these men and women are known for their steady devotion to our Lord through all the trials of oppression and invasion and for their readiness to die for their faith. (Daily 1956, 11)

This vision of an indigenous church built on steadfast devotion, demonstrated through all the trials within our painful history, was further developed by the first Korean Bishop Lee Chun-Hwan in his consideration of the relevance of inculturation for the unity of churches:

> The locality or local expression of church is not different from "the parts of one body" written in the Bible. Each part has its own different function. . . . The Church in Asia is different from the Church in Europe. Even in Asia, all churches in the different regions have different functions from each other. . . . While there are churches sticking to their own denominational traditions, there are also churches ignoring the old Christian traditions. In this situation, the way of true ecumenism is very far away. For these reasons, I would like to suggest the third way. It is the way to free ourselves from the elements of

unnecessary attachment to the past and to be churches expressed locally, which make possible for them to encounter with the changed situation of new era. . . . If we can cooperate with each other, we can reduce foreign influences from the so called mother churches, which are the background of our denominational division, and we have to do so. Those influences from overseas can easily become a kind of religious flunkeyism. . . . In this atmosphere, we cannot expect the true ecumenism. It is because the flunkeyism is deeply related with exclusivism and factionalism. (Chun-Hwan 1975, 350–1)

Bishop Lee Chun-Hwan loved Anglican traditions more than most. However, he recognized the negative function of denominational or confessional identities. Then and now, to speak about Anglican identity in the Korean context is a very dangerous and difficult task. It is a process that includes critical confrontation of various exclusive and factional elements.

With the industrialization that started in the 1960s, new social problems demanding Christian involvement emerged. Bishop John Daily, who had initiated the industrial mission in the mining areas in 1961, expressed a balanced view about mission and evangelism:

If we made a tremendous effort and concentrated all our energies we might be able to build a little central church and Sunday by Sunday we might attract a lively little congregation. But this would give us a cheap sense of achievement and we should very soon have lost all sense of adventure and zeal for the Kingdom. Our problem is how to preserve our sense of adventure and zeal and at the same time build a worshipping community. (Daily 1963, 4)

In the same article, he envisioned a church that realized a beautiful vision of ecumenism and inculturation:

In our completed picture we see the community center dominated by a beautiful church built to the honour and glory of God by the entire Christian population. We have the vision of a Korean royal pavilion, octagonal in shape, the premier divided into separate sanctuaries; one sanctuary would be furnished by the Anglicans, another to suit Presbyterian tastes; the Roman Catholics when using it for public worship would furnish their own and the Methodists theirs . . . (Daily 1963, 6)

In Bishop Daily's view of mission, the churches' solidarity with the margins, adventure, and zeal for the Kingdom of God, and building of the church are inseparably combined with the goal of one, united church. We still remember him as the person who said, "I do not want that sort of church members; I want Christians" (Daily 1963, 4). In the 1980s, the ACK's experiences with the margins developed into the Sharing House Movement (CSH 2006, 14–19), which encompassed the distinctive Anglican missionary activities for the excluded victims of industrialization and urbanization. The movement had a vision to build a sacramental community in the sharing of life and worship with the marginalized poor. Many young clergy and laypeople dedicated their ministry with the urban poor by living with them and helping them in their struggles.

Human rights and social justice were very important items on the ecumenical agenda during the military dictatorship. The military government did not allow any critical voice, and the raging wind of industrialization did not consider the basic human rights of the workers. In 1974, a group of Anglican clergy launched the Corps of Priests for the Realization of Justice. Their statement in the launch emphasized the churches' responsibility for social justice:

> We believe that the task of true church and the saving work of Christ in this context are just in the realization of social justice, the wellbeing of humanity and peace. We believe they are the cores of Christ's salvation. . . . Therefore, we insist that church should be the witness and protector of human conscience as the cross of Jesus Christ witnesses to us. (Jae-Jeong 1990, 342–3)

Bishop Lee Chun-Hwan's sermon in 1971 gave witness to the Anglicans' struggle for social justice and their faith in the cross and resurrection:

> The Cross is significant not because it is the implement of punishment, but because it is the cross of Christ saving the tragic history. This tragedy is in the land of Korea and in the mind of us now. We need to see the will of God behind the tragedy, not resigning to the tragic fate. . . . The cross of our Lord is a revolutionary boldness and victory realized in the midst of the outcry of villains. . . . The tragedy of Korean peoples is not different. One who knows the meaning of the tragedy of the Korean nation has to have such boldness and to be ready to risk his or her life. Our Lord could not surrender himself to the villains. . . . Therefore, his death on the cross was the sign of the victory against all the evils of the society. This is the message of resurrection. The Lord who had sacrificed himself in order to follow the will of God had to be raised. Let us wait for the blessing of resurrection for the Korean nation. But in order to receive the blessing of the resurrection, we need to have boldness to be able to overcome the tragedy of the cross with an indomitable spirit. If we do not do so, we can be the subject of tragic fate and useless sacrifice. (Chun-Hwan 1975, 246–7)

## The Anglican Church of Korea as a Province

Peace, reconciliation, and unity are the very pressing issues for Korean Christians. These issues, however, were considered to be taboo topics in the ideologically divided and conflicted peninsula. Although there was a deep concern for healing and reconciliation, it was not possible to express it publicly. It was in this situation that the biblical vision of peace and reconciliation was suppressed by the logic of the antagonistic balance of power. Hence, the missionary concern for peace and reconciliation was strangely expressed in the phrase "Mission to North Korea" (Jae-Jeong 1990, 364), which could be understood as the desire to recover lost territories and churches in the North. In the celebration of the centennial in 1990, Anglicans proclaimed that "true peace and reconciliation in the situation of division and conflict is possible with belief in Christ" (Jae-Jeong 1990, 366–7). The canons of ACK, proclaimed in the establishment of the province in 1992, recognized "the reconciliation and salvation of the nation" (Canons 2010, 4) as the main calling of the ACK province. "Come now, O Prince of Peace. Make us one body. Come O Lord, Jesus. Reconcile your people" (Geon-Yong 1990). This well-known hymn, composed by Anglican musician Lee Geon-Yong, was the most impressive Anglican voice produced in this paradoxical context where, despite the urgency of peace and reconciliation, merely dreaming of it was regarded as seditious or subversive.

Today, an Anglican initiative for peace and reconciliation is taking concrete shape with the establishment of the TOPIK (Toward Peace in Korea) Project, founded on the resolutions of the national synod and ACC 13 (Resolution 40). Humanitarian aid for North Koreans, the development of Christian network for peace in Korea and Northeast Asia, and peace and reconciliation education based on biblical vision are the main agenda of the project, with Japan and the neighboring countries around the Pacific also participating.

The issue of reconciliation is not only related to the problem of division in Korea. The sad history between Korea and Japan in colonial times also left deep scars that need sustained efforts for reconciliation. Since 1984, the Anglican Churches in Korea and Japan began a dialogue under the structure of the Committee for the Cooperation of Korea and Japan. The statement of this committee, published in 1984, recognized the importance of the proper understanding of history. The goal is to unlearn the history which had been distorted by the interests of dominant political powers in both countries and to redirect the peoples' vision towards the biblical goal for peace and reconciliation.

The preface of the 2006 Mission Plan of the Diocese of Seoul (DS 2006) summarizes the Anglican mission in the time of globalization. Sharing, peace, and life were suggested as the three keywords of the mission. While tackling the new socioeconomic conflicts and problems caused by economic neo-liberalism and globalization, the mission plan emphasizes that sharing, as the Bible teaches, once again, should be the principle of community and church life. The vision of peace and reconciliation suggested in this plan appeals to us to go beyond the ideas contaminated by political ideologies and to achieve reconciliation with all forms of life in this world.

## The Development of Canons and Prayer Book

The most important references for the theology and doctrine of the ACK are the prayer books and the Basic Declaration of Doctrine and Liturgy, which is attached as a preamble to the canons. Theological and doctrinal development comes after long experience of mission and ministry in a particular context, and after long theological reflection and discussion. While it is true that there were continued theological discussions and changes during the time of the missionary bishops, they can be evaluated as the reflections of individual theological tastes related to the diverse theological strands in the Church of England, rather than the contextual demands of Korea. With the installation of Korean bishops and establishment of the province, a more serious discussion on theology and doctrine in the ACK was started.

The Basic Declaration of Doctrine and Liturgy, which was revised with the canons in the process of preparing the establishment of the province in 1990, can be divided into three parts (Canons 2010, 4). The first part mentions the faith in the triune God, an ecclesiological belief that the church is "a family member" or a part of the One, Holy, Catholic, and Apostolic Church, and a position about unity. It speaks of the unity of churches that can be achieved through "the restoration of the faith and the unity principle of early church before division." This is "the Christian faith and order established by Jesus Christ and transmitted by the Apostles" and is "indispensable grace for the salvation of all up to the end of this world." In spite of its lack of theological explanations about concepts like the "unity principle" and faith of early church, it seems to reflect a typical Anglican tendency to emphasize antiquity.

The second part of the declaration deals with the four topics of scripture, creed, sacrament, and the three-fold order. The doctrinal descriptions are not different from the traditional Anglican formularies and articles. Nevertheless, the article about creed is extraordinary. Aside from expressing respect to the two creeds, namely the Apostles' Creed and the Nicene-Constantinopolitan Creed, it has also added the sentence: "[the Anglican Church of Korea] searches for the belief for the reconciliation and salvation of this nation from Christ's suffering and teachings revealed through his life." This sentence can be seen as an unnecessary addition in comparison with the general form of the articles. However, it should be understood as an expression of Korean Anglicans' will to re-interpret and re-appropriate the faith revealed in the Bible from their distinctive experiences of mission and ministry, in their hope for the reconciliation of their nation. Moreover, it is a pledge that their struggle for the reconciliation of the nation will be developed into a new creedal confession of biblical faith.

The third part of the declaration is not much different from the traditional Anglican understanding. It emphasizes the importance of the inculturation of liturgy and the reinterpretation of doctrines in the interaction with Korean culture and traditions.

The prayer book revised in 2004 summarizes the history of the revision of the prayer book in the ACK (PB 2004, 10–13). In the early period of the Anglican mission in Korea, prayer books and liturgies were based on the 1662 Book of Common Prayer of the Church of England. However, the revision in 1939 moved in a very high Anglo-Catholic direction. This High Church tradition was continued until 2004 despite several attempts to revise it. Then the 2004 prayer book made the observation that the liturgy in Korea was dominated by "one sided high church tradition . . . did not respond properly to the demands of diverse mission fields . . . and its function as the instrument of mission and ministry was seriously weakened" (PB 2004, 9). In order to achieve such goals as the restoration of the diversity of liturgy, and the strengthening of the liturgy's function for mission and ministry, the new prayer book included more diverse forms of liturgy and worship. The church calendar was also revised, particularly in consideration of the distinctive mission agenda and life cycles of Koreans. Many new prayers, collects, and prefaces were made and added in the process of revision.

## Lotus and Cross

I would like to conclude this chapter by introducing a very special cross, the lotus flower cross, which was produced through the Anglican mission in Korea. The seed of the lotus is placed at the bottom of a pond or a ditch, where all the wastes of life are heaped. The seed waits and endures for a long time in the cold bottom of the pond. It takes nutritive substance from the heaped wastes, like the wretched life of the weak and poor. It puts forth a bud under such bad conditions and grows a pipe breaking the depth of the water. At last, the pipe meets fresh air and bright sunshine, and a beautiful flower bursts into blossom. However, it never separates itself from the wretched bottom under the water. The flower lives in the mysterious connection between the wretched bottom and the fresh winds and rays of the sun coming down from heaven.

On the lotus flower cross covering the front wall of the chapel of SunKongHoe (Anglican) University, this traditional reflection on the life of a lotus flower encounters Christian faith in the cross and resurrection of Jesus Christ. According to the Rev. Dr. Lee Jae-Joung, who designed the flower cross in the chapel, it came from a pattern used in an early church built by missionaries following Korean traditional style in the 1900s. It is not known whether the early missionaries had an understanding or intention to connect the pattern and the image of the cross. Nevertheless, in many ways, it is the most evident symbol of Anglican faith and spirituality in Korea and of the educational motto of the university, which is a very precious fruit of the Anglican mission in Korea. The faith set forth in the life of a lotus flower may lead Anglicans and all the peoples in this peninsula toward the future of peace and reconciliation.

**Figure 26.1:**   Lotus Flower Cross of SungKongHoe (Anglican) University Chapel.

# Bibliography

Anglican Church of Korea (ACK). 2004. *PB (The Prayer Book of Sung Kong Hoe)*. Seoul: The Publishing Board of the ACK.

Anglican Church of Korea (ACK). 2010. *Canons of the ACK*. Seoul: The Provincial Office of the ACK.

Byung-Joon, Chung. 2009. A Study on the Structural Changes of the Church-State Relation before the Korean Liberation. *Mission and Theology*, vol. 23, 213–45.

Chun-Hwan, Lee. 1975. *Cross in the Land of Korea*. Seoul: The Publishing Board of the ACK.

Committee for Sharing Houses (CSH). 2006. *20 Years Mission History of Sharing Houses*. Unpublished.

Daily, John. 1956. Whatsoever He Saith Unto You, Do It. *Morning Calm*, no.38, 9–12.

Daily, John. 1963. Hwangchi. *Morning Calm*, no.66, 3–7.

Daily, John. 2010. *Four Mitres*. Trans. St. John's Mission Center in Kumi. Seoul: The Publishing Board of the ACK.

Diocese of Seoul (DS). 2006. Mission Plan of the Diocese of Seoul. *The Resource Book of the Diocesan Synod of Seoul*. Unpublished.

Geon-Yong, Lee. 1990. Come Now, O. Prince of Peace. *The Hymn Book of the Anglican Church of Korea*. Seoul: The Publishing Board of the ACK.

In-Cheol, Kang. 2006. The Korean Protestant Churches and the Overcoming of the Past, 1945~1960. *Korean Christianity and History*, no.24, 67–102.

Jae-Jeong, Lee. 1990. *The Centennial History of the Anglican Church of Korea*. Seoul: The Publishing Board of the ACK.

Man-Yeol, Lee. 1998. *The Study on the History of the Reception of Christianity in Korea*. Seoul: Duresidae.

Nak-Chong, Paek. 1998. *The Shaking System of Division*. Seoul: Changbi Publishers.

National Council of Churches in Korea (NCCK). 1988. Declaration of the Churches of Korea on National Reunification and Peace. http://warc.ch/pc/20th/03.html.

Society of the History of Christianity in Korea (SHCK). 2011. *A History of Christianity in Korea*, Vol. I. Seoul: The Christian Literature Press.

Sharpe, Charles E. 1906. Motives for Seeking Christ. *The Korea Mission Field*, vol. 2, no. 10, 182–3.

Turner, Arthur B. 1907. The Bishop's Letters. *Morning Calm*, vol. 18, no. 114.

CHAPTER 27

# The Church of the Province of Myanmar (Burma)

## Katharine E. Babson and Saw Maung Doe

## Introduction

The Anglican Church is a relative newcomer to the land long understood by its over 135 different ethnic groups and subgroups as being "myanmar," meaning "land of many peoples" in the Burmese language. Even after 1989, when Burma's military government officially renamed the country as the "Union of Myanmar" to mark its ancient multi-ethnic reality and distinguish its modern identity from that of its British colonial overlords, many have persisted in calling Myanmar "Burma." That it was simply the majority ethnic group – the predominantly Buddhist Bamar, or Burmans, whose ancestral homelands happened to lie in the south and central areas of Myanmar where British merchants established trading posts which the British military secured for England in three Anglo-Burmese Wars – after whom the British conveniently named their lucrative South Asian colony as "Burma" is an irony of history. In particular, this calls attention to the many complicating factors for the emergence of modern Myanmar and its native churches: the devastation during World War II, its official independence from Great Britain in 1948, its self-imposed isolation from the world following the Burmese military coup of 1962, and its pariah status after the junta placed Myanmar's best-known citizen, Daw Aung San Suu Kyi, under house arrest in 1994. The need for this ethnically diverse nation to form a unified native identity, develop sound self-government, and foster creative engagement with the world is a severe and continuing challenge.

It has been especially so for Myanmar's ethnic minority Christian groups and their mainstream Western-originated churches. Making up approximately 6 percent of the population, the largest among the churches are the Anglican, Baptist, Methodist, and

*The Wiley-Blackwell Companion to the Anglican Communion*, First Edition. Edited by Ian S. Markham, J. Barney Hawkins IV, Justyn Terry, and Leslie Nuñez Steffensen.

Roman Catholic. Adverse conditions for them became especially complicated after 1962 when the Burmese military, having been asked by the country's civilian government to stabilize the country in 1958, intervened again, this time in a coup to topple what they believed was another weak civilian government. One of the most draconian consequences of the takeover was that the churches began to wrestle with deprivations officially designed to privilege the much older, more deeply rooted Buddhist community and culture of the Burmese military leadership.

Yet, the Anglican Church has faced some of the most difficult challenges of all because it bears the additional burden of the colonial stamp in name, form, and connections with England's Canterbury and the worldwide Anglican Communion. Indeed, that there are still British-built churches in Myanmar with signage that declares them "The Church of England" demonstrates the necessity that any fair account of the Church of the Province of Myanmar's present circumstances and future hope take serious stock of its colonial history. Indeed, from its origins to its present within one of the most notorious nations in the world, the Anglican Church in Myanmar has been almost inextricably bound by its roots. Yet, notwithstanding challenges that might have confounded the less courageous, the faith and work of Myanmar's Anglicans have been constant and often brilliantly creative. Both lay and ordained members have made important contributions to people of all ethnicities and religious persuasions within their complex native society. Awareness of this witness might well stir the imagination of that inspirational faith which flourished under similar circumstances in the earliest days and years of the church under Roman rule as it secured and celebrated the revelation that even in death lies the assurance of resurrection wrought by an ever-faithful God.

## Colonial Years and British Inheritance: "Merchants, Military, and Missionaries"

The deepest root and most complicating factor of Myanmar's Anglican Church history lies not in the service of missionaries whom the Church of England sent out to work among the native peoples, but in the expansive trade interests of the British East India Company. As early Portuguese and French Roman Catholic missionaries had experienced before the British ever set foot in Myanmar, Christian missions that challenged majority Burmese Buddhist sensibilities had not always survived intact, for the Burmese kings zealously protected the Theravada Buddhism that had come into their lands from India in the eighth century and forbade any form of proselytization among their Buddhist subjects. Mindful of these lessons of history, when the British East India Company reached eastward from its established Indian trade center in Calcutta and succeeded in winning valuable western and southern coastland territories from the ethnic Burmans upon victory in the First Anglo-Burmese War in 1826, it introduced the same company policy in place in its India holdings: missionaries could not work among the natives in any company territory lest they offend native religious sensibilities and jeopardize the company's trade ambitions. In compliance with policy, the Church of England sent out priests who were in all respects merely company chaplains.

Even by then, the Anglicans were latecomers to the land of many peoples, for it had been almost over two and a half centuries since Portuguese Roman Catholics had ventured a mission in 1602 in Thanlwin, then known as Syriam, on Myanmar's southern coast. Later, in 1692, French friars of the Society of Foreign Mission in Paris had established a mission in the southern Burmese city of Bago, then known as Pegu. Later still, in the year 1807, the English Baptist medical doctor, Felix Carey, the eldest son of the noted missionary to India, William Carey, had opened a medical mission in the Burmese city of Rangoon. In 1813, Carey had welcomed the arrival of the American Baptist missionaries Anne and Adoniram Judson when they arrived in Rangoon after fleeing the British East India Company's trading outpost in Calcutta for fear that they would be arrested because of their missionary activities.

Even under threat of native attack, imprisonment, and death, the likes of which the British East India Company most feared, these non-nationalistic and less politically constrained Roman Catholic and Baptist missions had prevailed to achieve considerable success. Judson's own missionary approach is instructive in comprehending the comparative slowness of the British Anglicans to establish viable missions in Myanmar. Believing that missionaries should not focus their attentions on the spiritual needs of their own countrymen, Judson demonstrated his unusual gift for language by mastering Burmese and compiling a Burmese grammar book and a basic Burmese–English dictionary with which to work among the majority Burmese people. Later, in 1823 and 1834, respectively, he completed Burmese translations of the New and Old Testaments of the Bible that remain in use today. However, after six years of working among the Burmans, he recognized that Burmese identity and Buddhist belief were practically synonymous, as a saying still in parlance attests: "To be Burmese is to be Buddhist." Having also discovered for himself that the risks of working among the Burmans far outweighed the promises, Judson moved beyond the Ayeyarwaddy River basin that defined the Burmans' ancestral homeland, to introduce Christianity to the populous Sgaw subgroup of the Karen people, one of the largest of all Myanmar's 135 ethnic minority groups. Not only were all seven of the major Karen subgroups predominantly animist, and therefore more open to Christian teaching, they had also lived for centuries with variations on the belief that a light-skinned stranger would one day appear with the lost book of their ancestors. So it happened that when Judson appeared with the Bible, the Sgaw embraced it as their lost story and were baptized in great numbers, making the account of Judson's Baptist mission in Myanmar one of the most extraordinary chapters in the annals of Christian mission history.

In contrast, it was only after its successive victories in the First and Second Anglo-Burmese Wars which ended in 1826 and 1853, and by which it had secured the better part of the Burmans' southernmost ancestral homeland, that the British East India Company eased its restrictions on British missionary work among native peoples within its holdings. In 1854, the Society for the Propagation of the Gospel (SPG), having taken over the mission work that the Society for the Promoting of Christian Knowledge (SPCK) had begun in India, established its first official mission in Mawlamyine, one of the company's oldest and most developed southeastern coastal port cities. As the largest trading outpost and administrative center in the east of Burma, Moulmein, as the British called it, also had a large population of British residents, so the United Society for the Propagation of the Gospel (USPG) also planted its first Anglican mission school there. According to the culture long established by the British East India Company, the school was primarily intended to educate urbanized English and Eurasian students, though a few ethnic minority students also attended. Comparatively, the non-urban, upcountry areas of Burma continued to be the focus of Baptist missions and Baptist mission schools.

In 1857, when the shock of the Great Mutiny in India moved the British government to replace the British East India Company as the sole ruling authority in all its South Asian colonies, the way to unrestricted Anglican mission work finally opened in all British-held Burmese territories. Then, with all of Lower Burma already under British control, the last Burman prize lay north in Mandalay where the Burman king held court at Ava. In 1885, the British sent government gunboats steaming up the Ayeyarwaddy to capture King Thibaw and his family in residence in the Crystal Palace in the heart of the great Mandalay Fort. When the king and his immediate family were wheeled through the city to a waiting British ship and sent out of the country into cloistered exile in India, the Burmans were completely subjugated and their ancient culture suffered deep internal fractures.

Not only did this final victory in the Third Anglo-Burmese War render all the Burmans' ancestral lands to Britain, but non-Burman, predominantly animist, ethnic minority groups like the Karen, upland Shan, and Kachin, whose homelands were beyond those of the Burmans, and whom the Burmans held as cultural inferiors, began to cooperate with the British in new ways. These relationships allowed the British effectively to extend their influence and activity even more deeply into the land of many peoples. At the same time, as the American Adoniram Judson had experienced, many among the ethnic minority groups moved almost naturally toward the Christian faith, so their conversions further differentiated them from the majority Burman Buddhists.

However, even in the wake of territorial and relational victories like these, when compared to the efforts of the Baptists and the Romans before them, Anglican mission activity proceeded much more slowly, not only because of the abiding cultural affect of old British East India Company policies that had held them so long in abeyance, but because the Anglicans continued to concentrate their efforts within major colonial centers like Moulmein that were largely populated by the British and important allies, such as Indians whom they brought with them to help administer their businesses and government offices. Notwithstanding the evidence of their other-denominational brethren, the Anglicans also persisted in focusing their primary efforts on the Burmans, even though they had long demonstrated steadfast resistance to Christian ministrations, especially to missionaries of the Empire that had subdued them.

While there were some Burman conversions, the comparatively few ethnic Burmans who did convert to become Anglicans often won closer British partnerships that enabled them to establish significant influence within colonial society; yet most native converts came from ethnic minority groups and subgroups whose ancestral lands were peripheral to those of the Burmans. Aside from the Sgaw Karen who lived in the hilly areas north and east of Rangoon, one of the largest groups of converts came from the Pwo Karen. The Pwo's ancestral lands extended west and south of Rangoon into the rich delta lands of the Ayeyarwaddy River: by virtue of having their ancestral localities geographically proximate to the British trading hubs where the British also established their government and ecclesiastic centers, the Pwo rose to achieve significant native prominence in positions of colonial business and government. Like the Sgaw Karen, the Moe Karen, who lived north and east of Rangoon in mountainous jungle lands that extended east toward what is now Thailand, also converted in great numbers; also the Asho Chin of central Burma; the Mon people who lived to the southeast of Rangoon; and the Kumi and Arakan people who lived in the far west around coastal Sittwe. To a lesser degree, there were also the Shan, whose extensive princedoms lay north and east of Mandalay in Central Burma; and then in the far north there were the Kachin people whose lands extended from the Shan States all the way to China's southernmost borders in Yunnan.

Among these conversions, there were some unusual, even quirky advances in upcountry missionary success for the Anglicans, such as when an American Baptist missionary, one Mrs. Francis Mason, wife of the founder of the American Mission in Toungoo, chose to break with the Baptists in 1870, and take approximately 6,000 converts, together with Baptist-founded mission schools and other properties, with her to the Anglican side. The purported reason was that the Baptists and Roman Catholics, who were also active in the Toungoo area, believed each other to be heretics, a position Mrs. Mason decried, so she took her newly converted Baptist flock over to the Anglicans because they were Protestant and therefore considered to be both faithful and non-heretical by the Baptists. After several years of turmoil in which some of the Karen Baptists fell back to their animist traditions and others turned to the Roman Catholic Church, the Church of England decided to undertake mission work in the Toungoo area in earnest and officially accepted 5,000 Baptist schismatics who lived in 110 villages in the hills of Toungoo. To date, the Christian communities in the Toungoo area remain strongly Anglican, and the Anglican Diocese of Toungoo is the most populous of the Province of Myanmar's six dioceses, with upwards of 15,000 faithful belonging to over 60 parishes.

Overall, ethnic minority conversions and colonial alliances had the effect of further circumscribing the ancient primacy of the Burmans by allowing minorities enhanced access to advanced educational opportunities, entry into positions of authority in the British Civil Service, and lucrative trade and business affiliations. These developments reflected the British colonial divide and conquer strategy by which the vanquished Burmans were kept in check, but the stratagem also sowed tenacious seeds of Burman-ethnic minority acrimony and increasing distrust that were rooted not so much in Buddhist–Christian religious difference as in the distinction between viewing the British as conquerors and looking to them appreciatively as patrons.

From the start, the Anglican Church presence in Burma was met with harsh criticism from Burman detractors who charged that it was merely the outgrowth and expression of British colonial policies they summarized as "the Three M Movement." The adage refers to the historical sequence of British merchants, military, and missionaries who moved successively into Myanmar to trade, then to conquer and subjugate, and only afterward to serve its native peoples, all in what the Burmans hold to have been for British self-gain and expansion of their own particular expression of

Christianity. Throughout its history until today, this has been a difficult and challenging legacy with which the Anglicans in Myanmar have had to work.

## The Church of England in Burma: Foundation of the Province of Myanmar

Despite a slow start in mission due to the continuing effect of old British East India Company policies, setbacks from death and illness among missionaries, and departures from Burma's challenging climate for return to England, the Anglicans' mission work increased. Accordingly, on February 24, 1877, the newly established Diocese of Rangoon superseded the Diocese of Calcutta in overseeing Anglican work throughout the colony. Later that year, the Rev. Jonathan Holt Titcomb, an honorary canon of Winchester Cathedral in England, was consecrated to serve as Burma's first bishop. Bishop Titcomb's arrival in Rangoon in February 1878 to take up residence at "Bishopscourt," a Burmese-styled golden teak mansion in the outskirts of the city center, was a historic step toward the eventual birth of a truly native church, the Church of the Anglican Province of Myanmar.

In reviewing the history and circumstances of his new cure, Bishop Titcomb learned that, unlike Baptist missionaries who had translated the Bible into Burmese and other native languages with which to train native teachers and local preachers to work among their own people, the Anglicans had pursued a policy of bringing lay and ordained mission leaders to Burma from England. Given the perennial short supply of the willing, there had also been few converts. In 1878, in a decisive corrective initiative, the new bishop traveled to the strong mission center in Toungoo to consecrate St. Paul's Cathedral and confirm 70 Karen, 17 Burmans, and 11 English. He also ordained four Karen as deacons of the church: they were the first native clergy to serve the Church of England.

Having laid these foundations for the development of native lay and ordained leaders, Bishop Titcomb suffered an untimely fall that checked his work, and retired to England in 1882. He was succeeded by a sequence of six more British Bishops of Rangoon who were appointed in England for their service in Burma: John Miller Strahan (s. 1882–1903), A. M. Knight (s. 1903–1909), R. S. Fyffe (s. 1909–1928), N. H. Tubbs (s. 1928–1935), G. A. West (s. 1935–1954), and V. G. Shearburn (s. 1955–1966). Altogether, Burma's British bishops ruled Burma's Church of England for 68 years.

These men opened many new missions in Upper Burma after the last of the Burmans' lands were annexed in 1885 at the end of the Third Anglo-Burmese War. The church's first Bible School for training native teachers and catechists to evangelize in new mission fields throughout the expanding colony opened in 1883. With grants from both SPG and the SPCK, almost exactly 29 years after SPG had begun its work in Burma, St. Michael's Mission in Kyimyidine on the outskirts of Rangoon opened its doors to 12 native students who studied in the Burmese language. In 1893, St. Peter's Bible School in Toungoo was opened to train Karen converts in their own language to work as catechists in 110 Karen villages in the distant eastern Toungoo hills. To this day, St. Peter's

Bible School continues its mission to train catechists for work in churches throughout Myanmar.

In 1904, the Winchester Brotherhood was established in Mandalay. The Mission to the Seamen began its Burma ministry in Rangoon in 1907. To date, both these mission initiatives continue strong mission relationships with the Province of Myanmar. The church also pushed south from Rangoon into the Ayeyarwaddy Delta area to work among the Sgaw and Pwo Karen, Anglican centers that remain strong today. Missionaries from St. Michael's Bible School in Kyimyidine were inspired to go west of Rangoon into the Pyay area to work among the Asho Chin people. While more mission schools opened in all these new mission centers, the student composition was telling: of the natives, few were Anglicans, while economically advantaged Burmese Buddhists, to whom the schools were open, far outnumbered the Christians because they valued the expansive educational curricula taught in the mission schools compared with the more strictly religious education offered in the Buddhist monastery schools. Notwithstanding ethnic discrepancies like these, the native population was being advanced educationally, and many of the brightest won fellowships for higher study in England after which they returned to Burma with valuable professional and social skills with which to strengthen the native voice within the colonial government. For the Christians, these advances made it even more apparent that the only way to maintain mission strength, service the burgeoning number of mission centers and schools, and replace British clergy numbers persistently afflicted by high attrition was to ordain more natives to serve the native peoples in their own native languages. However, the reach back to England for missionary recruitment habitually continued with the effect that many mission ventures faltered because of inconsistency in leadership, and some failed.

The need for native clergy leadership thus became more and more apparent. To begin to meet need, in 1912, Rangoon began to send native graduates of Rangoon University and Rangoon's Judson College to Bishop's College in Calcutta for their Bachelors' Degrees in Theology, after which they were ordained to the priesthood. In 1914, with greater strength in native leadership the first annual Rangoon Diocesan Council was held. In 1919, a school for the blind was opened at St. Michael's Mission in Kyimyidine, and a school for the deaf and dumb opened in the city: the first principal of the latter was Mary Chapman, after whom the school took the name by which it is still known. Also, in 1919, a native evangelist was sent from the Toungoo mission to begin work among the Sgaw Karen in the more southern Hpa'an area, upriver from Moulmein. In 1924, the evangelical wing of the Church of England, the Bible Churchmen's Missionary Society (BCMS), initiated mission work among the Kachin people in the far reaches of Upper Burma: that mission tradition remains strong in Kachin State today. Three years later, in 1927, the BCMS opened a new Bible school for native catechists in Karmaing, one of the Kachin people's major towns. In 1929, the BCMS proceeded to open a Bible school among the Khumi people at Paletwa, north of Sittwe in far western Burma. By 1926, there were, throughout Burma, 105 Anglican Mission Schools with 229 natives teaching high-school-level courses. Many of these schools operated contiguous hospitals and clinics. As part of its own increasingly comprehensive approach to mission, SPG began to use its mission centers to deliver sound healthcare, aid to needy children, and assistance in agricultural development.

However, the increase in Anglican mission activity among the ethnic minority peoples also had the effect of further identifying them with the British against the Buddhist Burmans, who had never forgotten their defeat at the hands of the colonial overlords. These tensions, joined with the rising press for national independence, precipitated the creation of the predominantly Buddhist Burmese military under which the Burman voice for national independence from the British gained both strength and momentum. Simultaneously, with British support, the British-allied ethnic minority groups raised their voice for a federalist-styled arrangement within a new government, by which they anticipated being able to self-govern within the boundaries of their ancestral homelands and according to their own cultural traditions. Throughout the years of rising tension, the native Anglicans pitched their religious loyalty solidly with the Church of England, within which they enjoyed the security of faith coupled with guarantees of continuing top-down financial support according to English Anglican tradition. Yet, these identifications ultimately weakened them.

These political and ethnic tensions made it ever more difficult to attract British clergy to Burma, so in 1929 the Kokkine Bible School for advanced theological education for native clergy and church leaders opened in outer Rangoon, and the tradition of sending students to Calcutta's Bishop's College for study ended. In 1934, a more eminent setting for the school was secured on Inya Road next to Holy Cross Church, which sat across the road from Rangoon University; a cornerstone was laid and preparations to raise the standard of theological education to the bachelors' level began. After its church neighbor, the school was consecrated "the College of the Holy Cross," and is known today as Holy Cross Theological College (HCTC). Unfortunately, the intention to develop further the caliber of study to the postgraduate level did not materialize at that time because, when the Japanese invaded Burma in 1942, they commandeered churches all over the country for use as barracks and stables, granaries, and salt stores. Holy Cross Church was turned into a Japanese dining hall, and the college closed.

The war years seriously stalled the church's growth and development. As the Japanese advanced, the Bishop of Rangoon, Bishop George West, removed the church's offices to the British hill station at Simla in northern India, and many British missionaries followed suit. Yet, the ensuing years of harsh deprivation also necessarily advanced the rise of native leadership, albeit painfully, for those left behind had to maintain the church at a time when all Christians were suspect because of the faith that connected them with the enemy British. Many Christians were imprisoned and tortured; the British-allied Anglican Christians suffered in particular.

At the end of the war in 1945, Bishop West returned to Burma to encounter widespread devastation. One after-effect of the war was the more vocal Burmese press for national independence from the British, whom they viewed increasingly as the cause of all the misfortunes they had suffered from foreigners since British traders had first set foot in their land. In particular, they blamed the British for what they viewed as their war-sacrifice of Burma to save India, their "jewel in the crown." Simultaneously, the ethnic minorities began to agitate to ensure that their rights would be honored within any design for a future independent government. The Karen were the primary agitators. Being the most populous of all the minorities, and the one with the highest number of Christians, they became the focus of Burman antipathy.

As Burmese–Karen frictions escalated, Bishop West's work to reconstruct the war-torn church became more and more difficult. Being unusually short of British missionaries to assist him, in 1946, West chose to form three archdeaneries in the most heavily churched areas of Mandalay, Toungoo, and the Ayeyarwaddy Delta. To lead them, he reached for three native priests who became the first natives appointed to positions of higher ecclesial authority in the Anglican Church in Burma. West also began to send bright young laymen and women to England for advanced education in the fields of education and nursing, so they could return with professional skills to strengthen their broken communities at home.

Burma finally achieved independence in 1948, a year after British India won independence as the separate states of India and Pakistan. However, Burma's Anglican churches, known collectively as the Diocese of Rangoon, remained officially under the jurisdiction of the Church of the Province of India, Pakistan, Burma and Ceylon. In 1949, Bishop West selected two of the first native Anglican priests to serve as Assistant Bishops of Rangoon. The Rev. Saw Francis Ah Mya and the Rev. John Aung Hla helped lead the church through the fractious post-war years of nation-building and ongoing reconstruction. In addition, continuing inter-ethnic tensions had been exacerbated by the murder of General Aung San, the promising young Burman military founder and war hero who had been the arbiter of the Panlong Agreement that guaranteed the major ethnic minorities a ten-year exercise of the federalist state arrangement they had worked for. Aung San's murder finally sparked armed Karen insurrection against the Burmans. As a consequence, HCTC and most of the mission schools throughout the country closed their doors because they were seen as likely pockets of anti-Burman resistance.

The inter-ethnic wars raged for over three years. After the Karen almost took the Burman stronghold and national capital of Rangoon itself, the Burmans pushed back to retake the city and regain control over many other areas of resistance throughout the country, although to this day pockets of minority resistance exist all over Myanmar. The insurgencies fanned the long-simmering Karen–Burmese distrust to a bitter and enduring mutual hatred. Along with it, the Anglican Church in Burma was irrevocably stamped as suspect because of its British roots, strong Karen numbers, and British-trained and -elevated Karen leadership.

When the churches reopened at the end of the inter-ethnic war, the last British Bishop of Rangoon, V. G. Shearburn, stepped up the policy of sending young men and women abroad for advanced education and augmented local opportunity of leadership development by sending others to Rangoon University to earn bachelor's degrees in preparation for teaching at HCTC. This move proved vital to the church's stability, for the end of British primacy in the Burma Church began with a bang in 1962 when the Burmese Buddhist General Ne Win seized the government in a coup and began to author isolationist, self-protective policies designed to reinstate the primacy of the ethnic Burman majority in all quarters of national life. In 1966, the military cancelled visa extensions for all foreigners, forcing their departure from the country. They further advanced the Burmanization of the country by nationalizing all church-operated private schools, mission schools, and hospitals, which they turned into Burmese-operated schools, military barracks, and police stations. The junta also disenfranchised many among Burma's large population of ethnic Indians who had come with the British to help manage the colony in Burma. Given that the Indian community also comprehended many of the country's most highly educated and able managers and businessmen, many of whom were Anglicans, the church's financial stability and capacity for mission was simultaneously wounded at the grass roots. Further still, in 1965, the church's connection to the India-based provincial headquarters of the Church of India, Pakistan, Burma and Ceylon was truncated by the military's official imposition of a closed-door policy, thus making it impossible for the church in Burma to participate in any of the provincial councils in Calcutta. Foreign visas for entry into Burma immediately became harder to win, especially for reporting journalists and British citizens. Except for well-connected Burmans, success for any native seeking an exit visa for travel abroad became practically impossible.

Moves like these threw all of Burma's foreign-funded and connected churches into a dark age of almost 30 years duration when they had to reframe and remake themselves in practical isolation, and with scant benefit or active relationship with overseas companions in faith. For the Anglicans who had been relative latecomers in actively developing indigenous leadership and capacity, the sudden wholesale departure of their British patrons, clergy, doctors, nurses, mission school teachers, administrators, and managers, at all levels of church leadership, was a shock. The immediate need to design post-colonial ways and means to recombine the church's Anglican heritage with those of the distinctly different ethnic cultures represented within it compounded the severity of the church's difficulty. Later still, in 1993, when the Burmese military junta officially renamed Burma "Myanmar," it was as if the generals had managed the ultimate global disappearing act. Then, in 1994, the imposition of Daw Aung Su Kyi's house arrest brought down the ire of many nations, which refused to honor the new, but ancient Burmese name for the land of many peoples, so they resisted the country's new name and persisted in calling it by the old colonial name they knew.

In 1994, several nations followed the United States and England in imposing economic sanctions on Myanmar. Subsequently, when Daw Suu argued that foreign visitors should not travel to "Burma" because their dollars would only enrich the pockets of the ruling generals and their partners, many of the more intrepid visa seekers ceased from trying. Thus the country's isolation deepened, and the common people's poverty became more extreme. Even though the government's allowance of freedom of religious expression enabled the churches to remain open and able to receive remunerations from overseas, the churches' isolation and difficulty in communicating with their overseas companions quickly impacted the receipt of outside support. Much of the support for the British-identified Anglicans, in particular, came to a standstill, except from their original and steadfast supporter, USPG. However, the monetary value of USPG's support was grossly diminished by monetary exchange rates designed to advantage the military. Given the circumstances, it was not long before many churches in the Anglican Communion aside from the Church of England did not even know that an Anglican Church existed in Myanmar.

## The Post-Colonial Church: Provincial Leaders and Ministries

The years of isolation necessarily drove the rise of many new lay and ordained leaders whose ministries steadied the church and helped it develop a more secure native identity. Practically everything was needed. Among the most pressing were the training of native clergy to replace the foreigners who had departed, clergy and lay leadership training in administration and management, and Christian education for all ages. Other vital needs were the provision of education at all levels to enable job security for minority Christians disadvantaged by pro-Buddhist Burmese military policies; ways and means with which to provide comprehensive medical care to the people; development of supportive relationships with the church beyond Myanmar, especially toward provision of advanced theological study for clergy; development of infrastructure to support social services; authorization of indigenous language liturgies, prayer books, and hymnals; and revision of the church's constitution and canons to address its Asian, multi-ethnic reality context. Overall, it was critical that the church grow beyond its accustomed dependence on British patronage to become financially self-sufficient. Developing good stewardship practices and investment strategies was then, and remains, a challenge.

Of the many who rose up to recreate the church according to need, two of its six archbishops deserve special attention for the importance of their achievements: Archbishop Francis Ah Mya (s. 1966–1973) and Archbishop Andrew Mya Han (s. 1988–2001).

As the first native primate, Archbishop Ah Mya's ministry was foundational. In 1966, just before foreigners' forced departure from Burma, Bishop Shearburn, the last of the British Bishops of Rangoon, presided over the consecration of Bishop Ah Mya as the eighth Bishop of Rangoon. In all ways, the new bishop was ready for the gargantuan task before him. He had been one of Rangoon's first two native assistant bishops, one of the three native archdeacons appointed to head new deaneries established at the end of World War II, and one of the first natives sent to Calcutta for advanced theological education, although he had not completed his course before being called back to manage USPG's original mission school in Moulmein. In Moulmein, he had initiated self-supporting projects in animal husbandry, cash cropping, and orchard cultivation; he had opened a printing press to produce Christian education materials, a hymnal, and a Book of Common Prayer in the regional Sgaw Karen language; and he had built new churches and opened St. Peter's Bible School in Hpa'an to boarding students from distant country areas. Highly respected among his people, he had proven himself a most able administrator. He was above all an energetic visionary.

One of Bishop Ah Mya's first actions was to advocate the church's official transformation from the Diocese of Rangoon into an autonomous province independent of the Province of India, Pakistan, Burma and Ceylon, whose councils it could not attend, given the military government's draconian visa restrictions. In 1968, under the advisement of Canterbury and the provincial leadership in Calcutta, a formal proposal was made to form the Province of Burma. By this arrangement, Rangoon was divided into three dioceses to satisfy the requirement that a province have at least as many: Rangoon,

Hpa'an, and Mandalay were demarcated, and in the far west, Sittwe was designated a mission diocese. With plans in place to secure sufficient endowment to support the mission of the new province, in early 1970 the Church of the Province of Burma was officially established. While continuing to serve as the Bishop of Rangoon, Bishop Ah Mya simultaneously became the first Archbishop of Burma: this dual arrangement continues today.

Always a strong advocate of a self-supporting church, Archbishop Ah Mya presented the province with a plan for developing provincial self-support at all levels. It involved development of a mission-oriented holy order, promotion of ecumenical partnerships, and lay leadership development. To nurture the laity, he organized four lay-led associations that came to be known as "the Four Pillars" of the church: the Anglican Young People's Association (AYPA); the Religious Education Department (RE), specifically to attend to the needs of children; the Men's Association (MA); and the Mother's Union (MU), to organize women for a spectrum of vital support ministries throughout the church. These structures remain strong today. Archbishop Ah Mya also propagated self-supporting projects like those he had initiated in Hpa'an. He established financial self-supporting committees for Rangoon Diocese and instructed all dioceses and parishes to do the same. To improve parish management, he introduced a design for parochial councils of elected lay members to serve with their priest to organize annual all-parish meetings and to develop parochial mission and evangelism programs to engage parishioners. He oversaw the opening of a "Night Bible School" for lay Christian education, a Religious Education Committee, and Summer Sunday School Camps for young people.

In 1972, Archbishop Ah Mya established the Provincial Aid Board for collecting donations to fortify provincial endowment funds. He guided the church to make local securities investments to reap as much return as possible within Myanmar's military-connected banking institutions. However, these proved neither institutionally safe nor successful, so overall, the church necessarily had to continue its primary dependence on remunerations from its oldest patron, USPG. Occasional receipts for structural improvements from the United Thank Offering (UTO) of the Episcopal Church, grants for infrastructure development from Trinity Church, Wall Street, New York, and gifts from parishes and private individuals in England helped sustain them. Without the strength and integrity of the foundations that Archbishop Ah Mya laid for the newly independent, yet ill-prepared, Anglican Church in Burma, it may not have survived, for with some exception, his successors simply maintained the programs and leadership arrangements he had put in place.

The second most significant, but perhaps one of the least understood, yet most creative, of all the church's later leaders was Archbishop Andrew Mya Han, the 11th Bishop of Rangoon and fourth Archbishop of Burma. As a youth activist for student rights and academic freedom while a student, and president of the student union at Mandalay University during the last years of British rule, he became known as a poet whose published work under the pen name Maung Pauk Si evokes the depth and tenderness of his Christian faith. The young university graduate continued his concern for students' interests and demonstrated his skill as an educator while working as the headmaster of St. Peter's Bible School. Upon his early graduation from HCTC and his ordination to the diaconate and priesthood, he served as principal of Emmanuel Divinity School in Myitkyina from 1968 to 1972. Having served as general secretary of the province and archdeacon and secretary of the Diocese of Rangoon, he was appointed the general secretary of what became the Myanmar Council of Churches (MCC), and served there until his election as archbishop in 1988.

Archbishop Andrew Mya Han introduced twice-annual clergy seminars for the continuing education of the clergy. He successfully increased clergy salaries and introduced retirement pensions for clergy and lay provincial staff. He invited and welcomed overseas visitors. His family background as part Burman and part Karen allowed him to speak to each of these archenemies as one of their own and to act as a peace negotiator between them. When many of the church's properties continued to be diminished by the military, he was able to successfully negotiate the construction of a building complex to house the Rangoon diocesan offices, with generous meeting space as well as sufficient facilities for housing primary diocesan staff and some retirees. He also managed the construction of new buildings at HCTC, and a large new modern replacement for the old teak structure that had served as the church's Bishopscourt ever since it was built for the first British Bishop of Rangoon in 1877. This complex also has a suitable home for the primate and his family. Archbishop Andrew Mya Han's dual ethnicity also helped him win visas for overseas travel that connected the church in Burma with the world in ways it had not been able to do since the military initiated its closed-door policies.

Of all his innovations, undoubtedly the most important was his initiation of a new Order for Holy Communion, the church's first indigenous Eucharistic liturgy (Babson 2006). The poet and evangelist in him reached for the help of a skilled liturgist resident in the Diocese of Rangoon known as Father Felix. Working together, the two designed a liturgy that is a brilliant apology of Christian faith and a bold expression of evangelism for use within the church's majority Buddhist culture (Babson 2006, 406–10). The liturgy was formally introduced in 1999.

When Archbishop Andrew Mya Han was consecrated primate, his country's name was still Burma, and its capital city was still known as Rangoon. When he retired in 2001, Burma had become Myanmar, Rangoon had become Yangon, and the church had necessarily followed in name to become the Church of the Province of Myanmar (CPM). That Archbishop Andrew Mya Han was able to do as much as he did during the severely trying years of student challenge to the military's socialist government, which ended with the notorious crackdown and subsequent deepening of Myanmar's economic difficulty in 1988, should not be lost to any reading of his legacy as a leader of his church.

In addition to these two seminal leaders, each of the other four native primates must be credited for important achievements: John Aung Hla (s. 1973–1979), Saw Gregory Hla Gyaw (s. 1979–1987), Mahn Samuel San Si Tay (s. 2001–2008), and Mahn Stephen Thant Myint Oo (s. 2009–). Archbishop John Aung Hla blessed the matriculation of the first female student at HCTC, after which increasing numbers of women attended and graduated to take up important ministries in the MU and departments of Christian education throughout the province. Archbishop Saw Gregory Hla Gyaw entered the province into the Partnership in Mission (PIM) consultation, by which it engaged in rigorous self-examination to assess its mission strategies, financial needs, and general viability. Accordingly, individual parishes, dioceses, and the province as a whole began to commit their histories to writing instead of relying on oral history as they had in the past. Internally, this work also led to the articulation of new church-funding policies, and externally, to the identification of sources of support from new communion partnerships. By establishing a separate office for the Diocese of Rangoon, he also began to disentwine and attempt to distinguish between what had been the shared functions and practical simultaneity of his apostolic governance of the province and the Diocese of Rangoon. As general secretary of the MCC from 1993 to 2001, Archbishop Mahn Samuel San Si Tay had proven himself as a gifted ecumenical leader in difficult times when Myanmar's Protestant denominations had to share their resources with both creativity and discipline in order to make ends meet. During the tumultuous years following the 1988 student uprising, he strengthened partnerships with the Episcopal Church, the Church of Canada, and the Anglican Board of Mission, Australia (ABMA), to secure grants with which to upgrade significantly the province's internal communications facilities and put in place new diocesan structures to enhance provincial mission capacity. To build up excellence in leadership among women, he was strategic in sending Holy Cross's best female graduates overseas to earn advanced degrees in theological studies. Archbishop Mahn Samuel San Si Tay's most important legacy to his church was his institution in 2003 of the biennial Anglican family gather-ing, to which all Anglicans in the country come to celebrate their heritage and the hope of the future. Archbishop Mahn Stephen Thant Myint Oo's first test of leadership was management of the recovery from the horrific destruction caused by Cyclone Nargis. This effort required the appropriate distribution of vital gifts in aid sent to CPM from all over the communion.

Of all the laity, U Aung Hla Tun (b. 1935) may well be called the church's most eminent lay leader. Born into a Baptist family, he was inured in his youth with the understanding that grass-roots activism is a normal witness of faith within a healthy Christian community. After he became an Anglican when attending Anglican mission schools, he brought his example of voluntary activism and self-sacrificial leadership into his mature ministries, leavening the more hierarchical forms of his native culture and adopted church with another model of possibility needed in particular during the years of isolation when both clergy and lay leaders were scant in number and lean in training.

Highly educated in Burma, England, and Scotland, with excellent experience as a practitioner and educator of metallurgical engineering, U Tun brought discipline, imagination, creativity, and long-term vision to his many and varied ministries within the church. In 1961, together with several colleagues, he used his personal resources to open a much-needed clinic and pharmacy in Rangoon. A self-educated historian who restored many of the church's environmentally damaged records, in 1962 he was the primary force behind the creation of a printing press with which he self-published Burmese-language Christian educational materials, calendars, and cards. When in charge of the Ministry of Labour's Worker's Educational Broadcasting Programme, he proved himself a prodigious writer by authoring scripts and managing the production of weekly radio broadcasts. With these skills and those of a natural intellectual, he wrote a series of plays on Christian topics and points of Anglican Church history in Burma. He proceeded to produce and direct these with the help of volunteers who included members of the AYPA. The government allowed several his plays to be aired on national radio in the 1960s. Unfortunately, many of his manuscripts have been lost to record (Doe 2008, 252).

The Sunday School Summer Camps program he organized to engage parents and youth volunteers has proved to be an enduring contribution to the Christian education of provincial youth. Operating under the apt motto "Five Loaves and Two Fishes" (Luke 9:13b), the first camp operated without a budget, yet ended with a surplus of funds available to support the development of other ministries to children. Involving hundreds of children and young people in every diocese, they remain the summer highlight of Christian education and fellowship (Doe 2008, 232). Altogether, it was both a natural and graceful outcome that he became chairman of the Provincial Religious Education Committee in 1982.

U Aung Hla Tun also played a primary leadership role in organizing and developing the MA; and, together with the MU and AYPA leaders, he developed and led the Mobile Team Programme to train leadership skills in many of the most distant, less accessible areas in the province. He also promoted and wrote culturally appropriate materials for the Theological Education by Extension (TEE) program. Particularly active in his home Diocese of Rangoon where he held leadership roles on its standing committee, finance committee, Partnership in Mission (PIM) committee, and helped guide its evaluation and long-term planning processes, many of these ministries led to similar developments in Yangon's five sister dioceses.

One of the plays that U Aung Hla Tun wrote and directed addresses the need for shared service as a fundamental aspect of sound stewardship, a message seminal to the church's survival in Myanmar. Entitled *Hnang-da-lone*, which means "one seed of sesame" in Burmese, it develops the theme that a single seed of sesame cannot produce the cooking oil needed for many, so everyone must gather together to ensure that the hungry are fed (Doe 2008, 247, 252). U Aung Hla Tun himself might well be called such a seed, for throughout his years of leadership in his church, his ability to inspire people of all ages to join him in sacrificial service to others helped the church grow and made him a legend in his own time.

A young contemporary and apostolic complement to the gifted U Hla Tun is the Rt. Rev. Saw John Wilme. Bishop Wilme was consecrated the first bishop of the newly created Diocese of Toungoo in 1994.

Highly educated at Yangon University and HCTC, after which he was ordained to the diaconate and priesthood, he proceeded to Virginia Theological Seminary in Alexandria, Virginia, in the United States, to study for his M.Div. Returning to Yangon in 1989, he was named principal of HCTC, where he made several strategic innovations to strengthen the integrity of its course of study.

In 1994, after his election as the first diocesan bishop of Toungoo, which had been a missionary diocese of the province for two years prior, Bishop Wilme began the work of delivering to the people what respite was possible in their area, one of several border areas constantly wracked by ongoing Karen insurgencies against the military government. The bishop's development program included management of clean water supply to mountain villages, access to clinics supplied with bona fide pharmaceuticals with which to combat the scourge of killing diseases and afflictions common in the mountainous jungles of Myanmar, distribution of treated mosquito nets to check the spread of malaria, and delivery of basic health education, especially regarding maternal health and safe childbirth practice. He sent young village women to Yangon for education in nursing with which they are prepared to manage small clinics in distant villages. He has opened preschools to avail families of otherwise-inaccessible early-childhood educational opportunities for their children, constructed youth hostels to provide young boarders access to middle- and high-school education, and developed tuition programs to encourage success for students studying for national end-of-high-school graduate examinations. Technical training programs have helped young men and women develop wage-earning skills to enhance family incomes. Animal husbandry, fish-farming, and fruit orchard projects have built income capacity at the village level. English language training and computer skills-building programs help young people keep pace with global modernization so they may hold onto hope for the future. Bishop Wilme's development of a strong educational program at Toungoo's St. Peter's Bible School has also prepared theologically educated catechists from all over Myanmar to serve in villages where priests are able to celebrate Eucharist but occasionally on a rotational basis in the fashion of circuit riders.

To enable further the success of these programmatic developments, Bishop John Wilme has built structures to house them, inspired and educated young lay and ordained leaders to manage them, and won support from overseas friendships to finance them. Elected Dean of the Province three times by his fellow bishops, appointed to represent the Anglicans of the province on the MCC and the Association of Theological Education in Myanmar (ATEM), and having chaired the Provincial Education Committee, at all levels, Bishop John Wilme's leadership has demonstrated discipline, constancy, integrity, and vision. Named a Fellow of Virginia Theological Seminary's Center for Anglican Communion Studies, he meets annually with communion peers from around the world to share ideas and discern ways to advance reconciliation within the communion's culturally diverse sister provinces. The author of "Engaging with a Multi-Faith World 3" in the volume *Christ and Culture: Communion after Lambeth* (Wilme 2010), Bishop John Wilme addresses the Christian–Buddhist–Muslim relationships he knows in his native context where such conversation is the practical platform for a new order of national civility and hope. Altogether, Bishop John Wilme's leadership has demonstrated how one of the most challenged and less affluent churches in the Anglican Communion has been able to grow in number, capacity, and spirit when the authority of faith, courage, and vision uplifts and guides it.

## Contemporary Issues and Challenges Facing the Province

Since Daw Aung San Suu Kyi's release from house arrest in 2011 and the national elections of March 2012 that seated 43 members of the National League for Democracy (NLD) in Myanmar's new national parliament, freedom from long-debilitating fear has begun to open a new time of hope for Myanmar and its people. Subsequent political, economic, and social change is sweeping over the country like monsoon rain over parched ground, stirring the voice of free speech and greening popular opportunity unknown for almost three generations. In country, an explosion in the availability, affordability, and widespread popular use of cell phones is a visible sign of the reality of a communications revolution within which people converse without fear of surveillance or reprisal. The old government censorship office has been closed; journalists now write openly and independent daily newspapers have been given the green light to publish. When the new government cancelled the unpopular Myitsone dam project which it had undertaken in tandem with Chinese business investors at the confluence of rivers that originate the great Ayarawaddy River in upper Burma, it signaled its intention to listen to the people as never before and to push back against entrenched and unpopular Chinese interests that used the global vacuum to commandeer many of Myanmar's richest national resources for themselves. The world is suddenly investing in Myanmar as it moves to catch up with its advanced neighbors and satisfy its people's pent-up desires. For internationals, the concern that a visit to Myanmar would damage the strength and integrity of its democracy movement by putting dollars in the hands of the military need no longer keep companions in faith away.

Promising developments like these are beginning to unlock the will of the international community and the communion of churches to enter in more boldly with resources and skills assistance to help the church serve the people. Together, these changes now invite the Church of the Province of Myanmar to move beyond internal constraints it has wrestled with since the expulsion of its British helpmeets in the 1960s, and to meet long-tabled issues and challenges with bold re-creativity.

Nevertheless, enduring colonial era mindsets unleavened by open engagement with the world and the communion have diminished the Anglican Church's skill and confidence. Its vulnerabilities are most apparent at the leadership level where persistent colonial-era assumptions of privilege and prerogative check creative thinking and initiative at the grass roots that otherwise could help the church develop for the good of all. Hence, there is limited awareness as to how to engage international institutions and overseas churches eager to help support and develop native ministries; how to locate and make use of opportune grants possibilities; and within the communion, how gracefully to manage ecclesial differences without causing offense to any particular side of the apparent political divide.

Stewardship understanding and practice is also handicapped by these old notions of leadership privilege: unlike the Baptists who were nurtured at the start by democratically minded American missionaries, the Anglicans' origins in the Church of England accustomed them to a patronage system within which salaries, benefits, and advancement opportunities were bestowed from the top down, thus checking voice, creativity, and initiative among clergy and laity alike. A Burmese Buddhist cultural belief that any criticism of a monk invites grave misfortune fortifies a pattern of silence among colonially accustomed Anglicans even when a leader's actions may be questionable and potentially harmful to the integrity of the whole. The most unfortunate aspect of weak stewardship practice is that many clergy suffer from ministry overload because there are insufficient funds to support more ordinations.

By no means an urgent issue, but an increasingly pressing one as the Myanmar church is able to engage more openly with is sister churches of the communion, particularly those in Asia, is the ordination of women. There are many aspiring young women who are both highly educated theologically and already holding important leadership positions who continue to hope that their gifts and talents for ordained ministry will be recognized and affirmed in this way, especially as the country opens up and their church's ministries expand with increased international support. In any event, the possibility poses an unusual contextual challenge because the Anglicans' English words for "priest" and "ordination" convey kindred meaning with those used by Myanmar's Buddhists, for whom ordination and the spiritual authority – "pon" – it endows are strictly the privilege of men. Unlike the Myanmar Baptists, whose terms for clergy – "pastor" and "pastorate" – are not in linguistic conflict with those of the Burmese Buddhists, the Anglican leadership holds that the church must move toward women's ordination with unusual care.

Among the most demanding of challenges is how to manage the imminent repatriation of thousands of refugees, many of them Anglicans, who have been held in ghettoized camps on the Thai side of the Myanmar border where all their needs have been supplied by a consortium of non-government organizations (NGOs). There also is the issue of how to provide safe haven for thousands of internally displaced persons (IDPs) whose numbers have recently swelled because of inter-ethnic warfare between government forces and the Kachin Independence Army (KIA) in Upper Burma. All will need village homes and the wherewithal to earn a sustainable living inside Myanmar. The challenge is made more severe by the fact that many of the younger refugees were born in the camps and have no experience in the land they call "home." While the church has done its best to meet the spiritual needs of this population, it is not equipped for the task of supporting large-scale resettlement efforts minus substantial international help.

One of the most iconic of issues to be addressed stems from the colonial era when the Bishop of Rangoon simultaneously served as the Archbishop of Burma within the historic governing body of the Church of India, Pakistan, Burma, and Ceylon. Today, the enduring linkage and relative lack of distinction between the roles and position descriptions of the primate and the Diocesan of Rangoon confuse the clarity of authority and leadership in both quarters. Perhaps even tragically, the persistence of this dual governance arrangement effectively refuses more equal ethnic representation within the church since it has expanded beyond Rangoon into five additional dioceses, each located in different regional ethnic homelands and populated by different groups speaking different languages and celebrating different customs. Ironically, this structure allows the church's own internal inter-ethnic differences to languish rather than to bring strength to the provincial union, in a dynamic oddly similar to that within the nation itself.

## Conclusion

Given all the challenges that the church in the Province of Myanmar faces as it seeks to grow into the fullness of its autonomy, what remains most perplexing is its communion partners' almost mythical understanding of what has been involved in its historic struggle to be a recognized and involved church of the Anglican Communion. This is especially true concerning the years of military rule when a strong "lady" was kept under house arrest like a captive fairytale princess, years when her story trumped the people's stories and need for due notice and appreciation of their own most difficult situations. Though politically tantalizing and even a convenient mask from reality for powers and principalities both inside and outside Myanmar, it was always surprisingly tangential to the profound complexity of the Myanmar story, particularly in regard to the country's inter-ethnic issues. For the Church of the Province of Myanmar, it might even be said that the lady's drama depreciated the value of spirit alive and active among its tens of thousands of faithful, its greatest of all assets. So now more than ever, there is a need for companions in faith who will watch, visit, and truly listen to Myanmar's church so the clarity of its insight into how God in Christ has been abidingly present and alive to it in its wilderness will be honored for what it can offer a global church often faltering in faith that no money can buy.

"Three Baskets," a poem written by former Archbishop Andrew Mya Han, may best summarize the struggle, faith, and extraordinary spirit of this church:

> We have firewood,
> we have fire, but nothing to offer
> just nothing.
> Faith, hope, love:
> which basket have you filled?
> Before the sun sets on life's horizon
> have you prepared yourself?

## Bibliography

Babson, Katharine. 2006. The Province of Myanmar (Burma). In *The Oxford Guide to the Book of Common Prayer: A Worldwide Survey*, ed. Charles Hefling and Cynthia Shattuck. Oxford: Oxford University Press, pp. 406–10.

Doe, Saw Maung. 2008. A Critical Appraisal of Christian Education in the Diocese of Yangon: With a Special Focus on the Contributions of U Tun (1955–2003). A Doctoral Thesis Submitted to the Oxford Center for Mission Studies, 2008.

The Life and Mission of the Church of the Province of Myanmar AD 1970 Onwards. 2003. Pamphlet Prepared by the Office of the Archbishop for General Distribution at the Bi-Annual Provincial Council held in Myitkyina. Yangon, Myanmar.

The Order for Holy Communion. 2001. Prepared by the Liturgical Commission of the Church of the Anglican Province of Myanmar. Yangon, Myanmar.

Wilme, Saw John. 2010. Engaging with a Multi-Faith World 3. In *Christ and Culture: Communion After Lambeth*, ed. Martyn Percy, Mark Chapman, Ian S. Markham, and James Barney Hawkins IV. London: Canterbury Press, pp. 133–43.

CHAPTER 28

# The Church of North India (United)

## Dhirendra Kumar Sahu

**Figure 28.1:** The emblem of the Church of North India, designed by Frank Wesley.

## Introduction

The emblem of the Church of North India (CNI), a united and uniting church, was designed by Frank Wesley, and it captures the character of an indigenous but universal church. The circle symbolizes eternity, and is dominated by a golden cross against a red background, which symbolizes sacrifice. Behind the cross is a lotus, which is dear to every Indian as a symbol of purity, rising out of the dirt beneath the water. The chalice is set at the very center to focus on the point that worship and sacrament are at the center of Christian living. On the lower portion of the outer circle are embedded the three key words: "Unity," "Witness," and "Service." The story of the CNI is the journey of a people of God in search of identity. The search was entrenched within the mission in colonial era, in Indian nationalism, and in the desire to be Indian-Christian without

*The Wiley-Blackwell Companion to the Anglican Communion*, First Edition. Edited by Ian S. Markham,
J. Barney Hawkins IV, Justyn Terry, and Leslie Nuñez Steffensen.
© 2013 John Wiley & Sons, Ltd. Published 2013 by John Wiley & Sons, Ltd.

losing sight of the global lineage. The concurrence of colonialism and the modern missionary movement provided a challenging starting point for defining the distinctiveness of the Indian Christian community.

The vision of a united and uniting church within the ecumenical movement in North India had to journey through the experience of extensive years of debate, from the way the theological and non-theological factors interplayed during the negotiation. However, such a vision has to be true to its beginning and must be continuously open to rejuvenation in new embodiments in different contexts. The obvious issues are how to remain true to its distinctiveness, to retain continuity with its beginning, and, not the least, to respond to new contexts in order to be a witnessing Christian community. The vision was realized in the joyful reunion of six major denominations: the Church of India, Pakistan, Burma and Ceylon; the United Church of North India (merger of Presbyterian and Congregational); the Methodist Church (British and Australian Conference); the Church of the Brethren; the Church of the Disciples of Christ; and the churches connected with the Council of the Baptist Churches in Northern India that led to the inauguration of the CNI on November 29, 1970, in All Saints' Cathedral Campus, Nagpur. CNI's jurisdiction covers all states of the Indian Union, with the exception of the four states in the south (Andhra Pradesh, Karnataka, Kerala, and Tamil Nadu), and has approximately 1,250,000 members in 3,000 *pastorates*.

The formation of the CNI is the story of negotiation over 40 years (1929–1970). It was a transition from denominational identity to a corporate identity and the uniting churches adopting the ideal of organic union as a contemporary expression of the distinctiveness of the church. The strength of this new identity lies in the discovery of the richness of various traditions along with the way in which groups of people in different regions make their own contribution to the witness and service of the church. The CNI self-consciously admits plurality, which implies the underlying principle for the vision of a church where discipleship includes the irreducible diversity. The challenge has been to reconcile different convictions, castes, regions, and language groups into a unified church that becomes vulnerable to internal power politics. The integration of local worshipping groups has proved "easier said than done" in comparison to the unification of confessions, particularly when the union is based on the principle of freedom of conscience. Therefore, the plan of union categorically stated that "We do not desire that any one Church shall absorb other churches, nor that one tradition shall be imposed upon all; but rather that each Church shall bring the true riches of its inheritance into the united Church to which we look forward. We intend that it shall be a Church which, while holding to the fundamentals (Faith and Order of the Universal Church), shall assure to its members freedom of opinion in all other matters, and also freedom of action in such varieties of practices as are consistent with the life of the Church as one organic body" (The Plan of Church Union 1965, x).

## The Mission

The story of modern mission in India is the story of a community that embraced a faith which arrived with colonial power and was dependent on finance from the West. It was also made up of people drawn from various other religious communities and caste backgrounds. In the course of history, the visible Christian community in India as elsewhere has often failed to express the fruits of new life in Christ in a sense of renewal, freedom, and dignity. Caste or class still persists in the Indian Christian community in some form or other, and it will be right to admit this more openly than has perhaps been done usually.

Early in 1910, the World Missionary Conference at Edinburgh was the outgrowth and climax of earlier gatherings through which Protestants expressed their purpose to give the gospel to the world. The agreement in the mission was expressed quite early in the system of mutual adjustment known as "comity." Non-interference in one another's affairs, respect for each other's discipline, and adoption of a common standard and procedure were essential features of this system. Beaver argues that the territorial comity was intended first of all to sponsor responsible evangelistic cooperation everywhere and, secondly, to be a preliminary step toward a united and independent church in every land (Beaver 1962, 327). The arrangement of comity was a great advantage for the evangelistic task but not necessarily to address the issues of scandal of denominations.

The cooperation in mission did not exclude the obvious tension implicit in the relation between mission and church. The story of the Serampore controversy is one such example when the Serampore trio – Carey, Marsman, and Ward – did not succumb to stricter control by the new committee in England after the death of Fuller in 1815. The other example was the exact authority of the bishop over the missionaries and the controversy between High Church and Low Church. The church in the mission field had to wrestle with three issues: first was the experience of being surrounded by a majority non-Christian community, the second that of being in close relation with an older Christian community with whom it had parental relationship, and the third of all was the issue of caste. Initially, the missionaries had continued a tradition of tolerance to caste in the nineteenth century, but caste was later viewed as inconsistent with the fundamental principles of Christian fellowship. All Protestant missions with exception of the Leipzig mission were in agreement in holding that caste was a great evil and that it must be rooted out from the church (Madras Diocesan Record 1894, 79).

In the light of the lack of converts from high castes, the strategy of the mission turned to outcastes. The change of strategy began to witness growth through group conversions. In the mass movement, the decision to adopt the new faith was usually taken by the caste leaders. The mass movement had a great impact on Indian society and within the church. In that scenario, it was the most natural way of accepting Christ as personal savior because it helped people to preserve integration of the individual in his group, whereas individual conversion compelled the convert to break from the group. Therefore, the churches of the villages, which were predominantly the churches of the mass movement, were highly Indian in social pattern and customs, but at the same time the drawback was the import of the caste barriers and caste exclusiveness and undesirable caste customs into the church.

The Christian community has always tried to maintain its own identity in relation to other religious communities in India, while at the same time having relationships with Christians in other parts of the world. While the Hindu and Muslim communities have tried to protect their faith, the Indian Christians have made attempts to gain an identity through questioning their own faith, practice, and ecclesiastical control of the church. The distinct character of the Christian community was its complex nature in contrast to the homogeneity of the others. Religiously, it shared the spiritual outlook derived from all communities and added to it an equal variety of denominational attitudes adopted from the continents of Europe and America. The subtle issue was and is the issue of "conversion." The possibility of mobility within the caste system was closed to the untouchables, but conversion to Christianity provided an opportunity from a negative rejection to positive affirmation of new identity and equality of dignity. It resulted in developing a sense of solidarity among the converts (Forrester 1980), and both a challenge and tension within the fellowship of the church.

## Negotiation

The challenge in any scheme of union is to evolve an indigenous but ecumenical church that has to coexist alongside the denominational churches. The two schemes of union in South India and North India were almost parallel, but the Church of South India (CSI) was inaugurated on September 27, 1947, in St. George's Cathedral, Madras, with the South India United Church, the union between Congregationalists and Presbyterians, the South India Province of the Methodist Church, and the four dioceses of the Church of India, Pakistan, Burma and Ceylon. The inauguration of CSI and achievement of Indian independence in 1947 provided the stimulus for the negotiators in the north to move forward.

A formal discussion on church union began in May 1919 at Tranquebar. One of the main leaders of this conference and later negotiations was Bishop V. S. Azariah of the Dornakal diocese, the Indian bishop of the Anglican Church. The 33 visionaries, all but two of them Indian, and from different churches, issued the Tranquebar Manifesto:

> We believe that the challenge of the present hour in the period of reconstruction after the war, in the gathering together of the nations, and the present critical situation in India itself, calls us to mourn our past divisions and turn to our Lord Jesus Christ to seek in Him the unity of the body expressed in one visible Church. We face together the titanic of the winning of India for Christ – one fifth of the human race. Yet confronted by such an overwhelming responsibility, we find ourselves rendered weak and relatively impotent by our unhappy division – divisions for which we were not responsible, and which have been, as it were, imposed upon us from without; divisions which we did not create, and which we do not desire to perpetuate. (Sundkler 1954, 101)

The climate created at Tranquebar helped the various Congregational and Presbyterian Churches to come together and constitute the United Church of Northern India. The first assembly of this church, which met in 1924, sent out an urgent invitation to other churches to seek means of expressing the church's oneness in Christ. As a result of these developments, a Round Table Conference was called at Lucknow in 1929 to discuss the possibility of church union. Several Round Table Conferences were held subsequently, and many thorny problems and apparently irreconcilable differences were ironed out. It was possible to appoint a "definite Negotiating Committee," which met in Calcutta in 1951 and drew up the first plan of church union in North India. The plan was further revised in 1954 and 1957. It was then presented to the negotiating churches for them to decide whether or not they wished to join the union on the basis of the plan. However, four out of seven churches failed to get the majorities constitutionally required for entering the union. The plan was further revised to clear some of the difficulties encountered by the churches while voting on it.

The fourth revised edition of the plan was published in 1965. While issuing the latest edition of the plan, the Negotiating Committee passed the following resolution, emphasizing the need for a serious and urgent consideration of the plan:

> Resolved that the Negotiating Committee, in authorizing the issue of Fourth Edition of the Plan of Union, believes that the Churches should now take their decisions to unite or not on this basis with the least possible delay. While realizing that the time required for constitutional procedure varies in different Churches, the Committee requests the Churches to deal with this as a matter of urgency and to take all measures to awaken this sense of urgency among their people as a whole. Finally, the Committee would request that the decisions of the Churches regarding the Plan be taken and communicated to the Secretary by March 1969. (Minutes of the Negotiating Committee 1965)

One issue that is still persistent after 40 years of journey and celebration of being united is unfortunately the ignorance of the value of each other's tradition. Most members are only superficially acquainted, if at all, with the life of the other five. The impression is based frequently on caricatures or stereotypes, not unlike those in a story often told by the late Dr. Augustine Ralla Ram, one of the "founding parents" of the church union movement in North India. The story is that a traveler entering a city for the first time stopped to ask where the various Protestant churches were located. "You'll have no trouble in finding them," was the reply. "The Baptist Church is half a mile down the road, near a large pond. The Methodist Church is opposite the gas works, the Anglican Church next to the laundry, and the Presbyterian Church across the road from the ice factory" (Dharmaraj 1973). However, in defining and assessing the fourth plan, W. J. Marshall makes a succinct remark that one dominant insight as a whole was the dependence of the church on God which may sound obvious but which divisions in the church tend to obscure (Marshall 1975). The object of such affirmation is not to justify one's own position in stressing the rightness of own beliefs but collectively to seek from God the full expression of truth. The negotiators made the journey with open recognition of each other in Christ having one faith, one Lord, and one baptism.

## Issues Addressed and Resolved

### Baptism

The participation of Baptists in the negotiation process in North India had to address the question of baptism. The most intelligent way of addressing the issue was to accept the baptism in infancy to be followed by later profession of faith and to accept believer's baptism to be preceded by presentation and blessing in infancy as alternative, as well as equivalent, for entry into the household of God. The declaration of acceptance of Jesus Christ as personal savior and being baptized with water in the name of the Father, and of the Son, and of the Holy Spirit is to be made either at the time of baptism when it is believer's baptism or at the time of confirmation when it is infant baptism. One overriding principle that determined the negotiation was liberty of individual conscience. The baptism is considered in itself not a completed act but the beginning of a process which is God's saving and reconciling activity in the life of an individual within the fellowship.

## Lord's Supper

The sacrament of Lord's Supper reaffirms a weakness of witness at both individual and corporate levels when Christians cannot unite in full fellowship around the same table to eat the bread and drink from the same cup. The Supper is set at the heart of the fellowship with the unfailing use of Christ's words of institution. The United Church laid down thanksgiving, commemoration of Christ's life and work through the ministry of word and recitation of the Creed, pleading before the Father and invoking Christ's merit for the whole church, presenting ourselves as a living sacrifice, communion with God, and offering to God our sacrifice of praise to be basic components of the service. However, the United Church set the structure of Lord's Supper in two main divisions: the proclamation of the Word and Prayers, and the Communion with four actions of taking the bread and wine, the thanksgiving, the breaking of the bread, and sharing of the bread and wine. The fellowship at the table is seen not just as the goal of union but also as the source of power for witness of the church.

## Episcopacy

The threefold ministry of bishop, presbyter, and deacon is accepted as the pattern of ministry. It was also envisaged that it would be free to develop an appropriate diaconate as might be demanded by the needs and life of the church. The form of a permanent diaconate would be such as to free other ministers (presbyters and bishops) to perform the functions which more appropriately belong to their distinctive calling. The ministry of the diaconate might be undertaken for life by persons who have been accepted for this ministry by the diocesan authorities and have received due training, which might, in some respects, be different from the normal course of training for presbyters. However, there has been no progress even after 40 years of life in a united church.

Episcopacy in CNI is both constitutional and historic – "constitutional" in that bishops shall be appointed and perform their functions in accordance with the constitution of the church, and "historic" in that the episcopate is in historic continuity with that of the early church. It was accepted as a means of expressing the continuity of the church down the ages. However, the church is not committed to any one particular theological interpretation of episcopacy, nor does it demand the acceptance of such an interpretation from its ministers or members.

## Unification of ministry

The Episcopal and non-Episcopal ministries were accepted side by side as the ministries of the CSI. The CSI was expected to determine for itself whether to make any exception after 30 years of inauguration, and in fact they made the proclamation to have a fully unified ministry of Episcopal-ordained ministers in the CSI. However, the negotiators decided in North India to have the unification of ministry satisfactory to all the bodies concerned as a prerequisite for union. From the beginning, there was expected to be intercommunion between the united church and the churches of the Anglican Communion. Therefore, mutual recognition meant that all the ministers of uniting churches at the time of the inauguration of the CNI were brought into the ministry by the use of a common service of unification. However, the difficult task was to recognize the episcopate to be the witness to God's grace in this form of ministry without making a negative judgment on others. "The uniting churches pledge themselves and fully trust each other that any bishop or Presbyter officiating in the rite will do so with the sincere intention of placing himself unreservedly in the hands of God, to be used as He wills, as a channel of His grace, commission and authority" (The Plan of Church Union in North India and Pakistan 1965, 52).

## Unfinished Agenda

The pain of the last-minute withdrawal of a major negotiating church, namely the Methodist Church in Southern Asia (MCSA, now the Methodist Church in India), is not just a part of history now but also a constant reminder that human frailty in the name of church takes the precedence at the cost of most enduring challenges. The Juridical Council of the Methodist Church in 1972 had declared that the decision of MCSA in 1970, which reversed an earlier decision to join the union, was beyond its legal authority. The door was kept open for a union, but the union was not yet a reality. The CNI had sent the invitation to the CSI and Mar Thoma Syrian Church of Malabar to explore the ways and means of further cooperation and possibly organic union. Even adopting one common name in India has not been possible because of retaining the identity of three churches. The communion of churches in India has been constituted as the visible organ for common expression of the life and witness of the three churches while each remaining autonomous.

The founding parents had envisaged a united and uniting church on the basis of organic union to overcome the scandals of denominational identity in a particular place. Localization was one of the priorities. While locality, language, ethnic identity, and confessional traditions have been the determining factors in defining the form of the church, the relevance of being a sign of new creation needs to be addressed again and again. Therefore, there ought to be a community learning to be faithful to the call of God. The history of schism has been the history of Christianity's defeat, and the church accepted the divisions of the society it had hoped to transform and transcend (Niebuhr 1929, 264). The denominational character of the church depicts the conflicts of the society becoming just one social institution alongside many others. The caste and communal structures of Indian Christian congregations has been and is one of the main causes of its ineffectiveness as a church.

Religious pluralism is another reality of Indian society, and it is not an entirely new phenomenon because Indian people have lived with and witnessed the major religions of the world. However, the major concern in recent history in India is the number of conflicts between the communities. Orissa has been in the spotlight in recent times. It was the first state of independent India to enact legislation on religious conversions called "The Orissa Freedom of Religion Act, 1967," stipulating that no person shall "convert or attempt to convert, either directly or otherwise, any person from one religious faith to another by the use of force or by inducement or by any fraudulent means." Graham Stains, an Australian missionary working with the Evangelical Missionary Society of Mayurbhanj, was burned to death on the night of January 22, 1999, along with his two sons, ten-year-old Philip and six-year-old Timothy. Another instance is the violence that initially broke out on December 24, 2007, at 8.00 a.m. at Bamunigan village in Kondhmal district. It escalated after the murder of the octogenarian Swami Lakshmanananda Saraswati (a leader of Vishwa Hindu Parishad) at his Jalespata ashram in Kandhamal district in Odisha, along with four others on the evening of Saturday, August 23, 2008. The aftermath of the violence is now a history but it includes burning of 4,104 houses in 310 villages, 17 churches, and death of 38 people. More than 25,000 Christians were forced to flee their villages after their houses were attacked by rampaging mobs. India's Prime Minister Manmohan Singh called the Odisha violence a "National Shame."

The church as a community among the communities claims that, in Christ, God really did something decisive for the world. The question of Christian distinctiveness must not be confined within the supposed characteristics of just another communal group but has to come to terms with the full implications of the notions of church. The early history of India indicates that there was in existence multiple communities based on various identities. In pre-Islamic India, the religious identity seems to be related more closely to a sect than a dominant Hindu community. The notion of a Hindu community does not have as long an ancestry as is often presumed. There were a variety of communities, determined by location, occupation, and caste, none of which were necessarily bound together by a common religious identity. The community had one of its roots in location (Thapar 1989, 220). The idea of a Hindu community appears to be a concern of more recent times. Therefore, the obvious temptation in recent times is for loyalty to one's own community in competition with others. The communities assume political importance, and the relations between communities are embittered by their relevance to the balance of power. Therefore, conversion from one group to another means not only a change in spiritual allegiance but also shifts in political power.

The church throughout the ages has proclaimed the gospel as the story of God's relation with creation. The greatness, the finality, and the absoluteness of what God has done in Jesus Christ for the salvation of the whole world is proclaimed and affirmed.

The question of distinctiveness of a faithful community depends on communicating Christian faith in all sincerity. The United Church should not overlook the challenges of caste, poverty, communalism, and religious pluralism, all of which are overwhelming. While pragmatic considerations could not be ruled out altogether behind the journey, it is now pertinent to ask how far after 40 years of birth of a United Church have we been a witnessing community. The inequalities and discriminatory practices found in Indian society are very much operative in the church. God has reconciled the world to Himself through the death and resurrection of Jesus Christ, and this is not a fairy tale. The United Church must be prophetically self-critical so that the story of the church can now be a sign of the kingdom of God. The model of organic union is based on the principle that unity in diversity is an acceptable and ever-essential characteristic of a united church. However, the larger issue behind the principle is the interpretation of the principle of unity in diversity.

The church as a people of God is only a channel through which God's creating and redeeming love is witnessed. The important point is the contingent character of the church. The boundary of a united church is not a strategic concern for exclusion or in opposition to others, but must operate as a facilitating point for communication as a precondition for understanding and harmony. The family and community play a greater part in Indian life in comparison to the West. Therefore, it is possible to envisage in the church that type of life which perfectly reconciles the individual and community. The community that worships together and celebrates the Lord's Supper is reminded of a divine relationship where there is a correspondence between human rights and dignity with a unique place of every human being in the eternal will of God including the sick, weak, outcast, poor, and rich. The implicit character of this community is risk-taking love based on the self-emptying character of Christ being obedient unto death, even death on a cross. It is argued and justified in some circles that a communal church is ideal in India on the basis that the churches composed of homogeneous caste or tribal groups are among the strongest in India. They even carry over some of their old social cohesion intact. However, the question is whether that is or ought to be the ideal character of the church while it claims to be a witnessing community dealing with issues of justice and reconciling power of the gospel.

Institutional blindness has been a constant deterrent in deviating from the path of truth. The human tendency is to cling to the past and to a structure that makes people insensitive to the Lord's active visitation of His people in judgment and renewal. The eschatological dimension of our faith assists in challenging a community from generation to generation. It has a substantial component of the "already" and the "not yet." The church does not establish itself in final form at any given time but must learn to function as the pilgrim people of God. It also has to internalize the minority character not as a weak point but as a strength of the real church. The real church has often been a minority in many parts of the world, despite the claim to be numerical majority in one part of the world. The success of mission is not to play with number games in mission strategy but to proclaim God's love and justice through the reconciled community. The Incarnate Word enables through the Holy Spirit the personal and community identity to be fused with the narrative history of God's grace revealed through the life, death, and resurrection of Jesus Christ.

One major problem in the CNI, both at the synod and diocesan level, has been that on the one hand there is a dominant class, small in number but powerful, and on the other, a subordinate class which is predominantly rural and more numerous but in practice powerless and marginalized. The urban–rural divide of the congregations within and between the dioceses has not been able to address the issues of pastoral ministry and common mission witness despite the rhetoric of being one united church. This has brought a cleavage within the church similar to the struggles in the society in general. It reflects the ongoing struggle within and between leadership and broad-based participatory community. In fact, it is a question of communication and dialectics of giving–receiving. The church is constituted by the story of Israel and Jesus, which means it is a movement with the power of the Holy Spirit. In reality, it brings the conception of ministry, mission, and management not in opposition to each other but as a dynamic process entailing mutuality. The authority is based on the servanthood of God who became human for us. If the church wants to be true to its calling, then the ministry and mission need to be open to new forms in which "diakonia" and "witness" may find expression appropriate to the needs and conditions of the people. The church as an institution frequently squanders the full potential of human resources available to it because it does not inculcate a vision. The effectiveness of the mission of the church is not separable from the degree to which it can work within the culture of a society. One major weakness on the part of the church lies in its supposed attitude that "we have always done it in that way before." A constant reminder is the need to relate the triune God to the historical community in order to uncover the presence and action of God in the ongoing journey as a people of God.

## Bibliography

Beaver, R. Pierce. 1962. *The Ecumenical Beginnings in Protestant World Mission*. New York: Nelson.

Dharmaraj, A. C. 1973. General Secretary, CNI. October 22, 1973.

Forrester, Duncan B. 1980. *Caste and Christianity*. London: Curzon Press.

*Madras Diocesan Record*. 1894. Vol. VIII, no. 3, July.

Marshall, W. J. 1975. The Church of North India/Pakistan: A Theological Assessment of the Plan of Union, Ph.D. Thesis, Dublin University.

Minutes of the Negotiating Committee, Pachmarhi. 1965.

Niebuhr, Richard H. 1929. *The Social Sources of Denominationalism*. New York: Holt.

Sundkler, Bengt. 1954. *Church of South India: The Movement Towards Unity, 1900–1947*. London: Seabury Press.

Thapar, Romila. 1989. Imagined Religious Communities? Ancient History and Modern Search for a Hindu Identity. *Modern Asian Studies*, vol. 23 (May).

The Plan of Church Union, Fourth Revised Edition. 1965. Madras: CLS.

The Plan of Church Union in North India and Pakistan. 1965. Madras: CLS.

CHAPTER 29

# The Church of Pakistan (United)

## Azad Marshall

In South Asia, surrounded by China, India, Iran, and Afghanistan, with the Arabian
Sea in the south, lies the country of Pakistan, undersized in comparison to India and
China, but known for its nuclear power status, advanced missile technology, and
growing Islamic militancy that has affected the rest of the world. There is more to her
story, particularly in the rich history of her church.

Despite Islamization, the impact of refugee movements, and political instability, there
has been the constant presence of the Christian church, which has existed in the Indian
subcontinent since St. Thomas' arrival in 58 CE. The church continues to be an active
part of the country's social, religious, and cultural dynamic as salt and light.

This church has deep historic roots (Frykenberg 2010) with nearly 2,000 years of
history. In 1965, the churches of the newly emerging state, Pakistan, agreed to become
a Uniting Church in order to continue the story of indigenous Christian witness in the
subcontinent. By 1970, this union, which had been initiated and encouraged by the
Anglican Church (Marshall 2012), was complete, and was called the Church of
Pakistan.

The story of the Church of Pakistan is a bold one, of courageous and faithful witness
in the midst of challenges and difficulties. From the efforts of St. Thomas, to the work
of Jesuit priests who visited King Akbar (Strickland 2001), to the ministry of men such
as William Carey and Henry Martyn in the 1800s (Rhea 2010), this courageous witness
has been consistent across the country. In Pakistan, the church's witnessing to Christ
extends from the very north, on the border with Afghanistan, to the south, along the
coast, all while enduring violence, hostility, and persecution (Sookhdeo 2002).

The story of this church is one of growth, while being faithful to the gospel and
remaining relentlessly missionary at heart (Frykenberg 2010). The churches that

*The Wiley-Blackwell Companion to the Anglican Communion*, First Edition. Edited by Ian S. Markham,
J. Barney Hawkins IV, Justyn Terry, and Leslie Nuñez Steffensen.
© 2013 John Wiley & Sons, Ltd. Published 2013 by John Wiley & Sons, Ltd.

united into the Church of Pakistan had been established prior to the partition of India through the missionary work of churches in Europe, America, and Australia. They began work in India over different periods, beginning early in the eighteenth century with the missions of the Church Missionary Society (CMS) and the Society for the Propagation of the Gospel (SPG) (Moffett 1998). Both institutions were closely linked with the Anglican Church. Their labor left deep and unshakeable roots in the region. Two men who left an indelible mark on the history and identity of Christians in South Asia and Persia are William Carey and Henry Martyn. Carey was a Presbyterian missionary (Benge 1998) who set up the first printing press in the sub-continent to print scriptures and materials. Martin lived a short life and translated scriptures into Urdu and Persian. It was through the reading of scriptures and the incarnational ministry of Henry Martyn in India that Abdul Masih, an early Indian Muslim, was ordained to serve in the Anglican Church, marking a movement and a new identity emerging in the indigenous church.

The Church of Pakistan in the twenty-first century has grown from wave upon wave of mission movements, maintaining even now the mission and joy to proclaim the good news of the Kingdom, to teach, baptize, and nurture new believers. The church's response to human need is accomplished through loving service and long-term efforts to transform unjust structures of society.

Despite the differences with their neighbors and a global conflict challenged by new interpretation of scripture, the church has continued to follow the apostolic mission in faithfulness to those very scriptures. There has been a consistent effort of organizing them together in a specific order to maintain the historic mission of the church and nurturing through the Sacraments, the body of Christ, and her witness (Marshall 2012). This has encouraged and reaffirmed the identity of those parented by the Church of Pakistan, knit together by the Word of God and the liturgy of the Book of Common Prayer.

Historical mission movements are the roots of the present-day church in the region – a deeply apostolic movement.

a.  The bringing of Christianity to the subcontinent by the Apostle Thomas in the first century CE (Frykenberg 2010).
b.  The Mar Thomas traditions that exist from Thomas' time, as well as the sending out of missionary bishops from the Orthodox movements of Syria and the Middle East. These established the churches which would one day partner with later Christian mission movements like the CMS (Neil 1991).
c.  Church mission movements and other European mission movements during the British occupation and rule of India (Neil 1991).

While the very early presence of the church began with the Apostle Thomas in the first century CE, the church has journeyed through these events bringing it into an era of global communication, efficient travel, and advances in media. While the church in Pakistan tries to keep abreast with these developments, the realities of the situation, such as political instability, religious intolerance, and financial limitations, present barriers to Christian expression.

Since September 11, 2001, the Church of Pakistan has been affected by terrorist surveillance, the increased presence of militant Islamic activity over much of the country, and the tracking of men and money across borders. This threatens the anonymity of Christians and their activity in the region. The church also faces homegrown biases, such as being considered lower caste, agents of the West, or "kafirs" (infidels). Consequently, the church has to struggle to remain an indigenous movement with minimal help and aid from abroad.

The church walks a tightrope to constantly prove its national pride in its heritage and ethnicity, while seeing the local church as part of a global fellowship of the Anglican Communion, without whom they would become isolated and alone, spiritually and socially undernourished, and forgotten.

The church union of the 1970s coincided with changing identities, nationalism, growing religious fanaticism, and emerging political powers in the new political order. Pakistan, in particular, experienced the growing visibility of local Islamic extremists with which the rest of the world became well-acquainted via media, social networking, and other communications. The demographics of Pakistan have been influenced by the movement of Muslims to Pakistan, and Hindus and Sikhs to India. As of 2005, over 3 million refugees (approximately 81.5% being ethnic Pashtuns) remain in Pakistan as a result of the wars in Afghanistan, according to the United Nations High Commissioner for Refugees.

Within such a demographic, the local church has celebrated consistent church growth as well as witnessing the sad demise of a handful of mission efforts, the thwarted testimony of mission outlets, and the exodus of large numbers of Christians from the region to the West due to heightened persecution and reduced opportunities for Christians.

Pakistani Christians parented under the Church of Pakistan face constant challenges in the everyday routines of life, despite Mohammad Ali Jinnah's (the founder of Pakistan) promise of freedom of religion for all non-Muslim groups. The constitution acknowledges religious minorities but restricts and limits their role in leadership and their ambition to grow as a community. What is worse is the ever-present Blasphemy law, which calls it a crime for anyone to speak against Islam, its prophet, or its creed. This is a crime punishable by death or life imprisonment. While it is highly unlikely that even a small fraction of these cases are valid, charges such as these are often trumped up to intimidate Christians and acquire their properties. Significantly, the Church of Pakistan's efforts are hampered by the increased rejection and moving away from Holy Scriptures and Christian views on family and marriage by some Western churches. This raises questions by others concerning the local church's position on personhood, dignity, and life.

Time and again, the church faces class and social bias from the community around it. Ethnic and pre-existing caste and class biases slot Christians into low-caste groups and restrict them to domestic labor jobs. Because of the conflicts rife in the region, governments and authorities are more likely to deal with issues of national security and foreign policy while leaving minority issues and rights on the back burner. As a result, Pakistani Christians and their rights suffer as compared to their wealthier and more influential Muslim neighbors. Pakistan's Christians still face from their non-Christian neighbors the suspicion that the church, having been brought to the region by Europeans, is an agent of the West and of the war on terror, as well as endorsing a Western, postmodern, amoral lifestyle.

In the face of these difficulties, suffered by both the church as a whole and individual Christians, it is of significant value for the Christian identity to have a uniting church. The Union of 1970 brought the Church of Pakistan out of a time of isolation, and connected her to the wider fellowship. This uniting church was announced in the Anglican Cathedral of Resurrection in Lahore by the then Chief Justice Cornelius, bringing the Church of Pakistan into the membership of the Lambeth Conference and other instruments of the Anglican Communion. The current Church of Pakistan representative on the Anglican Consultative Council (ACC) is Bishop Humphrey Peters of Peshawar. All the presiding bishops have been members of the Primates Council. The Archbishop of Canterbury, as head of the Anglican Communion, has been called upon to resolve conflicts and intervene in difficulties in the church, bringing the Church of Pakistan into the global communion.

This concluded a period of isolation which had intensified for the church shortly after partition when the Church of North India and the Church of South India separated from the rest of the body in Pakistan (which then also included Bangladesh). India, Sri Lanka, and Burma were in relatively secular environments although this has seen waves of change since 1947.

The church in Pakistan perceived that their freer environment, larger numbers, and access to the global church made for church growth and freshness. In those early years of independence after 1947, there was a significant Anglican presence while other churches were smaller in number and isolated in difficult geographic locations within Pakistan, making it more difficult for them to survive.

In 1948, after the death of Jinnah, the constituent assembly passed the objectives resolution, laying the foundation for Islamization, making it mandatory that all laws be in keeping with Shariah and that no law be passed in contradiction to Islamic Shariah (Sookhdeo 2002). A unique Islamic identity in Pakistan began to emerge at the very birth of the nation. During the latter part of the twentieth century, Pakistan's Christians needed unity as well as a connection with the global church so that they could continue in the cause of the gospel.

Uniting has enabled the church for mission, serving the incarnational agenda of the great commission as presented in the gospel of Matthew. A united, indigenous Christian church was needed to ally with the mission-oriented and gospel-preaching global church; a church able to advocate for them when their voiceless-ness restricted the telling of their story.

However, faced with the challenges of credibility and uniting very diverse groups, the churches themselves began to work to reduce the scandal of disunity, seeking ways to overcome it. The Church of Pakistan came into being on All Saints Day, 1970, by official delegates from the following churches of Pakistan: the CIPBC (Anglican Communion in Pakistan), the UMCP (United Methodists in Pakistan) Conferences; the Indus River Annual Conference; the Karachi Provisional Annual Conference; the UCNIP (United Church of Pakistan); the PLC (Pakistani Lutheran Church); and the church councils of Rajshahi and Sialkot.

It is still very important to the church that the Government of Pakistan agreed to this emerging body and gave the Church of Pakistan legal authority and acceptance, so that she might become the spiritual heir and successor to each and all of the churches. This act of covenant was declared to be irrevocable, and the union was considered indissoluble.

Initially in 1970, there were four dioceses in the Church of Pakistan: Karachi, Multan, Lahore, and Sialkot. In 1980, four additional dioceses were created through a special resolution, for better ministerial work: Hyderabad, Raiwind, Faisalabad, and Peshawar. There are eight active diocesan bishops with an area bishop for the Gulf ministries. This appointment was made to take care of the pastoral and worship needs of Urdu-speaking workers in the Gulf. This was confirmed after a long consultation with the Diocese of Cyprus and the Gulf, and with the President Bishop of Jerusalem and the Middle East, Samir Kafity.

The presiding bishop and moderator for the Church of Pakistan has a three-year term and is currently the Most Rev. Samuel Azariah. The United Church of Pakistan is the second-largest church in the country after the Roman Catholic Church and works closely with the former on issues of advocacy. The Rt. Rev. Michael Nazir-Ali, former Bishop of Raiwind, then Bishop of Rochester in England, and now president of OXTRAD, continues to advocate for the church in Pakistan. He also encourages dialogue with other communities and encourages youth to overcome their difficulties. The Rt. Rev. Nazir-Ali has worked closely with the Rt. Rev. Azad Marshall, Bishop of Iran, to realize a vision for a theological institute that reaches into a united interdenominational Christian community across Pakistan and develop leadership for the Church of the Pakistan and other Southwest Asian countries.

Christians are some 3 percent of the population of Pakistan, which is approximately 180 million. Christians, even those who are able to access education and employment, face problems of identity and full participation in the social and political life of the country.

While there is no clear legal bar to evangelistic work, propagation of the gospel is not always welcome and is a matter of intricate Islamic jurisprudence. Most educational institutions went through nationalization and operate under the control and direction of the government. The Church of Pakistan initiated significant steps to continue her role in education in the light of the policy of nationalization. Some of the schools nationalized in 1972 have since been returned to the church. Significant institutions among these include United Christian Hospital, Gujranwala Theological Seminary, St. Thomas Theological College in Karachi, Edwards College in Peshawar, Mission Hospital in Sahiwal, Kinnaird College for Women in Lahore, and the Lahore College of Theology. The Lahore College of Theology works closely with the Gujranwala Seminary, a Presbyterian seminary.

One consistent difficulty has been the lack of reliable statistical information regarding the Christian population. The 1960 census put Christians down to 2 percent of the total population. According to the National Council of Churches, there are, as of 2011, at least 6–7 million Pakistani Christians. This is 3–4 percent of the population of Pakistan. This increase in percentage is attributed to the increased visibility of Christians, an increase in their seats in Parliament, and a recent allocation of seats in the senate.

The church is spread across the country with dioceses flourishing through mission activities and health and educational services. An example of this is the missionary diocese of Hyderabad that was established to enable outreach and ministry to countless unreached animistic tribes. The first bishop of this diocese, Bishop Bashir Jewan, worked faithfully to this end. This spirit of evangelism and development continues to be at the core of this diocese.

Political strife, local hostility and persecution, weak church leadership, poverty, and natural disasters are significant difficulties restricting church growth and development.

The Church of Pakistan has a rich heritage of courageous men and women, lay people, and ordained ministers, to whom credit ought be given as they stand up to adversity on behalf of the church, all the while raising her profile.

While political manipulations in the 1970s sought to nationalize church institutions, the church did not discontinue her efforts to influence society. Perhaps this is due to the strong missionary vein that runs through Pakistan's church. Under the auspices of the Bishop of Lahore, the Rt. Rev. Alexander John Malik, the support and expertise of the Rev. Smart K. Das, who later became Bishop of Hyderabad, and Mr. Khurshid Gil, the Diocese of Lahore has provided education for thousands of children through schools throughout the diocese. The cathedral school system has educated Pakistani students and has even expanded some schools into colleges. The cathedral school and its college facility, as well as the Kinnaird College for Women, have been strong Christian hallmarks on the education of thousands of Pakistanis, creating environments of learning and mutual respect. Women such Ms. Mangat Rai and Mrs. Mira Phailbus have shown a quality of leadership at Kinnaird for which the church can be proud.

In the early 1970s, when Prime Minister Zulfiqar Ali Bhutto nationalized all schools and hospitals, it was the religious extremist groups in the far north and south (Baluchistan), rebelling against nationalization, who allowed for Christian schools, colleges, and hospitals to maintain their identity and independence. As a result, schools such as St. Mary's in Quetta, Holy Trinity Girls' School in Karachi, and St. Denys' in Muree continued to function under the church's leadership.

However, in other areas like Faisalabad, Sialkot, and Multan, most of the schools were taken over. In the late 1990s, the Rt. Rev. John Samuel in Faisalabad supported 12 primary schools and hostels in the area. The Diocese of Multan has seen a slower growth in schools and educational institutions, because for a significant time they faced unique difficulties in locating appropriate leadership.

While some set up and ran schools and colleges, others responded to a unique call to minister to Pakistan's young Christians. Mrs. Tara James was one of those who was deeply involved in developing educational institutions despite an unfriendly environment, while earning the respect of thousands of students. She served as principal of Holy Trinity Girls' School in Karachi, and then upon retirement continued to serve young people by mentoring them in their Christian faith, and encouraging them to enter public life and serve with an incarnational vision.

These names are but a representation of those Christians whose hard work and tireless efforts influenced large numbers of young Christians.

Under the visionary leadership of the Rt. Rev. Azad Marshall, and the prophetic contribution of Dr. Anne Van der Bijl, also known as Brother Andrew, the IBADAT

(Institute for Basic Adult Development and Training) program was initiated. With their continued oversight and vision, this program was given into the care of lay leadership and managed and directed with excellence by Obaid Nasir Samuel serving since 2012 as a priest in the Diocese of Peshawar, encouraging unity and cooperation between dioceses as well as between dioceses and para-church organizations. The program not only partnered with a sister foundation for developing Christian literature (CFS Church Foundation Seminars), but has also trained about 100,000 Christians since 1987. The IBADAT has provided literacy and vocational skills and a basic Bible school education, bringing community churches in far-flung areas under the leadership and care of the church.

IBADAT and CFS work alongside the National Council of Churches in Pakistan and the Diocese of Raiwind, encouraging and educating Christians, with the belief that Christians who are well versed in holy scriptures are better able to advocate for their rights.

The Rt. Rev. Dr. Azad Marshall, in his role as Anglican Bishop of Iran, demonstrates the missional approach of the Church of the Pakistan and is looking beyond her borders and preparing pastoral care and leadership for the global church. Included in the Rt. Rev. Azad Marshall's efforts is the newly formed Lahore College of Theology, under the scholarly care of the Rev. Emmanuel Bahadur. It was formed to work alongside the only other seminary in the Church of Pakistan, St Thomas' Theological College in Karachi. The Gujranwala Seminary, although not yet affiliated with the Church of Pakistan, has been dedicated to training many Church of Pakistan priests and lay workers, as well as workers for many para-church organizations.

The Diocese of Lahore, also under the leadership of the Rt. Rev. Alexander John Malik, has been involved in advocating for rights, addressing injustices, and speaking out fearlessly, thus being a voice for millions of voiceless Pakistani Christians.

There have been dedicated lay and ordained members of the church involved in Christian mentoring and youth ministry to Christians in Pakistan. In the latter part of the 1970s, there was a move in the church to reach out to Christian young people, which coincided with the rallies of young people vying for political realization in Pakistan.

The late B. U. Khokhar remained a lay worker throughout his life despite his role as the general secretary of the Pakistan Bible Society. He reached out to young Pakistani Christians, working closely with the Pakistan Fellowship of Evangelical Students (PFES). The PFES is an evangelical fellowship which works among Christian students in and graduates of colleges and universities, sharing the good news of Jesus and making disciples of Christ. The PFES has been working in Pakistan for more than 60 years, producing leaders who are working toward an improved community profile. Khokhar, Mrs. Tara James, and the Rev. Iggulden, an Australian priest who came to Pakistan, trained the next generation of Pakistan's Anglican leadership. This included the Rt. Rev. Irfan Jamil, who, after years of ministry to students through PFES, came into ordained leadership and was then consecrated Anglican Bishop Coadjutor of Lahore in 2011. When the Rt. Rev. Irfan Jamil entered into ordained ministry, he handed over the ministry of PFES to the experienced and faithful co-worker, Philip Chandi.

Enormous dedication of Christian leaders has given the Church of Pakistan a strong leadership that currently steers the course for the Church of Pakistan. The former general secretary of the Pakistan Bible Society, B. U. Khokhar, prepared Mr. Anthony Lamuel, who, as a lay worker, had served the church as his predecessor, taking over as general secretary of the Pakistan Bible Society.

The year 2010 was the end of the decade of the Bible. Over that decade, the Pakistan Bible Society introduced new products for promoting the understanding of the Bible. The Urdu New Testament with Notes was the first publication of the decade, being introduced in 2001, and it won the hearts of many. Within 10 years, the Pakistan Bible Society has distributed 28,500 copies. Muslim scholars from the majority community have spoken highly of the Urdu Study Bible, thus encouraging a spirit of dialogue and interfaith communications between the two communities and recognizing the potential for peaceful witness and friendship. Other products brought out in this decade included: the Children's Bible, a synopsis of the four gospels, Sunday school portions, animated Bible stories, a computerized Bible, and a large print Bible. The Pakistan Bible Society has also been involved in producing the Urdu Interlinear Bible with Interpretation and translating the Word of God into Pashto, Yusuf Zai, Hindu Sindhi, and Siraiki.

Also active in areas of publishing, translation, and literature development are organizations such as MIK (Masihi Ishayat Khana) and CFS (Church Foundation Seminars a sister organization of IBADAT). Both organizations have strong leadership, with Peter Calvin heading the work at MIK and the Rev. Emmanuel Joseph at CFS. Joseph followed his predecessor John Maqbool. Maqbool was another lay worker who had a conversion experience that led him to give up a secular job and come into Christian ministry to serve Pakistan's church with his language skills and passion for God's Word. These are men who have led the way in perceiving the needs of the Pakistani church, keeping a keen eye out for literature and materials which will benefit the church, and working to make them available in Urdu.

The Church of Pakistan has been very appreciative of these efforts. These are just some of the efforts which have enriched the Church of Pakistan and helped it develop a clear understanding about these matters. Hence, the church is better equipped to function within its sometimes hostile environment.

Medical care has been an incredibly well-structured area of missions and outreach, showing the church's deep commitment to service to the community. In particular, the church has served those who are otherwise unable to seek medical care and pay for it. Across Pakistan, from the very north to the south, Christian mission hospitals were set up to share the heart of Christ and His compassion for people.

While sharing the gospel appears almost impossible by using traditional methods as understood by much of the Western church, sharing Christ and His gifts through service and the offering of social help to communities continues with great sacrifice and dedication. This evangelism creates local tensions if the compassionate ministry of the church is misunderstood or is seen as a threat to the local community. The continual risk of the accusation of blasphemy puts Christians at risk of being forced to leave or have their homes and properties taken over. The discourse is commonly of God's faithfulness and engagement with the church, and that the church is able to maintain a spirit of service through incarnational engagement, the sacraments, and the reading of God's word.

Some of the hospitals that have had significant impact on the communities around them are:

*United Christian Hospital* came into being in 1947 and by 1965 received much attention and acclaim for having performed the first open heart surgery in Asia. Almost 350 surgery cases were undertaken in those early years of the hospital. Until the early 1980s, this hospital was in its golden years, after which a decline began due to pressure from the hostile environment, large-scale exodus of medical personnel, and lack of finances (Zafar 2007).

The *Memorial Christian Hospital*, Sialkot, was established in 1886 by Dr. Maria White.

The *Christian Hospital*, Quetta was the first hospital to treat cases relating to eye disease. This hospital was the fruit of Sir Henry Holland's labor and received the very first *Quaid-e-Azad* award (a high national recognition) for its unique innovations in ophthalmology.

*Shilokh Mission Hospital* in Jalalpur Jatan in Gujrat district was founded by Dr. Taylor, a missionary of the Church of Scotland in the early 1900s. While the early work of the hospital was performed in a tent, it eventually became the first and most famous hospital in the region, testifying to a dedication to the country and people who frequented the area. Sadly, this hospital is no longer in church possession and has been lost to the community. This is one of the sad stories and consequences of restrictions on the Christian church, which results in unhealthy trends and insecurity within the church and can eventually lead to the difficulties associated with internal struggles, politics, and lack of funds.

The *Mission Hospital*, Peshawar, at the time of this writing has seen more than 100 years of service, serving the people of the Northwest Frontier Province (NWFP), Afghanistan, FATA, tribal areas, Kashmir, and Punjab. This hospital was famous for women's care and its excellent treatment of eye diseases, mental diseases, and leprosy. Dr. Anwar Ujagar worked as part of a dedicated team of doctors and medical care givers. This hospital, after the installation of Bishop Khairdin, became of critical importance to mission efforts to reach the refugees in the area. The hospital's involvement during times of crisis earned it an award of high order by the then president of Pakistan, Ghulam Ishaq Khan.

*Pennell Hospital*, Bannu, was a well-known Christian medical institution in the NWFP, now known as Khyber Pakhtunkhwa (KPK). It was founded by Dr. T. L. Pennell. He was known as the Afghan doctor, and he traveled into difficult places to treat and care for people during the tribal period. He promoted the teachings of Christ's love and was well loved by the people. Dr. Altaf carried on Dr. Pennell's vision, and for his continuation of services of love and medical care for the locals was awarded the *Satara-e Pakistan* by the government of Pakistan – another of the highest honors in the country.

*Christian Hospital Tank*, KPK, and the *Bagh Hospital*, also in the care of the Peshawar diocese, have been places where faithful and courageous witness has occurred. The staffs of these hospitals have performed the difficult task of administering health services to the local tribes.

*Christian Hospital Kunri* is well known in Tharpakkar district of the Sindh province. It started out initially as a mobile hospital, popularly known as the *Caravan Hospital*. The hospital worked in the far-flung desert areas, primarily as an eye hospital, although, like the other mission hospitals, catering with excellence to other medical needs as well. Dr. and Mrs. Hover were the founders of this mobile hospital.

*Christian Hospital Multan* is a more recent IBADAT hospital. Although small, it was the first ministry of compassion in Kashmir. It was set up as a response to the disaster of the 2005 earthquake in the northern parts of Pakistan.

While some of these hospitals have flourished and been a beacon of light, others have dwindled in size and performance, signifying the struggle of the Pakistani church to remain afloat, facing a myriad of difficulties. Other services have included ministering to communities through training and other services to initiate communities into an upward cycle rather than the heavily prevalent downward spiral. Dr. Khulda Namman, Dr. Marina Lamuel, and Dr. Reginald Zahiruddin are important Christian doctors and medical case workers who served as missionaries. They have made an important difference.

The Rev. Graham Burton is one of those who became involved with the local church. As a CMS missionary, he served in the late 1980s and early 1990s, and led a deeply spiritual life. His patient and generous heart was always on the look out for new ideas, and he worked well with the enthusiastic and enterprising young priest, the Rev. Christopher Edgar, who has since then gone on to serve parishes in the Gulf, and is currently an Anglican Priest in Iran. They worked together to acquire the land to build the present-day St. Thomas Church in Islamabad. The building process was holistic, with the spiritual and physical building being developed simultaneously. Their ministry involved practical understanding, guidance of the Word of God, effective and organized youth care, and counseling. In the slums of Islamabad, they developed, with great sensitivity to its residents, a program providing spiritual care for children, a teacher's training program, as well as basic health care programs. They recognized and reached out to address the need for rehabilitation for drug-affected individuals. The program for the drug addicts of Islamabad was initiated and hosted by St. Thomas Church and run through ecumenical cooperation. Additionally, they set up a program of intricately designed care and support for the refugees and the homeless.

The Raiwind Diocese has also worked with deep conviction for the needs of some of the most downtrodden members of Pakistan's social structure, giving of themselves to serve faithfully. Mrs. Khushnood Azariah has developed a successful educational system, alongside mainstream schools, for children with special needs. Ms Shunila Qaderbukhsh worked alongside Mrs. Alice Garrick, who is committed to seeing the role and profile of women raised. This is in a context of religious and gender bias, which leaves Christian women oftentimes at the bottom of the ladder.

To this effect, the Emmanuel Center for Renewal Empowerment Skill and Training (ECREST) in Lahore, under the direction and deeply compassionate efforts of Mrs. Lesley Marshall, has worked alongside the IBADAT projects mentioned earlier to raise the profile of women and children, encourage healthy families, and develop vocational skills and discipleship for women.

As the story of Pakistan's church is chronicled and documented, this chapter has tried to share the impact of Christian witness through the church union and to pay credit to those who are currently serving despite the challenges of the times. The story shows how the Church of Pakistan, as a united church within the Anglican Union, despite sometimes discouraging pressures and stories, evidences the body working to support, encourage, and work alongside one another to share the gospel (Chatterton 1924). Their goal is to be like Christ in Pakistan and to serve alongside the global church in keeping with Biblical scriptures, the Creeds, and the Lambeth Quadrilateral to ensure that we remain a church that lives by the inspired word of God.

As a bishop deeply rooted and still serving the church in Pakistan, and who received the prophetic call to serve beyond her borders, the writer of this chapter is confident of the indigenous expression of the local Pakistani church. The church is not made up of an external ethnicity, but of local believers. Nonetheless, her ties with the global fellowship of the Anglican Commission are there to strengthen her and uphold her as a member of Christ's body in the spirit of 1 Corinthians 12:12. This connection with the global communion bolsters her position and is a source of huge encouragement and prayer ministry.

While many challenges lie ahead in terms of the geopolitical context, it is in this that the church exists. The church will sculpt out a place in the comity of the region amidst the significant ideologies of Islam, Hinduism, Buddhism, and socialism. It will do so rooted in God's word in an unwavering and uncompromised tradition, encouraged on by the martyrs who laid down their lives for the scriptures and the Christian identity. While the church may remain persecuted and challenged, she is critically positioned in the midst of these ideologies. She is poised to flourish and become a vital influence in this region of emerging superpowers: India, China, and the Middle East.

This will draw together some of the most persecuted churches, uniting their heritage and their common experience of being rooted in God's word. The years ahead promise considerable geopolitical and economic shifts in Asia. Regardless of Pakistan's politics and the questions of the future of Islamic extremism, her church promises to remain intensely missionary and fervent in the zeal for God's word and the incarnational mission of Christ. This will secure the primary Christian identity of those parented by the Church of Pakistan into the next century and certainly beyond. The prayer of the writer of this chapter is this: *Secured Christian fervor of Pakistan's Christians for the Gospel and its Lord until Christ's coming again. Amen.*

## Bibliography

Benge, J. 1998. *William Carey: Obliged to Go (Christian Heroes: Then & Now)*. Edmonds, Washington: YWAM Publishing.

Chatterton, E. 1924. *A History of the Church of England in India . . . 1924*. ctd, http://anglicanhistory.org/india/.

Frykenberg, R. E. 2010. *Christianity in India: From Beginnings to the Present (Oxford History of the Christian Church)*. New York: Oxford Press.

Marshall, S. 2012. *Global Fellowship and the Anglican Communion in Pakistan and Iran*. Toronto: Clements Publishing.

Moffett, S. 1998. *A History of Christianity in Asia: Beginnings to 1500*. New York: Orbis.

Neil, S. 1991. *A History of Christian Missions*, 2nd ed. (History of the Church). UK: Penguin.

Rhea, S. 2010. *The Life of Henry Martyn, Missionary to India and Persia, 1781 to 1812*. New York: F Q Books.

Sookhdeo, P. 2002. *A People Betrayed: The Impact of Islamisation on the Christian Community in Pakistan*. UK: Isaac Publishing.

Strickland, W. 2001. *The Jesuit in India*. Charleston, South Carolina: Nabu Press.

Stock, E. 1913. *An Heroic Bishop: The Life-Story of French of Lahore*. Toronto: Hodder and Stoughton.

Zafar, E. 2007. *A Concise History of Pakistani Christians*. Pakistan: Hamsakhoon Publications.

CHAPTER 30

# The Episcopal Church in the Philippines

## Mary Jane L. Dogue-is

The Anglican Church came to the Philippine islands with the American soldiers during the Spanish–American War in 1898. The phrase "the cross and the sword" is an apt description of how the Episcopal Church found its way to the Philippine islands. That same year, the first Episcopal service was held for American soldiers and other English-speaking people by an American chaplain. A service for a Filipino congregation followed a few months later. Lay members of the Brotherhood of Saint Andrew assisted the American chaplains in the early missionary work, laying the ground for the mission of the Episcopal Church. The 1901 General Convention of the PECUSA created the Philippines as a missionary district and consecrated the Rt. Rev. Charles Henry Brent as its first missionary bishop.

Bishop Brent arrived in the Philippines in 1902 primarily as a missionary to the American soldiers. Although the Americans in the Philippines were Brent's first concern, it was also his intention "to create a Christian influence on the colonial government" (Norbeck 1996). Bishop Brent had a policy of "no setting of altar against altar," and focused his missionary work on the tribal communities of the Muslims of Mindanao in the southern part of the country, the Chinese migrants of Manila – the capital city, and the "Igorots" of the mountains in the northern part of the region. According to the Most Rev. Edward Malecdan, the current primate and a historiographer of the province, these were "the people that had fought against the subjugation and rule of the colonial Spanish regime for over 300 years, and had not fallen under the rule of Spain" (Episcopal Church in the Philippines 2012). It was to these unconverted communities that the Episcopal Church pursued its mission, seeking new members through conversions and baptisms. The same policy explains why most members of the Episcopal Church and most of its clergy are from tribal communities.

*The Wiley-Blackwell Companion to the Anglican Communion*, First Edition. Edited by Ian S. Markham, J. Barney Hawkins IV, Justyn Terry, and Leslie Nuñez Steffensen.
© 2013 John Wiley & Sons, Ltd. Published 2013 by John Wiley & Sons, Ltd.

Bishop Brent's missionary vision was to establish churches, schools, and hospitals in key areas such as Manila, Sagada, Bontoc, Baguio, and Zamboanga. It is common knowledge among Filipino Episcopalians that it was the Episcopal Church that first built schools, hospitals, and even roads in many remote communities in the country. Bishop Brent and the early missionaries who left the comfort of their homeland to serve in an unknown world sowed the seed of the gospel in Philippine soil that has developed into the autonomous province of the Episcopal Church in the Philippines (ECP).

In less than 100 years, the ECP grew from being a missionary district to a diocese of the then PECUSA. The church in the Philippines was finally weaned from her mother church in 1990 and inaugurated as an autonomous province in the Anglican Communion bearing the name the "Episcopal Church in the Philippines". Currently, there are about 130,000 members spread out in the seven Episcopal dioceses: the Episcopal Diocese of Southern Philippines (EDSP), the newly created Episcopal Diocese of Davao (EDD), the Episcopal Diocese of Central Philippines (EDCP), the Episcopal Diocese of North Central Philippines (EDNCP), the Episcopal Diocese of Northern Philippines (EDNP), the Episcopal Diocese of Northern Luzon (EDNL), and the Episcopal Diocese of Santiago (EDS). Another diocese in the Visayas region is being conceptualized, beginning with a new congregation in the heart of the city. The ECP also has two area missions; one in London and overseeing the rest of Europe with a Filipino clergy as canon missioner, and the other is the Filipino–Aussie area mission in Sydney. This latter mission was recently turned over to the Archdiocese of Sydney.

Serving both church members and all Filipinos are Episcopal institutions that were established to address the spiritual, physical, and educational needs of the people. In the mission center in Cathedral Heights Quezon City are the National Cathedral of St. Mary and St. John, St. Luke's Medical Center (known to be one of the best healthcare providers in South East Asia), Trinity-St. Luke's College of Nursing, Trinity University in Asia, and Saint Andrew's Theological Seminary (the lone seminary in the ECP). Other church institutions include the schools under the umbrella of Brent International School Inc. These schools are spread out in the different dioceses: Baguio, Manila, Laguna, Subic, Zambales, and Boracay.

The Most Rev. Edward P. Malecdan, the current primate of the ECP, has recently led the whole church in crafting a new vision for its future. The church had accomplished the ECP Vision 2007 which stated that "the Episcopal Church in the Philippines shall be a renewed church, fully self-supporting and reaching out to proclaim God's love throughout the nation" (Episcopal Church in the Philippines 2012). The newly crafted ECP VISION 2018 and the previous vision are both founded on how mission is understood in the Anglican Communion and as stipulated in the five marks of mission. The Vision 2018 states that "by the year 2018, we envision a dynamic and vibrant church of caring, witnessing, and mission-oriented parishes." The primate has this beautiful elucidation of the ECP vision. He explains:

> the word "parishes" describe the spirituality and the values that self-supporting congregations should embrace. Our being caring, witnessing, and mission-oriented parishes should take us beyond the confines of our communities, as it commands us to reach out not only to those within the church but perhaps more especially to those who require spiritual

nurture, community empowerment, companionship in many forms, and perhaps other services that we may be capable of providing. (Malecdan 2009)

With Vision 2018 and the strong advocacy of human rights and social justice, the ECP is challenged and confident enough to pursue its mission "to declare with integrity the fulfilling of God's mission in this world, by proclaiming the Good News of the kingdom of God; baptizing, teaching, and nurturing new believers; responding to human needs with loving service; and seeking to transform unjust structures of society" (Episcopal Church in the Philippines 2012).

## Bibliography

Episcopal Church in the Philippines. 2012. History. The Episcopal Church in the Philippines Website. Accessed August 12, 2012. www.episcopalchurchphilippines.com/1ecp2/index.php/history.

Norbeck, Mark Douglas. 1996. The Legacy of Charles Henry Brent. *International Bulletin of Missionary Research*, vol. 20, no. 4, pp. 163–8. *ATLA Religion Database with ATLASerials*. Web. Accessed August 12, 2012.

Malecdan, Edward. 2009. Prime Bishop's Message: From Covenant to Companionship. *The Philippine Episcopalian: The National Publication of the Episcopal Church in the Philippines*. Third Quarter. Found at http://www.episcopalchurchphilippines.com/1ecp2/files/3rd_Quarter_200911.pdf.

# CHAPTER 31

# The Church of the Province of South East Asia

## Justyn Terry

## Introduction

The Province of South East Asia was formed by the Archbishop of Canterbury, the Most Rev. Dr George Carey, on February 2, 1996 (Province 2006, 10). It consists of four dioceses: the Dioceses of West Malaysia, Kuching, and Sabah in Malaysia and Brunei, and the Diocese of Singapore. The Diocese of Singapore also has responsibility for the mission work of the deaneries in Indonesia, Vietnam, Nepal, Laos, Thailand, and Cambodia, giving the province a very wide reach. The Most Rev. Dr. Moses Tay, Bishop of Singapore, was consecrated as the first metropolitan archbishop of the province in 1996. He was succeeded by the Most Rev. Datuk Yong Ping Chung, Bishop of Sabah, in February 2000, and then by the Most Rev. Dr. John Chew Hiang Chea, Bishop of Singapore, in February 2006 (Province 2006, 11). In February 2012, the Most Rev. Datuk Bolly Lapok, Bishop of Kuching, became the metropolitan archbishop.

## History of the Anglican Church in South East Asia

Anglicanism was first introduced into the region of South East Asia with the establishment of the British East India Company's settlement of Penang Island, Malaya, now West Malaysia, in 1786. George Caunter, a local magistrate, was appointed as Acting Chaplain in 1799, under the See of Calcutta, India. Its first chaplain was appointed in 1805. In 1819, the first Anglican Church building, St. George the Martyr, was consecrated by the Bishop of Calcutta, Thomas Fanshawe Middleton (Diocese of West Malaysia 2007).

*The Wiley-Blackwell Companion to the Anglican Communion*, First Edition. Edited by Ian S. Markham,
J. Barney Hawkins IV, Justyn Terry, and Leslie Nuñez Steffensen.
© 2013 John Wiley & Sons, Ltd. Published 2013 by John Wiley & Sons, Ltd.

Anglican settlers arrived with the British East India Company in Singapore in 1819 (Diocese of Singapore 2010). The Church of England chaplains were forbidden to work among the "natives." For that, missionaries were needed (Ho 1996, 262f), and the mission chapel of the London Missionary Society (LMS) started services in Singapore in 1826. The first church building in Singapore was built in 1837. In 1842, Mrs. Maria Dyer, a missionary of the LMS, started the first girls' school in Singapore, now known as St. Margaret's School, to rescue girls from slavery. The St. Andrew's Mission was formed in 1856, and in 1870, St. Andrew's Cathedral was consecrated (Diocese of Singapore 2010).

The Borneo Church Mission was established in England in 1846 to send Anglican missionaries to Borneo (Diocese of Kuching 2012). The work on the island of Borneo itself started on June 29, 1848, when two missionaries, Francis Thomas McDougall and W. B. White, were invited by James Brooke, the Rajah of Sarawak (Poon 2012). McDougall arrived in Kuching as a 31-year-old surgeon and priest (Province 2006, 16). He encountered great difficulties. The McDougall's lost five of their children, one after another. His wife, Harriette, wrote, "The flowers all died along our way" (Thompson 1951, 395). In 1849, a wooden church was built in Kuching on land provided by the rajah, which was consecrated by Daniel Wilson, Bishop of Calcutta, in 1851, in honor of St. Thomas the Apostle. It served as a pro-cathedral for many years (Diocese of Kuching 2012). A school was started that developed into St. Thomas's and St Mary's School. McDougall also started a dispensary (Diocese of Kuching 2012). Converts were slow in coming, but in 1851 reinforcements arrived, and on September 7 that year, McDougall was able to admit the first five converts to Holy Communion (Neill 1986, 246).

A large part of McDougall's work was to provide chaplaincy to the European expatriates, but work was also begun among the Hakka Christians from Hong Kong and China. He wanted to use Labuan as a base to reach out to the Dusuns in the interior. On home leave in England in 1852, Francis McDougall spoke all over the country about his work, and Harriette sold 3,000 copies of her *Letters from Sarawak* (Thompson 1951, 395). Scores of missionaries were inspired to follow in McDougall's footsteps, some coming as deacons or priests, others as teachers (catechists) and medical personnel. Many of them were sent by the Society for the Propagation of the Gospel (SPG), which took over the work of the Borneo Church Mission in 1853 (Ward 2006, 268), while others were sent by the Church Missionary Society (CMS) (Diocese of Sabah 2010).

In the early 1950s, mission work began among the people in the interior of Sabah. Bruce Sandilands was a government surveyor. During his many trips to the jungle of Sabah (then North Borneo), he saw the needs of the local people for healthcare, education, and the gospel. He shared his concern with his priest in Sandakan, Fr. Frank Lomax. In 1956, they made a trip up the Kinabatangan River. They returned with a determination to start ministry among the people they met. The Sabah Anglican Interior Mission (SAIM) was born. Its specific task was to share the love of God in Jesus Christ with the people in the interior of Sabah. On January 6, 1958, the Epiphany Mission was officially opened in Tongud by Bishop Nigel Cornwall. Later, mission work began along the Labuk, Segama, and Sugut rivers. In the next 40 years, many people were baptized, churches were planted, and church workers were raised up. A large part of the Diocese of Sabah today consists of Christians and their churches in the interior of Sabah (Diocese of Sabah 2010).

The See of Calcutta extended from India to New Zealand and was unwieldy to manage. In 1855, the Diocese of Singapore, Labuan and Sarawak was created by Letters Patent to provide better administration for these outlying areas. The new diocese became a missionary diocese of the Archdiocese of Canterbury (Walters 2008, 74). McDougall was consecrated as the first bishop on October 18 of that year. He was also appointed the Bishop of Sarawak by the Rajah of Sarawak. In the political conventions of the day, no Anglican Diocese could be created outside of the British Empire, and Sarawak was then technically an independent kingdom. This practice continued until Sarawak became a Crown colony in 1946. In 1909, the united diocese was further divided into the Diocese of Singapore, the Diocese of Labuan, and the Bishopric of Sarawak. They developed independently from then onwards until the creation of the province.

The East India Company transferred Penang to the British Crown in 1867 and with that ended the chaplaincy of the Madras Presidency in Penang. The Anglican churches in Penang, Malacca, and Singapore were organized into the Church in the Straits Settlement while still under the jurisdiction of the See of Calcutta. At this time, the SPG began to take an active role in procuring chaplains for the Crown in its colonies. It led to a period of great missionary activity in the new diocese at a time of Chinese and Indian immigration (Diocese of West Malaysia 2007). The Constitution of the Synod of the Diocese of Kuching reflects on those early years: "The first sixty years of the Church in Borneo are a chronicle of heroic effort, much disappointment, long, faithful and lonely service by priests and lay missionaries. Asian workers played an increasing part, as the formation of a truly indigenous church had been intended from the beginning" (Diocese of Kuching 2012).

Between the division of the united diocese and the outbreak of World War II in the Pacific, missionary work continued. Increasing numbers of local clergy were ordained, and churches planted throughout Malaya and Singapore. Throughout the duration of World War II, most of the expatriate clergy and missionaries were interred by the Japanese, who occupied the peninsula between 1941 and 1945. The work of the church then fell on the shoulders of local clergy and church workers. Despite the great hardships and the war-time atrocities, Christian witness continued to thrive. Interracial services were held for the first time (Ward 2006, 269). Bishop Leonard Wilson proved a great example of godly leadership in a difficult season (Sng 2003, 194–7). It became clear that indigenous leaders urgently needed training for this developing part of the Anglican Church. Out of a discussion begun in the Changi prison by leaders of the Anglican, Methodist, and Presbyterian churches, a plan was hatched to create a theological college to train local men and women for service in the church. This led to the establishment of Singapore's Trinity Theological College in 1948, supported initially by the Anglican, Methodist, and Presbyterian churches (Sng 2003, 201).

There was a great deal of rebuilding to do after World War II. The Diocese of Labuan and the Bishopric of Sarawak were joined into the Diocese of Borneo, and Nigel Cornwall was consecrated bishop on November 1, 1949. His first task was to restore the ruins of churches, schools, and other mission property. The new St. Thomas's Cathedral was constructed in 1953 to replace the leaky, wooden edifice built by McDougall. The House of Epiphany provided nine new priests in 1956. By 1962, the Diocese of Borneo could be divided into the new Diocese of Jesselton (later called the Diocese of Sabah 2010), including Labuan, which came into being on July 24, 1962, and the remainder of the diocese, including Brunei, was reconstituted as the Diocese of Kuching on August 13, 1962. Nigel Cornwall continued as bishop (Diocese of Kuching 2012).

Malaya gained independence from British rule in 1957. In 1960, the diocese was renamed the Diocese of Singapore and Malaya. On September 16, 1963, the 11 states of the Malay Peninsula and the two states of Sarawak and Sabah, which gained independence from the British on August 31, 1963, was renamed Malaysia. Singapore was then a state of Malaysia but became independent on August 9, 1965. Then, in 1971, the churches in West Malaysia were separated from the diocese and reconstituted as the Diocese of West Malaysia by an Act of the Malaysian Parliament, and the diocese was renamed the Diocese of Singapore (Diocese of West Malaysia 2007).

These are the dioceses that came together as the Province of South East Asia in 1996. As we shall see in the following text, they have continued to grow and develop.

## The Story of the Contemporary Church

Since the formation of the province in 1996, much work has been done to consolidate and to equip the province for its life and mission. It promulgated its provincial canons in 1998, and published its provincial prayer book and song book in 1999 (Province 2006, 11). The Provincial Youth Network (PYNET) was set up to encourage the youth of the dioceses to fellowship, grow, and serve together (Province 2006, 11). In order to address the vast missionary challenge of reaching nine countries, the first archbishop, the Most Rev. Dr. Moses Tay, also set up the Province of South East Asia Mission Services (PROSEAMS) (Province 2006, 22).

This mission-minded approach has borne considerable fruit. Today, there are over 200,000 Anglicans out of an estimated population of 360 million in the province (Anglican Communion News 2000). Each of the four dioceses has experienced significant growth over recent years. The Diocese of West Malaysia reports the following:

> The Lord is a faithful God! Home to the oldest Anglican Church in South East Asia – St Georges Church, Penang (completed in 1818) – the Diocese West Malaysia still throbs with the life of our Lord Jesus Christ. In the cities as well as the rural villages, the Spirit is moving among His people. Historic churches are being renewed, established parishes are deepening and widening, new workers are being raised up and sent into the harvest field. The Gospel is being preached at new mission centres, souls are being won to Christ and new communities of faith are springing up where there were none before! Praise be to God! (Province 2006, 12)

The Diocese of Sabah reports very substantial growth:

> The past 15 years in the Diocese of Sabah have been years of exciting growth in the life and mission of the Church. We praise God that from 1990 to 2002, under the theme of

"Mission 113" focusing on evangelism, discipleship and church planting, the average Sunday attendance grew by more than 270% or 22.5% per year. This happened both in the urban churches as well as the rural ones, both English-speaking and otherwise. All glory to the God in salvation, who is not willing for *"anyone to perish, but everyone to come to repentance"* (2 Peter 3:9)! (Province 2006, 14)

It has also been a time of developing new leadership:

Not only did the church grow in attendance, God also raised up more clergy and laity to serve in the ministry, from 22 in 1990 to 102 in 2005. Significantly, in recent years, Sabah Diocese committed two missionaries to the overseas mission field, and look forward to even more in the near future. (Province 2006, 14)

The Diocese of Kuching enjoyed significant growth and consolidation in the first ten years of the province. They have had the joy seeing an average of about 4,000 candidates confirmed every year.

The last 10 years have seen the creation of three new parishes in our diocese namely: Siol Kandis, Engkilili and Lutong, and the construction of newer and bigger churches at Bintulu, Saratok, Serian and Batu Kawa. Many new chapels or extension centres have also been built to serve the kampongs and longhouses. (Province 2006, 16)

Eddie Ong ascribes this growth to three main factors: the external vulnerability to Islamization which has strengthened their sense of commitment to the Christian faith, charismatic renewal, and the family unity that the church enjoys (Ong 1998, 174ff).

The Diocese of Singapore likewise characterizes the first ten years in the province by "quantitative and qualitative growth" (Province 2006, 18). James Wong, writing about the church in Singapore, points out that in 1820 the percentage of Christians in Singapore was essentially zero. By the year 1900, it was approximately 1 percent of the population and, by the year 1990, it was approximately 15 percent of the population (Wong 1996, 305). He attributes this growth particularly to the charismatic renewal in the Anglican Church in the 1970s, the role of the Full Gospel Business Men's Fellowship and Women's Aglow, and policies aimed to evangelize and promote church growth. He also notes the importance of leadership training programs by the Fellowship of Evangelical Students, Campus Crusade, Navigators, Youth for Christ, and Youth with a Mission (Wong 1996, 300–7).

The Province of South East Asia has been very active in its social outreach. The Diocese of Singapore reports that it has strengthened its community service arm. It opened St Andrew's Centre in Tanjong Pagar, and remade the Singapore Anglican Welfare Council into the Singapore Anglican Community Services. It has built the St. Andrew's Community Hospital, the Hougang and Simei Care Centres for mental and psychiatric rehabilitation, as well as the St. George's Crisis Shelter, St. Andrew's Lifestreams counseling service, and the St. Andrew's Autism Center, which is an integrated and comprehensive facility serving people with Autism Spectrum Disorder (Province 2006, 18).

The Diocese of West Malaysia has recently opened a retirement home. It also runs a home for the visually impaired, an early intervention program, a food shelter, and several centers for hope and community care (Diocese West Malaysia). The Diocese of Sabah runs three preschools, eight primary schools, five secondary schools, and three academies (Diocese of Sabah 2010). The Diocese of Kuching reports working closely with Singapore to reach out to the needy in West Kalimantan of Indonesia. "As most of the tribal groups across the border from Sarawak speak the same local dialects, we are encouraging parishes to do cross-border outreach to the Dayak people" (Province 2006, 17).

The dioceses of the Province of South East Asia not only operate in close relation with one another, they are also connected with the wider Anglican Communion and with the worldwide Church. The province has been active in the work of the global south of the Anglican Communion. It hosted the second South to South Encounter in Kuala Lumpur in June 1997, and took an active role in the third Encounter in Egypt in October 2005 (Province 2006, 11). More controversially, Archbishop Tay, along with Archbishop Kolini of Rwanda, was involved with the consecration of Chuck Murphy and John Rodgers as bishops for the Anglican Mission in America on January 29, 2000, at St. Andrew's Cathedral, Singapore. This was in response to what were regarded as major theological and moral innovations in the Episcopal Church USA, and the Anglican Church of Canada.

The four dioceses participate in the ecumenical World Council of Churches via their respective national church councils: Council of Churches of Malaysia, for the Diocese of Kuching, Diocese of Sabah, and Diocese of West Malaysia, and the National Council of Churches of Singapore, for the Diocese of Singapore. Unlike many other Anglican churches, however, the Church of the Province of South East Asia is not a member of the World Council of Churches in its own right.

## Contemporary Issues Facing the Province

In *Christianities in Asia*, Edmund Kee-Fook Chia helpfully summarizes the challenges facing the Church in Malaysia and Singapore under the following headings: the challenge of an indigenous church, the challenge of Islamization, the challenge of ecumenism, and the challenge of church–state relations (Chia 2011, 84ff). Since Chia uses the term "ecumenism" to include inter-religious relations, we shall expand the title of this third category to make that clear.

### The challenge of an indigenous church

Chia points out that the first local bishop of the Anglican Diocese of West Malaysia was Roland Koh, who was elected in 1970. He also points out that there has been a history of the condescending attitude towards those from indigenous communities, and that use of the *Bahasa Melayu* (the Malay language) has been controversial from the start (Chia 2011, 84).

The complex mixture of cultures in South East Asia increases the challenge of forming an indigenous church there. For many, being Malay has become synonymous with being Muslim. Reaching out with the gospel of Jesus Christ to them will require attentiveness to their own culture. The Chinese Christians in the South East Asian Church have been influenced by Confucian, Buddhist, or Taoist backgrounds, whereas the Indian Christians tend to have Hindu, Sikh, or Jain backgrounds (Chia 2011, 85). Some have come out of animism, making the question of ancestor veneration important. So it is not a matter of adapting to one particular culture, but of reaching out to a cluster of very different cultures and seeking to draw a unity around the good news of Jesus Christ.

A recent study by Jonathan Wong identified the need for the church in Singapore to reach out more to the Chinese-speaking population. He recommends that it should do so by developing a more contextual theology. He calls for a prolegomena to be outlined for such a theology. It would need to examine the basis for its formulation and seek to justify the use of Chinese philosophical concepts for this work. One such concept is the Daoist, *Wu-wei* ("doing nothing"), which Wong sees as a potential parallel to Martin Luther's concept of passive righteousness (Wong 2008, 7). Such careful theological work will no doubt be necessary if this evangelistic task is to be properly fulfilled.

### The challenge of Islamization

The Constitution of Malaysia states that Islam is the official religion of the nation, but it also provides freedom of religion so that the interreligious relations may be peaceful. There are, however, strong pressures for a more explicitly Islamic state, especially from the Pan Malaysian Islamic Party, or PAS (Chia 2011, 85). A policy of Islamization was implemented in 1983, and since then Christian schools, some of which have been in existence for more than a century, are slowly being phased out as the government introduces Islamic education. Christians also have difficulty procuring land to build churches or for Christian burial grounds. Good Friday is no longer a public holiday. There are laws to guard against proselytizing Muslims. Some 25 words and ten expressions in Bahasa Malayasian are not allowed to be used by non-Muslims. Principal amongst these are: *Allah* (God), *injil* (gospel), *nabi* (prophet), *wahyu* (revelation), *insyallah* (God-willing), and *assailaimalaikun* (peace be to you) (Ho 1996, 266). Malay and Iban translations of the Bible are forbidden, although where the faith of Islam is not under threat these laws are seldom enforced. Evangelistic materials need to carry the warning, "For non-Muslims only" (Chia 2011, 86f).

### The challenge of Ecumenism and inter–religious relations

Christians represent 9.4 percent of the population of Malaysia (Johnstone 2010, 556). Generally speaking, they relate well to their Muslim, Buddhist, Hindu, and other neighbors. Over the years, members of different churches have come together with Christians of other denominations. In 1948, the Malayan Christian Council (MCC) was formed.

It included Anglicans, Methodists, Presbyterians, Mar Thoma, Syrian Orthodox, Lutherans, Salvation Army, and Brethren, as well as interdenominational organized nations
like the YMCA, YWCA, and the Bible Society. The MCC was renamed the Council of
Churches in Malaya and Singapore in 1961. Then, in 1974, it became two separate
councils: the Council of Churches in Malaysia (CCM) and the National Council of
Churches of Singapore (NCCS). In 1986, the CCM joined the National Evangelical Fellowship (NEF) and the Roman Catholic Church to form the Christian Federation of
Malaysia (CFM) (Chia 2011, 87). The churches are seeing each other increasingly as
partners rather than competitors (Ho 1996, 280). This is an important positive sign
for future mission (Kham 2003, 57).

One of the challenges currently facing the church in Malaysia is whether the Christians will be able to draw together people from so many different cultural and religious
backgrounds into one unified church (Ho 1996, 279). Bishop Stephen Neill has
expressed optimism about this. "If there is any place in the world where there is a case
for a united church, if it can be obtained without sacrifice of principle, it would seem
to be Malaya [West Malaysia]." (Neill 1965, 356).

There have also been some important initiatives to make formal relations with other
religious bodies. Several religious groups came together to inaugurate the Malaysian
Consultative Council for Buddhism, Christianity, Hinduism, and Sikhism (MCCBCHS)
in 1982. The Taoist community has also recently joined it. The council is acknowledged
to be the institution that speaks on behalf of the non-Muslims in Malaysia, and has
been able to speak out against policies that promote Islamization (Chia 2011, 87).

Despite the challenges faced by the Church in Malaysia, it has been clear about the
uniqueness of the person and work of Jesus Christ. Christians do not force others to
adapt to this view, but they do want to have the right and the freedom to express it, and
they are willing to reciprocate with people of other faiths (Ho 1996, 277f). It is very
important that care be taken with attitudes toward those of other religions. As Bishop
Roland Koh put it, "superiority and mere condemnation of other religions" harden the
hearts of many against Christianity (O'Connor et al. 2000, 183). Another of the challenges for the church identified by Ho is that of Christians simply keeping quiet about
their faith. The call to evangelism needs to be made afresh today, not only for corporate
outreach events, but also for personal evangelism (Ho 1996, 283f).

## The challenge of Church–State relations

The powerful governments in both Malaysia and Singapore have presented challenges
to the churches in these lands. Christian leaders have found themselves sometimes
having to choose between confronting the power of the state and the survival of their
churches. Urbanization in Malaysia has brought problems of inadequate housing and
infrastructure to cope with the influx of people. There also the problems of alienation,
powerlessness, loneliness, and displacement (Ho 1996, 280). Ann reports that Singapore faced the challenge of an economic downturn at the start of the new millennium,
and needed to address the problem of poverty (Ann 2000, 30f). Since then, the economy
has done well, but the distribution of wealth has remained uneven. Many Christians in

both countries have learned that it is safer to take a pro-government position. This has meant that they have been less free to operate prophetically in the nation (Chia 2011, 90). James Wong wants to stress how important it is that the church still speaks out in Singapore:

> [T]here is a great need in two areas which the Church can play a greater role – in its social service and as a prophetic voice to the nation. There are issues and developments in the nation which challenge the Church to be more proactive. A Christian response to the socio-economic and political arenas will help the Church to be more relevant and visible in national life. (Wong 1996, 307)

## Conclusion

As we have seen, the Province of South East Asia serves a large number of complex communities made up of people from enormously diverse backgrounds. We have also noted that the church in Malaysia and Singapore faces many substantial challenges. Yet, despite all that, the growth of the church in the province is exceptional. The British theologian and evangelist Michael Green sought to capture some of the lessons for the wider church in his book *Asian Tigers for Christ: The Dynamic Growth of the Church in South East Asia.* He focuses mainly, but not exclusively, on the Diocese of Singapore.

The first lesson to learn from the province, according to Green, is the importance of the appointment of an indigenous bishop. He points out that Bishop Chiu gave outstanding leadership. In his inaugural sermon, he stressed ideas that clearly proved fruitful. He looked for growth in prayer, evangelism, witness, and service (Green 2001, 4). The second is the stress on the Bible. Bishop Chiu made biblical literacy a priority and secured the assistance of Bishop Stephen Neill to provide an overview of the Bible and to equip Bible study leaders. The third lesson is the importance of strong youth work. In 1970, young people comprised 54 percent of the population of Singapore, 21 percent of those being between the ages of 12 and 21 years. To reach out to these young people with the gospel was an urgent priority, and has been treated as such. A fourth lesson is that of the ecumenical impetus that was gained by following the 1968 Lambeth Conference decision to open Holy Communion to those who were "duly baptized in the name of the Holy Trinity and qualified to receive Holy Communion in their own churches" (Green 2001, 5). Lastly, there is the importance of openness to the work of the Holy Spirit. Bishop Chiu read Dennis Bennett's *Nine O'clock in the Morning*, and prayed for the Holy Spirit to fill his life. He wrote afterwards, "When I woke up I was conscious of a great difference within me. God was suddenly very close. My heart was filled with life, joy and peace instead of anger, despair and gloom. I burst out with praise and thanked God through Jesus Christ" (Green 2001, 7). This led to a major renewal of his ministry. His successor and the first Archbishop of South East Asia, the Most Rev. Dr. Moses Tay, carried on in a similar direction. He emphasized the importance of well-trained and Spirit-filled leadership, mission and evangelism, community involvement, and holding strong convictions about the faith (Green 2001, 7–23), which was not just for the Diocese of Singapore, but for the whole province.

There are, no doubt, many other lessons that the wider church can learn from the Province of South East Asia, and Michael Green draws out many more in his book. Nevertheless, what we do see in this short overview is that a recently birthed province, focused on the scriptures, prayer, and the transforming life of the Holy Spirit, can promote vibrant witness even in difficult circumstances. This is evident in growing churches, people being won to Jesus Christ, and advances in social justice. There is, no doubt, still much to do. However, there is already a great deal for which to give thanks to God in this young province of the Anglican Communion.

## Bibliography

Anglican Communion News. 2000. Available at www.anglicancommunion.org/acns/news.cfm/2000/2/24/ACNS2044.

Ann, Lee Soon. 2000. The Church and Her Social Responsibility. *The Christian Church in 21st Century Singapore*, ed. Isaac Lim. Singapore: Millennium Publication of the National Council of Churches.

Chia, Edmund Kee-Fook. 2011. Malaysia and Singapore. *Christianities in Asia*, ed. Phan, Peter C. Phan. Chichester, UK: Wiley-Blackwell.

Diocese of Kuching. 2012. History. Available at kuching.anglican.org/main.htm, as of June 2012.

Diocese of Sabah. 2010. History. Available at www.anglicansabah.org/2010.1/aboutus.htm.

Diocese of Singapore. 2010. History. Available at http://www.anglican.org.sg/index.php/blog/comments/history, as of November 29, 2010.

Diocese of West Malaysia. 2007. History. Available at www.anglicanwestmalaysia.org.my/sub_page.aspx?catID=1&ddlID=36.

Green, Michael. 2001. *Asian Tigers for Christ: The Dynamic Growth of the Church in South East Asia*. London: SPCK.

Ho, Daniel K. C. 1996. The Church in Malaysia. *Church in Asia Today: Challenges and Opportunities*, ed. Saphir Athyal. Singapore: Asia Lausanne Committee for World Evangelization.

Kham, Chin Do. 2003. Partnership Issues and Challenges in Asian Mission. *Asian Church and God's Mission*, ed. Wonsuk and Julie C. Ma. Manila: OMF.

Neill, Stephen. 1965. *Anglicanism*, 3rd ed. London: Penguin.

Neill, Stephen. 1986. *A History of Christian Missions*, 2nd ed. London: Penguin.

Johnstone, Patrick. 2010. *Operation World*, 7th ed. Colorado Springs, CO.: Biblio Publishing.

O'Connor, Daniel, and others. 2000. *Three Centuries of Mission: The United Society for the Propagation of the Gospel 1701–2000*. London and New York: Continuum.

Ong, Eddie. 1998. Anglicanism in West Malaysia. *Anglicanism: A Global Communion*. New York: Church House Publishing.

Province of the Anglican Church in South East Asia. 2006. *Putting Our Hands to the Plough: The Province of the Anglican Church in South East Asia 10th Anniversary*. The Province of the Anglican Church in South East Asia.

Poon, Michael. 2012. *CSCA Society for the Propagation of the Gospel Archives on Borneo Mission. A Guide*. Available at www.ttc.edu.sg/csca/rart_doc/ang/spg.html, as of June 2012.

Sng, Bobby E. K. 2003. *In His Good Time: The Story of the Church in Singapore 1819–2002*, 3rd ed. Singapore: Bible Society of Singapore.

Thompson, H. P. 1951. *Into All Lands: The History of the Society for the Propagation of the Gospel in Foreign Parts, 1701–1950*. London: SPCK.

Walters, Albert Sundararaj. 2008. Anglican National Identity: Theological Education and Ministerial Formation in Multifaith Malaysia. *Journal of Anglican Studies*, vol. 6, no. 1, pp. 69–87.

Ward, Kevin. 2006. *A History of Global Anglicanism*. Cambridge: Cambridge University Press.

Wong, James. 1996. The Church in Singapore. *Church in Asia Today: Challenges and Opportunities*, ed. Saphir Athyal. Singapore: Asia Lausanne Committee for World Evangelization.

Wong, Jonathan. 2008. Contextualizing an Asian Evangelical Theology: A Prolegomena for the Church in Singapore. MDiv Thesis. Ambridge, PA: Trinity School for Ministry.

CHAPTER 32

# The Church of South India (United)

## Ian S. Markham

India is one of the most interesting countries in the world. It is the cradle of a great civilization that birthed the religions of Hinduism, Buddhism, Sikhism, and many more. It has a developing middle class as the economy starts to develop. It also has major challenges – poverty, population growth, and pollution. And it is a major geopolitical crossroads in the world.

According to the World Bank in 2012, the population of India is 1,214,491,960. According to the Ministry of Home Affairs in India, the population divides into the following religions: 80.5 percent Hindus, 13.4 percent Muslims, 2.3 percent Christians, and 1.9 percent Sikhs (Government of India 2012). The percentage of Christians might be small, but numerically it is still 24 million Christians. The majority of these Christians are Roman Catholics, but the next largest grouping is the Church of South India (United) (CSI).

## History

It was on December 31, 1600, that the English East India Company received a charter from Queen Elizabeth I, granting them exclusive British trade rights in Asia. This charter also included a commission that obligated the company to ensure that "prayers be said every morning and evening in every ship, and the whole company . . . may jointly with reverence and humility pray unto Almighty God to bless and preserve them from all the dangers in this long and tedious voyage" (Gibbs 1972, 3). This meant the initial Anglican presence was primarily linked with trade and with evangelical chaplains.

Much of the developments in India were linked with the legislation around the East India Company. Although, in 1858, sovereignty of India was under the British monarch,

*The Wiley-Blackwell Companion to the Anglican Communion*, First Edition. Edited by Ian S. Markham,
J. Barney Hawkins IV, Justyn Terry, and Leslie Nuñez Steffensen.
© 2013 John Wiley & Sons, Ltd. Published 2013 by John Wiley & Sons, Ltd.

the company's charter was reviewed every decade (and later every 20 years). It was the charter which determined whether missionaries had unhindered access to India. And there were opponents to mission, who feared that overt Christian missions would damage the trading relationship with the colony. Indeed, Lord Macaulay in 1835 wrote: "We abstain, and I trust shall always abstain, from giving any public encouragement to those who are in any way engaged in the work of converting natives to Christianity" (Harper 2000, 97).

It was William Wilberforce who led the campaign for the East India charter allowing missionary activity. On April 13, 1813, as a Member of Parliament, "Wilberforce made one of the greatest speeches of his career" (Gibbs 1972, 49). It is an interesting speech: he stressed the practices in India which, in his view, needed Christianity as the remedy. The caste system, polygamy, status of Indian women, the practice of infanticide, and the practice of widows leaping on the funeral pyre after their husbands had died. Wilberforce concluded, "Nothing but the absolute proof of the incompatibility with British rule in India could justify if at all the withholding of Christianity" (Gibbs 1972, 49). It was this legislation that led to the first appointment of a bishop. Gibbs helpfully summarizes the relevant section:

> One Bishoprick for the whole of the said British Territories in the East Indies and Parts aforesaid . . . and three archdeacons, one for each Presidency, with salaries to be paid out of the local revenues of £5000 a year for the bishop and £2000 a year for each archdeacon (Gibbs 1972, 51).

This was crucial legislation. This meant the British were in India. They were creating a structure to ensure the growth of Anglicanism in India. And they were opposed to various aspects of the indigenous culture.

Once the structure was in place, the country was opened to missionaries. The missionary groups started their work. They were led by the Church Missionary Society (CMS) and the Society for the Propagation of the Gospel (SPG). The first two CMS missionaries from England (there had been others from Germany) were Thomas Norton and William Greenwood. Thomas worked in Alleppey, while Greenwood started in Bengal. Much of the initial development of the church was in northern India.

Although an Anglican presence has been identified in Madras since 1647 (a chaplain from a ship celebrated the Eucharist at Fort St. George), it was not until 1815 that St. George's Church was built. And on October 28, 1835, Daniel Corrie was consecrated bishop and enthroned in St. George's Church (see Gibbs 1972, 133). This has been a pivotal diocese for South India. Some of the bishops anticipated its ecumenical future. So, for example, Bishop George Spencer, who became bishop in 1838, was responsible for ordaining Methodist and Congregational missionaries (Church of South India, Diocese of Madras 2012).

Interestingly, it was not until 1955 that the Diocese of Madras had its first Indian bishop, David Chellappa (bishop from 1955 to his death in 1964). The first Indian bishop in South India was Bishop V. S. Azariah, who was consecrated on December 29, 1912, at the young age of 38, for the new Diocese of Dornakal. Azariah lived through a dramatic period of Indian history. He was "influenced by, and felt broad sympathy for, the growing aspirations of his countrymen for freedom and self-determination" (Harper 2000, 354). Yet, as Susan Harper notes, his primary concerns were more with autonomy in ecclesiastical matters rather than with explicitly leading the charge on political independence. He tended to avoid the nationalist political movements in his country. Primarily, Azariah saw himself as a pastor to a flock and a leader in planting congregations: he did not see himself as a politician. He did lead the way in terms of teaching villagers songs in their own language about various Christian themes.

The fact that Gandhi considered "Azariah to be his 'Enemy Number One'" (Harper 2000, 7) reflects the difficult time this was for the Anglican Church in India. Although he was sympathetic to the nationalist movement, he was not considered sufficiently so. Yet, this spirit of nationalism did shape the CSI. As the church in India reflected on its needs, an ecumenical movement emerged which had a dramatic impact on the global church. It was the most successful and controversial ecumenical project ever. This resulted in the creation in 1947 of the CSI.

## The CSI

The emergence of the united church was a major issue. The Anglicans joined the Methodists and the South India United Church to form one church. It was an historic, dramatic, and controversial moment.

It was at St. George's Church in Madras, on September 27, 1947, that Bishop Chirakarottu Korula Jacob said the following:

> Dearly beloved brethren, in obedience to the Lord Jesus Christ, the Head of the Church, Who, on the night of His Passion, prayed that His Disciples might be one; and the by the authority of the governing bodies of the uniting Churches, whose resolutions have been read in your hearing and laid in prayer before Almighty God; I do hereby declare that these three Churches, namely: the Madras, Travancore and Cochin, Tinnevelly and Dornakal Diocese of the Church of India, Burma and Ceylon; the Madras, Madura, Malabar, Jaffna, Kannada, Telugu and Travancore Church Councils of the South India United Church; and the Methodist Church in South India, comprising the Madras, Trichinopoly, Hyderabad and Mysore Districts; are become one Church of South India, and that those bishops, presbyters, deacons and probationers who have assented to the basis of the Union and accepted the Constitution of the Church of South India and whose names are laid upon this holy table, are bishops, presbyters and deacons in this Church: in the name of the Father, and of the Son, and of the Holy Spirit. Amen

Naturally, there are many issues that emerge when three different polities come together. The various parties involved in this project worked hard to resolve the key questions. It is clear that there was considerable respect of the different views taken by different groups. There was also a strong desire, initially, to enable all members of the independent bodies to enjoy the services they were already familiar with. Dammers, an astute observer of the early days, describes the impact of the merger on the service on the

Eucharist when he notes that the differences between the English Book of Common Prayer and CSI liturgy were two principles:

> The first principle is a return to the Bible. The second principle is the participation of the whole congregation in the words and action of the Sacrament. . . . In the C.S.I. Liturgy, the Comfortable Words are placed between the Confession and the Absolution. Thus, after the Confession, the biblical basis of our belief in God's forgiveness is first declared as the necessary prelude to the presbyter's declaration of that forgiveness in the Absolution (Dammers 1958, 23).

Another rather attractive feature of the new church was the use of each other's resources. Dammers writes: "Such another gift is the Methodist Hymn Book" (Dammers 1958, 18). This was a time when resources across the traditions were shared to mutual benefit.

The best defense of the entire scheme is probably Leslie Newbigin's *The Reunion of the Church*. He was very close to the action (Newbigin 1960). And the revised edition is especially interesting. The first edition was tentative in its support; the second explains that the results on the ground have been so impressive. In the end, the challenges facing India need a united church. One cannot work in a setting of so much poverty as a small percentage of the total population without unity. It is almost as if disagreements between denominations are a luxury of affluence.

## Conclusion

There were plenty of skeptics about the united church. However, all the prophecies of failure have been refuted. The CSI is a remarkable success story within the communion. It is continuing to grow. The service in terms of hospitals and especially schools (which number over 10,000) is remarkable. Like Anglicans elsewhere in the world, the CSI is having a dramatic impact on society – well beyond its numerical numbers. For this gift to the region, the CSI is to be admired.

### Bibliography

Church of South India, Diocese of Madras. 2012. http://www.csimadrasdiocese.org/history.php accessed August 2012.

Dammers, A. H. 1958. *Great Venture: The Church of South India in Action*. London: The Highway Press.

Gibbs, M. E. 1972. *The Anglican Church in India 1600–1970*. New Delhi: ISPCK.

Government of India. 2012. Ministry of Home Affairs Website. Accessed August 2012. http://censusindia.gov.in/Census_And_You/religion.aspx.

Harper, Susan Billington. 2000. *In the Shadow of the Mahatma: Bishop V. S. Azariah and the Travails of Christianity in British India*. Grand Rapids, Michigan: Eerdmans.

Newbigin, J. E. Lesslie. 1960. *The Reunion of the Church: A Defence of the South India Scheme*, revised edition. London: SCM Press.

CHAPTER 33

# The Church of Ceylon (Extra-Provincial to the Archbishop of Canterbury)

## Duleep de Chickera

## Background

Sri Lanka (SL), known earlier as Amradipa, Taprobane, and then Ceylon, (Vimalananda 1970), is a small pearl-shaped island situated south of India, in the Indian Ocean. It is home to a population of over 20 million people, most of whom would claim allegiance with one of its four world religions. These religions were introduced by recurring waves of pilgrims, traders, missionaries, and invaders (Beven 1946). Buddhism is the majority religion, with Hinduism, Islam, and Christianity following in that order. Roman Catholicism is the largest Christian denomination, and Anglicanism comes next. An indigenous people pre-dates the arrival of these religions but has been assimilated into the dominant ethno-religious cultures.

## Early Beginnings

The earliest recorded presence of Christianity is of a sixth-century Persian Nestorian Community, including a presbyter and deacon, which lived in the north central province of the country and then petered out. A sixth-century Persian cross, embossed on rock, is today the emblem of the Church of Ceylon (CoC) (Fernando, C. 1948–1951). European colonization since the sixteenth century by the Portuguese, the Dutch, and the British, chronologically in that order, over a collective period of 450 years, led first to the occupation of the maritime areas and finally the whole island (Mendis 1932).

Anglicanism was introduced to SL in 1799 with the arrival of colonial chaplains, sent to serve the religious interests of the British colonial establishment. It was with the

*The Wiley-Blackwell Companion to the Anglican Communion*, First Edition. Edited by Ian S. Markham, J. Barney Hawkins IV, Justyn Terry, and Leslie Nuñez Steffensen.
© 2013 John Wiley & Sons, Ltd. Published 2013 by John Wiley & Sons, Ltd.

arrival of missionaries of the Church Missionary Society (CMS), the United Society for the Propagation of the Gospel (USPG), and the Zenana Missionary Society (ZMS), from the second decade of the nineteenth century, however, that Anglicanism took root among the indigenous population. These missionaries lived with the people, preached the gospel, built schools and churches, studied Buddhism and Hinduism, and translated the Bible into the Sinhala and Tamil languages. They also pioneered education for girls and groomed Sri Lankans for positions of leadership (Balding 1922).

Two women who are still household names stand out among these missionaries: Muriel Hutchins (CMS), who set up Karuna Nilayam (translated as "house of mercy"), a home for deprived girls in underdeveloped Kilinochchi in the northern province (Selvathurai nd), and Evelyn Karney (ZMS), who served the people of Talawa, a malaria-stricken village in the north central province and provided a safe home "House of Joy," for girls (Brohier nd). Both women imbibed the local cultures and generated hope and dignity among those they cared for. Their work continues to this day as a testimony to their compassion for the vulnerable.

Initially, Episcopal care of the Anglican community was from London, Calcutta, and Madras, chronologically in that order. The Diocese of Colombo (DoC) was established in 1845, with James Chapman as its first bishop. He was the ideal pioneer for the new diocese, traveling extensively and bringing cohesion to a scattered diocese. He also established a school for clergy training, St. Thomas' College for boys and Bishops College for girls, and built the first cathedral (Beven 1946). Much later, the late Cyril Abeynaike, tenth Bishop of Colombo and a saintly scholar, similarly steered the diocesan educational policy through difficult days, contributed immensely toward clergy formation, and completed the building of the new cathedral. The Diocese of Kurunegala (DoK) was founded as a missionary diocese in 1950. Lakdasa de Mel, its first bishop, later translated as metropolitan of the Province of India, Pakistan, Burma and Celyon (PIPBC), was a visionary who recognized the urgency of an indigenous church and worked tirelessly to blend the local cultures with the gospel. Kurunegala's second bishop, the late Lakshman Wickremasinghe, built on these foundations, vigorously championed the cause of the marginalized, and articulated an Asian spirituality (Wickremage et al. 1955).

## The Province

The widely spread Anglican Church in South Asia led to the establishment, in 1930, of the PIPBC with the Bishop of Calcutta as metropolitan. With this, the statutory link between the regional Anglican Church and the Church of England (CoE) ended. The formation of united churches in South India (1947), North India (1970), and Pakistan (1970) led to the dissolution of the province in 1970. Burma thereafter opted to become a province of its own, but the two Anglican dioceses of SL chose to remain extra-provincial with the intention of merging into the United Church of Sri Lanka (UCSL) (Fernando, K. 1995).

In December 2007, the DoC and DoK were incorporated as the CoC by an ordinance of Parliament and the adoption of the CoC constitution. This action removed the restrictions that prevailed under the previous provincial constitution and empowered the two dioceses to manage their own affairs independently. A general assembly and a presiding bishop are two enabling features of this collaboration. The Archbishop of Canterbury, who since 1970 performed metro-political functions, continues as such but with some of his authority delegated to the presiding bishop (Peiris 2011). This incorporation offers a third model of jurisdiction to the Anglican Communion (AC), different from the province and the extra-provincial diocese, yet to be recognized by the AC.

## Church Governance

Synodical governance was introduced in 1886. Ever since, these gatherings, now known as diocesan council and comprising the bishop, licensed clergy, and lay representatives of the congregations, have met to deliberate on the church's mission and temporal affairs (De Chickera 2011). The clergy of the dioceses meet annually with their respective bishops, either at clergy synod or clergy conference, and the respective standing committees, elected at diocesan council, exercise executive responsibility on behalf of the diocesan councils. The administration of the dioceses comes under separate diocesan secretaries, and honorary registrars advise on legal matters.

Today, the DoC has jurisdiction over the maritime and some interior regions while the DoK covers a landlocked region in the north central and central parts of the island. The two bishops ensure unity in diversity, exercise pastoral care, interact with state authorities, and facilitate mission and witness within their dioceses. They are assisted by archdeacons and area deans (Peiris 2011).

## Outreach

Outreach initiatives coordinated by the Board of Mission link the congregations with the center and generate an exchange of ideas and resources. The historically older initiatives include the Mothers' Union, the Medical Mission, the Missionary Council, the Board of Social Responsibility (BSR), the Board of Women's Work, the Youth Movement, the Board of Christian Education, and the Liturgical and Theological Commissions. Institutions provide care for vulnerable children and seniors, and vocational training centers equip needy youth. The Ceylon churchmen Pradeepana (meaning "brightness") and Thellivu (meaning "wisdom") publish church news, and a library and archives facilitate research, study, and the preservation of records. Initiatives which address more recent obligations are the Commission on Environment and Medical Ethics, and the Peace, Inter Faith, and Gospel and Culture Desks.

The CoC modestly demonstrates and attracts people to abundant life in Christ. This role is largely based on the model of "germination," the seed dying to bear good fruit, and highlights that mission is both costly and compatible with God's incarnation in Christ. The respect this model implies for the "soil," that which is out there, also created by God and without which germination is not possible, tempers mission in a multi-religious society. If this trend is to continue with integrity, however, the "harvest" model of mission, which clearly seeks the conversion of all, will have to be reviewed. This model tends to disregard the life-empowering spirituality of the sister religions (SR) and undermines inter-religious (IR) coexistence.

The work of the CoC in natural and human-caused disaster is commendable. Its response to war is described elsewhere. The tsunami of December 2004 which ravaged two-thirds of the coastal region killed nearly 40,000 people and brought chaos to more than a million. A CoC Task Force, set up overnight, worked professionally and speedily with support from the congregations and clergy to restore normalcy. The World Church offered generous funding, and Mission Partners sent volunteers to help. Welcoming centers, trauma counseling, housing, medical equipment, the twinning of church schools with affected state schools, and livelihood support were the thrusts of this work. The BSR took over this responsibility from the Task Force in the latter stages and coordinates the CoC's response to unprecedented natural calamities like floods, earth-slides, and drought.

## Children and Youth

Work with children has mostly centered around the Sunday school and the Christian day school. A recent commission on children recommended the physical and sexual protection of children and their fullest participation in the whole life of the whole church. While many youth are finding their place and sharing in the leadership of the church, an increasing number tend to keep away due to the pressure of careers or because they find the church irrelevant. Until these worrying concerns are addressed at depth, an investment in gospel values during childhood seems to be the best compromise that will equip these youth to remain faithful.

## Ministerial Training and Formation

Ministerial training first began in regional centers under the CMS (Balding 1922). Bishop Chapman set up a more structured course for clergy training at S. Thomas' College, Mutwal. The first principal of the formal Divinity School was the Rev. Dr. G. B. Ekanayake, a distinguished theologian and Hebrew scholar who had earlier taught at Cambridge and Cuddesdon, Oxford (Beven 1946). The Divinity School was thereafter moved to several sites until it was finally closed in 1964 when the two Anglican dioceses affiliated with three other churches set up the Ecumenical Theological College of Lanka (TCL), Pilimatalawa, as an investment toward a united church (Fernando, K. 1995). It was here in the 1970s and 1980s that the late Ven. Dr. Donald Kanagaratnam, a CoC lecturer and principal, made an impact on his students on the need for inculturation of the gospel. He later set up an informal ashram in the Vanni as a center for dialogue between communities.

Ecumenical theological formation has, from the beginning, posed a dual challenge to the churches. These are to draw out the core practices and beliefs of the respective churches for the enhancement of the whole, and to generate an enduring enthusiasm for the UCSL.

After some decades, the Colombo Divinity School was revived by Kenneth Fernando, the 13th Bishop of Colombo. Known today as the Cathedral Institute for Education and Formation (CIEF), it has become immensely useful in empowering the laity and lay workers. The CIEF also provides pre-TCL and post-TCL formation courses for Anglican ordinands (Fernando, K. 1995).

## Women in Ministry

The DoC ordained its first women presbyters in 2006, and the DoK ordained its first women deacons in 2011. These historic landmarks were a culmination of the faithful ministries and leadership of numerous women as Bible teachers, lay workers, religious sisters, teachers, educationists, and lay leaders. The achievement of women in secular life, including SL's achievement in producing the world's first female prime minister (the late Sirimavo Bandaranaike), also influenced this trend. Nevertheless, the way forward for these pioneering women is steep. The absence of role models and support mechanisms to enable women to develop a feminine spirituality are among the immediate challenges faced. The church's growing self-understanding that it is still very much a male-influenced institution that is yet to become a more equal community of men and women is, however, a sign of hope for the future (De Chickera 2002). One who did much to empower women in the CoC was its first ordained women presbyter, the late Rev. Canon Malini Devanda, who also distinguished herself as an Asian woman theologian.

## Lay Orders

Early batches of catechists were brought by the CMS from South India around the mid-nineteenth century to minister to the South Indians working on the plantations. The order was thereafter supplemented by locals and spread to other parts of the country. Many of today's vibrant congregations, especially in the plantation areas, are a testimony to the faithful endeavors of these catechists (Thomas nd). This exclusive male order is non-existent today, and some of its pastoral responsibilities have been absorbed by the Estate Community Development Movement which works for the socio-economic transformation of this historically exploited community. Another early lay order known as Bible Teachers taught the Bible and reading to women and children of rural communities (Beven 1946). They were financially supported by the Ceylon Bible Society and the CMS (Thomas nd).

Today the Order of Lay Worker is a merger of the two previous lay orders. Lay orders assist the clergy in practically all areas of pastoral ministry, and some, in the absence of a presbyter, are even authorized to administer the reserved sacrament at the Eucharistic gathering of the faithful. Lay workers receive a foundational training either at the TCL or the CIEF, and some of them are subsequently ordained. A discrepancy in the status of the lay worker when compared with the clergy can best be resolved by upgrading the order and appointing better-qualified and trained persons (De Chickera 2006).

*Religious communities*

A lesser known feature of the CoC are its religious communities which reflect a fusion of Western and Asian monasticism. The Sisters of St. Margaret's of East Grinstead began their work in Colombo in 1887. They engage in a cycle of work and prayer and offer support for children and women in need. In the past, they were associated with healthcare at the Kandy Hospital and education at Bishops College (Beven 1946). The Devasevikaramaya (meaning "ashram of the women servants of God") was founded as an indigenous community in Kurunegala in 1962 by the late Bishop Lakdasa de Mel. These sisters similarly work among women and children, visit the poor and the sick, and offer hospitality and counseling to those in need (Devananda 1995). Today, both orders face a crisis of vocations, indicating a bleak future.

The CoC has, in collaboration with the Methodists and the Jaffna Diocese of the Church of South India (JDCSI), been part of the ecumenical ashram movement in the Tamil areas. The Christa Seva Ashram (translated as "ashram of the servants of Christ") was established in the north in 1939 and was modeled on the Hindu tradition of residential celibate monks (called "Sevaks") whose spirituality generated an ethos of prayer, penance, and poverty and attracted pilgrims and seekers of truth. A branch was set up in Kiran, in the east, in 1959. The Ashram Fellowship, a non-residential support group, provides the link for entry into the residential Ashram Community. The late Sevaks Peri-Annan, Sinn-Annan (translated as "elder brother," and "younger brother," respectively), and Sam Alfred are remembered to this day for their saintly lives. Here, too, the absence of celibate monks requires modifications in its rules if the movement is to be sustained (Christa Seva Ashram nd).

Of the two ashrams located in the Sinhala areas: Devasaranaramya (translated as "ashram of divine refuge") was founded in 1957 by Sevak Yohan Devananda, an Anglican presbyter, and it relocated in 1960 to Ibbagamuwa. It engaged in Buddhist–Christian–Marxist dialogue, liturgical innovation, and a quest for human liberation. Changes both personal and structural have occurred here, too, and the ashram functions today under the two wings of contemplation and action (Wickremage et al. 1995). Two recent innovations are "Meth Piyasa" (translated as "home of compassion"), a community of women whose identities take shape as they journey, and the presence of a Sri Lankan Franciscan monk, Brother Lionel, who builds on Franciscan spirituality in IR peace and community initiatives. The Diviya Seva Ashramaya (translated as "ashram of divine service") at Urubokka, founded in 1962, began as an initiative to build community life under the pioneering leadership of Ms. Constance Jayawardene. Its mission interestingly combined evangelism with social care in the surrounding rural villages. Following the passing of its founder, the work of the Ashram went through a period of slumber but has recently been resuscitated through the founding of "The Friends of Urubokka" (Rebera nd).

## Liturgy and Worship

The Ceylon liturgy, the first indigenous Eucharist, based on eastern liturgical sources and written in the languages of the people, was approved for use in 1938. Prior to this, the 1662 Book of Common Prayer of the CoE was in use. Three significant changes occurred thereafter: the adoption of the 1960 Provincial Prayer Book, the adoption of the 1988 Eucharist, and the approval for experimental use of the 2009 liturgy (Wick-remasinghe 2011). Services for morning and evening prayer and the occasional serv-ices are still from the Provincial Prayer book, with a tendency for the Alternate Service Book of the CoE to be used when these services are conducted in English. Marriages between Anglicans and persons from the SRs occur frequently and are blessed at a service which offers vows, the blessing of rings and thali (marriage necklace), hymns, prayers, and sermon.

Worship in the CoC is solemn and participatory and includes cultural elements such as drumming, dancing, indigenous lyrics, the prostration, the use of the roti or chapatti as the host, and the lighting of the traditional oil lamp. Clergy preside barefooted, and Sesath (colorful banners on colorful poles which symbolize the presence of the monar-chy) are carried in liturgical processions and adorn the sanctuary to indicate that worship is directed to Christ the King. In some congregations and on special occasions such as ordinations, worship is tri-lingual. In several congregations, it is bi-lingual. Music is provided from either the pipe organ or eastern instruments such as the tabla, serpina, violin, and sitar. A contemporary feature in the canon of the Eucharist is the reference to "Sages" along with the Law and the Prophets as vehicles of God's revelation to humans (CoC Liturgy 1988).

Of late, there have been attempts to make the Eucharist less formal through the singing of choruses and offering of spontaneous prayer. This trend, popularly known as "praise and worship," has the potential to widen participation but needs to be liturgi-cally integrated.

The May Day Workers Mass is a radical rendering of the Eucharist by the Christian Workers Fellowship (CWF). Based on orthodox and contemporary liturgies, it has inputs from the SRs and is sung to a Sinhala pilgrim chant. Vestments in red depict workers' symbols and sacrifice (Weerasuriya 1995). Several lay persons of the CoC established the CWF and created the Workers Mass. Prominent among them is Vijaya Vidyasagara, a layman who advocates the inclusion of all at the Eucharist.

Several outstanding liturgists have been responsible for the rich and creative liturgi-cal journey of the CoC. The most distinguished include the late Deva Surya Sena who set the Ceylon liturgy into local Sinhala folk chants, the late Mr. and Mrs. Anandanay-agam who were responsible for the Tamil Karnatic setting, and Dr. Narme Wickremas-inghe, a layman who crafted the liturgy of 1988.

## Art and Architecture

A feature of Christian art in the CoC are the impressive murals that adorn the sanctu-ary walls of several school chapels. The distinguished Nalini Jayasuriya painted the mural at Bishops, and the murals at Trinity College and St. Thomas College were done by the world-famous David Paynter, who transferred the features of persons from the local community onto his characters. The mural in the Lady Chapel of the Colombo Cathedral commemorates the ordination of the first women presbyters of the CoC by depicting the miracle of the turning of water into wine. It is the work of the late Stanley Kirinde, one of SL's most creative Buddhist painters, and gives a contemporary interpretation to the event through a brown-skinned Christ and an inter-ethnic Sinhala-Tamil marriage. Similarly, Weerawardene's murals at the Kadalana Church give a contemporary interpretation of the compassion of Christ. Hewawickrema's paintings at Hevadiwela and his life-like sculpture of the busts of Bishops Chapman and Wickremasinghe are other significant aesthetic contributions of the CoC.

The two cathedrals, as well as some churches and chapels, display outstanding examples of indigenous architecture. A feature of the Kurunegala Cathedral is its three-tiered structure, borrowed from Kandyan Buddhist architecture which represents the Buddha, the Dhamma, and the Sangha, to demonstrate the Trinitarian God that Christians worship (Fernando, K. 1995). The Colombo Cathedral, also built at three levels, has a floor that slopes from the baptistery at the entrance toward a slightly elevated sanctuary, conveying that all baptized persons are equal before God. Its massive, bare, concrete columns are a reminder that our work for God is incomplete. The wall-less chapels with roofs supported by intricately carved columns, at locations such as the former Teacher Training Colony in Peradeniya, Trinity College Kandy, Nuffield School Kaitaidi, and Karuna Nilayam Killinichchi, convey the openness, beauty, and strength of the gospel as well as similarities in Buddhist and Hindu architecture.

Three other original works are the labyrinth and the open-air theatre in the cathedral gardens in Colombo, and the Peace Centre in Jaffna. The labyrinth, designed by the Architect Lyn Edrisinha, is built on a previous dirt dump with paths of sharp sand and stone, causes increasing discomfort to pilgrims traversing bare feet to highlight the paradox of transformation through the cross; the "Nuga Sevana" (translated as "shade of the Nuga tree") theatre built around a majestic Banyan tree inspires creativity; and the Jaffna Peace Centre, built on the ruins of a destroyed church, retains the marks of war as a reminder that peace is costly.

There is today a dearth of skills and a dying interest in art and architecture that threaten the rich legacy of structural design and visual beauty in the CoC. An appreciation that aesthetic expression is intrinsic to the mission of the church is necessary to arrest this situation.

## Ecumenism

Mission activity of the different missionary societies shows a mix of sensible cooperation with fierce rivalry. Formal conversations on church union (CU), however, began with an ecumenical conference in 1934. The scandal of division, known to cause confusion among the SRs and weaken the church's credibility in calling for national unity, was by then beginning to buttress the theologically correct rationale that those in the One Christ must be One. Thereafter, a joint committee of the uniting Methodists,

Baptists, Presbyterians, JDCSI, and Anglicans was set up to work on the modalities of CU. This work culminated with a scheme for CU in 1963, which received the endorsement of the uniting churches (Scheme of Church Union 1963) by the early 1970s. Just when the UCSL appeared within reach, these tireless efforts had to be put on hold due to litigation by a group of Anglicans from Colombo (De Chickera 1998).

This setback was re-addressed much later in 2008 when a fresh collaboration known as the Confederation of Churches brought together the same five uniting churches, with the Salvation Army and the Christian Reformed Church as observers. The objective of this confederation is to increasingly strengthen understanding and visible cooperation among the churches, hopefully leading to the UCSL.

Several ecumenical organizations such as the Ceylon Bible Society, YMCA, YWCA, SCM, Christian Literature Society, and the Ecumenical Institute for Study and Dialogue (EISD) have nourished Sri Lankan ecumenism. The CoC is statutorily affiliated with all these organizations, and Anglicans have contributed substantially to their life and growth. The National Christian Council of Sri Lanka (NCCSL), inaugurated in 1948, plays a much more formal ecumenical role. It provides a platform for ecumenical dialogue and common witness in the spirit of the Lund principle that the churches are "to do separately only what they cannot do together" (Lund Principle 1951). The CoC is a founder member of the NCCSL, which today comprises the Methodist, Baptist, Presbyterian, and Christian Reformed Churches; the JDCSI, Salvation Army, and the two CoC dioceses; as well as the ecumenical organizations named in the preceding text except for the EISD (De Chickera 1998).

A recent decision calling for the establishment of at least a third diocese and possibly a future province indicates the CoC's ambivalence with its future status (Diocesan Council 2009). While the logistical, financial, and temperamental challenges of implementing this decision involve significant hurdles, the more worrying concern is its repercussions on the CoC's time-tested commitment to the UCSL. Consequently, the CoC stands at a crucial juncture between a more visible Anglican identity with greater recognition in the AC and the transformation of its Anglican identity into a new identity of the UCSL with greater credibility to serve a torn and divided nation.

In either instance, and since ecumenism is wider than church union, an evaluation of the different emphases in mission methodologies that have developed in the churches since the 1970s is now timely. A step already taken in this direction is the recent endorsement of the revised statement on comity, an ecumenical covenant on cooperation and amity among the churches (Comity 2011); however, the process must continue. Another area in which greater consensus is required is the historic Episcopate. The concept of an ecumenical bishop, from the time of the undivided church, with emphasis on Apostolic teaching and traditions and inclusive of the threefold ministry of deacon, presbyter and chief shepherd, could turn out to be the best compromise.

Certain distinct contributions that the CoC will make to a future UCSL are the centrality of the Eucharist, the appreciation of incarnational mission, the affirmation of the SRs, and the CoC's core value of unity in diversity, whether cultural, theological, or ethical.

Three other ecumenical conversations enhance understanding and cooperation between the CoC and the other churches. The CoC–Roman Catholic conversations discuss more practical and cordial ways of working together; the Sri Lanka Association for Theology searches for an Asian theology through exposure and reflection; and the Inter-Church Fellowship seeks to build trust between the historically newer and older churches.

## Diocesan Link

Through the initiative of the late Bishop David Young, the two Sri Lankan dioceses and the Diocese of Ripon and Leeds established a link in 1988. Exposure visits, the sharing of resources, and exchange of personnel and programs on mutual educational learning have so far been the thrusts of the link.

## The World Church

The CoC has several links with the AC. It has representation on the Anglican Consultative Council and its various networks and activities; its bishops attend the Lambeth Conference; and it sustains strong connections with its historic mission partners, the CMS and the USPG, as well as the Canadian Anglican Church, and a more recent associate, the Episcopal Relief and Development Fund. The formal and informal movements of persons to and from the CoC enrich these bonds of affection. Very strong relationships have also been maintained with its longstanding ecumenical partners: the WCC, the Christian Conference of Asia, and the churches of the South Asian region. Interestingly, the CoC is not part of either the Asian Anglican Bishops Fellowship or GAFCON.

## Change and Challenge

Sri Lanka's national independence from British rule in 1948 introduced a combination of democratic governance and rapid social change. The new political leadership was eager to undo the discrimination suffered by the majority Sinhala community under colonial rule. The "Sinhala Only" Act of 1956 was one such attempt. It predictably led to reverse discrimination against the English- and Tamil-speaking population, sowed seeds of grievance among the Tamil community, and accelerated waves of emigration of hundreds of thousands over the next five decades.

With national independence, the CoC lost much of the privilege it enjoyed under British rule. Also, the emigration of thousands of Anglicans reduced its numerical strength and ironically made the CoC a "sending church," since those who left served with distinction elsewhere. They are far too many to be named, but the current Archbishop of Perth, the Most Rev. Roger Herft, may be identified as one such gift to world Anglicanism. These changes ironically made the CoC a "remnant community" and compelled those who stayed behind to wrestle anew with God's purposes for both church and nation.

## Schools

The Education Act of 1961 drastically cut state funding to the independent, denominational schools. One objective of the bill was to restrict the church's influence over young minds. Consequently, the CoC, along with several other religious groups, was compelled to hand over the majority of its vernacular schools, which served the lesser privileged, to the state. Eleven better endowed secondary schools as well as three special education schools for the blind and the deaf were however retained. Funding was obtained in the form of fees and donations from parents and other interest groups. In some instances a limited state grant was received toward the salaries of teachers. Today, these schools adhere to state educational policy, function in the national languages, and prepare their students for international exams. The requests for admissions come from people of all faiths. Two recurring challenges faced are inadequate funding for the special education schools and the scarcity of competent and qualified heads and teachers for all schools (De Chickera 1982).

## Sister Religions

The CoC's relationship with its SRs is paradoxical. On the one hand, they are cordial. Christians share life with adherents of the SRs at all levels of life including the family. Religious leaders sustain friendships and participate in each other's ceremonies, and bishops and presbyters help to motivate IR collaborations which speak and intervene on public issues. On the other hand, recurring IR tensions threaten the trust and goodwill built over the years. These tensions are usually provoked by a social perception that the church has its loyalties elsewhere and because of the insensitive evangelistic methods of some Christian groups.

The move to restrict religious conversions at the beginning of the twenty-first century is an example of how IR relations can take a turn for the worse in multi-religious societies. Appealing to majority religious sensitivities, the Jathika Hela Uramaya (translated as "national Sinhala heritage") party gained some seats in Parliament for the first time and introduced a bill to prevent the forcible conversion of persons as part of its mandate to protect Buddhists from alleged unethical conversions.

The CoC has offered three responses to this trend. These are a call for self-scrutiny, both intra-church and IR; the affirmation of the democratic right to conversion; and the proposal of an IR Body, instead of legislation, to monitor and resolve IR tensions. This last suggestion was subsequently proposed by the NCCSL and the Congress of Religions, and was well received by some moderate political leaders but made little further progress. The bill itself has been put on hold.

The long-term ideal for IR relations in a multi-religious society must however be the celebration of the other through mutual understanding and trust. The religions need each other as never before if the complex crises faced by the people are to be combated, and it is through a sharing of spiritualities and human resources that this will, if at all, be possible. Some Christian leaders have even advocated an apology by the church for its past cultural and religious insensitivity, as an indispensable gesture of healing in this process (De Chickera 2004).

This shift will be helped immensely through the dissemination of a theology of religions that God is one and creator of all, and consequently that respect for and cooperation with other religions amount to dealings with this same one, creator God.

## Just Peace

The ethnic conflicts of over 30 years have now escalated into a wider democratic issue. Contrary to populist political propaganda, the end to the civil war has not brought peace. Instead, the military victory has been exploited to caricature democratic dissent and entrench authoritarianism. Just peace for SL therefore includes accountability for the violations and atrocities of the past; the healing of memories; a return to good governance, law and order; economic justice for the poor; the devolution of political power; and the restoration of the autonomy of democratic institutions such as the media, judiciary, and parliament, with adequate constitutional safeguards. Concurrent steps are also necessary to strengthen democratic ideals and values in the people.

The minority CoC plays a continuing role for just peace in SL. The CoC's composition, which includes several ethnic groups, and its geographical location in all parts of the island enable the CoC to hear all and rise above bias to any. In practical terms, this work includes the pastoral care of victims, relief and rehabilitation, peace education, collaboration with civil society peace partners, dialogue with groups with different perspectives, and a prophetic voice on behalf of the vulnerable. Bishops, presbyters, and laypersons have provided courageous leadership in this work throughout the years, which has received both harsh criticism and profound appreciation. The late Bishop Lakshman Wickremasinghe and Bishop Kenneth Fernando are two visionary leaders who upheld the integrity of the church and worked courageously for a better SL. A summary of the CoC's stance on just peace for SL was submitted to the Presidential Commission on Lessons Learnt and Reconciliation (Submissions to LLRC 2010).

## The Anglican Communion

The current anxieties of the AC, such as the ordination of women Bishops, the Vatican Ordinariate, and human sexuality, have an impact to a lesser degree on the life of the CoC, engrossed with its share of human crises. Nevertheless, some comment is necessary.

It is unlikely that the CoC, which now ordains women presbyters, will resist the ordination of women bishops when the time is ripe. Ordained women are received well, and the prospect of women in the episcopate is likely to be seen as a logical consequence to this reception. While the Vatican Ordinariate is compatible with the democratic right of Anglicans to convert, it is at the same time a blatant denial of the validity of Anglican orders.

The issue of human sexuality received the formal attention of the CoC when the clergy synod of 2005 studied the Windsor report. On that occasion, some saw homosexuality as a sin; others called for a more welcoming church where gay/lesbian persons would not be caricatured; and some argued that the exclusion of homosexuals from positions of leadership in the Body of Christ was a justice issue. Building on these perspectives, the Bishop of Colombo, in his Lambeth Sermon of 2008, called for a more inclusive AC in which persons of different sexual orientation will be equal (De Chickera 2008).

If the AC, plagued with issues of human sexuality, the violation of Episcopal jurisdiction, the Vatican Ordinariate, and women bishops, is to experience reconciliation, however, another subtle grievance will have to be addressed. This is the frustration across the AC with the dominant Anglo-Saxon culture (Ward 2006). Even a cursory survey will show that persons of Anglo-Saxon origin hold positions of decision-making, influence, and authority disproportionate to their numerical strength. This discrepancy brought about by historical, educational, linguistic, and economic advantages requires urgent correction. Such a process will be long and painful, but it will also be rewarding since it will help create a less divisive and a more integrated communion.

## Conclusion

The story of the CoC is essentially the story of men, women, and children who, in the midst of disobedience and indifference, have strived to be faithful in Christ. Among them are the countless saints of the church, known and hidden, through whom the legacy of the restless and generous Christ has been passed on. Those who follow are called to build on this tradition by journeying from institutional interests to community compassion, the fear of challenge to courageous discernment, personal religiosity to social justice, and boundaries that enslave to the freedom of the Spirit (Wickremasinghe, L. nd).

## Bibliography

Balding, J. W. 1922. *One Hundred Years in Ceylon*. Madras: Diocesab Press, Vepery.

Beven, F. Lorenz. 1946. *A History of the Diocese of Colombo*. Colombo: The Times of Ceylon Co., Ltd.

Brohier, Christina. nd. Evelyn Karney. *Breaking the Alabaster Box*. Colombo. NCCSL Women's Commission.

Christa Seva Ashram. Twenty-Five Years. nd. Manipay: The American Ceylon Press.

Church of Ceylon Liturgy. 1988. *The Book of Common Worship, 1964*. London: Oxford University Press.

Code of Ethics for Mission. 2004. Colombo: National Christian Council of Sri Lanka.

Comity (revised). 2011. Colombo: National Christian Council of Sri Lanka.

De Chickera, Duleep. 1982. The Educational Policy of the Diocese of Colombo. Unpublished Msc. Dissertation, University of Oxford.

De Chickera, Duleep. 1998/99. Ecumenism in Independent Sri Lanka, Achievements and Failures. *A Critical Evaluation of the Post Independence Period 1948–1998*. Colombo: Ecumenical Institute of Study and Dialogue Colombo.

De Chickera, Duleep. 2002. Bishop's Address. Diocese of Colombo.

De Chickera, Duleep. 2004. Bishop's Address. Diocese of Colombo.

De Chickera, Duleep. 2008. Lambeth Sermon.

De Chickera, Duleep. 2011. Preface. *Salient Trends*. Colombo: Diocese of Colombo.

Devananda, Malini. 1995. Religious Communities Devasevikaramaya Kurunegala. *Church of Ceylon*, ed. Frederick Medis. Colombo: Diocese of Colombo.

Devananda, Malini. 1995. Devasaranaramaya. *Church of Ceylon*, ed. Frederick Medis. Colombo: Diocese of Colombo.

Diocesan Council Minute. 2009. Diocese of Colombo.

Fernando, Celestine. 1948–1951. *Early Christianity in Ceylon*. Colombo: University of Ceylon Review.

Fernando, Kenneth. 1995. Church of Ceylon 1945–1995. *Church of Ceylon*, ed. Frederick Medis. Colombo: Diocese of Colombo.

Lund Principle. 1951, in the minutes of Faith and Order Commission. World Council of Churches, Geneva 1952.

Mendis, G. C. 1932. *The Early History of Ceylon*. Calcutta: Y.M.C.A. Publishing House Calcutta.

Peiris, Thanja. 2011. Church Governance. *Salient Trends*. Colombo: Diocese of Colombo.

Rebera, Audrey. nd. Constance Jayawardena. *Breaking the Alabaster Box*. Colombo: NCCSL Women's Commission.

Scheme of Church Union in Ceylon (revised). 1963. *The Negotiating Committee*. Madras: Christian Literature Society.

Selvathurai, A. Gnanaponraj Eva. nd. Muriel Hutchins. *Breaking the Alabaster Box*. Colombo: NCCSL Women's Commission.

Submissions to Presidential Commission on Lessons Learnt and Reconciliation. 2010. Colombo: Church of Ceylon

Thomas, S. M. nd. *Tamil Church Mission*. Colmobo: Mortlake Press.

Vimalananda, Tennekoon. 1970. *The State and Religion in Ceylon Since 1815*. Colombo: M.D. Gunesena & Co. Ltd.

Ward, Kevin. 2006. *A History of Global Anglicanism*. Cambridge: Cambridge University Press.

Weerasuriya Godwin. 1995. Indigenisation of Church Worship. *Church of Ceylon*, ed. Frederick Medis. Colombo: Diocese of Colombo.

Wickremage, Upail, Rose Nicholas, and Devananda Yohan. 1995. Diocese of Kurunegala. *Church of Ceylon*, ed. Frederick Medis. Colombo: Diocese of Colombo.

Wickremasinghe, Lakshman. nd. *Anglicanism and the Emerging Church in Sri Lanka*. Kandy: Sithumina.

Wickremasinghe, Narme. 2011. Liturgy at the Synods/ Councils of the Colombo Diocese. *Salient Trends*. Colombo: The Diocese of Colombo.

# Australia and Oceania

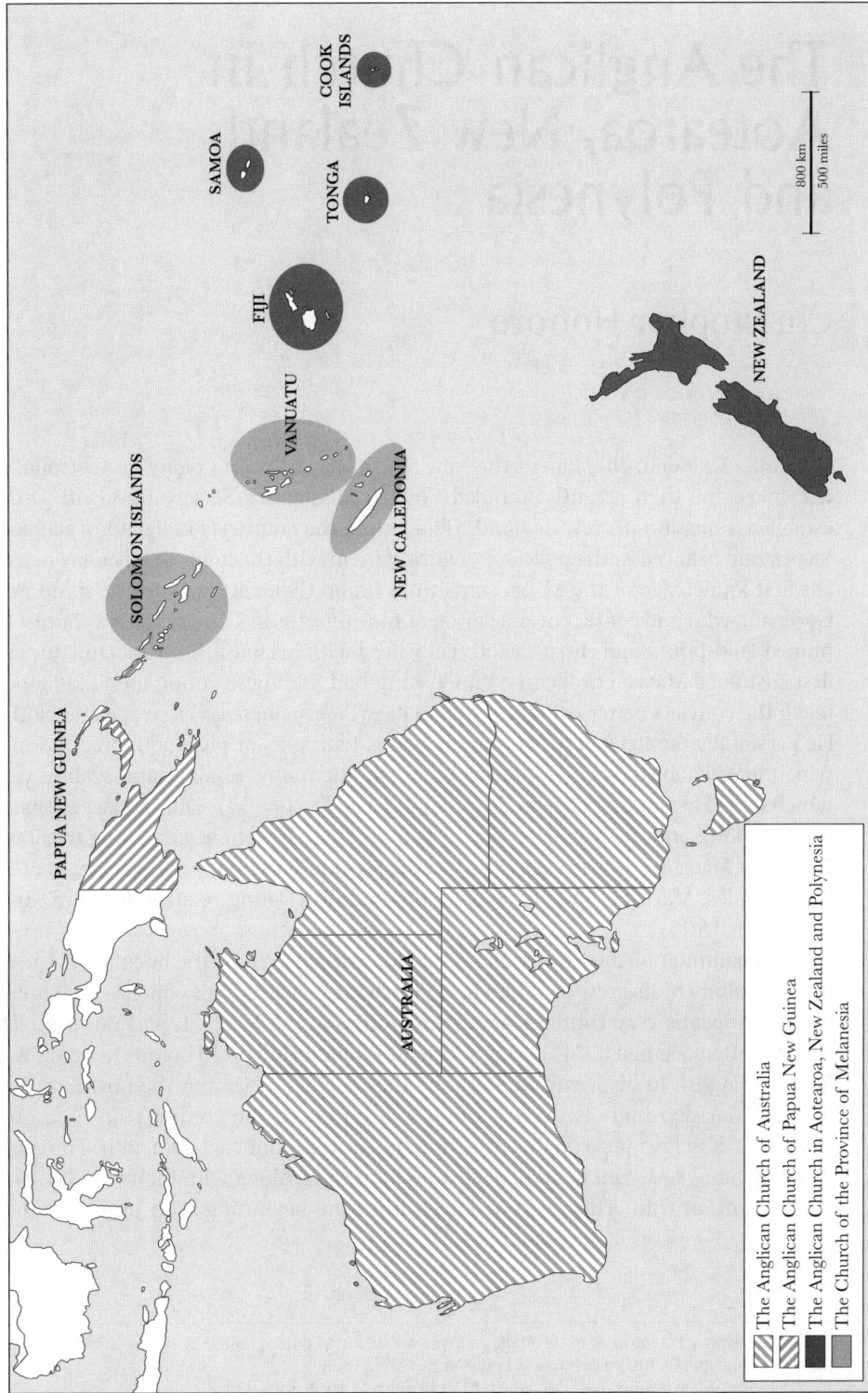

Map legend:

- The Anglican Church of Australia
- The Anglican Church of Papua New Guinea
- The Anglican Church in Aotearoa, New Zealand and Polynesia
- The Church of the Province of Melanesia

Labels on map: COOK ISLANDS, SAMOA, TONGA, FIJI, VANUATU, SOLOMON ISLANDS, NEW CALEDONIA, NEW ZEALAND, PAPUA NEW GUINEA, AUSTRALIA

Scale: 800 km / 500 miles

CHAPTER 34

# The Anglican Church in Aotearoa, New Zealand, and Polynesia

## Christopher Honoré

Samuel Marsden, chaplain of the New South Wales Prison Colony in Australia, convinced the then recently founded Church Missionary Society (CMS) in 1807 to establish a mission in New Zealand. He admired the country's indigenous people, the Māori, and believed in the policy of civilizing them with the help of skilled lay artisans. His first knowledge of the Māori came from Philip Gidley King, Norfolk Island Prison Governor, who had contact over a period of nine months in 1793 with two young chiefs named Tuki-tahua and Huru-kokoti. They lived with his family in what constitutes the first sustained Māori–European contact. King had had these young men kidnapped to teach the convicts better ways of dressing flax (*Phormium tenax*) for rope and clothing. He personally repatriated them to their home, with gifts of pigs, potatoes, and maize, which later enabled Northern Māori to supply the many whaling and sealing vessels which called at the Bay of Islands (Salmond 1997, 206–33). The rapport established between King and the Northern Bay of Islands chief Te Pahi began a long tradition of Northern Māori leaders traveling to Port Jackson to liaise with the governors of New South Wales. Marsden had also met Te Pahi and his young relative, Ruatara, in Port Jackson in 1805.

The beginning of the New Zealand mission was delayed by the burning of the *Boyd* and the killing of its crew at Whangaroa Harbour in 1809. This controversial incident made Europeans very cautious about encountering the Māori. It was not until 1814 that Marsden deemed it safe enough to send William Hall and Thomas Kendall, with a letter in English to his friend Ruatara, by then a chief at Oihi in the northern Bay of Islands. Marsden had discovered Ruatara ill on board the convict ship *Ann*, on the voyage back to Port Jackson in 1809, and had nursed him back to health. The mission began in late 1814 with Kendall, Hall, and John King, along with their wives and families, settling at Oihi. They were troubled from the beginning with inner dissension,

*The Wiley-Blackwell Companion to the Anglican Communion*, First Edition. Edited by Ian S. Markham, J. Barney Hawkins IV, Justyn Terry, and Leslie Nuñez Steffensen.
© 2013 John Wiley & Sons, Ltd. Published 2013 by John Wiley & Sons, Ltd.

lacked a regular supply of provisions, and suffered from isolation, fear, and uncertainty. Thomas Kendall recognized the demands of cultural adaptation, and although he had no philological training, he began to put the Māori language into a written form and attempted the first grammar and vocabulary. The Rev. John Butler, his family, and two lay workers, James Kemp and Francis Hall, joined the mission in 1819. Butler, based at Kerikeri, was appointed superintendent of the mission. The mission community was dependent upon Māori goodwill for their safety and survival.

Only months after Butler's arrival, Kendall took the chiefs Hongi Hika and Waikato to England without the consent of the local committee. Kendall sought ordination, which the CMS committee agreed to, albeit reluctantly. Kendall and the two chiefs ostensibly went to further the Māori language grammar and orthography project, which was seen as crucial for the establishment of Māori as a written language. The grammar was honed and published with the aid of CMS language consultant Professor Samuel Lee of Cambridge University. Hongi Hika and Waikato, while acting as linguistic consultants, were more preoccupied with obtaining armaments (Binney 2005, 69–70). The inter-tribal musket wars of the 1820s, in which Hongi played a leading part, resulted in many deaths and political and social instability.

A third mission station began at Paihia in 1823 when the Rev. Henry and Marianne Williams arrived, and Butler and Kendall were withdrawn for misdemeanors. The infusion of new talent enabled the mission to concentrate on the tasks associated with evangelism, while still dependent on Māori goodwill. Henry Williams was particularly diligent in seeking to reconcile warring tribes and earned much respect for his fearless interventions. In the late 1820s, the mission was augmented by Henry's brother William Williams, and William Yate, who both contributed to the translation of the New Testament from Greek into Māori. Robert Maunsell, a Hebrew Scholar, joined the mission in the mid-1830s, and played a major part in the translation of the Old Testament into Māori. An early adult convert was the chief Rawiri Taiwhanga, who worked with the missionary John Butler at Kerikeri as his foreman gardener and was baptized in early 1830. Maori prisoners of war from southern tribal areas were allowed to attend mission schools in the Bay of Islands. With the release of these prisoners and their repatriation in the early 1830s at the instigation of William Williams, the gospel message moved to places unvisited by European missionaries.

Missionaries had consistently reported on the progress of the mission, the rivalries of the tribes, and their occasional anxiety at the vulnerability of New Zealand to annexation by either France or the United States. With the growth of the whaling and sealing industries, ships of these nations were often in New Zealand waters, and occasionally their naval vessels visited. The CMS in the 1830s had influence in the British Parliament at a time when leading Anglican evangelicals had close associations with both the Colonial Office and the Parliament. In 1831, a Māori-owned ship was confiscated at Port Jackson and its cargo impounded as the vessel was unregistered and did not fly a flag of origin. The British Resident, James Busby, an official appointed by the British government in 1832 to liaise with Northern Maori chiefs, solved this issue by assisting the chiefs to choose a flag, and to issue certificates of registration under their names. The Māori were significant suppliers of necessary foodstuffs to the prison colonies of early Australia, and annual trade to Sydney alone has been calculated to be in the vicinity of £34,000 at the beginning of the 1830s. In 1835, Busby used Charles de Thierry's attempt to declare a sovereign state in the Hokianga to encourage chiefs to sign a declaration asserting their own sovereignty over New Zealand. While there was considerable doubt that the "confederation" existed as a political reality, the British government recognized the document as evidence of chiefly sovereignty, and therefore could not simply annex the country without reference to the rights of the local inhabitants. Although the British were reluctant to acquire further colonies, the actions of Edward Gibbon Wakefield's New Zealand Company led them to send a British naval officer, Captain William Hobson, with the commission to encourage Māori leaders to make a treaty with the British Crown. This simple document of three clauses was signed on February 6, 1840, with the active cooperation of the both Anglican and Wesleyan missionaries. Copies of the Treaty of Waitangi were taken to the other parts of New Zealand by Henry Williams and other missionaries, with some 500 chiefs and highborn Māori women signing the treaty.

The church of the missionaries, Te Hahi Mihinare, was evangelical in theology and Low Church in liturgical practice, and worship and preaching were conducted in the Māori language. It was missionary led, and by the late 1830s the missionaries perceived that, for the mission to develop into a church, episcopal leadership must be sought. Bishop Broughton of Australia had visited the Mission at Paihia in the Bay of Islands in 1838 at the request of the missionary community, and had ordained Octavius Hadfield to the priesthood on that occasion. Richard Davis wrote firmly on this subject to Dandeson Coates in 1839, "We want authority, and we want a head and above all, we want a system. The Wesleyans have a system and consequently proceed without difficulty. We have none" (Morrell 1973). George Augustus Selwyn offered himself as the first Bishop of New Zealand after his scholarly elder brother William declined the position for family reasons, and within a few days was appointed, aged only 32. After consecration in Lambeth Palace chapel on October 17, 1841, Selwyn sailed from the United Kingdom in late December on the ship *Tomatin* with his wife Sarah and son William, and five clergy, including two CMS members.

An immediate challenge for Selwyn was how to create a legislative structure for the Anglican Church in New Zealand. The structure needed to be separate from the state, true to the Church of England and the apostolic background of the undivided church; it needed to avoid monarchical episcopacy, and be led by bishop, clergy, and representatives of the laity, gathered in council. Selwyn began this process on September 26, 1844, when he gathered his clergy at Waimate in a synod in order to make rules for the better conduct of the mission. This was probably the first synodical meeting held by a Church of England bishop since the convocations of Canterbury and York were dismissed by King William in 1717. Some criticism was leveled at Selwyn for "breaching the Royal Prerogative" when he appointed senior missionaries as archdeacons, but it is important to note that Selwyn and his CMS colleagues were working to put the church on both a structural and mission-orientated footing which would enable it to grow robustly.

Selwyn's concerns for the health and mission of the colonial church were shared by leading laymen such as New Zealand Governor Sir George Grey, the first chief justice, William Martin, and the attorney general, William Swainson, who in 1848 presented the bishop with a petition signed by 257 laymen. Selwyn took this petition to a conference held in Sydney in September 1850, under the chairmanship of Bishop Broughton. Selwyn's views were expressed in his 1852 pastoral letter advocating synodical government of three houses, bishops, clergy, and laymen. Consent in each house being necessary for legislation to pass, the formularies of the church were to be enshrined in a way which was congruent with the Church of England, and included the authorized version of the Bible and the rites and ceremonies of the church as declared in the Book of Common Prayer. These proposals were sent to all the settlements, and responses encouraged. In 1857, the presence of senior CMS clergy was deemed to be sufficient to represent the Māori church. The constitution provided for episcopal leadership and governance by a general synod and an orderly way of dividing the Diocese of New Zealand into smaller, more manageable bishoprics. The dioceses of Wellington, Waiapu, and Nelson were created in 1858; Christchurch was inaugurated in 1856 with the beginning of the colony there; Dunedin was created from the rural deaneries of Otago and Southland and inaugurated in 1869; and the Diocese of Waikato was created from the southern portion of the Auckland diocese in 1926.

By the mid-1850s, there were a significant number of British immigrants to New Zealand who desired land, hoping for a better life, and eager to contribute to the creation of a new colony. Many of these settlers did not understand the Māori spiritual connection to land, and viewed the forests and swamps as empty for the taking. They wanted this allocated for settler occupation and, by 1858, the settler population had surpassed Māori. The church was divided between those settlers who wanted land no matter what and saw Māori as obstructive savages, and those who saw that natural justice should prevail and Māori customary rights be upheld as declared in the Treaty of Waitangi. The "responsible settler government," however, in their desire to provide for settlers and help the colony to become self sufficient, disregarded the provisions of the treaty concerning Māori land rights.

## Māori in Ministry

In 1842, a scant eight years after moving to Kaitaia, Joseph Matthews and William Puckey had 17 "native assistants" and enjoyed the cooperation of the Te Rarawa chief Nopera Panakareao, who was an active evangelist. Māori catechists were not uncommon in the missionary era. The first Māori to be ordained deacon, on May 22, 1853, was a man named Rota (Lot) Waitoa, who had accompanied Bishop Selwyn and his family for ten years, and is honored as the forerunner of all ordained Māori. The land wars of the 1860s affected Māori work, especially in the Waikato and Taranaki, and many left the Anglican Church as a result. Indigenous forms of Christianity grew up as a protest against both the missionary religion, and the unjust ways in which land was wrested from Māori ownership. From 1868, responsibility for Māori work was devolved to native church boards which were headed by Pākehā. In the northern part of the North Island, during Bishop William Garden Cowie's episcopate, reports show that many Māori were confirmed. Cowie also encouraged Māori work and, between 1870 and 1902, ordained 26 Māori men. His Diocese of Auckland included much of the northern part of the North Island. Māori clergy were paid much less than their European colleagues and often had to farm to live. The attitude of the settler church to the Māori in ordained leadership was paternalistic and dismissive, and the needs of the Māori church were often ignored. It was easy for the Māori "mission" to become invisible. Calls by Māori Anglicans for episcopal leadership of their own were voiced as early as the 1870s as Māori learned of the Yoruba bishop, Samuel Ajayi Crowther of Nigeria, through the CMS publication *The Missionary Record*. The bishops were reluctant to admit a Māori to the bench of bishops, and it was not until 1925 that the general synod debated the issue properly, a debate energized by the contribution of a number of notable Māori leaders, including Sir Apirana Ngata, a member of Parliament, and the Rev. Wiremu Netana Panapa, who was the first Māori graduate of St. Johns Theological College. In 1928, the bishops reluctantly agreed to appoint a suffragan Māori bishop in the Diocese of Waiapu, Frederick Augustus Bennett. He did not always have the consent of the Pākehā bishops to minister to Māori in their dioceses. He had no voice in the general synod, and his meager stipend and travel costs were paid for, not by the Church, but by the Māori-owned Waiapu Cooperative Dairy Company. The lack of proper representation pertained until, as a result of increased Māori political activism during the 1970s, the general synod granted the titular Bishopric of Aotearoa the status of a diocese like the European ones, and representation in the general synod. This greatly facilitated the Bishop of Aotearoa's work across the country, and money was raised to provide an endowment for the bishopric. During the 1980s, an Anglican Bicultural Commission was convened by the general synod, which resulted in the revision of the church's constitution, as Pākehā lay and ordained leaders began to attend to Māori arguments. This commission benefitted from the participation of the retired third bishop of Aotearoa, Dr. Manuhuia Bennett. Bishop Whakahuihui Vercoe, Bishop of Aotearoa from 1981, was the first bishop of Aotearoa to be elected by Māori rather than appointed (by Pākehā), and he was the first Bishop of Aotearoa to hold the office of Archbishop of New Zealand.

The 1992 revised constitution of the church is the fruit of a profound reflection on the Treaty of Waitangi, and seeks to describe the ordering of the church to engender the values of partnership, interdependence, self determination, and inclusivity. The three verities of Henry Venn, that missions should move to being self-governing, self-propagating, and self-funding, are part of the intellectual substructure of this unique arrangement. The provisions of ACC 6 are enshrined in the constitution, and a feature of the document is its preamble which rehearses relevant parts of the mission story in these islands. The seven dioceses of New Zealand form Tikanga Pākehā; the former bishopric of Aotearoa has undergone transformation into five regions known as Hui Amorangi, each with a bishop. The Diocese of Polynesia, with its vast distances and nine languages, forms the third part of the rearrangement. Each cultural stream conducts its business in a manner which is congruent with its culture and language. Each of the three is free to conduct its mission and ministry within its cultural norms. Representatives of each cultural stream meet in the general synod once every two years, and the committees of the general synod which have an ongoing life between sessions are likewise comprised of members from each Tikanga.

## Women in Ministry

It was not until the early 1890s that deaconesses and women religious emerged to do significant work among the poor and disadvantaged in New Zealand cities. The Diocese of Christchurch paved the way in 1892, and such work began in the Diocese of Auckland in 1894 with the Mission to Streets and Lanes. The Community of the Holy Name, which grew out of the Mission to the Streets and Lanes, operated until about 1957 when it amalgamated with the Order of the Good Shepherd, and the New Zealand sisters went to the headquarters of that order in Australia. Their property in Arney Road became Deaconess House under the leadership of Deaconess Glenys Lewis. Similar initiatives were taken in the Dioceses of Dunedin, Waiapu, and Wellington. The example of these pioneers of women's ministry facilitated the introduction of legislation to permit the ordination of women to the priesthood. Perhaps as important a factor was the church union negotiations and the already-accepted practice of ordaining women in Presbyterian, Methodist and Congregational Churches. In 1970, the ordination of women to the priesthood was given serious consideration in diocesan synods, but it was not until 1977 that the general synod passed the necessary legislation. The first Māori woman to be ordained to the priesthood was of a family from which more than one Anglican priest had emerged. She had to overcome a deeply held, tribally infused patriarchal reserve against women's ordination. The Rev. Puti Murray (née Kapa) was ordained to the priesthood at Te Kao in 1978 by Eric Gowing, Bishop of Auckland. Her highly successful ministry was particularly orientated toward poverty-struck urban Māori in Otara, South Auckland. The Rt. Rev. Penelope Jamieson, the first woman diocesan bishop of the Anglican Communion, was elected to the See of Dunedin in 1990 and served until her retirement in 2004.

The Women's Studies Centre was set up to advance the interests and needs of the women of this church, particularly those undertaking theological education.

Representatives from each diocese and Hui Amorangi have been chosen for their leadership ability to identify, gather, facilitate, resource, and encourage women in their educational preparation for ministry, whether lay or ordained. The issue of increasing numbers of women in representative positions across the councils and committees of the church is seen as a high priority, and the practice of intentional mentoring by those already in national and international representative roles is seen as a good way to encourage women of this church to fulfill their potential as leaders. Ensuring that women's voices and stories are heard now and in the future is also a continued aim, whether it be by traditional methods of publication or using more contemporary technologies like website publication. The Centre for Women's Studies helps ensure that the needs and aspirations of women throughout this province will continue to be valued and recognized.

From the earliest missionary days, schools and education have been high priority of the Anglican Church. There are nine Anglican Schools in the Diocese of Polynesia. In the Auckland diocese, there are five schools with an Anglican association, including the Diocesan School for Girls, and Kings College, which is among the oldest foundations. The Diocese of Waikato and Taranaki has five schools; there are five in the Diocese of Waiapu, including the two for Māori students, Hukarere Girls School and Te Aute Boys School, both of which have illustrious pasts. The Wellington diocese, including the regional city of Wanganui, boasts of 12 affiliated schools. The Diocese of Christchurch has eight schools, and the Diocese of Dunedin has one. What makes the education these schools offer different is the presence of Anglican chaplaincy and worship, and the care that each school takes to provide the best possible environment for learning.

## Melanesia and Polynesia

The association between what is now the Province of Melanesia and the fledgling colonial church began in 1849 when Bishop Selwyn sailed his schooner *Undine* to Melanesia to find men whom he could bring back to St. Johns Theological College and train as catechists and evangelists to work among their own peoples. Unfamiliar with the many languages in the islands and archipelagos of Melanesia, Selwyn struggled in his efforts to evangelize the people he encountered. In 1858, under the leadership of John Coleridge Patteson (consecrated Missionary Bishop of Melanesia in 1861), the mission training establishment was re-sited from St. Johns Theological College to Mission Bay on the Waitematā foreshore. In 1867, the training school and diocesan administration was relocated to Norfolk Island, which was warmer than Auckland, but the graveyard there around the beautiful Church of St. Barnabas testifies to the human cost of this enterprise. The nineteenth-century teacher and translator Elizabeth Fairburn Colenso taught at the mission school on Norfolk Island from 1876 to 1898, and translated works into the Mota language. Bishop John Coleridge Patteson, together with Joseph Atkin and Stephen Taroaniara, were martyred on the Island of Nukapu on September 20, 1871, while on one of their annual voyages. Following the patristic dictum that the blood of the martyrs is the seed of the church, it is likely that the deaths of Patteson and his companions did much to further the cause of mission in the Solomons. Initially, clergy for the diocese were recruited mainly from upper middle class, public school, Oxbridge-educated Englishmen, some of whom used their private incomes to support their missionary work. There were attempts to foster an indigenous clergy, but progress was slow in the early years, and the diocese was run on a system whereby the European clergy spent half the year in the Solomons, and the other half with Melanesian students at school on Norfolk Island. The aim was to teach these students to be evangelists and teachers. In the later nineteenth century and into the twentieth century, indigenization was slowed by the autocratic rule of monarchical bishops. Indigenization was seriously pursued from the 1930s, but the work of the church was hampered by the development of the Pacific theatre of war from 1939 to 1945. Until 1975, when the Province of Melanesia was formed, consisting of eight dioceses, Melanesia was part of the Province of New Zealand. The Melanesian Trust Board, which funds much of the operational costs of the province, is New Zealand based. The Province of Melanesia is led by indigenous bishops and clergy, and local theological education from Bishop Patteson Theological College, at Kohimarama on the island of

Guadalcanal, is supplemented by some clergy coming for further study either to New Zealand or Australia.

The Melanesian Brotherhood, the largest male religious order in the Anglican Communion, which was begun by Ini Kopuria, a Melanesian policeman, during the episcopate of John Manwaring Steward, is famous for its music and mission activity. During a period of civil unrest in the Solomon Islands, during the early 2000s the brotherhood was active in peacemaking work, and seven brothers lost their lives in the course of this reconciliatory and prophetic action. There are vibrant Melanesian orders of women religious, and the Society of St. Francis is represented both by first-order brothers and numerous third-order members.

The Anglican Church in Polynesia started rather differently, as it was an area evangelized initially by the London Missionary Society and the Wesleyan Missionary Society, dating from the late 1790s, during Samuel Marsden's era. Anglicans came later, in 1870 when William Floyd volunteered to live and work in Fiji, first as chaplain to planters and other expatriates, and later to the indentured laborers from the sugar plantations who came from Melanesia, and much later Anglican work was extended to include the indigenous peoples of Polynesia, Indian workers, and Chinese traders and shopkeepers. Indian workers came from Kerala, and among the Hindu and Muslim immigrants were some Christian families. Pastoral work and education have formed the main outreach to the Solomon descended community in Fiji. Originally landless, the diocese has assisted some of these people to obtain permanent leases of land in the Levuka region. A British Consul to Samoa arriving in 1890 began the first Anglican work on the Island in the consulate, and conducted regular services and instruction so that, in 1897, Bishop Willis, while he was bishop of Honolulu, was able to baptize eight persons and confirm 11 when he visited Apia. He came to Tonga to live in 1902 at the invitation of a group of Tongans. In 1913, Willis was appointed assistant bishop of Tonga by the Bishop of Polynesia, Thomas Clayton Twitchell. Willis served in this capacity until his death shortly after the 1920 Lambeth Conference, which he attended. Fine Halapua, the first Tongan priest, was ordained in 1956. By 1962, the year of the late Archbishop of Polynesia Jabez Bryce's ordination to the priesthood, Bishop John Charles Vockler reported to the synod that indigenous members outnumbered expatriates for the first time. Bishop Bryce, consecrated in 1975, was the first indigenous bishop of Polynesia. The diocese serves Anglicans in Fiji, Samoa, Tonga, and the Cook Islands. The current archbishop, Winston Halapua, is Tongan, and is assisted by bishops Apimeleki Qihilo, who is Fijian, and Gabriel Sharma, who is Indo-Fijian. The diocese has a theological college, St. John Baptist, in Suva, and hosted the 2012 general synod of the church in Aotearoa, New Zealand, and Polynesia. Presently, there is due attention being paid to the development of Anglican Youth work as the church continues its emphasis on ministry to youth and others under the age of 40. Historically, the church in New Zealand has assisted the missionary diocese of Polynesia with financial support, and with a number of clergy who served part of their career in Polynesia until indigenization became the main priority. There have also been teachers and nurses who have served the children and the sick as part of their Christian ministry. Since 1968, sisters of the Community of the Sacred Name have run St. Christopher's home for orphaned children. The diocese may have few monetary resources, but the life and faith of these Anglicans is inspirational.

## Contemporary Issues

The question of how to sustain smaller ecclesial communities in both rural and city contexts has resulted in the movement known in New Zealand as Local Shared Ministry, which may be known as Enabler Led or Collaborative Ministry in other parts of the communion. It seems to be working most effectively in the Auckland and Dunedin dioceses, where it is seen as a way in which communities which can no longer sustain a stipendiary ministry can, with the support of the diocese, develop and maintain a sacramental and missional life. In this model, a congregation calls a ministry support team, some of whom are ordained either to preside at Eucharist and other community gatherings, others ordained as deacons for the outreach and costly service of the faith community, and yet others called and licensed as lay ministers for other tasks related to the good order of a faith community. Those in the ministry support team are to promote the ministry of all the baptized. Specially trained ministry developers mentor the ministry support teams and provide a close link with the diocese. This way of ecclesial ordering was inspired by the experience of the Dioceses of Nevada and Northern Michigan and fuelled by the theological reflection of Roland Allen. New Zealand pastoral theologians have contributed to this work and reflected on the experience of the church. In Tikanga Māori, with the innovative leadership of Bishop Whakahuihui Vercoe, the same theology fuelled the minita-a-iwi (ministers of the people) movement, which envisaged each local Māori community (Marae) having its own priests and deacons chosen from among the people to serve the sacramental and pastoral needs of their area. These local non-stipendiary ministers are resourced by seminary-trained educators.

Some issues faced in the Anglican Church in Aotearoa, New Zealand, and Polynesia are common across the Communion, but the priority these issues receive can vary. For example, how to faithfully read and interpret scripture has been addressed in a series of "Theological Hui" where Anglicans from the Diocese of Polynesia, the bishoprics of Aotearoa, and the dioceses of New Zealand met for prayer, to study the scriptures, and engage in dialogue. There have been three of these since 2007.They have been valuable meetings, gathering Anglicans in one room to listen carefully and respectfully to one another. The study series will not conclude until early 2013. The related matter of lesbian and gay people in leadership is receiving attention at both diocesan and provincial levels, as is the question of whether it is time to recognize committed relationships other than Holy Matrimony, thus allowing the canonical definition of chastity to be expanded to include same-sex-covenanted relationships. There is wide divergence of attitudes toward LGBT people in the church, and this varies in accordance with cultural norms, and how scripture is interpreted. At the 2012 general synod, a commission entitled General Synod Commission on Same Gender Blessings and Ordinations – "Ma Whea/Mei fe Kei fe/Where to?" – was set up to talk to interested parties, and is charged with presenting "a summary of the biblical and theological work done by our church on the issues surrounding Christian ethics, human sexuality and the blessing and ordination of people in same sex relationships, including missiological, doctrinal, canonical, cultural and pastoral issues . . ." This commission is to report to the 2014 General Synod after work done in New Zealand and listening to a wide range of groups and individuals.

## Life in the Province

Since 1964, the Anglican Church in Aotearoa, New Zealand, and Polynesia has engaged in liturgical reform along with other churches of the Anglican Communion, with the inauguration of the Prayer book Commission, and the first modern language English liturgy was published in 1966. It was followed by the durable 1970 liturgy, and these two books ushered in the era of ongoing liturgical reform issuing modern English pastoral liturgies and orders for morning and evening prayer. A Māori translation of the 1970 liturgy was not available until 1977. The 1980s saw a flowering of liturgical experimentation and writing which culminated in the 1989 publication of *A New Zealand Prayer Book – He Karakia Mihinare o Aotearoa*. For the first time, the church in New Zealand was enriched by liturgies composed in both Māori and English within the one book, and one of the Eucharistic liturgies, composed by Māori scholars, used proverbial allusions from Māori poetry and oratory. Special pastoral liturgies were written by Māori liturgical scholars. The creative liturgical work continues, and a revision of the present book is being considered after nearly 25 years use.

The Society of St. Francis, first order, has been a part of religious life in the Anglican Church of Aotearoa, New Zealand, and Polynesia since 1969. They have undertaken inner city mission in Auckland Central, parish ministry in the suburb of Glen Innes, a return to inner city ministry while resident at Parnell in the cathedral precinct, and also administered the retreat facility at Vaughan Park on Auckland's North Shore from 1998. In 2001, the brothers moved at Bishop David Moxon's invitation to Hamilton to be part of Te Ara Hou, a social agency complex. The brothers offer retreats and parish visitations, seeking to display and enable a lived communal spirituality in the spirit of St. Francis of Assisi. The Second Order sisters, of the Community of St. Clare, maintained a small house in Auckland during the 1980s, where they witnessed to the contemplative life; they later returned to the United Kingdom, as the sisters were needed in their home province. There have been Third Order brothers and sisters in this church from 1962. They express community by means of daily prayer from the New Zealand Prayer Book and reading from the Principles of the Third Order, praying for the members of TSSF in New Zealand, Melanesia, and other parts of the communion. The order expresses community by monthly gatherings, either as a wider community or in smaller groups, meeting for Eucharist, study, and fellowship. A larger national convocation is held annually.

The Community of the Sacred Name has existed in Christchurch since the 1890s, and their members live in community and undertake teaching, pastoral work, and ecclesiastical embroidery. There is also a House in Fiji where the sisters run the St. Christopher's Home for Children. It is acknowledged that religious life is difficult to sustain in New Zealand, and the various orders have nearly always depended on overseas members and leadership to sustain the communities.

Anglican ministry to younger people has received greater priority since the creation of the first youth synod in the late 1970s, and is increasingly seen as a sector ministry in its own right. The Tikanga Toru Youth Commission belongs to the Anglican Church in Aotearoa, New Zealand, and Polynesia. Its purpose is to strengthen and support ministry to young people through advocacy, training, and fellowship. The commission governs the Three Tikanga youth structures, advocates for youth ministry throughout the church, acts as the standing committee for the Tikanga Youth Synod, and supports the Three Tikanga Youth Commissioner, the Rev. Michael Tamihere. The Order of St. Stephen provides the chance for young people between the ages of 16 and 30 to live in a dispersed vowed community, following a simple rule of life.

The Hikoi of Hope 1998 was an initiative sparked by a spirited discussion in the general synod over the effects of poverty and job loss engendered by the economic reforms enacted by the Labour government during the 1980s. The idea adopted by the general synod mobilized middle New Zealand. About 40,000 people walked from all parts of New Zealand to converge in front of the Parliament in Wellington as part of a protest about increasing poverty and the difficulties this was causing for low-income families in particular. The general synod of the church had identified creation of real sustainable jobs, measures to address poverty, especially child poverty, the provision of affordable housing, and a health system which delivered quality care to all segments of the population as the matters which the leaders of the Anglican Church were to bring to the attention of Parliamentary leaders. This began regular meetings of members of the government with church leaders, not only Anglicans.

Protest is never popular when it challenges the received wisdom and behavior of middle New Zealand, and it is a comparatively rare event when even part of the Anglican Church stands to protest. In 1968, a group of theological students from St. Johns College joined the Good Friday procession of witness in Auckland's main thoroughfare, Queen Street, bearing placards protesting New Zealand's involvement in the Vietnam War. This incurred the ire of the Bishop of Auckland, who was scandalized at co-opting a devotional witness for political purpose. His displeasure notwithstanding, Bishop Eric Gowing was one of the few bishops of the time to be critical of New Zealand involvement in the Vietnam War. In 1975, Dr. George Armstrong, lecturer in theology at St. Johns College, organized the peace squadron to protest the visit of nuclear-armed and powered ships and was part of the flotilla of little ships that met the USS Texas in 1983. This was not the action of fringe radicals, but that of Christians deeply concerned about the ongoing effect of militarism and the possibility of nuclear war, and the negative effects of such dangers on Pacific peoples. This action was part of a wider disenchantment with nuclear weaponry and contributed to the Labour government in 1987 declaring New Zealand to be nuclear free.

The 1981 Tour of the South African rugby team polarized the churches and the nation. The issue was the privileging of a white minority in that country at the expense of the rights and equality of the black majority. The protest was strong enough to halt the test match at Hamilton, and Anglicans were very much part of the event. This prophetic action sprang from concerns about New Zealand's own race relations, and it was about this time that both national and church debate settled on the status of the Treaty of Waitangi.

## Interfaith and Ecumenical Relationships

The Anglican Church has been formally engaged in ecumenical relationships since 1947, with the formation of the National Council of Churches. This important ecumenical group, including Anglicans, Methodists, Presbyterians, and Associated Churches of Christ, had a number of special committees which sought to establish common ground on faith and order, international ecumenical relationships, Christian work in broadcasting, Māori affairs, women and youth issues, and issues surrounding unity and theological differences. The council originally enjoyed the participation of the Roman Catholic Church and the Greek and Serbian Orthodox Churches. During the later 1960s, the Anglican Church was in serious negotiation over the plan for union which would have seen Anglicans, Methodists, Presbyterians, and Churches of Christ unite in one communion, not unlike the Church of South India. However, by 1976, the general synod regretfully informed the partner churches that the Anglican Church could not enter into the union. In the later 1970s, as the Anglican and Methodist Churches were cooperating closely in theological education, a plan for mutual recognition of ministries was mooted, but again this did not proceed. The Anglican Church in Aotearoa, New Zealand, and Polynesia has no formal links with Judaism or Islam, although there are Associations of Christians and Jews and Christians and Muslims which have significant Anglican membership.

## Participation within the Communion

The Anglican Church in Aotearoa, New Zealand, and Polynesia claim Bishop Selwyn of New Zealand and Lichfield as its forerunner who modeled participation in inter-Anglican conversations; he was one of those who worked to inaugurate the first Lambeth Conference in 1867, and was actively engaged in working to continue the Lambeth relationship until his death. He laid the foundations for the second Lambeth Conference and thereby the ongoing life of the Anglican Communion. In our own time, significant contributors to the Anglican Communion have included Bishop John Paterson, who served the communion as Chair of the Anglican Consultative Council. Archbishop David Moxon was chair of the Anglican Roman Catholic International Commission (ARCIC), and has been appointed the Archbishop of Canterbury's Representative to the Holy See and Director of the Anglican Centre in Rome. Canon Dr. Jenny Plane-Te Paa contributes to international Anglicanism through her involvement in theological education, and the International Anglican Women's Network. Archbishop Sir Paul Reeves offered significant leadership as bishop in Waiapu and Auckland and as archbishop, and in his role as Governor General of New Zealand and also as Anglican Observer at the United Nations. He was regarded as a skilled negotiator in his interventions with Fiji during their constitutional crisis in the 1980s. Bishop Victoria Matthews of the Christchurch diocese also serves on the Windsor Continuation Group. The late Rev. Canon Hone Kaa was part of the Indigenous Anglican Network for many years, and Bishop Winston Halapua had a significant organizational role in preparation for the last Lambeth Conference.

## Possible Future

John Bluck, Bishop of Waiapu (2002–2008), has observed that all participants in church-related conversations need to stay at the table, a metaphor which is vital for the future of a church which strives to be prophetic, radically inclusive, and true to the gospel. This means that our conversations around the matters which exercise us most need the will of all parties to stay in relationship. The question may well be, "How can we achieve these things and, in the process, become missional?" It would be good to see an Anglican Church in Aotearoa, New Zealand, and Polynesia which is deeply and radically biblically literate, liturgically innovative, and engaging with the local community in the places where people are hurting.

## Bibliography

Binney, Judith. 2005. *The Legacy of Guilt: A Life of Thomas Kendall*. Wellington, New Zealand: Bridget Williams Books Limited.

Davidson, Allan K. 2011b. *A Controversial Churchman: Essays on George Selwyn, Bishop of New Zealand and Lichfield, and Sarah Selwyn*. Wellington: Bridget Williams Books Limited.

Davidson, Allan K. ed. 2002. *Tongan Anglicans 1902–2002*. Auckland: College of the Diocese of Polynesia.

Davidson, Allan K. 2011a. *Living Legacy: A History of the Anglican Diocese of Auckland*. Auckland: Anglican Diocese of Auckland.

Elder, John Rawson. 1932. *The Letters and Journals of Samuel Marsden*. Dunedin: Coulls, Somerville, Wilkie.

Elder, John Rawson. 1934. *Marsden's Lieutenants*. Dunedin: Coulls, Somerville, Wilkie.

Glen, Robert. 1992. *Mission and Moko: Aspects of the Work of the Church Missionary Society in New Zealand*. Christchurch: Latimer Fellowship of New Zealand.

Morrell, William P. 1973. *The Anglican Church in New Zealand*. Dunedin: Church of the Province of New Zealand.

*Proceedings of the Sixtieth General Synod / Te Hinota Whanui*, Nadi, Fiji, July 7–12, 2012.

Salmond, Anne. 1997. *Between Worlds: Early Exchanges Between Māori and Europeans 1773–1815*. Auckland: Viking.

CHAPTER 35

# The Anglican Church of Australia

## Robert Tong

## Beginnings

When the American Revolutionary War (1775–1783) concluded with the loss of the "Thirteen Colonies," the government of the United Kingdom had to find alternative venues for the transportation of convicts. Captain James Cook's earlier discovery of Botany Bay (April 28, 1770) offered a solution (Clark 1968, vol. 1, 49, 59–72). On May 13, 1787, the British government dispatched a fleet (the "First Fleet") of 11 ships, carrying a human cargo of some 760 convicts and 550 ships' crew, military officers, marines, and their families, to far away New South Wales to found a new penal colony. On arrival, Botany Bay was deemed unsuitable owing to lack of water, so the fleet moved one inlet north to Port Jackson, and at Sydney Cove, on January 26, 1788, the new colony was proclaimed by the governor, Captain Arthur Phillip, Royal Navy.

The New South Wales settlement and the Church of England presence are located within the context of the phenomenon of the British Empire. The sequence of imperial progress, according to Hobson (1938, 204), was "first the missionary, then the Consul, and at last the invading army." In Australia's case, there was a different reason. Certainly, there were strategic reasons for establishing the colony (Clark 1968), but the transportation of convicts was the dominant motivation. Apart from those accompanying the early convict fleets, the first free settlers did not arrive until 1793. From the raising of the flag in 1788 to 1823, New South Wales was officially a penal colony comprised of convicts, marine guards and their wives, and government officials. Transportation of convicts to New South Wales ceased in 1840 but continued to some other Australian colonies until 1868. By that time, some 165,000 men and women had been relocated from the prisons of Britain and other parts of the British Empire to Australia. South Australia never accepted transportation.

*The Wiley-Blackwell Companion to the Anglican Communion*, First Edition. Edited by Ian S. Markham, J. Barney Hawkins IV, Justyn Terry, and Leslie Nuñez Steffensen.
© 2013 John Wiley & Sons, Ltd. Published 2013 by John Wiley & Sons, Ltd.

Prompted by John Newton, author of *Amazing Grace* and reformed slave trader, the Eclectic Society, assisted by William Wilberforce, persuaded Prime Minister William Pitt to appoint a chaplain to the new colony (Macintosh 1978; Judd and Cable 1987, 6; Kaye 2002, 9). On October 24, 1786, the Rev. Richard Johnson (1755–1827) was appointed "Chaplain to the settlement" at New South Wales. Thus, Christianity in its official Anglican expression, arrived on "Terra Australis" as part of the apparatus of government. Johnson's official position in the colony was unique: while a clergyman of the established church, he was on the payroll of the government and he was a military chaplain appointed by commission in the same way as the other senior officers. Johnson was bound "to observe and follow such orders . . . from our Governor . . . or any other of your superior officers, according to the rules and discipline of war" (Historical Records 1892).

Responsibility for religion was not solely Johnson's. The April 25, 1787, instructions to Governor Phillip stated: "And it is further Our Royal Will and Pleasure that you do by all proper methods enforce a due observance of Religion and good order among all the inhabitants of the new Settlement and that you so take such steps for the due celebration of public Worship as circumstances will permit" (Macintosh 1978, 15).

Other chaplains were appointed by the British government in succession to Johnson with similar duties and rights and they, like Johnson, were also appointed civil magistrates. Cable (1966, 21) says that the period 1770–1820 was the heyday of clerical justice in England and, on the whole, the contribution of these early chaplains as magistrates "was a notable one." Loane (1976) provides a comprehensive survey of clergy who served in New South Wales from Johnson to the close of the episcopate of Frederick Barker in 1882. Individual biographies exist for some of these early chaplains: Johnson (Bonwick 1898; Macintosh 1978); Marsden (Yarwood 1996); and Cowper (Bolt 2009). Fletcher (2000) has an illuminating article on the role of Christianity in the first 50 years of the colony.

When the Diocese of Calcutta was created in 1814, the Letters Patent restricted the jurisdiction of Bishop Middleton to India and, therefore, clergy in New South Wales remained under the ecclesiastical and spiritual jurisdiction of the Bishop of London (Giles 1929, 58). However, on October 2, 1824, Letters Patent were issued establishing the Archdeaconry of New South Wales and appointing as archdeacon Thomas Hobbes Scott, under the jurisdiction of the Bishop of Calcutta. When Scott resigned in 1829, William Grant Broughton (Shaw 1978) was appointed to replace him. Subsequently, Broughton was consecrated at Lambeth on February 14, 1836, as Bishop of Australia. The Letters Patent directed him to: "erect, found, make, ordain, and constitute all the Territories and Islands comprised within or dependent upon our Colonies of New South Wales, Van Diemen's Land, and Western Australia into a Bishop's See or Diocese, to be styled the Bishopric of Australia" (Clarke 1924, 39–44; Giles 1929, 219–25). While the colony of New South Wales (which incorporated present-day Victoria and Queensland) was the main area of his diocese, Broughton was responsible for the spiritual welfare of settlers in the colonies of Van Diemen's Land (later named Tasmania), the Swan River settlement in Western Australia, and South Australia.

## The Division of the Diocese of Australia

Tasmania was created as a separate diocese out of the Diocese of Australia in 1842, with the appointment of Francis Nixon (1842–1863) as bishop. On June 29, 1847, in Westminster Abbey, and with the benefit of a significant donation from Angelia Burdett-Coutts to the Colonial Bishoprics Fund, four bishops were consecrated for four new colonial dioceses: Robert Gray (1847–1872) for Cape Town, South Africa; Augustus Short (1847–1881) for Adelaide; Charles Perry (1847–1876) for Melbourne; and William Tyrrell (1847–1879) for Newcastle. On the creation of the three new Australian dioceses, the Diocese of Australia ceased to exist and the Bishop of Australia became the Metropolitan of Australasia and the Bishop of Sydney. The territory of the Adelaide diocese encompassed present-day South Australia and Western Australia. The Diocese of Perth was severed from Adelaide by Letters Patent in 1857. Newcastle covered the whole of present-day northern New South Wales and southern Queensland. The Diocese of Melbourne covered the whole of present-day Victoria. Further divisions of these vast dioceses occurred over the next 50 years.

## Colonial Church Issues

Several questions troubled Church of England congregations in the colonies of the British Empire. What was their legal status? In some colonies, the church was "established" and enjoyed a privileged position. In other colonies, the Church of England took its place with other Christian denominations. Addleshaw (1948) and Pearce (2000) survey this issue. A second question for the colonial church concerned the laws applicable to the colonial church. The laws governing the Church of England were part of the law of England and enforced as such in the king's courts. Did the law of England run in the king's dominions beyond the realm of England and, in particular, did the ecclesiastical laws applicable in England also apply in the colonies? McPherson (2007) provides a fascinating account of the process and the content of the English law which was received in the various colonies of the British Empire. In the early years of New South Wales, the governing authorities assumed that the Church of England was the established church in the colony. After all, the chaplains were on the government payroll, they served as civil magistrates, provision was made for lands to be set aside for church purposes, and the archdeacon was an ex officio member of the Legislative Council and ranked next after the lieutenant-governor. However, after the passage of a few years and some vigorous opposition, particularly from the Presbyterians and Roman Catholics, the local Church of England found itself in the same position as the other Christian denominations in the colony.

The middle years of the nineteenth century marked fundamental changes in the relationship between the Church of England and her daughter churches in the colonies. The pressing questions were being addressed by the English Crown, the Parliament, and departments of state. Daw (1977, 1) captures the central issues in these words:

In the mid-nineteenth century, the Anglican Church, established by law in England, Wales and Ireland, was widely believed to be similarly privileged throughout the empire. Whether it was in fact ever legally established, and hence part of the structure of the state, was something of a moot point; but in the late eighteenth century and the early decades of the nineteenth century, there was scarcely any dispute about it. The few colonial bishops who were sent out prior to 1840 were appointed, however reluctantly, by the imperial government, just as their brethren of the English episcopate were. They were treated as officers of the state, given status as such, and were generally supported financially by it. And yet, there was no adequate definition of the relations between church and state in the empire. Any such definition would have had to clarify the situation without separating the colonial church from the mother church; without encroaching upon apparent royal prerogatives; and without interfering in the colonies in matters of purely local concern.

In the same period, several Privy Council appeal cases from South Africa settled a number of the legal questions facing the colonial church: *Long v Bishop of Cape Town* (1863); *Re Lord Bishop of Natal* (1865); *Bishop of Natal v Gladstone* (1866); and *Merriman v Williams* (1882). (Hinchliff 1963 considers these cases from the Anglican Church of Southern Africa perspective and Ive 1992 from the perspective of the Church of England in South Africa.) In *Long* (at 774), it was held that:

> The Church of England, in places where there is no Church established by law, is in the same situation with any other religious body – in no better, but in no worse position; and the members may adopt, as the members of any other communion may adopt, rules for enforcing discipline within their body which will be binding on those who expressly or by implication have assented to them.

The cases also concluded that the coercive powers in the Letters Patent appointing bishops to their diocese were void of any effect.

Pestana (2011, 7), in a broad-scale treatment of the role of religion in the British colonial expansion in the eighteenth century, says that "English monarchs not only assumed that planters (as early settlers were frequently called) would introduce Protestant Christianity to far-flung Atlantic locations but also that their adherence to England's state church would help to make them loyal and effective representatives of the Crown." Carey's (2011b) groundbreaking *God's Empire*, sets nineteenth-century Anglican colonial church endeavors in the context of Christian mission in the settlement colonies of the British Empire.

## The 1850 Conference of Australasian Bishops

Broughton, as Metropolitan of Australasia, convened a month-long conference in Sydney, in October 1850. All the bishops of the province were in attendance: Perry (Melbourne), Short (Adelaide), Tyrrell (Newcastle), and George August Selwyn, Bishop of New Zealand (1841–1869). The constitutional arrangements for the colonial church, its legal status, the discipline of clergy and the ability to make local administrative decisions were matters of primary concern to the bishops.

Two matters formed the immediate backdrop to the conference: the failure of the Gladstone amendment to the Australian Colonies Bill 1850, and the *Gorham* judgment. From the late 1840s, there was general interest in England in reforming relationships with her colonial possessions. This interest included the relationship of the Church of England with its colonial manifestations. William Gladstone (1809–1898), a future prime minister, was drawn into this debate and his position as a founding member and treasurer of the Colonial Bishoprics Fund (founded 1841) gave him particular insights. The House of Commons debate on the Australian Colonies Bill on May 6, 1850, provided Gladstone with an opportunity to address a colonial problem. He proposed the addition of the "Colonial Church" clause, which would allow members of the Church of England in the Australian colonies to meet together by mutual consent "to make all such regulations as may be necessary for the better conduct of their ecclesiastical affairs and for the holding of meetings for the said purpose." Gladstone failed to persuade the House, by 187 votes to 102, to insert the clause. Had this amendment succeeded, it would have freed colonial churches to convene a representative assembly for local decision- making without running the risk of offending the ancient law requiring the king's consent to hold a convocation or synod (Powell [2008] recounts the colonial church clause episode).

The second issue cast a shadow over the conference, and the fault line it represented remains throughout the Anglican Communion today. George Gorham was an elderly clergyman who was suspected by his bishop, Phillpotts of Exeter, of not holding the correct doctrine on baptism, that is, baptismal regeneration. Gorham was indicted for heresy and found guilty by an ecclesiastical court (Court of Arches). He appealed to the judicial committee of the Privy Council and was acquitted. The Archbishops of Canterbury and York, sitting as assessors, concurred with the conclusion. This decision reverberated around the Empire, sparking the central question: is the "church" an autonomous body deciding its own doctrine and laws or is it dependent on the state to decide these questions? (Chadwick [1987, 250–71] provides an analysis of the crisis caused by this case. An evangelical view is argued by Holbrooke-Jones [2005]. Cockshut [1959] sets this case in the context of other controversies.)

The 1850 conference agreed that the canons of 1604 were "generally binding upon ourselves and the clergy of our respective dioceses. Where they cannot be literally complied with, in consequence of the altered state of circumstances since the enactment of the Canons, we are of [the] opinion that they must be, as far as possible, complied with in substance."

The bishops determined that it was now essential to establish provincial and diocesan synods, including laity as full members, to enable local rules to be made for ordering the common life of the church. The Letters Patent appointing each bishop purported to give him power to try their clergy for offences and to impose sanctions. The bishops disclaimed any desire to exercise this power and proposed the synod as the court for deacons and presbyters, and the bishops of the province as the court for the trial of a bishop. The Australasian Board of Mission was formed with a "Domestic" object, the "conversion and civilisation of the Australian Blacks," and a "Foreign" object: the "conversion and civilisation of the Heathen races in all the Islands of the Western Pacific." "Holy Baptism" was the only topic on which there was not unanimity. Perry, whose evangelical sympathies lay with Gorham, recorded his views separately. Carey (2011b, 167) states: "From this time, colonial Evangelicals feared that high church bishops would use their majority influence in the colonies to proscribe Evangelicals, dominate colonial synods and block their access to appeal to the Privy Council." The bishops were not free from criticism on their return to their dioceses (Cooper 2005). Minutes of the conference were sent to the "Archbishops and Bishops of the United Church of England and Ireland" and are reproduced in Clarke (1924, 96–105) and Giles (1929, 237–47). Kaye (2003) analyses the conference. Stephenson (1978, 13) notes a similar meeting of Canadian bishops.

Despite failing in 1850, Gladstone continued to raise the constitutional plight of the colonial church in the Imperial Parliament (see Carey's 2011a book chapter for Gladstone's colonial church initiatives). Agitation for reform also came from the colonial church. For example, the Canadian Diocese of Toronto, in 1853, petitioned the Queen "to remove all doubts about the legality of Synods in the colonial dioceses of the Empire" (Border 1962, 195). The Archbishop of Canterbury, John Bird Sumner, persuaded the House of Lords to pass the Colonial Church Regulation Bill, but the House of Commons rejected it in 1853 (Clarke 1924, 24 reprints the Bill). Thereafter, no further attempts were made in the Imperial Parliament to provide an Empire-wide constitutional framework for the colonial church.

In the decade following the 1850 conference, diocesan bishops in Australia had to take the initiative for local decision-making, whatever the uncertain state of English ecclesiastical law applicable in the colony. Each Australian diocese worked out its own constitution to create a synod with power to regulate the life of the diocese. The *Australian Colonies Act 1850* (UK) separated Victoria from New South Wales as an independent colony in 1851. Perry took advantage of this new colonial structure and, using Archbishop Sumner's failed 1853 Bill as a model, obtained the successful passage of the *Church of England Act 1854* (Vic) through the Victorian legislature. This Act allowed the church to convene assemblies for the management of church life in Victoria and was the first colonial legislation anywhere in the British Empire for the local regulation of the church (Robin 1967; Giles 1929, 247–51 reprints the Act). Tasmania followed suit in 1858. The dioceses in New South Wales (Sydney, Newcastle, and Goulburn) also obtained similar constitutional framework legislation from the New South Wales Parliament in 1866. Leaders of the dioceses in Queensland, South Australia, and Western Australia, as a matter of principle, felt that seeking legislation was too Erastian, and proceeded by way of consensual compact to convene assemblies for the purpose of internal management and regulation. Border (1962) tells the constitutional story in detail for the period 1788–1872. Clarke (1924) and Giles (1929) provide many of the relevant documents.

## A Constitution for the Australian Church

In 1872, Bishop Frederic Barker, as Metropolitan of Australia, convened a meeting of delegates from each diocese who agreed to form a general synod for the Australian

Church. It was to meet every five years, but "Determinations" of the general synod only became law in a diocese when adopted by the diocesan synod. This followed the New South Wales provincial synod arrangements where provincial ordinances did not take effect in a diocese until adopted by ordinance of the diocesan synod. Border (1962, 251) is highly critical of Barker's role in entrenching the primacy of the diocese over the general synod. The adoption of the 1872 constitution did not create a "new" church. Unlike the South African constitution of 1870, which did create a new church, no power was taken to alter the Thirty-Nine Articles of Religion, or the 1662 Book of Common Prayer, or to restrict the operation of English ecclesiastical law in church tribunals (cf. 1882 South African Privy Council appeal case *Merriman v Williams*, discussed in Clarke 1924, 329–34 and Hinchliff 1963, 122–8).

The unbroken connection or "nexus" with the Church of England was confirmed by a series of legal opinions given by eminent senior counsel in England (1911) and in Australia the following year (reproduced in *Canon Law* 1981, 112–46; summarized in Giles 1929, 158–67). The lawyers concluded that the Church of England churches in Australia were organized on the basis that "they are part of the Church of England," not churches "in communion with," or "in connection with" the Church of England. This meant that any changes to doctrine or practice in England were to be applied in Australia, unless the local situation made the change inapplicable.

Federation of the Australian colonies into the Australian nation in 1901 and the nexus opinions stimulated a desire for a new national constitution. Between 1920 and 1955, there were a number of draft constitutions considered by general and diocesan synods. The debates were often difficult, and there was much suspicion. Anglo-Catholics wanted to secure "catholic order," and evangelicals wanted to preserve the Elizabethan Settlement. Points of contention included the powers of the general synod, the composition of the Appellate Tribunal (only bishops or some lawyers), and constitutional safeguards for diocesan autonomy, and meant that no final form of a constitution was agreed to until 1961. The intervention of the Archbishop of Canterbury, Dr. Geoffrey Fisher, during his visit in 1950 reinvigorated the constitutional debate. A fresh draft was passed by the 1955 general synod, and all diocesan synods accepted this version. Enabling Acts, to which the constitution is a schedule, were passed by state and territory legislatures to come into effect on January 1, 1962. The South Australian Act contains an "escape clause" which allows the Diocese of Adelaide, and any diocese formed out of Adelaide, to withdraw from the constitution by resolution passed at two successive synods. Any diocese not assenting to the constitution remained in communion with the new church. Davis (1993) provides the best history for this whole period. Judd (1984) examines the politics till 1930.

The constitution begins with "Fundamental Declarations." The Australian Church is "part of the One Holy Catholic and Apostolic Church of Christ," affirms the Nicene and Apostles' Creeds, and receives the Old and New Testaments as "the ultimate rule and standard of faith . . . containing all things necessary for salvation." There is a commitment to obey the commands of Christ, teach his doctrine, administer the sacraments of Holy Baptism and Holy Communion, and preserve the orders of bishops, priests, and deacons. The "Ruling Principles" commit the church to the doctrine and principles of the Church of England embodied in the Book of Common Prayer, the Ordinal, and the Thirty-Nine Articles of Religion. The primate, chosen from the diocesan bishops by election, has a fixed term, limited constitutional responsibilities, and continues in office as diocesan bishop. Although the enabling Acts passed by state legislatures are similar, they are not identical, and this may affect the force of the constitution in each state. In *Scandrett v Dowling* (the 1992 "Women Priests" case), the New South Wales Supreme Court held that while decisions relating to property would be upheld by the courts, other obligations found in the constitution were binding *in foro conscientiae*.

In the 50 years since the commencement of the present general synod arrangements, the two significant positive outcomes have been the Australia-wide acceptance of *An Australian Prayer Book* in 1978 (Fletcher 1999) and the almost universal acceptance of the revision of the canons of 1604. On the negative side, the debilitating effect of the women's ordination question, stretching over a number of general synods, reduced the ability of the general synod to act as an instrument for unity. A number of dioceses have not adopted the canon authorizing the ordination of women as priests. As orders are not universally recognized across the whole Australian Church, there is a state of *impaired communion*. Additionally, the 1995 canon authorizing *A Prayer Book for Australia* was not adopted by the Diocese of Sydney as the book contained elements of Tractarian theology and ritual. This shattered the ideal of Australian "common prayer." Over the last two decades, there has been a gradual loss of confidence in principal organs of the general synod. All these factors reduce the ability of the general synod to speak with a unified voice for Australian Anglicanism.

## Missions

Because New Zealand, under Selwyn, had become a separate province in 1858, the inaugural general synod of 1872 reconstituted the Australasian Board of Missions as the Australian Board of Mission (ABM). In its heyday, ABM had a significant number of missionaries in the field, mostly in Northern Australia, the Pacific Islands, South East Asia, and present-day Papua New Guinea. ABM was the principal missionary agency providing Anglican ministry to Papua New Guinea. Philip Strong, as Bishop of New Guinea (1936–1962), gave highly respected leadership in that country, particularly during World War II. The church in Papua New Guinea was constitutionally part of the province of Queensland until its formation as a separate province in 1976, following independence from Australia in 1975. Strong was elected Archbishop of Brisbane in 1962 and Primate of Australia in 1966. An Australian, David Hand, succeeded Strong as Bishop of New Guinea before becoming Archbishop of Papua New Guinea on its formation as a separate province (Hand 2002).

In recent years, ABM has ceased to send missionaries and, instead, has partnership programs with local churches and agencies located in about ten countries, as well as Northern Australia. This change of direction may reflect the shrinking Anglo-Catholic base of ABM and the declining interest in traditional missionary endeavor from liberal Catholics.

A feature of Anglican Church life over the last two centuries is the existence of voluntary societies working within the official life of the denomination. One example is the Church Missionary Society-Australia (CMS-A). CMS-A traces its roots to the Church

Missionary Society (CMS) founded in 1799 by the leaders of the Eclectic Society, who were also prominent members of the Clapham Sect. The Rev. Samuel Marsden, who was instrumental in missionary efforts to the Maori in New Zealand, established a New South Wales Auxiliary of CMS in 1825 "primarily to help Australian Aborigines" (Bolt 2009, 243). Of particular note is the Australian connection with East Africa. CMS-A took responsibility for the finances and supply of missionaries in the new diocese of Central Tanganyika following a request in 1926 from CMS in Britain. The diocese was carved out of the diocese of Mombasa, which then comprised Kenya and much of Tanganyika territory. The first three diocesans were Australians: George Chambers (1927–1946) (Sibtain 1968), William Wynn-Jones (1947–1950), and Alfred Stanway (1951–1971) (Stanway 1991; Grant Forthcoming). CMS-A ensured a steady stream of missionaries. Welcome publicity was engendered by the returned missionary doctor, Paul White, with his "Jungle Doctor" stories (White 1977).

In 2013, CMS-A supports some 250 missionaries located in Northern Australia and in 35 other countries. They are engaged in strengthening local churches, theological education, caring ministries, and student work (Cole 1971; Paterson 1998; O'Brien 1999).

Christian ministry to rural Australia has presented a challenge from the early days of settlement. Isolated pastoral homesteads, small scattered communities, and mining towns often populated with itinerant workers are all features of this challenge. The Bush Church Aid (BCA) Society, founded in 1919, is another voluntary society working within the Anglican Church of Australia to take ministry to these communities. George Chambers, later Bishop of Central Tanganyika, was one of the founders. Its parent body, the Colonial and Continental Church Society, began life in the Swan River Colony in Western Australia in 1836. BCA works mainly in the Northern Territory, Western Australia, and South Australia (Caterer 1981; George 1993).

The Anglo-Catholic answer to the challenge of the outback was the formation of bush brotherhoods. On his appointment in 1892 as the first bishop of Rockhampton, Nathaniel Dawes had six clergy to cover an area four times that of England and Wales. He conceived a plan to bring Christian ministry to the outback. Young men would commit themselves to Christian ministry for five years in return for board, lodging, and a modest amount for personal expenses. This plan was modeled on Oxford House, where undergraduates worked during their vacation in the London slums. With the encouragement of Bishop B. F. Westcott of Durham, George Halford exchanged his living as vicar of St. Peter's Jarrow for that of "Bush Brother" in Longreach, Central Queensland (Frappell 1996). This initiative grew into several bush brotherhoods. At their height, there were over a dozen bush brotherhoods which ministered in rural areas in every state of Australia. Over the course of a century, some 19 brothers became bishops in the Australian Church. By the 1980s, settled parishes replaced the need for bush brothers and, with a marked fall in candidates and funding, the movement had run its course (Webb 1978).

Bringing the gospel to the original indigenous inhabitants of Australia has been a story of difficulty, disappointment, and hope. The story is told compellingly, comprehensively, and compassionately by John Harris (1994). The April 25, 1787, instructions to Governor Phillip stated: "You are to endeavour by every means possible to open an Intercourse with the Natives and to conciliate their affections, enjoining all Our Subjects to live in amity and kindness with them." Chaplains Marsden and Cowper were especially concerned about aborigines (Bolt 2009). For much of the nineteenth century, the prevailing anthropology was that the level of civilization had to be raised before the gospel could have significant impact. The failure to understand indigenous social structures and land tenure compounded the difficulties. Although the separate Australian colonies joined in a federation in 1901, the constitution of the new nation did not allow aborigines to be counted for census purposes, nor were they permitted to vote. The franchise issue was corrected in 1962 and the census in 1967. In the lead-up to the bicentenary of European settlement, there were calls for a national act of reconciliation for past injustices. On February 7, 1988, in St. Andrew's Cathedral, Sydney, at a service marking the first Christian service 200 years previously, the primate, Archbishop Sir John Grindrod, expressed to Aboriginal Bishop Arthur Malcolm, "our sorrow for the past and the seeking of your forgiveness." Bishop Malcolm responded, ". . . through the message of Jesus Christ we have learned to forgive. We have received his forgiveness, and now in turn we must also forgive" (Harris 1994, 867). A multiplicity of Aboriginal languages presented difficulties in Bible translation. The task was fragmented, and only in 2007 was a whole Bible available in Kriol, an Australian creole language widely spoken in Northern Australia. Since 1977, Nungalinya College has been a training establishment for indigenous Christian leaders. Some fundamental challenges remain, but the growing number of indigenous Christian leaders, lay and ordained, give hope that "God is working his purpose out as year succeeds to year."

## Diocesan Churchmanship

While Bishop Broughton (1836–1853) belonged to the old school of High Churchmen, the Oxford Movement greatly influenced him in his choice of clergy. The 1847 consecration of Augustus Short for Adelaide and William Tyrrell for Newcastle consolidated this new school of churchmanship in Australian Anglicanism. The first bishops of the dioceses located in the capital cities of the colonies of Tasmania (Nixon 1842), South Australia (Short 1847), Western Australia (Matthew Hale 1857), and Queensland (Edward Tufnell 1859) were all disciples of the Oxford Movement. Naturally, new dioceses carved out of these mother dioceses over the next century were Anglo-Catholic in outlook and temperament at their foundation. Episcopal appointments to these new dioceses were of the same theological stamp, as were most of the clergy appointed by them. For nearly 150 years, the majority of Australian dioceses were firmly placed in the Anglo-Catholic camp. However, from the 1970s, adherence to the theology of the Oxford Fathers fell away and the theological stance of many Australian dioceses is now more accurately described as "liberal catholic." The sesquicentenary of the Oxford Movement in 1983 was probably the last high point of organized diocesan Tractarian activity. In 2011, only a few smaller dioceses would identify themselves as "Catholic" in the Oxford Movement sense. *Colonial Tractarians* (Porter 1989) and *From Oxford to the Bush* (Moses 1997) are two collections of well-written and scholarly essays which capture the story of the Oxford Movement in Australia.

Evangelical interests secured the appointments of the early chaplains to New South Wales. Broughton's successor to the See of Sydney, Frederic Barker (1854–1882), "stood in the mainstream of strong Evangelical tradition and brought to life all that was best in the hopes and dreams of early Chaplains. No one man did more to mould the character of the Diocese or to lay down the lines for its future development" (Loane 1987, 63). During Barker's episcopate, the founding bishops appointed to the rural dioceses created out of Sydney were evangelicals: Mesac Thomas to Goulburn (1863) and Samuel Marsden to Bathurst (1869). Barker's successors have maintained the predominantly evangelical character of the Sydney diocese. Today, Armidale diocese and North West Australia are of a similar evangelical stamp. Melbourne, after Perry, did not continue in the evangelical fold. Bendigo (1902) and Gippsland (1902), both carved out of Melbourne diocese, had evangelical founding bishops, H. A. Langley and A. W. Pain, respectively (Kuan 2011). A number of current diocesan bishops would identify themselves as evangelical, but they lead dioceses with mixed churchmanship and theology.

## Education

In the early days of the New South Wales settlement, Church of England clergy included in their responsibilities the education of children. Archdeacon Scott was appointed in 1825 as King's Visitor to schools by the Colonial Office. To assist the Church of England discharge its responsibilities for religion and education, a Church and Schools Corporation was created in 1826 and endowed with one-seventh of the new lands of the colony. The scheme was strongly opposed by Presbyterians, Roman Catholics, and secular interests, and in 1833, the corporation was dissolved (Grose 1986). A similar reservation of land for "Protestant Clergy" had been made in Canada but by 1856, the "Clergy Reserves" had been sold and the proceeds applied for secular use (Carrington 1963). In both countries, the reservation of land was perceived as supporting the "establishment" of the Church of England. Governor Bourke's 1836 Church Act provided matching grants of money to the Church of England, the Church of Rome, and the Presbyterians for building churches and for stipends. The Act was later extended to other Christian denominations. When Victoria and Queensland became separate colonies, this form of state aid continued until finally withdrawn in 1871. In New South Wales, financial assistance for the maintenance of denominational schools continued until the 1880 *Public Instruction Act*, which gave the government primary responsibility for education. Turney et al. (1991, 15–25) details the fierce church and state struggle over education. The political resolution of this struggle in New South Wales did grant to clergy the right of regular access to teach their denominational faith to their flocks in the new public schools (Austin 1965). This access to public schools for scripture teaching continues to this day. It is in the area of secondary education that Anglican interests established successful independent schools in each state during the nineteenth and early part of the twentieth centuries. For example, in New South Wales: The Kings School (1831) and St. Catherine's School (1856); in Tasmania: Launceston Church Grammar School (1846); in Victoria: Melbourne Grammar School (1849); in South

Australia: St. Peter's College (1847); and in Western Australia: Hale School (1858). From the earliest days, there were always a small number of private schools not directly connected to any Christian denomination (Turney 1989). Federal government grants for science teaching in 1964 reintroduced state aid for non-government schools. Favorable government policies toward capital grants and interest subsidies over the last 20 years have enabled the establishment of a significant number of Anglican "low-fees" schools in many dioceses. Across Australia, nearly one-third of school children are educated in non-government schools. Some fresh thinking has begun about the Anglican contribution to education (Cairney et al. 2011).

Apart from Notre Dame (1989) and the Australian Catholic University (1991), Australian universities are secular foundations (Turney et al. 1991). Some have colleges of residence sponsored by Christian churches. Only a few universities offer divinity or theology as a separate discipline. Theological study for ordination had to be undertaken separately from the universities. To meet this need, a number of bishops established their own college for training ordinands. Carey (2011b, 247–86) has an illuminating survey on the training and supply of clergy during the nineteenth century. The creation of the Australian College of Theology by the general synod in 1891 as an examining body established the two-year Licentiate in Theology of the College as a minimum standard for ordination. Since the early 1970s, the level of theological education required for ordination has risen, so that a bachelor's degree is now the accepted standard. A consequence is that smaller colleges have closed or joined ecumenical theological colleges. Larger colleges have been granted degree-awarding status. In some dioceses, arrangements have been made with local universities to supply academic instruction, with ministerial formation remaining with the diocese. Moore Theological College is the only college which still requires full-time residence for degree students. With the demise of St. John's College, Morpeth, and St. Michael's House, Crafers, South Australia, there is no college in the Anglo-Catholic tradition in Australia. Trinity College, Melbourne (1872), is the leading liberal Catholic college while St. Mark's, Canberra, meets needs across the theological spectrum. Moore Theological College, Sydney (1856), Ridley College, Melbourne (1910), and Trinity Theological College, Perth (1997), are evangelical in foundation and purpose.

## Liturgy

Like many of the larger provinces of the Anglican Communion which produced their own prayer book after independence from the Church of England, the Australian general synod commissioned the production of a contemporary language revision of the Book of Common Prayer, together with some experimental services. Following extensive trial use, "An Australian Prayer Book for use together with the Book of Common Prayer 1662" was approved by the general synod in 1978, and all dioceses adopted the canon authorizing its use. The 1978 book is faithful to the constitution which enshrines the 1662 Book of Common Prayer and the Thirty-Nine Articles of Religion as "the authorised standard of worship and doctrine in this Church" (Fletcher 1999). A further revision, "A Prayer Book for Australia," was approved by the general synod after a contentious debate in 1995 and, as noted earlier, it is not approved for use in the Diocese of Sydney. Before the creation of the new Australian Church, liturgical experimentation was held by the High Court of Australia to be a breach of the trusts on which Church of England property was held (the "*Red Book Case*" 1948, Galbraith 1998). The new constitution permits a bishop to authorize variations to the Book of Common Prayer, and since 1992, the Canon Concerning Services allows a minister to make variations to authorized services. All variations must be edifying and "not depart from the doctrine of this Church."

## Statistics

The first national census in 1911 showed that 38.4 percent of the population of 4,455,000 identified themselves as Anglican, in contrast with 22.4 percent identifying themselves as Roman Catholic. The 2001 census had Anglicans at 20.7 percent and Roman Catholics at 26.6 percent of a total population of about 18.769 million. Apart from increases shown in the 1921 census and the 1946 census, attributable to increased migration from Britain, there has been a steady decline in the Anglican population to 18.7 percent out of 19,855,288 persons in 2006. The 2006 Australian census figures on *Religious Affiliations in Australia* show 63.9 percent Christian, 4.9 percent other religions; in 1996, the figures were 70.88 percent and 3.45 percent, respectively; in 1991, they were 73.98 percent and 2.64 percent, respectively.

Since 1991, the National Church Life Survey (NCLS) has collected information about church attendance in the same year as the national census. NCLS estimated weekly attendances for the Anglican Church of Australia in 2006 at approximately 178,000. The 2006 estimates for the mainland capital cities were: Adelaide – 8,000; Perth – 10,600; Brisbane – 19,000; Melbourne – 25,000; and Sydney – 52,000. A survey of active clergy numbers over the last 15 years suggests that only the dioceses of Armidale, North West Australia, and Sydney are ordaining sufficient numbers to replace losses through retirement or death. Unless there is significant change, the number of active clergy in eight dioceses will drop by half within the next 15 years. Grutzner (2011) is an annual listing of all clergy.

## Social Voice

Concern for the poor, initiating "good works," and engagement in issues of public policy have involved members of the church since the early days of European settlement. The Rev. William Cowper was a leading light in this for most of the first 50 years of the nineteenth century (Bolt 2009). Lawton (1990) has tellingly examined through "Sydney eyes" issues of divorce, Sabbath Observance, and alcohol abuse for the 30-year period preceding World War I. The Sydney archdeacon, Francis Bertie Boyce (1844–1931), was a leading agitator for reform in those areas. F. E. Maynard (1882–1973), vicar of Eastern Hill, was a Melbourne voice for Christian socialism. He fostered the work of the Brotherhood of St. Lawrence among the inner-city poor of Melbourne

(Holden 1996). Archdeacon R. B. S. Hammond (1870–1946) conducted a vigorous program of pastoral care and evangelism in the Sydney slums (Judd 1951). Welfare services in the various dioceses now cooperate under the generic name of *Anglicare* for the delivery of assistance to the needy. Leading Anglican critics of the social and political order during the Great Depression were Bishop E. H. Burgmann (Canberra and Goulburn 1934–1960) (Hempenstall 1993) and Bishop J. S. Moyes (Armidale 1929–1964). While Anglicans continue to be concerned about "church and society" issues, there is little attention given to this in the mainstream media. Notable exceptions are a speech by Archbishop Sir Marcus Loane in 1972, which stirred the federal government into commissioning the Henderson Report on Poverty (Reid 2004, 66), and Archbishop Jensen's 2001 call for compassion toward boat refugees seeking asylum in Australia.

## Literature

Given the diocesan nature of the Australian Church, most literature consists of diocesan histories, for example: Elkin (1955), Robin (1967), Hilliard (1986), Judd and Cable (1987), Porter (1997), Williams (1989), Le Couteur (2006), and Grant (2010), or biographies of bishops, for example: Cowper (1888), Loane (1960), Robin (1967), Brown (1974), Reid (2004), and Withycombe (2009). Other works have been cited earlier. A small number of contemporary books consider the phenomenon of Australian Anglicanism. Fletcher (2008) provides an assessment of the contribution of Australian Anglicans to the making of the history of Australia. Kaye's (2002) *Anglicanism in Australia* is the only national history of Anglicans in Australia. Frame (2007) explores current tensions in their historical context. Kaye (2006) edits a collection of essays which illustrate the breadth of Australian thought on ecclesiology, although no hint is given as to the number of adherents of each position. Kaye (2011) explores the contemporary relationship of church and state in Australia. Frappell et al. (1999) provides an index to the papers of successive Archbishops of Canterbury which relate to Australia. Most current "Anglican" literary output comes from theological college faculties. Significant internationally recognized contributions in the area of Bible commentary are connected with names such as Leon Morris, Peter O'Brien, Paul Barnett, William Dumbrell, David Peterson, Graeme Goldsworthy, and John Woodhouse. In the area of systematic theology, names such as T. C. Hammond, D. B. Knox, P. F. Jensen, and Mark D. Thompson are recognized. In addition, Macquarie University's Department of Ancient History, connected particularly with the name of Edwin Judge, continues to produce excellent research in the area of early Christianity.

## Anglican Communion

Australian bishops were present at the first Lambeth Conference in 1867 and at each conference since. The first chairman of the Anglican Consultative Council was Australian-born John Denton AM, OBE, and other Australians have served on the standing committee of the council. Over the years, there has been Australian membership of communion bodies such as the Anglican–Roman Catholic International Commission (ARCIC), the Inter-Anglican Theological and Doctrinal Commission, the International Anglican Liturgical Consultations, the International Anglican Women's Network, and the Archbishop of Canterbury's Panel of Reference. The Australian general synod standing committee made detailed submissions on the proposed Anglican Covenant, and the *St. Mark's Review*, number 220, is a themed issue "The Anglican Communion Covenant."

On issues of theological principle and in solidarity with many bishops from Africa and Asia, Archbishop Peter Jensen (Sydney) and his five assistant bishops, together with the Bishop of North West Australia, declined the invitation to Lambeth 2009 but, instead, attended the Global Anglican Future Conference (GAFCON) in Jerusalem. The events detailed in *The Windsor Report 2004* (Bolt et al. 2005, reviewed by Rees 2008) form the back ground to this decision. Declining an invitation to Lambeth is not without precedent. The Archbishop of York and a number of evangelicals did not attend the first conference of 1867 (Curtis 1942; Stephenson 1978).

## Diocese of Sydney

The Diocese of Sydney, the "mother diocese" of the Australian Church, played a primary role in establishing the constitutional shape of the Australian Church. The Bishop of Sydney held the primacy, almost without break, for the first 150 years. The predominant theological stance of the diocese is, at present, a minority one in the Australian Church. This theological outlook was established by the appointment of evangelical clergy as chaplains to the colony. The 27-year episcopate of Frederick Barker (1854–1882) allowed deep foundations to be laid, which consolidated this evangelical character; this was further reinforced by the long, twentieth-century episcopates of Howard Mowll (1933–1958) and Marcus Loane (1966–1982).

A generous bequest from a leading citizen, Thomas Moore (1762–1840), enabled Barker to found Moore College in 1856 (Loane 1955). Carey (2011b, 268) records some 170 students educated at Moore up to 1900. The college was central to Barker's goal of a home-grown supply of clergy. The academic leadership of D. B. Knox (principal, 1958–1985) (Cameron 2006) and D. W. B. Robinson (vice-principal, 1959–1972, later archbishop) enabled the college faculty to engage fully with the resurgence of evangelical scholarship in the 1960s. Knox was associated with the foundation of Tyndale House, Cambridge (Noble 2006), and was the founding principal of George Whitefield College, Cape Town (1989). Moore has strong connections with Ridley College, Melbourne, and Oak Hill College, London.

Sydney evangelicals understand the Book of Common Prayer through the eyes of Archbishop Cranmer, the Thirty-Nine Articles of Religion through W. H. Griffith Thomas (1930), and the proper place of evangelicals in the church from the writings of Bishop J. C. Ryle (1816–1900) (Ryle 1901). However, in the 1960s, fresh insights on the doctrine of the church from Knox and Robinson refocused attention on the text of the scriptures and served to weaken denominational loyalties (Knox

2000; Robinson 2008). In the same period, three overseas leaders nourished evangelical church life in Sydney. John Stott's writings and visits taught generations the art of expository preaching; Dr. Jim Packer published reformed evangelical theology; and the Billy Graham Crusades marked a spiritual turning point in the lives of thousands. Bible study and evangelism are two distinguishing marks of Sydney Anglicans.

The Sydney synod's 1922 *Women's Work in the Church Ordinance* "allowed women to preach when needed and to engage in other liturgical ministries" and put Sydney "at the forefront of women's ministry development" (Rodgers 1998, 78). Today, there are some 45 women deacons licensed in the diocese, as well as a much larger number of theologically trained laywomen in employed ministry in parishes. Moore College has established the Priscilla and Aquila Centre to encourage and promote the practice of Christian ministry by women, in partnership with men.

Two other elements in the synodical life of the diocese should be noted. First, the remarkable contribution of the Anglican Church League, an association of lay and clerical leaders founded in 1909, for "the maintenance of the reformed, protestant and evangelical character of the diocese of Sydney" (Robinson 1976). Secondly, the thorough and measured reports of the Sydney Doctrine Commission on topics such as women's ministry, administration of the Lord's Supper, and penal substitutionary atonement have given the synod a theological foundation for policy decisions.

Almost since the beginning, "Sydney" has attracted comment and criticism. Recent accusations of doctrinal error (Carnley 2004, 233–5) or warnings that Sydney is a threat to "worldwide Anglican unity" (Porter 2011) have not deflected diocesan leadership from giving strong support to the spirit and intent of the 1998 Lambeth Resolution 1.10 on human sexuality, the Global South Anglicans, and the GAFCON movement. (See Jensen 2012 for a response.) At the parish level, these criticisms only serve to strengthen the resolve of church goers to continue "making disciples of all nations."

## Current Issues Facing the Australian Church

There is recognition by bishops and synods of the long-term, downward trend of church attendance, the rising age of clergy, and the declining number offering for ordination. Due to post-World War II migration patterns, challenges of language and culture are now present in Australia. Cross-cultural mission is now an imperative in most urban churches. The impaired communion resulting from women's ordination remains a theological obstacle. The Sydney synod resolution which "affirmed that the Lord's Supper in this diocese may be administered by persons other than presbyters" raises questions of order and theology (Bolt et al. 2008 and 2010; Atherstone 2011). The long history of diocesan autonomy, having been set within a federal framework for the last 50 years, is now due for serious constitutional review. Questions on Anglican identity sharpened by the Global South, and given trajectory by the GAFCON Jerusalem Declaration, presently confront the church in Australia. National answers will be muted; the clearest answers will come from the dioceses which support the renewed missional articulation of Anglican identity.

Many names cited in this article have entries in the *Australian Dictionary of Biography*, which can also be accessed online. Websites are maintained by all dioceses, the General Synod Office, and most of the organizations cited.

## Bibliography

Addleshaw, George W. 1948. The Law and Constitution of the Church Overseas. In *The Mission of the Anglican Communion*, eds. E. R. Morgan and R. Lloyd. London: SPCK & SPG.

Atherstone, Andrew. 2011. *Lay Presidency: An Anglican Option?* Cambridge: Grove Books Limited.

*Australian Dictionary of Biography*. Melbourne University Press and Online.

Austin, Albert G. 1965. *Australian Education 1788–1900*. Melbourne: Issac Pitman & Sons.

Bolt, Peter G., Mark Thompson, Robert Tong, eds. 2005. *The Faith Once for all Delivered, an Australian Evangelical Response to the Windsor Report*. Sydney: Australian Church Record.

Bolt, Peter G., Mark Thompson, Robert Tong, eds. 2008. *The Lord's Supper in Human Hands*. Sydney: Australian Church Record.

Bolt, Peter G., Mark Thompson, Robert Tong, eds. 2010. *The Lord's Supper in Human Hands: Epilogue*. Sydney: Australian Church Record.

Bolt, Peter G. 2009. *William Cowper (1778–1858). The Life and Influence of Australia's First Parish Clergyman*. Sydney: Bolt Publishing Services.

Bonwick, James. 1898. *Australia's First Preacher*. London: Sampson Low, Marston & Company.

Border, Ross. 1962. *Church and State in Australia, 1788–1872*. London: SPCK.

Brown, Judith M. 1974. *Augustus Short, DD*. Adelaide: Hodge Publishing House.

Cable, Kenneth J. 1966. *The Churches and Local Government Finance: An Historical Survey*. Sydney: Ian J. Harvey.

Canon Law Commission. 1981. *Canon Law in Australia*. Sydney: Anglican Church of Australia Trust Corporation.

Cairney, Trevor, Bryan Cowling, and Michael Jensen. 2011. *New Perspectives on Anglican Education: Reconsidering Purpose and Plotting a Future direction*. Sydney: Anglican Education Commission, Diocese of Sydney.

Cameron, Marcia Helen. 2006. *An Enigmatic Life: David Broughton Knox: Father of Contemporary Sydney Anglicanism*. Victoria: Acorn Press.

Carey, Hilary M. 2011a. Gladstone, the Colonial Church and Imperial State. *Church and State in Old and New Worlds*. Leiden: Brill.

Carey, Hilary M. 2011b. *God's Empire, Religion and Colonialism in the British World, c. 1801–1908*. Cambridge: Cambridge University Press.

Carnley, Peter. 2004. *Reflections in Glass*. Australia: Harper Collins.

Carrington, Philip. 1963. *The Anglican Church in Canada-a History*. Toronto: Collins.

Caterer, Helen. 1981. *Australians Outback: 60 Years of Bush Church Aid*. Sydney: Anglican Information Office.

Chadwick, Owen. 1987. *The Victorian Church, Part One, 1829–1859*. London: SCM Press.

Clark, Manning. 1968. *A History of Australia*. Vol. 1. Melbourne: Melbourne University Press.

Clarke, Henry L. 1924. *Constitutional Church Government*. London: SPCK.

Cockshut, Anthony O. J. 1959. *Anglican Attitudes: A Study of Victorian Religious Controversies*. London: Collins.

Cole, Kenneth. 1971. *A History of the Church Missionary Society of Australia*. Melbourne: Church Missionary Historical Publications.

Cooper, Austin. 2005. The Bishops and Baptism: Colonial Reverberations of a Tractarian Controversy. *Pacifica*, vol. 18 (February).

Cowper, William M. 1888. *Episcopate of the Right Reverend Frederic Barker, D. D.* London: Hatchards.

Curtis, William R. 1942/1968. *The Lambeth Conferences*. New York: AMS Press.

Daw, E. D. 1977. *Church and State in the Empire, the Evolution of Imperial Policy 1846–1856*. Canberra: Faculty of Military Studies.

Davis, John. 1993. *Australian Anglicans and their Constitution*. Melbourne: Acorn Press.

Elkin, A. P. 1955. *The Diocese of Newcastle*. Australia: Australasian Medical Publishing Company Limited.

Fletcher, Brian. 1999. Re-shaping Australian Anglicanism 1962–1978: From Book of Common Prayer to An Australian Prayer Book. *Journal Royal Australian Historical Society*, vol. 85, no. 2, pp. 120–39.

Fletcher, Brian. 2000. Christianity and Free Society in New South Wales 1788–1840. *Journal Royal Australian Historical Society*, vol. 86, no. 2, pp. 93–113.

Fletcher, Brian H. 2008. *The Place of Anglicanism in Australia: Church, Society and Nation*. Victoria: Broughton Publishing.

Frame, Thomas R. 2000. *A Church for a Nation – A History of the Anglican Diocese of Canberra & Goulburn*. Alexandria: Hale & Iremonger.

Frame, Thomas R. 2007. *Anglicans in Australia*. Sydney: University of New South Wales Press.

Frappell, Ruth. 1996. The Australian Bush Brotherhoods and their English Origins. *Journal of Ecclesiastical History*, vol. 47, pp. 82–97.

Frappell, Ruth, Leighton Frappell, Robert Withycombe, and Raymond Knobbs. 1999. *Anglicans in the Antipodes. An Indexed Calendar of the Papers and Correspondence of the Archbishops of Canterbury, 1788–1961, Relating to Australia, New Zealand, and the Pacific*. Connecticut: Greenwood Press.

Galbraith, David. 1998. Just Enough Religion to Make Us Hate: An Historico-Legal Study of the Red Book Case. Unpublished PhD Thesis, University of New South Wales.

George, Peter. 1993. *BCA 75 Not Out! : 1919–1994: The Bush Church Aid Society Celebrates 75 Years of Ministry in Remote Australia*. Sydney: BCA Australia.

Giles, Robbie A. 1929. *The Constitutional History of the Australian Church*. London: Skeffington & Son.

Grant, Audrey. Forthcoming. *Running True Bishop Alfred Stanway*.

Grant, James. 2010. *Episcopally Led and Synodically Governed: Anglicans in Victoria: 1803–1997*. Melbourne: Australian Scholarly Publishing.

Grose, Kelvin. 1986. What Happened to the Clergy Reserves of New South Wales? *Journal of the Royal Australian Historical Society*, vol. 72, no. 2, pp. 92–103.

Grutzner, Angela. 2011. *The Australian Clerical Directory*. Melbourne: Publishing Solutions.

Hand, David. 2002. *Modawa: Papua New Guinea and Me 1946–2002*. Port Moresby: Salpress.

Harris, John. 1994. *One Blood. 200 Years of Aboriginal Encounter with Christianity: A Story of Hope*, 2nd ed. Australia: Albatross Books.

Hempenstall, Peter. 1993. *Meddlesome Priest: A Life of Ernest Burgmann*. St. Leonards NSW: Allen & Unwin.

Hilliard, David. 1986. *Godliness and Good Order: A History of the Anglican Church in South Australia*. Netley: Wakefield Press.

Hinchliff, Peter. 1963. *The Anglican Church in South Africa: An Account of the History and Development of the Church of the Province of South Africa*. London: Darton, Longman & Todd.

Historical Records of New South Wales. 1892–1901. Sydney: The Government Printer.

Hobson, John A. 1938. *Imperialism: A Study*, 3rd ed. London: Allen & Unwin.

Holbrooke-Jones, Stanley. 2005. The Triumph of Anglo-Catholicism Challenged. *The Churchman*, vol. 119, no. 2 (Summer), pp. 159–78.

Holden, Colin. 1996. *From Tories at Prayer to Socialists at Mass: St. Peter's Eastern Hill, Melbourne 1846–1990*. Melbourne: Melbourne University Press.

Ive, Anthony. 1992. *A Candle Burns in Africa*. Natal: Church of England in South Africa.

Jensen, Michael P. 2012. *Sydney Anglicanism An Apology*. Oregon: WIPF & STOCK.

Judd, Bernard G. 1951. *He that Doeth – the Life Story of Archdeacon R. B. S. Hammond, OBE* London: Marshall, Morgan & Scott.

Judd, Stephen. 1984. Defenders of their Faith: Party and Power in the Anglican Diocese of Sydney 1909–1938. Unpublished PhD thesis, University of Sydney.

Judd, Stephen and Kenneth J. Cable. 1987. *Sydney Anglicans*. Sydney: Anglican Information Office.

Kaye, Bruce, ed. 2002. *Anglicanism in Australia*. Melbourne: Melbourne University Press.

Kaye, Bruce, ed. 2006. *"Wonderful and Confessedly Strange": Australian Essays in Anglican Ecclesiology*. Adelaide: ATF Press.

Kaye, Bruce. 2011. From Anglican Gaol to Religious Pluralism: Re-Casting Anglican Views of Church and State in Australia. *Church and State in Old and New Worlds*. Leiden: Brill.

Kaye, Bruce N. 2003. The Strange Birth of Anglican Synods in Australia and the 1850 Bishops Conference. *The Journal of Religious History*, vol. 27, no. 2.

Knox, David Broughton. 2000. *Selected Works*. Kingsford: Matthias Media.

Kuan, Jonathan Wei-Han. 2011. A History of Evangelicalism in the Anglican Diocese of Melbourne, 1847–1937. Unpublished PhD Thesis, Australian College of Theology.

Lambeth Commission on Communion. 2004. *The Windsor Report*. London: The Anglican Communion Office.

Lawton, William. 1990. *The Better Time to Be. Utopian Attitudes to Society Amongst Sydney Anglicans 1855 to 1914*. Sydney: New South Wales University Press.

Le Couteur, Howard. 2006. Brisbane Anglicans: 1842–1875. Unpublished PhD Dissertation, Macquarie University, Australia.

Loane, Marcus L. 1955. *A Centenary History of Moore Theological College*. Sydney: Angus & Robertson.

Loane, Marcus L. 1960. *Archbishop Mowll: The Biography of Howard West Kilvinton Mowll, Archbishop of Sydney and Primate of Australia*. Sydney: Hodder & Stoughton.

Loane, Marcus L. 1976. *Hewn from the Rock; the Moorhouse Lectures 1976*. Sydney: Anglican Information Office.

Loane, Marcus L. 1987. *Men to Remember*. Canberra: Acorn Press.

Macintosh, Neil. 1978. *Richard Johnson, Chaplain to the Colony of New South Wales: His Life and Times, 1755–1827*. Sydney: Library of Australian History.

McPherson, Bruce H. 2007. *The Reception of English Law Abroad*. Brisbane: The Supreme Court of Queensland.

Moses, John A. ed. 1997. *From Oxford to the Bush. Catholic Anglicanism in Australia*. Adelaide: Broughton Press.

Noble, Thomas A. 2006. *Tyndale House and Fellowship: The First Sixty Years*. Leicester: Intervarsity Press.

O'Brien, Peter T. 1999. *God's Mission and Ours: The Challenge of Telling the Nations*. Sydney: Church Missionary Society Australia Inc.

Paterson, Cecily A. 1998. *Celebrate! 200 Years of Taking the Gospel to the World*. Sydney: Church Missionary Society Australia Inc.

Pearce, C. C. A. 2000. Public Religion in the English Colonies. *Ecclesiastical Law Journal*, vol. 5, pp. 440–54.

Pestana, Carla G. 2011. *Protestant Empire, Religion and the Making of the British Atlantic World*. Philadelphia: University of Pennsylvania Press.

Porter, Brian, ed. 1989. *Colonial Tractarians: The Oxford Movement in Australia*. Melbourne: Joint Board of Christian Education.

Porter, Brian, ed. 1997. *Melbourne Anglicans: The Diocese of Melbourne 1847–1997* Melbourne: Mitre Books.

Porter, Muriel. 2011. *Sydney Anglicans and the Threat to World Anglicanism – the Sydney Experiment*. England: Ashgate Publishing Limited.

Powell, John. 2008. Gladstone and the Colonial Church Clause: An Episode in Church-State Relations, 1849–1850. *Tradition and Formation: Claiming an Inheritance: Essays in Honour of Peter C. Erb*, eds. Michel

Desjardins and Harold Remus. Ontario: Pandora Press.

Rees, John. 2008. The Faith Once For All Delivered. *International Journal for the Study of the Christian Church*, vol. 8, no. 2 (May), pp. 171–6.

Reid, John R. 2004. *Marcus L. Loane: A Biography*. Brunswick East: Acorn Press.

Robin, Arthur de Quetteville. 1967. *Charles Perry Bishop of Melbourne*. University of Western Australia Press.

Robinson, Donald B. R. 1976. *The Origins of the Anglican Church League*. Sydney: Moore College.

Robinson, Donald B. R. 2008. *Donald Robinson: Selected Works*. Camperdown: Australian Church Record.

Rodgers, Margaret. 1998. The Ministry of Women. *A Real, Vet Imperfect Communion. The 1996 and 1997 Halifax-Portal Lectures.* Strathfield: St. Pauls Publications.

Ryle, John Charles. 1901. *Knots Untied: Being Plain Statements on Disputed Points in Religion from an Evangelical Standpoint*. London: Thynne.

*St. Mark's Review*. 2012. Issue 220. Themed Issue: The Anglican Communion Covenant.

Shaw, G. 1978. *Patriarch and Patriot, William Grant Broughton 1788–1853*. Melbourne: Melbourne University Press.

Sibtain, Nancy de S. P. 1968. *Dare to Look Up: A Memoir of Bishop George Alexander Chambers*. Sydney: Angus and Robertson.

Stanway, Marjory. 1991. *Alfred Stanway: The Recollections of a "Little M."* Melbourne: Acorn Press.

Stephenson, Alan M. 1978. *Anglicanism and the Lambeth Conferences*. London: SPCK.

Thomas, William Henry Griffith. 1930. *The Principles of Theology: An Introduction to the Thirty-Nine Articles*. London: Longmans.

Turney, Clifford. 1989. *Grammar, a History of Sydney Grammar School 1819–1988*. Sydney: Sydney Grammar School, in association with Allen & Unwin.

Turney, Clifford, Ursula Bygott, and Peter Chippendale. 1991. *Australia's First: A History of the University of Sydney, 1850–1939*, Vol. 1. Sydney: University of Sydney, with Hale & Iremonger.

Webb, Rex A. F. 1978. *Brothers in the Sun. A History of the Bush Brotherhood Movement in the Outback of Australia*. Australia: Rigby Ltd.

White, Paul. 1977. *Alias Jungle Doctor: An Autobiography*. Surry Hills, NSW: Anzea Books.

Williams, Albert E. 1989. *West Anglican Way*. Perth: Province of Western Australia of the Anglican Church of Australia.

Withycombe, Robert. 2009. *Montgomery of Tasmania: Henry and Maud Montgomery in Australasia*. Melbourne: Acorn Press.

Yarwood, Alexander T. 1996. *Samuel Marsden: The Great Survivor*, 2nd ed. Melbourne: Melbourne University Press.

## Legal Cases

*Gorham v Bishop of Exeter*. 1850. Moore's Special Reports 462.

*Long v Bishop of Cape Town*. 1863. I Moore NS 411; 15 English Reports 756.

*Re Lord Bishop of Natal*. 1865. III Moore NS 115; 16 English Reports 43.

*Bishop of Natal v Gladstone*. 1866. 3 Law Reports, Chancery Division 1.

*Merriman v Williams*. 1882. 7 Law Reports, Appeal Cases 484.

*Scandrett v Dowling*. 1992. 27 New South Wales Law Reports 483 ("*Women Priests Case*").

*Wylde v Attorney-General for New South Wales ex rel Ashelford*. 1948. 78 Commonwealth Law Reports 224 ("*Red Book Case*").

CHAPTER 36

# The Church of the Province of Melanesia

## J. Barney Hawkins IV

The Church of the Province of Melanesia was founded – by accident it seems – in late 1848. The story is told of George Augustus Selwyn, an Anglican bishop who journeyed to Melanesia:

> In his letters patent his jurisdiction was stated as extending as far as thirty-four degrees north latitude. This, it is said, was an error for thirty-four degrees south latitude. But the bishop accepted the position and determined to explore, as soon as he could, islands utterly unknown to missionaries, and only visited by sandal-wood traders and others, who bore, too often, the worst of reputations. Deeds done by white men to the blacks in those days are a disgrace to our nation. An immense improvement has now been effected; let us throw a veil over the past, and attempt rather to make what reparation we can in the name of Him who made of one blood all nations, and commanded us to preach His Gospel to all without distinction. (Montgomery 1904, 2)

The bishop found more islands than he could number. He realized that it would be impossible to secure enough English clergy for such a mission. In addition, Bishop Selwyn found the climate "unfit for Europeans as permanent residences" (Montgomery 1904, 3).

He concluded that:

> the natives themselves must be made to become missionaries to their own people. This idea was to be fostered in every possible manner. The number of the English clergy was to be more select than numerous. "They were to be the white floats to sustain the black net," which was to win the souls in the future in Christ's name. (Montgomery 1904, 4)

*The Wiley-Blackwell Companion to the Anglican Communion*, First Edition. Edited by Ian S. Markham,
J. Barney Hawkins IV, Justyn Terry, and Leslie Nuñez Steffensen.
© 2013 John Wiley & Sons, Ltd. Published 2013 by John Wiley & Sons, Ltd.

In many ways, Selwyn's vision has shaped the Church of the Province of Melanesia, an Anglicanism constantly experimenting with the indigenous people about Christian worship and practices. Let us consider the ecclesiastical structure of the Church of the Province of Melanesia; its liturgy and worship; and its respect for other cultures in a multicultural setting.

The Archbishop of the Province of Melanesia is a spiritual head who oversees the dioceses of the province with the assistance of a general secretary, chief chaplain, and general treasurer. The province encourages lay ministry through the "Melanesian Gulde of Servers of the Church of Melanesia." This "Gulde" is open to any communicant "who is a person of strong faith." In the Diocese of Malaita, for example, the members of the "Gulde" pledge:

1.  To say the Gulde collect on every Sunday and on the main holy days
2.  To say the appointed prayers before and after serving
3.  To take full responsibility to care for the church house and everything inside the church – e.g., vestments, vessels, etc., and to see that the church is well equipped
4.  To plan fundraising for the church
5.  To assist the parish priest in his ministry. (Church of the Province of Melanesia 1993)

The Church of the Province of Melanesia embraces the four orders of ministry which is common to the Anglican Communion: lay, deacon, priest, and bishop. The Book of Common Prayer is called "A Melanesian English Prayer Book." The prayer book remembers in its collects the pioneer martyrs, especially Bishop John Coleridge Patteson and his companions who were killed in 1871. Bishop Patteson died trying to combat slave traders in the South Pacific. His death motivated England to renew its efforts to stamp out slavery in the Pacific islands.

The Anglican missionaries who brought the Christian faith to Melanesia and its environs faced an indigenous culture which needed to be blended with the Anglican way of being Christian. "The interaction of Melanesians with European agents of change has produced a blending of cultures in a new form that is neither wholly Melanesian nor wholly European, but a blending of elements from each" (Whiteman 1983, 323). The Anglican "agents of change" decided what should be blended, what should be expunged, and what should be expanded. The liturgy and worship of the Anglican Church has attempted to incorporate the traditional culture – "dancing, singing, arts and crafts, language, social organization, etc." (Whiteman 1983, 323). From the beginning, the Anglicans spoke against traditional practices such as "headhunting, cannibalism, warfare, infanticide, widow strangling, sorcery, and other cultural values that idealized violence and aggression" (Whiteman 1983, 323).

Anglicans learned to work with the village structure in Melanesia. The parish priest talks to the "village headman and a village catechist" (Whiteman 1983, 329). European values have not been easily incorporated into Melanesian worldviews. Belief and practice have collided – as the rural has a tense relationship with the urban, and the Melanesian with the European.

# Bibliography

Church of the Province of Melanesia, Diocese of Malaita. 1993. DIOCESAN CANONS.

Montgomery, H. H. 1904. *The Light of Melanesia: A Record of Fifty Years' Mission Work in the South Seas*. London: Society for Promoting Christian Knowledge.

Whiteman, Darrell L. 1983. *Melanesians and Missionaries: An Ethnohistorical Study of Social and Religious Change in Southwest Pacific*. Pasadena: William Carey Library.

CHAPTER 37

# The Anglican Church of Papua New Guinea

## J. Barney Hawkins IV

Papua New Guinea gained its independence from Australia in 1975. The next year, the Anglican Church of Papua New Guinea separated from the Anglican province of Queensland, Australia, and became an autonomous province of the Anglican Communion. The first archbishop and primate was the Most Rev. Sir David Hand, the Bishop of Port Moresby. This chapter will focus on the Anglican Church's ecclesiastical structure in Papua New Guinea; its travails during World War II; and the ways liturgy and worship respect and honor the traditional religions.

The Archbishop of Papua New Guinea is both metropolitan and primate. The episcopal polity is ensured by the oversight of five diocesan bishops in five geographical areas: Aipo Rongo; the New Guinea Islands; Port Moresby, which includes what was British New Guinea; Popondota; and Dogura. The cathedral for the province is in Dogura. Early Anglican missionaries worked primarily in the north and the Milne Bay area of Papua – hence, the majority of the population in the north, or the Diocese of Port Moresby, is Anglican.

The first Anglican missionaries landed in the last quarter of the nineteenth century. The young Anglican mission in Papua New Guinea suffered a deadly season in 1942 when the war came to Papua New Guinea. In February 1942, Port Moresby was bombed, and the Anglican Church lost clergy, teachers, and medical missionaries. The Anglican Board of Mission of the Province of Australia has published a booklet in 2006, titled *I Wait for the Lord, My Soul Waits for Him: And in His Word Is My Hope, a Resource Book of the Martyrs of Papua New Guinea and Melanesia*, by Margaret Bride. The cover of the booklet has a photograph of the stained glass windows in St. Peter's Anglican Church, East Hill, Melbourne, which recalls the New Guinea mission and the martyrs of 1942. It was the northern province, which includes Port Moresby, which was invaded by the Japanese. The Japanese troops hoped to use this area as a beachhead or "stepping stone" for an invasion of Australia.

*The Wiley-Blackwell Companion to the Anglican Communion*, First Edition. Edited by Ian S. Markham,
J. Barney Hawkins IV, Justyn Terry, and Leslie Nuñez Steffensen.
© 2013 John Wiley & Sons, Ltd. Published 2013 by John Wiley & Sons, Ltd.

Most of the martyrs of 1942 were Anglican priests and laypeople. There was, however, one Papuan, Lucian Tapiedi, who was killed for his Christian faith. In 1988, Westminster Abbey in London installed in niches above the west door ten statues of twentieth-century martyrs. The martyrs of the Pacific region in World War II are represented by a statue of Lucian Tapiedi. The subtitle of the entry about Tapiedi states:

> In an age of aggression, Tapiedi was born in 1921 or 1922, in the village of Taupota, on the north coast of Papua. His father was a sorcerer who died when his sons were quite young. He was taught at mission schools and then, in 1939, he entered St. Aiden's teacher training college. Here Tapiedi became known as a diligent and cheerful presence, fond of physical recreation but also a musician. In 1941 he became part of the staff at Sangara as a teacher and evangelist. (Bride 2006, 6)

There is also a church dedicated to the memory of Lucian Tapiedi near Port Moresby. The Diocese of Papua New Guinea Prayer Book includes a prayer for the martyrs:

> Father, we thank you for your martyrs of Papua New Guinea; they obeyed the call of your Son Jesus Christ to take up the cross and follow him, and so they glorified you by their deaths. May their witness and their prayers make strong your Church in this land; and may we, your servants today, follow their example of faithfulness and courage, work for your kingdom, and be joined with them forever: through the same Jesus Christ Our Lord who lives and rules with you in the unity of the Holy Spirit, one God for ever and ever. Amen. (Bride 2006, 14)

The Anglican Church in Papua New Guinea had provided its dioceses and parishes a litany for the 12 Anglicans who died in 1942–1943. Two of the 12 were Papuan nationals. Other major churches also lost members in the invasion of 1942, including Roman Catholics, Lutherans, Salvation Army, and Seventh Day Adventists. On September 2 of each year, Papua New Guinea remembers the 333 Christian martyrs of World War II.

Anglican liturgy and worship in the province is largely Anglo-Catholic, with a celebration of the Holy Eucharist or the Mass as the principal Sunday service. Clergy are referred to as "Father." There are no women serving as Anglican priests in Papua New Guinea, even though the New Guinea Islands have a strong matriarchal culture. The Anglican Church has become increasingly sensitive to the rich multiculturalism of Papua New Guinea. Traditional religion with its magical and cult practices has been respected. Native arts, crafts, and music are incorporated in regular Anglican worship. The province's hymn book, for example, includes a number of hymns from other traditions.

## Bibliography

Bride, Margaret. 2006. *I Wait for the Lord, My Soul Waits for Him: And in His Word Is My Hope, a Resource Book of the Martyrs of Papua New Guinea and Melanesia.* Sydney: Anglican Board of Mission Australia.

# Europe

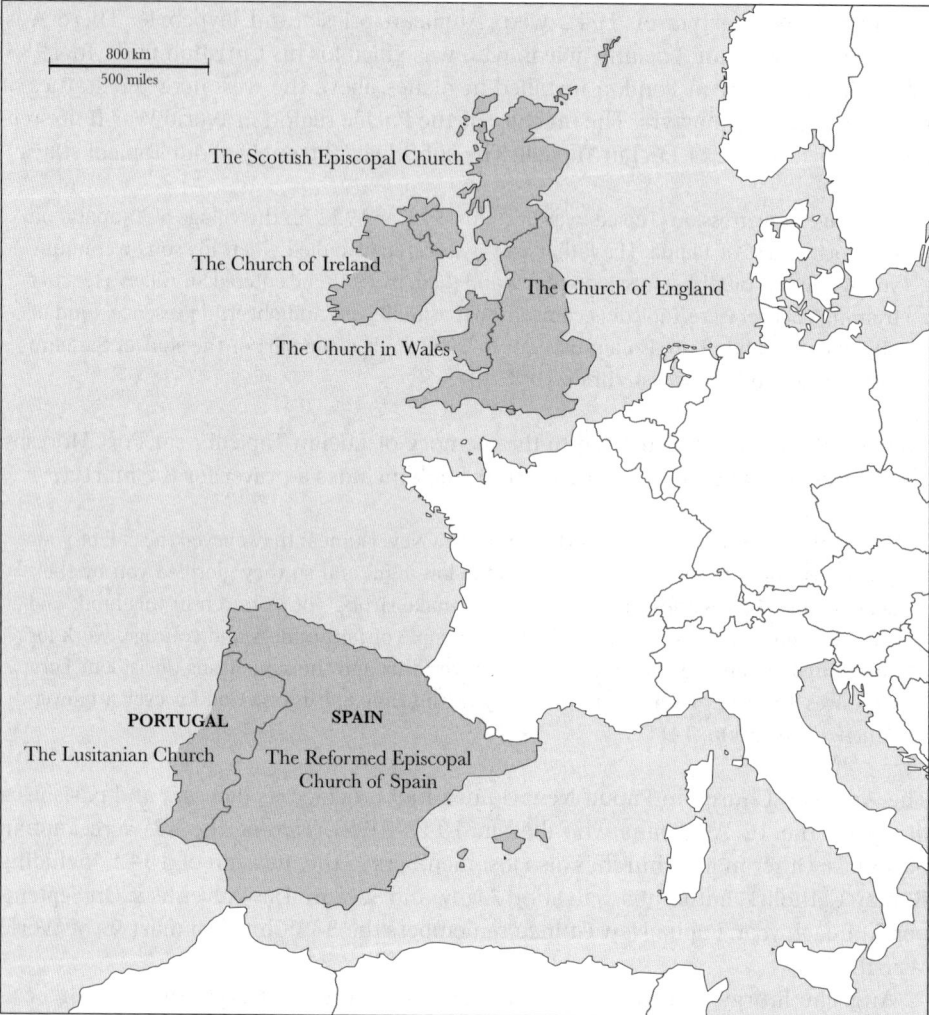

The Scottish Episcopal Church

The Church of Ireland

The Church of England

The Church in Wales

**PORTUGAL**

The Lusitanian Church

**SPAIN**

The Reformed Episcopal
Church of Spain

800 km
500 miles

FALKLAND
ISLANDS

800 km
500 miles

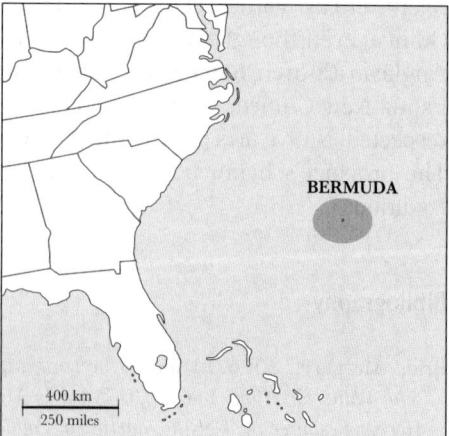

BERMUDA

400 km
250 miles

# CHAPTER 38

# The Church of England

## Mark Chapman

The history, theology, and practices of the Church of England have profoundly shaped the churches of the Anglican Communion, which have usually defined themselves in relation to the English Church, and which in part gain their identity as Anglican Churches by being in communion with the Archbishop of Canterbury, the "Primate of All England." The word "Anglican" simply derives from the Latin word for "English" and has been used to describe the English Church from at least as early as the reign of King John in the *Magna Carta* of 1215. However, the contemporary Church of England has changed beyond recognition from the early days of the Anglican Communion. Since the 1960s, it has declined rapidly and can no longer be regarded as the religious expression of the English people, even if it remains the strongest Christian voice in contemporary England and still enjoys the modest privileges of establishment. Every square inch of England remains divided up into about 16,000 parishes served by about 8,000 stipendiary clergy and 300 or so senior clergy. In addition, there are about 2,000 unpaid clergy. All people retain a right to marriage and baptism in their parish church, regardless of whether they are members of church rolls. In addition, the Church of England provides state-funded chaplaincies in hospitals, the armed forces, and prisons.

## History

The close links between the English nation and the Church of England date from the very foundation of Christianity in the British Isles. Although it is impossible to date the beginnings of Christianity in the territory now referred to as "England," there is clear

*The Wiley-Blackwell Companion to the Anglican Communion*, First Edition. Edited by Ian S. Markham, J. Barney Hawkins IV, Justyn Terry, and Leslie Nuñez Steffensen.
© 2013 John Wiley & Sons, Ltd. Published 2013 by John Wiley & Sons, Ltd.

evidence of Christian practice during Roman times: a well-preserved early-fourth-century chi-rho, a Christian symbol, was found in a mosaic pavement at Hinton St. Mary, Dorset. Mention was also made of Christians in Britain in the third- and fourth-century writings of Tertullian and Eusebius of Caesarea. At much the same time, three bishops from Britain, from York, London, and Caerleon (now in Wales), are reported as having attended the Council of Arles in 314. Before this time, the first English martyr Alban came to an untimely end either during the persecutions under the Emperor Severus around the year 209, or during the time of the Decian persecutions in the mid-century, or under Diocletian at the beginning of the fourth century. Gildas' sixth-century history of Britain, *On the Ruin and Conquest of Britain*, which claims that Christianity came to Britain perhaps as early as the year 37, provides the most important early text about the state of Christianity during the collapse of Roman rule. More fanciful myths about the arrival of Christianity developed later which identified the arrival of Christianity with a visit of Joseph of Arimathea to Britain. Mention had been made of this event in *Life of Mary Magdalene*, attributed to Rabanus Maurus (766–856), Archbishop of Mainz. These myths were associated with the great Abbey of Glastonbury, the legends of King Arthur, and the quest for the Holy Grail. In *The Chronicle of the English Kings*, composed in the 1120s, William of Malmesbury reported that the Apostle Philip sent Joseph to England. Later, this Romano-British tradition was used to distance the Church of England from Rome by Elizabeth I in her reply to the five Catholic bishops in 1559. Gildas, she stated, "testifieth Joseph of Arimathea to be the first preacher of the word of God within our realms. Long after that period when Austin [Augustine] came from Rome, this our realm had Bishops and Priests therein, as is well known to the wise and learned of our realm" (Harrison 1968, 30). Similarly, her archbishop, Matthew Parker, defended the antiquity of the English Church by arranging for ancient texts to be published, including Gildas, as well as compiling his own book on the antiquity of the English Church, *De antiquitate Britannicae ecclesiae* (1572). A distinctively English church, free from Roman "usurpations," was thus traced to the years immediately after the death of Christ.

Following the departure of the Romans in the early fifth century, however, there is little archaeological evidence for Christianity in much of Britain, although in western parts of the British Isles, Christianity survived among those who continued to speak the Celtic languages and who maintained some distinctive usages, such as the dating of Easter. The most important source for this period is the *Ecclesiastical History of the English Church and People*, written by the Venerable Bede (672/3–735), a monk at Monkwearmouth/Jarrow in the northeast of England who was keen to describe a unified people with a unified religion. The year 597 is usually dated as the arrival of Christianity in Anglo-Saxon England when Pope Gregory the Great sent the Benedictine monk Augustine to evangelize the people of England. The success of the Roman mission depended on the conversion of Æthelberht, the ruler of Kent, who had earlier married a Christian princess, Bertha, daughter of Charibert I, King of Paris. Augustine established his see in the old Roman center of Canterbury, and further sees were soon established in Rochester (604), London (604), and York (626). Other kingdoms soon followed, with sees established for East Anglia (628), Wessex (635), Mercia (656), and Sussex (685). Further north, Christianity spread through the influence of important royalty, especially King Oswald of Northumbria, who invited Aidan from Iona to become bishop in about 635. He was given the see of Lindisfarne, an island off the northeast coast, which became home to an important monastery and seat of learning before the Viking attacks from the end of the eighth century. These different strands of Christianity in England, which used different methods for calculating Easter, met under the influence of the powerful noble Abbess Hilda, probably at Whitby in 664. After debate between Colman for the "Celtic" side and Wilfrid for the Roman, the latter eventually triumphed. King Oswui of Northumbria is reported to have said: "I tell you that Peter is the guardian of the gates of heaven, and I shall not contradict him" (Bede 1968, 192).

Bede's emphasis on the unity of the English people, and the uniformity of its church, was reflected after the Synod of Whitby in the "golden age" of the archbishopric of Theodore of Tarsus (from 669 to 690). Theodore was able to institute a number of reforms, which improved the government of the church, in addition to establishing a school of learning at Canterbury which influenced other monastic schools across the country. He ensured the division of the unwieldy dioceses which were hitherto coterminous with kingdoms, and by the end of his time the English Church had achieved a coherent and unified diocesan structure. This also marked the beginnings of a more stable system of parishes distinct from the earlier model of itinerancy where, as Bede reports, "whenever a clerk or a priest visited a town, English folk always used to gather at his call to hear the Word, eager to understand his message and even more eager to carry out whatever they had heard and understood" (London: Penguin, 1968, Bk IV, 27, 260).

The Viking raids and political control through the ninth century led to significant periods of warfare, especially under the unifying King of Wessex, Alfred the Great (849–899). His military exploits were accompanied by a revival in learning and translations of classic texts, including Gregory the Great's treatise on pastoral care and Boethius's *Consolation of Philosophy*. In the following century, under the Archbishopric of Dunstan (960–88), the church experienced a period of renewal with the consolidation of many monasteries, the improvement of clergy education, as well as reforms of clerical abuses. In the eleventh century, King Edward the Confessor, who ruled from 1042 to 66 and who was canonized in 1161, sought to establish increased control over the church, building a new royal abbey at Westminster. Following the regime change after the defeat of Harold at Hastings, William I reformed the English Church by imposing Norman bishops and by re-establishing monastic houses under Norman control. The number of dioceses, which included four in Wales, was 21, whose bishops along with the heads of the major monasteries were also "Lords Spiritual," that is, members of the House of Lords. Their right to sit in Parliament, where they outnumbered the "temporal" peers, dated back to the very beginnings of Parliament in Anglo-Saxon times. Bishops frequently held important offices of state. Even in 2012, 26 peers still sit in the House of Lords, although their role is currently under discussion by the British government.

As in other parts of Europe, the increasingly centralized Roman Church was frequently in conflict with the civil authorities. This was exemplified in England during the twelfth century by Henry II's efforts to distance his church from Rome through the Constitutions of Clarendon which sought to make clergymen subject to the secular courts. After excommunicating the three senior bishops who had crowned the king without the archbishop's consent, Becket fell victim to the king's outburst which resulted in his murder in his own cathedral in 1170 by the king's agents. This martyrdom soon led to the development of one of the leading cults of the Middle Ages. Conflict between church and state continued to be a regular feature of medieval life, with particular pressure points during the reign of King John (1199–1216). In 1206, the pope refused John's choice as Archbishop of Canterbury and imposed his own choice of Stephen Langton. In turn, John seized the Canterbury estates, and the monks fled into exile. John had already confiscated property from the Archbishop of York, and when the pope protested, John confiscated all clerical property. By 1209, he had been excommunicated by Pope Innocent III, and the English bishops went into exile. John kept seven bishoprics and 17 abbacies vacant, thereby increasing his revenues.

Through the thirteenth century, the parish system, which had been regularized throughout Europe following the reforms of Pope Gregory VII in 1075, was consolidated as clerical incomes were stabilized often after appeal to Rome. Large amounts of church income were paid over to "rectors" of parishes which were frequently religious houses. These houses in turn ensured that some income was given over to the "vicar," who looked after services in the parish churches. This practice was particularly common in England, which means to this day the majority of English parochial clergy bear the title "vicar." Although the right to appoint clergy remained with the patron, following his appointment the clergyman had "freehold," which gave him absolute right to possess the church and its endowments, which meant the church's independence from the landowner was strengthened. Significant sums were also being paid over to Rome for dispensations from canon law, which led once again to conflict over the rights of the papal courts to exercise jurisdiction in England. By 1306, during the reign of Edward I, the Statute of Provisors (1306) made it illegal to pass any tax out of the country. A second Act of 1350 imposed further checks, and by the reign of Richard II the Statute of *Praemunire* (1353) made it illegal to appeal outside of England on any matter in the settlement of ecclesiastical cases. Fines levied on such appeals became another source of revenue for the Crown. While there was nothing unique about England, these Acts of Parliament reveal a high degree of conflict between church and state, which was to reach its climax during the reign of Henry VIII.

## The Reformation

The Church of England was fundamentally transformed during the 1530s, which saw its final separation from the Church of Rome. The need for papal dispensation to ensure an annulment of his marriage to Catherine of Aragon, in order to secure a male heir, led King Henry VIII to assume the pope's "usurped" powers and to assert his own imperial authority over the Church of England. The declaration in the Act in Restraint of Appeals of 1533 that "This realm of England is an Empire" meant that there could be no source of authority or law from beyond the "imperial" throne: the status of the Church of England as an independent church outside the jurisdiction of the pope was thereby declared by statute. This meant that the church *in* England – even one which was sometimes rather troublesome – became the Church *of* England. In the years following the Act of Supremacy in 1534, where the king was declared "head" over the church, Henry's chief advisor, Thomas Cromwell, set about a wholesale transformation of the English landscape, as all the monasteries were closed over the next six years. Despite some opposition, huge amounts of ecclesiastical endowments and property were effectively nationalized, many of them being redistributed to Henry's supporters. The rectories belonging to religious houses were "secularized" and frequently given to private individuals or to corporations such as Oxford and Cambridge colleges. Some church money was also used to endow six new dioceses. Unlike other churches of the time, the Church of England did not compel a strict form of theological education on its clergy: undergraduate theology did not exist until the late nineteenth century at Oxford and Cambridge, which meant that clergy were often well versed in other disciplines but surprisingly ignorant of theology. It was not until the 1920s that theological education began to be the norm for clergy, and not until after World War II that it became compulsory.

Despite the break from Rome, the doctrinal reforms in the English Church during Henry's reign were modest. The Ten Articles of 1536 show a degree of affinity to moderate Lutheranism, but only three years later these were replaced by a restatement of traditional Catholic teaching on the mass and purgatory. Services remained in Latin, although Henry's archbishop, Thomas Cranmer, produced an English-language litany in 1544. It was only in the reign of Henry's son, Edward VI (1547–1553), that the Church of England moved into the next stage of reform, as its services and doctrine were transformed. The publication of the first English-language Book of Common Prayer in 1549 was quickly imposed on all parish churches. Although probably intended as an interim prayer book and relatively conservative, it transformed worship by making it available in the vernacular, and by basing liturgy on the regular reading of scripture. While retaining simplified forms of earlier liturgy, it represented a significant development, especially in its theology of the Eucharist, which moved away from the theology of transubstantiation of the medieval church. Further discussions prompted in part by the conservative Bishop of Winchester Stephen Gardiner led Cranmer toward a revision of the prayer book under the guidance of a number of continental reformers, two of whom had been appointed as Regius Professors at Oxford (Peter Martyr Vermigli) and Cambridge (Martin Bucer). These resulted in a significantly revised prayer book in 1552, which became the basis for the modest later revisions of 1559 and 1662. It introduced changes which moved in a more thoroughgoing reformed direction: in the communion service, the remembrance of Jesus' death was stressed at the expense of the real presence of Christ in the bread and wine. In addition, church interiors were transformed by the removal of images and the simplification of ecclesiastical dress. The forms of service for the ordination of clergy were also modified to stress the proclamation of the word as the main task of the minister, even though the three traditional orders of ministry (bishops, priests, and deacons) were retained. Shortly before Edward's death, Cranmer published a collection of 42 Articles of Religion which were to function as the doctrinal statement of the English Church. These were drawn from other formularies of faith, both Lutheran and Reformed, although in certain areas, especially in relation to predestination and the Eucharist, they veered in a more reformed direction. They also stressed the importance of the civil authorities in maintaining order.

Following Edward's untimely death, his half-sister Mary sought to return the country to Roman obedience, which led to a degree of persecution of Protestants, many of whom were forced into exile, and others executed, including Cranmer, as well as Bishops Hooper of Gloucester, Ridley of London, and Latimer of Worcester. However, Mary's reign was too brief for a complete return to the old religion or to re-endow monasteries. The accession of Elizabeth in 1558 rapidly saw a return to the earlier religious settlement: the prayer book of 1552 was reintroduced with modifications which introduced greater ambiguity over the doctrine of the presence of Christ in the Eucharist. The Articles of Religion, in a revised version which reduced their number to 39, were reintroduced after 1563, although it took until 1571 for them to be formally agreed on, and even then subscription was required only for the clergy. Shortly after Elizabeth's accession, the first defense of the English Church against Rome was composed by Bishop John Jewel. His *Apology* of 1562 sought for as great a degree of comprehensiveness as possible by trying to prove the continuity of the Church of England with the church of the past. Many of the returning exiles, however, were dissatisfied with the Elizabethan Settlement, hoping that there might be further reform. Following a conflict over ecclesiastical dress in 1566 (the so-called vestiarian controversy), there were repeated demands for removal of such medieval trappings, further modifications to the prayer book, as well as a move toward a Presbyterian constitution for the church which would remove some of the power of bishops. Those who called for reform to the Church of England came to be labeled as "puritan," and had prominent spokesmen in such men as Thomas Cartwright and Walter Travers, who occupied important positions in the church. Some of Elizabeth's bishops, including John Whitgift, who became Archbishop of Canterbury in 1584, played a principal part in opposing puritan demands. The chief disputes rested in what precisely could be permitted in matters "indifferent" to salvation, which related principally to the ceremonies and structures of the church. Later in the sixteenth century, this dispute led Richard Hooker to write the eight volumes of his *magnum opus*, the *Laws of Ecclesiastical Polity*, which has come to be regarded as one of the key theological texts of the Church of England, although it had less impact at the time. Hooker's theology of law is a clear and sophisticated justification of the power of the prince over matters indifferent. By ensuring there was a large area in which scripture was silent and where God-given reason had thus to be used to make decisions, Hooker was able to defend a high view of royal supremacy.

Although the phrase "Supreme Head" was altered to "Supreme Governor" under Elizabeth, the Crown remained the sovereign authority over the church. Consequently, many of the controversies focused on the importance of authority and order in the church, and the need for conformity. While this period has sometimes been described as a *via media* between more extreme Protestantism and Roman Catholicism, it is perhaps best understood as a time of conflict between those who held to the authority of the Crown exercised through her bishops in an ordered and uniform church, and those who sought to give the church, including its lay members, a greater say in ordering its own affairs. Indeed, bishops survived chiefly as agents of the Queen's authority rather than divinely sanctioned successors to the apostles (even if some began to defend this idea by the end of the century). Despite the many conflicts over church order, however, there was remarkably little dispute over the nature of doctrine: Archbishop Whitgift, for instance, was responsible for drawing up a supplementary set of Articles in 1595 (the Lambeth Articles) which were unequivocal in their support for a strong form of Calvinist double predestination. By refusing her consent, the Queen did not sanction any additions to the church's teaching, which allowed for a modest degree of latitude for the Church of England.

After the accession of James I in 1603, there were efforts to try to ensure a degree of reconciliation between the factions. At the Hampton Court Conference of 1604 between puritans and conformists, a new standard translation of the Bible was com- missioned, and a number of abuses were addressed to try to improve the exercise of ministry. At the same time, a further set of canons was introduced which codified the various instructions and injunctions produced during Edward's and Elizabeth's reigns. These also sought to improve the state of the church. James, an astute politician, ensured that there was a degree of latitude in their interpretation, which meant that most puritans were able to remain within the Church of England. In addition, James promoted men of a range of opinions as bishops. George Abbot, for instance, who became archbishop in 1611, was a convinced Calvinist, while Lancelot Andrewes, Bishop of Winchester, had a quite different understanding of the thorny issue of grace. James summarized his policy in a speech to both Houses of Parliament in 1610: "I never found, that blood and too much severity did good in matters of religion" (*The Conclusive Part of the Parliamentary or Constitutional History of England* 1660, 30). While Calvinist theology dominated in the second decade of the century, with the Church of England sending a delegation to the Synod of Dort in 1618–1619, its formulations, however, were not added to the Thirty-Nine Articles.

By the 1620s, the church began to polarize between puritans and a number of "avant-garde conformists" who sought to impose the 1604 canons with greater force and to reorder churches and the worship of the church. Under the influence of William Laud, who became Archbishop of Canterbury in 1633, but who was already exercising considerable power beforehand, ecclesiastical policy became less tolerant of diversity. Given the strength of the puritan faction in parliament, there was increased tension between the factions. The attempt to impose a version of the English Prayer Book on Scotland in 1637 eventually led to the breakdown of law and order and the outbreak of Civil War: this resulted in the abolition of the prayer book and bishops as well as the drawing up of new forms of worship and a statement of belief at the Westminster Assembly from 1643. During the Commonwealth period, however, there was consider- able toleration of different understandings of Christianity, partly because Oliver Cromwell came from an Independent rather than a Presbyterian background.

## The Restoration and the Making of a Denomination

With the restoration of the monarchy in 1660, there was a great deal of expectation (which Charles II shared) that there would be a degree of "comprehension" which would allow a range of opinions, practices, and structures to survive alongside one another in the church. A meeting was set up at the Savoy in London to discuss differences where puritans such as Richard Baxter met with those, led by Gilbert Sheldon, Bishop of London, who sought a return to the previous religious settlement. It soon became clear that "comprehension" would not be achieved. By 1662, an Act of Uniformity restored the Book of Common Prayer of Elizabeth's reign, with minor amendments, and imposed episcopal ordination on all clergy. This had the effect of driving significant numbers of clergy, perhaps as many as 2,500, from the church and creating "non-conformists," many of whom sought refuge in the American colonies. After 1662, while some within the church, who came to be labeled "latitudinarian," tried to remain as inclusive as possible, others were far less inclusive. For the remainder of Charles II's reign, there was considerable persecution of non-conformists, but following the accession of his brother, the Roman Catholic James I in 1685, things quickly changed.

After the "Glorious Revolution" of 1688 when the Protestant William III was put on the throne with his Stuart wife Mary, there was official toleration of dissenters, even if they were deprived of holding office in the state. At the same time, a number of bishops refused to swear their oath to the new king ("non-jurors"), which led to a schism in the Church of England which lasted a number of years. The official church came to be increasingly under the control of Parliament through the influence of the "low" church Whigs, while the Tories promoted a more traditional "high" view of the church under the control of the monarch and bishops. In 1717, the old clerical parliament or convocation was prorogued permanently, and parliament effectively became the (predominantly lay) "synod" of the church. While the eighteenth-century church was not as moribund as was previously held to be the case, it nevertheless suffered from clerical poverty, pluralism (where clergy were forced to hold many parishes at the same time), and the consequent non-residence. Some effort was made to improve the lot of the clergy with the establishing of Queen Anne's Bounty in 1704 to help clergy in poor parishes.

At the turn of the eighteenth century, priest Thomas Bray founded the first two important mission societies for the Church of England. He was sent by the Bishop of London, who had oversight of churches outside England, to Maryland, and expressed a desire to "counteract the growth of vice and immorality" which was seen as resulting from the "gross ignorance of the principles of the Christian religion," especially among the native peoples. The Society for the Promotion of Christian Knowledge (SPCK) (1698) was established to provide cheap Christian literature principally for parish libraries, and the Society for the Propagation of the Gospel (SPG) (1701) quickly grew into a major mission agency. The gradual spread of the British Empire through the next two centuries led to the rapid expansion of the Church of England overseas, first in the American colonies and later in Canada, India, Australia, and Africa. While initially the English form of establishment meant that it was difficult to provide bishops for the colonies, this began to change with the expansion in the number of "Colonial Bishoprics" throughout the world from the 1840s. Conflict between these different parts of the expanded Church of England and the few independent churches of the "Anglican Communion" led to calls for a council of bishops from across the world. The Archbishop of Canterbury, Charles Longley, summoned the first Lambeth Conference in 1867, but resisted any claim to jurisdiction outside England. Because of the legal establishment of the English Church, the status of bishops from outside England remained unclear. Thus, almost by default, the "national" church ideal came to dominate Anglican theology. Establishment, however, survived only in England, despite attempts elsewhere (as in Canada and Australia). This meant that the other Anglican churches developed a completely different relationship with the civil authorities.

## Church Parties

The eighteenth century also saw the first major religious revival, which is traditionally dated to the conversion of John Wesley, a high church clergyman, in 1738. The Evangelical Revival promoted a strong experiential form of religion based on personal conversion and resulting in activism. The movement quickly spread among a number of clergy, including William Grimshaw and Henry Venn in West Yorkshire, who quickly attracted others and who began to reform parish life. Later in the century, a number of evangelicals were attracted to John Venn to form the "Clapham Sect," which promoted a number of missionary activities, including the founding of the Church Missionary Society (CMS) in 1799 – as an evangelical alternative to the SPG – and the campaign for the abolition of slavery under the MP William Wilberforce. Equally important in the Evangelical Movement was Charles Simeon of Holy Trinity Church, Cambridge, who was responsible for the acquisition of large numbers of "advowsons," or the right to present the incumbent to a parish, which ensured the future succession of evangelical clergy. While always under-represented at the leadership level, evangelicalism became a powerful force in parishes through the nineteenth century. As the century moved on, however, it tended to define itself increasingly in opposition to other groups, especially ritualists, and to seek to promote the "protestant" heritage of the Church of England using such means as publishing the works of the sixteenth-century reformers. By the early twentieth century, evangelicalism became increasingly divided and factionalized, which led to a split in the CMS.

With the rise of dissent, especially after the success of Methodism, as well as the removal of the bars on non-conformists entering public offices in 1828, and Roman Catholics the following year, the position of the Church of England was rapidly changing. These Acts led to the anomaly that the final authority over the church was no longer a purely Anglican body. While many high churchmen held to the old Tory ideal of a church maintained by a divinely anointed king, others, under the leadership of the Oxford scholars John Henry Newman, John Keble, and later Edward Pusey, sought to locate the authority of the Church of England in its bishops as successors of the Apostles. Their series of Tracts, which gave them the name "Tractarian," was deeply influential on generations of clergy. The effects of the Oxford Movement, as it is also known, were profound as they sought to distance the Church of England from the Reformation and to identify it with the church of the early Fathers. They published the writings of the Fathers as well as those of the earlier high churchmen. In the generations that followed, the Church of England became increasingly polarized between these parties. Often, the differences were represented by approaches to worship, as many Anglo-Catholics adopted ritual practices and symbolism through the nineteenth century.

Much energy was spent on litigation by Protestant evangelicals who formed organizations such as the Church Association to campaign against the ritualists who formed the English Church Union and other like-minded organizations.

Alongside these two parties was another group, later labeled "broad churchmen," who in some ways were the successors to the latitudinarians of the past. They tended to understand the church as part of the wider society involved with the quest for truth. This group, dominated by such figures as Thomas Arnold and Julius Hare, was particularly involved in education, establishing a number of schools where the Christian ethos was identified with the schoolboy's maturity into truth. Many of the leaders of the Church of England were headmasters and schoolmasters, including three successive Archbishops of Canterbury. This group kept alive the ideal of a broad national church despite the rise of non-conformity which, by the middle of the nineteenth century, had begun to rival the Church of England in terms of numbers. The English "public" school based on the principles of the (broad) Church of England provided a model for education outside England. Until the 1870s, the two ancient universities also remained Church of England institutions, where students had to subscribe to the Thirty-Nine Articles. Part of the impetus behind the Oxford Movement concerned the attempts to open up university education to non-Anglicans. Seminary education in England began in earnest only after the universities began to liberalize their curriculum and to reduce the requirement for compulsory theology in the 1850s. Since most diocesan institutions fell into the hands of Anglo-Catholics, evangelicals responded by creating their own distinctive institutions later in the century.

The mid-nineteenth century also saw the first serious efforts at reform of the structures and financing of the Church of England in a series of measures begun in the 1830s under an Ecclesiastical Commission. Clergy were made to reside in their parishes, and their incomes were made far more equal. Many of the huge resources of the cathedrals were redirected toward parish ministry by building up a central reserve. This meant that, for the first time since the Reformation, many parishes had a resident clergyman, many of whom sought to rebuild the church and reform the worship. Agricultural income, on which the church depended, remained high, and offered enormous financial resources to the church. Parish life revived with the introduction of choirs and parish guilds, and clergy came to understand their role more as religious professionals than as generalist "parsons." In addition, there was significant expenditure on elementary parochial schools sponsored by the National Society, which was founded in 1811. The church's role in education continues to be widespread, with about 25 percent of primary and middle schools remaining in the hands of the church, although government legislation and funding, and the church's diffidence, mean that there is often little overt Anglican religious teaching or practice. The revival of church life in the nineteenth century masked some of the other social changes which reduced the secular role of the churches: civil registration offered alternatives to the ecclesiastical monopoly, and the changes to the poor laws marked the end of the church's direct role in administering significant alms. With universal state provision in health and welfare in the twentieth century, the role of the Church of England in recent years has become insignificant in comparison to the huge sums expended by government, despite initiatives like the Church Urban Fund.

The twentieth century saw the numbers of those attending the Church of England continue to increase, although not in line with the population. As parliament became increasingly pluralist in its religious make-up and had less interest in and less time for ecclesiastical matters, the church began to see the need for its own representative institutions. This had already begun in the nineteenth century with the establishment of diocesan conferences as well as a restoration of convocation. By the time of World War I, a serious call to create self-government at every level of the church was led by William Temple, later Archbishop of Canterbury. This resulted in the Enabling Act of 1919 that established the Church Assembly, which included a House of Laity along with the convocations. Parochial church councils were also set up, establishing democratic accountability at the parish level. Following the perceived inadequacies of the prayer book, especially among the soldiers at the front, there were serious attempts to revise the prayer book in the 1920s. Parliament, however, having retained control over worship and doctrine, flexed its muscle in 1928 when it rejected the proposed new book. This precipitated something of a constitutional crisis, leading to further calls for church autonomy, and even complete disestablishment. Although the years following World War I saw the triumph of Anglo-Catholicism at the parish level, (which like evangelicalism had few representatives among church leaders), a benign form of state religion predominated. During the 1930s, the Church of England remained at the heart of English society, as was shown in the crisis in 1936 when Cosmo Gordon Lang played a prominent role in forcing the abdication of Edward VIII. The Church of England continued to fulfill an important function in World War II, particularly in the discussions which led to the creation of the welfare state under the influence of William Temple. In the years of austerity following the war, the Church of England continued to grow in numbers and to command general assent, as was symbolized by the part it played in the coronation in 1953.

## The Contemporary Church of England

From the early 1960s, "passive" Anglicanism went into rapid decline, with far fewer people seeking baptism or confirmation. Sunday school attendance plummeted, which meant all denominations found it difficult to educate the next generation. Ordination numbers collapsed, and many questioned the relevance of the English religious settlement for contemporary society. Even from within the church, there was a questioning of its traditional theology and ministry; Bishop John Robinson's *Honest to God* created an enormous stir in the media. An influential report on the payment and deployment of the clergy sought to redirect the resources of the church away from the countryside, where it was considered to be over-represented, toward the inner cities where there were few churchgoers. However, since the report was predicated on continued increase in numbers of clergy and churchgoers, it met with little long-term success. From the 1960s, parishes have been combined and clergy numbers continue to decline.

By the 1960s, liturgical renewal had affected many churches, with the Parish Communion replacing Morning Prayer for the main Sunday service. Efforts at liturgical reform led to a number of experimental booklets which were consolidated in the short-lived Alternative Service Book in 1980, which was replaced by the mix-and-match Common Worship in 2000. This new book partly reflected the changing balance within the Church of England. Evangelicalism moved away from its marginalized and fragmented status toward the center of church life, following the Keele Conference of Anglican evangelicals in 1967, where a decision was made by leaders including John Stott to participate in the institutional structures of the church at every level. Theological education was dominated by evangelical colleges, although the rise of part-time clergy training meant that partisan identity often became weaker.

Michael Ramsey, archbishop through the 1960s, was able to support some of the more radical social legislation, as well as to promote further reform of the structures of the church. This led to the creation of the general synod in 1970 which was given significantly greater powers than the Church Assembly. Later in the 1970s, the church was given a far greater say in the appointment of its bishops, and by the beginning of the new millennium the prime minister no longer played any role. Through the 1970s, under Donald Coggan, the church began to regroup around the need for mission, and by the 1980s, under Robert Runcie, it adopted a strong political role, particularly following the publication in 1985 of the *Faith in the City* report, which was derided by Conservative politicians as "Marxist." The vision of the report, however, was somewhat romantically based on the idea of the Church of England being the national church. It paid scant regard to the multicultural context of contemporary England.

Through the 1990s, the Church of England became increasingly dominated by a revitalized evangelicalism, which had frequently adopted forms of charismatic worship which questioned the uniformity of the prayer book and traditional forms of liturgy. At the same time, the church voted to ordain women, even if it offered alternative structures of oversight for opponents, which served to create a "church within a church." The decade also brought a dramatic decline in church attendance and numbers of baptisms and confirmations. Baptism rates have halved from about a quarter of all live births in 1992 to about one-eighth in 2010. Numbers on electoral rolls – the closest the Church of England has to "membership" – in 2008 was 1,179,100, or only about 2 percent of the population, with almost identical numbers attending church regularly. This means that the Church of England has become a small church, even if it retains some of its privileges from the past. There has been a significant change in the public perception of the role of the church, with the church looking increasingly out of touch with the public mood, particularly in its resistance to opening up its ministry to homosexuals and the continued opposition to women's ministry. Some of the divisions in worldwide Anglicanism, particularly over the question of homosexuality, are reflected in the internal strife in the Church of England, although as yet there have been very few splits. Similarly, although some clergy and a few laity have left the Church of England for the Roman Catholic "Ordinariate" in recent years, numbers have been extremely modest, and it seems as if most Anglicans are content to remain in the Church of England even if, as seems likely, it decides to ordain women as bishops. At present, the Church of England finds itself in a precarious position, with falling and aging congregations and a shortage of funds. It comes as little surprise that it has invested heavily in new mission strategies to try to boost its congregations. As yet, these efforts have yielded few concrete results. Like other churches of Western Europe, the Church of England appears to be sinking into terminal if managed decline.

## Bibliography

Avis, Paul. 2000. *The Anglican Understanding of the Church*. London: SPCK.

Bede. 1968. *A History of the English Church and People*. London: Penguin.

Chapman, Mark. 2006. *Anglicanism: A Very Short Introduction*. Oxford: Oxford University Press.

Chapman, Mark. 2012. *Anglican Theology*. London: T & T Clark.

Davie, Martin. 2008. *A Guide to the Church of England*. London: Continuum.

Harrison, G. B., ed. 1968. *The Letters of Queen Elizabeth*. Reprint 1935. New York: Funk and Wagnalls.

Podmore, Colin. 2005. *Aspects of Anglican Identity*. London: Church House Publishing.

Spencer, Stephen. 2010. *SCM Study Guide: Anglicanism*. London: SCM.

*The Conclusive Part of the Parliamentary or Constitutional History of England. From the earliest times, to the Dissolution of the Convention Parliament that restored King Charles II. Together with an Appendix of Several Matters relative to the foregoing History, which were either omitted in the Course of it, or have been sent in to the Compilers since the Publication of the former Parts of this Work*. Vol. 23. London, 1660.

CHAPTER 39

# The Church of Ireland

## Robyn M. Neville

## Introduction

Although the Anglican identity of the Church of Ireland may have officially germinated through the impositions of the English Reformation, the roots of this modern Irish church stretch deep into the traditions of early Christianity in Ireland, and it has blossomed into its own unique province in the worldwide Anglican Communion. Comprising at present some 390,000 members (approximately 257,800 in Northern Ireland, and 129,039 in the Republic of Ireland), the Church of Ireland today encompasses 12 dioceses in two archiepiscopal provinces, Armagh and Dublin (Macourt 2008; see also Central Statistics Office Ireland 2012, 104). Historically maintaining a generally "Low Church" tendency in ecclesiastical practice, the Church of Ireland nevertheless embraces an increasing number of "High Church" (or Anglo-Catholic) and evangelical congregations among its parochial units.

## Christianity in Ireland: Origins to the Reformation

Although the precise mechanisms by which Christianity arrived in Ireland remain obscure, evidence suggests three possible channels for its gradual introduction: a series of fifth-century migrations to and from Ireland; networks of trade and cultural exchange with Gaul; and the trade in prisoners of war, although references in the historical record indicate a series of evangelizing missions authorized by Rome and launched from Britain sometime in the early decades of the fifth century (Ó Corráin 1972, 14–23). A certain Palladius, for example, is mentioned by name by Prosper of Aqui-

*The Wiley-Blackwell Companion to the Anglican Communion*, First Edition. Edited by Ian S. Markham,
J. Barney Hawkins IV, Justyn Terry, and Leslie Nuñez Steffensen.
© 2013 John Wiley & Sons, Ltd. Published 2013 by John Wiley & Sons, Ltd.

taine as undertaking a fifth-century mission to the Irish, although the project was not as successful as had been hoped. This occasioned the mission made by Patrick, which tradition dates to the 430s (although the precise historical date remains contested). Elected for this assignment by a synod of British clergy, Patrick himself describes the tensions between the growing numbers of Christians and adherents to Ireland's indigenous religious culture in his *Letter to Coroticus*, detailing the particulars of his mission in his fifth-century *Confessio*. Although the legions of Rome never conquered Ireland, these early missions introduced religious practices and ecclesiastical organization structures that closely mirrored the Roman Christian tradition of the continent.

By the seventh century, Irish Christianity had developed its own distinct character; indeed, this was the beginning of a true florescence of early Irish Christian culture. Organized according to two systems of polity, the Irish church depended primarily on the parochial oversight of influential monasteries and their abbots; the authority of bishops, though considerable, was influential only in particular localities (Ó Corráin 1972). A complicating figure in the polity of the early Irish church was the abbot-bishop, whose influence extended both to monastic foundations and, in some cases, to the oversight of smaller, proto-diocesan units. Under the monastic system, a powerful abbot reigned over a series of daughter monastic houses in a *paruchia*, or federation, which drew both identity and practice from the legacy of an eminent founding figure (Hughes 1972, 71–75). Dynasties of monastic leadership, often related to the powerful ruling families of specific territories, dominated much of Irish church leadership in this early period.

The monastic life was highly significant for early Irish Christianity, as it was the great monastic houses that fostered a dazzling culture of education and produced such treasures as the great illuminated manuscripts of the eighth and ninth centuries (such as the Books of Kells and Durrow) and a plethora of early Christian texts, first in Latin through the seventh century, and then in the vernacular thereafter. Armagh was the ancient episcopal polestar of Irish Christianity, although as a cultic center, Kildare rivaled Armagh for primacy (Ó Crónín 1999). Liturgical practice was heavily influenced by continental forms, as attested by such documents as the Lorrha (also called Stowe) Missal, with particularly Irish additions, such as the invocation of native saints in apotropaic prayers and charms. The uniquely Irish genre of penitentials, handbooks for penance and ascetical practice, demonstrate the earliest Western application for private confession and a sensitive appreciation for the care of souls. A robust hagiographic tradition narrated the lively foundational activities of early Irish holy figures such as Patrick, Brigit of Kildare, and Columcille of Iona, whose sixth-century mission to the inhabitants of northwest Scotland (then under Irish control in the region known as the Dál Riada) included contact both with native Picts and Irish colonists. A few intrepid clerics and religious undertook *peregrinatio*, a form of voluntary exile, as a type of extended pilgrimage (or act of ascetical renunciation), and pioneering Irish *peregrini* (literally, "strangers") such as Columbanus traveled as far as Germany and Italy, establishing monastic centers according to Irish rules of life and influencing the development of monasticism on the European continent (Dunn 2003; Stancliffe 1982). A spirit of adventure, artistic and intellectual achievement, rigorous Biblical analysis, and an exuberant interest in preserving the expressive and ancient narratives of Irish identity and cultural history permeated this early period of Irish Christian writing and material production.

Ireland retained a thriving connection to English Christianity at this time, especially via the strong patterns of cultural and material exchange that occurred between Irish monasteries in modern-day Argyll and monastic communities in Northumbria (Cramp 1997). At the Synod of Whitby in 664, such associations came into conflict over the seemingly simple issues of monastic tonsure style and the dating of Easter (Abels 1983, 25). According to Bede, representatives of the Irish *paruchia* of Iona met in 664 with Northumbrian representatives who identified their practice directly with Rome; the synod resolved the Easter issue in favor of the Roman calculation. Far from being a uniquely Irish problem, this was an issue that had distressed many churches throughout Latin Christendom for centuries, and therefore had resulted in a number of local synods and councils (Harrison 1982, 307; see also Hughes 1981). It was only after the Reformation that the Synod of Whitby took on pronounced historic significance, when Irish Anglican apologists sought to justify the break with the papacy by referencing a so-called native "Celtic" aversion to Rome in historical precedent (Ford 1995, 2–3; see also O'Loughlin 2002, 55–58).

The last years of the eighth century witnessed the commencement of a new era as Viking raiders swept out of the North Sea and descended upon Ireland. Monasteries and churches that had flourished in the new age of Christian cultural abundance were favored targets because of their rich holdings in plate (Ó Corráin 1998). As the Scandinavians began to move further inland and settle in the ninth century, they created urban centers such as Dublin, and gradually established the coastal cities of Cork, Waterford, Wexford, and Limerick (Ó Corráin 1972). Initially, the native Irish fought to keep their lands from the invaders, but by the eleventh century, a period of relative stability was achieved through centuries of intermarriage and cultural exchange, and Viking settlers contributed felicitously to Ireland's trade economy (Valante 2008). Over time, the Vikings of Ireland were converted to Christianity, possibly by contact with the English church in York, and the first bishops of Viking Dublin were subject to the see of Canterbury rather than to Armagh (Watt 1998, 231–3).

An organized diocesan system emerged in Ireland by the beginning of the twelfth century as a consequence of a new, intensified model for papal authority that was achieved at the conclusion of the eleventh. Although first articulated in 1110–1111 at a synod at Rathbreasil in Tipperary, it was not until the Synod of Kells-Mellifont in 1152 that this structure was implemented for the whole of Ireland (McNeill 1974, 217). Canterbury's influence did not receive the same amplification, for in this same year, four Irish archbishoprics received the *pallium* directly from the papacy: Armagh, Cashel, Tuam, and Dublin. This solidified Ireland's growing relationship with continental European Christianity and with the papacy in particular (Watt 1998).

Such moves toward a more unifying effort of ecclesiastical organization proved important when, in the same century, Norman invaders from Britain and Wales began to colonize portions of Ireland, beginning with areas along the eastern coast. In Britain, the Anglo-Norman Crown used the church as an instrument for exerting greater control over its growing holdings in Ireland, and ecclesiastical reformers in Ireland sought to bring their practices in line with those of England. To this end, the Synod of Cashel in 1171 mandated that all offices of the Irish church should be performed according to English practice (Milne 2003, 28). Slowly, English clergy filled Irish ecclesiastical offices; by 1217, royal decree demanded that only Englishmen hold episcopal office or serve as cathedral deans, and native Irish clergy found themselves maneuvered to an increasingly marginalized position (Warren 1997). By the fourteenth century, Anglo-Norman control of the Irish church was complete: in 1367, the Statutes of Kilkenny were established for the express purpose of preventing Anglo-Norman cultural assimilation of native Irish customs, dress, and language; to prevent intermarriage between Irish and Anglo-Normans; and to preserve clear ethnic delineations between the new English and the native Irish (Richter 2005, 164–5). One of the stipulations prevented native Irish from holding leadership positions in any church that happened to be located in the area of English control, known as "the Pale."

Anglo-Norman nobility owned so much of the available land holdings by the sixteenth century that native Irish were all but excluded from positions of influence. A series of revolts and rebellions throughout the fifteenth and sixteenth centuries increased tensions between the Irish and the Anglo-Norman elites, although some Normans who intermarried with the Irish carved out their own local fiefdoms and adopted Gaelic culture and language (Richter 2005, 167–8, 174). Despite a long period of native Irish resurgence that developed in the wake of England's internal and foreign wars, by the reign of the Tudors, England sought to reclaim authority over Ireland. This had significant and long-reaching implications for the church.

By 1542, King Henry VIII was declared "King of Ireland" and head of the Irish church by acts of the Irish Parliament (the body of which was dominated by representatives sympathetic to the agenda of the king), and his daughter, Elizabeth I, staged a series of campaigns and occupations both to subdue native Irish rebellions to the Crown and to retake the country by conquest. Under Henry VIII, and continuing through the era of Cromwell's Protectorate, the English government issued permission for and encouraged the settlement of plantations, wherein large numbers of English and lowland Scottish settlers were imported to confiscated Irish lands to reestablish English language, culture, religion, and law, often displacing large groups of Irish in the process. In practice, this meant that Scottish colonists brought Presbyterianism with them and English colonists brought Anglicanism; indeed, the first book printed with movable type in Ireland was the English Book of Common Prayer, brought into use for the first time on Easter Day, 1551, at Christ Church Cathedral in Dublin (Mayne 2006, 202). In the wake of the English Reformation, church offices in Ireland were deliberately filled with English clergy, and public offices were staffed with English and Scottish officials, such that Irish Roman Catholics were now forced into a state of dependence on a ruling class of Protestants of either Anglican or Presbyterian affiliation. In the Ulster plantation, settled during the reign of James I, many colonists were Scottish Presbyterians, which led to later tensions with Irish Anglicans over the "true" articulation of Reformation ideals. The native Irish Roman Catholics of Ulster were forcibly displaced from their own lands, and the Church of Ireland was granted all the church properties in Ulster that had originally belonged to the Roman Catholic Church.

## The Church of Ireland: "No New Faith, No New Church"

The Tudor Reformation resulted in a gradual repopulation of clerical offices with English clergy and, under Edward VI, the declaration of Anglicanism as the official state religion of Ireland. The Act of Supremacy in 1534 had established the king as the head of the English church; two years later, the English Augustinian friar George Browne arrived in Ireland as the new Archbishop of Dublin (appointed by the king after the murder of the former archbishop), and the Irish parliament formally dissolved papal authority over the church in favor of the Crown. The dissolution of the monasteries under the Tudors produced a gradual disintegration of monastic influence, and tensions continued between the new English clergy that filled clerical vacancies and the people. Although native Irish and Hiberno-Norman Roman Catholics initially solicited the help of European powers such as Spain in resisting the English, and under Mary I a brief Roman Catholic resurgence enjoyed the benefits of official state recognition, by the reign of Elizabeth I, the Irish Act of Uniformity, passed in 1560, made attendance at Church of Ireland services compulsory and required an Oath of Supremacy of all holders of ecclesiastical and secular office.

Yet, Irish Anglican apologists such as Archbishop James Ussher (d. 1656) stressed the continuity of the Church of Ireland with more ancient forms of Christianity. A scholar of early Christian theology, Ussher insisted that Anglicanism preserved the true intention of early Christianity, and that the early medieval clashes between "native Celtic" and "Romish" Christian practices (as demonstrated at the Synod of Whitby) revealed the legitimacy of indigenous Irish resistance to Rome. Ancient Christian theologians ("the ancient Fathers," in Ussher's words) would look upon contemporary abuses of papal authority as deviating from the true church; Irish Anglicanism, then, was in keeping with ancient church understandings of authority and scripture. "We bring in no new faith, no new Church," Ussher insisted (Elrington 1847, 493; see generally Acheson 2002 and Bolton 1958). Under Ussher, a convocation of united Scottish, English, and native Irish (or Anglo-Norman) Church of Ireland clergy agreed to 104 Articles of Religion in 1615. On the whole, these offered a perspective fundamentally sympathetic to Calvinism, but by 1634, the church had returned to the 39 Articles (first ratified by English Anglicans in 1562) as the basis for "sound belief."

A general shortage of competent clergy, clerical absenteeism, and the paucity of viable incomes from the lands and rents of ecclesiastical benefices led to a period of decay and disorganization soon after the Tudor Reformation established Anglicanism in Ireland. Many churches of the seventeenth century that had fallen to neglect under the absenteeism of parish clergy and their bishops were in ruins; often, bishops followed nepotistic practices by granting parishes and parish glebes to their own sons, many of whom had received only the sparest training in theology and who used their titles merely for admittance into higher levels of society (McCafferty 2007).

A new era of episcopal reformers sought to restore discipline and education to the ranks of the clergy, and several enterprising bishops undertook efforts toward making the words of scripture and the prayer book available to the Irish in their own language. William O'Donnell (Uilliam Ó Domhnaill, d. 1628), Archbishop of Tuam, had translated the English Book of Common Prayer into Irish by 1608 (Pullan 1900, 126). The English provost of Trinity College Dublin, William Bedell (d. 1642), encouraged education in the Irish language at that institution, hoping to ensure that future priests would be able to relate to and converse with the people in their parochial charges. After his consecration as Bishop of Kilmore and Ardagh, Bedell appointed Irish-speaking clergy to parishes in his diocese, held services in Irish, and supervised the translation of the Old Testament into Irish Gaelic, a project that was not completed until 1685, 43 years after his death (an Irish translation of the New Testament had been available since 1603).

In the aftermath of the English Civil War (which extended to Ireland during the prolonged and ruthless conflict known as the Irish Confederate Wars or the Eleven Years War), Cromwell enacted a series of laws in Ireland that enforced a Puritan form of church practice and polity that rejected Anglican episcopal authority and outlawed the use of the Book of Common Prayer. Under the Restoration in 1660, the Church of Ireland was able to find its footing as a legal religious entity once more, aided by the Clarendon Code, a series of harsh laws aimed at limiting the freedoms and influence of religious nonconformists. The Church of Ireland adopted the English Book of Common Prayer of 1662, a version of which was published in Ireland in 1666 that essentially reproduced the English 1662 book with the addition of special prayers for prisoners, the Governors of Ireland, and a prayer in thanksgiving for the 1641 victory over an Irish Roman Catholic attack on Dublin Castle.

It was at this point, under the restored English monarchy of the Stuarts, that the Church of Ireland enjoyed a period of relative stability, scholarly renewal, and theological achievement. A number of influential seventeenth-century theologians, called "Carolines" because many of them wrote during the reign of Charles I and Charles II, articulated the unique character of Irish Anglican theology and piety. Although many emphasized the continuity of the Church of Ireland with the standards of Scripture and ancient Christian tradition, other Caroline theologians castigated Rome's departure from the standards of faith set forth in the early centuries of the church. As John Bramhall (d. 1663), Archbishop of Armagh, observed, "the Court of Rome would have obtruded upon us new articles of faith; we have rejected them; they introduced unlawful rites into the Liturgies of the Church and use of the Sacraments; we have reformed them for ourselves: they went about to violate the just liberties and privileges of our Church; we have vindicated them." On this view, the Church of Ireland was preserving the true spirit and practices of early Christianity. "We do not challenge a new Church, a new religion, or new holy orders: we obtrude no innovation upon others, nor desire to have any obtruded upon ourselves: we pluck up the weeds, but retain all the plants of saving truth," Bramhall argued (Bolton 1958, 68–9).

Another Caroline divine, Jeremy Taylor (d. 1667), agreed. Taylor, who eventually became Bishop of Down and Connor and who was known for both his preaching and his pastoral writings, emphasized the apostolic succession of Church of Ireland bishops and clergy, and contrasted their faithfulness with the papacy's "invasion" of the rights of bishops prior to the English Reformation (Bolton 1958, 69–70). He also affirmed the necessity for practical piety, constant prayer, the grounding of the soul in the words of scripture, and frequent communion. In addition to forging an identity distinct from that of Tridentine Rome, the Church of Ireland had to deal with the "Presbyterian question" – that is, the role of Presbyterian churches in an increasingly Anglicized Ireland, particularly in Ulster, where they often constituted a majority (Acheson 2002, 28). Taylor attempted to pacify the Presbyterian clergy in his diocese, but they refused to recognize the validity of his episcopal office, and Taylor was reduced to barring them from their own churches and installing Anglican clergymen in their place (Carroll 1990, 33).

The fortunes of the Church of Ireland were once again reversed when James II, a recent convert to Roman Catholicism, succeeded Charles II in 1685. For a period of four years, James enforced a policy that sought to restore Roman Catholic rule in both England and Ireland, with the result that many in Ireland who had once enjoyed the benefits of being counted among the Protestant "establishment" now found themselves deprived of titles and offices. In some cases, where the Crown found it convenient to fill vacant Church of Ireland episcopacies with favorites, Anglican Irish clergy found themselves serving under a Roman Catholic bishop.

James II was succeeded by the Protestant William of Orange and his English queen, Mary, and a period of prosperity followed in the Church of Ireland in the first half of the eighteenth century. Although the treaty of Limerick had ended the bloodshed in Ireland that had led up to William's accession, a new series of penal laws erected a system whereby education, employment opportunities, civic rights, attendance at Roman Catholic worship, and even the Irish language itself were denied to Irish Catholics. The era of Protestant Ascendancy thus provided the effect that Irish Roman Catholics were denied education and prevented from speaking their own language. Once again, Church of Ireland supporters found themselves benefitting from their status as members of the "established" religion. By the end of the eighteenth century, every bishop in Armagh was English by birth (Milne 2003, 55).

As its status increased during the rise of the House of Hanover, the Church of Ireland enjoyed a period of gradual rebuilding and development. Several notable bishops who were scholars and able leaders advanced a new program of ecclesiastical renewal. William King, dean of St. Patrick's Cathedral and later archbishop of Dublin (d. 1729), worked to restore clergy to their benefices, addressed widespread neglect of the sacraments, and demonstrated an interest in the Irish language by making services available in Irish (Acheson 2002). The translation work of John Richardson (d. 1747), rector of Belturbet in Cavan, produced an Irish version of the 1662 prayer book by 1712; Richardson also campaigned energetically to have catechisms and Bibles printed in Irish and distributed to lay people (Muss-Arnolt 1914). Jonathan Swift (d. 1745), the great satirist who wrote *Gulliver's Travels* and the incendiary *A Modest Proposal*, was Dean of St. Patrick's Cathedral, where he restored the practice of weekly Eucharist and endowed St. Patrick's Hospital for the mentally ill (Landa 1954). Similarly, George Berkeley (d. 1753), Dean of Derry and then Bishop of Cloyne, a sensitive scholar, imaginative philosopher, and philanthropist, supported a mission to Bermuda, where he hoped to establish a theological college. John Wesley, the great Anglican revivalist and preacher whose insistence on holy living so impressed Christians both in England and the American colonies, found the Anglicans whom he encountered during his extensive visits to Ireland to be quite disciplined in their own piety and "authentic in their fervor," although he remarked that penal laws and acts of Parliament were hardly the means for converting Roman Catholics to Anglicanism (Acheson 2002, 102). In this way, a renewed interest in devotion and the reforming work of several outstanding bishops and priests rehabilitated the flagging spirits of a struggling church.

The early nineteenth century saw tensions increase between the so-called "High Churchmen" and the evangelicals. Although the Act of Union in 1800 joined Anglicans in both Ireland and Britain under "one protestant episcopal church, the united church of England and Ireland," Irish Anglicans were often subordinated to favored English candidates in the practice of clerical appointments. The early decades thereafter witnessed a period of renewed attention to church buildings, including a "substantial programme" of new church construction and renovation (Acheson 2002, 111).

The development of voluntary church societies such as the Association for Promoting Christian Knowledge, or APCK, also characterized the early decades of the nineteenth century. Founded in 1792 and incorporated in 1800, from 1803 APCK established schools and funded their faculty (Acheson 2002, 122). Other societies, such as the Hibernian Bible Society (founded in 1806), undertook to distribute the Bible in Ireland as part of a growing evangelical program of mission. Women made significant contributions in support of these organizations and also volunteered time and resources in the education of Irish children, especially poor Catholics (Acheson 2002, 125). The United Society for the Propagation of the Gospel (renamed USPG Ireland in 2007), which had been founded in 1701, sent its first missionaries to India in 1820 and South Africa in 1821, and accepted its first female missionary, Sarah Coombes, in 1856. A period of evangelical revival in the late 1850s infused the work of such societies with renewed energy.

By the mid-nineteenth century, more pressing concerns at home consumed the Church of Ireland. The Great Famine, one of the most tragic and horrific eras in the history of Ireland, was responsible for the deaths of more than 1 million Irish and the emigration of a million more. The Irish Church Act of 1869 disestablished the Church of Ireland, effectively dissociating it from the Crown and the British state; legislation that took final effect in 1871 officially founded the Church of Ireland as an independent Anglican church. The first general synod was held in February of 1870 at St. Patrick's Cathedral in Dublin and ratified a new constitution, and a new preamble and declaration of faith and order (Church of Ireland 1870). In 1873, the Church of Ireland authorized and published its first hymnal after disestablishment; the first Book of Common Prayer after disestablishment was published in 1878.

The early twentieth century witnessed a growing concern with self-reliance in a climate of increased sectarianism (Acheson 2002, 216–19). In the wake of the Irish War of Independence and partition, the Church of Ireland displayed a strong commitment to pastoral activity and an increasing interest in advocacy for peace and reconciliation among opposing sides (Power 2007). Toward the end of the period known as "The Troubles," anguished clergy, weary of decades of terror and violence, called for stability and understanding (McMullan 1997). Under the leadership of the Most Rev. Dr. Robin Eames, Archbishop of Armagh and Primate of All Ireland from 1986 to 2006, a delegation of Church of Ireland bishops met with Sinn Fein in October 2006 to affirm the church's support of democratic procedure in the Irish Peace Process. Eames has discussed his personal experience with sectarianism in his 1992 book, *Chains to be Broken*.

In response to the 1920 Lambeth Conference appeal, the Church of Ireland formed the United Council of Christian Churches and Religious Communions in Ireland with other churches across the island in 1923, an organization that later developed into the Irish Council of Churches in 1966. The Book of Common Prayer was revised, and a new version was published in 1926. Irish Anglican women in the early decades of the twentieth century used their volunteer positions in charitable organizations to effect remarkable change in the areas of education, international philanthropic aid, and the shifting culture of Irish gender norms (Walsh 2005).

In the second half of the twentieth century, Irish Anglicans looked beyond their own borders for ecumenical connections (Davidson 2008; see also Power 2007). In 1963, the Church of Ireland established a relationship of full communion with the Lusitanian and Spanish Reformed Episcopal Churches and the Church of South India (Barkley 1983). In the same year, the Church of Ireland established formal talks with the Methodist, Presbyterian, and Congregational Churches in Ireland (Thompson 2007). Relations with the Methodists in Ireland were renewed via the establishment of a Methodist/ Church of Ireland Theological Working Party in 1989. This resulted in both churches signing a covenant in 2002, which stated that "there are no theological objections to full visible unity between our churches"; as a result, the joint Theological Working Party was replaced by a Covenant Council in 2003 (Thompson 2007). In 1995, the Church of Ireland entered into the Porvoo Communion, which established full communion with the Baltic–Nordic Lutheran Churches; the Church of Ireland also enjoys full communion with the Church of North India, the Church of Pakistan, and the Old Catholic Churches of Utrecht. A member of the World Council of Churches since 1948, the Church of Ireland joined both the Conference of European Churches at its foundation in 1959 and the Anglican Consultative Council in 1968. The Irish Inter-Church Meeting was founded in 1973 to include the Roman Catholic Church in ecumenical dialogue in Ireland.

The Church of Ireland also turned its attention to its institutions of higher learning in the second half of the twentieth century. In 1980, the Church of Ireland Theological College was reassembled from the former Divinity School at Trinity College Dublin during a period of transition and reorganization. Reforming efforts originating in the House of Bishops over the course of 2006–2007 resulted in a new entity, the Church of Ireland Theological Institute, with a revised curriculum, new governance, and a renewed partnership with Trinity College Dublin. The first courses under the new program were offered to matriculating students in 2008.

Founded in 1811 in Dublin by the Kildare Place Society to provide training to parochial school teachers, the Church of Ireland Training College gained status as a national institution of higher education in 1884 and incorporated Irish language courses after partition in the 1920s. Later affiliated with Trinity College Dublin and renamed the Church of Ireland College of Education, it continues to house an extensive collection of historic Kildare Place Society publications and archival material, which testify to the Church of Ireland's longstanding involvement in promoting literacy in the modern era.

A period of liturgical innovation and experimentation that first arose in the 1960s was brought to definitive expression with the publication of the Alternative Prayer Book 1984 and the Alternative Occasional Services 1993. The fifth edition of the

Church of Ireland Hymnal was revised and published in 2000. In 1997, the general synod authorized the Liturgical Advisory Committee to prepare a new edition of the 1926 Book of Common Prayer; this was issued in English in 2004. In the same year, Cumann Gaelach na hEaglaise, the Irish Guild of the church, published *Leabhar na hUrnaí Coitinne 2004*, a new translation of the Book of Common Prayer in Irish by Archdeacon Gary Hastings, Rector of St. Nicholas' Collegiate Church in Galway. A new translation of the New Testament into Irish was made by the Rev. Canon Coslett Quinn and published in 1970.

## The Contemporary Church of Ireland

By the latter half of the twentieth century, dramatic cultural changes in Irish society occasioned a number of landmark historical events in the Church of Ireland. Women's ordination was ratified in 1990, "before the Church of England, the Scottish Episcopal Church, and the Church in Wales decided to ordain women" (Acheson 2002, 245), although no women have been elected to episcopal office to date.

In 2004, the Book of Common Prayer was revised from the 1926 version, but this move was deemed by some to represent too drastic a departure from traditional expressions of Irish Anglicanism. In response, break-away Anglican churches such as the Church of Ireland, Traditional Rite (founded in 1991, primarily over objections to women's ordination and allied with the worldwide Traditional Anglican Communion), continued to use the 1926 Book of Common Prayer.

The Church of Ireland has not been immune to the controversy in the first decades of the twenty-first century over the blessing of same-sex unions, the legitimacy of same-sex civil partnerships among the clergy, and the ordination of persons in loving, same-gender relationships. When the Bishop of Limerick attended the Rt. Rev. Gene Robinson's consecration as Bishop of New Hampshire (Episcopal Church, USA), evangelical groups such as Reform Ireland and the Evangelical Fellowship of Irish Clergy were galvanized to make strenuous objections to same-sex unions and to express support for defending a "traditional" definition of marriage. Groups in support of a more "inclusive" church culture with regard to human sexual identity and sexuality, such as Changing Attitude Ireland, have contributed vocal advocacy for full equality and affirmation for LGBT/Q persons in the life of the Church of Ireland. In 2011, the same-sex civil partnership of the Very Rev. Tom Gordon, Dean of the Cathedral of St. Laserian in Leighlin in the Diocese of Cashel and Ossory, came to the attention of both the Church of Ireland and the media, precipitating an even more vehement clash of opinions and a sense of impending crisis in the months leading up to the general synod of 2012.

Although the Church of Ireland, broadly speaking, has generally maintained a cautious stance in regard to these issues, formal church decisions about human sexual identity have tended to be more conservative than those of the Church of England or the Episcopal Church, USA. In the period leading up to the general synod of 2012, the Church of Ireland engaged in a formal "listening" process for hearing arguments for and against the affirmation of a "traditional" understanding of marriage; this process included a conference on human sexuality held in March at the Slieve Russell Hotel in Ballyconnell, County Cavan. At the commencement of the general synod on May 10, 2012, at Christ Church Cathedral, Dublin, the Most Rev. Alan Harper, Archbishop of Armagh and Primate of all Ireland, urged the synod to listen to one another with "wisdom and humility," and quoted John Calvin on "the exercise of charity" (Harper 2012). Despite the efforts of some Church of Ireland members to engage in social media and Internet-based advocacy for a more expansive understanding of human sexuality and partnership, the general synod of 2012 nevertheless decided in favor of reaffirming a "traditional" definition of marriage. By a vote of 91 clergy (including 10 bishops) and 154 lay delegates in favor of a revised version of Resolution 8A (with an opposition vote of 55 clergy and 60 laity), the general synod of 2012 determined that "faithfulness within marriage is the only normative context for sexual intercourse" (Church of Ireland 2012). The resolution was proposed by the Archbishop of Dublin, the Most Rev. Dr. Michael Jackson, and seconded by the Bishop of Down and Dromore, the Rt. Rev. Harold Miller.

Despite this enduring conflict over human sexuality, the Church of Ireland in the twenty-first century has expanded its concern for other aspects of social justice to a global stage. The Church in Society Committee of the general synod of the Church of Ireland provides resources and advocates for social justice issues pertaining to ecology and the environment, medical ethics, and the growing concern with advancements in technology that intersect with human flourishing in Europe. The Church of Ireland also participates in the Anglican Alliance, a global Anglican relief and justice advocacy organization that was established in 2008.

A growing investment in working toward a more ecumenical Ireland has resulted in new conversations about sharing sacred space. In late 2011, the Very Rev. Dr. Robert MacCarthy, dean of St. Patrick's Cathedral in Dublin, argued for making St. Patrick's an ecumenical worship space, a "national cathedral for all Christians," although this suggestion elicited some controversy (McGarry 2011).

Finally, a burgeoning scholarly interest in the history of the Church of Ireland has resulted in a number of academic conferences and publications in the last two decades, as well as the founding of the Church of Ireland Historical Society in 1994. Recent research has focused on the role of the laity in the Church of Ireland (Gillespie and Neely 2002), the changing roles and initiatives of the clergy (Barnard and Neely 2006), and the role of women in Church of Ireland missions and relief organizations (Walsh 2005). It has also produced accessible histories (MacCarthy 1995; Milne 2003), comprehensive historical surveys (Acheson 2002), and bibliographies (Ford and Milne 1993).

## The Future of Anglicanism in Ireland?

For much of the latter half of the twentieth century, the Church of Ireland faced declining membership, similar to declining numbers in the Church of England but perhaps more statistically significant in light of smaller general populations in both Northern Ireland and the Republic (the population of which itself declined until the decade of economic resurgence that began in the late 1990s and consequently initiated a period of significant immigration that reversed that trend dramatically). Although an increasing tendency in the Republic of Ireland for people to gravitate toward more secular expressions of meaning rather than to religious institutions may be partially to blame for the late-twentieth-century decline in the membership of minority religions overall (Gillmor 2006, 117), the rise of new religious movements in Ireland over the same period may indicate a more nuanced geography of shifting religious affiliation and identity (Cosgrave 2011). Indeed, in the past decade, Church of Ireland membership in the Republic of Ireland has itself been on the rise, owing perhaps to increased immigration from the United Kingdom and other countries encompassing a strong Anglican presence, and to the repeal of the Roman Catholic *Ne Temere* decree (Macourt 2008). According to the 2006 Irish census, the Church of Ireland grew by 8.7 percent in the Republic over 2002–2006, "just ahead of the national increase in population" overall (at 8.2 %) (Central Statistics Office Ireland 2007, 31). Northern Ireland has witnessed a slight decline in Church of Ireland membership, from 22 percent in 1968 to 17 percent in 2008 (Hayes and Dowds 2010; see also Macourt 2008, 127). Worship attendance in Northern Ireland has also declined, "with just a third of the population currently reporting that they attend church on a weekly basis" in any denomination (Hayes and Dowds 2010).

Ireland's future stability in the wake of the 2008–2009 economic crisis will likely benefit from the full powers of the Church of Ireland's pastoral presence, necessitating new initiatives for the care of the poor and the unemployed, although the rate of Ireland's recovery may also have implications for the Church of Ireland's own internal financial resiliency (Wynne 2009). In Northern Ireland, where the effects of the European sovereign debt crisis have been felt in terms of intense recession, the Church of Ireland has partnered with other religious organizations to develop interdenominational community outreach programs, such as food banks and debt-counseling services. "On Our Doorstep," a report on poverty commissioned by the Rt. Rev. Harold Miller, Bishop of Down and Dromore, and produced by a special diocesan "Poverty Think Tank," was presented to the diocesan synod in June 2011. This sophisticated analysis paired theological reflection with practical suggestions for improved involvement at the parish level, including a call for individual parishes to undertake research on local poverty demographics and develop community resources in response (Diocese of Down and Dromore 2011).

A continuing issue for the Church of Ireland will be the question of full inclusion for LGBT/Q members at all levels of ecclesiastical participation and leadership. In the wake of the decision of the general synod of 2012 on Resolution 8A, several Church of Ireland members who identify as LGBT expressed dissatisfaction with the perceived homophobic position of the church as an institution (McGarry 2012). As with other Anglican churches contending with similar issues, the effects of the controversy may have some bearing on the Church of Ireland's future relationship with and participation in the Worldwide Anglican Communion. In the meantime, debates over human sexuality and the nature of marriage and partnership may continue to reveal the rift between evangelical and progressive perspectives in the Church of Ireland, although an enduring commitment to the processes of listening and mutual respect may also reveal unanticipated affirmations of common sympathy (Kennerley and O'Leary 2012, 7–9).

Finally, the Church of Ireland may expand the role of women to the highest levels of ecclesiastical leadership and polity in the near future. Although women have been appointed as canons and deans, by 2012 no woman has yet been elected to the episcopal office or consecrated bishop.

## Bibliography

Abels, Richard. 1983. The Council of Whitby: A Study in Early Anglo-Saxon Politics. *The Journal of British Studies*, vol. 23, no. 1, pp. 1–25.

Acheson, Alan. 2002. *A History of the Church of Ireland 1691–2001*, 2nd ed. Dublin: The Columba Press and APCK.

Akenson, Donald Harmon. 1971. *The Church of Ireland: Ecclesiastical Reform and Revolution, 1800–85*. New Haven and London: Yale University Press.

Barkley, John Monteith. 1983. *The Irish Council of Churches 1923–1983*. Belfast: ICC and Oikoumene.

Barnard, Toby and W. G. Neely, eds. 2006. *The Clergy of the Church of Ireland, 1000–2000*. Dublin: Four Courts Press.

Bolton, Frederick Rothwell. 1958. *The Caroline Tradition of the Church of Ireland, with Particular Reference to Bishop Jeremy Taylor*. London: SPCK for the Church Historical Society.

Brown, Terence. 1985. *Ireland, a Social and Cultural History, 1922 to the Present*. Ithaca, New York: Cornell University Press.

Brynn, Edward. 1982. *The Church of Ireland in the Age of Catholic Emancipation*. New York and London: Garland.

Carroll, Thomas K. 1990. *Jeremy Taylor: Selected Works*. Mahwah, New Jersey: The Paulist Press.

Central Statistics Office Ireland. 2007. *Census 2006: Principle Demographic Results*. Dublin: The Stationery Office.

Central Statistics Office Ireland. 2012. Table 36: Persons, Male and Female, Classified by Religious Denomination with Actual Percentage Change, 2006 and 2011. *This Is Ireland, Highlights from Census 2011, Part 1*. Dublin: The Stationery Office.

Church of Ireland. 1870. The Constitution of the Church of Ireland: Being Statutes Passed at the General Convention, 1870; with the Charter of Incorporation of the Representative Church Body and Resolutions with Reference to Finance. Dublin: Hodges, Foster, & Co.

Church of Ireland. 2012. Motion: Human Sexuality in the Context of Christian Belief. Proposed at the 2012 General Synod of the Church of Ireland, Christ Church Cathedral, Dublin, May 12.

Cochrane, Feargal. 2001. *Unionist Politics and the Politics of Unionism Since the Anglo-Irish Agreement*. Cork: Cork University Press.

Cosgrave, Olivia, Laurence Cox, Carmen Kuhling, and Peter Mulholland (eds). 2011. *Ireland's New Religious Movements*. Newcastle, UK: Cambridge Scholars Publishing.

Cramp, Rosemary. 1997. The Insular Tradition: An Overview. In *The Insular Tradition*, eds. Catherine E. Karkov, Michael Ryan, and Robert T. Farrell. Albany: State University of New York Press.

Davidson, Tony. 2008. Inter-Church Relations in a New Ireland. In *Inter-Church Relations: Developments and Perspectives*, ed. Brendan Leahy. Dublin: Veritas.

Diocese of Down and Dromore. 2011. *On Our Doorstep: The Report of the Bishop of Down and Dromore's Poverty Think Tank*. Belfast: Church of Ireland House.

Dunn, Marilyn. 2003. *The Emergence of Monasticism: From the Desert Fathers to the Early*

*Middle Ages.* Oxford: Blackwell Publishers, Ltd.

Eames, Robin. 1992. *Chains to Be Broken: A Personal Reflection on Northern Ireland and its People.* Belfast: Blackstaff Press, Ltd.

Elrington, Charles R., ed. 1847. *The Whole Works of the Most Rev. James Ussher, D. D,* vol. II. Dublin: Hodges and Smith.

Ervin, Spencer. 1965. *The Polity of the Church of Ireland.* Ambler, Pennsylvania: Trinity Press.

Ford, Alan. 1995. "Standing One's Ground": Religion, Polemic and Irish History Since the Reformation. In *As By Law Established: The Church of Ireland Since the Reformation,* eds. Alan Ford, James McGuire, and Kenneth Milne. Dublin: The Lilliput Press.

Ford, Alan and Kenneth Milne, eds. 1993. The Church of Ireland: A Critical Bibliography 1536–1992. *Irish Historical Studies,* vol. 28, no. 12 (November), pp. 345–84.

Gillespie, Raymond and W. G. Neely, eds. 2002. *The Laity and the Church of Ireland, 1000–2000: All Sorts and Conditions.* Dublin: Four Courts Press.

Gillmor, Desmond A. 2006. Changing Religions in the Republic of Ireland, 1991–2002. *Irish Geography,* vol. 39, no. 2, pp. 111–28.

Harrison, Kenneth. 1982. Episodes in the History of Easter Cycles in Ireland. In *Ireland in Early Mediaeval Europe: Studies in Memory of Kathleen Hughes,* eds. Dorothy Whitelock, Rosamond McKitterick and David Dumville. Cambridge: Cambridge University Press, pp. 307–19.

Hayes, Bernadette C. and Lizanne Dowds. 2010. Vacant Seats and Empty Pews. *Research Update,* vol. 65, no. 5 (February), pp. 1–4.

Hughes, Kathleen. 1972. *Early Christian Ireland: Introduction to the Sources.* Ithaca: Cornell University Press.

Hughes, Kathleen. 1981. The Celtic Church: Is This a Valid Concept? O'Donnell Lectures in Celtic Studies, University of Oxford 1975. *Cambridge Medieval Celtic Studies,* vol. 1, pp. 1–20.

Harper, Alan. 2012. Presidential Address Given at the Commencement of the General Synod of the Church of Ireland, May 10, 2012, Christ Church Cathedral, Dublin, Ireland. Belfast: The Church of Ireland Press Office.

Hurley, Michael, ed. 1970. *Irish Anglicanism 1869–1969.* Dublin: Allen Figgis.

Kennerley, Ginnie and Richard O'Leary, eds. 2012. *Moving Forward Together: Homosexuality and the Church of Ireland.* Belfast: Changing Attitude Ireland.

Landa, Louis A. 1954. *Swift and the Church of Ireland.* Oxford: Clarendon Press.

Macourt, Malcolm. 2008. *Counting the People of God? The Census of Population and the Church of Ireland.* Dublin: Church of Ireland Publishing.

Macourt, Malcolm. 2011. Mapping the "New Religious Landscape" and the "New Irish": Uses and Limitations of the Census. In *Ireland's New Religious Movements,* eds. Olivia Cosgrove et al. Newcastle-upon-Tyne: Cambridge Scholars, 28–50.

Mayne, Brian. 2006. Ireland. In *The Oxford Guide to the Book of Common Prayer: A Worldwide Survey,* eds. Charles Hefling and Cynthia Shattuck. Oxford: Oxford University Press.

McCafferty, John. 2007. *The Reconstruction of the Church of Ireland: Bishop Bramhall and the Laudian Reforms, 1633–1641.* Cambridge: Cambridge University Press.

MacCarthy, Robert B. 1995. *Ancient and Modern: A Short History of the Church of Ireland.* Dublin: Four Courts Press.

McCready, David. 2006. The Ordination of Women in the Church of Ireland. *Proceedings of the Royal Irish Academy, Section C,* vol. 106, no. 1 (January), pp. 367–94.

McDowell, Robert Brendan. 1975. *The Church of Ireland, 1869–1969.* Boston and London: Routledge and Kegan Paul.

McGarry, Patsy. 2011. Dean Seeks Backing for National Cathedral Plan. *The Irish Times,* Tuesday, October 25.

McGarry, Patsy. 2012. Traditional Teaching on Marriage Endorsed. *The Irish Times,* Monday, May 14.

McNeill, John T. 1974. *The Celtic Churches: A History, A.D. 200 to 1200*. Chicago: University of Chicago Press.

McMullan, Gordon. 1997. *Opposing Violence, Building Bridges: Words Written and Spoken in the Course of Ordained Ministry to a Suffering and Deeply Troubled Society: Ulster, 1969–1996*. Belfast: Down and Dromore Publications.

Milne, Kenneth. 2003. *A Short History of the Church of Ireland*. Blackrock: Columba Press.

Muss-Arnolt, William. 1914. *The Book of Common Prayer Among the Nations of the World: A History of the Translations of the Prayer Book of the Church of England and of the Protestant Episcopal Church of America; A Study, Based Mainly on the Collection of Josiah Henry Benton*. London: Society for Promoting Christian Knowledge.

Ó Corráin, Donnchadh. 1972. *Ireland Before the Normans. The Gill History of Ireland*. Dublin: Gill & Macmillan.

Ó Corráin, Donnchadh. 1998. Viking Ireland: Afterthoughts. In *Ireland and Scandinavia in the Early Viking Age*, eds. H. B. Clarke, Máire Ní Mhaonaigh and Raghnall Ó Floinn. Dublin: Four Courts Press.

Ó Cróinín, Dáibhí. 1999. *Early Medieval Ireland: 400–1200*. London and New York: Longman.

O'Loughlin, Thomas. 2002. "A Celtic Theology": Some Awkward Questions and Observations. In *Identifying the "Celtic": CSANA Yearbook II*, ed. Joseph Falaky Nagy. Dublin: Four Courts Press.

Power, Maria. 2007. *From Ecumenism to Community Relations: Inter-Church Relationships in Northern Ireland 1980–2005*. Dublin: Irish Academic Press.

Pullan, Leighton. 1900. *The History of the Book of Common Prayer*. London, New York: Longmans, Green and Co.

Richter, Michael. 2005. *Medieval Ireland: The Enduring Tradition*, 2nd ed. Dublin: Gill and Macmillan, Ltd.

Stancliffe, Clare. 1982. Red, White and Blue Martyrdom. In *Ireland in Early Mediaeval Europe: Studies in Memory of Kathleen Hughes*, eds. Dorothy Whitelock, Rosamond McKitterick and David Dumville. Cambridge: Cambridge University Press.

Thompson, Peter. 2007. Methodist-Anglican Dialogue. Paper Presented for the IICC Study Day, 22nd Meeting of the Irish Inter-Church Meeting, October 24, Dublin.

Valante, Mary A. 2008. *The Vikings in Ireland: Settlement, Trade and Urbanization*. Dublin: Four Courts Press.

Walsh, Oonagh. 2005. *Anglican Women in Dublin: Philanthropy, Politics and Education in the Early Twentieth Century*. Dublin: University College Dublin Press.

Warren, Wilfrid Lewis. 1997. Church and State in Angevin Ireland. *Chronicon*, vol. 1, no. 6, pp. 1–17.

Watt, John. 1998. *The Church in Medieval Ireland*, 2nd ed. Dublin: University College Dublin Press.

Wynne, Gordon. 2009. *Pastoral Care in the Recession*. Dublin: Church of Ireland Publishing.

CHAPTER 40

# The Scottish Episcopal Church

## Brian Smith

## Introduction

Canon One of the Code of Canons of the Scottish Episcopal Church reads:

> The Scottish Church, being a branch of the One Holy Catholic and Apostolic Church of
> Christ, retains inviolate in the sacred ministry the three orders of Bishops, Priests and
> Deacons, as of Divine Institution. The right to consecrate and ordain Bishops, Priests and
> Deacons belongs to the Order of Bishops only.

By this, the church takes its place within the Anglican family of churches; however,
certain features give it a distinctive place within that communion. These would include:

1. The church traces it origins back to missionary activity in Scotland in the fourth
   century. Distinctive features of pre-Reformation Christianity are reflected in its
   life today.
2. The church was influenced by the Scottish Reformation, not the English
   Reformation.
3. The church has a distinctive form of government. There is no archbishop. The
   bishops meeting in episcopal synod elect one of their numbers to be primus
   (*Primus inter Pares*).
4. The church is small in numbers and has no "established" status within the life
   of Scotland.
5. The Scottish Episcopal Church is one of *four* separate Anglican churches serving
   in the United Kingdom. The others are the Church of England, the Church in
   Wales, and the Church of Ireland. The Scottish Episcopal Church can suffer from

*The Wiley-Blackwell Companion to the Anglican Communion*, First Edition. Edited by Ian S. Markham,
J. Barney Hawkins IV, Justyn Terry, and Leslie Nuñez Steffensen.
© 2013 John Wiley & Sons, Ltd. Published 2013 by John Wiley & Sons, Ltd.

being regarded by persons outside the United Kingdom as simply being a branch of the Church of England which happens to be situated in Scotland.

The motto of the church is "Evangelical Truth and Apostolic Order."

(The Scottish Episcopal Church has been known by slightly different names at different points in its history. For simplicity, "Scottish Episcopal Church" is used throughout this chapter.)

## Historical Survey

The history of the Scottish Episcopal Church is bound up with the wider history of Scotland. The following sections seek to outline aspects of that history, particularly where past events still resonate within church life.

### Pre-Reformation

Scotland, like the Scandinavian and Baltic parts of Europe, was never formally subject to the Roman Empire. That Empire extended into southern Scotland. To the north were tribes who resisted the invaders. The land was mountainous with deep river valleys. It favored "guerrilla warfare," and provided few expansive plains upon which Roman Legions could maneuver.

Christianity is regarded as having become established in England through the mission, from Rome, of Augustine in Kent in 597. However, the development of Christianity in Scotland began as early as the fourth century with Ninian establishing a center of learning in Whithorn in southwest Scotland. In 563, Columba came from Ireland and his work, from the island of Iona, made a more lasting impression.

Christianity of a Celtic variety flourished in Scotland and began to move south into northern England. Christianity of a Roman variety was moving north. The crunch came in the seventh century when conflict concerning Celtic and Roman traditions needed resolution. The date of Easter and the issue of monks' tonsures were resolved in 664 at the Synod of Whitby. Scotland might have been set for assimilation into the mainstream developments in Europe, had not the Norse pagan invasion around the Scottish coast slowed down such integration.

Even after the Synod of Whitby, one matter remained unresolved concerning governance of the church in Scotland. Could archbishops in England claim any formal jurisdiction over a church in the separate Kingdom of Scotland? In 1176, Pope Alexander III confirmed the freedom of the Scottish Church from any subjection to England. In 1192, Pope Celestine III made the church a "special daughter of the Holy See," without an archbishop – its dioceses becoming directly responsible to the pope. However, the church was allowed to hold regular provincial councils presided over by a "conservator of the privileges of the Scottish Church" – one of the Scottish bishops elected by his peers.

This historical circumstance provides a background to the position later adopted in the post-Reformation Scottish Episcopal Church. In May 1732, the church adopted a proposal that the bishops should choose for themselves one of their number to be primus (*Primus Inter Pares*), for "convocating and presiding only," and that no bishop should claim jurisdiction other than within his own district. Such a position obtains to the present day. While in many provinces of the Anglican Communion, there exist archbishops, providing a final court of appeal in matters of dispute, in Scotland there is no such office. Matters on appeal are referred to the episcopal synod – the seven bishops meeting together in council. This tradition, asserted in 1732 and continuing into the present, reflects the papal enactment of 1192.

(There is no *direct* historical continuity from the arrangements of 1192 to the arrangements of the present day. In the fifteenth century, the office of archbishop was introduced into the pre-Reformation church in Scotland but ceased at the start of the eighteenth century.)

## The Reformation

Whereas the Reformation in England was achieved through the action of the sovereign severing formal connection with Rome, in Scotland the Reformation was animated by reformed thinking, hostile to papal claims, arising from within the church itself. The thought of Calvin, and his work in Geneva, was influential in Scotland through the activity of John Knox. Different emphases were present among the reforming parties. Some looked for modest reforms, correcting abuses, but preserving much continuity in the church life. Others looked for a "root and branch" reform, drawing upon ultra-Protestant and Puritan thinking from Europe.

Accordingly, from 1575 to 1690, the church in Scotland alternated between favoring a Presbyterian and favoring an episcopal policy in its governance. However, the church remained united as a Church of Scotland. The historian Gordon Donaldson commented, "the party that was for a period out of office did not go into schism, but remained within the church working for the restoration of the church order which it believed to be the better one."

Such "alternation" must be seen in the context of wider dynastic struggles taking place in the United Kingdom. The church was caught up in these. Indeed, ecclesiastical dispute was a major factor animating them.

Over the centuries, there had been periods of war between Scotland and England. By the time of the Reformation, Scotland and England had developed into two separate kingdoms, each with its own sovereign and its own parliament. The Scottish Reformation dates from 1560, when the Scottish Parliament abrogated the authority of the pope in Scotland.

Following the death of Elizabeth I of England in 1603, James VI of Scotland (of the Stuart line of kings) acceded also to that throne, becoming both James I of England and James VI of Scotland. By this "Union of the Crowns," Scotland and England continued as two separate kingdoms, each with a separate parliament, but with the one monarch.

James died in 1625. His son Charles I succeeded him. Charles created a new Diocese of Edinburgh in 1633, and established the Church of St. Giles as its cathedral.

## The Bishops' Wars

In 1637, Charles sought to achieve unity in the church in Scotland by introducing a new prayer book. This was badly handled and ignited what became known as the Bishops' Wars.

In 1638, a national covenant was signed. It demanded that matters such as liturgical change be approved through discussion in Assembly and Parliament, and not be imposed by the king. Although not formally part of the original document, later rejections of episcopal forms of church government became associated with that covenant. The national covenant and the activity of the covenanters passed into legend, leaving to later historians the task of disentangling truth from a developed mythology. Popular history came to speak of this period as being a time of conflict between the covenanters (who spoke for the "true Scotland") and the bishops (who were alien to true Scottish culture – on the side of an "English" monarch). Such popularization belied the fact that members of the episcopal party were as deeply rooted in the wider Scottish culture as were their adversaries.

This popularized understanding colors ecumenical discussion even into recent times. Episcopacy became seen by many as alien to Scotland and Scottish culture, and such perceptions caused schemes for union to flounder. In more recent discussions of a proposed Anglican covenant, some members of the Scottish Episcopal Church expressed unease about the word "covenant" being used to describe an instrument designed to introduce harmony into an episcopal church.

During the seventeenth century, the Bishops' Wars affected both England and Scotland. Charles I was executed in 1649. His son Charles II was proclaimed King of Scotland, but in England a Commonwealth was proclaimed under Oliver Cromwell. The monarchy was restored in England in 1660, and Charles II became king of both nations. After his death, the Stuart line continued through James II and VII until 1688. At that point, to prevent the throne passing to James' son (a Roman Catholic), the English Parliament, with the concurrence of a convention of estates in Scotland, invited William of Orange with his wife Mary to take the throne. James fled to France.

Many in the episcopal party had a strong loyalty to James and found it difficult to change allegiance when William came to the throne. When William visited London in 1688, he inquired of the loyalty of the Scottish bishops. Bishop Rose of Edinburgh visited him, assuring him that he would give the King such loyalty "as law, reason or conscience shall allow." This less-than-fulsome expression of support contributed to the marginalization of the episcopal party. They were seen as failing adequately to evince the required anti-catholic sentiments, making more certain the establishment of Presbyterianism in Scotland. In 1689, Rose was ejected from his cathedral and founded a congregation in a wool store off the Royal Mile in Edinburgh. In 1690, William agreed to a statute firmly establishing a Presbyterian polity in Scotland. The period of informal "alternation" came to an end.

## The Eighteenth Century

As the eighteenth century began, Scotland's national finances suffered a severe blow as a result of an unsuccessful attempt at colonization in the West Indies (the Darien Scheme). The merchant classes saw advantage in closer links with England. Scotland and England achieved a united Parliament in 1707. In 1712, the Toleration Act freed the Scottish Episcopal Church from subjection to Presbyterian Church Courts, giving it separate formal legal recognition. However, that Act also required clergy to swear allegiance to the Crown and abjure the Stuart line. Some did this; others (non-jurors) did not. The church was divided.

The accession in 1714 of George I (of Hanover) provoked "Jacobite" rebellions. In 1715, the son of James II and VII, James Stuart (the Old Pretender), sought to restore the Stuart line. In 1745, a further rebellion was led by his son Charles Stuart (the Young Pretender – "Bonnie Prince Charlie"). Episcopalian non-jurors were seen as supporting these. The church suffered accordingly. In 1746, penal laws restricting the ministry of Scottish episcopally ordained clergy led to further marginalization and persecution. In the words of the novelist Walter Scott, the church became "a shadow of a shade."

This period saw the rise of independent "qualified congregations," satisfying the requirements of the Toleration Act, served by clergy in English or Irish orders. These attracted episcopalians of Hanoverian sympathies and immigrants from England. The death in 1788 of Charles Stuart meant that episcopalians could no longer hope for an imminent restoration of the Stuart line. In 1792, the penal laws were repealed. The task of introducing order into the church, whose recent history had contained both strong Jacobite and Hanoverian loyalties, began.

Thus, at the end of the eighteenth century, the national Church of Scotland was Presbyterian in ecclesiology. The Scottish Episcopal Church was recognized as an independent church, also of Scottish origin, but governed by bishops elected by the church itself.

Meanwhile, in England, the national church was episcopal in ecclesiology. Its bishops swore allegiance to the monarch, who had responsibility for their appointment. This difference between Scotland and England had consequences for the Anglican Communion.

In the eighteenth century, the church in the newly independent United States of America wished to have its own bishop consecrated. Having broken away from Britain, it could not look to England for this. Without a dispensation from Parliament, that bishop would have to swear allegiance to the British Crown – something not possible for citizens of the new United States. They looked to Scotland where this would not be required. Samuel Seabury, having earlier studied medicine in Edinburgh, was elected Bishop of Connecticut and was consecrated by the Scottish bishops in Aberdeen in 1784. The Scottish Episcopal Church looks to the Episcopal Church in the United States as its offspring.

A similar situation arose in continental Europe. Around 1818, Dr. Matthew Luscombe was ministering to Americans and Britons in Paris. It was suggested that Dr. Luscombe be consecrated bishop with responsibility for Anglican congregations in

Europe. The British prime minister did not approve, so the Church of England could not consecrate him. However, the Scottish bishops agreed to do so. He was consecrated in Stirling in 1825. Soon after, in 1842, the Church of England established the Diocese of Gibraltar, and the need to continue this practice lapsed.

## The Nineteenth Century

Winds of change were felt in the Scottish Episcopal Church in the nineteenth century. The penal laws affecting episcopalian clergy had been repealed. In 1804, at the Convocation of Laurencekirk, the clergy agreed to subscribe to the Thirty-Nine Articles of Religion. This brought the Scottish Episcopal Church closer to the Church of England and Ireland in matters of doctrine and discipline, paving the way for a greater interchange of ministry.

The church was significantly influenced by the Oxford Movement. Members of the movement saw in the Episcopal Church, with its freedom from state "interference," a paradigm of what an apostolic church could be. New church-building took place. Religious communities were established. It was undoubtedly a period of growth for the church, though some see this as a time when what was distinctive about the Scottish Episcopal Church began to be eroded.

While the influence of the Oxford Movement encouraged a more "catholic" style of worship, the period also saw significant changes in evangelical Anglican life in Scotland. A number of evangelical congregations had been established in the cities of Edinburgh, Glasgow, and Aberdeen. The general synod of 1838 required more consistent use of the prayer book, and demanded the surplice as the customary vesture of ministers. Consequently, some evangelical congregations separated themselves from the normal diocesan structure and looked to England for their episcopal oversight. This anomaly was removed during the twentieth century. The latter part of the twentieth century and the twenty-first century have seen significant growth in these evangelical congregations.

In 1864, the Parliament removed the disqualification of priests ordained in Scotland from being appointed to an English benefice. Full communion with the Church of England was thereby achieved.

Significant building took place at this time. In 1848, in the Diocese of Argyll and The Isles, a set of collegiate buildings including a chapel (later raised to cathedral status) was built on the Island of Cumbrae in the Firth of Clyde. Also in that diocese, "Bishop's House" was built in 1894 on the Island of Iona to provide a religious presence on the island associated with Columba. Both continue as retreat houses to the present day.

Some see the nineteenth century as a time when the Scottish Episcopal Church began to flower and grow after the years of the penal laws. Others see the nineteenth century as a time when a distinctively Scottish vision of an episcopal church (high in its doctrine of the Eucharist and of ministry, but low on ceremonial and dress) got lost amidst the development of a high church ritual and architecture. However, despite such differing evaluations, the church entered the twentieth century with many fine new buildings and endowments, including a Theological College in Edinburgh. It entered the twentieth century in a spirit of confidence.

## The Twentieth Century

The twentieth century saw many changes. The seventeenth century had seen the Bishops' Wars and the struggles with the covenanters. The eighteenth century had seen the church under penal laws as a consequence of support given to the Jacobites. The nineteenth century saw the church growing free from these constraints, but developing in ways that were drawing much from its neighbor in England.

The century opened with the challenge of the Ecumenical Movement. The year 1910 saw the World Missionary Conference in Edinburgh. The history of the churches in Scotland would make ecumenism no easy task. The history of the Presbyterian and Episcopal Churches was one which, in popular imagination, contained bitter conflict. The contours within which ecumenical developments would be mapped over the years would be rough and craggy. It has led some to comment that the path to Christian unity is possibly more difficult in Scotland than in any other part of the world.

Activity in mission took place to gain the church a significant presence in new housing estates and in new towns. Clerical subscription to the Thirty-Nine Articles was removed in 1979. Non-stipendiary ministry was developed, and ordained ministry opened to women.

Despite the optimism as it opened, the twentieth century saw decline in membership. Over the century, membership declined by approximately 50 percent. Comparable figures were registered in the Church of Scotland and the Church of England. Communicant numbers show less of a decline.

Toward the end of the century, in 1982, a Partners-in-Mission consultation took place in Scotland. The partners, while recording thanks for their welcome and a sense of joy within the life of the church, claimed to note a deep sense of apprehension for the future.

As the twenty-first century begins, the church continues to be marked by diversity on many fronts. It feels the tensions currently affecting the Anglican Communion. It knows challenges both in terms of numbers and finance. It faces theological questions and spiritual demands from a secular culture. Some congregations exhibit growth, energy, and optimism; others test out new ways of maintaining a presence in their community. Challenges are recognized, but the spirit is positive.

## Diocesan Structure

The Scottish Episcopal Church consists of seven dioceses, each with a diocesan bishop. There are no suffragan bishops. The dioceses generally follow the boundaries and maintain the names of the pre-Reformation dioceses of Scotland. Some dioceses have been formed by a union of these ancient dioceses. The exception is the "new" Diocese of Edinburgh, created out of the Diocese of St. Andrews in 1633.

Each bishop appoints one of the clergy to the office of dean. The dean deputizes for the bishop in actions not requiring episcopal orders. The dean holds office alongside another appointment in the diocese. In each diocese, there is a cathedral whose ministry is overseen by the provost. (The Diocese of Argyll and The Isles has two cathedrals.) Each cathedral has a chapter of canons. The synod clerk is elected to the chapter by the clergy and may deputize for the dean. Bishops are appointed by a process of election by the diocese. In 1986, it became possible for women to be ordained as deacons, in 1994 as priests, and in 2003 as bishops.

Prior to 1982, the affairs of the church were shaped by two bodies. The provincial synod oversaw the legislative and spiritual affairs of the church. Over the years, this had grown in size, handling powers originally vested in the episcopal synod alone. In addition, the Representative Church Council (RCC), consisting of clergy and laity from every congregation in the province, had responsibility for administration and finance.

In 1982, the Scottish Episcopal Church chose to be governed by a single general synod of three houses – bishops, clergy, and laity. This meets once a year. The general synod enacts the canons of the church. Each diocese has its own diocesan synod.

## Ordination Training

A residential theological college, purchased in 1890, was established in Edinburgh at Coates Hall. Students shared in the "seminary" life, often completing theological degrees at other universities. In the second half of the twentieth century, training following a non-residential pattern also developed to address the needs of those entering a non-stipendiary ministry.

In 1993, the buildings of Coates Hall were sold, and the collegiate structure of training was replaced by a "distance learning" program across the province. This single program sought to address the training both of non-stipendiary and full-time stipendiary ministry. Patterns of training have continued to undergo revision over the years. Lay readers also train in this program.

## Mission

The Episcopal Church had, in the nineteenth century, taken up a responsibility for Overseas Mission work in Chanda in India, and Kaffraria in South Africa. In Home Mission, youth work in the second half of the twentieth century initially focused on the use of a large former rectory at Dalmahoy serving as a provincial youth hostel. Currently, residential youth work is focused on an annual summer conference at the episcopalian private school at Glenalmond. Services for older people were originally offered through the foundation of a number of residential homes for the elderly. These passed out of provincial responsibility during the twenty-first century. Currently, a project titled "Faith in Older People" seeks to address the spiritual needs of older people. The work of two Rural Commissions, in 1995 and 2009, has sought to highlight the particular needs of the rural areas of Scotland.

In 1996, a Home Mission initiative entitled *Mission 21* was established, drawing on insights from the Alban Institute in Washington (USA). This sought to make congregations more welcoming and to encourage development in their life. Arising within this were initiatives in Local Collaborative Ministry. This was grounded in the theology that all people had a calling to ministry by virtue of their baptism, and the church had a responsibility to discern how this ministry might be exercised. Patterns for lay education and training in discipleship have developed, often relating to significant current interest in spirituality and liturgy.

Much recent mission work has taken place through a large number of finite initiatives. A full record of these will be found in the book by the former primus, Dr. Edward Luscombe, *The Scottish Episcopal Church in the Twentieth Century*.

## Liturgy

The authorized liturgies of the Scottish Episcopal Church consist of the Scottish Prayer Book of 1929 (amended in 1952 and 1967), together with a number of recent revisions to various rites, published in booklet form. The complete list of authorized services is found in the Schedule to Canon 22 of the church's Code of Canons.

The history of liturgy of the Scottish Episcopal Church is tied up with the history of Scotland. However, it is useful to look back to the Prayer Book of 1637 (often called Laud's Liturgy) and the event that took place on July 23, 1637, in St. Giles Cathedral.

The 1637 liturgy was authorized for use in Scotland by Charles I, and on this day the legendary Jenny Geddes threw her prayer stool at the minister while he was conducting a service from that book. Her words "Daur ye say Mass in ma Lug?" (Dare you say the Mass in my ear?) passed into the tradition as being words that incited immediate rebellion, fanned the Civil War, and eventually led to the execution of Charles himself. It would be fair to say that this event was one for which some preparations had already been laid and was not simply a spontaneous outburst.

By that book, Charles sought to give order to worship in Scotland. It built upon the 1549 Prayer Book of Edward VI, but incorporated features drafted by the Scottish bishops. The manner of its introduction obscured its virtues. Its hostile reception caused it rapidly to disappear from general use. During the eighteenth century, Queen Anne made available in Scotland copies of the English book of 1662. Use of this was often supplemented by "wee bookies" (small booklets) containing elements from the 1637 rite.

The desire for a prayer book which could be a vehicle for a more "catholic" teaching and worship than was found in the 1662 book grew during the nineteenth century. While English proposals for a new prayer book in 1928 failed to win parliamentary approval, such approval was not necessary for a Scottish book. The 1929 book adopted some of the English revisions of 1928. The 1929 book makes prayer for the departed more explicit. While the 1662 liturgy invites prayer with the words "Let us pray for the whole state of Christ's Church militant here on Earth," the 1929 invitation is "Let us pray for the whole state of Christ's Church." The Eucharistic prayer in 1929 includes an *epiclesis*, adds the *Benedictus*, the *Peace*, and the *Agnus Dei*. However, the 1929 book as it was published did include the full text both of the 1929 Eucharistic Rite as well as that of the 1662 English Book of Common Prayer. The 1929 book also contains two "shorter litanies" and an office of Compline. The lectionary contains readings from the Apocrypha. The amendments of 1967 authorize a brief rite for the reconciliation of a penitent.

As in other Anglican provinces, thought toward a new structure of the Eucharist took place in the 1960s, resulting in the "Grey Book" of 1970 and the "Blue Book" of 1982 (with additional Eucharistic prayers authorized in 1996). This is the current text in general use in the Scottish Episcopal Church.

The twentieth century also saw revision of the Daily Office, the Marriage Liturgy, the Ordinal, the Funeral Rites, Rites of Initiation, and a service of Communion from the Reserved Sacrament (administered by a deacon or layperson). In 1993, the general synod agreed that, in future, printed editions of the authorized services would omit the *filioque* clause from the Nicene Creed.

## Ecumenism

Churches in Scotland meet together under the umbrella of the ecumenical instrument – ACTS (Action of Churches Together in Scotland). The two largest churches in Scotland are the Church of Scotland (Presbyterian) and the Roman Catholic Church. The legacy of past conflicts still makes itself felt in the life of Scotland. In the wider society, sectarianism, hostility between "protestant" and "catholic" groups, particularly when this is associated with rival football teams, can manifest itself in unpleasant ways. Combating such sectarianism is a major task facing the present Scottish government.

Within Scotland, there has long been a legacy of unease attached to the office of bishop, causing several schemes for reunion to flounder. Proposals advanced in 1957 failed to achieve support and were attacked in the press. Some even saw these discussions as having increased the animosity between the churches. Informal moves toward helping a growing together took place within the Scottish Episcopal Church over the following 40 years. The church opened the Communion Table to all baptized and communicant members of all Trinitarian churches. The canons were altered to allow an interchangeability of ministers within specifically designated local ecumenical partnerships.

Consequently, at the turn of the century, there was a further initiative for union – SCIFU – (Scottish Churches Initiative for Union) between the Scottish Episcopal Church, the Church of Scotland, the Methodist Church, and the United Reformed Church. Had this come into being, it would have involved the mutual recognition of all existing ministers, with the proviso that all future ordination would satisfy episcopal requirements. This was turned down by the general assembly of the Church of Scotland in 2003. This failure resulted in a tripartite covenant between the Scottish Episcopal Church, the Methodist Church, and the United Reformed Church (EMU), expressing a desire to work together without seeking interchangeability of ministers.

Despite the failure of the wider proposal for unity, working relationships between the Scottish Episcopal Church and the Church of Scotland remain very good. In addition, its bishops and the Roman Catholic bishops in Scotland meet together on a regular basis.

In 1992, the Scottish Episcopal Church with the other British Anglican churches entered into communion with Scandinavian and Baltic Evangelical Lutheran churches – the Porvoo Agreement.

Changes in Scottish society over the past 50 years have seen a greater presence of members of non-Christian religions, particularly in the cities. The Scottish government and city councils, when consulting with religious leaders, generally wish to do this at an inter-faith meeting, rather than at an ecumenical meeting only of church leaders. This has given greater prominence to inter-faith bodies. The church seeks to play an active part in relation to these developments.

## Bibliography

Bertie, David. 2000. *Scottish Episcopal Clergy, 1689–2000*. Edinburgh: T and T Clark.

Code of Canons of the Scottish Episcopal Church. (Available Online).

Donaldson, Gordon. 1960. *Scotland Church and Nation through Sixteen Centuries*. London: SCM Press.

Donaldson, Gordon. 1960. *The Scottish Reformation*. London: Cambridge: Cambridge University Press.

Goldie, Frederick. 1951/1976. *A Short History of the Episcopal Church in Scotland*. Edinburgh: St. Andrew Press.

Lawson, John Parker. 1843. *History of the Scottish Episcopal Church from the Revolution to the Present Time*. Edinburgh.

Lawson, John Parker. 1844. *The Episcopal Church of Scotland, from the Reformation to the Revolution*. Edinburgh.

Luscombe, Edward. 1996. *The Scottish Episcopal Church in the Twentieth Century*. Edinburgh: General Synod Office of the Scottish Episcopal Church.

MacLean, Colin, and Kenneth Veitch. 2000. *Scottish Life and Society: A Compendium of Scottish Ethnology. Vol. 12, Religion*. Edinburgh: John Donald in association with The European Ethnological Research Centre and the National Museums of Scotland.

# CHAPTER 41

# The Church in Wales

## Barry Morgan

The Church in Wales traces its roots back to the second century CE during the Roman occupation, and its catechism claims that it is the ancient Church of Wales, pre-dating the coming of St. Augustine to Canterbury in the sixth century. It was only in 1920, however, that it became a separate province of the Anglican Communion, following its disestablishment from the Church of England. The Church in Wales has its own distinctive history, which can be divided into four periods – namely, pre-Norman conquest; the Medieval period; the Reformation and later centuries; and dis-establishment up to the present day.

## Pre-Norman Conquest

The Christian faith was probably brought to Wales by tradespeople and soldiers at the time of the Roman occupation, for, by the third century, Julius and Aaron had been martyred for the faith at Caerleon in South Wales, and British bishops were present at the Council of Arles in France in 314 CE. After the withdrawal of the Romans toward the end of the fourth century, much of England was invaded by pagan Saxons, Angles, and Jutes, and Christianity disappeared from the areas they conquered. Christianity remained, however, in the West, in the Celtic lands of Wales, Scotland, Cornwall, and Ireland. This period is popularly known as the Age of Saints, for they were people who were deeply influenced by the eremitical and monastic movement of the East which came to Britain via Gaul, and they preached the gospel and formed Christian communities. They lived scholarly, monastic, mission-orientated lives, reflecting the essentially rural nature of the country.

*The Wiley-Blackwell Companion to the Anglican Communion*, First Edition. Edited by Ian S. Markham, J. Barney Hawkins IV, Justyn Terry, and Leslie Nuñez Steffensen.
© 2013 John Wiley & Sons, Ltd. Published 2013 by John Wiley & Sons, Ltd.

Among these early missionaries were people such as Dewi (who eventually became our patron saint, known in English as David), Teilo, Dyfrig, Cadog, Illtud, and Padarn in the south, and Deiniol, Beuno, and Asaph in the north. The churches which they established became associated with their names, and their jurisdiction was based on these churches, rather than on distinct territorial areas. From these mother churches, over which they were abbots, they evangelized the surrounding countryside, and their legacy is evidenced in the many Welsh place names with the prefix "Llan," meaning "church," followed by the name of its founder, often with the initial letter changed in accordance with the rules of mutation – for example, Llandeilo, Llanilltud, and Llanbadarn. Many saints travelled to and from Gaul and Ireland.

The Diocese of Bangor in the north-west of the country was probably the first territorial diocese, its boundaries coinciding in 546 CE with the kingdom of Maelgwyn, which was ruled by the King of Gwynedd, but that form of organization was the exception at this period in Wales's history.

## The Medieval Church

The Normans who conquered England in 1066 CE took much longer to conquer Wales (until around 1284 CE), because of its difficult terrain and the existence of territorial princes who resisted any form of centralization. Nevertheless, by the thirteenth century, Anglo-Norman lordships had been established in most of Wales. As a result, church and state became increasingly intertwined, and there was a determination to bring the Welsh Church under the authority of the Crown and the Archbishop of Canterbury.

By the end of the twelfth century, the four ancient dioceses of St. Davids, St. Asaph, Bangor, and Llandaff had become part of the Province of Canterbury. The bishops were political nominees of the Crown, often French, and, therefore, they favored Norman rule. Celtic practices such as the marriage of clerics were proscribed, and Welsh religious houses were replaced by Benedictine and Cistercian ones. The Normans also introduced a hierarchical system of parishes, rural deaneries, and archdeaconries. The church was part of Catholic Christendom owing allegiance to the pope and sharing devotional practices such as venerating relics, saints, and holy places. Futile attempts were made to establish an independent province in Wales with a metropolitan at St. Davids, especially by Gerald, Archdeacon of Brecon in the twelfth century.

## The Reformation

Wales, being an integral part of the Church of England, found itself cut off from European Catholic Christendom when the Church of England became a distinct national church. Acts of Parliament proscribed medieval teachings such as the invocation of saints, the veneration of relics, and belief in purgatory, masses for the dead, and transubstantiation. Emphasis was placed on the centrality of scripture. The Bible was translated into English and then Welsh, and vernacular prayer books replaced the Latin service books. The threefold order of bishops, priests, and deacons was, however, retained, as was liturgical worship, the two dominical sacraments and the Creeds.

Although monasteries were dissolved, cathedrals, parishes, and parish churches remained, but many images were removed. In spite of the fact that the Act of Union of 1536 absorbed Wales into England and gave no official status to the Welsh language, the Book of Common Prayer and the entire Bible were published in Welsh in 1567 and 1588, respectively, and these, paradoxically, did much to save the language from extinction. The forbidden Catholic rituals took longer to eradicate in Wales. Bishops continued to be appointed by the Crown, and from 1715 to 1870 no native Welsh speaker was appointed to a diocese in Wales. These bishops usually had no connection with Wales; some rarely visited their sees, and often they held them in plurality with other posts because they yielded little revenue. The clergy for the most part were poor and illiterate.

The centuries following the Reformation saw the emergence of a degree of religious toleration that gave birth to dissenting congregations, although most people were still Anglican in the eighteenth century. However, a strong strain of nonconformist religion began to pepper Wales with its distinctive buildings, greatly influenced by the Puritan theology of Luther and Calvin, emphasizing the Word rather than Sacraments, with ecstatic worship characterized by rousing hymns and long sermons. The established Anglican Church became the church of a minority, lacking the allegiance of most of the population of Wales by the mid-nineteenth century. The Calvinistic Methodists became a separate denomination in 1811, and other dissenting churches, such as the Congregationalists, Baptists, and Wesleyan Methodists, grew.

This process was accelerated by the increasing industrialization of Wales begun in the seventeenth century, reaching its zenith in the nineteenth century. The nonconformist chapels, with no reserved seating for the aristocracy and owners of industry, offered something akin to the primitive socialism of the gospels. The established church was seen as being linked to the most powerful and influential sectors of society, English in character and culture, while mine and quarry workers were, by and large, Welsh speaking and nonconformist.

The church also failed to respond quickly enough to the explosion of the population since its churches were often on remote hilltops, or in fields, not on valley floors where most people lived. Chapels could be built quickly and inexpensively, while the Anglican Church could create new parishes only with Parliamentary consent.

The religious census of 1851 recorded four out of five of the 50 percent of people attending any place of worship as nonconformist, increasingly objecting to the privileged position of an established church to which they were obliged to pay tithes and which was regarded as a symbol of the English domination of Wales. Since clergy were often English, absentee, and pluralists, the campaign for disestablishing an "alien church" was supported by the Liberal Party. It was bitter and long drawn out and opposed by every member of the church hierarchy. However, disestablishment and disendowment were agreed by Parliament in 1914 and 1919, and finally brought into effect in 1920 after World War I.


## The Disestablished Church in Wales

A traumatized Church in Wales began to set up structures to safeguard Anglicanism, replace the fiscal losses to which it had been subjected, and maintain the parochial system. Paradoxically, nonconformity began its slow decline, which has continued up to the present. This was a period of reconstruction for the Church in Wales.

The Church in Wales, a name decided at a 1917 church convention, from the 1950s onward began to shed its image of being the Church of England in Wales, and to take on a leading role as the guardian of the use of the Welsh language in worship as it produced bilingual liturgies. It created new parishes, restored churches, and built new ones. It had already been instrumental in supporting the Sunday school movement, and it continued establishing church schools, designed to nurture faith among young people. St. David's College, Lampeter, founded in 1822, trained clergy, and Trinity College, Carmarthen, founded in 1848, trained Anglican teachers.

Out of disaster had come opportunity, and the church saw it as its duty to minister to every community in Wales through its parochial system, with the clergy being available to offer pastoral care to anyone who sought it, not only to Anglicans.

Even after disestablishment, anyone residing in a parish had, and still has, a right to be baptized (7,787 in 2010), married (3,518 couples in 2010), and buried (6,987 in 2010) according to Anglican rites, and Anglican clergy remain registrars for marriages.

In 2010, the Church in Wales had 1,430 places of worship, two-thirds of which are listed (29 percent of the Grade I listed buildings in Wales), with an estimated 2 million people visiting them each year.

With disestablishment, Wales became an independent province of the Anglican Communion, not answerable to the Archbishop of Canterbury or the Crown in Parliament. The new province elected its own archbishop from among the bishops by means of an electoral college consisting of the bishops and three lay and three clerical elected representatives from each of the dioceses. The archbishop retained his see, combining the role of primate with that of a diocesan bishop, but the office of archbishop was not attached to any one diocese. A new Diocese of Monmouth (the former Archdeaconry of Monmouth) was carved out of the Diocese of Llandaff in 1921, and the Diocese of Swansea and Brecon came into being in 1923, created out of the Archdeaconry of Brecon and part of the Archdeaconry of Carmarthen in the Diocese of St. Davids.

After 1920, the bishops no longer sat in the House of Lords, and they were (and are) elected by electoral colleges, comprising their fellow bishops, 12 elected clergy, and 12 elected laity from the vacant diocese, and six elected clergy and six elected laity from each of the five other dioceses. Lay patronage was abolished at disestablishment, and incumbents were (and are) appointed by either the bishop, or a provincial, or a diocesan board in turn.

The Church in Wales adopted a written constitution, and its governing body, now meeting twice a year (for years it was once a year), consists of the diocesan bishops, elected laity, and clergy, with each diocese having equal representation, no matter what its population, with provision for co-opted members. The governing body has ultimate authority to approve liturgies, review organizational structures, and secure firm fiscal resources for the mission and ministry of the church. In partnership with the bishops, it appoints groups, officers, and commissions charged with oversight of ministry, liturgy, social responsibility, education, language, and ecumenical affairs.

The Church in Wales was one of the first provinces of the Anglican Communion to adopt synodical government, and any canon (usually matters concerning faith, order, discipline, and doctrine) requires a two-thirds majority in each of the three orders of laity, clergy, and bishops. In each diocese, diocesan conferences handle diocesan affairs, and each parish has its own parochial church council, overseeing the parish's own work and its outreach within the local community.

The church was also disendowed, but it was allowed to keep all endowments acquired since 1662, although it had to surrender endowments acquired prior to 1662. Eventually, £4.5 million were eventually transferred to county councils, the University of Wales, and the National Library, although the Welsh Temporalities Act of 1919 had returned £1 million to the church. Disendowment caused considerable financial hardship, and a Representative Body had been established in 1917 to hold most properties, churches, and endowments in trust for the bishops, clergy, and laity. It also administers the pensions and finances of the church.

By 1935, a special appeal had raised nearly £750,000 from church members, with a further Layman's Appeal in the 1950s raising another £600,000. These formed the church's capital base. Its present portfolio is over £400 million. This has enabled the Representative Body to subsidize the work of the dioceses – at one point 70 percent of its expenditure. In 2011, it still contributes 30 percent of diocesan costs, so that the parishes of the province are the most subsidized in the Anglican Communion. Dioceses are, however, being increasingly asked to fund their own ministerial costs, and it is likely that the subsidy will diminish in future.

Both governing and representative bodies were originally numerically large. Numbers were reduced slightly over the years, and there was a drastic reduction in membership of the Representative Body in January 2006 and of the Governing Body in 2008, since both were felt to be unwieldy and over-large. Lord Dafydd Elis-Thomas, a former presiding officer of the devolved Assembly in Wales and an Anglican, was once heard to remark that whereas a devolved Assembly had 60 members to govern Wales with a population of nearly 3 million, the Church in Wales needed more than 450 people to govern a church of fewer than 100,000 members (Governing Body membership is now 143 people). The reduced Representative Body consists of up to 26 members, meets three times a year, and oversees the church's business, property, churches, investments, and finances.

## Parish Life

In 2009, the Church in Wales produced a booklet titled *The Church in Wales: A Small Guide to a Big Picture*. In it, the beliefs of the Church in Wales were set out:

The Church believes in God as a loving creator, redeemer and inspirer.

The love of God is revealed uniquely in the person of Jesus of Nazareth and can be found in all people.

The values which flow from our beliefs mean that the Church in Wales:

- Cares about the things that really matter in people's lives
- Has a presence and purpose in every part of Wales through its parishes
- Works with and for people in communities and organisations within that parish area and beyond
- Is actively involved in local needs and opportunities and the wellbeing of people
- Encourages new kinds of involvement through social projects and partnerships
- Opens and shares its buildings for wider community use
- Welcomes people from whatever background and age in its worship and activities
- Responds to people's spiritual needs at times of great importance and change in their lives
- Provides primary, secondary and tertiary education with a distinctive Christian character

The church has 350 church halls and parish rooms, and 15,000 sessions per week of community work are carried out in Church in Wales' buildings. Churches, too, are being increasingly adapted to provide for a wide range of activities for communities, such as cafés, crèches, social clubs, surgeries, exhibitions, and galleries, and are discovering again that they can be focal points for community cohesion. Indeed, the church and its hall are often the only large public buildings remaining in many communities.

Through after-school clubs, disability groups, art projects, lunch clubs, Information Technology, and parenting classes, local churches are also attempting to contribute positively to the health and wellbeing of individuals and communities. Thousands of volunteers from congregations lead and support community groups as carers, listeners, reconcilers, advocates, mentors, coaches, friends, supporters, and funders. Without Christian involvement, many voluntary organizations in Wales would collapse.

## Church and Community

Social responsibility projects employing 160 staff, with 3,000 volunteers, work in Welsh dioceses, often in disadvantaged areas with vulnerable people. In 2009, 8,000 individuals were helped with an investment of £2.5 million. The church's concern for more affordable housing in Wales has seen a number of homes built on church land. Outreach projects in urban and rural areas alleviate homelessness, working closely with governmental and non-governmental agencies not only in this field but also in spheres such as rural affairs, the environment, and social problems like domestic violence and binge drinking. All parish clergy are provided with church houses so that they can live within the communities they serve. The clergy are often the only professional people living in some poorer communities, living among those they seek to serve and, therefore, experiencing the problems first hand.

A devolved Assembly in Wales since 1999, with new primary legislative powers gained in 2011, means more accessible government. For a number of years, the bishops of the Church in Wales have held symposia in partnership with the Welsh government and leaders in fields such as education, health, and the police, and the Governing Body has debated issues such as housing, broadcasting, embryology, nuclear weapons, and alcohol misuse.

Interfaith work has concentrated on building up good relationships with the Muslim Council of Wales, and the church has held a series of consultations in partnership with it, called "Finding a Common Voice."

The Church in Wales has an active presence within the life and structures of many different institutions, working with their staff and those they serve. Chaplains are appointed to the police, prisons, hospitals, the deaf, the armed services, seafarers, businesses, educational establishments, and fire brigades. A total of 20 Anglican chaplains in Further and Higher Education serve 340,000 students and 29,000 staff; 27 chaplains work in four prisons; and 61 chaplains offer pastoral care in hospitals. Chaplains serve on committees and project groups, making decisions affecting the whole life of organizations, as well as providing a range of services to particular individuals and groups and institutions as a whole.

The church has always been committed to education and lifelong learning and works closely with local authorities and the Welsh government to provide church schools across Wales. These schools offer education to churchgoers and non-churchgoers alike, and seek to be truly comprehensive in their intake and outlook to help all children to reach their full potential in an atmosphere of acceptance that gives direction and purpose to their lives. There are 168 Church in Wales' schools, with almost 3,000 teachers and other staff, and more than 2,000 governors, serving 21,000 pupils. In a recent document entitled "Faith in Education," the Welsh Government acknowledged the vital role of faith schools (Anglican and Roman Catholic) in the life of the nation.

Much of Wales is rural, and the church has always been integral to the farming community since 80 percent of parishes are in, or close to, the countryside. Each diocese has a rural life adviser who works with government and other agencies such as the farming unions, the Farm Crisis Network, and the Institute of Rural Health, as well as markets, food co-operatives, and tourism agencies. Farming is a key industry in much of Wales, although it accounts for less than 2 percent of the GDP. The Church in Wales helped to administer the Addington Welfare Fund set up during the outbreak of foot and mouth disease in 2001, offering support to farmers and communities. In 2010, it also set up a "Rural Hub" in partnership with the Welsh government to bring together rural agencies to address the challenges facing communities. The church has also tried to build up strong links with the business community by sponsoring the Leading Wales Awards for three years and forging links with the Cardiff Business Club and the Institute of Directors.

In much the same way, the Church in Wales seeks to care for the environment and organizes national conferences in partnership with others, dealing with controversial issues such as sustainable populations, nuclear energy, and climate change.

The church group called CHASE (Church Action on Sustaining the Environment) has representatives on a variety of national and international environmental bodies and seeks to guide church policy on this topic. A Parish Green Guide and an environment website have been produced to help take forward policies and procedures, and an award is given each year for green projects in each diocese.

The Church in Wales maintains more than 1,200 churchyards with little help from local authorities, and 125,000 hours of volunteer time is spent every year maintaining them. Unlike in England, closed churchyards cannot be returned to local authorities for maintenance, and it is estimated that £16 million of repair work is required for the churchyards of Wales. It is also estimated that, by 2020, two-thirds of these churchyards will have no further space for burials.

Many of the dioceses have links with other provinces of the communion – Bangor with Lango in Uganda and Dublin and Glendalough in Ireland, Monmouth with Highveld in South Africa, and Llandaff with both Uppsala in Sweden and Bangladesh. St. Asaph has a link with South West Tanganyika. The province has contributed much of the cost of maintaining a mobile dental clinic in Gaza and has organized visits to the Middle East in solidarity with its problems.


## Leadership

The Church in Wales has produced a number of outstanding leaders over the years. Archbishop Rowan Williams (Bishop of Monmouth, 1992–2002, and Archbishop of Wales, 1999–2002) is an obvious example of a brilliant theologian and a man of deep personal holiness, appointed to Canterbury in 2002 – the first time for the Archbishop of Canterbury to come from another province. Archbishop Glyn Simon (Bishop of Swansea and Brecon, 1954–1957, Bishop of Llandaff, 1957–1971, and Archbishop of Wales,s 1968–1971) was also highly regarded as a great national leader at the time of the Aberfan disaster in October 1966, when a coal tip slippage killed 116 schoolchildren. He was also a scholar who published important essays on episcopacy. Archbishop Gwilym Williams (Bishop of Bangor, 1957–1982, and Archbishop of Wales, 1971–1982) worked hard to ensure the setting up of a Welsh television channel, S4C. Over the years, the Church in Wales has produced poets of great standing such as Gwenallt and Euros Bowen writing in Welsh, and the internationally renowned R. S. Thomas writing in English (the last two being clerics); biblical scholars of the caliber of Margaret Thrall and Gareth Lloyd Jones; and historians such as David Walker, Owain Jones, and William Price. Patrick Thomas and Donald Allchin have researched Celtic spirituality, and Gwynn ap Gwilym has produced a metrical version of the Psalms in Welsh from the original Hebrew, while Professor Norman Doe, Professor of Canon Law at Cardiff University, has acquired an international reputation as the leading Anglican canon lawyer of his generation, whose services are availed both by Anglican provinces and the Roman Catholic Church.

## Contemporary Issues

As with any church, the Church in Wales faces enormous challenges in the third millennium. Although it seeks to engage with the national life of Wales, and 70 percent of its population in the census of 2001 claimed to be Christian, its membership, in common with other churches, has continued to decline, especially among young people. Its Easter Communicant membership was 60,827 in 2011, compared with 166,700 in 1923, with an average attendance at present of around 35,500 people per week; but it is still the largest single denomination in Wales. There are many buildings to maintain, and a strategy is needed to rationalize them, since 31 percent of all parish expenditure is spent on their maintenance. It is a church too reliant on its ordained ministers, and it must seek to involve all God's people in its mission and ministry. The laity look to the clergy to do this fundamental work, but the clergy also need to work more collaboratively, both with one another and with their congregations. The hope is that the church's acquisition of St. Michael's College, Llandaff, hitherto an independent theological college, will help in this enterprise. However, in spite of too heavy a reliance on the ordained ministry (the church still has 526 stipendiary and 124 non-stipendiary clerics), the church will face a shortage of clergy in the next decade as many are approaching retirement. Of these, 25 percent are between 61 and 65 years of age, 20 percent between 56 and 60 years of age, and 15 percent between 50 and 55 years of age. In 2011, there are only 25 candidates training for stipendiary ministry and 17 for non-stipendiary ministry. Fewer people under the age of 30 have been ordained in recent years, and there has been a reliance on people who enter the ordained ministry at a later stage in their Christian journey. Age is, of course, no barrier to effective ministry, but youth attracts youth, brings energy, is willing to take risks (not, of course, restricted to younger people), and gives fresh perspectives which can help revitalize the church. There is the need both to recruit younger people and also to use existing young people in the structures of the church.

The church also needs to settle some of the internal issues that have been discussed for decades without resolution. The diocesan boundaries are those of 1923 in spite of widespread acknowledgement that they need revision. Although women are ordained to the priesthood, an attempt to open the episcopate to women priests was defeated in 2008. There is no consensus about the setting up of a permanent archiepiscopal see, in spite of at least three commissions recommending it. That fact illustrates one of the church's major failings. It is often prepared to think radically, but it is reluctant to implement consequent recommendations. In the 1970s, a commission recommended the re-organization of diocesan boundaries, but this failed to win approval at the Governing Body in 1980; and even when the church takes decisive actions, it can fail to follow them through to their logical conclusions. Wales was one of the first provinces to ordain women to the diaconate, in 1980, but it was not until 1997 that the canon to ordain them priests was passed, having failed in 1994, and so Wales was the last Anglican province in the British Isles to ordain them. That was finally achieved in 1997 only by appointing a provincial assistant bishop offering episcopal ministry to those who could not accept the priestly ministry of women. After the retirement of that post-holder, the Bench of Bishops decided it would not appoint a successor in the role.

The Church in Wales was in the vanguard of liturgical reform in the 1950s, having used the 1662 and 1928 prayer books until then. Its 1984 prayer book, however, including the Eucharist and the Daily Offices, was hardly different from the experimental revised Eucharist and Daily Offices of 1966, which had been widely praised by liturgical scholars as innovative at the time. The 1984 book retained the "thou" form of addressing God and was conservative in its approach to liturgy. Alternative Eucharistic prayers were given full assent in 2004, and a new Book of Daily Prayer was printed in 2010. These services allow for far more diversity and choice and draw on the Celtic spiritual tradition, which was singularly lacking in the 1984 prayer book. These alternative books do not replace the 1984 book in the way that the 1984 prayer book replaced the 1662 Book of Common Prayer, although the services of Holy Communion and the Solemnisation of Matrimony in the 1662 Book of Common Prayer can still be used.

Although the Church in Wales is a bilingual church, many traditionally Welsh-speaking parishes find it difficult to attract native Welsh-speaking clergy. Yet, many clergy who have come to the province from outside Wales have learned the language, while the traditional heartlands which used to produce Welsh-speaking clergy no longer do so. All liturgical materials are published in both languages, but there are parts of the province that are mono-lingual in English. A working group is looking at how to foster the use of Welsh and how to provide a more effective ministry in the Welsh language.

Ecumenically, although the Church in Wales covenanted in 1975 with the Methodist Church, the Presbyterian (otherwise the Calvinistic Methodist) Church of Wales, the United Reformed Church, and some Baptist congregations, to work for organic unity, little progress has been made, apart from a limited number of ecumenical projects where interchange of ministers is possible. The Church in Wales has turned down, more than once, the chance for wider ecumenical integration. However, its relationship with the nonconformist churches has improved greatly over the last 50 years, and some buildings are shared and joint liturgies produced. It is a church, however, in full communion with the Old Catholic Church, the Philippine Independent Church, the Spanish Reformed Church, the Lusitanian Church, the Mar Thoma Syrian Church, and the United Churches of North and South India, Pakistan, and Bangladesh. It has signed the Porvoo Declaration and the Meissen Declaration.

The Church in Wales is a fairly traditional church. Although there are some Anglo-Catholic parishes, especially in the south-east, and also a growing number of evangelical parishes, neither wing is sufficiently numerous to cause enormous divisions. The challenge for the Church in Wales is the challenge to see tradition as a dynamic process, embracing creative innovation and challenging members to new ways of thinking, for the sake of the gospel.

In 2010–2011, the bishops of the Church in Wales, in consultation with the Governing Body, highlighted three particular challenges – those of leadership, resources, and structure. They asked:

1. How should effective leadership be provided and trained, both at local and national levels?
2. How could the church's human and financial resources be effectively deployed to support its mission?
3. How could its structures enable that to happen?

Three independent reviewers from outside Wales looked at these questions and made 50 significant recommendations, which were discussed at the Governing Body meeting in September 2012.

Compared with the problems faced by many provinces of the Anglican Communion, however, those of the Province of Wales fade into insignificance. Anglican churches in many parts of the world face persecution, civil unrest, famine, natural disasters, poverty, and war. The Church in Wales ought, therefore, to be a church that counts its blessings. Its history also ought to give it a sense of perspective and confidence to resolve successfully the issues which it faces as its leaders and members did in earlier times.

## Bibliography

Bowen, H. V., ed. 2011. *A New History of Wales.* Llandysul: Gomer Press.

Davies, John. 1990. *Hanes Cymru.* London: Allen Lane, Penguin Press.

Davies, John. 1994. (English translation) *A History of Wales.* London: Penguin Press.

Davies, E. T. 1970. *Disestablishment and Disendowment.* Penarth: Church in Wales Publication.

Edwards, Arthur J. 1986. *Archbishop Green: His Life and Opinions.* Llandysul: Gomer Press.

Harris, Christopher and Richard Startup. 1999. *The Church in Wales: The Sociology of a Traditional Institution.* Cardiff: University of Wales Press.

Jones, Owain W. 1981. *Glyn Simon: His Life and Opinions.* Llandysul: Gomer Press.

Jones, Robert B. 2001. *The Particularity of Wales.* Penarth: Church in Wales Publications.

Morgan, D. D. 1999. *The Span of the Cross: Christian Religion and Society in Wales 1914–2000.* Cardiff: University of Wales Press.

Morgan, Kenneth O. 1966. *Freedom or Sacrilege? A History of the Campaign for Welsh Disestablishment.* Penarth: Church in Wales Publications.

Morgan, Kenneth O. 1970. *Wales in British Politics 1868–1922.* Cardiff: University of Wales Press.

Morgan, Kenneth O. 1982. *Rebirth of a Nation: Wales 1880–1980.* Oxford: Oxford University Press and Cardiff: University of Wales Press.

Peart-Binns, John S. 1990. *Edwin Morris: Archbishop of Wales*. Llandysul: Gomer Press.

Price, David T. W. 1990. *A History of the Church in Wales in the Twentieth Century*. Penarth: Church in Wales Publications.

The Church in Wales Guide: A Small Guide to a Big Picture. 2009. Cardiff: Church in Wales Publications.

Walker, David, ed. 1976. *A History of the Church in Wales*. Penarth: Church in Wales Publications.

Williams, Glanmor. 1962. *The Welsh Church from Conquest to Reformation*. Cardiff: University of Wales Press.

Williams, Glanmor. 1991. *The Welsh and Their Religion*. Cardiff: University of Wales Press.

Williams, Glanmor. 1997. *Wales and the Reformation*. Cardiff: University of Wales Press.

# Extra-Provincial to Canterbury

CHAPTER 42

# Dioceses Extra-Provincial to Canterbury (Bermuda, the Lusitanian Church, the Reformed Episcopal Church of Spain, and Falkland Islands)

John A. Macdonald

## Introduction

There are three dioceses and one parish that are extra-provincial and come under the primatial authority of the Archbishop of Canterbury. The three dioceses are the Spanish Reformed Episcopal Church (Iglesia Española Reformada Episcopal), the Lusitanian Catholic Apostolic Evangelical Church of Portugal (Igreja Lusitana Católica Apostólica Evangélica), and the Diocese of Bermuda. The Falkland Islands is considered a parish and receives Episcopal attention from a bishop commissary appointed by the Archbishop of Canterbury.

## The Spanish Reformed Episcopal Church

While the Christian faith in Spain can be traced back to the first centuries after the birth of Christ, the Spanish Episcopal Church sees its roots in the Mozarabic liturgy of Spain and then the Spanish Reformation. While the Spanish Reformation was for all intents and purposes repressed, the theological foundations established there and elsewhere on the continent did provide the basis for the eventual formation of the Spanish Episcopal Church. A number of Spaniards were in direct contact with reformers in different parts of Europe, and some even traveled to England during the reign of Edward VI (see

*The Wiley-Blackwell Companion to the Anglican Communion*, First Edition. Edited by Ian S. Markham, J. Barney Hawkins IV, Justyn Terry, and Leslie Nuñez Steffensen.
© 2013 John Wiley & Sons, Ltd. Published 2013 by John Wiley & Sons, Ltd.

López-Lozano 1991). Throughout the seventeenth century, there were a number of Protestant Spaniards who sought refuge in England in order to avoid the Inquisition (López-Lozano 1991, 108).

The Spanish Episcopal Church itself, in its current form, goes back to 1868 when an English Anglican priest by the name of Lewen S. Tugwell went to Seville due to bad health which he developed while working as a missionary in North America. There was an English-speaking congregation there, but such was the atmosphere at the time that the expatriates had to worship with the windows and doors shut so that the sound of their services would not go out onto the street. Two policeman also stood watch to make sure that no Spaniards attended the services (Álvarez 2000, 21–2). Even still, there were a number of Spaniards who were aware of the services and had been secretly reading the Bible. After the Revolution of 1868, many of the religious liberties that had been taken away were restored and Protestant Spaniards were able to return to Spain from exile (Álvarez 2000, 7–8). Tugwell saw the need to find some way to support these people, and as a result was led to found a society that was called "The Spanish and Portuguese Mission."

At the time of the Revolution, the Rev. Juan S. Cabrera, a former Roman Catholic priest who had become a Protestant, was in exile in Gibraltar. It was at this time that Cabrera had a significant conversation with General Juan Prim, the Revolution's leader. General Prim promised Cabrera that there would be full religious liberty in Spain with the overthrow of Queen Isabella II and the re-establishment of a liberal government (López-Lozano 1991, 173–4). Cabrera summed up the conversation with Prim:

> After today there will be liberty in our country, true liberty; the tyranny has ended. Each man will be the owner of his own conscience, and will be able to profess the faith that best suits him. You can return to your country by means of the first ship that leaves and are at liberty to enter Spain with the Bible under your arm and to preach the doctrines contained in it (López-Lozano 1991, 174; translation mine).

Cabrera was born in Benisa near Alicante in eastern Spain in 1837. He studied for the Roman Catholic priesthood and was ordained in 1862. His private study of the Bible led him to doubt some of the teaching of the church, and he found he could no longer remain Roman Catholic. Upon taking this position, he realized that it would be unsafe to remain in Spain, so he went into voluntary exile for five years in Gibraltar. It was in Gibraltar that he founded with several others the Consistory of the Spanish Reformed Church, which would eventually become the Spanish Reformed Episcopal Church (Álvarez 2000, 54–5). He used his time in exile to study Protestant and Anglican theology, although, at the time, Cabrera was influenced more by Presbyterians. He was tolerant of their polity but not completely convinced by it (López-Lozano 1991, 178). When a window of religious freedom opened up after the 1868 Revolution, he founded the Spanish National Church in September of that same year and started a congregation which he named the Reformed Church of the Most Holy Trinity (Iglesia Reformada Santísima Trinidad) (Álvarez 2000, 55).

Under Cabrera's leadership, the Protestant movement in Spain began to grow and become consolidated. He produced a number of publications during this period that outlined the Reformed Church's position on various doctrines, including the translation of a commentary on the Thirty-Nine Articles (López-Lozano 1991, 179). The political situation during this period was very unstable, and in spite of the promise of religious liberty, the church suffered persecutions, and Cabrera was personally attacked from the Roman Catholic pulpit. It was also during this period that Cabrera and others made a concerted study to formalize and standardize the doctrines of the church and its worship practices. There was general agreement that the church should revive the Mozarabic Rite since it was an authentic Spanish liturgy (López-Lozano 2012a).

On March 2, 1880, the church held its first synod at the recently acquired St. Basil's Church in Seville. The synod took the following actions:

1. Elected Juan Cabrera as the first bishop.
2. Sent a letter to sister churches abroad, inviting those churches to be in communion with them and asking for their prayers and support.
3. Asked these sister churches to form a Provisional Council of Bishops in order to provide a spiritual union with the historic episcopate.
4. Solicited the consecration of the Spanish bishop by the Council of Bishops (López-Lozano 1991, 191).

The only bishops to respond to the call for the formation of a Provisional Council of Bishops were three bishops from Ireland: the Archbishop of Armagh, the Archbishop of Dublin, and the Bishop of Meath. The relationship between Ireland and Spain continued to grow and strengthen during these years, but it was not until September 23, 1894, that Cabrera was finally consecrated the first Bishop of the Reformed Church of Spain. The consecrating bishops were the then Archbishop of Dublin, who had been the Bishop of Meath, the Bishop of Clogher, and the Bishop of Down and Connor (López-Lozano 1991, 182). Bishop Cabrera's consecration was not accepted by all. Lord Halifax, an Anglo-Catholic, wrote to the Archbishop of Toledo and apologized for this unusual act "without the sanction of your Eminence and of the bishops of your Province of Toledo to consecrate a certain schismatic named Cabrera to the Episcopate" (Jacob 1997, 278).

In 1891, the cornerstone of the Iglesia del Redentor was laid in Madrid. This parish church was eventually to become the cathedral. Other churches were founded in towns and cities throughout Spain as the church extended its influence. Bishop Cabrera continued to serve, though in 1916 he had a hard winter and eventually died on May 18, 1916, at the age of 79. The first and most important stage in the establishment of the Spanish Reformed Episcopal Church came to a close (López-Lozano 2012a).

This stage is important because it established the church that was linked to an historic episcopate, affirmed the Thirty-Nine Articles of the Church of England, adopted a liturgy, and established a diocesan structure. Due to various circumstances, the church did not elect another bishop for many years. During this time, there was political instability, and when General Francisco Franco triumphed over the Republicans to end the Civil War in 1939, the Protestant churches suffered hardship and persecution. However, there was no interruption of services at the Cathedral in Madrid. The situation was more problematic in other areas of Spain. Episcopal oversight came from

Ireland, and various bishops during this period made occasional visits to confirm and ordain deacons. In 1952, the church made the decision to add "Episcopal" to the name of the denomination in order to distinguish it from other Reformed churches in Spain (López-Lozano 2012a).

Two years earlier, at the XVI Synod of the church, the Rev. Fernando Cabrera, son of Bishop Juan Cabrera, was elected bishop. He unfortunately died in 1953 before he could be consecrated (Álvarez 2000, 489). The XVIII Synod in 1954 elected the Rev. Santos Molina as the next bishop. In 1980, the Spanish Reformed Episcopal Church was accepted as a full member of the Anglican Communion (López-Lozano 2012a).

## The Spanish Reformed Episcopal Church Today

The church today has 24 congregations spread throughout Spain. Some of them go back to the earlier origins of the denomination in the mid-eighteenth century and have been in continuous operation since (López-Lozano 2012a). The current diocesan is the Rt. Rev. Carlos López-Lozano who was elected at the XLIII Synod on July 29, 1995. At the age of 33, he was the youngest bishop in the Anglican Communion. He was consecrated in November of that year by the Archbishop of Canterbury, the Most Rev. George Carey (Álvarez 2000, 529). Bishop López is now in the 17th year of his episcopate.

Churches in the diocese range from the Cathedral in Madrid, which has developed a very successful ministry to the immigrant population of Madrid, to small neighborhood churches in purchased or rented space. There have been some missionaries from the United Kingdom and the United States who have aided in the work, but the majority of the pastoral leaders are Spaniards. One of the newest churches is in Reus in Catalonia, and it is under the leadership of the Rev. Rafael Arencón Edo. La Iglesia del Buen Pastor in Móstoles, a working-class community on the outskirts of Madrid, is an earlier church plant that has also been successful in ministering to European, African, and Eastern European immigrants. In addition to the churches, there is a student center at the University of Salamanca and an ecumenical center in Alcocéber (López-Lozano 2012b).

## The Lusitanian Catholic Apostolic Evangelical Church of Portugal

*History*

Even though there had been an Anglican presence on the Iberian Peninsula for a long time – especially if Gibraltar is taken into consideration – these churches were composed of English-speaking expatriates that were directly tied to the Church of England. Although the climate in Portugal was mainly anti-Protestant, there were times when there was a relaxation of the restrictions against non-Roman churches, and it was then that two Anglican churches were founded in Lisbon (Jacob 1997, 277). One was founded in 1838 but closed in 1870, and a second was founded in 1868. The Rev. Angelo Mora, a Spanish Roman Catholic priest, was received into the American

Episcopal Church. Mora was able to attract a group of Portuguese evangelicals who wanted to start a Portuguese reformed church. The decisions of Vatican I with the decree of papal infallibility created consternation, however, and there was reluctance to establish a national church that would be Anglican in structure, practice, and doctrine (Jacob 1997, 277).

In 1878, both Spain and Portugal petitioned the Lambeth Conference for a bishop to oversee the emerging churches there, but the petition was denied (Jacob 1997, 277). In the petition, they stated, "In spite of the fact that many congregations in Spain and Portugal had adopted the title of Episcopal, they never had enjoyed the favor of Episcopal supervision or aid" (Álvarez 2000, 189). The Archbishop of Canterbury, Archibald Campbell, recommended that they be in contact with the Rt. Rev. Henry C. Riley, an American who had been consecrated Bishop of the Valley of Mexico, to have him visit Spain and Portugal and to "assess and to assist" the churches there (Álvarez 2000, 199). In spite of the rebuff, the Portuguese clergy and leaders were officially constituted in 1880 at a synod presided over by Bishop Riley (Jacob 1997, 277). The Synod stated:

> We do not desire to found a new religion, but simply to cleanse the Christian religion from the corruption of the ages, and to reconquer the ancient liberties of the early Lusitanian Church – so long subjected to the foreign yoke of Rome – and to spread through all this country a doctrine, which shall be Catholic and Apostolic, in a church that shall be Portuguese not Roman (Lusitana 2011).

In 1884, the Lusitanian Church finished its own liturgy that was based on the Roman Mass, the Anglican Book of Common Prayer and the Mozarabic rite. Much in the same way that the Church of Ireland assisted the Spanish Reformed Episcopal Church, assistance was provided to Portugal. Even though a petition for a bishop was denied again at the Lambeth Conference of 1888, the Archbishop of Dublin, Lord Plunkett, provided an Episcopal presence in the new church (Jacob 1997, 278). This arrangement continued for many years, and at times, the American bishop in charge of the Convocation of Episcopal Churches in Europe would also serve the Portuguese churches. It was not until 1958 that Portugal's first indigenous bishop was consecrated (Lusitana 2011). Full communion with the American Episcopal Church came in 1961, and in 1963 Portugal was brought into full communion with the Church of England and the Church of Ireland. In 1980, it became a member of the Anglican Communion worldwide (Lusitana 2011).

## The church today

The church is named "Lusitanian" since that is the ancient Roman name for the area. It is Catholic because it "professes the catholic faith that is sustained always for all and everywhere." It is Apostolic because it maintains the threefold ministry of bishops, priests, and deacons as part of the historic episcopate, and Evangelical because it considers the Holy Scriptures of the Old and New Testaments to be inspired by God and as the ultimate rule of faith and that they contain all that is necessary for salvation in Jesus Christ (Lusitana n.d., 5; translation mine).

The diocese is divided into the Prelature of the North and the Prelature of the South. There are two missions in the north, and eight parishes, including the Catedral do S. Paulo in Lisbon, in the south. The diocese is directly involved in three social ministries. The first is the Association of Schools that provides help to children, youth, families, and the elderly. The second is the Bolsa Diogo Cassels that provides books and educational material for needy children. The third is the Social Centre of the Holy Family that provides assistance in personal hygiene and distributes clothing and food (Lusitana n.d., 14). The current bishop is the Rt. Rev. Fernando Soares, who was elected bishop on June 16, 1979, and consecrated on May 1, 1980 (Evangelista 2012).

## The Diocese of Bermuda

Bermuda has been settled by Europeans since the early part of the seventeenth century. The oldest Anglican Church in Bermuda and the first non-Roman church in the New World is St. Peter's, which is found on St. George's Island. It was founded in 1612 by English settlers who were shipwrecked on the island in 1609 on their way to the Virginia colony (Hook 1990, 284). Later, additional settlers arrived who were actually Puritans, and the clergy who ministered to them until Bermuda became a Crown colony were mostly Presbyterian or Congregationalist (Nelson 1995, 514). After 1683, the clergy were predominantly Anglican. Except for one parish, this transition apparently did not have any of the tensions or disruptions that would have been expected, and Bishop Henry Compton of London, Governor Benjamin Bennett, and the vicar, the Rev. Andrew Auchinleck, are identified as being instrumental in this regard. The dissenting parish was Christ Church in Warwick, which preferred to receive its ecclesiastical oversight from New England instead of London (Nelson 1995, 515).

For the better part of the eighteenth century, it appears that the Anglican churches did not flourish. Some of the Bermudians were becoming Methodists, and having only one clergyman to serve the parishes would have limited their effectiveness. By the early part of the eighteenth century, there were nine Anglican churches that were served by one priest. It was not until 1822 that the Society for the Propagation of the Gospel began work there (Higgins 1942, 111). This must have improved the situation because it introduced a period when the church buildings were improved and expanded (Nelson 1995, 515). In 1826, Bishop Spencer of Nova Scotia became the first bishop to visit the archipelago. He worked with the Colonial Legislature to establish eight parishes and four livings for the clergy working there. The population of Bermuda was 10,000, and Bishop Spencer confirmed over 1,200 while he was there. Ten mission schools were also started, and according to John Higgins, when emancipation came in 1838, the social and pastoral response to the freed slaves put a tremendous financial burden on the churches there (Higgins 1942, 111). There was no formal Episcopal oversight until 1839 when Bermuda was made part of the Diocese of Newfoundland – an arrangement that lasted until 1917. The Anglican Church continued to grow and reached 10,000 in number, again with five clergy by the end of the nineteenth century. Due to security issues during World War I, it was not possible for the Bishop of Newfoundland to travel, but even so, the Bermudan Church grew to 16,000 with 15 clergy. The Diocese of Bermuda was created in 1917, but there was no bishop there until 1925 (Higgins 1942, 111).

In 1975, Bermuda came under the full jurisdiction of the Church of England as extra-provincial to the Archbishop of Canterbury. The Rt. Rev. Patrick G. H. White is the current bishop. There are nine parishes in the archipelago that conform to the original historic parish boundaries (Bermuda 2012). These parishes are:

- Christ Church, Devonshire
- Holy Trinity, Hamilton
- St. Paul, Paget
- St. John with St. Monica's Mission, and St. Augustine, Pembroke
- St. Peter and St. Peter's West with Chapel-of-Ease, St. George's
- St. James, Sandys
- St. Mark, Smiths
- St. Anne, Southampton
- St. Mary, Warwick

## The Parish of the Falkland Islands

### History

The history of the Anglican Church in the Falkland Islands begins with the first missionary expeditions of the Patagonian Missionary Society under the leadership of Captain Allen Gardiner. Gardiner, anxious to reach the native peoples of Tierra del Fuego, arrived in December 1850 with a team of six additional men. The trip ended in failure with the death of all from starvation and scurvy, but the discovery of Allen Gardiner's diary and the report of their deaths in the London *Times* prompted renewed interest in the mission, and the Patagonian Missionary Society received the funds necessary to continue Gardiner's work (Hazlewood 2000, 158–60). A second effort was initiated, and it was decided that the Falkland Islands would be used as a base. Not only would it provide a suitable outpost from which to reach Tierra del Fuego, but it also could be used as a training center for those preparing to do the work. Initial contact was made with a Fuegian who had traveled to England 25 years previously named Jemmy Button. Button and his family would prove to be invaluable as they taught the missionaries their local language on Keppel Island in June 1858 (Thompson 1983, 194). The settlement on Keppel Island was to be a "durable centre of operations, a place of rendezvous for the Missionaries, a safe depot for stores, a model community for the natives, a refuge for the Missionaries in winter, where they might do printing and writing, and finally it was hoped that Keppel would produce a considerable revenue" (Macdonald 1929, 44).

The Patagonian Missionary Society, which then became the South American Missionary Society, continued to expand its work in South America. By the 1860s, it was apparent that there needed to be an Anglican Episcopal authority. On December 21, 1869, the Rev. Waite Hockin Stirling was consecrated bishop in Westminster Abbey. Stirling had already been a missionary to Tierra del Fuego and had to be called back to England for his consecration from Ushuaia (Macdonald 1929, 119). Bishop Stirling was enthroned at St. Thomas's Church in Port Stanley on January 14, 1872 (Macdonald 1929, 126). This church was very primitive in its construction and was eventually destroyed by a peat slide in 1886 (Millam 1997, 2). The administrative office for the new diocese was located in Buenos Aires. The diocese included not only the Falkland Islands but all of South America as well. Bishop Stirling remained Bishop of the Falkland Islands until the year 1900. During that time, Christ Church Cathedral was built in Port Stanley at a cost of £10,080 and consecrated by Bishop Stirling on February 21, 1892. The Bishop's Chair was made from oak from Canterbury Cathedral (Every 1915). Upon his return to England, Bishop Stirling became canon and assistant bishop at Wells Cathedral, finally retiring in 1920 at the age of 91 (Millam 1997, 2).

The Rev. Edward Every was then appointed the next bishop and served from 1902 to 1910. It was during his episcopate that the Diocese of the Falklands was divided into two: the east coast and the west coast. Bishop Lawrence Blair had jurisdiction over the Falklands and the west coast countries of Chile, Bolivia, and Peru. He resigned in 1914, and Bishop Every regained pastoral oversight until Bishop Norman de Jersey took over in 1919. He served until 1934.

Bishop John Weller started his episcopacy in the Falkland Islands, but financial pressures required him to move to Argentina. He had pastoral oversight of the Falkland Islands, but the diocese was technically without a bishop until 1946. Bishop Daniel Evans, who had previously been in Rio de Janeiro, became bishop, and the diocese once again included most of South America. He died suddenly while traveling in Chile in 1962 (Millam 1997, 2).

Following a convention in Cuernavaca, Mexico, in 1963, the diocese was once again divided, this time into three. A single bishop, Cyril Tucker, served two of the three dioceses: the Falklands, Argentina, and Eastern South America. As additional dioceses were formed in South America in the 1970s, they formed the Anglican Council of South America, which included the Falklands. The other dioceses did their work and ministry primarily in Spanish, and this did not sit well with the Falkland Islanders. In light of this, the Archbishop of Canterbury, F. Donald Coggan, assumed oversight of the Falklands and appointed the Bishop of Argentina as commissary (Millam 1997, 3). It was reduced to a single parish, and the subsequent clergy who served there do so under the title of "rector." As a result of the Falklands War in 1982, the Bishop to the Forces has provided an Episcopal presence, and this has meant that the archbishop now gives his commission to any visiting bishop (Millam 1997, 3).

## Bibliography

Álvarez, Francisco Serrano. 2000. *Contra Vientos y Mareas: Los Sueños de la Iglesia Reformada Hecha Realidad*. Barcelona: Editorial CLIE.

Bermuda, Anglican Church of. 2012. The Anglican Church of Bermuda. Anglican Diocese of Bermuda. April 4, 2012. http://www.facebook.com/anglicanbda?sk=info.

Evangelista, Paróquia S. João. 2012. Bispo D. Fernando Soares. April 3, 2012. http://www.igrejadotorne.org/index.php?option=com_content&task=view&id=526&Itemid=1.

Every, Edward Francis. 1915. The Anglican Church in South America, p. 3. April 4, 2012. http://anglicanhistory.org/sa/every1915/02.html.

Hazlewood, Nick. 2000. *The Life and Times of Jemmy Button.* New York: Thomas Dunne Books of St. Martin's Press.

Higgins, John. 1942. *The Expansion of the Anglican Communion.* Louisville, Kentucky: The Cloister Press.

Hook, Donald D. 1990. The Oldest Non-Roman Church in the New World: St. Peter's Anglican Church, St. George's, Bermuda. *Anglican Episcopal History*, vol. 59, no. 2 , p. 5.

Jacob, W. M. 1997. *The Making of the Anglican Church Worldwide.* London: SPCK.

López-Lozano, Carlos. 1991. *Precedentes de la Iglesia Española Reformada Episcopal.* Seville: Iglesia Española Reformada Episcopal.

López-Lozano, Carlos. 2012a. Nuestra Historia. Madrid. Iglesia Española Reformada Episcopal. March 31, 2012. http://www.anglicanos.org/web_iglesia_anglicana/g_general/g_nh_historia_iglesia_anglicana.html.

López-Lozano, Carlos. 2012b. Quienes Somos. Iglesia Española Reformada Episcopal. April 2, 2012. http://www.anglicanos.org/web_iglesia_anglicana/g_general/g_qs_iglesia_espanola_reformada.html.

Lusitana, Igreja. 2011. History of the Lusitanian Church of Portugal. April 3, 2012. http://www.igreja-lusitana.org/index.php?option=com_content&view=article&id=73&Itemid=475&lang=en.

Lusitana, Igreja, ed. n.d. *Igreja Lusitana Católica Apostólica Evangélica.* April 3, 2012. http://www.igreja-lusitana.org/ilcae.

Macdonald, Frederick C. 1929. *Bishop Stirling of the Falklands.* London: Seely, Service and Co.

Millam, Peter J. 1997. The Falkland Islands – The World's Largest Diocese. Port Stanley, Falkland Islands. The Falkland Islands Association. April 4, 2012. http://www.falklands.info/history/histarticle18.html.

Nelson, John K. 1995. Review of Chronicle of a Colonial Church: 1612–1826 by A. C. Hollis-Hallett. *Anglican Episcopal History*, vol. 64, no. 4, p. 3.

Thompson, Phyllis. 1983. *The Unquenchable Flame.* London: Hodder and Stoughton.

# North America

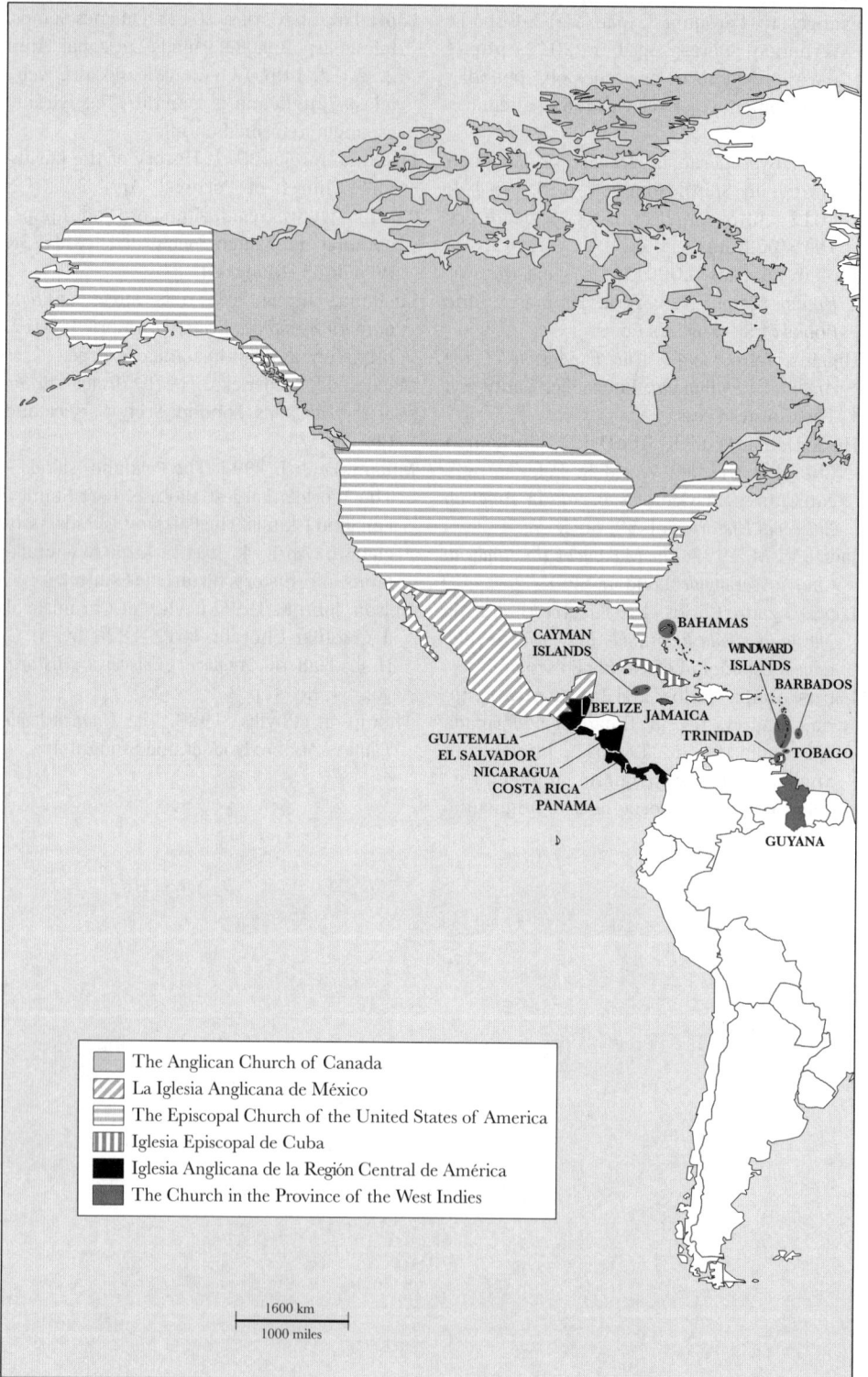

BAHAMAS

CAYMAN
ISLANDS

WINDWARD
ISLANDS

BARBADOS

BELIZE JAMAICA

GUATEMALA
EL SALVADOR
NICARAGUA
COSTA RICA
PANAMA

TRINIDAD

TOBAGO

GUYANA

| | |
|---|---|
| | The Anglican Church of Canada |
| | La Iglesia Anglicana de México |
| | The Episcopal Church of the United States of America |
| | Iglesia Episcopal de Cuba |
| | Iglesia Anglicana de la Región Central de América |
| | The Church in the Province of the West Indies |

1600 km

1000 miles

# CHAPTER 43

# The Anglican Church of Canada

## Alan L. Hayes

The Anglican Church of Canada (ACC), as it is now called, was organized in 1893 under the name Church of England in Canada. It was a "consolidation" (to use the term used then) of most of the country's existing Anglican parishes, dioceses, and provinces. The ACC thus became the Canadian national branch of the Anglican Communion, with its own primate and general synod. Organizationally, the ACC was modeled on Canada, and its development paralleled the process of Canadian nation-building. Canada is a confederation of former British colonies that entered into union between 1867 and 1948. As Canada's territory expanded to its present boundaries, so did the ACC. Both Canada and the ACC are characterized by robust regional identities, held together by a relatively remote national governance. However, ACC's central governance has nothing like Canada's powers of coercion and direct taxation and remains weak.

There are a few very small Anglican bodies in Canada, but these are regarded by the ACC as schismatic and are not formally recognized by the Archbishop of Canterbury as part of the Anglican Communion.

## General Characteristics

### Roots in English church establishment

In modern times, the ACC has functioned as a denomination; that is, it is an organized voluntary association accustomed to operating in a religiously pluralistic society, applying minimal standards of membership, and sometimes cooperating, sometimes competing with other denominations. In colonial times, however, its predecessor components

*The Wiley-Blackwell Companion to the Anglican Communion*, First Edition. Edited by Ian S. Markham,
J. Barney Hawkins IV, Justyn Terry, and Leslie Nuñez Steffensen.
© 2013 John Wiley & Sons, Ltd. Published 2013 by John Wiley & Sons, Ltd.

functioned as overseas branches of the Church of England, often assuming its estab-lishmentarian ethos, and sharing in some of its privileges, symbols, mentalities, and burdens. Relics of this establishmentarian ethos survive here and there, for example, in the coats of arms and Union Jacks in older church buildings, the survival of colonial financial endowments, prayers for the Queen, the taste for patriotic songs such as "Jerusalem," and the propensity of visiting members of the Royal Family to worship in Anglican churches. Similarly, although the ACC now has a multi-cultural membership, there is little mistaking its British ethnic roots.

### Doctrine

Theologically, the ACC is very diverse (Hayes 2004). There are no doctrinal tests on membership, except that persons being baptized, or their sponsors, profess the Apostles' Creed. In addition, by participating in liturgy, Anglicans implicitly express their comfort with its doctrinal statements and assumptions. Until the 1960s, ordinands were required to assent to the Thirty-Nine Articles of Religion of the Church of England, but no longer. Perhaps reflecting its roots in an English church establishment that sought to keep peace by comprehending difference, the ACC allows a practically unlimited lati-tude in matters of belief, while more vigorously enforcing standards of church order, canonical obedience, and liturgical conformity.

The ACC umbrella covers conservative evangelicals, charismatics, liberal protes-tants, post-liberals, conservative Anglo-Catholics, proponents of creation spirituality, and doctrinal agnostics. Probably the largest theological grouping in the ACC is liberal catholics, who favor a sacramental spirituality, a modernist theology, and progressive social and personal ethics.

### Organization

There are four principal levels of governance in the ACC, each with its own executive leader and conciliar structure: the national church, with a primate and general synod; four geographically defined ecclesiastical provinces, each with a metropolitan and pro-vincial synod; 29 dioceses, each with a bishop and a diocesan synod; and, according to the ACC website (http://www.anglican.ca/about/history), about 1,700 parishes, each with an incumbent and vestry or parish council. Synods and councils in the ACC include both ordained and lay members. A 30th diocese was forced into bankruptcy in 2001, but continues as a "family of parishes" overseen by a bishop; and a national indigenous ministry, also overseen by a bishop, is moving toward a form of self-govern-ment. Something approaching half the members of the ACC live in the three southern Ontario dioceses of Toronto, Huron, and Niagara. The northern dioceses, though very large in area (the Diocese of the Arctic alone is 15 times the size of the United Kingdom), are very sparsely populated, and require the financial support of the southern dioceses, via grants from the general synod to a grouping called the Council of the North.

National governance is weak. Although in 1893 the new general synod received jurisdiction over doctrine, worship, clergy education, pensions, social issues of national importance, relations with other churches, and missionary work, in practice its work in these areas is modest, and dioceses operate more or less vigorously and with impunity in most of these areas. A general synod staff of about 60 persons, assigned mostly to financial affairs, the monthly denominational newspaper the *Anglican Journal*, and communications, is headquartered at 80 Hayden Street, Toronto.

By contrast, dioceses are relatively independent and powerful. Diocesan bishops wield considerable authority since they hold office without term of years and are almost impervious to removal; they have the power to veto the acts of their synod, have considerable clout in appointing clergy to parishes, exercise sole patronage in diocesan appointments such as honorary canonries, archdeaconries, and regional deanships, administer clergy discipline, and can exploit the prestige of office. The dioceses employ most of the clergy and own most of the denomination's property. Diocesan bishops have received from general synod a virtually unfettered latitude to authorize alternative liturgies within their dioceses, and, invoking their *ius liturgicum*, several have permitted blessings of same-sex unions despite a national policy prohibiting them (as most recently enunciated by the national House of Bishops in 2008).

## Worship

The most common form of worship is the Sunday Eucharist according to the Book of Alternative Services (BAS), which was authorized by general synod in 1985. The BAS closely reflects the Book of Common Prayer of the Episcopal Church (1979), and presents a Canadian expression of the theology of the Liturgical Movement. According to its introductory material, it works from "the theological principle *lex orandi: lex credendi*, i.e., the law of prayer is the law of belief," which it dubiously calls a principle "particularly treasured by Anglicans." The statement reflects a liberal catholic perspective, in distinction from both the Roman Catholic view that, conversely, the rule of faith determines the rule of prayer (*Mediator dei* 1947), and the classical Protestant value that scripture alone is the authority for matters of faith. The other principal nationally authorized liturgical book, the Canadian Book of Common Prayer (1962), though no longer widely used, formally remains the official liturgy of the ACC. This was the last prayer book in the Anglican Communion to be revised in the tradition dating back to the Reformation versions of 1549 and 1552. Many bishops authorize alternative and local forms of worship for parish use. Not only liturgical texts, but ceremonial, use of space, leadership style, and mood can vary significantly from church to church.

Generally, any baptized person can receive communion in an Anglican church, although some parish priests exclude children. Confirmation has been removed from the order of Christian initiation, and the BAS has placed it in a section of "episcopal offices" following the blessing of oil. Some parishes welcome un-baptized persons to receive communion, although the national House of Bishops has rejected this practice. Services of Morning and Evening Prayer, which were very common before the 1970s, are now largely confined to seminaries, religious communities, and those parish churches that see themselves as very traditional.

## Architecture

Most church buildings in the ACC were constructed between 1845 and 1960 in a Gothic revival style of architecture, which for a century was a visible international badge of Anglican identity. An early and satisfying example is Christ Church Cathedral, Montreal (1859). However, a few prominent churches from this period are in a central-plan style of either Richardsonian Romanesque or Byzantine inspiration. An important example of the latter is St. Anne's, Toronto (1908), decorated by three members of the Group of Seven, Canada's best-known school of painters. Surviving church buildings from before 1845 are usually neoclassical in style, though most of these have been Gothicized in later renovations. Architectural styles of churches built after 1960 are diverse but typically express congregational community by stressing horizontal lines.

## Membership

The ACC's peak year of membership was 1964, when it recorded 1,365,313 persons on parish rolls. By 2012, according to its website (http://www.anglican.ca/about/history), membership had shrunk to approximately 500,000 members. (In this same period, the population of Canada increased from 19 million to 34 million.) Reasons for declining membership include deaths in an aging church population, schisms, dissatisfaction, increased religious competition and non-Christian immigration, and, more disputably, "secularization." Declining participation has influenced the ACC's agenda. On the one hand, it has led to dispiriting reductions in denominational budgets, downsizings of staff complements, closures of parish churches, and the narrowing of mission goals. On the other hand, it has inspired some creative approaches to Christian evangelism, mission, community, and outreach (Clarke and Macdonald 2010).

The most recent Canadian census to ask questions about religious affiliation was also in 2001, and it found 2,035,495 self-identified Anglicans. This was the fourth-largest religious grouping in Canada, after Roman Catholic (12,793,125), "no religious affiliation" (4,900,054), and United Church of Canada (2,839,125).

## Ethnicity

Through the 1950s, the ACC was dominated by people of English, Irish, and Scottish background, and these identities likely remain in the majority.

Not just an ethnic group but a diverse set of founding nations whose aboriginal rights are constitutionally recognized, Indigenous peoples constitute a significant Anglican population. Of about 1 million First Nations people (Indians) in Canada, an estimated 25 percent identify as Anglicans; and of 45,000 Inuit (formerly called

Eskimos), an estimated 85 percent are Anglicans. Among First Nations groups with strong Anglican connections are the Mi'kmaq, Cree, Mohawk, Blackfoot, Tsimshian, Kwakiutl, Haida, and Gwich'in. About 225 congregations have all or nearly all Indigenous membership. Most Aboriginal Anglicans who live off-reserve, however, avoid church, where they often feel unwelcome. There are signs of new spiritual vitality in Aboriginal Anglicanism. Factors include an effective Indigenous leadership (there have been native bishops since 1989 and a national Indigenous bishop since 2007, and there are about 130 native clergy), the inculturation of theology, liturgy, and church music, and a recovery of native ways after many decades of repression under the Indian Act.

Finally, since 1962, when racial restrictions were largely eliminated from Canada's immigration regulations, the ACC has become significantly more multi-cultural. West Indians are particularly well represented; other ethnicities include sub-Saharan African, Chinese (particularly from Hong Kong), Filipino, Hispanic, Japanese, Korean, Tamil, and Sudanese. However, in Quebec, where French is the dominant language, francophone ministry is limited to two or three very small congregations. In Vancouver, which has a large Asian population, the ACC since 2003 has lost its Japanese and Chinese Anglican parishes to more conservative Anglican groupings.

### Women

Women were largely though not entirely excluded from church governance until the 1960s. They were conspicuously involved in lay ministries, however. The Women's Auxiliary to missionary society had active branches in most parishes, sponsored female missionaries for domestic and foreign service, and undertook educational and social ministries. The first women's religious orders were founded in the 1870s; the most active today is the Sisters of St. John the Divine. The first deaconesses were "set aside" in 1895 and were used mainly for missionary, educational, and inner-city social work; their order gradually disappeared when women began to be ordained as deacons after 1969. A proposal to ordain women to the priesthood was raised, discussed, agreed, and implemented between 1968 and 1976. Despite some protest, the change was absorbed relatively quickly and painlessly. The first woman bishop, Victoria Matthews, was ordained in 1993 (Knowles 2008).

## History

The history of the ACC can be divided into three periods: (1) origins to 1863, (2) 1863–1963, (3) since 1963.

### Colonial church, to 1863

Anglican Christianity came to what is now Canada in the wake of British exploration, military enterprise, resource exploitation, and settlement. Some of the earliest Anglican activity in the various parts of colonial British North America (BNA) includes the following.

- *The Arctic.* In 1578, an Anglican Eucharist was celebrated near present-day Iqaluit, Nunavut, during an adventuring expedition under Martin Frobisher.
- *Newfoundland.* (Millman and Kelley 1983). In 1583, the regulations for a settlement that proved short-lived in Newfoundland provided for an Anglican establishment. The country's oldest Anglican parish (1699) is St. John the Baptist, in St. John's, Newfoundland, a settlement which supported the cod-fishing industry on the Grand Banks. Its parish priest was one of the first to receive funding from the Society for the Propagation of the Gospel (SPG), an English mission society founded in 1701 that would become immensely important as a sponsor and regulator of Anglican missions in BNA.
- *Nova Scotia and New Brunswick.* (Millman and Kelley 1983). In 1750, the country's oldest Anglican church building still in use was erected in Halifax, Nova Scotia, with the name St. Paul's. A statute of the colonial legislature in 1758 declared the Church of England the established church; a similar act was passed in New Brunswick in 1786 after it was partitioned from Nova Scotia. (These statutes would be repealed in the 1850s.) The population of Nova Scotia expanded significantly after the American Revolution, building pressure for an innovation that had been controversial for decades: an Anglican colonial bishop. Many non-Anglicans had come to the New World precisely to escape bishops. But for loyalist Anglicans, a bishop appointed by the Crown would forcefully promote Paul's teaching in Romans 13, beloved of Tories, that "the powers that be are ordained of God," and thus help secure the loyal colonies from the threat of American republicanism. In 1787, the king created an Anglican diocese for virtually all of BNA and appointed as its bishop Charles Inglis, the former rector of Trinity Church, New York. Since then, the diocese has been divided many times.
- *Prince Edward Island.* An Anglican rector was appointed to Charlottetown in 1769. Four years later he had still never set foot on the island, and he was dismissed. His successor was the son of the lieutenant governor.
- *Quebec.* When England took control of Quebec in 1763, at the end of the Seven Years War, the governor received royal instructions "that the Church of England may be established both in Principle and Practice." However, neither he nor his successor was willing to disrupt the religious practices of the province's 70,000 French-speaking Roman Catholics, a wise policy confirmed by the Quebec Act of 1774. Instead, they made a minimal provision for Anglican services for the tiny British population.
- *Ontario.* After the American Revolution, loyalist refugees, including Mohawks and others in the Six Nations Confederation, began settling around Lake Ontario and its watershed. An Anglican chapel was built in 1785 for the Mohawks in Brantford; this is the oldest surviving church in the province.
- *Rupert's Land.* (Boon 1962). This vast territory, named for the first governor of the Hudson's Bay Company (HBC), which claimed title to it from 1670 to 1870, has since been divided among Manitoba, Saskatchewan, Alberta, Northwest

Territories, Nunavut, Yukon, Ontario, Quebec, Minnesota, and North Dakota. It prohibited missionaries and clergy until 1811. The first Anglican missionary, John West, was sent there from England in 1820 by the evangelical Church Missionary Society (CMS). He made it his special concern to marry couples who had been living *à la façon du pays*. He created Canada's first Indian residential school and led Anglican worship at Upper Fort Garry (now Winnipeg). With growing settlements and increased numbers of clergy, Rupert's Land was created as a diocese in 1849 with funds from the HBC and one of its executives.

- *First Nations missions.* (Peake 1989). Henry Budd (Sakashuwestam), an orphaned Cree child baptized by John West, grew up to be the first First Nations person to be ordained an Anglican priest (1853). He was highly effective as a missionary and made translations of the Bible and the prayer book into the Cree language. Even more influential was Robert McDonald, the *métis* son of a Scottish father and Ojibwe mother, who was ordained a priest in 1852. He learned several Aboriginal languages, published a grammar of Tukudh, translated the Bible and prayer book, and ministered widely across the north for 60 years, particularly among the Ojibwe and Gwitch'in.
- *British Columbia.* (Peake 1959). Before gold was discovered on the Fraser River in 1858, the CMS had a mission to the Tsimshian, and two HBC settlements provided for Anglican services. In that year, with an explosion of population, a diocese was endowed and a bishop was appointed.

During the colonial period, Anglican religious affairs were controlled by the Colonial Office (normally working through local governors and councils), the Bishop of London and colonial bishops, and the SPG. These authorities did not always work together harmoniously. The aura of church establishment was palpable, and several "High-Church" leaders (most notably John Strachan, archdeacon of York and later Bishop of Toronto) argued that the constitutional entrenchment of the Church of England in the mother country spilled over into the colonies and was essential to a healthy body politic (Fahey 1991). The general tasks of the colonial Church of England were to form congregations, frequently in remote places; build and furnish churches; supply missionaries; organize schools, parish libraries, and colleges of higher learning; sponsor religious groups; and develop lay leadership. Since tithes, which were legally required in the Church of England, were not imposed in BNA, and since Anglicans had no tradition of giving voluntary financial support, colonial Anglican leaders learned to curry government largesse, plead for help from the SPG, and sometimes try their hand at fundraising. In Nova Scotia, the English government gave Anglicans a generous landed endowment in glebe and rectory lands, and in what are now Ontario and Quebec it gave an estimated 3 million acres in a landed endowment called "the clergy reserves." Governments also gave the colonial Church of England such advantages as college and university charters, educational subsidies, authority to administer marriages, and appointments to powerful colonial councils and agencies.

Predictably, non-Anglicans opposed these privileges, but so did many Anglicans. The Low-Church Anglicans of the whiggish type, then very common south of the border, thought that Anglican establishment had no place in a religiously diverse society.

Church of Ireland Anglicans, who flooded into Canada between 1830 and 1860, were no more favorable to English ecclesiastical hegemony in Canada than they had been in Ireland (Vaudry 2003). And, from the 1830s, a new group, Anglo-Catholics, stressed the divine authority of the church in a way that challenged its captivity to the state. Some Anglo-Catholics were fast-tracked to leadership in the colonies through the efforts of a fund-raising group called the Colonial Bishoprics Council, founded in 1841. In BNA, two of its earliest beneficiaries, John Medley, Bishop of Fredericton, and George Hills, Bishop of British Columbia, publicly opposed a colonial church establishment.

Given the opposition of both the friends and foes of Anglicanism, official privilege for colonial Anglicans could not persist. Local legislatures dismantled the church's special status from the 1830s to the 1850s; the clergy reserve lands were secularized in 1854. The arguments among High-Church, Low-Church, evangelical, and Anglo-Catholic Anglicans continued through the nineteenth century in other contexts.

With endowments threatened and government largesse terminated, and with the SPG wanting to withdraw its support from the older colonies, Anglicans needed mechanisms for self-finance and self-government. Taking the initiative, and theoretically running the risk of prosecution for acting without the Queen's approval, Bishop Strachan in Toronto in 1853 created a synod of bishop, clergy, and lay delegates with the power to govern diocesan affairs (Hayes 1989). Similar bodies, called "diocesan conventions," existed in the Episcopal Church in the USA, but Strachan's venture was the first of its kind in the British Empire. (George Selwyn in New Zealand had convened a synod in 1844, but it was all clergy.) The idea quickly spread to other dioceses and became the standard form of Anglican self-government in Canada. A self-governing ecclesiastical province of Canada was created in 1860, bringing together the dioceses of Nova Scotia, Fredericton, Quebec, Montreal, Toronto, and Huron.

In 1863, the unwelcome liberation of colonial Anglicanism from its dependence on the English government came abruptly (Hayes 2004). The highest court in the British Empire decided, in *Long v. Gray*, that England had no authority in church matters in self-governing colonies. In the several parts of BNA that already had their own legislatures, Anglicans could no longer turn to England to create their dioceses, appoint their bishops, make their rules, or set theological, liturgical, or canonical standards. Anglicans in these colonies now constituted only one voluntary religious association among others.

## Satellite church, 1863–1963

Thus, in 1863, Anglicans in BNA were no longer formally privileged, though they remained an influential minority in Ontario and points east. They had no national organization. They had few formal institutional connections with other Anglicans in the British Empire. Nevertheless, they understood themselves as morally connected to the Church of England, and for another century they were royalist and anglophilic, proud to be held securely within England's gravitational field (Westfall 1989).

The Canadian bishops were appalled by the implications of *Long v. Grey*. The legal fragmentation of the Empire-wide Church of England left each provincial church free to go its own way in theology, liturgy, discipline, and ethos, spelling the end of a sense of Anglican Communion. The Canadian bishops petitioned the Archbishop of Canterbury to invite all Anglican bishops worldwide to discuss the "distress." Despite resistance from many English and American bishops who feared losing control to foreigners, a conference was held in 1867 at Lambeth Palace, the London residence of the Archbishop of Canterbury. This proved to be the first of a series of decennial Lambeth Conferences, now considered a major instrument of the unity of the Anglican Communion.

For the next half century, the missionary agenda of Canadian Anglicans was dominated by the North West. In 1868, Canada bought Rupert's Land from the HBC. Learning from the bad example of the Indian wars in the United States, Canada signed treaties with the First Nations, promising to reserve land for their use and to educate their children. The government contracted out the latter obligation to four Christian denominations, including Anglicans. When the Canadian Pacific Railway was completed across the continent in 1885, the North West was flooded with immigrants of European descent – 2 million in 35 years. As First Nations people were pushed into ever-more remote reserves, where CMS missionaries followed, Anglicans organized mission strategies for the settlers, raising funds, building churches, recruiting and training clergy. The principal overseer of this immense enterprise was Robert Machray, the second Anglican Bishop of Rupert's Land. He developed lay leadership, created parish vestries, promoted financial self-support, marshaled experienced missionaries to challenging tasks, began parish schools, and organized higher education. He envisioned an indigenous First Nations church (which did not materialize) and supported native missionaries. He upgraded his diocese into an ecclesiastical province, and then subdivided the original diocese by persuading the CMS and SPG to endow episcopal salaries.

British Columbia entered Canadian Confederation in 1871. In 1879, two new dioceses were formed, one for the settler population of the lower mainland and one for native ministries in the north.

From the 1860s to the 1890s, hostilities among the church parties dominated Anglican politics in Canada as elsewhere. The focal controversy was unauthorized liturgical ceremonial, which could range from modest physical signs of reverence to lavish medievalism. Evangelicals aggressively sought to suppress such ceremonial as un-Anglican, un-Protestant, un-Scriptural, and "Papist." Two opposing camps emerged, called "the Church party" and "the evangelical party." The former typically championed clerical and episcopal authority, while the latter spoke out for "the rights of the laity." Each party developed its own newspapers, Sunday school curricula, hymn books, theological schools, and mission societies. Synods became political battlegrounds. Much of the ceremonial that was controversial then is common in the ACC today.

By the 1880s, most Canadian Anglicans wanted to unite the ecclesiastical provinces of Canada and Rupert's Land into an integrated national structure. Western Canadian dioceses hoped that "church consolidation" would inspire more generous financial support from eastern Canada. Many hoped that it would strengthen resources for global mission, which Canadian Anglicans were tentatively embracing. Some eastern High-Church dioceses, however, feared a national forum where they would be outvoted by a combination of the evangelical western dioceses and the evangelical eastern dioceses of Toronto, Montreal, and Huron. However, the completion of the national railway in 1885 made consolidation all but inevitable, and in 1893 Anglican delegates met in Toronto, published a "solemn declaration" of their intent to remain connected theologically and liturgically with the Church of England, and created the national general synod. Robert Machray was elected primate.

At first, the general synod had no budget for staff members or office space. Not until 1905 was a missionary society functioning effectively. Later, a Sunday School Commission and a Council for Social Service were established. A Toronto office building was purchased for a national headquarters in 1920. However, the dioceses ensured that national structures would remain under-budgeted and restricted. By far, most of the denomination's mission budget came from the federal government in the form of funding for Indian residential schools.

The scenery of church partisanship changed with the rise of theological liberalism. By the early 1900s, disputes about ritual had given way to arguments about the theological implications of modern science and scholarship. At first, a few liberal clergy and professors were disciplined for accommodating doctrine to modern science, but from World War I to the 1950s the dominant theology of the Church of England in Canada was a liberal evangelicalism that affirmed both modernity and religion, and tried to avoid conflicts by evading doctrinal complexities and stressing individual religious experience (Katerberg 2001). The liberal agenda included modernizing the church in communication, educational techniques, governance, and administration (Carrington 1963). In 1931, an Anglican National Commission (1931) made dozens of recommendations to make "organized religion" more respectable, responsive, and relevant to "our modern civilization."

Many Anglicans were attracted to the "social gospel movement," a form of Protestant liberalism that understood Jesus' teaching of the "kingdom of God" to be a call to build a just and compassionate social order. The church lent its weight to legislation and measures for social reform, including temperance laws, Sunday observance, the prohibition of child labor, workers' compensation, film censorship, and, in the 1940s, welfare legislation (Hayes 2004). Unfortunately, many Anglican interventionists thought that social improvement also included the cultural assimilation of Indians, racial restrictions on immigration, and eugenic sterilizations of undesirable classes of women. The tragic results have brought more recent Anglicans to make vicarious repentance.

Throughout the period of the satellite church, the Church of England in Canada saw itself as an expression of the mother church, as reflected in architecture and decorations, liturgy and music, literature and conversation. By contrast, the larger United Church of Canada, formed in 1925, stressed its Canadian national identity and destiny. However, as the wider Canadian society after World War II gathered an independent sense of national identity, as reflected, for example, in the creation of Canadian citizenship, Canadian passports, and a Canadian flag, the ACC increasingly saw itself as a Canadian church in the Anglican tradition, not an English church in a former colony. In 1955, the church adopted the name Anglican Church of Canada, the first national church in the communion to use the word "Anglican" in its title.

## Post–Christendom church, since 1963

The third (and, so far, still the last) Anglican Congress, held in Toronto in 1963, symbolized the ACC's coming of age. The ACC presented itself as giving leadership to the Anglican Communion by hosting 1,000 delegates, 400 official guests, and many others at a carefully organized, wonderfully energizing 11 days of provocative theme speakers, panel discussions, group discussions, and common worship on an epic scale. This was the first occasion when the Anglican Communion could not be seen as spiritually rooted in Britain and the assumptions of Christendom. That is because British Africa and Britain's other territories had entered post-colonialism, and their churches were now domiciled, not in Britain, but in home countries where they were often outnumbered by non-Christian religions. (The importance of this change was not evident to everyone at the time.) A document prepared the week before by the primates on "Mutual Responsibility and Interdependence" (MRI) was informally endorsed. Its vision of the Anglican Communion as an egalitarian, collegial family of churches united in a single mission would replace the old system in which paternalistic "have" churches took care of the "have not" churches. More or less directly, though not immediately, MRI generated the Anglican Consultative Council and the Partners in Mission program.

From the 1960s, Christian symbols and practices were increasingly removed from the Canadian public sphere, including legislatures, government offices, schools, communications media, and public space. Most formal and informal privileges for churches and clergy were withdrawn. Canada no longer saw itself as a Christian nation, and the ACC no longer saw itself as a necessary spiritual bulwark of English Canadian life. It began looking for other ways to prove its relevance and usefulness. A powerful expression of the change in mood was the ACC's choice of Lenten reading for 1965. *The Comfortable Pew*, by a journalist and self-proclaimed atheist named Pierre Berton, was intended to tell Anglicans as clearly as possible why the modern world found them unnecessary. The book was actually commissioned by the ACC. A secularizing mood could be discerned also in the new denominational hymn book of 1971, which jettisoned traditional hymns such as "Amazing Grace" in favor of more modern hymns such as "God of Concrete, God of Steel." Liturgical reformers purged medieval elements from new forms of worship, simplified theological language for a post-Christendom audience, and accommodated modern sensibilities. ("Shorter and fewer readings . . . are all most active people are likely to be able to deal with," said the BAS of its lectionary.)

Advocating for social justice was one way for a church to be relevant in post-Christendom, and the ACC supported numerous progressive social causes in the 1970s and 1980s, frequently in collaboration with other mainline churches. Indeed, its voice was surprisingly effective in important ways, including corporate social responsibility, the discrediting of apartheid in South Africa, protecting the environment, and supporting a fair resolution of First Nations land claims. The primate, Ted Scott, personable, authentic, passionate for justice, was the public face of this Anglican social advocacy. Predictably, however, it provoked negative reactions from business interests, conservative media, and many Anglicans. After 1990, the ACC seemed to lose much of its energy for social justice, perhaps because of its declining (and aging) membership, its impaired credibility in the wake of scandalous clergy behavior, the indifference of the media, and competition for staff time from such other demands as defending the church from lawsuits. Moreover, many Anglicans concluded that they could work more effectively for social justice and world development by giving their time and money to non-governmental organizations with greater focus, expertise, and resources. For instance, thanks in significant part to its Anglican president, staff members, directors, and donors, World Vision Canada waxed while the Primate's World Relief and Development Fund waned.

In the 1990s, it became known that many children had been abused in Indian residential schools administered in earlier years by the ACC under agreements with the government of Canada (Miller 1996). By the end of 2002, claims and lawsuits had been filed by about 1,350 Anglican residential school survivors against the ACC and Canada. The denomination felt conflicted between its concern for persons whom it had injured and its desire to survive financially. In 2003, the ACC and Canada struck a deal on the sharing of liability that protected the ACC financially but was not entirely equitable to the survivors, who would be required to navigate a complex, slow, and sometimes humiliating claims process, if indeed their claims were qualified at all. Before reaching this agreement, ACC officials did not consult the Anglican Council of Indigenous People. The agreement was revised in 2006 and wrapped into an omnibus Indian Residential Schools Settlement Agreement, the largest class action settlement in Canadian history. The federal government has assumed most of the responsibility for restoration and reconciliation under this settlement.

Discussions gained traction in the 1970s as to whether the ACC should ordain gay and lesbian clergy and bless same-sex unions (after 2005 in Canada, same-sex marriages), and by the 1990s these had become principal topics at meetings of general synod, the House of Bishops, and the Primate's Theological Commission, as well as in the denominational press. Not only was it impossible for Anglicans to reach consensus on the issues, but they could hardly agree on the proper arenas and procedures for discussion, or on how far the views of the wider Anglican Communion should be taken into account. Conversations were further complicated by the fact that disagreements on sexuality frequently camouflaged other, perhaps deeper disagreements on religious identity and authority, theological method, culture, styles of leadership, and personality. In 2003, the Diocese of New Westminster, on its own accord, publicly authorized the blessing of same-sex unions, provoking the separation of some parish churches (including St. John's, Shaughnessy, Vancouver, reputedly the largest and wealthiest in the country), and widening fissures in the worldwide Anglican Communion. Since then, 50 parish churches, dissatisfied with liberal trends in the ACC, perhaps particularly in matters of sexuality, have seceded, and have joined a breakaway diocese called the Anglican Network in Canada, part of the Anglican Church in North America (http://www.anglicannetwork.ca/member_parish.htm). Court decisions to settle competing claims of property between ACC and former parishes have consistently favored the ACC.

Today, the ACC faces many of the same challenges and opportunities as it did in 1963. The Toronto Anglican Congress exposed numerous fault-lines running through the ACC and across the Anglican Communion: between maintaining Anglican traditions and moving out ecumenically; between British–American dominance and Third

World equality; between top-down ecclesiologies and bottom-up ecclesiologies; between liturgical tradition and liturgical updating; and between the two missionary visions of changing the world and changing the individual. Disagreements in matters of sexuality have revealed further fault-lines. One involves the ACC's relationship to the Anglican Communion. While there are intermediate positions, a line separates those who affirm the ACC's national identity, cultural context, independence, and mission, and would be pleased for the ACC to take its own path apart from the Anglican Communion, and those who believe that only a greater accountability to the Anglican Communion can counter the ACC's historic drift to cultural assimilation.

In past disputes, the ACC has been able to comprehend diversity in the long run, but in the short run the contesting of Anglican identity has very often led to bad feeling, institutionalized division, or schism (Katerberg 2001). If the way forward is to confront disagreement, then effective leadership, theological wisdom, and ample room for prayerful conversation will be necessary. However, Canadian Anglicans may decide that the problems of Anglican identity and policy are, in the end, too subsidiary and self-referential to justify devoting so much energy to them. Another way forward may be to raise the ACC's sense of the critical needs of the wider world and the demands of mission, which was the direction taken by the Toronto Anglican Congress. Another way forward may be through a spiritual broadening of horizons which, in Canada, may come from First Nations Anglicans.

# Bibliography

Anglican Church of Canada. 1985. *Book of Alternative Services*. Toronto: Anglican Book Centre.

Anglican Book of Canada. 1962. *Book of Common Prayer*. Toronto: Oxford University Press.

Anglican National Commission. 1931. *The Report of the Field Commissioners*. Toronto: Church of England in Canada.

Boon, Thomas C. B. 1962. *The Anglican Church from the Bay to the Rockies*. Toronto: Ryerson Press.

Carrington, Philip. 1963. *The Anglican Church in Canada*. Toronto: Collins.

Clarke, Brian and Stuart Macdonald. 2010. "Working Paper – Anglican Church of Canada Statistics." http://individual.utoronto.ca/clarkemacdonald/clarkemacdonald/Welcome_files/anglicanchurch.pdf

Fahey, Curtis. 1991. *In His Name: The Anglican Experience in Upper Canada, 1791–1854*. Ottawa: Carleton University Press.

Hayes, Alan L., ed. 1989. *By Grace Co-Workers: Building the Anglican Diocese of Toronto, 1780–1989*. Toronto: Anglican Book Centre.

Hayes, Alan L. 2004. *Anglicans in Canada: Controversies and Identity in Historical Perspective*. Urbana and Chicago: University of Illinois Press.

Katerberg, William. 2001. *Modernity and the Dilemma of North American Anglican Identities, 1880–1950*. Montreal and Kingston: McGill Queen's University Pres.

Knowles, Norman, ed. 2008. *Seeds Scattered and Sown: Studies in the History of Canadian Anglicanism*. Toronto: Anglican Book Centre.

Miller, J. R. 1996. *Shingwauk's Vision: A History of Native Residential Schools*. Toronto: University of Toronto Press.

Millman, Thomas R. and A. R. Kelley. 1983. *Atlantic Canada to 1900: A History of the Anglican Church*. Toronto: Anglican Book Centre.

Peake, Frank A. 1959. *The Anglican Church in British Columbia*. Vancouver: Mitchell Press.

Peake, Frank A. 1989. *From the Red River to the Arctic: Essays on Anglican Missionary Expansion in the Nineteenth Century*. Toronto: Canadian Church Historical Society.

Shortt, Adam and Arthur G. Doughty. 1918. *Documents Relating to the Constitutional History of Canada, 1759–1791*. Ottawa: J. de L. Taché.

Vaudry, Richard. 2003. *Anglicans and the Atlantic World: High Churchmen, Evangelicals, and the Quebec Connection*. Montreal and Kingston: McGill Queen's University Press.

Westfall, William. 1989. *Two Worlds: The Protestant Culture of Nineteenth-Century Ontario*. Toronto: McGill-Queen's University Press.

CHAPTER 44

# Iglesia Anglicana de la Región Central de América

## Ricardo F. Blanco-Beledo

## History of the Anglican Church in the Province

The Province of the Central Region of America occupies the territory between the North of Colombia and the South of Mexico. It covers the following countries that by themselves are independent dioceses: Costa Rica, El Salvador, Guatemala, Nicaragua, and Panama. Even though Belize and Honduras are geographically located within the area, they do not belong to the province. As a matter of fact, during the IV Provincial Synod of IARCA celebrated during April 15 and 16, 2010, the Most Rev. Martin de Jesus Barahona, primate bishop of the region at the time, hoped that both Belize and Honduras would become part of the Anglican Church in the Central Region of America, precisely because of their location.

The Church of England's influences on the origins of the Province of the Central Region of America are diverse and, in some cases, common. The arrival of African people during the eighteenth and nineteenth centuries, many of whom were English speakers and educated in the Church of England, led to the presence of the church in the region. Another influence during the nineteenth century was groups of British who settled in the area mainly for commercial reasons. Mostly, there was neither integration nor good relationships between these two original large groups. Caribbean groups migrated primarily from Barbados, Belize, Jamaica, and other islands influenced by the British Empire either political or economically. The most important non-English-speaking exception was the Misquito people, who constituted an independent kingdom in the present Nicaragua. The economic reasons for these migrations arose with the onset of railroad and agricultural activities in the Central Region of America, as well as the start of the activities for the construction of the Panama Canal.

*The Wiley-Blackwell Companion to the Anglican Communion*, First Edition. Edited by Ian S. Markham,
J. Barney Hawkins IV, Justyn Terry, and Leslie Nuñez Steffensen.
© 2013 John Wiley & Sons, Ltd. Published 2013 by John Wiley & Sons, Ltd.

In 1957, the administration of the church in the region changed from the Church of England through the West Indies to the Protestant Episcopal Church in the United States of America (ECUSA). This event coincided with the growth of economic and political interests of the United States in Central America. In 1998, ECUSA granted autonomy to the region of Central America, provided that the standards and working criteria that were controlled by the ECUSA for more than 40 years were maintained.

We shall briefly comment on the particular history of the Church of England in each of the countries that are part of this province.

## Costa Rica

In 1851, the Church of England began a ministry to serve the English-speaking migrants in Costa Rica. This chaplaincy ended in 1947 when it was transferred to ECUSA. The Diocese of Costa Rica was later founded as an extra-provincial diocese in 1970.

Here, there is a long history of chaplaincies. The year 1864 is pointed out as the beginning of the first Protestant church services in the country. Dr. Richard Brealey and Captain William Le Lacheur may be acknowledged, in 1837 and 1843, respectively, among the precursors of this movement. The services started, as usual, in private houses, which led to the founding of the Congregation of the Good Shepherd in 1865, which is considered the first Protestant church in Costa Rica.

In 1896, the Bishop of Belize (who later exercised episcopal jurisdiction over Costa Rica) appointed two clergymen, one for San Jose and one for the province of Limón. In 1909, he suggested that the Diocese of Costa Rica be placed under the jurisdiction of Panama. However, it was not until 1930 that this process began. It lasted until 1947 when the missionary responsibility of the Episcopal Church in Costa Rica was transferred to the ECUSA. The presiding bishop in the United States then delegated responsibility to the Bishop of Panama. In 1958, missionary David Richards was appointed to take charge of the missionary district of Central America, settling in San Jose, Costa Rica.

Several achievements were accomplished during this period, among which the opening of a seminary for theological education in the Municipality of Siquirres, which played a key role in the process of autonomy, must be highlighted. Its origin is set in 1957, when the Diocese of Central America came under the ecclesiastical jurisdiction of the ECUSA and subsequently formed the Missionary District of Central America. In 1967, dioceses were established corresponding to the countries which make up the region.

## El Salvador

Anglicanism has a relatively short history in El Salvador. The antecedents were established during the year 1931. The Mission of San Juan Evangelista, established on March 15, 1957, was the first one set up by ECUSA.

There were two congregations, "Saint John" for foreigners and "San Juan" for the locals. In the meantime, parishioner wives of businessmen and diplomats founded the CREFAC (Educative, Family and Christian Reorientation Center), which was in charge of providing the needy with help and support, raising funds for scholarships, and providing clothing, among other activities. The Rev. Ramiro Chávez was a member of the CREFAC board for more than ten years. By the end of the 1960s, the CREFAC became independent from the church, and now its name is Centro de Reorientación Familiar y Comunitaria.

The Rev. Edward Haynesworth, now bishop, was the first who administered the church – from 1961 until December 1963, when the Rev. Jess Petty took his place, to be followed in 1972 by the Rev. Luis Serrano.

In 1971, the Rev. Onell established in San Salvador the provincial office of the ninth province of the Episcopal Church. There were only two priests, Father Soto and Luis Serrano Onell, without any bishop in charge.

Politically speaking, it was a very troubled time. The Rev. Luis Serrano created CREDHO (Concientización para la Recuperación Espiritual y Económica del Hombre) with the aim to establish the beginning of a path to liberation, through raising awareness about certain life conditions. Hacienda la Florida in Santa Ana, which still exists, provided psychological care. In 1975, CREDHO obtained legal authority and legal independence from the church.

As part of the military offensive that hit the country, in 1989 Rev. Luis Serrano suffered 45 days in prison for merely exercising his ministry. By the 1990s, with the signing of the Peace Treaties, the country changed; the church focused more than ever on the marginalized and pastoral work. In 1991, Martin Barahona was ordained the first Bishop of Salvador, with his episcopate continuing to this day.

# Guatemala

In 1867, English-speaking chaplaincies began in this region. The next phase of development was in 1957, when administrative jurisdiction was transferred from the Antilles to the missionary district of the Episcopal Church in Central America.

New missions were initiated: San Juan del Trébol in 1963, the Espíritu Santo mission in 1965, San Pedro y San Pablo in 1970, and San Juan Bautista in 1972. In 1975, the Thomas Cranmer Elementary School was founded.

A noteworthy project to mention is LIFE, which began in 1971, for thousands of Kekchi Indians and mestizos living in conditions of extreme poverty, to supply land (bought with the help of the visiting Bishop of California), and to produce cassava, corn, and sugar cane for sustenance and community development. Many farms and living spaces were built, as well as a medical clinic and places of worship.

In 1974, the construction of the first permanent church, San Esteban, began in the lake zone of Mariscos. In 1975, the church of San Marcos was founded.

The Most Rev. Armando Guerra Soria has been Bishop of Guatemala for 30 years.

# Nicaragua

The Moravians were very successful in establishing a protestant structure in this country. Many immigrants from different countries have settled here, many of them Anglicans; as a result, a priest was requested from the ECUSA. The Anglican Church in Nicaragua officially became part of the ECUSA in 1946. In 1967, the five republics of Central America created one united diocese under the care and jurisdiction of Bishop David Richards. After 11 years, Nicaragua became its own independent missionary diocese in province IX of the Episcopal Church.

# Panama

In 1853, the construction of the church of "Cristo a la Orilla del Mar" began. It was completed and consecrated in 1865.

In 1872, the railroad company changed its policy and withdrew its economic support for the chaplaincy; as a result, the church suffered a major setback. After 1876, priests were not sent to Panama for a long period of time, which contributed to local mistrust of the style of Anglican work.

Towards 1882, with a high presence of African Caribbean English-speaking workers, the Bishop of the Antilles requested that the Church of England send them a minister. This petition resulted in the transfer of two missionaries of the South American Missionary Society from Jamaica to Panama the following year.

Until 1903, the work of the Anglican Church was under the direction of the Church of England. In 1903, all missionary work was transferred to the supervision of the ECUSA. In 1919, nine new missions were established.

In 1947, the missionary district was expanded in a way that included the work of the Church of England in the rest of Panama, Costa Rica, and Nicaragua, and, in 1956, Guatemala, Honduras, and El Salvador were added to this jurisdiction. However, the jurisdiction was too wide because it came to include the Republic of Colombia as well. In 1964, the boundaries were redesigned to be more manageable and the diocese only extended to the Panama Canal region.

In 1971, the Venerable Lemuel B. Shirley was elected as the fourth missionary bishop, the first native Panamanian, and the first of African descent.

The implementation of the Panama Treaty made it possible for the church to go from the Missionary District of the Panama Canal to the Missionary Diocese of Panama and Canal Zone, and finally reach the current status of the Diocese of Panama.

# Relationship of the Church with Indigenous/Traditional Cultures and Religions

As indicated, the history of the Anglican Church begins with chaplaincies and churches established to meet the spiritual needs of foreigners and immigrants. This, without a doubt, limited the influence of the church with the indigenous cultures and local traditions where churches were settled. It often resulted in mistrust of the church, which led to questioning of the influence of Britain and the United States, and above all questions of foreign political interference in the area.

However, many good works were carried out in the Central American region – projects such as schools, literacy programs, and vocational training – to give marginalized populations access to the work. This allowed the poor and indigenous in the region to achieve a higher standard of living and bridge the cultural and societal gaps of the region.

In the initial years, Anglican chapels only offered religious services in English; for obvious reasons, this separated the church from new possible local converts.

Between 1958 and 1969, with the support of Lambeth, new and serious efforts to create an indigenous, self-governing national church were undertaken.

Today, there are not only religious services in English, but also in Spanish; in indigenous Mayan languages such as Quiché, Kekchí, and Carchiquel; and also in Garúfuna, an African language of the Caribbean.

## Story of the Contemporary Church

A covenant between the Iglesia Anglicana of the Central Region of America (IARCA) and the Protestant ECUSA, signed in July 1997, created the foundations for true autonomy for the Province of Central America.

The requirements for autonomy were established by the general convention, among them being a provincial constitution and canons approved by the convention and the support of the ECUSA.

The metropolitan authority for the Diocese of the Central Region of America was transferred from the general convention to the general synod of the Anglican Church of the Central Region of America (IARCA).

This autonomy does not mean sacrificing the support set out in the mission of the IARCA and the ECUSA, which agreed to participate together actively in evangelism, Christian education, theological and liturgical studies, stewardship training, and a diverse number of programs for minorities, women, youth, and children. Ecumenical participation was also established and strengthened in these countries and for the rest of the world.

The autonomy granted is only possible with economic independence; in this sense, the covenant establishes six basic points:

I.    The ECUSA will continue to contribute to the general budget of the IARCA for a period of 40 years with a gradual reduction of 1% to 5%, according to the yearly appropriation of 1994. This reduction would be effective in the set date of the autonomy, established for July 1, 2001.

      This resolution can be revised as stated by current situations by the Executive Committee of the ECUSA and the Provincial Council of the IARCA.

II.     As with the ECUSA, the IARCA, with the advice and cooperation of the Church Pension Fund will create a pension plan for clergy and lay employees.

III.    ECUSA will reimburse the IARCA with the funds and interest proportioned from the property sale of the Episcopal Seminary of the Caribbean, as well as the sale of books from its library preserved in the Episcopal Seminary of the Southwest in Austin, Texas.

IV.     ESUSA will assist the IARCA and its dioceses technologically to develop the administration of its programs and the growth of capital for the expansion of missionary work.

V.      The Anglican Church of the Central Region of America will establish rules in each diocese for financial maintenance, to draft budgets, audits, restrictions, and reports to set procedures for the account organization of the Province.

VI.     The Anglican Church of the Central Region of America will draft annual financial reports to the ECUSA until only 50% of its appropriations are provided by the ECUSA.

Canon I, section 3, with respect to organization and administration, establishes "This Anglican Church of the Central Region of America . . . will have a synod made up of a House of Bishops, and a House of Priests, Deacons and Laity that will meet and deliberate together or separate when it is necessary."

The IV Synod of the IARCA met in Panama on April 15 and 16, 2010.

## Leadership and Description of Services and Outreach

Until the year 2010, the IARCA was presided over by His Grace, the Most Rev. Martin Barahona. In his administration, he attended the primates meeting held in Brazil and the general convention of the ECUSA in July and August of 2003. The present primate, since 2010, is His Grace, the Most Rev. Armando Guerra Soria, Bishop of Guatemala.

During the provincial council's regular meeting (Managua, Nicaragua, June 8 and 9, 2004), support and power were given to the Anglican Center for Superior Theological Studies (CAETS), which has a mission to "form, in an integral manner, leadership from clergy and laity, providing certification in accordance to the courses that are offered."

In the IV Synod (Panama, April 15 and 16, 2010), the Most Rev. Armando R. Guerra Soria was elected as primate and the Most Rev. Julio Ernesto Murray Thompson as vice president of the House of Bishops in the provincial council.

The current provincial council has the following members – Nicaragua: the Rt. Rev. George Porter and Mrs. Carolina Salgado Castillo; Guatemala: the Rev. Ramón Ovalle and Mr. Henry E. Martinez; Costa Rica: the Rev. Pedro Mendez; El Salvador: the Rev. Julio Rivera and Mrs. Ana Emilia Gomez; and Panama: the Rev. Nelson Edwards and Juris Doctor Mycol Morgan.

With respect to current situations and achievements in each diocese of the province, it is necessary to refer to each situation individually.

The Episcopal Church in Costa Rica has three provinces: San José, Heredia, and Limón. It has three full parishes and 17 congregations.

The mission of the Heredia province was founded on June 30, 2004. Each parish has a rector, and there are priests-in-charge at each church and mission.

The Diocese of Costa Rica is headed by the Most Rev. Héctor Monterroso, who attended the regular meeting of the provincial council of the IARCA, held in Managua, Nicaragua, on June 8 and 9, 2004, and presented the report of his diocese. The Most Rev. Monterroso has worked diligently in the expansion of the church and has attempted to increase its reach across the entire country.

One of the most difficult challenges is confronting the financial deficit, which in the past years has resulted in the diocese's lack of support for CAETS, the capitalization fund, and the inability to meet provincial quotas.

This report led to the creation of a commission during the meeting. Mrs. Ana Emilia Gomez, member of the commission and representative of Costa Rica, presented the resolution submitted, which included the proportioning of a loan of solidarity to the diocese mentioned.

This was a major step in connecting the diocese with the rest of the Province of the Central Region of America, because it affirmed solidarity and mutual support in difficult times, and since the province functioned as a team, it made it possible for the Diocese of Costa Rica to get through this difficult period.

On March 26, 2012, in the church of Buen Pastor, the Rev. Arturo Morales became the first minister in the Diocese of Costa Rica to receive the honorary title of canon.

Also notable is the work of Mrs. Martha Davis, who until May 14, 2012 (being one year in office), acted in the position of senior fellowship program director for maintaining the Diocese of Costa Rica and North Carolina.

At the regular meeting mentioned in the preceding text, the Most Rev. Monterroso's report mentioned the visit of six groups from the Diocese of North Carolina, making it clear how this companionship has flourished between the dioceses.

Also notable is the work of Father Ricardo Bernal, who led the CAET. Last April, the CAET held a graduation of ten participants in the pastoral counseling program, which is a course program of two years, and which works with Latin American Biblical University to provide corresponding diplomas and degrees based on the work accomplished.

The Most Rev. Martin Barahona presented El Salvador's report. El Salvador has eight clergy serving four diocesan-assisted congregations, two organized missions, and 16 missionary centers. The dollarization and the high cost of living have decreased the incomes of the majority of parishioners. One of the hopes of the church of El Salvador is to create a university-level school of theology. A director would be needed for the school. Another goal is to be present in three more provinces of the country. El Salvador has also established a companion diocese relationship with four dioceses of the United States, and there are two legal institutions that support the work in the missionary fields of El Salvador.

The Most Rev. Armando Guerra presented the report of the Diocese of Guatemala. In 2004, an English-speaking mission was established in Antigua. The average income of the lay members was presented, a goal to stabilize the finances of the church was established, and an audit was carried out with the support of the Episcopal Church headquarters in New York. The final goal was to explore the idea of creating two more dioceses. The diocese was in the process of investing in the rubber industry to increase its economic resources. Also presented was the creation of a pilot project for a school at an elementary level and the eventual aim of establishing a university. Each region of the diocese has a theological education coordinator. The national priesthood council maintains a good relationship with the Roman Catholic Church.

In the 43rd convention of the Episcopal Church Diocese of Guatemala, held in Xelajú, Quetzaltenango, on November 20 and 21, 2009, a resolution was passed to create two new dioceses (which came in time to be represented in the fourth synod of the IARCA). The Diocese of Guatemala has regionalized its work as follows: South Central (Guatemala, Escuintla, Santa Rosa, and Suchitepéquez), West (Quetzaltenango, Totonicapan, Solola, Quiche, and Chimaltenango), and Northeast (Izabal, Zacapa, and Chiquimula). With the success of the decentralization of the diocese, the central southern region was maintained as the original diocese of the country.

Along with the diocesan convention, several committees were presented which organize work in addressing, developing, and accelerating the achievement of development strategies of the diocese. The following committees currently work in the diocese: Finances, Theological Education, Clerical Counseling, Ministry, Women of the Central Region, Women of the Northwest, PREPIFEM, Women's Presidency and Leadership, Emergency Council, Global Commission, and Local Commission of IARCA. As seen here, the Diocese of Guatemala is the most organized within the province in terms of its structure, and this is even evident in its website.

In the report to the Council of the Anglican Province of the Central Region of America, presented in San Salvador, El Salvador, April 7–10, 2008, the Episcopal Church of Guatemala cited lack of economic resources (a common issue for this region) as one of the reasons why the commissions had implemented cuts of 60 percent of planning and 50 percent of congregational budgets. As a result, finances had to be adjusted by various measures including the reduction and elimination of subsidies for diocesan institutions and a freeze on hiring personnel, except for those positions deemed essential.

Among many companion diocese relationships, Pennsylvania and Belize were mentioned as the strongest.

Also mentioned were the implementation of the Ecumenical Forum for Peace and Reconciliation as a non-profit organization and the achievement of legal recognition under the Christian Ecumenical Council. Also, the Diocese of Guatemala continues as a witness of unity through the Latin American Council of Churches.

Among the associated institutions with the church, the following were mentioned: St. Stephen Episcopal Camp, Canterbury High School, and Episcopal School of Laity and Seminary.

In the global plan and development strategy of the diocese for the period from 2011 to 2013, the following regional correspondents were established in each area: clerical motivation: the Most Rev. Armando Guerra; music: the Rev. P. Ramon Ovalle; family ministry: the Rev. P. Miguel Salanic; Anglican identity: Suffragan Bishop Carlos Enrique

Lainfiesta; leadership: the Rev. P. Juan Jose Salazar; stewardship: Laura Sandova; and publicity: Juris Dr. Juan Jose Hernandez Molina.

The Anglican Church of Nicaragua is presided over by the Most Rev. Sturdie Downs. In the report that was presented in the regular meeting of the provincial council in 2004, the necessity to increase the number of ordained ministers was emphasized. A scholarship is available to university students who are active in the church. San Marcos Academy is, without a doubt, one of most noteworthy achievements; also mentioned was the increase in tuition at the academy. The first cathedral of the diocese is San Marcos in Bluefields. In the northern pacific region, medical service is provided. Academies are equipped with computer laboratories. Stewardship is a subject of interest, and new missions are always being established.

The Diocese of Panama is headed by the Most Rev. Julio Murray. In the report presented to the appointment meeting, the establishment of the six regions was emphasized. In each region, there is a coordinator and a co-coordinator. The Nehemiah program offers help to construction projects, whether in full or partial erection of buildings. With this assistance, the repairs of the chapel and parish house were carried out in Bocas del Toro. The subject of healthcare is very important in the region; for this reason, doctors perform medical tours to bring clean and safe healthcare to those who, for a variety of reasons, do not have access to adequate medical attention. A medical clinic was established. On April 15, 2004, contracts were signed for new properties in the area of the Panama Canal. Mrs. Elsa Shambo, motivated by the need for economic resources for the church, led a collection of empty cans and their sale. With this initiative, environmental concerns were promoted, as well as support for recycling and the obvious monetary gains. Two new deacons have been ordained. The Rev. Luis Felipe Cáceres is in charge of family pastoral care in three congregations.

## Contemporary Issues Facing the Province

Many of the situations faced by the Province of the Central Region of America are not foreign to what is faced by the Anglican Communion as a whole. As it is always necessary to bring the church closer to the community, the following issues are often the focus of the church: support for marginalized sectors; promoting education, whether it be religious or secular; participation in current societal issues; participation in the debate of ideas and projects that affect present-day society; working with infants; addressing the lack of education and career opportunities for youth; fighting discrimination against women and the homosexual community; and support for the elderly.

Nevertheless, taking as a reference the resolutions and recommendations given during the IV Provincial Synod (Ciudad de Saber-Antiguo Fuerte Clayton, Panama, Republic of Panama, April 15 and 16, 2010), we can see the points that are most worrisome to society today.

Among them, without a doubt, is the concern over lack of economic resources. It is, therefore, important to develop stewardship activities and training for congregational treasurers, create and share accounting material and the maintenance of finances, as well as to develop greater commitment of clergy and education about tithing. Ecological stewardship is also important, by implementing environmental projects and promoting unity with other organizations that work with these concerns.

The education of the faithful should be promoted and be continuous. The CAETS should expand on the necessary content and provide the materials. The objective is to involve the ordained ministry with the laity.

Minorities such as women, youth, migrants, and elderly are also on the agenda of the IARCA. With respect to women, the promise to continue to support them has been maintained, seeking to give them a voice and integration into ordained ministry in the church.

The youth deserve their space and to be heard. It is logical to attempt to integrate them into the church because the majority of the local population presently consists of young people. Therefore, it should be a primary concern to reinitiate programs of youth ministry. Also, it was resolved that CAETS will provide education and training for leaders with a focus on developing youth ministry. A request was sent in 2012 to CETALC in a Latin American regional meeting to initiate more involvement with the youth ministry.

Since 2004, the Rev. Lainfiesta has raised the issue of gaps and unforeseen issues in the constitutions and canons of the IARCA and has since advocated that the commission of canons, presided over by the chancellor of the province, perform all respective revisions and add all the necessary modifications. This work is difficult and therefore requires constant updating.

The Most Rev. Primate Armando Guerra, in a public interview with "Episcopalians in Action, 5th edition" (2001), mentions some of the objectives over the course of the next four years – the major integration of the province, new forms of finances and budgets, pastoral visits to every diocese, consolidation of the province, and greater participation in areas such as social life, ethics, and the economy.

## Connection with the World-Wide Anglican Communion

Resolution X adopted by the IV Provincial Synod is based on the importance of communication between provinces. In this regard, it insists that each diocese update and revise its web pages. It proposed the creation of a province-wide bulletin that serves to present the province to the greater Anglican community. Additionally, it included the management of a provincial radio stream by the end of 2012 at the latest.

Each diocese of the IARCA has established contact with its companion dioceses, has worked together with their partners, and has received the necessary support.

With regard to the covenant between the Episcopal Church and the Church of Central America (TEC-IARCA), the Primate Bishop Armando Guerra expressed a sentiment of frustration to the authorities of the Episcopal Church to honor their end of the agreement.

The Diocese of Guatemala has close fraternal relations with Pennsylvania and Belize. In November 2010, representatives of the Diocese of Newark visited the Diocese of Panama. The Episcopal Church of Costa Rica has maintained for over 12 years a relationship of close fellowship with North Carolina, which has taken part in various missionary programs.

## Conclusion / Possible Future

The Province of the Central Region of America is a relatively new organization. The province is working on organizational and financial systems that will bring more members to the church, and continuing to promote activities and events that help the needy. The differences and diversities that exist even among the member countries of the region make the task even more arduous. There is consensus that there should be first a strong bond of union among the member countries to present a cohesive institution to the rest of the Anglican Communion, a goal that is still present and is highlighted in each regular meeting. There is high regard for this province from the other provinces in the Latin American subcontinent.

## Bibliography

A Covenant between the Anglican Church of the Central Region of America (IARCA) and the Protestant Episcopal Church in the United States of America (ECUSA), July 1997.

Acta del IV Sínodo Provincial de IARCA, Panamá 15 y 16 de Abril 2010.

Brooks, Ashton J., ed. 1990. *Eclesiología, presencia anglicana en la Región Central de América.* Editorial DEI, Costa Rica.

Guerra, Armando R. 2005m. Un análisis de la presencia del Anglicanismo en Latinoamérica. In *La Globalización y sus implicaciones en América Latina: Un desafío para la Iglesia Episcopal Anglicana.* Ed. CETALC, Memorias del Congreso de Teología de Panamá.

Iglesia Anglicana de la Región Central de América; Reunión Ordinaria del Consejo Provincial, Managua, Nicaragua, 8 y 9 de Junio de 2004.

Iglesia Anglicana de la Región Central de América; Reunión Ordinaria del Consejo Provincial, Panamá, 16 y 17 de agosto 2005.

Informe al Consejo de la Provincia Anglicana de la Región Central de América, San Salvador, El Salvador Abril 7-10 2008. Iglesia Episcopal de Guatemala.

Informe Secretaría Provincial. 2011. IARCA Marzo 15 y 16, San Salvador.

Las Resoluciones y Recomendaciones, IV Sínodo Provincial, 2010, 15 y 16 de Abril 2010.

Milmine, Douglas. 1993. *La Comunión Anglicana en América Latina.* Talleres Banca Gráfica (sin datos de país).

Plan de Trabajo 2006, IARCA, 2005, Costa Rica.

Plan Global de Estrategia y Desarrollo Diocesano 2011 a 2013. Diócesis de Guatemala.

Resolución I, Iglesia Episcopal de Guatemala Noviembre 2009

Sykes, Stephen and John Booty, eds. 1988. *The Study of Anglicanism.* UK: SPCK.

Ward, Kevin. 2006. *A History of Global Anglicanism.* Cambridge: Cambridge University Press.

# CHAPTER 45

# The Anglican Church of Mexico (La Iglesia Anglicana de México)

## John A. Macdonald

Location:  Mexico
Dioceses:  Diocese of Mexico (1874): The Most Rev. Carlos Touché Porter
           Diocese of Northern Mexico (1973): The Rt. Rev. Francisco Moreno
           Diocese of Western Mexico (1973): The Rt. Rev. Lino Rodríguez Amaro
           Diocese of Cuernavaca (1989): The Rt. Rev. James H. Ottley (Interim)
           Diocese of the Southeast (1989): The Rt. Rev. Benito Juárez Martínez (México)

The Anglican Church of Mexico is comprised of five dioceses, each with its own diocesan bishop, one of whom is the province's presiding bishop. The provincial boundaries are defined by the boundaries of the country of Mexico.

## Early History

Anglican worship first took place in 1869 when North Americans and British personnel arrived to work in the railroad and mining industries. They requested that Anglican worship services be offered in English. In 1882, Christ Church in Mexico City was organized. In the subsequent years, additional English-speaking congregations were started. By 1904, there were enough churches that they were organized into the Missionary District of Mexico. The focus of these churches remained on the English-speaking, expatriate communities (Porter 2012).

During the same period, another significant theological movement was taking place. In 1857, Mexico passed the Laws of Reform and the Political Constitution, which gave religious liberty to the entire country. No longer were Mexicans required to be exclusively Roman Catholic. A group of Roman Catholic priests, known as the Constitutional Fathers, publicly supported the reforms and were therefore excommu-

*The Wiley-Blackwell Companion to the Anglican Communion*, First Edition. Edited by Ian S. Markham, J. Barney Hawkins IV, Justyn Terry, and Leslie Nuñez Steffensen.
© 2013 John Wiley & Sons, Ltd. Published 2013 by John Wiley & Sons, Ltd.

nicated. Part of their motivation for leaving the Roman Catholic Church was because they were not politically aligned with the conservatives who backed the traditional socio-political order (Miller 2008, 43). The Liberals, under the leadership of President Benito Juárez, produced a constitution in 1857 that severely restricted the Roman Catholic clergy and eliminated many of the legal privileges they had enjoyed for centuries. Two years later, Juárez had many church properties sold off at auction, which introduced a decade of political instability (Miller 2008, 45). Such was the climate at the time that the group was able to purchase the Roman Catholic Church building, San José de la Gracia, with funds from the United States. This church building eventually became the Episcopal Cathedral in Mexico City (*The Reformation in Mexico* 1894, 6).

The Church of Jesus, which was the name they more consistently used, formed their own church in 1861. The church was also known at times as the Mexican Episcopal Church (Porter 2012) and the Mexican Catholic Apostolic Society (Smith 2000). At their start, they numbered 7,000 members (Johnson 1963, 356). In their manifesto published in the liberal newspaper *Monitor Republicano*, the founders attacked the Roman Catholic Church, calling it an "erroneous sect," that they had suffered the abuse of its prelates and high-ranking clergy who had "sordid interest" in temporal goods which had caused the loss of prestige in the church. The group of clergy requested that President Juárez protect them from the attacks of the church and that reform and security be established (Mondragón 2005, translation mine). The aim at the time was to create a Mexican Catholic Church, but this apparently failed because the leaders contacted various Protestant denominations for funding to assist them in the establishment of new congregations under the protection of the Laws of Reform. The church that provided the most sympathy for the Mexican clergy was the Episcopal Church (Mondragón 2005). President Juárez, recognizing the important place of this group, commented, "I would like that there be a Mexican expression of Protestantism in order to improve the quality of life [The word used is *conquistar*, which is translated directly as 'conquer.' However, the meaning intended is to express an improvement of the quality of life – not subjugation by conquest.] for the Indians. They need a religion that obligates them to read and does not require them to spend their savings in votive candles for the saints" (Mondragón 2005).

In an unpublished paper produced in the year 2000, Jim C. Smith notes that, nearly from the beginning, the society had ties to the American Episcopal Church and Anglicanism. They used the Bible as the doctrinal base, allowed clergy to marry, and held services in Spanish using the Book of Common Prayer (Smith 2000). The current Presiding Bishop and Bishop of Mexico, Carlos Touché Porter, writes, "This brought about that the Mexican Church, then independent and isolated, learned more about the Anglican tradition and subsequently decided to become fully joined" (Porter 2012, translation mine).

One of the leaders of the reform movement was the Rev. Manuel Aguas. Aguas had been canon at the Roman Catholic Cathedral in Mexico City and a popular preacher. He had been asked to do what he could to stifle the reform movement. Instead of stifling it, he was converted and took over the leadership of the nascent church in 1871. In a public letter, he wrote:

> I . . . dedicated myself to the study of all the Protestant books and pamphlets that I could lay my hands on. I carefully read the *History of the Reformation of the Sixteenth Century* by Merle D'Aubigne, and, above all, I commenced to study the Bible. . . . This study, from the moment that it was accompanied by earnest prayer, led me to true happiness. I commenced to see the light. The Lord had pity on me, and enabled me to clearly understand the great truths of the Gospel (Aguas 1871).

Aguas not only organized the church, his preaching and public witness led to many new members joining and new congregations being founded (*The Reformation in Mexico* 1894, 7–8). Aguas was strongly evangelistic in his work, and while that contributed to church growth, it also increased the tensions with the Roman Catholic Church, some of whose members responded violently (Smith 2000). That year, he was elected the first bishop of the church with the expectation that he would be consecrated by the Americans. However, this did not take place, and Aguas died unexpectedly the following year (*The Reformation in Mexico* 1894, 8). The American Church Missionary Society took responsibility for supporting the church and the American missionaries who were there. While there was intercommunion, it was not until the early years of the twentieth century that full integration between the Church of Jesus and the Episcopal Church took place (Porter 2012).

The Episcopal Church in the United States remained interested in what was going on in Mexico. The House of Bishops formed a Mexican Commission in 1879, and the Acting Chairman was the Bishop of Delaware, Alfred Lee. The bishop reported that the Church of Jesus in Mexico had "grown up into an important community of Christians, who worship the Lord in spirit and truth. Two Dioceses have been organized, one in the vale of Mexico and the other with its centre in Cuernavaca" (Lee 1879, 1). There were six Presbyters, six ministers who were ready for ordination, and several other candidates for the ministry. Each congregation had a lay reader. He reported that there were about 3,500 members (Lee 1879, 1). The bishop added that the Bible and the prayer book were becoming more prevalent in Mexican homes and that the church seemed to be more suited for rural members than urban ones (Lee 1879, 2). The commission's final recommendations were that the Church of Jesus submit their constitution and to "be instant in prayer on behalf of the persecuted Church in Mexico and its Bishops elect . . ." (Lee 1879, 4).

An American priest who had spent considerable years in Chile, the Rev. Henry C. Riley, gave substantial assistance to the Church in Mexico, not only in terms of his time and presence but also in financial support. In 1874, the church had asked for a bishop to be consecrated. As a result of the report given by the Bishop of Delaware five years later, the Rev. Henry C. Riley was consecrated the first bishop of the autonomous Church in Mexico (Creighton 1929, 1). Once consecrated in the United States, Bishop Riley did not return to Mexico for two years. Upon his return, he found the church in disarray. For the next five years, his poor administration nearly caused the demise of the church. In the end, he resigned, and the church came under the jurisdiction of the American Episcopal presiding bishop (Creighton 1929, 2).

By 1894, the Mexican Church had only seven priests, two deacons, and 22 congregations. There were ten parochial schools with that same number of teachers for 400 students, 60 percent of which were girls. It is reported that there were about 1,000 communicants (*The Reformation in Mexico* 1894, 17).

In 1904, more Americans settled in Mexico, and the House of Bishops of the American Episcopal Church sent Bishop Henry D. Aves to be the first bishop of the missionary district. His focus was to serve the English-speaking congregations there, but he was given permission to work with the Church of Jesus, should that be considered necessary. The Church of Jesus at that time had three bishops-elect who were waiting to be consecrated, but the Americans were reluctant to do this (Johnson 1963, 358). Even though the Church of Jesus had been in communion with the Episcopal Church for more than a quarter of a century, the feeling was that their departure from the Roman Catholic Church was much too recent, and that they had not yet had the opportunity to become fully Anglican in their theological and ecclesiastical orientation (Johnson 1963, 356). This cautious approach most likely caused the loss of a good opportunity to establish a strong indigenous Anglican presence in Mexico. Howard A. Johnson quotes his friend Gordon Charlton on the results of this decision: "In the face of this final disappointment, the *Iglesia de Jesús* gave up its high hopes of becoming a genuine Mexican National Catholic Church and of reforming the entire Christianity of its country. It surrendered its autonomy and begged to be included as a part of the Missionary District of the American Episcopal Church" (Johnson 1963, 359).

At the same time, the majority of Mexicans in the missionary district meant that it was much more of a Mexican church than an American one, which set the stage for the election of the first Mexican bishop in 1931. Bishop Efraín Salinas y Velasco was the first Spanish-speaking bishop in the Anglican Communion (Porter 2012). His election was also probably due to the strict laws that Mexico had passed earlier that prohibited the presence of foreign missionaries and ecclesiastical leaders. This prohibition allowed for the development of national leaders and limited North American paternalism. Bishop Frank W. Creighton, who had been consecrated in 1926, stated: "When I visit our Mexican congregations I am unable to conduct the service. Our Mexican people may not receive the Sacrament at the hands of their bishop, and furthermore I am unable to confirm candidates in native churches" (Miller 2008, 56).

The connection between political reform and the protestant churches remained strong. Well into the twentieth century, the Mexican Church saw the humanitarian benefits of socialism in contrast with the apparent abuses of an autocratic government. Bishop Salinas y Velasco commented:

> We have faith that socialist education is trying precisely to prepare the future generations for the conscious enjoyment of those goods that must be collective; to illuminate their minds in such a manner that the darkness of fanaticism, of superstition, and of ignorance will not be able to cloud the moral and intellectual development of our people along the paths of new goals and methods by which the Mexican people are directing themselves (Miller 2008, 60).

The first Mexican bishop to be consecrated in Mexico was the Rev. José G. Saucedo in 1958. Under his episcopate, there was a period of growth (Porter 2012). In 1963, at the Anglican Congress in Toronto, the Anglican leaders meeting encouraged "mutual

responsibility and interdependence" (Brown 1963), which called for increased awareness, participation, and support of Anglican churches around the world. Anglican and
Episcopal Churches around the world were to be more fully integrated and included in
the Anglican Communion in order to strengthen their identities and mission in their
respective countries. Interdependence was preferable to dependence. Even though
Mexico was still part of the American Episcopal Church at the time, the goal would be
for the Mexican Church eventually to become autonomous.

In 1972, Bishop Saucedo led the decision to divide the church into three dioceses,
and in 1973 two additional dioceses were formally constituted: the Diócesis del Norte,
based in Monterrey, and the Diócesis del Occidente, which is headquartered in Guad-
alajara. Bishop Saucedo remained Bishop of the Diócesis del Centro y Sur with its
cathedral and diocesan offices in Mexico City. Cuernavaca and the Diócesis del Sureste
were added in 1989 (Porter 2012).

## The Formation of an Autonomous Province

Up until 1992, Mexican laws controlled religious activity and placed restrictions on
religious groups. The constitutional reform of that year granted the right for churches
to incorporate and be designated "religious associations." This change in the law made
it possible for the Mexican Church to expand its mission, witness, and service in the
country (Porter 2012).

At the 1994 General Convention of the Episcopal Church, held Indianapolis, Indiana,
the five Mexican dioceses were released from the American church and allowed to form
their own autonomous Anglican province ("First Anglican Synod in Mexico Convened"
1995). At their first general synod, held in Mexico City from February 25 to 26, 1995,
Bishop José G. Saucedo was elected the first primate. The Rev. Benito Juárez-Martínez
was elected the first secretary; the constitution and canons were ratified; and the 1979
American Book of Common Prayer was accepted for worship ("First Anglican Synod
in Mexico Convened" 1995). In light of their independence, the church was officially
named and incorporated as the "Iglesia Anglicana de México." Bishop Porter writes
that autonomy "implies full authority to govern its internal life within the theological,
liturgical and practical framework of Anglicanism" (Porter 2012, translation mine).
On May 13, 1995, Bishop Saucedo was enthroned at the San José de la Gracia Cathedral
in Mexico City by the Episcopal Church's presiding bishop, Edmond L. Browning ("First
Anglican Synod in Mexico Convened" 1995).

Even though the Anglican Church of Mexico was granted autonomy in 1995, it
continued to receive substantial financial support from the Episcopal Church in the
United States. The bishops and presiding bishop were always welcome to attend
the general convention, but without a vote. In 2002, however, it came to light that two
of the Mexican bishops, one from the Diocese of Western Mexico and one from the
Diocese of Northern Mexico, had misused funds that had been designated for the work
and ministry of their dioceses. An investigative committee was formed, and it was discovered that a total of US$1.4 million had been misappropriated. The committee, which

was comprised of members from the Anglican Church in Mexico and the Episcopal Church, saw the need for "greater mutuality in mission and ministry." The two bishops charged with the misappropriation of funds were inhibited (Episcopal News Service 2003).

The Anglican Church of Mexico remains fully active in the work of the overall Anglican Communion. In response to the crisis in the Anglican Communion over human sexuality and the inclusion of homosexual persons in the leadership and ministry of some of the Anglican provinces, Mexico participated in the Indaba Listening Process that was started in 2005 to investigate how Anglicans around the communion felt about this issue. Since the Anglican Church in Mexico had always been associated with liberal and reform movements in Mexico since its beginnings in the nineteenth century, the province responded that even though it is not the right time to consider the blessing of same-sex unions, they want to be an "open, welcome and inclusive Church which takes its Baptismal Covenant seriously" (Anglican Communion News Service 2007).

Also in 2005, in light of the divisions that existed between certain Anglican provinces that were fully inclusive in their ordination of partnered homosexual persons to the presbyterate and the episcopate, a number of Latin American dioceses met to pray, reflect, and prepare a statement that expressed their position in regards to the crisis. This gathering was called together by the Theological Education Commission for Latin America and the Caribbean. The purpose of this gathering was to arrive at a theological and moral consensus that reflected the position of the Latin American Anglican churches. The result was a document that was named the Panama Declaration. The Panama Declaration states, in part, thus: "Our commitment will emphasize the renewal of respect to the plurality, diversity and inclusivity that have been a permanent sign of Anglicanism and our spirituality based on the Holy Scriptures, the Creed, and the primary teachings of our doctrine" (Group 2005) This meeting also served as a starting point for enabling the Latin American dioceses and provinces to "initiate an organizing process that will help us in the missionary expansion, common strengthening and joint reflection of the Church in the Latin American region" (Group 2005). The Most Rev. Carlos Touché Porter, Presiding Bishop of the Iglesia Anglicana de México, was one of three primates who signed the declaration along with the primates of Brazil and Central America and 22 diocesan bishops (Group 2005).

## Theological Education

The Iglesia Anglicana de México has a seminary named the Seminario San Andrés, which is located in the Diocese of Mexico's diocesan center. The seminary's roots go back to the latter part of the nineteenth century when the Episcopal Theological School in Cambridge, Massachusetts, provided resources and the impetus for the Mexican Church to develop their own theological program in Spanish for the purpose of training its clergy. It is now a fully accredited institution and has been consistently training and producing clergy and Christian leaders for over 100 years. Its web page states: "In this,

its second century of life, the Seminario San Andrés renews its commitment with Christ
and His church and by the grace of God will continue to push forward as an initiator
of the ministry of reconciliation formed in the theological, spiritual, liturgical and
sacramental tradition of Anglicanism, above all in the Anglican spirit of liberty, inclusivity, flexibility, and respect to the mind and the conscience of all members of the
people of God" (Andrés, translation mine).

## The Future

The province continues to move forward in its mission and increase in membership in
spite of continuing financial difficulties and the challenges presented in its own history.
In spite of these difficulties, there is the potential for a strong church if it develops even
further its evangelistic witness and its prophetic presence in Mexico. Bishop Porter
states:

> The actual Iglesia Anglicana de México represents the union of the two sources that gave
> it its beginning. This reality demonstrates that even though our Church, equally with the
> Roman Church in the Sixteenth Century, came from another part of the world, it is in no
> way a foreign church distant from the Mexican mentality, but on the contrary: It is a
> Church with which our people is capable to identify itself fully without having to renounce
> its historic and cultural roots (Porter 2012).

## Bibliography

1995. First Anglican Synod in Mexico Convened. *Christian Century*, vol. 112, no. 10, p.
322.

Aguas, Manuel. 1871. *Letter from Manuel
Aguas. Pages.* New York: T. Whittaker.
Available at http://www.anglicanhistory.
org.

Andrés, Seminario San. 2012. Seminario San
Andrés. Iglesia Anglicana de México. Web.
March 31, 2012.

Anglican Communion News Service. 2007.
*Reports from the Provinces: La Iglesia Angli-
cana de México.* [cited March 30, 2012].

Anonymous. 1894. *The Reformation in Mexico.*
Hartford: Junior Auxiliary Publishing Co.

Brown, Dr. Terry, transcriber. 1963. Mutual
Responsibility and Interdependence in the
Body of Christ. http://anglicanhistory.org/
canada/toronto_mutual1963.html. March
31, 2012.

Creighton, Frank W. 1929. The Church in
Mexico: An Address Delivered before the

Church Historical Society at its Meeting in Philadelphia, November 14, 1928.
Philadelphia.

Episcopal News Service. 2003. Mexican Bishops Rebuked: $1.4 Million US Misappropri-
ated. *Anglican Journal*, vol. 129, no. 1.

Group, Latin American Theological. 2005.
The Panama Declaration. Anglican Communion News Service. http://www.anglican
communion.org/acns/news.cfm/2005/
10/21/ACNS4054. March 30, 2012.

Johnson, Howard A. 1963. *Global Odyssey: An
Episcopalian's Encounter with the Anglican
Communion in Eighty Countries.* New York:
Harper and Row.

Lee, Alfred. 1879. Statement of the Acting
Chairman of the Mexican Commission of
the House of Bishops of the Protestant Episcopal Church in the United States of
America. Canterbury Project.

México, Iglesia Anglicana de. 2012. Quienes
Somos. Anglican Church of Mexico. http://

www.iglesiaanglicanademexico.org/anglimain.html. March 29, 2012.

Miller, Daniel R. 2008. Protestantism and Radicalism in Mexico from the 1860s to the 1930s. *Fides et Historia*, vol. 40, no. 1.

Mondragón, Carlos. 2005. Protestantes y Protestantismo en América Latina: Reflexiones en Torno a la Variedad de Experiencias en su Introducción. *Espacio de Diálogo*, vol. 2 (April). http://www.cenpromex.org.mx/revista_ftl/ftl/textos/carlos_mondragon.htm. April 12, 2012.

Porter, Carlos Touché. 2012. Historia: El Anglicanismo en México. Iglesia Anglicana de México. http://www.iglesiaanglicanademexico.org/anglimain.html. March 29, 2012.

Smith, Jim C. 2000. Report on the Seminario San Andrés in Mexico City. Church Divinity School of the Pacific.

CHAPTER 46

# The Episcopal Church in the United States of America

## J. Barney Hawkins IV

We live in a world which is often described as "post-modern." Without doubt, this is becoming a dominant perspective in the first world. Being "post-modern," however, does not mean we are "post-historic." History and tradition matter to Anglicans in a so-called "post-modern" world. In the United States, the Episcopal Church is the primary placeholder for Anglicanism. Anglicanism and the Anglican Communion are the historical context of the Episcopal Church in the United States of America. This chapter will consider the Anglican Church's initial relationship with indigenous or traditional cultures. A selective history of the Episcopal Church (TEC) will be the backdrop for a review of the contemporary Episcopal Church, issues facing its province, and its connection with the worldwide Anglican Communion.

The first articulation of Anglicanism is in the reign of Elizabeth I, not Henry VIII or Edward VI. Under Queen Elizabeth I, there was found a way forward between the polarities of Rome and Geneva. Anglicanism became the "via media," a political solution which produced a doctrinal system or an Anglican Theology. The golden age of Anglicanism may have been the seventeenth century. The truth of Christianity was found in scripture and tradition, and both were regarded as authoritative and grounded in the first four centuries of Christian history. Anglicans decided what Anglicanism should be. Ecclesiastical polity was framed, and the oversight of bishops was established. It was decided that Anglicanism would have certain continuity with England's Catholic past. The Book of Common Prayer defined liturgical forms and practices. The Thirty-Nine Articles became normative. Anglican tolerance, in its fledgling state, accepted other Christian denominations or communions in the British Isles. England, through persecutions and the "Glorious Revolution," emerged by the end of the century as a Protestant land, shaping its own religious destiny.

*The Wiley-Blackwell Companion to the Anglican Communion*, First Edition. Edited by Ian S. Markham,
J. Barney Hawkins IV, Justyn Terry, and Leslie Nuñez Steffensen.
© 2013 John Wiley & Sons, Ltd. Published 2013 by John Wiley & Sons, Ltd.

Seventeenth-century Anglicanism had its inspiration from Thomas Cranmer in liturgical reforms which were anchored to an emerging theology that was anti-Roman, sympathetic to Puritan moral piety, and rationalistic. Anglican was a "via media," which resisted dogma and was open to the intellectual renderings of John Locke and the Enlightenment, as set forth by the Cambridge Platonists. Anglicanism was "reasonable" – even as it was deeply rooted in the Bible, particularly the King James Version. Preachers like Lancelot Andrews, George Herbert, and Jeremy Taylor provided wisdom for the practical application of Anglican theology.

England settled upon Anglicanism in the seventeenth century, a century which began with the transplanting of this new understanding of the Christian faith to the new world. After several failures, three ships with 105 "colonists" landed at what would become Jamestown in Virginia, a royal colony. Soon after the landing at Jamestown, the Rev. Robert Hunt celebrated Holy Communion, and the story of Anglicanism began in this outpost of England. Soon there were English settlements in New England. The pilgrims with their Puritan faith became part of American religious history. Baptists and Quakers became part of the early colonization of the new world. In the Middle Colonies, the Dutch (New York) joined the English in the commerce and religion of the new world experiment. George Calvert had a grant from James I to settle the colony known as Maryland. Calvert was a Roman Catholic, and so was Maryland. William Penn was a man who followed Quaker principles – and Pennsylvania became a tolerant colony and may have prefigured the democracy which would be articulated in the Constitution of the United States of America. Maryland and Pennsylvania, with their Roman Catholic and Quaker leanings, respectively, keep the record straight. Anglicanism, while dominant in the colonial period of American history, was never established in the new world. Establishment came closest in the southern colonies, particularly Carolina and Virginia.

The colonial period in American religious history has a blind spot about indigenous or traditional cultures. "America became the Great Frontier of Western Christendom in 1492" (Ahlstrom 1972, 17). The first Americans, the Indians, were seen as heathen tribes in need of conversion. Their civilization was disregarded. Moreover, the Indians were not impressed with the conversion attempts of the "white man." The Indian way of life did not fit with Puritan premises, such as hard work and individual advancement. Anglicanism was at odds with the animism of Indian religion and culture. The colonial period of Anglicanism in the new world is stained with the blood and conflicts between the settlers and the first Americans.

In the seventeenth century, Anglicanism in America saw triumphs and tragedy. The success of Anglicanism was very evident in the connection which Anglicans made to education. James Blair was a representative of the Bishop of London in Virginia. He had a commission as commissary for Virginia and thereby was the highest ecclesiastical officer in the colony. Blair secured a charter in 1693 for a college, naming it in honor of England's sovereigns, William and Mary. If educating colonists was the nobler side of Anglicanism, its darker side in Virginia was its uncritical connection to the institution of slavery. Blacks were brought unwillingly from Africa to support the economic expansion of the new world, particularly the cotton and tobacco cultures. Colonies like Virginia and South Carolina became dependent on slave labor, and the

Anglican Church was largely silent on the human tragedy. Economic interest trumped religious conviction – in the south and in the north. It must be noted that Anglicanism in seventeenth-century America was the strongest in the colonies most dependent of slave labor.

Let us now look at the achievements of eighteenth-century Anglicanism in the colonies of what would become North America. Early Anglicanism in the colonies was not self-governed. The Bishop of London, living at Lambeth Palace, was the diocesan bishop for the American colonies. In many ways, there was not an American Church until the last decades of the eighteenth century. Rather, there was a Church of England in the new world. The English bishop had a representative, known as a commissary. The commissary derived his authority solely from his commission from the Bishop of London. With no bishop at hand, some of the colonies struggled with how best to make Anglicanism work in such a far-flung outpost. James Blair in Virginia understood the role of the commissary – and he used his power and authority to commence higher education in the colony.

In South Carolina, there emerged the church acts of 1704 and 1706 (guaranteeing conformity to and establishment of the Church of England), and the commissary in South Carolina was more interested in governance than education. These acts provided for local ecclesiastical government in the elected vestries, which emerged as strong and powerful entities. "While the authority of the vestry and parish rector was insured, the church acts failed to address a provincial government for the established church" (Hawkins 1981, 207). Garden was called upon "to interpret Anglican establishment to a New World which was not wholly inclined to apply all of English canon law" (Hawkins 1981, 207). In due course, Anglicanism in South Carolina became a blend of English episcopacy and American congregationalism. Early on, the seeds of American democracy were in the largely lay initiative of American Anglicanism.

In 1701, the Society for the Propagation of the Gospel concluded that there were 43,000 Anglican Church members and about 50 clergymen in all of the colonies (Pascoe 1901, 86–87). As England came to see that a national church for all English Christians was not possible, so Anglicans in the American colonies were beginning to see a religious landscape, rich and diverse. The Great Awakening was the "outward" sign of what was emerging as American Protestantism. Revivals were part of eighteenth-century America. Baptists and Methodists became very much part of the religious narrative. Commissary Garden in South Carolina encountered George Whitefield – with the tradition of reasonable Anglicanism challenged by the fervor of religious awakening. The Anglican emphasis on awakening, education, and congregational governance would serve the eighteenth-century church well as it moved closer and closer to revolution and independence.

America's war of independence was tied to its desire for religious revival. If the new nation had a destiny and was chosen, then that special identity had a deep religious connection. The Great Awakening paved the way for revolution in church and state. Revival preaching spoke of the "hand of God" in America – and so in the political leaders who were designing a new nation (Prichard 1991, 73–74).

By the middle of the eighteenth century, the American colonies were restless. The relationship with England was deteriorating. Independence was in the air. An American culture was coming into being. The colonies had been a success. By 1776, there were nearly 3 million "Americans." The colonies were a great melting pot and a new world of immigrants. The area of the land seemed without end, and the economic strength of the new world called out for independence and expansion. A form of "American" education was emerging. Only Anglican clergy continued to be educated in England.

Perhaps in the last analysis, the American Revolution was connected to English taxes and the lack of representation by the colonists. The Stamp Act in 1765 produced a crisis, and a revolutionary spirit took hold of the colonies. In 1776, the British were sent home. Suddenly, there were American heroes and patriots, not kings and queens. The Church of England in the new world was untethered from its cultural and theological moorings. It became one more denomination in the first years of a new, fledgling nation.

In the years that followed the American Revolution, there was disarray for Anglicans in America. Non-Anglicans worried about the loyalty of Anglicans to the new nation. It was finally not left to the places where Anglicanism was the strongest for the decisions to be made that led to the Protestant Episcopal Church in the United States. Why did leadership not emerge from Virginia where the most Anglicans were located? Or South Carolina with a strong Anglican Church headquartered in Charleston? There was an Anglican Church peculiar to the southern colonies. Another manifestation of Anglicanism existed in the middle colonies. In New England, still another form of the Church of England had expression and interaction with other more strongly identified congregational churches.

In 1783, Samuel Seabury was elected by the clergy of Connecticut as their bishop. Not being able to be consecrated in England because the colonies or states were independent and because he could not take the Oath of Allegiance, bishops of the Church of the Scotland laid holy hands on Seabury in Aberdeen on November 14, 1784. Seabury later cooperated in the consecration of Bishop T. J. Claggett in Maryland – thereby uniting Scottish and English episcopal succession. Bishop Seabury became the first bishop of the Protestant Episcopal Church of America. William White of Pennsylvania had served as de facto bishop for about two months. For a long time, the "presiding bishop," not archbishop, was the senior diocesan bishop in the House of Bishops. In 1919, the office became an elected one. In the 1940s, it was deemed necessary for the presiding bishop to resign any other jurisdictions for which he might have responsibility. In 1982, the presiding bishop was also given the title of "primate."

It is noteworthy that the Protestant Episcopal Church in America did not choose to have an archbishop. The spirit of the new democracy would not allow such a religious monarchy. Indeed, with the consecration of Seabury, there was another revolution of sorts. The new Church of England in the new United States of America had strong lay representation in its governance, not surprising with the strong vestries which had always been part of the colonial Anglican Church. There were two houses of ecclesiastical government (House of Bishops and House of Deputies) to mirror the new national, federal government. Furthermore, bishops were elected, not appointed.

The eighteenth century ended with a new nation finding its way in the family of nations. For Christian churches, it was becoming a land of many Christian churches and sects. Denominationalism was part of the fabric of the United States. There was also a high-pitched reverence for the national life. Patriotism was alive and well in church and state. The century ended with the beginning of the Second Great Awakening. The Protestant Republic was finding a new spirit for a new century. Unitarians were finding their voice in New England. A democratic ideal was emerging from the pulpits and in pews of American churches. Humanitarian concerns were raised by churches as America sought to be the New Jerusalem. As the century closed, the day seemed to belong to Methodists, Presbyterians, Baptists, and other "popular" denominations. You could conclude that a democratic theology was coming into view. The Protestant Episcopal Church was becoming one voluntary church among others.

At the beginning of the nineteenth century, the Protestant Episcopal Church was adrift. Democratic sensibilities may have been at cross-purposes with a monarchical institution which was being transformed by revolution and revival. It was reported that bishops were not making visitations. Many Anglican clergy departed the church after the Revolution. The clergy seemed unmotivated. By 1810, however, the Protestant Episcopal Church received an infusion of energy as evangelicals debated high churchmen. Theological issues were discussed with new energy. The Protestant Episcopal Church needed seminaries to train its clergy for the lively faith it was expressing. In 1817, the general convention of the church established the General Theological Seminary in New York. In 1823, vestrymen at St. Paul's Church in Alexandria founded the Virginia Theological Seminary, a seminary committed to the evangelical heritage of the Protestant Episcopal Church.

In the nineteenth century, the Protestant Episcopal Church faced the sin of slavery; the Civil War; its reputation as a church for the rich; and the Social Gospel movement in the waning decades of a century which saw the United States become richer and stronger as it assumed leadership in the first American Century.

The rise of abolitionism in the United States involved American churches at its core. The Protestant Episcopal Church was not of one mind on the matter of slavery. In the south, church and society were segregated, and discrimination was a pattern of life. However, the north was not pure and on the side of the angels. Economic interest in south and north impacted decision-making and prolonged the agony of human beings who had been hunted down in Africa for servitude in America. During the Civil War (1861–1865), the southern dioceses of the Protestant Episcopal Church formed itself into separate body – but this was largely informal and not about doctrine. Some Episcopalians were committed to slave churches – separate buildings for segregated worship. If not separate, then balconies in white churches where African slaves were consigned. It is strange that schism did not threaten the whole of the Episcopal Church. In fact, the church was rather passive about the issue of slavery.

After the long and bloody national war, the Protestant Episcopal Church reconciled south and north. During reconstruction, the church continued its silence about the sin of slavery. Rather than addressing the aftermath of the war and need for reparations and restoration at home, the Protestant Episcopal Church turned to a season of missionary zeal. The nation was becoming more visible on the stage of nations; so the Protestant Episcopal Church became a force in the worldwide church – sending missionaries to South America and Asia. In 1821, the Protestant Episcopal Church founded the Domestic and Foreign Missionary Society. Indeed, the official name of the church

until 1964 was the Domestic and Foreign Missionary Society of the Protestant Episcopal Church. In 1964, Protestant and other designations were dropped, and it became
the Episcopal Church.

After the Civil War and before the divisions in American society were healed, the
Protestant Episcopal Church began sending missionaries to Africa – and receiving students from Africa in at least one of its seminaries, the Protestant Episcopal Seminary
in Virginia. As the Protestant Episcopal Church engaged in missionary work, it also saw
the need to connect with the Anglican Communion. In a 1990 report commissioned
by the Archbishop of Canterbury, it was said that the Protestant Episcopal Church was
the first Anglican Province outside of the British Isles. Since 1867, the church has
attended all of the Lambeth Conferences. Perhaps it is not accidental that the Episcopal
Church flexed its muscle in the last half of the nineteenth century. The country was
becoming richer and richer, and so was the Episcopal Church. Impressive Gothic
churches were being built, designed by great architects like Ralph Adam Cram and
Richard Upjohn. In the evangelical Catholic tradition of the Episcopal Church, there
was a besetting concern: is the Episcopal Church for the rich only? This was a good
question as the country faced the problems of industrialization and urbanization. Many
"Robber Barons" found a home in the Episcopal Church. More and more financiers
and titans of commerce and industry were receiving Holy Communion from Episcopal
priests. Care for the poor and the dispossessed have always been the vocation of the
church. However, in late-nineteenth-century America, that vocation, some surmised,
was carried out as nothing more than an act of *noblesse oblige* – a noble obligation of
the rich and powerful in the Episcopal Church. An age of philanthropy was born – but
was Christian charity part of the motivation?

In the first half of the twentieth century, the Episcopal Church faced a changing
social order in America: urbanization, an economic depression, and two World Wars.
The end of slavery did not ensure civil rights for all. The long struggle for the right of
women to vote in the United States culminated in the nineteenth amendment to the
Constitution in 1920. The Episcopal Church embraced women in leadership roles at a
much slower pace, with women priests not being "allowed" until 1976.

By 1950, the Episcopal Church could claim one-quarter of all presidents of the
United States. That power and influence, however, was under stress as the Episcopal
Church increasingly found itself one among many Christian churches in a nation
which was becoming more populated and more diverse. Urbanization provided the
Episcopal Church growth in numbers, as its social and political influence waned on
the national stage. In the first decades of the twentieth century, great wealth accumulated in the hands of very few. As cities grew and became more populated, poverty
increased and the gulf between rich and poor increased. The stock market in the
United States crashed in 1929 and the Great Depression which followed left the Episcopal Church and its sister churches bewildered as resources for ministry and mission
dried up. Two World Wars took its toll in many ways as the country gave its young for
wars on European soil. Episcopal seminaries had smaller classes, and for many years
there was a shortage of clergy. The Vietnam War was also a difficult season in church
and nation. The war divided the Episcopal Church, as it did the nation. The twentieth
century was a time of upheaval and change for the tradition-rooted Episcopal Church.

By the end of the century, the church was giving up the numerical strength it enjoyed mid-century.

On the eve of the Great Depression in 1929, the Episcopal Church adopted its third Book of Common Prayer. The 1928 Book of Common Prayer had been preceded by prayer books in 1789 and 1892. In 1979, the General Convention of the Episcopal Church approved a new version of the Book of Common Prayer.

Two of the distinguishing characteristics of the Episcopal Church in the Anglican Communion are the way General Convention works and the process of electing bishops in the American Episcopal Church. In General Convention with its bicameral legislation and as bishops are elected in the Episcopal Church, the Episcopal Church honors the orders of ministry – and in particular the role of laypeople in its governance, polity, and practice. The full inclusion of laypeople has deep historical roots. Strong vestries were part of the Anglican Church in the colonial period. There has always been a strong democratic inclination in the American Episcopal Church. The voices of the laity matter and are often decisive as the Episcopal Church finds its way. In many ways, the local church is "the seat of authority and power in the American version of a somewhat 'dethroned' Anglicanism" (Hawkins and Markham 2008, 21). In revising the prayer book, in electing bishops, as well as in its daily life, the Episcopal Church in the United States takes seriously the authority and voice of the laity. In 2003, this often-overlooked reality was put to the test for the Anglican Communion when the clergy and laity in New Hampshire elected a new bishop who was openly gay. Because the people of New Hampshire had spoken, many in the Episcopal Church's House of Bishops and House of Deputies believed it reasonable to consent to his consecration.

Finally, the present-day Episcopal Church is shaped by the civil rights' discourse of the 1960s and its emerging center. For the Episcopal Church, the national spokesman for the long and bitter discourse about civil rights for the children of slavery was the Most Rev. John E. Hines, the 22nd Presiding Bishop of the Episcopal Church. Bishop Hines heard Martin Luther King talk about the "white moderate" clergy who were slow to embrace King's campaign for justice. As American cities were burning in the 1960s, Bishop Hines decided to be anything but "moderate." Hines may have been the first to declare that, because of Dr. King and his followers, a new generation of leaders would claim new possibilities for their society and their church. So it is now with the current leadership of the Episcopal Church. Because of King and Hines, the late-twentieth- and early-twenty-first-century Episcopal Church in the United States has been "about revolution not the status quo" (Hawkins and Markham 2008, 21). Perhaps this explains the historical roots of the Episcopal Church's current leadership about the rights of gays, lesbians, bisexuals, transgenders, and others whose voices have long been relegated to the margins of the church's conversation and practice.

The Episcopal Church was born out of a revolution, the War of Independence in 1776. Early-on, it declined an archbishop at its helm and chose rather a presiding bishop. Its bishops have never truly been princes of the church. Its laity has always embraced almost revolutionary authority and voice. It is a church both Catholic and Protestant. The Episcopal Church has always pushed back when fundamentalists insisted that every word of Holy Scripture be taken literally. Likewise, it has been a church which has understood the Christian tradition as the context for conversation, and not the focus of authority. The Episcopal Church's relationships in the worldwide Anglican Communion have been stretched by the church's revolutionary, restless way of being Anglican in a fast-paced, global church.

## Bibliography

Ahlstrom, Sydney E. 1972. *A Religious History of the American People*. New Haven: Yale University Press.

Hawkins, James Barney IV. 1981. *Alexander Garden: The Commissary in Church and State*. Ph.D. Dissertation. Department of Religion. Duke University, Durham, North Carolina.

Hawkins, Barney and Ian Markham. 2008. The Episcopal Church and the Anglican Communion. *Modern Believing: Church and Society*, vol. 49, no. 3. The Modern Churchpeople's Union.

Pascoe, C. F. 1901. *Two Hundred Years of the SPG*. London: SPG.

Prichard, Robert W. 1991. *A History of the Episcopal Church*. Harrisburg, Pennsylvania: Morehouse Publishing.

CHAPTER 47

# The Church in the Province of the West Indies

## Noel Titus

The islands of the West Indies were first settled by the Spaniards toward the end of the fifteenth century, as granted to them by papal bull in 1493. Their monopoly in the islands came to an end in the seventeenth century as their rivals from Europe moved into the region. The advent of the French caused no change in religion; but change came with the Dutch, and especially the English. In the islands, the English settled residents were expected to be Protestants, or more precisely, members of the Church of England. In the eighteenth and nineteenth centuries, other denominations entered from England.

The advent of the Church of England coincided with the period of political and religious conflict in seventeenth-century England. The rivalry between Roundheads and Cavaliers played itself out in Barbados in 1650. This was partly inevitable, since migration and civil wars caused many of them to relocate to Barbados. In a small "frontier" society such as this was, the situation naturally became volatile and led to armed conflict orchestrated largely by the Cavaliers, who adopted "Loyalty and Piety" as their slogan (Harlow 1926, 45–6). Loyalty of course was to the monarch. Piety expressed itself through the use of the Book of Common Prayer. Those with contrary views supported both the Parliament and the banning of the prayer book. The Church of England had been strongly influenced by the Puritan movement of the previous century and reflected a mixture of Episcopal and Presbyterian ideas. As a result, one cannot be quite sure that those who planted the church were completely "orthodox," as this term was later used. When the commissioners sent out by Cromwell banned the prayer book in Barbados in 1652, after a successful siege of the island, only the minister of All Saints' Church resisted the ban (Harlow 1926, 96). Either those who adhered to the ban were supporters of Parliament and possibly Presbyterian in their sentiments, or

*The Wiley-Blackwell Companion to the Anglican Communion*, First Edition. Edited by Ian S. Markham, J. Barney Hawkins IV, Justyn Terry, and Leslie Nuñez Steffensen.
© 2013 John Wiley & Sons, Ltd. Published 2013 by John Wiley & Sons, Ltd.

they were lacking in conviction about the retention of the book. Following the capture of Jamaica in 1654–1655, Cromwell appointed seven chaplains to the island (Bridges 1968, 538; Long 1970, 234). These were neither royalist nor episcopalian in outlook; however, some of them retained their tenure after the restoration of the monarchy. From 1661 onward, there was agitation in both colonies to replace existing incumbents with "orthodox" clergy of the Church of England (C.S.P. 1661–68, No. 24; No. 489). The church, therefore, had a shaky start in the West Indies.

The clergy who first came to the region could be described as freelancers – persons whose functions were not under the auspices of any ecclesiastical authority. Persons like Nicholas Leverton, John Featley, and Thomas Lane came and went as circumstances dictated. The lack of any authority or pastoral supervision resulted in some indiscipline, such as Archbishop Laud himself found unacceptable in England. Ironically, the first complaint to a bishop against conditions in the church was made to Laud, the Archbishop of Canterbury (C.S.P. 1574–1660, No. 70). Lack of coordination or of episcopal control characterized the church in the early years; the malaise would be slightly modified later on. Those who eventually served in the West Indies in the eighteenth century represented a cross section of persons in the society – governors' favorites, sons of planters (graduates from English institutions), "civil servants," and others. Beginning in the late seventeenth century, such persons needed to be licensed by the Bishop of London; however, having licensed them, the Bishop of London played no further role in their service as clergy. The result was that, even when they were of poor character, it was not easy to move them. Part of the problem had its origin in the secular control of the church. The governor was the *de facto* authority, functioning as Ordinary on the prevailing belief that he was the monarch's deputy. However, once the governor had collated someone to the office, he seemed to play no further role regarding the performance of that individual.

## Bishops of London

While it is true that bishops of London played a part in the life of the West Indian Church, that part began much later than is usually allowed. The influence of that prelate began in 1676, when Bishop Compton became a member of the Board of Trade and Plantations – a forerunner of the Colonial Office. In this capacity, the bishop from time to time made recommendations to the board for the improvement of the work of the church. These proposals were usually accepted by the board and transmitted to the various governors for implementation. Even so, the bishops of London were not as energetic as one would have expected, with some harboring doubts about their jurisdiction. In the 1720s, the Law Officers of the Crown determined that the Bishop of London had no jurisdiction in the West Indies; that jurisdiction was subsequently conferred by the legislatures between 1726 and 1748.

The inability of the bishops of London to be present in what was considered part of their jurisdiction was partially addressed by the appointment of commissaries, who were the bishop's representatives. Among the first commissaries were men like Alexander Gordon and Thomas Bray for the American colonies. For the West Indies, some of the early commissaries were William Gordon for Barbados and William May for Jamaica. Lacking any real authority, the commissaries relayed to the clergy such instructions as they received from the bishop, collecting and transmitting to the latter such information as he requested. Commissaries sometimes came into conflict with governors and legislators when they tried to establish ecclesiastical courts. Moreover, since they were incumbents of parishes in the chief town in the territory, and given the fact that parishes had both civil and ecclesiastical functions, the commissaries had little or no time to visit other parishes. Because many parishes were large and widely scattered, consultations with clergy were also difficult and were not attempted (Fulham Papers, Vol XVII, 211–35). Separation from a leader, and separation from one another, compounded to render united action impossible.

## The Structures

The organization of the church followed the general pattern of the Church in England. Parishes were quickly demarcated, each having: a church for worship, a rectory for the rector's residence, a portion of land as glebe, with such fees as were considered necessary for various pastoral occasions. The supervision of the activities of the parish was the responsibility of a body called the vestry, which consisted of the principal property owners and rate payers in the parish. These persons were not required to be members of the church, except in a rather Erastian interpretation of the church. According to one complainant, this body had the authority to "hire and fire," and the clergy were very much at their mercy. The clergy were not usually members of the vestry until 1680, when a recommendation of the Bishop of London enabled them to become members (C.S.P. 1677–80, No. 488). Through consanguinity or common interest with legislators elected by the parishes, these vestry members became parochial magnates, and the church was dependent on them. This dependence marked the real status of the church, which was therefore firmly under their control. In small insular societies, their power was real. Thus, the stipends granted to the clergy were often withheld if the rector were to challenge the sometimes blatant immorality of vestry members. In some cases, the stipends were withheld for as long as three years, a circumstance which did nothing to enhance the performance of clergy (Fulham Papers, Vol. XVI, 44–5).

For most of the seventeenth and eighteenth centuries, the social issue of greatest concern was chattel slavery, with all its attendant evils. Critical among these were the failure of the leaders to encourage marriage or stable family life; the rejection of slave evidence against whites, thus allowing major crimes to escape punishment if the only witnesses were slaves; and the failure to instruct the slaves in the basic tenets of the Christian faith. For this latter, the church was partly to blame, but a great share of the blame rested with slave owners who stoutly opposed such instruction and were able to control the clergy to such an extent that they could not function. The failure of the church was cruelly exposed as a result of Bishop Gibson's investigation in 1723 (Fulham Papers, Vol XV, 203–14; XVI, 211–35; XIX, 16–20). Responses to his query about pastoral ministration to the slaves were not complimentary to the clergy. Yet, if one looked at other responses from the clergy, it becomes evident that not much was going on generally. This is only partly explained by the size of the parishes – some in Jamaica being larger than the island of Barbados, and some like Harbour Island in the Bahamas forming part of the parish of the island of Eleuthera. It is also to be explained by the general atmosphere of insecurity and uncertainty in which clergy often functioned, as well as the habit of industry or otherwise of individual clergy.

Change was slow in coming to the West Indian islands and resulted partly from the efforts of Bishop Porteus, who paid careful attention to the selection of persons for ordination, and who prescribed a program of study for all such persons. During his tenure in the late eighteenth century, there came into being a society whose focus was on the conversion and religious instruction of the West Indian slaves. The work of that society was extremely limited, as its agents functioned in the Leeward Islands and Jamaica. And despite the fact that the Codrington bequest also targeted the slaves in Barbados, cumulatively their effect left much to be desired (Bennett 1958 is still the best single text on the subject; see also Titus 2002).

A militant evangelicalism in the late eighteenth and early nineteenth century helped to promote the abolition of the slave trade and, some time later, the abolition of slavery. The former was achieved in 1807, but the latter would occupy the attention of the English Parliament and people for another 25 years or so. A large part of this period, 1823–1833, would be taken up with attempts to ameliorate the system of slavery. An analogy might easily be drawn between this period of the church's development and the era of its entry into the region. The implanting of the church began in an atmosphere of conflict, with the struggle of Englishmen for certain rights against a determined monarch. In 1823, the West Indies was caught up in a struggle for basic human rights by and for the majority of the population. The difference was that, whereas the fight in England was against a single monarch, in the West Indies the prevailing social and economic system produced many monarchs. Each slave owner had absolute control over his or her slaves, and whenever the authority of the slave owner was challenged by a court action, slave-owning juries could be depended on to acquit the accused – even for the murder of a slave. These were the evils the English government sought to correct by a process of amelioration of slavery, sometimes referred to as "gradual abolition."

## Beginning of the Episcopate

At the height of this process, the government in London proposed the establishment of two Episcopal Sees in the West Indies. Their decision was based on the conviction that religious instruction was vital to the success of the program of amelioration then being initiated. Not prepared to commit this important function to dissenting missionaries, the government secured the appointment of two bishops to mobilize the clergy to perform this task more effectively. Consecrated in July 1824, both bishops arrived in the West Indies early in 1825. William Hart Coleridge arrived in Barbados on January 29, to preside over a diocese stretching from Tortola in the North to Guyana in the South. Christopher Lipscomb arrived in Jamaica on February 5, his diocese comprising that island, the Bahamas, and Belize (then British Honduras).

On their assumption of duty, the bishops were faced with a variety of challenges, the most critical being the challenge of church order. It became necessary to establish the norms in the church, so that clergy and laity understood what was expected of them. One of the first issues which evoked firm action on the part of both bishops concerned the operations of the Church Missionary Society (CMS). In each case, the bishop was forced to make clear the respective roles of the bishop and the missionary societies. The CMS tended to control its missionaries in the West Indies in a way neither bishop approved. The society also had difficulty on the issue of ordination, Lipscomb in particular insisting on the need for acceptable titles. After some negotiations, this matter was eventually resolved (Cnattingius 1952, 156–7).

Major tasks facing the bishops concerned the increase in the number of places for worship and education. Coleridge embarked on a building program across his diocese, where he was fortunate to have the resources of several governments, as opposed to Lipscomb who had to depend mostly on Jamaica and the perennially poor Bahamas together with British Honduras. The massive increase in the number of churches and schools necessitated a comparable increase in the number of clergy and teachers. On the whole, the bishops looked to England to provide persons in both categories, Codrington College in Barbados helping that diocese to meet its needs. In the prevailing slave society of those days, neither bishop considered recruiting colored clergy; education was the most obvious deterrent. Coleridge was insistent on ordaining only graduates of Oxford or Cambridge, an insistence which led to conflict with the CMS. The bishops' successors were equally cautious. Thus, the first colored person from the West Indies to be ordained was probably ordained in England, the second in Sierra Leone.

While schools were very quickly built, the appointment of teachers was unplanned, depending completely on available personnel. A school was usually headed by a member of the church, whose major qualification was not in the area of pedagogy, but rather in faithfulness as a member of the church. Using the Bell system, the more advanced students were responsible for passing on to their juniors what they had learned. This method of proceeding made it possible for one person to be *the* teacher of a large school. More often than not, the teacher was English or white creole. Yet, the system enabled some other persons to emerge as good teachers, and to make significant contributions to education.

The main reason for the appointment of bishops was to give direction to the clergy in facilitating the slave amelioration program. On their arrival, they found that some work had already been in progress. Parliamentary papers included reports of clergy detailing the work they had been doing among the slaves. Their efforts were not as extensive as they might have been, nor were the clergy effective in resisting the opposition of slave owners to the evangelization of the slaves. Anglicans of that age tended to be conformists. On the other hand, while their instructions warned Baptists, Methodists, and others against attempting to teach the slaves without their owners' consent, what they witnessed often caused them to be in breach of those instructions.

## Mission

Toward the middle of the nineteenth century, a missionary interest emerged among the leadership of the West Indian Church. One aspect of that interest represented the church as carrying the gospel to distant lands, Africa being the destination of immediate concern. The idea originated in Jamaica. The man responsible for initiating it in our church was J. M. Trew, who argued that a colossal injustice had been done to Africa by the removal of so many millions of her children and that an evangelistic effort from the West Indies would be a worthy, though partial, reparation (Trew 1843, 40–41). It is one of the injustices of history that so much of the scheme has been attributed to Richard Rawle, while hardly any mention is made of Trew. While Rawle must be acknowledged as the man who helped to make the mission a reality, he added nothing to Trew's conception of it (Titus 1980, 95–7).

The enterprise was intended to recognize the dynamic character of Christianity as a missionary movement which thrives on growth and activity. Specifically, the effort strove to show that the injustice perpetrated on Africa needed some conscious effort on the part of those who profited by the labor of Africans. It may well be regarded as the local challenge to the view that emancipation had brought the issue of slavery to an end. Compensation had been paid to those who had exploited their slaves, and who ultimately became the beneficiaries of the cruel system. This venture was the token compensation of the West Indian Church to Africa.

One of the defects of this approach lay in the conviction that mission meant going far away, ignoring the tremendous significance of Acts 1:8: "You shall be my witnesses in Jerusalem and in all Judea and Samaria and to the end of the earth." Some leaders of the church were prepared to leave a field of mission on their doorstep, to forego witness in their own location, and to engage in mission elsewhere. Neither Trinidad nor Guyana took any active part in this enterprise. A more crucial defect was that the mission was not intended to have African leadership. Thus, an Englishman, Hamble J. Leacock, led the mission and John Duporte of St. Kitts went to Africa as his lay assistant. And yet, were it not for John Duporte, the mission could not have survived; for 17 years, he was, metaphorically speaking, its foundation and buttress. He was ordained in Sierra Leone, not in the West Indies.

Happily, any distortion in missionary perspective was corrected in other parts of the province. The church in Trinidad and Guyana saw the demands of mission close at hand, and both made determined efforts to grapple with those needs. In Trinidad, Richard Rawle (bishop since 1872) pioneered the work among the indentured Indians. Rawle was uneasy at the influx of East Indians whose language, in his view, rendered them inaccessible. Rawle endeavored to acquire knowledge of Hindustani and also wrote to the SPG seeking help. One factor which exacerbated the difficulty Rawle perceived was the fact that the Indian population was essentially transitory. People were always arriving from and returning to India, so that attempts at evangelization constituted a series of new beginnings.

In Guyana, there was similar work among the indentured Indians from 1861. So enthusiastically did Bishop Austin commit himself to this work that he quickly secured the services of a missionary from Calcutta. Schools were built for them very rapidly, thus adding education to evangelization (Titus 1999, 351–8). Even before this, the church had begun work among the Amerindians, progressing slowly but methodically, under the superintendence of William Henry Brett. Brett was significant less for his length of service than for his diligence in translating the scriptures into one of the languages of the Amerindians. It was the kind of work not done in our part of the world, and which was the distinctive contribution of John Duporte who labored in West Africa. This work, which evoked great enthusiasm under the leadership of Bishop Austin, seems to have declined early in the twentieth century, as it proved difficult to enlist persons for that enterprise. The local church may not have accepted the challenge as its own.

## Dis-Endowment

In the early 1870s, the church in the West Indies faced perhaps its sternest test. With an eye on the economy, the British government began to reduce the funds it granted to the hierarchy and other ministers in the West Indies. Except for the Diocese of Barbados, the Anglican Church in the region was left to provide its own funding. Though it continued to enjoy "most favored status" on the whole, it never received anything beyond the capitation grants given to other churches. In the new Diocese of Trinidad, the bishop began his ministry at the end of what must have been the shortest establishment in history. The church had been established in 1844 and was disestablished in 1870. It was therefore not as well off as its sister dioceses, which had at least secured sound church buildings and schools before the axe fell. Barbados enjoyed status and funding for another 100 years before disestablishment. The kind of planning needed at the change had not been done, so that for many years thereafter the church's finances were shaky and bishops were often seeking to recoup their deficits by appeals to contacts in England. The Methodists and Moravians had similar problems, but they had resorted to the employment of colored persons as a means of effecting economy. The Anglicans did not do this; they never actively recruited colored clergy.

## Formation of the Province

It was at this time that the thought of forming a province was born. At a meeting of the bishops in Guyana in 1873, a resolution was passed to the effect that this end be actively pursued. It was ten years before this was finally achieved, and the first provincial synod was held in November 1883. That inaugural synod comprised the Bishop of Guyana, William Piercy Austin, who was elected primate; the Bishop of Jamaica, Enos Nuttall; the Bishop Coadjutor of Antigua, C. J. Branch; the Bishop of Barbados, Herbert Bree, and the Bishop of Nassau, Addington Vanables. Those absent were the Bishop of Trinidad, Richard Rawle; and the Bishop of Antigua, W. W. Jackson. The diocese of the Windward Islands was administered from Barbados. Originally, the provincial synod was composed solely of the bishops, though there was an early desire for extension of the membership to comprise three houses. It took the province just over three-quarters of a century to attain that goal, so that 1959 marks a significant milestone in our provincial history.

One of the failures of the church in our region was the absence of any conscious effort to train persons for leadership at the highest level. The Anglican Church, emanating from England, seemed always to see its leadership arriving by boat or airplane from the same location. The first colored bishop, Perceval Gibson, was elected in 1947 as the Suffragan of Kingston in Jamaica, becoming diocesan in 1955. The first colored archbishop, G. C. M. Woodroffe, was elected in 1980, by which time almost the entire bench was West Indian and colored. This important development was long in coming even though a white West Indian creole had become a bishop in the nineteenth century. It was a rapid change in 30 years, but one which even English clergy were calling for.

## Ecumenism

It is now necessary to say a word on the ecumenical dimension of church life in the Caribbean. Not long ago, a letter written in support of a candidate for election as bishop contained these words: "He is ecumenical but not ecumaniac." Those words suggested that the candidate was willing to work with other churches, but not to the extent of throwing himself fully into that development. The task which may face us in the future is that of recognizing that we are Anglicans and knowing why we are Anglicans. And then, there will be the additional task of making an Anglican contribution to the ecumenical movement. This point is worth stressing because of a tendency on the part of some people to be so much "one with everybody" that they fail to be anything at all. That would appear to be ecumaniac. It fails to enrich the ecumenical dialogue, and it robs our partners of the opportunity to see and to share what we have. In emphasizing what we have in common, our differences can enhance the dialogue and enlighten those of other traditions. It was as convinced Anglicans that the dioceses of the province participated in the formation of the Caribbean Conferences of Churches, with members of the hierarchy serving in the executive of that body. The dioceses continue to engage in ecumenical dialogue, and, in some areas, in inter-religious dialogue.

## Theological Education

At a very early stage, theological education was seen as a major desideratum. This took different forms. On the one hand, it entailed education for persons in the ordained ministry, the focus of Codrington College from 1830 onward, facilitating the Eastern Caribbean. Later on, the church in Guyana started a program of training, which lasted only for a short period. In Jamaica, following a number of false starts, St. Peter's College gave valuable training to ordinands for some 90 years before its program was merged with that of the United Theological College of the West Indies in 1967. Programs were also run in Guyana and Jamaica for the training of catechists. Lack of resources, however, proved an almost insurmountable obstacle, which Codrington College has barely avoided because of its bequest.

Under Richard Rawle, the college made considerable contribution to education with its training program for teachers; this continued for several years under Arthur Anstey.

In the later part of the last century, Sehon Goodridge, the first West Indian principal, introduced a program for lay leaders which has proven its worth over many decades. the author was the college's second West Indian principal. During my tenure, I initiated a number of important thrusts. One of these entailed the broadening of the student body to embrace persons who were not preparing for ordination, and who paid their way, eventually with support from the government of Barbados. The second was the introduction of post-graduate degrees in theology, awarded by the University of the West Indies. This has proven to be a valuable development, which has been used by ministers of different denominations. By way of support for this work, another initiative entailed the repatriation of original documents on various churches, as far as this was possible. Thus, the CMS, SPG, Baptist, Presbyterian, and Moravian records form part of the college's microform collection. The last initiative was the promotion of courses on Anglicanism, including an in-depth study of the Lambeth Conference reports. Following my introduction of online services, the new principal, Dr. Ian Rock, is hoping to expand the offering of courses using this format. It is a serious challenge for the limited resources of the institution, but it is an inevitable necessity, given the scattered nature of the islands.

## Looking Toward the Future

In 1989, the House of Bishops led by Archbishop Lindsay produced, for debate in that year's provincial synod, a document titled "The Way Forward." Deficient in some vital areas, the document identified ten strategies as the way to take the church forward. Unfortunately, there was never an agreed process of implementation or an identification of priorities. After 11 years, in 2000, there followed a provincial congress, led by Archbishop Gomez, in which work on these issues was not evaluated so that outstanding work could be addressed. This pattern of proceeding tends to be characteristic, so that there is a tendency to pass on to the next item before knowing whether the last was successful. The result is inevitable lack of direction and continuity. Two major tasks have been completed by the province. These are the preparation of a Book of Common Prayer and a hymnal. These are first steps, but indicate the willingness and the ability to execute such work. The perennial worry of the provincial leaders is the lack of funds to make good the desires of the province, and hopefully our small steps will get us where we want to go.

### Bibliography

Baxter, Thomas R. 1913. Caribbean Bishops: The Establishment of the Bishoprics of Jamaica and of Barbados and the Leeward Islands, 1824–1843. *Historical Magazine of* *the Protestant Episcopal Church*, vol. XXXII, no. 3, pp. 189–209.

Bennett, J. H. 1958. *Bondsmen and Bishops*. Berkley: University of California Press.

Bridges, G. W. 1968. *The Annals of Jamaica* (1828), vol. I, Appendix, Section II. London: Frank Cass & Co., Ltd.

Caldecott, A. 1970. *The Church in the West Indies*. London: Frank Cass & Co., Ltd.

Calendar of State Papers. 1661. No. 24. Minutes of the Council for Plantations. February 11, 1661. CD-ROM.

Calendar of State Papers. 1663. No. 489. Instructions to Francis, Lord Willoughby. January 16, 1663. CD-ROM.

Calendar of State Papers. 1637. No. 70. Thomas Lane to Archbishop Laud. October 6, 1637. CD-ROM.

Calendar of State Papers. 1680. No. 488. Memorandum of the Bishop of London Concerning the Church in Barbados. April 28, 1680. CD-ROM.

Campbell, Peter D. 1982. *The Church in Barbados in the Seventh Century*. Bridgetown, Barbados: Barbados Museum and Historical Society.

Cnattingius. 1952. *Bishops and Societies*. London: SPCK.

Ellis, J. B. 1913. *The Diocese of Jamaica*. London: SPCK.

Evans, E. L. n.d. *A History of the Diocese of Jamaica*. n.p.

Fulham Papers. 1723. Answers to Queries Addressed to the Clergy. Vol. XV, pp. 203–14; Vol. XVI, pp. 211–35; Vol. XIX, pp. 16–20. Lambeth Palace Library. Microfilm.

Fulham Papers. 1723. Size of Parishes in Jamaica. Vol. XVII, pp. 211–35. Lambeth Palace Library. Microfilm.

Fulham Papers. 1733. William Johnson to Bishop Gibson, Bridgetown. June 22, 1733. Vol. XVI, pp. 44–45. Lambeth Palace Library. Microfilm.

Harlow, V. 1926. *Barbados, 1625–1685*. Oxford: Clarendon Press.

Long, Edward. 1970. *The History of Jamaica* (1774). Vol. II. London: Frank Cass & Co. Ltd.

Minter, R. A. 1990. *Episcopacy without Episcopate*. Upton upon Severn, Worcester: Self Publishing Association.

Reece, J. E. and C. G. Clark-Hunt. 1925. *Barbados Diocesan History*. London: West India Committee.

Titus, Noel. 1980. The West Indian Mission to Africa: Its Conception and Birth. *Journal of Negro History*, vol. LXV, no. 2 (Spring), pp. 93–111.

Titus, Noel. 1999. Missionary Challenges in Guyana, 1842–1892. *Anglican and Episcopal History*, vol. LXVIII, no. 3 (September), pp. 345–71.

Titus, Noel. 2002. Concurrence without Compliance: S.P.G. and the Barbadian Plantations, 1710–1834. In *Three Centuries of Mission*, ed. Daniel O'Connor. London: Continuum.

Trew, J. M. 1843. *Africa Wasted by Britain and Restored by Native Agency*. London: J. Hatchard and Son.

Williams, Fay Aileen. The Work of the Anglican Church in Education in Jamaica, 1826–1845. Unpublished MA paper.

## CHAPTER 48

# The Episcopal Church of Cuba

## A. Hugo Blankingship, Jr.

A brief review of the history of Cuba is helpful in developing an understanding of the status of Christianity and the role of Anglicanism on that island. Such a review reveals the role of wars and the political consequences of those wars affecting the spread of Christianity. Spain played the predominant part in Cuba's development.

Fifteenth-century Spain was still a divided part of Western Europe, with the Moors in control of much of that country. The uniting of Castile and Aragon with the marriage of Ferdinand and Isabella brought into being a sufficient force to drive the Moors out of Spain. Their cultural influence remains, but they had abandoned their final stronghold of Granada by 1492. This gave the monarchs the opportunity to plant Spain in the New World.

Christopher Columbus had been unsuccessful in persuading the Portuguese to sponsor his intended explorations, because they were concentrating on North and Western Africa, but in 1492 he found a friendly ear in Spain. By midyear, he was on his way with three small ships, westward on a journey that would change the history of the world.

After several other stops, he landed in Cuba on October 27, 1492. He is widely quoted as having described the physical beauty of what he had found as "the most beautiful land that human eyes have ever seen."

Columbus did not circumnavigate the island believing it to be a peninsula. It was not until some years later that the land mass was determined to be an island.

Cuba is the largest island in the Caribbean. It extends from east to west a length of approximately 750 miles and covers approximately 44,000 square miles. It is quite close to the Florida Keys and the Yucatan Peninsula, and hence a gateway to Mexico and Central America (Jaime Suchiliki 1997).

*The Wiley-Blackwell Companion to the Anglican Communion*, First Edition. Edited by Ian S. Markham,
J. Barney Hawkins IV, Justyn Terry, and Leslie Nuñez Steffensen.
© 2013 John Wiley & Sons, Ltd. Published 2013 by John Wiley & Sons, Ltd.

From the beginning, the Spanish were military conquerors. The Indians native to Cuba were the Guanahatabey, the Ciboneyes, and the Tainos. Spain dealt cruelly with the original inhabitants. Many were killed or pressed into slavery. Today, there is barely a trace of any of those tribes. The conquest was quickly over and, within a few years, Spain began to colonize the island and the City of Havana, with its excellent harbor. Early searches for gold were not successful so the conquerors began the development of the island as a major camp from which the conquest of Mexico was launched.

Agriculture grew rapidly, with sugar and tobacco being the primary crops. Some mining was also found to be profitable. At an early stage of its history, African slavery became a part of Cuban life, and its influence today is significant. The Spanish brought their language, culture, architecture, ambition for wealth, and their religion. The Africans brought their own customs, music, and religions. The blend of these two cultures is evident today.

The dominant religion in Cuba has always been Roman Catholicism. As the two cultures blended, a syncretistic religion known as "Santeria" developed and remains an active force to this day – tolerated by the Catholics.

In Europe, Martin Luther nailed his 95 theses on the church door in 1517. The early stages of Anglicanism were slowly developing by the mid-1500s. Henry VIII divorced his first wife, Catherine of Aragon, who was the daughter of Ferdinand and Isabella, and when he could not get papal approval he separated the English Church from Rome and took over its leadership. England and Spain were enemies and in time became rivals in the New World. The defeat of the Spanish Armada in 1588 kept England Protestant.

The Church of England became established in the New World in the American colonies and those islands in the Caribbean occupied by the British. The first recorded Anglican worship in America occurred in 1607 in Virginia.

In the eighteenth century, Spain allied itself with France during the Seven Years War in an effort to protect its Caribbean possessions, which proved to be a mistake. The British Navy was too powerful. In 1762, the British seized Havana and occupied part of Cuba for about 11 months. It is possible that some Anglican worship may have occurred during this period. Spain, however, recovered Cuba in exchange for Florida as a result of the Treaty of Paris.

The British occupation of Cuba provided significant economic and commercial opportunities for Cuba. The slave uprising in Haiti and the destruction of its sugar industry allowed Cuba to become the dominant exporter of sugar in the world.

By the 1790s, Anglicanism had developed a new, independent province in the form of the Protestant Episcopal Church in the United States, with its own bishops. It was the first of the many provinces that developed through the mission work of the English church. Anglicanism spread from England in two stages. First, through its colonial enterprises, and later, in the nineteenth century, through its missionary efforts.

The preface to the American version of the Book of Common Prayer, adopted in 1789, notes that "this Church is far from intending to depart from the Church of England in any essential point of doctrine, discipline or worship, or further than local circumstances require." At the same time, Article XXXIV of the Articles of Religion makes clear that "It is not necessary that traditions and ceremonies be in all places one or utterly alike" (Book of Common Prayer 1789). United in the essentials and flexible in non-essentials became an important characteristic in the spread of Anglicanism throughout the world. Bishop Colin Bazley, the Presiding Bishop of the Anglican Church of the Southern Cone, writing the foreword to *History of Anglicanism in Latin America* (see Ward 2006), noted that "a church with a solid basis in the essentials and flexibility in the non-essential allows the Holy Spirit to produce that kind of unity which reflects something of the New Testament which ought to be seen in every Christian community."

The nineteenth century saw immigration into Cuba from the United States, Britain, and Canada. The increase of commerce also brought frequent shipping from these countries. Bishop Whipple of Minnesota visited Cuba in 1871 and found a need for Anglican chaplaincy on behalf of the growing English-speaking population in Cuba. In his academic thesis on the history of the Episcopal Church in Cuba in 1868 to 1933, the Rev. Juan Ramon de las Paz Cereso makes special note that, when Bishop Whipple returned to the United States convinced of the need for a chaplain to serve the American community in Cuba, he met with resistance from American and Canadian bishops who felt that there should be no such effort in a country where there was already established another Christian church of long standing. The Roman Catholic Church had been the exclusive provider of Christian ministry for well over 300 years. Bishop Whipple prevailed, however, and the Rev. Edward Keeney went to Cuba where he established an effective ministry to English-speaking colonists for a period of 11 years. His written reports back to the Episcopal Church in the United States detail the struggle that he had with problems in Cuba, including yellow fever and a hostile Spanish regime.[1] Keeney was followed by the Rev. Edward Edgerton.

It is important to note that, despite the early American efforts in Cuba, intended mainly to serve the American and British colonials, Anglican ministry to Cubans began first by the creation of Anglican congregations among Cuban immigrants to the United States. Congregations in New York, Philadelphia, and New Orleans were organized and led by native Cuban clergy ordained by American bishops. In time, Cuban clergy left their cures in the United States and founded congregations of Cubans in Cuba. Among those early leaders were the Rev. Pedro Duarte, who was born in Matanzas and ordained by Bishop Whitaker in New York, and the Rev. Manuel Moreno, who was born in Havana and ordained to the priesthood by Bishop H. C. Potter in New York. In time, these congregations and their clergy, as well as many Cuban communities in the United States, became strong supporters of the independence movement that was rapidly developing in Cuba. Among other early Cuban leaders were the Rev. Joaquin de Palma and Juan Bautista Mancebo in the City of Santiago.

This early mission work of Cubans to Cubans came under the general sponsorship of the American Church Missionary Society, acting as an auxiliary of the Board of Missions. The year 1884 saw the confirmation of no less than 116 new members by Bishop John F. Young of Florida (Milmine 1993, 77). By the time of the election and

---

[1] A plaque in the Cathedral in Havana is dedicated to "Presbyter Edward Keeney, Precursor of the Anglican and Evangelical work in Cuba 1871–1880. The Episcopal Church in Cuba offers tribute to his memory. 1971 The Centenary year" (translation).

consecration of the first Missionary Bishop of Cuba, the Rt. Rev. Albion W. Knight in 1904, *The Journal of the Episcopal Church* reports five clergy, five missions and churches, and 149 communicants.

Bishop Knight had come to Cuba from Florida. He saw his ministry principally devoted to having the church serve as a chaplaincy to North Americans working in Cuba and other English-speaking residents, but also to lapsed Catholics who might find Anglicanism an acceptable alternative. During his stay, the church grew, a cathedral was built in downtown Havana, a seminary was started, and schools built. The 1913 *Living Church Journal* reports 22 clergy, of which 11 were foreign and 11 were Cuban. There were 53 parishes and missions and 1,734 communicants. Bishop Knight resigned in 1913 to accept the office of vice chancellor at the University of the South.

There were two other American-born Missionary Bishops of Cuba. Bishop Hiram Richard Hulse served from 1915 until his death in 1938. He was followed by Bishop Alexander Hugo Blankingship of Virginia in 1939, who had been serving as Dean of the Cathedral in Havana for 11 years before his consecration. The church continued to grow; emphasis was placed on a strong group of clergy, well trained, and mostly Cuban, who aided greatly in establishing a domestic church for the Cuban people. A new cathedral in the suburbs of Havana was built at the end of World War II with a school, two residences, and a playground. New churches were built in numerous places throughout the island. Church schools were successful and the source of new Anglicans and future clergy. At the convocation in 1961, at which he announced his intended retirement, Bishop Blankingship declared that the church in Cuba must go forward with a Cuban bishop. A brief summary of the ministry of these three bishops can be found in the section on Cuba in Milmine's *History of Anglicanism in Latin America* (see Milmine 1993, 77f).

By 1962, the *Living Church Annual* reported 33 clergy, 45 churches and missions, 9,454 communicants, and 71,765 baptized members.

On January 1, 1959 a dramatic change occurred in the political structure of the government. Fulgencio Batista, who had ruled for many years (as a result of a coup), fled the country on New Year's Eve, representing the collapse of his regime and the success of the Revolution led by Fidel Castro. As the Castro government secured its position of total control, the implementation of a socialist/communist system gradually came into being and has dominated Cuban life ever since.

Businesses, banks, and other commercial enterprises, many of which had been foreign owned and operated, were either taken over or closed down. This, in turn, created a gradual economic decline which Russian, Chinese, and Venezuelan assistance could not overcome.

Fidel Castro's bad health in 2012 led him to turn over control of the country to his brother Raul. It appears that reality has been finally recognized and the government has most recently allowed limited private enterprise to enter the economic scene, prompting Teo Babura to report: "Cuba, right now, is in a state of great confusion between shifting from purely a socialist–communist system to a quasi-market system" (see Milmine 1993).

Bishop Blankingship and his wife were forced to leave Cuba several months before his intended retirement date because of the anti-American feeling which developed following the unsuccessful Bay of Pigs invasion in April of 1961. His call for the election of a Cuban bishop as his successor was met with the election of Romualdo Gonzalez y Agueros, a highly educated Spanish-born Cuban to whom fell the responsibility of leading the Cuban Episcopal Church into its life under the Castro regime.

Just as the Cuban clergy had assumed patriotic roles against Spain and its abuses, some Cuban clergy and many Cuban Episcopalians had become part of the resistance against the Batista regime. Not all supported Castro, however, and gradually many Cuban Episcopalians left Cuba and relocated to the United States. Those who remained continued to be led by competent Cuban bishops who bravely forged a life "to witness in all things which would not compromise its commitment to Christ, to win respect from the State and a recognition that the Church could contribute to the general good of the people of Cuba."[2]

## The Castro Revolution and the Church in Cuba

Fulgencio Batista held a tight rein on Cuba that gradually generated popular dissent. The presence of North American mafia added to the corruption that prevailed everywhere. Those opposed to Batista were prosecuted, and many dissidents were killed. It was not hard to discern how things were going to develop.

Castro rose to leadership when he launched a small force from Mexico and attacked a military barracks in eastern Cuba. The operation was not successful as a military venture, but it helped galvanize the beginning of a revolution that was to last for four years before Batista fled the island on New Year's Eve, 1958.

A swift but still bloody mop-up operation followed, and Castro soon reached Havana to take charge of the country.

The stated principles of the Revolution were social and land reform, clean up of all corruption in government, expulsion of undesirable elements of the prior regime, universal education, and economic change, all of which received wide appeal among people.

Religious bodies, and especially young people, both Catholic and Protestant, became associated with the Revolution. This included members of Cuban Episcopal clergy. From their standpoint, their actions were intended to be similar to the patriotic efforts of Cuban clergy in the mid-1800s against the tyranny of Spain and consistent with Christian goals.

As the new government began to implement changes, concern began to develop, especially in the United States, that the Revolution had taken a socialist Marxist turn. At first, most Protestant clergy in Cuba were quick to defend the Revolution, to support its reforms and to deny that there was any Communist influence involved.

The first group to offer opposing comment was the Roman Catholics. Castro was busy opening new schools all over the island, but at the same time he began to close church schools. In response to their complaints, Castro invalidated the academic

[2] Author unknown.

degrees of persons graduated from Catholic universities. Since the Protestants had no universities, they were silent.

The first two years of the government take-over or closing down of institutions, businesses, newspapers, and the like went rather smoothly for Castro. Many foreign residents left the country only to be followed by many Cubans, mostly from the upper economic classes. In time, over a million Cubans fled the island, causing serious problems for all the churches.

The public debate over whether or not Castro was a Communist continued with concerns now being expressed by many Cubans.

In 1961, a group of Cuban dissidents undertook a counter-revolutionary invasion of the island landing at an area known as the Bay of Pigs. In retrospect, the invasion was not well planned or executed, although it had support of the American Central Intelligence Agency. Air support from the United States was not forthcoming. The expectation that a large portion of the population would rise in an effort to be rid of Castro was just that, an expectation which never materialized.

The invasion failed. Many of the invaders were killed or captured. At that point, for the first time, Fidel Castro announced that the Revolution was indeed Socialist–Marxist inspired, and suddenly the tough times in Cuba began. Castro committed publicly to establishing an atheistic society. The Soviet Union saw an opportunity for the spread of Communism in the Western world and undertook a program of support, with financial, technological, and military assistance from Russia. This led to the Cuban missile crisis and the other efforts by the Soviets, ultimately bringing the Cuban economy to a standstill.

The Episcopal Church in Cuba was confronted with a major problem. Some still supported the Revolution, some opposed the Revolution, and some sought a position of neutrality. It caused an internal division which in time prevented the church from agreeing on the election of a bishop.

Castro attempted to undermine Christian missions in Cuba. Christian holidays were abandoned in favor of secular festivities celebrating the Revolution and its heroes. A good account of the difficulties experienced by Protestant churches in Cuba can be found in a work by Theron Corse, an assistant professor of Latin American history at Tennessee State University, entitled *Protestants, Revolution and the Cuba–U.S. Bond* (see Corse 2007).

The Revolution had the salutary effect of advancing ecumenism in Cuba. Before the Revolution, a seminary, Seminario Evangelico de Teologia, was established in Matanzas by the Methodists, Presbyterians, and Episcopalians,. Protestant churches founded the Council of Evangelical Churches in Cuba (Concilio Cubano de Iglesias Evangelicas), to which many churches belonged. These groups sought accommodation with the Revolution but gradually experienced the divisions which have already been mentioned.

Theron Corse notes the sudden increase of house churches to which the Pentecostals and Afro-Cuban religions, including Santeria, have claimed the greatest growth. This is consistent with reports of the rapid growth of Pentecostalism elsewhere in Latin America, and today the Pentecostals are well established in Cuba. With the collapse of the Soviet Union, things began to change in Cuba.

The Roman Catholics had been severely persecuted by Castro in the early years of the Revolution. In time, Castro seems to have realized that these pursuits were not politically wise. In November 1996, Castro visited Pope John Paul II in Rome and invited him to come to Cuba. This he did in January 1998. As a prelude to the visit, Castro restored Christmas as an official holiday for the first time since 1960. Subsequently, he declared that his government was secular (not atheistic). The pope's visit was widely acclaimed as a hope for better relations between all the churches and the government.

In earlier times, the Catholic Church had sought to marginalize the Protestants. That practice seems to have disappeared, and cooperation among all churches in Cuba is on the rise.

## The Future of Anglicanism in Cuba

Charles Henry Long, in *Who Are the Anglicans*, notes: "It has been said that the Anglican Communion is rapidly outgrowing its Englishness but has not yet established its own identity as a multi-raced, multi-lingual, multi-cultural family" (*Who Are the Anglicans* 1998).

The year before Long's work, which was prepared for the 1988 Lambeth Conference, the Episcopal Diocese of Panama conducted a "Symposium on Latin American Anglicanism" and John Kater edited and published a number of essays delivered at or resulting from that conference. The Spanish version of the texts appeared under the title *Somos Anglicanos* in 1987. Kater, who was the Education Officer of the Diocese of Panama, was responsible for the translation of the texts into English, which were published by the Diocese in 1989.

Although no essay was available from a Cuban writer, there is merit in examining these texts since Anglicanism elsewhere in Latin America has developed in patterns similar to that in Cuba. Kater quotes with approval from an earlier work by Bishop Jose Gonzalez, a retired Bishop of Cuba, from his *La Communion Anglicana en America Latina* (1986), as follows:

> Our mission, the same one passed on to the disciples by the Lord, is that of proclaiming the Good News, which we will do within our theological, liturgical, missionary, ecumenical and administrative structure, without feeling obligated to give any excuses. . . . This mission includes ministering to the millions of Latin Americans who do not have a shepherd, anywhere and everywhere, to those who prefer our church . . . where the ancient Christian traditions can and should be enriched by the cultural contributions of each place . . . (Gonzalez 1986)

Elsewhere in *We Are the Anglicans*, we read from Jose Vilar of Puerto Rico:

> We cannot look with certainty at the different components of Latin America and point out without ambiguities what is manifest as a clearly defined Latin American Anglican. The

most we can say is that we must look up close, not at Anglicanism but at Anglicans. It is Anglicans as persons who, when we gather together their characteristics, worries and occupations, little by little will contribute to the collectivity of people and structure which we call "Anglicanism." (see *Who Are the Anglicans* 1998)

It follows that in considering the future of Anglicanism in Cuba we need to get close to the Cuban people their culture, their history, and their problems.

Anglicanism in Cuba has developed and continues to develop its own local identity. Seen as an alternative to Roman Catholicism, it has retained its ancient Christian roots and catholicity. Faithful to the biblical truths on which it was founded, it has adopted itself to the character of the Cuban people.

Milmine, in his *History of Anglicanism in Latin America*, recites a comment from the Ven. Juan Ramon de la Paz Cereso, a retired priest of the Episcopal Church in Cuba and the designated historian of the Diocese.

The history of the Episcopal Church of Cuba constitutes the original effort of a church which has always been small and poor and sometimes decimated, but which has a prophetic spirit expressive of patriotism and universal Christianity, bountiful, liberal, original and creative which has aroused the affection, passion and surrender of a small but significant number of men through its history. (Milmine 1993, 81)

John Westerhoff, writing in *The Essential Guide to the Anglican Communion*, outlines his view of the Anglican temperament as follows, "Temperament refers to a tradition's characteristic ways of thinking and behaving. The Anglican Temperament is comprehensive, ambiguous, open-minded, intuitive, aesthetic, moderate, not unrealistic, historical and political."

He goes on to discuss each of his listed attributes. It is interesting to note how a Latin American Anglican views the makeup of Anglicans:

In the North, the bishop continues to be the liturgical center on which everyone leans. Although the form of electing bishops is the same, the experience is greater. The electors generally look more at aptitudes for administration, communication, public relations and leadership than for aspects more related to gifts and charisma. The diocesan tradition, the social status of the candidate and the programmatic projections of the diocese are factors which influence an election. In the United States and England, there are always many who are qualified to be bishops.

The Church in Latin America seems to be more charismatic; it wants to trust more in the Holy Spirit than in its own capacity. It is Biblical and practical. A smile often converts more people than a sermon. In the North, a Church which aspires to academic excellence with high intellectual interest is still evident; particularly among the leadership, we can note the preference for theologians and able administrators. (*The Essential Guide to the Anglican Communion* 1998)

Protestantism has grown significantly in Latin America since the 1990s. All mainline denominations are present, and they seek mutual cooperation through membership in the Latin American Council of Churches, the Caribbean Conference of Churches, and other similar organizations. The Cuban Council of Churches boasts 14 different denominational members, of which the Episcopal Church is one.

The Evangelical and Pentecostal churches seem to have acquired the strongest foothold. Pentecostals represent the most rapidly growing sector of Latin American Protestantism. It is said that about 73 percent of Protestants in South America are Pentecostals.

Kevin Ward, in his *A History of Global Anglicanism*, cites Bishop David Leane's comment that Anglicanism in Latin America is "an empty bus desperately needing to be filled." Ward goes on to comment:

> There has always been a strong optimism among people involved in mission in South America that there is an Anglican-shaped gap in Latin American spirituality just waiting to be filled. Anglicans have consistently noted that Latin America is "not as Roman Catholic" as would seem at first glance, with perhaps only 20 per cent of the total population having more than a superficial encounter with Catholicism (figures vary, but all are more or less based on subjective criteria). The general Catholic shaping of culture is acknowledged. Anglicanism seems perfectly designed to appeal to those dissatisfied with the Catholic Church, but for whom colour and liturgy and a sacramental approach to life are more appealing than Protestant alternatives. Unfortunately for this optimistic view, the evidence seems to point to a great increase in Protestantism, particularly in its Pentecostal forms, rather than to the modified forms of Catholic worship and the cerebral literary (biblical) focus which many see as typical of Evangelical Anglicanism. (Ward 2006)

Early in the life of the American Episcopal Church, Bishop John Henry Hobart, the founder of General Theological Seminary, in his *Companion for the Festivals and Feasts of the Protestant Episcopal Church* (1804), made a carefully worded defense of the use of a prescribed liturgy, noting that "The Lessons, the Creeds, the Commandments, the Epistles and Gospels contain the most important and impressive instructions on the doctrines and duties of religion; while the Confession, the Collects and Prayers, the Litany and Thanksgivings lead the understanding and the heart through all the sublime and affecting exercises of devotion."

The Book of Common Prayer, as adapted for local usage, is able to draw many a searching person into the reach of Anglicanism. In fact, a number of Pentecostal groups have found it very appealing and, recalling the earlier comment that "the Church in Latin America seems to be more charismatic," it may well be that the advance of Anglicanism can be enhanced by means of a closer link with the Pentecostals. God works in wondrous ways.

In Cuba today, the Cuban Pentecostal Church reports 191 congregations, 49 ordained ministers, 87 preachers, and 108 lay workers. It has been active in Cuba for less than 50 years. By contrast, the Episcopal Church reports 45 churches, 27 presbyters, three deacons, two bishops, and 16,233 confirmands (see Ward 2006 and Report of Juan Ramon de le Paz Cerezo 2012).

In the Episcopal Church, the collapse of the Cuba–United States relations created the need to separate from the Episcopal Church USA. In 1996, the church in Cuba became an autonomous, extra-provincial diocese under the authority of a metropolitan council composed of the Primate of Anglican Church in Canada, the Primate of the West Indies, and the President of Province 9, now the Presiding Bishop of the Episcopal Church in the United States.

In late 1965, Bishop Romualdo Gonzalez stepped down as the Bishop of Cuba. Suffering a serious illness, he moved to New Orleans, where he died shortly thereafter. He was succeeded by two other Cuban bishops, Jose Augustin Gonzalez, followed by Emilio Joaquin Hernandez. During that period, the Episcopal Church participated in extensive ecumenical activity with other Cuban Protestants. A degree of liberalism as to politics and religion, local and international, created or exacerbated internal divisions within the church to a point where clergy and laity could not elect another bishop. The metropolitan council appointed the Bishop of Uruguay, the Rt. Rev. Miguel Tamayo, who was a Cuban, to serve as acting Bishop of Cuba. The inability to elect a bishop continued for a number of years, so the council in 2007 appointed two suffragan bishops to assist Bishop Tamayo – Nerva Cot Aguilera and Ulises Aguero Prendes. One was the first female bishop ever to serve in Cuba. When Bishop Tamayo announced his intention to retire, the council, in 2010, appointed the first female diocesan Bishop of Cuba, Griselda de Caprio, who was born in Bolivia but had served as a priest in Cuba for many years. She was consecrated in February 2011 and has wide support among the clergy and laity as she leads the church forward.

In recent years, there has been another Anglican missionary effort in Cuba. A small group of believers in eastern Cuba, led by a Canadian, made contact through the Internet with a Canadian bishop located in western Canada. They invited Bishop Charles Dorrington to come for a visit. Canadian visitors had free access to Cuba during the Cuban–American difficulties so the Bishop and his wife accepted the invitation in 2003. That visit let to the establishment of a significant missionary effort under the auspices of the Reformed Episcopal Church, of which Bishop Dorrington is a diocesan.

The Dorringtons have returned to Cuba each year since their initial visit to start and support new churches; baptize and confirm new members; and to raise up new clergy. Today, La Iglesia Episcopal Reformada has constitutional and canonical structure with approximately 20 congregations under the care of dedicated clergy. Its mission does not clash with that of the Episcopal Church, it being clear that there are abundant candidates, especially among young people, hungry to hear and abide by the Word of God.

In his report to the first council of La Iglesia Episcopal Reformada de Cuba, the late Archdeacon Ramon Batista stressed the prospering of ecumenical relations with numerous other Protestant churches, including La Iglesia Episcopal de Cuba. He outlined the approach to ministry as follows:

> We focus our attention on the significance of local congregations as principal agency of our mission. If we are to reach many Cubans with Jesus Christ's transforming love the main way to do it is through local churches, missioning with the fourfold responsibility imperative of:
>
> 1. Being faithful to the Sacred Scriptures, living and speaking of the faith according to them as the Apostle Peter said 1 Peter 4:11;

2.  Keeping the great Anglican Tradition of authentic orthodox faith;
3.  Becoming people committed to personal sanctity of life under the power of the Spirit of Trust, (Heb 12:14) and, finally,
4.  Producing a testimony that transforms the families and communities in which we carry out our ministry.
5.  The understanding of these things is an outstanding achievement in itself.

Cuba is going to change. It has learned the failures of Communism, and the old regime is getting older. Economic pressures as well as opportunities will, in time, bring adjustments we have seen elsewhere where Communism has failed.

Mission trips to Cuba from churches, largely from the United States, are increasing each year. Financial assistance will follow. A number of Episcopal congregations in the United States have adopted "companion" relationships with churches in Cuba.

It is beyond the scope of this chapter to discuss the conflicts and changes that have been taking place within the Anglican Communion, especially in recent times. Anglicans in the Global South have significant issues with their fellow Anglicans in the North and the West. These pending problems and potential divisions present some uncertainty over how Anglicanism is to develop and grow in those areas of the world, like Cuba, where the church since its early days has been small and poor.

The Archbishop of Canterbury, speaking at Gimnasio Nuevo in Panama in 1996, referred to a thought expressed much earlier by Bishop Edward King, Bishop of Lincoln in the Church of England:

> I long to see a real and simple imitation of the life we have shown to us in the Gospels. It seems to me that if people go on allowing themselves to shape their lives so much more by the circumstances of the world than by the Gospel, they will be in danger of disbelieving the truths of the Bible itself.

These words of Bishop King are prophetic and offer a sober warning to Anglicans the world over. The circumstances confronting the Cuban people and those confronting the Anglican Church elsewhere can determine the future of Anglicans anywhere. It all depends on how firm their foundation is and how well it will be maintained. With God's help and guidance, Anglicanism in Cuba will go forward.

## Bibliography

Batista, Ramon. Report to the First Council of La Iglesia Episcopal Reformada de Cuba.

Corse, Theron. 2007. *Protestants, Revolution, and the Cuba-U.S. Bond*. Gainesville: University Press of Florida.

Episcopal Church, The. 1789. *The Book of Common Prayer*. New York: T. Allen.

Episcopal Church, The. 1979. *The Book of Common Prayer*. New York: Seabury Press.

Episcopal Church, The. 1904. *The Journal of the Episcopal Church*. New York: Winthrop Press.

Hobart, John Henry. 1804. *A Companion for the Festivals and Fasts of the Protestant Episcopal Church in the United States of America*. New York: Stanford and Swords.

Gonzalez, Jose. 1986. *La Communion Anglicana en America Latina*.

Kater, John L., trans. and ed. 1987/1989. *Somos Anglicanos (We Are Anglicans)*. Diocese of Panama: Morehouse Publishing.

Living Church Journal, The. 1913.

Living Church Annual, The. 1962.

Long, Charles Henry. 1988. *Who Are the Anglicans? Profiles and Maps of the Anglican Communion*. Cincinnati, Ohio: Forward Movement Publications.

Milmine, Douglas. 1993. *The History of Anglicanism in Latin America*. Tunbridge Wells, Kent: South American Missionary Society.

Pew Forum on Religion and Public Life.

Report of Juan Ramon de le Paz Cerezo. 2012.

Rosenthal, James, ed. 1998. *The Essential Guide to the Anglican Communion*. Harrisburg: Morehouse Publishing.

Sermon of the Archbishop of Canterbury, Sunday, October 13, 1996 as seen in *Being Anglican*. Morehouse Publishing.

Suchiliki, Jaime. 1997. *Cuba from Columbus to Castro and Beyond*, 4th ed. Washington, DC: Brassey's, Inc.

Ward, Kevin. 2006. *A History of Global Anglicanism*. Cambridge, UK: Cambridge University Press.

World Christian Database.

# South America

**Legend:**
- La Iglesia Anglicana del Cono Sur
- Igreja Episcopal Anglicana do Brasil

PERU

BRAZIL

BOLIVIA

PARAGUAY

CHILE

ARGENTINA

URUGUAY

1600 km

1000 miles

CHAPTER 49

# Igreja Episcopal Anglicana do Brasil (The Anglican Episcopal Church of Brazil)

## Gustavo L. Castello Branco and Marcus Throup

The genesis of Anglicanism in Brazil comprises one of those chapters in the history of Christianity which reminds us that the Triune God frequently acts in unexpected ways, accomplishing his wonderful plans through ordinary people made extraordinary by his Spirit. As Jesus himself put it, "The Spirit blows wherever it wills; we know neither from where it comes nor where it goes" (Jn 3.8).

In contrast to the advent and advance of Anglicanism in other parts of South America, Brazilian Anglicanism did not grow out of the work of a missionary organization, nor did it result from the missional stratagem of a particular province or diocese. Again, it was the spiritual insight of neither bishops nor seasoned clergy which perceived, beyond the veil of nominal Catholicism, the deep spiritual thirst of the Brazilian people. Rather, the rise of Anglicanism in Brazil is associated with the efforts of a few young seminarians in the late nineteenth century who, inspired by the missionary revival in the Theological Seminary of Virginia, in the United States, took it upon themselves to further the gospel in *terra brasilis*. However, before we retrace the missionary steps of Lucien Lee Kinsolving and James Watson Morris, a word must be said in relation to what may be termed the *prehistory* of Brazilian Anglicanism.

## The Prehistory of Anglicanism in Brazil

As far as the records show, the first Anglican to set foot in Brazil was the famous English missionary Henry Martyn. Martyn reached Brazil in November 1805, when the country was still a colony of Portugal. En route to India, Martyn's ship docked in Salvador, Bahia, affording him the opportunity to converse with Roman Catholic priests, slave

*The Wiley-Blackwell Companion to the Anglican Communion*, First Edition. Edited by Ian S. Markham,
J. Barney Hawkins IV, Justyn Terry, and Leslie Nuñez Steffensen.
© 2013 John Wiley & Sons, Ltd. Published 2013 by John Wiley & Sons, Ltd.

traders, and dignitaries. Although he remained in Brazil for just a fortnight, that was time enough for Martyn to lament what he perceived to be a superficial religiosity on the part of the Brazilian people. His diary entry for November 12, 1805, reads as follows:

> What happy missionary shall be sent to bear the name of Christ to these Western regions? When shall this beautiful country be delivered from idolatry and spurious Christianity? Crosses there are in abundance, but when shall the doctrine of the Cross be held up? (Smith n.d., 108; compare the verdict of the Edinburgh Conference on World Mission in 1910 which, on account of the Roman Catholic presence in Brazil, found it unnecessary to view Brazil as a "mission field").

Notwithstanding the urgency in Martyn's impassioned appeal, a concrete response would not be forthcoming for some time. Staunchly Roman Catholic, Brazil had expressly and uniformly prohibited the presence on its soil of Protestant missions. This prohibition continued even after the nation won its independence from Portugal on September 7, 1822. There was, though, a single qualified exception. In February 1810, not long after Henry Martyn had visited Brazil, a Treaty of Navigation and Commerce between Portugal and Great Britain opened the way for business and the sojourn in Brazil of British citizens who were ordinarily members of the Church of England. Thus, in the interests of trade, Portugal granted the subjects of the British crown freedom to practice their own religion while resident in Brazil.

Accordingly, the twelfth article of the treaty made provision for the building of Anglican places of worship and cemeteries (Kickhöfel 1995, 202). Nevertheless, the Anglican chapels were not to have the appearance of churches, rather they were to be built on the model of private residences! Again, the chapels were denied the use of bells, since these were used in Catholic parishes as a call to worship. Despite these restrictions, the concession made to the immigrant British workforce resulted in the erection of the first Protestant church in Brazil, the Anglican chapel Christchurch built in 1819, and inaugurated in 1822, which continues to this day as an English-speaking church in the heart of Rio de Janeiro. After Christchurch, further Anglican chapels, hospitals, and cemeteries were built in the major cities on the Brazilian coast.

Although the Anglican chaplaincies arrived in Brazil more than 60 years before the missionaries from Virginia, the roots of Brazilian Anglicanism are generally traced to the latter rather than the former. While the Brazilian Anglican churches planted by US missionaries were outward looking and mission focused, experiencing exponential growth and forming themselves into dioceses and electing bishops, the British chaplaincies were of essence parochial (Kickhöfel 1995, 209–13). Indeed, the chaplaincies were established with the specific aim of providing religious services for the British residents. Moreover, until transferred to the Bishop of the Falkland Isles in 1869, the chaplaincies were under the jurisdiction of the Bishop of London (Kickhöfel 1995, 203). Even with the eventual consolidation of religious liberty in Brazil, the British chapels remained true to their original remit, showing little if any missionary initiative. While it must be borne in mind that the chaplaincies felt a certain legal obligation to maintain a low profile, in later years with new legislation, their apparent reluctance to broaden frontiers and share fellowship with Brazilians would be interpreted unfavorably by subsequent generations of Brazilian Anglicans.

Prior to the successful missionary campaign of the Episcopalian seminarians in 1889, there were two other attempts to establish Anglican Christianity in Brazil. First, William Cooper was sent by the missionary society of the Protestant Episcopal Church of the United States (ECUSA) in 1853, in response to an appeal from an American Episcopalian resident in Rio de Janeiro. However, on account of a shipwreck which forced him to return home, Cooper would never set foot in Brazilian territory. The second attempt was more fortuitous. During the years 1860–1872, Richard Holden ministered in Brazil. Holden was a Scot, born in 1828 into an Episcopalian family. At the age of 21, he was converted and went to study in the Theological Seminary of the Diocese of Ohio. Holden learned Portuguese and began work in Belém, Pará state, supported by the mission division of the ECUSA and also by the American Bible Society. Like Martyn before him, Holden was a critic of the Brazilian religious scenario, particularly in regard to what he perceived to be the corruption within the Roman Catholic ranks. In his diary, after a year and a half working in Pará, Holden wrote: "I'm yet to meet a single Catholic priest who appears sincere or who is at all interested in matters divine" (Kickhöfel 1995, 35).

Holden was unable to plant a church in Brazil on account of strong opposition from the Catholic Bishop of Belém, who spread abroad the notion that Holden advocated "a masonic, protestant movement seeking to destroy the Roman Catholic Church, the first step in a planned invasion of the Amazon by the United States" (Kickhöfel 1995, 35). Nevertheless, Holden's missionary endeavors made a positive impression and bequeathed an important legacy: the translation of the prayer book into Portuguese. Again, Holden brought Bibles and Christian literature to small towns on the Amazon River, proclaimed the gospel in articles published in newspapers in Pará, Bahia, and Rio de Janeiro, and wrote various hymns which retain their place in Brazilian hymnody. Holden was in many respects the precursor to the definitive establishment of Episcopalian Anglicanism in Brazil.

## Episcopalian Missionaries and the Rise of the National Church: Anglicanism in Brazil from 1889

Described by one church historian as the "Antioch of the North American Episcopal Church" (Kickhöfel 1995, 40), in the nineteenth century the Theological Seminary of Virginia trained a generation of leaders whose evangelistic zeal would change the world. Missionaries were sent to Greece, China, Africa, Japan, and Brazil. L. L. Kinsolving and J. W. Morris were commissioned in the seminary and sent to Brazil in 1889. On arrival in Rio de Janeiro after a stormy sea voyage, Kinsolving and Morris set about learning the language and the culture, fixing residence in São Paulo. Moving south, the duo founded a church in Porto Alegre in 1890, where, on the first Sunday of June, an inaugural church service was held in Portuguese for Brazilians (Aquino 2000, 28).

The arrival of a second pair of missionaries, William Cabel Brown and John Meem, served to reinforce and further the missionary efforts of Kinsolving and Morris. New church plants were built up, and by 1893 the number of converts was so great that it was necessary to send for a bishop to minister the confirmation rite. Bishop George W. Peterkin travelled from West Virginia to the South of Brazil to perform the rite. However, in 1899, Kinsolving was consecrated as the first Episcopalian bishop sent to Brazil but accountable to the ECUSA. In a ministry spanning 27 years, Kinsolving, who eventually retired due to ill health, baptized no less than 13,535 people, confirmed 4,997, and built 25 churches (Aquino 2000, 28).

While initially a "missionary district" of the Episcopal Church of North America, the consecration of the first Brazilian bishop in 1940, D. Athalício Theodoro Pithan, opened the way for the creation of an independent national church. Brazil claimed its status as an autonomous province of the Anglican Communion in 1964, and in 1965 became known as the *Igreja Episcopal do Brasil* (The Episcopal Church of Brazil); nevertheless, in practice it would continue to be heavily dependent on US funding in the following decades. The Episcopal Church of Brazil became the "Anglican Episcopal Church of Brazil" (Igreja Episcopal Anglicana do Brasil [IEAB]) in 1990. Today, the IEAB is made up of several dioceses which span the entire territory of Brazil, although the number of active members is probably no more than 10,000.

In common with the mainstream North American Episcopalian spirituality, but in contrast with Anglican spirituality in other South American nations, Brazilian Anglicanism exhibits rigid and conservative liturgical tendencies. Vestments are worn even in the more evangelical congregations, and even in tropical regions where a simple clerical shirt would surely be more practical! Though the liturgical approach is traditional, the theology espoused is not. Given the historical ties with the ECUSA, it is perhaps unsurprising that the IEAB has shadowed the former on theological issues. For example, following the sanctioning of women's ordination in the Episcopal Church, the IEAB ordained its first female deacon, Carmem Etel Alves Gomes, in 1985. More recently, the IEAB has stood shoulder to shoulder with the Episcopal Church in the United States (TEC) on questions pertaining to human sexuality and the ordination of practicing homosexual clergy, an issue to which we now turn.

## A Microcosm of the AC: Anglicanism in Brazil from Lambeth 1998 to Recife 2011

Following the consecration of practicing homosexual Gene Robinson in New Hampshire, United States, in November 2003, the *phony war* in the Anglican Communion came to an end and *civil war* ensued. However, the first major confrontation in the struggle for the soul of the communion took place neither in Canterbury nor in New York. As is wont to happen in the history of the church, in times of crisis, little-known places and persons come suddenly to center stage as localized disputes take on deeper significance in virtue of the political agendas and theological positions represented. It is thus that the Diocese of Recife, Brazil, and its diocesan bishop, Edward Robinson de Barros Cavalcanti, emerged from relative obscurity to assume a place in the ecclesiastical annals. Although Bishop Cavalcanti and his wife were killed by his son in February 2012, Bishop Cavalcanti took a distinctive stance in the debate over homosexuality.

In a sense, the writing was on the wall at the Lambeth Conference 1998. Allied with the pro-homosexual majority of the ECUSA, with one exception, the Brazilian bishops voted against the controversial Resolution 1.10, which declares homosexual practice to be incompatible with the scriptures. Bishop Cavalcanti, a founder of the Lausanne Movement and a former IFES leader, was the only Brazilian bishop to vote for the resolution, making it an official diocesan precept on his return to Recife. Since its inauguration in 1976, the Diocese of Recife had always stood apart from the Brazilian Province (IEAB), both geographically (Recife is some 1,850 miles from the Provincial See, Porto Alegre!), and in terms of churchmanship: the IEAB, influenced theologically by the North American Church, is predominantly liberal catholic, whereas the Diocese of Recife was planted as an evangelical and charismatic diocese under the auspices of North American missionary Bishop Edmund Sherill. Post Lambeth 1998, however, prior tensions would resurface with new force, as differing theological positions became entrenched.

In December 2000, in the spirit of Lambeth 1998, Resolution 1.10, the evangelical Diocese of Recife passed a rubric designed to prevent the ordination of (a) practicing homosexuals; (b) heterosexuals who consider homosexual practice "normal"; and (c) homophobic persons. Then, in June 2003, following Bishop Michael Ingham's authorization of a blessing for same-sex couples in New Westminster, Canada, and Canon Gene Robinson's election as the first openly gay bishop of the Anglican Communion, Bishop Cavalcanti, his suffragan Filadelfo Oliveira, and the diocesan standing committee published a statement suspending communion with New Westminster and New Hampshire, reaffirming the commitment of the diocese to Resolution 1.10 of Lambeth 1998.

The consecration of Gene Robinson in November 2003 was headline material on Brazilian national TV. In Recife, despite attempts to clarify the unprecedented and anomalous character of this occurrence, evangelical clergy found that church attendance dropped as several parishioners abandoned the diocese, ridiculed by peers and members of other churches as those belonging to the "gay church." Little wonder, then, that at synod in December 2003, the Diocese of Recife deliberated to maintain communion exclusively with entities who had undersigned Resolution 1.10, voting to annul its partnership with the Diocese of Central Pennsylvania. In contrast, Brazilian Archbishop Orlando Oliveira sent a letter to the North American Primate in support of the consecration of Gene Robinson (Cavalcanti 2007, 36–7). Thus, on issues concerning human sexuality, in a somewhat symmetrical configuration, a single diocese espousing the majority position of the communion entered on a collision course with its province, an advocate of the communion's minority position.

In September 2004, the Diocese of Recife received notification from the Brazilian House of Bishops that a "special episcopal oversight" would take effect in the diocese. Accused among other things of "profound intolerance with regard to those who think differently," illegal border-crossing without provincial authorization, "the diffusion of concepts which contradict the doctrine of the Church and the notion of comprehensiveness," and "anticanonical behaviour," Bishop Cavalcanti was suspended by Brazilian primate Orlando Oliveira, who proceeded to designate suffragan bishop Filadelfo Oliveira (no relation to the primate) as the "diocesan authority." While a handful of Recife clergy backed the province, siding with the suffragan against the diocesan bishop, 35 parishes and church plants and 32 clergy, representing 90 percent of the members of the Diocese of Recife, rejected the provincial measures and, in the Setubal Letter, reaffirmed their loyalty to the "legitimate diocesan bishop," Bishop Cavalcanti (Cavalcanti 2007, 41–2).

In a situation which to some extent prefigured what would eventually take place in North America, two rival entities thus claimed to be the Diocese of Recife. The parting of the ways became acrimonious as the IEAB moved a canonical and later a civil lawsuit against Bishop Cavalcanti and the diocese; the civil case against the diocese is ongoing at the time of writing. For remaining loyal to their diocesan bishop, several evangelical clergy were unceremoniously dismissed by the Brazilian province, as the *Church of England Newspaper* reported on September 2, 2005:

> The Anglican Church of Brazil has deposed 37 members of its clergy in what observers claim is a bid to "to exterminate" the only evangelical diocese in the province.
>
> It is the latest clash in the Anglican Communion over the decision of the North American Churches to consecrate a gay bishop and authorise rites for same-sex blessings. The plight of the clergy is set to come before the Panel of Reference, set up by the Archbishop of Canterbury to intervene in cases where there has been a breakdown of pastoral relationships.
>
> They have had their licences taken away for pledging their loyalty to the Bishop of Recife, the Rt Rev Robinson Cavalcanti, who has been deposed for breaking communion with North American dioceses that have pushed the gay agenda.
>
> The clergy serve 40 parishes, representing over 90 per cent of the diocese's communicants. Among those deposed are English priests who work for the South American Missionary Agency.

The article explains that Archbishop Oliveira had deposed the priests without trial or a right to appeal because he said they abandoned the communion of the church with their refusal to retract their allegiance to Bishop Cavalcanti. The article continued with reactions from those who were concerned about the deposed priests:

> Bishop Cavalcanti described it as a calculated political move to seize control of the diocese. He said it was "part of a plot to have a quorum for an irregular diocesan synod" next month called to "re-create a new diocese, destroying the existing orthodox one."
>
> Evangelicals around the world will be concerned at what many see as a form of persecution for upholding traditional teaching on homosexuality. The Rev Chris Sugden, a spokesman for Anglican Mainstream, expressed deep concern at the move. "This is a systematic attempt to rid the province of its one evangelical diocese. They are determined to oust the evangelicals because they want to show that the whole of Brazil, which is strongly funded by ECUSA, is united in its support of revisionist teachings."

He said that the "assault" on evangelical clergy in Brazil needed to be urgently addressed by the Archbishop of Canterbury's Panel of Reference.

Canon John Sutton, the General Secretary of SAMS, said: "We are greatly disturbed by the events in Recife diocese because of the precipitous action in which over 30 workers have been dismissed, some of whom are mission partners and national workers supported by SAMS. We are also concerned that no allowance is made for freedom of conscience for those whose theological position differs from that of both the imposed diocese and the province."

Despite frequent appeals from the Brazilians, Archbishop of Canterbury Rowan Williams would not be drawn into their dispute, and the Panel of Reference did not become involved in any public sense. While in Cavalcanti's camp Canterbury is generally thought to have been negligent, in fairness, the archbishop had no *de facto* power to intervene in the affairs of an autonomous province of the communion. Again, an inquiry was launched, and envoy bishops Patrick Harris and William Godfrey heard both the Diocese of Recife and the Brazilian province. The findings contained in their report were submitted to the Archbishop of Canterbury, but have never been made public. Eventually, in consultation with Canterbury, Archbishop Gregory Venables, Primate of the Province of the Southern Cone of America, did intervene, reinstating deposed bishop Cavalcanti and the Recife clergy who had been dismissed by the Brazilian province, placing them under his extra-provincial oversight. Politically, this remains the arrangement at the time of writing, though the fact that the Diocese of Recife ordains women to the priesthood and also candidates who have divorced and remarried sets it at odds with the Province of the Southern Cone, which takes a more conservative stance on these issues.

From an institutional point of view, the implications of what took place in 2004–2005 in Brazil would be felt in 2008, a significant year in the life of the communion. Bishop Cavalcanti did not receive an invitation to the Lambeth Conference in 2008, whereas his IEAB counterpart Bishop Sebastian Gamaleira was a full participant. On the other hand, Cavalcanti and a delegation of six clergy (Miguel Uchoa, Marcio Meira, Fred Souto, Mauricio Coelho, Manoel Moraes, and Marcus Throup) participated in the GAFCON conference held in Jerusalem in the same year, a global conference for theologically orthodox Anglicans which voiced some concerns regarding the leadership of Archbishop Rowan Williams and his handling of the crisis in the communion. Since 2008, the institutional situation in Brazil has remained much the same, although Bishop Cavalcanti's diocese has now taken on provincial proportions insofar as it is now present in the majority of the Brazilian states in a "missionary capacity."

With the recent decision taken by the Brazilian Supreme Court to officially recognize homosexual unions and to treat such unions from a civil and juridical perspective as equivalent to marriage, the diametrically opposite positions of the two Brazilian Anglican entities have resurfaced. Whereas the Primate of the IEAB, Bishop Mauricio Andrade, published a note of approval and support for the government initiative, posted on the province's website (www.ieab.org.br, accessed at 14.30 on May 23, 2011), Bishop Cavalcanti and his diocese have publicly objected to these measures, which they believe undermine traditional family values. It is clear that on this issue the two entities espouse two antithetical doctrinal positions, where no amount of Hegelian optimism is likely to reconcile that which is irreconcilable. The best which might be hoped for is *tolerance*, reconciliation on a personal level between injured parties, and for the Brazilian province to drop the lawsuits against Bishop Cavalcanti and the people of the Diocese of Recife. Such would be an advert not only for Anglicanism but for Christianity.

## Bibliography

Aquino, Jorge. 2000. *Anglicanismo: Uma in-trodução*. Recife: Perfilgráfica e Editora.

Cavalcanti, Robinson. 2007. *Reforçando as Trincheiras*. São Paulo: Editora Vida.

Kickhöfel, Oswaldo. 1995. *Notas para uma História da Igreja Episcopal Anglicana do Brasil*. Porto Alegre: Projeto Memória.

*The Church of England Newspaper*. September 2, 2005.

Smith, George. n.d. *Henry Martyn Saint and Scholar: First Modern Missionary to the Mo-hammedans 1781–1812*. New York: Fleming H. Revell.

CHAPTER 50

# La Iglesia Anglicana del Cono Sur (The Anglican Province of the Cono Sur[1])

John A. Macdonald

## Early History

The early history of the Anglican Church of the Cono Sur is inextricably linked with the missionary efforts of Captain Allen Gardiner, the founder of the Patagonian Missionary Society that later became the South American Missionary Society after his untimely death in Spanish Harbor in Tierra del Fuego on or about September 6, 1851 (Thompson 1983, 184). His death and the subsequent publishing of his diary in the London *Times* excited a nation and spurred them on to support further missionary work. "This is not the end," wrote George Pakenham Despard, who was general secretary of the Patagonian Missionary Society, "With God's help the mission will go on" (Thompson 1983, 191).

A second influence in the eventual formation of the province was the establishment as early as the mid-nineteenth century of English-speaking congregations in various South American cities. One of the first leaders in this was the American David Trumbull, who had a ministry to sailors in Valparaíso, Chile. His efforts and presence there enabled the ratification by the Chilean government of the Law of Religious Tolerance (Milmine 1993, 6). Anglican services started in Valparaíso in 1825, and in 1858, St. Paul's Church was built (Every 1915). Anglican chapels were also built in Buenos Aires (1825), Montevideo (1845), and Lima (1849) (Ward 2006: 103). Some of the Anglican churches that were started were the result of negotiations that took place between the British government and the host country (Milmine 1993, 7). Others were started spontaneously by English speakers who wanted to worship in their own tongue. It was not only Anglican work that was taking place; other Protestant groups were

---

[1] At the Provincial Executive Council meeting held in Montevideo, Uruguay, on May 24–25, 2012, "Cono Sur" was chosen as the preferred name – even when writing the name of the province in English.

*The Wiley-Blackwell Companion to the Anglican Communion*, First Edition. Edited by Ian S. Markham, J. Barney Hawkins IV, Justyn Terry, and Leslie Nuñez Steffensen.
© 2013 John Wiley & Sons, Ltd. Published 2013 by John Wiley & Sons, Ltd.

active as well, establishing footholds in a continent that had been traditionally Roman Catholic for over 300 years (Milmine 1993, 6). The establishment of other Protestant centers facilitated future Anglican missionary work on the continent.

Expansion of Protestant mission started off slowly, however, because of the long-time presence of the Roman Catholic Church. At the Edinburgh Missionary Conference of 1910, there were no Latin American Protestant delegates. In fact, the region was not recognized as a legitimate area of missionary activity. In Volume I of the *Report of the Commission* (World Missionary Conference 1910), the only discussion of those who needed to be evangelized in South America was about the Indians (World Missionary Conference, Commission I, 246). There is mention of Asians working in South America, and the assumption is that they are non-Christian (World Missionary Conference, Commission I, 247). The Edinburgh Commission did recognize SAMS's work among the Enxet (Lengua) Indians in the Paraguayan Chaco and the work among the Mapuche in Southern Chile (World Missionary Conference, Commission I, 248). In spite of the narrow definition by which mission work in South America was to be defined, the South American Missionary Society did send two representatives to Edinburgh, so there was at least some partial recognition that work was going on in South America (Stanley 2009, 64, n55).

While discussion of South America is brief – especially the part of the continent that now comprises the Province of the Cono Sur – the Edinburgh Commission did state that South America "may still well be called the Neglected Continent" (World Missionary Conference, Commission I, 249). They described a number of obstacles placed in the way of Protestant missionary work by the Roman Catholic Church. Additional obstacles described were the numerous Indian languages that would have to be learned, the remoteness of many of the tribes, and the hostile environment (World Missionary Conference, Commission I, 249). In 1928, the International Mission Council met in Jerusalem and affirmed that Latin America should be included in the regions of the world that needed the gospel, thus correcting the oversight of the Edinburgh Commission of 1910 (Milmine 1993, 7).

This did not deter missionary efforts among the Indians of South America. Allen Gardiner, prior to his ill-fated expedition to Tierra del Fuego, spent two years trying to establish a missionary presence among the Mapuche Indians (Milmine 1993, 24). Each attempt at finding a suitable location was frustrated, and he finally turned his sights on Tierra del Fuego. He writes in his diary that he would use the Falkland Islands as his base as a means to prepare for the eventual mission to the Yahgan (Yamani) Indians (Thompson 1983, 73–4). He had already heard of the Yahgan Indians who had been brought to England by Captain FitzRoy of the *Beagle* in 1830, and then returned to Tierra del Fuego. He thought that if he could get in touch with one of them, Jemmy Button, he would have a point of contact with the Indians there that would facilitate his work (Hazlewood 2000, 157). In spite of his untimely death, Gardiner's initial missionary work did prompt further attempts to reach the Yahgans, and the work of the South American Missionary Society grew. One biographer wrote about Allen: "The life of such a man never really ends . . . but with undiminished force it sprang on again, to animate and inspire thousands of other lives in the years to come" (Page 1929, 7).

A second expedition was launched to reach the Yahgans in Wulaia in Tierra del Fuego at the beginning of November 1859.[2] On November 6, the team started worship services and then were suddenly attacked and killed. The relationship between the Yahgans and the missionaries had been deteriorating for reasons that still remain unknown, and the mission party was beaten with clubs and stoned to death (Hazlewood 2000, 253). This was a second tragic setback for the then Patagonian Missionary Society.

At the mission station on Keppel Island in the Falklands, the Rev. Thomas Bridges and his wife stated that they wished to remain and continue the work. They had made a good study of the Yahgan language and felt capable of communicating the gospel to them in spite of the failures of the first two efforts. Bridges was the adopted son of George Pakenham Despard, the general secretary of the Patagonian Missionary Society. The Bridges established a base in Ushuaia and through their efforts the majority of the Yahgans present became Christian. Some years later, the Yahgans rescued mariners from an Italian ship that had sunk and provided them with food and blankets. The King of Italy was so impressed by their response to the tragedy that he issued a medal in honor of the Yahgans and Thomas Bridges. It appeared as though the Christian faith had become permanently established in Tierra del Fuego (SAMS-USA 2012).

It is unfortunate to read, however, in the report of the Edinburgh Commission in 1910 that the fruits of their labors were coming to an end due to the near-extinction of the tribe (World Missionary Conference, Commission I 1910, 248). The first cause was an outbreak of measles that reduced the Yahgan population by 75 percent. When the Argentine government began to take an interest in the area and the land began to be settled by herdsmen, miners, and opportunists, Yahgans were not only slaughtered by the settlers, but they themselves got into bloody disputes (Hazlewood 2000, 349–50).

At the same time, it had been Allen Gardiner's wish that not only Tierra del Fuego but also the Mapuche Indians in the Araucanian region of Chile and the Gran Chaco in Paraguay and Argentina should receive the message of the Christian gospel. The Rev. Allen Gardiner, Jr., did extensive work in Chile with the Mapuche (Ward 2006, 104). The Rev. Wilfred Barbrooke Grubb of Scotland also brought the gospel to the Enxet (Lengua) Indians of the Paraguayan Chaco beginning in 1888 (Ward 2006, 105). And while the Yahgan work has come to an end, work in these areas has been expanded and continues to this day.

In 1862, the Rev. Waite Hockin Stirling arrived in the Falklands to carry on the missionary work in Tierra del Fuego and elsewhere. It was during this time that the Patagonian Missionary Society became the South American Missionary Society, because the reach of the missionaries was extending beyond Patagonia. Five years later,

[2] Hazlewood states that the date was November 6, 1859, although Page states the date as October 6, 1859. Hazlewood quotes Captain Robert Fell's diary, which should be considered a reliable source. Fell was in the group of eight who were killed and his diary was recovered later (Hazlewood, Nick. 2001. *Savage: The Life and Times of Jemmy Button.* New York: Thomas Dunne Books/St. Martin's Press, p. 251). It is possible that Page did not have access to Fell's diary at the time he wrote his biography of Allen Gardiner.

Stirling was consecrated Bishop of the Falkland Islands (Page 1929, 169). He was "fully commissioned by the Archbishop to exercise the functions of his office throughout the continent of South America" (Macdonald 1929, 119). Not only did Bishop Stirling supervise the work of the missionaries from the Society, he also had episcopal oversight of the various chaplaincies that were being founded by British and American expatriates in South America. One of the characteristics of his work was that not only did the chaplaincies serve the English-speaking communities, but several of them also ministered to Spanish speakers (Milmine 1993, 12). In 1904, two years after Bishop Stirling's retirement as Bishop of the Falklands, the South American Missionary Society listed a total of 12 clergy, 61 laymen, 58 women, 19 stations, and 35 out-stations (The Churchman 1909, 46).

In 1910, the Diocese of the Falklands and South America was divided into two due to the growth of the Anglican Church in the country and the huge distances that had to be travelled. The "mother diocese" of the Falklands retained oversight of Argentina and Chile below the 46th parallel (Tierra del Fuego), and parts of Bolivia, Peru, Ecuador, and Colombia. Argentina and Chile north of the 46th parallel, Uruguay, Paraguay, and the Bolivian Chaco formed the second diocese. St. John's Church in Buenos Aires became the cathedral for this diocese (Scampini 2009).

While these British chaplaincies helped in the establishment of the Anglican Church on the continent, sadly a number of them were closed during the 1930s due to the worldwide economic depression and the collapse of trade (Higgins 1942, 123). These middle years of the twentieth century – apart from the ongoing work with the Indians in Paraguay, Argentina, and Chile – were particularly sparse in terms of church attendance and new church work.

## Later Years

In 1969, the Diocese of Northern Argentina was created, and in 1977, the Diocese of Peru came into existence, which added Bolivia to its territory in 1981. Uruguay broke off from the Diocese of Argentina in 1988. Bolivia then became its own diocese in 1995 (Scampini 2009, 7).

For much of this time, the dioceses that were being formed in South America were extra-provincial to the Archbishop of Canterbury. However, in 1973, a process began that eventually resulted in the formation of an independent Anglican province. The Anglican Consultative Council held a meeting in Huampani outside of Lima, Peru, in March of that year. The meeting consisted of bishops, clergy, and lay representatives, along with observers from the Roman Catholic Church. After ten days of meeting, the Concilio Anglicano Sud Americano (South American Anglican Council) was formed, and started functioning as a province-in-formation. The Rt. Rev. Bill Flagg, Bishop of Northern Argentina, was elected the first president of the council (Milmine 1993, 40). Ten years after the formation of the Anglican Council on April 30, 1983, the Province of the Southern Cone was formed out of the five dioceses of Argentina, Northern Argentina, Paraguay, Peru, and Bolivia (Milmine 1993, 44).

## The Province of the Cono Sur Today

The Presiding Bishop of the Province of the Cono Sur is the Most Rev. Hector "Tito" Zavala, who also serves as the Bishop of Chile. He was elected in 2010 to succeed the Rt. Rev. Gregory Venables, Bishop of Argentina since 2002 and the former (and first) Bishop of Bolivia. The province is made up of seven dioceses: Argentina, Bolivia, Chile, Northern Argentina, Paraguay, Peru, and Uruguay. At their most recent Provincial Executive Council meeting held in Montevideo, Uruguay, at the end of May 2012, plans were further solidified for applying to the Anglican Consultative Council for permission in 2012 to form a second province out of the western dioceses of Chile, Peru, and Bolivia. A second diocese would need to be created in Chile in order to meet the minimum number of dioceses required in order to form a province.

Due to its founding for the most part by Anglican evangelical missionaries from the South American Missionary Society, the province is strongly evangelical in character and theology in most of the dioceses. Chile, Argentina, Northern Argentina, and Paraguay would be more Protestant in their expression, while Bolivia, Peru, and Uruguay would be more Catholic. Even with these differences, there is strong unity and a common vision for reaching out with the gospel. The province has contributed much to the expansion of the gospel throughout South America, and its influence extends even beyond the province itself. Ministries such as Marriage Encounter, which began in the Diocese of Chile, have gone on to numerous countries in South America and to Spain.

Work with various indigenous groups continues. There are strong churches among the Mapuche in Chile. In Northern Argentina, there are 124 Wichi congregations.[3] Work with the Enxet (Lengua) and Guaraní in the Paraguayan Chaco continues. With massive migration from the countryside to the cities, Peru especially has been doing exemplary work reaching out to the indigenous groups that live in the marginal communities of Lima and Ica.

Ministry in the urban areas is also strengthening. Chile, Peru, Argentina, Bolivia, and Uruguay all have growing urban churches, with Chile taking the lead with their systematic and strategic church planting. To facilitate the preparation of national clergy for the various Christian ministries, Peru and Chile have their own theological programs in place. Peru has two theological centers in Lima and Arequipa, and Chile has their CEP (Center for Pastoral Studies) program in Santiago.

Even though there have been numerous challenges – earthquakes, revolutions, wars, poverty, and governmental corruption and interference on the one hand – the province is making a good transition toward having more and more national leadership with less dependence on foreign missionaries and outside financial support. There is still a long way to go, but as the gospel is proclaimed and the ministries continue, the Province of the Cono Sur along with other Christian churches is fulfilling Allen Gardiner's original dream of reaching the continent of South America for Christ.

---

[3] Conversation with Bishop Nick Drayson, Bishop of Northern Argentina, May 2012.

**Table 50.1:**    Bishops of the dioceses of the Cono Sur.

| | |
|---|---|
| The Diocese of Chile | The Most Rev. Hector Zavala, Primate and Bishop |
| | The Rt. Rev. Abelino Manuel Apeleo, Suffragan Bishop |
| The Diocese of Argentina | The Rt. Rev. Gregory Venables, Bishop |
| The Diocese of Northern Argentina | The Rt. Rev. Nicholas James Quested Drayson, Bishop |
| The Diocese of Bolivia | Vacant |
| The Diocese of Paraguay | The Rt. Rev. Peter John Henry Bartlett, Bishop |
| The Diocese of Peru | The Rt. Rev. William Godfrey, Bishop |
| | The Rt. Rev. Michael Chapman, Suffragan Bishop |
| The Diocese of Uruguay | The Rt. Rev. Miguel Eudaldo Tamayo Zaldívar, Bishop |
| | The Rt. Rev. Gilberto Abdulio Porcal Martínez, Suffragan Bishop |

## Bibliography

The South American Opportunity. 1909. *The Churchman*, vol. 99, no. 2. p. 46.

Commission I, World Missionary Conference. 1910. *Report of the Commission: Carrying the Gospel to all the Non-Christian World*, vol. I. 8 vols. Edinburg, New York: Fleming H. Revell Company.

Every, Edward Francis. 1915. The Anglican Church in South America, p. 3. Web. April 4, 2012.

Hazlewood, Nick. 2000. *Savage: The Life and Times of Jemmy Button*. New York: Thomas Dunne Books/St. Martin's Press.

Higgins, John.1942. *The Expansion of the Anglican Communion*. Louisville, Kentucky: The Cloister Press.

Macdonald, Frederick C. 1929. *Bishop Stirling of the Falklands*. London: Seely, Service and Co.

Milmine, Douglas. 1993. *La Comunión Anglicana en América Latina*. Santiago de Chile: Banka Gráfika Ltda.

Page, Jesse. 1929. *Captain Allen Gardiner of Patagonia*. London: Pickering and Inglis.

SAMS-USA. 2012. SAMS History. Web. June 11, 2012.

Scampini, Jorge. 2009. El anglicanismo: historia, identidad y presencia en Argentina. *Vida Pastoral*, vol. XLIX. Web. June 28, 2012.

Stanley, Brian. 2009. *The World Missionary Conference, Edinburgh 1910*. Studies in the History of Christian Missions. Grand Rapids: William B. Eerdmans.

Thompson, Phyllis, ed. 1983. *An Unquenchable Flame: The Compelling Story of the Founding of the South American Missionary Society*. London: Hodder and Stoughton and the South American Missionary Society.

Ward, Kevin. 2006. *A History of Global Anglicanism*. Cambridge: Cambridge University Press.

PART IV
# Themes

CHAPTER 51

# Theology in the Anglican Communion

## Justyn Terry

A nglican theology is both a distinctive tradition in Christian thought and one that
is so deeply bound up with many other such traditions that it is notoriously hard
to define or distinguish. Without one towering figure like Augustine of Hippo, Thomas
Aquinas, Martin Luther, or John Calvin, but instead drawing heavily on all of these and
many others, it is difficult to describe what Anglican theology is. There is no magiste-
rium to determine what should or should not be deemed properly Anglican. Even the
1662 Book of Common Prayer and Ordinal and the Thirty-Nine Articles of Religion
that once provided the benchmarks for Anglican theology are no longer universally
seen as binding on all Anglicans. Archbishop William Temple went so far as to deny
the existence of a distinctively Anglican theology, a suggestion that was strongly rebut-
ted by Bishop Stephen Sykes (Sykes 1978, 55). More positively, Anglican theology is an
ecumenical theology that seeks to bring the insights of the Reformation to bear on the
tradition of Catholic thought and practice, and to do so with particular attention to
the scriptures, the creeds, and the patristic era of the undivided church. As such, Anglican theology is perhaps best described as "reformed Catholicism."

Seeing Anglican theology in this way not only reminds us of the formation of the
Anglican movement in Tudor England but also provides a brief description of its character and breadth. There are Anglicans who wish to stress their catholic heritage and
others their reformed or protestant ancestry; still others deliberately maintain a critical
distance from both of these positions. The common descriptors of these three broad
streams of thought are: catholic, evangelical (reformed), and liberal. Any such categories are bound to have their limitations, but they are unavoidable if we are to describe
the tradition in more detail. The designations should be understood more as archetypes
than labels to be applied to individuals, since many Anglicans do not fit neatly under

*The Wiley-Blackwell Companion to the Anglican Communion*, First Edition. Edited by Ian S. Markham,
J. Barney Hawkins IV, Justyn Terry, and Leslie Nuñez Steffensen.
© 2013 John Wiley & Sons, Ltd. Published 2013 by John Wiley & Sons, Ltd.

any one of them, or combine elements of two or even all three. It is also important to notice that, in all of these streams, there are charismatic expressions that would, in various ways, stress the work of the Holy Spirit, who continues to speak, heal, and bring renewal today.

Many attempts have been made to describe the overarching shape of Anglican theology. Bishop Lancelot Andrewes, who was appointed by King James I to help compile the Authorized Version of the Bible of 1611, gave the following overview: "One canon, reduced to writing by God himself, two testaments, three creeds, four general councils, five centuries, and the series of fathers in that period – the centuries, that is before Constantine, and two after, determine the boundary of our faith" (Andrewes 1629, 91). We notice here the importance of the first four ecumenical councils which the English and European reformers regarded as those whose canons were fully aligned with biblical teaching. This has important implications for making distinctions from doctrinal decisions made at later councils, such as the transubstantiation of the elements at Communion at the Fourth Lateran Council (1215), and the condemnation of Wycliffe and Hus at the Council of Constance (1414–1418).

Another important outline of Anglicanism is the Chicago-Lambeth Quadrilateral, initially suggested by William Reed Huntington in 1870 and endorsed by the bishops of the Episcopal Church, USA, in Chicago in 1886 as a basis for ecumenical dialogue. It has come to be widely used in attempts to define Anglicanism. Resolution 11 of Lambeth Conference 1888 states the four-fold commitment in the following terms:

(a)   The Holy Scriptures of the Old and New Testaments, as "containing all things necessary to salvation," and as being the rule and ultimate standard of faith.

(b)   The Apostles' Creed, as the Baptismal Symbol; and the Nicene Creed, as the sufficient statement of the Christian faith.

(c)   The two Sacraments ordained by Christ Himself – Baptism and the Supper of the Lord – ministered with unfailing use of Christ's words of Institution, and of the elements ordained by Him.

(d)   The Historic Episcopate, locally adapted in the methods of its administration to the varying needs of the nations and peoples called of God into the Unity of His Church.

The phrase in the first of these, "containing all things necessary to salvation" refers to Article VI of the Thirty-Nine Articles, to which we shall come later. We also notice that the three creeds to which Andrewes alludes are here reduced to two, with the Athanasian Creed omitted. We shall return later to the questions raised about the number of sacraments and the role of the historic episcopate.

More recent attempts to define the official teaching of the Anglican Communion, such as the Jerusalem Declaration (2008) and the Anglican Communion Covenant (2009), neither of which has achieved communion-wide support, draw directly or indirectly on Church of England Canon C15, of the Declaration of Assent. In its preface, we find:

The Church of England is part of the One, Holy, Catholic and Apostolic Church worshipping the one true God, Father, Son and Holy Spirit. It professes the faith uniquely revealed in the Holy Scriptures and set forth in the catholic creeds, which faith the Church is called upon to proclaim afresh in each generation. Led by the Holy Spirit, it has borne witness to Christian truth in its historic formularies, the Thirty-Nine Articles of Religion, the Book of Common Prayer and the Ordering of Bishops, Priests and Deacons.

This provides a helpful outline for a fuller consideration of Anglican theology.

## Sources of Theology

The Anglican commitments to the Holy Scriptures, the catholic creeds, and to the historic formularies of the Church of England supply a basis for shared reflection and discussion, but they also allow differences to emerge according to the emphasis placed on these various authorities and to the way in which appeals are made to them. In particular, the extent to which received interpretations of the Bible and Christian tradition are to be maintained or reconsidered in the light of developments in such disciplines as science and philosophy plays an important part in understanding differences between more traditional (e.g., evangelical and catholic) and progressive (e.g., liberal) voices in the communion.

The liberal tradition seeks a constructive engagement with the leading thinkers of the day and is willing to rework previously held doctrinal and ethical positions in their light. Important texts that show how this tradition has developed from what might today seem quite conservative positions are: *Essays and Reviews* (1860), *Lux Mundi* (1889), *Foundations* (1913), *Essays Catholic and Critical* (1926), *Soundings* (1963), *Honest to God* (1963) by Bishop John A. T. Robinson, *Principles of Christian Theology* (1966) by John Macquarrie, *Christ, Faith and History* (1972), and *The Myth of God Incarnate* (1977), although the tradition extends back even earlier to the Latitudinarians of the later seventeenth century. One of the characteristics of this liberal stream is a commitment to social justice, which is perhaps best displayed in the work of Archbishop Desmond Tutu, whose campaigning for all people to be treated as creatures made in God's image irrespective of the color of their skin played a vital part in the fall of apartheid in South Africa in 1994.

Richard Hooker, probably the most celebrated theologian of the Anglican tradition, has provided an important contribution to the question of how sources of theology should be treated in his eight-volume work, *Of the Laws of Ecclesiastical Polity*. Here, he carefully distinguished his position from that of the Roman Catholic Church, which he felt deferred to tradition even where it contradicted scripture, and from the Puritans, whose desire to justify doctrine and practice solely from the Bible he found to lay inappropriate burdens on scripture. Hooker drew on Thomas Aquinas and John Calvin, among others, to consider a right use of scripture, reason, and tradition. It has become widely known as a "three-legged stool," suggesting the three sources demand equal attention. However, this is in contrast to Hooker's own position which was to see scripture as primary: "[W]hat Scripture doth plainly deliver, to that the first place both of credit and obedience is due; the next whereunto is whatsoever any man can necessarily conclude by force of reason; after these the voice of the Church succeedeth" (Hooker 1597, V, viii, 2). This biblical primacy is affirmed, as we have seen, in the Chicago-Lambeth Quadrilateral. It is to recall, with John Webster, "the centrality of Scripture to the entire enterprise of Christian theology" (Webster 2003, 108). As Archbishop Rowan Williams notes, "Scripture, with all its discord and polyphony, is the canonical text of a community in which there are limits to pluralism" (Williams 2000, 56).

The "historic formularies" are listed in Canon C15 as: the Thirty-Nine Articles of Religion, the Book of Common Prayer, and the Ordering of Bishops, Priests, and Deacons, the set of ordination services that accompanied the 1662 Book of Common Prayer. Here, we see the more general commitments to scripture and creeds which are held in common with Trinitarian Christians around the world supplemented by more specifically Anglican positions.

The Thirty-Nine Articles of Religion of 1571 were developed from the Forty-Two Articles written under the direction of Archbishop Thomas Cranmer in 1553. These in turn owed much to the Lutheran Augsburg Confession of 1530. They were intended to bring peace to the church and were, according to their title, "for the avoiding of diversities of opinions and for the establishing of consent touching true religion." They affirm the three Creeds (VIII), justification by faith alone (XI), and the marriage of priests (XXXII). They also reject works of supererogation (XIV), purgatory (XXII), and the doctrine of transubstantiation (XXVIII). In addition, Article XXXV gives equivalent authoritative status to two books of Homilies written by Archbishop Thomas Cranmer, Bishop Hugh Latimer, Bishop John Jewel, Archbishop Matthew Parker et al. Cranmer's "Homily on Justification" (Homily III, "On the salvation of all mankind") is given special mention in Article XI, stressing again the importance of justification by faith alone. For Cranmer, God's gracious offer of forgiveness of sin, received by faith, was to evoke the response of gratitude that manifested in lives orientated to love of God and neighbor by the Holy Spirit. These homilies were intended to be used, like those written by Martin Luther, to spread the Protestant message, and to promote reformed Catholicism in the Church of England. They elaborate many of the commitments of the Thirty-Nine Articles.

Ever since the Latitudinarians of the later seventeenth century, like Bishop Simon Patrick and Archbishops John Tillotson and Thomas Tenison, there have been advocates for a looser interpretation of the Thirty-Nine Articles. For instance, Article XVIII, "Of Obtaining eternal Salvation only by the Name of Christ" is controversial in a pluralistic society:

> They also are to be had accursed that presume to say, That every man shall be saved by the Law or Sect which he professeth, so that he be diligent to frame his life according to that Law, and the light of Nature. For Holy Scripture doth set out unto us only the Name of Jesus Christ, whereby men must be saved.

Liberals who wish to learn from modernity and post-modernity think that such commitments put unnecessary stumbling blocks on the path of contemporary people who are considering the Christian faith. It is, however, just such articles that evangelicals and Catholics wish to affirm to ensure that Anglicans bear faithful witness to the gospel of Jesus Christ and not be conformed to the spirit of the age.

The Articles proved contentious for the Oxford Movement of the early nineteenth century, during which John Henry Newman wrote a Tract (90) seeking to reinterpret them to be more compatible with the ancient church and the Council of Trent, rather than the reformers. It provoked such strong opposition that it brought the series of tracts to an end. Despite these challenges, the Articles retain a place as an historic witness to Anglican positions, and remain fully authoritative in many provinces of the Anglican Communion.

The 1662 Book of Common Prayer and the Ordinal are also historic formularies of the Church of England with continuing implications for the theology of the Anglican Communion. We see here the integral connection between doctrine and prayer, the principle of *lex orandi, lex credendi* ("the law of prayer is the law of belief") of Prosper of Aquitaine (c.390–c.455). It is a sign of the continuing influence of Thomas Cranmer, whose theological and liturgical skills are evident in the Book of Common Prayer and Ordinal. It is in the Daily Offices of Morning and Evening Prayer, and in the services of Baptism, Confirmation, Holy Communion, Marriage, and Burial, as well as in the Making of Deacons, Ordaining of Priests, and Consecration of Bishops, that we see Anglican theology at work.

## Distinctive Theological Commitments: Church

The theological commitments of Anglicanism with regard to the church, ministry, and sacraments reveal doctrinal differences from other Christian denominations. Let us consider each in turn.

Questions about how the church should be understood have been a concern from the days when the Church of England first separated from the Church of Rome in the sixteenth century. Apologists like John Jewel, Richard Hooker, and Lancelot Andrewes wanted to be clear that the Church of England was not now a sect but remained fully Christian and continued to bear all the marks of the one, holy, catholic, and apostolic church, and to have valid orders and sacraments. Those who remained in the Church of England had not lost their salvation even though they were no longer in communion with the Roman Catholic Church. Indeed, it was only when John Henry Newman came to doubt this claim that he left for the Roman Catholic Church in 1845, saying, "My one paramount reason for contemplating a change [to Roman Catholicism] is my deep unvarying conviction that our Church is in schism, and that my salvation depends on my joining the Church of Rome" (quoted Carrick 1984, 34). Jewel, Hooker, and Andrewes were also defending their positions from those of the Puritans who were calling for more radical reforms and for closer adherence to the teaching of reformers like John Calvin.

In *An Apology or Answer in Defence of the Church of England* (1564), John Jewel made his case by showing that the Church of England was being true to the scriptures and to the church fathers. It was the Church of Rome that had gone astray, not the Church of England. Article XIX from "Of the Church" affirms this position:

> The visible Church of Christ is a congregation of faithful men, in which the pure Word of God is preached, and the Sacraments be duly ministered according to Christ's ordinance, in all those things that of necessity are requisite to the same.

> As the Church of Jerusalem, Alexandria and Antioch, have erred; so also the Church of Rome hath erred, not only in their living and manner of Ceremonies, but also in matters of Faith.

Richard Hooker followed the same line of argument as Jewel. When he was asked whether the Church of England was a new church, he answered that it was not. He saw the church as both a political and supernatural society with a divine purpose. It was a true fellowship with God united by calling on the same Lord Jesus Christ. "One Lord, one faith, one baptism" (Eph 4:5, ESV) was his defining text (Hooker 1593, III, i, 7). He preferred to employ the category of "mystical Church" rather than Calvin's "invisible Church," since it was not strictly invisible even though its membership was known to God alone. Despite the strident polemics of the day, Hooker included Roman Catholics in the "mystical Church." Heretics, schismatics, and the excommunicated were in the "visible Church," but as "imps and limbs of Satan" unless they repent (Hooker 1593, III, i, 7).

Lancelot Andrewes made the case for the Church of England by saying that it was not sectarian but "reformed Catholic." This "reformation" was needed because the Roman Catholic Church was in a state of "deformation" (Andrewes 1610, 159). He was willing to describe the Church of England as "Protestant" as a temporary convenience, awaiting the reform of the Church of Rome. The Church of England was, after all, being true to the scriptures and the fathers.

Two movements raised questions about the nature and role of the church in England as it entered the nineteenth century. One was Latitudinarianism for which reason was, "the very voice of God" (Benjamin Whichcote 1703, no. 76). This was seen as a corrective to what they regarded as overconfident dogmatism, and was coupled with a concern for moral reform in a dissolute age. The other was the evangelicalism of John and Charles Wesley, George Whitefield, and Charles Simeon, who stressed the need for personal conversion and the priesthood of all believers. Both of these movements raised questions about how the church was to be understood in society. In particular, how was the Erastianism affirmed by Richard Hooker that gave the state ascendency over the church in ecclesiastical (not theological) matters to be understood as the values of the Enlightenment and Romanticism grew in influence?

John Keble, Professor of Poetry at Oxford, preached an Assize Sermon on July 14, 1833, at the University Church, proclaiming a state of national apostasy in protest against the British parliament suppressing ten Irish bishoprics without reference to the United Church of England and Ireland. He said that the state was overreaching itself in making such a decision and that the church needed to regain a sense of its own God-given authority in order to resist such moves and live up to her high calling. The "Oxford Movement" that was birthed that day led to a new stress on the visible church, including decoration of the house of God, and to a higher regard for the ancient church. It drew heavily on seventeenth-century Caroline Divines like Lancelot

Andrewes, George Herbert, John Donne, Bishop Jeremy Taylor, and Archbishop William Laud, who had promoted a high view of the church. Edward Bouverie Pusey, Professor of Hebrew and one of the main leaders of the Oxford Movement, expressed a desire for the Church of England to be a *via media* between Roman Catholicism and reformed Protestantism.

The Anglo-Catholicism that arose from this movement placed greater emphasis on the apostolic succession of bishops, the authority of the threefold order of deacons, priests, and bishops, and on the sacraments. They introduced the weekly Eucharist in moderate parishes and daily Eucharist in high-church (catholic) ones; wore Roman vestments including the alb, stole, and chasuble, and the miter for bishops; used candles and wafers; genuflected; rang bells at consecration; crossed themselves; fasted before communion; invoked the intercession of saints; offered masses for the departed; and used incense and Latin texts. There was a considerable missionary drive with this movement, which meant these teachings were rapidly spread to Scotland, New Zealand, and the United States, and to East, Central, and South Africa, India, China, and Japan through the University Mission to Central Africa, the Society for the Propagation of the Gospel, and other smaller societies. Anglo-Catholic theology, promoted by such notable thinkers as Bishop Charles Gore, Edwin Hoskyns, Archbishop Michael Ramsey, E. L. Mascall, Austin Farrer, and more recently Bishop Geoffrey Rowell, came to dominate the Church of England before declining in influence due to the rise of liberalism and evangelicalism in the twentieth century, the changes made to Roman Catholicism at Vatican II (1962–1965), and the ordination of women priests and bishops in some parts of the Anglican Communion.

Another important contribution to ecclesiology has come from the Radical Orthodoxy movement, led by high-church Anglicans like John Milbank, Catherine Pickstock, and Graham Ward. Their aim is to "reclaim the world [from secularism] by situating its concerns and activities within a theological framework" (Milbank et al. 1999, 1). They stress the importance of the church and the Eucharist, along with the Trinity and Christology, by promoting embodiment and participation, using an Augustinian view of all knowledge as divine illumination, and developing a more Platonic vision of Christianity. It is their hope that this project will lead to overcoming many polarities, including those between conservatives and liberals.

## Distinctive Theological Commitments: Ministry

The role of the laity and of the ordained in Christian ministry was another concern of the magisterial reformers and as such the subject of considerable theological discussion at the beginning of reformed Catholicism in England. Martin Luther's desire that the vocation of all the baptized be recognized and encouraged came alongside a call to reform the medieval priesthood from its sacerdotal accretions. The prime function of the ordained minister was to preach and teach the scriptures. English reformers like Thomas Becon, Cranmer's chaplain, stressed the need for biblically educated pastors at a time when university-trained clergy were usually not resident in parishes. By 1552, the pre-Reformation giving of the newly ordained priest a chalice and/or paten with the charge "Receive the power to offer sacrifice to God" had been replaced by the giving of a Bible with the exhortation, "Take thou authority to preach the Word of God, and to minister the holy sacraments in the congregation." It was a major reworking of the theology of ordained ministry from one based on the mediation of an Aaronic priesthood to one more explicitly centered on the ministry of a New Testament "presbyter," a transliteration of the Greek, meaning "elder."

Cranmer retained the threefold order of ordained ministry of deacons, priests, and bishops. This was welcomed by those who were more catholic-minded, but raised strong objections from the Puritans who protested the use of the term "priest." Even though it was, strictly speaking, a contraction of the term "presbyter," it was widely associated with the mediatory cultic function of the *sacerdos*, and as such was insufficiently reformed. Hooker responded to this complaint by suggesting the term be understood to signify eldership or leadership in the congregation and, as an allusion, to identify "that which the Gospel has *proportionable* to ancient sacrifices, namely the Communion of the blessed Body and Blood of Christ, although it have properly no new sacrifice" (Hooker 1597, V, lxxviii, 2). Puritans like Thomas Cartwright also thought the distinction between priests and bishops was unsupported biblically, and objected to reserving ordination to bishops. Their objections were overruled by the 1662 Act of Uniformity which required episcopal ordination for all who would hold a benefice in the Church of England, resulting in what became known as the "Great Ejection" of many Puritans on St. Bartholomew's Day 1662, creating "non-conformity."

The first half of the eighteenth century saw a decline in ministerial practice, with many incumbents not resident in their parishes, leaving daily ministry to their curates. Two initiatives served to change both the theology and the practice of ministry at that time. One came from the Oxford Movement, which called upon clergy to "magnify your office" and "act up to your profession" (Newman, Tract 1). The other was the Evangelical Revival of the later eighteenth and early nineteenth century, which stressed the function of the Christian minister as preacher and teacher, especially of the gospel message. Charles Simeon, who served at Holy Trinity Church, Cambridge, from 1782 to 1831, made his goal to expound the Bible, saying, "I love the simplicity of the Scriptures; and I wish to receive and inculcate every truth precisely in the way, and to the extent, that it is set forth in the inspired Volume" (quoted Moule 1948, 77). During his 49-year ministry, he inspired and trained many men for ordained ministry and has continued to be an inspiration for evangelicals like C. F. D. Moule, J. I. Packer, and John Stott. This was also a time of great missionary expansion, with Simeon being one of the founders of the Church Missionary Society, which worked in East, Central, and West Africa, India, Pakistan, Sri Lanka, China, Japan, the Middle East, Canada, and New Zealand. Simeon also helped found what became the "University and College Christian Fellowship," "Inter-Varsity Christian Fellowship," in the United States and Canada, and the "Church's Ministry among Jewish People."

John Wesley travelled widely on horseback, often preaching in the open air, following the example of George Whitefield, and saw the world as his parish. Wesley summarized his message as follows:

That without holiness no man shall see the Lord; that this holiness is the work of God, who worketh in us both to will and to do; that he doeth it of his own good pleasure, merely for the merits of Christ; that this holiness is the mind that was in Christ; enabling us to walk as he also walked; that no man can be thus sanctified till he is justified; and, that we are justified by faith alone (Wesley 1872, para. 13).

The Methodist movement grew rapidly in the United States, but when many Anglican clergy returned to England during or after the Revolutionary War (1775–1783), many people were left without the sacraments. The Bishop of London was unwilling to ordain poorly educated Methodist lay preachers, and in 1784 Wesley himself ordained Richard Whatcoat and Thomas Vasey as presbyters for North America. He did so partly on the basis of Latitudinarian Bishop Edward Stillingfleet's *Irenicum* (1659), which argued that, in the "primitive" church, ordination had sometimes been carried out by presbyters. It was a decision that provoked strong criticism from many in the Church of England. Wesley also had women office-bearers and preachers, which was significant for later advocates of the ordination of women.

The questions raised by Wesley and others about the ministry of priests and bishops were brought into sharp relief by the Oxford Movement and the Anglo-Catholics. For them, bishops are required for a true church; they are of the *esse* (essence). It is through them that a line of succession can be traced back to the Apostles, and it is only by them that priests can be validly ordained. The ministry of word and sacrament, through which God brings salvation, is thus contingent upon bishops, so no bishops, no church (Keble, Tract 4). Richard Hooker had discussed the role of bishops in his seminal work on *Ecclesiastical Polity* and affirmed the benefit of having bishops as the successors of the Apostles, but he did not consider them as being essential to the church. There could be the "exigence of necessity," such as a group of Christians washed up on an island without a bishop, that could still properly claim to be the church in that place (Hooker 1662, VII, i, 4 and VII, xiv, 11). For him, bishops were *bene esse* (for the benefit of the church). A third alternative was developed in 1954 by Bishop H. W. Montefiore and Kenneth M. Carey as part of a response to the formation of the Church of South India. This unified church of episcopal and non-episcopal churches would not re-ordain those who were already ordained, but would make all future ordinations episcopal. Montefiore and Carey decided that the *esse* view claimed too much for episcopacy and the *bene esse* position too little. They proposed that the bishop be understood as being *plene esse*: not indispensible, nor preferable, but necessary for the full expression of the church (Carey 1954, 105ff).

The Chicago-Lambeth Quadrilateral makes the historic episcopate one of the elements of Anglican identity. As Michael Ramsey argued in *The Gospel and the Catholic Church* (1936, 219f), bishops have an important place in securing the faithful proclamation of the gospel in the world. However, the provision in the Quadrilateral for the episcopate to be "locally adapted in the methods of its administration to the varying needs of the nations and peoples called of God into the Unity of His Church" makes it clear that the goal is not to "unchurch" non-episcopal bodies, but to allow for a variety of applications with a view to a growing ecumenism.

In the second half of the nineteenth century, debates about the validity of Anglican orders were intensified through historical studies by scholars like J. B. Lightfoot and F. J. A. Hort that called into question the claim in the preface to the Ordinal that "it is evident unto all men diligently reading holy Scripture, and ancient authors, that from the Apostles' time there hath been these orders of ministers in Christ's Church: Bishops, Priests, and Deacons." It was only possible to trace the roots of the threefold order back to the later part of the second century. There was also an objection to Anglican orders in the papal bull *Apostolicae Curae* in 1896, which declared that "ordinations carried out according to the Anglican rite have been and are absolutely null and utterly void." The bull was firmly repudiated by Archbishop Frederick Temple in a reply that "agreed with the Pope that matter, form and intention were vital in sacramental actions, but went on to claim that the Anglican ordinal met these requirements in every way" (Avis 2007, 135ff). It was only with the ecumenical openness of the Second Vatican Council in which other churches were seen as "subsisting in" the Roman Catholic Church (*Lumen Gentium* 1964, 8, 2) that a new spirit of cooperation emerged, and studies like those of the Anglican–Roman Catholic International Commission (ARCIC, from 1967) and the World Council of Churches' Lima Document on *Baptism, Eucharist and Ministry* (1982) could be achieved.

## Distinctive Theological Commitments: Sacraments

The 1662 Catechism defines a sacrament as "an outward and visible sign of an inward and spiritual grace given unto us, ordained by Christ himself, as a means whereby we receive the same, and a pledge to assure us thereof." Here, we see the use of the wider definition of sacrament as "an outward sign of an inward grace" that had emerged in the patristic era more tightly defined with the additional phrase "ordained by Christ himself" introduced by the reformers. As such, the focus of the sacraments is on God's purposes of salvation rather than on wider means of grace.

The effectiveness, number, and use of sacraments are described in Article XXV of the Thirty-Nine Articles:

Sacraments ordained of Christ be not only badges or tokens of Christian men's profession, but rather they be certain sure witnesses, and effectual signs of grace, and God's good will towards us, by the which he doth work invisibly in us, and doth not only quicken, but also strengthen and confirm our Faith in him.

There are two Sacraments ordained of Christ our Lord in the Gospel, that is to say, Baptism, and the Supper of the Lord. Those five commonly called Sacraments, that is to say, Confirmation, Penance, Orders, Matrimony, and Extreme Unction, are not to be counted for Sacraments of the Gospel, being such as have grown partly of the corrupt following of the Apostles, partly are states of life allowed in the Scriptures, but yet have not like nature of Sacraments with Baptism, and the Lord's Supper, for that they have not any visible sign or ceremony ordained of God.

There has been much debate in Anglican theology about sacramental grace, and several positions have been taken. The *ex opere operato* ("by the work worked," i.e., by the action being performed) view of sacraments approved at the Council of Trent has advocates among catholic Anglicans. Evangelicals have objected that this renders the sacraments too mechanical, giving insufficient place to the necessity of receiving them by faith. The *ex opere operato* position can, however, be understood to affirm that right dispositions are needed by the recipient, making the distinction less sharp than it might at first appear.

Anglicans affirm infant baptism (Article XXVII) for the children of believers, but there are many views as to what it accomplishes. For instance, the "effectual sign of grace" position on sacraments and the use of the phrase in the 1662 Order of Public Baptism after the sacrament is administered, "seeing that this child is regenerate," seem to affirm a catholic position that the baptized infant is born again. Evangelicals have objected that this overstates what baptism achieves, and affirm the phrases only on the "charitable supposition," as Bishop J. C. Ryle called it (1874, 145), that the promises made in the baptismal service about the candidate coming to confirmation to express his or her own repentance and faith would be fulfilled.

This issue was a source of conflict in the church as evangelicals grew in number and influence in the nineteenth century. In 1847, the Bishop of Exeter, Henry Phillpotts, was unwilling to institute George Gorham as vicar of the parish of Brampford Speke, Devon, because Gorham rejected the doctrine of invariable baptismal regeneration. Gorham challenged the decision and won the case when it went to the judicial committee of the Privy Council, which included the Archbishops of Canterbury and York. Their decision, which affirmed the legitimacy of both doctrinal opinions regarding baptism, led to the secession to Rome of Henry Manning and Robert Wilberforce but, as Bishop Colin Buchanan points out, "preserved evangelicalism within the Church of England" (Buchanan 2006, 202).

What happens at a service of Holy Communion has also been much debated. Article XXVIII, "Of the Lord's Supper," states that, "to such as rightly, worthily, and with faith, receive the [Sacrament of Redemption], the Bread which we break is a partaking of the Body of Christ; and likewise the Cup of Blessing is a partaking of the Blood of Christ." Clarification is then made that, "The Body of Christ is given, taken, and eaten, in the Supper, only after an heavenly and spiritual manner. And the mean whereby the Body of Christ is received and eaten in the Supper, is Faith." Article XXIX then states that:

> The Wicked, and such as be void of a lively faith, although they do carnally and visibly press with their teeth (as Saint Augustine saith) the Sacrament of the Body and Blood of Christ; yet in no wise are they partakers of Christ: but rather, to their condemnation, do eat and drink the sign or Sacrament of so great a thing.

The presence of the ascended Christ at communion is being affirmed, but not as a change of the substance of the bread and wine (transubstantiation), as the Fourth Lateran Council claimed.

No single theory has replaced transubstantiation. Instead, a range of views has emerged which may be categorized under the three broad headings of virtualism, receptionism, and real presence. By virtualism is meant that the bread and wine are unchanged at consecration but the faithful communicant receives with these elements the power or virtue of the body and blood of Christ. Receptionism claims that the bread and wine remain unchanged at consecration but the faithful communicant receives with these elements the true body and blood of Christ. Real presence suggests that the bread and wine are changed at consecration so that, in some sense, the body and blood of Christ are present in the consecrated elements. This real presence position is understood in many different ways but generally as a spiritual rather than bodily presence. As Cranmer says:

> And although Christ in his human nature substantially, really, corporeally, naturally and sensibly, be present with his Father in heaven, yet sacramentally and spiritually he is here present in water, bread and wine, as in signs and sacraments, but he is indeed spiritually in the faithful Christian people, which according to Christ's ordinance be baptized, or receive the Holy Communion, or unfeignedly believe in him (Cranmer 1550, 40)

Jeremy Taylor explains: "We, by the real spiritual presence of Christ, do understand Christ to be present, as the Spirit of God is present in the hearts of the faithful, by blessing and grace; and this is all which we mean besides the tropical and figurative presence" (Taylor 1828, 15). So the exact location and mode in which Christ is present at Holy Communion is left undefined by Anglicans, although his presence by virtue of the Holy Spirit in the service would be variously affirmed.

Understanding that Anglicans are not asserting a corporeal presence of Christ at the Eucharist sheds light on questions regarding the sense in which Holy Communion is a sacrifice. There is no explicit reference to the Last Supper as a sacrifice in the Bible, as Bishop Kenneth Stevenson points out (McAdoo and Stevenson 1995, 129), but as a memorial of the one sacrifice of Jesus Christ on the cross and the new covenant that it established, sacrificial language has been deployed by Anglican theologians. John Jewel, Simon Patrick, and John Johnson used the term "unbloody sacrifice," and Charles Gore, "bloodless sacrifice" (McAdoo and Stevenson 1995, 163f), making clear that no fresh sacrifice was being offered but that the one sacrifice of the risen Christ was being presented to be received by faith. Evangelicals and Anglo-Catholics have been divided on this issue, with the latter wanting to assert a stronger sacrificial component to communion. Leading representatives of these movements worked together to agree on the following statement:

> Sacrifice means offering. What, then, do we offer at the Eucharist? Christ offered himself on the cross in our stead and without our aid, and we certainly cannot repeat that offering. We do, on the other hand, offer not merely "the fruit of the lips"; not merely undefined "spiritual sacrifices"; not even ourselves in Christ if that is seen in separation from our feeding on Christ; but ourselves as reappropriated by Christ (Buchanan et al. 1970, 191).

## Conclusion

Anglicanism has a rich and varied theology and has produced numerous world-class theologians. Not having one central figure to guide the discourse does make describing and maintaining an Anglican theology more challenging, with the ever-present danger of losing elements of the tradition if it fails to remember its own history. It does, however, mean that there is the capacity to overcome the limitations of any one individual, to work in collaboration with people of different commitments, and to provide a generosity to a range of opinions that can properly claim to be Christian.

Despite the diversity embodied in Anglicanism, certain family characteristics do emerge. There is the integration of faith and life seen in the work of pastor–scholars like Richard Hooker, John Donne, and George Herbert; and the willingness to leave undefined things that the scriptures and tradition of the church leave open, as seen in S. T. Coleridge, Thomas Arnold, William Porcher DuBose, and Keith Ward. There is the desire to construct a pastorally oriented theology that leads to prayer, epitomized in Thomas Cranmer, Evelyn Underhill, and Sarah Coakley, and the impetus to social action, like that seen in William Wilberforce, F. D. Maurice, Bishop Festo Kivengere, and Kathryn Tanner. Anglicanism has also raised up outstanding apologists for the Christian faith like Bishop Joseph Butler, William Paley, C. S. Lewis, Dorothy L. Sayers, Alister McGrath, Bishop N. T. Wright, and Oliver O'Donovan. If there is one overarching theme that could be said to characterize Anglican theology, it might be the quest for holiness identified by Geoffrey Rowell et al. (2001, xxiv), the very quest that first drew Cranmer's attention to the grace and gratitude dynamic of the Lutheran reformation.

There are many doctrinal areas in need of further consideration. Most pressing at the moment is the question of whether Anglicanism should be more deliberately confessional, so that, without losing the distinctive characteristics of the provinces, the communion may maintain a clearer shared identity. Related to that is the work of developing an Anglican ecclesiology that is genuinely true to itself while at the same time maintaining that the communion is part of the one, holy, catholic, and apostolic church. Questions remain about the ordination of women as priests and bishops and whether ordination should be open to men and women who are gays, lesbians, bisexuals, or transgendered. In some parts of the communion, there are also questions about whether ordination is required for someone to preside at communion. There are also the ongoing questions about whether "priest" is the best term to denote those ordained as "presbyter," and about the formal recognition of "men and women of prayer, teachers, or evangelists," which has been raised by John Webster (Webster 1998, 332). Many more issues might be added, but we have reason enough to recognize that this is a vibrant school of thought. It is a tradition with an important part to play in the mission of God in a world that is increasingly looking elsewhere than the church for meaning and hope, and needing the very rootedness in Jesus Christ, empowerment of the Holy Spirit, and graciousness of our heavenly Father that many have found in the Anglican way.

## Bibliography

Andrewes, Lancelot. [1610] 1851. *Responsio ad Apologiam Cardinal Bellarmine*. Vol. 4. Library of Anglo-Catholic Theology, Oxford: J. H. Parker.

Andrewes, Lancelot. [1629] 1852. *Opuscula Quaedam Posthuma*. Vol. 1. Library of Anglo-Catholic Theology, Oxford: J. H. Parker.

Avis, Paul. 2007. *The Identity of Anglicanism: Essentials of Anglican Ecclesiology*. London and New York: T&T Clark.

Buchanan, Colin. 2006. *The A to Z of Anglicanism*. Lanham, Toronto, Plymouth UK: Scarecrow Press.

Buchanan, Colin, E. L. Mascall, J. I. Packer and The Bishop of Willesden. 1970. *Growing into Union: Proposals for Forming a United Church in England*. London: SPCK.

Carey, Kenneth. 1954. *The Historic Episcopate*. Westminster: Dacre Press.

Carrick, John 1984. *Evangelicals and the Oxford Movement*. Bridgend, Wales: Evangelical Press.

Cranmer, Thomas. [1550] 1825. *A Defence of the True and Catholic Doctrine of the Sacrament of the Body and Blood of Our Saviour Christ*. London: C. J. Rivington.

Hooker, Richard. 1593/1888. *Of the Laws of Ecclesiastical Polity*. Vol. III. *The Works of that Learned and Judicious Divine Mr. Richard Hooker with an Account of His Life and Death by Isaac Walton*. Vol. 1. Arranged by John Keble. 7th edition revised by R. W. Church and F. Paget. Oxford: Clarendon Press.

Hooker, Richard. 1597/1888. *Of the Laws of Ecclesiastical Polity*. Vol. V. *The Works of that Learned and Judicious Divine Mr. Richard Hooker with an Account of His Life and Death by Isaac Walton*. Vol. 2. Arranged by John Keble. 7th edition revised by R. W. Church and F. Paget. Oxford: Clarendon Press.

Hooker, Richard. 1662/1888. *Of the Laws of Ecclesiastical Polity*. Vol. VII. *The Works of that Learned and Judicious Divine Mr. Richard Hooker with an Account of His Life and Death by Isaac Walton*. Vol. 3. Arranged by John Keble. 7th edition revised by R. W. Church and F. Paget. Oxford: Clarendon Press.

McAdoo, H. R. and Kenneth E. Stevenson. 1995. *The Mystery of the Eucharist in the Anglican Tradition*. Eugene UR: Wipf and Stock.

Milbank, John, Catherine Pickstock, and Graham Ward, eds. 1999. *Radical Orthodoxy*. London and New York: Routledge.

Moule, H. C. G. 1948. *Charles Simeon*. London: IVP.

Ramsey, Michael. [1936] 1990. *The Gospel and the Catholic Church*. Eugene, Oregon: Wipf and Stock.

Rowell, Geoffrey, Kenneth Stevenson and Rowan Williams. 2001. *Love's Redeeming Work: The Anglican Quest for Holiness*. Oxford: OUP.

Ryle, John Charles. [1874] 2000. *Knots Untied*. Moscow: Charles Nolan.

Sykes, Stephen W. 1978. *The Integrity of Anglicanism*. London and Oxford: Mowbray.

Taylor, Jeremy. 1828. *The Real Presence and Spiritual of Christ in the Blessed Sacrament*. London: C. and J. Rivington.

Webster, John. 1998. Ministry and Priesthood. *The Study of Anglicanism*, eds. Stephen Sykes, John Booty and Jonathan Knight. Rev. edn. London: SPCK.

Webster, John. 2003. *Holy Scripture: A Dogmatic Sketch*. Cambridge: CUP.

Wesley, John. [1872] 1996. Sermon 63 on The General Spread of the Gospel. *The Works of Rev. John Wesley*, 7 Vol., ed. Thomas Jackson. Grand Rapids, MI: Baker Book House.

Whichcote, Benjamin. [1703] 1930. *Moral and Religious Aphorisms*. London: E. Mathews & Marrot.

Williams, Rowan. 2000. *On Christian Theology*. Oxford: Blackwell Publishing.

# CHAPTER 52

# The Anglican Communion and Ecumenical Relations

## Michael Nazir-Ali

It has often been said that Anglicanism is but an expression of the Western, Latin tradition of Christianity (see Platten 2003). Indeed, the formularies of the Church of England, the foundation documents of Anglicanism, explicitly lay claim to continuing with the medieval church, where this could be done without endorsing unnecessary accretion and corruption (*First and Second Prayer Books of King Edward VI* 1968, 3f, 286f, 292, 321f, 438; see also Article 34 of the Articles of Religion). This continuity was affirmed not only in diverse primers and catechisms but also in piety and devotion (see Nazir-Ali and Sagovsky 2007, 131ff). There was, however, innovation as well as continuity. If the first prayer book reflected continuity with the Old Sarum rite, the second clearly showed the influence of Martin Bucer and other continental reformers. On the one hand, Anglicans, like Richard Hooker, refused to unchurch Roman Catholics, even if they engaged in controversy with them; on the other, they recognized the reformed churches of the continent as truly churches, even though they lacked the threefold ministry of bishop, priest, and deacon (see Avis 1989, 31ff, 51ff and *passim*).

Although the pattern of theological thought, forms of ministry, and ecclesiastical life in the Church of England remained that of the Western type, the Reformation and its aftermath brought more contact with the Eastern churches. This is shown already in Cranmer's use of the Liturgy of St. Basil in the 1549 Eucharistic rite and in Lancelot Andrewes' borrowing from the liturgies of SS Chrysostom and James (Nazir-Ali and Sagovsky 2007, 136f; see *The First and Second Prayer Books of King Edward VI* 1968, x). While the Articles declare that the Eastern churches have erred, early Anglican theologians, like Richard Field, are not prepared to unchurch them or to say that they have been deprived of the gospel of salvation. Rather, their separation from Rome is evidence that communion with that see cannot be a necessary sign of belonging to the Catholic Church (Avis 1989, 71f).

*The Wiley-Blackwell Companion to the Anglican Communion*, First Edition. Edited by Ian S. Markham, J. Barney Hawkins IV, Justyn Terry, and Leslie Nuñez Steffensen.
© 2013 John Wiley & Sons, Ltd. Published 2013 by John Wiley & Sons, Ltd.

The first sustained ecumenical contact with the Orthodox churches came, however, with the non-jurors. The non-jurors were bishops and clergy who could not conscientiously take the Oaths of Allegiance and of Supremacy to the newly arrived William and Mary, after the Glorious Revolution of 1688, because they had already taken such Oaths to the exiled James II. They became, in effect, an *ecclesiola*, surviving, in one way or another, for over 100 years. Because they were a relatively small body, they sought wider fellowship and although, through James, they had contact with Rome, their attention was really focused on the Eastern churches. For nearly ten years, they were engaged in negotiations with the various patriarchs of the Eastern churches, addressing several "humble supplications" to them and receiving, in reply, some very haughty letters making a number of demands of them.

In the end, the negotiations proved abortive for reasons which bear rehearsal as they have some contemporary significance. The non-jurors were mostly High-Church Anglicans who believed the church to be a spiritual society with its own laws and who emphasized the importance of liturgical worship in the life of the church. In this, they provide the link between the Caroline divines of the seventeenth century and the Tractarians of the nineteenth. In spite of their High-Church tendencies, they could not accept patriarchal demands that they should put tradition on the same level of authority as the Holy Scriptures. While they honored Mary the Blessed *Theotokos*, they were afraid of excessive Marian cults in Orthodoxy as much as in Rome. Again, although they believed firmly in the communion of saints, they had scruples about the necessity of invoking them. They readily acknowledged the presence of Christ in the Eucharist but were wary of cults of Eucharistic adoration and, finally, they could not agree to the worship of icons as a matter of faith. To this, we might add the grand question, as Hooker put it, that hangs between Rome and Anglicans: the doctrine of justification by faith alone. The fates of Cyril Lucar, Patriarch of Constantinople in the seventeenth century, and of others, suggest that this has also been the case with the Orthodox. While Roman Catholic–Lutheran, and, to some extent, Anglican–Roman Catholic dialogue has directly tackled this question, it is difficult to find evidence of direct discussion in this area as far as Anglican–Orthodox dialogue is concerned, especially in view of the often-repeated Orthodox insistence on "free cooperation with God's grace" and working for our salvation (Nazir-Ali 1996, 87f; see also Anglican-Orthodox Dialogue 1984; the Church of the Triune God 2006; Joint Declaration of the Justification 2000; Salvation and the Church 1987; and Ware 1973, 226f).

The eighteenth century was also, of course, the beginning of the Evangelical Revival which radically altered many of the landmarks in church life, including the uneasy, and sometimes downright hostile, relationship between Anglicans and dissenters or nonconformists. As the historian of Evangelicalism, D. W. Bebbington, has shown, all of this was changed by the Revival. Evangelicals were prepared not only to lower denominational barriers to intercommunion, for instance, but also to join with one another in a common cause and to establish organizations for its fulfillment. Thus, the British and Foreign Bible Society was created for the better dissemination of the scriptures at home and abroad, and the London Missionary Society for cooperation in overseas mission, another favorite object of the Evangelicals, and one which was to produce significant challenge as well as opportunity for ecumenism (Bebbington 1989, 66).

Across the Atlantic, a vision for unity would arise in a very different context. Already in the second half of the nineteenth century, an Episcopal priest, William Reed Huntington, had formed a local clergy fellowship, along with the local Roman Catholic priest. It was here that his ideas about church unity in the United States developed. These can be found most conveniently in his book *The Church-Idea: An Essay Towards Unity*, first published in 1870. Huntington distinguished between the Anglican system and the Anglican principle. The latter had become obscured by the former, which included surplices, spires, choirs, important-sounding titles for church officials and the like. For Huntington, it also included the Church of England's relationship to the State which, in his opinion, compromised its adherence to the Anglican principle. According to him, the Anglican principle could be articulated in terms of a common adherence to scripture as the Word of God, the Catholic Creeds as the Rule of Faith, the Sacraments ordained by Christ himself, i.e., Baptism and Holy Communion and the Episcopate as a means of and a focus for unity. This was the first public airing of the now-famous Quadrilateral which has been so influential in ecumenical discussion including Anglicans and, indeed, beyond that (Huntington 1989).

For Huntington, the principle involved the right and the duty of every local church to be and to become the catholic church in that place. There is here both the pole of locality and that of catholicity. The local church must take its own culture and context seriously; for Huntington, this meant that the situation in the United States was markedly different from that of the Elizabethan Settlement in England. Proposals for the greater unity of Christians could, for example, be better explored because there was no pressure in terms of the church's relationship to the state. At the same time, Huntington knew well enough that the local church could only be truly catholic in relationship with all the other local churches. In this, he can be said to have anticipated the World Council of Churches (WCC) New Delhi Assembly's call for unity which involves "all in each place united with all in every place."

Huntington's somewhat intra-American and pan-Protestant vision was adapted and given a more "Catholic" direction by the House of Bishops at the 1886 Chicago Convention of the Episcopal Church. It was, more or less, in this form that the Quadrilateral was adopted by the 1888 Lambeth Conference, although that conference sought to bring it into greater conformity with the Articles of Religion (Wright 1988, 8ff; see also Nazir-Ali 1989, 117f).

Even the 1888 Lambeth Conference, however, saw the Quadrilateral not in fully Catholic terms but only as applying to "Home Reunion" or to "the English-speaking peoples." It was not until the 1920 Conference's *Appeal to All Christian People* that its remit was extended to the whole world. Since then, it has been hugely influential in negotiations for church unity on a regional or national basis. The many schemes of union that mushroomed in different parts of the world could not have been imagined without the Quadrilateral. Certainly, the ones that came to fruition, such as that of South India, North India, and Pakistan, owe a great deal to the vision of the church as set out in the Chicago-Lambeth Quadrilateral. The influence of the Chicago-Lambeth Quadrilateral on the so-called "Lima Text" or the WCC's Faith and Order agreement on Baptism, Eucharist, and Ministry is also apparent and has been noted (*Baptism, Eucharist and Ministry* 1985; see also Wright 1988, 13).

The Quadrilateral, has, however, been criticized for being minimalist and anti-confessional, and even non-liturgical. The charge of minimalism was met already by the American House of Bishops in 1886 when they not only deepened its content but also declared that it was a basis for serious study rather than being sufficient for unity as such. The various plans for union also had to flesh out the theological and ecclesiological implications of organic unity among the churches. As to being anti-confessional, Huntington was certainly not a fan of the Thirty-Nine Articles. Whether Anglicanism is confessional or not has been a subject of debate for many years, not least at this time of fresh challenges to its unity. On the one hand, it does not possess the great confessions of the churches of the Reformation, such as the Westminster for the Presbyterians or the Augsburg for the Lutherans. On the other, it is most emphatically a credal church with all three of the catholic creeds, the Apostles', Nicene, and Athanasian, being regularly used in the liturgical worship of the church.

We have noted earlier the ecumenical significance of the Quadrilateral but it was also, from almost the beginning, seen as being related to Anglican identity, to what was regarded as essential for the church's faithfulness. At this time of crisis in the Anglican Communion, it cannot be said too strongly that the bare bones of the Quadrilateral are not only insufficient for pursuing an ecumenical vocation but also for our self-understanding as Anglicans. Both the wider Global South movement and GAFCON have shown interest in developing a "confessing," if not "confessional" aspect to Anglicanism which is based on its traditional formularies: the Book of Common Prayer, the Ordinal, and the Articles of Religion (see Gomez and Sinclair 2001, and the Jerusalem Declaration at gafcon.org).

The Quadrilateral does not mention the concern, for example, of the 1930 Lambeth Conference about the nature of the church's unity and how this unity is to be maintained. The so-called Instruments of Unity, i.e., the office of the Archbishop of Canterbury, the Lambeth Conference of Bishops and its standing committee, which evolved into the Primates' Meeting, and the Anglican Consultative Council, were seen as maintaining and promoting this unity. In the current crisis, all have, however, proved unequal to the task, as set out by the 1930 Lambeth Conference, of sustaining mutual loyalty through the common counsel of bishops in conference. Successive Lambeth Conferences have guided the communion in important ecumenical, moral, and doctrinal areas, but the last conference (a) could not gather all the bishops, and (b) did not produce any resolutions or teaching documents, relying on the so-called *Indaba* process for continuing deliberations on difficult questions in the communion. Again, both the 1988 and 1998 Conferences asked for an enhanced role for the primates in resolving particularly thorny issues. Such a role was certainly envisaged in the earlier drafts of the Anglican Covenant, proposed by the Windsor Report, but has been progressively marginalized in the subsequent drafts. The latest draft has an excellent theological and ecclesiological preamble, but the section on the implementation of any covenant has been rendered virtually toothless by outlining a process of consultation which is unlikely to lead to a decision which is effective (The Truth Shall Make You Free 1988, Res 18:2a, 216; The Official Report of the Lambeth Conference 1998, Res III:6b, pp396f; see also the draft of the Anglican Covenant at www.anglicancommunion.org/commission/covenant/ridley_cambridge/draft_ text.cfm).

Alongside the Quadrilateral then, there is a need to develop the credal, confessing aspect of Anglicanism as also its need for a functioning conciliarity which, on the one hand, acknowledges the Anglican genius for a synodality which gathers together representatives of the whole *laos* of God but, on the other, provides for a differentiated understanding of how responsibilities are exercised, in such gatherings, according to biblical and historic patterns found in the church. These steps are necessary not only for Anglicanism's own self-understanding and proper functioning but also for ecumenical credibility, so that our partners can have confidence in our rootedness in the scriptures and the Apostolic tradition.

If the Quadrilateral was one kind of encouragement toward seeking greater unity with Christians of other traditions, the different arrangements for cooperation among mission agencies in Africa and Asia was certainly another. In Kenya and India, for example, various kinds of "comity" agreements had emerged which recognized the mission agencies, of different denominations, as having particular spheres of influence. Such arrangements were, undoubtedly, instrumental in bringing about, for example, the Kikuyu Conference in Kenya which went beyond cooperation in missionary work and proposed steps toward a united church. This led to a fully developed scheme of church union, modeled on that for the Church of South India. Although it did not result in the uniting of the churches, it laid the foundations for greater cooperation in matters of social and political justice, for instance, and to the emergence of the National Council of Churches in Kenya (NCCK), which has been of some significance in the national life of that country (see Neill 1960, 379ff and Hewitt 1971, 142ff). Since then, there have been many schemes for church union in which Anglicans have been involved. Apart from the schemes in South Asia, none of the others have come to fruition. Although church union schemes have continued to emerge (e.g., the Welsh scheme in the 1980s), the failure of the Anglican–Methodist Scheme in 1970 marks a watershed for Anglican involvement in this model for unity (The Emmaus Report 1987; Buchanan et al. 1970).

The entry of the Roman Catholic Church, following the Second Vatican Council, into the Ecumenical Movement has changed the entire topography of ecumenical relations. From this time on, the emphasis has been on bilateral dialogue between world communions rather than between denominational expressions within a particular country or region. The aim then is not so much united churches at this level but, rather, reconciliation at the universal level although, of course, with local implications. The bilateralism of this approach has, however, been complemented by multilateral work, for example, in the preparation by the WCC's Faith and Order Commission's report, with full Roman Catholic participation, on Baptism, Eucharist, and Ministry, and on a common confession of the Apostolic Faith (*Baptism, Eucharist and Ministry* 1985; Towards a Common Confession of the Apostolic Faith 1991; and Towards Sharing the One Faith 1996).

Before we enter into a detailed discussion of Anglican–Roman Catholic relations, however, we must return to relations with the Orthodox, both "Eastern" and "Oriental," or, if you like, Chalcedonian and non-Chalcedonian, and with the Assyrian Church of the East.

The 1920 Lambeth *Appeal to All Christian People* coincided with an encyclical from the Ecumenical Patriarch regarding Christian unity. Two years later, the patriarch and his Holy Synod set out a statement on the validity of Anglican Orders which is notable for its clarity and charity. This led to the well-known visit by an Orthodox delegation to the 1930 Lambeth Conference and to a positive resolution requesting further dialogue on doctrinal issues which unite or divide the two communions. Other Orthodox churches, such as Alexandria, Jerusalem, Cyprus, and Romania, agreed with the judgment of Constantinople on the recognition of Anglican Orders. There was an air of optimism about Anglican–Orthodox relationships throughout the 1930s and 1940s, but from 1948 there was increasing recognition that serious obstacles remained to inter-communion between the two families of churches. For example, as Bishop Kallistos Ware points out, while Anglicans thought that the judgment on Orders had to do with the *present* status of Anglican clergy, the Orthodox view had more to do with what would happen if Anglicans and Orthodox reached sufficient doctrinal agreement to warrant the restoration of communion: would Anglican clergy need to be re-ordained (see Neill 1960, 370f; Stephenson 1978, 166f; Coleman 1992, 77f; and Ware 1973, 324f)?

After Archbishop Michael Ramsey's visit to the Ecumenical Patriarch, Athenagoras I, there was a new "spring" in relations between Anglicans and Orthodox with the coming into being of the joint Anglican–Orthodox Doctrinal Commission. However, no sooner had the commission issued its first agreed statement (Moscow 1976) than it was plunged into a first-class row over the ordination of women in some parts of the Anglican Communion.

Some Orthodox churches and theologians, in the light of this development, wished to downgrade the dialogue to an educational exercise which no longer aimed at mutual recognition and organic union. In the end, however, and partly as a result of efforts by Robert Runcie, then the Anglican co-chairman of the dialogue, it was decided to continue the dialogue as before, though with a fresh realization of the disagreements and obstacles in the way of unity (The Emmaus Report 1987, 89ff; Anglican-Orthodox Dialogue 1984, 1ff). While the consecration of women to the episcopate in some Anglican provinces did not cause quite the furor among the Orthodox which some were expecting, the consecration of an active and partnered homosexual to the episcopate in the Episcopal Church, once again, brought Anglican–Orthodox relations to a point of crisis. A number of Orthodox churches have declared that they are unable to continue dialogue with the Anglican Communion. An example of such unease is the frank speech delivered by Metropolitan Hilarion Alfeyev to the Church of England's Nikaean Club, which promotes ecumenical relations. In this, he declared that the dialogue is doomed to closure if the unrestrained liberalization of Christian values continues in many communities of the Anglican world. Given that Metropolitan Hilarion is the head of the Moscow patriarchate's Department for External Relations, this has been recognized as a serious declaration indeed (see www.mospat.ru/en/2010/09/10/news25819/).

On the other hand, the Anglican–Orthodox International Commission was able to publish an agreed statement on the *Church of the Triune God*, which explores ecclesiological and cultural issues at some length, but does not directly address a number of the concerns raised by Metropolitan Hilarion in his speech.

Anglican contact with the Ancient Oriental Churches dates, in the main, from the nineteenth century as commerce, empire, and missionary activity brought these churches to Anglican attention. Within the Ottoman domains, these communities had long lived as *dhimmis*, or protected minorities, with all the disabilities that entailed. British diplomats, scholars, and travellers often found them living in parlous conditions. Their reports back home created pressure for the Church of England to come to the assistance of these beleaguered Christians (Hill 1988).

In India, the situation was different. At the dawn of the nineteenth century, the East India Company did not permit Christian mission in British territories. (It was compelled to change this policy as the century progressed.) This meant that Anglican and other mission agencies, such as the Society for the Propagation of the Gospel (SPG) and the Church Missionary Society (CMS), were forced to locate either in territories held by other European powers or even to operate in the areas still ruled by native princes. CMS thus found itself in the state of Travancore on a "mission of help" to the Syrian Orthodox Church there. This expression was to characterize much Anglican involvement with the oriental churches. As distinct from Roman Catholic or other Protestant efforts, it was felt that the emphasis should not be on converting local Christians to Anglicanism and establishing an Anglican church, but on the revitalization of the existing church and its members. Among the "St. Thomas Christians" of South India, this took the form of encouraging theological education, assistance with the translation of the Bible into Malayalam (since the liturgy of the church remained in Syriac), and in education more generally. The early missionaries were discreet and patient but some of the later ones wanted change in the church at a faster pace. The result of this was increasing friction between the hierarchy and the missionaries, eventually bringing CMS involvement to an end but not before some of the "Syrian" Christians had separated themselves into an Anglican Syrian Church. Ultimately, this led to the formation of the Anglican diocese of Travancore and Cochin. The impetus for reform did not cease, however, within the ancient church, and the reforming party was able to secure the consecration of a bishop by the Patriarch of Antioch. After years of litigation and dispute, the result was the emergence of the Mar Thoma Syrian Church, an oriental church in liturgy and church order but reformed along Anglican lines. The churches of the Anglican Communion, including the United Churches of South Asia, are in communion with this church, and its bishops attend representative Anglican gatherings (Hill 1988, 82f; Mar Thoma 1986).

The dispute within the Malankara Church in South India had brought the Patriarch of Antioch, Peter III, to Britain in hope that the Church of England might mediate between the two sides. This was not to be as the Archbishop of Canterbury clearly supported the reforming party and its bishop, Mar Athanasius. The visit did result, however, in an educational "mission of help" for the Syrian Orthodox Church's schools in Turkey. Because of the tension in India, it was not as significant as that among the Assyrians. George Badger's work among the Assyrians (also called the Church of the East and, erroneously, the Nestorians) led to the Archbishop of Canterbury's mission to the

Assyrians. This was largely an educational initiative run by a number of clergy and the Sisters of Bethany. Not only did they establish schools and a seminary, they were also responsible for much scholarship on the language, manuscripts, and liturgy of this ancient church.

In Ethiopia too, Anglican missionaries, largely from evangelical mission agencies such as the Bible Churchmen's Missionary Society (BCMS, now Crosslinks) and the Church's Ministry Among Jewish People (CMJ), have refused to proselytize among Orthodox Christians. They have sought to assist in the renewal of the Ethiopian Ortho-dox Church and to integrate any converts, resulting from their work, into the Ethiopian Church. With Armenians, likewise, there have been warm relations with cooperation in education, especially theological education. Anglicans have, for long, supported the Armenian people in their search for justice and security in their homeland and in the diaspora. There has also been collaboration in pastoral care and the sharing of church buildings (see Nazir-Ali 1990, 57ff).

As with the Chalcedonian Orthodox, recognition of Anglicans as perhaps the nearest among Western-type Christians to the Oriental churches has been seriously affected by the ordination of women to the priesthood and the episcopate and, even more seriously, by the decision in some provinces of the Anglican Communion to permit the blessing of same-sex unions and the ordination of openly homosexual persons to the priesthood and the episcopate.

A very significant development, which must be noted, has been the *rapprochement* between the Chalcedonian Orthodox and the non-Chalecdonian. Under the auspices of the WCC, these ecclesial families have now produced agreements on the Christological questions which have divided them since the fifth century. This, in turn, has led to ecumenical cooperation in the areas of mission, liturgy, the life of women in the church, and the development of spirituality. The Roman Catholic Church has also come to important agreements with the Oriental Orthodox and the Assyrians on Christological issues (Gregorios et al. 1981; Fitzgerald and Boutenoff 1998; see also the Information Service of the Pontifical Council for Promoting Christian Unity for progress in dialogue between the Roman Catholic and the Oriental Churches, e.g., Nos 76, 90, 117, 127).

It is clear that some effort is required to restore the confidence of the Ancient Orien-tal churches in the apostolicity and orthodoxy of the Anglican Communion. This is also true, of course, of the Chalcedonian churches and of the Roman Catholic Church, to which we now turn.

Pope Pius the Fifth's excommunication of Elizabeth and his releasing of her English subjects from any allegiance to her set the tone for Anglican–Roman Catholic relations in the latter part of the sixteenth century. In such a situation of open hostility, where recusant Catholics were regarded *ipso facto* as traitors, any discussions could only be polemical and adversarial. It was not until the next century that any positive evaluation could be made and influence acknowledged which was beyond mere controversy (see Chadwick 1990, 286f; Avis 1989, 23ff). There were, of course, friendlier contacts, such as those that William Wake, Archbishop of Canterbury in the eighteenth century, had with the Gallicans and, indeed, through his wider writing on the positive nature and status of the Roman Catholic Church. The Tractarian revival, which sought a recovery of the Church of England's "Catholic" heritage, also brought renewed contact and fresh interest on both sides which could not be dampened by Leo XIII's negative judgment on Anglican Orders in *Apostolicae Curae* (1896) and the "Responsio" by the Archbishops of Canterbury and York known as *Saepius Officio* (texts can be found in Anglican Orders: A century of *Apostolicae Curae* 1996, 127ff). In the end, this interest led to the abortive Malines Conversations which did, nevertheless, provide the groundwork for the future.

The present state of Anglican–Roman Catholic dialogue can be traced back to the historic meeting between Archbishop of Canterbury Michael Ramsey and Pope Paul VI in 1966, which followed the Second Vatican Council's recognition, in the Decree on Ecumenism, that elements of Catholic faith and order (*fidem et structuram ecclesiasticam*) continued to exist within the Anglican Communion. The two leaders' joint declaration agreed upon a dialogue based on "the Gospels and on the ancient common traditions." A preparatory commission then, with remarkable speed, issued the Malta Report, which resulted in the appointment by the two churches of the first Anglican–Roman Catholic International Commission (ARCIC). In just over a decade, it completed ground-breaking agreements on the Eucharist, Ministry, and Authority. These were then submitted to the authorities of the churches for reception. It is interesting, in this connection, to note that while the Church of England and the Anglican Communion (in the shape of the 1988 Lambeth Conference) were able to recognize the agreements "as consonant in substance with the faith of Anglicans," the Roman Catholic Church's Congregation for the Doctrine of the Faith (CDF) could only give it a warm, but qualified, welcome (see Hill and Yarnold 1994, 12ff, 111ff, 153ff, and 156ff). Perhaps some of the emerging fault lines could already be seen. The Roman Catholic bishops of England and Wales wished to see a stronger evangelical voice in the dialogue, especially on the doctrine of justification by faith and the importance of the Word of God for the church. The CDF's response raised the question about the ordination of women and pointed out that correspondence with the Archbishop of Canterbury had mentioned this point in the context of any Roman Catholic re-evaluation of the question about Anglican Orders in the light of the agreement on ministry (Hill and Yarnold 1994, 109, 163f).

As if in response to the Catholic Bishops Conference of England and Wales, the second ARCIC began its work with a consideration of the doctrine of justification. Here, they themselves acknowledge the work already being done on this subject by the Lutheran–Roman Catholic dialogue. It is clear that the Anglican–Roman Catholic agreement, "Salvation and the Church," must be read in the light of the subsequent Lutheran–Roman Catholic Declaration which makes this doctrine a touchstone or measure of the Christian faith and a criterion which orients all the church's teaching and practice to Christ (Salvation and the Church 1987; Joint Declaration on the Doctrine of Justification 1999).

The commission continued its work with "The Church as Communion," "Life in Christ: Morals Communion and the Church," and "The Gift of Authority and Mary: Grace and Hope in Christ." Although there have been debates and discussions about these reports in different provinces in the Anglican Communion, and the Roman Catholic Church has responded to some of this work, there has not been the kind of authoritative response which was seen in respect of ARCIC I. This may well be because of the changed relationship between the communions and the lower expectations that they now have of one another. The final phase of ARCIC II's work was seriously affected by developments in the Anglican Communion following the ordination of a partnered and active homosexual to the episcopate in the United States.

In spite of the difficulties already looming, Anglican and Roman Catholic bishops, meeting together at Mississauga in Canada in 2000, felt sufficiently optimistic to call for a new commission of bishops which would be able to implement the ARCIC agreement in different parts of the world. As it points out, however, the work of the new commission (known as the International Anglican–Roman Catholic Commission for Unity and Mission, or IARCCUM) was affected by the situation in the Anglican Communion almost from the beginning, and it felt unable to take the two churches on to another stage in their relationship. In the end, it contented itself with summarizing the ARCIC agreements and commenting on them, as well as setting out some more practical areas for ecumenical cooperation (see Growing Together in Unity and Mission 2007).

A number of Anglican groups have felt that the Bishop of Rome alone can guarantee their continuance in historic orthodoxy and have petitioned the Vatican for some kind of "corporate union." This has led Rome to provide for Ordinariates which recognize Anglican liturgical, theological, and pastoral "patrimony" to some extent. Such concessions seem based on the recognition by Paul VI, at the canonization of the English Martyrs in 1970, that when the Roman Catholic Church is able to embrace her ever-beloved sister, the Anglican Communion, in the fullness of unity, "there will be no seeking to lessen the legitimate prestige and worthy patrimony of piety and usage proper to the Anglican Church" (see Hill and Yarnold 1994, 148). It is noteworthy that what had been said about the reconciliation of two communions is now being used to receive individuals and groups from one communion to the other. There is also some provision for the continuing ordination of married men, even if the norm of clerical celibacy is upheld, and for special formation for all candidates for Holy Orders in the Ordinariates. While much of this can be welcome, there are important ecclesiological and practical questions which remain: the ecclesial form of the Ordinariate is "presbyterian" in the sense that it does not provide for a bishop. It is strange that one episcopally ordered church should provide for the reception of those from another episcopally ordered church in this way. It seems also to go against the spirit of the teaching in *Sacerdotalis Caelibatus* that sacred ministers from other churches, who are received into the communion of the Catholic Church, may be able to continue the exercise of their ministry. There is the danger, as has happened with many Eastern Catholic churches, of gradually being Latinized, in this case because of a necessary recourse to a Latin episcopate. Again, while the continuing ordination of married men is welcome, will the "objective criteria" required for it include the Anglican experience of married clergy or will they just be about matters like "scarcity"? The provisions for formation also could lead to Latinization unless there is robust attention given to distinctive programs and institutions for the transmission of Anglican patrimony. At best then, it seems the Ordinariates are only a step along the ecumenical path and not the final fruit of Anglican–Roman Catholic dialogue (Apostolic Constitution *Anglicanorum Coetibus* along with its Complementary Norms can be found at www.vatican.va/holy_father/benedict_xvi/apost_constitutions/documents/hf_ben-xvi_apc_20091104_anglicanorum-coetibus_en.html).

The serious setbacks in the last few years have not brought the dialogue to an end. There is a new ARCIC, and it has been charged with the very subject which has gripped the Anglican Communion over the last decade: how do moral aspects of living the Christian life relate to communion? Because of the severity of the difficulties, however, there seems to be a sense, as with the Anglican–Orthodox dialogue noted earlier, that the dialogue is now about the better understanding of each church's beliefs and practices and, therefore, of difference rather than being a focused endeavor to achieve the restoration of communion. It may be that God, in his mercy, will overrule, and the churches will, once again, be able to return to a common quest for that unity in faith and life for which Christ prayed.

At the same time, it must be noted that just as relations with the historic churches of the East and with the Roman Catholics have encountered new obstacles, Anglicans have, in different ways, got closer to the mainline Protestant denominations. One of the expressions of this must be the far-reaching agreement between the British and Irish Anglican churches, on the one hand, and the Nordic and Baltic churches on the other. The so-called Porvoo Declaration, building on past agreements between, for example, the Church of England and the Church of Sweden or the Church of Finland, in effect, creates a communion of churches in Northern Europe. This has happened without full agreement about the nature of episcopal ministry and whether those churches which lost the historic line of succession (perhaps for good reason) were willing to regain it within the new context created by the agreement. It is interesting that this declaration did not create any of the sharp disagreements which occurred when the Church of South India was inaugurated, with the incorporation of non-episcopally-ordained ministers in an episcopally ordered church. There was a guarantee then that future ordinations would all be episcopal by bishops in historic succession. Such a guarantee was not forthcoming at the time of the Porvoo agreement, only that ordinations would be carried out in an overall episcopal context and with episcopal authority. Although the Anglican Communion was asked to comment on the statement only after it was issued, the 1998 Lambeth Conference welcomed it in fulsome terms (Together in Mission and Ministry 1993; *The Official Report of Lambeth Conference 1998*, Res IV:16, 411f; see also Synodical Opinion of the Bishop of Rochester 1995).

Since then, new obstacles have emerged even in this communion of churches with the removal of reference to gender in the marriage service of the Swedish church and the election of a same-sex partnered female bishop in that church. Once again, there was nothing like the anguish caused by similar developments within the Anglican Communion. This raises the question as to whether the agreement is of sufficient "thickness" to warrant the grand title of "Communion of Churches" given to those who are a party to it.

The Lutheran theologian Prof. Michael Root has pointed out the similarities and differences between the Porvoo process and the attempts at a closer relationship between the Episcopal Church in the USA and the Evangelical Lutheran Church of America. He notes that, while the Porvoo churches share a history of establishment in Europe, the American churches are part of the great denominational mix of American Christianity. The other big difference is the absence of episcopacy in the American Lutheran churches until fairly recent times. Even when it was introduced, there was no claim, as in Europe, to stand in some kind of historic succession. Historic episcopacy would then gradually be absorbed by the ELCA as TEC bishops participated in the consecration of its bishops (as Lutheran bishops would in the consecration of TEC bishops). In the meantime, and despite the frequent description of the relationship as one of "full communion," there would be inevitable restrictions on the complete interchangeability of ministries (Root 1994, 138ff).

In England, the collapse of the Anglican–Methodist scheme of union in 1972 was a shock to ecumenists and was, particularly, regarded by the Methodists as having been left at the altar. This undoubtedly created a crisis of trust between Anglicans and Methodists, at least in Great Britain. International dialogue between the two communions has continued, nevertheless, and those who had opposed the scheme, mainly Anglo-Catholics and Evangelicals, were quick to set out their own views on how a union could be achieved which was theologically coherent, locally driven, and gradual (on international dialogue, see, for instance, Sharing the Apostolic Communion 1996; on the English situation, see Buchanan et al. 1970).

Since 1995, conversations have resumed between the Church of England and the Methodist Church, leading to a covenant for unity. Once again, it is unclear whether there is a real agreement on matters like the place of the Bible in the life of the church, the sacraments, and ministry. From the point of view of some conservative evangelicals, the Methodist doctrine of "perfection," i.e., the possibility that sin can be eradicated from a believer's life, has continued to cause problems of conscience (on the Methodist doctrine of perfection, see Bebbington 1989, 153f; on the conversations and the problems involved, see An Anglican-Methodist Covenant 2001).

We have seen how Anglicans came to be in communion with the Mar Thoma Church, an oriental church in the Syrian tradition. They have also established communion with Old Catholic churches, which emerged from eighteenth- and nineteenth-century movements against papal supremacy in the Roman Catholic Church, and with the Philippines Independent Catholic Church, which has roots in the war of independence against Spanish rule in that country. As in other cases, already noted, some of these relationships have been threatened either by developments in the Anglican Communion or, indeed, within these churches themselves. The Lambeth Conference of 1998 recommended that ways should be found for taking counsel and making decisions together. As with the Anglican Communion itself, it is doubtful whether, without a coherent ecclesiology and an effective ecclesial structure, such relationships can flourish (The Emmaus Report 1987, 38ff; Report of the Lambeth 1998, Res IV.6, 407f).

There have been many other significant ecumenical encounters and agreements in which Anglicans have been involved, not least, of course, the structures and instruments of the ecumenical movement itself. Since the Edinburgh Missionary Conference of 1910, Anglicans have been involved in the Mission, Faith and Order, and Life and Work aspects of the movement. The *Appeal to all Christian People* of the 1920 Lambeth Conference gave the movement a much-needed impetus. Anglican relationships with the Orthodox contributed to the eventual participation of the Orthodox in the ecumenical movement. Faith and Order and Life and Work were, in due course, merged into the WCC, which was inaugurated in 1948. Anglicans have always participated vigorously, if sometimes critically, in the life and institutions of the WCC. They have also been active in local and regional expressions of ecumenism. In some cases, as in Britain and Ireland,

and in the Middle-East, they have worked toward more comprehensive councils that could include the Catholic, Orthodox, Protestant, and Pentecostal families of churches (on the Ecumenical movement and its various bodies, see Lossky et al. 1991; on Anglican perspectives on ecumenism, see Evans and Wright 1991; also see The Emmaus Report 1987).

Since 1978, at least, the Anglican Communion, as other churches, has been aware of the emergence and growth of a whole spectrum of newer churches. Some of these are so-called African Independent churches. Two Anglicans in particular, David Barrett and John Padwick, have been at the forefront of bringing their extent and importance to the attention of mainline Christianity. There has also been a veritable explosion of Pentecostalism in South America, the Caribbean, Africa, and East Asia; with Pentecostals now numbering some 400 million, and claiming large sections of the population in countries like Brazil and Korea, they cannot be ignored. Another Anglican, the sociologist David Martin, has shown how Pentecostalism is changing the social, economic, as well as the spiritual situation in a number of countries on different continents. Timothy and Rebecca Samuel Shah are also Anglicans who have been researching how Christian faith, including its Pentecostal expressions, is affecting communities in terms of changing their social status and economic standing (Report of Lambeth 1978, 111f; Report of Lambeth 1988, Res ii, 213; Report of Lambeth 1998, Res IV:21, 415; The Emmaus Report 1987, 142f; see also Barrett and Padwick 1989; Martin 2002; Shah and Shah 2011).

All of the preceding facts mean not only that the Anglican Communion, as such, and the various provinces need to engage with Pentecostalism and Independency in terms of dialogue but also that local, regional, and international structures will have to be found which can accommodate such traditions without undue obstruction from those with vested interests in keeping them out. The ecumenical scheme "Not Strangers but Pilgrims" of the churches in Britain and Ireland, set out to be as inclusive as possible in the establishing of new ecumenical instruments for the nations involved and proposals at the WCC's Eighth Assembly in Harare, envisaged the development of a "forum" which would include churches and other bodies that could not, for the time being, belong to the WCC. With the latter, the question remains, of course, why a new ecumenical instrument should not emerge at the world level, in ways similar to the emergence of such instruments at regional or local levels, which would, in fact, replace the WCC rather than being in addition to it (Not Strangers But Pilgrims 1987; Churches Together in Pilgrimage 1989; Kessler 1999). From experience and conviction, Anglicans have an important contribution to make in the re-forming of ecumenical instruments at this and at other levels.

On the one hand, Anglicans have always claimed to be *part* of the One, Holy, Catholic, and Apostolic Church and, on the other, they have sought to seek a greater and deeper expression of its unity. Again and again, they have claimed that Anglicans have no distinct doctrine or theology, but they have also themselves wished to preserve that patrimony of which Pope Paul VI spoke so warmly. If asked about the specific content of this patrimony, they might say that while Anglicans have no distinct doctrine, they *do* have distinctive methods and approaches to the doing of theology and of interpreting the Christian tradition in all its richness. There is a rich liturgical, literary, and devotional tradition which is admired, sometimes by those not Anglicans, and sometimes even by non-Christians. Approaches to pastoral work, a commitment to the wider community, local or national, and involvement of clergy and laypeople in decision-making are other features of a distinctive Anglicanism (see Avis 1989, 36ff; Evans and Wright 1991).

Anglicans have been wont to say that Anglicanism is "provisional," in the sense that Anglicans are prepared for a distinct Anglican Church to disappear in the greater cause of Christian Unity – for its churches to be less and less Anglican so they could be more and more catholic. This has, at least partially, been demonstrated in the United Churches where Anglicans have united with Christians of other traditions. At the same time, there has been a sense that Anglicans also have certain gifts to bring to the wider unity which they seek. (The tension is seen clearly in the *Appeal to All Christian People* of the 1920 Lambeth Conference and an encyclical of the same conference, as well as in the well-known Resolution of the 1930 Conference on the Anglican Communion, No 49. See Evans and Wright 1991, 377f, 380f and 380f; Coleman 1992, 45f, 83f.)

As we have seen, however, a more fundamental question has arisen recently about Anglican identity itself. It is vital for Anglicans to know who they are and to have effective instruments to sustain their fellowship, one with another. It is clear that previous Lambeth Conferences have emphasized, as Archbishop Robert Runcie put it in his opening address at the 1988 Lambeth Conference, *interdependence* rather than independence (The Truth Shall Make You Free 1988, 15). Their understanding of the autonomy of particular or national churches has been called "autonomy in communion" by the Windsor report of the Lambeth Commission on Communion (The Windsor Report 2004, 81ff). The report points out that, as long ago as the 1920 Lambeth Conference, it was said that churches were not free to deny the truth or to ignore the fellowship (The Windsor Report 2004, 51). The 1930 Conference declared that, as in antiquity, councils of bishops were the proper instruments to maintain the church's unity (Evans and Wright 1991, 389f; Coleman 1992, 83f). The 1988 and 1998 Conferences both requested that the primates of the communion be given "enhanced responsibility in offering guidance on doctrinal, moral and pastoral matters" (Report of Lambeth 1988, Res. 18; Report of Lambeth 1998, Res. III.6). It is crucial that Anglican structures reflect such an understanding of the communion for the sake of Anglican identity itself, and so that our ecumenical partners may be clear about what kind of ecclesial body they are dealing with. Anglican involvement in the search for unity has mostly been honorable and principled. Let us keep it that way.

## Bibliography

An Anglican-Methodist Covenant. 2001. Peterborough: Methodist Publishing House.

Anglican Orders: A Century of *Apostolicae Curae*. 1996. *Anglican Theological Review*, vol LXXVIII, no. 1 (Winter), Evanson, Ill.

Anglican–Orthodox Dialogue: The Dublin Agreed Statement. 1984. London: SPCK.

Avis, Paul. 1989. *Anglicanism and the Christian Church*. Edinburgh: T & T Clark.

*Baptism, Eucharist and Ministry*. 1985. Geneva: WCC.

Barrett, Daniel and John Padwick. 1989. *Rise Up and Walk! Conciliarcism and the African Indigenous Churches 1815–1987*. Nairobi: OUP.

Bebbington, D. W. 1989. *Evangelicalism in Modern Britain*. London: Unwin Hyman.

Buchanan, C. O., E. L. Mascall, J. I. Packer and G. Leonard. 1970. *Growing into Union: Proposals for Forming a United Church in England*. London: SPCK.

Chadwick, Owen. 1990. *The Reformation*. London: Penguin.

Churches Together in Pilgrimage. 1989. London: British Council of Churches and Catholic Truth Society.

Coleman, R., ed. 1992. *Resolutions of the Twelve Lambeth Conferences 1867–1988*. Toronto: Anglican Book Centre.

Evans, G. R. and J. R. Wright. 1991. *The Anglican Tradition: A Handbook of Sources*. London: SPCK and Minneapolis: Fortress.

*First and Second Prayer Books of King Edward VI*. 1968. London: J. M. Dent.

Fitzgerald, Thomas and Peter Boutenoff, eds. 1998. *Turn to God Rejoice in Hope: Orthodox Reflections on the Way to Harare*. Geneva: WCC.

Gomez, D. W. and M. W. Sinclair, eds. 2001. *To Mend the Net: Anglican Faith and Order for Renewed Mission*. Carrollton, Texas: Ekklesia.

Gregorios, Paulos, W. H. Lazareth and N. A. Nissiotis, eds. 1981. *Does Chalecdon Divide or Unite?* Geneva: WCC.

Growing Together in Unity and Mission: An Agreed Statement of IARCCUM. 2007. London: SPCK.

Hewitt, Gordon. 1971. *The Problems of Success: A History of the Church Missionary Society 1919–1942*. London: SCM.

Hill, Christopher and Edward Yarnold, eds. 1994. *Anglicans and Roman Catholics: The Search for Unity*. London: SPCK/CTS.

Hill, Henry, ed. 1988. *Light from the East: A Symposium on the Oriental Orthodox and Assyrian Churches*. Toronto: Anglican Book Centre.

Huntington, W. Reed. 1989. *The Church-Idea: An Essay Towards Unity*. New York: Scribner and Sons.

Joint Declaration on the Doctrine of Justification. 1999. Grand Rapids: Eerdmans.

Joint Declaration of the Justification: LWF and RCC. 2000. Grand Rapids: Eerdmans.

Kessler, D., ed. 1999. *Together on the Way: Official Report of the 8th Assembly of the WCC*. Geneva: WCC.

Lossky, N., J. M. Bonino, J. S. Pobee, T. F. Stransky, G. Wainwright and P. Webb, eds. 1991. *Dictionary of the Ecumenical Movement*. Geneva: WCC.

Mar Thoma, Alexander. 1986. *The Mar Thoma Church: Heritage and Mission*. Thiruvalla, India: Christava Sahitya Samithy.

Martin, David. 2002. *Pentecostalism: The World Their Parish*. Oxford: Blackwell.

Moscow, The agreed statement. 1976. Found at: http://www.anglicancommunion.org/ministry/ecumenical/dialogues/orthodox/docs/the_moscow_statement.cfm (accessed December 2012).

Nazir-Ali, Michael. 1989. The Vocation of Anglicanism. *Anvil*, vol. 6, no. 2.

Nazir-Ali, Michael. 1990. *From Everywhere to Everywhere: A World View of Christian Mission*. London: Collins.

Nazir-Ali, Michael. 1996. Scripture in Ecumenical Dialogue. *The Anglican Communion and Scripture*. John Stott and Others. Oxford: Regnum/EFAC.

Nazir-Ali, M. and N. Sagovsky. 2007. The Virgin Mary in the Anglican Tradition in the 16th and 17th Centuries. In *Studying Mary: The Virgin Mary in Anglican and Roman Catholic Theology and Devotion*, eds. A. Denaux and N. Sagovsky. London: T & T Clark.

Neill, Stephen. 1960. *Anglicanism*. Harmondsworth: Penguin.

Not Strangers But Pilgrims. 1987. London: British Council of Churches and Catholic Truth Society.

Platten, S., ed. 2003. *Anglicanism and the Western Christian Tradition*. Norwich: Canterbury Press.

Root, Michael. 1994. *A Commentary on Concordat Agreement*, eds. J. Eniffiss and D. Meitosen. Minneapolis: Augsburg.

Salvation and the Church. 1987. London: ACC/RC Secretariat for Promoting Christian Unity.

Shah, T. and R. Shah. 2011. Pentecost Amid Pujas: Charismatic Christianity in the Lives of Dalit Women in 21st century Bangalore. In *The Hidden Form of Capital: Spiritual Influences in Societal Progress*, eds. Peter L Berger and Gordon Redding. London: Anthem Press.

Sharing the Apostolic Communion. 1996. North Carolina: World Methodist Council.

Stephenson, Alan. 1978. *Anglicanism and the Lambeth Conferences*. London: SPCK.

Synodical Opinion of the Bishop of Rochester at his Diocesan Synod, 11 February 1995.

The Church of the Triune God: The Cyprus Agreed Statement. 2006. London: ACO.

The Emmaus Report: A Report of the Anglican Ecumenical Consultation 1987. 1987. London: ACC/CHP.

The Official Report of the Lambeth Conference 1998. 1999. Harrisburg: Morehouse.

The Report of the Lambeth Conference 1978. 1978. London: Church Information Office.

The Truth Shall Make You Free, Report of the 1988 Lambeth Conference. 1988. London: CHP.

The Windsor Report. 2004. London: ACO.

Together in Mission and Ministry: The Porvoo Common Statement with Essays on Church and Ministry in Northern Europe. 1993. London: CHP.

Towards a Common Confession of the Apostolic Faith, Confessing the One Faith. 1991. Faith and Order Paper NO153. Geneva: WCC.

Towards Sharing the One Faith. 1996. Faith and Order Paper NO153. Geneva: WCC.

Ware, Timothy. 1973. *The Orthodox Church*. Harmondsworth: Penguin.

Wright, J. R., ed. 1988. *Quadrilateral at One Hundred*. Cincinnati: Forward Movement.

# CHAPTER 53

# Music in the Anglican Communion

## William Bradley Roberts

## Tradition and Diversity

Anglican music in the early twenty-first century finds itself with more glorious variety than at any other time in its history. At the same time, diversity expands at a pace that challenges – and sometimes bewilders – practitioners. As the music of Thomas Tallis, Henry Purcell, Charles Villiers Stanford, Herbert Howells, and Benjamin Britten has migrated around the world, it has gathered local musical languages that enrich and enliven and occasionally supplant its historic legacy. Because of its expanding diversity, defining Anglican music is increasingly difficult, and performing the kaleidoscope of its present-day styles a mounting challenge.

The English cathedral tradition, as well as the collegiate choral school, continues to thrive in the motherland though, in some quarters, beset with financial challenges. The widely known service of Advent Lessons and Carols has radiated in all directions from its apotheosis, King's College, Cambridge. Indeed, the service has been adapted and replicated all over the globe, strengthening the fame and appeal of the annual King's College service. Historic English liturgies also flourish abroad, as will be discussed in the following text.

## Sub-Saharan Africa

Equally as remarkable as the persistence of the Anglican tradition is the proliferation of diverse local practice. While organ and vested choirs continue as the norm in England's worship (except in small parishes with limited resources), at an Anglican parish in rural South Africa, for example, one is likely to encounter only three instruments: the human voice, clapping hands, and, curiously enough, a cowbell. In the small town

*The Wiley-Blackwell Companion to the Anglican Communion*, First Edition. Edited by Ian S. Markham, J. Barney Hawkins IV, Justyn Terry, and Leslie Nuñez Steffensen.

of Davies outside Johannesburg, South Africa, this observer found delight in the intense fervor of singing in a three-hour service, as well as amazement at the ease with which even modestly educated worshippers sing in a half-dozen tongues. (In this nation of 11 official languages, to be a citizen is to be a polyglot.) Hymnody among black South African Anglicans is more likely to reflect indigenous cultures than it is to imitate English heritage.

In other parts of Africa, however, congregations commonly sing nineteenth-century British and American gospel music rather than indigenous music, reflecting the practice of the era in which their region was evangelized and the philosophy of the missionaries who introduced Christianity to the area. In some cases, the missionaries were eager to separate the natives from their "pagan" culture, including their indigenous music, in order to spread the faith. Other early missionaries probably just taught converts the hymns they themselves knew from their homeland, unaware of other options. One contemporary African reported that pioneering missionaries described Africans as having no sense of rhythm, an observation that is even more remarkable for its utter inaccuracy than for its Euro-centricity. The truth is that the African rhythms they encountered were so fabulously complex that the Europeans couldn't comprehend them. Therefore, African rhythm sounded completely cacophonous to the untutored ears of the missionaries. Modern mission work, however, is more committed to affirming the local culture and benefitting by the incorporation of indigenous music into the liturgy.

In contrast with the small-town Davies parish, music at the cathedral in Cape Town gravitates toward the traditional British repertoire; indeed, the cathedral's music, like its architecture, might easily be found in the British Isles of an earlier century, and the quality of the choral offerings is not unlike that of the music of English collegiate chapels or cathedrals. Hymnody and choral literature in this setting closely reflect the values and practices imported from the motherland. This juxtaposition in South Africa – traditional Anglican music and indigenous music – is repeated in many countries around the world.

## Ecuador and Latin America

Moving westward across the southern Atlantic Ocean and crossing the continent of South America to Ecuador, one hears further examples of indigenous music. Here, it is highly unlikely that one will experience traditional tunes like *Westminster Abbey* (Henry Purcell's tune most often sung with the text "Christ is made the sure foundation") or *Michael* (Herbert Howells' tune sung with "All my hope on God is founded"). Instead, lively, local Latin rhythms abound, incorporating African dance rhythms. One is also likely to hear many tunes whose harmonic structures sound "minor," because they adopt the ancient-sounding modal scales of the Quechua Indians. Western ears experience these tunes as attractive, exotic, and displaying a somewhat plaintive character. This observer has heard Quechua street musicians in New York, Paris, and Rome, playing songs that are immediately recognizable as music of the Andes Mountains. A type of indigenous pan-flute (hollow tubes of different lengths, bound together like handheld organ pipes), the *samponia*, often carries the melody. (Originally fabricated from hollowed-out cane, these instruments now are frequently made of plastic, or PVC pipes. Though some of the charm of the natural materials might be lost, plastic is probably easier to obtain as well as easier to fashion into flutes, the sound of these synthetic instruments being quite pleasant.)

Preparing for a regional worship service at the cathedral in Guayaquil, on the Pacific coast of Ecuador, I asked the diocesan bishop if we might use the harmonium (a "pump organ" with reeds producing the sound instead of pipes) found in the rear of the nave. He replied, "You're welcome to do so, if you can get it to work." Upon closer inspection, sure enough, the harmonium seemed not to have uttered a sound in decades. "What about guitars?" I asked. "Will people bring them?" Shaking his head, the bishop explained that no one could afford such a luxury. This saddened me, since excellent local guitars could be bought at a price that was astonishingly inexpensive by North American standards.

When the people from this coastal region assembled in the Anglican cathedral (a modest building with a concrete floor and a corrugated tin ceiling), there were two great surprises: first, my "leading" the music meant simply starting a familiar song, then getting out of the way of the sonic tsunami that rolled through the room; second, had there been instruments, one would never have heard them above the high decibels of human voices, passionately and exuberantly praising God. In stark contrast to this experience, a lay leader from rural Virginia recently reported to me that his parish never sang, because they had no one to lead them on an instrument. (In reality, what is missing from that situation is leadership that empowers people to sing without reliance on an instrument.) Naturally, the hard surfaces of the Ecuadorian cathedral amplified the singing, but that did not totally account for the powerful sound. Their faith did.

The Ecuadorians' ecstatic singing reminded me of a conversation from years earlier. I was showing a local California organ builder our church with its miserably dead acoustics. He surmised that, given the acoustically dry room, the congregational singing was probably not very good. "On the contrary," I replied, "their singing is extraordinary." "Well," he concluded, "they must have something to sing about." Those words echoed in my mind as I listened with amazement to the Ecuadorian congregation. Yes, they had something to sing about. In fact, their faith was palpable and infectious; it was the closest I could imagine to what must have characterized the fervor of the first-century church. Faith, full pews, and discipleship were very much in evidence in Anglican churches throughout Ecuador. Local Christians should be sending missionaries to North America instead of the other way around. Since they customarily consider how much they lack in comparison to North Americans, they expressed confusion. Their curiosity led me to explain that many of our churches display an attitude of nonchalance and complacency. Because faith is so crucial in their lives, this was a surprise to them.

## Anglican Tradition in North America

In North America, as in South Africa, one is more likely to hear traditional and classically based contemporary Anglican music in large parishes and in cathedrals in major cities, and simpler music in small towns and rural areas. However, that is not wholly descriptive. Where the resources exist – a good pipe organ, funds to invest in trained singers, creative leadership – one might hear superb renditions of William Byrd, Henry Purcell, or Tarik O'Regan from the choir, great works of organ literature, and traditional hymnody from the congregation. Traveling to the small parish of Good Shepherd in the small city of Rocky Mount, North Carolina, for example, one might be startled to hear a superb organ by English builders Harrison & Harrison, lending a very traditional, Anglican sound to worship. Out on the Great Plains of Nebraska, a lively English choral tradition thrives at the cathedral in Omaha. Along the eastern seaboard of the United States, one is most likely to hear undiluted English music at Trinity, Copley Square, in Boston; St. Philip's Cathedral, Atlanta; St. Thomas, Fifth Avenue, New York; and the Washington National Cathedral. (Small wonder that, in these last two places, immigrant musicians from England exert powerful leadership and oversee superb choir schools easily comparable with those in the United Kingdom.) Other large cities boast major Anglican music programs as well: Chicago, Dallas, Houston, Los Angeles, San Francisco, Seattle, Minneapolis, and Phoenix, among others.

Likewise, in smaller cities of the United States, one hears superb traditional music at Princeton, Ashmont (Boston environs), Asheville, Jackson, Memphis, Albuquerque, Tucson, Phoenix, Indianapolis, Portland (in both Maine and Oregon), Akron, Milwaukie, and other locales.

In some of these places, excellent choral music derives from a lively faith community whose financial contributions support fine music, while in other settings residual endowment funds from former eras or the gifts of contemporary patrons allow for ambitious programs. Superb offerings of choral evensong persist in the major capitals of North America, preserving what many people consider to be the splendor of Anglicanism.

Alas, near-empty naves often discourage the Herculean efforts of those who mount these impressive services. One frequently hears singers somberly depict gatherings where the choir outnumbers the congregation. Leaders demonstrate two divergent attitudes in response to this situation: (1) they question whether evensong is worth the effort and expense when so few attend; (2) they insist that it is vital to preserve our tradition, and so we must faithfully persist. One parish priest recently explained his parish's evensong practice in this way: we live in an age that does not regard highly matters of the spirit, but it is critical that we keep our skills up so that we are prepared for the day when people do begin to recognize their need for spiritual sustenance. This bit of philosophical probity was an unnecessary rationalization in his own particular parish, where the evensong congregation is large and enthusiastic.

## Ethnic Diversity

In still other places, the Anglican tradition survives, but is combined with a strong admixture of the prevailing local culture. In the southwestern United States, for example, one is likely to hear a Native American paean to the four winds with drumming, followed by a choral and organ-led *Gloria in excelsis Deo*. In the Southern United States, American gospel music, reflecting late-nineteenth-century hymnody, as well as spirited, black-gospel choral renditions, enliven the worship landscape. Many Episcopalians (as Anglicans are known in the United States) convert from other, more evangelical branches of Christendom, owing to the more open theology and polity of the Episcopal Church, or because they are attracted to the rich tradition of liturgy and music. When they do, they bring with them a knowledge and love of evangelical hymnody, especially those from the Southern United States, whether they are African Americans or European Americans. Even in predominantly European American congregations, the hymnody of African Americans has come to be seen by many as endemic to all US culture, and is likely to be sung in worship. Likewise, Latino culture, expanding exponentially in numbers and significance in North America, is influencing Anglican church music in North American worship services.

It is important to note, however, that among both African Americans and Latino Americans, there are congregations who prefer traditional Anglican music to indigenous music. I was surprised to hear a respected Latino church musician refer disparagingly to indigenous songs from Latin America as "mariachi music." On a similar note, when a parish I served scheduled a Black Gospel Mass, led by an expert in this genre, some African American parishioners reported that they would not attend, because this was not their music. The people who display this negative response to indigenous music from their own cultures usually fall into two categories: (1) those who have left behind their culture as they moved into another socio-economic and/or educational environment, wanting to avoid reminders of the modest beginnings associated with the music of their indigenous culture; and (2) those who were never exposed to the indigenous music of their own ethnic group, because they grew up in traditional Anglican churches with Western European music. (This is seen, for example, in Afro-Caribbean Americans whose worship roots are based in those islands where British culture predominates.)

Sometimes when liturgies haphazardly combine music from different cultures in the interest of cultural diversity, a jarring mixture occurs, combining elements that seem to spite each other. In others situations, however, where careful, creative planning is in the hands of sensitive leaders, contrasting elements are combined with meaningful and effective results. Often, the argument is heard that stylistic unity must be preserved for the integrity of the liturgy. The counter-argument, however, seems more convincing: Anglican music is already eclectic. The only remaining question is "has the canon of acceptable styles closed, or is it still feasible to add new genres of music?"

Evidence of eclecticism may be found in a resource as iconic and traditional as the *Hymnal 1940*, the American Episcopal hymnal that set the standard for congregational music for 45 years. In this collection, even though conservative by today's standards, one is likely to find secular folk tunes of the British Isles and North America, Negro spirituals (the first mainline denominational hymnal to include them), German chorales, plainsong, folk hymnody, cathedral hymns, etc. The current *Hymnal 1982* stretched the envelope of musical styles to an even greater extent, incorporating more ancient music (Gregorian chant and Greek hymns), contemporary music ("I am the bread of life"), and American hymnody ("Come, thou fount of every blessing"). Even worshippers with reserved tastes would scarcely blink when asked to sing "For all the saints" (*Sine nomine* by Ralph Vaughan Williams) and "Come, thou fount" (*Nettleton*, an anonymous US folk tune) in the same service. Placing the latter two hymns in a hardbound collection likely to be used over several decades often leads to an assumption that they are both standard, traditional hymns of the same genre, when in fact they are markedly disparate in origin and expression.

## The Primary Source of Controversy and Challenge

Church musicians, when asked about their greatest challenge, often point to the rapidly expanding diversity of musical styles required of them. This dilemma primarily concerns two broad categories of music: music from ethnic minorities (or global cultures), and music in popular styles.

"Popular Religious Song," a term created by church music scholar Carol Doran, is a moniker that covers any type of music written in a folk style or in the style of any commercial popular music. It is a useful term, because it carries no implicit judgment. (This is in stark contrast with the outdated label "legit" music that confines all other music to an unspoken category of "illegitimate." This term assumed the natural superiority of classical, Western European music. Fortunately, scholars have discarded this limited Eurocentric perspective.)

Nothing causes musicians' anxieties to mount, fears to rise, and blood pressures to soar like the issue of Popular Religious Song. These emotional anxieties derive from easily identifiable causes. Classically trained musicians fear that easily performed tunes, often as catchy as commercial radio jingles, will supplant traditional hymn repertoire that usually requires a greater investment of time and energy to learn. This fear is not without foundation. Indeed, there are individual churches that have banished the classical music of their heritage in favor of a steady diet of Popular Religious Song.

A second source of these fears, however, is less easily identified. Classical musicians, if they are honest, also will admit to not knowing how to perform Popular Religious Song with any degree of accuracy or integrity. (Books such as *Playing Gospel Piano* (2003) by Carl MaultsBy help the classical musician to gain proficiency in Black Gospel style.) Indeed, confronting music that is beyond the scope of musicians' conservatory education exacerbates their fear of newer styles. While some musicians are eager to expand their knowledge of music styles, others rely solely upon the education they received in their youth, educations that often focused exclusively on traditional materials. (It should be noted that music programs in large universities increasingly incorporate non-Western music.) Not only do the overly crowded curricula of some traditional conservatories prohibit adding non-European styles of music, but faculty often display antipathy toward non-classical music and deem it unworthy. Unsurprisingly these attitudes are adopted by students, eager to please their mentors.

In many parishes, Popular Religious Song and/or global music are relegated to their own separate liturgy. Often, this practice divides a parish into separate congregations. Loyalties and financial resources are divided, often resulting in unhealthy competition. In addition, those who attend a service with exclusively popular or global music never hear or sing the great traditional music of the church that was forged in the crucible of history and personal spiritual experience; those choosing the service with traditional music are never exposed to popular or global music that their sisters and brothers consider essential to their spiritual journey.

Elsewhere (*Music and Vital Congregations: A Practical Guide for Clergy*, published in 2009), I have compared stylistically segregated liturgies to a bizarre family reunion in which separate seatings are offered according to culinary preference. In this odd approach, those who prefer chicken as a main course would be seated at 1:00, while those who like pork dine at 3:00. In a healthy family reunion, the focus is on the mutual engagement of those who care for each other and cherish the opportunity to celebrate family relationships, not the menu. Likewise, in healthy worship, we are not dealing with consumers whose demands for disparate styles of music must be met, but worshippers belonging to a spiritual family who see their unity as vital. Surely we can tolerate – better yet, learn to appreciate – styles which do not necessarily satisfy us, but which bring joy or nourishment to other members of the worshipping community. Often, when we open our minds and hearts to new possibilities, unexpected blessings arise. In the words of eighteenth-century English hymnist William Cowper, "Sometimes a light surprises the Christian while he [or she] sings."

There is another dismaying consequence of dividing the parish into stylistically discrete musical congregations. Often, the classically trained musician leads music in the traditional service, while the musician using popular or global music is a person with less skill. Sometimes this decision is made in deference to the feelings of the principal musician who is eager to avoid popular or global music. Among the unhappy results that occur from this practice is this: the musical enrichment that the classically trained musician might lend to the popular or global music is missing.

This is not to imply that classically trained musicians are necessary to the successful performance of non-classical music. Au contraire. There are effective performances of music occurring every day that do not employ classically trained musicians. I recall, however, attending services with popular style music that had been relegated to well-meaning amateur musicians who had not diligently perfected their craft even to the point of knowing how to tune their instruments effectively. Likewise, classically trained musicians might well learn a kind of ease and spontaneity that comes naturally to performers of popular music. No matter what style of music is sung in a service, the worship of God surely deserves the best of that style we can present, and urges us constantly to improve and expand our skills.

## Contextual Decisions

Planning and preparing music for Anglican worship is not likely to become a simpler proposition any time in the near future; in all probability, complexity will increase as more styles are added. In the face of this, making wise decisions about music becomes a greater and greater challenge. Contextual questions about the worship at hand are critical to the decision-making: Who are the people who will hear and sing the music? What is their musical heritage? Are several cultural identities present in the same service, or only one? Are the musicians available able, with some work, to lead the music with accuracy and stylistic integrity? Above all, do the texts of the music reflect the theme of the liturgy, based on the lectionary texts and the liturgical season? Are the worshippers adequately prepared for the particular music to be sung, or will they find it stylistically shocking or musically impossible to perform? Will the music call undue attention to itself, or will it enrich and enhance the overall worship? Music that is entirely appropriate in one worship setting may well be entirely out of place in another.

Discernment, wisdom, and prayer are vital to liturgical and musical planning. When those are present, clashes over musical style are likely to diminish in importance.

## Alternatives to Popular Religious Song

In some cultural contexts, Popular Religious Song is not an acceptable choice. Sometimes Popular Religious Song, particularly of the commercially produced variety, will simply not enhance worship in a particular place, but, in fact, will detract from the worshippers' spiritual encounter. Nonetheless, leaders might sense a need for alternatives to traditional classical hymnody. Several options pertain.

Global music, that is, indigenous music that fairly represents the identity of the people of cultures other than one's own, often greatly enriches worship. Increasingly publishers make this music available. Several publishing houses in the United States are good sources of such music. The Global Praise Series of the United Methodist Church (New York City) makes available several volumes of songs that are easily learned by congregations. Choristers Guild (Dallas) has a number of global music collections, several of them edited by Michael Hawn. Some of these provide pronunciation guides for congregations wishing to sing in languages other than their own, as well as background information on the songs. Earthsongs (Corvallis, Oregon) publishes choral music from a variety of nations and cultures. Singing music from other lands unites us with Christians around the globe, giving us a natural affinity for people who might have heretofore been foreign to us, reminding us of our common humanity under one God.

The music of two religious communities, Taizé (France) and Iona (Scotland), is in a simple and, especially in the case of Taize, repetitive style that is easy to sing, has musical interest, yet provides some of the delights accessible in Popular Religious Song. Many parishes in the Anglican Communion have discovered that music from these communities provides a contrast to the more complex, textually dense hymns from classical Anglican repertoire. In addition, the songs of Taizé and Iona draw from the resources of a number of different nations, affording some of the same advantages as global music.

## The Unfolding Riches of Anglican Music

Stylistic diversity, described earlier, when approached with pastoral sensitivity, can serve to enrich and enliven Anglican worship. At the same time, the music of our historic heritage continues to bring delight and spiritual sustenance to large populations of the world as well as to local Anglican congregations. The attitude of both leaders and worshippers demonstrates whether we are self-serving or concerned for the common good, regardless of whether the musical style is monolithic or diverse. The church is at its worst when worshippers believe themselves (or are thought by their leaders) to be consumers, whose tastes and wishes must be discerned and satisfied in the crass, commercial manner of market research. Where prayerful and discerning wisdom guides the planning and practice of worship, however, Anglican music in all its rich diversity – historic and contemporary, traditional and innovative – continues to attract new worshippers and bless the people of Christ's church.

## Bibliography

Churchhill, John. 1966. *Congregational Singing: The Church's Part in Public Worship*. Croydon: Royal School of Church Music.

Dakers, Lionel. 1980. *The Psalms: Their Use and Performance Today*. Croydon: Royal School of Church Music.

Doran, Carol. 1995. Popular Religious Song. In *The Hymnal 1982 Companion*, vol. I, ed. Raymond F. Glover. New York: Church Publishing, pp. 13–28.

Hawn, Michael. 2000. *Halle, Halle: We Sing the World Round*. Dallas: Chorister's Guild.

Hawn, Michael and John Witvliet. 2003. *Gather into One: Praying and Singing Globally*. Grand Rapids, Michigan: Wm. B. Eerdmans.

Hustad, Donald P. 1993. *Jubilate II: Church Music in Worship and Renewal*. Carol Stream, Illinois: Hope Publishing.

MaultsBy, Carl. 2003. *Playing Gospel Piano*. New York: Church Publishing.

Pulkingham, Betty Carr. 2011. *This Is My Story, This Is My Song: A Life Journey*. Bloomington, Indiana: West Bow.

Richardson, Paul A. and Timothy W. Sharp. 2009. *Jubilate, Amen: A Festschrift in Honor of Donald Paul Hustad*. Hillsdale, New York: Pendragon Press.

Roberts, William Bradley. 2009. *Music and Vital Congregations: A Practical Guide for Clergy*. New York: Church Publishing.

Ross, Alex. 2007. *The Rest Is Noise: Listening to the Twentieth Century*. New York: Farrar, Strauss and Giroux.

Routley, Erik. 1967. *The Church and Music*. London: Duckworth.

Routley, Erik. 1968. *Words, Music and the Church*. Nashville: Abingdon.

Routley, Erik and Lionel Dakers. 1997. *A Short History of English Church Music*. London: Mowbrays.

Routley, Erik, edited and expanded by Paul A. Richardson. 2005. *A Panorama of Christian Hymnody*. Chicago: GIA.

Westermeyer, Paul. 1997. *The Church Musician*. Minneapolis: Augsburg Fortress.

Westermeyer, Paul. 1998. *Te Deum: The Church and Music*. Minneapolis: Augsburg Fortress.

Wilson-Dickson, Andrew. 1992. *The Story of Christian Music: From Gregorian Chant to Black Gospel*. Minneapolis: Fortress Press (published in the UK by Lion-Hudson, Oxford).

# CHAPTER 54

# Liturgy in the Anglican Communion

## Nancy Carol James

## Meaning of Liturgy

From time immemorial, people have gathered together to worship the power they called God and named this act "liturgy." For Christians, this worship or liturgy is a multi-faceted experience that enables people's engagement with the living presence of Christ. This worship can evoke feelings, call forth memories long buried, and awaken faith in a way that makes the world new. Worshippers invite the Holy Spirit by prayerfully responding with their heart, mind, and soul to the divine influence and welcoming the immediacy of Christ's presence. Theologian Dom Gregory Dix (1945, 393) defines this liturgy as "the worshipping act of the Body of Christ towards God, by which His eternal kingdom 'comes' in time." Also, Archbishop of Canterbury Rowan Williams expresses a spiritual understanding of liturgy that supplements Dix's definition. In the context of discussing St. Antony of Egypt and the Desert Father's spirituality, Williams (2003, 65) describes their "clear suggestion that exercising a public role in the church's worship involved standing in the furnace of divine action which unites earth and heaven." In this liturgy rooted in the divine furnace of God, the boundaries between terrestrial meaning and divine revelation are opened, so that heavenly realities become the living fire of worship. In authenticity and truth, the liturgy speaks from the heart of God and, replete with awe and wonder, leads human beings to worship. In liturgy, the mighty acts of God spring into present experience.

Yet, from its earliest use, both the word and experience of "liturgy" have had a complex meaning. A Greek word, λειτουργίας, "liturgy" was combined from two words "people" and "work" and originally was defined as "work for the people." Pre-Christian Greece's liturgy meant a public service at a private cost, with military duty as one

*The Wiley-Blackwell Companion to the Anglican Communion*, First Edition. Edited by Ian S. Markham, J. Barney Hawkins IV, Justyn Terry, and Leslie Nuñez Steffensen.

example of liturgy. In fourth century BCE, if a Greek person had some form of "individual and personal excellence," special contributions were expected beyond the duties of simple democratic participation (Ober 2011, 153). These extraordinary contributions included such diverse offerings as funding artistic events, paying occasional extraordinary taxes, as well as using individual talents, such as athletic or musical gifts.

These forms of liturgy were not purely a one-way offering to the populace but included expectations of some return in the form of special honors or privileges given to them by judges, politicians, or society as a whole. For example, honors, remembrances, and legal benefits could be given to them as a fulfillment of liturgy.

Contemporaries of the fourth-century-BCE Greek philosopher Socrates applied the word "liturgy" to his life and thinking. Beyond his expected involvement in the political system, he fulfilled his ministry or liturgy in his intense, public dialogues that raised moral awareness in Athenian society. Yet, even as he understood the debt owed to him by Greek society for his dialogues, Socrates believed that he owed them more because of the vast benefits he derived from his participation in the Athenian world. Hence, when he received the guilty verdict from the Greek court for charges of impiety, he refused to flee in order to save his life. Instead, he fulfilled his liturgy by drinking hemlock, surrounded by his disciples, while discussing the afterlife.

Another example of an ancient Greek liturgy lies in the Olympic Games. An athlete came from a particular family and world in which his or her special gifts were recognized and developed. The triumphant athlete offered back to others the sight of a human glorified in skill and strength; in success, the person received the olive wreath placed in honor on his or her head. Yet, the two-way flow of power and thanksgiving between the honoring populace and the honored athlete created a deep communion called "liturgy."

Therefore, the early use of the word "liturgy" involved a circular movement between a person offering his or her special gifts while receiving back from those benefitting from his or her actions. This movement called liturgy creates a sense of wonder, love, and praise, to which the word "worship" has been applied. In this form of worship, the furnace of divine action unites earth and heaven.

The Hebrews also recognized the use of liturgy in their temple. The priest received the sacrificial animal from the person or family who had a special thanksgiving or need. While offering this animal, the gift of renewed life poured upon the waiting persons, transforming and purifying their lives. This powerful motion created a new opening between heaven and earth so that people could find a deep and truthful foundation.

Another example of Hebrew liturgy comes from Hannah in First Samuel. She and her husband Elkanah had just sacrificed at Shiloh, but she still remained deeply troubled. Her fervent prayers bridged the gap between the holy and profane, and after the conception of Samuel, she cried out, "My heart exults in the Lord; my strength is exalted in God" (I Samuel 2:1). Hannah's liturgy connected the actions of heaven and her life on earth.

Those writing the first Christian scriptures used the Greek word "liturgy" to reference Jesus' life, death, and resurrection. In its precise use, the New Testament use of the word "liturgy" refers to the sacrifice of Christ on the cross. Jesus had offered his very life to God in order to save all humanity, which was the supreme public sacrifice at a high, private cost. His resurrection freed him, and all faithful humans with him, from the power of death. Hebrews 8:6 describes the ministry or liturgy of Jesus Christ, "But now He has obtained a more excellent ministry (λειτουργίας) by as much as He is also the mediator of a better covenant, which has been enacted on better promises."

This theme of sacrificial liturgy continues in Philippians. Paul said, "But even if I am being poured out as a drink offering upon the sacrifice and service (λειτουργία) of your faith, I rejoice and share my joy with you" (2:17). Later in the same letter, Paul writes about Epaphroditus, "Because he came close to death for the work of Christ, risking his life to complete what was deficient in your service (λειτουργίας) to me" (2:30).

The author of Acts of the Apostles identified the worshipping early church as a liturgy in describing them as "ministering and fasting to the Lord" (3:12). Once again, the circle of liturgy between serving the Lord and receiving from the Lord opens up the furnace of divine action. Rooted and grounded in God, liturgy is also an outward expression of an interior confidence in the loving will of God. As he was dying, Jesus cried out, "Father, into thy hands I commit my spirit" (Luke 23:36). With this same trust, worshippers commit themselves to the liturgy of Christ.

Hence, Christ's obedience unto death on the cross is the one liturgy ultimately honored in the Christian faith. In Christian worship, all people participate in the central revelatory experience or liturgy of Christ's death and resurrection. The furnace of divine action uniting heaven and earth is open to all faithful people in Jesus' completed liturgy.

Early Christian worship reflected the freedom of this divine furnace. Reginald Fuller (1969, 2) describes the early church saying, "For there were no fixed forms of service in the Church anywhere, as far as we know, until somewhere about 200 A.D." Yet, the early church recognized three active commandments of Christ and lived into these commands. Two commands are expressed as, "Go into the world and preach the gospel to the whole creation baptizing them in the name of the Father and of the Son and of the Holy Spirit" (Matthew 28:19). Jesus expressed the third command about the celebration of the Eucharist (also called communion or Lord's Supper), "Do this as a memorial of Me" (Luke 22: 19). He enabled the fulfillment of these commandments under the power of the promise, "Lo, I am with you always, even to the end of the age." The church then responded in faith to the commandments and promise of Christ. This liturgy then presented the saving act of God in Christ and became the first Anglican liturgy.

In about year 200 CE, Hippolytus (Easton 1934, 35) wrote words for the worship service that the Anglican Communion still use. He described a dialogue flow, called the Sursum Corda, between a bishop and a congregation:

> The Lord be with you.
> *And with thy spirit.*
> Lift up your hearts.
> *We lift them up unto the Lord.*
> Let us give thanks unto the Lord.
> *It is meet and right.*

This Eucharistic service continued with the Sanctus "Holy, holy, holy." The subsequent Eucharistic prayer was spoken by the priest as a faithful response to the promises of God in Christ.

The freedom of writing different words for worship in fulfillment of the commandments of Christ continued in the ministry of the first Archbishop of Canterbury, Augustine. In about year 600 CE, he sent Bishop Gregory of Rome a letter expressing concern about the many and varied liturgies in England. Gregory wisely told Augustine not to be too tied down to a Roman liturgy but to make a new liturgy for the Church of England, "an English one" (Hook 1882, 62). Hence, in Anglican worship, there is a clear continuity of liturgy from the church of the earliest times.

## Growth of Liturgy in the Middle Ages

During the Middle Ages, worship services grew in complexity with the development of intricate rituals which made the symbolic understanding of the worship services difficult to interpret. Over the centuries, the Latin Mass grew to consist of a combination of mainly Egyptian and Syrian liturgical forms based on written Eucharistic prayers.

The problems associated with the Mass were manifold. Dix described the growth of the liturgy in the Middle Ages as a deformation following the Roman proclamation of Christianity as the official religion. Indeed, this devaluation of the original power of liturgy primarily occurred because of the baptism of large groups of people without spiritual preparation, as well as priests speaking Masses without congregational involvement. The medieval liturgy became a heavy burden that was alienated from a majority of the common people.

Problems with the Eucharist proliferated. The people did not receive the Eucharistic cup and usually only received the bread at Easter. Many believed the theology of transubstantiation in which the accidents (that which is seen by the eye) do not change but the substance changes to the real body and blood of Christ. This could be interpreted as a magical transformation rather than a faithful response to Christ's presence.

Baptism also evolved away from its original roots. Initially, the rite of baptism was a public and festive celebration for both adults and children after a lengthy period of preparation. During the Middle Ages, virtually every adult had been baptized, and people quickly baptized newborn babies out of a fear of death and hell.

The practices of the early church were now no longer followed. Preaching was not required or regularly done in the Eucharistic service, and because of this, the gospel message was not applied to life's challenges. The Daily Office no longer was widely used but only said in monasteries with its short and non-consecutive scripture readings. To find the correct worship services for any particular day became a time-consuming burden.

Priests conducted the worship liturgy in Latin. Because most could not understand this language, the service devolved into a performance by the priests that the congregation watched without understanding the words. The Christian faith was becoming only available for the highly educated, while the uneducated suffered exclusion from the benefits of the gospel message.

The congregation's experience of worship had declined from the power of the early church as worship for the people had become reduced to adoration of a distant and strange power. The congregation could look with devotion upon the Mass, yet they could not enter fully into the liturgy to praise, to give thanksgiving, to offer their own lives, and to receive the full benefits of Christ's redemption. Hence, the worship services had become preoccupied with themselves and an "autonomous route according to its own logic, rather than as subject to the free working of the Holy Spirit" (Price and Weil 2000, 2).

In the Middle Ages, the word "liturgy" itself was transformed. Initially, liturgy meant a deep and profound involvement of divine power shared with humanity. After centuries of use though, the word "liturgy" became a derivative meaning as a term specifying the actual words spoken at services. In this meaning, liturgy was not the power of participating in Christ's death and resurrection, but became a technical term for the cultic or ritualistic words spoken in worship services.

## Archbishop Thomas Cranmer and the Sixteenth-Century Liturgical Reform Movement

In the sixteenth century, reformation thinkers Martin Luther, John Calvin, Ulrich Zwingli, and others spoke out boldly against these late-Middle Age worship practices and the theology supporting them. The sixteenth-century liturgical movement sought to regain both the original power and the authentic words from the early church by researching the scriptures and history. One example of the early liturgy comes from the Acts of the Apostles. "Day by day, as they spent much time together in the temple, they broke bread at home and ate their food with glad and generous hearts, praising God and having the goodwill of all the people" (Acts 2:46–7). In this scripture, one sees the mutual involvement circulating among people and the divine.

Although King Henry VIII had broken relations with the pope in 1534, he did not wish a liturgical review; however, soon after his death, this liturgical reform began. During the reign of Edward VI, the task fell to Archbishop of Canterbury Thomas Cranmer to write the Christian faith in a new Anglican prayer book. Cranmer finished writing this in a room on an upper floor of Lambeth Palace, and proved himself a "great liturgical artist" (Dix 1945, 728). Cranmer hoped to gather all people, both nobility and common, learned and unlearned, into the liturgy of Christ. This distinctive Anglican liturgy emphasized the scriptures, preaching, and the Eucharist, so that the newly empowered gospel message would reach all people. His inner vision reflected the original use of the word "liturgy" as he grounded the worship service in the death and resurrection of Jesus Christ.

To capture in his Eucharistic prayer the full power and magnificence of Christ's work on the cross, Cranmer (1910, 222) wrote, "O God heavenly father, which of thy tender mercies didst give thine only son Jesus Christ to suffer death upon the cross for our redemption, who made there (by his one oblation once offered) a full, perfect, and sufficient sacrifice, oblation, and satisfaction for the sins of the whole world." With his timeless words, Cranmer changed centuries of medieval worship and theology, and reclaimed the one liturgy of Christ's death and resurrection. At this intersection of Greek, Hebrew, and Christian thought, Cranmer reclaimed the existential significance of Christ's once-for-all liturgy. The liturgy of Christ was hence memorialized forever, and made Christ's redemption fully available and present for Anglican worshippers.

Christians could then understand Christ's liturgy through the intersection of three strains of thought: the Greek use of the word "liturgy" as a public ministry at a private cost; the Hebrew use of the word "liturgy" as a pure sacrifice that brings blessings; and the early Christian thought that Christ's redemption is brought into time with a united earth and heaven.

In the completed 1549 Book of Common Prayer, Cranmer thus preserved the real presence of the Lord himself in the sacrament without affirming transubstantiation. At the distribution of the sacrament, the priest said, "The body of our Lord Jesus Christ which was given for thee, preserve thy body and soul unto everlasting life" (Cranmer 1910, 225).

## Thomas Cranmer's 1549 and 1552 Prayer Books

In both the 1549 and 1552 prayer books, Cranmer's belief in the "one, perfect and sufficient sacrifice" was highlighted by the increasing simplification of the rites and ceremonies. Cranmer's 1549 liturgy was a streamlined version of the Roman Catholic Mass. In his preface, Cranmer writes, "So that here you have an order for prayer (as touching the reading of the holy Scripture), much agreeable to the mind and purpose of the old fathers" (Cranmer 1910, 4). He reduced the number of worship books needed to this one prayer book and rejected the four previous books: the Missal, the Breviary, the Manual, and the Pie. Cranmer wrote, "Moreover, the number and hardness of the Rules called the Pie, and the manifold changings of the service . . . was so hard and intricate a matter, that many times, there was more business to find out what should be read, than to read it when it was found out" (Cranmer 1910, 4).

This new book in English was available to both clergy and laity. The liturgical calendar only contained New Testament saints. The book's lectionary included many Bible readings, all read in English or the common language. Cranmer wrote that the worship services should be conducted in a "language understanded by the people" (Cranmer 2001, 179).

Baptism was restored to its original usage. Unless it was an emergency, as Cranmer wrote, "When great need shall compel them" (Cranmer 1910, 242), all baptisms were now to be done publicly in the gathering of a worshipping congregation. Several elements of the medieval baptism were omitted, including the naming by godparents, signing of the candidates' forehead and breast, and the exorcism of unclean spirits. Furthermore, the use of all holy things such as ashes, palms, and holy water were eliminated.

Cranmer honored the Reformation emphasis on preaching and encouraged a revival of preaching. Indeed, in the 1549 prayer book, the Eucharist required a sermon.

Following an act of Parliament, on June 9, 1549, the Church of England introduced the first Book of Common Prayer to the parishes. Yet, even with these far-reaching changes, the people wanted greater reform. After the introduction of this prayer book, people rioted in London and other places of Protestant influence. Many wanted an intensified Protestant prayer book, so Cranmer wrote the 1552 prayer book.

In the 1552 prayer book, Cranmer continued his Reformation efforts. He deleted what is called the epiclesis or invocation, a medieval concept that at a certain moment the words call the Holy Spirit down to become the body and blood of Christ. The altar became known as the table and the elements were set on the table before the service. Long paragraphs including self-offering and anamnesis were omitted in the 1552 version. One example of a prayer omitted in the 1552 book is the following: "Command these our prayers and supplications, by the Ministry of thy holy Angels, to be brought up into thy holy Tabernacle before the sight of thy divine majesty" (Cranmer 1910, 223).

In the 1552 prayer book, the words spoken at the passing out of the bread and wine lost their abstract statement and became personally directed to the recipient. It read, "Take and eat this in remembrance that Christ died for thee, and feed on him in thy heart by faith, with thanksgiving" (Cranmer 1910, 389). On All Saints' Day, 1552, the Second Prayer Book of Edward VI began its use in the Church of England.

After King Edward VI died and the Catholic Queen Mary came to the throne, she killed many Protestants, including Archbishop Cranmer. At his trial, the Bishop of Gloucester, Dr. Brookes, sat below an ornate altar with the Catholic reserved sacrament exposed to affirm the doctrine of transubstantiation and let Cranmer know that his guilty judgment had already been decided. Thomas Cranmer was burned at the stake on March 21, 1556.

Yet, Cranmer's 1552 prayer book survived and increased in use. In later revisions, the Church of England only made minor changes from the 1552 Book of Common Prayer. The Elizabethan prayer book in 1559 allowed the use of increased number of vestments, including albs, chasubles, and copes. The 1604 Book of Common Prayer required that baptism be performed by a lawful minister. The 1662 Book of Common Prayer came out after the translation of the King James Bible and used its translation for the epistles and gospels. It also allowed the offering of bread and wine in the communion service. The 1662 Book of Common Prayer is still in use in the Church of England.

Episcopal authors Price and Weil (2000) write, "From one end of the Prayer Book to the other, in Daily Office, Eucharist, Pastoral Offices, and Ordinal, the English liturgy has vividly proclaimed the great deliverance God has brought to us through his people Israel, and most of all, through his Son Jesus Christ."

## Continuing Liturgical Issues

Even with the advent of these English prayer books, issues later arose about both theological meaning and worship services practices. The sixteenth-century reformation movement had the unintended side effect of a diminished value for the sacraments. As they placed a strong emphasis on the Word of God in scriptures and sermons, the Eucharist began to be received less frequently.

Also, an unwanted theological understanding grew. Until the invention of the printing press, consistent and invariable liturgies were a literal impossibility. Because of the newly published words, people frequently assumed that this was the only correct way of celebrating the Eucharist. After widespread printed liturgies became possible, a subsequent value grew that placed an emphasis on particular words and phrases as if these called down or invoked the Holy Spirit. In previous Christendom, the liturgy was celebrated with more of a regional flavor with some spontaneity allowed in the words chosen by the priest.

Yet, the Anglican Thirty-Nine Articles of Religion established under Archbishop of Canterbury Matthew Parker in 1662 do not require liturgical regularity. Article XXXIV reads, "It is not necessary that Traditions and Ceremonies be in all places one, and utterly alike; for at all times they have been divers, and may be changed according to the diversities of countries, times, and men's manners, so that nothing be ordained against God's Word" (Book of Common Prayer 1979, 874).

Moreover, the Eucharist still had theological problems about meaning as well as participation. One reason behind this was the growth of philosophical nominalism in Western Europe that detached the world of meaning from particular objects and hence made the comprehension of the meaning of the sacraments difficult. One way of understanding nominalism is through Gertrude Stein's quote, "A rose is a rose is a rose." Because of this reigning nominalism and the concomitant culture, the meaning of the Eucharist was still in question. To paraphrase Stein, is a piece of bread only a piece of bread? Or is it the body of Christ? With the rise of nominalism, most parishes in the Church of England began receiving communion only about five times a year.

As people struggled to understand the meaning of the Eucharist, some understood it as only a symbol that is first a literal thing that obtains a "spontaneously formed and immediately significant" meaning (Ricoeur 1967, 18). Hence, a symbolic understanding of the Eucharist would be first a piece of bread and a cup of wine that a person or group spontaneously understands actually represents the body and blood of Christ. Yet, this Eucharistic understanding depends on the revelatory reception and symbol-creating abilities of people. This symbolism may lack participation in divine reality and hence makes the Eucharist a mere memorial, detached from the original power of the Christ's death and resurrection.

On the other hand, in transubstantiation with its philosophical basis in Aristotle, the priest recreates the sacrifice of Christ, with the substantive change in the Eucharistic elements. In the sixteenth century, the Church of England officially rejected this belief.

Some tried to correct these problems of the infrequent reception of the Eucharist as well as the lack of clarity about its meaning. After both John Wesley's evangelical movement in the eighteenth century and the Oxford Movement's Anglo-Catholic movement in the nineteenth century, parishes again celebrated communion more frequently but the struggle to keep balance between the spoken Word of God and the Sacraments continued in Anglican parishes.

## Twentieth-Century Liturgical Reform

In the twentieth century, an ecumenical liturgical movement began that carried power-ful consequences. The Roman Catholic Vatican II, along with a similar movement in the Anglican Communion and Protestant churches, reassessed the effectiveness of the church's worship services. One question addressed by this movement was how to recover the power of the early church's liturgy, while another question addressed the relationship between liturgy and life. Archbishop of Canterbury William Temple elo-quently expressed this when he wrote, "People are always thinking that conduct is supremely important, and that because prayer helps it, therefore prayer is good. That is true as far as it goes; still truer is to say that worship is of supreme importance and conduct tests it. Conduct tests how much of yourself was in the worship you gave to God" (Temple 1944, 19).

The liturgical movement sought to regain the initial meaning of the word "liturgy" and to widen the perception of liturgy as God's presence in historical life. The appropria-tion of the Greek term "anamnesis," which is usually translated as "remembrance" or "recollection," brought a new era into liturgical thought. Liturgy and worship moved once again into the center of human life, as a powerful experience of God's actions in the present time. Dom Gregory Dix (1945, 161–2) describes anamnesis in the following words:

> In the scriptures both of the Old and New Testament, *anamnesis* and the cognate verb have the sense of 're-calling' or 're-presenting' before God an event in the past, so that it becomes *here and now operative by its effects*. . . . . Justin and Hippolytus and later writers after them speak so directly and vividly of the Eucharist *in the present* bestowing on the communicants those effects of redemption—immortality, eternal life, forgiveness of sins, deliverance from the power of the devil, and so on.

As the old spiritual hymn said, "Were you there when they crucified my Lord?" Under the reality of anamnesis, the answer is "yes."

Under the influence of this idea of anamnesis, the original power of the Greek, Hebrew, and Biblical word "liturgy" was reclaimed. When a congregation gathers, through anamnesis all time is present to God, and because of that, all events are acces-sible in that moment. The congregation remembers the mighty acts of God, and in remembering through anamnesis, the acts are present. When freed from the con-straints of time and space through the power of the Holy Spirit, the worshipping people would experience the original wonder of the revelatory acts of God in the crossing of the Red Sea, in the law given on Mt. Sinai, and, most importantly, the cross and resur-rection of Jesus Christ.

Now with anamnesis, this connection between the original revelation and the worship services became strong. Responding to God's promises, worshippers as the Body of Christ offer themselves and receive the Kingdom of God into time. Earth and heaven are united, as the Lord's Prayer says, "Thy Kingdom come. Thy will be done on earth as it is in heaven."

Hence, this twentieth-century movement attempted to strike a middle ground between the Middle Age idea of the Mass offered from humans as a gift to God and the sixteenth-century reformation movement emphasizing the human as receiver of God's gift. In the new idea of offering in some parts of the Anglican Communion, the person offers everything, including the bread and wine, as thanksgiving.

Episcopal theologian Charles P. Price stated that twentieth-century liturgical revisions used the two criteria of flexibility and enrichment that were needed to restore anamnesis in the Greek form to the Eucharistic prayer. Because of anamnesis, the mighty redemption of Jesus of Nazareth becomes accessible and "the cross and resurrection are present in their dread power" (Price 1994, 10).

Moreover, the idea of anamnesis provides theological support for new ecumenical relationships. The twentieth-century ecumenical movement wanted to restore unity among the divided denominations. The theology of remembrance in the Eucharist had previously divided denominations at the time of the Reformation as theologians failed to agree on what remembrance means. Anamnesis now helps ground the varying Eucharistic theologies. In particular, the lengthy Eucharistic Prayer D in the Episcopal 1979 Book of Common Prayer achieved agreement among denominations for common use. The hope was that liturgy could help forge some theological and structural unity among the denominations, though much of this desired unity is still unrealized.

## Further Revisions in Anglican Liturgy

Liturgy is frequently used to solidify and cement social changes. While the practice of liturgy reflects the religious hungers and thirsts of an era and responds to them with revelation, it is not developed in a world entirely separated from political power, and certain liturgies become connected with particular political movements. In the Reformation, for example, certain liturgical words and phrases would identify particular political movements. For example, during the reign of Elizabeth I, if a priest conducted a Latin Mass, the political implication would be that they rejected the theology of the leading Anglican reformers. Also, after the 1776 American Revolution, the Episcopal Church rewrote the prayer book to eliminate allegiance to the King of England and turned to the Scottish liturgy for a model for the first American prayer book. Changes in liturgy are frequently used to connect with popular and newly ascending spiritual convictions. After the environmental movement began in the mid-twentieth century, more prayers were initiated for the safe care of the Earth.

Liturgical changes frequently bring intense and even violent reactions in their wake. Ill-planned changes can lead to protest, disenfranchisement, schism, and even death. When discussing the reluctance of some to change the liturgy, Dom Gregory Dix (1945, 614) writes, "These things go deep behind us. Two archbishops of Canterbury have lost their lives and a third his see, in these quarrels. One king has been beheaded and another dethroned; many lesser men have suffered all manner of penalties from martyrdom downwards on one side and another." Or as the current Archbishop of Canterbury Williams (2003, 65) writes about leading public worship in the divine furnace, "If we can't see that this is a dangerous place, we have missed something essential."

Yet, even with full awareness of the difficulties of liturgical revision, the twentieth and twenty-first centuries became a time of global revisions.

The Church of England under the leadership of Archbishop of Canterbury Randall Davidson attempted to revise its prayer book in 1928, but Parliament narrowly defeated this measure. The controversy surrounding the 1928 prayer book included the invocation in the Eucharist, the different position of the Prayer of Oblation, and the reserve sacrament. This prayer book was approved by the House of Lords, but in the House of Commons, concern was raised about the Anglo-Catholic worship possibilities and that the church was being led toward Rome. Hence, Parliament did not approve the 1928 prayer book.

In 1974, Parliament however passed the Worship and Doctrine Measure that gave to the general synod of the Church of England the power to control its liturgies and doctrines, so that any future revisions would only be approved by the Church of England. No future revisions have been proposed, and the Church of England still uses the 1662 prayer book.

The Episcopal Church in the United States revised its prayer book in 1892, 1928, and 1979. Yet, after the 1979 Book of Common Prayer was accepted, several Episcopal organizations sprang up in protest and some parishes left over this issue. The 1979 Book of Common Prayer re-appropriated some of the liturgy from the Middle Ages, such as the imposition of ashes on Ash Wednesday, the procession with palms on Palm Sunday, and the Great Vigil of Easter.

In recent years, some concern over male pronouns for God has sparked informal liturgical revisions. Some priests avoid the use of male words for God in traditional words of blessing, "In the name of the Father, Son and Holy Spirit." Instead they substitute non-gender words such as, "In the name of the Creator, Redeemer, and Sanctifier." Controversy over American liturgy approached again when the 2012 General Convention of the Episcopal Church decided to allow the development of liturgies for the blessing of same-sex unions.

The 1662 English prayer book has gone around the world, and in due time, was translated in many different languages and cultures. Some new prayer books are noted here to give an idea of the flavor and enthusiasm for the reception of this 1662 prayer book: Scotland, 1637 and 1929; America, 1789, 1928, and 1979; Canada, 1918 and 1962; South Africa, 1924 and 1954; Ireland, 1878 and 1926; South India, 1963; Kenya, 2002; Nigeria, 1954; Australia, 1978; New Zealand, 1989; Melanesia, 1938; West Indies, 1978; Mexico, 1894; Philippines, 1999; Japan, 1959 and 1990; Hong Kong, 1957; Korea, 2004; Myanmar, 2001; and Wales, 1567, 1662, and 1984 (Hefling and Shattuck 2006).

As the prayer book moves into new countries, every new rendition of it enriches the global Anglican Communion. The original intention of liturgy as bringing God's actions into the present time remains as it seeks the power of Christ and helps bring the Kingdom of God into history. With Cranmer's enriching liturgy of Christ expressed as "a full, perfect, and sufficient sacrifice, oblation, and satisfaction for the sins of the whole world," the Anglican Communion led Christianity into a deeper involvement with the divine that has impacted the entire globe (Cranmer 1910, 222). In public worship, as congregations from every country stand in the furnace of Christ's divine action, heaven and earth become closer and even united. The liturgy of Christ's death and resurrection takes new forms and words, and within these active translations and interpretations, the power of the Christian vision lives.

## Bibliography

*The Book of Common Prayer*. 1979. New York: The Church Hymnal Corporation.

Cranmer, Thomas. 1844. *Writings and Disputations of Thomas Cranmer Relative to the Sacrament of the Lord's Supper*. Cambridge: Cambridge University Press.

Cranmer, Thomas. 1910. *The First and Second Prayer-Books of King Edward the Sixth*. London: J. M. Dent & Sons.

Cranmer, Thomas. 1907. *Defence of the True and Catholic Doctrine of the Sacrament of the Body and Blood of Our Saviour Christ*. London: Thynne.

Cranmer, Thomas. 2001. *Writings and Disputations Relative to the Lord's Supper*, ed. John Edmund Cox. Vancouver: Regent College Publishing.

Dix, Dom Gregory. 1945. *The Shape of the Liturgy*. London: Dacre Press.

Easton, Burton Scott. 1934. *The Apostolic Tradition of Hippolytus*. New York: The Macmillan Company.

Fuller, Reginald H. 1969. *Lent with the Liturgy*. London: SPCK.

Hefling, Charles and Cynthia Shattuck, ed. 2006. *The Oxford Guide to the Book of Common Prayer: A Worldwide Survey*. New York: Oxford University Press.

Hook, Walter Farquhar. 1882. *Lives of the Archbishops of Canterbury*, vol. I. London: Richard Bentley & Son.

Jasper, Ronald C. D. 1989. *The Development of Anglican Liturgy 1662–1980*. London: SPCK.

Ober, Josiah. 2011. *The Cambridge Companion to Socrates*, ed. Donald R. Morrison. New York: Cambridge University Press.

Price, Charles P. 1994. New Life for Old: Christian Sacrifice. *Virginia Theological Seminary Journal*, vol. XLVI (December), pp. 2–19.

Price, Charles P. and Louis Weil. 2000. *Liturgy for Living*. Harrisburg, Pennsylvania: Morehouse Publishing.

Ramsey, Michael. 1991. *The Anglican Spirit*, ed. Dale Coleman. Boston, Massachusetts: Cowley.

Ricoeur, Paul. 1967. *The Symbolism of Evil*. New York: Harper and Row.

Shepherd, M. 1950. *The Oxford American Prayer Book Commentary*. New York: Oxford University Press.

Temple, William. 1944. *The Church Looks Forward*. New York: Macmillan.

Williams, Rowan. 2003. *Silence and Honey Cakes: The Wisdom of the Desert*. Lion Publishing: Oxford.

CHAPTER 55

# Preaching in the Anglican Communion

George L. Carey

It is questionable whether there is, or ever has been, such a generic thing such as "Anglican preaching." At the very least, we may concede that, in its most basic form, Anglican preaching is that form of communication by Christian ministers within the tradition known as Anglicanism. Anglican preaching therefore is co-terminus with the Reformation, and reflects many of the elements it shares with Reformation churches of the same period. The enormous upheaval of continental Christianity, known to us as the Reformation, destroyed the unity of the Western Church and led to the formation of national churches, each identified by its relationship with the Church of Rome.

It is a mistake to conclude that the pre-Reformation period was devoid of good preaching. The High Medieval period was well known for great oratory accompanied by deep devotion and learning. The Reformation led to many reforms, and preaching was one of the most notable, with a shift from an allegorical and florid form of preaching to one that was scriptural and more dependent upon the theology and teaching of the Patristic Fathers. This was certainly central to the teaching of such reformers as Martin Luther, John Oecolampadius, Ulrich Zwingi, and John Calvin. A great influence upon the Reformers was the teaching of John Chyrsostom, whose emphasis upon preaching systematically, called *lectio continua*, was followed by Zwingli and popularized by him.

England was not far removed from the developments on the mainland. The corruption and abuses so very clearly manifest in the church made England ripe for Reformation also. There were many in England who longed for change, and for young men like Thomas Cranmer, Latimer, Ridley and John Jewell, Reformation could not come quickly enough.

However, preaching is never done in isolation from political and social factors of the time. While there were, of course, factors in common that made England one

*The Wiley-Blackwell Companion to the Anglican Communion*, First Edition. Edited by Ian S. Markham,
J. Barney Hawkins IV, Justyn Terry, and Leslie Nuñez Steffensen.
© 2013 John Wiley & Sons, Ltd. Published 2013 by John Wiley & Sons, Ltd.

with continental Christianity, the presence of the sovereign, Henry VIII, was to be a determining element that created particular difficulties for English preachers. The English monarch, of course, was no ordinary ruler. Henry VIII was intensely interested and learned in theological issues and, although reform of the English church was important to him – as far as independency from Rome was concerned – he was conservative in many other matters of theology. Preaching while he was sovereign was exceedingly risky business, and woe to the man who chose to challenge the theology of the king.

Preaching, of course, is an arm of reformation, and English reformers were no less determined to change the hearts and minds of the people. Thomas Cranmer's grasp of the task of reforming the national church was profound. He realized that edification could only be achieved through sound preaching and knowledge of scripture. And because there was such a deficiency of preaching among the clergy, a Book of Homilies was issued to them containing sermons authorized to be preached in parish churches. Cranmer understood the doxological place of preaching in worship and knew that it had to be balanced by the sacraments. Perhaps this was Cranmer's greatest contribution to preaching – to make it one arm of a bond that we call "Word and Sacrament." As Thomas Becon said later: "A sacrament without preaching of the word is but a dumb ceremony: a glass offered to a blind man or a tale offered to a man who is deaf" (Ayre 1845, 255).

Hugh Latimer was an accomplished orator who used his natural skills to great effect. Whereas excellent preaching on the continent was extensive, the same could not be said for England. Latimer's sardonic quip that "preachers were like strawberries, they came but once a year and then only for a short time" (Chester 1986, 32) hit home as a perceptive comment on the paucity of good preaching. Bernard Gilpin paints a dark picture of church life in England in the middle of the century: "A thousand pulpits in England are covered in duste, some have not had four sermons these fifteen or sixteen years, since the Friars left their limitations, and fewe of those were worthy of the name of sermons" (Moorman 1983, 38). Latimer used this deficiency with great effect by using all the skills of the late medieval form to communicate the faith. In his sermon "Sermon on the Cards," he pulled a deck of playing cards from his preaching gown; an illustrative flourish that would have been at home in the twenty-first century as it would have been on the continent in the early sixteenth century.

John Jewell was certainly Latimer's equal when it came to preaching, but he added an extra dimension of focusing on an apologetic method that was to prove effective. In November 1559, Jewell preached a famous sermon at St. Paul's Cross in which his challenge to his Roman Catholic opponents took the form of calling upon them to prove the legitimacy of Catholic practices from the scriptures and the Fathers of the Church. The force and intellectual strength of this address became, in the words of Mark Chapman, "the standard work in defining Anglican theology" (Chapman 2012, 59). However, for Jewell and other English preachers, it was scripture that was normative, the "very sure and infallible rule" (Chapman 2012, 60). The Fathers of the Church were very important, to be sure, but it was conformity to the witness of the Bible that mattered. Hence, Jewell was puzzled that anyone could call the Church of England a new church when its theology was a return to the faith of the early church. For him, the reformed church "had washed its face clean" and was the very same church as it was intended to be by Almighty God.

Hand in glove with preaching went the translation of scripture, and it was the versions of the Bible such as William Tyndale's great translation of 1527, Coverdale's version of 1535, and the Great Bible of 1538 that gave impetus to preaching. With the daily lectionary reading at morning and evening prayer, clergy and people heard four chapters of the Bible a day. This was a rich and steady diet that helped to prepare the way for informed communication. Little wonder that, within a few decades, literacy in England soared.

However, the English reformers were also clear that if preaching was formed by its relationship to the sacraments, it was no less in a relation to tradition and reason. Important though the Bible was for English reformers, conformity to tradition and reason were also important to the theologian and preacher. Our faith has to relate to the past as well as to contemporary rational argument. This is where we must acknowledge the enormous contribution of Richard Hooker who, in his *Laws of Ecclesiastical Polity*, more than any other churchman laid the foundation stone of the Anglican tradition.

Hooker's concern, however, was focused upon the problem of Puritanism. Whereas the desire of the Church of Rome was to crush the Church of England, the many different groups that arose from the breakup of the English church dreamed of transforming it. That Hooker wrote at such length to give structure to the church is indicative of the strength of nonconformity in the nation, and the power of its preaching. Men like Robert Browne who around 1580 formed a separatist congregation at Norwich; Henry Barrow in London; or Thomas Cartwright of Cambridge were powerful preachers who drew many to follow their practices. Their conviction was that the English Reformation was far from complete, and that defiance of the establishment must continue.

Thus, as the seventeenth century dawned, the unruly yet conscientious anti-establishment forces of Puritanism and non-conformity continued to clash with Anglicanism.

It is sometimes said that the seventeenth century was the high point of Anglican theology. While that is questionable, there is little doubt that the century was very special in terms of great Anglican preaching; Lancelot Andrews, Jeremy Taylor, George Herbert, John Donne, and John Cosin are but some of the luminaries of the period.

Lancelot Andrewes (1555–1626) was one of the chief translators of the King James Bible and was well known as an outstanding linguistic and Biblical scholar, and this was essentially the basis of his preaching. A very popular preacher at the court of King James I, his style of preaching was designed to appeal to hearers learned in languages, with sophisticated knowledge of the classics, as well as knowledge of Hebrew and Greek. T. S. Eliot, an admirer of Andrewes, says that "Andrewes takes a word and derives the world from it; squeezing and squeezing the word until it yields a full juice of meaning which we should never have supposed any word to possess" (Cooper 1995, 19). Brilliant as Andrewes was in such company (and, rightly, we should salute his prowess because there were very few other preachers at the time able to minister to such a congregation), his sermons are rarely read these days, whereas that of John Donne are still readable and quotable today. John Donne (1573–1631) could hardly be more different from Andrewes, his contemporary. Where Andrewes was reserved, shy, and distant, Donne was passionate, moody, and volatile. Even today, Donne's sermons strike home with their directness and relevance. Just as his poetry, whether secular or religious, moves from earthly, even erotic, themes to spiritual, so we find the same ingredients of passion and earthiness in his preaching. For Donne, it is not enough to contemplate God; his concern was to "enflesh" the themes he preached and to lead his hearers into a deeper penitence to a holy God, but also into the joy of the love of God.

A person often overlooked in discussions of seventeen-century preaching is George Herbert (1593–1633). So admired are his poems that his contribution to preaching is missed. Herbert is important for reminding us that most of the preaching that went on in England at his time was to country congregations. His sole prose work, *A Priest to the Temple*, is a glorious tribute to the ordained ministry. However idealistic we might consider his writing to be, Herbert's goal was a praying church leading to the conversion of hearts and minds. The sermon was an important element in achieving the vision. Thus, he tells us: "The country parson preacheth constantly, the pulpit is his joy and his throne . . . the character of his sermon is holiness, he is not witty, or learned, or eloquent, but holy." And Herbert reminds us to take into account the level of ability of our hearers: "Sometimes he tells them stories and sayings of others . . . for them also men heed, and remember better than exhortations; which, though earnest, yet often die with country folk who are thick and heavy and hard to raise to a point of zeal and fervency, and need a mountain of fire to kindle them, but stories and sayings they well remember" (Herbert 1652, Ch. 4).

As we have already observed, preaching never occurs in a vacuum, it is an activity that has a context to which preaching must either challenge or affirm. This is particularly so with respect to Jeremy Taylor (1613–1667). Ordained before his 21st birthday, Taylor had gifts that marked him out as a person to note: tall, handsome, clever, well educated, and with a deep love of God. News of his accomplishments reached the ears of Archbishop William Laud who was constantly looking for catholic clergy with ability. It was Laud who arranged for Taylor to study in Oxford and who subsequently secured him a position as chaplain to King Charles I. Taylor was a gifted preacher and a prolific writer whose contribution through pen and pulpit was largely the blend of spiritual insight and its practical application in personal and church life. Taylor shared with his famous patron a love of order but he added to it a deep desire for the unity of the church; moderation was his call.

However, the seventeenth century was a violent and polemical age. Significant numbers of puritan folk looked longingly for opportunities to live their Christian lives without persecution and the threats of Archbishop Laud and others. It is here that the story of Anglican preaching takes us across the ocean to New England and to other parts of a virgin land, where restrictions on preaching and teaching were few in number. Here, the story of the flourishing of preaching in Anglican and nonconformist contexts continued. Sadly, our knowledge is very scant of the effectiveness of such preaching, or even the individuals concerned, but central to it was the King James Bible. The result, in the words of Diarmaid MacCulloch, was that the Bible made the new communities of New England "possibly the most literate society then existing in the world" (Ferguson 2011, 67).

In England, the fierce tussles between the king and Parliament, into which the church was drawn, and none more unwisely than Archbishop Laud, led to the Civil War and to a general disillusionment with the controversies of religion. The post-1660 world was one in which new ideas were stirring. There was a shift from notions of authority to that of reason. In 1662, the Royal Society for Improving Natural Knowledge was incorporated by charter. Robin Boyle and Isaac Newton, among its members, though both convinced Christians, encouraged the development of science. The motto of the society, *Nullius in Verba* (take nobody's word for it), summed up the new spirit of the age. All things should come before the bar of reason.

Against this background, a handful of Christian thinkers emerged, known as the Cambridge Platonists, who sought to find harmony between faith and philosophy. The group sought to transcend the polemics of the past and to restore thoughtful discussion, harmony, and reason to the church. The name often applied to this group of thinkers is "latitudinarians," the characteristic of which is broadness of mind, mildness in temperament, and rejection of dogmatism.

If we take John Tillotson as an example of this style of preaching, we find the style of communication thoughtful and reasonable. Certainly, Tillotson in his preaching caught the spirit of the age. His sermons are as far from emotional as they could be. Tillotson sought to show that, far from religion being redundant, it was essential for the cohesion of society because of its inextricable link with moral formation. The shortcomings of latitudinarianism are seen in its elevation of morality above dogma. Deism, which was to be a major force in the eighteenth century, is the younger sister of the latitudinarian movement and influential on the thinking of Thomas Jefferson and others. Joseph Butler (1692–1752), the Bishop of Bristol, was an effective communicator in the Tillotson tradition in combating Deism. A learned and very clever man, in his *Fifteen Sermons* and *The Analogy of Religion, Natural and Revealed*, Butler sought to show the truth of God's revelation of himself and Christ through nature and through scripture. Joseph Butler is an excellent example of the type of preacher who, working within the ideas and concepts of his own culture, seeks to show the relevance of faith – which he did with great ability and learning.

If Deism was a constant thread in the intellectual life of the eighteenth-century Anglo-Saxon world, so we find it challenged by an unexpected visitor to the thought forms of an age known to us as the "enlightenment." Evangelical Anglicanism seems to have come from nowhere, but it had been an important element within Puritanism that had refused to separate from the Church of England into nonconformism. From this tradition within English Anglicanism arose several great preachers whose legacy lives on in the church.

George Whitefield (1714–1770), also known as George Whitfield, was a remarkable clergyman who helped to spread the Great Awakening in the United States with Jonathan Edwards, and the Evangelical Revival in England with the Wesley brothers. Born of poor parents in Gloucester, England, he soon realized that he had great talent for acting, and the theatre became for him his earliest ambition. He was educated at the Crypt School in Gloucester, and academic success ensured him a place in Oxford University where he met the Wesley brothers at the Holy Club. A dramatic experience of conversion led him to the conviction that his vocation was to lead others to his Lord.

Always unorthodox and moving on the fringes of the Church of England, Whitfield was happiest when he was preaching in the open air and using his gifts of acting. Whitfield divided his time between the United States and England to such a degree (making 13 Atlantic crossings in all) that he was equally known on both sides of the Atlantic and respected for his propensity in moving people to accept the truths of the Christian faith. Benjamin Franklin was a critical admirer of Whitfield, impressed by his ability to preach to so many in the open air and by the impact his preaching made on people's behavior and life.

An overlooked American preacher in the Episcopal tradition was Devereux Jarratt (1733–1801), whose evangelistic preaching in the State of Virginia made a great contribution to the Great Awakening. In 1773, Jarratt united with Methodist preachers in a campaign to bring the gospel to as many people as possible. This led to a major revival of faith which resulted in the growth of many congregations and the building of several others. The Methodist Bishop Francis Asbury wrote in 1776 that he believed that Jarratt was the most effective of the preachers taking part in this campaign. Jarratt is a fine example of a man whose natural gifts of speech, wit, and knowledge of the scriptures coincided with the needs of the age.

The Wesley brothers were no less significant than their friend Whitefield as preachers, although they were more firmly embedded in the Anglican tradition than was Whitfield. Indeed, in many respects, the Wesley brothers were catholic Anglicans. They valued the sacrament of Holy Communion and received it regularly, often daily. As young clergymen, they left England for Georgia to minister to English congregations, only to return from the experience shaken by the apathy of their congregants. However, contact with the Moravians in America was enough to convince John Wesley that his religious experience was deficient. A visit to Moravian congregations in Germany was the prelude to his "conversion" experience at a meeting room in Aldersgate Street, which rekindled his faith. This was to lead both brothers on a journey that was to rejuvenate evangelicalism and create a wholly new denomination known as Methodism.

As always, the context is important. England was changing fast. The Industrial Revolution created massive social upheaval, with people pouring from the countryside into the fast-growing cities, leading to vast slums. The established church was ill-equipped to cope with the needs of the time, and the character of its latitudinarian theology was inappropriate for the mission. John Wesley saw the need and responded with energy, conviction, and zeal. Scorning the spirituality of his time, he turned to wholehearted preaching of repentance and faith. "God deliver me from being a half-Christian" was his cry (Wesley 1931, 169). That was the last thing he could ever be accused of. No one could have been more indefatigable in his work or more zealous in preaching. So began a ministry of preaching that lasted a half-century, often preaching three or four times a day, and sometimes starting at 5 AM. It is estimated that, in his lifetime, John Wesley covered 250,000 miles in England, preaching in excess of 40,000 times.

What was the character of John Wesley's preaching? He was by far a simplistic communicator. He read constantly on horseback and was continually reflecting on the task of ministry. He preached an urgent gospel, calling on his hearers to "turn to Christ" and repent of their sins. His theology developed into a rejection of Calvinism toward an Arminianism which took seriously the free will of the hearer. This led him to part company from the theology of his friend George Whitfield. The response to Wesley's preaching was staggering, with hundreds at each meeting turning to faith and with corresponding scenes of hysteria and emotion. The impact upon the established church took different forms. Some clergy were encouraged and saw the opportunity to learn from the style of Wesley. Others were disturbed by the emotional response and regarded any form of religious enthusiasm as distasteful. Bishop Butler was certainly concerned. To the youthful Wesley, he said: "Sir, the pretending to extraordinary revelations and gifts of the Spirit is a horrid thing, a very horrid thing." For Wesley, there was no pretence whatsoever, neither was he worried whether people disapproved or not. John Wesley continued his way, preaching his heart out and calling for people to follow the Christ he knew. As he did so, he formed new communities of believers who, unwelcomed by the established church, gradually found fellowship outside it. It is to the shame of the Church of England that bishops and parish priests of the time were so blind to the effective ministry of the Wesley brothers.

And we should not forget Charles Wesley. The irony is that, although John is better known, very few can recall a sentence of what the older brother said, but thousands can instantly recall a snatch of a hymn composed by Charles. It is estimated that Charles wrote as many as 9,000 hymns, of which some 400 are in use today. The hymns balanced the rhetoric of his brother and continued the force and yearning of God that the preaching had opened up. As Richard Schmidt argues, "It was Charles Wesley who popularised the first person pronoun" in hymnody (Schmidt 2002, 130), thus making personal the impact of John Wesley's preaching.

We pass now from preachers who were always on the move to someone who never left his beloved parish of Holy Trinity, Cambridge. Charles Simeon (1759–1836) has every reason to be called the outstanding preacher of his day. He was only 23 when he was invited to be rector of Holy Trinity, and he remained there until his death in 1836. At a time when the sermon was not valued and where most clergy dipped into the homilies of others, Simeon revolutionized the concept of the sermon by making it central to worship itself. He regularly arose at 4 AM to begin preparation for his Sunday addressing, spending no less than 12 hours on the message. He used his learning and intelligence to bring to his hearers a powerful message of God's love. In a letter to his friend John Berridge, he clarified his goal as a preacher: "To bring pardon to the broken heart, the spirit of prayer to the prayer-less heart, holiness to the filthy heart and faith to the unbelieving heart" (Moorman 1983, 150). The most distinctive feature of his preaching was its scriptural nature and his emphasis that the preacher should not get in its way: "My goal," he said, "is to bring out of scripture what is there and not what I think might be there" (Simeon 1832, preface). However, for Simeon, preaching should never be isolated from the worship of the church. He loved the Book of Common Prayer and remarked: "The finest sight short of heaven is a whole congregation using the prayers of the liturgy in the spirit of them" (Moorman 1983, 150). Simeon also considered preaching as a vital element within a pastoral ministry that necessitated visiting the sick and families of the parish. He was constantly visible, and thus his preaching was able to feed from regular contact with people in the town. By his devotion to the church and his love of the liturgy, Simeon did more than most evangelical leaders in encouraging evangelicals and others to stay rooted in the established church.

In spite of effective evangelical preaching and the way it strengthened the church, there was much that was wrong with church life at the beginning of the nineteenth century. Two things especially stood out: a weak doctrine of the church and an even weaker theology of Holy Communion. It was this deficiency that theologians of the Oxford Movement were to correct, and three in particular stand out – John Keble (1792–1866), John Newman (1801–1890), and Edward Bouverie Pusey (1800–1882). These three men were part of a close and small group of learned Christian men who were troubled by the times in which they lived and the worldliness of the church. It was John Keble who struck the first blow in a famous sermon on July 14, 1833, in St. Mary's Church, Oxford. Although it is called the Assize sermon because it was preached on an occasion when the king's judges were present, Keble himself entitled it National Apostasy. It caused little upset at the time, but within a short while was seen as a prophetic and urgent call for repentance and new life. The sermon, preached by a quiet man unused to controversy and discord, went to the heart of the spiritual malaise in the country. Keble raised two questions: How does one tell if a nation has alienated itself from God, and what should faithful Christians do when that happens? (Lock 1893, 79). When a parishioner was asked if he thought Keble a great preacher, he replied: "Well, I don't know what a great preacher is . . . but he (Keble) always made us understand him."

Keble's trumpet call for return to the faith of the church was the beginning of what is called the Oxford Movement, or, as it is sometimes called, the Tractarian Movement, because in the few years following the sermon, tracts were written by leaders of the movement to galvanize the church into action.

Keble may have launched the new ideas, but it was undoubtedly John Henry Newman who was the leader of the movement and the one who now took up the cause. Curiously, Newman's roots were in the evangelical movement, and he had professed a conversion experience at the age of 15. Although the Tracts continued to be an important element in making the movement for change known, hundreds of students and others flocked to St. Mary's to hear the brilliant sermons of John Henry Newman. A central theme to his preaching was God's call for the holiness of life. Familiar evangelical undertones may be detected in his addresses. "What is a Christian?"' he asks again and again. His response is: "It is to make Christ the very centre of our lives" (Newman 1840, 75–6). There was always a sense of urgency to Newman's preaching, because, for him and his contemporaries, death was an ever-present reality. But where Wesley might have put emotion, Newman's focus was on reason and theology. His delivery was often quiet but with exquisite diction and with power. His sermons must be numbered among the most effective sermons of the nineteenth century, and were aimed at the minds of intellectuals who were moved by ideas. In a perceptive comment, Newman once observed that "People are drawn and moved, not simply by what is said but how it is said and who says it" (Hughes 2007, 363). However, it does seem that Newman, brilliant though he was as a communicator, did not view the sermon as a very important element in worship. For him, the Eucharist was by far more significant and the kerygmatic element less so.

The third person of this great triumvirate was Edward Bouverie Pusey, the youngest of the three. Though his preaching and teaching was not in Newman's league, he was seen as a great communicator of the faith and committed to the reforms of the Oxford Movement. He too drew many to his pulpit, but it was Newman's defection to Rome that led to a great call upon Pusey's leadership to keep the adherents together. Newman's decision to leave the Church of England was a huge shock and a great disappointment to his friends. Pusey's great fear was that this would lead to a large-scale drift to Roman Catholicism. It is to Pusey and Keble's credit and leadership that nothing like this occurred. However, Pusey's preaching often got him into trouble with university authorities and illustrates that honest, brave preaching may have personal costs and consequences beyond our realization.

Today, the Oxford Movement is often associated with innovations in liturgy and ceremonial matters. However, its true significance lies in what it achieved in restoring the Church of England and, later, other parts of the Anglican Communion to a more developed and catholic understanding of Christianity. We owe this particularly to the preaching of these three great men.

The Victorian period reveals other significant Anglican preachers. Charles Kingsley (1819–1875) stands in the tradition of Christian social reformers. Although from a privileged background, he was appalled at the social conditions of so many and was an activist for change. A "broad churchman," his sermons were very popular, and a selection was published in *Twenty Five Village Sermons*, which reveal a witty, simple style within the reach of most hearers. His was a rugged, "muscular" Christianity. Henry Parry Liddon (1829–1890), Dean of St. Paul's, was another great preacher but, unlike Kingsley who had no love of the Oxford Movement, he drew his spirituality from this source. Liddon's sermons were often very long and he was not noted for his oratory, but he drew thousands because of his passion for truth.

In the United States, Anglican preaching was also alive and well. As we have already observed, lively, entertaining, and bold preaching was very common in nonconformist circles, and it must be confessed that this was not always true of the Episcopal Church of the United States (ECUSA). However, there were some significant exceptions. Bishop John Henry Hobart (1775–1830), who was the third Episcopal bishop of New York, founded the General Theological Seminary and Geneva College. A well-educated Christian in the High Church tradition, he soon made his mark as a teacher and preacher. Controversy often followed his forceful sermons. He was a strong opponent of dissenting congregations and was not afraid to preach against anything that challenged the unity of the church or its mission. Although sometimes impetuous, he was fearless in his preaching and a speaker of much eloquence and learning. Mission was a central concern of Hobart, whether it was for the Oneida Indians or for the building up of his diocese. His commitment to theological education was an aspect of his vision for a growing, confident Episcopal Church.

A younger contemporary of John Hobart was Gregory Townsend Bedell (1817–1892), whose life and ministry was conducted against a background of suffering and illness that could only have been done in the power of the Holy Spirit, as he saw it. Whereas Hobart was a High Churchman, Bedell never disguised his leaning toward an evangelical faith. It showed in his preaching where an urgent appeal was ever present.

He was the first incumbent of St. Andrew's, Philadelphia, and much of his success rested on the popularity of his preaching. Earnestness marked his style, accompanied by a freshness about his biblical exegesis. Although he wrote out in full his addresses, he had mastered them so fully that they came across as *ex tempore*, vigorous, personal, and challenging. He died at the age of 41, an example of preaching graced by much dignity in suffering.

One of the giants in Anglican preaching was Bishop Phillips Brooks (1835–1893), a man of many talents and learning whose powers of communication were highly regarded in his own day, and who is highly respected today for his reflections on the nature of preaching. His definition of preaching as "truth through personality" sums up his understanding of the symbiotic relationship between content and the person delivering the address. For him, there was no modest withdrawal of the personality and talents of the preacher. The content had to be "enfleshed" through the physical contact of preacher to congregation. Anything else in Christian terms is less than truth. Ironically, Brooks by all accounts was shy, spoke too rapidly, and hardly had eye contact with his audiences. He often stared at the sounding board above his head. However, he overcame these handicaps by the mastery of his material, the conversational tone of his addresses, and the way he knew his congregation through his visiting program.

Twentieth-century Anglican preaching is contextualized by two fundamental realities: a much harsher secular world in which confidence in the ability of human beings to control their environment dominates, and the worrying social conditions in many industrialized nations that became the theme of many preachers. William Temple (1881–1944) was a highly respected thinker whose social thought was admired by political leaders and whose sermons were penetrating and influential. As Bishop of Manchester, his interventions in discussions between trade unions and business leaders by way of personal contact and sensitive preaching led to his greatly admired book *Christianity and the Social Order*. However, through his hugely popular *War Sermons*, Temple helped to settle the nation, giving hope and faith to a Britain that needed the commanding voice of a great prophet of God.

We have to acknowledge frankly that twentieth-century Anglican preachers of outstanding quality cannot be compared with nonconformist preachers such as Leslie Weatherhead, William Sangster, George W. Truett, Norman Vincent Peale, Peter Marshall, E. Stanley Jones, Donald Barnhouse, Ralph Seckman, Billy Graham, and Gardner Taylor. This is, as observed earlier, most likely because Anglicanism has focused on the balance between Word and Sacrament, the beauty of worship in which the grandeur of God replaces the cult of the personality. Nevertheless, if by great preaching what is meant is the influence that a preacher has had on the church and wider society, then we can pick out individuals who, by their powers of communication, have been leaders in their generation. From the African continent, Bishop Festo Kevengere (1921–1988), Bishop of Kigeze in Uganda, was a powerful electrifying preacher in the evangelical tradition. His abilities were so widely admired that he was asked by the Billy Graham organization to become an associate evangelist to Billy Graham. Festo refused, knowing that he was called to serve his own church. From South Africa, Archbishop Trevor Huddlestone (1913–1998), author of *Naught for Your Comfort*, was a key personality in the overcoming of apartheid in South Africa. A forceful, commanding, and intelligent preacher, he gave the Anglican Province of South Africa great leadership. Desmond Tutu (1931–) was also a leader in the struggle to overcome apartheid. His sermons, laced with humor, reveal a faith that is nurtured by three streams: African spirituality, a love of the Bible, and a gospel of forgiveness.

John Stott (1921–2011) spent most of his Christian ministry in one church, All Souls', Langham Place, London. A learned conservative evangelical, he was one of the most influential evangelicals of the twentieth century. His sermons were strictly biblically based and always deeply thoughtful and engaging. Always critically loyal to the Church of England, his example led to many evangelicals staying within mainstream Anglicanism.

This short summary of Anglican preaching reveals that Anglican teachers have often been at the center of national events when a trumpet call has been needed to call God's people into battle. A departure from this would not only be cowardice; it would be betrayal of our tradition.

## Bibliography

Ayre, John, ed. 1845. *Prayer and Other Pieces of Thomas Becon.* Parker Society.

Chapman, Mark. 2012. *Anglican Theology.* London: T&T Clark International.

Chester, Allan G. 1986. *Hugh Latimer, Selected Sermons.* Charlottesville: University of Virginia.

Cooper, Xiros John. 1995. *T. S. Eliot and the Ideology of Four Quarters.* Cambridge: University of Cambridge.

Ferguson, Niall. 2011. *Civilisation: The West and the Rest.* Allen Lane. Harmondsworth: Penguin Books.

Herbert, George. 1652. *A Priest to the Temple.* London.

Hughes Oliphants Old. 2007. The Modern Age. Vol. 6. Grand Rapids: Eerdmans.

Lock, W. 1893. *Keble: A Biography.* Boston: Houghton Mifflin.

Moorman, John R. 1983. *The Anglican Spiritual Tradition.* London: Darton Longman and Todd.

Newman. J. H. 1840. *Parochial Sermons.* Vol. I. London: J. G. F. & J. Rivington.

Schmidt, Richard. 2002. *Glorious Companions.* Grand Rapids: Eerdmans Publishing Co.

Simeon, Charles. 1832. *Horae Homilecticae,* The Preface. London: Holdsworth and Ball.

Wesley, J. H. 1931. *Letters,* Vol 1, ed. J. Telford.

CHAPTER 56

# Women in the Anglican Communion

## Janet Trisk

The church has been the major opponent of the suffragists' demand for full personhood.
The church provides the ideologist underpinning for women's' inferior status (Matilda
Gage 1893, quoted in Swart-Russell and Draper 1991, 221).

Being a woman in the church with this kind of awareness is not easy. I often feel alienated
(Ackermann 1998, 63).

Almost 100 years after Matilda Gage reflected on the church's role in sidelining
women, Denise Ackermann expresses her own experience of alienation in the
church – this despite the almost unbelievable changes in church and society over that
period, including the acquisition of women's political suffrage in practically every part
of the Anglican Communion. Even in the last decade, there have been further advances
in the inclusion of women in church life. Indeed, the inclusion of this chapter in this
volume may be seen as progress – recognition of the different situations of women and
men in the churches of the Communion and an improvement on the silence surrounding the failure to afford their full personhood to women. For example, the 1998 book
(revised edition of the 1988) *The Study of Anglicanism* (Sykes et al. 1998) contains not
a single reference to the Mothers' Union, and only eight references in nearly 500 pages
to the ordination of women. In some parts of the Communion, the ordination of
women to the priesthood and to the episcopate has been approved and, to some degree,
implemented. The Anglican Communion is represented in the United Nations by a
woman. Women hold important positions in the Anglican Communion, for example,
as deans of theological institutions, as the director of Theological Studies for the Anglican Communion (at the time of writing), and as the Anglican Networks Coordinator.
Is it therefore somewhat outdated to ask questions about the current status of women
in the Anglican Communion? Is this a question of historical interest only? Or does the
teaching and praxis of the churches of the Anglican Communion still offer a basis for

*The Wiley-Blackwell Companion to the Anglican Communion*, First Edition. Edited by Ian S. Markham,
J. Barney Hawkins IV, Justyn Terry, and Leslie Nuñez Steffensen.
© 2013 John Wiley & Sons, Ltd. Published 2013 by John Wiley & Sons, Ltd.

discrimination against women? Do women still feel alienated as Ackermann did just over ten years ago?

In this chapter, I shall be suggesting that alienation is still the experience of many women. In addressing this question, I shall survey the history of the ordination of women as one of the ways of assessing the place of women in the churches of the communion. I shall also note the ambiguous place of the Mothers' Union as both "a powerful expression of female solidarity . . ." (Goedhals 1998, 93) and "closely associated with narrow definitions of Christian family and marriage" (Gaitskell 2002, 384). I shall also note the formation and role of the International Anglican Women's Network and note other leadership roles played by women in the communion, particularly in the role of theological education. In addition, I shall also highlight practices and attitudes displayed by some members and some churches in the communion which still render women "aliens in the household of God" (the evocative title of a book edited by Paul Germond and Steve de Gruchy [1997] on the experience of homosexual people in the church).

## Changing Roles of Women in the Anglican Communion

To focus only on the debates surrounding the ordination of women to the priesthood and episcopacy is to miss the significant contribution of women from far further back in the history of the Anglican Communion. As Kwok Pui-Lan points out, women were, for example, both missionaries and funders of mission in the nineteenth century (Kwok 1996, 250). However, the role of women in missions illustrates the complex and overlapping positions of both privilege and disadvantage of women in the church and mission field. From these early days of the Anglican Communion, women from the Western world occupied both subservient and authoritative positions. While undermined at home, women missionaries found "unexpected authority and power" (Kwok 1996, 252) in the mission field. In addition, it allowed them to train as doctors or teachers, leading to the kind of independence not possible at home (Kwok 1996, 252). However, the women of the colonies were frequently infantilized, referred to as "children" by the white women (Kwok 1996, 253). Women missionaries failed to translate their experience of oppression and desire for independence into a liberating praxis for women from the colonies.

The intertwining of colonial expansion and mission by England (from the early 1600s) and, to a lesser degree, from North America (from the mid-1800s) to the mission fields of Africa and Asia ensured the export of not only Anglican theology and worship but also English cultural and societal norms and attitudes in the various Anglican churches around the world. Hence, in the early years of the Anglican Communion, the Victorian ideal of women as homemakers, wives, and mothers was exported to the colonial churches (Goedhals 1998, 88–9). Despite this (or perhaps as an extension of the attitude that it is "women's work to care"), Goedhals describes three groups of women engaged in church work: ". . . the wives, daughters and sisters of the clergy; single women who received a stipend; and members of religious communities" (Goedhals 1998, 89). In all three of these groups, women, almost exclusively white women, and usually English women, worked under male patronage and supervision. Hence, for example, in the early years of the South African province, single and religious women cared for the poor and sick; ran schools, orphanages, and hospitals; and carried out the work of mission. However, there was a considerable difference in the work and status between white English and black African women. "Although African women played an important part in the daily life of missions, the possibility of including them in policy-making bodies was not even considered," and those African women who lived on the mission stations were often outcast by their own communities (Goedhals 1998, 91).

Over the course of the twentieth century, women's roles in both society and the church have changed, so that whereas at the opening of the century women were restricted in the ways described by Goedhals, over time women became eligible for every office in the church – from members of parish councils and diocesan synods to bishops. Even into the second decade of the twenty-first century, women face very different conditions in the various parts of the communion, and their opportunities for involvement in ministry vary enormously.

However, Goedhals' observation is an important reminder not to generalize women and their experiences. There is no single experience of women in the Anglican Communion. Those differences, in very complex ways, persist to this day. For example, as Brigalia Bam laments as she describes the contradictions and challenges of wanting to be loyal to the church in which her great-grandfather was baptized and yet wanting to be free to be a black African woman with a voice and equal recognition: "I am Anglican. But I am not English and I am not male" (Bam 1998, 349).

## The Ordination of Women

The debate about the ordination of women has intensified in the Communion since the 1960s, but the issue has a far longer history. Swart-Russell and Draper (1991, 221) note two factors which led to the increasing role of women in the Church of England from the late 1800s. First, women who had been active in the mission field returned to England only to find their attempts to minster there stifled. Second, the Anglo-Catholic revival resulted in the establishing of religious communities of women. The order of deaconesses was revived in 1862 and was recognized at the Lambeth Conference of 1897 (Swart-Russell and Draper 1991, 221). In the twentieth century, the contribution of women in World War I, and, later, in the civil rights movement (in particular in the United States) and the emergence of feminism all led to an increasing awareness of the place of women in society. In turn, there has been an increase in pressure for recognition of the place of women in the church too (Rakoczy 2004, 13). In some places, ordination is now commonplace. In others, still, women are not even "consulted in the running of events, but are merely expected to carry out orders" (Wild 1998, 286).

Florence Li Tim-Oi was the first woman to be ordained priest in the Anglican Communion. Born in Hong Kong and the daughter of a priest, she had been made a deacon in May 1941. On January 25, 1944, she was ordained priest in response to a crisis which had resulted from the Japanese invasion of China. The occupation meant that Anglican priests were prevented from crossing to the unoccupied colony of Macau to officiate at the celebration of the sacraments of Anglicans living there. Without consultation with bishops in the rest of the Communion, Bishop Ronald Hall therefore ordained Florence Li Tim-Oi as a priest and licensed her to officiate at the sacraments. The ordination caused a storm of protest, but Bishop Hall refused to revoke her license. After the war, with the end of the crisis, Florence however, decided to hand in her license in order to alleviate pressure on her bishop. When, in 1971, the newly formed Anglican Consultative Council (ACC) narrowly voted (by 24 to 22 votes) to allow the diocese of Hong Kong to ordain women, Florence was again officially recognized as a priest in the diocese. She subsequent moved to Canada (where the ordination of women was recognized) and exercised her ministry there until her death in 1992.

The debate about the ordination of women as priests was raised at the Lambeth Conference of 1968. The bishops were of the opinion that the theological reasons for and against women's ordination were, at that stage, inconclusive, but also requested the soon-to-be-formed ACC to advise on the matter (http://www.lambethconference.org/resolutions). Three years later, in 1971, the first meeting of the ACC took place at Limuru in Kenya. The ACC not only assented to the request from Hong Kong that women be ordained to the priesthood in South East Asia, but also recognized the urgent nature of the question and called on all provinces to consider the matter and report back to ACC 2 in 1963 (http://www.anglicancommunion.org/communion/acc/meetings/acc1/resolutions.cfm#s28). Despite this request, no resolution was passed regarding the ordination of women at either of the next meetings of ACC in 1973 and 1976. However, at the next Lambeth Conference in 1978, the bishops resolved that each province should respect the choice of every other province to make its own decision regarding the ordination of women. They also recommended that no decision to consecrate a woman as a bishop be taken without both overwhelming support in the member church and in the diocese concerned and consultation with the bishops of the communion through the primates "lest the bishop's office should become a cause of disunity instead of a focus of unity" (http://www.lambethconference.org/resolutions/1978/1978-22.cfm). It was also recommended that those churches which at that time had not yet taken steps to allow the ordination of women as deacons do so now (http://www.lambethconference.org/resolutions/1978/1978-20.cfm).

After the ordinations in Hong Kong in 1971, further ordinations followed in Canada in 1976, and in the United States in 1974 (although these were deemed "irregular") and subsequently in 1977. Currently, women may be ordained to the priesthood in 28 of the 39 provinces of the communion. Of these, 16 provinces also permit the ordination of women bishops, although only six provinces in fact have ordained a woman bishop. (Information supplied by the Rev. Terrie Robinson, Anglican Communion Networks Coordinator and Women's Desk Officer, in response to a question addressed by e-mail on February 14, 2011. She notes in her response that "provinces don't always let us know automatically when they change their canon law or begin de facto to ordain women. So it may not be one hundred percent accurate.")

The first woman bishop to be consecrated in the Anglican Communion was Barbara Harris, who was consecrated Suffragan Bishop of Massachusetts in the Episcopal Church of the United States in 1989. Consecrations of women followed in the Provinces of Aotearoa/New Zealand and Polynesia in 1990 (Penny Jaimeson) and in Canada in

1994 (Victoria Matthews). More recently, women have been consecrated in Cuba in 2007 (Nerva Cot Aguilera) and in Australia in 2008 (Kay Goldsworthy), and most recently, Southern Africa (Ellinah Wamukoya and Margaret Vertue). The only woman primate is Katharine Jefferts Schori, presiding bishop of the Episcopal Church. She was elected in 2006 (http://www.guide2womenleaders.com/bishops.htm).

A fascinating study of the conditions of service of women clergy in the Episcopal Church was recently released. Entitled *Called to Serve*, it examines the inequalities between conditions of service of clergywomen and clergymen in the Episcopal Church, 35 years after the first ordinations. The study notes that there are now almost 4,000 female priests in the Episcopal Church, and that women represent over 40 percent of ordinations to the priesthood. However, "(D)espite the presence of women clergy in the Church for over thirty years, there are still significant gaps when comparing compensation and years of service between male and female clergy, pointing to the significant obstacles that women clergy face" (Matthew Price in *Called to Serve*, 2). Even in a province where women's ordination has a long history, women are still in some senses "aliens" in God's household.

## The Mothers' Union

The Mothers' Union was started by Mary Sumner in England in 1876. Fostering Christian motherhood was seen as its priority. It had three central objects listed in its Royal Charter granted in 1926, namely, to uphold the sanctity of marriage; to awaken in all mothers a sense of their great responsibility in the training of their boys and girls (the so-called Fathers and Mothers of the future); and to organize in every place a band of mothers who will unite in prayer and seek by their own example to lead their families in purity and holiness of life (Gaitskell 2002, 377). From its inception, its express purpose is to preserve the status quo of traditional (English) family life. Unmarried women, divorced women, and women who had not been married in accordance with Christian rites were (and in some places, still are) excluded. Wild, for example, notes the role of the Mothers' Union in the Congo: ". . . the older women organise seminars for teenage girls in which they learn how to be good wives and mothers" (Wild 1998, 283). Such training is unlikely to result in women being equipped and given confidence to challenge the patriarchal practices of the church. As Goedhals observes, from inception, each branch of the Mothers' Union fell under the direction of the (male) parish priest, and she goes on to note that "(I)n many ways, the Mothers' Union was yet another manifestation of the ideology of home and family . . ." (1998, 93).

Observing meetings of the Mothers' Union, Gaitskell notes a "fervent, vocal style of their own" (2002, 377) in which women, more often than not silenced in both preaching and decision-making in church affairs, come into their own. She also notes the "stress on uniforms as a sign of female zeal and marital respectability" (2002, 377). For many women, membership in the Mothers' Union offers a place and status in a church which otherwise offers little in terms of participation apart from sitting on a pew on Sunday. However, this membership may come at a cost. Esther Mombo points out the ambiguous role of the Mothers' Union in contemporary Kenya. The wife of the archbishop is the head of Mothers' Union, thus ensuring that the organization is integrally entwined with the hierarchical structures of the church. Furthermore, because of its strong focus on traditional family values, members conceal issues such as marital rape or domestic abuse (Mombo 1998, 221).

Nevertheless, the Mothers' Union claims a large and active membership. By the year 2000, the Mothers' Union was active in 59 countries with a membership of almost 1 million (Gaitskell 2002, 384). Today, 80 percent of the membership of the Mothers' Union lives outside Britain – mostly in sub-Saharan Africa (Lawes and Vincer 1998, 377).

## Leaders in Theological Education

Because theological education is so often connected with training for ordination, women have been under-represented in this arena too. However, there is an increasing contribution being made by women in this field. As of 2011, there are a number of women in key roles in theological education. For example, Jenny Plane Te Paa was principal of Te Rau Kahikatea, College of St. John in Auckland, New Zealand; Esther Mombo is academic dean of St. Paul's United Theological College, Limuru, Kenya; and Kwok Pui-Lan is professor of Christian Theology and Spirituality at the Episcopal Divinity School. In 2003, Clare Amos was appointed director of the Theological Education for the Anglican Communion working party established by the Anglican primates. She has now left this position for work at the WCC in Geneva. Interestingly, none of the four is ordained. Perhaps even more significantly, three of the four are women from indigenous non-Western communities. Most recently, Helen-Ann Hartley has been appointed Dean for the New Zealand dioceses at the College of St. John the Evangelist, Auckland.

In 2009, a consultation for 35 woman educators was held in Canterbury. Women came from around the communion, including as diverse places as Myanmar, Sri Lanka, Mexico, Kenya, South Africa, Uganda, Brazil, China, Fiji, India, Philippines, Jamaica, Zambia, Argentina, New Zealand, Britain, and the United States. That meeting discerned a number of key concerns to be taken up, including the mentoring of new woman theological scholars and educators, establishing a network of woman theological educators, and mainstreaming women's issues in theological education (http://www.anglicancommunion.org/acns/news.cfm/2009/3/3/ACNS4584).

This conference is just one indication of a rising interest in all aspects of theological education and formation, particularly in formerly colonized countries. An example of this focus is the series of articles in *Journal of Anglican Studies* (Volume 6.1, June 2008) where contributors note the concern with questions of theological education as it relates to gender (Galgalo and Mombo 2008) context (Trisk and Pato 2008) and indigenous communities (Te Paa 2008).

## Women and the Networks of the Anglican Communion

Much of the work of the communion is done through a series of networks, each with its own focus and steering group, though coordinated through the communion office in London. Not only is the present coordinator of the networks a woman (Terrie Robinson), but there is one network specifically designed to address women's issues, and three others place women's issues on their agendas.

In 1996, the International Anglican Women's Network (IAWN) was formed "to enable women's concerns to be voiced in the councils of the church, particularly the ACC and the Joint Standing Committee of the ACC and the Primates" (http://iawn. anglicancommunion.org). The IAWN is a particularly active group, mainly taking on an advocacy role. Hence, for example, at the encouragement and instigation of the IAWN, at its meeting in 2005, the ACC passed Resolution 13–31, which included the acknowledgement of Millennium Development Goal number three for equal representation of women in decision-making at all levels; a request to provinces to consider the establishment of a women's desk; and a recommendation that the standing committee should undertake a study of the place and role of women in the structures of the Anglican Communion. Four years later, at the next meeting of ACC, Resolution 13–31 was endorsed and, again at the instigation of IAWN, ACC stated its support for the elimination of all forms of violence against women and girls (including trafficking), encouraged provinces to participate in activities promoting the rights and welfare of women, and recommended the implementation of the principles of gender budgeting (Resolution 14–33).

IAWN has set as its immediate goals the elimination of all forms of violence against women and children, especially trafficking; the elimination of extreme poverty, by ensuring access to health care, safe water, and employment opportunities; the promotion of gender equality throughout the Anglican Communion; the combating HIV/ AIDS, malaria, and tuberculosis; and the promotion of gender budgeting (http://iawn. anglicancommunion.org).

The Anglican Justice and Peace Network (AJPN), founded in 1985, includes among its aims the championing of the role of women, striving to assist them (along with young people, indigenous communities, and other marginalized groups) "to have full voice and representation in the official councils of the Church as a matter of justice" (http://apjn.anglicancommunion.org/index.cfm). The AJPN also aims to "advocate human rights (especially for women and children), environmental justice and peacemaking to the Anglican Communion, civil society and governments wherever there are injustices" (http://apjn.anglicancommunion.org/index.cfm).

Two other networks, the International Anglican Youth Network and the International Anglican Family Network, have as one of their principal foci the addressing of family violence. The former has developed a five-point study guide for groups who wish to address violence against women and girls (http://iayn.anglicancommunion. org/resources/docs/ending_violence.cfm   and   http://iafn.anglicancommunion.org/ index.cfm).

## Conclusion: At Home or Aliens?

What then can we say about women in the Anglican Communion in the early years of the twenty-first century? In many parts of the Communion, women are ordained and take leadership roles. Indeed, it is interesting to note that women have, since the very first meeting of ACC in 1971, been members of this body – one of the four instruments of communion. However, as we noted earlier, even in the Episcopal Church, where women have been ordained for over 35 years, there is a disparity in working conditions for male and female clergy. In conclusion, I wish to note three areas of concern, issues which, to some degree, continue to render women aliens in the churches of the communion. I shall briefly note the role of culture and tradition, the prayer book, and divisions around the place of lesbian, gay, bi-sexual and trans-gendered, and inter-sexed ("LGBTI") people in the churches of the communion.

Cultures and traditions, especially (but not exclusively) in the two-thirds world, continue to undervalue women and to exclude them from leadership roles. Wild notes that, in the Congo, "Women's participation in leadership and decision-making is dismissed on the grounds that these are natural roles of men" and that clergy "defend the status quo by saying innovations are contrary to African culture" (1998, 284–5). As we noted in the earlier discussion on the Mothers' Union, the church often reinforces rather than challenges the exclusion of women from leadership, and instead promotes "traditional" roles for women. It is interesting, for example, that the 1998 Lambeth Conference, when calling for justice for women and children in society, omitted mentioning the possibility of injustice in the church (see resolution 1998-1-3. http://www.lambethconference.org/resolutions/1998/1998-1-3.cfm).

It is commonplace to observe that the prayer book and liturgy are central to Anglican spirituality and theology. Where other denominations have councils or confessions, Anglicans point to the Book of Common Prayer and its derivatives. As Marjorie Proctor-Smith suggests, "When Christians gather for worship, their identity as Christians is established or reinforced" (Proctor-Smith 1996, 175). The problem is that, in the English-speaking world, the prayer books of the communion, until the 1980s, always referred to humanity in masculine terms, and this exclusive practice continues today in many churches. Furthermore, almost all liturgical language for God is masculine, usually referring to God as Father, and, as Mary Daly memorably pointed out, where God is Father, the father is god (Daly 1973). However, the problem goes even deeper than that of the language used to describe human beings and God. As Proctor-Smith notes, the liturgy values obedience and humility, and the lections selected reinforce this (1996, 175–6). She analyzes the texts selected for the Sunday readings and concludes that the majority of texts make no mention of women at all and, where they are included, it is not to focus on them, but either to note their relationship to the men in the text (180) or because the text deals with marriage (181). She concludes: "It is evident that the lectionary's hermeneutical principles fail to take women seriously as active, significant agents in salvation history" (183). She thus exposes a fundamental "alienation" of women in the very heart of liturgical practice founded on sexist and patriarchal theology.

The third area of concern regarding the leadership of women in the churches of the communion is linked to what is frequently termed "recent developments" in the Anglican Communion, and which refers to discussions and actions around the place of LGBTI people in the clergy. The 1998 Lambeth Conference was the first to place questions of human sexuality on its agenda (http://www.lambethconference.org/resolutions/1998). Subsequent developments have included the consecrations of Gene

Robinson and Mary Glasspool, as well as cross-diocesan interventions, to minister to Anglicans offended by a diocesan policy of ordaining LGBTI people in same-sex partnerships. Without rehearsing the history and details of these developments, we might note an increasingly vocal call for a neo-conservative reading of scripture and church praxis. In effect, this has also sometimes included at least an exclusion, and, on occasions, a reversion of efforts to include women in leadership. There has been a linking of women's issues with debates concerning homosexuality. There is, of course, good reason for this. All issues of liberation are connected. However, the effect has been to exclude women again. As Esther Mombo trenchantly observes, the human sexuality debate is carried out by "some heterosexual male church leaders . . . at the expense of the far more pressing issues of mission and ministry . . ." (Mombo 2007, 77).

We have come a long way since Matilda Gage's lament in 1893, but we have yet to realize the full personhood of women, many of whom are still aliens in their own household.

## Bibliography

Ackermann, Denise. 1998. "Both and Neither": Letter to Robert Gray from a Troubled Woman in Cape Town. In *Change and Challenge: Essays Commemorating the 150th Anniversary of the Arrival of Robert Gray as First Bishop of Cape Town*, eds. John Suggit and Mandy Goedhals. Marshalltown, Johannesburg: CPSA Publishing, pp. 63–70.

Bam, Brigalia. 1998. All about Eve: Woman of Africa. In *Anglicanism: A Global Communion*, eds. Andrew Wingate, Kevin Ward, Carrie Pemberton and Wilson Sitshebo. London: Mowbray, pp. 347–3.

Butler, Perry. 1998. From the Early Eighteenth Century to the Present Day. In *The Study of Anglicanism*, revised edition, eds. Stephen Sykes, John Booty and Jonathan Knight. Minneapolis: Fortress Press, pp. 30–51.

Daly, Mary. 1973. *Beyond God the Father: Toward a Philosophy of Women's Liberation*. Boston: Beacon Press.

Gaitskell, Deborah. 2002. Whose Heartland and Which Periphery? Christian Women Crossing South Africa's Racial Divide in the Twentieth Century. *Women's History Review*, vol. 11, no. 3, pp. 375–94.

Galgalo, Joseph and Esther Mombo. 2008. Theological Education in Africa in the Post-

1998 Lambeth Conference. *Journal of Anglican studies*, vol. 6, no. 1, pp. 31–40.

Germond, Paul and Steve De Gruchy, eds. 1997. *Aliens in the Household of God: Homosexuality and Christian Faith in South Africa*. Cape Town & Johannesburg: David Philip.

Goedhals, Mandy. 1998. Devotion and Diversity: Anglican Women 1848–1998. In *Change and Challenge: Essays Commemorating the 150th Anniversary of the Arrival of Robert Gray as First Bishop of Cape Town*, eds. John Suggit and Mandy Goedhals. Marshalltown, Johannesburg: CPSA Publishing, pp. 88–97.

Kwok, Pui-Lan. 1996. The Image of the "White Lady": Gender and Race in Christian Mission. In *The Power of Naming: A Concilium Reader in Feminist Liberation Theology*, ed. Elisabeth Schussler Fiorenza. London: SCM, pp. 250–8.

Lawes, Barbara and Louise Vincer. 1998. The Mothers' Unions of the Future. In *Anglicanism: A Global Communion*, eds. Andrew Wingate, Kevin Ward, Carrie Pemberton and Wilson Sitshebo. London: Mowbray, pp. 377–84.

Mombo, Esther. 1998. Resisting *Vumilia* Theology: The Church and Violence Against Women in Kenya. In *Anglicanism: A Global*

Communion, eds. Andrew Wingate, Kevin Ward, Carrie Pemberton and Wilson Sitshebo. London: Mowbray, pp. 219–24.

Mombo, Esther. 2007. The Windsor Report: A Paradigm Shift for Anglicanism. The Anglican Theological Review, vol. 89, no. 1, pp. 69–78.

Proctor-Smith, Marjorie. 1996. Images of Women in the Lectionary. In The Power of Naming: A Concilium Reader in Feminist Liberation Theology, ed. Elisabeth Schussler Fiorenza. London: SCM, pp. 175–86.

Rakoczy, Susan. 2004. In Her Name: Women Doing Theology. Pietermaritzburg, South Africa: Cluster Publications.

Rao, Krupaveni Prakash and Julie Lipp-Nathaniel. 1998. Women within Church and Society in India. In Anglicanism: A Global Communion, eds. Andrew Wingate, Kevin Ward, Carrie Pemberton and Wilson Sitshebo. London: Mowbray, pp. 258–63.

Swart-Russell, Phoebe and Jonathan Draper. 1991. A Brief History of the Movement for the Ordination of Women in the Church of the Province of Southern Africa. In Women Hold Up Half the Sky: Women in the Church in Southern Africa, eds. Denise Ackermann, Jonathan Draper and Emma Mashinini. Pietermaritzburg, South Africa: Cluster Publications, pp. 220–37.

Sykes, Stephen, John Booty, and Jonathan Knight, eds. 1998. The Study of Anglicanism, revised edition. Minneapolis: Fortress Press.

Te Paa, Jenny Plane. 2008. Anglican Identity and Theological Formation in Aotearoa New Zealand. Journal of Anglican Studies, vol. 6, no. 1, pp. 49–58.

Trisk, Janet and Luke Pato. 2008. Theological Education and Anglican Identity in South Africa. Journal of Anglican Studies, vol. 6, no. 1, pp. 59–68.

Wild, Emma. 1998. Working with Women in the Congo. In Anglicanism: A Global Communion, eds. Andrew Wingate, Kevin Ward, Carrie Pemberton and Wilson Sitshebo. London: Mowbray, pp. 281–6.

## Online resources

Called to Serve – A Study of Clergy Careers, Clergy Wellness, and Clergy Women. Available at http://www.download.cpg.org/home/publications/pdf/CalledToServe. Accessed on March 7, 2011.

http://www.anglicancommunion.org/communion/acc/meetings/acc1/resolutions.cfm#s28. Accessed on March 21, 2011.

http://apjn.anglicancommunion.org/index.cfm. Accessed on March 7, 2011.

http://iafn.anglicancommunion.org/index.cfm. Accessed on March 7, 2011.

http://iawn.anglicancommunion.org. Accessed on February 7, 2011.

http://iayn.anglicancommunion.org/resources/docs/ending_violence.cfm. Accessed on March 7, 2011.

http://www.anglicancommunion.org/acns/news.cfm/2009/3/3/ACNS4584. Accessed on February 28, 2011.

http://www.guide2womenleaders.com/bishops.htm. Accessed on February 28, 2011.

http://www.lambethconference.org/resolutions. Accessed on March 21, 2011.

## Personal interviews and correspondence

E-mail correspondence with the Rev. Terrie Robinson, Anglican Communion. Networks Coordinator and Women's Desk Officer on February 14, 2011.

CHAPTER 57

# Human Sexuality in the Anglican Communion

Godfrey Mdimi Mhogolo

## Introduction

I am aware that when one writes about human sexuality, it is not just a matter of theology and ideology; it is basically a matter of human life and dignity. It touches the very lives of real people as they live and express their lives in this world, in the context of their faith and belief in Jesus Christ.

The ethical/moral concerns about sexuality have revolved around the right way to propagate the human race in marriage. Ethical norms try to control conception by abstinence and contraception. The study of human sexuality in the Anglican Communion has been characterized by the issues of marriage and divorce, contraception, polygamy, and homosexuality.

As it was during the reformation period of the fifteenth and sixteenth centuries when sexuality played a major role (e.g., Martin Luther marrying Katharina von Bora, and King Henry VIII marrying six wives), the Anglican Communion is being threatened again by sexuality issues.

It seems the "Western church" has always been fascinated with and influenced by sexual issues. It is no wonder that all the issues relating to human sexuality were brought to the Lambeth Conferences by the "Western church" – dragging the rest of the Anglican Communion into the debates.

Human sexuality in the Anglican Communion has been discussed as part of the "moral or ethical" theology. Instead of developing a positive human sexuality theology, the Anglican Communion has studied the issue from a negative response to the moral/ethical issues of divorce, contraceptives, polygamy, and homosexuality. The Anglican Consultative Council (ACC) and the Primates' Meetings have given responses to some of the issues, and after wrestling with them, have offered resolutions and statements in the hope of settling the Anglican way of life.

*The Wiley-Blackwell Companion to the Anglican Communion*, First Edition. Edited by Ian S. Markham, J. Barney Hawkins IV, Justyn Terry, and Leslie Nuñez Steffensen.
© 2013 John Wiley & Sons, Ltd. Published 2013 by John Wiley & Sons, Ltd.

As these "organs" or "instruments" of the Anglican Communion are by nature consultative and do not adequately represent the whole communion participation, the communion itself is now beset by the problem of "reception."

The value of reception has always depended on the effectiveness of bishops and primates in sharing and explaining the resolutions and statements of their meetings to their constituencies. The official language of print and spoken materials has been English which, over the years, has been used less and less by the majority of Anglicans in the communion. Coupled with the modest use of Internet facilities in many parts of the Anglican Communion, the knowledge and discernment of resolutions has become known by very few Anglicans in the communion. To date, there has been no effective communication mechanism in the Anglican Communion that guarantees information reaching most Anglicans in the communion. Consequently, the issues became hobby-horses for a very few.

The problem of theological reflection and conclusions on the issues has always been a challenge. Each region or province in the Anglican Communion has studied scripture and theology in isolation from the rest of the communion. There is, therefore, no consensus on applying hermeneutics in the Anglican Communion.

For this reason, I will not draw on the contributions of regional theologians as representing the Anglican Communion; instead, I will use the resolutions of Lambeth Conferences, the Anglican Consultative Council, and the pastoral letters of the Archbishop of Canterbury and the Primates' Meetings as representing the general mind of the Anglican Community on human sexuality.

The scope of this study will also be limited to the issues and concerns that the organs of the Anglican Communion have discussed and to which they gave direction. I will trace the history and meaning of human sexuality as it appeared in the resolutions and pastoral letters of the Anglican Communion organs. The major concerns on human sexuality touched on divorce, marriage, sex, contraceptives, and homosexuality.

## Divorce

Human sexuality as touching marriage was articulated for the first time in the third Lambeth Conference [1888] because of the divorce problem that was troubling the church. The conference made a resolution on divorce "forbidding divorce except in the case of fornication or adultery" (Lambeth Conference 1888, Resolution 4). Divorce was allowed on condition of fornication. The guilty party in a divorce case could marry under civil sanction but his/her marriage would not be recognized by the church. It was also argued that because scripture was "silent" on the innocent party marrying again in the church, it was advised to leave the matter to the discretion of the clergy.

This stance of the conference was reiterated at the following Lambeth Conference of 1908. The conference was very concerned about the prevalence of disregard for the sanctity of marriage and called for "active and determined" people to cooperate with "all right-thinking and clean-living men and women in all ranks of life in defense of family life and social order which rest upon the sanctity of marriage tie" (LC 1908, Res. 37). The conference also lamented the "terrible evils which have grown up for the creation of facilities for divorce" (LC 1908, Res. 37) – presumably by state laws. Instead of the innocent party who wished to marry obtaining clergy approval, the conference stated that the innocent person who "by means of a court of law divorced a spouse for adultery" should not receive the blessings of the church (LC 1908, Res. 40).

The conference also gave option to adopt "native forms of marriage" and consecrate them for Christian use, provided that "the form used explicitly states the marriage is life-long and exclusive," that the form should have no "heaven and idolatrous taint," and that provisions are made for registering such marriages according to the law of the land (LC 1908, Res. 25).

The Lambeth Conference of 1920 defined marriage as "a life-long and indissoluble union for better or worse, of one man and one woman, to the exclusion of all others on either side," and called all Christian people to maintain and bear witness to that standard (LC 1920, Res. 67). The conference, being aware that governments create marriage laws for their citizens, stated that in every country the church should remain true and bear witness to its standards and laws on marriage (LC 1920, Res. 67). The Lambeth Conference recognized its limitations and complied with and recognized the meaning of marriage as enacted by governments. The conference recognized the rights of governments to create marriage laws for its peoples and how those laws could also be reflected in and adhered to by the Christian church (LC 1920, Res. 67).

The Lambeth Conference of 1930 declared the functions of sex as "a God-given factor in human life as essentially noble and creative" (LC 1930, Res. 9). Resolution 10 went even further, agreeing with some of the teachings of the secular understanding of marriage which included "the sacredness of personality, equal partnerships of men and women, and the biological importance of monogamy" (LC 1930, Res. 10).

On divorce, the conference affirmed the previous Lambeth Conference position of life-long union and indissolubility. The conference, without passing judgment, prohibited the marriage of divorced persons in churches (LC 1930, Res. 11); and where an innocent person has remarried, the admission to Holy Communion was for the bishops concerned to decide, according to provincial regulations (LC 1930, Res. 11).

The conference also noted that sexual intercourse between people who are not legally married was "a grievous sin" (LC 1930, Res. 19). The conference also rejected all "illicit and irregular unions" for the well-being of Christian communities (LC 1930, Res. 19).

On bringing up a family, the Lambeth Conference of 1948 declared that it was a "human rights issue" (LC 1948, Res. 7). However, the conference noted that marriage and motherhood remained the normal vocation of women, and argued the importance of fostering in girls a sense of dignity of "this calling" and preparing them for it (LC 1948, Res. 48).

The conference promoted the life-long union and obligation of marriage and advised provincial and regional churches to give the best pastoral care possible for people who would not conform to "our Lord's standards" (LC 1948, Res. 95). Marriages that were officiated "contrary to Church law" were to be subjected to church discipline by withdrawing their rights to receive Holy Communion. Their admittance to Holy Communion was left to the discretion of bishops, subject to provincial or regional regulations (LC 1948, Res. 96).

The Lambeth Conference of 1958 defined family life as "rooted in the Godhead" and stated that marriage was regarded as "a vocation to holiness" through which "men and women share in the love and creation purposes of God." "Sexual love," the conference declared, was "not an end in itself nor a means to self-gratification," but that "self-discipline and restraint" were essentially conditions of "the freedom of marriage and family planning" (LC 1958, Res. 116).

For the first time, the conference noted the importance of forgiveness and reconciliation in marriage and family life (LC 1958, Res. 116, 121). The conference also noted that secular authorities in many lands granted divorce on the grounds that the church did not approve or recognize. It encouraged provinces and regional churches to define marital status on the issue (LC 1958, Res. 118).

The Lambeth Conference of 1968 had nothing new to say about marriage, except to reiterate the resolution on marriage of the Lambeth Conference of 1958.

The Lambeth Conference of 1988, referring to pre-marital sex and the adoption by many people of life-styles different from traditional Christian teaching, both within and outside the church, called "on provinces and dioceses to adopt a caring and pastoral attitude to such people." It also affirmed the "traditional Biblical teaching" that sexual intercourse was an "act of total commitment which belonged properly within a permanent married relationship" (LC 1988, Res. 34).

On the meaning of human sexuality, the Lambeth Conference of 1998 had nothing new to say other than reiterating what other conferences had insisted: marriage was a life-long union between a man and a woman, and abstinence was right for those who were not called to marriage.

On dealing with human sexuality in marriage, Lambeth Conferences have studied and issued statements on marriage from the divorce issue, which dominated all Lambeth Conferences. The problem of divorce called Lambeth Conferences to think about the meaning of marriage.

As years went by, the problem of divorce became a challenge for the churches (LC 1948, Res. 97). Lambeth Conferences lamented that national or state laws provided divorce for many reasons other than adultery.

It was held by Lambeth Conferences that the act of marriage and the provision for divorce were prerogatives of governments. The church was then a government agent for officiating marriages according to country or state laws. The church had no power to grant its own marriage certificates.

With the divorce issue, the church also had no authority to issue divorce certificates. The conference recognized state governments' rights to provide divorce judgments for their citizens. The only sanction the church could inflict on its divorced people was to refuse them Holy Communion.

The theology of marriage restricted sexual intercourse to take place within married life. Abstinence was promoted for both married and unmarried people. Christian marriage was between a woman and a man to the exclusion of all others.

As Lambeth Conferences proceeded, a change of mind was clearly seen over the years. Divorce that was allowed on account of adultery was later challenged when the church introduced the idea of forgiveness and reconciliation in estranged marriages. Adultery was subjected to the Christian idea of forgiveness and reconciliation. Again in later days, divorce was accepted by the church, and a "blessing" would be given to the "innocent" parties.

Sex outside marriage was seen as "a pastoral" challenge, and people living without marriage should be handled with sensitivity, care, and Christian charity.

What made marriage "Christian" was its life-long intent and living a monogamous life.

The Lambeth Conferences' understanding of Christian marriage depended heavily on the teaching as found in Matthew 19.1–12. It was taken for granted that Matthew's teaching satisfied all that it takes to have a Christian marriage. There has been no significant study of marriage and divorce which takes into account all Old and New Testament materials. Approaching human sexuality from "a missionary problem of divorce" did not do justice to the positive contribution to human sexuality in general.

## Contraception

The Lambeth Conference of 1920 was the first to mention and be concerned about contraception. It stated:

> We utter an emphatic warning against the use of unnatural means for the avoidance of conception, together with the grave dangers – physical, moral and religious – thereby incurred, and against the evils with which the extension of such use threatens the race. In opposition to the teaching that, under the name of science and religion, encourages married people in the deliberate cultivation of sexual union as an end in itself, we steadfastly uphold what must always be regarded as the governing considerations of Christian marriage. One is the primary purpose for which marriage exists, namely the continuation of the race through the gift and heritage of children; the other is the paramount importance in married life of deliberate and thoughtful self-control.

> We desire solemnly to commend what we have said to Christian people and to all who will hear (LC 1920, Res. 68).

The Lambeth Conference of 1930 was not as harsh as the previous one. It allowed some use of contraception according to "Christian principles" and condemned all other uses, as it stated:

> Where there is a clearly felt moral obligation to limit or avoid parenthood, the method must be decided on Christian principles. The primary and obvious method is complete abstinence from intercourse (as far as may be necessary) in a life of discipline and self-control lived in the power of the Holy Spirit. Nevertheless in those cases where there is such a clearly felt moral obligation to limit or avoid parenthood, and where there is a morally sound reason for avoiding complete abstinence, the Conference agrees that other methods may be used, provided that this is done in the light of the same Christian principles. The Conference records its strong condemnation of the use of any methods of conception control from motives of selfishness, luxury, or mere convenience (LC 1930, Res. 15).

The Lambeth Conference of 1948 reversed the previous resolutions and stated emphatically that "The Conference welcomes the great advance in scientific discovery characteristic of our age, and repudiates the suggestion that any check should be placed upon it. But we insist that the consequent growth of man's knowledge increases his moral responsibility for the use he makes of it" (LC 1948, Res. 3).

Subsequently, the Lambeth Conference of 1958 had this to say:

> The Conference acknowledges gratefully the work of scientists in increasing man's knowledge of the universe, wherein is seen the majesty of God in his creative activity. It therefore calls upon Christian people both to learn reverently from every new disclosure of truth, and at the same time to bear witness to the biblical message of a God and Savior apart from whom no gift can be rightly used (LC 1958, Res. 8).

The conference went further to say: "In view of the lack of understanding which can develop in consequence of the different thought and language of the Bible and the modern world, the Conference urges Christian scholars and leaders to co-operate with men of science and other kinds of modern learning in the study of their respective modes of thought and speech" (LC 1958, Res. 9).

Even though the Lambeth Conference 1958 did not comment specifically about the use of contraceptives, it supported the responsibility of married people to decide upon the number and frequency of children. The means by which couples would do this was left unsaid but inferred (LC 1958, Res. 115).

Examining these resolutions of the Lambeth Conference of 1958, one can see a shift toward accepting scientific truth and values as not being contradictory to Christian truth.

The Lambeth Conference of 1968 restated the resolution of Lambeth 1958 with the special emphasis that "the responsibility for deciding upon the number and frequency of children has been laid by God upon the consciences of parents everywhere; that this planning, in such ways as are mutually acceptable to husband and wife in Christian conscience, is a right and important factor in Christian family life and should be the result of positive choice before God" (LC 1968, Res. 115).

It is very interesting to see how Lambeth Conferences changed their minds on this issue from one conference to the next. The first conference to deal with the issue condemned outright the use of contraceptives. The following conference reiterated the previous Lambeth resolution and proceeded to refute any scientific contribution to the debate. Later Lambeth Conferences accepted scientific developments and affirmed the use of contraceptives and the rights of human beings to determine the number of children.

## Polygamy

The all-white Lambeth Conference of 1888, which made the first resolutions about divorce, also made a resolution on polygamy, banning the baptism of polygamists, while allowing that their wives could be baptized at the discretion of "the local authorities of the Church" (LC 1888, Res. 5).

The Lambeth Conference of 1908 recognized some forms of "native" marriages and resolved that those forms of marriage could be consecrated to be Christian marriages as long as they were monogamous (LC 1908, Res. 25).

The Lambeth Conference of 1920 called it a "missionary problem." In the resolution, the conference said:

> In dealing with the large number of persons in their colonies and dependencies who profess different faiths, the policy of the British and American governments has always been that of strict religious neutrality. We heartily endorse this policy, having no desire to see any kind of political influence brought to bear upon people to induce them to change their religion.

The conference went on to say:

> The Church would be failing in her work if the acceptance of the truth did not awaken in her converts a higher sense of their dignity as human beings, of their rights as well as their duties, and any government which has the real interest of subject races at heart will be glad of such awakening even though, in civil life, it raises new problems to be solved.

> We hold it to be the duty of missionaries to look at their work from the government point of view, as well as from their own, and to adapt their methods, as far as is consistent with Christian morality and justice and with the faith and order of the Church, to the policy which the government is following in dealing with such peoples (LC 1920, Res. 41).

The Lambeth Conference of 1958 still rejected polygamy but it began to understand that "the introduction of monogamy into societies that practice polygamy involves a social and economic revolution and raises problems which the Christian Church has as yet not solved" (LC 1958, Res. 120).

Resolution 23 of the Lambeth Conference of 1968 on polygamy stated that polygamy poses one of the sharpest conflicts between faith and a particular culture. The conference asked "each province to re-examine its discipline in such problems, in full consideration with other provinces in a similar situation" (LC 1968, Res. 23).

Taking the issue of faith and culture, Lambeth 1988 (which now had many black bishops) recognized that culture is the context in which people find their identity (LC 1988, Res. 22) and recommended:

> that a polygamist who responds to the Gospel and wishes to join the Anglican Church may be baptized and confirmed with his believing wives and children on the following conditions:

> (1) that the polygamist shall promise not to marry again as long as any of his wives at the time of his conversion are alive;

(2) that the receiving of such a polygamist has the consent of the local Anglican community;

(3) that such a polygamist shall not be compelled to put away any of his wives, on account of the social deprivation they would suffer;

(4) and recommends that provinces where the Churches face problems of polygamy are encouraged to share information of their pastoral approach to Christians who become polygamists so that the most appropriate way of disciplining and pastoring them can be found, and that the ACC be requested to facilitate the sharing of that information (LC 1988, Res. 26).

The way the issue of polygamous marriages was treated by Lambeth Conferences showed how a Western understanding of marriage dominated the debates and the Lambeth resolutions until such time as the college of bishops reflected different cultural backgrounds.

Polygamy was not recognized as a type of marriage. A study of the Old Testament would have shown that the polygamous lives of Abraham, Jacob, Moses, David, and many more were recognized and accepted by their contemporaries as "real marriages" even though in the Christian understanding of marriage, they came short of the ideal of one man and one woman.

It took the Lambeth Conference of 1968 to recognize polygamous marriages as that which came short of the Christian ideal, but nonetheless were also a form of marriage. The conference also resolved that people who become Christians through faith could be sealed in baptism. The conference changed all the previous resolutions which demanded a monogamous marriage as necessary for salvation and baptism.

None of the Lambeth Conferences studied deeply the meaning of human sexuality in polygamy and the use of the term "polygamous marriages."

"Consistent polygamy" (many wives at one time) was always condemned by all Lambeth Conferences, whereas serial polygamists (many wives or husbands over time) was accepted in societies where the divorce rate was high. This showed how one's understanding of truth can have a huge impact on other affirmations of the same truth, and that those who win the mind of the conference are those who can have political advantage over others. A deep study of scriptures on polygamy has never been undertaken by the deliberations of the Lambeth Conferences.

## Homosexuality

The first Lambeth Conference to discuss the issue of homosexuality was the conference of 1978. The conference encouraged the communion to study the issue of sexuality "in such a way as to relate sexual relationships to that wholeness of human life which itself derives from God, who is the source of masculinity and femininity" (LC 1978, Res. 1.10).

The conference also noted: "While we reaffirm heterosexuality as the scriptural norm, we recognize the need for deep and dispassionate study of the question of homosexuality, which would take seriously both the teaching of Scripture and the results of scientific and medical research. The Church, recognizing the need for pastoral concern for those who are homosexual, encourages dialogue with them. We note with satisfaction that such studies are now proceeding in some member Churches of the Anglican Communion" (LC 1978, Res. 10.3).

The Lambeth Conference of 1988 restated Resolution 10.3 of the 1978 Lambeth Conference and argued for "such study and reflection to take account of biological, genetic and psychological research being undertaken by other agencies, and the socio-cultural factors that lead to the different attitudes in the provinces of our Communion." It also called "each province to reassess, in the light of such study and because of our concern for human rights, its care for and attitude towards persons of homosexual orientation" (LC 1988, Res. 64.2,3).

The Lambeth Conference of 1998 resolved that all provinces comply with the United Nations Universal Declaration on Human Rights (LC 1998, Res. 1.1) and urged churches to encourage their governments to do so (LC 1998, Res. 1.2).

Then the conference made the historic statement:

> This Conference recognizes that there are among us persons who experience themselves as having a homosexual orientation. Many of these are members of the Church and are seeking the pastoral care, moral direction of the Church, and God's transforming power for the living of their lives and the ordering of relationships. We commit ourselves to listen to the experience of homosexual persons and we wish to assure them that they are loved by God and that all baptized, believing and faithful persons, regardless of sexual orientation, are full members of the Body of Christ;
>
> . . .
>
> d.  while rejecting homosexual practice as incompatible with Scripture, calls on all our people to minister pastorally and sensitively to all irrespective of sexual orientation and to condemn irrational fear of homosexuals, violence within marriage and any trivialization and commercialization of sex;
> e.  cannot advise the legitimizing or blessing of same-sex unions nor ordaining those involved in same-gender unions;
> f.  requests the Primates and the ACC to establish a means of monitoring the work done on the subject of human sexuality in the Communion and to share statements and resources among us;
> g.  notes the significance of the Kuala Lumpur Statement on Human Sexuality and the concerns expressed in Resolutions IV.26, V.1, V.10, V.23 and V.35 on the authority of Scripture in matters of marriage and sexuality and asks the Primates and the ACC to include them in their monitoring process (LC 1998, Res. 1.10).

Though the Lambeth Conference 1978 called on the communion for a "dispassionate study of the question of homosexuality using Scripture and scientific and medical research," only a few provinces had the courage to take up the challenge. This was for reasons that varied from deeming it a "non-issue" in one's locality, as not a serious issue which should take precedence over other main local issues, to outright dismissal as "sin" that deserves condemnation.

The Lambeth Conference 1988 called for all provinces to "reassess" their attitudes "towards persons of homosexual orientation"; and, apart from using scripture and scientific and medical research, the conference added the notion of "human rights" into the debate as provinces came to grips with the homosexuality issue (http://www.episcopalarchives.org/cgi-bin/acts/acts_resolution-complete.pl?resolution=1976-A068).

There was also a force to be recognized within the Anglican Communion which came to be known as the Global South, which studied the issue using scripture; it issued the Kuala Lumpur Statement condemning homosexual practice as sinful and therefore under God's judgment, prior to Lambeth 1998 (http://www.globalsouthanglican.org/index.php/comments/the_kuala_lumpur_statement_on_human_sexuality_2nd_encounter_in_the_south_10).

From Lambeth 1998 till now, homosexuality has become a burning issue in all meetings of the three main Anglican Communion organs, namely the Archbishop of Canterbury, the ACC, and the Primates' Meetings.

## The Contribution of the Archbishop of Canterbury on Human Sexuality in the Anglican Communion

In responding to the crisis caused by the consecration of Gene Robinson, apart from chairing ordinary and ad hoc meetings for the Primates' Meetings, ACC, and later the Lambeth Conference, the Archbishop of Canterbury has been using the Internet to write pastoral letters to mainly the primates and moderators of the Anglican Communion before Lambeth 2008. In preparation for and immediately after the Lambeth Conference 2008, the archbishop wrote two letters to all bishops of the communion. After Lambeth 2008, the archbishop started writing pastoral letters to bishops, clergy, and the faithful of the Anglican Communion. With his Lent 2011 letter, the archbishop reverted to writing to the primates of the Anglican Communion (www.archbishopofcanterbury.org/689?q=Pastoral+letters).

Reading the letters, we see how the archbishop tried to play the mediator or the center between two opposing parties. He set the Windsor Commission from the Lambeth Conference 1988 resolution to try to hold the two opposing factions together and initiated the "covenant" process, hoping that the covenant might solve the "crisis." Pulled by the two forces, the archbishop helped the bishops at the Lambeth Conference to speak to one another through the indaba process.

The archbishop's main arguments have been drawn from the recommendations of the Windsor Report (http://www.anglicancommunion.org/windsor2004), and the concern to see that a covenant is established and endorsed. On human sexuality, the Windsor Report does not offer us any new insights, but endorses the Lambeth Conference of 1998 Resolution 1.10 and applies to and draws proposals on how to solve the "crisis." For this reason, the archbishop's contribution to the theology of human sexuality is very modest.

## The Contribution of the ACC to Human Sexuality

ACC Six prepared the Lambeth Conference of 1988 on the issue of polygamy by asking CAPA to study the issue theologically, pastorally, and culturally, and present its findings to Lambeth 1988 (www.anglicancommunion.org/acc/resolutions/downloads). The study helped the Lambeth Conference of 1988 to resolve the inclusion of polygamists in baptism and church life (LC 1988, Res. 26).

ACC Six commissioned a study on Christian marriage and family life which was also presented to the Lambeth Conference 1988 resulting in Resolution 34 of the Lambeth Conference 1988 (LC 1988, Res. 34).

ACC Eleven welcomed the Virginia report commissioned by the Archbishop of Canterbury and "requested" the primates to monitor its study in every province (ACC. 11. Res. 13).

ACC Thirteen endorsed the primates' communiqué from Dromontine on the Windsor report, especially paragraphs 156 and 157 of the report (ACC. 13 Res. 11).

## The Role Played by the Primates' Meeting on the Human Sexuality Issue in the Anglican Communion

As stated by Archbishop Coggan, the purpose of the primates meeting was for "leisurely thought, prayer and deep consultation" (http://www.anglicancommunion.org/communion/primates/press/index.cfm).

The primates' council, since its inception in 1978, did not touch the issues of divorce, contraceptives, and polygamy. These issues were regarded as having been settled in the previous Lambeth Conferences. The main occupation of the Primates' Meetings since Lambeth 1988 has been around the issue of homosexuality.

The primates' communiqués and "pastoral" letters to the Anglican Communion reflect "actions" to be taken for certain "offenders" of Resolution 1.10 of the Lambeth Conference 1998 and/or the recommendations of the Windsor Report (http://www.archbishopofcanterbury.org/91;http://www.anglicancommunion.org/acns/newscfm/2005/2/24/ACNS3948; http://www.archbishopofcanterbury.org/542; http://www.anglicancommunion.org/communion/primates/resources/downloads/Pastoral%20Letter.pdf).

The problem of "reception" of the primates' pastoral letters became an issue in many provinces where English is not the primary language of communication, and information sharing through the Internet is non-existent or is available only to very few Anglicans.

The judiciary type of interdependence, shared responsibility, and accountability of the primates' pastoral letters have not helped the communion to discuss homosexuality so deeply and theologically as to reach some consensual conclusions. Instead, Anglicans have been forced to take divergent positions, enforcing divisions and factions in the communion. The pastoral letters also show a move from a "consultative" mode to a judicial accountability mode.

This "crisis" in the communion did not come as a surprise. The issue of homosexuality was noted by Lambeth 1978, and the Anglican Communion was called to study the issue. A few provinces and regions took up the challenge; the majority ignored the call.

Again at Lambeth 1988, the issue was mentioned and a resolution made reiterating the previous resolution of Lambeth 1978. Again, a few provinces took note of the resolution. When some provinces wanted to make a favorable resolution on homosexuality at Lambeth 1998, it backfired and Resolution 1.10 was born after a very rough and brief discussion.

In response to the ordination of Gene Robinson to the episcopate, the primates met again, after the ad hoc meeting earlier during the year, in Lambeth Palace on October 15–16, 2003, to discuss the crisis and issued a statement which, among many other things, said:

> We feel the profound pain and uncertainty shared by others about our Christian discipleship in the light of controversial decisions by the Diocese of New Westminster to authorise a Public Rite of Blessing for those in committed same sex relationships, and by the 74th General Convention of the Episcopal Church (USA) to confirm the election of a priest in a committed same sex relationship to the office and work of a Bishop.

> These actions threaten the unity of our own Communion as well as our relationships with other parts of Christ's Church, our mission and witness, and our relations with other faiths, in a world already confused in areas of sexuality, morality and theology, and polarise Christian opinion.

> . . .

> We re-affirm the resolutions made by the bishops of the Anglican Communion gathered at the Lambeth Conference in 1998 on issues of human sexuality as having moral force and commanding the respect of the Communion as its present position on these issues. We commend the report of that Conference in its entirety to all members of the Anglican Communion, valuing especially its emphasis on the need "to listen to the experience of homosexual persons, and . . . to assure them that they are loved by God and that all baptised, believing and faithful persons, regardless of sexual orientation, are full members of the Body of Christ"; and its acknowledgement of the need for ongoing study on questions of human sexuality.

> . . . we call on the provinces concerned to make adequate provision for episcopal oversight of dissenting minorities within their own area of pastoral care in consultation with the Archbishop of Canterbury on behalf of the Primates (http://www.archbishopof canterbury.org/91).

The primates met at the Dromantine Retreat and Conference Center in Newry, Northern Ireland, between February 20 and 25, 2005, and issued a very strong statement that:

6. . . . in our discussion and assessment of the moral appropriateness of specific human behaviours, we continue unreservedly to be committed to the pastoral support and care of homosexual people. The victimisation or diminishment of human beings whose affections happen to be ordered towards people of the same sex is anathema to us. We assure homosexual people that they are children of God, loved and valued by him, and deserving of the best we can give of pastoral care and friendship (vii).

. . .

8. We believe that the Windsor Report offers in its Sections A & B an authentic description of the life of the Anglican Communion, and the principles by which its life is governed and sustained. . . . We therefore request all provinces to consider whether they are willing to be committed to the inter-dependent life of the Anglican Communion understood in the terms set out in these sections of the report.

The primates, while affirming the role of the Archbishop of Canterbury as primus inter pares, were wary of the establishment, or even the implication of such establishment, of an international body that could override provincial autonomy. They continued:

12. We as a body continue to address the situations which have arisen in North America with the utmost seriousness. Whilst there remains a very real question about whether the North American churches are willing to accept the same teaching on matters of sexual morality as is generally accepted elsewhere in the Communion, the underlying reality of our communion in God the Holy Trinity is obscured, and the effectiveness of our common mission severely hindered.

With this, the primates requested that the Episcopal Church (USA) and the Anglican Church of Canada voluntarily recall their representatives from the Anglican Consultative Council until the following Lambeth Conference. Additionally, they recommended that the Archbishop of Canterbury appoint a panel to ensure that provisions for the pastoral care of a province's dissenting minority members, as recommended by the primates' statement of October 2003, were adequate. Finally, the primates agreed to:

17. . . . pledge ourselves afresh to [Resolution 1.10 of Lambeth 1998] . . . and request the Anglican Consultative Council in June 2005 to take positive steps to initiate the listening and study process which has been the subject of resolutions not only at the Lambeth Conference in 1998, but in earlier Conferences as well (http://www.anglicancommunion. org/acns/newscfm/2005/2/24/ACNS3948).

The primates met in Dar es Salaam, Tanzania, in February 2007, and issued a statement, continuing to note and take some actions against TEC. In its communiqué, it stated:

8. We agreed to proceed with a worldwide study of hermeneutics (the methods of interpreting scripture). . .

9. Since the controversial events of 2003, we have faced the reality of increased tension in the life of the Anglican Communion – tension so deep that the fabric of our common life together has been torn.

The communiqué noted that it agreed with statements made at the Dromantine Primates' Meeting. It demanded that:

the Episcopal Church (USA) be invited to express its regret that the proper constraints of the bonds of affection were breached in the events surrounding the election and consecration of a bishop for the See of New Hampshire, and for the consequences which followed, and that such an expression of regret would represent the desire of the Episcopal Church (USA) to remain within the Communion; (2) the Episcopal Church (USA) be invited to effect a moratorium on the election and consent to the consecration of any candidate to the episcopate who is living in a same gender union until some new consensus in the Anglican Communion emerges.

Also, it called:

for a moratorium on all such public Rites, and recommend that bishops who have authorised such rites in the United States and Canada be invited to express regret that the proper constraints of the bonds of affection were breached by such authorisation.

The communiqué continues:

24. The response of The Episcopal Church to the requests made at Dromantine has not persuaded this meeting that we are yet in a position to recognise that The Episcopal Church has mended its broken relationships.

. . .

31. Three urgent needs exist. First, those of us who have lost trust in The Episcopal Church need to be re-assured that there is a genuine readiness in The Episcopal Church to embrace fully the recommendations of the Windsor Report.

32. Second, those of us who have intervened in other jurisdictions believe that we cannot abandon those who have appealed to us for pastoral care in situations in which they find themselves at odds with the normal jurisdiction. For interventions to cease, what is required in their view is a robust scheme of pastoral oversight to provide individuals and congregations alienated from The Episcopal Church with adequate space to flourish within the life of that church in the period leading up to the conclusion of the Covenant Process.

33. Third, the Presiding Bishop has reminded us that in The Episcopal Church there are those who have lost trust in the Primates and bishops of certain of our Provinces because

they fear that they are all too ready to undermine or subvert the polity of The Episcopal Church. In their view, there is an urgent need to embrace the recommendations of the Windsor Report and to bring an end to all interventions (http://www.archbishopofcanterbury.org/542).

The Primates' Meeting which met in Egypt in 2009 reiterated many of the decisions taken in the previous meetings and noted the work of the Windsor Continuation Group and stressed that consultation with the primates be establish at the earliest opportunity, such that a professionally mediated conversation would emerge at which all the significant parties could be gathered. The aim would be to find a provisional holding arrangement which will enable dialogue to take place and which will be revisited at the conclusion of the Covenant Process, or the achievement of long-term reconciliation in the communion.

The sample of recommendations and statements made in the Primates' Meetings demonstrates the lack of deep theological and hermeneutical engagement in dealing with the theology of human sexuality. The suggestions about exploring biblical hermeneutics for the communion and for the need to have a comprehensive theology of human sexuality suggest a lack of sufficient theological and hermeneutical input into the decisions made in those meetings. Decisions were made, and then theological and biblical hermeneutics called for to justify the statements.

## Conclusion

The way the Lambeth Conferences have been dealing with human sexuality should make us more cautious when we respond to new situations.

Divorce was once regarded as incompatible with scripture. The Lambeth Conferences later accepted it as a necessity for individual welfare and rights. Contraception was regarded as incompatible with scripture, but it was allowed later by the subsequent Lambeth Conferences. Polygamy was regarded as incompatible with the Christian life, but was later tolerated.

Homosexuality, for the majority of Anglicans, is incompatible with scripture; but for some Anglicans it is tolerated and accepted as a human rights issue. The only difference now is the threat that it would cause schism within the Anglican Communion, unlike other previous contentious issues.

Other concerns have complicated and contributed to the Anglican Communion scenario today. The political and religious power struggle between the Liberals and Conservatives has now come to a bitter end. Human rights and scientific and medical truth, which were recommended by the Lambeth Conferences and which the Liberals had incorporated into their theological reflections, have exacerbated the debates in the communion.

The differences in the cultural expressions of national ethics have also dominated and alienated the responses of Anglicans to each other with regard to human sexuality.

## Bibliography

For Lambeth Conference resolutions, see: www.lambethconference.org/resolutions/downloads (accessed August 2012).

Lambeth Conference. 1888. Resolutions 4, 5.

Lambeth Conference. 1908. Resolutions 25, 37, 40.

Lambeth Conference. 1920. Resolutions 41, 67, 68.

Lambeth Conference. 1930. Resolutions 9,10, 11, 15, 19.

Lambeth Conference. 1948. Resolutions 3, 7, 48, 95, 96, 97.

Lambeth Conference. 1958. Resolutions 8, 9, 115, 116, 118, 120, 121.

Lambeth Conference. 1968. Resolutions 23, 115.

Lambeth Conference. 1978. Resolutions 1.10, 10.3.

Lambeth Conference. 1988. Resolutions 3, 22, 26, 34, 64.2, 64.3.

Lambeth Conference. 1998. Resolutions 1.1, 1.2, 1.10.

See also Resolutions 1976-A069; 1976-A071; 1979-C035; 1982-B061; 1985-D082; 1988_A085; 1988-A090; 1988-D100; 1988-D102; 1994-C019; 1994-C026; 1994-C042; 1994-D006; 1997-C003; 1997-D011.

http://www.anglican.ca/faith/files/2010/10/hsrh.pdf (accessed August 2012).

http://www.archbishopofcanterbury.org/1452?q=Pastoral+letters (accessed August 2012).

http://www.archbishopofcanterbury.org/2635?q=Pastoral+letters (accessed August 2012).

http://www.archbishopofcanterbury.org/436?q=Pastoral+letters (accessed August 2012).

http://www.archbishopofcanterbury.org/2631?q=Pastoral+letters (accessed August 2012).

http://www.archbishopofcanterbury.org/1792?q=Pastoral+letters (accessed August 2012).

http://www.archbishopofcanterbury.org/1942?q=Pastoral+letters (accessed August 2012).

http://www.archbishopofcanterbury.org/media/word/j/k/Anglican_Communion_Pentecost_letter_2010.doc (accessed August 2012).

http://www.archbishopofcanterbury.org/1942?q=Pastoral+letters (accessed August 2012).

http://www.archbishopofcanterbury.org/media/word/j/k/Anglican_Communion_Pentecost_letter_2010.doc (accessed August 2012).

http://www.archbishopofcanterbury.org/3175?q=Pastoral+letters (accessed August 2012).

http://www.gafcon.org/news/gafcon_final_statement (accessed August 2012).

ACC. 11. Resolution 13.

Anglican Communion. ACC 13. Resolution 11.

See Primates communiqués available at http://www.anglicancommunion.org (accessed August 2012).

# CHAPTER 58

# Theological Education in the Anglican Communion

## Leon P. Spencer

In the church universal, the term *theological education* has encompassed a variety of things, such as *Christian education* (largely referring to programs for laity), *training* (specialized preparation for distinctive activities by laity or clergy), *Christian formation* (implying a vision of the whole person throughout a lifetime, applied to laity as well as clergy), and *ministerial formation* (often a synonym for *theological education*, both terms usually limited to those being formed for the ordained ministry).

Refreshingly, many parts of the Anglican Communion now embrace a larger role for laity in the life of the church. Still, Christian formation for laity remains quite secondary to ministerial formation for clergy. Reflecting that reality, this chapter mainly but not exclusively addresses theological education as formal preparation for the ordained ministry.

There are three sections to the article: The first considers conceptual approaches to theological education which influenced developments in Anglicanism; the second, historic developments in global Anglicanism; and the third, issues facing Christian formation for Anglicans today.

## Conceptual Approaches to Theological Education

David Kelsey, at Yale Divinity School, has made a helpful distinction between "Athens" and "Berlin" in theological education. "Athens" considered schooling to be a "process of 'culturing' the soul," engaging the "whole person," which the church embraced for the formation of church leadership. "Berlin," so named because the University of Berlin introduced the concept of a research university in 1810, represented a schooling with "orderly disciplined critical research" on the one hand and "professional" education for ministry on the other. With the "Athens" model, the teacher provided the context

*The Wiley-Blackwell Companion to the Anglican Communion*, First Edition. Edited by Ian S. Markham,
J. Barney Hawkins IV, Justyn Terry, and Leslie Nuñez Steffensen.
© 2013 John Wiley & Sons, Ltd. Published 2013 by John Wiley & Sons, Ltd.

for the student to deepen "self-knowledge" and "God-knowledge"; with the "Berlin" model, the teacher took the student on a journey from the acquisition of data to the development of theory to the application of theory to practice (Kelsey 1993, 6–24).

While Anglicans did not readily embrace the Berlin model in the nineteenth century, Berlin did have its appeal, and over time this model prompted academic accreditation standards, expectations that faculty would engage in research, and the value of significant library holdings (Kelsey 1993, 18–19, 29). Theological educators, Anglicans included, have spent much of the last couple of centuries negotiating their way between Athens and Berlin and displaying the tension between formation in community and professional training for church leadership. Was the church *forming* persons into priests, or instead providing defined knowledge and skills so that seminarians might leave much as they came except that they were now "equipped for specialist tasks" (Towler and Coxon 1979, 118)?

The shift toward theological education as professional study, academically legitimized by the emergence of formal disciplines – for example, the late eighteenth century's "Fourfold Pattern" of biblical studies, systematic theology, church history, and "practical" theology (Farley 1983, 49) – left Anglicans and others grappling as much with curricula and specialization as with the *faith* question of how a given course or subject contributed to the Christian witness (Kelsey 1993, 213). To the extent that theology was seen to constitute "a cluster of studies pertinent to the church's leadership" (Farley 1983, 131), the church risked both separating laity from deepening their lives of faith and measuring ordinands by academic achievement alone, with potentially ominous implications for the formation of both.

## The Historical Evolution of Theological Education in the Anglican Communion

There is a general presumption that, from the very beginnings of the Church of England, Anglicans have displayed a deep commitment to a well-educated clergy. Edward VI said as much in 1547: "Every parson, vicar, curate [etc.], being under the degree of a bachelor of divinity, shall provide and have of his own . . . the new Testament both in Latin and in English . . . and diligently study the same. . . . And the bishops . . . shall examine the said ecclesiastical persons how they have profited in the study of holy scripture" (in Cox 1846, 501). One scholar, though, has written that clergy in the 1550s and 1560s were a "mass of ignorant, vocationally unsuitable men" (O'Day 1976, 56). This poor state might only mean that the realities of the period contrasted vividly with the desire. With the Reformation, the dissolution of the monasteries had removed the educated clergy – the monks – from the picture; the sons of the upper classes now found university education to be a route to secular careers; bishops had limited control over the appointment of poorly educated clergy; and there was a severe shortage of priests (O'Day 1976, 56–64; Towler and Coxon 1979, 5–6; Webster 1998, 322). That said, a more educated clergy was essential, both to preach and pastor and to be "upholders of the political and religious establishment" (O'Day 1976, 62). Toward these ends, as the following centuries advanced, large proportions of clergy became university graduates. This pattern sustained the Church of England well into the 1800s.

What did it mean for clergy to be university educated? Oxford and Cambridge, the dominant source of clergy, attended to a "broad" academic education, not "practical" training. Ordinands were to be "socialized," to learn to mix well with those who would be leaders in other realms. That began to change as the nineteenth century advanced. With industrialization, if clergy were to be effective in ministering to "professional" classes, they needed a more "professional" theological education (Dowland 1997, 1, 204–5; O'Day 1976, 63, 75; Towler and Coxon 1979, 17–18).

Oxford and Cambridge responded to demands for more advanced theological education with new professorships in ecclesiastical history, pastoral theology, and biblical exegesis. In the 1870s, two specifically Anglican colleges were established at Oxford (Keble) and Cambridge (Selwyn). The universities also established several large graduate theological schools: Westcott House and Ridley Hall at Cambridge, St. Stephen's House and Wycliffe Hall at Oxford. Their curricula, however, remained traditional; ordinands, for example, could only engage in study of missions voluntarily and informally (Walls 1996, 200–7), a reality that disturbed participants at the Edinburgh Conference in 1910. They reported that "the theological curricula would be enriched for all students [i.e., missionary and "home"] by fuller treatment of missionary subjects" (in Walls 1996, 209). In 1842, Cambridge introduced a theology exam for postgraduate ordinands, with tests in Greek, the Church Fathers, ecclesiastical history, liturgy, and the Articles of Religion. Within a decade, both universities had ordinands sit for exams on the four gospels in Greek and "evidences of Christianity" (Dowland 1997, 5, 181–2; Towler and Coxon 1979, 19).

All of this, however, failed to address the question of preparation for the practice of ministry. Enter new Anglican theological colleges, intended to serve the lower-middle classes, those unable to attend university, and potential clergy in remote areas, though some came to serve university ordinands who felt the need for "specialist clerical training" as well. St. Bees in Cumbria was the first, in 1816, followed by institutions such as Wells (1840), Cuddesdon (1854), and Lincoln (1874). Some were created by the revival of religious communities, notably the Mirfield Fathers' College of the Resurrection (1902). King's College, London (1829), created a clergy-training department and appealed to university graduates to develop their "professional skills" as clergy there. There remains some debate about the academic standards of these colleges, and they offered diplomas, not degrees. However, they offered some pastoral training, regular worship, residential community life, and more courses in theology than Oxford and Cambridge. And, the fact that the church established a centralized system of exams for ordinands in the 1870s provided some reassurance that products of the colleges had academic integrity.

As English colonists headed to North America, Australia, New Zealand, South Africa, the West Indies, and elsewhere, so too did clergy from the Church of England. One source of clergy was the first Anglican missionary society, the Society for the Propagation of the Gospel in Foreign Parts (SPG), established in 1701. Its principal mandate at the outset was to send priests to what was to become the United States to provide ministry for the British colonists. Later in the century, SPG missionaries could be found in Australia and New Zealand, and after the American Revolution, in Canada (Nelson 2001, 123; O'Connor 2000, 27, 262).

SPG missionaries in the 1700s were from "the excessive numbers of poorer clergy" who rested at the bottom of "the Church's essentially class-determined structure" (O'Connor 2010, 28–9). Thomas Bray, key to the establishment of the SPG, provided them with books, some 52 volumes, from the Church Fathers to Hooker. With no formal missionary training provided, Bray personally took in a number of ordinands for preparation; they would study "the whole System of Theology, Positive, Practical and Pastoral" (O'Connor 2010, 24–9).

These priests would naturally have experienced an England-based theological education. However, as the colonies developed, a shortage of priests and the desire of some colonists to be ordained brought the question of local training to the fore. Virginians, for example, soon became convinced that they had to educate their own to serve in colonial parishes. This led to the establishment of the College of William and Mary (1693), created in part to train "native-born clergy for the colony's established church." Its trustees declared that "we have . . . all reason to believe it will prove the Seminary of the Church of England in this part of the world" (Bond and Gunderson 2007, 183). By 1775, over half of the Anglican clergy in Virginia had attended the school, educated "within a Christian worldview" but, much as in England, without professional training. Others, from Virginia and from elsewhere in North America, had similar training experiences at Harvard and Yale (Bond and Gunderson 2007, 192; Nelson 2001, 112; O'Connor 2000, 25–9).

Seminaries in the emerging Anglican Communion paralleled the rise of theological colleges in nineteenth-century England. The Episcopal Church in the United States chartered the General Theological Seminary in 1817 with a vision to serve the entire Episcopal Church, but theological differences during the century led also to the evangelical Virginia Theological Seminary (1823) and the High Church Nashotah House (1841). By the twentieth century, there were 11 such seminaries. In Canada, Newfoundland's first bishop established the Queen's College (1841), and Anglican evangelicals founded the Wycliffe College (1879) in Toronto. In Australia, the Diocese of Sydney established the Moore Theological College (1856), and in Melbourne, the Trinity College Theological School (1877). However varied their curricula, they marked the shift from a general education to professional training, principally for ordinands. In cases where colonists had to journey to England to be ordained, the Bishop of London arranged for their examination in biblical knowledge, the Thirty-Nine Articles, the Book of Common Prayer, the ordinal, Latin, and the ability to read the New Testament in Greek (Nelson 2001, 116).

Soon after its founding, the SPG expanded its mission to include evangelization of slaves and indigenous inhabitants, not only in North America but also in the West Indies. In 1799, it was joined by the Church Missionary Society (CMS), founded as an evangelical Anglican endeavor, which focused on indigenous peoples in Africa and "the East." Both expanded with the advance of the British Empire throughout the 1800s, in India and throughout Africa (and elsewhere as well, including Japan and China), and the CMS initiated work among the aborigines in Australia and the Maori in New Zealand. Australia and New Zealand soon established their own CMS "branches."

Meanwhile, the Episcopal Church in the United States created its own official mission-ary apparatus, focusing upon Liberia, the Philippines, and South America.

At first, the CMS hoped that university-educated men would come forward as missionaries. Instead, many "of humbler station," yet to be ordained, came forward. Andrew Walls, the preeminent scholar of non-Western Christianity, observes that the formal education of the early-nineteenth-century missionary would not have been high, and if an Anglican, "his social and educational attainments were not such as would have brought him ordination to the home ministry" (1996, 199). The CMS tried scattering their candidates among clergy around England for their theological training, but that proved less than satisfactory. Hence, in 1825, the CMS created a training college at Islington (Stock 1899, I, 244). By the end of the century, it offered a course emphasizing theological study but also providing technical, basic medical, and practical missionary training. It remained an institution for non-graduate men (Hodge 1971). Meanwhile, in 1848, the SPG was helped in its training by the establishment of St. Augustine's College in Canterbury, independent of the SPG but with its support, to be a college to educate missionary clergy, where those unable to attend university could be trained (O'Connor 2000, 64).

Universities began to provide more missionaries as the great missionary century progressed. David Livingstone's appeal in his Cambridge lecture in 1857 for his listeners to "carry out the work which I have begun" (Hastings 1994, 252) struck a chord, one of the results of which was a new Anglican society, the Universities' Mission to Central Africa, founded in 1860. Meanwhile, across the Atlantic, in 1888, the Student Volun-teer Movement called upon university and seminary students to sign a pledge to become missionaries under the banner "The Evangelization of the World in this Generation" (in Thomas 1995, 74). It too influenced the growth of university graduates in foreign missions.

The formation of missionaries is one aspect of Anglican theological education; the formation of indigenous leaders is another. To secure autonomous churches, local leaders needed to be prepared, and mission societies established a variety of educational institutions, including Codrington College in Barbados (1745), Bishop's College in Cal-cutta (1820), Fourah Bay College in Sierra Leone (1827), and St. John's College in Auckland (1847) (Yates 1998, 484). However, missionary leadership viewed these developments with some misgivings. The Bishop of Calcutta might argue that such institutions as Bishop's College were needed to prepare "the Native Mind to comprehend the importance and the truth of the doctrines proposed to them" (in O'Connor 2000, 58), Fourah Bay College might well boast that the gifted Samuel Crowther was among its first students (Stock 1899, I, 336), and Bishop George Selwyn might insist that Maoris should learn Greek and English before ordination, but Henry Venn, the CMS secretary, was not alone in advising that "simple" programs to train local pastors while they continued doing their catechetical work was much to be preferred over colleges (Williams 1990, 7, 20).

Mission societies were working out their educational strategy as they went along. For example, after the deaths of their first missionaries along the Zambezi, the UMCA decided instead to train Africans for mission work from their base in Zanzibar, then sent their students out, arguing that thereby they would be helping to create "a really native, home-grown Christianity" (O'Connor 2000, 330–2). The CMS in India created the "Tinnevelly system," by which missionaries would choose two or three promising students from their village schools, take them to their boarding school, and if the students seemed "called" would send them on to become catechists, and a few for ordination (Stock 1899, I, 194–5, and II, 521–52). As for theological study overseas, it was a rare occasion for indigenous peoples until well into the twentieth century.

True, Philip Quaque, from modern-day Ghana, went to England under SPG auspices, trained in theology, and was ordained in the Church of England in 1765 before his return to West Africa (O'Connor 2000, 414). Others studied abroad, too, but missionaries remained instinctively opposed to what they considered the risk of "detribalization," and in any case it was expensive. Thus, missions established more seminaries, such as the important Bishop Tucker Theological College in Uganda (1913) and the ecumenical St. Paul's United Theological College in Kenya (1903). As colonial education advanced and independence movements gained strength, it became clear, as the Africanist scholar Roland Oliver wrote in the 1950s, that Africa was likely to have well-educated citizens amidst a "peasant clergy" if more attention was not given by the churches to leadership training (1952). Recognizing this reality, Anglicans and Methodists came together to found Immanuel College of Theology (1958) in Ibadan, Nigeria; and rapid growth of the church in the half-century or so after independence led Anglicans to expand established institutions. Bishop Tucker Theological College, for example, became Uganda Christian University, St. Paul's in Kenya did much the same, and new university initiatives are taking place in Tanzania and elsewhere, stimulated by a desire for degrees rather than diplomas.

In the last century, the array of theological colleges in England faced similar pressure to offer degrees, and this led some to associate with nearby universities. With the decline in ordinands in the 1960s and 1970s, others closed. In 1961, the Church of England had 26 theological colleges; in 1977, only 15 (Hastings 1991, 603). The United States also experienced retrenchment. Elsewhere, federations of schools of theology – the Wycliffe College joining the Toronto School of Theology in 1969, for example – offered a cooperative solution to the challenges that seminaries were facing in the West. Conversely, the ecumenical Trinity Theological College (1948) in Umuahia, Nigeria, became Anglican. In South Africa, at the end of apartheid, the black theological college, St. Bede's in Mthata, and the white St. Paul's in Grahamstown merged into the College of the Transfiguration (1993).

However, in the midst of restructuring and retrenchment, there were some creative initiatives. The end of empire stimulated the College of the Ascension, an SPG institution at Selly Oak, to set as its goal "to sensitize mission candidates to the 'hopes and aspirations' of the new nations" (O'Connor 2000, 168). The CMS shifted its training to Selly Oak with its new Crowther Hall. Toward the end of the century, the Selly Oak colleges sought to reflect the post-colonial world, studying world religions, new religious movements, Third World theologies, and so on, with students from both Western and non-Western nations. They developed an impressive series of short courses within the Centre for Anglican Communion Studies in 1992. In Latin America, there are efforts to advance an Anglican Center of Superior Theological Education (CAETS), to include Costa Rica, Guatemala, El Salvador, Nicaragua, and Panama. In Brazil, after a century of struggle over ministerial formation, the church established a Center for Anglican Studies (CEA) in 1997 to creatively coordinate diocesan and provincial efforts. And the United Society for the Propagation of the Gospel (USPG; a merger of UMCA and SPG) supported the creation of St. Simon of Cyrene Theological Institute (1989) in London to help prepare blacks in England for ordination (Calvani 2008; Dowland 1997; Hastings 1991; O'Connor 2000; Towler and Coxon 1979).

So much for ministerial formation for priests. The diaconate in many Anglican provinces is merely a transitional step, so theological education for the priesthood has defined preparation. However, as some dioceses have chosen to return to the vocational diaconate, deacon formation programs have sprung up, mainly on the diocesan level, offering useful but relatively limited theological study.

Some laity are licensed for particular ministries, notably lay readers. The modern history of readers began in the 1850s when the Church of England concluded that "a class of persons is now needed to assist incumbents." By 1866, the Church of England began licensing. In this early period, readers only needed to have "moral character, religious knowledge, and efficiency." As the twentieth century proceeded, along with increased responsibilities, readers undertook rigorous training, including scripture, doctrine, worship, mission, ethics, preaching, pastoralia, and spirituality (Rawling and Gooder 2009, 16–22, 65). The West Indies and some places in Africa duplicated the Church of England's seriousness in reader training.

For the laity, generally and historically, the Anglican Communion has sadly not taken Christian formation seriously. The Sunday school movement may have begun in the Church of England in the late eighteenth century, but the schools were designed for slum children and largely grew outside the established church. When Sunday schools truly became Christian education for laity, their appeal to adults never quite caught on among Anglicans. (The notion of basic Christian education for children is, in contrast, widely held.) As a result, the concept of lifelong Christian formation through theological study has been seen far more as an optional activity for Anglican laity to whom it might appeal. This reality has had serious implications for biblical knowledge and for an appreciation for the heritage of the church in general and the Anglican tradition in particular.

There have, though, been moments where the church made serious efforts at adult lay education. Interested adults have entered into such programs as theological education by extension (TEE) and Education for Ministry (EfM). TEE originated in Latin America under the pioneering leadership of Ross Kinsler in the 1960s (see Kinsler 1983). Although it was never intended simply to be a program for laity, for some years it had to fight for its legitimacy against the view that only residential studies were suitable for ordinands (Spencer 2001). Still, "TEE was founded on the belief that ministry was given to the people through baptism, not through ordination" (in McCoy 2006). Many Anglican laypersons in the Global South, especially in East and South Africa, have embraced that view, and TEE. So too did the School of Theology at the University of the South (Sewanee) in the United States through its EfM program. Since 1975, EfM, an intensive local four-year undertaking, has reached over 70,000 persons in groups not only in the United States but also in Canada, Britain, Australia, New Zealand, and elsewhere. Meanwhile, within the Church of England, proposals have emerged for an

Education for Discipleship initiative, "so that, within the context of a church engaged in the ongoing task of encouraging all Christians in their growing discipleship, opportunities are available to . . . lay Christians" (Church of England 2005, 3). Whether they, and laity throughout the communion, will do so depends largely upon the will of church leadership, particularly at the parish level. History, unfortunately, is not an encouraging indicator that "theological education for all" has become an Anglican priority (see Amos 2010, 647–8).

## Issues in Theological Education Facing the Anglican Communion

Theological education issues facing those called to ordination are categorized here as *conceptual, contextual, topical*. and *financial. Conceptually*, the fundamental question remains what constitutes well-trained priests. In practice, the church generally tries to both *form* and *educate* priests for specialized ministry. How? In the midst of current controversies, one conceptual train of thought is that ordinands are to be taught the "truth", and seminarians are to receive biblical knowledge as the church has traditionally accepted it, not encouraged to examine the diverse strains of biblical interpretation. An alternative train of thought is that seminarians are invited to question, even to doubt, as they seek to understand God at work in the world throughout history and in the present. Ultimately, of course, the church needs to be confident in the depth of understanding ordinands possess about their faith and tradition, but what constitutes soundness may vary greatly around the communion.

Process is also a conceptual issue. How does the community of faith teach and learn? How does it *do* theology? The American Episcopal Church may well have helpfully published Paulo Freire's *Pedagogy of the Oppressed* in English (1968), but the vision of empowering participatory adult education has hardly been realized in the church. Partnership, an oft-used term in missiological circles dating from 1947, is also a deeply theological process. Anglicans captured the partnership theme when, at a Congress in Toronto in 1963, they used the phrase "Mutual Responsibility and Interdependence" (Bayne 1963). Over the years, the communion has identified "Ten Principles of Partnership" (MISAG-II 1992, 16–19), perhaps one of the most valuable and, in practice, least honored documents before the church. With prescience, the Toronto Congress observed that "we must everywhere ask ourselves . . . what we have, what we need, and where we are called of God to share in major partnership with our fellow Christians" (Bayne 1963, 23). Authentic partnership is difficult, and companion links in particular have foundered in the effort. Seminaries have also found it problematic (Spencer 2010), but the calling remains.

*Contextually*, the Anglican Communion remains ambivalent as to whether *all* theologies are contextual. The historical expansion of the communion brought to the Global South English and Western theology, and with it what John Pobee calls the "Anglo-Saxon captivity of Ecclesia Anglicana" (1998, 450). Theological education presented this singular theology as the norm. However, from liberation theology in Latin America to contextual theology as a challenge to apartheid South Africa, from African theology to "water buffalo" theology from South East Asia, theologians from the Global South have challenged the Western model. The "translation theologies" from scholars such as Lamin Sanneh, the theologies of reconstruction articulated by scholars such as the Anglican layman Jesse Mugambi, the African feminist theologies made visible through the work of Mercy Oduyoye and the Circle of Concerned African Women Theologians, and the Dalit theology in India (Maluleke 2007, 419) – these "adjective" theologies call out for recognition of contextual theology as reflective of the search by people to understand their faith in their life situations (Institute for Contextual Theology, 1980).

Western seminaries need to study theologies from the Global South, and the reverse. As the Ibo proverb teaches, a rooster may belong to the family, but its crowing belongs to the neighborhood. However, "the theological sector," Andrew Walls observes, "has not yet come to terms with the fundamental shift in the centre of gravity of the Christian world whereby the Southern continents have become the heartland of the Christian faith" (1996, 149). As a result, few Anglican seminaries grant contextualization a central place, in the West because they continue to define theology by its Western "truths" and contextual theology as merely interesting, and in the Global South because "seeking the truth, come whence it may, cost what it will" may be, simply put, dangerous. Contextual theology grounds itself in grassroots community-based theological reflection and a "fearless way in which everything is questioned" (Institute for Contextual Theology, 1980), and this can be threatening to a church steeped in authority.

There are exceptions, however. From Aotearoa in New Zealand, Jenny Plane Te Paa has called for "quality bicultural theological education" (2008), and the Episcopal Divinity School in the United States has directed considerable energy to cross-cultural studies. The Tamilnadu Theological Seminary in Madurai and the United Theological College in Bangalore, India, offer striking field education opportunities, from a program where students live in rural areas to one where students work with urban street dwellers (Razu 2002; Wingate 1999, 12). A group of Anglican theologians, meeting in South Africa in 2004, sought to affirm contextualization, suggesting that the church could wisely do contextual theology by beginning with common ground, identifying differences, and "engaging in interpretation as a dialogue with one another" (ACTs 2 e-diary 2004).

Teaching about the rich theological answers found contextually throughout the church universal is but one aspect of *topical* issues. Theological disciplines combine to form a unity, but emphases may need re-examination. Five examples are presented in the following text.

1. Arguably the teaching of ethics, especially Christian social ethics, is often weak at Anglican institutions worldwide, to the detriment of the Christian witness. The Anglican Communion's "Five Marks of Mission" (see MISAG-II, 15) include "responding to human need by loving service," "transforming unjust structures of society," and "striving to safeguard the integrity of creation and sustain and renew the life of the earth." The church has a distinguished if sometimes paternalistic history regarding human need, has often been tentative with unjust structures, and is still grappling with the new dimension of integrity of creation. In the process, the church needs to answer the question as to "whether theological education is primarily to serve the church as it is, or is intended to challenge

the church to be what it might be, as a sign of God's kingdom, but also as an instrument of service" (Wingate 1999, 8).

2.  Some may debate how well seminaries give attention to the other two marks – "proclamation of the Good News" and "teaching, baptizing and nurturing new believers" – but in one form or another there is a curriculum history. In addition, some new institutions – for example, the Trinity School for Ministry (1976), an evangelical seminary in the Anglican tradition in the United States – have treated these subjects very seriously indeed. Still, Anglican seminaries have often neglected courses on church growth or church planting (Markham 2010).

3.  Anglicans historically demonstrate significant ecumenical involvement, but Anglican theological education rarely directs energy toward teaching about the one Body of Christ. It needs to be on the agenda.

4.  Anglicans in the Global South have known for many years that "Christians can no longer expect to live purely in 'our own' community" (Conway 2010, 25–6), and that a deeper understanding of inter-faith relationships is needed.

5.  Missiology "has never gotten the space it required in theological education" (Oborji 2006, 41). At a time when the communion reminds the church again and again that mission is at the center, few seminaries are staffed by missiologists, and an approach in which mission is simply incorporated into the traditional theological disciplines seems inadequate. In his classic *Transforming Mission*, David Bosch wrote that mission is "the good news of God's love, incarnated in the witness of a community, for the sake of the world" (1991, 519). That powerful definition demands critical disciplinary study.

For subjects such as biblical studies, well represented in seminary curricula, how the Bible is taught reveals the great diversity within the Anglican Communion relating to biblical interpretation. The communion's Bible in the Life of the Church project recognizes this. Partly seeking understanding as to "how we, as Anglicans, actually use the Bible," the project may result in identifying "the principles of Anglican hermeneutics" (Anglican Communion 2011). As for church history, also well represented, Andrew Walls rightly argues that "the global transformation of Christianity requires nothing less than the complete rethinking of the church history syllabus" (1996, 145).

The Theological Education in the Anglican Communion (TEAC) working party has given valuable attention to "the Anglican Way" (2006b). Anglican heritage has generally not been effectively taught. There are reasons for this. A tradition that embraces *lex orandi, lex credendi* (the law of prayer is the law of belief) lacks the doctrinal clarity that other traditions have, and Anglicanism also lacks a central historical figure around whom its identity might be focused. Moreover, current controversies have called into question the Anglican *via media* as a key element of who Anglicans are, leading to definitions that exclude perspectives, and rendering clarity all the more difficult. All the more reason, then, to look toward theological education to "strengthen the sense of why we are Anglicans" (Amos 2010, 645).

Finally, there are *financial* issues, raised here because they point to fundamental questions as to how programs in ministerial formation may meet the missiological needs of the Anglican Communion and the church universal. How many residential seminaries does an Anglican province need to have, especially when enrollment at some is so reduced that the institution ceases to be viable financially? What kind of program might come into being in a national diocese such as Botswana which, being numerically small, cannot afford a traditional residential model, but wants training to be local? And, what are the dangers when bishops, their dioceses' facing financial limitations, opt for the least expensive method, regardless of whether it produces the kinds of priests the diocese requires?

The last question takes us to further considerations about TEE. Although widely seen as valuable for laity, TEE originally came into being as an alternative to residential training for ordinands. Not only was it less expensive, TEE could claim to be valuable because it kept ordinands within their local environment and urged them to reflect upon theological and ecclesiological course content contextually. Much can be made of those qualities, but unfortunately TEE – offered at diploma and degree levels – became a temptation not because it provided the desired priestly formation, but simply because it was affordable. Similarly, some non-denominational training programs offered internationally to the Global South at very modest expense have been accepted as adequate formation in some dioceses, even though their theology may be at serious odds with Anglican perspectives. The absence of ordination exams in some provinces further complicates the picture.

The key point is that the church needs to keep before it the purpose which theological education programs serve, namely, to form persons for lives of faith and for particular ministries in the Anglican tradition. TEAC has helped immeasurably by creating "grids" addressing benchmarks for laity, vocational deacons, licensed lay readers, priests, and bishops. For priests, for example, the grids name benchmarks at a candidate's selection, at ordination, after ordination, and in ongoing ministry. At the time of ordination, TEAC suggests that ordinands should, among numerous other qualities, "have successfully completed some form of formal theological training," be rooted in "a disciplined life of prayer shaped in Anglican common prayer and life," "have developed skills to recognise gifts in others and to equip them to serve," be aware of the distinctiveness of their own context, and "demonstrate a growing critical engagement with the Scriptures and the traditions of Christian thought, characterised both by faithful obedience and openness to new insights" (TEAC 2006a). Later, TEAC speaks of continuing education, which "remains patchy and grossly inadequate" widely throughout the communion (MISAG-II 1992, 26). Properly utilized, the grids provide not only a reminder of the agenda before the church but also serve as an instrument of evaluation that will indicate what programs truly serve the interests of the Anglican Communion and where provinces and dioceses need to strengthen their programs (see also Scully 2008).

This chapter has offered one Anglican's perspectives about Anglicanism's heritage and a present-day agenda in ministerial formation. Theological colleges and seminaries have some serious work to do to form leaders. The church's institutions also have some serious Christian formation work to do to "support the life of all the baptized" (TEAC 2005). The Anglican Andrew Wingate captured these tasks when he commented that "I will be forever thankful for my British academic training in biblical languages and biblical criticism, but it was in Tamilnadu Theological Seminary that I became excited about applying the Bible to life" (1999, 106). That represents a vision for ministerial formation that strikes at the heart of Anglicanism. Valuing biblical and theological knowledge, how do Anglicans ensure depth of understanding while, also valuing a faith that is *lived* in God's service, they "excite" the people of God to advance God's mission? One might also add, at a time of divisiveness, how do Anglicans *do* theology, together?

For a full list of theological institutions in the Anglican Communion, go to http://www.wiley.com/go/markham/anglicancommunion.

## Bibliography

ACTs 2 e-diary. 2004. *ANITEPAM Bulletin*, vol. 43 (August), p. 3.

Amos, Clare. 2010. Theological Education in Anglican Churches. In *Handbook of Theological Education in World Christianity*, eds. Dietrich Werner, David Esterline, Namsoon Kang, and Joshva Raja. Oxford: Regnum Books, pp. 641–51.

Anglican Communion. 2011. Theological Education – The Bible in the Life of the Church. www.anglicancommunion.org/ministry/theological/bible/index.cfm.

Bayne, Stephen F., Jr. 1963. *Mutual Responsibility and Interdependence in the Body of Christ*. New York: Seabury Press.

Bond, Edward L. and Joan R. Gunderson. 2007. The Episcopal Church in Virginia, 1607–2007. *Virginia Magazine of History and Biography*, vol. 115, no. 2, pp. 163–344.

Bosch, David J. 1991. *Transforming Mission: Paradigm Shifts in Theology of Mission*. Maryknoll: Orbis Books.

Calvani, Carlos Eduardo. 2008. Theological Education in the Brazilian Context. *Anglican Theological Review*, vol. 90 (Spring), pp. 239–54.

Church of England: Ministry Division of the Archbishops' Council. 2005. *Shaping the Future: New Patterns of Training for Lay and Ordained*. London: Church Publishing House.

Conway, Martin. 2010. Key Issues for Theological Education in the 21st Century. In *Handbook of Theological Education in World Christianity*, eds. Dietrich Werner, David Esterline, Namsoon Kang, and Joshva Raja. Oxford: Regnum Books, pp. 23–29.

Cox, John Edmund. 1846. *The Works of Thomas Cranmer*, vol. 2. Cambridge: Cambridge University Press.

Dowland, David. 1997. *Nineteenth-Century Anglican Theological Training*. Oxford: Clarendon Press.

Farley, Edward. 1983. *Theologia: The Fragmentation and Unity of Theological Education*. Philadelphia: Fortress Press.

Freire, Paulo. 1968. *Pedagogy of the Oppressed*. New York: Seabury Press.

Hastings, Adrian. 1991. *A History of English Christianity, 1920–1990*, 3rd edition. London: SCM Press.

Hastings, Adrian. 1994. *The Church in Africa: 1450–1950.* Oxford: Clarendon Press.

Hodge, Alison. 1971. The Training of Missionaries for Africa: The Church Missionary Society's Training College in Islington, 1900–1915. *Journal of Religion in Africa*, vol. 4, pp. 81–96.

Institute for Contextual Theology. 1980. *What Is Contextual Theology?* Braamfontein, South Africa: ICT.

Kelsey, David H. 1993. *Between Athens and Berlin: The Theological Education Debate.* Grand Rapids: Eerdmans Publishing.

Kinsler, F. Ross, ed. 1983. *Ministry by the People: Theological Education by Extension.* Geneva: World Council of Churches.

McCoy, Mike. 2006. TEE Pioneer Challenges Theological Education to Deliver Good News for the 21st Century. *ANITEPAM Bulletin*, vol. 50 (May), pp. 1–3.

Maluleke, Tinyiko Sam. 2007. Half a Century of African Christian Theologies: Elements of the Emerging Agenda for the Twenty-First Century. In *African Christianity: An African Story*, ed. Ogbu U. Kalu. Trenton: Africa World Press, pp. 420–9.

Markham, Ian S. 2010. Theological Education in the Twenty-First Century. *Anglican Theological Review*, vol. 92 (Winter), pp. 157–65.

Mission Issues and Strategy Advisory Group II (MISAG-II), Anglican Communion. 1992. *Towards Dynamic Mission: Renewing the Church for Mission* (final report). www.anglicancommunion.org/ministry/mission/resources/documents/towardsdynamicmission.pdf.

Nelson, John K. 2001. *A Blessed Company: Parishes, Parsons, and Parishioners in Anglican Virginia, 1690–1776.* Chapel Hill: University of North Carolina Press.

Oborji, Francis Anekwe. 2006. *Concept of Mission: The Evolution of Contemporary Missiology.* Maryknoll: Orbis Books.

O'Connor, Daniel. 2000. *Three Centuries of Mission: The United Society for the Propagation of the Gospel 1701–2000.* London: Continuum.

O'Day, Rosemary. 1976. The Reformation of the Ministry, 1558–1642. In *Continuity and Change: Personnel and Administration of the Church in England 1500–1642*, eds. Rosemary O'Day and Felicity Heal. Leicester: Leicester University Press, pp. 55–75.

Oliver, Roland Anthony. 1952. *The Missionary Factor in East Africa.* London: Longmans, Green.

Razu, John Mohan, ed. 2002. *On the Way to Critical Praxis: Field Education as a Relevant Theological Pedagogy at the United Theological College, Bangalore.* Bangalore: United Theological College.

Pobee, John S. 1998. Non-Anglo-Saxon Anglicanism. In *The Study of Anglicanism*, revised edition, eds. Stephen Sykes, John Booty and Jonathan Knight. London: SPCK, pp. 446–59.

Rawling, Cathy and Paula Gooder. 2009. *Reader Ministry Explored.* London: SPCK.

Scully, J. Eileen. 2008. Theological Education for the Anglican Communion: The Promises and Challenges of TEAC. *Anglican Theological Review*, vol. 90 (Spring), pp. 199–221.

Spencer, Leon P., ed. 2001. Understanding TEE: A Course Outline and Handbook for Students and Tutors in Residential Theological Institutions in Africa. *ANITEPAM Journal*, vol. 31 (November).

Spencer, Leon P. 2010. Not Yet There: Seminaries and the Challenge of Partnership. *International Bulletin of Missionary Research*, vol. 34 (July), pp. 150–4.

Stock, Eugene. 1899. *The History of the Church Missionary Society*, Vols. 1–3. London: CMS.

Stock, Eugene. 1916. *The History of the Church Missionary Society.* Supplementary vol. 4. London: CMS.

Te Paa, Jenny Plane. 2008. How Diverse is Contemporary Theological Education? Identity Politics and Theological Education. *Anglican Theological Review*, vol. 90 (Spring), pp. 223–38.

Theological Education for the Anglican Communion (TEAC). 2005. Principles of

Theological Education. www.anglican
communion.org/ministry/theological/teac/
principles.cfm.

Theological Education for the Anglican Communion (TEAC). 2006a. Outcome Based
Grids Relating to Theological Education.
www.anglicancommunion.org/ministry/
theological/teac/docs/index.cfm.

Theological Education for the Anglican Communion (TEAC). 2006b. Working Briefs and
Process of Target Groups. www.anglican-
communion.org/ministry/theological/teac/
docs/briefs080206.pdf.

Thomas, Norman E., ed. 1995. *Classic Texts in
Mission and World Christianity*. Maryknoll:
Orbis Books.

Towler, Robert and A. P. M. Coxon. 1979. *The
Fate of the Anglican Clergy: A Sociological
Study*. London: Macmillan Press.

Walls, Andrew F. 1996. *The Missionary Movement in Christian History: Studies in the Transmission of Faith*. Maryknoll: Orbis Books.

Webster, John. 1998. Ministry and Priesthood.
In *The Study of Anglicanism*, revised edition,
eds. Stephen Sykes, John Booty, and
Jonathan Knight. London: SPCK, pp.
321–33.

Williams, C. Peter. 1990. *The Ideal of the Self-
Governing Church: A Study in Victorian Missionary Strategy*. Leiden: E. J. Brill.

Wingate, Andrew. 1999. *Does Theological Edu-
cation Make a Difference? Global Lessons in
Mission and Ministry from India and Britain*.
Geneva: WCC Publications.

Yates, T. E. 1998. Anglicans and Mission. In
*The Study of Anglicanism*, revised edition,
eds. Stephen Sykes, John Booty and Jonathan
Knight. London: SPCK, pp. 477–96.

CHAPTER 59

# Interreligious Relations in the Anglican Communion

## Ian S. Markham

## Introduction

Approximately 33.2 percent of the world's population is Christian. The next largest group is the Muslims, at 20.4 percent. Both Christianity and Islam are global religions. The Hindus are the next group, with 13.3 percent; they are more localized, yet thanks to the global mobility are still found in 116 countries. The Chinese universists (the current preferred term for the distinctively Chinese combination of yin/yang cosmology with appropriate dualities, ancestor cult, Confucian ethics, and other folk religion features) are at 5.9 percent, closely followed at 5.8 percent by the Buddhists. Indigenous religious traditions (now more often called "ethnoreligionists" because of the tribal emphasis and focus) continue to be significant, with approximately 4 percent of the world's population (see Markham 2009).

Christians do not have this world to themselves. We are required to share this planet with a whole range of different religions and worldviews. Inevitably, this does pose some challenges. Along with language, religion is an important part of a person's identity. As conflicts between groups arise, the religious identity can sometimes come to the fore. In particular, Africa has been a good place for both Christians and Muslims to grow; as a result, there are significant tensions between Christians and Muslims on that continent.

Beyond the practical challenge of coexistence, there is also a theological challenge. How best do we make sense of religious diversity theologically? Why does God allow so many religious traditions to thrive in the creation? Many Anglican theologians have been at the forefront of the debate around religious diversity.

As we examine these two important areas, it will become increasingly clear that, in my judgment, the future of interreligious relations needs strong "tradition-constituted"

*The Wiley-Blackwell Companion to the Anglican Communion*, First Edition. Edited by Ian S. Markham,
J. Barney Hawkins IV, Justyn Terry, and Leslie Nuñez Steffensen.
© 2013 John Wiley & Sons, Ltd. Published 2013 by John Wiley & Sons, Ltd.

accounts of how to handle and relate to religious diversity. While the twentieth century was more dominated by "global" accounts of religious diversity, the twenty-first century needs more localized accounts.

This chapter will develop the discussion under the three headings of "interreligious challenges," "interreligious theology," and "the future of interreligious relations." However, before doing so, we shall touch briefly on two main global conversations facing the Anglican Communion – one of which tends to be liberal, and the other which tends to be conservative.

## Main Global Conversations

Although it is a little more complex, it generally remains true that Anglicanism was linked to the growth of the British Empire. Sometimes the church anticipated the arrival of the British machine; sometimes it came afterwards. Nevertheless, there was always a connection.

The first global conversation developed in India. In the early nineteenth century, the East India Company was the primary vehicle of British rule in India. The East India Company had an awkward relationship with missionaries. William Carey, the famous Baptist missionary, was not welcomed into India by the company until the "Pious Clause" was added by Parliament into the company's Charter Renewal Act of 1813. This clause did succeed in opening the door to significant numbers of missionaries.

However, interestingly, many of the missionaries had very ambiguous attitudes to colonialism. As R. E. Frykenberg observes: "Indeed, pre-colonial, non-colonial and anti-colonial missionaries, taken together, outnumbered those British missionaries of the Anglican establishment who might have wanted to make India into another fiefdom for their own Christendom" (Frykenberg 1999,183).

This lack of overt Anglican presence was partly due to the sheer numbers of Roman Catholic missionaries (from countries such as France and Italy) and evangelical missionaries (many of whom were from North America). As a result, the Christian presence in India was very diverse. Anglicans were one group among many.

Anglicans did bring a distinctive approach to interreligious relations in India. As early as 1875, Krishna Mohan Banerjea argued that Hindus did not have to abandon their Hindu cultural and social traditions when they became Christians. And it was Jack Winslow who created a Christian ashram called *Christa Seva Sangha* – Christian Service Society – in 1922. There was a "liberal" stress in these movements. The emphasis was on inculturation. Some of the finest educational institutions were a result of this approach. St. Stephen's College, in Delhi, is a good illustration.

Although numerically significant, as a percentage of the population of India the total number of Christians is small. For many years, Christians have been seen as a "foreign" and "alien" religion, which is unfair given the presence of Thomas Christians (who claim to have arrived in India in 52 CE). And more recently, with the emergence of the Bharatiya Janata Party (BJP), some Christian groups have had a difficult time. The result of this distinctive interreligious context is that Christians in India have been more ecumenically sympathetic (given Christians are a small minority, they do not fixate on doctrinal differences) and more accommodating to other religious traditions. Anglicans played a major role in shaping both the ecumenical and interreligious focus.

This interreligious conversation tended to be anti-colonial and more liberal (in the sense that it is strongly committed to both ecumenism and interreligious dialogue). The Anglican approach in India was heavily influenced by the sense of being a small minority. Turning now to the second, we shall see that the competition for adherents between Christianity and Islam produced a very different approach to religious diversity.

This second interreligious conversation is found in Africa. As Christianity started to spread, North Africa (especially Ethiopia) was a key area of growth. And when Islam started to develop, North Africa proved to be an important area of development. Muslim historians record the approach by Muhammad to the Christian king of Ethiopia, where the king declares that the new faith of Muhammad is virtually the same as his own (Ibn Isḥāq 1955, 146–53). In Africa, Islam has been in conversation with Christianity since the birth of the Islamic movement.

These two monotheistic faiths were both seeking to define themselves against each other and win converts from African traditional religions. Both religions were successful. Eliza Griswold's *The Tenth Parallel* (the circle of latitude which is ten degrees north – i.e., 700 miles north of the equator) describes the growing conflict between Islam and Christianity. She notes how the tenth parallel provides the fault line in terms of demographics. She writes, "Due to the explosive growth of Christianity over the past fifty years, there are now 493 million Christians living south of the tenth parallel – nearly a fourth of the world's Christian population of 2 billion. To the north live the majority of the continent's 367 million Muslims; they represent nearly one quarter of the world's 1.6 billion Muslims" (Griswold 2010, 9).

Griswold goes on to document how the tensions around the tenth parallel are deep. Violence is commonplace. In Nigerian elections, people tend to vote with their religious affiliation. At the 2002 Miss World pageant, a Christian journalist who implied that Muhammad would have taken a wife from one of the participants triggered riots, which led to people being killed. In the Nigerian town of Yelwa, Christians resented the way wealthy Muslim males take poor Christian females as their second or third wives, reducing the possibility of a large family among the Christians. Hence, an initial edict by Christian pastors that intermarriage is forbidden led to the killing of 78 Christians at a church in 2004. For the recently retired Primate of Nigeria, Archbishop Peter Akinola, Christianity is in a battle with Islam. In 2006, Archbishop Benjamin Kwashi (a contributor to this book) had his home invaded by some Muslim men who "knocked his nineteen-year-old son unconscious, and blinded his wife" (Griswold 2010, 55). For Kwashi, this is "a global conflict playing out locally here in Nigeria" (Griswold 2010, 55).

Sudan is facing a comparable challenge, which finally expressed itself in the birth of a new "Christian" nation. In both cases, the situation is generating an approach to interreligious relations that sees the "other" as a problem and any "liberal" overtures to the other as part of the problem.

There is an irony here: the form of Islam that developed in northern Africa should be more dialogical than other forms of Islam. It is no coincidence that the two forms of faith that flourish most effectively in Africa are Pentecostal Christianity (with its passionate worship and occasional flirtation with the prosperity gospel) and Sufi Islam (with an equally intense form of worship). Sufi Islam was able to accommodate more indigenous practices and is less doctrinaire than many other forms of Islam. However, it is clear that the extent and depth of the mistrust is such that all language of accommodation and peace is being displaced by talk of war and eradication.

These two illustrations demonstrate that, in the communion, Anglicans are facing two contrasting directions. To oversimplify a bit, Asian Christians tend to stress the need for dialogue and learning from the "other," while African Christians (especially in the north) tend to stress the threat and the need to be uncompromising. It is with this background that we now examine the interreligious challenges.

## Interreligious Challenges

It is clear that the precise nature of the challenge partly depends on context. To take one illustration, the Anglican relationship with Judaism varies, depending on whether you are in Europe or in the United States. For the Church of England, the history of European anti-Semitism and the enormous tragedy of the Holocaust still shape the outlook of the church. Hence, when the Church of England's Interfaith Consultative Group to the Archbishops' Council produced a report called *Sharing One Hope: the Church of England and Christian–Jewish Relations – a contribution to a continuing debate*, the line on the state of Israel was interesting:

> In a new relationship between Judaism and Christianity, Christian attitudes must start from an understanding of Jews as a people, and not simply as a religion. For most Jews attachment to the land of Israel is an essential aspect of their personhood, although some may regard emphasis on the Israeli State as a diminution of the heart of Jewish faith (The Archbishops' Council 2001, 14).

For the Church of England, Christians should recognize the fundamental validity of the state of Israel as an intrinsic part of Jewish sensitivities. It then deals with the "Palestinian issue," stressing the complexity of the problem and how Christians in England need to tread carefully. So the authors conclude: "While members of the Church of England can and do hold strong opinions on these issues, their readiness to express their views should be tempered by the recognition that they do not have to live directly with the consequences, as do Arabs and Jews in the Middle East" (The Archbishops' Council 2001, 16).

Compare this outlook with the position that the Episcopal Church in the United States has taken. The Episcopal Church has deep links with the Christian sites, most of which are in the Occupied Territories; as a result, they tend to almost always use the language of equivalence. Hence, this statement by Presiding Bishop Katherine Jefferts Schori is typical: "For Palestinians, the challenges and burdens of life under occupation, and a shrinking footprint for a future Palestinian state, are untenable. For Israelis, the fear that changes in the region will lead to increased violence and hostility from all directions after a decade of relative harmony is equally untenable" (Katherine Jefferts Schori, 2011).

For the US church, Israel must stop the settlements and let the Palestinians create a viable state, and the Palestinians must guarantee the security of Israel. The Episcopal Church has been involved in the debates around disinvestment from Israel (or, more precisely, in companies that are directly or indirectly involved in the oppression of the Palestinian people). Broadly speaking, the Church of England is more sympathetic to the predicament facing the Jewish people in Israel, while the US church is more sympathetic to the pain of the Palestinians.

Continuing the theme of context, there are certain interfaith relations that are deeply local. Certain provinces are preoccupied with the conversation between the indigenous traditions. The conversations in the United States with the Native Americans, in Australia with the Aboriginal peoples, and in Africa with the traditional African religions are all important. The Anglican Communion made these conversations more formal when the "Anglican Indigenous Network" was formed in 1991.

The most constructive and innovative conversations are to be found between Anglicans and Hindus and Anglicans and Buddhists. India has produced a plethora of leaders who wanted to recognize the deep insights embedded in these traditions. Many of these Christians leaders have come out of the Roman Catholic tradition, inspired by the likes of Bede Griffiths, who was the Benedictine monk who became a *sannyasi* (one who renounces the world entirely and dedicates himself to spiritual pursuits). When the Church of South India was formed in 1947, there was a lively debate about its constitution and a fear that the terminology shaping the Indian church would be too Western. As a result, the governing principles of the Church of South India include the explicit hope that the church must conserve "all that is of spiritual value in its Indian heritage, to express under Indian conditions and in Indian forms the spirit, the thought and the life of the Church Universal" (Boyd 1975, 207). Many of the Hindu converts to Christianity proved to be highly innovative in their interpretation of Christianity in the light of their Hindu upbringing. Interestingly, as time passes, the leading theologians are now cradle Christians who lack this first-hand knowledge of Hinduism. Perhaps as a result, Indian theology is becoming a little more traditional.

The dominant challenge and the most complex interreligious relation is the one with Islam. There are many dynamics at work in this relationship. Minorities in any country can have a difficult time. Christian minorities in well-established Muslim countries are no exception. Pakistan's Blasphemy Law has been used against Christians, leading to tragic consequences. In August 2009, at Gojra, Pakistan, a simple rumor that Christians might have defiled the Qur'an led to a rampage that led to 100 Christian homes being burned and looted, as well as seven people killed. One important dynamic is the sense of powerlessness felt by many Muslims in Pakistan (*New York Times* 2009). From their perspective, as they hear about Western forces killing women and children in Afghanistan or Iraq (and how powerless Muslim countries are to respond), they express their outrage by exercising their limited power against the even more powerless Christian minority.

While in Pakistan the dynamic is primarily one of a minority coping with a majority, in Africa the dynamic is much more even and competitive. Leaving South Africa aside, the most encouraging African country at handling the dynamic between Muslims and Christians is probably Tanzania. The countries which find it harder are Nigeria, Sudan, and Somalia.

## Interreligious Theology

Many of the dynamics documented have focused on the sociological challenge of "living with difference." In this section, we need to examine briefly the theological interpretations of religious diversity.

It was an Anglican theologian, Alan Race, who proposed the now famous taxonomy of "pluralism, inclusivism, and exclusivism" (Race 1993 and Jones 2004). And it is this taxonomy that has dominated the theology of other religions' debate – not simply for the Anglican Communion, but for the entire mainline. Pluralism is the position which affirms that the reality of "God" (or, given that certain forms of Buddhism would not talk about a creator God, the Real) is the mystery beyond all cultural religious accounts. This is best understood through the famous image of the large mountain that has many routes to the top. Although the different routes appear to be different, the reality is that it is one mountain, and no single route captures the entire complexity of the mountain. In this view, the doctrines of the Trinity and the Incarnation are Christian interpretations of the divine; they are not descriptive of the way the divine really is. The best statement of this position is the work of John Hick.

Inclusivism is the official position of the Roman Catholic Church. It was affirmed at Vatican II, and the inspiration behind the position is the Roman Catholic theologian Karl Rahner. Rahner suggested that it is essential to recognize that the saving act of God in Christ does not depend on conscious knowledge of that saving act. In the same way that the heroes of the Old Testament are saved by Christ but were in their consciousness no more than faithful Jews, so this same divine action may apply to the faithful Muslim or Buddhist or Hindu. The great advantage of inclusivism is that it holds together a commitment to the truth of the Trinity and the Incarnation and a generosity to those of other faiths.

Exclusivism is the position of the conservative evangelicals. This position insists that the Biblical witness is clear: conscious knowledge of the saving work of Jesus is essential for salvation. The Biblical witness does not answer the question: what about those who haven't heard? Hence, at that point, we must simply trust that the "Judge of the earth will do right." However, for those who are not saved, the message of the Bible is that hell is a reality that looms as a consequence of our sinfulness.

Recent discussions have modified this taxonomy. The favored term of Paul Hedges is "particularities." This fourth option describes the largely postliberal, postmodern position that rejects the possibility of tradition-independent taxonomies and invites each tradition to struggle with religious diversity within the parameters of that tradition. According to advocates of this position, the problem with the first three is that they are attempts to provide overarching theories of religious diversity, which ignores our locatedness and place within traditions.

The center of gravity in the communion is probably around Inclusivism, with Archbishop Rowan Williams tending to combine inclusivism with particularities. It combines the Anglican sensitivity to generosity with a faithfulness to the tradition which is attractive to Anglican culture. However, in the United Kingdom, Canada, Australia, and the United States, you will find plenty of pluralist sympathizers; and in Africa, the exclusivist approach is more dominant.

## The Future of Interreligious Relations

Interreligious relations can and should be an area where the Anglican Communion can make distinctive contributions to global Christianity. We have the advantage of being a truly global family, which means that we have the full range of viewpoints within the family, from the liberal mainline to the almost fundamentalist conservative evangelical. In addition, as we have seen in this chapter, Anglicans are present in many different contexts and cultures. For all these differences of viewpoints and contexts, we also have a shared history, prayer book, and ethos. This combination of differences and shared resource provides a powerful resource which can bring a distinctive perspective to interreligious conversation.

Four features are emerging that could shape a distinctively Anglican approach to interreligious relations. The first is a recognition that the church will want to address interreligious relations in different ways in different contexts. We should support the Christian minorities in Pakistan; we should invite the leadership of the Middle East to move beyond toleration of their (often significant) Christian minorities, but also allow them to proselytize, build churches, and participate fully as citizens of their countries. Meanwhile, in Europe and America, where the minority of Muslims have to cope with Islamaphobia (often running parallel with an anti-immigration narrative), we should identify with and support our neighbors. Our support for a Christian minority in a Muslim country should run parallel with support for the Muslim minority in a predominantly secular or Christian country. We should both support the state of Israel and, at the same time, work to see a strong, viable Palestinian state emerge. We should commit to dialogue with all the major religions of the world.

The second is that we should continue to witness to the Lordship of Christ and the affirmation of scripture that "every knee will bow and every tongue confess Jesus is Lord" (Phillippians 2). Anglicanism is a tradition that connects the theological dots; we believe that God has spoken in Jesus Christ and that the Word made flesh is our control on our theology. Although some Anglicans are sympathetic to the pluralist hypothesis of John Hick, most are not. In the United States, there is a risk of a nondescriptive, generic mainline approach emerging that has no sense of authority; this approach has no basis on which it can justify its talk about God and what God wants; instead, it simply invites the membership to construct a God that fits their desires and aspiration.

While some traditions, for example, forms of Buddhism that have development in the West, might understand this generic mainline approach, the vast majority of religions find such an approach incoherent. Muslims, for example, are not interested in elaborate conversations about different projections of God. When the Turkish Muslim theologian Beduizzaman Said Nursi talks about dialogue with Christians and Jews, he assumes a shared revelation – the people of the Book – and a shared quest for truth (see Markham 2009).

There is no question that the global family of Anglicanism has sufficient safeguards built in to prevent it moving to the generic mainline approach. There is in Anglicanism a recognition that ultimately the Word made flesh, which is captured in the text of scripture, is the authority for all Christian action and conversation.

The third is that reasons for dialogue should be grounded in our tradition, not derived from principles transcending our tradition. One temptation of modernity is to seek for tradition-transcendent reasons for dialogue; hence, for example, we dialogue out of a commitment to "peaceful relations" or "mutual love." Such reasons do not persuade a person who is deeply committed to a particular tradition. The reasons for dialogue will be different, depending on the tradition one belongs to. Hence, Muslims might develop their reasons for dialogue because of the Qur'anic category of the "People of the Book"; Jews might find it helpful to develop the Noachide covenant; and Christians might talk about the agency of the Holy Spirit which can reveal insights about the nature of God which are compatible with scripture and found in other faith traditions. These are tradition-specific reasons for dialogue.

An Anglican witness to the importance of developing tradition-specific reasons for dialogue would be powerful.

The fourth is that we need to create systems and mechanisms for conversation. It was Autosh Varsney who pointed out that dialogue needs systems and organizations. Indeed, there is ample evidence that a diverse city where there are such mechanisms are much more likely to withstand some social tension between religious groups than those cities where there are no such organizations.

However, there is a significant difficulty here. The impact of the 2008 global recession has depleted resources for denominational and communion activities. National churches are being starved of resources, and intercommunion activities are also in a season of contraction. Yet, this is important. Probably the best hope is the larger congregations, the stronger seminaries and theological colleges, and the occasional diocese which sets in to provide such organizations.

## Conclusion

The Anglican Communion is part of a tradition that is both faithful and generous. It is faithful in that the connecting text – *The Book of Common Prayer* – is primarily scripture, which witnesses to a deep, contextual, incarnational, and creedal faith. It is generous in that it also recognizes that the Holy Spirit is active in other faith traditions. Unlike some other branches of Christendom, it is a tradition placed to play a constructive role in interreligious relations.

In addition, it is a global family. Hence, there are mechanisms which ensure that the challenges facing one part of the family (e.g., in the Sudan) reach the rest of the

Anglican family. This interconnectedness, both in terms of information and support, is a real strength of the communion.

To conclude, this is an area of strength. It needs to be an appropriate priority as we find our way forward as a communion.

## Bibliography

Boyd, Robin. 1975. *An Introduction to Indian Christian Theology*, revised edition. Delhi: ISPCK.

Church of South India Constitution II, 2 as Quoted in Robin Boyd. *An Introduction to Indian Christian Theology, Revised Edition*, Delhi: ISPCK.

D'Costa, Gavin, Paul Knitter, and Daniel Strange. 2011. *Only One Way: Three Christian Responses on the Uniqueness of Christ in a Religiously Plural World*. London: SCM Press.

Frykenberg, R. E. 1999. India. In *A World History of Christianity*, ed. Adrian Hastings. Grand Rapids, Michigan: Eerdmans.

Griswold, Eliza. 2010. *The Tenth Parallel: Dispatches from the Fault Line Between Christianity and Islam*. New York: Farrar, Straus, and Giroux.

Hastings, Adrian, ed. 1999. *A World History of Christianity*. Grand Rapids, Michigan: Eerdmans.

Ibn Ishāq. 1955. *The Life of Muhammad: A Translation of Ibn Ishāq Sīrat Rasūl Allah*, trans. A. Guillaume. Lahore: Oxford University Press.

Jones, Gareth. 2004. *The Blackwell Companion to Modern Theology*. Oxford: Blackwell.

Markham, Ian with Christy Lohr, eds. 2009. *A World Religions Reader*, 3rd edition. Oxford: Wiley Blackwell.

*New York Times*. 2009. Hate Engulfs Christians in Pakistan.

Race, Alan. 1993. *Christians and Religious Pluralism*. London: SCM Press.

Schori, Katherine Jefferts. 2011. A Pastoral Letter on Israeli Palestinian Peace, October 3, 2011. As found at http://www.episcopalchurch.org/page/pastoral-letter-israeli-palestinian-peace. Accessed June 30, 2012.

The Archbishops' Council. 2001. *Sharing One Hope: the Church of England and Christian–Jewish Relations – A Contribution to a Continuing Debate*. London: Church House Publishing.

CHAPTER 60

# Globalization of the Anglican Communion

## Grant LeMarquand

It seems almost an oxymoron to use the words "Anglicanism" (i.e., a church which is distinguished by its "Englishness") and "globalization" in the same sentence.[1] How can one speak of a "national" church being at the same time "global"? The vocation of Anglicanism, it seems, is to live in a tension between its historical rootedness in the British Isles and its particular manifestations in 38 provinces which extend to virtually every country in the world. Of course, the reason for Anglicanism's presence in much of the world could be simplistically associated with the British Empire. There was a time when "the sun never set on the British Empire," and although that time is now passed, it did not pass before the English imperial project had carried its distinctive form of church life to many parts of the globe. Some parts of the world which were relatively untouched by British Anglican presence were impacted by the presence of England's imperial successor, the United States, whose own Anglican missionaries followed their leaders to various corners of the earth (e.g., Brazil, Liberia, and Japan).

The reality of the mixing of imperial aspirations with missionary endeavors is not unique to Anglicanism. The great Roman Empire gave birth to the great Western church known as the *Roman* Catholic Church. The Orthodox churches, likewise, have been identified closely with their places of origin (e.g., Greece, Russia, Egypt, and Ethiopia), even if branches of those bodies can be found in Canada, Scandinavia, and Jamaica.

However, the global reach of the Anglican Communion (or, indeed, other communions) cannot be explained merely as the religious dimension of an imperial project. Although churches built in the colonial period in Nairobi, or Singapore, or Addis Ababa,

[1] The term "globalization" will be used in a non-technical sense in this chapter, as a synonym for "internationalization."

*The Wiley-Blackwell Companion to the Anglican Communion*, First Edition. Edited by Ian S. Markham, J. Barney Hawkins IV, Justyn Terry, and Leslie Nuñez Steffensen.

may appear English in their architecture and may use English as their language of worship, these churches, which were founded as chaplaincies for English-speaking expatriates, do not explain the emergence of indigenous Anglicanism within and indeed beyond former British or American colonies. Indigenous Anglican churches can be found in places around the world where there has never been a British or American colony. Angola, the Congo, Rwanda, Burundi, and Nepal, for example, never had a colonial English-speaking congregation. In places like Singapore, Ethiopia, Chile, and Peru, the first Anglican church was an English-speaking congregation, but those congregations are now a tiny minority within a church indigenous to that place. In short, Anglicanism on the ground, although not yet in its official structures, is moving beyond and away from its colonial heritage. This movement away from a center, and toward a multiplicity of contexts, raises sharp questions for the meaning of the common life of Anglicans.

What does it mean for a family of churches historically identified with the Church of England that the majority of Anglicans today are from the south, with very different cultures from that of the English? What does it mean that contemporary global Anglicanism is increasingly moving away from the cultural, political, and economic hegemony of Anglo-American colonialism (Douglas and Pui-Lan 2001, 11)?

## How Did Anglicanism Become Globalized?

Few attempts have been made to trace the history of the Anglican Communion. Volumes on Anglican Church history have, until recently, been studies of the church in England or the British Isles, sometimes including the English church before the Reformation (Bede 1999; Kaye 2008), some beginning the story with the Reformation period (Moorman 1963). A current standard textbook on Anglicanism includes only one 12-page chapter on "Non-Anglo-Saxon Anglicanism" in a volume of more than 500 pages (Pobee 1998). The impression one has from a quick glance at the secondary sources on Anglicanism is that the communion is a British church with a few rather small outposts. The writing of "communion history" *per se* is still in its infancy.

A truly comprehensive history of the communion would need to take into account the multiplicity of studies of Anglicanism in particular places (e.g., Karanja 1999; Tucker 1938; Carrington 1963), accounts of particular personalities, both missionaries and indigenous (e.g., Billington Harper 2000; Shenk 1983; Maynard Smith 1926; Li 1996; Crombie 2006), including, perhaps, those who felt compelled to leave Anglicanism to pursue ministry unhindered by its constraints (Shank 1994; Singh 2000), and records and studies of important events or crises (Stephenson 1978; Fairweather 1963; Lambeth Commission 2004). Since missionary societies were involved in the founding of Anglican churches in various parts of the world, the records and histories of those organizations are also crucial (e.g., the Protestant Episcopal Church of the United States published a magazine for over 100 years, beginning in 1836, entitled *Spirit of Missions*). The writing of such a history is daunting and has been rarely attempted. Although Stephen Neill's *Anglicanism* appeared in 1958, the next real

attempt to produce a full-fledged history of the communion was not until the publication of *A History of Global Anglicanism* by Kevin Ward in 2006.[2]

The existence of the Anglican Communion is a kind of accident of history. Before
the colonial period, the Protestant churches of Europe basically considered themselves
to be *the* church in their particular place. Since the German and English churches were
closely identified with the politics and the culture of those places, non-Roman Catholics
gave little thought to global mission. The Roman Church, on the other hand, a body
which considered itself "catholic" (universal), had long been involved in establishing
churches globally (Neill 1964). However, ironically, those Christian bodies associated
with the Reformation, which so emphasized the great doctrine of justification by grace
through faith, were blind to the missiological implications of their own central doctrine
(Bosch 1991, 239–61).

The age of exploration transformed both the modern view of the world and the
Protestant view of mission. As European explorers and merchants began to establish
bases in various parts of the globe, they brought chaplains with them to attend to the
spiritual needs of the ships' crews and of the settlers. The presence of chaplains brought
the church into two contrasting, indeed contradictory, realities; the church became
complicit with unjust trading practices, including the evils of the slave trade, and, at
the same time, the church began to awaken to the existence of millions of people
around the world who had not heard the good news of Jesus Christ. In some cases,
chaplains became directly involved in the slave trade; in other cases, the chaplains
began to reach out with the gospel beyond the confines of their companies' settlements
to the native populations of Africa, Asia, and Latin America.[3]

As settlements turned into colonies, Anglican churches began to be built in territory
claimed by Great Britain, as well as in places where Britain maintained trading centers.
In some places, like India, the trading companies resisted the attempts of missionaries
to evangelize the native peoples, worrying that the planting of indigenous churches
would lead to religious tensions and therefore hamper trade.

In Britain, however, there emerged a growing interest in the mission of the church.
The Society for Promoting Christian Knowledge was founded in 1698, primarily to
foster education. The Society for the Propagation of the Gospel in Foreign Parts, a High
Church society, was established in 1701, working first in North America and then in
West Africa. The Church Missionary Society (CMS), an evangelical society, came into
existence in 1799, founded by the same circle of acquaintances which spent years
lobbying the British government to end the slave trade. Indeed, one of the primary
motivations for the formation of the CMS was to do restitution to the continent of Africa
on behalf of the British people by bringing the gospel to Africa. The Tractarian movement also formed its own society, the Universities' Mission to Central Africa. Other
societies, both evangelical and High Church, were formed later to focus on particular
areas of the world. The formation of these organizations reveals a growing missionary

[2] Two rather popular, even journalistic, accounts appeared in the mid-twentieth century: Higgins and
Johnson. Both were members of the American clergy.

[3] For a brilliant cinematic portrayal of this tension, albeit in a Roman Catholic context, see the beautiful 1986
film directed by Roland Joffé, *The Mission*, starring Jeremy Irons and Robert De Niro.

consciousness among Anglicans in England, a growing desire to spread the gospel in an Anglican form to parts of the world which came under the British sphere of influence.

As colonies began to grow into nations, so also did Anglican bodies outside of the British Isles begin to desire a greater autonomy from the parent body. In some cases, like in Kenya, an English settler church and an African "native" church were kept separate for a time – a situation which simply exacerbated the tensions which were developing on the political front. In other cases, like in the United States, Anglicanism had to survive without episcopal leadership for a time because of the constraints of the English church's legal position under the British Parliament. In Nigeria, an indigenous bishop (Samuel Adjai Crowther) was ordained relatively early, but then, due to opposition from a generation of foreign missionaries who opposed his leadership, was replaced by a British bishop. It was decades before Nigeria once again received indigenous episcopal leadership. Such ugly incidents still linger in the background of contemporary Anglican relationships (Ward 2006, 124–5; Kwashi 2007).

With a few exceptions (e.g., the United States and Canada), indigenous, autonomous Anglican bodies only began to develop communal structures in the late nineteenth century when a pastoral and theological crisis forced bishops from around the world to meet together for the first Lambeth Conference in 1867. In 1863, under the leadership of Bishop Robert Gray of Cape Town, the church in South Africa declared the Bishop of Natal, John Colenso, a heretic. Gray was a High Church bishop in the Tractarian tradition; Colenso was a modernist, influenced by F. D. Maurice and German biblical criticism. Having been removed from his see, Colenso protested, not to a South African body, but to the English Privy Council. Anglicans in South Africa were still governed by British law, and Colenso won his case before the council. However, a new bishop had already been appointed for Natal, and so the church found itself in schism. Seeing a looming international crisis, a synod of the Canadian church called for an international conference of bishops. Not everyone in the emerging communion was happy with this idea (e.g., the Archbishop of York boycotted it), but the first Lambeth Conference did meet in 1867.

Over the next century or so, the Lambeth Conference became a significant marker in the communion's life, being considered (at least since the Virginia Report) as an Instrument of Unity, or Instrument of Communion, together with the Archbishop of Canterbury, the Primates' Meeting, and the Anglican Consultative Council.

## Aspects of Contextualization

Globalization implies contextualization. An important result of Anglicanism becoming globalized is not that there are English-speaking or English-looking churches in many corners of the world (although there are), but that there are now "contextualized" churches in the Anglican tradition all over the world. The word "contextualized" needs some discussion. It is being used here as a synonym for what others (especially Roman Catholics) call "inculturation." Contextualization is more than simply "indigenization" – ministry being done by people who are native to a particular place, although that is one important aspect. Contextualization means what Articles XXIV and XXXIV of the Thirty-Nine Articles were pointing toward. Article XXIV ("Of speaking in the Congregation in such a Tongue as the people Understandeth") reads, "It is a thing plainly repugnant to the Word of God, and the custom of the Primitive Church, to have public Prayer in the Church, or to minister the Sacraments, in a tongue not understanded of the people." That is, the good news of Jesus Christ must be given in a language which can be understood. Language, of course, can be understood on a literal level. One should not preach in English when the congregation understands only French. One must not celebrate the Eucharist in Ge'ez when the people understand only Amharic. However, "language" also points to the deeper reality of culture. Culture shapes and is shaped by language. To give a simple example, in northern Canada, where the Inuit peoples have many words for "snow," the problem of translating a biblical verse which mentions snow will be a problem of what particular word for snow the translator chooses. Among the Jieng people of Sudan, who do not have a word for snow, the translator faces a different kind of choice – what word can one choose which expresses the idea that the biblical verse wishes to convey (the answer, by the way, is that Jieng translators chose a word which means a white rock). To say that the gospel must be conveyed in the language of the people is to say, at the same time, that it must be conveyed in the culture of the people.

Similarly, Article XXXIV states, in part, "It is not necessary that Traditions and Ceremonies be in all places one, or utterly like; for at all times they have been divers, and may be changed according to the diversity of countries, times and men's manners, so that nothing be ordained against God's will." In other words, in order for the will of God to be done, culture must be taken into account. That is, "countries, times and . . . manners" must be accommodated – not in such a way that the gospel is compromised, but in such a way that the gospel is communicated, received, and honored. And so, English choir music need not be introduced in Anglican churches in Pakistan; heavy black vestments are probably not appropriate in Melanesia. Structures and traditions appropriate to the area need to be and have been developed, although this is always an ongoing process.

There are at least four ways in which Anglican provinces, dioceses, and parishes can measure whether they are becoming appropriately contextualized. Three of these go back to the great mission leader Henry Venn of the CMS, whose goal was that churches planted outside of England become self-propagating, self-governing, and self-supporting. To these "three selfs" we must add a fourth – self-theologizing.

As we look back over the last 200 years of Anglican missionary activity, the goal of self-propagation has evidently been the easiest of the "four selfs" to achieve. Andrew Walls' description of the present reality of the Christian world – that it has undergone a "shift in the centre of gravity" (Walls 2001, 85) – is as true of Anglicanism as it is of other Christian bodies. The vast majority of church-going Anglicans live in the southern hemisphere. Foreign missionaries are a part of the story of this shift, but they are a relatively small part of the story. As has now been documented repeatedly (for just one example, see Karanja 1999), the majority of primary evangelistic activity has been and is being accomplished by local agents. The only question, which the statistics force us to ask, is whether the Anglican churches in the Western world will once again become self-propagating – will Western Anglicans recover the zeal to reach the lost with the good news of the grace of God in Christ in such a way that lives will be transformed and vital churches planted?

Sadly, many Anglican provinces are not yet self-supporting. The realities of the global economy have made many countries dependent on foreign aid. The same is true of many churches. In order to function within contexts of poverty and powerlessness, many Anglicans in the non-Western world have turned to Anglicans in richer countries for financial support. More must be done to move these provinces out of situations of dependency to self-sufficiency. This is especially true since there is also a temptation on the part of richer churches to attach strings to donations. Such "strings" do not seem to be ideologically one-sided – both "conservatives" and "liberals" have been accused and are probably both guilty of using money to sway poorer churches to one side or the other in our current Anglican culture wars. There is also, of course, a temptation on the part of poorer churches to capitulate theologically or ideologically to northern demands. The ideal, articulated at the 1963 Anglican Congress in Toronto, is that the communion should live in "Mutual Responsibility and Interdependence" (Fairweather 1963, 117–22). Such an ideal is difficult to attain in a fallen and sinful world, and in a fallen and sinful church.

As nations around the world have been freed from colonial bondage, the churches in those places have likewise become self-governing. It is not always the case, however, that independence from colonial power always means true freedom. As in politics, so in the church, groups or individuals who rise to power do so for a variety of motivations. Ethnocentrism (often misleadingly referred to as "tribalism") frequently affects who is considered capable of governing. Neo-colonialism, the use of outside money to influence policy, still has the power to influence whether local leaders will be puppets of trans-local causes. It must be always kept in mind that these pressures shape Western leadership patterns just as much as they do non-Western patterns.[4]

The fourth "self," self-theologizing, may be the most crucial of all of the various aspects of contextualization. Self-theologizing will include how worship and liturgy are shaped and therefore how Christian communities understand themselves in relation to God and the world around them. A Christian community which worships in a foreign language (using the term "language" inclusively here to mean more than words, but music, movement, sacramental actions, modes of prayer, and spirituality) will remain foreign to the culture in which they live. To take just one obvious example, if an Anglican church in some part of Asia has a prayer book which includes prayers for the British royal family, but no prayers for the political leadership of its own country, how will the Christians in that place understand themselves in relation to their own nation? Such an example may seem far-fetched; more interesting may be a situation in which new Anglican churches are being formed with converts coming directly from African traditional religion in the Sudan. It has become common for families coming to faith among the Jieng to have their compounds exorcized. Rituals have been developed for such an event. These rituals are common and known at a popular and oral level, but have not

---

[4] As a citizen of Canada and a native Quebecer, I am deeply aware that language and culture can become contentious issues, and that the negotiation of these subjects can leverage the influence of political power.

yet been written down as stable liturgies. Should they be? Why, or why not? Would writing them down rob them of the power of their spontaneity, or would the process of reducing them to writing enable these liturgies to be tested and refined? Pastoral issues in particular, such as marriage, family, politics, land and the environment, violence, the press, religious freedom, the media, poverty, health care, and a plethora of other subjects, require theological reflection at the local level. Theology, however, is not merely local.

It has also become clear that decisions made in one place affect the church everywhere. Along with local theologizing, there must be international, trans-cultural consultation, so that the mind of Christ can be discerned corporately, and enacted in such a way that the actions of the church in one place are not perceived as repugnant either to scripture, or to the church in another place. Such Anglican, trans-cultural theological consultation is fraught with difficulty, especially since the churches of the Western world still hold most of the power and the money. It is too easy to marginalize the churches of the non-Western world, and examples of how this has been done and is being done are legion.[5]

## Is the Communion "One"?

The life of the Anglican Communion can be considered a gift of grace. The communion's existence implies the possibility that we can learn the gospel from one another. Areas of the Christian life which Christians in one place had been blind to can be understood and opened up by Christians from other places. Would the Nippon Sei Ko Kai (the Holy Catholic Church of Japan) have repented its idolatrous policy of support for the veneration of the Japanese Emperor if it were not for consultation with communion partners (LeMarquand 1996)? At the same time, any international body can be manipulated; the possibility of deception and abuse of power and money are genuine temptations. The fact that one Anglican parish in New York City has more money than several Anglican provinces makes the temptation real that the leaders of those provinces may want to say things that please a potential wealthy patron, even if the people of that province do not agree. Likewise, rich Christians in the West may be tempted to use money to gain power and influence in the communion. Our theological and ideological differences are often worked out with the use of ungodly manipulation and the exercise of worldly power. These realities are leading to the stressing and tearing of the communion. The question must be asked: Can the communion hold together? Many would already consider that question anachronistic and immediately ask, "which communion?"

---

[5] The recent appointment of Anglicans to ARCIC III is a case in point – only one African, but several Westerners, including members of churches from Canada and the United States, were appointed against the protests of southern churches. Likewise, the primate who was supposed to represent all the primates on the Crown Appointments Committee to recommend the successor to Rowan Williams as Archbishop of Canterbury was a Western primate. The hegemony of the Western churches appears to be tightening, rather than loosening.

It is ironic that just in the period of history in which we have become aware of the reality of the Anglican Communion, we are faced with the real possibility of its non-existence – at least in the form that we thought it has existed for the last 100 years or so. It was often repeated in the twentieth century that Anglicanism should be seen as "provisional" (see, especially, Runcie 1993, 13). The reason Anglicanism was first considered provisional was because Anglicanism made no claim to *be* the church, but considered itself only a branch of the greater church. Now we must ask whether Anglicanism can be seen as coherent at all, or are the Anglican churches associated only because of a common history, a story in which the next chapters will include further and further division?

The question, then, is: if there is such a thing as "Anglicanism" after "globalization," what is it that holds it together?

For a time, it appeared that Anglicanism was a form of reformed Catholicism held together by a form of prayer, "common prayer," encapsulated in a liturgy. Certainly, the Book of Common Prayer, as it emerged from the Reformation period, did much to keep more Protestant-minded and more Catholic-minded Anglicans together. The liturgical renewal movement of the 1970s and the books which developed from that movement have looked less and less like the classic Book of Common Prayer, calling into question whether the Anglican Communion still has "common prayer."

More vaguely, Anglicans have often spoken of "bonds of affection" which tie together various parts of the international body. Such a romantic notion may have carried more weight in the past, and there may still be a kind of affection which most Anglicans around the world have for the English church. However, such relations are now fragile, if not completely severed. Have the Nigerian church and the Episcopal Church of the USA said anything "affectionate" about each other in the last decade? Do most Anglicans in Wales even know that there are Anglicans in Papua New Guinea? Desmond Tutu was once asked what holds Anglicanism together and he apparently said, "we meet." However, the contentious 2008 Lambeth Conference, what some consider the scandalous behavior of the ACC-14 meeting in Jamaica in 2009, and the boycott of the 2011 Primates' Meeting in Dublin, have tested the idea that "we meet." *We* don't – at least at the moment, we don't.

The so-called "Instruments of Communion" have already been mentioned. It is considered by most of the spokespeople of the southern provinces that all four of these instruments have failed (Nazir-Ali 2012; Wabukala 2012). Perhaps new instruments will appear which will have more effectiveness. Some had hoped that the Anglican Covenant would be such a device. At the time of writing, this seems less and less likely.

We come back to an issue which a few have argued can hold the communion together – at least the communion as it is presently constituted. Can the Anglican Communion fashion a theological statement which can form an adequate basis for unity? The creeds seem to have been able to function this way in the ancient church. It is doubtful whether they alone are adequate to our current situation, since many who hold divergent opinions on almost everything still claim a common allegiance to the creeds. The Thirty-Nine Articles were once considered a doctrinal standard, but have been rejected by many provinces. The Chicago Lambeth Quadrilateral is both minimalistic and not conceived of as a statement which could carry the weight that any current statement may need. Under current discussion are two statements: the Anglican Covenant and the Jerusalem Declaration. Some have declared the covenant dead. That may or may not be so. Is the covenant to be rejected by the rest of the communion simply because England has rejected it? Does England, therefore, hold a veto in the communion? Some have said that this leaves the Jerusalem Declaration formed at the Global Anglican Futures Conference as "the only game in town" (Nazir-Ali 2012).

Perhaps one way forward is to check conversation which implies that Anglicans "cannot" have a common theological statement. It has often been said in the modern period that "Anglicans have never had a confession or a theological system." It is true that we Anglicans have not been as focused on doctrinal definition as, say, the Roman Church or Lutheran or Reformed bodies. That does not mean that we have *no* theological formulae. Neither does it mean that we *should not* have more precision. Our rather loose and flexible way of dealing with doctrine may have worked in the past, when Anglicanism was more or less confined to one island. As we attempt to negotiate life as a communion which spans multiple contexts, some articulation of what holds us together as a church (not just "bonds of affection," they are torn; not just "meetings," they are boycotted and overly politicized) needs to find a consensus. It is true that there is no one doctrinal statement which at present is accepted by all. And it is doubtful that one will be found which will be acceptable to every part of Anglicanism. It seems inevitable, then, that some consensus must be reached by some majority, and that this will mean that boundaries will be established by some which will exclude others. This is not necessarily a bad thing. To use a hypothetical example: if the church of the Province of South Africa had capitulated to apartheid ideas and not allowed the ordination of non-white priests, or not allowed inter-racial marriages to take place in their churches, the communion would probably have had to exclude that province from its communion life. We may be facing a situation now in which the Instruments of Communion might, because of the political power available to those who wish for such a change, agree to allow certain new forms of marriage (same-gender unions). Such a decision would exclude those provinces which believe that such an action is beyond what is allowed by scripture, Christian tradition, and scripture-and-tradition-led reason. Similarly, the decision not to allow such a practice in some provinces would lead either to perpetual political lobbying by those provinces until the rest of the world capitulated, or else to a distancing of the relationship between provinces which must (in the words of the Windsor Report) "learn to walk apart."

Is there, then, actually an Anglican Communion? Perhaps not in the same sense that there is a Roman Catholic Church. Perhaps we are more like the Orthodox, with a multiplicity of autocephalous churches, not all in communion with each other. If so, is this a desirable thing? What does seem clear is that the population trajectory of the communion is still moving in a southward direction. If that trend continues, the continuing hegemony of the West will not. The call to seek common theological and moral commitments is now urgent. What is needed is a church which is truly catholic and truly reformed. It is doubtful that any statement can be formulated which will make every side happy. One way or another, deliberately or by default, choices will be made in the next years which will shape the future of Anglicanism and the Anglican Communion.

# Bibliography

Bede. 1999. *Bede: The Ecclesiastical History of the English People (Oxford World Classics)*, eds. Judith McClure and Roger Collins. Oxford: Oxford University Press.

Billington Harper, Susan. 2000. In the Shadow of the Mahatma: Bishop V. S. Azariah and the Travails of Christianity in British India. *Studies in the History of Christian Missions*. Grand Rapids: Eerdmans.

Bosch, David. 1991. Transforming Mission: Paradigm Shifts in Theology of Mission. *American Society of Missiology Series*, no. 16. Maryknoll: Orbis. [Especially Ch. 8, "The Missionary Paradigm of the Protestant Reformation."]

Carrington, Philip. 1963. *The Anglican Church in Canada: A History*. Toronto: Collins.

Crombie, Kelvin. 2006. *A Jewish Bishop in Jerusalem: The Life Story of Michael Solomon Alexander*. Jerusalem: Nicolayson's.

Douglas, Ian T. 1996. *Fling Out the Banner! The National Church Ideal and the Foreign Mission of the Episcopal Church*. New York: The Church Hymnal Corporation.

Douglas, Ian T. and Kwok Pui-Lan. 2001. Introduction. *Beyond Colonial Anglicanism: The Anglican Communion in the Twenty-First Century*, eds. Ian T. Douglas and Kwok Pui-Lan. New York: Church Publishing, pp. 9–21.

Fairweather, Eugene R. 1963. *Anglican Congress 1963: Report of Proceedings*. Toronto: Anglican Book Centre.

Hassett, Miranda K. 2007. *Anglican Communion in Crisis: How Episcopal Dissidents and Their African Allies Are Reshaping Anglicanism*. Princeton: Princeton University Press.

Higgins, John. 1942. *The Expansion of the Anglican Communion*. Louisville: Cloister.

Johnson, Howard A. 1963. *Global Odyssey: An Episcopalian's Encounter with the Anglican Communion in Eighty Countries*. New York: Harper & Row.

Karanja, John. 1999. *Founding an African Faith: Kikuyu Anglican Christianity 1900–1945*. Nairobi: Uzima.

Kayanga, Samuel E. and Andrew C. Wheeler, eds. 1999. *"But God Is Not Defeated": Celebrating the Centenary of the Episcopal Church of the Sudan 1899–1999*. Nairobi: Paulines.

Kaye, Bruce. 2008. *An Introduction to World Anglicanism*. Cambridge: Cambridge University Press.

Kwashi, Benjamin. 2007. The Anglican Communion: An African Perspective. http://www.globalsouthanglican.org/index.php/blog/printing/the_anglican_communion_an_african_perspective.

Lambeth Commission on Communion, The. 2004. *The Windsor Report 2004*. London: The Anglican Consultative Council.

LeMarquand, Grant. 1996. Nippon Sei Ko Kai: Essays on the Church in Japan. *Anglican and Episcopal History*, vol. 65, no. 4.

Li, Florence Tim Oi. 1996. *Raindrops of My Life*. Toronto: Anglican Book Centre.

Maynard Smith, H. 1926. *Frank Weston: Bishop of Zanzibar*. London: SPCK.

Moorman, J. R. H. 1963. *A History of the Church in England*, 3rd edition. Harrisburg: Moorehouse.

Nazir-Ali, Michael. 2012. Jesus, Lord of His Church and the Church's Mission. http://gafcon.org/news/jesus-lord-of-his-church-and-of-the-churchs-mission.

Neill, Stephen. 1958. *Anglicanism*. Harmondsworth: Penguin.

Neill, Stephen. 1964. *A History of Christian Missions*. The Pelican History of the Church 6. Harmondworth: Penguin.

Pobee, John. 1998. Non-Anglo-Saxon Anglicanism. *The Study of Anglicanism*, revised edition, eds. Stephen Sykes, John Booty and Jonathan Knight. Minneapolis: Fortress, pp. 446–59.

Runcie, Robert A. K. 1993. The Nature of the Unity We Seek. *The Truth Shall Make You Free: The Lambeth Conference 1988*. London: Anglican Consultative Council, pp. 11–24.

Shank, David. 1994. *Prophet Harris, the "Black Elijah" of West Africa*. Studies of Religion in Africa 10. Leiden: Brill.

Shenk, Wilbert R. 1983. *Henry Venn – Missionary Statesman*. Ibandan: Daystar.

Stephenson, Alan M. G. 1978. *Anglicanism and the Lambeth Conferences*. London: SPCK.

Singh, Sadhu Sundar. 2000. *Wisdom of the Sadhu: Teachings of Sundar Singh*. Compiled and edited by Kim Comer. Plough: Farmington, PA.

Tucker, Henry St. George. 1938. *The History of the Episcopal Church in Japan*. New York / London: Scribner's.

Wabukala, Eliud. 2012. A Global Communion for the Twenty-first Century. http://gafcon.org/news/a-global-communion-for-the-twenty-first-century.

Walls, Andrew. 2001. Africa in Christian History: Retrospect and Prospect. *The Cross-Cultural Process in Christian History: Studies in the Transmission and Appropriation of Faith*. Maryknoll: Orbis, pp. 85–115.

Ward, Kevin. 2006. *A History of Global Anglicanism*. Cambridge: Cambridge University Press.

# CHAPTER 61

# Missionary Work in the Anglican Communion

## Timothy J. Dakin

## Becoming Missionary

This chapter is about the strategic work of becoming missionary rather than the work of those who are called "missionaries." The term "missionary work" is traditionally explored by emphasizing either the word "missionary" or the word "work." Indeed, in the history of the Anglican Communion, there is a lot to celebrate from either perspective. Thus, much of the literature on mission has been focused on those who have been sent – the missionary heroes of faith. Anglican mission *work* is now better appreciated through the Five Marks of Mission: proclaiming the good news, nurturing the faith, enabling loving service, promoting social justice, and advocating environmental care. However, neither of these two approaches is taken here; rather, I have interpreted the word "missionary" as an adjective. I therefore believe the primary work of the Anglican Communion is to become missionary.

I thus offer this chapter not as an alternative to a new outline of missionary history or an updated overview of the shape of mission work; rather, I offer it precisely because the literature on mission history now includes the question of the missionaries' worldview and motivation; and because the reflection on missionary work has moved on to explore the deeper missiological grounding of the Five Marks of Mission (I deal with some of these issues in the following section on the church as "holy"). The fact is that we are in a new era of world mission which coincides not only with the post-colonial context, but also with the globalization of Christianity. This new phase may well be the kind of change that only takes place every 500 years (see the outline of such a suggestion in Phyllis Tickle 2008). We are therefore in a new phase of Anglicanism: the emergence of global Anglicanism in which the focus is on the work of becoming missionary.

*The Wiley-Blackwell Companion to the Anglican Communion*, First Edition. Edited by Ian S. Markham,
J. Barney Hawkins IV, Justyn Terry, and Leslie Nuñez Steffensen.
© 2013 John Wiley & Sons, Ltd. Published 2013 by John Wiley & Sons, Ltd.

## Changing Mission

Hence, in this chapter, I suggest that there is now a new era of mission in which *fresh missional expressions* of church need to be considered within the widest context of what is happening in *global Christianity*. For example, while many have acknowledged the growth of the southern churches and have paid lip-service to the need to "learn from the south," the reality is that there does not seem to be a coherent theological framework for understanding how northern/Western fresh expressions of church are linked with, or should be linked with, or learn from, what is happening elsewhere, and vice-versa. In other words, there is a need to explore how mission truly is a matter of mutual reciprocity.

Three factors come together in recent global changes, summarized by Justo Gonzalez as follows: "the growth of a truly universal church; the post-Constantinian character of our times; the failure of the promises of the North" – these factors are disruptive and "confront Christians everywhere, not just in the Third World" (Gonzalez 1999, 132). Thus, the global south church is now huge, the decline of Western Christianity invites re-evangelization, and the resources of the north are limited. In confronting these factors, Western Christians experience the reality of decentering, decline, and disempowerment; also, unsurprisingly, some demotivation.[1]

Hence, Westerners from a declining church with diminishing resources are confronted by a post-colonial world in which a majority of Christians are post-Western and yet poor. These changes disrupt old mission relationships, so we can no longer maintain the former sending model of mission, i.e., from the West to the rest. We can no longer avoid the deep cultural and social changes that have diminished Western Christendom, revealing the need for the re-evangelization of these former Christian heartlands. And we can no longer take for granted and use the power of northern/Western resources to sustain mission work.

## Refounding Anglicanism: "The Analogy of Mission"

The twenty-first century thus requires of Anglicanism nothing less than a refounding process.[2] The Anglican tradition has been forged out of the ancient mission to England

---

[1] These changes require a paradigm shift in mission thinking and practice, particularly by northern/Western Churches and mission societies. The partnership pattern of mission had done a holding job, but had effectively allowed post-colonialism to continue. During my time in CMS, we attempted to move beyond the "partnership pattern" of mission. This paradigm shift included three changes: first, CMS became more locally rooted and was recognized by the Church of England as an "acknowledged community" with its own rule of life and episcopal visitor; second, it established new autonomous CMSs in former mission fields with whom it could relate in an inter-dependent worldwide network, i.e., CMS Africa, Asia CMS, and (forthcoming) Latin CMS; third, it embraced a prophetic mission perspective which includes a renewed confidence in Jesus' historical and continuing mission and a dialogical commitment to social transformation.

[2] On refounding, see G. Arbuckle's books, particularly Arbuckle, G. 1996. *From Chaos to Mission: Refounding Religious Life Formation*. London: Geoffrey Chapman. See also the articles by Dunn, T. 2009. Refounding Religious Life: A Choice for Transformational Change. *Human Development*, vol. 30, no. 3 (Fall); and Wittberg, P. 2009. The Challenge of Reconfiguration: New Opportunities for Religious Congregations. *Human Development*, vol. 30, no. 3 (Fall); and Bevans, S. B. *Towards a Mission Spirituality* (available online).

which was reformed in the sixteenth and seventeenth centuries, renewed by revival in the eighteenth century, and reorganized by diocesan renewal in the nineteenth century. The nineteenth and twentieth centuries saw this Anglican Faith and Order spread around the world by mission movements.[3]

This refounding could be approached from a number of perspectives, but one way would be to reverse the order of the classic marks of the church, i.e., to begin with Apostolic (see Richard R. Gaillardetz 2008). Apostolic would here refer to the missionary (missional) nature – mission-shape – of the church grounded in the eternal, historic, and continuing mission of Jesus: "As the Father sent me so I send you . . . Receive the Spirit" (John 20: 21–2).[4]

This would have major implications for what it might then mean to describe the church as Catholic, Holy, and One. In this chapter, I suggest that beginning with Apostolic, as the analogical participation in the mission of God revealed in Jesus, challenges us to revisit how mission opens up the human cultural question regarding catholicity, helps us to see holiness as a missiological set-apartness, which nevertheless enables a greater vision of unity as revealed in Jesus the One, who is of ultimate significance for all peoples.

David Runcorn (2006, 18; *emphasis mine*) suggests that the founders of the Church of England "believed that they were part of the 'One, Holy, Catholic and Apostolic church'. But they were exploring a *fresh expression* of its particular life and calling." If so, I hope the founders would be delighted with what is emerging: a *mission-shaped church*, encouraging all kinds of fresh expressions of a global/local church!

In this chapter, I sometimes use the term "capital," deploying it in a wide-ranging way, in exploring theological and mission perspectives. By capital, I mean the mission resource available to us; both revealed and constructed. At one level, it is "the boundless riches of Christ" (Ep 3:8); at another level, it is the social capital constructed in the administration of this rich mystery in the dynamics of the bonding, bridging, and linking of Christian mission.

---

[3] Arthur Burns, in his essay "English 'church reform' Revisted, 1780–1840" in Burns, A. and J. Innes, eds. 2003. *Rethinking the Age of Reform*. Cambridge: Cambridge University Press, pp. 136–62, points out that the term "church reform" is not applied to the kind of major changes in the church which reflected the reforms in wider society, and the term is never applied to mission. The transformation, the reform, of the polity of the Church of England by mission is one still taking place but hastened now by the kind of social pressures, for example, globalization, which created the diocesan renewal of which Burns writes (see preceding text). For the impact of globalization and its "elective affinity" with world mission, see Goheen, M. and E. G. Glanville, eds. 2009. *The Gospel and Globalization*. Vancouver: Regents College. Texts supporting the significance of the missionary movement or the value of the prophetic within mission include: the 2002 report by the Mission Theology Advisory Group: *Presence and Prophecy: A Heart for Mission in Theological Education*. London: CHP; Bartlett, Alan. 2008. *A Passionate Balance: The Anglican Tradition*. London: DLT; Chapman, Mark. 2006. *Anglicanism: A Very Short Introduction*. Oxford: Oxford University Press; Spencer, Stephen. 2007. *Christian Mission*. London: SCM; Spencer, Stephen. 2010. *Anglicanism*. London: SCM. See also Hivdt, N. C. 2007. *Christian Prophecy*. Oxford: Oxford University Press.

[4] On the "analogy of mission" of the Son and the church, see Barth: CD IV. 3.2 p. 768, for an exploration of this two sendings. In proposing an analogy of mission, I am developing Barth's own approach to *analogia fidei* and developing a theme first explored by Aquinas.

# APOSTOLIC

## The missionary God

Having thus recognized that, in the twenty-first century, there is a paradigm shift in our understanding of the Christian faith, mission is no longer left to the missionaries and evangelists. The word "missionary" (or missional), as an adjective, applies to the whole church, both locally and globally; all Christians are called to a daily every-member mission. Thus, missionary work in the Anglican Communion is the responsibility and the calling of all. *We are a communion in mission, participating in God's worldwide mission through Christ by the Spirit for the glory of God the Father.*

Having said this, it is not clear that our theology has caught up with the emerging reality and perspective of the global church. We need both a new theology and new approaches to Anglican Faith and Order that explain and complement this emerging paradigm.[5] Something radical is called for; something which recognizes that it is only when we understand God as a missionary God that we will truly understand the church as a missionary church. As John Flett says, "God's movement into his redemptive economy, while a deliberate act, is not an ancillary second step alongside an otherwise defined perfection. The attribute missionary narrates the very nature of God's perfection" (2010a, 226).

For both Catholic and evangelical traditions, the permanent priority of evangelistic mission is a given. Yet, if the permanent priority of evangelization is seen as only a temporal priority; it will always, whatever importance it is given in the life of the church, be seen as secondary to the activities and dimensions of the Christian life which are understood as having eternal significance, for example, worship. The permanent priority of evangelization needs to be undergirded by a theology of eternal mission, i.e., eternal mission as the eternal obedience of the Son to the Father in the Spirit, *in which we participate analogically.*

If evangelistic mission is seen as coming within the sphere of the interim horizon of the Christian life, an activity in time that will pass away into a life of the eternal worship of God, then there remains an abiding dualism. This dualism emerges in Anglican thought and practice in the reductionism implied, but not always intended, in the pragmatic use of the Five Marks of Mission and the utilitarian place given to the missionary societies in the life of the church. It seems that Anglicans take pride in being a pragmatic tradition rather than a theological one when it comes to mission. Compare this with the way we prioritize liturgy and worship and articulate the eternal significance of worship. Yet, is the Eucharist not the celebration of the eternal mission of the Son, which is his eternal obedience of the Father revealed in Jesus' historical mission?

---

[5] The Church of England's *Mission-shaped Church* report is an example of the change in perspective and practice and offers some theological reflection to accompany the change; and the *Anglican Covenant* can be seen as one contribution to providing a complementary new framework for faith and order in the Anglican Communion. See also Mark Chapman's concluding chapter in Chapman, Mark. 2012. *Anglican Theology*. London: T&T Clark.

(For a review of the relationship between mission and worship, see Alan Kreider and Eleanor Kreider [2009].) Flett states the issue in a challenging way:

> Instrumental approaches to the community of the church are one clear result of an inadequate mission theology. But can mission be understood as the eschatological end and purpose of creation? It is on this constructive question that matters run aground. Every tradition falls prey to the dichotomy of church and mission for this single reason: mission, it is assumed, is a temporary act undertaken in relation to the contingency of sin and subject to terminus in the final judgment. The church, the community of worship, by comparison, waits in hope for its final redemption, for the fulfillment of the Lord's Supper in the wedding feast of the Lamb (2010b, 22).

Pragmatism about mission is not something confined to Anglicans. There is a deeper pattern that relates to the whole separation between mission and theology. One way of exploring this is through the development of theology where the theoretical disciplines were separated from the practical ones. Many might argue that there has been an attempt to overcome this through the grand schemes or localizing perspectives of philosophical hermeneutics or contextual theology. However, my sense is that there is a need for a new confidence in the historical and eternal mission of Jesus, grounding our analogical participation in the *missio Dei*.[6]

This move expresses the missionary character of God as an adjectival reality, rather than an interim necessity. God's economic mission is to share, with creation, the eternal missional life and glory he shares with himself. Speculatively, therefore, he would have sent his Son to fulfill this mission and would have given his Spirit to glorify creation even if we had never sinned. Our sin only reveals more of his eternal mission. We have been invited to share in God's eternal sending of himself as Son, expressing his greater self which is glorified by the Spirit in the fellowship of the Trinity. God is unfolding this mission in creation, through redemption, and in recreation. We, as created beings, are invited to share in this eternal mission, through the redemption of the cross and in the hope of the new heavens and earth that are filled with the glory of God by the Spirit as revealed in the resurrection. We may participate in that mission now in all that we do. This is our mission which is analogous to the mission of God – the analogy of mission: "As the Father sent me, so I send you . . . Receive the Spirit" (John 20:21–2).

## Jesus' Prophetic Mission

The confidence to talk about the eternal mission of the Son only comes from a renewed understanding of the historical mission of Jesus. The eternal Word has become flesh in

---

[6] An authentic use of the theology of *missio Dei* requires not only a reevaluation of the prophetic mission of Jesus (see Flett, John. 2010. *The Witness of God: The Trinity, Missio Dei, Karl Barth, and the Nature of Christian Community*. Grand Rapids: Eerdmans), but also a proper understanding of the relationship between Jesus and the Spirit. See Yong, Amos. 2005. *The Spirit Poured Out on All Flesh*. Grand Rapids: Baker. Yong draws on Spirit-Christology; for an overview of Spirit-Christology, see Habets, Myk. 2010. *The Anointed Son: A Trinitarian Spirit Christology*. Eugene: Pickwick.

Jesus the Prophet, who continues his prophetic mission through the Spirit in church and world. Summarizing for the general reader, N. T. Wright (2011, 55) says this of Jesus' mission:

> He took upon himself (this is one of the most secure starting points for a historical investigation of Jesus) the role of a prophet, in other words, of a man sent from God to reaffirm God's intention of overthrowing the might of pagan empire, but also to warn Israel that its present way of going about things was dangerously ill-conceived and leading to disaster. And with that, the sea is lashed into a frenzy; the wind makes the waves dance like wild things; and Jesus himself strides out into the middle of it all, into the very eye of the storm, announcing that the time is fulfilled, that God's kingdom is now at hand. He commands his hearers to give up their other dreams and to trust his instead. This at its simplest, is what Jesus was all about.

At a more academic level, Wright (1996, 150) outlines Jesus' mission as follows:

> . . . Jesus habitually went about from village to village, speaking of the kingdom of the god of Israel, and celebrating this kingdom in various ways, not least sharing meals with all and sundry. These actions and words must therefore be seen not as incidental behaviour, irrelevant to his worldview or mindset, but as part at least of the praxis through which we can bring that worldview into focus. . . . What sort of worldview, then, might such praxis reveal? And what sort of mindset begins to emerge as Jesus' own variant on that worldview? I want now to argue that the best initial model for understanding this praxis is that of a prophet; more specifically, that of a prophet bearing an urgent eschatological, and indeed apocalyptic, message for Israel.

According to Luke 4:14–30, when Jesus returned from the desert, he was recognized to be full of the Spirit. The Spirit of prophecy had returned. Jesus was invited to speak at his home synagogue at Nazareth. He read three verses from parts of Isaiah, beginning with "The Spirit of the Lord is upon me," and then outlined all that these meant in terms of good news for the poor, the captives, the blind, and the oppressed. He then declared that this scripture was fulfilled in himself and would be fulfilled in his ministry. This was Jesus declaring that he was beginning the prophetic mission of the reign of God.

Jesus was no Levite, priest, scribe, or official rabbi, but, effectively, he announces that he is a prophet, and more: that the Spirit of prophecy has returned and so has God's reign and favor. Hence, Jesus was actualizing what was promised in the revelation of the prophecies of Isaiah. He does this without official title or recognition. He does this as a prophet who will make real for people God's reign through deeds and words. "Jesus is the revelation of God precisely as the man anointed by the Spirit of God to herald and usher in the reign of God" (Yong 2005, 86) (Yong draws on Spirit-Christology, for an overview, see Myk Habets 2010). Supremely, he will do this through his death and resurrection as the critical challenge and energizing new imagination of his prophetic mission.

The content and function of prophecy has been defined as "the dynamic actualization of revelation" (Hvidt 2007, 126). Jesus "dynamically actualizes" (!) in his mission the revelation of who God is for us and who God is in himself, Father, Son, and Spirit. Full of the Spirit of prophecy, Jesus not only prophesies about God, but is also himself the Word of God as revealed in his mission as a man fulfilling Israel's story. He does this in his life, death, and resurrection and in sending the Spirit. Jesus continues his prophetic mission through the Spirit.

The prophetic mission of the church is the call to the "dynamic actualization" of *this* revelation of Jesus by the power of the Spirit of prophecy. Prophetic mission is a cross-shaped mission filled with resurrection power. Guided by the Spirit, and shaped by the revelation of Jesus, prophetic mission actualizes the gospel for our place and time – the kingdom come. Making revelation real is not a comfortable calling. Those who dynamically actualize the revelation of God are challenging people. They listen to what God is saying about how, where, and when to actualize the good news, and they do it – they prophesy.

The confidence we can now have about Jesus and his mission can be set out as follows:

1. In compiling a reliable interpretation of Jesus' mission, the big-picture memories of Jesus are more important than detailed investigations of verses and passages.
2. Jesus needs to be interpreted in the context of Second Temple Judaism (its apocalyptic eschatology), without the mediation of our own metaphysics, mysticism, or social–political patterns of Christianity.
3. Jesus' worldview influences the big-picture memories about him because these big-picture worldviews were part of the early mission of Jesus which he shaped; they were also part of the mission of the disciples when they were with Jesus and which they carried over into the Christian mission after Pentecost in continuing the mission of Jesus.
4. The New Testament tradition of Jesus' mission is the governing motif of Christian mission. As such, Jesus the Prophet proclaims the message, becomes the message, and continues to proclaim the message that he has become, i.e., post-Easter, by the Spirit.
5. Jesus' big-picture worldviews of mission are to be interpreted in our time and context as part of prophesying the good news, bearing in mind the diversity of mission traditions and their host cultures. Prophetic mission is the actualizing of the apostolic God of Jesus.

Prophetic mission must be able to confidently affirm the gospel, but it needs to be able to do this in a dialogical way that incorporates the importance of worldview and way of life: "Mission must by all means be dialogical, since it is nothing else finally than the participation in the dialogical nature of the triune, missionary God. But it must be prophetic as well, since, at bottom, there can be no real dialogue when truth is not expressed and clearly articulated" (Bevans and Schroeder 2004, 398).

Yet, this prophetic affirmation of the gospel also needs to be done holistically to represent the holistic nature of the good news. Hence, as two leading missiologists, Bevans and Schroeder, suggest, and as shown in Table 61.1, there are at least six components to mission: the first three are practical (and condense the Anglican five marks of mission); and the second three set the new mission context and its theological challenges. The second three indicate the need for deeper theological reflection about the context of the Five Marks of Mission.

**Table 61.1:**    The Six Components and Five Marks of Mission of Jesus' Prophetic Mission.

| | |
|---|---|
| "Mission must by all means be dialogical since it is nothing else finally than the participation in the dialogical nature of the triune, missionary God. But it must be prophetic as well, since, at bottom, there can be no real dialogue when truth is not expressed and clearly articulated." (p.398) | "Mission goes out from God. Mission is God's way of loving and saving the world . . . .. So mission is never our invention, or choice." Lambeth Conference 1998 |

| SIX COMPONENTS | FIVE MARKS OF MISSION |
|---|---|
| 1.  Witness and Proclamation | 1.  To proclaim the good news of the Kingdom |
| 2.  Liturgy, prayer, and contemplation | 2.  To teach, baptize, and nurture new believers |
| 3.  Justice, peace, and integrity of creation | 3.  **To respond to human need by loving service** |
| 4.  Interreligious dialogue | 4.  To seek to transform unjust structures in society |
| 5.  Inculturation | 5.  To strive to safeguard the integrity of creation, and sustain and renew the life of the earth |
| 6.  Reconciliation | |

An accessible exploration of a theology that might resource a new prophetic but dialogical approach to mission is found in S. B. Bevans and R. P. Schroeder's *Prophetic Dialogue: Reflections on Christian Mission Today*, which builds on their concluding chapter in *Constants in Context: A Theology of Mission for Today*. Prophetic dialogue has an internal pluralism, reflecting the untidy nature of history and human interaction and reciprocity. It offers a vision for a mixed economy of *mission*, and not just "the mixed economy of church"[7]. This mixed economy of mission has a rationale, a grammar[8], which allows for the kind of flexibility needed for relational mission that

---

[7] The term "the mixed economy church" was first used by Rowan Williams when he was Archbishop of Wales. Here, I am suggesting that we need to take this further and talk of a mixed economy of mission: an economy that is fundamental and more than merely instrumental, having its roots in the nature of God's own mixed economy of Trinitarian mission. I would also want to suggest that a more robust understanding of a mixed economy of church would also require more than the recognition of temporary "fresh expressions" of parochial church in new networks or worship styles; there needs to be a thorough embracing of both modality (parochial) and sodality (associational/mission society) structures as a pattern inherent and necessary for an effective mission-shaped church – as has been seen throughout the centuries. In Anglican ecclesiology, I would add that the historic episcopacy offers a way of holding together the modality and sodality structures in a relational unity, i.e., the episcopacy as "nodality." See Winter, Ralf. 1999. Two Structures of God's Redemptive Mission. *Perspectives on the World Christian Movement*, 3rd edition. Pasadena: William Carey Library, pp. 220–30.

[8] Here, grammar refers to more than the rules of the language of faith; it also suggests that our language enables us to refer to the world in relation to God. Yet, to recognize that we have a grammar is to acknowledge that we have a particular perspective on how we see the world, but as Christians we believe that our grammar not only coheres with the world but is also the grammar for God's knowledge of us through the revelation of his relationship with us in Jesus. There is for some, therefore, an asymmetrical relationship in revelation that would lead to an asymmetry in the analogy of mission. See Thacker, Justin. 2007. *Postmodernism and the Ethics of Theological Knowledge*. Aldershot: Ashgate, p. 44.

crosses the barriers of cultural diversity. It has the potential to provide the basis for the "deep theology" that is needed for new mission.

Deep theology is the reworking of the great traditions which, in normal times, are used as a ready-to-hand resource for reflection and practical wisdom. In times of great change, these resources (mission capital), and the traditions from which they are drawn, are remade in dialogue with culture and other faiths and with a vision and practice for reconciliation in all aspects of life. We are in such a time. Bevans and Schroeder offer one approach to what this might mean for exploring the constants of faith: for Christ, eschatology, salvation, church, humanity, and culture. Table 61.2 is a summary of their overview, indicating the level of theological reworking taking place in the apostolic capital.[9]

**Table 61.2:**   Bevans and Schroeder: Approaches to mission.

| Constants in Context Part III: Chaps 9–12 | A. Law: Mission as Proclamation [Minister?] Preaching | B. Truth: Mission as Participation [Priest?] Witness | C. Mission as Liberation [Parson?] Service | B/C &A: Prophetic Dialogue Missionary-M/P/P 6 mission practices |
|---|---|---|---|---|
| Christ | High Christology Atonement: Substitutionary; Exclusivist | Spirit-Christology Atonement: Exemplary Inclusive/ pluralist | From Below Atonement: deep symbol, liberation Pluralist/ inclusivist | Spirit-Christology Atonement: Exemplary liberation Modified inclusivist |
| Eschatology | Future and now but started; individualist | Started and historical; history & individual | Started and historical | Historical and communal |
| Salvation | Spiritual – personalist and/ or thru church | Holistic including creation | Holistic liberation of creation | Holistic and all of creation |
| Church | Hierarchical and/ or voluntarist mission community | Body of Christ & people of God; missional symbol | Chaplain: servant sacrament – God's pilgrim people | Communion-in-Mission; missional pilgrim people |
| Humanity | In God's image but sinful; individualist | God's image marred; all things | Fulfillment of potential by Spirit | Communal and cosmic |
| Culture | 'translate' gospel and need to be counter-cultural | Critical but positive need for inculturation | Reflects God's goodness but needs challenging | Critically positive inculturation and alternative models |

[9] This chart is based on a compilation of a number of charts found in Bevans and Schroeder. It also draws on Billings, Alan. 2010. *Making God Possible*. London: SPCK for the ministry headings to which I have added "missionary." On the relevance of the prophetic perspective for interpreting the meaning of "missionary" in the English context, see Peter Sedgwick's chapter on "Anglican Theology" in Ford, D. and R. Muers, eds. 2005. *The Modern Theologians*. Oxford: Blackwell, pp. 178–194, and Chapter 2 in Plant, Raymond. 2001. *Politics, Theology and History*. Cambridge: CUP, pp. 25–43.

# CATHOLIC

While the vision of global Christianity is invigorating, relating this to the processes of globalization is disconcerting. I begin with some summary definitions of globalization and then explore the sharp critique of globalization from the perspective of postcolonial studies.

## Globalization and postcolonialism

In sum, globalization can best be understood as a set of transforming processes, driven primarily by economic and technological impulses but having an impact on virtually every sphere of life, including politics, culture, education, religion, and the family. These processes generate networks of interaction that transcend the previous boundaries between the spheres. The intensification and institutionalization of global interconnectedness through new global and regional infrastructures of control and communication is unprecedented. As such, globalization marks a new era in human affairs (Heslam 2002, 13).

Whatever else, the reality of globalization means that any faith aiming to be a global faith is going to be changed. The question is how global faith can itself contribute to and critique other aspects of globalization in the emerging new patterns of human affairs. One of the givens of the globalization of interaction is that there is no longer an essential core to cultural identity – something an older paradigm of mission took for granted in its approach to inculturation. As Steger (2003, 76) argues, "hardly any society in the world today possesses an 'authentic' self-contained culture." Along with this, we also see the delinking of identity with territory as communication between people becomes global through technology and travel. Yet, this change is paradoxically combined with a resurgence of the importance of place as the focus of the local. Localization goes with globalization.

One way of addressing the significance of globalization is to explore how the interaction that is now possible between people and cultures has led to a critique of the colonial era, when European cultures and nations dominated much of the southern hemisphere. Postcolonial studies look at what colonialism did and is still doing, and what is happening to cultures north and south as globalization enables interaction.

There are three streams of postcolonialism: "The first carries the notion of invasion and control; the second places enormous investment in recovering the cultural soul; and the third stresses *mutual interdependence and transformation*" (Sugirtharajah 2001, 248, *emphasis mine*). The third stream is the one which offers the most positive way to engage with colonialism, though this does not imply that this stream lacks the concerns of the other two streams; rather, the third integrates these concerns in a discourse that offers more hope for our future.

## Some definitions

It is important to distinguish between describing what is happening globally and evaluating it. Steger suggests that we should differentiate between the social condition of globality, the social processes of globalization, and the ideology of globalism:

> *Globality:* "a *social condition* characterised by the existence of global economic, political, cultural, and environmental interconnections and flows that make many of the existing borders and boundaries irrelevant" (Steger 2003, 7).

> *Globalization:* "a *set of social processes* that are thought to transform our present social condition into one of globality. At its core, then, globalization is about shifting forms of human contact" (Steger 2003, 8).

> *Globalism:* "an *ideology* that endows the concept of globalization with neoliberal values and meaning" (Steger 2003, 94).

That is, globalism uses globalization to establish a certain form of globality that is said to be inevitable, liberal, anonymous, beneficial, and democratic.

From a Christian point of view, globality is something that could be seen as very much in line with the vision of mission: that all should know the One who fills all in all – the Lord Jesus Christ – and in knowing him find themselves in fellowship with all others. That there are social processes, resulting in another form of globality, is what the term "globalization" identifies; and that there is clear apology for these processes is how some see globalism as an ideology that defends powerful interests. In relation to globalization and globalism, the Christian faith will have a range of responses, from critique and challenge to welcome and its pragmatic use (e.g., Internet technology).

For some, the ideology of globalism is the focus of the postcolonial critique of globalization. As Robert Young (2003, 4) suggests:

> . . . postcolonialism involves first of all the argument that the nations of the three non-Western continents (Africa, Asia and Latin America) are largely in a situation of subordination to Europe and North America, and in a position of economic inequality. Postcolonialism names a politics and philosophy of activism that contests that disparity, and so continues in a new way the anti-colonial struggles of the past. It asserts the right of African, Asian, and Latin American peoples to access resources and material well-being, but also the dynamic powers of their cultures, cultures that are now intervening in and transforming the societies of the West.

For some, this intervention from the south in the north will take a militant tone; for others, who follow in the third stream of mutual independence and transformation, there is the possibility of creating something positive out of the conditions of globalism which are not necessarily the processes of globalization or the ideology that goes with it. Nevertheless, there is a need to redress the imbalance of power and influence, and so it is true to say that postcolonialism, as a movement, is always an insurgent one: "Postcolonialism, or triconninentalism, is a general name for [these] insurgent knowledges that come from the subaltern, the dispossessed, and seek to change the terms and values under which we live" (Young 2003, 20).[10]

This critique can be applied to the past analogous relationship between the mission theology and colonialism. The present writing on mission history includes a reevaluation of the worldview, or ideology, that goes with mission (see, e.g., Andrew Porter's (2004, 11) *Religion versus Empire*, which aims to take seriously the "sources of mission inspiration" as part of the exploration of mission history). However, this new concern for worldview can be seen to cut both ways. For some, mission had an ideology that went with colonialism, but for others, mission had a worldview (and an accompanying process) that was against colonialism. Therefore, there may be a continuity between mission in the former colonial period and that of today, in that there is a shared worldview that cannot be tied to colonialism or postcolonial globalism.

It was Lamin Sanneh's research on the impact of mission which began to open up the question of intentionality. Sanneh focused on the seemingly unintentional consequences of the Christian commitment to transmit the gospel to another culture, particularly through the translation of the Christian Scriptures. Sanneh (1980, 11) noted that in contrast with Islam, "Christianity seeks to take shelter in the flowering of local culture and tradition which in the independent African churches assumes eruptive force but which nevertheless exists even in the historic churches under the agency of African recipients." Developing his thesis further, Sanneh (1991, 1) went on to expound his great insight into the nature of Christian mission and the character of God's relation to us:

> . . . Christianity, from its origins, identified itself with the need to translate out of Aramaic and Hebrew, and from that position came to exert a dual force in its historical development. One was the resolve to relativize its Judaic roots, with the consequence that it promoted significant aspects of those roots. The other was to destigmatize Gentile culture and adopt that culture as a natural extension of the life of the new religion. This action to *destigmatize* complemented the other action to *relativize*. Thus it was that the two subjects, the Judaic and the Gentile, became closely intertwined in the Christian dispensation, both crucial to the formative image of the new religion.

### Reconstructing Catholic ecclesiology

From the perspective of globality, ecclesiology is going to look different now than it did during colonialism when the European universals appeared to be imposed and were forced to become other people's absolutes. However, as we have seen in Sanneh's work,

---

[10] One way of interpreting the crisis in the Anglican Communion is that it expresses the insurgency of tricontinental Anglicans who in the cause of "righteousness" have sought to change the values and terms of Northern Anglicans and to challenge the ongoing imposition of postcolonial causes of "liberal justice."

this mono-cultural perspective on what is universally significant was challenged by the processes of mission itself by those who received the gospel. To develop an ecclesiology in global perspective will require an approach which is able to include the changes implied in the postcolonial critique of the use of knowledge and the use of power (and both in combination), but also include the wider better intentions of the gospel and of those who share the gospel.

There are a number of ways in which theological perspectives are developed. Hunt (2005) suggests that three of these are analogy, the "mysteries of faith," and eschatology.[11] Hunt uses the strategy of the interconnection of the mysteries in her own writing as the one most appropriate to the global context of twenty-first century theology. Yet, as she hints, it may be that the third strategy is equally able to bear the load of developing an appropriate approach for a global perspective (Hunt 2005, 230). I tend toward prioritizing the third strategy, but using the logic of analogy and including the mysteries of faith. This method provides the most open approach to the relationship between God and history, and between the church and the future of humanity, i.e., the constants (mysteries) of faith.[12] Such an approach coheres, I believe, with Taylor's and Allen's proposals for a mission spirituality which I will review later.

Hence, in reconstructing ecclesiology in global perspective, I suggest that, first, we need to recognize that all theological language is going to be analogous – with a proviso about the limits of human language and yet a confidence in affirmations of theological truth (see I. U. Dalferth 1988, 200f, on the rule of analogy). Second, we can follow Hunt in using the mysteries of faith as *constants* which, in their variety of interconnectedness, can form a framework for the diverse expressions of faith in *contexts* across the world and throughout history. This strategy is taken up by Bevans and Schroeder (2004) in their overview of the theology and history of mission, where, as we have seen, they suggest six constants – Christology, ecclesiology, eschatology, salvation, anthropology, and culture – and three theological types of interconnection. (For an extended reflection, see my "Discipleship: Marked for Mission" in Andrew Walls and Cathy Ross [2008].)

However, third, my suggestion is that we must integrate an eschatological strategy in developing ecclesiology in global perspective. As was indicated earlier, a renewed Christology, following the Enlightenment, will require a return to the eschatology of the Biblical sources. Here, we may also add the weight of Karl Barth's own rediscovery of eschatology which led him to affirm in his second commentary on *Romans* that:

---

[11] Hunt explains these three approaches as follows: The three strategies that we dare to speak with a measure of confidence about the sacred mysteries are thus: (1) by analogy with the truths known naturally; (2) from the interconnection of the mysteries with one another; and (3) in reference to our final end and ultimate destiny (Hunt 2005, 2).

[12] There is an interesting correlation here between Hunt's three strategies and the three types of theology, called simply A, B, and C, which Bevans and Schroeder identify (*op cit*, 35–7) as persisting throughout the mission history of the church. Type A began in Carthage, its key word is Law, and it is more "conservative"; Type B began in Alexandria, its key word is Truth, and it is more "liberal"; and Type C began in Antioch, its key word is History, and it is more "radical." (For a recent view on the latter, see Braaten, C. E. and R. W. Jensen. 1984. *Christian Dogmatics*. Philadelphia: Fortress Press.

"Christianity which is not entirely and completely eschatology . . . is entirely and completely contrary to Christ" (quoted in Dalferth 1988, 113).

What we need is a missional eschatology which affirms the possibility of an analogy of mission grounded in the historical mission of Jesus. This would acknowledge the complexity of the mysteries of God's mission, but relating these to the break in history and social order of Christ's coming. Introducing eschatology into this dynamic implies that God is open to history and history to God, and that provides an analogical knowledge of how God is mysteriously known through participation in the *missio Dei*, i.e., the analogy of mission.

Theological knowledge in this approach is orientational knowledge for interpreting God's mission through the call, the vocation, to practical participation in mission based on a vision of what humanity might be in Christ. As Rowan Williams (2005, 18) says, "The discovery that occurs in the practice of mission is that he [Jesus] is both native and stranger in all human contexts." Or, as he says elsewhere, "Christian theology celebrates a divine stranger who creates a common world; and in so doing it establishes once and for all the possibility of a humanity that does not depend for its harmony on any transient human alliances or definitions of common interest or purpose" (Williams 2005, 114).

# HOLY

## Set apart for mission

"It [is] necessary to go back to the biblical vision that conceives mission as God's initiative coming from God's love for his creation and from his design in choosing some instruments to use for the salvation and blessing of all of humankind" (Escobar 2003, 24). What the preceding requires is a fresh expression of God's "instruments" – the church – in the new context of today's world and twenty-first-century mission. In Anglican terms, this may lead to changes as significant as those of the Reformation and the "Faith and Order" developments that culminated in the Hanoverian period of the Church of England. I believe that the proposed Anglican Covenant provides this opportunity (see my article "Covenant for Communion in Mission" on the Anglican Communion Institute website: www.anglicancommunion institute.com [articles 2007]). In simple terms, I propose this necessary fresh expression is the conscious integration of the modern missionary movement into Anglican identity. Crucial to this is the recognition that there would be no Anglican Communion today without evangelistic mission on the part of mission societies and intentional outreach by mission boards.

The "eschatological breakthrough" of these initiatives into the ecclesiastical structures of Anglican churches (notably the Church of England and the Protestant Episcopal Church of the United States) cannot now be overlaid by a renewed affirmation of the structures which, in and of themselves, did not produce the mission which created the Anglican Communion (see Chapman 2006, Chs. 1, 4, 5, 6 and 7).

There needs to be a fresh expression of church which integrates the motivational and practical resources of the mission societies, which were part of the means by which the global Anglican Communion was generated, in today's context of globality and globalization. I suggest this will require an orientational knowledge, or a mission spirituality, based on an analogy of mission, leading to a confidence to make sense of twenty-first-century globality in and through the church locally and more widely.

Fresh expressions of the mission-shaped church arise as the church becomes the means by which people gain some orientation on the complexity of the world and are enabled in that complexity to have the confidence to take notice of, to focus on, some things and not others. You might call this a missionary spirituality. "The complexity of our world is thus reduced by selecting some of the available information and ignoring others, and the resulting *orientational knowledge* helps our actions by allowing us to locate ourselves in our world and to order the world with respect to us. Only knowledge with these kind of *localizing* and *organizing* functions is orientational knowledge" (Dalferth 1988, 204).

## Mission/ary societies and ecclesiastical structures

Andrew Porter (2004, 50) suggests that there are four patterns for how mission societies related to the church: "A society might organise itself on a basis at once voluntary and non-denominational, as did the LMS [London Mission Society]"; "Alternatively a society might be identified with a single strand or denomination of Christianity, but, while existing within the church, remain as a separate voluntary body in no way controlled by any church authorities" (like the Church Missionary Society, CMS); "Then again, a missionary society might be constituted as a formal arm of the church or denomination, subject to church leaders and those whom they delegated their authority" (like Society for the Propagation of the Gospel, SPG); "Finally and often equally constraining, there was the Wesleyan Methodists' arrangement in which their missionary society was in a very real sense one with the denomination."

Missional expressions of church can take any of these four approaches, but in Anglican terms the most successful have been options two and three.[13] However, what connects these approaches to missional expressions of church and the current need for a global perspective on ecclesiology is not the ecclesiastical arrangements, but two other things. The first is a recognition that these missional expressions are fresh expressions of *church*, i.e., that they are ecclesial communities. The second is a confidence that, in their participation in mission, these communities are in fact participating in God's mission; they are analogies of the *missio Dei* in seeking to make known the coming

---

[13] I have suggested, in footnote 7, that a thoroughgoing mixed economy of a mission-shaped church would need to embrace both modality and sodality structures. In *The Mission and Ministry of the Whole Church* (London: General Synod, 2007, 34), the modern missionary movement, of which the USPG, CMS, and other mission societies are a part, is recognized as having influenced the development of the Church of England's ministry and order in three ways: mission is now central, new ministry is pioneered creatively, and laypeople and women are being included.

Kingdom. (Interestingly, Philip Jenkins [2007, 73–86], in his book titled *God's Continent: Christianity, Islam, and Europe's Religious Crisis*, recognizes the importance of new ecclesial movements.)

### Missionary spirituality: Taylor (CMS) and Allen (SPG)

Allen and Taylor were two Anglican mission leaders and thinkers who asked: Why we do the things we do in ministry? They made suggestions about fresh expressions based on the vision of a mission-shaped church. They came at this question from the angle of having been convinced that one of the keys to developing a new perspective on the church was to take seriously the work of the Holy Spirit. They adopted different approaches to the Holy Spirit, but their perspectives are surprisingly similar. Their proposals about fresh expressions of a missional church are summarized in two phrases "the least possible withdrawal" of Christians from mission in the world (Taylor 1972, 148), and "Do you deliver?" – both the Christian tradition and its effective mission (Allen) (Long and Rowthorn 1998, 388).

*Taylor's theology* is rooted in a well-developed doctrine of the Trinity in which the inter-penetration of the Persons (their one-another-ness or perichoresis) is enabled by the Go-Between Person of the Holy Spirit.[14] This one-another-ness is reflected in the nature of creation, the salvation made possible in Jesus, and the recreation by the Spirit in the renewal of all things, moving toward a final consummation. In the meantime, we live and suffer in the Spirit in the long wait between Pentecost and Parousia:

> To be the very power of God yet to wait in frustration and hope until the whole be brought to fulfilment, might be called the kenosis, or self-emptying, of the Holy Spirit. For him it has been so from the beginning. If now we are caught up into his being, we must share his humiliation as well as his power (J. Taylor 1972, 115).

A key insight from Taylor (1972, 133) is that "Our theology would improve if we thought more of the church being given to the Spirit than the Spirit being given to the church." This view results in putting the Spirit's mission first and then asking how the church participates in this mission by the Spirit and what the best way is of doing that. For Taylor, the mission of the Spirit is focused on the recreation of the wider world. This is therefore the sphere of the church in mission. "For the church is essentially scattered, like seed in the earth, salt in the stew, yeast in the dough. The Christian's milieu is the world because that is the milieu of the Holy Spirit" (J. Taylor 1972, 147). For Taylor, this does not mean letting the world set the agenda; it means developing an authentic discipleship:

[14] For a review of the different patterns for interpreting the Holy Spirit, see MacIntyre, J. 1997. *The Shape of Pneumatology*. Edinburgh: T&T Clark, Ch. 1. MacIntyre offers three basic types: Biblical/Definitional Model, Hypostatic Model, and Dynamic Model. Taylor falls into a variant of the Hypostatic Model, whereas Allen seems to include bits of both the Biblical/Definitional and the Dynamic Models.

Irrelevance and cheap relevance are equally caused by my failure to visualise what it will mean to respond to Jesus Christ in the real world in which I, with others, do a job, enjoy a home, think and interact. The disciples waiting in the upper room in Jerusalem had an uncomfortably clear idea of what it would mean if they started to live the life of Jesus in that city. But somewhere along the road the church stopped being so specific about its appeal to men (J. Taylor 1972, 115).

The purpose of Christian fellowship, "one-another-ness," is therefore to keep alive the vision and expression of "the most characteristic forms of the action of the Spirit as Creator Redeemer." As Taylor goes on to explain, these forms of action are three: "the constant pressure towards greater personhood, the creation of new occasions for choice, and the principle of self-surrender in responsibility for others. These are the marks of any evangelism which is truly Christ's evangelism" (J. Taylor 1972, 136).

*The local is the global*    This leads Taylor (1972, 148) to articulate a fundamental prin-ciple: "the ideal shape of the church is such as will provide this 'one-another-ness' with *the least possible withdrawal of Christians from their corporateness with their fellow men in the world.*" The mission shape of the church, in which there is the least possible with-drawal from the world, is found, suggests Taylor, in "little congregations." These "Chris-tian cells and house-churches" are not meant to be the means by which the uncommitted are drawn back into parish life or as interim structures that will grow into a full-orbed parish. Rather, these groups have the responsibilities of the local church and are called to express the fullness of Christ. The parish church may be the cathedral gathering for these groups, "But it is the 'little congregations' which must become normative if the church is to respond to the Spirit's movements in the life of the world" (1972 149).

To these little congregations are given the responsibilities of being church: reflection (or teaching), service, worship (including the sacraments), and evangelism. While there are dangers in fragmentation and the question of the universal nature of the church, Taylor (1972, 151) believes that this local church is worth the risk: "Through the apostolate of a continual interchange of persons the separate groups are linked and mutually responsible, being open to the life of the world they find in their mission their meeting place with one another."

We might see in Taylor a strong commitment to contextual mission – local church.

*Allen's theology* could almost start (except that he came earlier) where Taylor's ends up. In *The Spontaneous Expansion of the Church,* he argues that the New Testament Church grew as little groups sprang up as a result of Christians witnessing to their faith:

The Church expanded simply by organizing these little groups as they were converted, handing on to them the organization which she had received from her first founders. It was itself a unity composed of a multitude of little churches any one of which could propagate itself, and consequently the reception of any new group of Christians was a very simple matter (Allen 1927/2006, 143).

Similar to Taylor, Allen (1927/2006, 10) suggests that it is in the daily life of disciple-ship that the church expands: "Spontaneous expansion begins with the individual effort of the individual Christian to assist his fellow, when common experience, common difficulties, common toil have first brought the two together." What generates this voluntary expression is the Holy Spirit who creates missionary zeal. However, this happens when, as Allen argues, we follow the two principles of St. Paul's missionary method: "St. Paul was a preacher of a Gospel, not of a law" and "He practised retirement, not simply by restraint, but willingly" (Allen 1912/2006, 149f). Both of these principles recognize that it is the Spirit who is promised and given by Christ in the hearing of the gospel, and it is the Spirit who will lead believers into all truth as they seek to follow Christ in their local context. Allen therefore radicalizes the "three-self" strategy (churches should become self-supporting, self-governing, and self-extending) and proposes an extreme reliance on the Holy Spirit with minimalist post-mission contact with others.

However, this does not mean that little groups of Christians are abandoned: "To watch and assist spontaneous expansion is certainly not to abandon converts to their own devices" (Allen 1927/2006, 154). In fact, the "little group must be fully equipped with spiritual power and authority; and the bishop ought to deliver to them the Creeds, the Gospel, the Sacraments and the Ministry by solemn and deliberate act. It is to do that work that we have missionary bishops" (Allen 1927/2006, 147). Allen believed that the Spirit would take the newly planted church beyond even the three-self strategy of planting churches which are self-supporting, self-governing, and self-extending. The Spirit, if relied upon, would ensure that such churches would not stagnate but continue to expand spontaneously.

*The global is the local*    This then is what it means to answer Allen's question, "Do you Deliver?" And in the book which provided the basic perspective for *Spontaneous Expansion* and *Missionary Methods*, Allen outlines the fundamental principles of missionary zeal, or mission spirituality. Zeal is based on the life of the Spirit in the believer and not on following a rule or a law or supporting a mission society. It is as the Spirit is received in relation to a growth in the knowledge of the revelation of hope in Christ (for the individual, the church, and the world through the church) that true missionary zeal is born. "Missionary life begins with an act of reception; missionary zeal grows upon the knowledge of the Spirit so received; missionary work is the expression of the Spirit in activity" (Allen 1913/2006, 59). Some words of Allen's could have been written for us today:

> Only in the last few years have we begun to grasp what a world-wide communion might mean. Already we are expecting new ideas of virtue, new aspects of the Truth of Christ. We begin to understand what the foundation of native Churches in China or in Japan, in India and in Africa may mean for us all, bringing to us new conceptions of the manifold working of the Spirit of Christ. We begin to understand that a world-wide communion does not involve the destruction of local characteristics, that a world-wide communion is a communion, a unity, catholic, apostolic, not a loose federation of mutually suspicious societies. This sense of the corporate unity has come to us late, and we have scarcely begun to see what it is; but we see that it is the manifestation of Christ (Allen 1913/2006, 51).

As we face the crisis in the Anglican Communion, let us ask whether we are being given the opportunity to discover the communion for what it truly is and could become: a fresh expression of church as a communion in mission (see *Communion in Mission* [ACO 2006], Chapter 2, for an exploration of this theme in an official report). In order for this to happen, we shall need all the missionary zeal and the risk-taking experiments that Allen and Taylor have encouraged us to explore. They do not offer us a blueprint for the church in an era of globalization, but they do challenge us to be bold with our fresh expressions because there is so much more of Christ for us to discover as we are led by his Spirit.

I have reviewed the possibilities of a new perspective of the church by beginning with Apostolic, and then in the context of Catholic globalization. Here, I have considered those who have, in previous years, sought to pursue missional expressions of church within the wider hope of the Holy Spirit's work through Christ in a global context. From this exploration, we may draw the courage to face the challenges which will come to us as we seek to orient ourselves in a complex and fast-changing world. I conclude this section with words from William Taylor. May they envision us as we go forward in God's Holy mission.

> We stand at the start of this uncertain new century, this new millennium. New language and categories have entered our lives. We speak of globalization, and we witness the world-view transitions from pre-modernity to modernity to post-modernity with their respective blessings and curses. Regardless of our culture, our gender, our geography, and our ministry, the times have radically changed, requiring a serious *re-evaluation of why we do the things we do in ministry whether personal or organizational* (W. D. Taylor 2000, 8, *emphasis mine*).

## ONE

"Considering Christianity as a global reality can make us see the whole religion in a radically new perspective, which is startling and, often, uncomfortable" (Jenkins 2002, 215). Fresh expressions of church are making us aware of things we have taken for granted about our church culture – the wallpaper to which we have become accustomed. It makes us think again about those things we take for granted which have provided the glue, the oneness, a particular perspective, tradition, or culture.

> We have long been used to a Christian theology that was shaped by the interaction of Christian faith with Greek philosophy and Roman law. We are equally accustomed, though not usually so conscious of its origins, to ecclesiology and codes of practice shaped by Christian interaction with the traditional law and custom of the German and Slavic tribes beyond the Roman frontiers. These forms have become so familiar and established that we have come to think of them as the normal and characteristic forms of Christianity (Walls 2002a, 1).

Exploring missional expressions of church in a Western context encourages us to become conscious of presuppositions, and so helps us to make sense of local church in the context of the church worldwide. However, this deeper awareness of our own context also highlights how in the West we are alienated from the past. It is like another culture, and yet it is the culture in which our understanding of faith in Christ is rooted. With the collapse of the ancient synthesis of church and culture in Christendom, we are now "resident aliens" in a post-Enlightenment culture:

> The three pillars of orthodox Christology (mysticism, metaphysics and a socio-political settlement), upon which both a common religion and a common culture were built, collapsed. Consequently, Christology suffered a series of ignominious defeats, the most obvious of which was the equivocation that now surrounded the socio-political status and function of religion. The privatisation of religion and the construction of a new political settlement, based on the persuasive idea of the social contract, entailed that a universal common religion (i.e., one, holy, catholic and apostolic church) gave way to the notion of a universal common humanity (Greene 2003, 350).

It is disconcerting to be confronted like this, but perhaps it is the only way to truly connect with others who have another understanding of faith, Jesus, and life. Missionary or missional church should therefore connect us with the principle and the possibility of a new *Christian* vision of a common humanity – we are members of a *global* faith: "Global Christianity is a recent phrase, but not a recent idea. It expresses what has always been the Christian *principle*. The early church reflected it" (Walls 2006, 36, *emphasis mine*).

Walls (2006, 37, *emphasis mine*) suggests that those same possibilities present themselves today, reflecting what the early church looked like in following the principle of a global faith: "Curiously enough, the conditions of the twentieth and twenty-first centuries have brought about the *possibility* of renewing both the apostolic model of the church that first arose in Antioch and the catholic model of active participation in a worldwide multicultural church in ante-Nicene times."

Elsewhere Walls (2002b, 78) explains what he means, with particular reference to Ephesians:

> If I understand what Paul says in Ephesians correctly, it is as though Christ himself is growing as the different cultures are brought together. The Ephesian moment – the social coming together of people of two cultures to experience Christ – was quite brief. In our day the Ephesian moment has come again, and come in a richer mode . . . since the first century. Developments over several centuries . . . mean that we have innumerable cultures in the church.

While this new vision for a global faith may be emerging – for Europeans from the refinement of the Enlightenment – there remain great challenges in developing a global perspective on the church and in the practical outworking of a global faith: "The church in the twenty-first century faces the dual challenge of a non-Christian West and a non-Western Christianity, and the complex relationship between the two" (Laing 2006, 165).

However, once again, Walls sees here a pattern that has emerged before in the history of mission. Christianity rises and falls rather than retains territory in the way that Islam seeks to do. That Christendom was such a territorial expression of faith means that the decline of European Christianity may be disconcerting but also liberating. However, for Walls, the Lord is at work:

> The recession of Christianity among the European peoples appears to be continuing. And yet we seem to stand at the threshold of a new age of Christianity, one in which its main base will be in the Southern continents, and where its dominant expressions will be filtered through culture of those countries. Once again, Christianity has been saved for the world by its diffusion across cultural lines (quoted in Escobar 2003, 13).

To hold to such a view requires a reconstruction of our belief in Jesus that is beyond the limitations of one particular cultural perspective; it requires a return to an eschatological interpretation of Jesus. An interpretation in which eschatology is understood, in Greene's words, "as a set of metaphors that refer to climatic events (most notably the exile and the crucifixion/resurrection) that tear the fabric of history apart. Consequently they offer proposals and possibilities for a new social order" (Greene 2003, 355).

## Jesus is the ONE

Christianity has always been a religion on many continents which has ebbed and flowed and come again in fresh expressions. This pattern has been generated largely by migrational mission, but has been sustained by intentional evangelism. Thus, the "faith and order" of the church has emerged out of mission, not vice-versa. Or, as Bevans and Schroeder (2004, 13) say, "mission . . . is prior to the church, and is constitutive of its very existence," so "as mission takes shape so does the church." Hence, the mission-shaped church is foundational to all fresh expressions: ". . . a missional church ecclesiology stresses that the church's very existence has been sent into the world. It fulfills its sent-ness as much by its presence and the quality of its life in the gospel as it does by its actions and communications" (Hunsberger 2003, 110).

Yet, it is easy for discussions about church to be conducted purely in the "ecclesiastical" sphere without using missional ecclesiology, i.e., without taking into account the fundamental issue at stake: that it is *through mission itself* that the fullness of Christ is expressed, and it is in that expression that the hope of a new humanity is revealed.

We pursue mission, because it is in the practice of mission that we find the full truth of Christ for ourselves as, we hope, for others; and we go on doing Christology because it makes sense of mission. In both, we discover who we are and who we can be in relation to Jesus, the incarnate word – members of the new humanity, at peace with itself and its maker, dependent on one another for our good, living from the grace of Christ as we live in the community of mutual creative service. Of this reality, this marriage of heaven and earth, there will always be more to find and more to celebrate (Williams 1994, 23f).

The celebration of this "more" includes the conversion and renewal of cultures in Christ as each one, through the variety of Christian communities within a culture, expresses the ultimate significance of Jesus. Thus, mission has no less an issue at stake than the ultimate significance of Jesus:

> It is the Lordship of Christ which is in question. Either he is the Lord of all possible worlds and cultures, or he is the Lord of one world and one culture only. Either we must think of the Christian mission in terms of bringing the Muslim, the Hindu, the Animist into Christendom, or we must go with Christ . . . and watch with him . . . as he becomes – dare we say it – Muslim, Hindu or Animist, as once he became Man and a Jew (J. Taylor 1963, 105).

The fresh expression of the church as Apostolic, Catholic, Holy, and One church is an important opportunity because it is one of the means that God is using to help Christians rediscover God's overriding concern for mission revealed in the historical mission of Jesus. It offers Christians the opportunity to taste pioneer missionary life and work for themselves, and to go back to basics. In going back to the basics, Christians can ask the fundamental questions of faith, particularly about the revelation of Christ in mission – about the ultimate significance of Jesus for all peoples.

## Bibliography

Allen, Roland. 1912/2006. *Missionary Methods – St Paul's or Ours?* Cambridge: Lutterworth.

Allen, Roland. 1913/2006. *Missionary Principles – and Practice.* Cambridge: Lutterworth.

Allen, Roland. 1927/2006. *The Spontaneous Expansion of the Church – and the Cause which Hinder it.* Cambridge: Lutterworth.

Bevans, Stephen B. and Roger P. Schroeder. 2004. *Constants in Context: A Theology of Mission for Today.* Maryknoll: Orbis.

Braaten, C. E. and R. W. Jensen. 1984. *Christian Dogmatics.* Philadelphia: Fortress.

*Communion in Mission.* 2006. London: Anglican Communion Office.

Chapman, Mark. 2006. *Anglicanism: A Very Short Introduction.* Oxford: Oxford University Press.

Dakin, Timothy J. 2007. Covenant for Communion in Mission. www.anglicancommunioninstitute.com articles 2007.

Dakin, Timothy J. 2008. Discipleship: Marked for Mission. In *Mission in the Twenty-First Century: Exploring the Five Marks of Global Mission,* eds. Andrew Walls and Cathy Ross. Maryknoll: Orbis.

Dalferth, Ingolf U. 1988. *Theology and Philosophy.* Oxford: Blackwell.

Escobar, Samuel. 2003. *The New Global Mission.* Downers Grove: IVP.

Flett, John G. 2010a. *The Witness of God: The Trinity, Missio Dei, Karl Barth, and the Nature of Christian Community.* Grand Rapids: Eerdmans.

Flett, John G. 2010b. A Bastard in the Royal Family: Wither Mission? *Princeton Theological Review,* vol. xvi, no. 1 (Spring), pp. 17–31.

Gaillardetz, Richard R. 2008. *Ecclesiology for a Global Church: A People Called and Sent.* Maryknoll: Orbis.

Gonzalez, Justo. 1999. *Christian Thought Revisited.* Maryknoll: Orbis.

Greene, Colin. 2003. *Christology in Cultural Perspective: Marking out the Horizons.* Carlisle: Paternoster.

Habets, Myk. 2010. *The Anointed Son: A Trinitarian Spirit Christology.* Eugene: Pickwick.

Heslam, Peter S. 2002. *Globalization: Unravelling the New Capitalism*. Cambridge: Grove.

Hunsberger, George R. 2003. Evangelical Conversion towards Missional Ecclesiology. In *Evangelical Ecclesiology*, ed. John Stackhouse. Grand Rapids: Baker.

Hunt, Anne. 2005. *Trinity*. Maryknoll: Orbis.

Hvidt, N. C. 2007. *Christian Prophecy: The Post-Biblical Tradition*. Oxford: Oxford University Press.

Jenkins, Philip. 2002. *The Next Christendom: The Coming of Global Christianity*. Oxford: Oxford University Press.

Jenkins, Philip. 2007. *God's Continent: Christianity, Islam, and Europe's Religious Crisis*. Oxford: Oxford University Press.

Kreider, Alan and Eleanor Kreider. 2009. *Worship and Mission after Christendom*. Milton Keynes: Paternoster.

Laing, Mark. 2006. The Changing Face of Mission: Implications for the Southern Shift in Christianity. *Missiology*, vol. xxxiv, no. 2 (April).

Long, Charles H. and Ann Rowthorn. 1998. Roland Allen 1868–1947. In *Mission Legacies*, eds. G. Anderson et al. Maryknoll: Orbis.

McIntyre, John. 1997. *The Shape of Pneumatology: Studies in the Doctrine of the Holy Spirit*. Edinburgh: T&T Clark.

Porter, Andrew. 2004. *Religion versus Empire? British Protestant Missionaries and Overseas Expansion, 1700–1914*. Manchester: MUP.

Runcorn, David. 2006. *Spirituality Workbook*. London: SPCK.

Sanneh, Lamin. 1980. The Domestication of Islam and Christianity in African Societies. *Journal of Religion in Africa*, vol. 11, no. 1, pp. 1–12.

Sanneh, Lamin. 1991. *Translating the Message*. London: DLT.

Steger, Manfred B. 2003. *Globalization: A Very Short Introduction*. Oxford: Oxford University Press.

Sugirtharajah, R. S. 2001. *The Bible and the Third World: Precolonial, Colonial and Postcolonial Encounters*. Cambridge: Cambridge University Press.

Taylor, John V. 1963. *The Primal Vision: Christian Presence amid African Religion*. London: SCM.

Taylor, John V. 1972. *The Go-Between God: The Holy Spirit and the Christian Mission*. London: SCM.

Taylor, William D. 2000. Setting the Stage. In *Global Missiology for the 21st Century: The Igaussu Dialogue*, ed. W. D. Taylor. Grand Rapids: Baker.

Tickle, Phyllis. 2008. *The Great Emergence: How Christianity is Changing and Why*. Grand Rapids: Baker.

Walls, Andrew. 2002a. Eusebius Tries Again: The Task of Reconceiving and Re-envisioning the Study of Christian History. In *Enlarging the Story: Perspectives on Writing World Christian History*, ed. W. R. Shenk. Maryknoll: Orbis.

Walls, Andrew. 2002b. *The Cross-Cultural Process in Human History*. Edinburgh: T&T Clark.

Walls, Andrew. 2006. Evangelical and Ecumenical: The Rise and Fall of the Early Church Model. In *Evangelical, Ecumenical and Anabaptist Missiologists in Conversation*, eds. J. R. Krabill et al. Maryknoll: Orbis.

Williams, R. D. 1994. *Christology and Mission*. CMS Wales.

Williams, R. D. 2005. *Why Study the Past? The Quest for the Historical Church*. London: DLT.

Wright, N. T. 1996. *Jesus and the Victory of God*. London: SPCK.

Wright, N. T. 2011. *Simply Jesus: Who He Was, What He Did, Why It Matters*. London: SPCK.

Yong, Amos. 2005. *The Spirit Poured Out on All Flesh*. Grand Rapids: Baker.

Young, Robert J. C. 2003. *Postcolonialism: A Very Short Introduction*. Oxford: Oxford University Press.

# CHAPTER 62

# Cross-Communion Organizations

## Julian Linnell

## Introduction

As an inherently global entity, the Anglican Communion today exists in over 160 countries, with over 80 million adherents, among 44 member churches. The shift from being a state church to a global communion over the past 300 years has led, inevitably, to cross-communion organizations (CCOs). This chapter will report on the Society for the Propagation of Christian Knowledge (SPCK), the British and Foreign Bible Society (BFBS), Church Missionary Society (CMS), and Anglican Frontier Missions (AFM).

CCOs have a precedent both in the New Testament and in early church history. Even at the beginning, the soon-to-be global church was supported and expanded as churches from one area served as resources to each other. Antioch, for example, provided a missionary base for outreach both to the Jewish Diaspora and to Gentiles throughout the Roman Empire (Acts 13). Alexandria and Carthage became hubs for church networks in Africa during the early church (Oden 2007). Nestorian and Jacobite church networks were developed by the sixth century across the Middle East (Jenkins 2008).

Global Christian trends today indicate that independent, post-denominational ecclesial bodies represent about 20 percent of all Christians and are growing faster than Catholic, Protestant, and Orthodox groups (2.55 percent per year versus 0.89 percent, 1.46 percent, and 0.74 percent, respectively). Anglican growth rates (1.21 percent) are less than half the independent rate (Barrett et al. 2008). Combine this with increased nationalism, ethnic consciousness, and post-colonialism in the majority world, and modernist skepticism and post-modern subjectivism in the Western world, and we might argue that CCOs are embarrassing leftovers from the era of the British Empire. However, neither glossing over these realities nor swallowing them whole will provide us with a realistic basis to understand the shortcomings as well as the potential of CCOs.

In this chapter, we will see the pioneering spirit that brought some revitalization to a complacent Anglican Church in the British Isles. Such a spirit is relevant for today's

*The Wiley-Blackwell Companion to the Anglican Communion*, First Edition. Edited by Ian S. Markham, J. Barney Hawkins IV, Justyn Terry, and Leslie Nuñez Steffensen.
© 2013 John Wiley & Sons, Ltd. Published 2013 by John Wiley & Sons, Ltd.

majority world centers of Christian growth. Hopefully, new centers of Anglican growth in Africa and Asia can learn lessons from the mixed 300-year history of a uniquely "English" variety of colonialism, individualism, ethnocentrism/Eurocentrism, and paternalism (Gitari 1999). Perhaps such lessons can be beneficial in their own cross-cultural evangelism and church planting.

Our contention in this chapter is that CCOs can provide not only some sense of historical perspective, but also a genuine opportunity for mutuality in global mission, evangelism, and church planting. This will not exist in the tired old clothing of Anglican imperialism, but in new outfits suited to diverse ethnic, political, economic, religious, and ecumenical realities of today. If mission and evangelism is a spark plug to ignite new life, then CCOs have the potential to enable individual parishes and dioceses to do together what they are unable to do alone. They can offer training, support, partnership, logistics, consulting and technical aids, but also offer opportunities for Christian friendship, as Bishop Azariah of India noted over 100 years ago at the Edinburgh Conference. At a time when globalization and Internet connectivity simultaneously unite and divide us, CCOs have potential for intensifying the church's witness to Jesus Christ who alone can reconcile and restore what is broken (Ephesians 2:14–18).

## Society for the Propagation of Christian Knowledge (SPCK)

*Origins*

SPCK formally began in March 1699 at Lincoln's Inn, London, where Lord Guilford, Sir Humphrey Mackworth, Mr Justice Hooke, and Colonel Colchester met to consolidate the ministry of Rev. Thomas Bray. SPCK had four original aims: to promote Christian knowledge on plantations in North America, to recruit clergy as missionaries ordained by Bishop of London, to establish libraries on plantations, and to provide financial support for missionaries. The urgency for a new Christian organization was fueled by the rise of Deism and a decline in morality.

*Developments in the 1700s*

SPCK began as a direct outcome of overseas missionary experience. In 1696, the Bishop of London appointed the Rev. Thomas Bray as his official representative (called a "commissary") to Maryland. Due to legal difficulties, he departed in 1699. Bray was to recruit Anglican clergy as missionaries, provide libraries for parishes, and secure funding for Christian work among the 25,000 settlers and 30 parishes. He used publications such as "Proposals for encouraging learning and religion in the foreign plantations" (1695) and "Catechetical lectures' (1696) to make his case. Many bishops supported him, and Bray enjoyed some early successes. By 1698, 21 clergy had been recruited as missionaries, 70 libraries had begun, and, in 1695, Princess Anne donated £44 toward a library (subsequently built in Annapolis, named in her honor). By 1701, Bray had sent out 129 missionaries. He founded the Society for the Propagation of the

Gospel (SPG) in that year as a related, yet distinct missions agency to consolidate the work begun by SPCK.

The development of charity schools, which provided free education for working-class children, was also a major aspect of SPCK's rise. Often under a parochial system, the schools provided instruction equally for girls and boys in the Bible, the Book of Common Prayer, as well as in basic literacy, numeracy, and practical skills such as sewing and spinning. Charity schools began in Britain but expanded to America and India. They were funded through subscriptions, endowments, legacies, parish support, and specific fund-raising events. Teachers were licensed by the local bishop, and the schools were governed through a board of Trustees, usually with the local clergy and wardens in leadership roles.

SPCK's historic relationship with Indian Christianity began in 1705. It helped to support two German Lutherans sent out by the King of Denmark in a remarkable international and ecumenical mission project. No Danish or English missionaries were available, but German Lutherans were ready to evangelize India. In 1709, SPCK stepped in when requests from the missionaries to the SPG went unheeded. SPCK set up a "Malabar Committee" in 1710 to fund protestant missionaries in India as arranged through the King of Denmark. A small charity school and church were established in Tranquebar, a Danish trading settlement in South India. SPCK had friendly relations with the East India Company and admitted the two Lutherans, Ziegenbalg and Plutschao, as members of SPCK. By 1711, they had translated the New Testament into Tamil. By 1743, versions of the Bible were available in Telugu and Hindi, and over 20 schools had been established.

While the Indian work progressed, SPCK began printing Bibles and prayer books in other parts of the world. The society's preference was mostly for High Church rather than evangelical books and tracts. Also, SPCK tended to select materials from existing rather than new publications. Spanish tracts were available in 1710 and, later on, both the Spanish Bible (1862) and Book of Common Prayer (1839) were published. The King of Denmark donated £500 in 1720 for the publication of the New Testament and Book of Common Prayer in Arabic. These were distributed to missionaries in Persia, Russia, and India. In 1727, SPCK printed the first Welsh Bible, and later the Bible in Gaelic (1803).

### Growth in the 1800s

Two political and social trends played a significant role in SPCK's growth in the 1800s, especially in India. In 1812, William Wilberforce MP drafted a plan for the British government to protect Christianity in India. When the East India Company became the governor of certain territories, Wilberforce feared that the company might become negative toward mission work. This could even lead to the persecution of new converts. In 1813, an Act of Parliament established the Bishop of Calcutta, plus three archdeacons, to be financed by the East India Company. Bishop Middleton was consecrated as Bishop of Calcutta in 1814, and SPCK provided £1,000 for the "Colonial Bishoprics Fund." In 1829, SPCK petitioned the government to elevate Calcutta to an archiepiscopate and establish Madras, Delhi, and Bombay as episcopates. Another boost came when Queen Victoria became patron of SPCK in 1839.

Emigration in the 1800s also helped SPCK to grow. In 1836, W. E. Gladstone MP asked SPCK to provide Bibles, prayer books, and tracts for emigrants. This led to new ministries for chaplains aboard various ship routes to Australia, United States, Canada, and New Zealand. In addition to helping emigrants learn to read, they also promoted family prayers and daily Bible reading.

Not all the expansion was successful. SPCK had to restrict itself. Its growth into new areas such as training medical missionaries (1885) was later judged to be outside its original aims. The provision of Arabic and Armenian prayer books (1880, 1883) as part of the experiment to revive the ancient church in Kurdistan also proved to be misguided.

### Adaptation in the 1900s

World War I significantly affected SPCK and reshaped many of its practices and goals. Negatively, publishing had to be curtailed, as paper was in short supply. Positively, women's involvement was increased. In 1915, the first woman was hired on staff, and, in 1919, women could become "full members" rather than "lady subscribers." After the war, SPCK became more of a middleman for Bibles, prayer books, and hymnals, rather than a producer. SPCK grants were allocated more to people (such as ordinands) than to buildings. Criteria for disbursing grants were revised. In 1933, SPCK established bookshops in the precincts of Canterbury Cathedral and expanded a network of shops that proved financially successful.

After World War II, SPCK faced the economic reality that British churches did not have the cash to support mission. Reconstruction, diocesan quotas, and other concerns took priority. SPCK reviewed its mission and decided that it needed to return to Dr. Bray's original goals. Their work in medical missions and among Braille publications was therefore disbanded. There was a greater need for collaboration with national publishers and Christian literature organizations. This was especially true in India. An independent Indian SPCK (ISPCK) was formed in 1958. Its aims were similar to SPCK in London, but included a major emphasis on Indian languages. ISPCK eventually became the vehicle for Christian publications of the newly formed Church of North India (CNI) (1968). ISPCK had close relationships with dioceses and actively promoted Bibles and Christian literature in Indian languages. In 1973, the CNI provided a grant to ISPCK which published liturgy and translations in Gujarati, Mundari, Punjabi, Assamese, and other languages. By the 1980s, ISPCK had bilateral agreements with other Christian organizations such as the Hindi Theological Literature Committee and the Christian Institute for Sikh Studies. Similarly, the Joint Council of CNI, Church of South India (CSI), and the Mar Thoma Church has continued to provide new opportunities for ISPCK.

### Refinement of the 2000s

SPCK's mission statement (2011) builds upon Dr. Bray's original aims: "Communicating the Christian faith in its rich diversity, helping people to understand it and to develop their personal faith, equipping Christians for mission and ministry." Its publishing arm continues to supply resources for both clergy and laity, but with a diverse range of titles including both academic and popular topics in fields such as theology and science. Its global work (SPCK Worldwide) supplies books for Anglican and other ordinands from Africa, Asia, and Latin America, as well as books for the poor. The third arm of SPCK today (called Diffusion) develops innovative and new titles for special interest groups. SPCK has international offices in Ireland (1996), Australia (1972), and the United States (1983) today, but these function largely in a fund-raising capacity.

## The British and Foreign Bible Society (BFBS)

*Origins*

"Surely a society might be formed for the purpose," said the Rev. Joseph Hughes. He was speaking at the Religious Tract Society in London in December 1802. The purpose in question was an initiative to provide more Bibles for the Welsh. "But if for Wales," he continued, "why not for the kingdom? Why not for the world?" (Canton 1904, 5).

The impetus had come from the poignant story of a young Welsh girl, Mary Jones. In 1800, Mary walked 26 miles to buy a Bible, only to discover none were available. BFBS was founded in March 1804 to meet a need for Welsh Bibles that the prevailing organization of the day, the SPCK, had been unable to meet.

The founding of BFBS was unremarkable. Others were being founded like SPG (1701), Naval and Military Bible Society (1790s), and the French Bible Society (1792). However, given the challenges of its time, its success is startling. England faced military threats from France. No bishops, MPs, or peers were physically present. It was not a sectarian organization, but ecumenical and international from the start. The founding committee had 36 lay Anglicans, Foreigners, and Dissenters, with three ordained secretaries from each category: Rev. Owen, Rev. Hughes, and Rev. Steinkopf.

Their aim was "To encourage the wider circulation of Holy Scriptures, without note or comment." Rather than duplicate the efforts of others, BFBS tried to "add its endeavors to those employed by other Societies for the circulating the Scriptures" (Law 2, BFBS Constitution). Their distinctive would be to distribute Bibles in "heathen" countries. The Bishop of London wrote to Lord Teignmouth, the first president of BFBS, about the "Moors of Africa, pagans, and Mohammedans, wherever they can be come at, [who] are unquestionably the objects that demand our first and principal attention" (October 10, 1806) (Temple 1859, 218).

*Rapid growth: 1804–1854*

The rise of an "auxiliary system" outside London was a major factor behind BFBS' rapid growth. Prices were fixed by BFBS in London, but sold in an expanding network of sellers throughout the country who remitted the purchase price in addition to other donations to the London committee. Supporters paid annual subscriptions which entitled them to discounted rates for Bibles. Although BFBS distributed Bibles, printing was outsourced to commercial printers.

BFBS was also aided by the effective leadership provided by Rev. Steinkopf and Dr. John Paterson. As foreign secretary for BFBS, Steinkopf spent five years diligently working in Germany, Switzerland, and Scandinavia. Paterson's presence in Russia in 1812 led to Czar Alexander I himself becoming a member of an indigenous society, the St. Petersburg Bible Society (1813). By 1854, BFBS had issued nearly 28 million Bibles in 152 languages and dialects.

### Expansion east: 1854–1904

The London Bible House was opened with much fanfare in 1866, but after the Governor of Tokyo had visited and accepted a copy of the Chinese Bible and an English Reference Bible, there was no Japanese Bible to give him. This had to wait until 1875 for the Gospel of Luke and some other New Testament books in 1876 (Steer 2004, 254). Slowly, BFBS expanded its work into Korea, China, and Japan.

### War and nationalism: 1904–1954

By 1904, the BFBS network was truly global. The society had distributed 180 million Bibles in 89 languages, with portions available in 207 other languages. By the mid-1920s, it had depots in 100 cities around the world. Over half a million Bibles were being printed in Korea, and 4 million in China.

BFBS was also innovative in its approach. Military personnel in World War I had access to discounted Bibles in 50 languages. Indian college students in the 1920s were offered a copy of the four gospels and the book of Acts upon entry.

After World War II, BFBS faced new challenges. As the British Empire was dismantled, cooperation rather than competition became increasingly important for translation and publication. In July 1946, several leading Christians called for a "global federation of Bible societies." The growth of national Bible societies meant that BFBS no longer reigned supreme.

### Globalization: 1954–present

In 1967, the United Bible Societies (UBS) around the world distributed over 100 million scriptures for the first time. The Apocrypha was printed (1969) over some reservations, and UBS revised "no note and comment" to "no doctrinal note or comment" (1971). By 2003, a network of 130 Bible societies worldwide distributed the scriptures in over 2,300 languages. Despite such a globalized reach, as Archbishop Rowan Williams has noted, the worldview of many countries was deeply "unreceptive" to the Bible (Batalden et al. 2004, xii). In Britain, for example, BFBS responded to the general public's reluctance to read the Bible with easy-to-read versions such as the Good News Bible (1976) and with adaptations for specific audiences.

BFBS and UBS could be criticized as more business than mission and more as an exporter of Eurocentric colonialism than a respecter of local cultures, but this would be simplistic. Their historic, international role in the standardization and development of national languages, as Lamin Sanneh (1989) has argued, was foundational for the cultural and religious identity of many indigenous peoples. Where Bible translation failed to meet genuine indigenous needs, as in the case of the Russian Orthodox in post-Soviet Russia, then full indigenization was not accomplished (Batalden et al. 2004).

## The Church Mission Society (CMS)

*Origins*

Several evangelical Anglicans started the Society for Missions to Africa and the East on Aldersgate Street, London, in 1799. The name was changed to "The Church Missionary Society" (and, in 1995, to "The Church Mission Society"). CMS was a product of eighteenth-century revivals across Britain and was viewed somewhat suspiciously by the Anglican establishment in its early years. Its leaders, men like Henry Thornton, William Wilberforce, and John Venn, were vital forces for the abolition of slavery, social reform, and global evangelism. At their inaugural meeting, Venn laid down principles that have enduring value today: (1) Follow God's lead, (2) Recruit the best people, (3) Start small, and (4) Money follows mission. Classic accounts of CMS can be found in Stock (1899, 1902, 1916), Hewitt (1971, 1977), and Murray (1985), but more critical perspectives are presented by Ward and Stanley (2000) and Gitari (1999).

The rise of the Anglican Communion as a global entity is in large part due to CMS; however, today, CMS is not just an Anglican agency, but also a dynamic ecumenical partner with non-Anglican organizations for mission and evangelism. CMS's overseas work started in Sierra Leone (1804), but expanded to India, Canada, New Zealand, and to Mediterranean regions. The lion's share of CMS's focus has been in Africa (Sierra Leone, Nigeria, Kenya, Tanzania, Uganda, Congo, Rwanda, and Sudan), though CMS has had significant service in India, Pakistan, Sri Lanka, China, Japan, as well as in Middle Eastern countries such as Egypt, Palestine, and Iran. CMS also pioneered work in Australia (1825) and New Zealand (1809–1914). Canon Max Warren (general secretary from 1942 to 1963), a dominant figure in twentieth-century missiology, defined the growth of CMS in four historic stages.

*Proclamation: 1799–1851*

Anglicans in the late 1700s had few models and even fewer recruits for international mission work. CMS initially turned to German Lutherans trained at the Basel Missionary Institute as its first missionaries. In Sierra Leone, the focus was on former slaves; in

Australia and New Zealand, it was on aboriginal peoples. Some success was experienced in West and East Africa, India, the Middle East, China and Japan; but failure was evident in Turkey, Greece, Abyssinia, Zululand, Madagascar, Guiana, Jamaica, and Hudson Bay. By 1815, 15 missionaries had been sent out. This year was also significant because, up until this time, English bishops were unwilling to ordain men who were to serve overseas unless they committed to a curacy in Britain first. Bishop Ryder of Gloucester was willing to break this tradition. By 1824, 100 men had been commissioned as CMS missionaries, of which one-third were Germans, one-third English laity, and one-third English clergy.

### Construction: 1851–1900

High Church Anglicans advocated the bishop as the leading edge for mission, but CMS adopted more of a grassroots approach to build up churches and to add structures later. This was in keeping with the evangelical Anglican ethos of CMS as epitomized by Henry Venn (1842–1872), the general secretary for half of this period. Murray argues that he was ". . . in the truest sense a father of the worldwide Anglican Communion" (Murray 1985, 40). His strong convictions about churches being self-supporting, self-governing, and self-propagating are well known. He considered missionaries as temporary necessities until indigenous churches were established. Indigenous pastors, on the other hand, were permanent fixtures.

The influence of women as missionaries and as missionary wives, daughters, and widows was increasingly significant. Ward reports that, between 1820 and 1885, 99 women missionaries were sent (as distinct from missionary wives), but, by 1990, 485 women had been commissioned overseas. Overall, numbers of CMS missionaries had virtually doubled between 1889 and 1899 – from 630 to 1,238 (Ward and Stanley 2000, 29–31).

Yet, in reflecting upon this colonial era, one twentieth-century general secretary, Bishop Simon Barrington-Ward, noted that there was much to repent of: "Christians were often trained to detach themselves from political and social issues and to adopt a rather inward and individualistic gospel with disastrous results even today. Unconsciously they became part of the economic process whereby the 'North' profited from the impoverished 'South', while politically the 'South' was subordinated to the interests of the 'North' and was drawn into its catastrophic wars" (CMS 1999).

### Stabilization: 1900–1955

CMS worked to consolidate the growth of the previous 100 years or so. However, there were a number of challenges (Ward and Stanley 2000, 32): Should the mission strategy be top down or bottom up? In other words, should CMS educate elites whose Christian influence would hopefully trickle down to lower social groups, or bottom up and make the education of the masses their priority? Should British government continue to give grants to CMS rather than directly to the indigenous church? Should the government be involved at all? Should CMS define biblical orthodoxy in conventional Anglican terms or not? CMS remained evangelical rather than High Church, but not as self-consciously precise as Bible Churchmen's Missionary Society (1922).

### Interchange: 1956–present

After World War II, CMS started to hand over institutions to local authorities and reshape itself for a post-colonial era. Christian growth in the global south became the engine for expansion rather than British migration and diplomacy overseas. Dramatic economic inequalities between north and south became painfully evident. With the end of the Cold War and the rise of al Qaeda and other forms of fundamentalism, global mission faces uncertainty and instability as never before. Countries that formerly received missionaries are now sending missionaries back to the motherlands. New organizational relationships are being forged. CMS and the South American Missionary Society merged into a new entity 2010. The Faith2Share network, which consists of Anglican, non-Anglican, and indigenous mission organizations, is another promising indication of the potential that CCOs have for new types of partnering in mission and evangelism.

## Anglican Frontier Missions (AFM)

### Origins

On All Saints' Day 1990, about 20 mission leaders from Episcopal Church USA met in Richmond, Virginia, at the global strategy room of the International Mission Board. Led by Tad de Bordenave and Dr. David Barrett, these Episcopal mission leaders felt there ought to be an Episcopal response to the 1.6 billion people in the world who were unevangelized and ignored by the Anglican Communion. This huge segment of the global population was labeled "World A" by missiologists, who defined it as less than 50 percent evangelized. In contrast, "World B" was already evangelized over 50 percent and basically consisted of people who had heard the gospel but had not necessarily converted. "World C" was essentially the Christianized world, already evangelized over 50 percent and with the majority defined as Christian in some shape or form.

As result, a smaller group met monthly with support from Overseas Missions Committee of the Diocese of Virginia. Tad de Bordenave remembered: "In the spring of 1991, as I was reading Stephen Neill's book *The History of Christian Mission*, it became very clear to me that frontiers were broken by people who were willing to say, 'I will cut my ties and I will go out there'. I heard the Lord saying to me, 'Cut your ties and go out there' (Stockdale 1996). In the Fall of 1993, he left St. Matthew's Episcopal Church, Richmond, after 17 years of ministry, and Anglican Frontier Missions began. Based on Matthew 28:19–20, AFM's vision was to see indigenous churches planted among the 25 largest, least evangelized people groups. These had populations over 1 million and had no viable Christian church and fewer than five mission agencies active in evangelism.

Unlike traditional approaches to mission that viewed an Anglican province or diocese as the unit of evangelism, AFM regarded entire people groups as their focus for church planting. A people group shares a common ethnolinguistic identity and is the largest-sized group within which the gospel can spread without facing problems of comprehension or acceptance. AFM was ecumenical in its approach of collaborating with different denominations and mission agencies to achieve the goal of indigenous church planting, but faced two hurdles.

First, the Anglican Communion policy of only sending missionaries at the request of a bishop had failed to address the spiritual and humanitarian needs of the unevangelized. Hence, without an Anglican bishop in Tibet or Algeria, for example, there was no chance that missionaries would be called. Second, clergy attitudes, particularly among American Episcopalians in the 1990s, were parochial and generally dismissive toward the unevangelized: "We've got too much on our plate (e.g., heresies, squabbles, etc.)," they would say, "to get anything going among one billion people in places we've never heard of" (Stockdale 1996, 365).

As de Bordenave noted, "We need to remind ourselves that the church is nothing more than a servant" (Stockdale 1996, 368). As a result of AFM's work at both Lambeth 1998 and Lambeth 2008, there were some initial signs that Anglicans might wake up to the evangelistic needs of 1.7 billion people; however, this was largely through the response of African and Asian Anglicans rather than through Westerners.

### Nigeria

Following Lambeth 1998, Nigerian Bishop Nathan Inyom coordinated an effort to evangelize unreached people groups inside and outside Nigeria. Subsequently, AFM Nigeria was established in the diocese of Makurdi. Bishops Inyom, Chukwuma, Akanya, Omole, Ibadan, and Kattey received strategy coordinator training in Singapore in 2000 and 2003. This led to further Nigerian outreach in three directions.

First, in 2004, 12 Nigerian priests were commissioned to evangelize several tribal groups inside Nigeria (Manga Kanuri, Adamawa Fulani, Dakakari, Hausa, Sokoto Fulani), as well as the Gangam (Togo), Baka Pygmies (Cameroon), Fang (Equatorial Guinea), Futa Toro Fulani (Senegal), and Zema (Niger). One Nigerian evangelist went farther, even to Iran and the United Arab Emirates, with the aim of awakening Anglican churches to pray and to evangelize the unreached there. Each Nigerian missionary was paired with Episcopal parishes in the United States, who provided some financial and prayer support.

Second, in 2006, Bishop Segun of Ibadan established the Nigerian College of Intercultural Missions as a direct outcome of World A and people group thinking. Though small, the college has trained 30 Nigerian evangelists to work among unreached people groups in remote, tribal areas in Nigeria.

The third outcome for AFM Nigeria was to mobilize Nigerian church planters to work among unreached people groups. Strategy coordinator training provided in Abuja (2004), Jos (2007), and Central Nigeria (2011) has continued the effort to point the church to truly unevangelized peoples.

## India

Tad de Bordenave worked closely with Bishop Jason Dharmaraj of the CSI to increase awareness of unevangelized people groups. Bishops Dharmaraj, Khanna, and Matthews from CSI were trained as strategy coordinators in 2001 in Singapore. A series of mission conferences in Ajmer and Jodhpur, Rajasthan, were organized to focus on the Marwari people (10.2 million population, 99.9 percent Hindu). Further training and mission awareness was achieved through a cross-cultural mission conference in Noida/ Delhi (2005) that assembled 81 bishops from CSI, CNI, Bangladesh, and the Mar Thoma Church (Pradhan et al. 2006).

AFM also developed a partnership with an indigenous mission network in the state of Bihar in North India. Known as the graveyard of missions, Bihar has presented many challenges to the gospel. AFM has partnered in a small way with Bihar Outreach Network's director, Rev. S. D. Ponraj, to support evangelism to its population of 90 million. Through the strategic coordinator approach, over 5,000 churches have been planted in the past 15 years among many unreached people groups (Ponraj and Sah 2008).

## Al-hazadis

Southern Baptists trained a non-residential missionary (NRM) to serve the Al-hazadis (pseudonym for security reasons) (Garrison 1992). After extensive research, the NRM discovered that the 1 million Al-hazadis were Sunni Muslims. They originated in one country, but their diaspora stretched across several nations. Due to severe restrictions, it was not possible to engage in direct evangelism. The NRM devised 100 ways to get the gospel heard by the Al-hazadis. After surveying their needs and identifying resources within the wider body of Christ, including both Anglican and ecumenical partners, the NRM was able to coordinate medical and humanitarian services. A combination of short- and longer-term teams were able to serve the Al-hazadis. The New Testament was published in the Al-hazadi language. When the NRM began, it was estimated that fewer than 20 believers existed; yet, by 2010, possibly 1,000 believers existed. A global prayer network was established, and an embryonic church has been birthed.

## Qashqa'i

In the early 1990s, de Bordenave joined with an ecumenical group from Asian and Western countries to focus on the Qashqa'i. Their research pointed them to 1 million of this semi-nomadic people in Iran. Astonished, they learned that there were no known Christians, no scripture, and no missionary work. In 1995, they sent out prayer requests globally for Qashqa'i, and, by 1996, remarkably, the first known Qashqa'i was converted, a man living in India. The coordinating team visited him in 1997, recorded his conversion story, and initiated a Bible translation and recordings. Their first visit to Qashqa'i areas led them to a "man of peace," which subsequently led to the distribution of cassettes and a full translation of the New Testament in 1998. By 2000, reports of new believers and of house churches had reached the coordinating team. However, the mobile lifestyle of the Qashqa'i makes church-planting a major challenge.

### Welho

There are 1.4 million Welho (pseudonym) in South East Asia, among whom 95 percent are non-Christian – either ancestor-worshippers, Buddhists, or animists. The Welho straddle several countries and have different names in each location, but are ethnolinguistically the same people group. Unfortunately, they are generally poverty-stricken and suffer high rates of infant mortality and illiteracy. In the early 1990s, over 80 percent had never heard the gospel.

AFM workers discovered that the Bible had not been translated into their language and Jesus Film was not available, so they cooperated with Christians from other mission agencies. As about 80 percent of the Welho are illiterate, oral Bible stories were deemed important. AFM workers converted their home into a recording studio for the Jesus Film project and began a ministry to train Welho as church planters. Over 400 new believers emerged, with 70 leaders trained and 80 house churches established, and 50 Bible stories and 30 songs in Welho. Despite challenges today from police harassment and squabbles among Christian workers, the gospel continues to expand among them.

## Conclusion: Future Roles for CCOs

What is the future for CCOs? If they cannot reconfigure themselves to serve Jesus Christ in economically turbulent, politically unstable, and religiously intolerant regions, then there is no reason for them to exist. However, if CCOs today can adapt to new global conditions, then there is a bright future. Their value will be felt in three areas: spiritual dynamism, inter-church aid, and evangelistic strategy.

First, in terms of spiritual dynamism, CCOs have the potential to widen the impact of revival and renewal in Africa, for example, to reach complacent and dying parts of the communion in the West (Johnson and Ross 2009, 53). After all, it was through mission that German pietism was used by God to renew some British Anglicans.

Second, inter-church aid can play an important, highly selective role in indigenous Christian movements in the majority world. If CCOs can avoid promoting financial dependency, paternalism, and cultural arrogance, then they can encourage isolated and often persecuted churches through links to the wider body and to the historic faith. CCOs can also help to birth new indigenous mission organizations.

Finally, CCOs could have value in the future by making the evangelization of people groups a priority. Anglican churches and dioceses are scattered in many parts of the world that could become hubs for church planting and renewal. However, this may be controversial for a number of reasons. Many Anglican dioceses in Muslim countries, for example, can serve expatriates but are forbidden to evangelize indigenous peoples. Other dioceses have people groups where it is legal to evangelize, but their present mission strategy ignores them. Some provinces have the capacity to evangelize groups that are outside their ecclesial boundaries, but such boundary crossing may be frowned upon. In each case, CCOs could help dioceses and provinces rediscover an ecclesiology based on the great commission rather than church politics. It will be their faithfulness to the gospel and sensitivity to ethnic contexts that will ultimately determine their fruitfulness for the global body of Christ.

## Bibliography

Anglican Frontier Missions. 2011. Entire Site. Accessed August 31, 2012. www.anglicanfrontiers.com.

Barrett, David, Todd Johnson, and Peter Crossing. 2008. Missiometrics 2008: Reality Checks for Christian World Communions. *International Bulletin of Missionary Research*, vol. 22, no. 1, pp. 27–38.

Bible Society. 2011. Entire Site. Accessed August 31, 2012. www.biblesociety.org.uk.

Canton, William. 1904. *The Story of the Bible Society*. London: John Murray.

Church Mission Society. 2011. Entire Site. Accessed August 31, 2012. www.cms-uk.org.

Clarke, William. 1959. *The History of the SPCK*. London: SPCK.

De Bordenave, Tad. 2008. *Light to the Nations: God's Covenant with Unreached Peoples*. Chennai, India: Mission Educational Books.

Garrison, David. 1992. A New Model for Missions. *International Journal of Frontier Missions*, vol. 9, no. 2, pp. 67–9.

Gitari, David. 1999. *Church Mission Society Annual Sermon: On the Occasion of CMS' Bicentenary Celebration*. London: CMS.

Hewitt, Gordon. 1971. *The Problems of Success: A History of the Church Missionary Society, 1910–1942. Vol. 1 – In Tropical Africa, the Middle East, At Home*. London: SCM.

Hewitt, Gordon. 1977. *The Problems of Success: A History of the Church Missionary Society, 1910–1942. Vol. 2 Asia and Overseas Partners*. London: SCM.

Jenkins, Philip. 2008. *The Lost History of Christianity: The Thousand-Year Golden Age of the Church in the Middle East, Africa and Asia and How It Died*. New York: Harper Collins Publishers.

Johnson, Todd and Kenneth Ross. 2009. *Atlas of Global Christianity*. Edinburgh: Edinburgh University Press.

Koilpillai, Victor. 1985. *The SPCK in India 1710–1985*. Delhi: ISPCK.

Murray, Jocelyn. 1985. *Proclaim the Good News: A Short History of the CMS*. London: Hodder and Stoughton.

Oden, Thomas. 2007. *How Africa Shaped the Christian Mind: Rediscovering the African Seedbed of Western Christianity*. Downers Grove, Illinois: InterVarsity Press.

Ponraj, S. D. and Chandan Sah. 2008. *From Graveyard to Vineyard: The Story of the Transformation Movement in Bihar*. Chennai: Mission Educational Books.

Pradhan, Enos, Sudipta Singh, and Kasta Dip, eds. 2006. *Uniting in Christ's Mission*. Delhi, India: ISPCK.

Roe, James. 1965. *A History of the British and Foreign Bible Society 1905–1954*. London: The British and Foreign Bible Society.

Sanneh, Lamin. 1989. *Translating the Message: The Missionary Impact on Culture*. Maryknoll, New York: Orbis Books.

SPCK. 2011. Entire Site. Accessed August 31, 2012. www.spck.org.uk.

Steer, Roger. 2004. *Good News for the World: The Story of the Bible Society. 200 Years of Making the Bible Heard*. Oxford : Monarch Books.

Stephen Batalden, Kathleen Cann, and John Dean. 2004. *Sowing the Word: The Cultural Impact of the British and Foreign Bible Society 1804–2004*. Sheffield: Sheffield Phoenix Press.

Stock, Eugene. 1899. *The History of the Church Missionary Society, Vols. 1–3*. London: CMS.

Stock, Eugene. 1902. *The Centenary Volume of the Church Missionary Society for Africa and the East*. London: CMS.

Stock, Eugene. 1916. *The History of the Church Missionary Society, Vol. 4*. London: CMS.

Stockdale, Sharon, ed. 1996. *New Wineskins for Global Mission*. Pasadena, CA: William Carey Library.

Temple, Richard. 1859. *Memoirs of the Rt. Hon. John Lord Teignmouth, Governor-General of India, and First President for the British and Foreign Bible Society*. New York: Protestant Episcopal Society for the Promotion of Evangelical Knowledge.

*200 Years. The CMS 1799–1999*. London: CMS.

Ward, Kevin and Brian Stanley. 2000. *The Church Mission Society and World Christianity 1799–1999*. Grand Rapids, Michigan: William B. Eerdmans Publishing Company.

CHAPTER 63

# The Spirituality of the Anglican Communion

## Elizabeth Hoare

It is sometimes claimed that there is nothing distinctive about Anglican spirituality, and if we were to ask people who worship regularly at an Anglican church what distinguishes their spirituality from other Christians, we may be met with puzzlement. For all Christians, spirituality has to do with how we live out what we believe about God as he is revealed in scripture. It is certainly true that Anglicans can have characteristics without these being distinctive. So it is characteristic of Anglicans to practice liturgical worship and say the creeds, for example, but these are not unique to Anglicanism.

The website of the Anglican Communion reveals a number of elements that are of the essence of Anglican spirituality. They include structures, ministries lay and ordained, news, networks, and topics for prayer. They concern the shared faith, common life, and mission of Anglicans around the world and as such offer a basis on which to build a spirituality that is both local and universal.

## Prayer and Living

Prayer and living are at the heart of all Christian spirituality. It has been claimed over and over that the response to the question of what Anglican believe is *lex orandi, lex credendi*, that is: "if you want to know what we believe, come and pray with us."

In just a single city in the United Kingdom, however, we could attend numerous examples of Anglican churches that all pray in very different ways. There is a church that proclaims it is Bible-based and relies on the preaching of God's word to feed the congregation; nearby we could go to a church where the emphasis is on the present experience of the Holy Spirit and gifts and ministries are exercised during worship. Close to that church is another Anglican congregation where ritual and ceremony are practiced meticulously and seem a little different from the local Roman Catholic Church.

*The Wiley-Blackwell Companion to the Anglican Communion*, First Edition. Edited by Ian S. Markham,
J. Barney Hawkins IV, Justyn Terry, and Leslie Nuñez Steffensen.
© 2013 John Wiley & Sons, Ltd. Published 2013 by John Wiley & Sons, Ltd.

There is also a "family-friendly" church where liturgy is very low-key and the atmosphere is informal to the point of chaotic, while down the road is an Anglican church offering the beauty of holiness through liturgy and stillness. And there is more, for further on is an Anglican church where issues of the day are wrestled with in an atmosphere of inquiry, and the prayer book firmly adhered to. Other churches offer a varied menu that might be Common Worship one week and Book of Common Prayer the next, with Taize services and Celtic liturgies in between.

How can all these be Anglican? If we were to widen the picture to take in the worldwide Anglican Communion, we would soon discover that these distinctive types of spirituality would increase in number in some places, while in others they would seem meaningless. Where simply being a Christian is a matter of life and death, people do not have the luxury of choosing what type of spirituality they prefer. Yet, it matters to most Anglicans that they adhere to a form of Christian faith that calls itself Anglican, and while labels like comprehensive, open-minded, and ambiguous seem to suggest that looking for qualities that stand out is a hopeless task, there is a distinctiveness that has sustained Anglicans for over 450 years and makes for an identifiable spirituality, even if it exerts a weaker hold on the Anglican Communion today. The importance of such roots for maintaining a sense of cohesion and for nourishing a common Anglican spirituality in the future is crucial.

## Beginnings and History

The beginnings of Anglican spirituality did not emerge *ex nihilo* at the time of the Reformation, though this was a momentous time, and from it emerged the Book of Common Prayer that has had such a formative influence on Anglican spirituality, worship, and so much else besides. The coming of Christianity to the British Isles shaped the faith as it was passed on down the generations until the break with Rome in the middle of the sixteenth century. The Celtic and Roman missions both had a part to play in how Christian faith was practiced among the people who lived in Britain, and they in their turn were formed by the scriptures and the early Church Fathers. The Reformers consciously looked back to the Early Church and maintained firmly that they remained part of the "one, holy, catholic and apostolic church" despite the changes wrought by the Reformation. Thus, just as the Anglican Church saw herself as catholic and reformed, so her spirituality has been influenced by aspects of both strands of the Christian tradition. Although Anglicans are divided by different traditions, prayer remains at the heart of spirituality for all, from high Anglo-catholics to conservative evangelicals. The latter have always emphasized the importance of a personal faith in Christ nourished by a daily quiet time involving Bible reading and prayer from the heart. Catholics have been encouraged to attend early-morning communion and a daily office of morning and evening prayer. If the first is a more individualistic spirituality, the latter has a more church-based emphasis. Both ways of praying are important aspects of Anglican spirituality, and both have grown difficult to sustain in the modern Western world where constraints of work and family life make ever-increasing demands. There is therefore all the more need to recover the riches of the tradition, so that people can find fresh ways to sustain their spirituality through prayer that encourages rather than defeats them.

## Thomas Cranmer and the Book of Common Prayer

While often being self-deprecating, the Anglican Church has produced a number of key individuals who have influenced not only their own church but also impressed those of other denominations. William Tyndale, for example, could hardly be called an Anglican since the Anglican Church had not as yet been defined, but his translation work of the Bible laid the foundations for the activities of Archbishop Thomas Cranmer, the architect of the Book of Common Prayer. Cranmer's aim was to enable every person to be able to worship in their own language, to hear the scriptures proclaimed in a systematic and comprehensible way, and to go to church and experience rites that were rooted in tradition but were also accessible. Its influence on the emerging Anglican spirituality was deeply formative. As a book to enable people to pray, its literary form was key in shaping Anglican spirituality. Anglican spirituality thus has no problem with prayers written down as a means of addressing God. Indeed, there are written prayers that have stood the test of time and that unite Anglicans across the world. *An African Prayer Book*, compiled by Archbishop Desmond Tutu, contains a selection of prayers ancient and modern, including prayers by the North African bishop Augustine that are as well known in England as anywhere in the world and have been included in anthologies of prayers since they were first used. Cranmer's strategy has also helped Anglican spirituality to remain firmly connected with the church universal. Many of its collects, for example, stem from the ancient church in the East and the West. Cranmer sought to hold on to the best of earlier practices in worship while reforming those aspects that had strayed far from scripture and clarity concerning faith in Jesus Christ. Public reading of scripture, for example, had formed the basis of daily communal prayer from earliest times, and so he made this the basis of morning and evening prayer when he reformed the liturgy. Thus, the Book of Common Prayer, along with the King James Bible, from the mid-seventeenth century, shaped the language of personal prayer and devotion of most Anglicans, clergy, and lay until well into the second half of the twentieth century.

The Book of Common Prayer, as its title suggests, was intended to be a prayer book for the entire nation. The reformers desired everyone to have access to the Bible in their own language and to be able to come to God in prayer, confident of access to him through grace. Spirituality was no longer to be regarded as the preserve of a few. High and low, rich and poor, the parish gathers everyone together, and people have to learn to live with each other. This feature is still true of most English parishes today, especially in rural areas where choice may be limited to the one village church. Cranmer wanted everyone to hear the scriptures read when they came to pray and to recite the prayers themselves, not listen to someone else do it for them. It is a spirituality for laypeople as well as ordained. He also wanted people to receive communion regularly as a means of sustaining their spirituality, and Anglican spirituality has always been firmly sacramental in both a narrow and a broad sense.

Cranmer's emphasis was on the Psalms as the basis for morning and evening prayer, and the Book of Common Prayer covers the entire Psalter each month. Every emotion is embedded in the Psalms from exuberant joy to the depths of despair, from quiet trust to furious anger, and gives permission for all of life to be part of a lively spirituality.

The Psalms continue to be a prominent part of how Anglicans are formed spiritually, rooting them in scripture and experience.

Cranmer's aforementioned collects are a good way of exploring the fundamentals of Anglican spirituality. They include ancient prayers which Cranmer adopted wholesale, new ones specially composed, and others that were adapted to bring out the reformed emphases of grace and providence. They are designed to teach as well as express Christian belief corporately. They cover every aspect of the Christian faith: the doctrinal framework of belief, the highpoints of the Christian year, and the everyday nature of spirituality that finds "heaven in ordinary." Collects in Anglican prayer books around the world now number about 1,000, having increased substantially in the last 100 years from Cranmer's original collection (Dudley 2002).

## Everyday Spirituality

Here is a further defining feature of Anglican spirituality: it is a spirituality for everyday life. When the reformers took spirituality out of the cloister, they did not try to water it down for lay consumption. William Tyndale was inspired by Erasmus' vision of the poorest ploughboy being able to read the scriptures for himself as he worked in the fields. The prayer book contained everything required from cradle to grave. There were prayers for harvest, for those at sea, for rain, for peace, and so on. It might be argued that, today, we need prayers for computers, for protection from nuclear fallout, for air travel, and so on, but the fundamental principle is the same: prayer is for the whole of life. Stripped of the protective buffers that Western Christians have provided for them, human need for food, safety, and peace are the same the world over. Indeed, one of the benefits of the Anglican Communion is that the over-developed West is reminded by her brothers and sisters in the developing world that, while we may be cushioned from the harsher aspects of life, we still need God's providential care and we have a responsibility to act to relieve those in need. The Anglican cycle of prayer continues to remind Anglicans of their brothers and sisters in different parts of the world.

## Spirituality Shaped by Doctrine

Creation and Redemption are celebrated side by side in Anglican spirituality. Hence, the General Thanksgiving from the Book of Common Prayer: "We bless thee for our creation, preservation and all the blessings of this life; but above all for thy inestimable love in the redemption of the whole world by our Lord Jesus Christ, for the means of grace and the hope of glory." Moreover, life has seasons, and the Christian year connects with our own personal journeys of faith in a challenging as well as sustaining fashion.

Like Eastern Orthodoxy, Anglicanism at its best sees the potential within heaven and earth for glory waiting to be revealed. The whole world has sacramental value. Anglican spirituality, though firmly rooted in the redemptive work of the cross, has a strong sense of the goodness of creation and its place as the theatre of God's grace. It may be said to be a thoroughly this-world spirituality in that it refuses to separate sacred and secular. Confident of the Christian hope, it remains firmly engaged with the world, and it was William Temple, an Anglican archbishop of the last century, who famously described the Christian faith as "the most material of all religions." Canon Henry Scott Holland, another Anglican, this time in the nineteenth century, commented that "the more one believes in the Incarnation, the more interested one becomes in drains." Anglican spirituality has led and continues to lead its adherents to be in the forefront of efforts to improve the people in this world, as well as to look forward to eternal hope. The five marks of mission are the natural outcome of such a spirituality as well as informing it for today.

## Time

Cycles of prayer, the arrangement of the Collects, Christian festivals (which, for Cranmer, had to be based in scripture), and the movement of the seasons point to the importance of time in Anglican spirituality. There is a rhythm to life which is reflected in the patterns of spirituality we follow. Both the annual cycle of the Christian year and the motif of human life as a pilgrimage from cradle to grave mean that time, in God's sight, is hallowed, and each time we revisit a particular point in the Christian year, there is the opportunity to deepen our understanding and experience of Christ in our lives. Common Worship emphasizes this still further with its rich variety for days of the week, seasons of the year, and liturgies for various rites of passage.

Given the close relationship between Creation, the Incarnation, and Redemption, it is not surprising that, in addition to producing high-flown poetry and prose, Anglican spirituality should be down-to-earth and practical. It values "sanctified common sense." It has learned how to consecrate the ordinary. The prayer book synthesizes scripture and daily life, prayer and morality. Spirituality is as much to do with how we live alongside others and how faith influences this.

## Incarnational Spirituality

The Incarnation lay at the basis of one of Anglicanism's earliest apologists and theologians, Richard Hooker. In his position of offering a middle way, and through his theological method based on scripture and reason, Hooker is recognized as providing something distinctively Anglican. He is important for understanding Anglican spirituality, in that he never forgot the pastoral and practical in his search for theological truth. He was first and foremost a parish priest who lived and prayed his faith as well as thought about it, and thereby exemplifies the best of Anglican spirituality. In his great work *The Laws of Ecclesiastical Polity*, Hooker wrote about the sacraments of baptism and communion as being the means whereby we participate in the life of Christ. Sacraments are, for Hooker, a visible sign of God's grace. They underlie the world-affirming ethos of Anglican spirituality and its incarnational character expressed in worship. The sacraments both presume faith and articulate it. They must be linked to the inner core of the Christian's life so that they enable us to make connections between what we do in worship and our daily lives. Hooker is also important for the conviction that word and sacrament belong together. Although the English reformers shared with their continental counterparts a deeply held suspicion of the mass, they never replaced the altar with the pulpit, nor reduced the sacraments to mere symbols. While local practice and theological emphasis will vary considerably, the principle holds true for the regular nourishment of spirituality in the Anglican tradition. Wherever bread is broken and wine outpoured, there Christ is present and makes himself known. This is beautifully expressed in the second post-communion prayer in the Alternative Service Book:

> Lord when we were still far off you met us in your son and brought us home. Dying and living he declared your love, gave us grace and opened the gate of glory. May we who share Christ's body live his risen life; we who drink his cup bring life to others; we whom the spirit lights give light to the world. Keep us firm in the hope you have set before us, so we and all your children shall be free and the whole earth live to praise your name.

Here is the biblical underpinning of how spirituality is shaped and expressed, doctrine expressed in poetic language, and the plea that we might be Christ to the world in what we do and say. All is of grace and the eschatological thrust of the prayer provides a counter-balance to complacency or any tendency to become too rooted in this world. Centuries before this prayer was composed, the non-juror and spiritual writer William Law (1686–1761) wrote about "the process of Christ" by which he meant the daily encounters Christians have with the risen Christ in events and circumstances as well as through word and sacrament that mold us in Christ's likeness. For many today, this is a very costly experience, and spirituality for them is cross-shaped in every way. When an indigenous spirituality has to be worked out in the face of hostile opposition, as it does in parts of Nigeria, for example, there is little room for complacency or nostalgia.

## Local

The local nature of indigenous Anglican spirituality is an essential aspect of how it should be understood. Cultural differences between, say North America and the Sudan, mean that searching for similarities between them is a tenuous business. Early on in the history of the Christian faith in Britain, parishes and dioceses became the way the church practiced its mission. Everyone belonged to a parish and could expect pastoral care from the cradle to the grave. Most Anglican churches across the communion still have a sense of continuity with the past and an identity that is rooted in the local area, though the English concept of the parish may not be present. Just as God in Christ took flesh and was born in a particular place at a particular time in history, that same incarnational principle is at work in Anglican spirituality. This has important consequences for how spirituality should be expressed locally.

As the preface to the Book of Common Prayer in "Of ceremonies" puts it: "And in these our doings we condemn no other nations, nor prescribe any thing but to our own people only. For we think it convenient that every country should use such ceremonies as they shall think best to the setting forth of God's honour and glory, and to the reducing of the people to a most perfect and godly living, without error or superstition." Local difference is perfectly in keeping with Anglican self-understanding. From the sixteenth century, Anglicans have seen themselves as the local embodiment of the catholic or universal church. They have never set out to claim that they are the best or the only church. Hooker wrote of God's harmonious dissimilitude of types of church. An early example before the era of Anglican expansion abroad is Wales, which has had its own Bible and prayer book in Welsh since the sixteenth century.

The impact of the sixteenth century on the Church of England has meant that there is a close relationship between church and state in the United Kingdom that is not evident elsewhere. The fact that, in England, the established church was so closely bound up with its political life had important consequences for its spiritual life, and often changes in the church were as a result of social or political change. Inevitably, there were knock-on effects that impacted people's spirituality, and this continues today.

While this has had its serious drawbacks, in terms of its spirituality it has meant that the church has never shied away from getting involved in the structures of society. Reaching out for the love of Christ has led Anglicans to challenge injustice and campaign on behalf of the weak and voiceless at a high level, as well as encourage its members to care for their neighbors in small but vital ways. It is indicative of this characteristic that one of the most influential bodies in the Anglican Communion has been the Mothers' Union. Founded by an Anglican woman, Mary Sumner, the movement currently has 4 million members in 81 countries around the world, and in many ways demonstrates the growing and changing nature of the Anglican Communion. It also exemplifies the essence of Anglican spirituality in the way it celebrates something fundamental to our common humanity while expressing a grounded spirituality through prayer, programs, policy work, and community relationships that effect change and express the love of Christ. Their work has the same quality of practical spirituality described earlier that nurtures, sustains, and effects change in the lives of many.

Mention of the Mothers' Union is a reminder of the part played by women in the Anglican Communion in helping to shape Anglican spirituality. The story of Anglican spirituality in the United Kingdom has many unsung female characters, as well as a handful of missionaries, social reformers, and prayer warriors who are better known. There have been efforts taken in recent decades to raise the profile of women throughout the church, and spirituality is an area where they have made a huge contribution behind the scenes through prayer and nurture. The report *Making Women Visible*, published in 1988, is indicative of women's role needing to be taken seriously, not least in the area of spirituality. It has often been women such as Evelyn Underhill, for example, who have led the way in the ministry of spiritual direction.

## Elitist?

It is sometimes claimed that Anglican spirituality is elitist. A spirituality that often refers to poetry, literary figures, and church architecture seems to suggest that this is the case. It is also true that a great deal of cultural and historical baggage has been exported along with the gospel and superimposed on other cultures, as if to say that spirituality can be adopted as a readymade commodity. Greater respect for local context, both at home and abroad, is enabling Anglican spirituality to put down roots and grow in response to the indigenous situation, as well as offering challenge where necessary.

Anglican spirituality may conjure up images of high-flown poetry and prose, but mention of the Mothers' Union reminds us that it is essentially practical in nature. At its best, it is a way of life that flows out of going to church and joining in formal worship in word and sacrament. Personal prayer, public worship, and community service are intimately linked because God is involved in the whole of life. Prayers for rain, for those at sea, and for the sick, contained in the Book of Common Prayer but reproduced in principle and form all around the world, remind us of spirituality's all-encompassing nature.

## Settled?

The spirituality of the Book of Common Prayer was an expression of life in the sixteenth century when it was assumed that all people were Christians. Therefore, there was no mention of mission or going out to spread the gospel because to be Anglican was to be English, and vice versa. Even in the sixteenth century, however, this proved impossible to sustain. The spirituality which the Book of Common Prayer expressed was focused on helping people to grow in prayer and holy living. Yet, the prayer book has been exported around the world and is still held in high regard as a spiritual resource. Indigenous forms of worship have developed alongside it, however, which express the local spirituality more fully and authentically. Appropriate ways of praying that reflect the context in which they are prayed can only encourage and deepen local expressions of spirituality and enable the Anglican Communion to be more fully itself amidst great diversity.

Historically, the Anglican Church has been caricatured as "the British Empire at prayer," implying that its spirituality is suitable for the English alone. Few in the United Kingdom would assent to this image today. While there is no longer a British Empire, the Anglican Communion remains and consists of churches that are increasingly indigenous and independent. How strong the family likeness continues to be will depend in part on acknowledgement of the value of the principles of Anglican spirituality in the past and the ability to translate them into something meaningful for a variety of present contexts. In parts of the world where persecution is a reality, most adherents to the Christian faith will think of themselves as Christian before being Anglican. The Anglican Communion is growing even here, however. What it will look like to future generations is still an open question. One formative influence is the growing family of indigenous prayer books issued as a result of the Liturgical Movement, whereas in previous generations the Book of Common Prayer had been the standard resource, regardless of context. Whereas worship once relied on one book, there are now many other possibilities. Liturgical renewal and cultural adaptation are helping to forge a characteristically Anglican spirituality in different parts of the communion. They will enable the Christian gospel to be seen more clearly through the culture in which it is being spread and a subsequent native spirituality to deepen in culturally appropriate ways.

## Fellowship

Anglican spirituality is not an individualistic affair. Worship draws us into fellowship with other believers across the world and through time. The Book of Common Prayer reinforced this sense of continuity and, while this unifying factor has been seriously eroded, the importance of the word of God in Anglican liturgies continues to connect us with God and with one another. Moreover, the basis of Common Worship, while seeking to provide variety, continues to be built upon a clear structure with a liturgical shape that provides common ground for liturgical prayer. Prayer and scripture sustain all Christian spirituality, and do so for Anglicans in a particular way.

A number of influences besides politics and local culture that influence worship in a global church also affect her spirituality. These include developments in information technology, new approaches to music and visual presentation, the charismatic movement, increased lay leadership within scattered communities, and a stress on individual choice.

Anglican worship seeks to lead people to God, to feed the spiritual life of individuals, and to shape the mission of the church. It can look very different in different parts of the Anglican Communion but behind the diversity is a desire to foster a common understanding and approach.

## Vision

The Anglican vision of the world encompasses the broad sweep of Creation, Incarnation, Redemption, and the Consummation of all things. This big vision means that we may know God as one who acts in the present moment and is encountered in our daily existence, but we are also made aware that he cannot be domesticated or shrunk to our small horizons. It is a vision that reminds us that God goes before us and has a concern for all his creation. He is not confined to the Christian church. Historically, Anglican spirituality had its roots in the parish, the local congregation where all were welcome and the church had a duty to baptize, marry, and bury all within its boundaries. While this is breaking down in the United Kingdom today and does not appertain to other parts of the communion at all, the principle of openness toward outsiders remains, however. Many have begun their spiritual journey because they have been allowed to hover at the edges of the body of Christ until they feel ready to commit themselves in response to God's call on their lives. This is less true in those parts of the world where a clear identity and commitment has been necessary for survival.

Anglicans are intentionally inclusive, though there have been times when they have squeezed out those who are deemed too far beyond the bounds of the Anglican way. However, even in the sixteenth century, when Puritans and conservatives struggled to take the church in one or other direction, many church leaders worked hard to maintain a middle way that would hold on to as many as possible.

## Diverse

Today, breadth and diversity characterize Anglican spirituality, and this is increasing all the time. The Church of England has never stood still in this respect. Historically, the English Tractarians were instrumental in the growth of the Anglican Communion worldwide through their demand that the church should be free to order its internal affairs without state interference. Christians the world over are less interested in denominations than they were a few generations ago. Anglicanism has often been seen as a bridge connecting widely diverse parts of the Christian church. Bridges are only required when there are divides. Moreover, as its catalogue of poets, writers, artists, and musicians demonstrates, Anglicanism values creativity, so who can complain if diversity continues to blossom? The recognition of the central role played by context for theology and spirituality suggests that such diversity is here to stay.

Above all, Anglican spirituality articulates the biblical truth that the church consists of a pilgrim people. The word *parakoia* from which we gain the word "parish" originally meant a Christian community in any place, that is, sojourners. When we regard spirituality as something settled and permanent, we lose something that is vital regarding its essence. People learn by participation to speak with one another in the idiom of their own churches, and this involves a host of factors including unspoken assumptions, tone, ways of relating, and attitudes toward common structures, to name a few. The long and varied history of the Anglican Church means that there is a great treasure house of spiritual resources to draw upon. Ironically, the richer and more diverse the communion becomes, modern Anglicans may well be less aware of the riches of their tradition.

## A Balanced Spirituality

Balance is found in the Anglican way of doing theology and also in her understanding of discipleship. Anglican spirituality involves the heart as well as the mind, the body as well as the soul.

The seventeenth-century pastor and poet George Herbert, like Hooker before him, combined pastoral sensitivity with theological acumen. Through meditation on the daily office and the Eucharist, Herbert wrote his poems to give meaning to his own life and the ordinary lives of those people to whom he ministered. He has been held up as the perfect parish priest (which probably does not correspond to reality), an ideal that most in the West have found impossible to emulate. Herbert, however, did not set himself up as the model for all Anglicans to follow, but his spirituality as expressed through his poetry has inspired many who have experienced the contrary nature of so much of the life of faith. This paradoxical "on the one hand . . . and on the other" characteristic of faith is evident also in the prayer book in which Herbert's spirituality was steeped. On the one hand, we are abject sinners not worthy to pick up the crumbs from under that table, while on the other grace abounds and we rejoice in the invitation to intimacy with the living God. Life has to be lived within these parameters, the daily experience of both being an ever-present reality. Herbert understood and articulated the struggles of the spiritual life. He described his poems as a "picture of the many spiritual conflicts that have passed between God and my soul, before I could subject mine to the will of Jesus my master, in whose service I have now found perfect freedom." As such, they embody the constant conflict of Romans: 7, which is the conflict of self-will. In this, he embodies much that may be deemed the Anglican spirit: striving for balance, reason, contrition, but having nothing to do with despair. Grace will have the last word every time. Herbert may seem a far cry from the twenty-first century, yet in the West at least, we have entered what has been called an age of spirituality, and it may be the poetic that offers the key to spiritual revival here. Herbert is a reminder that it is possible to teach Christian truth in ways that are both practical and memorable and that spirituality can stay connected to truth and speak to people where they are.

## All the Saints

Cranmer, Hooker, and Herbert, the liturgist, the thinker, and the poet, respectively, were all in their different ways offering windows into the spiritual life. All were deeply rooted in scripture, used reason to negotiate the world, and, in addition to being rooted in the Christian tradition, were instrumental in taking it forward for a new age. Prayer and spirituality were integral to their aims: Cranmer seeking to make God accessible to the people through a liturgy that could be prayed and lived; Hooker who reflected long and hard on how scripture informs the way we order our lives; and Herbert who wrestled through carefully chosen words with sinful humanity transformed by grace. It is interesting but not perhaps surprising that Anglicans of all traditions appeal to them as authoritative. All three left room for ambiguity, leaving room for further light to be shed. They gave English-speaking people a way of talking about God that was not confined to those who shared their theological convictions, and they were able to do this because they did their theology less by systematically examining doctrinal structures as by reflecting on the shape of the Christian life as it was lived in the ordinary. The principle remains true for the spiritual life, wherever it is lived. It is perhaps a good way of describing the heart of Anglican spirituality to say it is about what a human life looks like when it is transformed by grace. This flexibility means that Anglican spirituality is difficult to pin down and is easily lost underneath political battles within Anglicanism. Yet, it may be that the key to the survival of a lively and relevant Anglican spirituality is that same flexibility that can be adapted to different contexts.

Anglican spirituality holds many great figures in high esteem as examples of the faith besides these three notables. There are other poets besides literary figures and statesmen, people who have made their mark in the world. However, perhaps one of the most characteristic features of Anglican spirituality is that it is equally valid to point to the unknowns, the nobodies, the young, the old, and the ordinary folk who follow Christ and see them as examples of the spiritual life, too. Prayer and scripture, worship, and seeing "heaven in ordinary" would probably constitute the essence of their spirituality. With over 85 million adherents in 160 countries, this will inevitably be expressed in a myriad different ways as each one seeks to live out in their daily lives what it means to trust and obey the risen Christ.

## Bibliography

Dudley, M. R. 2002. Collect. In *The new SCM Dictionary of Liturgy and Worship*, ed. P. Bradshaw. London: SCM.

# CHAPTER 64

# Views of Colonization Across the Anglican Communion

## Robert S. Heaney

This chapter will outline both positive and negative views of colonization before beginning to envisage practices for a critically post-colonial Anglican Communion. Prior to this task, it is important that the way in which key terms are used in this chapter be outlined. It should be noted that these concepts and practices are more complex than these initial definitions would suggest (Young 2001). Nonetheless, they are submitted at the outset to orientate the reader quickly for what follows.

Within the purposes and scope of this chapter, colonialism is the practice of foreign settlement on stolen land. Colonization goes beyond geographical incursion to include also the importation of, for example, custom, education, ideology, culture, law, and religion, which is often viewed by the colonizers as superior to the previous practices of the colonized. Empire is a collection of colonies under the sovereignty of a centralized foreign power. Imperialism refers to a vision or impulse for hegemonic control over territory, peoples, and cultures beyond a metropolitan center, purportedly for the benefit of that center and the peripheries to which the vision is directed. Globalization has been used more recently to explain practices which have ancient precedent (Hatton 2011). It is used especially to focus attention on the apparent decline in the power of nation states and the rise of the influence of international capitalism, international media, international political organizations, and international economic organisms driven by the logic of the market.

## Viewing Colonization as Providential

Anglican concern for empire and colonization is missional. It might be seen to begin with the foundation of the Society for the Propagation of the Gospel in Foreign Parts (SPG) in 1701 (Strong 2007, 6, 32). From that time, a consistently religio-imperial

*The Wiley-Blackwell Companion to the Anglican Communion*, First Edition. Edited by Ian S. Markham,
J. Barney Hawkins IV, Justyn Terry, and Leslie Nuñez Steffensen.
© 2013 John Wiley & Sons, Ltd. Published 2013 by John Wiley & Sons, Ltd.

discourse emerges and is sustained, to greater or lesser degrees, until the era of decolonization. If, as is too often the case, the theological nature of the engagement with Anglicanism's enmeshment with colonization is overlooked or reduced, much misunderstanding follows. This is not to say that all or even a majority of Anglicans were interested in theologizing about the British Empire. It is simply to say that, for Anglicans interested in engagement with the emergence of such an empire overseas, the engagement took place through a theological lens.

An Anglican theological construction of empire begins with a conviction in divine providence (Strong 2007, 32). Consequently, Bishop Blomfield in an 1827 sermon could ponder:

> An empire so vast, so interspersed amidst the different nations of the world, so unaccountable in its growth, so singular in its structure, as fully to justify a belief that Providence has ordained it for some purpose of vast importance to mankind; and . . . a commerce so wonderfully extended and extending that we may seem to discern the finger of the Most High (O'Connor et al. 2000, 52–3).

Such theologizing was not only evident in the metropole. It was also evident among those who experienced colonization as missionaries. Johann Rebmann of the Church Missionary Society (CMS), who had 30 years' experience of working in the absence of European political governance, concluded that ". . . where the power of a Christian nation ceased to be felt, there is also the boundary, set by Providence, to missionary labor" (Strayer 1978, 33).

For imperial Anglicanism, the *missio dei* is not abstract. It is grounded in historical realities. The British Empire is determined, or allowed, by God to be the means of blessing for the world. Consequently, that which is outside the providential work of God is Other and to be resisted and remade. That England is a nation favored by God includes the notion, and requisite practices which emerge from it, that the Church of England is herself a peculiar vessel for God. Both indigenous peoples and unregenerate colonialists had, therefore, to be rescued from perdition. In 1709, Sir William Dawes (Bishop of Chester) asks:

> As to our holy religion: When doth that ever appear as glorious, as when it is enlarging its Borders, and extending its Conquests over the World? As when it is beating down Ignorance, Superstition, Errour, Profaneness and Irreligion? As when it is triumphing over the Prejudices, Lusts, Passions, and Vices of Mankind, and setting up its rational and holy Empire upon the Ruins of them? (Strong 2007, 61)

Imperial Anglicans conceive of empire in providential terms and see its function in missional terms. It is, therefore, theologically reductionist and historically simplistic not to differentiate them within British imperialism. The relationship between Anglican mission and colonization was both co-operative and conflictual.

Anglican mission and colonization co-operated when the aims and/or practices of both colonizers and missionaries were similar or perceived to be similar. This resulted in, for example, education and evangelization being provided by missionaries, which colonizers sometimes regarded as bringing pacification. Anglican missionaries also mirrored practices which colonizers adopted. The SPG had two Barbadian plantations bequeathed to it in 1710 (Ward 2006, 86). Apparently, providence deigned that the SPG become a slave-owning mission. Unsurprisingly, the SPG did not promote abolition in the Caribbean (Ward 2006, 87).

Conflictual relationships between colonizers and missional Anglicans could arise both at the metropolitan center and in the colony. Anglican missional understandings of imperialism could clash with colonial and/or settler policy. In some contexts, evangelism might be seen to bring pacification. In other contexts, it might be seen as creating subversive emancipatory expectations. Conflict can be seen also when, during the 1750s and 1760s in North America, colonial bishops, in succession with British sees, were sought. Such succession was considered suspect in a pluralist context where Congregationalists and Independents feared for their liberty. Such fears were not to be exacerbated by any decision in London, and the government would not support local bishops. Imperial Anglicanism could not, in this case, bring about its envisaged end precisely because it was enmeshed with the empire (Strong 2007, 112–15, 283–94).

In the colonies, missionaries sometimes lobbied, with debatable effectiveness, against colonial policies which were disadvantageous to those colonized (Mbiti 1999, 10–11). Missionaries sometimes acted as "buffers" between "rulers and citizens" (Mugambi 2004, 18). John Colenso (SPG) in South Africa and James Long (CMS) in India exemplify such conflictual relationships. Colenso and Long opposed colonial malpractice, were involved in controversial political campaigns for indigenous peoples, and sought to correlate Zulu and Indian traditions and practices with the Old Testament (Sugirtharajah 2002, 49–52). Despite such conflict, there is little evidence that those involved in it ever questioned the colonial paradigm itself. These counter-discourses are voiced within the framework of colonialism. Colenso and Long recognized the brutality of colonization and sought a more humane empire. They were imperial Anglicans because they remained committed to the theological conviction that God had ordained, providentially, the British Empire for God's good (missional) purposes.

By the first half of the nineteenth century, evangelical Anglicans had become part of the religio-imperial discourse (Strong 2007, 33). A well-distilled articulation of evangelical theologizing on colonization is found in the Reinecker Lectures given by Max Warren at the Virginia Theological Seminary in 1955. Warren was general secretary of the CMS from 1942 to 1963. These lectures were later published as *Caesar the Beloved Enemy: Three Studies in the Relation of Church and State*:

> ... the expansion of Christianity as an influence and a creed, as a civilization and a Gospel, has in fact been intimately related to political realities of which imperialism has been one of the most important. From Constantine to Mao-tse-tung this intimate relationship has been an embarrassment and a scandal but also a testimony and an adventure of faith (Warren 1955, 11).

Warren is conscious that his "theology of imperialism" is being developed in a context where those who have experienced colonization are rejecting foreign domination.

It is imperative . . . that those concerned with the Christian Mission in the world should
have a theology of imperialism which can at once distinguish the place of imperialism in
the providence of God and at the same time recognize its ambiguous character as affording
material both for theology and demonology (Warren 1955, 13–14).

Despite a rejection of domination "making every necessary qualification as to the sinfulness of those who exercise power," it is possible to theologically (and biblically) justify
the subordination of one group of people by another. Indeed, it is possible to ". . . envisage circumstances in which imperialism has a place in the purpose and providence of
God." As with Warren's imperialist Anglican forebears, imperialism is only ever theologically justified according to its missional efficacy. Colonization is legitimate if it serves
". . . the purpose of God in history . . . to bring mankind to a true knowledge of Himself
who is Love, Power and Justice" (Warren 1955, 24). For Warren, that justification will
include at least three characteristics: law bringing unity, vocation, and greater goods.

Colonization can establish a rule of law and unity among formerly disparate peoples.
These qualities, argues Warren, are theologically significant because they correlate
with eschatological realities. Those colonized move from being citizens of tribes to
become citizens of the world, which is a step toward becoming citizens of God's eternal
kingdom (Warren 1955, 26–8). "Imperialism would then appear to have a function as
a *preparatio* for God's good will for the world. At least, up till today, no other method has
been devised for so successfully keeping the peace and making progress possible"
(Warren 1955, 28).

Warren draws on Paul Tillich's understanding that power is not only physical but
also symbolic. This symbolic power, exercised often through language and culture, is
"spiritual" and can engender a sense of special vocation. Such special vocation can be
ignoble (as in the concept of *Herrenvolk*), but it can also be noble, inspiring selfless and
societal service (Warren 1955, 29–31).

Colonization and subordination limit the freedom of subject peoples. However,
Warren argues, greater goods may become apparent. For example, the greater goods
delivered to India by Britain include legislation predicated on the equality of all before
the law, democracy, cities, unity, and an integration of the country into a community
of nations (Warren 1955, 31–41). Unlike earlier imperial Anglicans, Warren is more
prepared to acknowledge resistance against colonization. However, it seems, Warren
does not take seriously the possibility that there may exist theological counter-
discourses against any missional interpretation of colonization.

## Viewing Colonization as Heresy

Anglican counter-imperial discourses exist. In order both to present the Anglican
nature of such counter-discourse and begin to point toward post-colonial Anglican
practice, the present section will be viewed through a familiar theological lens. Consequently, experience, Bible, reason, and tradition will begin to be interrogated and seen
to provoke wider post-colonial concerns and practices of marginalized agency, power
analyses, hybridity, and decolonization.

The Three Combined Bodies: Missionaries, Government, and Companies or Gainers of money do form the same rule to look on a Native with mockery eyes. It sometimes startles us to see that the Three Combined Bodies are from Europe, and along with them there is a title "CHRISTENDOM." And to compare or make a comparison between the MASTER of the title and His Servant it pushes any African away from believing the Master of the title. If we had the power enough to communicate ourselves to Europe, we would have advised them not to call themselves "CHRISTENDOM" but "Europeandom" . . . the title "CHRISTENDOM" does not belong to Europe, but to future BRIDE. Therefore the life of the Three Combined Bodies is altogether too cheaty, too thefty, too mockery (Isichei 1995, 142).

Because of his *experience* of foreign Christianity, Charles Domingo penned these words in Malawi in 1911. The "mockery eyes," and attendant violence, undermine a gospel which declares all are made in the image of God and redeemed in Christ. For him, foreign malpractice abrogates any missional justification for colonization. His wish for "power enough" to communicate with Europe would eventually become a reality as published theological counter-discourses, especially since the 1960s, began to emerge from former colonies. These discourses from beyond the metropole, along with theologizing influenced by post-colonial criticisms and theories from within the metropole, challenge theological justifications for colonization. Correlation between colonial subjugation and Christianity is assessed as "a scandal" by colonized theologians (Mugambi 2003, 70). "During the colonial period Christianity tended to be used for the theological justification of colonial domination. There was a tendency to bless and sanctify imperial domination as a positive experience for colonial subjects. How can a liberating God condone oppression?" (Mugambi 1989, 147).

Such counter-discoursing gives voice and vision to those who experience marginalization. They are not objects of mission but theological subjects. Such theological agency begins with imagination. Imagining, as part of a decolonizing of the mind, is vital because without envisaging a different reality it will be impossible to struggle for or live toward such a reality. Consequently, "stepping outside" Eurocentricism for Kwok Pui-Lan is achieved by historical imagining (hearing voices of marginalized women), dialogical imagining (problematizing the liberal notion of diversity and recognizing asymmetrical power relations), and diasporic imagining (undermining the assumptions that Christianity is normatively Western) (Kwok 2005, 29–51).

The God of the *Bible* appears to be both *conquistador* and liberator. For those theologically resisting colonization, the biblical text itself is colonized ground. A variety of power relations, both liberative and oppressive, seem to be embedded and sanctioned by scripture. God liberates the people from slavery. God calls the people to steal (colonize) the land of others. A retreat to the authority of the liberal self or a retreat to the authority of the text conserved without criticism will not change this. Consequently, a post-colonial appeal to the Bible will need to do more than recognize that there is a plurality of cultural contextualizations in the communion. An appeal to the Bible will mean active recognition of power relations within the text and in the interpretation of the text. Indeed, there is evidence that just this kind of criticism is impacting Anglican thought and practice.

Musa Dube raises the issue of how the Bible is to be read by Africans, given its role in imperialism. Because the coming of the text to Africa is inextricably linked to the colonizing of African lands and African minds, the Bible must prove its liberating and decolonizing potential (Dube 2000, 4, 19). Gerald West rightly notes that it is not only the Bible that affects Africa. Africa is an "actor." The Bible then is the object of the actions of African interpreters. There is a transactional relationship between the Bible and its interpreters. The Bible in colonial contexts is not always a gift. Africans have paid dearly for it and continue to negotiate with it. Power analysis in the task of interpretation is, therefore, necessary. "Ordinary" readers and "ordinary" exegesis play a part in a critically post-colonial approach to the biblical text. West observes, "African biblical scholars have revelled in the unravelling of the masters' mystical and exclusive academic empire, unprivileging the dominant discourses and thereby admitting, at last, the contributions of ordinary Africans to the task of critical discourse" (West 2000, 43).

An anti-imperial discourse will critique Anglican *reason*. R. S. Sugirtharajah rightly complains that much published theology is done in light of the Reformation, the Counter-Reformation, the Enlightenment, modernity, the Holocaust, and postmodernity while ignoring the theological causes and effects of colonization (Sugirtharajah 2002, 25, 28). For example, Paul Avis acknowledges that Anglicanism has spread largely because of empire (Avis 2008, 52). The significance he, and many others, draw from such history is the cultural competition between assimilation and inculturation or contextualization. Questions of how imperial practices affect visions of God are ignored. This large-scale failure remains a challenge to the purported critical nature of Anglican theologizing. The challenge is compounded when it is recognized that theologies emerging in colonial and post-colonial contexts explicitly critique so-called Western theologizing and exclusionary reason. Eurocentric reason, shaping and being shaped by colonization, delivers much Anglican theological practice. However, Enlightenment certainties and rationalism are questioned (McGrath 1993, 131–3). The universality of the Enlightenment is an attempt to globalize "the" European "Man." The post-colonial point here is not that Eurocentric rationalism fails simply because the universalist assumptions arose from particular traditions and cultures. The point is that such rationalism explicitly excludes others and uses them to define modernist rationality over against the "irrationality" of the Other. Colonized peoples, argues Kant, have displayed a passivity more akin to animals than to rational European men. They will be raised from their irrational indolence only through a civilizing mission. Theologies built upon such understandings of rationality are exclusionary not as a by-product of history. They are exclusionary philosophically (Serequeberhan 1997; McCarthy 2009). Post-colonial theologizing will not, therefore, be fixated with the aims of coherency or with answering the rational skeptic. Rather, what might be termed the "moral skeptic" and the "transformative function of theology" will be in view.

Attention is drawn to the experiences of colonialists (and missionaries) and colonized (and converts) which problematize, hybridize, and undermine such polar distinctions as self/other, pure/impure, sacred/profane, and rational/chaotic. Post-colonial scholars seek to identify the underlying subjugating agenda which sustains such differences (Bhabha 1994, 2–12). More constructively, post-colonial theologies identify and affirm the apparent hybridities present in Christian theology which will serve a multilingual, multiracial, multicultural world better. Christianity itself emerges as a "great hybrid," intermixing metaphysics, philosophies, and identities at the "urban crossroads of the Roman Empire" (Keller et al. 2004, 13–14).

It is widely assumed that Anglicanism is a (living) *tradition*. It emerges in the actions and reactions of Christians in the sixteenth century. It might be assumed that, throughout the communion and wherever else Anglicanism is taught, its "proximity to the castle" (*aban mu asor*) remains (Pobee 1998, 450). That is to say, Henry VIII, Cranmer, Elizabeth I, Jewel, Hooker et al. are part of the story passed on. This, along with claims to apostolic and biblical tradition, is the assumed historic and theological substructure of a globalized Anglican Communion. However, tradition has not only meant connections to the past. Tradition has been a globalizing imposition of foreign categories and, its corollary, the debasement of others. Missionaries and their converts often exhibited a "bulldozer mentality" which assumed that indigenous traditions were demonic and, therefore, needed to be "swept aside." Too often, missionaries ". . . scandalized, vandalized, and brutally tor[e] cultural life apart . . ." (Mbiti 1994, 12, 138). If evidence was found of converts involved in "devilish" rites such as sacrifice, dances, and circumcision, they could be suspended from Christian instruction or fellowship. For many colonized people, it seemed that colonizers took their land and missionaries took their identity (see Brokenleg 2008, 281–3). Colonization is, therefore, both physical and epistemic violence.

Rejecting the hegemonic intent of imposed foreign traditions provokes the possibility, in post-colonial Anglicanism, of theological decolonization. Post-colonial criticism is a movement which seeks to undermine so-called "Western" hegemony. Hegemony, as it is especially associated with Antonio Gramsci, might be seen as the ideological dominance (or attempt at dominance) of one social group over others. For Gramsci, and tellingly for Anglicanism, the superiority of social groups is seen in domination *via* the organs of the state and in "intellectual and moral leadership" objectified in and practiced through education, religion, and associational institutions. This intellectual superiority is what constitutes hegemony (Femia 1975, 31; Gill and Law 1989; Said 2003, 6–7).

Given such a critique focusing on the issues of marginalized agency, the Bible's part in colonization, the oppositional nature of modernist reason, and the Eurocentric and hegemonic impulse of Anglican tradition, the final section will seek to provide a more constructive theological move toward practices for a post-colonial communion.

## Re-envisaging a Post-Colonial Communion

As has been seen, Anglican justification and resistance to colonization are theological. It is not an oversimplification, therefore, to submit that how colonization is viewed is shaped by how God is viewed, and how God is viewed is shaped by how colonization is experienced. If much Anglican theologizing, by its active justification or passivity, justifies the *status quo*, this section will examine the nature and implications of the God who resists human imperialisms. Consequently, this final section will begin to identify certain

Anglican post-colonial practices by addressing the issues of God and power, God and marginalization, God and hybridity, and God and decolonization.

## God and power

Today, human beings live in a world where superpower and hyperpower exist. The genealogy of imperialism, especially as it touches Anglicanism, is Eurocentric. However, its present potency is not limited to region. Its "logics of rule" function also in chronologically post-colonial contexts (Hardt and Negri 2000, xvi). Imperialist practice is still a desire for the extension of geographical, political, economical, as well as intellectual, emotional, psychological, spiritual, cultural, and religious control (Padilla 2004). It is control exhibited in top down power, disallowing alternative realities or alternative purposes (Rieger 2007, 2–3, 276; Williams 2011).

Rowan Williams, reflecting on the significance of the Nicene settlement, reminds Christians that God is not an individual. God's will is, therefore, not about "self-assertion" or "contest" for control (Williams 2002, 3578). The Trinity is non-individualistic, non-hierarchical, and differentiated. Consequently, such inherent ontological pluralism becomes a threat to the hegemonic processes of imperialism (Rieger 2007, 96). Most evocatively, Williams writes, "God does not compete with us for space" (Williams 2002, 3578). Humans colonize. God does not. The implications of such a vision of God "for ethics and for prayer and spirituality are enormous; and we are still discovering them" (Williams 2002, 3586). It should be added that this revelation of God has enormous implications, not only on Anglican biblical hermeneutics in making this the starting place for reading the text, but also for the Anglican Communion which we are, at best, only beginning to discover.

The divine does not compete for space. God's grace creates space for creation and fellowship with and between creation. A kingdom of eternal expansive grace stands in contrast to the expansionist over-reach of all human imperialism. Because of the Trinitarian revelation of God, particularisms of faith-responses, faith-communities, faith-traditions, and faith-stories emerge. Indeed, such pluralist particularisms are too often suppressed so that orthodoxy and catholicity are presented as homogeneous against the relativist pluralisms of heterodoxy. Yet, even Nicene Christianity is pluralist, and theological categories are elected (particularly *homoousios*), which one might describe as spacious (see Ayres 2004, 98–100; Rieger 2007, 94–5). A post-colonial Anglicanism will shun any strategies or impulses to contract or centralize the communion. The particularisms of provinces, dioceses, and parishes make up the story of the communion. These along with the variant theological traditions and methodologies, apparently at odds with each other, are part of the spaciousness of God's grace grounded in Anglicanism (Hooker *EP*, V, lxviii:6 [Keble 1876, 36]).

## God and marginalization

Divine power, as revealed in Christ, is witnessed in the marginalization of the Son at the hands of imperialism. Caesar pushes Christ beyond the margins of empire and life only to find that, beyond death, Christ subverts and converts the margin into a threshold. The empire's marginalizing of God in Christ becomes the threshold for renewed life, renewed community, and the reign of God. Caesarian power is subverted by divine power from the margins. Cruciform power does not emanate from the center, nor is it exercised from the top down. This liminal subversive power might be seen to have certain practical implications for a re-envisaged communion. Not least among such re-envisaged practice is a continued commitment to the margins and a practice of porosity because of the boundary-crossing risen Christ. It seems the so-called Anglican Covenant is particularly concerned with boundaries and centralizing authority. A covenant polices boundaries which, if not impermeable, are gated. The danger here is that the bureaucratizing of center and margin stands in tension with a more Christologically functioning center and margin. The center is Christ who needs no gatekeepers (John 10:9).

Practically, the communion faces a dilemma. It seems that many want the communion policed. There are, however, other ways. One way would be to abandon the practice of covenanted Anglicanism in favor of storied Anglicanism. Such communion would expect of believers and leaders regular testifying. At parish, diocesan, provincial, and international gatherings, Anglicans would be invited to testify to how their experiences and practices relate to biblical and Anglican traditions. Testifying to how Christ is central to the practices of the church would then be the communion Anglicans share. Centering on Christ and Christ's mission, in the stories of scripture, tradition, and contemporary believers, turns the attention of Anglicans away from border-making to the threshold-creating Christ. Because Christ practices lordship on the margins, Christ is the center of the church. Centering on Christ means turning our backs on border-policing while simultaneously being confronted by the margins of human experience in the broken body and poured-out life of Christ. In the Spirit, Word and sacrament push us to the margins where, in interstitial perspective, we network ("from the bottom up") in missions of particularities and localisms. The extent to which such networks can exist will depend, in part, on the recognition that ecclesiological boundaries are porous (mystical). The church is "mixed" (Hooker *EP*, III, xxiv:2 [Pollard 1990, 112–13]). It is hybridized fellowship.

### God and hybridity

The "primary characteristic" of a post-colonial text is hybridity (Ashcroft et al. 2002, 182). A transformative and decolonizing practice is recognized, in large part, to the degree in which it erases binary oppositions. Transformation is not the replacement of old binaries of opposition, such as colonizer versus colonized, with new binaries of opposition, such as liberated versus oppressor. It is largely for this reason, though some acknowledge their indebtedness, that post-colonial theologians distinguish themselves from liberationists. Post-colonial theology is about recognitions, readings, analyses, and practices which undermine rationalistic systems, clearly demarcated categories, and apparent simple causal relations.

For Kwok, "[t]he most hybridized concept in the Christian tradition is that of Jesus/Christ" (Kwok 2005, 171). The attempt to fix the space between "Jesus" and "Christ" for systematic, missiological, or rationalistic reasons results in a denial of the pluralist and hybrid contexts which shape gospel, and it simultaneously mollifies imperialism. It is because of the inherent hybrid nature of Jesus/Christ and the space ("contact zone" or "borderland") between Jesus and Christ that marginal Christologies exist. Consequently, Christ is Black, Corn Mother, Feminine Shakti, Theological Transvestite, and Bi/Christ (Kwok 2005, 174–85). Regardless of the merits of these Christologies, they do demonstrate what Homi Bhabha calls "interstitial perspective" (Bhabha 1994, 4). It is the conviction that God has come to us in hybridity (God-human) that makes such commitment to Christ possible in the first place. In Christ, humanity is opened to divinity and divinity to humanity. If Anglicanism codifies the binary of "covenanted" and "non-covenanted" believers, from a critically post-colonial perspective, it may be in danger of solidifying boundaries which God in Christ makes porous.

Hybridity in itself for itself does not necessarily hold theological value. Even cultural hybridity does not necessarily deliver transformative theological practice. An emphasis on hybridity can disempower attempts at transformative action if it is assumed that all oppositional stances are now comprised of people and circumstances that are partly good and partly bad. Does not the message that, to some extent, we are all colonizers and colonized veil ongoing oppression? It is possible that such danger can be undercut if it is recognized that practices of hybridity are predicated on "differentials of power not just on difference in general." It is because of the differentials of power that the potentially revolutionary and decolonizing effects of hybridization exist. Hybridizing only has decolonizing effect if powers are pushing for the erasure of local differences in favor of some kind of uniformity (Rieger 2010, 31).

The issues surrounding power differentials and the possible liberative function of hybridity pushes us back to the very issue we began this section with: God and power. According to Christian theology, there is a power differential between creator and creature. The danger is that this theological (ontological) power differential ultimately undermines all decolonizing action. Worse, the omnipotent lordship and sovereignty of God may, in the end, be justifiable theological ground for human empire building.

## God and decolonization

A possible riposte might be to stress the kenotic (self-emptying) exercise of divine power as both theologically well founded and practically decolonizing. However, Christian tradition may obstruct this very move. Under the influence of Cyril of Alexandria, *kenōsis* becomes in no sense a loss of power. Contrary to the apparent plain meaning of the text of Philippians 2, *kenōsis* becomes ". . . divine force that takes on humanity by controlling and partly *obliterating* it." While Sarah Coakley does not frame her analysis in post-colonial terms, it is possible to see how it can be extended to include such concerns (Coakley 2002, 15–16).

Coakley deals with several Anglican scholars who seek to respond constructively to the problems of such an "Alexandrian" reading. For present purposes, the approach of the colonial bishop of Zanzibar, Frank Weston, will be of particular interest. Weston seeks to elucidate an incarnated power where Christ submits voluntarily to the "law of self-restraint" (Weston 1914, 149–53). Christ is like St. Francis de Sales acting "merely" as confessor to his parents and relating to them as their son. Christ is a defeated African leader made "a king in slavery." Christ is a favorite son of an officer transferred to his father's regiment. The son possesses both "self-consciousness" as a son and, now, "limited consciousness" as a subordinate rank (Weston 1914, 166–72). Weston's chosen analogies deserve more analysis than can be provided here. Two of the analogies emerge directly from the crucible of colonization. Further, it is the African king alone who suffers not so much from self-limitation but from forced limitation. The white priest and, it might be assumed, the white soldier have the freedom to abandon their limitations through resigning from holy and military orders. However, even viewed Christologically, the emancipation of an African is unlikely. Decolonization, it appears, is not served by this incarnational kenoticism.

Coakley argues that true divine "empowerment" may occur "most unimpededly in the context of a *special* form of human 'vulnerability'." Her proposal assumes an understanding of *kenōsis*, which means choosing never to have "worldly" (colonizing) forms of power. Responding to the God who does not compete for space (Williams), believers make space for God in "defenceless" and "wordless" prayer (Coakley 2002, 31–4). Such worship is displacement. It is de-centering discipleship. It is human kenoticism in response to divine kenoticism. However, there is danger that such practice will be seized as a female and/or "non-Western" and/or lay "complement" in defining the roles and power of legions of male deacons, priests, and bishops (see Said 2003, 96, 105–10; Oduyoye 1995, 190–1). Yet, the interstices between this space-making prayer and space-making God are sacred. It is not possible to occupy potentiality. Consequently, this vulnerable *askēsis* is never an invitation or opportunity to be battered or silenced (Coakley 2002, 35; see Davis 1985, 95). Exercising such vulnerability inverts and undoes male and imperialist binaries of opposition. The call to prayer is a call to be undone. It is a call to be remade. In the current context, it is the Holy Spirit's call to a re-envisaged, vulnerable, and dangerous practice of Word and sacrament within a vulnerable communion.

In conclusion, across the communion in terms of history and theology, Anglicans view colonization as providential and as heresy. Accepting that colonization is sin, and ought not to be justified theologically, initial directions for a critically post-colonial communion are submitted. A re-envisaged Anglican Communion affirms particularisms which create a spacious Anglicanism. A re-envisaged communion is storied and not covenanted, thus leaving ecclesiological and theological boundaries, transformed by the risen Christ, porous and potentially thresholds to God's mission. A re-envisaged communion practices interstitial perspectives envisioning and identifying resistant and liberative potential for hybridities against hegemonic power. A re-envisaged communion practices a dangerous worship which makes us vulnerable, but in vulnerability we participate in the self-emptying, subversive power of God.

# Bibliography

Ashcroft, Bill, Gareth Griffiths, and Helen Tiffin. 2002. *The Empire Writes Back: Theory and Practice in Post-Colonial Literatures*, 2nd ed. London and New York: Routledge.

Avis, Paul. 2008. *The Identity of Anglicanism: Essentials of Anglican Ecclesiology*. London: T&T Clark.

Ayres, Lewis. 2004. *Nicea and its Legacy: An Approach to Fourth-Century Trinitarian Theology*. Oxford: Oxford University Press.

Bhabha, Homi K. 1994. *The Location of Culture*. London and New York: Routledge.

Brokenleg, Martin. 2008. Themes in Contemporary Native Theological Education. *Anglican Theological Review*, vol. 90, no. 2, pp. 277–83.

Coakley, Sarah. 2002. *Powers and Submissions: Spirituality, Philosophy and Gender*. Oxford: Blackwell.

Davis, Kortright. 1985. Third World Theological Priorities. *Scottish Journal of Theology*, vol. 40, pp. 85–105.

Dube, Musa W. 2000. *Postcolonial Feminist Interpretation of the Bible*. St. Louis: Chalice Press.

Femia, Joseph. 1975. Hegemony and Consciousness in the Thought of Antonio Gramsci. *Political Studies*, vol. 23, no. 1, pp. 29–48.

Gill, Stephen R. and David Law. 1989. Global Hegemony and the Structural Power of Capital. *International Studies Quarterly*, vol. 33, pp. 475–99.

Hardt, Michael and Antonio Negri. 2000. *Empire*. Cambridge and London: Harvard University Press.

Hatton, Peter. 2011. "Age after Age . . ." The Old Testament and Empire. *Soma: An International Journal of Theological Discourses and Counter-Discourses*. http://www.sjut.org/journals/ojs/index.php/soma/article/view/3/pdf_5. Accessed February 17, 2012.

Hooker, Richard. [1594–1662] 1876. *The Works of That Learned and Judicious Divine, Mr. Richard Hooker: with an Account of His Life and Death*. Edited by John Keble. Oxford:

Clarendon Press. http://anglicanhistory.org/hooker/. Accessed January 28, 2012.

Hooker, Richard. [1594–1662] 1990. *Ecclesiastical Polity*. Edited with an introduction by Arthur Pollard. Manchester: Carcanet Press.

Isichei, Elizabeth. 1995. *A History of Christianity in Africa: From Antiquity to the Present*. Grand Rapids: Eerdmans and Lawrenceville: Africa World Press.

Keller, Catherine, Michael Nausner, and Mayra Rivera, eds. 2004. *Postcolonial Theologies: Divinity and Empire*. St. Louis: Chalice Press.

Kwok, Pui-Lan. 2005. *Postcolonial Imagination and Feminist Theology*. Louisville: Westminster John Knox Press.

Mbiti, John S. 1994. Confessing Christ in a Multifaith Context, With Two Examples from Africa. *Metanoia*, vol. 4, no. 3–4, pp. 138–45.

Mbiti, John S. 1999. When the Right Hand Washes the Left Hand and the Left Hand Washes the Right Hand, the Two Will Be Clean: Some Thoughts on Justice and Christian Mission in Africa (and Madagascar). Paper presented at the Conference on Justice and Global Witness: A Biblical Foundation for Action, Washington, DC, July 8–10, 1991.

McCarthy, Thomas. 2009. *Race, Empire, and the Idea of Human Development*. Cambridge: Cambridge University Press.

McGrath, Alister. 1993. *The Renewal of Anglicanism*. London: SPCK.

Mugambi, J. N. K. 1989. Christological Paradigms in African Christianity. In *Jesus in African Christianity: Experimentation and Diversity in African Christology*, eds. J. N. K. Mugambi and Laurenti Magesa. Nairobi: Initiatives, pp. 136–61.

Mugambi, J. N. K. 2003. *Christian Theology and Social Reconstruction*. Nairobi: Acton.

Mugambi, J. N. K. 2004. Religion and Social Reconstruction in Post-Colonial Africa. In *Church–State Relations: A Challenge for African Christianity*, eds. J. N. K. Mugambi, and Frank Küschner-Pelkman. Nairobi: Acton, pp. 13–34.

O'Connor, Daniel, et al. 2000. *Three Centuries of Mission: The United Society for the Propagation of the Gospel 1701–2000.* London and New York: Continuum.

Oduyoye, Mercy Amba. 1995. *Daughters of Anowa: African Women and Patriarchy.* Maryknoll: Orbis Press.

Padilla, C. René. 2004. United States Foreign Policy and Terrorism. In *Terrorism and the War in Iraq: A Christian Word from Latin America.* Buenos Aires: Kairos Ediciones.

Pobee, John. 1998. Non-Anglo-Saxon Anglicanism. In *The Study of Anglicanism*, revised edition, eds. Stephen Sykes, John Booty, and Jonathan Knight. London: SPCK and Minneapolis: Fortress Press, pp. 446–59.

Rieger, Joerg. 2007. *Christ and Empire: From Paul to Postcolonial Times.* Minneapolis: Fortress Press.

Rieger, Joerg. 2010. *Globalization and Theology.* Nashville: Abingdon Press.

Said, Edward. 2003 [1978]. *Orientalism.* London: Penguin Books.

Serequeberhan, Tsenay. 1997. The Critique of Eurocentrism and the Practice of African Philosophy. In *Postcolonial African Philosophy: A Critical Reader*, ed. Emmanuel Chukwudi Eze. Oxford: Blackwell, pp. 141–61.

Strayer, Robert W. 1978. *The Making of Mission Communities in East Africa: Anglicans and Africans in Colonial Kenya, 1875–1935.* London: Heinemann.

Strong, Rowan. 2007. *Anglicanism and the British Empire c. 1700–1850.* Oxford: Oxford University Press.

Sugirtharajah, R. S. 2002. *Postcolonial Criticism and Biblical Interpretation.* Oxford: Oxford University Press.

Ward, Kevin. 2006. *A History of Global Anglicanism.* Cambridge: Cambridge University Press.

Warren, M. A. C. 1955. *Caesar The Beloved Enemy: Three Studies in the Relation of Church and State.* London: SCM Press.

West, Gerald O. 2000. Mapping African Biblical Interpretation: A Tentative Sketch. In *The Bible in Africa: Transactions, Trajectories, and Trends*, eds. Gerald O. West and Musa W. Dube. Leiden: Brill, pp. 29–53.

Weston, Frank. 1914. *The One Christ: An Enquiry into the Manner of the Incarnation*, revised edition. London: Longmans, Green and Co.

Williams, Rowan. 2002. *Arius: Heresy and Tradition*, 2nd ed. Grand Rapids: Eerdmans. Kindle Electronic Edition (references are to location not page number).

Williams, Rowan. 2011. "Kingdom" and Empire: A Biblical Orientation. *Soma: An International Journal of Theological Discourses and Counter-Discourses.* www.sjut.org/journals/ojs/index.php/soma/article/viewFile/2/pdf_4. Accessed January 25, 2012.

Young, Robert J. C. 2001. *Postcolonialism: An Historical Introduction.* Malden: Blackwell.

CHAPTER 65

# The Global Anglican Future Conference (GAFCON)

## Mark D. Thompson

In June 2008, 1,148 men and women met in Jerusalem for the Global Anglican Future Conference (GAFCON). The attendees were Anglican leaders from around the globe, including 291 bishops, who represented more than two-thirds of the world's Anglicans. Most of these bishops had decided not to attend the upcoming Lambeth Conference, choosing instead to meet in this way to talk about the mission of Christ and the future of confessional Anglicanism in the post-colonial, aggressively secular world of the twenty-first century. The organizers had insisted that, while a crisis in the Anglican Communion had been the catalyst for the conference, its real focus would be the future, the biblical faith, and global mission. This was the beginning of a worldwide movement (the Fellowship of Confessing Anglicans, FCA), a network of Anglicans committed to the authority of scripture and joining together to see Christ proclaimed as the only hope for lost men and women. The statement of faith drafted at the conference (the Jerusalem Declaration) has been embraced by many around the world as a powerful affirmation of Anglican orthodoxy. It represents the first expression of a rejuvenated Anglicanism that takes the Thirty-Nine Articles seriously as a confessional standard and is more clearly focused on faithfulness to the teaching of scripture than on acceptability in contemporary secular Western culture.

## The Anglican Crisis at the Turn of the Century

The catalyst for GAFCON was a realization that the official instruments of the Anglican Communion were either unwilling or unable to act decisively to deal with departures from Anglican doctrine and practice on the part of the Episcopal Church (USA) and the Anglican Church of Canada. These departures were in fact simply further steps along a trajectory extending back many decades, even centuries, and involving much more than the presenting issue of human sexuality. Different conceptions of authority,

*The Wiley-Blackwell Companion to the Anglican Communion*, First Edition. Edited by Ian S. Markham, J. Barney Hawkins IV, Justyn Terry, and Leslie Nuñez Steffensen.
© 2013 John Wiley & Sons, Ltd. Published 2013 by John Wiley & Sons, Ltd.

different assessments of the human predicament and its remedy, indeed mutually exclusive accounts of the Christian gospel, had driven a wedge between members of the communion which grew into an open breach as the result of decisions made in the two decades straddling the turn of the millennium. Despite the continuing rhetoric of unity and communion, a fork in the road had been reached, and members of the denomination had already embarked on one or other of two radically divergent paths. However, the decision to hold GAFCON is caricatured if the catalyst is considered in isolation from long-term and deep-seated theological and ecclesiological tensions in the communion.

## A longstanding divide

The roots of the crisis at the beginning of the twenty-first century are very deep indeed. At one level, it would be possible to trace them back to the very beginnings of Anglicanism as a distinctive form of Christian corporate life. Born out of controversy in the middle of the sixteenth century, unresolved tensions from that earliest period have to a certain extent shaped the course of its history ever since. However, in the second half of the twentieth century, new elements were added which threatened the future of the denomination.

Anglicans around the world were scandalized by a series of public challenges to core Anglican doctrine made by individuals with leadership responsibilities within the various Anglican provinces. This was not entirely new, of course, but it did seem to be on an entirely new scale. In 1963, John Robinson, the then Bishop of Woolwich, published his book *Honest to God* (Robinson 1963). It called for a radical "break with traditional thinking" on such central doctrines as our understanding of God, Christ, and salvation. Unsurprisingly, it generated heated comment. In 1984, there was outrage at what David Jenkins, newly appointed Bishop of Durham, had said – or at least was understood to have said – about the resurrection of Jesus.[1] Robinson and Jenkins would soon be joined by John Shelby Spong, who campaigned for radical change in Anglican practice and doctrine throughout his time as Bishop of Newark. He eventually produced a list of 12 theses which called for the abandonment of (among other things) theism, Christology, any view of Christ's death as a sacrifice of atonement, the bodily resurrection and ascension of Christ, and prayer as "a request made to a theistic deity to act in human history in a particular way."[2] Less prominent but just as radical, Bishop Michael Ingham of New Westminster insisted, "It's time for Christians to drop the idea that Christ is the one sure way to salvation" (Ottawa Citizen 1997). These are simply a few of the most prominent examples. However, while such public questioning of the doctrinal standards of traditional Anglicanism raised serious concerns, these remained the personal views of individuals. The positions of leadership within the communion held by such figures might have drawn their ideas to public attention, but more conservative Anglicans could still distinguish them from the official teaching of the church.

---

[1] The reference is to a television interview on the BBC radio program *Poles Apart*, recorded at Auckland Castle in October 1984. See also Harrison (1985).
[2] See Spong, J. S. (1998, 2000).

It was in the last few decades of the twentieth century that a very significant new development took place: a number of decisions were taken by provincial and diocesan synods, which were seen by others to compromise the teaching of scripture and the doctrine taught by Anglicans on the basis of the Articles, the Book of Common Prayer, and the Homilies. Chief among these were decisions to ordain women to the presbyterate and later to the episcopate, and decisions which, one way or another, sought to endorse homosexual activity as consistent with Christian discipleship. For the first time in the 500-year history of Anglicanism, its orders of ministry were not universally recognized across the communion. Similarly, it seemed that, for the first time, moral teaching explicit in scripture and accepted by Anglicans of every theological complexion was being deliberately and officially set aside. This was no longer simply a matter of eccentric individual opinion. The character of the communion, its structure, and the nature of its appeal to scripture was being transformed. Unsurprisingly, high-profile voices began to call for decisive action to preserve authentic Anglicanism.

## The catalyst

As the issue of human sexuality began to become more prominent in Anglican discussions in the 1990s, attention began to be increasingly focused on the decisions and actions of the Episcopal Church (USA). On December 16, 1989, John Spong ordained a practicing homosexual man in Hoboken, New Jersey. This action directly contravened Resolution AO53 of the 1979 general convention of the Episcopal Church. In August 1994, Spong and 67 other bishops in the general convention published *A Statement in Koinonia*, which stated unequivocally "we believe that homosexuality and heterosexuality are morally neutral, that both can be lived out with beauty, honor, holiness, and integrity and that both are capable of being lived out destructively." It went on to insist that "gay and lesbian clergy . . . [b]y their willingness to accept and acknowledge their own sexual orientation and by the very witness of the committed nature of the lives they live with their partners . . . have brought the hope and love of Christ to communities of people long oppressed . . ."[3]

These developments were viewed with concern both in America and throughout the Anglican Communion. On November 30, 1995, a group of academics gathered by the Church of England Evangelical Council produced *The St Andrews Day Statement*.[4] This document attempted to illumine the theological ground upon which discussions about human sexuality in general, and homosexuality in particular, might proceed. A little over a year later, in February 1997, the Second Anglican Encounter in the South produced *The Kuala Lumpur Statement*, which expressed concern about moves to accommodate homosexual practice and even to endorse homosexual unions: "We are deeply concerned that the setting aside of biblical teaching in such actions as the ordination

[3]The text can be found online at http://www.integrityusa.org/samesexblessings/a_statement_in_koinonia. htm. Accessed December 14, 2011.
[4]The text can be found online at http://www.aco.org/listening/book_resources/docs/St%20Andrew's%20 Day%20Statement.pdf. Accessed December 14, 2011.

of practicing homosexuals and the blessing of same-sex unions calls into question the authority of the Holy Scriptures. This is totally unacceptable to us."[5] Nevertheless, in May 1998, the Diocese of New Westminster in the Anglican Church of Canada voted to authorize same-sex unions. On this first occasion, the diocesan bishop withheld his consent. The stage was set for confrontation over the issue when George Carey convened the Thirteenth Lambeth Conference in July 1998.

The debates about human sexuality overshadowed the entire conference. When at last the final form of a resolution on the matter was put, it was passed with an overwhelming majority (526/70, with 45 abstentions). Resolution 1.10 upheld "faithfulness in marriage between a man and a woman in lifelong union" and affirmed that "abstinence is right for those who are not called to marriage" (1.10[b]). While it called for compassion toward those who experience "homosexual orientation," it declared unequivocally that the conference rejected "homosexual practice as incompatible with Scripture" (1.10[d]).[6] The response was immediate. Strong dissenting voices spoke to the press on both sides of the Atlantic. Within a month, 146 bishops present at Lambeth published an open letter which insisted "We must not stop where this Conference left off."[7] At the next meeting of its general convention, the Episcopal Church resolved to acknowledge that "the issues of human sexuality are not yet resolved" (Resolution 2000-D039). Despite the huge majority it had gained, Resolution 1.10 was not going to end the debate or ease the tensions in the communion.

The controversy took a new turn at the very end of the decade. A request for alternative episcopal oversight by those American Anglicans who felt alienated from the stance the Episcopal Church had taken on this and other issues was considered but shelved at a meeting of Anglican primates and archbishops in Kampala in November 1999. However, the request itself was evidence of the deep divide in the Episcopal Church over matters of doctrine and appropriate Christian living. Just two months later, action was taken by Archbishop Moses Tay of South East Asia and Archbishop Emmanuel Kolini of Rwanda. On January 29, 2000, they, with a number of others including two Americans, consecrated Charles Murphy and John Rodgers in Singapore as missionary bishops to serve disaffected Anglicans in America. These consecrations were greeted with alarm, not only by the Presiding Bishop of the Episcopal Church, Frank Griswold, but also by the Archbishop of Canterbury, George Carey, and many other Anglican leaders.

The next scheduled meeting of the primates of the communion was held a little over a month later in Oporto, Portugal. The primates "noted with deep concern the recent consecrations in Singapore intended to provide extended episcopal oversight for Anglicans in the USA . . . such action taken without appropriate consultation poses serious questions for the life of the Communion." However, they also recognized that "clear and public repudiation of those sections of the Resolution [Lambeth 1.10] related to

---

[5]The full text of the Kuala Lumpur Statement can be found online at http://www.globalsouthanglican.org/index.php/blog/printing/the_kuala_lumpur_statement_on_human_sexuality_2nd_encounter_in_the_south_10. Accessed December 14, 2011.

[6]The text of the resolution can be found online at http://www.lambethconference.org/resolutions/1998/1998-1-10.cfm. Accessed December 14, 2011.

[7]The text can be found at http://www.whosoever.org/v3i2/lambeth2.html. Accessed December 14, 2011.

the public blessing of same-sex unions and the ordination of declared non-celibate homosexuals, and the declared intention of some dioceses to proceed with such actions, have come to threaten the unity of the communion in a profound way."[8] In March 2001, the primates met again, this time in Kanuga, North Carolina, and the pastoral letter issued from that meeting mentioned specifically "the difficulties of those who are estranged from others because of changes in theology and practice – especially with regard to the acceptance of homosexual activity and the ordination of practicing homosexuals – that they believe to be unfaithful to the gospel of Christ."[9] Caution was urged on all sides.

However, in June 2002, the Diocese of New Westminster resolved for the third time to authorize the blessing of same-sex unions, this time receiving the consent of the bishop. A number of parishes withdrew from the synod when that decision was made. Pointedly, the Anglican Consultative Council, when it met in Hong Kong in October that year, called on dioceses and individual bishops "not to undertake unilateral actions or adopt policies which would strain our communion with one another without reference to their provincial authorities" (Resolution 34). Despite this call for calm, caution, and consultation, on May 20, 2003, Richard Harries, the Bishop of Oxford, announced his intention to appoint Jeffrey John, a self-styled non-practicing homosexual, as the next Bishop of Reading. Jeffrey John would later withdraw his name after a meeting with the new Archbishop of Canterbury, Rowan Williams.

What proved to be the decisive move was made on June 7, 2003, when a practicing homosexual man, V. Gene Robinson, was elected as Bishop of New Hampshire. His election was confirmed by the 74th general convention of the Episcopal Church in August. Upon news of the election, the Archbishop of Canterbury called an emergency meeting of the primates, to be held in Lambeth Palace in October. The statement issued at the conclusion of that meeting spelled out the consequences of continuing down this path:

> If his consecration proceeds, we recognise that we have reached a crucial and critical point in the life of the Anglican Communion and we have had to conclude that the future of the Communion itself will be put into jeopardy. In this case, the ministry of this one bishop will not be recognised by most of the Anglican world, and many provinces are likely to consider themselves out of Communion with the Episcopal Church (USA). This will tear the fabric of our Communion at its deepest level, and may lead to further division on this and further issues as provinces have to decide in consequence whether they can remain in communion with provinces that choose not to break communion with the Episcopal Church (USA).[10]

---

[8] The full text of the communiqué can be found online at http://www.americananglican.org/final-communiqu-from-the-primates-meeting-in-march-2000-in-portugal/pageprint. Accessed December 14, 2011.

[9] The full text of the pastoral letter can be found online at http://www.americananglican.org/pastoral-letter-and-call-to-prayer-from-the-march-2001-primates-meeting-kanuga-nc/pageprint. Accessed December 14, 2011.

[10] The full text of the communiqué can be found online at http://www.globalsouthanglican.org/index.php/blog/comments/a_statement_by_the_primates_of_the_anglican_communion_meeting_in_lambeth_pa. Accessed December 14, 2011.

Nevertheless, Gene Robinson's consecration took place on November 2, 2003, in the Whittemore Center in Durham, New Hampshire. In the words of the primates, the fabric of the Anglican Communion was now torn at its deepest level.

The meeting of the primates at Lambeth had also called for a commission to investigate how the communion might function, given the pressures of increasing diversity and even serious disagreement between its provinces. A year later, this commission would produce the *Windsor Report*, which proposed, among other things, an Anglican Covenant. The report itself received a mixed response, and subsequent drafts of a proposed covenant have failed to win widespread support. Yet, the work of the commission and the report itself were testimony to a mounting sense of crisis even among the most ardent supporters of Anglican comprehensiveness. Meanwhile, the determination of the American revisionists to continue on their path was evident. In March 2004, the Diocese of Washington began to develop rites for blessing same-sex unions, and, in April 2004, retired bishop Otis Charles of Utah "married" Felipe Paris in Saint Gregory of Nyssa Episcopal Church in Mariposa, San Francisco. In a very real sense, the separation had already happened, and what was left was a decision about how to live with the consequences.

A new question now emerged. To what extent could those who had brought about this state of affairs continue to participate in the various boards, bodies, and conferences of the communion they had so seriously disrupted? The primates, meeting in Dromantine, Ireland, in February 2005, requested that "the Episcopal Church (USA) and the Anglican Church of Canada voluntarily withdraw their members from the Anglican Consultative Council for the period leading up to the next Lambeth Conference" (para. 14), although it did also request an opportunity for representatives of both provinces to be heard at the upcoming ACC meeting in Nottingham (para. 16).[11] Later that year, at the Third Anglican South to South Encounter in Egypt, the participants insisted that "Unscriptural and unilateral decisions, especially on moral issues, tear the fabric of our Communion and require appropriate discipline at every level to maintain our unity."[12] At their meeting in Dar es Salaam in February 2007, the primates set a deadline of September 30, 2007, for the House of Bishops of the Episcopal Church to "make an unequivocal common covenant that the bishops will not authorise any Rite of Blessing for same sex unions" and "confirm that a candidate for episcopal orders living in a same-sex union shall not receive the necessary consent."[13] The deadline would pass without any such undertaking.

This was the context in which the invitations to the Fourteenth Lambeth Conference were delivered. A number of bishops made clear that they would have difficulty accepting the Archbishop of Canterbury's invitation if such an invitation was also extended to those who had repudiated the Anglican Communion by pursuing a revisionist course

---

[11] The full text of the communiqué can be found online at http://www.anglicancommunion.org/communion/primates/resources/downloads/communique%20_english.pdf. Accessed December 24, 2011.

[12] The full text of the communiqué issued by this gathering can be found online at http://www.globalsouthanglican.org/index.php/blog/printing/third_trumpet_communique_from_3rd_south_to_south_encounter. Accessed December 24, 2011.

[13] The full text of the communiqué can be found online at http://www.aco.org/communion/primates/resources/downloads/communique2007_english.pdf. Accessed December 14, 2011.

in matters of doctrine and ethical practice, especially since this course had been pursued in defiance of explicit and repeated entreaties made by the primates and other Anglican leaders throughout the world. Direct representations were made to the Archbishop of Canterbury himself, seeking to make clear the serious consequences of such invitations. However, in May 2007, the Anglican Communion Office announced that invitations had been issued to 800 bishops, excluding Gene Robinson but including those who consented to and participated in his consecration. This was taken by many as a sign that the Communion Office simply proposed a "business as usual" approach and had rejected any discipline of the Episcopal Church (USA) or the Anglican Church of Canada.

Hence, the catalyst for GAFCON was not simply the consecration of a practicing homosexual as Bishop of New Hampshire, though this action was considered a defining moment in the new doctrinal and ethical direction the Episcopal Church had been taking throughout the twentieth century. It was that this action, and the departure from fellowship in biblical teaching of which it was only the presenting issue, had been taken very deliberately in the face of publicly expressed concern and explicit requests from Anglican leaders around the world to refrain from acting in this way. Furthermore, the traditional structures of world Anglicanism were either unable or unwilling to respond decisively. To many, the American and Canadian actions appeared as schismatic repudiations of the rest of the communion in order to follow an agenda many considered deeply suspect. It was not a matter of seeking to avoid a schism. The schism had already happened. This was a tragedy the vast majority of Anglicans around the world could not afford to ignore.

## The Global Anglican Future Conference

### *The decision to meet in Jerusalem*

In late December 2007, Archbishops Peter Akinola of Nigeria, Justice Akrofi of West Africa, Emmanuel Kolini of Rwanda, Donald Mtelemela of Tanzania, Benjamin Nzimbi of Kenya, and Henry Orombi of Uganda, all primates of the Anglican Communion, met to address the continuing crisis. Presiding Bishop Greg Venables, Primate of the Southern Cone, was represented at the meeting by Bishop Bill Atwood. Also attending were Archbishops Nicholas Okoh of Nigeria and Peter Jensen of Sydney; Bishops Bob Duncan, Donald Harvey, and Martyn Minns; and Canons Vinay Samuel and Chris Sugden. Together, these men represented the vast majority of Anglicans worldwide. They determined to convene a meeting of bishops and other leaders to consult on the future of Anglican life, ministry, and mission. Peter Jensen's press release of December 27, 2007, spoke of the proposed conference as:

> a meeting which accepts the current reality of a Communion in disarray over fundamental issues of the gospel and biblical authority. It therefore seeks to plan for a future in which Anglican Christians worldwide will increasingly be pressured to depart from the biblical norms of behaviour and belief. It gives an opportunity for many to draw together to

strengthen each other over the issue of biblical authority and interpretation and gospel mission.

Jerusalem was chosen as the venue for the conference because of its significance as the city which witnessed the ministry of Jesus and became the launching pad for world mission (Acts 1:8). Archbishop Akinola described it as "returning to our biblical roots." The choice proved to be somewhat controversial, due to opposition from the Bishop of Jerusalem. However, consultations revealed no insurmountable barriers, and so the conference was scheduled for Jerusalem from June 22 to 29, 2008.

As invitations were organized, a Theological Resource Group was set up under the chairmanship of Archbishop Nicholas Okoh of Nigeria. Its brief would be to provide theological material that would assist the conference in charting a course for the future of confessional Anglicanism. Its first publication, entitled *The Way the Truth and the Life*, was published with the aid of the Latimer Trust just prior to the conference.

### The conference itself

The conference organizers, together with keynote speakers, workshop leaders, and other advisers, met in Jordan immediately prior to the main conference. This planning meeting had to be aborted when official permission to meet was withdrawn without explanation. As a result, the group transferred to Jerusalem, after meeting Archbishop Akinola in Jericho.

The Global Anglican Future Conference opened on the evening of Sunday, June 22, 2008, in the Renaissance Hotel in Jerusalem with an address from Archbishop Akinola entitled "GAFCON – A Rescue Mission." Earlier in the day, delegates had attended a variety of Christian church services in the city, and the leaders and speakers at the conference attended a prayer service in St. George's Cathedral, where they were welcomed by the Bishop of Jerusalem, Suheil Salman Dawani.

The conference program contained a mixture of biblical expositions outlining the sweep of biblical theology, small group prayer and Bible study, workshops to explore key subjects in detail, and opportunities to visit key sites associated with the life and ministry of the Lord Jesus Christ. The workshops covered gospel and culture, gospel and leadership, biblical authority and interpretation, family and marriage, Anglican identity in the twenty-first century, evangelism and church planting, and theological education. There was also a special workshop stream for bishops' wives. A significant amount of the time was devoted to more informal fellowship. On a number of the afternoons, a "focus topic" was addressed either through a panel of specialists or by an individual presentation. These included "The Gospel and Secularism," "The Nature and Future of the Anglican Communion," "The Gospel and Religion," and "Enterprise Approaches to Poverty."

The program of the conference reflected the larger concerns which had brought these leaders together. Repeatedly, delegates were given the opportunity to reflect on the gospel taught in the scriptures and on how best this gospel might be proclaimed and embodied in the twenty-first century. The range of speakers and workshop leaders (from Africa, Asia, Australia, Europe, and North and South America), together with the content of the various addresses, Bible studies, discussions, and workshops, belied any suggestion that the conference's agenda could be narrowly construed as a response to Western Anglican revisionism on human sexuality. This was even more obvious in the official statement released at the end of the conference, at the heart of which lay the Jerusalem Declaration.

## The Jerusalem Declaration

The conference had always been intended to culminate in the release of a statement which could provide the basis for future Anglican mission in the twenty-first century. Throughout the week, individuals and provinces were encouraged to make submissions to a drafting group. A first draft of a statement was then prepared and submitted to the entire conference. Later that day, the delegates met in provincial groups to consider the draft and to submit their reactions and suggestions for amendment. Finally, on Sunday, June 29, 2008, Archbishop Henry Orombi of Uganda read the final text of the Jerusalem Declaration to a plenary session. It was endorsed with sustained and thunderous applause.

In the name of God the Father, God the Son and God the Holy Spirit:

We, the participants in the Global Anglican Future Conference, have met in the land of Jesus' birth. We express our loyalty as disciples to the King of kings, the Lord Jesus. We joyfully embrace his command to proclaim the reality of his kingdom which he first announced in this land. The gospel of the kingdom is the good news of salvation, liberation and transformation for all. In light of the above, we agree to chart a way forward together that promotes and protects the biblical gospel and mission to the world, solemnly declaring the following tenets of orthodoxy which underpin our Anglican identity.

1. We rejoice in the gospel of God through which we have been saved by grace through faith in Jesus Christ by the power of the Holy Spirit. Because God first loved us, we love him and as believers bring forth fruits of love, ongoing repentance, lively hope and thanksgiving to God in all things.
2. We believe the Holy Scriptures of the Old and New Testaments to be the word of God written and to contain all things necessary for salvation. The Bible is to be translated, read, preached, taught and obeyed in its plain and canonical sense, respectful of the Church's historic and consensual reading.
3. We uphold the four Ecumenical Councils and the three historic Creeds as expressing the rule of faith of the one holy catholic and apostolic Church.
4. We uphold the Thirty-Nine Articles as containing the true doctrine of the Church agreeing with God's word and as authoritative for Anglicans today.
5. We gladly proclaim and submit to the unique and universal Lordship of Jesus Christ, the Son of God, humanity's only Saviour from sin, judgement and hell, who lived the life we could not live and died the death that we deserve. By his

atoning death and glorious resurrection, he secured redemption of all who come to him in repentance and faith.

6.  We rejoice in our Anglican sacramental and liturgical heritage as an expression of the gospel, and we uphold the 1662 Book of Common Prayer as a true and authoritative standard of worship and prayer, to be translated and locally adapted for each culture.

7.  We recognise that God has called and gifted bishops, priests and deacons in historic succession to equip all the people of God for their ministry in the world. We uphold the classic Anglican Ordinal as an authoritative standard of clerical orders.

8.  We acknowledge God's creation of humankind as male and female and the unchangeable standard of Christian marriage between one man and one woman as the proper place for sexual intimacy and the basis of the family. We repent of our failures to maintain this standard and call for a renewed commitment to lifelong fidelity in marriage and abstinence for those who are not married.

9.  We gladly accept the Great Commission of the risen Lord to make disciples of all nations, to seek those who do not know Christ and to baptise, teach and bring new believers to maturity.

10. We are mindful of our responsibility to be good stewards of God's creation, to uphold and advocate justice in society, and to seek relief and empowerment of the poor and needy.

11. We are committed to the unity of all those who know and love Christ and to building authentic ecumenical relationships. We recognise the orders and jurisdiction of those Anglicans who uphold orthodox faith and practice, and we encourage them to join us in this declaration.

12. We celebrate the God-given diversity among us which enriches our global fellowship, and we acknowledge freedom in secondary matters. We pledge to work together to seek the mind of Christ on issues that divide us.

13. We reject the authority of those churches and leaders who have denied the orthodox faith in word or deed. We pray for them and call on them to repent and return to the Lord.

14. We rejoice at the prospect of Jesus' coming again in glory, and while we await this final event of history, we praise him for the way he builds up his Church through his Spirit by miraculously changing lives.

## The Fellowship of Confessing Anglicans

Throughout the conference, it was insisted that GAFCON was not just a moment but a movement. The conference itself was only a critical first step in the rejuvenation of Anglicanism by a return to its biblical moorings in the gospel of Jesus Christ and faithful discipleship as outlined in the teaching of scripture. As a result of the conference, plans were made and realized to endorse an alternative American province (ACNA) for those alienated and disenfranchised by the actions of the American and Canadian leadership. The Fellowship of Confessing Anglicans was formed as a network of Anglicans committed to the teaching of scripture and the authentic Anglican expression of that teaching in the Thirty-Nine Articles, the Book of Common Prayer, and the Homilies. Membership of the FCA now spans six continents, and efforts are underway to provide practical support to those under pressure "to depart from the biblical norms of behavior and belief."

Meanwhile the Episcopal Church (USA) and the Anglican Church of Canada have continued on their course unabated. On May 15, 2010, an openly lesbian woman, Mary Glasspool, was consecrated as suffragan Bishop of Los Angeles in the Long Beach Arena by the new presiding bishop, Katherine Jefferts Schori. This, like the consecration of Gene Robinson, was not a random act. The presiding bishop spoke of it as a settled and determined course, "a prayerful and thoughtful decision." It has proven to be a decision to walk apart.

A second international conference has been announced (GAFCON II), to meet in 2013. As the primatial leadership among the GAFCON provinces has passed to another generation, the resolve has not diminished. Many Anglicans in Western provinces have faced more intense opposition since GAFCON. Litigation against dioceses, parishes, and individuals in the United States and Canada, in particular, has created genuine hardship for many. Yet, the fruit of the GAFCON movement is already evident and, under God's good hand, seems set to multiply greatly in the decades ahead.

## Bibliography

Robinson, J. A. T. 1963. *Honest to God.* London: SCM.

Harrison, T. 1985. *The Durham Phenomenon: What Does Today's Most Controversial Bishop Really Believe?* London: Darton, Longman and Todd.

Spong, J. S. 1998. *Why Christianity Must Change or Die: A Bishop Speaks to Believers in Exile.* San Francisco: HarperCollins.

Spong, J. S. 2000. *Here I Stand: My Struggle for a Christianity of Integrity, Love, & Equality.* San Francisco: HarperCollins, pp. 453–4.

*Ottawa Citizen 1997.* September 26, 1997.

# Index

Akinola, Peter, 175–9, 659, 745–6
Andrewes, Lancelot, 419, 556, 559–61, 569, 608–9
Anglican Communion Covenant, 43, 51–2, 58–64, 75–6, 103, 119–32, 556, 572–3, 636, 673–4, 734–5
Anglican Consultative Council, 42, 47–8, 51, 96, 105–17, 485, 572, 743
apartheid, 24, 30, 40, 101, 194, 196–8, 485, 557, 615–16
Archbishop of Canterbury, office of, 49–50, 67–72, 76–7, 105
Augustine of Canterbury, 16, 70–1, 414, 442, 452, 597

Becket, Thomas, 69, 72, 77, 416
Bede, 414–15, 428
Bible
  authority of, 112, 190, 216, 258–9, 557–8, 731
  in local language, 5, 17, 24, 82, 170, 201, 207, 258–9, 265, 280, 291, 305, 330, 336, 350, 360, 396, 430–2, 454, 481, 521–2, 575, 702, 704–6, 710–11, 716, 720
  King James Version, 17, 419, 509, 608–9, 716

Book of Common Prayer,
  1662, 559, 598–600, 604, 748
  in Anglicanism, 17, 57, 81–9, 99, 202, 417–18, 516, 534, 664, 673, 716–17, 721–2
  local versions, 21, 196, 259, 263, 297, 310, 398–9, 408, 431, 433–5, 449–50, 461, 477, 514, 524, 604–5, 703
Bray, Thomas, 7, 18, 34, 420, 517, 646, 701, 703–4

canon law, 11, 48, 50, 53–8, 64, 121
Caroline divines, 10, 431–2, 560–1, 570
Caswell, Henry, 4, 11
Chicago–Lambeth Quadrilateral, 37–8, 59, 100, 121, 216, 556, 563, 571–3, 673–4
Church Missionary Society (CMS), 19, 21–5, 28, 30, 35, 38, 41, 137–8, 149–50, 159, 163, 165–71, 184–5, 199, 204, 206–7, 221–5, 227, 233, 241, 246, 254, 264, 274, 278, 280, 330, 338, 345, 356, 360, 374–7, 394–5, 421, 481, 483, 520, 562, 575, 646–8, 668, 691, 706–8, 727
Clapham sect, 19, 35, 395, 421
Coakley, Sarah, 567, 735–6